West's Law School Advisory Board

Sexual Identity Law in Context

CASES AND MATERIALS

Second Edition

■ ■ ■

By

Shannon Gilreath

Wake Forest University

Lydia E. Lavelle

North Carolina Central University School of Law

AMERICAN CASEBOOK SERIES®

WEST®

A Thomson Reuters business

Mat #41225483

610 Opperman Drive
St. Paul, MN 55123
1–800–313–9378

Printed in the United States of America

ISBN: 978–0–314–27922–4

This second edition is dedicated to the memory of Derrick Bell, for his example, but most especially for his kindness.

Preface to the Second Edition

The fast pace of change in the area of gay rights law necessitates a second edition of this casebook. What hasn't changed is that gay people still must fight for their rights, and the battle isn't easy. Many improvements must be acknowledged, of course; still, there is much important work to do. This casebook is designed to teach students how to represent gay clients, and how to challenge the law to change in response to their unique needs. Our students today will ensure in which direction the future moves.

Professor Gilreath's Acknowledgments

My thanks go to student research assistants Trevor Ostbye, Amy Shafer, and Rory Agan. Thanks also to Wake Forest University reference librarian, Liz Johnson, and to my assistant, Cynthia Ring.

Professor Lavelle's Acknowledgments

During my ten-plus years working in administration at the North Carolina Central University School of Law, I created and taught a "Sexual Identity and the Law" course. I found that I enjoyed teaching so much that after a few years, I pursued a position as an assistant professor. I was honored that my colleagues voted to have me join the faculty. I am so appreciative of this opportunity that has been given to me, to teach our students to understand the important issues of our day, and how to go about effecting change in the world.

I used the first edition of this book while teaching my course, and am grateful to Shannon for allowing me to co-author this second edition. I have tried to offer a "woman's touch" to this updated text. Further, because I am also an elected official (I currently serve as a board member of the Carrboro, North Carolina Board of Aldermen), I have included material in this edition that I know first-hand will help with grassroots advocacy by students who choose to get active in the local political arena in the area of LGBT rights. I am fortunate to serve on a Board and in a community that sees LGBT rights as human rights.

Many students have helped enhance my contributions to this book. I would like to thank my research assistants, Melenia Jackson and Jordan Ford, currently third-year students at North Carolina Central University School of Law, who helped me enormously with gathering and condensing material for the book. Thanks also to my former research assistant, Mary Jane Cook, a 2010 graduate of North Carolina Central University School of Law, for her work which helped inform my thinking about inclusion of various materials in the parenting chapter. Thanks also to Cole Phelps, currently a second-year student at North Carolina Central University School of Law, for help with proofing and reviewing the material.

Upon request, the students in my "Sexual Identity and the Law" course the past few years have given me helpful critiques of the first edition of the book, and their thoughts on how it could be improved when it was updated. Many of their suggestions have been incorporated into this edition, and I believe they would be pleased.

I would be remiss if I did not acknowledge two North Carolina mentors who impacted my legal career and, thus, have their stamp on this work: Clifton E. Johnson (former judge on the North Carolina Court of Appeals, for whom I clerked) and Dean Janice L. Mills (former Dean of the NCCU School of Law, with whom I worked for many years). You are both greatly missed.

Finally, I want to acknowledge my family, my partner Alicia and our children Riley and Avery. Thank you so much for your support in this venture and in life in general. It is my great hope that the work I do will ultimately make our lives and the lives of those that follow better.

PREFACE TO THE FIRST EDITION

When I began teaching courses on sexual orientation and law, there were precious few text offerings in the field. William Rubenstein, now settled at UCLA, wrote the pioneering casebook in the area, while teaching the subject as an adjunct professor at several schools. I used Professor Rubenstein's book the first year I taught the subject. Shortly after I began teaching, William Eskridge and Nan Hunter published their magisterial casebook, broadly surveying gender and sexuality law. Arthur Leonard and Patricia Cain added a third alternative with the publication of their "Sexuality Law." When West gave me the opportunity to author a fourth casebook in the area, I was already teaching from materials that I had been compiling and editing for two years.

I have endeavored to create a casebook that fits an upper-level, two- or three- credit-hour discussion seminar. The law in this area has exploded in recent years, with many lawyers and most courts called upon to answer complicated legal questions concerning gay privacy, gay sex, gay families, gay speech, and the incorporation of lesbians, gays, bisexuals, and transgender people into the fabric of American everyday life.

The rapid growth of the law made selecting and editing the cases for this volume a challenge. Like Dean Langdell, the originator of the casebook method, I found myself wondering if "there was any satisfactory principle upon which such a selection could be made."

I think that I found it.

This book examines the law of sexual orientation and sexual identity in the way the Supreme Court suggested in *Lawrence:* from and within the context of the society in which lesbian, gay, bisexual, and transgender individuals live. Much of this book is comprised, of course, of cases edited to present the law of sexual identity in a clear and understandable manner. But the book includes much more.

If the progression from *Bowers v. Hardwick* to *Romer v. Evans* to *Lawrence v. Texas* (the three truly landmark cases in the area of sexual orientation/identity) teaches us anything, the lesson is that the courts are often not the leaders in this area of the law. The courts are often followers of the changing societal ethos concerning lesbian and gay people. Students are disserved when they are merely offered the black letter regulation without an exploration of the reasons for such regulations. By presenting cases only (or even primarily), we omit the material needed to understand factors that shape the law.

Therefore, a primary purpose of this book is to put the law into its social context. I do this by including excerpts from various non-case materials: personal stories, excerpts from political platforms, law review articles, journal articles from other disciplines, journalism and traditional prose, history, science, religious studies, philosophy, and comparative law materials. The inclusion of comparative international cases, typically from the European Court of Human Rights, is important because it shows, as *Lawrence* suggested, that recent developments in United States lesbian/gay law are part of a wider international trend. Decisions from state courts on state constitutional grounds also show the Supreme Court cases to be part of a larger national trend. Both of these observations were made in *Lawrence*.

The law of sexual identity is often treated only as a matter of constitutional law. But the subject is much, much broader. It includes a mix of several areas including property, contract, domestic relations, and constitutional law. Because constitutional law is centrally important, however, and also because the other areas of law are just now widely grappling with the subject, the law regarding sexuality is still composed of relatively little "settled" law and a lot of theory as to the direction the law should or may take.

As with the story of any human struggle—which the story of the law inevitably is—there are gaps and discrepancies. As editor, my job was to offer, within rigorous space limits, what was to me the most revealing and pertinent material. Every casebook editor is under the compulsion to omit things he would like to include, particularly when new cases are being decided at a dizzying pace; my experience has not been exceptional in that regard. In many instances, some of the most recent legal developments appear in the "Analysis" section of a chapter, rather than as full text reproductions. For example, the New Jersey Supreme Court decision holding that same-sex couples must be afforded rights equal to those of heterosexual married couples appears in brief in the "Analysis" section of Chapter 9, as the catalyst to a question asking students to weigh the efficacy of the approaches of the Vermont (*Baker*) court (the approach largely followed by the New Jersey court) and the Massachusetts (*Goodridge*) court.

The basic pedagogy of the book breaks each main chapter topic into subparts. The first part (the "Context") provides the necessary background discussion and supplies the context necessary to understanding the area of the law. The second part (the "Law") contains the cases. The third part (the "Analysis") provides further consideration of the concepts explored in the preceding two parts.

In the Analysis, I pose a series of questions asking the student to reflect on or to apply the concepts gleaned from the reading. The idea is to prompt students to incorporate knowledge not only from the chapter at hand, but from the preceding material as well, making learning the law less episodic, and more like logically progressing discussion.

Each subsection of the book can stand alone, allowing professors to shorten or lengthen discussion of a particular topic as class time permits or to delete sections entirely. For example, if there is not enough time to cover all the materials on "outing," a professor could omit the cases and merely assign the "Context" to give an overview of the issue.

Authoring a casebook is no solitary enterprise. So many acknowledgments are due that I am sure to leave out some important person. First, I must thank the authors and publishers from whom I have reprinted the material which provides the all-important Context sections of the book. I have done my best to ascertain all necessary permissions. You may bring any inadvertent omissions to my attention by writing to me in care of West Publishing.

Thanks go to a number of people who read portions of the text, made comments, provided beneficial conversation, or otherwise contributed: Professors Michael Kent Curtis, J. Wilson Parker, Suzanne Reynolds, Ronald Wright, Derrick Bell, James Strammel, Mr. Jonathan Katz, and Professors William Rubenstein, Bryan Wildenthal, Michael J. Perry, Libby Adler, Brian Chase, Paul Siegel, Richard Mohr, Sidney Shapiro, David A.J. Richards, Russell Weaver. Steve Nickles, professor at Wake Forest Law School, has been enormously supportive of this book. He and Bill Leonard, Dean of the Wake Forest Divinity School, were the first people at Wake Forest to see the value of a course specifically dealing with sexuality and law. Dr. Perry Patterson, and Drs. Anne Boyle, former director of the Women's and Gender Studies program at Wake Forest, and Wanda Balzano, the current director, were also instrumental. Deans Robert Walsh, H. Miles Foy, Marian Parker, Susan Montaquila and the faculty of the Wake Forest Law School have been supportive of my courses and of this book. They have my thanks for research funds and for other crucial support.

The unsung heroes of a project like this are the support staff who make it possible. My secretaries at the Wake Forest University School of Law, Rosemary Sigmon and Connie Cashin, provided invaluable clerical aid. Ms. Sigmon was also a most efficient copy editor. Arlene McClannon and Beth Malone provided equally invaluable computing support.

A number of student researchers aided me. Stacy Gomes, now an alumna of Wake Forest Law, provided invaluable assistance in the editing process. Rick Rutledge, a second-year law student, was an extraordinarily able and resourceful assistant. Rick performed feats of wonder with Microsoft Word, and he and student Karlyn McManus double-checked cites, ferreted out elusive material, and helped with some chapter introductory language. Law student Elizabeth Goodwin is an organizational dynamo. She helped coordinate the permissions effort and, on more than one occasion, kept me from losing my sanity.

Certainly, the students in my sexuality and law, sexuality and religion, and women's and gender studies courses at Wake Forest Law School, Divinity School, and Wake Forest College have all contributed to my understanding and to my life in the law. Their contribution to this book is indelible.

Finally, I would be remiss if I did not add a mention of how personally important this work has been to me. I am not yet thirty years old, and this is my third book; but creating this book—and teaching from it—have definitely been the most rewarding projects I have undertaken. As a gay man and as a lawyer, I have been more than academically interested in the issues in this volume—I have been *existentially* interested in them.

The overarching theme of this book is discrimination. In the new preface to his best-selling *Faces at the Bottom of the Well*, Derrick Bell tells the story of Mrs. Biona MacDonald from the black hamlet of Harmony in the Mississippi delta. Bell met her as she and a group of other African–Americans organized to ensure the desegregation of their schools as mandated by a court order. Bell inquired of Mrs. Macdonald what it was that kept her going, kept her agitating in the face of near crushing reprisal by the white bigots. Mrs. MacDonald replied with a nugget of wisdom that should echo in the struggle for equal rights for gays as well: "I can't speak for everyone, but as for me, I am an old woman. I lives [sic] to harass white folks."

The pure wisdom in Mrs. MacDonald's response comes as much from what she doesn't say: she doesn't believe she is personally winning the war. Instead, she is fighting a battle. This old woman does not believe that "harassing" the white folks will bring an immediate end to white oppression of blacks; she simply intends to use determination and moxie as a weapon against the smothering domination. Her tactic of making small dents in the edifice of discrimination, as opposed to totally obliterating it, ensures that she does not know defeat. She knows victory simply by setting out to and having the courage to agitate against the machine.

Gay people are a distinct socio-political minority in this country, and the cases and materials collected here represent a minority's struggle for equality—for justice. In some cases the gay litigants win; in many they lose. This text is a teaching tool not a work of advocacy. Nevertheless, although I have tried to present both sides of the issues, I make no apologies for my own viewpoint—evidenced by the inclusion of some of my own published contributions to the debate—that discrimination against gay people is wrong. As the twenty-first century is shaping up to be the century of the sexuality line, eventually every student—every person—will have to come to her own conclusion on the matter.

–EDITOR'S NOTE–

In general, the materials selected for this book have not been heavily edited. This is so because of my preference for teaching from materials that have not been severely pruned, and also because it is important that the reader see how the legal claims gay people make relate and meld together. So while I may use a case chiefly to illustrate a First Amendment point, I may also retain the portions of the opinion that deal with equal protection or due process. The additional sections illustrate the interrelation of First Amendment, equal protection, and due process claims and may also provide additional material to consider when, say, the equal protection unit is taken up later.

Where portions of the opinions and other materials have been omitted, the omissions are indicated by ellipses (. . .). Footnotes or endnotes supplying authority citation, as well as explanatory footnotes deemed unnecessary, are often omitted from the materials without indication. Remaining notes were sometimes renumbered.

I made no effort to correct grammar, punctuation, or citation errors in any original material.

SHANNON GILREATH
Wake Forest University

Summary of Contents

Table of Contents

Table of Cases

The principal cases are in bold type. Cases cited or discussed in the text are in roman type. References are to pages. Cases cited in principal cases and within other quoted materials are not included.

Sexual Identity Law in Context

CASES AND MATERIALS

Second Edition

Chapter 1

Sexual Identity

■ ■ ■

The materials comprising this chapter sketch the struggle for gay identity and provide a framework for the legal discussion of the following chapters. The chapter opens a discussion of the historical progression from "conversion" (the medicalization of homosexuality and attendant compulsory heterosexuality) to "passing" (the phenomenon of hiding in the "The Closet" and refusing to identify as homosexual in a hostile, heterocentric society). Additional materials in this section elaborate the social and scientific debate over sexual identity.

I. A BRIEF OVERVIEW OF THE GAY RIGHTS MOVEMENT

A study of legal issues facing the gay community cannot be properly understood unless one is also familiar with an accompanying timeline of events, many of which are discussed in more detail elsewhere in this casebook. The unknowing student is usually astounded to realize that the modern gay rights movement did not begin until 1969 (it was not until 1973 that the American Psychiatric Association removed homosexuality from the official list of mental disorders). Prior to 1969, gay rights groups did exist, but somewhat under the radar. The Mattachine Society, formed in 1950, was the first national gay rights organization. It was formed by Harry Hay, often noted as the founder of the gay rights movement. The first lesbian organization was formed in 1955 and was known as The Daughters of Bilitis. After 1969, however, activist groups formed with a vengeance. 1969 is known as the year of Stonewall.

The Stonewall Inn in Greenwich Village in New York City was a gay bar like many others. Since homosexuality was illegal everywhere, these bars were often located in inconspicuous places, and usually required one to be a "member" or a guest of a member to enter. Known as places where patrons could go to drink, dance and socialize, drag shows were usually held late at night. These bars provided somewhat of a safe haven where gays could be themselves.

In the early morning hours of July 28, 1969, the New York City police conducted a police raid at The Stonewall Inn. The policemen started to confiscate liquor and beer at the unlicensed club, rumored to be owned by the Mafia, and to arrest employees and drag performers. While police raids were a commonplace occurrence at the gay bars in the city, this time the patrons as a collective had had enough and spontaneously fought back against the police raid. Several hundred more supporters of the bar showed up in the streets in protest. Fires were set, windows were broken and items from the bar were smashed to pieces. Various riots continued for three days.

The aftermath of the riots was felt across the country. Stonewall set off a movement that changed the world. Within months, activists and supporters around the nation began working to organize grass roots efforts to continue the equal rights effort that had begun at Stonewall. On the one-year anniversary of the bar raid, the first gay pride parade in the United States took place, fittingly in New York City. Although the Stonewall riots had received scant media attention, the one-year anniversary efforts garnered national coverage; *The New York Times* reported on its front page that the marchers took up the entire street for about 15 city blocks. Gay Pride marches took place that same year in Los Angeles and Chicago. The next year, Gay Pride marches took place in Boston, Dallas, Milwaukee, London, Paris, Berlin, and Stockholm. By 1972 the participating cities included Atlanta, Buffalo, Detroit, Washington D.C., Miami, and Philadelphia. Within a few years of the Stonewall riots, there were gay rights groups in every major American city, as well as Canada, Australia, and Western Europe.

1978 was another landmark year for the gay rights movement. That year, two horrific murders took place in San Francisco, California as Board of Supervisors member Harvey Milk and the mayor of San Francisco (George Moscone) were slain by a former Board of Supervisors member in Town Hall. Milk, who lived in the city's Castro District, is known as the first openly gay man to be elected to public office in California. A gay activist later in his life, Milk helped the city pass a stringent gay rights ordinance shortly before his death. His brief tenure as an activist and politician and the events leading up to his death have been the subject of many books and a 2008 movie, *Milk*, starring Sean Penn.

The Democratic Party, in 1980, for the first time addressed gay rights in its adopted party platform: "All groups must be protected from discrimination based on race, color, religion, national origin, language, age, sex or sexual orientation." The party continues to include reference to the gay community in its current platform. The Republican Party made condemnation of homosexuality a plank in its platform. The early 1980s also marked the start of the AIDS epidemic, first diagnosed in a group of homosexual men in Los Angeles, California. Because the then-fatal illness was found to be prevalent in the homosexual community, it was initially known as the "gay disease." Throughout the 1980s, many high profile figures died of AIDS, and as a consequence many were "outed," some posthumously. This was a terrifying time for the gay community, as many lost lovers and friends to AIDS. It has been argued that the popular (although counterfactual) association of AIDS almost exclusively with the gay community contributed to lackluster efforts to seek a cure. Nevertheless, as AIDS became a bigger problem for the heterosexual world (well-known prominent figures, such as Arthur Ashe, succumbed to the illness), efforts to find a cure increased. Although funding for prevention and treatment of AIDS has come a long way since the 1980s, even in today's climate, some politicians insist on playing hardball with AIDS funding.

As local governments started to provide protections for their gay and lesbian citizens, former beauty queen, singer and orange juice spokeswoman, Anita Bryant, became an outspoken gay rights opponent. Bryant's crusade against a local ordinance prohibiting discrimination on the basis of sexual orientation that had been passed in 1977 in Dade County, Florida, is legendary. As the leader of the "Save Our Children," campaign, Bryant's efforts led to the repeal of the ordinance by the voters the same year it was passed. She also supported Florida's efforts that same year to write into state law that homosexuals were not permitted to adopt children. As a direct response to Bryant's efforts, a boycott of the Florida orange juice industry ensued, effectively ending Bryant's lucrative endorsement deal and eventually ending her career.

Legal protections were first made available on other fronts in the 1980s. In 1982, Wisconsin became the first state to outlaw discrimination on the basis of sexual orientation. While this might seem strange, given that the state passed an anti-gay marriage amendment in 2006, commentator William B. Turner argues that this "is quite consistent with a long history of profound ambivalence about lesbian/gay civil rights claims in the American public. Historically, support for equal employment rights for lesbians and gay men—one of the key provisions of Chapter 112, 1981 Wisconsin Laws 7—has been high, while support for recognition of lesbians' and gay men's families, including marriage and adoption, has been much lower." He notes that "for many years after passage of Chapter 112, Wisconsinites would appear at national LGBT [lesbian, gay, bisexual and transgender] civil rights events with signs declaring Wisconsin to be 'The Gay Rights State.' " See William B. Turner, *"The Gay Rights State": Wisconsin's Pioneering Legislation to Prohibit Discrimination Based on Sexual Orientation*, 22 WIS. WOMEN'S L.J. 91 (2007). 1984 was the first year that domestic partnership benefits were affirmatively considered by a local government, when the City of Berkeley, California enacted a policy to offer these benefits to their city and school district employees. The registry, however, was not created until 1991. The gender-neutral policy was open to gay and heterosexual couples.

President Clinton's disappointing 1993 "Don't Ask, Don't Tell" military policy was effectively dissolved in December 2010, clearing the way to allow gays and lesbians finally to serve openly in the U.S. military. Another disappointment during President Clinton's tenure was the passage of the federal "Defense of Marriage Act (DOMA)," in 1996, in response to early marriage efforts in Hawaii. However, in 1998 President Clinton did issue Executive Order 13087, which banned the federal government from discriminating on the basis of sexual orientation in employment. Not surprisingly, the order was controversial.

Other legal milestones include the United States Supreme Court trilogy of gay rights cases: *Bowers v. Hardwick*, 478 U.S. 186, 106 S.Ct. 2841, 92 L.Ed.2d 140 (1986); *Romer v. Evans*, 517 U.S. 620, 116 S.Ct. 1620, 134 L.Ed.2d 855 (1996); and *Lawrence v. Texas,* 539 U.S. 558, 123 S.Ct. 2472, 156 L.Ed.2d 508 (2003). Current litigation as this edition goes to press in 2011 involves questions of relationship recognition, including challenges to the constitutionality of DOMA.

DISCUSSION

1. What makes the gay rights movement similar to (or different from) the civil rights movement for African Americans? To the movement for women's liberation?

2. Do you think that the history of the gay rights movement should be included in textbooks for school children?

II. PASSING, COMING OUT, AND THE STRUGGLE FOR GAY IDENTITY*

For much of this nation's history, the passing norm was not even available for contestation. While the demand to convert was in place, it would have been foolhardy for gays to contest the demand to pass, as coming out would only have exposed the individual to the more stringent demand to convert. The painful irony of early gay activism is that its most prominent actors were pseudonymous or anonymous. Hungarian writer Karoly Benkert coined the word "homosexual" in 1869 writing as "Dr. M." Activist Edward Sagarin penned the first American tract for gay equality in 1951, as Donald Webster Cory, a pseudonym that may have been an oblique reference to Andre Gide's pro-homosexual *Corydon*. The names of the pre-Stonewall gay rights organizations were similarly obscure. The Mattachine Society, founded in 1950, was modeled on a group of medieval French bachelors of the same name. The Society identified itself as "a group of persons (not necessarily variants), interested in doing research, education and conducting social action for the benefit of the variant minority and, in turn, for the benefit of society as a whole." Its publication, *One,* referred to a Thomas Carlyle quotation—"A mystic bond of brotherhood makes all men one." The Daughters of Bilitis, a lesbian organization founded in 1955, took its name from *Songs of Bilitis,* a collection of prose poems by Pierre Louys.

Straights similarly shrouded homosexuality in a stigmatizing silence that drew on a long tradition of treating homosexuality as unspeakable. To take but one of many examples, the sodomy statutes regulating same-sex sexual conduct, which until 1961 were on the books in every state,

* Excerpted from Kenji Yoshino, *Covering*, 111 YALE L. J. 769 (2002) (internal citation omitted).

often referred to the proscribed activity no more specifically than as a "crime against nature." Silence in this era did not signify tolerance for homosexuality, but was rather a means of sexual regulation. The nexus between silence and disgust has long been captured in the preteritive formulations of the homosexual possibility—sodomy was the "sin which should neither be named nor committed," or the "detestable and abominable sin, amongst Christians not to be named" or the "sin so odious that the fame of it will fright the damned in the darksome pit."

It is true that straights in the pre-Stonewall years would sometimes loft gays into visibility by ferreting homosexuals out of their closets. Perhaps the most famous of these witch hunts were those conducted in the Navy in the 1920s, and in the federal civil service in the late 1940s to 1950s. Such witch hunts, however, were not sustained, in part because they inevitably revealed more than the hunters cared to know, outing individuals they did not wish to classify as gay. More to the point, even as they broke the code of gay silence, the witch hunts only served to strengthen it. The pressure on gays to pass became stronger when mainstream society disrespected the closet door. In an age of conversion, the closet door opened only from the outside.

As conventionally told, all of this changed with the Stonewall riots in 1969. When the police raided the Stonewall Inn, gay patrons of the bar refused to go quietly. Barricading themselves in the bar, they alternately hurled out beer bottles and slogans like "Gay Power ..." The riots did not last the week, and the mainstream press accorded them no great significance. Yet the riots imaginatively inaugurated the gay rights movement. As Cindy Patton describes it, "Stonewall divides a timeless time of oppression from the entry into the Time of History. *Before 1969:* we could only chafe and give up our fullest possibilities. *After 1969*: we could say who we are and in the unifying power of our speech, fight back."

What made Stonewall loom so large was that it dramatized a systematic resistance to the passing demand. The bar itself could be seen as a symbolic closet, over which gays had finally wrested control. In denying the police access to this space, gays emphasized the closet's protective rather than its confining dimensions. Yet in publicizing that space, gays paved the way for other anti-passing events by making themselves visible in unprecedented ways. The riots called forth a new set of gay activist organizations, including the Gay Liberation Front, Radicalesbians, and the Third World Gay Revolution. These groups unabashedly identified themselves as "gay." There was no talk among these new activists of disguising their mission with ambiguous titles—no homophile, no Mattachine, no Bilitis. These groups brought a militant visibility to gay rights politics. Proclaiming the necessity of "coming out of the closet" as the first essential step toward freedom, these groups acted on their beliefs by being as visible as they could in every sphere of life. They conducted sit-ins in the offices of newspapers and magazines that purveyed demeaning images of homosexuals; they marched in the street to protest police harassment; they disrupted the conventions of psychiatrists who proclaimed them to be sick; they occupied campus buildings to win concessions from university administrators. On the one-year anniversary of Stonewall, these activists organized the first gay pride march in New York, which drew out between five and fifteen thousand marchers. This march was by far the city's biggest gay demonstration, and, unlike Stonewall itself, made the front page of the *New York Times.*

The 1973 *DSM* deletion[1] also marked a watershed in the fight against passing norms. The deletion demonstrates how conversion norms and passing norms are intricated with each other. On the one hand, passing norms had to be sufficiently eroded to enable the political mobilization that would permit the contestation of the medical establishment's conversion norms. On the other hand, the formal retirement of this conversion norm created the analytic license further to contest passing norms. As Roy Cain has noted, "When homosexuality was considered pathological, secretiveness about one's homosexuality was widely viewed as normal and desirable; openness, conversely, was seen as an expression of personal and social pathology and as a political liability to gays in general. Yet 'when homosexuality was normalized, openness about one's homosexual preferences came to be viewed as desirable, while secretiveness came to be seen as problematic.' " If homosexuality was not a sickness, it became hard to justify why homosexuals should have to keep silent about their condition.

Many of the post-Stonewall developments that contested the passing norm were more diffuse than the Stonewall riots or the *DSM* deletion, including the recuperation of gay history, the flowering of gay publications, and the coming out of public and private figures. Beginning with Jonathan Ned Katz's *Gay American History* in 1977, professional and amateur historians sought to make homosexuality visible in the past as well as in the present. These efforts were embodied not only in scholarly and popular books, but also in the grass-roots gay history projects that sprang up in various American cities in the late 1970s—perhaps most notably New York City's Lesbian Herstory Archives. . . .

Other grass-roots publications spoke to the contemporary situation of gays. Rodger Streitmatter takes the proliferation of gay-themed publications during the 1970s as an indication that disparate strands of gay rights had finally coalesced into a movement. These publications included the following: *GAY*, *Come Out!*, *Gay Times*, and *Gay Flames*, in New York City; *Gay Sunshine* and the *San Francisco Gay Free Press* in San Francisco; *Lavender Vision* in Boston; *Gay Liberator* in Detroit; and *Killer Dyke* in Chicago. Again, these publications made explicit reference to homosexuality in their titles, in contrast to earlier homophile publications such as *One* or *The Ladder*. This new emphasis on visibility was also at the substantive core of these journals. Thus the first issue of *Come Out!* sounded a clarion call to its readers:

1. In 1973, the American Psychiatric Association deleted 'homosexuality' from its *Diagnostic and Statistical Manual of Mental Disorders*.

> Come out for freedom! Come out now! Power to the people! Gay power to gay people! Come out of the closet before the door is nailed shut! *Come Out!* COME OUT to fight for the freedom of the homosexual; to give voice to the rapidly growing militancy within our community; to provide a public forum for the discussion and clarification of methods and actions necessary to end our oppression.

These publications not only exhorted their readers toward visibility but also performatively enacted that visibility, demonstrating the existence of a gay community of writers and readers. While none of these publications was national in scope, they opened up discursive spaces populated by an imagined community of readers. Particularly in a pre-Internet age, these publications were doubtlessly a significant medium through which closeted individuals caught their first glimpse of life on the outside.

One function served by both scholarly and popular publications was the naming of names. Englishman A.L. Rowse's *Homosexuals in History* might stand as the best-known academic book of this genre, sketching famous "gay" historical figures from Richard the Lionhearted to Oscar Wilde. Popular publications similarly provided a running tally of contemporary gay names: *Gay Sunshine* reported that "1976 saw the public coming out of a number of writers and other public figures: culture analyst Charles Reich, . . . footballer Dave Kopay, painter Paul Cadmus, . . . Olympic skating champion John Curry, [and] poets Adrienne Rich and Walter Rinder." The post-Stonewall decades also saw the emergence of numerous volumes of "coming out" narratives, which gave eloquent first-person testimony to the power of self-identification. Thus, Adrienne Rich wrote in her foreword to *The Coming Out Stories:*

> I keep thinking about power. The intuitive flash of power that "coming-out" can give: I have an indestructible memory of walking along a particular block in New York City, the hour after I had acknowledged to myself that I loved a woman, feeling invincible. For the first time in my life I experienced sexuality as clarifying my mind instead of hazing it over; that passion, once named, flung a long, imperative beam of light into my future. I knew my life was decisively and forever different; and that change felt to me like power. In "coming-out" over and over to others—to old friends, in the classroom, in print, at a poetry reading, in the study hall of the girls' school I had long ago attended—each time, both fear and the renewal of that sense of power. And I ask myself, what is the fear about? That I can no longer "pass"? that I will see expressions alter, walls go up between my students and me, my old friends and me, some audience and me—that I will be dismissed, discredited, seen as monster?—or is it the fear of that old/new power, perhaps even some genetic imprinting of what was done to us of old, when we acted on our power?
>
> I don't know. But I think "coming-out"—that first permission we give ourselves to name our love for women as love, to say, I am a lesbian,

> but also the successive "comings-out" to the world ... is connected with power, connects us with power, and until we believe that we have the right not merely to our love but to our power, we will continue to do harm among ourselves, fearing that power in each other and in ourselves.

This passage captures how coming out is simultaneously an intensely personal and an intensely political act; indeed, a way of transforming the personal into the political. For this reason, in the post-Stonewall years, much pressure was placed on politically conscious gays to come out. As John D'Emilio puts it, "Among activists, coming out of the closet became the gay equivalent to a biblical injunction. Those who remained in the closet had a shadow cast over their moral character. Their integrity was suspect, their courage lacking, their identity uncertain."

Given these many years of anti-passing activism, one might ask why passing norms have remained so robust. For there is no doubt that the passing norm has survived post-Stonewall activism....

... The endurance of the norm cannot be understood without reference to the relational aspect of passing, in which both the performance of the gay individual and the literacy of the straight audience are implicated. On the gay side, two aspects of passing have made it particularly difficult to contest. First ... passing can occur in a selective manner.... [T]here are individuals in one's audience: "[E]very encounter with a new class full of students, to say nothing of a new boss, social worker, loan officer, landlord, doctor, erects new closets [that] ... exact from at least [some] gay people new surveys, new calculations, new draughts and requisitions of secrecy or disclosure." The multiplicity of gay closets means that gays can choose to be open to pro-gay audiences while remaining closeted to anti-gay ones. That gays have exercised this choice is unsurprising, as many entitlements can turn on selective closeting. Yet while this selectivity might be empowering for individual homosexuals, it has inhibited the ways in which the gay rights movement has been able to resist the passing norm. This collective action problem is what gives color to the wish expressed by gay activists that all gays would turn blue, a transformation that would make gays, like most racial minorities, unable to pick and choose among their audiences.

. . .

Straights have also contributed to the intractability of the passing norm. Much of this contribution has taken the form of generic anti-gay bias that increases the costs of gay self-disclosure. Yet some aspects of it are specific to passing. In his discussion of passing, Erving Goffman observed that passing depends not only on the performance of the individual attempting to conceal the trait, but also on the "decoding capacity" of her audience. Passing norms are thus maintained not only by gays who do not come out, but by straights who do not recognize a homosexual when they see one.

It may be difficult to see how such ignorance about gays could subordinate them. The Enlightenment equation of knowledge with power tends to underscore how ignorance has diminished the power of straights to regulate homosexuality. Yet this should not obscure how a studied ignorance has also increased that power. Survey after survey has demonstrated that straights who know homosexual individuals are much more likely to be pro-gay suggesting that anti-gay animus is much easier to preserve when its purveyors are ignorant of homosexuality. It should thus not surprise that a homophobic society should strive to keep its members willfully ignorant of homosexuality, as exemplified by the substance of "no promo homo" statutes and the rhetoric of "crime against nature" statutes. Ignorance of homosexuality is an ignorance into which straights have been laboriously schooled.

The passing norm has thus proved so powerful because it has been secured by a bilateral social contract between gays and straights. Not until the formulation of the military's policy in 1993 was this contract dubbed "don't ask, don't tell." Yet the arrangement long predated the military policy. The military policy did not spring from the head of Congress, but grew organically out of an underlying culture, taking its strength from the depth of that culture. What did it mean, after all, for Spitzer and Powell to say that they knew no homosexuals? In a post-Kinsey age, these individuals should surely have confronted the claim that such a statement was statistically unviable. That no such cognitive reconciliation occurred suggests that these individuals did not wish to have that knowledge, even as they deployed power that would have enormous consequences over those they sought not to know. It also suggests that there were gay individuals who did not seek to educate them into that knowledge. In this sense, "don't ask, don't tell" did not create, but rather diagnosed, an underlying convention that pervaded the culture.

. . .

Three decades after Stonewall, passing norms still have a grip on American society. It is true that more and more gays are coming out of the closet, and that straight literacy about gay culture has increased significantly. Yet the modality through which gays come out is still selective and individual, and the privilege of unknowing is still powerfully deployed by straights. It continues to be true that "for many gay people [the closet] is still the fundamental feature of social life; and there can be few gay people, however courageous and forthright by habit, however fortunate in the support of their immediate communities, in whose lives the closet is not still a shaping presence."

One might counter that even if passing norms endure, the fact that they have replaced conversion norms in many areas reflects significantly decreased animus toward gays. Unlike conversion, passing is something that all gays are assumed to be able to do. Moreover, replacing the demand to convert with the demand to pass seems to create a zone of privacy in which gays can maintain their identities so long as they do not make them public.

. . .

... But it may be that conversion and passing are tightly intertwined concepts, such that social actors can sometimes achieve the same ends under either regime. Indeed, Janet Halley has argued that passing is a form of conversion. She maintains that when individuals pass, the "result is no mere fib: it is a change." She continues: "To be sure, what has changed is not the supposed essence of sexual orientation, but the representation of it available for social interpretation. But essences, conceding for a moment their existence, are not visible to legislatures, judges, employers, or police. Social agents work with social meaning...."

Halley here suggests that like Bishop Berkeley's tree, gays may not exist in at least some senses unless they are perceived. To be homosexual is, in part, to be acknowledged and interpellated by others as such. This is the import of the gay rights slogan "I am out therefore I am." In other work, I have posited for this reason that gay identity may be linguistically performative, such that "I am gay" is akin to formulations like "I promise," "I contract," or *"J'accuse,"* in creating the substance it may seem only to describe. This may explain the transformation—a kind of ontological shudder—that some gays describe on intoning these words for the first time.

One might resist this conflation of passing and conversion by observing that many homosexuals routinely pass without feeling that they have converted. Yet this is not strictly a distinction between conversion and passing, but one between audiences. Gays do not feel as if they have converted even when passing to others because they are not passing *to themselves*. For individuals who do not know what they are in their own eyes, the acquisition of particular forms of knowledge may be experienced as change. The assumption of "no promo homo" is that such sexual waverers might, through knowledge about homosexuality, come to know themselves as homosexuals, and, in that instant, become homosexuals.

This convergence between conversion and passing should lead us to question the extent to which a shift in rhetoric from the demand to convert to the demand to pass actually signifies a change in the status hierarchy between straights and gays. For many third parties, after all, the distinction between converted and closeted homosexuals is no distinction at all. In the eyes of such third parties, neither the converted nor the closeted homosexual registers as a homosexual, thereby permitting such third parties entirely to ignore the existence of homosexuality.

III. PLACE AND MOVEMENT IN GAY AMERICAN HISTORY: A CASE FROM THE POST–WORLD WAR II SOUTH*

Difficulties in researching and uncovering the history of lesbians, gay men, and bisexuals in the United States are compounded when the inquiry is focused on a section that has been particularly hostile to sexual difference—the American South. Archivists and university administrators often express reservations about the validity of the field; families seeking to preserve the "good name" of their relatives routinely deny access to materials; and, as in any other part of the country, traditional historical sources remain largely silent with regard to homosexuality prior to the 1960s. Thus, oral history serves a vital role in reclaiming the lesbian, gay, and bisexual past, especially in the South.

Barry Kline (not his real name) is one of only a handful of older Alabamians who, given the state's persistent legal and societal strictures, is willing to discuss frankly his experiences as a gay man of the South. A resident of Birmingham since his birth in 1917, Kline "came out," as he terms it in retrospect, at the age of twenty-eight just after returning home from serving in World War II. Kline's story exemplifies many of the major themes outlined by gay historians. As in other parts of the U.S., urbanization, economic independence, public space, the gay bar, friendship networks, casual sex, and intimate relationships all were central to the formation of gay cultures and gay identities in Birmingham. However, the events from Kline's life complicate some of the leading assumptions surrounding U.S. gay life in the twentieth century, particularly the significance of the religious and medical professions.

Race, class, gender, and the attendant levels of social and physical mobility figure prominently in Kline's description of mid-twentieth-century gay life. The ability to travel, both to nearby rural areas and to other cities, provided a means of escape from familial pressure and police persecution—factors that, though prevalent in other parts of the U.S., were especially restrictive in the Deep South in the postwar period. Moreover, and perhaps most significantly, Kline's story encourages us to re-think the role of place and movement in U.S. gay history....

. . .

Upon his return in 1946 from Europe, where he served as a lieutenant in the U.S. Army, Barry Kline began to build a friendship with a boyhood acquaintance, Robert Holley. "Here I had 120 days of [paid] leave and all of that," says Kline, "so I wasn't anxious to get down to work." Holley, who was employed in his family's dry goods business, "didn't go to work until ten o'clock in the morning," so the two were free to stay out late into the evening and explore the nightlife of a postwar Southern city.

---

* John Howard, *Place and Movement in Gay American History: A Case from the Post–World War II South, in* BRETT BEEMYN, CREATING A PLACE FOR OURSELVES (1997).

Kline recalls how his friendship with Holley suddenly developed into a romance:

> We eventually, one night, wound up out by what was Edgewood Lake and got in a very serious discussion. And I had no idea what it all amounted to. But somehow or other I began to shake.... It wasn't because I was cold. It had to do with what we were talking about. I don't remember. But he took the bull by the horn and says, "I'm going to kiss you." And I didn't object.

Though he had experienced several homosexual encounters during his youth and early adulthood, Kline views that particular night as his coming out. Holley differed in important ways from Kline's previous partners, who typically were strangers he met during his travels or childhood pals of a lower socioeconomic class.

The fact that class distinctions structured Kline's own sense of identity is evident in his description of Robert as compared to two sex partners from his youth, a flamboyant set of twins. The twins, according to Kline, "really never did earn a good living. I mean, they were never successful. They did menial jobs, odd jobs." Their open avowal of homosexuality inevitably led Kline to ponder his own sexual orientation: "It was a great big question in my mind as whether I was or wasn't [But] I just couldn't be like those twins." Robert, on the other hand, represented a type and class of person with whom Kline could readily identify:

> Well, ... I was older. I was twenty-eight by that time, twenty-seven. I was doing this thing with somebody who was, I guess, a respected member of the community. And I began to meet other people who were doing the same sort of thing. It made me realize that I was not the only one in the world.

Indeed Holley, who at age thirty-three had long since accepted his gay identity, was able to introduce Kline to the white gay male culture that was emerging in and around Birmingham.

Gay life existed on the margins of so-called mainstream culture in Alabama. A small, select circle of Kline's friends, "circumspect I guess you would say," would occasionally gather for parties in homes or apartments, usually late at night. If they ventured into more public realms, gay white men frequented straight establishments only outside of regular or peak operating hours, or they found clubs that catered to a homosexual clientele but that typically were located on the outskirts of town. In downtown Birmingham, the Bouvet and the Jewel Box at the elegant Tutwiler Hotel, the Red Room at the Redmont Hotel, and the Stirrup Cup at the Thomas Jefferson Hotel all tolerated groups of gay men, provided they understood the primacy of heterosexual patrons. According to Kline, the Stirrup Cup, for example, would become a hub of activity only after a measure of secrecy and safety was assured:

> I remember one Saturday. You know everybody would go in there and have drinks and sit around the tables. Had two black waiters who

didn't know what was going on. One Saturday night I remember, ... I guess it was around ten o'clock. Well, the last straight couple left out of there, and somebody stood up and said, "The meeting will come to order. Will the secretary read the minutes of the last meeting?" Up until that time, everybody was only involved in talking to their immediate companions. And then of course after that everybody got chummy-chummy.

Kline remembers an unnamed, tarpaper shack honky-tonk southwest of the city on the Bessemer Superhighway "where the owner would let us dance together." And "from time to time, there were things over the mountain in Homewood," including the Little Southerner, which featured a lesbian pianist from New Orleans who played classics and boogie-woogie. But such bars were short-lived, says Kline, and most, like the Little Southerner, eventually "changed ownership, and gradually they ran everybody away."

As in other Southern cities during the late forties and fifties, men also congregated in public parks after dark to find friends or sex partners. In Woodrow Wilson Park (later renamed Linn Park), situated between City Hall and the Public Library, a man out walking might subtly proposition another by asking for a match. Or a man circling the park in his car might first establish prolonged eye contact with a passerby, then stop to strike up a conversation. Kline says that "any and all kinds" of people could be found in the park, but this diversity was largely limited to white men of varied socioeconomic classes. Many women were reluctant to walk downtown after dark unless escorted, and blacks would not have been found there, as city parks were racially segregated by law. Thus "cruising," like so much of homosexual interaction in and near Birmingham, was predicated on a complex web of forces, not the least of which were gender and race.

. . .

... Medical authorities also were critical agents in the expanding discourse on homosexuality during the Second World War, when millions of U.S. armed service recruits were asked about the nature of their sexual relations in routine pre-induction interviews, and numerous enlisted women and men were interrogated in occasional post-induction purges. Yet doctors might have had less influence than previously thought on the lives of individual lesbians, gay men, and bisexuals. Barry Kline recalls only once mentioning his perceived sexual problems to a physician, a military doctor, when he considered getting married prior to leaving the U.S. for active duty:

> I met a girl ... in Alexandria [Louisiana] that I liked very, very much, and we dated and carried on.... It was Camp Livingston, which was north of Alexandria.... I said, "You know, I don't know what's going to happen with this war." Maybe it was after Pearl Harbor that I said, "No, I'm not going to get married because I just don't know what's going to happen." This was early '42. I did talk to one of the

battalion physicians. I said, "Hey Doc, you've met Ella Barnes. You know I like her very, very much, but the idea of getting a hard-on—it just doesn't get to me." And he says, "Oh, ... there's nothing wrong." He says, "If we were back in Philadelphia, I'd know who to send you to, but ... I wouldn't worry." He says, "You're away from home. It's a different life. You don't have big pectorals. So you're not queer."

Kline placed little faith in such assessments. Eventually, he grew to ignore the pronouncements on homosexuality made by medical professionals. Although he might have self-identified as gay within the broader context of an extensive scientific discourse, it was without the advice, counsel, or consternation of any particular physician or psychiatrist.

Unlike many other gay men of the postwar South, Kline also seemed unaffected by the region's pervasive religious fervor, which is especially distinctive in the Southern lesbian, gay, and bisexual experience. An upper-middle-class Jew in a historically poor and Protestant state, Kline never mentions having consulted a rabbi or other cleric. He doesn't recall any religiously based condemnations of homosexuality in sermons or in the press. Nor does he remember any concerted efforts by the churches and synagogues of Birmingham to persecute lesbians, gays, and bisexuals.

Foremost among the concerns of Barry Kline were being arrested by the police and being discovered by his and his friends' relatives. The fear of disclosure often persisted even after death. Such was the case with Kline's longtime partner, Robert Holley: "We were a thing for several years there," according to Kline. And while the two suffered their share of lovers' quarrels, resulting primarily from Kline's dalliances while Holley was away on business in New York, the two remained close until Holley's life was cut short in 1957.

Even today, Kline's anxiety over the events surrounding Holley's funeral continues, reflecting the clandestine, conspiratorial nature of homosexual relationships vis-a-vis families:

> Robert died. [He] Had a cerebral hemorrhage in a hotel in New York on one of his trips. I don't know what his family thought. You know, the times he used to leave the Cadillac convertible for me to drive.... But when he died, they didn't ask me to be a pallbearer. His sister [Susie] couldn't stand me. She tolerated me but she could not stand me until the day she died. Although one, her youngest son ... calls me Uncle Barry to this day. And Susie's husband was very cordial to me, Robert's brother was cordial to me, but Susie and his mother were not that cordial. I think they figured out what was going on and resented it very much....

* * *

Despite the safeguards they took, like locating many gay establishments outside of the city limits, gay men nonetheless ran up against law enforcement officers who were determined to thwart the growth of gay social networks and maintain the marginalization of sexual deviants. In the early fifties, after neighbors burned down a suburban house noted for its late night parties in the ironically named Queenstown Lake development, Barry Kline and his friends began to frequent a private-home-turned-gay-hotspot in Shelby County, roughly forty miles southeast of the city. County officials raided the property, arresting the owner and citing several patrons for liquor violations. As Kline describes it:

> [A] young fellow came here as an automobile salesman. He was not making a living, and he rented a house down in Shelby County. He says, "Well I'm going to throw some Saturday night parties and see if I can't make ends meet by charging a dollar," which he did. I went down there a couple of times. . . .
>
> [One night,] probably around eleven thirty, I ran into somebody who said, "Let's go down to Biff's in the next county, Shelby County, to the house for a party." And I said, "Oh, I don't know." But then I said, "Okay, I'll go. . . . Let me get some alcohol." I carried a flask of Canadian Club in my glove compartment. I said, "I don't know whether I want a drink, but I'll just take it in case I do." So I put it in my coat pocket and got in Scott's car, and we drove down there. And the minute we turned off of Highway 280, there was a car parked. He flagged us down. Turned out to be the sheriff and his men. Well, they opened the trunk and poured out all Scott's whiskey—he had about five quarts in there—and gave him a ticket. If I hadn't had that flask on me, I wouldn't have gotten a ticket. But they took my flask and poured out the whiskey and gave me the flask back and gave me a ticket. . . . Of course, that was the end of Biff's place down there. [The sheriff] had been there before. And they had already made the raid. . . . [T]hey arrested Biff, . . . he [got] out on bond, [and] he skipped town.

But it wasn't until several years later, the summer of 1962, that Kline was involved in a police action that he says "changed [his] life." Two men from Nashville, who had been contracted to renovate a dwelling on 31st Street on Birmingham's more affluent Southside, decided to give an after-hours party in the house, where they lived while construction was under-way. On that hot Saturday evening, neighbors heard the noise through open windows and called the police. A paddy wagon arrived and carried four loads of men, thirty-eight in all, to jail. Arrested along with the others on charges of disorderly conduct and visiting a disorderly house, Barry Kline was freed after posting a bond. He later paid a fine. But the most damaging result of the incident happened a few days later with the listing of the arrestees' names and addresses in a local daily newspaper. . . .

Birmingham's infamous police chief and politician Eugene "Bull" Connor turned the event to his advantage, publicly boasting that the police force had successfully squelched a homosexual "convention." Apparently noticing that the hosts were Tennesseans and a few of the party guests were out-of-state residents—mostly former Birminghamians who had moved on—Connor concluded that the queer gathering was the work of outsiders, just as he mistakenly construed civil rights unrest as the stirrings of the ubiquitous "outside agitators." Nevertheless, the police crackdown on homosexuality had lasting repercussions for natives such as Barry Kline, who feels "it traumatized [him]." Afterwards, even when he traveled to relatively safe havens such as Chicago, he would be "scared to death" that the gay bars he visited would be raided and his sexuality would be exposed to the folks back home.

. . .

Traveling extensively from a young age, Kline met gay men from other cities as early as the 1930s, when as a teenager he and his family spent their summers in Miami. As an adult, Kline took regular trips out of town thereby reducing—if only temporarily—the pressures of life in a hostile environment. After World War II, he regularly made at least one major excursion out of Birmingham each year. Though many of these were business trips, as he became a board member and then an officer of a national trade association, he made time during the meetings and conventions to explore the gay nightlife of his destinations, and met a number of men with whom he developed satisfying, if fleeting, sexual relationships. In the late forties and fifties alone, he visited Miami, Orlando, Richmond, Philadelphia, Atlantic City, New York, Boston, Buffalo, Cleveland, Chicago, New Orleans, Dallas, Los Angeles, and San Francisco, among other cities. In addition, with groups of friends he often drove down to the Gulf Coast of Florida.

Such excursions, and the sexual opportunities they enabled, were direct functions of Kline's race, class, and gender. Whereas scholars Elizabeth Kennedy and Madeline Davis found that working-class lesbians' "defiant," nothing-to-lose attitudes fostered a direct, combative "community of resistance" in 1950s Buffalo, a significant segment of white gay male culture in Birmingham—the monied elite—utilized class prerogatives wherever possible to sidestep confrontations with intrusive police officers, irksome family members, and acrimonious townspeople. Most poorer gays in Birmingham could not have afforded the automobile that allowed men like Barry Kline to patronize gay establishments on the city's outskirts, much less could they have borne the cost of train or plane fares to distant cities or paid the rent on a "trick house." Lesbians in Birmingham faced not only economic marginalization, but also gender obstacles, including limits on their mobility which made the development of a women's community along the lines of the gay male culture unthinkable. And blacks in the Jim Crow South were burdened with oppression of a different sort; the police and the media focused on the Civil Rights Movement and the heroic attempts to overturn racial segregation, while the struggles of the African–American community's lesbians, gays, and bisexuals were further eclipsed, made even more marginal. Kline and his friends built one of the Deep South's early homosexual cultures upon a foundation of white, male, upper-middle-class privilege. With legal and political persecution of lesbians, gays, and bisexuals widespread throughout the U.S., these strategies appear to have been very effective for the few who could pursue them.

. . .

Barry Kline did not move to the city for economic or sexual reasons, as was the case with many gay migrants. Born in Birmingham, his need for mobility arose out of a need to free himself of family obligations and the possible threat of police persecution. Yet Kline's identity as a gay man was established and reinforced by his connection to his hometown and friends, most of whom belonged to the same socioeconomic class. Kline insists that he accepted his homosexuality after discovering, through Robert Holley and his social circle, that he was "not the only one in the world." But surely Kline had known this before. He had had sporadic homosexual liaisons for over ten years in various parts of the world. Significantly, however, the ability to categorize himself as gay and to identify with other gay men came only after an intense attachment to a fellow Birmingham native, Robert Holley, and an increasing involvement in a structured, localized gay community. While others found community by moving to the city, Kline found it, after traveling the globe, only by returning home. Yet home, as always, became transformed as a result of experiences in different places.

The prevalent theoretical model among lesbian and gay historians—a model that is distinctly modernist in its totalizing, linear construction—would have us view cities as centrifugal forces, magnets that pull isolated individuals from the hinterlands into large urban centers, where they could recognize their sexualities, find one another, and become a community. This causal schema, a long-term historical trajectory mirroring innovations in transportation and communication, denies rural people the ability to act and think—that is, to attach meanings to their sexual desires and behaviors.

Barry Kline's life suggests the need for a new postmodern gay history in which cities would be seen as centripetal forces—locations from which emanate any number of forays and journeys, many which were short-term, leading to a variety of opportunities for encounters, meetings, and rendezvous. Of course, such movements and interpersonal connections need never involve cities at all, such that we can begin to see avenues rather than venues, spokes rather than hubs. Certainly for those friends of Barry Kline who relocated to Birmingham from small-town and rural Alabama, life did not begin with the move. Their wanderings and wonderings preceded the rural-to-urban exodus and likely included a number of different sexual situations.

In the mid-century South, there functioned a sense of space markedly at variance from that of the dense, congested landscape of the East Coast, for example, and these instances of coming together, often one-on-one, regularly involved automobiles. Cars thus were conduits—tangible, material manifestations of a more accurate sexual mapping of the United States.

While class privilege eased movement and greatly facilitated the construction of gay identity for Kline and his friends, economic advantage cannot be construed solely as a means for circumventing oppressive forces or for avoiding confrontations. In Birmingham, throwing a party, patronizing a bar, driving the roads, or even walking the streets could precipitate a contentious encounter with the police. As a result, resistance in the 1950s often took subtle, but still empowering, forms.

IV. THE KINSEY STUDIES: SEXUAL BEHAVIOR IN THE HUMAN MALE*

In the total male population, single and married, between adolescence and old age, 24 per cent of the total outlet is derived from solitary sources (masturbation and nocturnal emissions), 69.4 per cent is derived from heterosexual sources (petting and coitus), and 6.3 per cent of the total number of orgasms is derived from homosexual contacts. It is not more than 0.3 per cent of the outlet which is derived from relations with animals of other species.

Homosexual contacts account, therefore, for a rather small but still significant portion of the total outlet of the human male. The significance of the homosexual is, furthermore, much greater than the frequencies of outlet may indicate, because a considerable portion of the population, perhaps the major portion of the male population, has at least some homosexual experience between adolescence and old age. In addition, about 60 per cent of the pre-adolescent boys engage in homosexual activities, and there is an additional group of adult males who avoid overt contacts but who are quite aware of their potentialities for reacting to other males.

The social significance of the homosexual is considerably emphasized by the fact that both Jewish and Christian churches have considered this aspect of human sexuality to be abnormal and immoral. Social custom and our Anglo-American law are sometimes very severe in penalizing one who is discovered to have had homosexual relations. In consequence, many persons who have had such experience are psychically disturbed, and not a few of them have been in open conflict with the social organization.

It is, therefore, peculiarly difficult to secure factual data concerning the nature and the extent of the homosexual in Western European or American cultures, and even more difficult to find strictly objective presentations of such data as are available. Most of the literature on the homosexual represents either a polemic against the heinous abnormality of such activity, or a biased argument in defense of an individual's right to choose his patterns of sexual behavior.

* Excerpted from ALFRED KINSEY, WARDELL POMERY & CLYDE MARTIN, *Homosexual Outlet, in* SEXUAL BEHAVIOR IN THE HUMAN MALE 610 (1948). Reprinted by permission of the Kinsey Institute for Research in Sex, Gender, and Reproduction, Inc.

Until the extent of any type of human behavior is adequately known, it is difficult to assess its significance, either to the individuals who are involved or to society as a whole; and until the extent of the homosexual is known, it is practically impossible to understand its biological or social origins. It is one thing if we are dealing with a type of activity that is unusual, without precedent among other animals, and restricted to peculiar types of individuals within the human population. It is another thing if the phenomenon proves to be a fundamental part, not only of human sexuality, but of mammalian patterns as a whole. The present chapter is, therefore, wholly confined to an analysis of the data which we now have on the incidence and the frequencies of homosexual activity in the white male population in this country.

. . .

Definition

For nearly a century the term homosexual in connection with human behavior has been applied to sexual relations, either overt or psychic, between individuals of the same sex. Derived from the Greek root *homo* rather than from the Latin word for man, the term emphasizes the *sameness* of the two individuals who are involved in a sexual relation. The word is, of course, patterned after and intended to represent the antithesis of the word heterosexual, which applies to a relation between individuals of different sexes.

The term homosexual has had an endless list of synonyms in the technical vocabularies and a still greater list in the vernaculars. The terms homogenic love, contrasexuality, homo-erotism, similisexualism, uranism and others have been used in English (Legman in Henry 1941). The terms sexual inversion, intersexuality, transsexuality, the third sex, psychosexual hermaphroditism, and others have been applied not merely to designate the nature of the partner involved in the sexual relation, but to emphasize the general opinion that individuals engaging in homosexual activity are neither male nor female, but persons of mixed sex. These latter terms are, however, most unfortunate, for they provide an interpretation in anticipation of any sufficient demonstration of the fact; and consequently they prejudice investigations of the nature and origin of homosexual activity.

The term Lesbian, referring to such female homosexual relations as were immortalized in the poetry of Sappho of the Greek Isle of Lesbos, has gained considerable usage within recent years, particularly in some of the larger Eastern cities where the existence of female homosexuality is more generally recognized by the public at large. Although there can be no objection to designating relations between females by a special term, it should be recognized that such activities are quite the equivalent of sexual relations between males....

If the term homosexual is restricted as it should be, the homosexuality or heterosexuality of any activity becomes apparent by determining the sexes of the two individuals involved in the relationship. For instance, mouth-genital contacts between males and females are certainly heterosexual, even though persons may think of them as homosexual. And although one may hear of a male "who has sex relations with his wife in a homosexual way," there is no logic in such a use of the term, and analyses of the behavior and of the motivations of the behavior in such cases do not show them necessarily related to any homosexual experience.

On the other hand, the homosexuality of certain relationships between individuals of the same sex may be denied by some persons, because the situation does not fulfill other criteria that they think should be attached to the definition. Mutual masturbation between two males may be dismissed, even by certain clinicians, as not homosexual, because oral or anal relations or particular levels of psychic response are required, according to their concept of homosexuality. There are persons who insist that the active male in an anal relation is essentially heterosexual in his behavior, and that the passive male in the same relation is the only one who is homosexual. These, however, are misapplications of terms, which are often unfortunate because they obscure the interpretations of the situation which the clinician is supposed to help by his analysis.

These misinterpretations are often encouraged by the very persons who are having homosexual experience. Some males who are being regularly fellated by other males without, however, ever performing fellatio themselves, may insist that they are exclusively heterosexual and that they have never been involved in a truly homosexual relation. Their consciences are cleared and they may avoid trouble with society and with the police by perpetrating the additional fiction that they are incapable of responding to a relation with a male unless they fantasy themselves in contact with a female. Even clinicians have allowed themselves to be diverted by such pretensions. The actual histories, however, show few if any cases of sexual relations between males which could be considered anything but homosexual.

Many individuals who have had considerable homosexual experience, construct a hierarchy on the basis of which they insist that anyone who has not had as much homosexual experience as they have had, or who is less exclusively aroused by homosexual stimuli, is "not really homosexual." It is amazing to observe how many psychologists and psychiatrists have accepted this sort of propaganda, and have come to believe that homosexual males and females are discretely different from persons who merely have homosexual experience, or who react sometimes to homosexual stimuli. Sometimes such an interpretation allows for only two kinds of males and two kinds of females, namely those who are heterosexual and those who are homosexual. But as subsequent data in this chapter will show, there is only about half of the male population whose sexual behavior is exclusively heterosexual, and there are only a few percent who are exclusively homosexual. Any restriction of the term homosexuality to individuals who are exclusively so demands, logically, that the term heterosexual be applied only to those individuals who are exclusively heterosexual; and this makes no allowance for the nearly half of the population which has had sexual contacts with, or reacted psychically to, individuals of their own as well as of the opposite sex. Actually, of course, one must learn to recognize every combination of heterosexuality and homosexuality in the histories of various individuals.

It would encourage clearer thinking on these matters if persons were not characterized as heterosexual or homosexual, but as individuals who have had certain amounts of heterosexual experience and certain amounts of homosexual experience. Instead of using these terms as substantives which stand for persons, or even as adjectives to describe persons, they may better be used to describe the nature of the overt sexual relations, or of the stimuli to which an individual erotically responds.

The Heterosexual–Homosexual Balance

Concerning patterns of sexual behavior, a great deal of the thinking done by scientists and laymen alike stems from the assumption that there are persons who are "heterosexual" and persons who are "homosexual," that these two types represent antitheses in the sexual world, and that there is only an insignificant class of "bisexuals" who occupy an intermediate position between the other groups. It is implied that every individual is innately—inherently—either heterosexual or homosexual. It is further implied that from the time of birth one is fated to be one thing or the other, and that there is little chance for one to change his pattern in the course of a lifetime.

It is quite generally believed that one's preference for a sexual partner of one or the other sex is correlated with various physical and mental qualities, and with the total personality which makes a homosexual male or female physically, psychically, and perhaps spiritually distinct from a heterosexual individual. It is generally thought that these qualities make a homosexual person obvious and recognizable to anyone who has a sufficient understanding of such matters. Even psychiatrists discuss "the homosexual personality" and many of them believe that preferences for sexual partners of a particular sex are merely secondary manifestations of something that lies much deeper in the totality of that intangible which they call the personality.

It is commonly believed, for instance, that homosexual males are rarely robust physically, are uncoordinated or delicate in their movements, or perhaps graceful enough but not strong and vigorous in their physical expression. Fine skins, high-pitched voices, obvious hand movements, a feminine carriage of the hips, and peculiarities of walking gaits are supposed accompaniments of a preference for a male as a sexual partner.

It is commonly believed that the homosexual male is artistically sensitive, emotionally unbalanced, temperamental to the point of being unpredictable, difficult to get along with, and undependable in meeting specific obligations. In physical characters there have been attempts to show that the homosexual male has a considerable crop of hair and less often becomes bald, has teeth which are more like those of the female, a broader pelvis, larger genitalia, and a tendency toward being fat, and that he lacks a linea alba. The homosexual male is supposed to be less interested in athletics, more often interested in music and the arts, more often engaged in such occupations as bookkeeping, dress design, window display, hairdressing, acting, radio work, nursing, religious service, and social work. The converse to all of these is supposed to represent the typical heterosexual male. Many a clinician attaches considerable weight to these things in diagnosing the basic heterosexuality or homosexuality of his patients. The characterizations are so distinct that they seem to leave little room for doubt that homosexual and heterosexual represent two very distinct types of males.

The Terman–Miles scale for determining the degree of masculinity or femininity of an individual (Terman and Miles 1936) is largely based upon these preconceptions. Some other psychology scales have utilized very much the same principles. While these scales have made it [more] apparent that there may be gradations between exclusively heterosexual and exclusively homosexual individuals, or between the extremes of masculinity and the extremes of femininity, the implication is always present that an individual's choice of a sexual partner is closely related to the masculinity or femininity of his personality.

It should be pointed out that scientific judgments on this point have been based on little more than the same sorts of impressions which the general public has had concerning homosexual persons. But before any sufficient study can be made of such possible correlations between patterns of sexual behavior and other qualities in the individual, it is necessary to understand the incidences and frequencies of the homosexual in the population as a whole, and the relation of the homosexual activity to the rest of the sexual pattern in each individual's history.

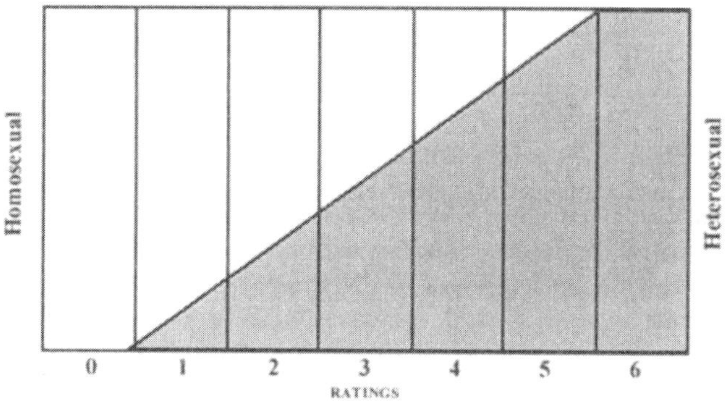

Figure 161. Heterosexual-Homosexual Rating Scale

Based on both psychologic reactions and overt experience, individuals rate as follows:

0. Exclusively heterosexual with no homosexual
1. Predominantly heterosexual, only incidentally homosexual
2. Predominantly heterosexual, but more than incidentally homosexual
3. Equally heterosexual and homosexual
4. Predominantly homosexual, but more than incidentally heterosexual
5. Predominantly homosexual, only incidentally heterosexual
6. Exclusively homosexual

The histories which have been available in the present study make it apparent that the heterosexuality or homosexuality of many individuals is not an all-or-none proposition. It is true that there are persons in the population whose histories are exclusively heterosexual, both in regard to their overt experience and in regard to their psychic reactions. And there are individuals in the population whose histories are exclusively homosexual, both in experience and in psychic reactions. But the record also shows that there is a considerable portion of the population whose members have combined, within their individual histories, both homosexual and heterosexual experience and/or psychic responses. There are some whose heterosexual experiences predominate, there are some whose homosexual experiences predominate, there are some who have had quite equal amounts of both types of experience.

Some of the males who are involved in one type of relation at one period in their lives, may have only the other type of relation at some later period. There may be considerable fluctuation of patterns from time to time. Some males may be involved in both heterosexual and homosexual activities within the same period of time. For instance, there are some who engage in both heterosexual and homosexual activities in the same year, or in the same month or week, or even in the same day. There are not a few individuals who engage in group activities in which they may make simultaneous contact with partners of both sexes.

Males do not represent two discrete populations, heterosexual and homosexual. The world is not to be divided into sheep and goats. Not all things are black nor all things white. It is a fundamental of taxonomy that nature rarely deals with discrete categories. Only the human mind invents categories and tries to force facts into separated pigeon-holes. The living world is a continuum in each and every one of its aspects. The sooner we learn this concerning human sexual behavior the sooner we shall reach a sound understanding of the realities of sex.

While emphasizing the continuity of the gradations between exclusively heterosexual and exclusively homosexual histories, it has seemed desirable to develop some sort of classification which could be based on the relative amounts of heterosexual and of homosexual experience or response in each history. Such a heterosexual-homosexual rating scale is shown in Figure 161. An individual may be assigned a position on this scale, for each age period in his life, in accordance with the following definitions of the various points on the scale:

0. Individuals are rated as 0's if they make no physical contacts which result in erotic arousal or orgasm, and make no psychic responses to individuals of their own sex. Their socio-sexual contacts and responses are exclusively with individuals of the opposite sex.

1. Individuals are rated as 1's if they have only incidental homosexual contacts which have involved physical or psychic response, or incidental psychic responses without physical contact. The great preponderance of their sociosexual experience and reactions is directed toward individuals of the opposite sex. Such homosexual experiences as these individuals have may occur only a single time or two, or at least infrequently in comparison to the amount of their heterosexual experience. Their homosexual experiences never involve as specific psychic reactions as they make to heterosexual stimuli. Sometimes the homosexual activities in which they engage may be inspired by curiosity, or may be more or less forced upon them by other individuals, perhaps when they are asleep or when they are drunk, or under some other peculiar circumstance.

2. Individuals are rated as 2's if they have more than incidental homosexual experience, and/or if they respond rather definitely to homosexual stimuli. Their heterosexual experiences and/or reactions still surpass their homosexual experiences and/or reactions. These individuals may have only a small amount of homosexual experience or they may have a considerable amount of it, but in every case it is surpassed by the amount of heterosexual experience that they have within the same period of time. They usually recognize their quite specific arousal by homosexual stimuli, but their responses to the opposite sex are still stronger. A few of these individuals may even have all of their overt experience in the homosexual, but their psychic reactions to persons of the opposite sex indicate that they are still predominantly heterosexual. This latter situation is most often found among younger males who have not yet ventured to have actual intercourse with girls, while their orientation is definitely heterosexual. On the other hand, there are some males who should be rated as 2's because of their strong reactions to individuals of their own sex, even though they have never had overt relations with them.

3. Individuals who are rated 3's stand midway on the heterosexual-homosexual scale. They are about equally homosexual and heterosexual in their overt experience and/or their psychic reactions. In general, they accept and equally enjoy both types of contacts, and have no strong preferences for one or the other. Some persons are rated 3's, even though they may have a larger amount of experience of one sort, because they respond psychically to partners of both sexes, and it is only a matter of circumstance that brings them into more frequent contact with one of the sexes. Such a situation is not unusual among single males, for male contacts are often more available to them than female contacts. Married males, on the other hand, find it simpler to secure a sexual outlet through intercourse with their wives, even though some of them may be as interested in males as they are in females.

4. Individuals are rated as 4's if they have more overt activity and/or psychic reactions in the homosexual, while still maintaining a fair amount of heterosexual activity and/or responding rather definitely to heterosexual stimuli.

5. Individuals are rated 5's if they are almost entirely homosexual in their overt activities and/or reactions. They do have incidental experience with the opposite sex and sometimes react psychically to individuals of the opposite sex.

6. Individuals are rated as 6's if they are exclusively homosexual, both in regard to their overt experience and in regard to their psychic reactions.

It will be observed that this is a seven-point scale, with 0 and 6 as the extreme points, and with 3 as the midpoint in the classification. On opposite sides of the midpoint the following relations hold:

0 is the opposite of 6; 1 is the opposite of 5; 2 is the opposite of 4

It will be observed that the rating which an individual receives has a dual basis. It takes into account his overt sexual experience and/or his psychosexual reactions. In the majority of instances the two aspects of the history parallel, but sometimes they are not in accord. In the latter case, the rating of an individual must be based upon an evaluation of the relative importance of the overt and the psychic in his history.

In each classification there are persons who have had no experience or a minimum of overt sexual experience, but in the same classification there may also be persons who have had hundreds of sexual contacts. In every case, however, all of the individuals in each classification show the same balance between the heterosexual and homosexual elements in their histories. The position of an individual on this scale is always based upon the relation of the heterosexual to the homosexual in his history, rather than upon the actual amount of overt experience or psychic reaction.

Finally, it should be emphasized again that the reality is a continuum, with individuals in the population occupying not only the seven categories which are recognized here, but every gradation between each of the categories, as well. Nevertheless, it does no great injustice to the fact to group the population as indicated above.

From all of this, it should be evident that one is not warranted in recognizing merely two types of individuals, heterosexual and homosexual, and that the characterization of the homosexual as a third sex fails to describe any actuality.

It is imperative that one understand the relative amounts of the heterosexual and homosexual in an individual's history if one is to make any significant analysis of him. Army and Navy officials and administrators in schools, prisons, and other institutions should be more concerned with the degree of heterosexuality or homosexuality in an individual than they are with the question of whether he has ever had an experience of either sort. It is obvious that the clinician must determine the balance that exists between the heterosexual and homosexual experience and reactions of his patient, before he can begin to help him. Even courts of law might well consider the totality of the individual's history, before passing judgment on the particular instance that has brought him into the hands of the law.

Everywhere in our society there is a tendency to consider an individual "homosexual" if he is known to have had a single experience with another individual of his own sex. Under the law an individual may receive the same penalty for a single homosexual experience that he would for a continuous record of experiences. In penal and mental institutions a male is likely to be rated "homosexual" if he is discovered to have had a single contact with another male. In society at large, a male who has worked out a highly successful marital adjustment is likely to be rated "homosexual" if the community learns about a single contact that he has had with another male. All such misjudgments are the product of the tendency to categorize sexual activities under only two heads, and of a failure to recognize the endless gradations that actually exist.

From all of this, it becomes obvious that any question as to the number of persons in the world who are homosexual and the number who are heterosexual is unanswerable. It is only possible to record the number of those who belong to each of the positions on such a heterosexual-homosexual scale as is given above. Summarizing our data on the incidence of overt homosexual experience in the white male population ... and the distribution of various degrees of heterosexual-homosexual balance in that population ... the following generalizations may be made:

37 per cent of the total male population has **at least some overt homosexual experience** to the point of orgasm between adolescence and old age. This accounts for nearly 2 males out of every 5 that one may meet.

50 per cent of the males **who remain single until age 35** have had overt homosexual experience to the point of orgasm, since the onset of adolescence.

58 per cent of the males who belong to the group that goes into **high school** but not beyond, **50 per cent of the grade school level**, and **47 per cent of the college level** have had homosexual experience to the point of orgasm if they remain single to the age of 35.

63 per cent of all males **never have overt** homosexual experience to the point of orgasm after the onset of adolescence.

50 per cent of all males (approximately) **have neither overt nor psychic** experience in the homosexual after the onset of adolescence.

13 per cent of the males (approximately) react erotically to other males **without having overt** homosexual contacts after the onset of adolescence.

30 per cent of all males **have at least incidental homosexual experience** or reactions (*i.e.*, rate 1 to 6) over at least a three-year period between the ages of 16 and 55. This accounts for one male out of every three in the population who is past the early years of adolescence.

25 per cent of the male population **has more than incidental homosexual experience** or reactions (*i.e.*, rates 2–6) for at least three years between the ages of 16 and 55. In terms of averages, one male out of approximately every four has had or will have such distinct and continued homosexual experience.

18 per cent of the males have at least **as much of the homosexual as the heterosexual** in their histories (*i.e.*, rate 3–6) for at least three years between the ages of 16 and 55. This is more than one in six of the white male population.

13 per cent of the population **has more of the homosexual than the heterosexual** (*i.e.*, rates 4–6) for at least three years between the ages of 16 and 55. This is one in eight of the white male population.

10 per cent of the males are **more or less exclusively homosexual** (*i.e.*, rate 5 or 6) for at least three years between the ages of 16 and 55. This is one male in ten in the white male population.

8 per cent of the males are **exclusively homosexual** (*i.e.*, rate a 6) for at least three years between the ages of 16 and 55. This is one male in every 13.

4 per cent of the white males are **exclusively homosexual throughout their lives,** after the onset of adolescence.

None of those who have previously attempted to estimate the incidence of the homosexual have made any clear-cut definition of the degree of homosexuality which they were including in their statistics. As a matter of fact, it seems fairly certain that none of them had any clear-cut conception of what they intended, other than their assurance that they were including only those "who were really homosexual." For that reason it is useless to compare the 2 or 3 per cent figure of Havelock Ellis, or the 2 to 5 per cent figure of Hirschfeld, or the 0.1 per cent figure of the Army induction centers with any of the data given above. The persons who are identified as "homosexuals" in much of the legal and social practice have rated anything between 1 and 6 on the above scale. On the other hand, there are some persons who would not rate an individual as "really homosexual" if he were anything less than a 5 or 6. Nevertheless, it should be emphasized again that there are persons who rate 2's or 3's who, in terms of the of the number of contacts they have made, may have had more homosexual experience than many persons who rate 6, and the clinician, the social worker, officials, and society in general are not infrequently concerned with persons who rate no more than 2's or 3's. Many who rate only 1 or 2 are much disturbed over their homosexual experience, and they are frequently among those who go to clinicians for help.

Finally, it should be emphasized that the social significance of an individual's history may or may not have any relation to his rating on the above scale. An older male who has never before had homosexual contact, may force a sexual relation with a small boy; and although he rates only a 1, he may so outrage the community that the full force of the law may be stirred up against him. On the contrary, most persons who rate l's have histories which do not disturb anybody. At the other end of the scale, some of the exclusively homosexual males may so confine their overt contacts that no social problems are raised, while others who also rate 6 are active wolves who are in continual trouble because of their open affronts to social conventions.

Bisexuality

Since only 50 per cent of the population is exclusively heterosexual throughout its adult life, and since only 4 per cent of the population exclusively homosexual throughout its life, it appears that nearly half (46%) of the population engages in both heterosexual and homosexual activities, or reacts to persons of both sexes, in the course of their adult lives. The term bisexual has been applied to at least some portion of this group. Unfortunately, the term as it has been used has never been strictly delimited, and consequently it is impossible to know whether it refers to all individuals who rate anything from 1 to 5, or whether it is being limited to some smaller number of categories, perhaps centering around group 3. If the latter is intended, it should be emphasized that the l's, 2's, 4's, and 5's have not yet been accounted for, and they constitute a considerable portion of the population.

In any event, such a scheme provides only a three-point scale (heterosexual, bisexual, and homosexual), and such a limited scale does not adequately describe the continuum which is the reality in nature. A seven-point scale comes nearer to showing the many gradations that actually exist.

As previously pointed out, it is rather unfortunate that the word bisexual should have been chosen to describe this intermediate group. The term is used as a substantive, designating individuals—persons; and the root meaning of the word and the way in which it is usually used imply that these persons have both masculine qualities and feminine qualities within their single bodies. We have objected to the use of the terms heterosexual and homosexual when used as nouns which stand for individuals. It is simply untenable to imply that these "bisexual" persons have an anatomy or an endocrine system or other sorts of physiologic or psychologic capacities which make them partly male and partly female or of the two sexes simultaneously. . . .

On the other hand, as applied to human sexual behavior, the term indicates that there are individuals who choose to have sexual relations with both males and females; and until it is demonstrated, as it certainly is not at the present time, that such a catholicity of taste in a sexual relation is dependent upon the individual containing within his anatomy both male and female structures, or male and female physiologic capacities, it is unfortunate to call such individuals bisexual. Because of its wide currency, the term will undoubtedly continue in use among students of human behavior and in the public in general. It should, however, be used with the understanding that it is patterned on the words heterosexual and homosexual and, like them, refers to the sex of the partner, and proves nothing about the constitution of the person who is labeled bisexual. . . .

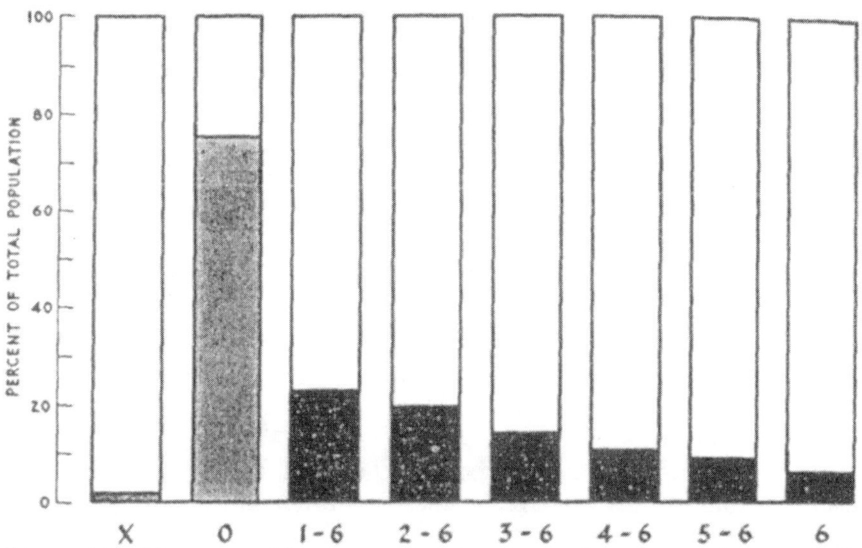

Figure 169. Heterosexual-homosexual ratings in total male population (single and married) in any single year

Based on U.S. Corrections data. . . . Passing experiences eliminated from data by showing only ratings which have involved a period of at least three years after the males turned 16. Percent shown as "X" have no socio-sexual contacts or reactions.

NOTE: ALFRED KINSEY'S STUDIES ON SEXUAL BEHAVIOR IN THE HUMAN FEMALE

Kinsey's findings published in *Studies on Sexual Behavior in the Human Female* were gleaned from a sample of 5940 white females, the majority of participants being younger white adults with some college education. In an attempt to compensate for volunteer bias in his sample, Kinsey interviewed 100% of the individuals available in a given organization or group.

According to Kinsey, an estimated 2% to 6% of females, aged 20–35, were more or less exclusively homosexual in experience/response, and 1 to 3% of unmarried females aged 20–35 were exclusively homosexual in experience/response. Additionally, 13% of females had had at least one same-sex orgasm.

In his studies on bisexuality, Kinsey found only a very small portion of females with exclusively homosexual histories. He reported that between 6% and 14% of females (ages 20–35) had more than incidental homosexual experience in their histories. 7% of single females (ages 20–35) and 4% of previously married females (ages 20–35) were given a rating of 3 (about equal heterosexual and homosexual experience/response) on the 7–point Kinsey Heterosexual–Homosexual Rating Scale for this period of their lives.

After Kinsey's death in 1956 his successors at the Institute for Sex Research in Indiana conducted a study of U.S. homosexual males and lesbians. The study was comprised of 979 male and female homosexuals and a comparison group of 477 heterosexuals. The study concluded that lesbians are less sexually active than male homosexuals; three quarters of the women were involved in relatively stable relationships and the majority had fewer than ten homosexual partners over a lifetime. Lesbians were also found to be nearly as well adjusted as heterosexual women, though they scored slightly lower on self-esteem and were more prone to thoughts of suicide. Twenty percent of the gay men had attempted suicide, versus 4% of the heterosexual males. Five percent were listed as "dysfunctional"—those tormented by their homosexuality and plagued with severe psychological, social and sexual problems.

V. MODERN SCIENTIFIC DEVELOPMENTS*

Based on the research of Kinsey and others, it is estimated that between 3 and 10 percent of the population identifies as exclusively homosexual (Kinsey, Pomeroy, & Martin, 1948; Levay, 1996; Pillard & Bailey, 1995). Many studies use some form of the Kinsey Scale to have research participants self-identify their sexual orientation. The Kinsey Scale is a seven-point scale that represents a continuum of human sexual behavior. The scores range from zero (exclusive heterosexuality) to six (exclusive homosexuality). Although Kinsey argued that there is a continuum of human sexual behavior, researchers have historically used his scale to dichotomize samples into heterosexual and homosexual/nonheterosexual groups. In response to this binary treatment, several researchers

* Excerpted from William J. Jenkins, *Can Anyone Tell Me Why I'm Gay? What Research Suggests Regarding the Origins of Sexual Orientation*, 12 N. AM. J. OF PSYCH. 279–296 (2010) (used with permission).

have been prompted to develop their own scales to better capture the continuous nature of human sexuality and allow for legitimate discussion of those individuals who identify as bisexual to be considered in their own right (for a more complete discussion see Klein, 1993; Rodriguez Rust, 1999).

Given prevailing social mores, we should approach the scientific literature regarding sexual orientation with some caution for a number of reasons. First, individuals willing to identify themselves as homosexual or bisexual may not be the most representative sample of their respective populations as a whole. Despite his enormous impact on the study of human sexual behavior, Kinsey received vocal criticism of the representativeness of his samples because of their willingness to participate in his studies and because of a presumed overreliance on prisoners and prostitutes (for examples see Cochran, Mosteller, & Tukey, 1954; Maslow & Sakoda, 1952), and some of these concerns continue to resonate today. Second, as previously mentioned, researchers have often imposed a dichotomy upon their samples so that individuals are grouped as either heterosexual or homosexual. This practice may not capture the true continuum of human sexual orientation and behavior and potentially confounds interpretations by treating bisexuals and homosexuals uniformly, despite research that suggests that bisexual individuals are distinct from both hetero-and homosexuals (Klein, 1993; Rodriguez Rust, 1999; Van Wyk & Geist, 1995). Finally, we should be cognizant of the motives for engaging in research focusing on the origins of sexual orientation. In reading this literature, it is clear that personal bias and opinion have colored the presentation of scientific findings and their potential implications (for a more detailed discussion see LeVay, 1996).

Researchers interested in the development of sexual orientation have often taken either a physiological or a psychosocial approach. It would be truly naive to argue that either of these perspectives could operate entirely independently of the other, and neither side is making that argument.... [B]ased on their own backgrounds and expertise, scientists are approaching the question of the etiology of sexual orientation from multiple perspectives and levels of analysis in the hope that the truth will emerge from the convergence of their findings. In the following pages, some of the major ideas and hypotheses that are considered include: studies of prenatal development, brain morphology and function, behavioral genetics, environmental factors, early childhood/adolescent experiences, and stability/plasticity of sexual orientation.

Prenatal Development

. . .

Male homosexuality has long been hypothesized to result from some sort of prenatal testosterone deficiency. While the cause of such a deficiency is unclear, some have investigated maternal stress during gestation as a possibility. There is evidence from the animal literature to suggest maternal stress during pregnancy demasculinizes and feminizes male sexual behavior and brain morphology (Kerchner & Ward, 1992; Ward, 1972). This demasculinization may be due to a delay in a surge of testosterone necessary for sexual differentiation of the brain (Ward & Weisz, 1980).

In the human literature, a number of retrospective studies have resulted in contradictory findings regarding the role of maternal stress in male homosexuality. When homosexual, bisexual, and heterosexual men were asked to estimate the amount of stress experienced by their mothers while they were pregnant with them, non-heterosexuals estimated higher levels of stress than heterosexuals (Domer, Schenk, Schrniedel, & Ahrens, 1983). Furthermore, when mothers were asked directly about the amount of stress they had experienced while pregnant with their sons, Ellis (1988) found that mothers of homosexuals were more likely to report stress than mothers of heterosexuals (especially during the second trimester of pregnancy). However, Bailey, Willerman, and Parks (1991) failed to find any difference in the amount of stress experienced by mothers of heterosexuals and non-heterosexuals in a very similar study.

While delays in or a deficiency of androgen activity is a compelling argument for those who view male homosexuals as somehow intermediate to male and female heterosexuals, this idea is in direct opposition to observations that both male and female homosexuality may be associated with hyper-masculinization, perhaps as a function of excess androgen exposure during early development (for examples see Bogaert & Hershberger, 1999; McFadden & Champlin, 2000). There is also some evidence to suggest that females prenatally exposed to diethylstilbestrol (DES), a synthetic estrogen, are more likely to identify as bi-or homosexual compared to those females not exposed to DES (MeyerBahlburg et al., 1995), presumably as a function of estrogen's role in the defeminization of the central nervous system.

Some researchers have suggested that a maternal immune response to the H–Y antigen in developing male fetuses may contribute to the development of male homosexuality (Blanchard, 2001; Blanchard, 2004; Blanchard & Klassen, 1997). This hypothesis stems from the observation of what is described as the "fraternal birth order effect." In 1996, Blanchard & Bogaert observed that male homosexuals were much more likely to have older male siblings than their heterosexual counterparts. Furthermore, evidence suggests that this effect only applies to biological, rather than adopted siblings (Bogaert, 2006). While this particular observation is compelling, more recent research suggests that earlier studies conflated issues of gendered-typed behaviors and sexual orientation. Specifically, the birth order effect only seems to apply to those individuals who exhibit high degrees of feminine behavior (Bogaert, 2005).

In rodents, the surge in leutinizing hormone (LH) in response to estrogen seems to be sex specific; however, it is unclear whether this pattern is as absolute in humans. Gladue, Green, and Hellman (1984) found that the pattern of LH secretion in response to an injection of premarin (an estrogen derivative) of homosexual men was intermediate to that of heterosexual men and heterosexual women. In addition, homosexual and heterosexual men differed in terms of the duration of lowered testosterone after the injection. This response was proposed to serve as a biological marker of homosexuality that is indicative of organizational differences in hypothalamic-pituitary-gonadal (HPG) axis between hetero- and homosexual men (Gladue et al., 1984). However, Gooren (1986a) found no difference in the LH secretion pattern between hetero- and homosexual men. Furthermore, Gooren (1986b) determined that LH secretion patterns in the human can be changed as a result of gonadectomy and cross-gender hormone treatment, suggesting this particular response is not due to an organizational difference in the HPG axis. However, in male-oriented rams, it appears that LH secretion pattern is indistinguishable from that of female-oriented rams and that both are defeminized compared to ewes, suggesting that sexual attraction is not related to organizational differences in the hypophyseal portal system (Stormshak, Estill, Resko, & Roselli, 2008).

Brain Morphology and Function

In 1978, Gorski, Gordon, Shryne, and Southam described a sexually dimorphic area of the medial preoptic nucleus of rats. Specifically, this area was found to be larger in males than in females and this difference arises as a function of perinatal hormonal milieu. In the case of the medial preoptic area, it is clear that this structure is critical for the normal display of sexual behavior in the male rat (De Jonge, Louwese, Ooms, Evers, & De Poll, 1989; Everitt, 1990; Hull & Dominguez, 2006; Hull & Dominguez, 2007).

Structures that display sexual dimorphism in the human brain have received attention as sites of interest among scientists interested in finding morphological correlates of sexual orientation as well. Swaab and Fliers (1985) identified an area of the human hypothalamus that appears to be analogous to the sexually dimorphic nucleus of the rat medial preoptic area described by Gorski and colleagues. Allen, Hines, Shryne and Gorski (1989) were unable to replicate the sexual dimorphism of this area which they referred to as the interstitial nucleus of the anterior hypothalamus-l (INAH–1); however, they did identify two other sexually dimorphic nuclei in the preoptic-anterior hypothalamus which they labeled INAH–2 and INAH–3. Levay (1991) conducted a study investigating how and if the anterior preoptic hypothalamus differed between heterosexual and homosexual men. Levay conducted a postmortem analysis of tissue obtained from women, heterosexual men, and homosexual men. While he observed no differences between men and women in the size of INAH–1 or 2, Levay did observe that INAH–3 was sexually dimorphic (larger in men than in women) and that this area was significantly larger in heterosexual men than in homosexual men. More recent research suggests that this size difference is due to cell density rather than cell number (Byne et al., 2001).

Levay's findings have recently received corroboration from researchers investigating the brains of a naturally occurring population of male-oriented rams. An area of the hypothalamus dubbed the "ovine sexually dimorphic nucleus" is larger in male rams than in female sheep, and it is larger in female-oriented rams than in male-oriented rams (Roselli, Larkin, Resko, Stellflug, & Storrnshak, 2004). These converging lines of evidence definitely point to sexually dimorphic hypothalamic areas under the influence of hormones as sites of great importance in an individual's sexual orientation, and this particular animal model is especially intriguing because these rams represent a naturally occurring population that displays not only same-sex behavior but also what seems to be a true preference for same-sex interactions (Roselli, Larkin, Schrunk, & Stormshak, 2004; Roselli & Stormshak, 2009a,b).

Differences in brain morphology and function are not limited to sexually dimorphic areas, however. The suprachiasmatic nucleus is larger in homosexual men than in heterosexual men, but this area does not appear to be sexually dimorphic (Swaab & Hofman, 1990). The anterior commissure also varies in size as a function of sexual orientation (Allen & Gorski, 1992) without differing between women and men.

Global, morphological differences in brain structure as a function of sexual orientation are related to differences in the ways in which homosexual and heterosexual brains function. Male and female homosexuals differ from their heterosexual counterparts in their performance on a variety of tasks that assess cognitive functions including: spatial memory, mental rotation, verbal fluency, and recognition of facial expressions of emotion (Rahman, Abrahams, & Wilson, 2003; Rahman & Wilson, 2003a,b; Rahman, Wilson, & Abrahams, 2003; Rahman, Wilson, & Abrahams, 2004a,b).

Furthermore, different neural circuits are activated in the visually evoked sexual arousal of heterosexual and homosexual men. While a number of structures are similarly activated in hetero- and homosexual participants, activation of the left caudate, left angular gyrus, and right pallidum is exclusive to homosexual subjects and activation in the left and right lingual gyri and right hippocampus and parahippocampal gyrus is exclusive to heterosexual subjects. (Hu, et al., 2008). Furthermore, sex-partner preference specific activation of certain regions of the reward circuitry of the brain (the ventral striatum and centromedian thalamus in this case) lead some to propose that there is a "functional endophenotype" indicative of the individual's sexual orientation (Ponseti et al., 2006), and recently, it has been demonstrated that this endophenotype has excellent predictive validity for an individual's sexual orientation (Ponseti et al., 2009).

Behavioral Genetics

Pillard and Weinrich (1986) found that homosexual men had about four times more homosexual brothers than would be expected given prevalence rates of male homosexuality, and Bailey and Pillard (1991) found that concordance rates for male homosexuality were 52% among monozygotic twins, 22% among dizygotic twins, and 11% for adopted brothers. After reviewing a number of studies like those mentioned above, Rodriguez–Larralde & Paradisi (2009) concluded the heritability of male homosexuality was somewhere in the range of 0.27 to 0.76. In 1993, a study was published that demonstrated a linkage between male homosexuality and a portion of the X chromosome (Hamer, Hu, Magnuson, Hu, & Pattatuci, 1993), however, subsequent studies have been unable to replicate this result (Mustanski et al., 2005; Rice, Anderson, Risch, & Ebers, 1999).

More recently, Hamer's group has conducted a genome-wide scan of male sexual orientation which identified several markers that are associated with genes important for organization and sexual differentiation of neural tissues and the HPG axis (Mustanski et al., 2005). It has been suggested that the candidate genes may confer increased fecundity upon the relatives of homosexuals (Lemmola & Camperio, 2009; Rahman et al., 2008) or that these genes may be associated with increased altruism and empathy that could be directed towards close relatives most likely to reproduce (for example see Salais & Fischer, 1995). So, even if one accepted the flawed (Dickemann, 1995) assumption that male homosexuals are less likely to successfully reproduce than heterosexuals, there are a number of potential explanations for the maintenance of the gene(s) that might contribute to homosexuality.

There is evidence that differential patterns of gene expression and/or the resultant *in utero* hormonal milieu that mediate developmental pathways are different between heterosexuals and homosexuals. For instance, Rahman & Wilson (2003a) demonstrated differences in finger length ratios between heterosexuals and homosexuals. Differences in handedness (for example Lippa, 2003), dermal ridge patterns (Hall & Kimura, 1994), hair whorl (Klar, 2004), and functional and structural aspects of the auditory system between heterosexuals have all been observed (LoeWin & McFadden, 2003; McFadden & Champlin, 2000; Mcfadden & Pasanen, 1998), although replicating some of these effects consistently has proven to be problematic (as discussed in Schwartz, Kim, Kolundzija, Rieger, & Sanders, 2010).

Environmental Factors

A behavioral pattern and identity as complex as sexual orientation is subject to an interaction of the individual's physiology with his or her environment, and researchers have proposed sundry environmental factors that may contribute to the development of sexual orientation. However, the results of these efforts have been somewhat equivocal. For instance, Bieber and colleagues (1962a) claimed that male homosexuality resulted more commonly among families with a domineering mother and a weak father. Research investigating this possibility, however, has not provided consistent evidence to support this hypothesis. While Milic and Crowne (1986) report differences in terms of lovingness and rejection by parents of homosexual versus heterosexual men, others have found no difference in parenting styles experienced by heterosexual and homosexual men (Bell, Weinberg, & Hammersmith, 1981; Ross & Arrindell, 1988).

Increasing numbers of homosexual individuals are having children either through adoption, marriage, or artificial inseminations; and many wonder whether their children are more likely to develop a homosexual orientation. Imitating the homosexual parent, being socialized by the homosexual parent to adopt a homosexual orientation, or viewing homosexuality as an acceptable alternative to heterosexuality-an option that might not be as obvious to children of strictly heterosexual parents, could all play a role in the development of a homosexual orientation. However, the vast majority of children of homosexual parents are heterosexual (Bailey, Bobrow, Wolfe & Mikach, 1995; Golombok & Tasker, 1995). It should be pointed out, however, that a concordance rate of 9% for non-heterosexual behavior of the sons of homosexual fathers has been observed, which is slightly larger than would be expected given overall prevalence rates of male homosexuality (Bailey et al., 1995). In this particular study, however, genetic influences could not be controlled for and there was no correlation between the sexual orientation of these children and the amount of time spent with their fathers.

Early Childhood Development and Adolescence

One of the most consistent, robust findings among homosexuals has been that they exhibited behaviors during childhood that are considered gender nonconforming (Bell et al., 1981; Bieber et al., 1962b), and recently, this observation has been replicated through the analysis of childhood videos obtained from male and female homosexual and heterosexual research volunteers. Pre-homosexual children, regardless of gender, displayed more gender non-conformity in the videos than their pre-heterosexual counterparts, and this pattern of behavior continued through adulthood (Rieger, Linsenmeier, Gygax, & Bailey, 2008).

Homosexual individuals have reported that they were aware from a very early age of their gender nonconformity and erotic attraction towards the same sex (Bell et al., 1981; Rieger et al., 2008). There is some evidence to suggest that masturbation and fantasy may play a role in integrating early feelings into the development of their sexual orientation (Money & Tucker, 1975; Van Wyk & Geist, 1984). It is unclear, however, whether these behaviors are involved in the development of a homosexual orientation or whether they are products of an already established homosexual orientation.

Theories of the development of a homosexual orientation often concentrate on adolescence as a critical period in this process because of the changes in physiology, psychological functioning, and social conditions occurring during this time (Savin–Williams, 1988). Frequently, adolescents engage in homosexual behavior at a higher rate than the rest of the population; however, this is often viewed as a natural phase on the way to developing a heterosexual orientation. However, for some, these activities are a part of a developing homosexual identity (Savin–Williams, 1990). Troiden (1988) describes adolescence as a time when homosexuals first become aware of their same sex attraction and begin to act on these attractions, and he proposed that male homosexuals generally begin to accept the fact that they are homosexual between the ages of 19 and 21. In this framework, adolescence may reflect the acceptance and recognition of an individual's homosexual orientation, rather than the development of it, per se.

. . .

Stability/Plasticity of Sexual–Orientation

Some individuals have claimed that they led an exclusively heterosexual life until they had a given homosexual experience after which point they were exclusively homosexual (as described in Meijer, 1993). Certainly, many homosexuals have tried to change their sexual orientation through various "reparative" therapies. In fact, there are reports suggesting that such programs are successful (for example, see Spitzer, 2003), though the rigor of the science assessing these therapeutic techniques described in such studies is often called into question (Ford, 2001; Haldeman, 2002). Aside from any legitimate evidence of the efficacy of the reparative therapies, the ethical grounds for providing such treatment have also been called into question, given that homosexuality is not an illness (Halpert, 2000).

While reparative therapies are largely eschewed by the scientific community, there is some evidence of malleability of sexual orientation because both homosexual men and women may have at one time identified as either heterosexual or bisexual. However, it is very uncommon to see individuals that once identified as homosexual to identify as heterosexual later in life. Thus, this plasticity may in fact reflect the "coming out" process undertaken by many gay men and lesbians (for a more detailed description see Levay, 1996). It should be noted, however, that with regards to "erotic plasticity" women are generally thought to be more malleable than men; and there are compelling arguments made about women "switching" sexual orientations at various points in their lives (as discussed in Baumeister, 2004). There have also been numerous reports of individuals who experience changes in sexual interests, sexual orientation, and even perception of the gender of themselves and others as a function of brain injury in the temporal lobes (Cheasty, Condren, & Cooney, 2002; Kasper, Kerling, Graf, Stefan, & Pauli, 2009; Miller, Cummings, McIntyre, Ebers, & Grode, 1986).

Conclusions

. . . This area of research is dynamic and researchers have attempted to address a variety of perspectives in their studies and for a variety of reasons. Despite decades of research, the ultimate answer to the question posed in the title of this paper, "Can anyone tell me why I'm gay?" is a resounding "Not yet."

. . .

Few areas of research can match the social implications associated with investigating the etiology of sexual orientation. From "Don't Ask, Don't Tell" to the ongoing debate about legalization of gay marriage in the United States, this is an issue that is politically and socially divisive and that generates social stigmas that can be personally devastating. Nearly 6,000 hate crimes motivated by sexual orientation were reported to have occurred in the United States between 2005 and 2008 (Johnson, 2008), and perhaps as a function of stigmatization and discrimination, homosexual/bisexual individuals are at higher risk for attempted suicide, suicidal ideation, substance abuse, and several mental disorders (King et al., 2008).

It is not inconceivable that we may one day fully understand the origins of sexual orientation and be faced with the implications that such an understanding engenders. Despite compelling arguments to the contrary (Greenberg & Bailey, 2001), this author believes we have a moral imperative to use that information in a socially responsible and positive way....

DISCUSSION

1. *What does sexual orientation mean to you? Is it biological or a product of one's environment?*

2. *What are your overall impressions of the Kinsey studies? What do you think about Kinsey's sliding scale of sexuality?*

3. *What about the percentages Kinsey posits for people who have had at least some homosexual contact in their lives? If they are true, how do we explain society's generally hostile reaction to homosexuality?*

4. *What, in your view, makes one homosexual (or heterosexual)?*

   a. *Does engaging in particular sex acts define one's sexuality?*

   b. *Does self-identification?*

5. *What is the importance of finding a scientific "cause" for sexual orientation? Are there dangers?*

6. *In a highly publicized and criticized article, entitled "Recruit, Recruit, Recruit," lesbian activist Donna Minkowitz wrote the following:*

> Since Anita Bryant's day, 'phobes have claimed that we "recruit" children. Of course we don't—if the phrase is taken to mean we sexually abuse the young in order to make converts for our community. But I am increasingly impatient with the old chestnut that our movement for public acceptance has not increased and will not increase the number of gay men and lesbians in existence. "There are *more of us* than there used to be," historian John D'Emilio has written. Firmly believing this, I wanted to go on the [Montel Williams' show] to argue the morality of

> teaching kids that gay is OK even if it means that some will join our ranks.
>
> . . .
>
> Let's take the offensive for a change, whether the issue is promiscuity or recruiting the previously straight. Remember that most of the line about homosexuality being one's nature, not a choice, was articulated as a response to brutal repression. "It's not our fault!" gay activists began to declaim a century ago, when queers first began to organize in Germany and England. "We didn't choose this, so don't punish us for it!" One hundred years later, it's time for us to abandon this defensive posture and walk upright on the earth. *Maybe you didn't choose to be gay—that's fine. But I did.** (emphasis added)

In your view, is Minkowitz really a lesbian? How do you feel about her criticism of the biological determinism argument?

---

* The Advocate, Dec. 29, 1992.

CHAPTER 2

TREATMENT OF LGBT, QUESTIONING, AND GENDER NON-CONFORMING YOUTH

■ ■ ■

For much of our country's history, admitted gay youth or children suspected of being gay were subjected to untold horrors in an effort to "cure" their aberration. After the horrors of medicalization, LGBT* youth have been the target of anti-gay violence and abuse in schools and elsewhere, from other children and even from adult school officials. This chapter chronicles the efforts of LGBT youth to combat abuse and efforts to silence them in schools. Materials about gay youth, psychiatric cure efforts, and even Anita Bryant's religious-right antigay campaign, waged under the banner of child welfare, mix with cases describing the battle for survival still facing many gay youth today.

I. OVERVIEW OF THE PROBLEM**

At its root, homophobia is ignorance, yet the vast majority of schools are unwilling or unprepared to do anything about it. Other harmful prejudices are regularly challenged, in the interest at least of practical harmony if not of true multiculturalism. Yet a stubborn double standard prevails. It is easy to find schools, even some that are otherwise progressive, where "kids notice that when a racial slur is written on a wall, there is a fuss, but 'fag' on a locker remains for days, unremarked." The consequences for students of the failure to address such issues are serious: a distorted view of human nature, bigotry, self-hatred, and violence.

Teaching about gays and lesbians and the diversity of their community would help reduce these problems. Yet school-based tolerance programs are almost always restricted to religious, racial, and ethnic understanding. Although teachers might draw attention to the links among other prejudices, they often see homophobia as separate, unrelated, and beyond the scope of the K–12 syllabus.

---

* *LGBT* is a common inclusive acronym for "lesbian, gay, bisexual, and transgender." It is occasionally expanded to encompass "questioning" youth—those who are exploring their sexuality but who have not yet identified themselves with a common label—as "LGBTQ."

** Excerpted from Arthur Lipkin, Understanding Homosexuality (Westview Press, 1999).

Few school leaders recognize how homophobia is related to student promiscuity, substance abuse, academic problems, and suicide. Nor do they acknowledge its connection to violence among heterosexual youth: that is, boys often beat other boys and batter girls to distance themselves from gayness. The vast majority of juveniles arrested for violent crime are male. They take foolish personal risks and shun academic success to prove they are not faggots.

Some Facts*

[A] 2009 survey of 7,261 middle and high school students found that at school nearly 9 out of 10 LGBT students experienced harassment at school in the past year and nearly two-thirds felt unsafe because of their sexual orientation. Nearly a third of LGBT students skipped at least one day of school in the past month because of safety concerns.

An analysis [of survey data] over 10 years showed that since 1999 there has been a decreasing trend in the frequency of hearing homophobic remarks; however, LGBT students' experiences with more severe forms of bullying and harassment have remained relatively constant.

[Key findings of the survey included the following:]

- 84.6% of LGBT students reported being verbally harassed, 40.1% reported being physically harassed and 18.8% reported being physically assaulted at school in the past year because of their sexual orientation.
- 63.7% of LGBT students reported being verbally harassed, 27.2% reported being physically harassed and 12.5% reported being physically assaulted at school in the past year because of their gender expression.
- 72.4% heard homophobic remarks, such as "faggot" or "dyke," frequently or often at school.
- Nearly two-thirds (61.1%) of students reported that they felt unsafe in school because of their sexual orientation, and more than a third (39.9%) felt unsafe because of their gender expression.
- 29.1% of LGBT students missed a class at least once and 30.0% missed at least one day of school in the past month because of safety concerns, compared to only 8.0% and 6.7%, respectively, of a national sample of secondary school students.
- The reported grade point average of students who were more frequently harassed because of their sexual orientation or gender expression was almost half a grade lower than for students who were less often harassed (2.7 vs. 3.1).
- Increased levels of victimization were related to increased levels of depression and anxiety and decreased levels of self-esteem.

* This summary is from the 2009 National School Climate Survey released by GLSEN, the Gay, Lesbian and Straight Education Network. Reprinted with permission of GLSEN.

• Being out in school had positive and negative repercussions for LGBT students; outness was related to higher levels of victimization, but also higher levels of psychological well-being.

[The survey indentified positive intervention and support mechanisms:]

• Having a Gay–Straight Alliance in school was related to more positive experiences for LGBT students, including: hearing fewer homophobic remarks, less victimization because of sexual orientation and gender expression, less absenteeism because of safety concerns and a greater sense of belonging to the school community.

• The presence of supportive staff contributed to a range of positive indicators including fewer reports of missing school, fewer reports of feeling unsafe, greater academic achievement, higher educational aspirations and a greater sense of school belonging.

• Students attending schools with an anti-bullying policy that included protections based on sexual orientation and/or gender identity/expression heard fewer homophobic remarks, experienced lower levels of victimization related to their sexual orientation, were more likely to report that staff intervened when hearing homophobic remarks and were more likely to report incidents of harassment and assault to school staff than students at schools with a general policy or no policy.

• Despite the positive benefits of these interventions, less than a half of LGBT students (44.6%) reported having a Gay–Straight Alliance at school, slightly more than half (53.4%) could identify six or more supportive educators and less than a fifth (18.2%) attended a school that had a comprehensive anti-bullying policy.

[The survey also studied school climate over the time period from 1999–2009:]

• There was a steady decline in the frequency of hearing homophobic remarks from 1999 to 2003. In recent years, between 2005 and 2009, student reports of hearing these types of remarks have not decreased significantly.

• LGBT student experiences of harassment and assault have remained relatively constant over time. However, there were small but significant decreases in frequencies of verbal harassment, physical harassment and physical assault from 2007 to 2009.

• There has been an increase over time in the presence of several LGBT-related resources and supports in school, specifically: Gay–Straight Alliances or other student clubs that address LGBT issues in education; school staff who were supportive of LGBT students; and LGBT-related materials in school libraries.

II. GROWING UP GAY

A. A QUEER'S OWN STORY*

Brooklyn isn't the easiest place to grow up, especially if you're a homo.

My cousin Marilu (short for Maria Lucia) was my best friend when I was five. It was perhaps through her, at that young age, that I realized I was queer. I use "queer" in the most traditional sense of the word, because I discerned that I was very *different* from most other little boys in the neighborhood. Like Marilu, I had felt affection toward boys as far back as I could remember. She and I used to talk about the ones we had crushes on. I sensed at that age that I wasn't supposed to be like Marilu in this regard, but still, it felt natural. And Marilu, bless her heart, didn't mind....

I remember always perceiving that Marilu and I were the same. I knew that she was a "girl" and I was a "boy," but I didn't understand the difference and certainly didn't feel it. And yet, even when I was five it seemed that the world was already trying to separate us, condemning our playing together and demanding that we be interested in different things. She was supposed to like dolls. I was supposed to like baseball. But I refused to follow those rules. I had something powerful in common with Marilu and it was something intrinsic. I wanted to play with her—and if that meant playing with dolls, then so be it.

My father didn't like that idea. After the first time I got caught dressing Barbie, I remember, I had to sneak play sessions, playing during the day, when my father wasn't around. My father was much more stern about my playing with dolls than my mother was. But I got caught again and again. Soon he became quite alarmed.

"Only sissies play with dolls," he angrily said, and punished me by not allowing me to ever go down to Marilu's again to play with her dolls.

What's a sissy? I thought to myself. Whatever it was, I concluded, I must be one. I also remember wondering why, if I was this thing called a sissy, everyone couldn't just accept that I was a sissy and let me play with Marilu and Barbie.

At the same age, I was discovering that I was left-handed. I remember being told that left-handedness was uncommon; yet people seemed to accept it. But things weren't always that way. My parents and aunts and uncles told me stories of how, just one generation before mine, nuns in Catholic schools used heavy wooden rulers to smash the left hand of anyone they caught trying to write lefty; sometimes they hit hard enough to make the pupils' hands bleed or fracture their bones. Lefties were

* Excerpted from *A Queer's Own Story,* Michaelangelo Signorile, Queer in America: Sex, the Media, and the Closets of Power (U. Wisconsin Press 2003), pp. 18–35. © 2003. Reprinted by permission of the University of Wisconsin Press.

forced to write with their right hands because left-handedness had for centuries been associated with the Devil in the eyes of the church. It wasn't until the late fifties (at least in Brooklyn) that Catholic schools had accepted lefties, decades after science had decided that left-handedness was natural and normal.

I remember asking myself, when I was five why, if they could look at being a lefty as uncommon but acceptable, they couldn't view being a sissy in the same way. I soon realized that when it came to religion, especially Roman Catholicism, logic didn't matter. I also discovered that in the culture in which I was being brought up, preserving *la famiglia* was more important than anything else. And being a lefty was one thing, but being a sissy just didn't fit in with preserving *la famiglia*. . . .

One of my cousins at one point began dating a Jewish boy. That caused an uproar like I had never seen before. Difference was not acceptable in my family—not at that time. And I knew that I was even more different. I was truly afraid, though I didn't know what it was I feared: I didn't know what homosexuality was. There was never any talk of it at the table, except for the occasional homo joke or antigay slur. One of my cousins had married a man who was effeminate, and the men in the family poked fun at him. The words "queer" and "fag" and "quiff" (an antigay slur prevalent in the outer boroughs of New York City) were thrown around a lot. But there was never any serious discussion—certainly there were no yelling matches—about homosexuality in those days. It was completely in the closet, especially in the church. Cardinal O'Connor may rail against homosexuals today, but back then there was no antigay rhetoric coming from the Roman Catholic pulpit, at least not at Holy Name, our local parish. There was no need for it. Gays weren't a threat because they weren't visible. As far as the church was concerned, there were no homosexuals. And homosexual acts were *sins* of the worst kind—the kind you never discussed, not even in confession. . . .

I had excellent grades and was a generally happy kid. With sandy-blond hair, blue eyes, and a button nose that everyone tweaked, I knew I was cute and played it to the hilt. I was a loudmouth too, always trying to be the center of attention and always managing to be popular. But by third or fourth grade things began to change: Suddenly, the boys were calling me a faggot. My happy nature grew more subdued.

It wasn't that I was particularly effeminate, but I hung around mostly with girls, rarely with boys. Just as I had with my cousin Marilu, I'd found that I had something powerful in common with the girls. Kids are extraordinarily perceptive: They know who's queer at a very young age. Little gay boys seem to find refuge with little straight girls: They bond, perhaps because both the girls and the gay boys feel oppressed by the straight boys. For young lesbians, it must be more awful than for the young gay boys: Baby dykes are ostracized not only by the boys, but by the girls as well.

I couldn't understand why I was being called names. It was devastating. "Sissy!" "Faggot!" "Queer!" The boys were cruel. I *wasn't* those things, I kept telling myself. Still, that word "sissy" stuck out in my mind because my father had used it, too. I realized that this sissy thing must be alot worse than I'd thought at first; it must be absolutely unacceptable. I would have to prove that I was just like the other boys. I would have to prove that I was a man, not a sissy, a faggot, or a queer.

In the working-class Brooklyn Italian tradition, my father had taught me that if anyone used an ethnic slur, hurling a remark at me like "wop" or "greaseball," I was supposed to punch that person in the face. He'd taught me how to fight.

I decided to transfer this strategy to being queer—even though I wasn't accepting, or even admitting to myself, the fact that I was such a ghastly thing—and so I began hitting whoever called me names. That got me in a lot of trouble in the early years. Worse yet, I wasn't only hitting the kids who were calling me names. I was going after *other* kids who'd been called faggot too, so that I could prove that I agreed they were freaks and distance myself from them. I became a queer-basher to prove I wasn't queer.

Still, the name-calling continued. My personality development was stunted and deformed. I had been a bubbly, smart kid when I entered school, but *now* I *was* defensive and belligerent. Whereas I might have developed into one of those kids who was funny, irrepressible, and well liked, instead I was a "faggot," laughed at and ostracized. All my time and energy were consumed with trying to prove I wasn't this horrible thing, this sissy-faggot-queer.

As we got older, entering the fifth and sixth grades, and people began hitting puberty, the girls also started to call me a fag. They now had to distance themselves from me because they wanted to date boys who made fun of me. I, in turn, to prove my manhood, asked out just about every pretty girl in my grade. All of them turned me down. I was a laughing-stock.

The name-calling got worse. Every day was hell, and I began to dread going to school. I did everything I could to avoid being noticed. I stayed quiet and tried not to answer questions. I didn't even laugh at jokes. At home, I had my few friends on the block who'd always been my pals. I spent some time with them but I spent more and more time alone, in my room or walking in the woods. I would fantasize about other places, other worlds. I started writing these ideas down, and was soon writing science fiction stories thirty and forty pages long. Escaping into those worlds kept me going. But I always had to come back to reality.

I felt myself becoming distant from my mother. We'd always been close. She was like my best friend, and I thought I could tell her anything. But I couldn't tell her *this*. If I told her the kids were calling me names, she'd want to know why. Even I was refusing to face the true reason. I couldn't just say, "Well, actually, Mom, maybe there's something to it.

You see, I do have these feelings I can't explain, and I don't think that fact should be seen as any different from being left-handed, and I just wish the kids would stop." No, I knew my mother wouldn't be able to accept my telling her any of this at that age, and I was afraid of what action might be taken. Would I be put in a home? Would I be punished? Would I be taken to a priest for some sort of ritual? Both the larger culture we lived in and the subculture I grew up in were homophobic. I was like an outsider in the family, an alien—something the family didn't like. As long as I could stay in disguise, however, I was safe. I had to stay that way to protect myself; since there was no telling what they might do. I was absolutely amazed that life had turned out this way—that there could be something about me that I couldn't tell to a soul, not even my mother; that I could be blamed and shamed for something I had no control over.

It was all very hard to comprehend. I knew that somehow the name-calling was tied to these feelings I'd always had toward boys. On top of it all, I realized that these feelings were sinful—they just *had to* be—and I felt dirty for having them. I alternately asked God for forgiveness and cursed him for making me this way. That, in turn, made me feel even more guilty. I pleaded with God, begging him to change me, to make me normal. *Why,* I asked him over and over again, *did you do this to me?* But I couldn't blame God. After all, he was flawless, I was told. I concluded, time and time again, that this was all my fault and that I was simply a bad Christian. I felt that the only way to redeem myself was to confess it all. But I wouldn't dare tell this to a priest. I was literally afraid for my safety, so I lived with the shame.

By sixth grade, people were pairing off. All the girls who had once been my friends were now dating the boys who'd always called me a faggot. The boys' attacks got worse. Sometimes they would gang up on me and beat me up. Many times I thought about going somewhere else, to a place where people weren't so mean and vicious. I often fantasized about running away. At the end of my fantasy there was almost always a reunion with my family and all the kids at school. I didn't really want to run away; I just wanted to get attention, to show everyone how horrible this was.

One day I raised my hand in class and asked one of my teachers, Mr. Reed (in the higher grades there were lay teachers because of a shortage of nuns), if I could go to the bathroom. It had been a particularly rough day; earlier, a group of kids had spat on me while shrieking "Queer!" I went into the bathroom and began crying and banging the walls. I then tore out of the building and walked around the school grounds for a while, eventually hiding in some bushes. About two hours later, I came back. The entire faculty was in a panic. They had been searching the building and were just about to call my parents. My whole class was concerned, too. Mr. Reed saw that I'd been crying. We went for a walk outside.

"Did something happen at home?" he said.

"No," I replied. "It's the kids at school."

"I think I know what it is."

I began to cry.

"Are they calling you names?" he asked.

"They call me a faggot and a sissy," I answered. "I just can't take it anymore. I don't know what to do. It drives me crazy. Everyone hates me."

He looked me in the eye and said, "Listen to me. I'm going to go inside and talk to the class before you come in. But I'm warning you, that's not going to change things too much. This is going to go on for quite some time. It's horrible. I know. But you have to be strong. Do you understand me?"

I nodded.

"One day," he continued, "everything will be fine. You will be happy. But that may be a long time from now. You've got to endure this. I promise you, if you do, everything will be great. But you've got to be strong, okay? Do you promise?"

I nodded, although I didn't really understand what he meant at the time. Years later, of course, I realized that Mr. Reed, a forty-year-old "bachelor" at the time, was also queer. He was trying to reach out to me but was limited in doing so for fear of losing his job, especially then. If only he could really have spoken frankly with me about this. If only there had been some older person—a teacher or a counselor—with whom I could have openly discussed these feelings. I'd have been spared so much pain and suffering. But, of course, there wasn't such a person.

When I went back into the classroom, Mr. Reed had chastised the class for being hateful and calling me ugly names. Everyone was nice. People came up to me separately and told me they were sorry. Some actually said they'd never realized it bothered me. Others said that if I ever wanted to talk to them about it, they would be there for me.

But within a month, the vicious name-calling resumed.

I was forever a "faggot."

Not too long after that incident, at the age of twelve, I had my first sexual experience. It was with a thirty-year-old man who worked in a bagel store near my house. I wasn't forcibly abused or otherwise coerced. On the contrary, I sought him out. I had heard about him from a friend in my neighborhood—a friend who was warning me about the man because he'd been propositioned by him. The tale intrigued me. My own hormones were beginning to rage. I was an early developer, with hair on my chest as I turned twelve. I found myself hanging around the bagel shop, hoping to be propositioned. Finally, I was.

While I willfully sought out sex with this man, some people would say he, as an adult, was grossly irresponsible. That may very well be true; certainly I, as an adult, would never have sex with a twelve-year-old and would consider anyone, straight or gay, who did so as behaving irresponsibly. But if it hadn't been him, it would have been someone else—most likely another twelve-year-old. I was curious and wanted to experiment.

Although I enjoyed the encounter, when it was over I ran home, crying. I promised myself—and God—that it would never happen again. The guilt was insurmountable. I was physically ill for days, throwing up, disgusted over being such a bad Catholic and doing such grotesque things. In the ensuing months and years, I developed an extreme weight problem, losing weight by starving myself and then gaining it by binging out of control. My sexual habits would later develop the same pattern: I'd go for long periods—months—without sex, only to gorge out of control at some point. And always I was racked with guilt. Somehow, I knew that all this was tied up with my hating myself.

At that time, I sought out some information on homosexuality. I was desperately hoping to be offered a "cure." Our family encyclopedia told me that this "deviant behavior" was difficult to root out after the individual had engaged in it for a long time, and it blamed mothers for the "problem." It said that homosexuality was caused by environmental factors, and there was a reference to the "homosexual-producing mother"—who, the encyclopedia said, was more prevalent among Italians and other Latins than among other ethnic groups. At first I was devastated, but I soon became suspicious of the information. It wasn't that I knew at that time how false and misogynistic the analysis was; I simply knew that my mother had nothing to do with this. However, I grew extremely depressed. There was no accurate information available to me.

In another attempt to prove my manhood, I joined the Pee Wee football league at thirteen. To keep in shape, I began running on the Franklin D. Roosevelt Boardwalk at nearby South Beach. This was about eight months after my first sexual encounter, after I'd sworn to myself that I would never have another homosexual experience. But in the dark, cool recesses under the boardwalk, I found a whole new world.

There, dozens of Italian boys, my age and a little bit older, regularly met in the afternoons and had sex. Sometimes it was group sex; most times it was one-on-one. The boys were all in the same boat as I was: None of them would ever have called themselves gay. They were all kids who were trying to deal with this madness that had seemingly taken over their bodies. Most would have said they hated it and wished they weren't that way; all would have said this was just a phase, a time that was going to pass. None of us were ever going to be homos when we got older. We were all going to get married, just like everyone else.

Actually, we didn't speak to one another about homosexuality all that much, except when the bashers came. Every now and then straight guys with baseball bats would show up under the boardwalk. Everyone would run, and a lot of times someone would get his head bashed in. The bashing was worse at night, I was told. Some said that people had been murdered under there. This danger was really the only thing that had us talking to one another; otherwise we'd just meet discreetly, have sex, and leave each other.

In the beginning, after each visit to the world under the boardwalk, I'd go home and cry. Each time, I'd not go back for quite a while. But eventually the guilt subsided. I started to accept this thing, whatever it was, as something manageable. It was my secret world and—well, yes, it was fun. But of course I could never tell anyone about it—and I could never let it become my whole life. It could only be a phase.

I felt I had to date girls to prove not only to everyone else, but to myself, that I was a heterosexual. I began seeing a girl at school, a new girl who'd transferred in. The affair helped my image. I was in the eighth grade by then, and the guys stopped calling me names, it seemed, out of respect for my girlfriend. It appeared as if I'd proven my heterosexuality to them.

Karen was a pretty blond girl but she didn't really interest me. More than that, I didn't really enjoy being physical with her. Kissing was okay, but I had no desire to have intercourse with her. After a while, she got bored and dumped me.

I was devastated—not because I'd lost her, but because I'd lost my cover. Some of the guys actually started saying Karen had left me because I was a fag. Thank goodness I was graduating that year. High school would be a whole new world, a clean slate. No one would know anything about me. And I'd make sure that I appeared completely heterosexual. I would not hang around with girls, and I would keep playing football—even though I hated it.

I was enrolled in Monsignor Farrell High School, a private, Catholic, all-boy school. It was the best school on the island and one of the finest in the state; it accepted only those who scored highest on the entrance exams. Farrell was a competitive school that prepared students for the top universities in the country, and it had the best high school football team in New York State.

I spent weeks trying out for the football team. I was a good player, but two conflicting forces were battling inside of me. One part of me wanted with every fiber and bone in my body to get on that team so that I could prove I was a man; the other part—the true me—hated the game and didn't want any part of it. I sabotaged myself, making slip-ups in tryouts, and didn't make the team. But the other side of me—the false me—pushed me to go to football camp anyway, as a second-stringer, so that I could still be part of the team and would of course be playing the next year.

Surprisingly, at football camp, a two-week preseason ordeal out in East Hampton, New York, it seemed that everyone became queer. Well, not everyone, but a lot of boys who were probably straight were experimenting with homosexuality, as usual in any all-male environment, especially when all the males are teenagers. Others probably were queer. I had sex with a few of the guys on the team.

But when we got back from camp, *everyone* was again heterosexual. I had actually developed a crush on one of the players with whom I'd had sex, and I kept pushing to be with him when we were back at school. He, of course, labeled me a queer. Suddenly, once again, I was the class fag, reviled by everyone. I got into a lot of fights.

But football had beefed me up. Now I was beating people up everywhere—in the cafeteria, in the library, in the bathroom. Anyone who called me a fag received a punch in the face. I had learned one thing: how to shut them up. I was a strong kid with a powerful left hook, and I could take on guys twice my size. My temper would rage, and I'd pummel my enemies to the ground and then sit on them, claiming victory. It was humiliating for them because a "fag" had beaten them up in front of everyone. But they'd never say anything nasty to me again because they were afraid I'd go crazy on them. However, no matter how vicious and mean they were to me, no matter how ugly their taunts, I felt terrible after beating them up, after that aggression dissipated. Each time, I'd cry myself to sleep that night, upset that I had hurt someone else.

This went on for almost two years. Then I got into one fight too many and was called into the principal's office. He said if my fighting didn't stop I'd have to leave the school. He wanted to know why I was always in fights, but I refused to tell him. After an hour or so, he called in one of the brothers to counsel me. This was a man who I always suspected was gay. In fact, there had been some rumors about him.

I told him, in private, that I was fighting the other guys because they were calling me a queer.

"You know," he said, "because this is an all-boy school, and because people are so envious of the students who attend, many on the outside say cruel things, I know, in order to intimidate the students here."

That was true. If you attended Farrell, you were a "Farrell fag." It was a running joke all over the island.

"Because of that," the brother continued, "many of the students here internalize that name-calling and take it out on each other. They're so afraid of being called these things themselves that they attack others in the school first."

"Well," I responded, "it's not entirely untrue."

"What's not entirely untrue?"

I was getting up the gumption to actually tell someone about myself, someone who I felt understood the situation.

"I do have these feelings," I continued. "And things have happened."

"What are you saying?" He seemed to become incensed. I suddenly realized he was not the person to tell.

"Nothing, sir. Forget it."

"Wait right here," he told me.

He went back out and spoke with the principal for quite some time. I then was called into his office. The dean of students, Father Finn, was also there.

"Mike," the principal said, "we don't think you're happy here. We think you would be better off on the outside, at a public school. We're not going to expel you. It's up to you. But I think you should go."

My mother was then called in and was told that I wasn't happy at Farrell, that I'd been in fights and that this type of disciplined environment wasn't right for everyone. They told her that I'd suggested I'd like to leave and that they had agreed.

I was enrolled in the local public high school, New Dorp High. Public school was much rougher, I knew. There were lots of tough kids, the kind who formed gangs and hated queers and enjoyed pouncing on them. I had to survive. I sensed that once high school was over, a lot of the nightmare would stop. Somehow I just had to get through this, as Mr. Reed had told me back in sixth grade. Of course I wasn't yet admitting to myself that I was really homosexual. I was still going to the beach, under the boardwalk, regularly. But that was my secret world, and it didn't mean anything. All of the years of name-calling had taken their toll: I hated myself. *Why, I* began to ask myself over and over, *do I want to live any longer? Why do I want to go through any more of this? I* contemplated suicide. Over and over I'd go through the scenarios: Take all the pills in the medicine cabinet. Jump off the Staten Island Ferry into the harbor. Run into oncoming traffic. Slit my wrists.

I couldn't go through with it. I vowed that I was going to make it—any way I could. I had to make sure that I'd never be labeled a fag again, so I sought out the toughest crowd in the school. I figured if I hung around with them, I'd be considered macho. I beat up a lot of boys over the silliest things, showing my new friends that I could handle myself. Then I got into drugs, to prove to the guys that I could take it. We were doing the hallucinogen mescaline a lot. When I was high, everything was easier to deal with. I found myself doing more drugs as time went on.

Another way to show the guys that I was heterosexual was bashing queers, just like they did. There was a skinny, quiet kid named Vinnie, one of those nerdy guys who rarely said a word to anyone and always took whatever abuse was hurled at him. And there was plenty. Everyone called him a fag and a queer. Lots of the tougher, meaner guys pushed him around a lot, sometimes punching and kicking him. He just took it all, never uttering a sound. Everyone laughed at him all the time, pointing and cackling.

In gym class, Vinnie always sat on the bleachers, participating in sports as little as possible. While he sat against the wall, the other boys hurled basketballs at him, as a sort of target practice. His glasses flew off most of the time, or broke. Still, he just sat through it. I knew Vinnie was living a hellish existence. So was I. Yet my way of dealing with it was to hurl basketballs at him too, to show everyone that I wasn't at all a fag like him. I remember vividly how the guys would egg me on and laugh, having a grand time as I whipped those basketballs at Vinnie. His head, over and over again, smashed against the wall. Still, he never moved. He never did anything. Passivity was his way of getting through the nightmare. And beating him up was mine. Each time, I went home and cried.

At the same time, I began to fall in love with my friend Jim. It was not a physical relationship. Jim was straight for all I knew, but I felt a powerful emotional bond with him. I was so emotionally disturbed, so messed up, that I was looking up to this tough, muscled guy, who really was a loser. His grades were lousy; he treated people terribly, using them for all of their money and anything else they could give him; and he was on drugs every day. I was easily taken in by him, partly because I was attracted to him physically and partly because he was telling me that I was a great guy. He was lying, scamming me. I think I knew that but I didn't care. Anyone who treated me well and told me that I was wonderful could manipulate me.

Jim and I did a lot of drugs, almost every night. I was a senior in high school by then, and we were hanging out with the rest of my gang in a nearby park. The drugs were costing a lot of money, and I was buying them for Jim too. He slept over at my house a lot, in my basement. I always fantasized about having sex with him, but I never dared to try anything. Soon, I began selling drugs in order to make money to fund our habits.

At home, things had hit rock bottom. Since I'd turned twelve, my parents had caught me with cigarettes several times and had punished me—which only made me more rebellious. I still did every thing I could to get them mad, it seemed, to prove to them that I was straight—which, to me, meant doing macho things and standing up to your parents. I was very defiant, running out on them, not coming home on time, saying the nastiest things to them. My mother was a nervous wreck. When she finally found my stash of pills, all hell broke loose. She and my father sat me down.

"I need help," I said. "I need someone to talk to about things." My mother called the pediatrician and got the name of a psychiatrist. Within two weeks I was in therapy.

Dr. Simmons knew that the drugs were not the problem, but rather were a symptom of a larger dilemma. I had no identity. My personality was stunted and damaged.

Therapy went well. I was more positive, thinking more about myself and what I wanted to do with my life. As a result, I pulled myself away from unhealthy influences and I was happier. But strangely, we never discussed my being gay, even though I was starting to feel good about that fact.

During therapy, which went on for almost two years, I graduated and enrolled at Brooklyn College, still unsure of what I wanted to do for a career.

During that time, I dated a woman and had sex with her several times. In terms of sheer enjoyment, the sex didn't compare to sex with men. But there was also something else missing. While I had always looked to girls rather than boys to be my best friends, I didn't bond emotionally with women in the same way that I did with men; there wasn't a sexual edge. But I had never bonded with any of the men I'd had sex with; that feeling was always reserved for the straight friends on whom I had crushes. The men I had sex with were quick encounters, men I met at the beach or on the subway, at the library or in cafés. I never attempted to see these people again or to have a conversation of any depth with them, because I was afraid of getting involved, afraid that it would mean I was a homosexual.

Now, toward the end of therapy, I started to think that I wanted to experience a bond with a man that was both emotional and sexual. For the first time, I felt good about being queer. It was exciting. Looking back, I realize that just dealing with my lack of confidence and repairing my damaged sense of self had equipped me to come to terms with my homosexuality. However, I didn't dare discuss that at length with Dr. Simmons because I knew that he was homophobic—even though I didn't know that word at the time. What had me leery of frankly discussing my homosexuality with him was his response after I'd first tested him on the issue. I told him that I'd had a sexual experience with a man I met outside his office, and he told me that it probably meant nothing.

"That's normal," he said. "Everyone has one or two homosexual experiences. I'm sure it's nothing. If it becomes something more, let me know."

"But what about people who are gay?" I asked. "People who live a gay life? Do they have some sort of problem?"

"Ninety-nine percent of homosexual men just have a fear of women," he said. "It's a fear of something different, since a woman has a different organ. It's easier to deal with the familiar and so they stick with men. All they really need to do is get over their fear."

I knew that wasn't it. My whole life was getting better because of therapy, and I was also feeling better about being gay. I didn't want to go into this with Dr. Simmons because I figured it would keep me in therapy much longer for something that I wasn't feeling so bad about and that I didn't think he had a handle on. I sensed that he was going to try to tamper with an aspect of my life that he shouldn't be tampering with. I wanted to pursue this—this homo thing—and see what happened.

On leaving therapy, I decided to study journalism. I transferred to the S.I. Newhouse School of Public Communications at Syracuse University. I also knew that if I wanted to be happy and live my life, I needed to move away from Staten Island.

At Syracuse, for the first time in my life, I was completely out of the closet in my day-to-day activities. I socialized in a gay environment. All of my friends were gay, and much of my life revolved around exploring my sexuality and exploring the rich gay culture I'd been denied. With distance, I realized how corrupt my church was. It wasn't preaching love and respect—it was ordering its members to hate and to exclude. So much of the madness I had lived through for twenty years was caused by the church's teachings on homosexuality. I discarded Roman Catholicism entirely. However, I would always retain my spirituality.

I was the happiest I'd ever been, as if I'd finally found that fantasy world I'd always dreamed about. But I also realized how lucky I'd been to make it through those rough years: Thirty percent of the teen suicides in America, I came to learn, are among lesbian and gay adolescents who feel that life has nothing to offer them and that they are freaks. I'd only made it, perhaps, because I was strong and because I had parents who loved me and cared about me enough to stick by me and get me help when I sent them a message—even though it would be years yet before I told them about my being queer.

I thought about the kids whose parents didn't send them to therapy. I thought about the kids whose parents sent them to therapists who tried to "cure" them. What about the kids whose parents were troubled themselves? What about children from broken homes or children of alcoholics? What about the kids who weren't strong enough, who weren't survivors?

I thought a lot in those years about Vinnie and the others whom I had pummeled. Had they made it? How badly had I hurt them? Still, I wasn't at all political and had no interest in gay politics at that time. I was filled with a lot of unhealthy ideas about homosexuality, and I was at the beginning of a road that would take years to travel.

At that time I told two close straight male friends from home that I was gay. John and Paul were great guys—typical macho Italian guys—who had been my constant companions during my two years at Brooklyn College. I wasn't sure how they'd react, but they accepted it well. I also told my cousin Marilu. Incredibly, she was shocked—but very supportive, and even delighted. "That's great," she said. "At least *someone* in the family is doing something exciting." And I had my first relationship, a one-year-long, intimate affair, while I was at Syracuse. Then I had another that lasted just as long. I graduated and decided to explore this new life. I'd been denied a real adolescence, even a real childhood, in which I could grow and learn.

Growing up is hard, especially if you're a homo. . . .

NOTE: HEALTH ISSUES

Signorile's essay highlights some of the destructive consequences of harassment, bullying, and internalized homophobia for gay youth. Although computations vary from study to study, nearly all reported studies reveal serious negative mental and physical health issues facing LGBT youth. For example:

- 1 in 5 HIV-positive men were apparently infected during their adolescent years.
- 68% of adolescent gay males use alcohol (26% or more at least once a week); 44% use other drugs.
- 83% of adolescent lesbians use alcohol and 56% use other drugs.
- 31% of LGB students have used cocaine as opposed to 7% of non-LGB students.
- 62% of LGB students smoke as opposed to 35% of non-LGB students.
- 32% of LGB students have gotten pregnant or gotten someone pregnant as opposed to 12% of non-LGB students.
- 30% of gay and bisexual adolescent males attempt suicide at least once.

Gay and lesbian youth represent 30% of all completed teen suicide: extrapolation shows this means a successful suicide attempt by a gay teen every 5 hours and 48 minutes.

LGB students are four times more likely to attempt suicide than non-LGB students.

B. THE REV. IRENE MOORE'S PERSONAL STORY*

"I ain't raising no goddamn bulldagger up in my house. Before I do that I'll send your ass right back to that damn agency where I got you."

Whenever my behavior revealed the slightest hint of masculinity, my foster mother always used those words to threaten me with expulsion from her house. My infraction one Saturday morning was getting caught playing an aggressive game of handball in the August heat with our neighbor's boys. . . .

My residency in my foster mother's house was always tenuous. It hinged precariously on my being a number of things for her, one of which was a dainty little girl. I desperately tried to be that little girl. However, sometimes I failed her. And in those times, before I learned to censor my undainty ways, the wild and happy and athletic butch girl in me would break loose. And I realized, in those wondrously fleeting moments, that not only did I enjoy competitive rough-and-tumble sports with boys, but also the sexual exploration that came with the sensuous joy of a touchy-feely game of "doctor" with girls.

* Excerpted from, MITCHELL GOLD, CRISIS: 40 STORIES REVEALING THE PERSONAL, SOCIAL, AND RELIGIOUS PAIN AND TRAUMA OF GROWING UP GAY IN AMERICA (2008). Used with permission of Mitchell Gold and Rev. Irene Moore.

At age six, my behavior was easily explained as precocious and cute; I was a tomboy who would outgrow this preadolescent phase once I learned cultural norms. However, by age sixteen I showed no signs of changing. Instead of precocious and cute, I was seen as a developmentally arrested teenager. The slang word for my "illness" was *bulldagger*, a colloquialism once commonly used in the African–American community to denote a masculine lesbian. This pejorative term had both tremendous sting and stigma, and my foster mother used it not only to spew her venom about my behavior but also to evoke fear in the hopes that it would straighten me out. It didn't. I like women! The realization of my attraction to them was affirmed weekly as I delighted in looking at the voluptuous mocha-colored to honey-brown complexioned centerfolds in *Jet* magazine. Oh how I dreamed of being sexy like those women *so* that they would lust and long for me the way men lusted and longed for them. And with my nightly fantasies of *Jet* centerfolds eyeing me, finally, I thought, I would make things up to my foster mother: Since I hadn't been able to be her dainty little girl, I would become her ultra-fem teenager.

I probably shouldn't have told my foster mother the reason why I wanted to become ultra-fem—so other women would like me. She yelled at me for my twisted thoughts, warning me that I would be homeless if I didn't take her demands that I become a normal girl seriously. My minister said I would go to hell if I didn't rebuke the homosexual demon in me and be spiritually treated by him.

As a ward of New York State, I had a third authority figure in my life: a social worker assigned to me by the Bureau of Child Welfare. And of the three—my mother, my minister, and my social worker—it was my social worker who showed the greatest optimism for my becoming a healthy heterosexual.

According to her, my sexual confusion was a textbook case. Having lived with my birth mother for six months before she abandoned me in a trash can in Fort Greene Park in Brooklyn, my behavior was merely an expression of my continuing search for her. In her usual distant and clinical tone, my social worker explained that the "tactile deficit" experienced by a child deprived of a parent's touch during infancy is often expressed sexually with someone of the same gender as the missing parent. I interrupted her to point out that I was missing both parents. Annoyed, she snapped back that it was the gender of the parent I missed most or who had hurt me most. Both my foster mother and my minister accepted her explanation.

So they sent me to weekly psychotherapy sessions, but I showed no progress. The child psychiatrist and my social worker seemed to realize I was incurably gay, incapable of modeling societal gender norms, and the frustration showed in their faces. At that point, my social worker gave me some advice: pretend to be straight.

Here was her reasoning: In those days, before there were group homes and interracial adoption, African–American and Latino foster kids were the hardest to place (and still are). With many more children in need than foster homes available, my being a troubled African–American homosexual teenager assured me neither long-term housing nor permanent placement.

Her stories of the many foster children thrown out of foster homes for lesser infractions than being homosexual scared me enough to act straight. Moreover, she believed in behavior modification to change dysfunctional behavior patterns and remediate damaged thinking so one can better interact with the world. With her advice, I began accessorizing myself with the outward accoutrements of heterosexual culture. Being captain of the girls track and volleyball teams kept the question of my sexual orientation on the front burner for my foster mother, minister, and social worker, so I became a cheerleader. My biggest and best cover-up was my six-foot-three high school basketball-playing boyfriend. And while the cover-up worked beautifully Monday through Friday at school, I never felt comfortable with the lie I had created when I was in church on Sunday.

The centrality of the black church in African–American communities shapes the attitudes and mores of both its "churched" and "unchurched" residents. I joined my church at age five, was baptized at six, and served on the junior usher board from ages six until sixteen, becoming president of the junior board by fifteen.

I still remember the first day my minister called me into his study to share Jesus's special love for children. He read the Bible passage in Mark 10:13–16:

"People were bringing little children to Jesus to have him touch them, but the disciples rebuked them. When Jesus saw this, he was indignant. He said to them, 'Let the little children come to me, and do not hinder them, for the kingdom of God belongs to such as these. I tell you the truth, anyone who will not receive the kingdom of God like a little child will never enter it.' And he took the children in his arms, put his hands on them and blessed them."

He told me no other place in the world so welcomes all children—especially orphans—as the church. And since my church, a pillar of the community, was so welcoming, it was a nod for the larger community to welcome me, too. Growing up in the church was a refuge from the hostile and violent worlds of my environment and foster home, feeding and clothing me both physically and spiritually. To me, aside from Martin Luther King, Jr., my minister was one of the best representations of doing God's work in the world and an exemplary disciple of Jesus because he, like Jesus, loved me. Therefore I took his advice and admonitions about unjust acts and ungodly behavior seriously.

Over the years, I frequently met with him in his office—to sign an embarrassing report card, explain receiving detention for cutting class, discuss why I wanted to join the Dance Theater of Harlem instead of going to college, debate scripture or world events, and get advice on how to be a good Christian.

I will always remember my last visit to his office, when I was sixteen. It was my desire to be a good Christian that led me to make the appointment. When we met, I told him that my boyfriend wanted to have sex but the feeling wasn't mutual. I also confessed that if there were anyone I'd want to be with in that way, it would be my girlfriend.

As always, he listened attentively. Then he came around the desk with his Bible in hand and told me to open my Bible. He read Leviticus 18:22: "Do not lie with a man as one lies with a woman; it is an abomination." Next he told me to read aloud Romans 1:26–27 in which Paul writes, "Because of this, God gave them over to shameful lusts. Even their women exchanged natural sexual relations for unnatural ones. In the same way the men also abandoned natural relations with women and were inflamed with lust for one another. Men committed shameful acts with other men, and received in themselves the due penalty for their error."

When I finished reading, he slammed his Bible shut, knocked mine out of my hands, and said not only was I causing God's wrath, but also his own. Like my social worker, he too believed in behavior modification: He explained that if I pretended to like natural sexual relations with men I would eventually come to love it. However, he said, the best person to teach me was not my boyfriend, but him—and he was going to teach me now, once and for all.

The scuffle that ensued caught the attention of two male deacons, who ran frantically down the hall and knocked on the door. When my minister swung the door open, the deacons could see furniture overturned and the contents of his desk on the floor. Noticing that my minister and I were both straightening our clothes, the deacons asked what was the matter. My minister said, "I was fighting this harlot off me. After all these years of being a father figure to her I couldn't imagine anything like this."

News spread through the church and the community, with most people, even my foster mother, questioning the veracity of the story because there had been rumors of his predilection for young girls. Nevertheless, because I brought shame to the minister, in less than a week, with a black garbage bag of my worldly possessions in tow, I was an emergency placement in another foster home. When I told my new foster family what had happened, they threw me out of their house for fear that my homosexuality would lead me to prey on their other female foster kids or cause them to "catch it" from me.

With no place to go—no help from the foster care agency and the loss of both my community and my church—I would have attempted to take my life were it not for the help of my high school guidance counselor and teachers.

When I left for college in the 1970s, I was the beneficiary of three civil rights movements—black, women's, and gay. I assumed my choice of school—renowned liberal Massachusetts women's college, Wellesley—would be the most open and affirming. It wasn't. Although Wellesley had many white openly lesbian students, the African–American ones were closeted. Controlled by the homophobic ethos of black nationalism, as well as the social isolation and cultural intolerance of the campus milieu, many of us African–American lesbian sisters performed our requisite black heterosexual roles in order to be part of the black community. I played my role so well that by my senior year, I was elected president of the black student governing body.

After college, I decided to attend seminary. I wanted to go to an African–American seminary because I felt there was no better place to learn about the black church. But by this time I had come out, and the two African–American seminaries to which I applied had rejected me because of my sexual orientation. Instead I attended Union Theological Seminary in New York and then Harvard Divinity School, where as a doctoral student my focus became gay rights. In recent years, the black church has yet again rejected me. Because I am openly lesbian, I have not found a home church in my faith tradition from which to do AIDS ministry—and black heterosexual women are the new face of HIV/AIDS, so there is much work to be done.

So I have become a public theologian. I have found a home and my ministry on the streets, with Boston's gay, lesbian, bisexual, and transgender community. The foundation for my life's work is in what Jesus said in Matthew 25:45: "In truth I tell you, in so far as you failed to do it for the least of these, however insignificant, you failed to do it for me."

My work is a public theology in tandem with a struggling community. While it is easy to see how economic disadvantage because of racial bias leads people of color to the streets, it is less determinable as to how many gay people are forced into homelessness. Abandoned by family and friends because of their sexual orientation, many have only the streets.

Part of my outreach ministries is reporting on religion in the news for gay and mainstream publications. In this era of dominance by the Christian Right, I try to inform the public of the role religion plays in discrimination against gay people. And because homophobia, like other prejudices, is a hatred of the "other," and usually acted upon in the name of religion, my writing allows me to highlight how intolerance and fundamentalism not only hurt the gay community but also perpetuate other forms of oppression such as racism, sexism, classism, and anti-Semitism. And in the process, prejudice and intolerance in the name of religion also shatter the goals of American democracy: life, liberty, and the pursuit of happiness for every citizen.

C. PAST MEDICALIZATION*

On November 13, 1964, a young man, who will here remain anonymous, was involuntarily committed by his parents to a private mental

* Reprinted from *1974: ANONYMOUS; Electroshock "The agony of the years after,"* in JONATHAN KATZ, GAY AMERICAN HISTORY (HarperColophon). Reprinted by permission of Jonathan Katz.

hospital in a Southern state. There he was given what one of his doctors termed "a course of electroconvulsive treatment"—electric shock. After hospitalization of two and a half months, the patient was discharged to his parents. In an interview with the present writer on April 29, 1974, the subject indicated that his parents' desire to "cure" his homosexuality was the reason for his confinement and shock treatment. This is verified by a number of incidents recalled by the subject, as well as by a recent correspondence with his parents concerning their reason for committing him.

Anon.: I was born in 1940, and I lived in one Southern state for my first eighteen years, till I graduated from high school. Then I went to art school in a neighboring state, stayed two and a half years there, and quit. Then I went to a nearby city and stayed about three years. During that time I visited my parents off and on, and they even came to visit me. At the end of one particular visit, they asked why I didn't go to a psychiatrist. I said I didn't think there was any reason to. I didn't think they were serious. They never came out and asked about my Gay life. That was a taboo subject with them. They said they just thought I might need psychological help. Even when I was sixteen they had taken me to a psychologist to have tests; they didn't want me to go to art school unless the doctor thought I was worth it.

In 1962, I was twenty-two. 1962 is the first commitment. I was living in this state near my parents and I'd gotten a job. I understood later that they came to that state to arrange this commitment.

In the United States, it's not hard for your nearest relatives to commit you, especially if they can pay for it. And this was very cheap. This was a state hospital, so it was only $37.50 a week.

The policemen came for me at work. They said, "We're not allowed to explain anything. You have to come with us." That was it. I realized what was happening when they drove me through the hospital gates and I saw the sign: —STATE HOSPITAL. I said to myself, "Well, they did it. I guess my parents are more concerned than I realized—for my well-being."

What made them commit me was a postcard I had gotten from an older friend. My mother asked, "What man writes to another man, 'there are many pretty boys on board ship but I don't touch a one'? Now what does he mean by that?" My mother brought it up to the psychiatrist when she committed me the first time.

I stayed in that state hospital and I just got bored. There were 2,700 patients, and I saw a doctor twice. They did ask about my ideas about sexuality. I had this German female doctor. I told her what I thought—that sex expressions could not be limited to one sex, and peoples' sex expression could be what they wished; I said a homosexual or a heterosexual act, it doesn't matter. She said, "Don't you think that's abnormal?" I said, "No." They let it go at that. I stayed there until I got tired of it. After seven weeks I decided I would leave. I walked away.

J.K.: Didn't they come after you?

Anon.: I went to live in a city about sixty miles away. I kept clear of anyone my parents might contact, anyone I'd known before. I called my parents after six months.

J.K.: Your parents hadn't tried to track you down?

Anon.: I don't know. They didn't say anything about it.

Almost two years went by. I did odd jobs and things. In 1964, I came to New York and stayed five months doing temporary work, typing mostly. Then my former art teacher, who was retiring, offered me her class—back in my hometown. I had never tried teaching, so I said OK. I went back there in September of 1964, and I started giving art lessons. On November 13, my parents committed me again.

J.K.: When you went back home, weren't you afraid that your parents might commit you again?

Anon.: I didn't have any fear of that; I should have. It came as a total surprise when they committed me again, just like the first time. I thought my parents had gotten over feeling that I was sick.

This was a much more sophisticated hospital. It was like a resort. During the time I had shock treatment it cost $350 a week.

J.K.: How did you get committed that time?

Anon.: I don't remember the actual details, but I do have copies of the letters I wrote from the hospital. In one I said, "The same thing happened that happened before." So it must have been the same procedure: they just went to the police and signed the papers.

J.K.: Was it specifically because you were Gay?

Anon.: I didn't know until I was out. I actually asked afterward. I was visiting my sister-in-law, and I asked her, "Why did they commit me? Did they really think I needed help?" She said, "Oh, you know; it was all over the Gay bit. That's all they were concerned about. They don't think you should be Gay." My brother, her husband, was the third signature on my commitment that time. He knew I was Gay. I met him at a Gay party once. He said to me, "What are you doing here?" I said, "What are you doing here?" He said, "I won't write home if you don't." He was already married at the time. Maybe he was guilty about some Gay activity. I had no feeling of guilt. After my commitment my brother said, "If I known what they were going to do, I would never have signed the paper. But I thought it was the best thing to do at the time. Our parents were so concerned."

J.K.: Do you remember what state of mind you were in the month before you were committed in November 1964?

Anon.: I've gone back to my notes and letters from that time thinking maybe I was totally flipped out. But I wasn't. I found notes and letters I wrote the day of my commitment that indicate I knew what I was doing. There were a few depressing times. There were arguments with my parents about why I was continuing relationships with people who they considered abnormal. I wrote a note to myself the day before my commitment about an argument we'd had. It was about writing to my friends who were obviously homosexual. I must have told my mother it was none of her business.

J.K.: Your parents were reading your mail?

Anon.: They read a few things.

J.K.: Do you think your parents feel guilty now about committing you, and about the shock treatment?

Anon.: A person who has become a close friend of theirs is a psychologist, and he asked them, "Why did you ever commit him for that?" My mother answered, "We just didn't know." Now she says they shouldn't have done it. I realize that they did what they thought was right at the time. They felt responsible, the typical attitude of intelligent parents. If they weren't so intelligent I think it wouldn't have happened. They didn't know that shock treatment was so bad. My mother said, "We didn't know what we were doing. The doctors convinced us to do it. We never would have done it if we knew the result."

J.K.: What was it like in the institution that time? Were there other Gay people there?

Anon.: I think so, but then you really never knew. Everyone was undergoing the same kind of shock treatment, both males and females.

They give you sodium pentothal beforehand, but I do remember being taken to one particular shock treatment. You're in your pajamas, and you just lie down on a table. Then you don't remember any more because they give you a shock. The shock itself erases anything you were experiencing before, any memory of it. I had seventeen shock treatments did have awareness enough to ask one of the nurses how many times I had had it, and she said, "I'll look it up." She said "seventeen."

J.K.: When you come out of the shock treatment, what is it like?

Anon.: I remember being shaved with an electric razor and thinking, "Isn't that strange? I can't move." I thought, "Why is he shaving me, and where am I, and why can't I do it myself, and why can't I stand up, and why can't I move my arms? Then I probably lost consciousness again. You're not aware of much."

I do remember after my own shock treatment listening to other people having shock treatment. I don't think that should be allowed. I was in the next ward. You hear that horrible scream. There's one loud scream—"Ahhhhh!!!"—very loud, each time they give you a shock, as the lungs are being evacuated. You hear what sounds like hundreds of people having shock treatment. They always did it in the morning, it went on all morning, three hours of those loud, single screams, one person at a time.

I do remember being very affectionate in the hospital during the time I had shock treatment. I thought I knew everyone. I would hug anyone.

J.K.: That seems to be the opposite of what was intended.

Anon.: Right, it was like making out with everyone, it didn't make any difference, male or female. I was going around feeling very close to everyone. They didn't respond with any affection. But I would do it anyway.

In the hospital I made copies of all my letters. I had a feeling at that time that I wouldn't remember, or that they wouldn't send them. I found out later that they hadn't sent some of them. John, who had been my lover in New York, told me later that he got no mail from me. He said he kept writing letters to someone who didn't answer. Another person, a friend, did get my letters. There's a gap in my letters in December '64. I always say I had shock treatment for Christmas that year. But I don't know if I actually had one on December 25.

The two doctors I had just weren't very hip people. One was a more aware, advanced person, a younger man. He was a very intelligent and much more involved person than the other. I remember what he said—These were his very words, I remember this very well. He said, "I don't see any reason why you should have been here. I've read through your files, I've read your whole case history, and you should never have been here." He said, "There's nothing wrong with being Gay. That's up to you. There's certainly no reason for you to stay." He had just come to the hospital, he was new. The very morning he said that, my other doctor had said something quite different. I don't know how many times I had discussed with him my ideas of sexuality, but finally he screamed out, "Then you're *sick* and I will not see you again! This is your last interview."

The same day, the new doctor said I could go home. I told him, "I'm in no state to go home." At that time I was so disoriented I didn't want to leave. He said, "Well, you can get out. I could let you go today if you want." I thought, "Is he just saying this? Maybe this is just another game." I became wary of their games. You don't trust anyone at that point. At the same time I wanted them to release me. When you're confined, you do have this sense that you want freedom more than anything. I said, "I'll go in a few days." I said I'd have to call my parents to come and get me. So we made all the arrangements and I left.

I was still in no state to be at home. My mother would ask me, "Well, what do you want to do?" She still felt very concerned. She said, "Your mail and Christmas gifts are in there from all your friends in New York." I said, "What friends in New York?" "I was never in New York." She gave me this look and said, "Don't talk like that! You know you were in New York. You were there for five months. How can you be so silly?" You're very sensitive at that point and you think, "My God, what's happened to me?" You don't remember anything.

Then another time we got to discussing homosexuality. I said I still felt it didn't make any difference which sex I had a feeling for if I liked someone. She screamed, "$6,200 for nothing! You haven't changed a bit." She said, "It was a total waste of time and money. The psychiatrists, they're stupid people; they don't know what they're doing."

I had group therapy with my parents after the shock treatment. The psychologist who didn't agree with my ideas of sexuality conducted this group, with the parents and outpatients, fifteen to eighteen people, once a week. In the group I was the only Gay one. At one session they brought up the Gay issue. We always went to the main problems we were supposed to be there for. I said it was not a problem for me. They said, "Don't you think you're abnormal, thinking you can have feelings for males as well as females?" I said, "No. I think you could be subnormal for not being able to have those feelings." The doctor says, "I'm afraid we got him too late." That was his explanation. Right in front of me he says, "He should have had therapy earlier and it would have been different." I remember the doctor saying he had had a homosexual in group therapy, "and now he's married."

After that particular session, on the way home, this horrible fight erupted in the car. My mother started hitting me. She hit me first so I figured I'd hit her back. I kicked her in the face, from the back seat of the car. Usually shock treatment makes you docile, and at the time I was taking these heavy tranquilizers, too. My father was upset. He wouldn't get involved in the screaming and yelling. He just kept out of it and said we should calm down. I don't think he ever felt as responsible as my mother did for my homosexuality. She really thought she'd created a monster.

I only went to about six sessions of group therapy, and then I came back to New York. I wanted to see who this person was who was writing to me, and to see all these other people I was supposed to know. I was fascinated to find out about an experience I was supposed to have had which I had absolutely no memory of. When I had come home from the hospital, I had read all of these letters from total strangers. I had no memory of them. One person was obviously my lover; he wrote me these wonderful letters. I thought, "I have to see who he is." He planned to meet me when I finally decided to go back to New York. I thought, "How will I recognize him?" Well, he recognized me, of course. When I met the other people I had known, I didn't remember them at all. But I pretended I did. I went along with everything. I became a very good actor then, by acting like I had a memory, which I didn't. I had absolutely none. It was extremely difficult.

I told my lover after about three months. I said, "I didn't remember you when I came back." It upset him so much that I didn't tell anyone else after that. He said, "How did you do what you did?" He meant—make love. I said, "I just did it. I must have done it before, so I did it." Sometimes people would see me and say, "Hi! Where have you been? I haven't seen you for years." That's a weird experience when you have no recollection of them at all. You act like you remember them because you don't want to offend them. I did explain a few times, but the explanation was so long it just wasn't worth it, and people got so upset hearing it that they didn't want to talk.

I had the most extreme depressions after shock treatment for the next three years. During these periods of depression it just seemed so hopeless, like I didn't have the strength to go on. Yet I'd resolved I'd never commit suicide. The depressions came from realizing that I didn't have my full faculties and from not knowing how long my memory would take to come back. I'd think: "It's going on and on and on; it's been five years, six years, eight years." You think it will never end. The depressions resulted from an accumulation of things, from it seeming such a struggle to concentrate. To accomplish any little thing seemed such an effort. I became almost immobile.

Other times I'd be very spicy, very up. After the shock treatment the doctor told me, "You're supposed to take these heavy tranquilizers for at least two years." After I was home for a while I took a drink my parents offered me, and I realized I was drooling. I couldn't even hold my mouth shut. I said, "I'm not taking these pills. This is dangerous." I threw the pills out. Maybe I wouldn't have spaced if I had taken the tranquilizers. I figured I'd rather space than not be able to function.

After shock treatment, it's like you've gotten stoned, like you're spacing. For the first eight years after shock treatment, I never knew if I would be able to connect my thoughts. I'd be walking down the street in New York and would have these flashes—and there would be nothing. I'd suddenly not know where I was. I'd think, "My God, I have to find out where I am. Why doesn't anything look familiar?" I would be typing at work and suddenly not be able to remember what city I was in. I'd think, "I have to remember!" A lot of times I'd forget my name and address. That might last for an hour and a half. But that's a long time when your mind is really going. The feeling was panic. But then I always said to myself, "Sit down and it'll come back." I always had awareness enough to think, "It's going to be temporary." When I left the hospital the doctor had said, "You'll have times when you won't know where you are—you'll feel disoriented, but it'll he temporary." I was told that much.

The fear of loss of memory is one of the worst experiences I had after shock treatment, the fear that I might at any point experience this amnesia. That amnesia happened maybe a thousand times. And you never know how long it will last, and you'll just forget where you are, for a few seconds, or minutes, or an hour. It could happen anywhere. You don't remember what you were doing or saying. And you don't want to show that you're upset, that you don't know where you are. Those memory lapses are over now, mostly. I noticed a definite change in January, 1972. Almost suddenly my thoughts connected. It was a wonderful feeling.

On the street a couple of years ago a woman said, "Sir!" and she reached out and grabbed my hand. She said, "Would you just stand by me for a few minutes? I want to get my bearings, I just want someone to be here. I don't know where I am. Will you tell me where I am?" I told her and she said, "Oh, thank you." I asked her later if she'd had shock treatment. She said, "Yes." I asked, "How long were you in the hospital?" She said, "Oh, I don't remember—a long time, many months. I just got out of the hospital, and I don't want to go back." She said, "My son thinks I shouldn't have left." She calmed down, then she remembered what she had to do. I had coffee with her and talked to her for about twenty minutes. I was on my lunch hour.

I think the people who prescribe shock treatment don't know what it can do to you—for years afterward. They know what the temporary result is. The doctor emphasized that there would be a memory loss. He said the treatment "rearranges your memory bank"—I think that's the terminology he used. But it doesn't rearrange it. For a while it removes it.

The main thing about shock is not the treatment itself, it's the agony of the years after—always having this sense that you will forget exactly where you are. That's bad, you know?

D. SAVING THE CHILDREN

America's youth have always been important capital in the culture wars surrounding sexuality and sexual orientation. In 1977, Dade County,

Florida passed a human-rights ordinance that prohibited discrimination on the basis of sexual orientation. Anita Bryant, at the time a highly visible star of television commercials, led a much publicized campaign to repeal the ordinance. Bryant asserted that the campaign against the ordinance was about "Christian beliefs regarding the sinfulness of homosexuality" and the likelihood that homosexuals would "recruit" children to the gay lifestyle.

This fear about the subversive effects of gay people on children led Bryant to found her political organization, *Save Our Children*. Among Bryant's assertions during the campaign were, "As a mother, I know that homosexuals cannot biologically reproduce children; therefore, they must recruit our children," and "If gays are granted rights, next we'll have to give rights to prostitutes and to people who sleep with St. Bernards and to nailbiters." On June 7, 1977, Bryant's campaign led to a repeal of the anti-discrimination ordinance by a margin of 69 to 31 percent.

The following day, Bryant stated, "In victory, we shall not be vindictive. We shall continue to seek help and change for homosexuals, whose sick and sad values belie the word 'gay' which they pathetically use to cover their unhappy lives."

Following is an article based on an interview with Anita Bryant, shortly after the initial success of *Save Our Children*. This piece is followed by a brief description of Bryant's life after her 1970s heyday.

"I'd Rather My Child Be Dead Than Homo"

By: Millie Ball*

Anita Bryant leaned forward, her elbows on her knees, and said,

"I'd rather my child be dead than be a homosexual.

"But I'll tell you something," she added, smiling. "I'd never disown my own child. I'd never condone what he did, but I'd love him. I've seen the effects homosexuality has on people, emotionally, spiritually, in every way, and I wouldn't wish it on anybody.

"When I think of young people of America today accepting this as an alternative lifestyle, it breaks my heart."

These comments from the singer who has turned part of her life into a crusade against what she believes are the evils of homosexuality and a successful fight against an anti-discrimination ordinance in Miami, Fla. came near the end of an almost two-hour interview at the Fairmont Hotel. They were in response to a direct question about what she'd do if one of *her* children were gay. Her first reply was that such a thing couldn't happen.

"Gay" is a word she doesn't use when talking about homosexuals. "It's an arbitrary word," she said. "It doesn't describe the sad lifestyle these people live."

She and her manager husband Bob Green decided to talk with the local news media because of the furor surrounding her appearance at the Summer Pops concerts Friday and Saturday nights at Municipal Auditorium, and because of a gay-rights rally sponsored Saturday night by Human Equal Rights for Everyone (HERE), a local civil rights group.

The 37–year old mother of four frequently quoted the Bible. At one point she went back to the bedroom of her suite to get her red Bible and read from the heavily underlined verses in the first chapter of Romans.

She ignored her room service avocado stuffed with seafood to proselytize about Jesus Christ, who she said is "on the throne of my life," and about God's will for our lives.

"I have no hate. I have no vendetta," she said. "My concern is for our children and us as a nation. I feel if we don't turn around soon, we will have to face judgment. Billy Graham said God would have to apologize to Sodom and Gomorrah if things don't get better here." She smiled at the little joke.

She said she has suffered an economic loss from a 70 per cent cancellation in bookings. But the Florida orange juice boycott by gay rights supporters didn't work. In fact, sales went up 25 per cent because of the backlash, said Miss Bryant.

The "silent majority" is speaking, she said. Out of the 1,000 or so letters her "Save the Children" organization gets daily, only six or seven are against her, according to Green.

The Save Our Children group does plan to go national he said, but no definite plans have been made yet. "We're waiting to hear from the public as to what direction to go into," she said. "Child pornography will probably be one."

Her husband brought out an often thumbed through gay travel guide (which incidentally recommended toilets in several local college university centers) and a guide to gay citizen's band radio lingo. "Read that last page," said Miss Bryant, referring to a section which graphically described a homosexual encounter. "I never knew that existed until I got into all of this," she said. "I never realized how sick it all is. It's against nature."

Rain started batting against the window. A roar of thunder momentarily stopped conversation. The gay rights rally was an hour away. "Do you think God made it rain because of the rally?" she was asked. Miss Bryant laughed and said, "No comment. I'll leave it up to you."

Excerpt From "Bankruptcy, Ill Will Plague Bryant."

By: Thomas C. Tobin
St. Petersburg Times, April 28, 2002

Anita Bryant, who turned her runner-up status as Miss America 1959 into a successful career as a singer and spokesperson for Florida orange juice, filed for Chapter 11 bankruptcy in Tennessee in 2001, the latest in a series of bankruptcy filings and mounted debts in four states. The former 1970's Good Housekeeping Magazine's "Most Admired Woman in America" staged a comeback through small entertainment capitals across the Bible Belt, the latest being Pigeon Forge, TN, where she purchased the "Music Mansion" to put on her show, a combination of music and Christian preaching called, "Anita With Love". "Anita with Love" did not draw crowds, in fact during its heyday the 2,040 seat theater was only 25% full, with staff often filling the empty seats to boost crew morale. This is 25 years after her famous anti-gay crusade ended a high-flying career. Many of her die hard supporters turned their backs on Bryant following her divorce from first husband, labeling her a sinner. Amongst those she owes are many of her employees, like Margaret Cole, whom she owes $6,400 in back pay. Cole, a 58–year–old Baptist used to thank God every night for having a Christian place to work, but who now thinks that Bryant leads anything but a Christian lifestyle. The troubles don't appear to have had the same effect on Bryant and her second husband, Charlie Dry, who have made their lease payments for their $350,000 home on time. Dry claims that everyone will be paid in a few months after they divest themselves of partners whom they blame for their troubles. Many of their employees doubt that, particularly after looking at the debt trail the couple has left behind in three other states.

The ACLU recently launched a campaign against the Florida ban on gay adoptions, placing the blame for its 1977 passage on the antigay fervor Bryant generated in Miami during her opposition to a gay rights bill. Some of the dancers in Bryant's show happened to be gay, but tolerated working for Bryant for a paycheck. Bryant's reputation has not been good for the Pigeon Forge, TN (billed as the "Hillbilly Vegas") tourism industry. The final straw came when an Irish dance troop showed up in August 2000 to perform at the Music Mansion and Dry refused to pay their full fee or provide an adequate per diem, leaving the dancers stranded. The community raised money and provided the dancers with food and clothing to pick up Bryant's slack. Church groups who booked her show months in advance show up to a closed theater. Other area theaters have chipped in free tickets to try to salvage Pigeon Forge's reputation. Bryant owes over $172,000 in unpaid state and federal taxes in Arkansas, $116,000 in Missouri, and now in Tennessee her creditors include $112,000 to over 40 employees, $80,000 to the IRS, $410,000 to local and state governments, $250,000 to contractors and commercial lenders and $200,000 to 60 retailers and small companies.

E. THE RELIGIOUS RIGHT'S "EX–GAY" MOVEMENT*

From his seat in the rear of a sparsely furnished room on the second floor of Miami Shores Baptist Church, the immaculately groomed Joe

* Excerpted from *Scared Straight: The religious right's ex-gay movement is scouting local recruits*, By Joanne Green, published July 12, 2007; Reprinted with permission of the *Miami New Times*.

Alicea—a self-described former homosexual—leans back, kicks up a shiny black shoe, and crosses one starched navy pinstripe pant leg neatly over the other.

. . .

Six men and three women, perched on folding plastic chairs encircling him, are completely still. They all "struggle" with same-sex attraction: the cave-eyed, overly thin female student; the married Hispanic man with three kids; the clean-cut Midwestern boy in an orange baseball cap; the bubbly young Latino; and the stocky, guilt-ridden Sarah.

Eyes closed, chin nestling on her white cotton shirt, 24–year–old Sarah (*New Times* has changed her name to protect her privacy) nods her head in agreement: "Yes, yes," she mutters—more for her own benefit than to be heard. "Amen." Balling her thick hands into tight fists and digging them into her black slacks, the five-foot nine-inch Sarah raises her face and gives her fellow struggler a sympathetic glance. She knows firsthand the arduous journey from gay to straight. The confusion. The frustration. The denial. The rage. The regret. The self-hatred.

At age 10 Sarah lusted after the players on her school's girls' softball team. At 17 she had her first sexual encounter, with a female. At 21 she met the love of her life—a woman. But for God to love her, Alicea teaches and Sarah believes, she must live righteously. And that means becoming "clean," stopping the scythe of shame slicing and scarring her life. She must wipe the stain of homosexuality from her soul.

Five years ago Sarah, who lives in North Miami Beach, entered the welcoming arms of Fort Lauderdale-based Worthy Creations, an interdenominational organization that shepherds gay men and women toward heterosexuality.

Since its inception in 1986, Worthy Creations has been an active member of what has been dubbed the ex-gay movement.

Champions of the nationwide campaign consider homosexuality a moral or mental condition that can—and should—be treated. They say same-sex attraction is caused by early-childhood sexual abuse, or trauma brought on by lack of same-sex parental affection that causes homosexuals to seek attention from members of their own sex.

Supporters of the movement fiercely reject the idea that people are born gay, arguing that homosexuality is a learned behavior. Above all, they regard it as an abominable sin.

The crusade to make gay people straight coalesced in the mid-Seventies, but it has picked up steam in recent years. Today it includes a Catholic group financially supported by the Archdiocese of New York, Courage International, which counsels gays to be abstinent; Homosexuals Anonymous, a Pennsylvania-based Christian fellowship patterned after Alcoholics Anonymous, which charges that homosexuals lead "failed lives" and calls their sexuality a "character defect" that can be treated with a fourteen-step program; and the nation's mother ship of the ex-gay movement, Exodus International.

From its Orlando headquarters, Exodus acts as a spiritual umbrella for an estimated 150 predominantly evangelical ministries across the country. Worthy Creations is Exodus's South Florida affiliate.

. . .

Thomas purports the "hundreds of thousands" of homosexuals Exodus has treated found "freedom" through prayer-based counseling and reparative therapy, a controversial technique supported by the National Association for Research and Therapy of Homosexuality (NARTH), a 1000–member, California-based coalition of secular psychiatrists.

Cases of reparative therapy (also referred to as conversion therapy) documented by Mel Seesholtz, Ph.D., in the *Online Journal*, involve attaching electric sensors to the genitals and then administering a shock at any sign of arousal by same-sex images. Other cases cite exorcism, sedation, isolation, physical restraints, and hypnosis.

NARTH was founded in 1992 by Joseph Nicolosi (who also declined an interview with *New Times*). Its Website provides links to medical studies that show statistical data in support of reparative therapy. Among them is a paper presented by the American Psychological Association's Dr. Robert Spitzer at a 2001 APA convention. Spitzer claims 66 percent of men and 44 percent of women who received reparative therapy for his study achieved "good heterosexual functioning."

Yet many reparative therapy studies NARTH cites are filled with methodological ambiguities and questionable results, according to psychiatric experts outside the organization. Indeed Spitzer's was discredited. Immediately following his study's publication, the APA issued an official disavowal of the paper, noting it had not been peer-reviewed and bluntly stating, "There is no published scientific evidence supporting the efficacy of reparative therapy as a treatment to change one's sexual orientation."

"One of the reasons there isn't any data," says Thomas, "is because the APA has a lot of internal politics determined by gay activists within their own ranks. There are plenty of people in the APA who are willing to ignore my reality and use their own bias to stop studies that would actually prove that change is possible."

Dr. Gerald Schoenewolf, a member of NARTH's Science Advisory Committee, agrees. He recently published a report on NARTH's Website that states the APA, to which he belongs, "has been taken over by extremist gays." He also claims Africans were "better off" in slavery and that the civil rights, women's rights, and gay rights movements are "irrational" and "destructive."

On a recent Tuesday evening, as she has done almost every week for the past five years, Sarah joins Joe Alicea and the Worthy Creations crew in Miami Shores for a strugglers' support group.

With each meeting, Sarah says, she inches further along the road to change, loosening her ties to homosexuality and nudging her closer to breaking free from the shackles of sin.

In the half-decade since joining the ex-gay ministry, Sarah has not had any sexual contact with a man. She hasn't felt an urge to kiss one yet, either. In fact she hasn't even reached the point of wanting to go out on a date with a guy. But she is convinced she will someday.

"I'm not there yet, that's all. It's a process; it takes time," she says with a half-hearted smile. "Am I attracted to men? Of course," she adds. Asked what kind of physical traits she finds attractive in men, she repeats the question and then pauses. "It's more about who the person is inside."

Sarah is more effusive about her former attraction to women. "What kind of girls did I like? All types, you name it. They ran the gamut from curly hair, straight hair, blond hair, dark hair, olive-skinned, white, blue eyes, brown eyes," she bubbles. "I like athletic girls, ones who like sports. Thin, tough, physically fit, in shape. And confidence—I loved girls who knew what they wanted and weren't afraid to show it.... Yeah, confident girls."

Tonight she must purge all thoughts of lithe, athletic, confident females. At the Worthy Creations meetings, the shy girl, who confesses she doesn't really have any good friends, must become an army of one, readying for battle before a crowd of peers. The enemy: her own tortured soul.

"The Lord can deliver us from our sexual brokenness," intones Alicea, who says he left the gay lifestyle half a decade ago and credits his sexual awakening to the healing powers of Jesus....

"It's not easy," scoffs Alicea, recrossing his legs and clasping his hands over a knee. "But we are not born into homosexuality and we do have a choice," he adds, shifting his attention to Sarah. "Would you like to go next?"

Sarah inhales, smiles awkwardly, and casts her eyes to the floor. Confession time.

"This has been a hard week for me," she mutters, "but I've realized some things. I became attracted to women because I didn't get the love I needed from my mom. I know that now." Clenching her fists, she digs them into her thighs and begins jiggling her right leg. "I craved female attention because I never got it from her...."

Clench, dig, jiggle.

"She was emotionally absent...."

Mom was reserved, dominating, and cold, Sarah says. Grandma was bipolar, and Sarah thinks Mom was abused: "She alluded to it, but she never gave me specifics." When Sarah was a baby, Mom divorced Sarah's biological father and then remarried. The little girl who always tried to please inherited five stepsiblings.

Clench, dig, jiggle.

And a sexually deviant male neighbor.

Clench, dig, jiggle.

"I was eight years old," she says. "I went to get the mail and I had to pass his house, and he called me over ... lured me in with Christmas presents.... He was handicapped, in a wheelchair. He started kissing me, holding me, hugging me ... lifted up my shirt ... made me touch him...."

Clench, dig, jiggle.

"After, I ran back into our house. I felt dirty, ashamed. I cried. I was mad—at my mom. She should have stopped it, should have been there."

"Did you tell your mom you were sexually abused?" prompts Alicea.

Lifting her chin toward the ceiling, Sarah shakes her head no and digs her white knuckles further into her thighs. She opens her mouth to respond, but nothing comes out.

"Have you told her since?" he pushes.

Clench, dig, jiggle. She shakes her head again, red hair swaying limply around broad shoulders.

She takes a deep breath. "I felt very alone when I first came here." Voice quivering, thick with shame, she is syllables away from tears. "When I realized after coming here I wasn't born this way, that the things that have happened to me in my life made me this way, that I could change ... I'll do whatever it takes for God's love.

"He's my best friend."

Alicea finds her eyes from across the room and holds her gaze. "God does love you," he says tenderly to his disciple, "very much."

Tears stream down her pale face.

"All these events play a part in our struggle," Alicea continues. "You must understand that."

Sarah is quiet. She looks bled dry.

. . .

When Exodus was just three years old, cofounder and ex-gay Michael Bussee fell—for Exodus volunteer and fellow ex-gay Gary Cooper. The two left their wives, shacked up, and exchanged wedding bands. This past month, on BeyondExGay.com, Bussee issued a formal apology for creating an organization he calls a fraud that hurts people and promotes self-hatred. "One [ex-gay] got drunk and deliberately drove his car into a tree," Bussee wrote. "Another told me that he had left Exodus and was now going to straight bars—looking for someone to beat him up ... made him feel less guilty. One of my most dedicated clients ... took a razor blade to his genitals, slashed himself repeatedly, and then poured drain-cleaner on the wounds, because after months of celibacy, he had a 'fall.' "

. . .

A slender, tan young girl in hot pink shorts jogs past Sarah. She pretends not to notice, but the slight tilt of her chin belies her stab at deception. Seconds later she stomps up a ramp that leads to a makeshift construction office near the project she presides over in North Miami Beach.

Sarah is an engineer. Dressed in dark jeans and a blue V-neck T-shirt, she is getting ready to leave work and lock up for the night. Her listless strawberry hair, carelessly parted in the middle, hangs limply around her shoulders.

"I'm not too big on dresses, either," she jokes, her thick shoulders moving up and down stiffly. "Thinking about it, I never have been." She got this gig almost two years ago, after graduating with a bachelor's degree from an Ivy League school. She is earning a healthy living and stashing some money away for the future—for the family she hopes to have one of these tomorrows. Today, though, she is still puzzling over her lust for women.

"I remember feeling attractions to women very early—10 years old—and not knowing what it was. I just knew it was there, but I didn't spend too much time thinking about it because I knew it wasn't normal."

As a youngster, Sarah preferred hanging out with the girls on her school softball team instead of going to the Episcopalian church her family attended in Pembroke Pines.

"It wasn't one in particular I was attracted to. It was all of them," she says, laughing. "I liked the fact that they were thin. They had these amazing athletic bodies. . . ."

In 1999 Sarah's sister Chrissie returned from military service in Guam. "She's older than me by 10 years, and she would always be the one drinking, taking drugs, having sex, sneaking out at night," Sarah recalls. "I was the quiet one; she was the fun one. When she came home that year, she said, 'Let's find a Bible study!' I was floored."

Big sis took Sarah to Calvary Chapel in Fort Lauderdale. "I began to realize that someone [God] really loved me. Things just began to make sense," says Sarah. "How do you describe the role your best friend plays in your life?"

She went to college in upstate New York and fell out of favor with God when she fell in love with a woman. "We met at an ice-cream social or something. We were both 17, in our freshman year. She was attractive, into sports and running like me. We got to know each other, and for the whole year we were hanging out 24/7. We would sleep together in the same bed; I would be all wrapped around her. We would stay like that all night. We never actually had sex, though. I tried, but she said she wasn't gay."

Sarah kept her feelings secret and pretended to like boys, even going on a few dates. But inside she was growing increasingly frustrated. Shortly after parting ways with the young woman she considered to be her girlfriend, one summer afternoon in 2001, she snapped.

"I started screaming at God because I felt completely and utterly alone and abandoned," she says. "I couldn't understand why if being gay was wrong, why He had made me this way. I felt like I'd been given a raw deal and I wasn't equipped to handle it."

Sarah recalls a time of confusion and loneliness: "The idea is to make God love us, and you go to whatever lengths you can to please him. So I finally told Him: 'You have got to help me.' "

God pointed her to Worthy Creations, Sarah says, and He has stuck by her ever since. "I now know I'm not a complete oddball," she says with a chuckle, explaining her gratitude for the program. "Obviously God didn't create me this way. I now realize that it's because I didn't get the love that I needed from my mom. That's all."

The ex-gay movement bolsters Sarah's conviction—one she did not hold when she lived a gay life—that homosexuality is not indelible. As she wanders back to the construction site on a blustery afternoon, a raven-haired girl passes by on Rollerblades and smiles. Sarah smiles back.

"It's not bad to admire attractive women, because being homosexual is like being an alcoholic," she says, reciting almost verbatim what Joe Alicea said in a recent group session. "Even when you're not drinking, you still have the desire to drink. But an alcoholic limits that desire to drink. I also limit my desires based on what, and who, I associate with.

"I can convert, sure. But it's not a quick fix, even if you believe in it with all your heart. And I do."

. . .

After two hours of worship, Bible study, and confession, Joe Alicea brings the Worthy Creations meeting in Miami Shores to a close with a prayer.

Palms are joined, fingers interlaced, eyes shut, heads bowed. Cheeks are stained with tears; emotionally drained bodies slump lifelessly over knees.

Alicea gives thanks, asks the Lord to bestow courage, and calls on Him to bring grace and truth to a world riddled with homosexuality. After a resounding "Amen," chairs scrape along the wooden floor and the members slowly clamber to their feet.

"Don't forget," he adds, "it's not too late to register for the Exodus Freedom Conference." For the past 32 years, Exodus has united approximately 1000 people at a week-long annual conference. Its purpose: to disseminate ex-gays' inspirational tales of conversion as well as religious leaders' (such as the late Jerry Falwell, who appeared in 2005 and 2006) insight into homosexuality. This year's event would be held in Irvine, California, in June. And, according to Alicea, it would be life-changing: "The testimonies alone are worth the $400."

Nodding her head, Sarah turns to the student standing beside her. "I went to one once and it was amazing," she tells the girl. "Really powerful." In May 2004 Sarah attended what she describes as a Worthy Creations church conference in Key West.

"I know, Key West is such a hotbed for gay activism," she says, laughing.

But Sarah did experience a life-changing event. She fell in love with a 30–year–old olive-skinned Italian woman who lived locally.

"She was short, with dark curly hair," Sarah recalls, "and she was funny. She used to make me laugh." The two women dated for nearly 10 months; their relationship became sexual during the last few weeks. Sarah describes her former flame as "the love of her life."

"It was wonderful," she says with a grin, "but it came with a high price tag, because it wasn't God's design." Feeling bad because "the electrical sockets just didn't work," Sarah ended the relationship two years ago. She has been "clean" ever since.

She regrets the affair. "I ruined what could have been a really good friendship," Sarah laments. "There are some people that you know from the get-go you should stay away from because deep down you know you won't be able to say no."

III. LAW

A. EXPRESSION: PROM CASES

FRICKE v. LYNCH

491 F.Supp. 381 (D.R.I. 1980)

OPINION: PETTINE

Most of the time, a young man's choice of a date for the senior prom is of no great interest to anyone other than the student, his companion, and, perhaps, a few of their classmates. But in Aaron Fricke's case, the school authorities actively disapprove of his choice, the other students are upset, the community is abuzz, and out-of-state newspapers consider the matter newsworthy. All this fuss arises because Aaron Fricke's intended escort is another young man. Claiming that the school's refusal to allow him to bring a male escort violates his first and fourteenth amendment rights, Fricke seeks a preliminary injunction ordering the school officials to allow him to attend with a male escort.

Two days of testimony have revealed the following facts. The senior reception at Cumberland High School is a formal dinner-dance sponsored and run by the senior class. It is held shortly before graduation but is not a part of the graduation ceremonies. This year the students have decided to hold the dance at the Pleasant Valley Country Club in Sutton, Massachusetts on Friday, May 30. All seniors except those on suspension are eligible to attend the dance; no one is required to go. All students who attend must bring an escort, although their dates need not be seniors or even Cumberland High School students. Each student is asked the name of his date at the time he buys the tickets.

The principal testified that school dances are chaperoned by him, two assistant principals, and one or two class advisers. They are sometimes joined by other teachers who volunteer to help chaperone; such teachers are not paid. Often these teachers will drop in for part of the dance. Additionally, police officers are on duty at the dance. Usually two officers attend; last year three plainclothes officers were at the junior prom.

The seeds of the present conflict were planted a year ago when Paul Guilbert, then a junior at Cumberland High School, sought permission to bring a male escort to the junior prom. The principal, Richard Lynch (the defendant here), denied the request, fearing that student reaction could lead to a disruption at the dance and possibly to physical harm to Guilbert. The request and its denial were widely publicized and led to widespread community and student reaction adverse to Paul. Some students taunted and spit at him, and once someone slapped him; in response, Principal Lynch arranged an escort system, in which Lynch or an assistant principal accompanied Paul as he went from one class to the next. No other incidents or violence occurred. Paul did not attend the prom. At that time Aaron Fricke (plaintiff here) was a friend of Paul's and supported his position regarding the dance.

This year, during or after an assembly in April in which senior class events were discussed, Aaron Fricke, a senior at Cumberland High School, decided that he wanted to attend the senior reception with a male companion. Aaron considers himself a homosexual, and has never dated girls, although he does socialize with female friends. He has never taken a girl to a school dance. Until this April, he had not "come out of the closet" by publicly acknowledging his sexual orientation.

Aaron asked Principal Lynch for permission to bring a male escort, which Lynch denied. A week later (during vacation), Aaron asked Paul Guilbert who now lives in New York to be his escort (if allowed), and Paul accepted. Aaron met again with Lynch, at which time they discussed Aaron's commitment to homosexuality; Aaron indicated that although it was possible he might someday be bisexual, at the present he is exclusively homosexual and could not conscientiously date girls. Lynch gave Aaron written reasons for his action;[11] his prime concern was the fear that a

11. Principal Lynch sent the following letter to Aaron's home and handed it to him in person:

I am denying your request for the following reasons:

1. The real and present threat of physical harm to you, your male escort and to others;

disruption would occur and Aaron or, especially, Paul would be hurt. He indicated in court that he would allow Aaron to bring a male escort if there were no threat of violence.

After Aaron filed suit in this Court, an event reported by the Rhode Island and Boston papers, a student shoved and, the next day, punched Aaron. The unprovoked, surprise assault necessitated five stitches under Aaron's right eye. The assailant was suspended for nine days. After this, Aaron was given a special parking space closer to the school doors and has been provided with an escort (principal or assistant principal) between classes. No further incidents have occurred.

This necessarily brief account does not convey the obvious concern and good faith Lynch has displayed in his handling of the matter. Lynch sincerely believes that there is a significant possibility that some students will attempt to injure Aaron and Paul if they attend the dance. Moreover, Lynch's actions in school have displayed a concern for Aaron's safety while at school. Perhaps one cannot be at all sure a totally different approach by Lynch might have kept the matter from reaching its present proportions, but I am convinced that Lynch's actions have stemmed in significant part from a concern for disruption.

Aaron contends that the school's action violates his first amendment right of association, his first amendment right to free speech, and his fourteenth amendment right to equal protection of the laws. (The equal protection claim is a "hybrid" one that he has been treated differently than others because of the content of his communication.)[12]

The starting point in my analysis of Aaron's first amendment free speech claim must be, of course, to determine whether the action he proposes to take has a "communicative content sufficient to bring it within the ambit of the first amendment." *Gay Students Organization v. Bonner*, 509 F.2d 652 (1st Cir. 1974) (hereinafter *Bonner*). As this Court has noted before, the "speech pure"/"speech plus" demarcation is problematic, both in logic and in practice. *Reilly v. Noel*, 384 F.Supp. 741 (D.R.I.1974); see cases cited therein. This normally difficult task is made

2. The adverse effect among your classmates, other students, the School and the Town of Cumberland, which is certain to follow approval of such a request for overt homosexual interaction (male or female) at a class function;

3. Since the dance is being held out of state and this is a function of the students of Cumberland High School, the School Department is powerless to insure protection in Sutton, Massachusetts. That protection would be required of property as well as persons and would expose all concerned to liability for harm which might occur;

4. It is long standing school policy that no unescorted student, male or female, is permitted to attend. To enforce this rule, a student must identify his or her escort before the committee will sell the ticket.

I suspect that other objections will be raised by your fellow students, the Cumberland School Department, Parents and other citizens, which will heighten the potential for harm.

12. The plaintiff has not advanced the plausible arguments that homosexuals constitute a suspect class, *see* L. Tribe, American Constitutional Law (1978) at 944–45 n. 17, or that one has a constitutional right to be a homosexual, *see, e.g.*, *Acanfora v. Board of Education*, 359 F.Supp. 843 (D.Md.1973), aff'd on other grounds, 491 F.2d 498 (4th Cir. 1974). The first amendment aspect of the case makes it unnecessary for me to reach these issues, although they may very well be applicable to this kind of case.

somewhat easier here, however, by the precedent set in *Bonner*, supra. In that case, the University of New Hampshire prohibited the Gay Students' Organization (GSO) from holding dances and other social events. The first circuit explicitly rejected the idea that traditional first amendment rights of expression were not involved. 509 F.2d at 660. The Court found that not only did discussion and exchange of ideas take place at informal social functions, id. at 660–61, but also that:

> beyond the specific communications at such events is the basic "message" GSO seeks to convey that homosexuals exist, that they feel repressed by existing laws and attitudes, that they wish to emerge from their isolation, and that public understanding of their attitudes and problems is desirable for society.

Here too the proposed activity has significant expressive content. Aaron testified that he wants to go because he feels he has a right to attend and participate just like all the other students and that it would be dishonest to his own sexual identity to take a girl to the dance. He went on to acknowledge that he feels his attendance would have a certain political element and would be a statement for equal rights and human rights. Admittedly, his explanation of his "message" was hesitant and not nearly as articulate as Judge Coffin's restatement of the GSO's message, cited above. Nevertheless, I believe Aaron's testimony that he is sincerely although perhaps not irrevocably committed to a homosexual orientation and that attending the dance with another young man would be a political statement. While mere communicative intent may not always transform conduct into speech, *United States v. O'Brien*, 391 U.S. 367, 376, 88 S.Ct. 1673, 1678, 20 L.Ed.2d 672 (1968), *Bonner* makes clear that this exact type of conduct as a vehicle for transmitting this very message can be considered protected speech.

Accordingly, the school's action must be judged by the standards articulated in *United States v. O'Brien*, 391 U.S. 367, 88 S.Ct. 1673, 20 L.Ed.2d 672 (1968), and applied in *Bonner*: (1) was the regulation within the constitutional power of the government; (2) did it further an important or substantial governmental interest; (3) was the governmental interest unrelated to the suppression of free expression; and (4) was the incidental restriction on alleged first amendment freedoms no greater than essential to the furtherance of that interest?

I need not dwell on the first two *O'Brien* requirements: the school unquestionably has an important interest in student safety and has the power to regulate students' conduct to ensure safety. As to the suppression of free expression, Lynch's testimony indicated that his personal views on homosexuality did not affect his decision, and that but for the threat of violence he would let the two young men go together. Thus the government's interest here is not in squelching a particular message because it objects to its content as such. On the other hand, the school's interest is in suppressing certain speech activity because of the reaction its message may engender. Surely this is still suppression of free expression.

It is also clear that the school's action fails to meet the last criterion set out in *O'Brien*, the requirement that the government employ the "least restrictive alternative" before curtailing speech. The plaintiff argues, and I agree, that the school can take appropriate security measures to control the risk of harm. Lynch testified that he did not know if adequate security could be provided, and that he would still need to sit down and make the necessary arrangements. In fact he has not made any effort to determine the need for and logistics of additional security. Although Lynch did not say that any additional security measures would be adequate, from the testimony I find that significant measures could be taken and would in all probability critically reduce the likelihood of any disturbance. As Lynch's own testimony indicates, police officers and teachers will be present at the dance, and have been quite successful in the past in controlling whatever problems arise, including unauthorized drinking. Despite the ever-present possibility of violence at sports events, adequate discipline has been maintained. From Lynch's testimony, I have every reason to believe that additional school or law enforcement personnel could be used to "shore up security" and would be effective. It should also be noted that Lynch testified that if he considered it impossible to provide adequate security he would move to cancel the dance. The Court appreciates that controlling high school students is no easy task. It is, of course, impossible to guarantee that no harm will occur, no matter what measures are taken. But only one student so far has attempted to harm Aaron, and no evidence was introduced of other threats. The measures taken already, especially the escort system, have been highly effective in preventing any further problems at school. Appropriate security measures coupled with a firm, clearly communicated attitude by the administration that any disturbance will not be tolerated appear to be a realistic, and less restrictive, alternative to prohibiting Aaron from attending the dance with the date of his choice.

The analysis so far has been along traditional first amendment lines, making no real allowance for the fact that this case arises in a high school setting. The most difficult problem this controversy presents is how this setting should affect the result. *Tinker v. Des Moines Independent Community School District*, 393 U.S. 503, 89 S.Ct. 733, 21 L.Ed.2d 731 (1969), makes clear that high school students do not "shed their constitutional rights to freedom of speech or expression at the schoolhouse gate."

. . .

In order for the State in the person of school officials to justify prohibition of a particular expression of opinion, it must be able to show that its action was caused by something more than a mere desire to avoid the discomfort and unpleasantness that always accompany an unpopular viewpoint. Certainly where there is no finding and no showing that engaging in the forbidden conduct would "materially and substantially interfere with the requirements of appropriate discipline in the operation of the school," the prohibition cannot be sustained. *Burnside v. Byars* (363 F.2d 744).... *Tinker* at 508–09, 89 S.Ct. at 737–738.

... *Tinker* did, however, indicate that there are limits on first amendment rights within the school:

A student's rights, therefore, do not embrace merely the classroom hours. When he is in the cafeteria, or on the playing field, or on the campus during the authorized hours, he may express his opinions, even on controversial subjects like the conflict in Vietnam, if he does so without "materially and substantially (interfering) with the requirements of appropriate discipline in the operation of the school" and without colliding with the rights of others. But conduct by the student, in class or out of it, which for any reason whether it stems from time, place or type of behavior materially disrupts classwork or involves substantial disorder or invasion of the rights of others is, of course, not immunized by the constitutional guarantee of freedom of speech.

It seems to me that here, not unlike in *Tinker*, the school administrators were acting on "an undifferentiated fear or apprehension of disturbance." True, Aaron was punched and then security measures were taken, but since that incident he has not been threatened with violence nor has he been attacked. There has been no disruption at the school; classes have not been cancelled, suspended, or interrupted. In short, while the defendants have perhaps shown more of a basis for fear of harm than in *Tinker*, they have failed to make a "showing" that Aaron's conduct would "materially and substantially interfere" with school discipline. *See Tinker* at 509, 89 S. Ct. at 737. However, even if the Court assumes that there is justifiable fear and that Aaron's peaceful speech leads, or may lead, to a violent reaction from others, the question remains: may the school prohibit the speech, or must it protect the speaker?

It is certainly clear that outside of the classroom the fear however justified of a violent reaction is not sufficient reason to restrain such speech in advance, and an actual hostile reaction is rarely an adequate basis for curtailing free speech. Thus, the question here is whether the interest in school discipline and order, recognized in *Tinker*, requires a different approach.

After considerable thought and research, I have concluded that even a legitimate interest in school discipline does not outweigh a student's right to peacefully express his views in an appropriate time, place, and manner.[13] To rule otherwise would completely subvert free speech in the

13. The second reason relied upon by the *Bonner* court in finding the GSO social events to be speech-related was the interpretation placed upon those events by the community. There the university prohibited the gay social events because the community considered them "shocking and offensive," "a spectacle, an abomination," an "affront" to townspeople, "grandstanding," inflammatory, "(undermining) the university within the state," and distasteful. The first circuit concluded that "(w)e do not see how these statements can be interpreted to avoid the conclusion that the regulation imposed was based in large measure, if not exclusively, on the content of the GSO's expression." *Bonner* at 661. I quite agree that these statements of community outrage indicate that the content, i.e. the homosexual-ness, of the GSO's activities led to the strong reaction and the prohibition, not the fact that they were dances. With all due respect, however, I am puzzled by how this reaction proves the expressive nature of these activities. Community outrage per se does not transform conduct into speech, or even indicate that it is speech; communities have reacted with outrage similar to that of the citizens of New Hampshire to such

schools by granting other students a "heckler's veto," allowing them to decide through prohibited and violent methods what speech will be heard. The first amendment does not tolerate mob rule by unruly school children. This conclusion is bolstered by the fact that any disturbance here, however great, would not interfere with the main business of school education. No classes or school work would be affected; at the very worst an optional social event, conducted by the students for their own enjoyment, would be marred. In such a context, the school does have an obligation to take reasonable measures to protect and foster free speech, not to stand helpless before unauthorized student violence.

The present case is so difficult because the Court is keenly sensitive to the testimony regarding the concerns of a possible disturbance, and of physical harm to Aaron or Paul. However, I am convinced that meaningful security measures are possible, and the first amendment requires that such steps be taken to protect rather than to stifle free expression. Some may feel that Aaron's attendance at the reception and the message he will thereby convey is trivial compared to other social debates, but to engage in this kind of a weighing in process is to make the content-based evaluation forbidden by the first amendment.

As to the other concern raised by *Tinker*, some people might say that Aaron Fricke's conduct would infringe the rights of the other students, and is thus unprotected by *Tinker*. This view is misguided, however. Aaron's conduct is quiet and peaceful; it demands no response from others and in a crowd of some five hundred people can be easily ignored. Any disturbance that might interfere with the rights of others would be caused by those students who resort to violence, not by Aaron and his companion, who do not want a fight.

Because the free speech claim is dispositive, I find it unnecessary to reach the plaintiff's right of association argument or to deal at length with his equal protection claim.[14] I find that the plaintiff has established a

---

non-expressive activities as Hester Prynne's adultery, the dumping of chemicals into Love Canal, and the Son of Sam murders. It is hard in *Bonner* to separate the community's opposition to the GSO's acts from its opposition to its message (if the acts had a message); surely they opposed both. Same-sex dancing may have an expressive element, but it is also action, and potentially objectionable as such.

Insofar as *Bonner* directs me to consider community reaction in assessing expressive content, I conclude that the community disapproves of the content of Aaron's message and that the vehemence of their opposition to his intended escort is based in part on this disapproval of what he is trying to communicate. The school here professes to be unconcerned with the content of the plaintiff's message, but their concern with townspeople's reaction is, indirectly, content-related.

14. This case can also be profitably analyzed under the Equal Protection Clause of the fourteenth amendment. In preventing Aaron Fricke from attending the senior reception, the school has afforded disparate treatment to a certain class of students those wishing to attend the reception with companions of the same sex. Ordinarily, a government classification need only bear a rational relationship to a legitimate public purpose; only where the classification encompasses a suspect class or burdens a fundamental right is the government held to a stricter standard of justification. Counsel have conceded that homosexuals are not a suspect class sufficient to trigger a higher standard of scrutiny. As noted above, however, there is a significant first amendment component to Aaron's desire to attend the reception with another male. Where, as here, government classification impinges on a first amendment right, the government is held to

probability of success on the merits and has shown irreparable harm; accordingly his request for a preliminary injunction is hereby granted....

*NOTE: AARON FRICKE'S PERSONAL STORY**

The simple, obvious thing would have been to go to the senior prom with a girl. But that would have been a lie—a lie to myself, to the girl, and to all the other students.

What I *wanted* to do was to take a male date. But as Paul Guilbert had shown the year before when he had attempted to take another man to the prom, such honesty is not always easy. There was an important difference between Paul's case and mine, though. Paul had not been able to fight for his rights because he was seventeen at the time. I was now eighteen and legally able to make my own decisions. If I wanted to go to the prom with a male escort and the school tried to stop me, I could take the case to court.

But should I do that? This would require a lot of thought if I was to make a decision without being selfish, uncaring, or irrational.

If I went to the prom with another guy, what would be the benefits? For myself, it would mean participating in an important social event and doing so with a clear conscience and a sense of wholeness. But how would it affect the rest of the people involved?

I believed that those who had themselves faced discrimination or prejudice would immediately understand what I was doing and its implications for human rights. There would be others who may never have had direct experiences with prejudice but who would recognize my right to the date of my choice. These people may have been misled to believe that homosexuality is wrong, but they could still understand that my rights were being denied.

At the opposite end of the spectrum were the homophobics who might act violently. But the example I set would be perfect for everyone. We would be just one more happy couple. Our happiness together would be something kids could relate to. I would be showing that my dignity and value as a human being was not affected by my sexual preference.

l concluded that taking a guy to the prom would be a strong positive statement about the existence of gay people. Any opposition to my case (and I anticipated a good bit) would show the negative side of society—not of homosexuality.

To attend the prom with a girl would not be unenjoyable, but it would be dishonest to my true feelings. Besides, most kids now knew I was gay. If I went with a female, I would probably have received more taunts than from going with a male. By going with a male I would win some respect from the more mature students, and I would keep my self-esteem.

---

a higher level of scrutiny. *Chicago Police Department v. Mosley*, 408 U.S. 92, 92 S.Ct. 2286, 33 L.Ed.2d 212 (1972); *Reilly v. Noel*, 384 F.Supp. 741 (D.R.I.1974).

I find that Principal Lynch's reason for prohibiting Aaron's attendance at the reception the potential for disruption is not sufficiently compelling to justify a classification that would abridge first amendment rights.

* Aaron Fricke, *One Life, One Prom, in* THE CHRISTOPHER STREET READER 21 (Michael Denneny et al. eds., 1983.)

I tried not to worry about the possibility of violence. Certainly I would face opposition. It was inevitable given the rampant prejudice against homosexuals today. But the threat of violence was not enough to change my mind, since I encountered that every day to some degree. Perhaps such threats would diminish in the future as people saw more homosexuals participating openly in everyday life.

My biggest concern was for my parents. Although the entire student body and administration of Cumberland High School knew or assumed I was gay, my family had remained blissfully blind to this reality. The news could be heartbreaking to them. Plus, it might get them ostracized by the neighbors, banned from town social gatherings ... from church ... from Tupperware parties! Was I willing to take this risk? No! As much as I believed in my rights, I valued my relationship with my parents too much to have it abruptly severed. After all, for years I had hidden my sexuality for fear of losing my parents' love. As a child it had been *the* most important thing to me. Now, as a man, it was just as important as before. I wanted to go to my prom, but it was not as important as eighteen years of love.

I decided to tell my parents of my homosexuality first, then ask them how they would feel about my going to the prom. If it seemed like too much for them to accept, I would forget the prom and just be happy that I no longer had to be secretive with my parents. But if they rejected me merely because I was gay, then I would still pursue my rights, even at the prom, realizing that my parents were good people but were horribly misled.

Until now, I had never spoken to them about my homosexuality. Like many adolescents I had drifted away from my parents lately. Now I had an impetus to improve my communication with them. I decided to approach my parents separately; a thousand times I rehearsed what I would say.

It began, "Ever since I was a kid ..." and ended, "I hope you love me enough not to reject me." But when the moment of truth came, I felt more self-confident and said, "I don't know if you've had any suspicions, but I'm gay."

Long pause. My mother replied, "I'm so glad you were finally able to be honest with me." She had long suspected. My father had not; when I told him he broke down and cried. Yet they both loved me unconditionally. When I explained why I wanted to go to the prom, they were supportive. I was my own man, they each said, and I would have to make my own decisions.

It felt great to be able to talk to my parents about this. Their reaction was encouraging, and I decided to go ahead. I would invite Paul Guilbert to the prom.

Anne Guillet wrote me a note in environmental science class when I asked for her advice about the prom, she wrote:

> Dear Aaron,
>
> Last year, Paul's attempt to bring a guy to the prom was seen by most people, in fact I think by all, as a grab at publicity. That was because no one knew Paul, he just showed up out of a clear blue sky (and raised a ruckus). Since you've been in Cumberland much longer and

have more close friends, people won't suspect you of such ill motives so easily, but this is what they will think.

Paul made you do it.

You're crazy.

You believe in gay rights.

In that order. Now I know you did it for reason 3, but you should think about how other people are going to react and I think you should make an effort to explain what you believe. I respect any decision you make, as long as you really think about it carefully.

Love, Anne

I took her advice and painstakingly wrote a letter to the school newspaper, explaining why I decided to go to the prom with a male date. The letter said that I hoped no one would be hurt by what I was doing, that a victory in court would be a victory for every Cumberland High student because it would be a blow against prejudice. The next issue of the school paper had space for all sorts of trivia, but my letter never appeared.

Later in April, the school theater group took its annual bus trip to New York City. Our teacher, Miss Frappier, was an exceptionally warm and friendly person, and we were a tightly-knit bunch—one of those rare groups of thespians whose members had no pent-up distrust or jealousy toward each other. On the bus Miss Frappier gave out the spring awards; I received one of them for an outstanding performance in *A Thurber Carnival*.

In New York we went to the Guggenheim Museum and to the Broadway production of *They're Playing Our Song*; then when the group returned to Rhode Island, I stayed in New York to spend time with Paul, who had moved there from Cumberland.

Paul seemed to be getting happier in the city. Our friendship had not faded, although Paul and I had not seen each other in months. We took a long walk through the Village, bringing each other up to date on what we'd been doing, and enjoying the feeling of the trees in bloom and spring in the air.

By evening I had settled any doubts I still had about who I wanted to invite to the prom. And so, with sweaty palms and butterflies in my stomach, I finally asked Paul: "I was wondering, um, do you have a date for the Cumberland High prom this year?"

Paul began laughing. "I'd love to attend the senior prom with you," he finally said. My feeling of happiness lasted all the way back to Rhode Island.

In Cumberland, prom tickets were on sale. Rather than go through the motion of trying to buy tickets in the cafeteria, where they would want the name of my date and would refuse to sell me the tickets anyway, I went right to the main office and asked Mrs. Dunbarton to tell Mr. Lynch, the principal, that I wanted to speak with him. She courteously took my name, leaned over the intercom, and buzzed Mr. Lynch. I couldn't hear much of what she said, but my imagination filled in the silence: "Oh, Mr. Lynch, that little faggot is here to see you."

Mr. Lynch soon appeared and, on my insistence, granted me the privacy of his office to speak to him. His office was familiar to me by now. I'd sat in it the year before when Mr. Lynch gave me that in-house suspension for cutting gym. But this time things were different.

Without mentioning Paul by name, I explained that I wanted to take a male escort to the prom. Mr. Lynch listened politely, then did exactly what I had assumed he would do.

He said no.

[Aaron Fricke appealed to the National Gay Task Force for help and got it. He was advised to sue his school in federal court; NGTF would cover legal fees.

After several weeks in court, Judge Pettine ruled in favor of Fricke, on the grounds that the social context of an act can represent a political statement, which is therefore protected by the First Amendment.

National media attention focused on Aaron Fricke, Paul Guilbert, and Cumberland High School.]

When we arrived at the prom site on the night of May 30, 1980, we were greeted with a glare of television lights. Flash bulbs were popping and everybody was talking and trying to ask questions as we walked toward the building. The reporters broke down the velvet ropes that were supposed to hold them back. I was too full of anticipation and excitement to think of anything to say. So a second before walking in the door, in a grand gesture of looniness, camp, and high drama, I turned to the reporters, waved, and stuck out my tongue.

Once inside, Mr. Lynch quickly ushered Paul and me away from the door so that the reporters would be unable to see us. We were shown to an empty table, which neither of us enjoyed because there were no kids to talk to. My ninth-grade Spanish teacher, Mrs. Noelte, eventually sat with us. Dinner was soon served. It was chicken cordon something or other and consisted of mushed chicken encased in oil. My piece looked like a monster from the film Alien. The salad looked better, but when I bit into the cherry tomato, it splattered right onto my pants. I did my best to ignore the stain, but it kept showing up in the pictures people took.

After dinner was cleared away, many students began coming by to offer us a few good words. There was more good feeling than I would ever have anticipated. One after another, students came by and expressed their happiness that we could share the prom with each other.

I wandered over to a big picture window and stared out. Several reporters were talking outside on the lawn. For a moment I thought of all the people who would have enjoyed going to their proms with the date of their choice, but were denied that right; of all the people in the past who wanted to live respectably with the person they loved but could not; of all the men and women who had been hurt or killed because they were gay; and of the rich history of lesbians and homosexual men that had so long been ignored. Gradually we were triumphing over ignorance. One day we would be free.

The dance music came on. Kelleen Driskell came over and asked me to dance the first song with her. I was happy to accept. I'd known Kelleen in elementary school, but I had drifted away from her, as from so many other people, during my fat years. We fast-danced for that song and just through our physical movements together, without exchanging words, it felt as if we were reestablishing a communication.

After the dance I had to use the bathroom. Throughout the evening, Paul and I would see all kinds of defense mechanisms from the other guys whenever we went to the bathroom. Some of them made a beeline for the door as soon as we walked in. Others stayed, their desire to escape temporarily overcome by their curiosity about how gay people go to the bathroom.

When I got back to the dance floor, Paul asked me if I wanted to slow-dance. I did. The next song was Bob Seger's "We've Got the Night," and we stepped out onto the dance floor.

The crowd receded. As I laid my head on Paul's shoulder, I saw a few students start to stare at us. I closed my eyes and listened to the music, my thoughts wandering over the events of that evening. When the song ended, I opened my eyes. A large crowd of students had formed a ring around us. Probably most of them had never before seen two happy men embracing in a slow dance. For a moment I was uncomfortable. Then I heard the sound that I knew so well as a B–52's fan. One of my favorite songs was coming up: "Rock Lobster."

Paul and I began dancing free-style. Everyone else was still staring at us, but by the end of the first stanza, several couples had also begun dancing. The song has a contagious enthusiasm to it, and with each bar, more dancers came onto the floor.

More students were coming onto the floor to dance. I doubt that any two people were dancing with the same movements: the dancing was an expression of our individuality, and no one felt bad about being different. Everyone was free to be themselves.

A quarter of the way into the song, thirty people were on the dance floor. "Down, Down, Down," commanded the lyrics. Everyone on the dance floor sank to their knees and crouched on the ground. I lifted my head slightly to look around. Dozens of intertwining bodies crouched on their knees as if praying. We were all one; we shared a unity of pure love. And those who did not want to share it sat on the sidelines.

"Red snappers snappin"

"Clamshells clappin"

Everyone jumped to their feet again and resumed dancing. Many more kids had joined us and there must have been sixty or eighty people on the dance floor now. As Paul and I danced, we had gradually drifted from our original space on the floor. "Down, Down, Down," cried the B–52's again, and we all went down. The feeling of unity among us permeated the air again. There were at least a hundred people on the dance floor. The tempo became more frenetic and everyone danced faster.

"Let's Rock!!!" bellowed from the speakers, and to my surprise, when I looked up, I saw that Paul had disappeared. I looked around; several other guys were dancing with each other, and girls were dancing with girls. Everybody was rockin', everybody was fruggin'. Who cared why? Maybe they were doing it to mock me and Paul, maybe they were doing it because they wanted to, maybe one was an excuse for the other ... I didn't know and I didn't care. It was fun. Everyone was together. I danced with girls, I danced with guys, I danced with the entire group.

Then the music stopped. "Rock Lobster" has an abrupt ending, and no one was quite ready for it to stop. I had been having so much fun that I lost track of time; I had also lost track of Paul and had to look around the room for him.

I could see that everyone felt a sense of disorientation. For six minutes and forty-nine seconds, the students on the dance floor had forgotten about their defenses, forgotten about their shells. We just had fun.

I do not blame my torments on heterosexuality. I have been friends with many loving, open-minded heterosexuals. The thing I blame has no sexuality. It is the nameless, faceless entity of prejudice and oppression. Often that oppression has taken a physical form in people who are straight; perhaps those people are themselves just pawns, trapped in a vicious cycle of oppression. I am only reporting their actions as I have experienced them.

The prom case brought about many good changes. It exposed people to the gay rights issue. It encouraged them to look at it more rationally than they might have otherwise. The hatred that many people feel when they hear the word gay must have diminished after the fourteenth time they heard it on the six o'clock news.

The media often handled this case well. The day Judge Pettine's ruling was announced, reporter Bob Blanchard came on the news and said, "Those who support equal rights for gay people say today's decision is a major victory.... In reality, however, it was not because the much larger question of rampant discrimination gay people face in housing and the job market remains."

Although the prom case is a bit more serious than the Village People's song "YMCA," its main value was to bring the issue to the attention of the public and make them aware that there is a problem, a problem that remains to be solved.

Parents sometimes teach their children that homosexuality is a disease, whereas homophobia is not. Actually, it is the contrary. Homophobia is a degeneration of respect for humans, and it is contagious. One person exhibits hatred toward a gay person, impressionable people see it, and they recreate those actions. Parents who teach their children to hate or fear homosexuals do not realize that their children could be homosexuals. Prejudiced attitudes serve only to confuse the children, whether they have homosexual tendencies or not.

My last day at Cumberland High School ended on a particularly sad note. As I walked off the football field after commencement, now escorted by several uniformed policemen, two children approached me before I stepped into my car. "Faggot!" one said. "You queer," said the other. I had never felt so defenseless. They were only about ten years old, and I felt no hostility toward them. But I pity the society that sits back and encourages children to feel bitterness and hatred toward anything.

I live with pride every day of my life now—pride in the idea that my openness can set an example for all people about the benefits of being open. My memories of the oppression I felt will not be forgotten, nor will my awareness that people continue to experience these emotional deprivations. But I am now confident that I can overcome the barriers that heterosexual prejudice will present.

Even so, I will be reminded daily of the torments gay people face. My writing will hopefully serve as a vehicle to make others more actively aware. I will remind heterosexuals that we are human. And I will remind gay people struggling for a positive identity that, in the words of André Gide, "it is better to be hated for what one is than loved for what one is not."

B. HARASSMENT: CONSTITUTIONAL CLAIMS

NABOZNY v. PODLESNY

92 F.3d 446 (7th Cir. 1996)

OPINION: ESCHBACH

Jamie Nabozny was a student in the Ashland Public School District (hereinafter "the District") in Ashland, Wisconsin throughout his middle school and high school years. During that time, Nabozny was continually harassed and physically abused by fellow students because he is homosexual. Both in middle school and high school Nabozny reported the harassment to school administrators. Nabozny asked the school officials to protect him and to punish his assailants. Despite the fact that the school administrators had a policy of investigating and punishing student-on-student battery and sexual harassment, they allegedly turned a deaf ear to Nabozny's requests. Indeed, there is evidence to suggest that some of the administrators themselves mocked Nabozny's predicament. Nabozny eventually filed suit against several school officials and the District pursuant to 42 U.S.C. § 1983 alleging, among other things, that the defendants: 1) violated his Fourteenth Amendment right to equal protection by discriminating against him based on his gender; 2) violated his Fourteenth Amendment right to equal protection by discriminating against him based on his sexual orientation; 3) violated his Fourteenth Amendment right to due process by exacerbating the risk that he would be harmed by fellow students; and, 4) violated his Fourteenth Amendment right to due process by encouraging an environment in which he would be harmed. The defendants filed a motion for summary judgment, which the district court granted. Nabozny appeals the district court's decision. Because we agree with the district court only in part, we affirm in part, reverse in part, and remand.

. . .

II.

From his birth in 1975, Nabozny lived in Ashland, Wisconsin. Throughout his childhood, adolescence, and teenaged years he attended schools owned and operated by the Ashland Public School District. In elementary school, Nabozny proved to be a good student and enjoyed a positive educational experience.

When Nabozny graduated to the Ashland Middle School in 1988, his life changed. Around the time that Nabozny entered the seventh grade, Nabozny realized that he is gay. Many of Nabozny's fellow classmates soon realized it too. Nabozny decided not to "closet" his sexuality, and considerable harassment from his fellow students ensued. Nabozny's classmates regularly referred to him as "faggot," and subjected him to various forms of physical abuse, including striking and spitting on him. Nabozny spoke to the school's guidance counselor, Ms. Peterson, about the abuse, informing Peterson that he is gay. Peterson took action, ordering the offending students to stop the harassment and placing two of them in detention. However, the students' abusive behavior toward Nabozny stopped only briefly. Meanwhile, Peterson was replaced as guidance counselor by Mr. Nowakowski. Nabozny similarly informed Nowakowski that he is gay, and asked for protection from the student harassment. Nowakowski, in turn, referred the matter to school Principal Mary Podlesny; Podlesny was responsible for school discipline.

Just before the 1988 winter holiday, Nabozny met with Nowakowski and Podlesny to discuss the harassment. During the meeting, Nabozny explained the nature of the harassment and again revealed his homosexuality. Podlesny promised to protect Nabozny, but took no action. Following the holiday season, student harassment of Nabozny worsened, especially at the hands of students Jason Welty and Roy Grande. Nabozny complained to Nowakowski, and school administrators spoke to the students. The harassment, however, only intensified. A short time later, in a science classroom, Welty grabbed Nabozny and pushed him to the floor. Welty and Grande held Nabozny down and performed a mock rape on Nabozny, exclaiming that Nabozny should enjoy it. The boys carried out the mock rape as twenty other students looked on and laughed. Nabozny escaped and fled to Podlesny's office. Podlesny's alleged response is somewhat astonishing; she said that "boys will be boys" and told Nabozny that if he was "going to be so openly gay," he should "expect" such behavior from his fellow students. In the wake of Podlesny's comments, Nabozny ran home. The next day Nabozny was forced to speak with a counselor, not because he was subjected to a mock rape in a classroom, but because he left the school without obtaining the proper permission. No action was taken against the students involved. Nabozny was forced to return to his regular schedule. Understandably, Nabozny was "petrified" to attend school; he was subjected to abuse throughout the duration of the school year.

The situation hardly improved when Nabozny entered the eighth grade. Shortly after the school year began, several boys attacked Nabozny in a school bathroom, hitting him and pushing his books from his hands. This time Nabozny's parents met with Podlesny and the alleged perpetrators. The offending boys denied that the incident occurred, and no action was taken. Podlesny told both Nabozny and his parents that Nabozny should expect such incidents because he is "openly" gay. Several similar meetings between Nabozny's parents and Podlesny followed subsequent incidents involving Nabozny. Each time perpetrators were identified to Podlesny. Each time Podlesny pledged to take action. And, each time nothing was done. Toward the end of the school year, the harassment against Nabozny intensified to the point that a district attorney purportedly advised Nabozny to take time off from school. Nabozny took one and a half weeks off from school. When he returned, the harassment resumed, driving Nabozny to attempt suicide. After a stint in a hospital, Nabozny finished his eighth grade year in a Catholic school.

The Catholic school attended by Nabozny did not offer classes beyond the eighth grade. Therefore, to attend the ninth grade, Nabozny enrolled in Ashland High School. Almost immediately Nabozny's fellow students sang an all too familiar tune. Early in the year, while Nabozny was using a urinal in the restroom, Nabozny was assaulted. Student Stephen Huntley struck Nabozny in the back of the knee, forcing him to fall into the urinal. Roy Grande then urinated on Nabozny. Nabozny immediately reported the incident to the principal's office. Nabozny recounted the incident to the office secretary, who in turn relayed the story to Principal William Davis. Davis ordered Nabozny to go home and change clothes. Nabozny's parents scheduled a meeting with Davis and Assistant Principal Thomas Blauert. At the meeting, the parties discussed numerous instances of harassment against Nabozny, including the restroom incident.

Rather than taking action against the perpetrators, Davis and Blauert referred Nabozny to Mr. Reeder, a school guidance counselor. Reeder was supposed to change Nabozny's schedule so as to minimize Nabozny's exposure to the offending students. Eventually the school placed Nabozny in a special education class; Stephen Huntley and Roy Grande were special education students. Nabozny's parents continued to insist that the school take action, repeatedly meeting with Davis and Blauert among others. Nabozny's parents' efforts were futile; no action was taken. In the middle of his ninth grade year, Nabozny again attempted suicide. Following another hospital stay and a period living with relatives, Nabozny ran away to Minneapolis. His parents convinced him to return to Ashland by promising that Nabozny would not have to attend Ashland High. Because Nabozny's parents were unable to afford private schooling, however, the Department of Social Services ordered Nabozny to return to Ashland High.

In tenth grade, Nabozny fared no better. Nabozny's parents moved, forcing Nabozny to rely on the school bus to take him to school. Students on the bus regularly used epithets, such as "fag" and "queer," to refer to

Nabozny. Some students even pelted Nabozny with dangerous objects such as steel nuts and bolts. When Nabozny's parents complained to the school, school officials changed Nabozny's assigned seat and moved him to the front of the bus. The harassment continued. Ms. Hanson, a school guidance counselor, lobbied the school's administration to take more aggressive action to no avail. The worst was yet to come, however. One morning when Nabozny arrived early to school, he went to the library to study. The library was not yet open, so Nabozny sat down in the hallway. Minutes later he was met by a group of eight boys led by Stephen Huntley. Huntley began kicking Nabozny in the stomach, and continued to do so for five to ten minutes while the other students looked on laughing. Nabozny reported the incident to Hanson, who referred him to the school's "police liaison" Dan Crawford. Nabozny told Crawford that he wanted to press charges, but Crawford dissuaded him. Crawford promised to speak to the offending boys instead. Meanwhile, at Crawford's behest, Nabozny reported the incident to Blauert. Blauert, the school official supposedly in charge of disciplining, laughed and told Nabozny that Nabozny deserved such treatment because he is gay. Weeks later Nabozny collapsed from internal bleeding that resulted from Huntley's beating. Nabozny's parents and counselor Hanson repeatedly urged Davis and Blauert to take action to protect Nabozny. Each time aggressive action was promised. And, each time nothing was done.

Finally, in his eleventh grade year, Nabozny withdrew from Ashland High School. Hanson told Nabozny and his parents that school administrators were unwilling to help him and that he should seek educational opportunities elsewhere. Nabozny left Ashland and moved to Minneapolis where he was diagnosed with Post Traumatic Stress Disorder. In addition to seeking medical help, Nabozny sought legal advice.

On February 6, 1995, Nabozny filed the instant suit pursuant to 42 U.S.C. § 1983 against Mary Podlesny, William Davis, Thomas Blauert, Steven Kelly, and the District alleging, among other things, that the defendants violated his Fourteenth Amendment rights to equal protection and due process. By an agreement between the parties, Steven Kelly was dropped from the suit.[15] The remaining defendants moved for summary judgment.

The district court ruled in favor of the defendants. The court dispensed with Nabozny's gender equal protection claim, holding that Nabozny failed to produce evidence to establish that the defendants discriminated against him based on his gender. The court did not specify its basis for deciding Nabozny's sexual orientation equal protection claim. It appears from the order, however, that the court intended the reasoning that it applied to Nabozny's gender claim to apply to the sexual orientation claim as well. Regarding Nabozny's due process claims, the court concluded that Nabozny failed to produce evidence to establish that the defen-

15. Kelly was Superintendent of the Ashland Public School District at the time that the suit was filed. He was not, however, Superintendent at the time that the events at issue occurred.

dants either created or exacerbated the risk of harm to Nabozny posed by other students. The court also concluded that Nabozny could not prevail on his claim that the defendants' policies encouraged a climate in which Nabozny suffered harm because none of Nabozny's assailants were state actors. In the alternative, the court granted qualified immunity to all of the defendants against all of Nabozny's claims. Nabozny now brings this timely appeal. We have jurisdiction pursuant to 28 U.S.C. § 1291.

III.

We will begin our analysis by considering Nabozny's equal protection claims, reserving Nabozny's due process claims for subsequent treatment in the opinion. Wisconsin has elected to protect the students in its schools from discrimination. Wisconsin statute section 118.13(1), regulating general school operations, provides that:

> No person may be denied ... participation in, be denied the benefits of or be discriminated against in any curricular, extracurricular, pupil services, recreational or other program or activity because of the person's sex, race, religion, national origin, ancestry, creed, pregnancy, marital or parental status, sexual orientation or physical, mental, emotional or learning disability.

Since at least 1988, in compliance with the state statute, the Ashland Public School District has had a policy of prohibiting discrimination against students on the basis of gender or sexual orientation. The District's policy and practice includes protecting students from student-on-student sexual harassment and battery. Nabozny maintains that the defendants denied him the equal protection of the law by denying him the protection extended to other students, based on his gender and sexual orientation.

The Equal Protection Clause grants to all Americans "the right to be free from invidious discrimination in statutory classifications and other governmental activity." *Harris v. McRae*, 448 U.S. 297, 322, 65 L.Ed.2d 784, 100 S.Ct. 2671 (1980). When a state actor turns a blind eye to the Clause's command, aggrieved parties such as Nabozny can seek relief pursuant to 42 U.S.C. § 1983. *Cf. Muckway v. Craft*, 789 F.2d 517, 521 (7th Cir. 1986) (noting that a § 1983 claim is a tort action, requiring proof of duty, breach, causation, and damages). In order to establish liability under § 1983, Nabozny must show that the defendants acted with a nefarious discriminatory purpose, *Personnel Adm'r of Massachusetts v. Feeney*, 442 U.S. 256, 279, 60 L.Ed.2d 870, 99 S.Ct. 2282 (1979), and discriminated against him based on his membership in a definable class. *Albright v. Oliver*, 975 F.2d 343, 348 (7th Cir. 1992), *aff'd*, 510 U.S. 266, 114 S.Ct. 807, 127 L.Ed.2d 114 (1994); *Falls v. Town of Dyer*, 875 F.2d 146, 148 (7th Cir. 1989).... A showing that the defendants were negligent will not suffice. Nabozny must show that the defendants acted either intentionally or with deliberate indifference. *Archie v. City of Racine*, 847 F.2d 1211, 1219 (7th Cir. 1988), *cert. denied*, 489 U.S. 1065, 103 L.Ed.2d 809, 109 S.Ct. 1338 (1989); *Jackson v. City of Joliet*, 715 F.2d 1200, 1203

(7th Cir. 1983), *cert. denied*, 465 U.S. 1049, 79 L.Ed.2d 720, 104 S.Ct. 1325 (1984); *Shango*, 681 F.2d at 1104; *Cf. Muckway*, 789 F.2d at 522 (holding that a violation of a state law does not establish an equal protection violation absent proof that the defendant intentionally discriminated against otherwise similarly situated persons). To escape liability, the defendants either must prove that they did not discriminate against Nabozny, or at a bare minimum, the defendants' discriminatory conduct must satisfy one of two well established standards of review: heightened scrutiny in the case of gender discrimination, or rational basis in the case of sexual orientation.

The district court found that Nabozny had proffered no evidence to support his equal protection claims. In the alternative, the court granted to the defendants qualified immunity. Considering the facts in the light most favorable to Nabozny, we respectfully disagree with the district court's conclusions.

A. Gender and Equal Protection.

. . .

The record viewed in the light most favorable to Nabozny, combined with the defendants' own admissions, suggests that Nabozny was treated differently from other students. The defendants stipulate that they had a commendable record of enforcing their anti-harassment policies. Yet Nabozny has presented evidence that his classmates harassed and battered him for years and that school administrators failed to enforce their anti-harassment policies, despite his repeated pleas for them to do so. If the defendants otherwise enforced their anti-harassment policies, as they contend, then Nabozny's evidence strongly suggests that they made an exception to their normal practice in Nabozny's case.

Therefore, the question becomes whether Nabozny can show that he received different treatment because of his gender. Nabozny's evidence regarding the defendants' punishment of male-on-female battery and harassment is not overwhelming. Nabozny contends that a male student that struck his girlfriend was immediately expelled, that males were reprimanded for striking girls, and that when pregnant girls were called "slut" or "whore," the school took action. Nabozny's evidence does not include specific facts, such as the names and dates of the individuals involved. Nabozny does allege, however, that when he was subjected to a mock rape Podlesny responded by saying "boys will be boys," apparently dismissing the incident because both the perpetrators and the victim were males. We find it impossible to believe that a female lodging a similar complaint would have received the same response.

More important, the defendants do not deny that they aggressively punished male-on-female battery and harassment. The defendants argue that they investigated and punished all complaints of battery and harassment, regardless of the victim's gender. According to the defendants, contrary to the evidence presented by Nabozny, they aggressively pursued each of Nabozny's complaints and punished the alleged perpetrators whenever possible. Like Nabozny, the defendants presented evidence to support their claim. Whether to believe the defendants or Nabozny is, of course, a question of credibility for the fact-finder. In the context of considering the defendants' summary judgment motion, we must assume that Nabozny's version is the credible one. If Nabozny's evidence is considered credible, the record taken in conjunction with the defendants' admissions demonstrates that the defendants treated male and female victims differently.

. . .

Our inquiry into Nabozny's gender equal protection claim does not end here, because the district court granted to the defendants qualified immunity. The District itself clearly is not entitled to qualified immunity. *See Owen v. City of Independence, Mo.*, 445 U.S. 622, 650–51, 63 L.Ed.2d 673, 100 S.Ct. 1398 (1980) (denying to municipalities qualified immunity based on good faith constitutional violations). Therefore, we need only consider whether the individual defendants are immune from suit.

In *Harlow v. Fitzgerald*, 457 U.S. 800, 73 L.Ed.2d 396, 102 S.Ct. 2727 (1982), the Supreme Court held that "government officials performing discretionary functions generally are shielded from liability for civil damages insofar as their conduct does not violate clearly established statutory or constitutional rights of which a reasonable person would have known." *Id.* at 818. If the law was not "clearly established," no liability should result because "an official could not reasonably be expected to anticipate subsequent legal developments, nor could be said to 'know' that the law forbade conduct not previously identified as unlawful." *Id.* Thus, the critical questions in this case are whether the law "clearly establishes" the basis for Nabozny's claim, and whether the law was so established in 1988 when Nabozny entered middle school. *Sherman v. Four County Counseling Ctr.*, 987 F.2d 397, 401 (7th Cir. 1993).

The Fourteenth Amendment provides that a State shall not "deny to any person within its jurisdiction the equal protection of the laws." In 1971, the Supreme Court interpreted the Equal Protection Clause to prevent arbitrary gender-based discrimination. *See Reed v. Reed*, 404 U.S. 71, 76, 30 L.Ed.2d 225, 92 S.Ct. 251 (1971) ("To give a mandatory preference to members of either sex over members of the other ... is to make the very kind of arbitrary legislative choice forbidden by the Equal Protection Clause....") A few years later, in *Weinberger v. Wiesenfeld*, 420 U.S. 636, 43 L.Ed.2d 514, 95 S.Ct. 1225 (1975), the Court held that discrimination based on "gender-based generalizations" in society runs afoul of the Equal Protection Clause. *Id.* at 645.

In *Mississippi University for Women v. Hogan*, 458 U.S. 718, 73 L.Ed.2d 1090, 102 S.Ct. 3331 (1982), building on its earlier precedents, the Court went further in requiring equal treatment regardless of gender.... It is now well settled that to survive constitutional scrutiny, gender based discrimination must be substantially related to an important governmental objective. *See Bohen v. City of East Chicago, Ind.*, 799 F.2d 1180, 1185 (7th Cir. 1986).

. . .

The question is whether they are required to give male and female students equivalent levels of protection; they are, absent an important governmental objective, and the law clearly said so prior to Nabozny's years in middle school.

B. Sexual Orientation and Equal Protection.

. . .

Our discussion of equal protection analysis thus far has revealed a well established principle: the Constitution prohibits intentional invidious discrimination between otherwise similarly situated persons based on one's membership in a definable minority, absent at least a rational basis for the discrimination. There can be little doubt that homosexuals are an identifiable minority subjected to discrimination in our society. Given the legislation across the country both positing and prohibiting homosexual rights, that proposition was as self-evident in 1988 as it is today. In addition, the Wisconsin statute expressly prohibits discrimination on the basis of sexual orientation. Obviously that language was included because the Wisconsin legislature both recognized that homosexuals are discriminated against, and sought to prohibit such discrimination in Wisconsin schools. The defendants stipulate that they knew about the Wisconsin law, and enforced it to protect homosexuals. Therefore, it appears that the defendants concede that they knew that homosexuals are a definable minority and treated them as such.

In this case we need not consider whether homosexuals are a suspect or quasi-suspect class, which would subject the defendants' conduct to either strict or heightened scrutiny. Our court has already ruled that, in the context of the military, discrimination on the basis of sexual orientation is subject to rational basis review. *See Ben–Shalom v. Marsh*, 881 F.2d 454, 464 (7th Cir. 1989), *cert. denied*, 494 U.S. 1004, 110 S.Ct. 1296, 108 L.Ed.2d 473 (1990). The rational basis standard is sufficient for our purposes herein.

Under rational basis review there is no constitutional violation if "there is any reasonably conceivable state of facts" that would provide a rational basis for the government's conduct. *FCC v. Beach Communications, Inc.*, 508 U.S. 307, 113 S.Ct. 2096, 2101, 124 L.Ed.2d 211 (1993). We are unable to garner any rational basis for permitting one student to assault another based on the victim's sexual orientation, and the defendants do not offer us one. Like Nabozny's gender claim, the defendants argue that they did not discriminate against Nabozny.

. . .

Therefore, although it presents a closer question than does Nabozny's gender claim, we hold that reasonable persons in the defendants' positions in 1988 would have concluded that discrimination against Nabozny based on his sexual orientation was unconstitutional.

IV.

Now we turn to Nabozny's due process arguments. We believe that in order to clarify the nature of Nabozny's due process theories, it is necessary to specify what Nabozny does not argue. However untenable it may be to suggest that under the Fourteenth Amendment a state can force a student to attend a school when school officials know that the student will be placed at risk of bodily harm, our court has concluded that local school administrations have no affirmative substantive due process duty to protect students....

Nabozny argues that the defendants should be liable because they enhanced his risk of harm, and because their policies encouraged a climate in which he suffered harm. We will consider each theory in turn. First, Nabozny argues that by failing to punish his assailants the defendants exacerbated the risk that he would be harmed, or even encouraged the students to harm him. Nabozny relies on our opinion in *Reed v. Gardner*, 986 F.2d 1122 (7th Cir.), *cert. denied*, 510 U.S. 947, 126 L.Ed.2d 337, 114 S.Ct. 389 (1993). In *Reed*, we considered a case in which police officers arrested the driver of an automobile, but left an intoxicated passenger on the side of the road with the keys to the car. *Id.* at 1124. After the police left, the intoxicated passenger drove the car onto the road and caused a serious accident. *Id.* The victims of the accident sued the police officers pursuant to § 1983 for leaving the intoxicated passenger on the side of the road, arguing that the officers' conduct deprived the victims of their Fourteenth Amendment right to due process. 986 F.2d at 1124–25. We reversed a lower court's dismissal of the complaint, ruling that state actors have a duty to care for citizens if the state actors' conduct "creates, or substantially contributes to the creation of, a danger or renders citizens more vulnerable to a danger than they otherwise would have been." *Id.* at 1126. But we noted that the plaintiffs would lose on summary judgment if the defendants could show that the arrested driver was also intoxicated: "the reason is simple: without state intervention, the same danger would exist." *Id.* at 1125.

We agree with Nabozny in principle that the defendants could be liable under a due process theory if Nabozny could show that the defendants created a risk of harm, or exacerbated an existing one. After a thorough review of the record, however, we must agree with the district court that Nabozny's claim suffers from a paucity of evidence. Nabozny has presented evidence to show that the defendants failed to act, and that their failure to act was intentional. But, as we noted, *Alton Community* held that the defendants had no affirmative duty to act. The defendants' failure to act left Nabozny in a position of danger, but nothing suggests that their failure to act placed him in the danger, or increased the pre-existing threat of harm. Nabozny has presented "wrenching" facts, but there is insufficient evidence from which a reasonable factfinder could conclude that the defendants' conduct increased the risk of harm to Nabozny beyond that which he would have faced had the defendants taken no action. *See Reed*, 986 F.2d at 1125.

. . .

Conclusion.

We conclude that, based on the record as a whole, a reasonable fact-finder could find that the District and defendants Podlesny, Davis, and Blauert violated Nabozny's Fourteenth Amendment right to equal protection by discriminating against him based on his gender or sexual orientation. Further, the law establishing the defendants' liability was sufficiently clear to inform the defendants at the time that their conduct was unconstitutional. Nabozny's equal protection claims against the District, Podlesny, Davis, and Blauert are reinstated in toto. We further conclude that Nabozny has failed to produce sufficient evidence to permit a reasonable fact-finder to find that the defendants violated Nabozny's Fourteenth Amendment right to due process either by enhancing his risk of harm or by encouraging a climate to flourish in which he suffered harm. Our disposition of Nabozny's due process claims renders the district court's award of qualified immunity as to those claims moot. The decision of the district court is affirmed in part, reversed in part, and remanded.

C. HARASSMENT: TITLE IX

MONTGOMERY v. INDEPENDENT SCH. DIST.

109 F.Supp.2d 1081 (D. Minn. 2000)

OPINION: JOHN R. TUNHEIM

MEMORANDUM OPINION AND ORDER

Plaintiff Jesse Montgomery brings this action against Independent School District Number 709 (the "School District") based on its failure to prevent harassment by other students that he experienced during approximately eleven years of education in defendant's schools. Plaintiff asserts that the other students harassed him both because of his gender and his perceived sexual orientation.... This matter is before the Court on defendant's motion for judgment on the pleadings against plaintiff's claims under the United States Constitution and Title IX....

Background

Plaintiff attended three of defendant's schools from kindergarten through the tenth grade, including Lakewood Elementary School, Ordean Middle School, and East High School. Plaintiff alleges, and defendant does not dispute, that while he was a student in defendant's schools he experienced frequent and continual teasing by other students beginning in kindergarten and recurring on an almost daily basis until the end of the tenth grade, when he transferred to another school district. While some of these taunts were more general in nature, many of them appear to have been directed at plaintiff because of his perceived sexual orientation, including, "faggot," "fag," "gay," "Jessica," "girl," "princess," "fairy," "homo," "freak," "lesbian," "femme boy," "gay boy," "bitch," "queer," "pansy," and "queen." A review of plaintiff's allegations, assuming them to be true for purposes of these motions, reveals that the verbal abuse to which his peers subjected him was severe and unrelenting throughout his entire tenure in defendant's school system.

According to plaintiff, the students' misconduct escalated to the point of physical violence beginning in the sixth grade, when several students punched him, kicked him, and knocked him down on the playground. Another student later super-glued him to his seat. Plaintiff claims that as he entered middle school and progressed on to high school, the harassment became noticeably worse. While the verbal taunts continued unabated, the physical threats and assaults intensified. Students threatened to beat him up on several occasions. A group of students pushed him down in the hallway in front of his family when they were at the school to attend a choir concert. Another student unzipped his backpack, threw his books to the floor and smashed his calculator. Plaintiff also states that during a gym exercise one of the students charged him and sent him flying several feet through the air, and that during hockey drills the offending students deliberately tripped him or knocked him down on several occasions, causing bruises. Plaintiff further alleges that students frequently kicked or tripped him on the school bus, and that while he was riding the bus or in art class students would throw objects at him such as crayons, paper, popcorn, water, chunks of clay, paint brushes, pencils, pen caps, trash, and other small things.

In addition to these incidents, plaintiff claims that on some occasions the physical threats and assaults he experienced were of a more sexual nature. He specifically contends that a student in his middle school choir class grabbed his legs, inner thighs, chest, and crotch. He states that the same student grabbed his buttocks on at least five or six occasions. Later another student approached him and asked to see him naked after gym class. Plaintiff states that he experienced similar incidents when he was in high school. According to plaintiff, students in his ninth and tenth grade choir classes sometimes put their arms around him or grabbed his inner thighs and buttocks while calling him names targeted at his perceived sexual orientation. Plaintiff states that one of the students grabbed his own genitals while squeezing plaintiff's buttocks, and on other occasions would stand behind plaintiff and grind his penis into plaintiff's backside. The same student once threw him to the ground and pretended to rape him anally, and on another occasion sat on plaintiff's lap and bounced while pretending to have intercourse with him. Other students watched and laughed during these incidents.

Plaintiff alleges that the harassment he experienced deprived him of the ability to access significant portions of the educational environment. During his tenure in defendant's schools, plaintiff generally achieved average to above average grades. Nonetheless, plaintiff states that he stayed home from school on approximately five or six occasions while he was in middle school in order to avoid the harassment. He further states that he did not participate or try to participate in intramural sports because his harassers were participants, that he avoided going to the school cafeteria unless absolutely necessary, and that he avoided using the school bathroom except in emergency situations. When plaintiff was in high school he stopped using the school bus in order to circumvent the continuous harassment he experienced there, requiring his parents and other family members to drive him to school.

Plaintiff states that he reported the students' misconduct to a variety of School District officials, including teachers, bus drivers, principals, assistant principals, playground and cafeteria monitors, locker room attendants, and school counselors. Plaintiff further states that on several occasions when he was in middle school, he and his parents reported the incidents of misconduct to the office of the School District's superintendent.

The officials to whom plaintiff reported the misconduct responded with a variety of measures. Defendant gave plaintiff access to school counselors, and he made appointments with them on a regular basis. Moreover, when plaintiff was in middle school defendant required him to attend a number of group sessions with other boys to discuss strategies for responding to harassment. According to plaintiff, defendant removed him from some of his favorite classes and required him to attend these sessions involuntarily.

Defendant also implemented several disciplinary measures against the offending students, although it appears that School District officials applied such discipline inconsistently. Plaintiff's teachers responded to many of his complaints by verbally reprimanding students or sending them to the principal's office. When students harassed plaintiff on the school bus, the driver sometimes stopped the bus and reprimanded the students. Defendant asserts that it assigned special seats to students on the bus at least temporarily in an attempt to circumvent the misconduct, although plaintiff claims that these seating assignments were not adequately enforced. On some occasions the cafeteria monitor responded to plaintiff's lunchtime complaints by requiring the offending students to stand in a designated area. On two occasions plaintiff's middle school counselor and principal required the offending students to meet with plaintiff and apologize to him. Plaintiff asserts that these sessions were unhelpful and ultimately resulted in a significant amount of retaliatory harassment.

In connection with the incidents of sexual touching he experienced, plaintiff alleges that he made multiple complaints to his choir teacher about the student who repeatedly grabbed his thigh, buttocks, and crotch and pretended to have intercourse with him. The teacher responded to plaintiff's complaints by verbally reprimanding the student, sending him out into the hallway, or sending him to the principal's office. There is no evidence in the record as to whether or how School District officials ultimately disciplined this student once he arrived in the principal's office.

With the exception of one occasion, defendant has not shown that any of the students whom teachers sent to the principal's office in response to plaintiff's reports ever received discipline stronger than a verbal reprimand. The disciplinary measures that defendant took on that occasion were precipitated by a formal complaint that plaintiff's mother filed with the School District in March 1995. At that time plaintiff had been experiencing almost daily harassment on the school bus and in his art class by a particular group of students who called him names, kicked him, or threw objects at him. The principal eventually referred plaintiff's complaint to Terri Kronzer ("Kronzer") with the School District's Human Resources Department. Kronzer conducted an investigation and determined that plaintiff had been sexually harassed. Based on her recommendations, defendant suspended one of the harassers for five days and another for one day. Other harassers received lectures on the School District's sexual harassment policy. Defendant also revoked the bus privileges of two of the students, who were brothers, and transferred the most egregious offender out of plaintiff's art class. Defendant further instructed the hall monitor to "keep an eye" on plaintiff.

Within one week after defendant implemented these measures, the students whose bus privileges had been revoked returned to the school bus. According to defendant, the students lived in a rural area, and their father complained to the principal that driving them to school each day would be a significant hardship. Defendant states that it permitted the students to return to the school bus on the condition that they sit directly behind the bus driver each day.

Plaintiff thereafter ceased riding the school bus altogether in order to avoid his harassers, but did not notify defendant that he had done so. Plaintiff and his parents were unhappy with defendant's decision to permit the students to ride the bus again. Plaintiff's mother thereafter filed charges against the School District with the Minnesota Department of Human Rights ("MDHR") based upon its allegedly inadequate response to plaintiff's formal harassment complaint, and this lawsuit followed from those charges. Eventually, after plaintiff finished the tenth grade, he transferred to another school district altogether for his last two years of secondary education.

Analysis

. . .

D. Title IX claims

Defendant also argues that plaintiff's Title IX claims must be dismissed because Title IX does not protect individuals from discrimination based on sexual orientation or perceived sexual orientation. Title IX provides in relevant part that "no person in the United States shall, *on the basis of sex*, be excluded from participation in, be denied the benefits of, or be subjected to discrimination under" federally-funded educational programs or activities. 20 U.S.C. § 1681(a) (emphasis added). Thus, unlike the Fourteenth Amendment, Title IX prohibits only discrimination based on sex and does not extend to any other form of invidious discrimination. For these reasons the Court concludes that, to the extent that plaintiff asserts Title IX claims based on discrimination due to his sexual orientation or perceived sexual orientation, these claims are not actionable and must be dismissed.

Plaintiff nevertheless contends that he has been a victim of harassment based upon sex or gender as well as harassment based upon his sexual orientation or perceived sexual orientation. In *Davis v. Monroe County Bd. of Educ.*, 526 U.S. 629, 631, 143 L.Ed.2d 839, 119 S.Ct. 1661 (1999), the Supreme Court recognized that student-against-student sexual harassment may give rise to a cognizable claim under Title IX in appropriate circumstances. No federal court appears to have addressed, however, whether the kind of conduct to which plaintiff was subjected constitutes discrimination "on the basis of sex" within the meaning of Title IX. In contrast with the claims recognized as viable in *Davis*, this case primarily involves same-sex harassment by students who, through name-calling and other forms of verbal abuse, repeatedly indicated that they perceived plaintiff to be homosexual. Thus, plaintiff's harassers do not appear to have been motivated by any sexual desire towards plaintiff, but rather, by hostility based upon his perceived sexual orientation.

Plaintiff contends that the students engaged in the offensive conduct at issue not only because they believed him to be gay, but also because he did not meet their stereotyped expectations of masculinity. The facts alleged in plaintiff's complaint support this characterization of the students' misconduct. He specifically alleges that some of the students called him "Jessica," a girl's name, indicating a belief that he exhibited feminine characteristics. Moreover, the Court finds important the fact that plaintiff's peers began harassing him as early as kindergarten. It is highly unlikely that at that tender age plaintiff would have developed any solidified sexual preference, or for that matter, that he even understood what it meant to be "homosexual" or "heterosexual." The likelihood that he openly identified himself as gay or that he engaged in any homosexual conduct at that age is quite low. It is much more plausible that the students began tormenting him based on feminine personality traits that he exhibited and the perception that he did not engage in behaviors befitting a boy. Plaintiff thus appears to plead facts that would support a claim of harassment based on the perception that he did not fit his peers' stereotypes of masculinity.

Whether such harassment is actionable under federal law has been the subject of significant controversy among federal courts. Although no court has addressed this issue in the context of a Title IX claim, several courts have considered whether same-sex harassment targeting the claimant's failure to meet expected gender stereotypes is actionable under Title

VII. The Court looks to these precedents in analyzing plaintiff's Title IX claim, noting that Title VII similarly requires that the discrimination resulting in the plaintiff's claims be based on his or her sex. *See, e.g., Schmedding v. Tnemec Co.*, 187 F.3d 862, 864 (8th Cir. 1999). Moreover, the Supreme Court relied upon Title VII precedents in first recognizing a private cause of action for sexual harassment under Title IX. In *Davis*, 526 U.S. at 643, the Supreme Court clearly distinguished Title IX from Title VII in connection with the use of agency principles and the requisites for institutional liability under each statute. Nevertheless, the same opinion cited Title VII precedents in connection with the issue of what constitutes gender-oriented harassment. Furthermore, no logical rationale appears to exist for distinguishing Title VII and Title IX in connection with the issue raised here regarding the circumstances under which abusive or offensive conduct amounts to harassment "based on sex." The Court accordingly applies Title VII precedents in analyzing plaintiff's Title IX claim.

. . .

The Court's determination on this issue is buttressed by the Eighth Circuit's recent decision in *Schmedding*, 187 F.3d at 865. The misconduct alleged in *Schmedding* is strikingly similar to that plead in this case. In that case the claimant alleged that his co-workers taunted him about being a homosexual and spread rumors about his perceived sexual orientation, as well as subjecting him to other offensive harassment such as patting him on the buttocks, asking him to perform sexual acts, and forcing him to observe offensive exhibitions of sexually inappropriate behavior. *See id.* Although these acts are indicative of harassment based upon sexual orientation or perceived sexual orientation, the court held them sufficient to support a Title VII claim. In this case, plaintiff alleges that his harassers called him names targeted at homosexuals and spread rumors about his sexual orientation, as well as subjecting him to more severe forms of misconduct such as asking him for sexual favors, grabbing his buttocks and inner thighs, and subjecting him to acts of pretended anal rape. The Court finds these alleged acts to be at least as indicative of harassment based on sex as those asserted in *Schmedding*. The Court accordingly denies defendant's motion for judgment on the pleadings against plaintiff's Title IX claim.

II. The Parties' Motions for Summary Judgment

. . .

E. Title IX Claim

. . . In challenging plaintiff's Title IX claim, defendant also contends that under the Supreme Court's decision in *Gebser v. Lago Vista Ind. Sch. Dist.*, 524 U.S. 274, 141 L.Ed.2d 277, 118 S.Ct. 1989 (1998), plaintiff failed to notify the appropriate authorities about the alleged harassment. *Gebser* involved a claim of sexual misconduct against a student by a teacher. *See id.* In that case, the Court held that the school district did not have actual notice of the misconduct when the only official who knew about it was the offending teacher himself. *See id.* at 291. The Court further held that in order to state a claim for damages under Title IX, a student must be able to prove that an official with sufficient authority to address the alleged harassment and to take corrective measures on the student's behalf has actual knowledge of it. *See id.* at 290.

Defendant argues that under these holdings, a Title IX claimant may never prevail unless a principal or higher official has actual knowledge of the alleged discrimination. Defendant contends that knowledge by a teacher is therefore insufficient. This argument fails for two reasons. First, plaintiff plainly alleges that he did inform the principals in his schools about the student misconduct, and furthermore, that on at least one occasion he informed the office of the School District's superintendent. Moreover, defendant stretches the Supreme Court's holdings in *Gebser* beyond recognition in arguing that actual knowledge by a teacher is always insufficient. In this case, unlike *Gebser*, the alleged harassers were students and not teachers. Because teachers ordinarily maintain at least some level of disciplinary control over their students, it is reasonable to infer that they had authority to take disciplinary action and to institute other corrective measures to end the harassment. Indeed, the School District's sexual harassment policy imposes upon teachers a duty to convey reports of sexual harassment to the school principals. It is therefore clear that teachers had the authority to take at least this minimal corrective measure which, if effectively carried out, would impart knowledge of the harassment to higher School District officials with even greater authority to act.

Defendant also challenges plaintiff's Title IX claim on the ground that he has failed make any showing of damages as a result of the harassment he experienced. Defendant cites *Price v. City of Charlotte*, 93 F.3d 1241, 1250 (4th Cir. 1996), and *Patterson v. PHP Health Care Corp.*, 90 F.3d 927, 939 (5th Cir. 1996), for the proposition that plaintiff's claim must be dismissed on this ground. Upon reviewing these authorities the Court finds that they do not support defendant's position. Rather, these cases stand for the proposition that in section 1983 cases, a plaintiff claiming emotional distress who fails to produce actual proof of injury is entitled to no more than nominal damages. *See Price*, 93 F.3d at 1250. They do not hold, as plaintiff suggests, that a failure to prove actual damages at the summary judgment stage constitutes grounds for dismissal on the issue of liability.

Finally, defendant challenges plaintiff's cause of action under Title IX on the ground that, as plead in his complaint, he bases this particular claim only on sexual harassment by female students. Defendant notes that plaintiff's evidence of such harassment is quite sparse. The Court agrees with defendant's characterization of the evidence. Nevertheless, when asked about the peculiar limitation on plaintiff's Title IX claim to harassment by only female students, plaintiff's counsel acknowledged that this was a mistake and stated that the focus of plaintiff's claim has always been on harassment by both male and female students. Counsel further suggested that plaintiff would be amenable to amending his complaint in order to correct this error.

Ordinarily the Court does not permit parties to amend their pleadings at this late stage in the process. Nevertheless, it does appear that defendant had ample notice of plaintiff's intent to litigate this matter on the basis of harassment by students of both sexes. Moreover, the parties conducted extensive discovery pertaining to plaintiff's allegations of harassment by male students in conjunction with his other claims. Permitting plaintiff to amend the complaint thus would not result in a need for further discovery. Although defendant argues that it would be prejudiced by an amendment to the pleadings at this point in time, it fails to articulate how such prejudice might arise. For these reasons, the Court concludes that plaintiff should be permitted to amend his complaint for the limited purposes of broadening his Title IX claim to include harassment by male as well as female students.

For all of these reasons, the Court denies defendant's summary judgment motion against plaintiff's Title IX claim. Nevertheless, because there are genuine factual issues remaining, the Court also denies plaintiff's cross-motion for summary judgment on this claim....

D. GAY/STRAIGHT ALLIANCES

Gay/Straight Alliances, especially in middle and high schools, have become important vehicles by which gay students seek support among their peers and raise awareness of the issues they face. The groups are sometimes bitterly opposed by school boards, parents, and administrators. The following case illustrates some of the difficulties students face in organizing such groups at schools as well as how the law responds.

COLIN v. ORANGE UNIFIED SCH. DIST.

83 F.Supp.2d 1135 (C.D. Cal. 2000)

OPINION: DAVID O. CARTER

GRANTING PLAINTIFFS' MOTION FOR PRELIMINARY INJUNCTION

Before the Court is Plaintiffs' Motion for Preliminary Injunction. Plaintiffs are students who wish to form a "Gay–Straight Alliance Club" at their high school. They claim that Defendants, the Orange Unified School District and its Board of Education and administrators, have violated their rights under the Equal Access Act and their First Amendment rights of expression and association when they voted to deny Plaintiffs' application to form the club. At issue is whether Plaintiffs are likely to prevail on these claims and whether an injunction should issue prohibiting Defendants, while this action is pending, from continuing to deny Plaintiffs the same access to El Modena facilities that is accorded to other student groups.

I. Statement of the Facts

There are limited factual disputes in this case. The parties have stipulated to the authenticity of all exhibits submitted, except for newspaper articles. Out of an abundance of caution, the Court heard testimony at the preliminary injunction hearing in order to address some of the limited factual disputes.

In late August 1999, Anthony Colin ("Colin") and his friend Shannon MacMillan ("MacMillan") decided to form a "Gay–Straight Alliance Club" ("GSA") at their school, El Modena High School in Orange, California. Colin, a tenth-grade student, had the idea after Matthew Shepherd, a young man from Wyoming, died after being brutally assaulted due to his homosexuality. Colin testified that he wanted to form the club to promote acceptance among and for gay and straight students at the school. After discussing the idea with friends and family, Colin submitted a club constitution in compliance with school policy during the week of September 7, 1999, the first week of the school year. The application stated that the purpose of the club was "to promote interest in a supportive community amongst our peers." Colin Decl., Ex. B.

Shortly thereafter, Colin submitted a mission statement for the club that had been written by MacMillan, a twelfth grade student. The group's mission statement is:

> Public schools have an obligation to provide an equal opportunity for all students to receive an education in a safe, nonhostile, nondiscriminatory environment. Our goal in this organization is to raise public awareness and promote tolerance by providing a safe forum for discussion of issues related to sexual orientation and homophobia. We wish to stress the need for people to put aside their personal prejudice and agree to treat everyone with respect when the situation calls for it. We invite ALL students, gay or straight, to join us in discussions, field trips, lectures, and social activities that will counterattack unfair treatment and prejudice. We respect privacy and require NO one to make disclosures regarding his or her own sexual orientation.
>
> This is not a sexual issue, it is about gaining support and promoting tolerance and respect for all students.

Colin Decl., Ex. C. Colin asked Mrs. Maryina Herde, a drama and English teacher at the school, to serve as the faculty advisor and she accepted. The application was turned in to the teacher in charge of student activities at the high school, who passed the application on to the Principal, Nancy Murray.

Colin and the other founders of the Gay–Straight Alliance had reason to believe that their application would be accepted. Consistent with the policy of the Orange Unified School District's Board of Education ("the Board"), their high school had a policy of allowing student-initiated groups to meet on school grounds during lunch period and to use school facilities to publicize their meetings and activities. A recent list of the clubs on campus, of which there are 38 in total, includes the following noncurriculum related student groups: the Asian Club, Black Student Union, Christian Club, Gentlemen's Club, Girls' League, Koinonia (for Catholic students), MECHA (Movimiento Estudiantil Chicano de Aztlan), and Red Cross/Key Club. *See* Colin Decl., Ex. D. Plaintiff's application was not approved, however. Principal Murray had been instructed by Assistant Superintendent Neil McKinnon ("McKinnon") in the spring of 1998 to keep him informed of the formation of any gay-straight alliance-type group. She was told the Board may want to make a decision on the application, contrary to its custom of leaving the decision to the administration, because the Board may not approve it. Principal Murray therefore forwarded the policy to the Assistant Superintendent. McKinnon gave the application to the Superintendent, Barbara Van Otterloo, who then forwarded it to the Board.

Because the Board had not yet acted on their application, Plaintiffs asked Principal Murray to participate in "Club Rush," a one day informational fair about student groups, during the first week of October 1999. It was only after they asked to participate in the club fair that Principal Murray informed Colin that the group's application had been passed on to the Board and the group would not be permitted to participate in "Club Rush." As Plaintiffs' mission statement was being scrutinized by the Board, all the other clubs displayed their banners and distributed their mission statements at "Club Rush." Though there was no Gay–Straight Alliance table at the event, approximately 58 students signed a petition in support of the GSA. At the end of Club Rush, on October 7, 1999, the Board decided to delay action on Plaintiff's application and voted to have a public forum on whether the Gay–Straight Alliance should be permitted. Weeks before the public forum, Principal Murray informed Colin that the name of his club was inappropriate and suggested alternate names such as the "Tolerance Club," the "Acceptance Club," or the "Alliance." *See* Colin Decl., P 12. No other club at El Modena has been approached by the Principal or the Board with suggestions to change the name that they chose for their club. By the end of October, a representative of the Gay Lesbian Straight Education Network of Orange County ("GLSEN"), a volunteer group that tries to end anti-gay bias in schools, contacted Herde and the Plaintiffs after learning of their struggle due to the publicity it had generated. "Gay–Straight Alliance" is a name recommended for clubs by the national GLSEN. Since, October, Luis Torres, the co-chair of the Orange County chapter of GLSEN, has had three meetings with students interested in the GSA as a means of providing them with moral support.

On November 9, 1999, the Board held the public forum. After hearing arguments both for and against the GSA, the Board decided to postpone the vote until November 18, 1999. At the November 18, 1999 meeting, Defendant Board Member Bill Lewis said, "The Bible says we're all sinners, but this, in my opinion, is asking us to legitimize sin." Codell Decl., Ex. A. Board Member Linda Davis said, "We know the law is on their side, but our community members don't want it." *Id.* Plaintiff Heather Zetin, an eleventh grade member of the student group, explained to the Board that she believed in sexual abstinence and again assured the Board that the GSA would not discuss sex. Still, the Board postponed its decision for a third time. After three months of delays, Colin, Zetin, and the GSA filed this action. Although there are about six hundred gay-straight alliance clubs at high schools across the country, this is reportedly only the fourth lawsuit against school districts by students seeking to form such clubs.

On December 7, 1999, the Board unanimously, seven to zero, approved a motion by Defendant Kathy Ward to deny Plaintiffs' application to form the Gay–Straight Alliance Club. The Board objected to the appropriateness of what they claimed was a sexually charged club. The decision was publicly announced as opponents of the club stood by with pickets, some of which stated, "GRADES NOT AIDS." Ward's motion was grounded on the following four reasons:

> (1) the proposed GSA has a subject matter related to sexual conduct and sexuality; (2) the District and El Modena High School offer courses that address sex, sexual conduct, sexual abstinence, and sexual transmission of diseases; (3) the State of California in the Education Code imposes strict requirements on how, when and by whom sex education and related courses are taught; and (4) the Board should consider that unrestricted, unsupervised student led discussion of sexual topics is age inappropriate and is likely to interfere with the legitimate educational concerns of the District in this sensitive area of sex education. Codell Decl., Ex. E. The Board further stated that it would not foreclose the submission of a revised mission statement "for a tolerance club with an appropriate name and a mission statement that clearly states that sex, sexuality, [and] sex education ... will not be the subject of discussion in club meetings."

Id.

On December 16, 1999, at 9:40 a.m., Superintendent Van Otterloo and Principal Murray pulled some of the students interested in the GSA, including Colin and Zetin, out of their classes to discuss this matter. Although Principal Murray believes that there is value in a club that allows harassed students to discuss issues of homophobia and would have approved the club if it were her decision, she edited the group's name and MacMillan's Mission Statement in a way that might meet the Board's concerns. She proposed a "Draft" that deleted any references to "gay," "straight" or "sexual orientation." Her changes included crossing out the name of the club and replacing it with "Tolerance For All," and deleting "sexual orientation and homophobia" and replacing it with "intolerance in all of its forms." Finally, Murray added a statement that "sex, sexuality, [and] sex education" will not be discussed at the meetings. Colin testified under oath that Principal Murray was "tearing my rights down" when she made these edits. Similarly, Zetin testified that adding the language from the Education Code "would communicate that gay people are inherently more sexual or sexually promiscuous when they're just people."

. . .

A. *The Equal Access Act*

Plaintiffs are suing under a federal law, the Equal Access Act. An understanding of how the law came into being is helpful in order to understand its operation and whether or nor it has been violated.

The Equal Access Act was passed to fit within the Constitutional limits that the Court has placed on school control over student speech. Some discussion of the First Amendment is therefore necessary to explain the somewhat surprising notion of federal courts requiring local school officials to recognize a student group that they did not choose to recognize. In general, "the education of the Nation's youth is primarily the responsibility of parents, teachers, and state and local school officials, and not of federal judges." The "daily operation of school systems" is traditionally reserved to the States and their local school boards.... Federal courts do intervene, however, when decisions of local school boards run afoul of the Constitution....

Public school students do not "shed their constitutional rights to freedom of speech or expression at the schoolhouse gate." *Tinker v. Des Moines Independent Community School Dist.*, 393 U.S. 503, 511, 89 S.Ct. 733, 21 L.Ed.2d 731 (1969). Students do not, however, have all the First Amendment rights of adults in other settings because their rights must be "applied in light, of the special characteristics of the school environment." *Id.* at 506. In *Tinker*, students were suspended until they removed their armbands protesting the Vietnam War. The Court found that school censorship of student expression was unconstitutional unless the speech "materially disrupts classwork or involves substantial disorder or invasion of the rights of others." *Id.* at 513. The "material disruption" standard is very similar to the one adopted by Congress in the Equal Access Act. Though school officials in *Tinker* may have disapproved of the war protesters' beliefs, official suppression of student speech in high schools could not be justified by the "mere desire to avoid the discomfort and unpleasantness that always accompany an unpopular viewpoint." *Id.* at 509.

The reason for the First Amendment's ban on official censorship is because in a free society we rely on the "marketplace of ideas." *See Abrams v. United States*, 250 U.S. 616, 630, 40 S.Ct. 17, 63 L.Ed. 1173 (1919) (Holmes, J., dissenting). Though the state education system has the awesome responsibility of inculcating moral and political values, that does not permit educators to act as "thought police" inhibiting all discussion that is not approved by, and in accord with the official position of, the state. The danger is that public education could transform schools into "enclaves of totalitarianism" and convert students into "closed-circuit recipients of only that which the State chooses to communicate." *Tinker*, 393 U.S. at 511. Though it may educate many of Orange's students, the Orange Unified School District must not become an Orwellian "guardianship of the public mind," *Thomas v. Collins*, 323 U.S. 516, 545, 65 S.Ct.

315, 89 L.Ed. 430 (1945) (Jackson, J., concurring), that can "strangle the free mind at its source." *Barnette*, 319 U.S. at 637.

The only way to maintain the "independence and vigor of Americans who grow up here" is through tolerating speech that school authorities may vehemently disagree with. *Tinker*, 393 U.S. at 509. "Our history says that it is this sort of hazardous freedom—this kind of openness—that is the basis of our national strength." *Id.* at 508–509. The democratic response to speech that people disagree with is more speech: by allowing students to express both the popular and unpopular viewpoints society can foster "enlightened opinion." *Cantwell v. Connecticut*, 310 U.S. 296, 310, 60 S.Ct. 900, 84 L.Ed. 1213 (1940). "Secondary school students are mature enough and are likely to understand that a school does not endorse or support student speech that it merely permits on a nondiscriminatory basis." *Board of Education of the Westside Community Schools v. Mergens*, 496 U.S. 226, 250, 110 S.Ct. 2356, 110 L.Ed.2d 191 (1990).

The Supreme Court found in 1981 that when state universities make their facilities generally available for use by registered student groups, they could not single out religious groups and prevent them from meeting. *See Widmar v. Vincent*, 454 U.S. 263, 102 S.Ct. 269, 70 L.Ed.2d 440 (1981). Though the presence of religious groups raised concerns about possibly violating the separation of church and state, the Court found that the religious speech and association rights of a Christian group at the University of Missouri at Kansas City were protected by the First Amendment. The *only* reason that the idea of religious groups using public facilities did not violate the Establishment Clause of the First Amendment (which provides that "Congress shall make no law respecting an establishment of religion") was because under an "equal access" policy, a school is not endorsing any particular viewpoint, either for or against religion in general or for or against any particular religion. *See id.* at 270–76. The Court did not decide in that case if high schools with an "equal access" policy, as well as universities, were prevented from excluding certain student groups on the basis of the content of their speech. *See id.* at 274 n.14.

In the 1984 Equal Access Act, Congress extended the rule in *Widmar* to public high schools. Under the Act, schools that allow student groups whose purpose is not directly related to the curriculum to meet on school grounds during lunch or after school cannot deny other student groups access to the school due to the content of the students' proposed discussions. *See* 20 U.S.C. §§ 4071(a), (b). In the words of the Act:

> It shall be unlawful for any public secondary school which receives Federal financial assistance and which has a limited open forum to deny equal access or a fair opportunity to, or discriminate against, any students who wish to conduct a meeting within that limited open forum on the basis of the religious, political, philosophical, or other content of the speech at such meetings.

The Act was intended to counteract perceived discrimination against religious speech in public schools and overturn two appellate court decisions that had held that allowing student religious groups to meet on campus before and after classes would violate the Establishment Clause. *See Mergens,* 496 U.S. at 239, 110 S.Ct. 2356. The Act was "passed by wide, bipartisan majorities in both the House and the Senate." *Id.* at 239, 110 S.Ct. 2356. As in the *Widmar* case, allowing religious groups on campus was constitutional only because an "equal access" policy does not endorse any particular viewpoint, does not give direct benefits to religion to such a degree that it tends to establish a state religion, or coerce students to participate in a religious activity. *See id.* at 247–253, 110 S.Ct. 2356 (plurality holding regarding endorsement) (O'Connor, J.); *id.* at 258–62, 110 S.Ct. 2356 (concurring opinion regarding establishing a state religion or coercing students) (Kennedy, J.). The constitutionality of the law therefore hinged on its openness and neutrality: if a school that accepts federal funds allows some "noncurricular" student groups, it can not deny others "on the basis of the religious, political, philosophical, or other content of the speech" at the student meetings. 20 U.S.C. § 4071(a).

When Congress passed the Equal Access Act, it "made a matter once left to the discretion of local school officials the subject of comprehensive regulation by federal law." *Mergens*, 496 U.S. at 259 (Kennedy, J., concurring). As Justice Kennedy pointed out, "one of the consequences of the statute, as we now interpret it, is that clubs of a most controversial character might have access to the student life of high schools that in the past have given official recognition only to clubs of a more conventional kind." *Id.* It's true that when courts enforce the Act, they remove control from local school boards; "(t)his decision, however, was for Congress to make, subject to constitutional limitations." *Id.* Due to the First Amendment, Congress passed an "Equal Access Act" when it wanted to permit religious speech on school campuses. It did not pass a "Religious Speech Access Act" or an "Access for All Students Except Gay Students Act" because to do so would be unconstitutional.

. . .

1. The Board has Established a "Limited Open Forum" at El Modena High

A school has a "limited open forum" whenever it "grants an offering to or opportunity for one or more noncurriculum related student groups to meet on school premises during noninstructional time." 20 U.S.C. § 4071(b). "Even if a school allows only one 'noncurriculum related student group' to meet, the Act's obligations are triggered and the school may not deny other clubs, on the basis of the content of their speech, equal access to meet on school premises during noninstructional time." *Mergens*, 496 U.S. at 236.

Many schools encourage the growth of a "limited open forum," recognizing that clubs "participate in the intellectual give and take of campus debate ..." *Healy v. James*, 408 U.S. 169, 181, 92 S.Ct. 2338,

2346, 33 L.Ed.2d 266 (1972). Indeed, the El Modena Board "believes that curriculum-and noncurriculum-related student organizations have an important place in students' lives ... [and] enhance school spirit and students' sense of belonging." BP 6145.5(a). Recognizing the value of student groups on a high school campus, the Orange Unified Board has provided for a "limited open forum" in both, word and deed. The Board's written policy states that it has a "limited open forum in accordance with provisions of the federal Equal Access Act" because the district allows student groups "not directly tied to the curriculum." BP 6145(a). The Board's policies track the language of the Equal Access Act. *See* BP 6145(a), (b). Whether or not a school has a "limited open forum" is determined by looking at "a school's actual practice rather than its stated policy." *Mergens*, 496 U.S. at 246. Like its policy, El Modena's actual practice is that of a "limited open forum," as it recognizes many noncurriculum clubs including the Asian Club, Black Student Union, Chess Club, Christian Club, Earth Club, Eighties Club, Girls' League, Koinonia (for Catholic students), Juggling Club, Mountain Bike Club, Red Cross/Key Club, and Ski Club. *See* Colin Decl., Ex. D. El Modena has created a "limited open forum" and is therefore precluded from discriminating against student groups seeking access to that open forum.

2. The Gay–Straight Alliance is a "Noncurriculum Related Student Group"

Defendants contend that the Gay–Straight Alliance is not protected by the Act because it is related to the curriculum. Specifically, Board Member Kathy Ward stated in her motion that "the District has a curriculum on sex education, which deals with human sexuality, sexual behavior and consequences, and prevention of sexually transmitted diseases. To the extent that the proposed GSA club intends to discuss these issues related to sexual orientation, the club is a 'curriculum related' club, not covered by the Equal Access Act." Codell Decl., Ex. E. The District contends that these subjects are taught in the following classes: Health (which is required for all ninth grade students); Biology and Life Sciences (students are required to take one of the two to graduate); and Family Planning (which is an elective). The District has specific guidelines for instruction on family life, sex education, and AIDS prevention. *See* BP 6142.1; 6142.1 (a), (b); 6142.2(a), (b). The topics covered in the Sex Education curriculum include "physiology of the reproductive system; conception through birth; prevention of pregnancy and sexually transmitted diseases; the benefits of abstinence, including it being the only totally effective prevention method; issues related to dating, marriage and parenting; and sexual assault and prevention." AR 6142.1.

According to Colin, Zetin, and the Mission Statement of the Gay–Straight Alliance, however, they do not intend to discuss topics that are covered under the sex education curriculum. According to the Mission Statement, their goal was to talk about "tolerance," "issues related to sexual orientation and homophobia," the need to "treat everyone with respect," and counterattacking "unfair treatment and prejudice." Colin Decl., Ex. C. The Mission Statement emphasizes, in a one-sentence paragraph at the end, that "this is not a sexual issue, it is about gaining support and promoting tolerance and respect for all students." *Id.* Both Colin and Zetin state in their declarations that the club did not propose to talk about the things that were covered in sex education. Furthermore, none of the classes at El Modena covered discrimination and harassment based on sexual orientation. Zetin testified that "the word homosexual is never even mentioned in our classes." Colin testified that the club was about "acceptance" for gay and straight people, and about helping people deal with being called "fag" or "dyke." Both Colin and Zetin laughed on the stand at the thought of the group discussing the "physiology of the reproductive system" and the other issues covered in Health class. What the students *did* want to talk about is best expressed in their own words. Echoing the Mission Statement, Zetin testified "I want us to talk about the experiences that gay, lesbian and bisexual kids go through in their everyday lives such as harassment, coming out of the closet or telling people that they are gay: the fear and the emotions such as self-hatred or denial that a lot of kids go through and the harassment they get and how to deal with that."

In order to establish that issues regarding homophobia were discussed in the curriculum, the Defendants introduced into evidence a Teacher's Edition of a *Human Sexuality* textbook. Principal Murray testified that part of the book was used by some teachers in the required Health class. Under cross-examination, however, Murray admitted that she was not sure if the section on homophobia in that book was given to students. She also did not think that other sections in the book had ever been given to students. Plaintiffs' counsel pointed out the ridiculousness of the notion that everything in the book was taught in Health class, as the book included sections on "sadism," "sado-masochism," "fetishism," "transvestitism," "obscene phone calls," "exhibitionism," and "pedophilia." These subjects would hardly be offered as a normal part of any secondary school curriculum. Plaintiffs amply demonstrated that the fact that El Modena had the Teacher's Edition of this book on a shelf in its media center did not mean that the subjects were necessarily taught in class. After reviewing the evidence submitted during the briefing and listening to testimony at the preliminary injunction hearing, the Court finds as a matter of fact that the subject matter of the proposed Gay–Straight Alliance was not covered in the curriculum at El Modena High School.

Even if there were some overlap between what the students wanted to talk about and a subject covered in the curriculum at El Modena, a greater nexus is required or else the club is still considered "noncurriculum related" under the Equal Access Act. Congress did not define the phrase "noncurriculum related" in the Act. It did define the "meetings" that must be accommodated under the Act as activities of student groups that are "not directly related to the school curriculum." 20 U.S.C. § 4072(3). This "implies that student groups directly related to the subject matter of courses offered by the school do not fall within the 'noncurriculum related' category." *Mergens*, 496 U.S. at 237. The Supreme Court found that this made sense in light of the Act's purpose: "Because the purpose of granting equal access is to prohibit discrimination between religious or political clubs on the one hand and other noncurriculum-related student groups on the other, the Act is premised on the notion that a religious or political club is itself likely to be a noncurriculum-related student group." *Id.* at 238. A curriculum-related student group is "one that has more than just a tangential or attenuated relationship to courses offered by the school" and "must at least have a more direct relationship to the curriculum than a religious or political club would have." *Id.* Thus, if a Christian Club prays for abstinence, it is still "noncurriculum related" even though abstinence is a topic covered in the curriculum. Indeed, Zetin testified that she believed in abstinence. Just as with the Christian Club, if discussion of abstinence were to arise at one of the meetings of the Gay–Straight Alliance, the club would still be "noncurriculum related."

The Supreme Court found that the term "is best interpreted broadly to mean any student group that does not directly relate to the body of courses offered by the school." *Mergens*, 496 U.S. at 239. The Court defined four ways in which a student group "directly relates to a school's curriculum:"

> [1.] if the subject matter of the group is actually taught, or will soon be taught, in a regularly offered course; [2.] if the subject matter of the group concerns the body of courses as a whole; [3.] if participation in the group is required for a particular course; or [4.] if participation in the group results in academic credit.

Id. at 239–40. According to the Court, "this limited definition" was "consistent with Congress' intent to provide a low threshold for triggering the Act's requirements." *Id.* at 240. As stated earlier, the Court finds as a matter of fact that there is no overlap between the curriculum and the GSA's proposed discussions. It takes a significant leap of the imagination to believe that the same board that voted unanimously against permitting this group on campus has also included the subject matter of what Plaintiffs intend to discuss in the curriculum. But even if there were some small nexus between what is taught in some classes and what the group proposes to discuss, it would require considerably more for the Gay–Straight Alliance to be considered curriculum related under *Mergens*. The subject matter of the group, dealing with their personal experiences of homophobia and seeking to improve relations among and between gay and straight students, is not "actually taught ... in a regularly offered course" at El Modena. *Id.* at 239.

. . .

4. The Gay–Straight Alliance has been Denied Access to the "Limited Open Forum" and the Accompanying Benefits of Being a School–Recognized Club

Because the Board has created a "limited open forum," it must give Plaintiffs all the same rights and privileges that it gives to other student groups. Once recognized, student groups are permitted to meet on campus during noninstructional time, publicize the group at "Club Rush," post flyers, make announcements over the public address system, and have a group picture in the yearbook. Defendants argue that Plaintiffs' First Amendment rights have not been harmed or abridged because they can still meet informally. Defendants claim that being denied official recognition by the school and the privileges that flow from recognition does not constitute First Amendment harm. Instead, Defendants contend no "limited open forum" has been created with respect to the benefits of recognized club status because the Defendants control the "time, place, manner, and *content* of expressive activities using these privileges, to the extent allowed by the Equal Access Act and all other applicable laws." Def's. Opp. 18 n.4 (emphasis in original). This is exactly the type of content-based restriction that is forbidden by the Equal Access Act. To the extent that the Board opens up its school facilities to any noncurriculum related group, it must uniformly open its facilities to *all* student groups. *See Ceniceros v. Board of Trustees of the San Diego Unified School District*, 106 F.3d 878 (9th Cir. 1997) (finding that allowing a religious club to meet before and after school but not during lunchtime was not sufficient to satisfy the Equal Access Act when other student groups were allowed to meet during lunchtime).

The Board also argues that the application has only been conditionally denied. According to the statement of Kathy Ward at the Board Meeting voting down the club's application, the student group could be approved if (1) they agreed not to discuss sex education topics covered under the California Education Code; and (2) their club was renamed with a different title that was less "divisive" and less likely to be perceived as "derogatory" or affiliated with an outside adult organization. As detailed above, the Board's objections in regard to the outside adult organization are not factually justified or valid under the Act. The Board's allegedly "modest" proposal to require the group to change its name is also not permissible.

A group's speech and association rights are implicated in the name that it chooses for itself. The Board is not allowed to require the student group to change its name merely because the Board finds that it would be less "divisive." The Board's suggested alternatives include the "Tolerance Club" and "Tolerance for All." Zetin and Colin testified that these name changes would attack the very core reason for having the club. Colin said that if he had to change the name, he "would feel my constitutional rights are useless." With the revised name change, Colin felt the emphasis of the club would not be on counteracting homophobia, the core mission of the group. He said that the use of the word "Gay" in the title is important to announce that "being gay or homosexual is not bad, it's who you are." Zetin testified that the Board's proposed revisions "take the whole purpose of the club and change it." She said that taking the word gay out would take the focus away from the issues people face and would imply that there's something wrong with the word "gay." In addition, Colin does not even like the word "tolerance" because it is not as affirming as the word "alliance" or "acceptance." To him, "tolerance" means "to put up with" in the sense that "Jews" and "Blacks" used to be "put up with" until they were finally "accepted." Though the group's mission statement includes the word tolerance, Colin had objected to the word's use to McMillan when she drafted the mission statement (even though it was not ultimately changed). Because Colin does not believe in "tolerance" and instead believes in "acceptance," the Board's suggested name change would indicate a club that is not only more general than the one he wants, but also a club that merely promotes "tolerance," far less than he hopes to achieve. For all of the reasons that Zetin and Colin mentioned when talking about being forced to change the club's name, the Board's suggested name change clearly infringes on profound expressive meaning that the group attaches to its name.

Similarly, the suggestion that the group incorporate a statement that it will not talk about sexual activities, while not requiring other groups to add a similar statement, was hurtful according to Colin and Zetin. Even though they had no plans to talk about sexual activities in the group, singling their group out by requiring their mission statement to include a prohibition on discussion of sexual activities would harm their freedom of expression. Zetin said that adding the requirement when no other groups have the requirement would intimate that "gay people are inherently more sexual than others." She testified that you can talk about being gay without talking about having sex, just as you can talk about being heterosexual without talking about sex. Plaintiffs' counsel sensibly analogized it to requiring a Catholic group to add a statement that it would not be intolerant of other religions. Even if the Catholic group would gladly state that it did not intend to be intolerant of other religions, singling that student group out to add a statement based on a stereotype that Catholics are intolerant of other religions, and requiring the group to add a disclaimer to their mission statement, would be forced speech that could greatly harm their expressive rights. Furthermore, Colin and Zetin have stated to Defendants and under oath in court that the group does not intend to talk about sexual activity, and would readily accept a statement in their mission statement that they will not talk about it if *all* groups are required to include the statement.

. . .

If this Court were to allow the School Board to deny recognition to the Gay–Straight Alliance, it would be guilty of the current evil of "judicial activism," carving out an exception from the bench to the statute enacted by the politically accountable Congress. If this Court were to interpret the Equal Access Act differently than courts have in the past when applying the Act to Christian groups, it would be complicit in the discrimination against students who want to raise awareness about homophobia and discuss how to deal with harassment directed towards gay youth.

The Board Members may be uncomfortable about students discussing sexual orientation and how all students need to accept each other, whether gay or straight. As in *Tinker*, however, when the school administration was uncomfortable with students wearing symbols of protest against the Vietnam War, Defendants can not censor the students' speech to avoid discussions on campus that cause them discomfort or represent an unpopular viewpoint. *See* 393 U.S. at 509. In order to comply with the Equal Access Act, Anthony Colin, Heather Zetin, and the members of the Gay–Straight Alliance must be permitted access to the school campus in the same way that the District provides access to all clubs, including the Christian Club and the Red Cross/Key Club. Plaintiffs have shown a strong likelihood of succeeding on their claim that Defendants have violated their rights under the Equal Access Act.

. . .

E. Plaintiffs Will Be Irreparably Injured Absent Preliminary Relief

"The loss of First Amendment freedoms, for even minimal periods of time unquestionably constitutes irreparable injury." *Elrod v. Burns,* 427 U.S. 347, 373, 96 S.Ct. 2673, 49 L.Ed.2d 547 (1976). Even though the Court does not reach the First Amendment issue, the same presumption of irreparable harm arises in the case of violations of the Equal Access Act because it protects "expressive liberties." *Hsu v. Roslyn Union Free School Dist. No. 3,* 85 F.3d 839, 872 (2nd Cir.1996) (finding that the denial for one year of an after-school Bible group constituted "irreparable injury" and issuing a preliminary injunction). Plaintiffs have already missed an entire semester, which is a significant portion of the time that they will spend in high school. Because Zetin is a junior, she has only a year and a half left before she graduates. By the time this matter is resolved in court, Zetin may have graduated.

Plaintiffs have been injured not only by the Board's excessive delay, but also by the inability to effectively address the hardships they encounter at school every day. Some students at El Modena do not even feel safe using the school's restrooms. Zetin is often harassed by students calling her a "dyke." While such harms may not be cured by a preliminary injunction, "gay-straight alliance clubs provide a safe place for students . . . [and] create a respectful environment where students realize that they have a place at the table . . ." Gogin Decl., PP 7–9. Without official recognition for nearly six months, the students have not had the same privileges as other student groups and have been burdened by having to meet across the street from their school. Thus, even without the presumption of irreparable harm in the area of free speech, the urgency of this matter and the inadequacy of legal remedies mandates preliminary relief.

. . .

Granting a preliminary injunction would also be in the public interest. Recent California legislation confirms that it is state public policy to prevent discrimination on the basis of sexual orientation. In passing the California Student Safety and Violence Prevention Act of 2000, the

California Legislature found that "violence is the number one cause of death for young people in California and has become a public health problem of epidemic proportion" and "the fastest growing, violent crime in California is hate crime." 1999 Cal. A.B. 537, Stats. 1999, ch. 587 § 2. The Legislature felt that "it is incumbent upon us to ensure that all students attending public school in California are protected from potentially violent discrimination." *Id.* The California Penal Code already contained a prohibition on hate crimes based on sexual orientation. *See* Cal. Penal Code § 422.6 (barring injury "because of the other person's race, color, religion, ancestry, national origin, disability, gender, or sexual orientation"). In passing ch. 587, however, the Legislature added sexual orientation to the list of prohibited forms of discrimination in public schools. *See* 1999 Cal. A.B. 537, Stats. 1999, ch. 587 § 3. In addition to protecting students from hate crimes, the Legislature was also concerned about suicide. According to the preamble:

> We must strive to reverse the increase in teen suicide. The number of teens who attempt suicide, as well as the number who actually kill themselves, has risen substantially in recent years. Teen suicides in the United States have doubled in number since 1960 and every year over a quarter of a million adolescents in the United States attempt suicide. Sadly, approximately 4,000 of these attempts every year are completed. Suicide is the third leading cause of death for youths 15 through 24 years of age. To combat this problem we must seriously examine these grim statistics and take immediate action to ensure all students are offered equal protection from discrimination under California law.

. . .

In addition to demonstrating a strong likelihood that Defendants have violated the Equal Access Act, Plaintiffs have also shown a significant threat of irreparable injury, greater hardship to Plaintiffs than Defendants, and that the public interest favors granting the injunction. The Court finds that a preliminary injunction is warranted under these circumstances.

DISCUSSION

Consider the ruling in Colin. *Then consider another high school gay/straight student alliance that maintains a website with links to outside content, including frequently asked questions about safer sex practices. The content includes discussion of anal sex, "rimming" and "fingering." Though the group states that it does not discuss sex acts during group meetings, the web content can be accessed by all students. The same content can be easily accessed through a "Google" search. May a school system ban the student group under these circumstances? Why or why not? See* Caudillo v. Lubbock Indep. Sch. Dist., 311 F.Supp.2d 550 (N.D. Tex. 2004).

E. HOMOPHOBIC SPEECH IN SCHOOLS

As statistics in this chapter attest, LGBT youth face significant harassment at school, including homophobic speech by fellow students that marginalizes and dehumanizes them. Schools respond in different ways, but when a school does decide to punish or otherwise limit negative speech that targets LGBT students, it is often met with a legal challenge in which it is claimed that the school has infringed the First Amendment right to free speech/expression of anti-gay students. How do you think the law should respond? Consider this question as you read the following opinion. For an expanded discussion of homophobic speech campaigns targeting school youth, see Shannon Gilreath, *"Tell Your Faggot Friend He Owes Me $500 for My Broken Hand": Thoughts on a Substantive Equality Theory of Free Speech* 44 WAKE FOREST LAW REVIEW 557–615 (2009). Professor Gilreath criticizes Judge Posner's answer to the question in *Nuxoll ex rel. Nuxoll v. Indian Prairie Sch. Dist. No. 204*, 523 F.3d 668, 671–72 (7th Cir. 2008) (following) and analyzes the 9th Circuit's response in *Harper v. Poway Unified Sch. Dist.*, 445 F.3d 1166 (9th Cir. 2006), in which the court upheld a high school's ban of a T-shirt which read "Homosexuality is Shameful." Judge Reinhardt, writing for the majority, held that the shirt would "impinge upon the rights of other students," under the *Tinker* test. In dissent, Judge Kozinski argued that the messages on the T-shirt were not "so offensive and demeaning that they interfere with the ability of homosexual students to partake of the educational environment," and could not be banned consistent with *Tinker*. After you read *Nuxoll*, ask yourself whether you think Judge Posner in *Nuxoll* or the majority in *Harper* came to the better decision. *(*Harper* was vacated as moot by the U.S. Supreme Court at 549 U.S. 1262 (2007)).

NUXOLL EX REL. NUXOLL v. INDIAN PRAIRIE SCHOOL DISTRICT

523 F.3d 668 (7th Cir. 2008)

Before POSNER, KANNE, and ROVNER, CIRCUIT JUDGES.

OPINION: POSNER

The plaintiff, a sophomore at Neuqua Valley High School, a large public high school in Naperville, Illinois, has brought suit against the school district and school officials contending that they are violating his right to free speech by forbidding him to make negative comments at school about homosexuality. He moved for a preliminary injunction, which was denied, and he appeals the denial. The parties tacitly agree that he is entitled to a preliminary injunction if he has shown a reasonable probability that his right to free speech is being violated. The Supreme Court believes that "the loss of *First Amendment* freedoms, for even minimal periods of time, unquestionably constitutes irreparable injury." *Elrod v. Burns,* 427 U.S. 347, 373, 96 S. Ct. 2673, 49 L. Ed. 2d 547 (1976) (plurality opinion); see also *Christian Legal Society v. Walker,* 453 F.3d 853, 859 (7th Cir. 2006); *Connection Distributing Co. v. Reno,* 154 F.3d 281, 288 (6th Cir. 1998); *Tunick v. Safir*, 209 F.3d 67, 70 (2d Cir. 2000). The school has not tried to show that the grant of a preliminary injunction, at least if narrowly drafted, would cause irreparable harm to it. So the balance of harms inclines toward the plaintiff, and therefore the school can prevail only if his claim is demonstrably weak.

A private group called the Gay, Lesbian, and Straight Education Network promotes an annual event called the "Day of Silence" that is intended to draw attention to harassment of homosexuals. See www.dayofsilence.org (visited Apr. 5, 2008). The idea behind the name is that homosexuals are silenced by harassment and other discrimination. The goal of the "Day of Silence" is not to advocate homosexuality but to advocate tolerance for homosexuals. A student club at Neuqua Valley High School called the Gay/Straight Alliance sponsors the "Day of Silence" at the school. Students participate by remaining silent throughout the day except when called upon in class, though some teachers, as part of their own observance of the "Day of Silence," will not call on students participating in the observance. Some students and faculty wear T-shirts that day with legends such as "Be Who You Are." None of the legends advocates homosexuality or criticizes heterosexuality. Indeed, opposition to harassment of persons who happen to be homosexual is consistent with disapproval of homosexuality itself.

The plaintiff is one of the students who disapprove of homosexuality. Some of them participate in a "Day of Truth" (see www.dayoftruth.org (visited Apr. 5,2008)) held on the first school day after the "Day of Silence." They recommend that supporters wear a T-shirt that reads "day of truth" and "The Truth cannot be silenced." Two years ago a coplaintiff (who has since graduated and as a result is no longer seeking injunctive relief) wore a shirt that read "My Day of Silence, Straight Alliance" on the front and "Be Happy, Not Gay" on the back. A school official had the phrase "Not Gay" inked out. Last year neither plaintiff wore a shirt that contained the phrase, or otherwise tried to counter the Day of Silence, for fear of being disciplined.

None of the slogans mentioned so far has been banned by the school authorities except "Be Happy, Not Gay." The school bases the ban on a school rule forbidding "derogatory comments," oral or written, "that refer to race, ethnicity, religion, gender, sexual orientation, or disability." The school deems "Be Happy, Not Gay" a derogatory comment on a particular sexual orientation. The school's position is that members of a listed group may comment favorably about their own group but may not make a derogatory comment about another group. The rule does not apply to comments made outside of school.

The plaintiff challenges the rule, as well as its application in this case. He believes that the First Amendment entitles him to make, whether in school or out, *any* negative comments he wants about the members of a listed group, including homosexuals (a group defined of course by sexual orientation), provided they are not inflammatory words-that is, not "fighting words," words likely to provoke a violent reaction and hence a breach of the peace. The Supreme Court has placed fighting words outside the protection of the First Amendment. *Chaplinsky v. New Hampshire,* 315 U.S. 568, 572–73, 62 S. Ct. 766, 86 L. Ed. 1031 (1942) (Jehovah's Witness called a government official "a God damned racketeer" and "a damned Fascist"). Although subsequent invocations of the doctrine have failed, e.g., *R.A.V. v. City of St. Paul,* 505 U.S. 377, 386, 112 S. Ct. 2538, 120 L. Ed. 2d 305 (1992); *Texas v. Johnson,* 491 U.S. 397, 409–10, 109 S. Ct. 2533, 105 L. Ed. 2d 342 (1989); *Cohen v. California,* 403 U.S. 15, 20–21, 91 S. Ct. 1780, 29 L. Ed. 2d 284 (1971); *Collin v. Smith,* 578 F.2d 1197, 1204–05 (7th Cir. 1978); *Sandul v. Larion,* 119 F.3d 1250, 1255 (6th Cir. 1997), the plaintiff concedes its continued validity and further concedes that he could not inscribe "homosexuals go to Hell" on his T-shirt because those are fighting words and so can be prohibited despite their expressive content and arguable theological support. *R.A.V. v. City of St. Paul, supra,* 505 U.S. at 386.

The concession is prudent. A heavy federal constitutional hand on the regulation of student speech by school authorities would make little sense. The contribution that kids can make to the marketplace in ideas and opinions is modest and a school's countervailing interest in protecting its students from offensive speech by their classmates is undeniable. Granted, because 18–year–olds can now vote, high-school students should not be "raised in an intellectual bubble," as we put it in *American Amusement Machine Association v. Kendrick,* 244 F.3d 572, 577 (7th Cir. 2001), which would be the effect of forbidding all discussion of public issues by such students. But Neuqua Valley High School has not tried to do that. It has prohibited only (1) *derogatory* comments on (2) unalterable or otherwise deeply rooted personal characteristics about which most people, including-perhaps especially including—adolescent schoolchildren, are highly sensitive. People are easily upset by comments about their race, sex, etc., including their sexual orientation, because for most people these are major components of their personal identity—none more so than a sexual orientation that deviates from the norm. Such comments can strike a person at the core of his being.

There is evidence, though it is suggestive rather than conclusive, that adolescent students subjected to derogatory comments about such characteristics may find it even harder than usual to concentrate on their studies and perform up to the school's expectations. See David M. Huebner et al., "Experiences of Harassment, Discrimination, and Physical Violence Among Young Gay and Bisexual Men," 94 *Am. J. Public Health* 1200–01 (July 2004); Michael Bochenek & A. Widney Brown, Human Rights Watch, "Hatred in the Hallways: Violence and Discrimination Against Lesbian, Gay, Bisexual, and Transgender Students in U.S. Schools" 1–3 (2001), www.hrw.org/reports/2001/uslgbt/toc.htm (visited Apr. 15, 2008); American Association of University Women Educational Foundation, "Hostile

Hallways: Bullying, Teasing, and Sexual Harassment in School" 37 (2001), www.aauw.org/research/upload/hostile hallways.pdf (visited Apr. 14, 2008). Neuqua Valley High School is huge—4200 students—and the potential for wounding speech concerning the personal characteristics listed in the school's rule is great. Nor, on the benefits side of the First Amendment balance, is uninhibited high-school student hallway debate over sexuality—whether carried out in the form of dueling T-shirts, dueling banners, dueling pamphlets, annotated Bibles, or soapbox oratory—an essential preparation for the exercise of the franchise.

A judicial policy of hands off (within reason) school regulation of student speech has much to recommend it. On the one hand, judges are incompetent to tell school authorities how to run schools in a way that will preserve an atmosphere conducive to learning; on the other hand the suppression of adolescents' freedom to debate sexuality is not one of the nation's pressing problems, or a problem that can be solved by aggressive federal judicial intervention. A far more urgent problem, the high dropout rates in many public schools, United States Department of Education National Center for Education Statistics, "Dropout Rates in the United States: 2005" 3–5 (June 2007), nces.ed.gov/pubs200712007059.pdf (visited Apr. 14,2008), will not be solved by First Amendment free-for-alls, though happily the drop-out rate at Neuqua Valley High School, serving as it does the wealthy city of Naperville, is negligible.

It may not be obvious to an outsider how a T-shirt on which is written the slogan "Be Happy, Not Gay" will poison the school atmosphere, but the outsider is—an outsider. And of course the plaintiff doesn't want to stop there. He wants to wear T-shirts that make more emphatically negative comments about homosexuality, provided only that the comments do not cross the line that separates nonbelligerent negative comments from fighting words, wherever that line may be. He also wants to distribute Bibles to students to provide documentary support for his views about homosexuality. We foresee a deterioration in the school's ability to educate its students if negative comments on homosexuality by students like Nuxoll who believe that the Bible is the word of God to be interpreted literally incite negative comments on the Bible by students who believe either that there is no God or that the Bible should be interpreted figuratively. Mutual respect and forbearance enforced by the school may well be essential to the maintenance of a minimally decorous atmosphere for learning.

But we cannot accept the defendants' argument that the rule is valid because all it does is protect the "rights" of the students against whom derogatory comments are directed. Of course a school can—often it must—protect students from the invasion of their legal rights by other students. But people do not have a legal right to prevent criticism of their beliefs or for that matter their way of life. *R.A.V. v. City of St. Paul, supra,* 505 U.S. at 394; *Boos v. Barry,* 485 U.S. 312, 321, 108 S. Ct. 1157, 99 L. Ed. 2d 333 (1988). There is no indication that the negative comments that the plaintiff wants to make about homosexuals or homosexuality names or otherwise targets an individual or is defamatory. Anyway, though *Beauharnais v. Illinois,* 343 U.S. 250, 72 S. Ct. 725, 96 L. Ed. 919 (1952), has never been overruled, no one thinks the First Amendment would today be interpreted to allow group defamation to be prohibited. *American Booksellers Ass'n v. Hudnut,* 771 F.2d 323, 331 n. 3 (7th Cir. 1985), aff'd without opinion, 475 U.S. 1001, 106 S. Ct. 1172, 89 L. Ed. 2d 291 (1986); *Abramson v. Pataki,* 278 F.3d 93, 102 (2d Cir. 2002); *Dworkin v. Hustler Magazine Inc.,* 867 F.2d 1188, 1200 (9th Cir. 1989).

The school is on stronger ground in arguing that the rule strikes a reasonable balance between the competing interests—free speech and ordered learning—at stake in the case. But the plaintiff tells us that the Supreme Court has placed a thumb on the balance—that it has held that a school unable to prove that student speech will cause "disorder or disturbance," *Tinker v. Des Moines Independent Community School District,* 393 U.S. 503, 508, 89 S. Ct. 733, 21 L. Ed. 2d 731 (1969), can ban such speech only if it either is lewd, *Bethel School District No. 403 v. Fraser,* 478 U.S. 675, 685, 106 S. Ct. 3159, 92 L. Ed. 2d 549 (1986) ("a sexually explicit monologue directed towards an unsuspecting audience of teenage students"), or advocates the consumption of illegal drugs. *Morse v. Frederick,* 127 S. Ct. 2618, 2626–27, 168 L. Ed. 2d 290 (2007). He notes that Justice Alito's concurring opinion in *Morse* (joined by Justice Kennedy) disparages invocation of a school's "educational mission" as a ground for upholding restrictions on high-school students' freedom of speech; the opinion warns that such invocation "strikes at the very heart of the First Amendment," *id.* at 2637, though one may doubt just how close debate by high-school students on sexual preferences really is to the heart of the First Amendment.

The plaintiff calls Justice Alito's concurrence the "controlling" opinion in *Morse* because Justices Alito and Kennedy were part of a five-Justice majority, so that their votes were crucial to the decision. But they joined the majority opinion, not just the decision, and by doing so they made it a majority opinion and not merely, as the plaintiff believes (as does the Fifth Circuit, *Ponce v. Socorro Independent School District,* 508 F.3d 765, 768 (5th Cir. 2007)), a plurality opinion. *McKevitt v. Pallasch,* 339 F.3d 530, 531–32 (7th Cir. 2003). The concurring Justices wanted to emphasize that in allowing a school to forbid student speech that encourages the use of illegal drugs the Court was not giving schools carte blanche to regulate student speech. And they were expressing their own view of the permissible scope of such regulation.

If the schoolchildren are very young or the speech is not of a kind that the First Amendment protects (both features of our decision in *Brandt v. Board of Education of City of Chicago,* 480 F.3d 460, 465–66 (7th Cir. 2007), which, as the plaintiff correctly notes, distinguishes that case from this one), the school has a pretty free hand. See *id.; Muller by Muller v. Jefferson Lighthouse School,* 98 F.3d 1530, 1538–39 (7th Cir. 1996); *Baxter by Baxter v. Vigo County School Corp.,* 26 F.3d 728, 738 (7th Cir. 1994); *Blau v. Fort Thomas Public School District,* 401 F.3d 381, 389 (6th Cir.

2005); *Walker–Serrano ex rel. Walker v. Leonard,* 325 F.3d 412, 416–17 (3d Cir. 2003); *Lovell by Lovell v. Poway Unified School District*, 90 F.3d 367, 373 (9th Cir. 1996). But it does not follow that because those features are missing from this case the school must prove that the speech it wants to suppress will cause "disorder or disturbance," or that it "materially disrupts classwork or involves substantial disorder" or "would materially and substantially disrupt the work and discipline of the school." All three formulas are found in *Tinker v. Des Moines Independent Community School District, supra*, 393 U.S. at 513, but that was a quite different case from this. The school was discriminating against a particular point of view, namely opposition to the Vietnam war expressed by the wearing of black armbands. *Id.* at 510–11. The parallel to *Tinker* in this case would be a rule that forbade negative comments just about heterosexuality or just about homosexuality. And *Tinker* preceded *Fraser* and *Morse.* Taking the case law as a whole we don't think a school is required to prove that unless the speech at issue is forbidden serious consequences will *in fact* ensue. That could rarely be proved. (*Scott v. School Board of Alachua County,* 324 F.3d 1246, 1249 (11 th Cir. 2003), and *West v. Derby Unified School District No. 260*, 206 F.3d 1358, 1365–66 (10th Cir. 2000)—cases that involved the display of the Confederate flag in racially mixed schools—illustrate the rare case.) It is enough for the school to present "facts which might reasonably lead school officials to forecast substantial disruption." *Boucher v. School Board of School District of Greenfield,* 134 F. 3d 821, 827–28 (7th Cir. 1998); *Walker–Serrano ex rel. Walker v. Leonard, supra,* 325 F.3d at 416; *LaVine v. Blaine School District,* 257 F.3d 981, 989 (9th Cir. 2001).

This tells us what the standard of proof is. But what is "substantial disruption"? Must it amount to "disorder or disturbance"? Must classwork be disrupted and if so how severely? We know from *Morse* that the Supreme Court will let a school ban speech—even speech outside the school premises—that encourages the use of illegal drugs, without the school's having to prove a causal relation between the speech and drug use. We know too that avoiding violence, if that is what "disorder or disturbance" connotes, is not a school's only substantial concern. Violence was not the issue in *Morse,* or in *Fraser,* the lewd-speech case. In fact one of the concerns expressed by the Supreme Court in *Morse* was with the *psychological* effects of drugs. 127 S. Ct. at 2628–29; see also *Canady v. Bossier Parish School Board,* 240 F.3d 437, 443 (5th Cir. 2001); *cf. Vernonia School District 47J v. Acton,* 515 U.S. 646, 656, 661–62, 115 S. Ct. 2386, 132 L. Ed. 2d 564 (1995). Imagine the psychological effects if the plaintiff wore a T-shirt on which was written "blacks have lower IQs than whites" or "a woman's place is in the home."

From *Morse* and *Fraser* we infer that if there is reason to think that a particular type of student speech will lead to a decline in students' test scores, an upsurge in truancy, or other symptoms of a sick school—symptoms therefore of substantial disruption—the school can forbid the speech. The rule challenged by the plaintiff appears to satisfy this test. It seeks to maintain a civilized school environment conducive to learning, and it does so in an even-handed way. It is not as if the school forbade only derogatory comments that refer, say, to religion, a prohibition that would signal a belief that being religious merits special protection. See *Lamb's Chapel v. Center Moriches Union Free School District*, 508 U.S. 384, 394, 113 S. Ct. 2141, 124 L. Ed. 2d 352 (1993); *R.A.V. v. City of St. Paul, supra*, 505 U.S. at 391–92; *Hedges v. Wauconda Community Unit School District No.* 118, 9 F.3d 1295, 1298 (7th Cir. 1993). The list of protected characteristics in the rule appears to cover the full spectrum of highly sensitive personal-identity characteristics. And the ban on derogatory words is general. Nuxoll can't say "homosexuals are going to Hell" (though he can advocate heterosexuality on religious grounds) and it cannot be said back to him that "homophobes are closeted homosexuals." The school's rule bans "derogatory comments that refer to race, ethnicity, religion, gender, sexual orientation, or disability."

We grant that a rule which forbids *any* class of remarks, however narrowly defined and whatever the justification, restricts free speech. But that observation is the beginning of the constitutional analysis, not the end. The number of restrictions on freedom of speech that have survived constitutional challenge is legion. This particular restriction, it is true, would not wash if it were being imposed on adults, *id.* at 390; *Rosenberger v. Rector & Visitors of University of Virginia*, 515 U.S. 819, 829, 115 S. Ct. 2510, 132 L. Ed. 2d 700 (1995), because they can handle such remarks better than kids can and because adult debates on social issues are more valuable than debates among children. It probably would not wash if it were extended to students when they are outside of the school, where students who would be hurt by the remarks could avoid exposure to them. It would not wash if the school understood "derogatory comments" to embrace *any* statement that could be construed by the very sensitive as critical of one of the protected group identities. (That may, as we'll see, be a problem with the school's application of its rule to the facts of this case.) But high-school students are not adults, schools are not public meeting halls, children are in school to be taught by adults rather than to practice attacking each other with wounding words, and school authorities have a protective relationship and responsibility to all the students. Because of that relationship and responsibility, we are concerned that if the rule is invalidated the school will be placed on a razor's edge, where if it bans offensive comments it is sued for violating free speech and if it fails to protect students from offensive comments by other students it is sued for violating laws against harassment, as in *Nabozny v. Podlesny,* 92 F.3d 446, 457 (7th Cir. 1996).

We are mindful that the Supreme Court said in *Tinker* that "if a regulation were adopted by school officials forbidding discussion of the Vietnam conflict ... it would be obvious that the regulation would violate the constitutional rights of students, at least if it could not be justified by a showing that the students' activities would materially and substantially disrupt the work and discipline of the school." 393 U.S. at 513. But to ban all discussion of the Vietnam war would in reality have been taking sides—would have delighted the government—because the debate over the war was started, maintained, and escalated by the war's opponents.

So the plaintiff is not entitled to a preliminary injunction against the rule. And, his lawyer conceded at oral argument, neither is he entitled to a preliminary injunction against the defendants' forbidding his making "negative comments" about homosexuality short of "fighting words." Not only are such terms too vague to be the operative terms of an injunction, which must contain a detailed and specific statement of its terms, *Fed. R. Civ. P. 65(d)(1)(A), (C); Schmidt v. Lessard,* 414 U.S. 473, 475–77, 94 S. Ct. 713, 38 L. Ed. 2d 661 (1974) (per "Curiam); *Hispanics United of DuPage County v. Village of Addison,* 248 F.3d 617, 619–20 (7th Cir. 2001); *Burton v. City of Belle Glade*, 178 F.3d 1175, 1200–01 (11th Cir. 1999), but the plaintiffs lawyer did not propose *any* language to the district judge. A litigant has a feeble claim for a preliminary injunction when he can't articulate what he wants enjoined. *Cf.* IIA Charles Alan Wright & Arthur R. Miller, Federal Practice and Procedure § 2949, pp. 212–13 (2d ed. 2007); cf. *Wolgin v. Simon,* 722 F.2d 389, 394–95 (8th Cir. 1983). The plaintiff concedes, therefore, that the most he is entitled to is an injunction that would permit him to stencil "Be Happy, Not Gay" on his T-shirt on the "Day of Truth" because forcing deletion of "Not Gay" stretches the school's derogatory-comments rule too far. We must consider the argument carefully, because the term "derogatory comments" is unavoidably vague. (If a clearer formulation could be substituted, the rule might be invalid because of its vagueness, but the parties do not suggest alternative formulations.)

The expression "Be Happy, Not Gay" is a play on words, since "gay" used to be an approximate synonym for "happy" but now has been appropriated to designate homosexual orientation. One cannot even be certain that it is a "derogatory" comment; for "not gay" is a synonym for "straight," yet the school has told us that it would not object to a T-shirt that said "Be Happy, Be Straight." It wouldn't object because to advocate *X* is not necessarily to disparage *Y*. If you say "drink Pepsi" you may be showing your preference for Pepsi over Coke, but you are not necessarily deriding Coke. It would be odd to call "Be Happy, Drink Pepsi" a derogatory comment about Coke. But context is vital. Given kids' sensitivity about their sexual orientation and their insensitivity about their preferences in soft drinks, the Pepsi–Coke analogy misses the mark. The plaintiff, like the students who participate in the "Day of Truth," is expressing disapproval of homosexuality, as everyone knows. No one bothers to talk up heterosexuality who isn't interested in denigrating homosexuality. The plaintiff himself describes "Be Happy, Not Gay" as one of the "negative comments" about homosexuality that he considers himself constitutionally privileged to make. He is in a better position than we are to interpret the meaning of his own comment.

Nevertheless, "Be Happy, Not Gay" is only tepidly negative; "derogatory" or "demeaning" seems too strong a characterization. As one would expect in a school the size of Neuqua Valley High School, there have been incidents of harassment of homosexual students. But it is highly speculative that allowing the plaintiff to wear a T-shirt that says "Be Happy, Not Gay" would have even a slight tendency to provoke such incidents, or for that matter to poison the educational atmosphere. Speculation that it might is, under the ruling precedents, and on the scanty record compiled thus far in the litigation, too thin a reed on which to hang a prohibition of the exercise of a student's free speech. We are therefore constrained to reverse the district court's order with directions to enter forthwith (the "Day of Truth" is scheduled for April 28) a preliminary injunction limited however to the application of the school's rule to a T-shirt that recites "Be Happy, Not Gay." The school has failed to justify the ban of that legend, though the fuller record that will be compiled in the further proceedings in the case may cast the issue in a different light.

And further proceedings there will be. The plaintiff will not be content with the limited relief that we are ordering. This is cause litigation. He will press for a broader injunction as permanent relief, though one that will fall short of permitting him to use fighting words in his fight against homosexuality, for he has conceded that the school can ban fighting words. The district judge will be required to strike a careful balance between the limited constitutional right of a high-school student to campaign inside the school against the sexual orientation of other students and the school's interest in maintaining an atmosphere in which students are not distracted from their studies by wrenching debates over issues of personal identity.

ROVNER, CIRCUIT JUDGE, *concurring in the judgment.* I agree that we should reverse and remand this case to the district court with instructions to enter an injunction allowing Nuxoll to wear a shirt bearing the slogan "Be Happy, Not Gay" on the school day following the Day of Silence. I view this as a simple case. We are bound by the rule of *Tinker v. Des Moines Indep. Cmty. Sch. Dist.*, 393 U.S. 503, 89 S. Ct. 733, 21 L. Ed. 2d 731 (1969), a case that the majority portrays in such a convoluted fashion that the discussion folds in on itself like a Mobius strip. *Tinker* straightforwardly tells us that, in order for school officials to justify prohibition of a particular expression of opinion, they must be able to show that this "action was caused by something more than a mere desire to avoid the discomfort and unpleasantness that always accompany an unpopular viewpoint." 393 U.S. at 509. Under *Tinker,* students may express their opinions, even on controversial subjects, so long as they do so "without 'materially and substantially interfer[ing] with the requirements of appropriate discipline in the operation of the school' and without colliding with the rights of others." 393 U.S. at 512–13 (quoting *Burnside v. Byars,* 363 F.2d 744, 749 (5th Cir. 1966)).' The school district has "not demonstrate[d] any facts which might reasonably have led school authorities to forecast substantial disruption of or material interference with school activities," and no such disruption occurred two years earlier when Nuxoll's co-plaintiff wore such a shirt to school following the Day of

Silence. *Tinker,* 393 U.S. at 514. Therefore, this particular expression must be allowed.

Contrary to the majority's characterization, *Tinker* is not a case about viewpoint discrimination and is not distinguishable from the instant case. *Supra* at 8. *Tinker* involved students who wished to wear black armbands to protest the Vietnam war. School officials would not allow the armbands although they did allow students to wear other symbols of political or controversial significance, including political campaign buttons and the Iron Cross, a symbol that is associated with Nazism. The Court concluded that "the prohibition of expression of one particular opinion, at least without evidence that it is necessary to avoid material and substantial interference with schoolwork or discipline, is not constitutionally permissible." *Tinker,* 393 U.S. at 511. *Tinker* reveals nothing about whether the school allowed symbols or other expressions of opinion favorable to U.S. involvement in the Vietnam war, and so there is no reason to read *Tinker* as a case about viewpoint.

It is more appropriately characterized as a discussion about subject matter discrimination, although the opinion is not limited to the circumstance where the school has banned all discussion of a particular subject. The majority attempts to turn *Tinker* into a viewpoint case by stating that a school ban on "all discussion of the Vietnam war would in reality have been taking sides," *supra* at 11, because the debate over the war was initiated by those opposed to it. And here is the Mobius strip. Under the majority's reasoning, allowing open debate on any subject would constitute taking the side of the *anti-status quo.* Open debate could never simply be open debate; it would constitute "taking sides," in particular taking the side of the party opposed to the *status quo.* Open debate is the very value preserved by the First Amendment and yet the majority reduces it to stealth viewpoint expression. The majority expends much ink trying to strike a balance between the interests of free speech and ordered learning, a discussion which sounds remarkably similar to the rule of *Hazelwood Sch. Dist. v. Kuhlmeier,* 484 U.S. 260, 108 S. Ct. 562, 98 L. Ed. 2d 592 (1988), where the Supreme Court set a balancing rule for school-sponsored speech. This case does not involve school-sponsored speech, and there is no need for us to strike a new balance; the Supreme Court has already set the applicable standard in *Tinker.*

Moreover, I heartily disagree with my brothers about the value of the speech and speech rights of high school students, which the majority repeatedly denigrates. *Supra,* at 4, 5, 7 and 10. Youth are often the vanguard of social change. Anyone who thinks otherwise has not been paying attention to the civil rights movement, the women's rights movement, the anti-war protests for Vietnam and Iraq, and the recent presidential primaries where the youth voice and the youth vote are having a substantial impact. And now youth are leading a broad, societal change in attitude towards homosexuals, forming alliances among lesbian, gay, bisexual, transgendered ("LGBT") and heterosexual students to discuss issues of importance related to sexual orientation. They have initiated a dialogue in which Nuxoll wishes to participate. The young adults to whom the majority refers as "kids" and "children" are either already eligible, or a few short years away from being eligible to vote, to contract, to marry, to serve in the military, and to be tried as adults in criminal prosecutions. To treat them as children in need of protection from controversy, to blithely dismiss their views as less valuable than those of adults, *supra* at 10, is contrary to the values of the First Amendment. Justice Brennan eloquently stated this for the Court more than forty years ago, and his words ring especially true today:

> The vigilant protection of constitutional freedoms is nowhere more vital than in the community of American schools. The classroom is peculiarly the marketplace of ideas. The Nation's future depends upon leaders trained through wide exposure to that robust exchange of ideas which discovers truth out of a multitude of tongues, rather than through any kind of authoritative selection.

Tinker, 393 U.S. at 512 (quoting *Keyishian v. Board of Regents,* 385 U.S. 589, 603, 87 S. Ct. 675, 17 L. Ed. 2d 629 (1967)) (internal citations and quotation marks omitted). *See also Hodgkins ex rel. Hodgkins v. Peterson,* 355 F.3d 1048, 1055 (7th Cir. 2004) ("The strength of our democracy depends on a citizenry that knows and understands its freedoms, exercises them responsibly, and guards them vigilantly. Young adults ... are not suddenly granted the full panoply of constitutional rights on the day they attain the age of majority. We not only permit but expect youths to exercise those liberties to learn to think for themselves, to give voice to their opinions, to hear and evaluate competing points of view-so that they might attain the right to vote at age eighteen with the tools to exercise that right.") The majority also treats the subject matter of sexual orientation as lacking importance, apparently failing to notice that, for the last decade or two, state and national legislatures have been awash with debates over the limits placed on the rights of LGBT persons, and that presidential candidates are often subjected to litmus tests on these very issues. Finally, there may be no more important time than adolescence for individuals to contemplate issues relating to their sexual identity. These are important issues and the voices of young adults add much to the discussion.

My brothers also wonder whether this slogan is actually derogatory, noting that it is a play on the words "happy" and "gay." *Supra* at 12. That it is a play on words does not change its ultimate meaning, however. Nuxoll tells us that he intends the slogan to convey the message that "homosexual behavior is contrary to the teachings of the bible, damaging to the participants and society at large, and does not lead to happiness." Throughout his brief, he claims to be criticizing homosexual "conduct" and "behavior" although his four-word polemic "Be Happy, Not Gay" does little to convey this message and instead seems to attack homosexual identity. Nonetheless, the statement is clearly intended to derogate homosexuals. Teenagers today often use the word "gay" as a generic term of disparagement. They might say, "That sweater is so gay" as a way of insulting the look of the garment. In this way, Nuxoll's statement is really a double-play on words because "gay" formerly meant "happy" in common usage, and now "gay," in addition to meaning "homosexual" is also often used as a general insult. Nuxoll's statement easily fits the school's definition of "disparaging" and would meet that standard for most listeners. Moreover, the idea that "not gay" is a synonym for "straight," *supra* at 12, fails to recognize the many nuances of sexual orientation that have been apparent since 1948, when Alfred Kinsey first set forth his zero-to-six Kinsey Scale, defining a continuum of sexuality from exclusively heterosexual on one end to exclusively homosexual on the other end. I scarcely know where to begin with the Pepsi/Coke analogy and even the majority seems to realize the comparison misses the mark. I would add that it misses the mark by a rather wide margin. In any case, there is no doubt that the slogan is disparaging. That said, it is not the kind of speech that would materially and substantially interfere with school activities. I suspect that similar uses of the word "gay" abound in the halls of Neuqua Valley High School and virtually every other high school in the United States without causing any substantial interruption to the educational process. There is a significant difference between expressing one's religiously-based disapproval of homosexuality and targeting LGBT students for harassment. Though probably offensive to most LGBT students, the former is not likely by itself to create a hostile environment. Certainly, this is not a case like *Nabozny v. Podlesny,* 92 F.3d 446 (7th Cir. 1996), where students repeatedly called a gay classmate a "faggot," struck him, spit on him, threw him into a urinal, beat him to such a degree that he suffered internal bleeding, and subjected him to a mock rape in a classroom while a few dozen people looked on and laughed at him. So severe and constant and enduring was his classmates' abuse, that Nabozny twice attempted suicide. The defendants here are unlikely to find themselves on the "razor's edge" of *Nabozny, supra* at 11, as a result of Nuxoll's t-shirt.

And what lesson would we teach young adults about the importance of our Constitutional rights if the judiciary took the "hands off" approach to school regulation of speech favored by my brothers? *Supra* at 5. This time I turn to Justice Jackson, speaking for the Court more than sixty years ago:

> The Fourteenth Amendment, as now applied to the States, protects the citizen against the State itself and all of its creatures—Boards of Education not excepted. These have, of course, important, delicate, and highly discretionary functions, but none that they may not perform within the limits of the Bill of Rights. That they are educating the young for citizenship is reason for scrupulous protection of Constitutional freedoms of the individual, if we are not to strangle the free mind at its source and teach youth to discount important principles of our government as mere platitudes.

West Virginia State Bd. of Educ. v. Barnette, 319 U.S. 624, 637, 63 S. Ct. 1178, 87 L. Ed. 1628 (1943) (quoted in *Tinker,* 393 U.S. at 507). The First Amendment provides the school with an opportunity for a discussion about the values of free speech and respect for differing points of view but it does not grant a license to shut down dissension because of an "undifferentiated fear or apprehension of disturbance." *Tinker,* 393 U.S. at 508. Contrary to the majority's view that "free speech and ordered learning" are "competing interests," *supra* at 7, I would argue that these values are compatible. The First Amendment as interpreted by *Tinker* is consistent with the school's mission to teach by encouraging debate on controversial topics while also allowing the school to limit the debate when it becomes substantially disruptive. Nuxoll's slogan-adorned t-shirt comes nowhere near that standard. For all of these reasons, I respectfully concur in the judgment.

CHAPTER 3

FREEDOM OF EXPRESSION

■ ■ ■

I. INTRODUCTION: OUTING AND OTHER CONTROVERSIES

This discussion of freedom of expression begins with a discussion of "outing." "Outing" is the practice of "making publicly acknowledged the sexual orientation of a homosexual without regard to whether the person is willing to have this information publicly acknowledged. It is making publicly acknowledged what most lesbians and gay men wish to be kept secret—their identity, what they are, possibly who they are." (Richard Mohr, *Gay Ideas*, p.11). Outing reached its zenith in the 1990s, stirring controversy and outrage, including vehement opposition in the gay community. Most outings were of celebrities or other high profile people, like gay journalist Michelangelo Signorile's outing of music producer David Geffen (who promoted various performers and groups with anti-gay lyrics) and assistant secretary of defense under the George H. W. Bush administration, Pete Williams. Outing continues today, and continues to be controversial, from Barbara Walter's pointed question to singer Ricky Martin about his sexual orientation (Martin later came out), to the high profile outings of former Republican party chair Ken Mehlman and anti-gay evangelist Ted Haggard. The outings of conservative politicians and preachers tend to look retributive, adding to the controversy surrounding outing as a practice.

Professor Richard Mohr vigorously defends outing as necessary for the dignity of gay individuals and the gay community.[1] To the frequent argument that outing violates the outed person's right to privacy, Professor Mohr responds that there is a normative difference between privacy and "secrecy" and that "there simply is no normative privacy, no content to the right to privacy, that covers the secret that is the closet." Mohr explains that "when I tell someone that someone else who does not want to be known as a homosexual is a homosexual, I convey a secret. That which is hidden is revealed. Metaphorically, I open the person's closet door

1. RICHARD D. MOHR, GAY IDEAS: OUTING AND OTHER CONTROVERSIES (ch. 1). Mohr specifically disavows retributive or vengeful outing, as such actions are necessarily diminutions of the dignity of the outer and the outed.

to another, who sees the person inside as homosexual. It is the person's sexual orientation that I am revealing. I am saying that the person is someone whose erotic energies and sexual desires are directed toward members of the same biological sex as the person."

"But the door that I open is not the door to the person's bedroom or to a cubicle at the baths. I am not revealing, making unhidden, the secrecy of the person's sexual behavior. I am not reporting, for instance, what could only have been gotten through spying, stealth, or coercion...."

"It is sexual acts, and derivatively talk of them, not sexual orientations, that are protected by privacy. The reporting of sexual orientation does not violate any senses of privacy that are legitimately invoked in sexual matters. ... [I]t does not violate privacy in its most central dimension as what is not to be spied on. Nor obviously does it, like rape, violate rights to bodily integrity, which constitute another central part of our conception of normative privacy."

Finally, Mohr believes that, ultimately, the right to privacy is about the right "*not to be coerced by others* to do something or not do something." As Mohr sees it, the outee is not forced to do anything: he or she can continue to deny his or her sexual orientation, for example. Moreover, for Mohr, a prohibition on outing would amount to a gag order on the outer's right to speak. Mohr argues that "the alleged 'no outing' right, unlike any common immunity right, is asserted as a positive demand-claim, that is, a right to coerce others to do or not do something. Specifically, the alleged right is a demand-claim that a specific person keep from repeating what he in fact knows about the closet case's identity—a right, that is, morally to place a gag order on someone. That the right asserted has both the general structure of a positive demand-claim and the specific form of a gag order should make it highly suspect."

DISCUSSION

Do you agree with Professor Mohr? Is there a right—if not a legal right, then a normative moral right—of homosexuals not to have their homosexuality divulged against their wishes? Would you out someone? Would it make a difference, assuming you are an ally of gay rights, that the closeted person actively works to undermine gay equality or incites hatred toward gays in some way? What considerations might most inform your decision? If you think you would out someone, an anti-gay politician for example, because of his or her hypocrisy on the issues, how far would you be willing to go? HIV/AIDS activist Larry Kramer has called for the "outing" of the HIV status of politicians who vote against AIDS initiatives. Would you agree? Are privacy rights that one is otherwise bound to respect somehow waived by hypocrisy?[2]

A. DIGNITY-BASED OUTING: WHEN IS OUTING PERMISSIBLE (OR EVEN DESIRABLE)?

Below is an excerpt from Professor Mohr's defense of dignity-based outing. It is followed by a rebuttal from Professor James Stramel. Do these

2. Professor Mohr doesn't think so. See Mohr, *Gay Ideas*, p. 22.

arguments change your perspective on outing? Who has the more persuasive argument?

THE OUTING CONTROVERSY: PRIVACY AND DIGNITY IN GAY ETHICS

Richard D. Mohr*

Any field anthropologist examining the folkways of the gay community would easily notice that among all the variety in the gay community—just for starters divisions of life-styles between lesbians and gay men—The Secret is the social convention that most centrally defines the community. That The Secret is the gay social convention explains why outing is so highly charged. To those committed to The Secret, which is to say virtually all gay people, the outer is a traitor. Thus is explained outers being called "terrorists" and "cannibals." Outing hits the bedrock of the gay community. To the extent that the convention of The Secret is the structuring element, the DNA, the constitutive convention of the gay community, outing is not simply a problem in gay ethics but the problem in gay ethics.

Yet what a strange convention The Secret is. That which binds the community together is a commitment to a belief in the community's worthlessness. The very structuring principle of the community functions as a denial that the community exists—indeed, a denial that it should exist. The convention is a complete capitulation to the general social belief that the only good gay is a nonexistent one. In this regard, gays are dissimilar to blacks and women traditionally considered, in that blacks and women have at least had a perceived legitimate presence in traditional society through their roles as slaves and servers. In this respect, gays are much more like Native Americans, about whom society holds the belief, as given voice by General Philip Sheridan, that the only good one is a dead one. The definitional work that gays perform in society is accomplished from their position in Non-being, the fearsome Just Beyond. In this evacuating milieu, for gays to maintain The Secret—the dirty little secret of their socially abject status—is like Native Americans knowingly handing out to their own people smallpox infected blankets provided by General Sheridan. Each time one gay person insists that other gay people, whether open or not, keep his identity as gay hidden in conformity with society's belief that gays are to society what shit is to the body and should, like shit, be eliminated from the body politic—each time he insists that the others go along with society's values in these matters—he is requiring the other gays to degrade themselves as gay, to sink to the level of abjection dictated for gays by the dominant culture.

---

* Excerpted from RICHARD MOHR, GAY IDEAS (Beacon Press 1992) (The Outing Controversy: Privacy and Dignity in Gay Ethics (pp. 11–25)).

The Secret's requirement that its keeper degrade himself means that, even if one could argue that the closet is a form of legitimate self-defense against unjust discrimination—could argue, that is, that there is no *duty* to come out, so that I cannot insist that you on your own come out—you still cannot insist that I keep your secret. For to require that keeping is to require that the out person do a double injustice to himself—to degrade himself and to force him to commit his life to the very values that keep him oppressed. The gay person who keeps another gay person's dirty little secret degrades himself, does an injustice to himself by going along with rather than resisting the values that oppress gays.

The web of omissions and commissions entailed in maintaining The Secret does not leave its keeper as an innocent bystander, who merely observes the immorality of others without participating in or enhancing it. The openly gay keeper of The Secret is morally not like those who, working the fields, simply observed in the distance trains carrying Jews to the East; rather, the keeper is like those who, while not setting the trains in motion, nevertheless voluntarily serviced the trains on their way to the East.

An examination of the types of values variously lost and protected by the closet will show all the more clearly the moral permissibility of outing and the expectation that the gay person, living morally, will indeed out others. . . .

What the closet case does in maintaining his closet is to barter away his self-respect, his worthiness for respect, his dignity, for happiness, regard, and nonrespectful love. To accept the closet is to have absorbed society's view of gays, to accept insult so that one avoids harm. Thereby one becomes a simulacrum—a deceptive substitute—of a person. One seems to be a moral agent with ends of one's own and an ability to revise them, but one really is simply a puppet to the values of society—the equivalent of the perpetually deferential "housewife" (of stereotype) who has no views but her husband's and who eventually loses even the ability to see things through any other eyes than his. To accept the closet is to be at best the "happy slave" (of stereotype) committed to the institution of slavery in the way a dog is committed to his food bowl.

Life in the closet is morally debased—and morally debasing. It frequently requires lying, but it always requires much more. Dan Bradley, president of the Legal Services Corporation under President Carter, elaborates:

> Always there was the coverup: Arranging for women with whom I was friendly and had shared my secret to brag about my virility to F.B.I. agents making a routine background check; keeping up a macho front with male colleagues; making sure I had a female escort for parties, and worrying about how to deal with homosexual issues in the legal services program. . . .
>
> The web of deceit I had so consciously and meticulously woven over the years made it possible for me to rationalize whatever I had to do

> to protect myself. You can rationalize the lies, the deceptions or whatever. There is no end of it.

The life as lie chiefly entails a devolution of the person as person, as moral agent. The whiteness of the individual lies might be forgiven as self-defense, but the dirtiness of the secret that the lies maintain cannot be. The dirt is the loss of self, of personhood, the loss of that which makes human life peculiarly worth protecting to begin with.

The secret that the closet case wants to force on others is not a secret that is unique or peculiar to the individual (say, the secret that he really is the author whose nom de plume graces the dust jacket of many a mystery novel). Rather, the imposed secret is about his status, a status that he views as abject and that he shares with the others who are supposed to keep the secret for him. So, in abiding by the convention to keep the secret, the keeper commits to the view of gays that the convention presupposes: that gays are loathsome and disgusting, to be kept from sight, nauseating if touched or seen, filth always in need of being flushed away.

This abject condition is quite remote from valued privacy. The philosopher Ferdinand Schoeman has pointed out that violations of privacy are experienced similarly to violations of sacred objects and that the sharing of a privacy is like the revelation, in ritual, of a sacred object. Outside their religious context sacred objects may be quite humble, say, mere dollops of flour or a few bound twigs, the commercial value of which may be as little as nothing. Still, their violations are experienced as affronts, defilements, and pollutions." But the closet case inverts this moral structure. The closet case and the society whose values he accepts do not view his violation as a defilement and pollution. Rather, he and society view his very existence—him—as an affront, as defilement and pollution. And his revelation of himself to his sacred band—his blood family—is not a wonderment but (he supposes) a horror.

The convention of The Secret would commit the openly gay person to a similar vision of gay people and so commit him to give up his own dignity for the happiness of the closeted gay person. To do that is the very inversion of moral life, in which nobility of character, as in the case, for example, of Freedom Riders, lies in sacrificing one's happiness so that dignity—one's own or others'—might be asserted. This is what civil disobedience does, yet the inverse does not hold. A person cannot be morally compelled to be debasedly servile, to sacrifice his dignity for the happiness of others. I cannot be morally compelled to eat dog shit even if to do so would comfort the lives of those who otherwise would commit suicide.

There are two exceptions to dignity-based outing. The first is if the outing violates some right of the outee. I cannot legitimately advance my dignity at the expense of other people's rights.... And this is crucially important: even if my actions in outing someone are a necessary condition for someone else violating the outee's rights—say, his right not to be harmed or his right not to be discriminated against—still, my actions are not violations of his rights any more so than are his great-great-grandfather's siring actions, which were also a necessary condition for the violations. Minus the siring or minus the outing, true, the violation would not have occurred, but the violator of the outee's rights is the bigoted employer, or whoever caused the violation, not those who merely provided some of the millions upon millions of necessary conditions for the violation.... Still, if it were the case (as it currently is not) that the government was shooting gays, I would morally be expected to suspend my dignity temporarily so that the current and prospective dignity of others is made possible.

Although outing is a morally expected activity, still there are a number of bad reasons for outing. When the motivation for outing is something other than the perpetuation of self-respect, the reasons for outing are likely to be morally dubious. When for a cool six-figure sum a has-been porn star outs his alleged ex-lover, a Hollywood movie idol, in the *National Enquirer*; this act does not bestir or enhance the outer's dignity. One can hardly cheer its motives. They are shameless and reflect badly on the outer's character.

Still more troubling is vindictive outing—outing that is analogous to Pete's "outing" of Julie as black in Showboat. Indeed, the vindictive outing of gays contributes to the very values that oppress gays. Vindictive outing of gays by straights occurs, for instance, when newspapers print names and addresses of men busted in police raids on tearooms—when a colleague outs you to higher management because you got a promotion he wanted. Vindictive outing has the same moral structure as the shouting of anti-gay invective, like calling someone a "faggot" or "bulldyke." These are imprecations. Imprecations call down evil on a person or group from an independently existing reservoir of cultural values, as though invoking God or the devil to destroy someone. At the same time, however, imprecations amplify, strengthen, and ritualistically affirm these values by pledging allegiance to them, just as one strengthens the symbolic power of the flag each time one salutes or pledges allegiance to it. Vindictive outing calls on the cultural repository of anti-gay forces to destroy a gay person and at the same time strengthens that repository's power by exercising and admiring its muscle.... But the sort of outing that I have been advocating does not invoke, mobilize, or ritualistically affirm anti-gay values; rather, it cuts against them, works to undo them. The point of outing, as I have defended it, is not to wreak vengeance, not to punish, and not to deflect attention from one's own debased state. Its point is to avoid degrading oneself. The outer who outs as an incident of her gay pride, not shame, does not pledge allegiance to the phobia-driven cyclone of hate that admittedly is sometimes a foreseeable consequence, of outing. However, that outing has a foreseeable bad consequence does not make it morally wrong any more than the foreseeable consequence of a reduced GNP would make my taking a vacation morally wrong. What is troublesome is the doubt, the possibility, that some outing is indeed motivated by lingering self-hatred on the part of the outer.

In not leading a life of lies, in simply "living in the truth," one will make known the sexual orientation of others because one does not think, and rightly does not think, that there is anything wrong with being gay and because one will not play along with conventions that degrade gay existence, even if they are the conventions of gays themselves as a community of self-hating and self-oppressing persons. Self-hatred is the glue that holds together the convention of The Secret, which in turn generates the shame that underwrites self-hatred.

The core question in the outing debate is, "Whose values shall count?" Are the bigot's values to count—even or especially when bigots are the overwhelming majority? Or are the values of pride and dignity as registered in the lives of openly gay people to count?

Vito Russo puts the core question thus: "What [outers are] saying is that if being gay is not disgusting, is not awful, then why can't we talk about it? After all, it's not an insult to call someone gay. Is it?" Similarly: "The principle is really very simple. Either being gay is OK or it isn't. And allowing homosexuality to take its place as a normal part of the human sexual spectrum requires ceasing to treat it as a dirty little secret."

Like civil disobedience, outing violates a community's conventions so that the community may come to live more morally....

Some have claimed that, far from supporting outing, the concept of dignity provides grounds for opposing it. The argument succinctly is that outing someone prevents him or her from achieving the dignity that attaches to the coming-out process.... This argument misunderstands several things: the scope of dignity, the possible materials of liberty, and the complexity of the coming-out process. First, dignity can be achieved in many ways, and it is not a property that can be maximized because the various ways to it will get in each other's way if one tries them all. The relevant question is, Can a person, although outed, still have access to enough dignity to be outstandingly dignified? Second, being free—being the author of one's own character—does not require that a person begin as a blank slate and that every future be indeterminate but for her actions and choices. The relevant question is, Are conditions for the outed person such that she can achieve a richly textured life of her own making given the cussedness of circumstance both social and material? Finally, coming out is not a one-step, single-stage, mechanical process of being publicly known as gay; rather, it is a complex process of self-reflection, self-recognition, and self-acceptance leading to and partly effected by a public presence as gay. The relevant question is, Does the outed person retain the possibility of having a robust, positive, dignifying relation to his sexual orientation? The answer to all these questions is yes.

The evidence is provided by Congressman Gerry Studds. In the summer of 1983, at the age of forty-six, Studds was outed to the nation by a special counsel to the House Ethics Committee for an affair Studds had

had with a male page a decade earlier. Unlike many outed people, Studds embraced, rather than denied, his sexual orientation. In its acceptance by him, in his self-acceptance, he found for the first time the capacity to love and a sense of freedom and serenity. In his pride, he has taken up a special role in gay projects, heading up congressional opposition to the ban on gays in the military. In an interview with *The Advocate* soon after he was outed, Studds answered the question, "How do you feel now that you have publicly declared you are gay?" with words that do not sound like those of a man bereft of freedom, dignity, pride, and self-definition:

> Better than I've ever felt in my life. I suspect that's something that would be easy for your audience of gay people to understand. But I've found that in giving that response to the media in general, to folks who have not had this experience themselves, that it requires a great deal of explanation as to how in the midst of what for a lot of reasons appears to be a disastrous situation, one can candidly say, "I've never felt better in my life." Any person who has ever gone through the experience of coming out will understand that. I feel as if the remaining seven cylinders had just kicked in for the first time in 46 years. And that's a powerful feeling.

It is evident from this statement that nothing was robbed from Studds and that opportunity for dignity was not preempted. Despite the fact that his sexual orientation was involuntarily made public, and despite the fact that the circumstances that occasioned the revelation were objectively embarrassing—a sexual affair with an underling in his non-age—Studds still speaks of the "experience" as of his own making, as *his*, coming out. And to be sure, in its morally and psychologically important dimensions, it was....

It is true that, if outing becomes widespread, those who are tentatively thinking of coming out socially into the gay community may not do so owing to increased fear of what the gay community might do to them—make them more publicly gay than they want to be. In an era of gay radiance, shadows for hiding will be fewer but darker; the price of admission to the gay community will be higher. But only at the higher price is the community one worth joining, one within which, not in spite of which, individual dignity is possible.... The comfort that the closet provides society stokes the convention of The Secret, by which in turn gays do most of the maintenance work in their own oppression. It is the shame-inducing Secret that is the chief dynamo of the closet's magnetic attraction. As long as The Secret is intact, the few people who are out are aberrant (even by gay standards) and are easily managed by society through the mechanisms of more and less subtle discriminations (a queer bashing here, a grant not given there, whatever does the trick). Being out, although necessary for gay progress, is nowhere near sufficient to achieve gay progress as long as the machinery by which gays are oppressed is left in place. Being out voluntarily is good. But no substantial gay progress will be made until the shame-enhancing Secret is abandoned. So gay progress requires both being publicly out and living in the truth, a necessary concomitant of which is that closet cases will be outed.

OUTING, ETHICS, AND POLITICS: A REPLY TO MOHR

James S. Stramel*

Does Outing Violate the Right to Privacy?

Outing has often been condemned as a violation of the right to privacy. However, Richard Mohr and others following him have ridiculed this claim as "a lot of hot air" and a "phony belief." ... I [will] briefly summarize the main reasons why the privacy objection to outing cannot be summarily dismissed.

Sex and sexuality have long been regarded as paradigmatically private matters, both morally and legally.... The right to privacy protects individual identity, autonomy, and dignity by shielding the individual (in body and mind) from various forms of unwanted access—both informational and physical—whether by the state or by other individuals. One of the basic and most important functions of this right is to maximize our opportunities to be self-determining, especially with respect to matters of fundamental importance to individual personality (including one's body, sexuality, home, and marital, reproductive, and family decisions). This includes a large measure of individual control over the division between publicity and privacy, rather than having this determined by others. Given the intimate and volatile character of sexual identity and its importance in our lives, gay people have a strong prima facie interest in being free from unwanted public disclosures. Unwanted and untimely exposure jeopardizes all the benefits of self-disclosure and can do real damage to one's identity interests—not to mention the significant consequential harms an outee may suffer at the hands of intolerant others.

It is sometimes argued that a person's heterosexual orientation is clearly not private; so, by parity, neither is homosexual orientation. But this obviously overlooks radical differences in the meaning and value attached to different sexual orientations. Whether—and the extent to which—sexual orientation is appropriately public is a contingent matter, depending on the personal and social meanings and values of sexual orientation in a given social context. Homosexual orientation is normatively private, not because it is an inherently private fact, but because privacy protects against the material and spiritual damage that unwarranted access to or distribution of sensitive personal information can do to individual identity, dignity, and autonomy.

Does appealing to privacy commit one to the repugnant and false view that gayness is bad and shameful, something to be kept hidden? Not at all; the right to privacy protects the individual against unwarranted public portrayals, not just the shameful ones. The right to privacy immunizes against the wrongful transformation of a private life into a public life open to scrutiny and judgment. To say that a public disclosure of homosexuality is offensive is not to say that homosexuality is offensive or shameful. Compare outing with the publication of a rape victim's identity: that a particular woman has been raped, while deplorable, is not a shaming fact about her, yet it is routinely and rightly regarded as privacy-protected information. In both cases, it is the disclosure itself—and not necessarily the fact disclosed—that is offensive and damaging.

While I have been arguing for a prima facie privacy right against outing, I do not mean to suggest that outing is never justified. A number of competing interests may be sufficiently important to override a person's privacy interests. One such case is that of elected officials who pursue antigay policies and legislation as a cover for their own homosexuality. The voting public has a strong democratic interest in knowing what motivates an official's actions; hypocritical behavior, lying, and deception also bear on the person's character and fitness for office. Note, however, that such outings are not justified by hypocrisy alone, nor as vindictive punishment for voting "improperly." Nor is this a utilitarian defense of the practice: political outing fosters voters' abilities to make informed and autonomous choices, while it may or may not produce better overall outcomes.

Mohr's Dignity-Based Outing

. . . If there is a prima facie privacy right against outing, then (as Mohr admits) even dignity-based outing would not be justified; but I also find Mohr's position troubling on its own terms. Outing may diminish gay dignity, both individual and collective, because the public regards homosexuality as bad or immoral and sees outing as punishment. Rather than serving to dismantle antigay attitudes, outing utilizes and reinforces the notion that homosexuality is shameful. Even when conscientiously motivated, the practice can look petty and vindictive.

Perhaps the most repugnant feature of all outing is that it steals from the outee a major opportunity to take control of and assume responsibility for his identity, integrity, and dignity—to come out on his own principles. Mohr complains that this argument—"dressed up in the finery of liberal cant"—misunderstands the scope and possible materials of dignity and the complexity of coming out. Shifting attention to the outee, Mohr says the relevant questions are: (1) Can a person, though outed, still have access to enough dignity to be highly dignified? (2) Are conditions such that individuals can achieve a rich life of their own making given the cussedness of their social and material circumstances? (3) Can the outee still have a positive, robust, dignifying relation to his sexual orientation? I agree that the answer to each question is yes. But none of this refutes the claim that outing wrongly diminishes the dignity of the outee.

It is certainly possible to imagine situations in which a failure to identify a person as gay would involve the loss of one's own dignity. But it is simply not plausible to claim that a person who decides not to out another out of respect for her autonomy and dignity necessarily regards homosexuality as shameful or has committed her life to the oppression of gays. Except in unusual circumstances, the threat to my dignity of your closetude—and my leaving you there—is negligible. As Mohr observes, dignity has many sources, and I can still be highly dignified despite forgoing the opportunity to out you. To see this, we can stand Mohr's questions on their heads to inquire whether a gay person can have access to enough dignity to be highly dignified, a rich life of his own making, and a robust dignifying relation to his sexual orientation—all without engaging in outing. Here too, the answer is yes.

Like many other groups, gay people are faced with a situation in which society unfairly and severely stigmatizes them for having a particular characteristic. One's dignity as a given type of person does not require outing every person one knows to share the relevant characteristic. Compare again the situation of gays to that of women who have been raped. Through no fault of their own rape victims are saddled with a status that is not inherently disrespectable, but that often prompts disrespectful treatment. Suppose that Anne was a victim of rape but has been able to rid herself of the shame and stigma rape victims often internalize; she now works actively in rape-prevention programs, counseling women and giving public talks in which she "comes out" as herself a victim of rape. If Anne knows that Brenda was also raped but remains "closeted," how does Anne's failure to out her cause a loss of Anne's dignity?

Mohr grants that outing can diminish the outee's dignity, but he holds that this will rarely outweigh the dignity gained for all gays by outing because the indignity bred by the secret of the closet is so great and pervasive. I think Mohr too readily trades concrete and significant individual harms and indignities for a hypothetical and incremental increase in the abstract quantity of overall dignity.

It is important to realize that objecting to outing does not require defending the closet. Lesbians and gays should certainly be encouraged to come out as a matter of moral virtue. But as long as homosexuality is stigmatized in ways that heterosexuality is not, being publicly gay will be personally dangerous and politically volatile. Except in unusual circumstances, individuals should have the freedom to decide for themselves whether to join the sociopolitical fray, rather than being made political footballs by others professing to know better the proper course for their lives.

There is no one way—certainly no correct way—to be gay, although some gays speak as if there were. What being gay means to a person and whether, when, and to what extent one shall be publicly identified as gay are decisions properly left to the individual. Tyranny takes many forms—wherever a person is victimized by coercive power. Outers, who know well that information is power, commit a tyranny of the few. In doing so, they betray one of gay activism's fundamental values: the right to pursue one's life free from domination and interference by others.

B. FURTHER REFLECTION ON OUTING

Many of the cases in this chapter deal with the state-sponsored violation of a gay person's right to speak about his or her sexuality when he or she wants to speak. But the case of *Sipple v. Chronicle Publ.* involves a newspaper's large-scale disclosure of the gay sexual orientation of Oliver W. Sipple. The case is particularly interesting because Sipple was, in fact, "out" within the relatively-closed gay community of San Francisco. As you read the *Sipple* case and the account of Sipple's life that follows it, consider again the arguments about outing offered by Mohr and Stramel. Doesn't journalist Herb Caen's proffered justification for writing about Sipple's sexual orientation sound a lot like Mohr's dignity-based justification for outing in general? Should it have been relevant that Sipple's sexual orientation was an "open secret"—already known to a substantial number of people?

SIPPLE v. CHRONICLE PUBL.

154 Cal.App.3d 1040, 201 Cal.Rptr. 665 (1984)

Opinion by CALDECOTT, P. J., with POCHE and PANELLI, JJ., concurring.

On September 22, 1975, Sara Jane Moore attempted to assassinate President Gerald R. Ford while the latter was visiting San Francisco, California. Plaintiff Oliver W. Sipple (hereafter appellant or Sipple) who was in the crowd at Union Square, San Francisco, grabbed or struck Moore's arm as the latter was about to fire the gun and shoot at the President. Although no one can be certain whether or not Sipple actually saved the President's life, the assassination attempt did not succeed and Sipple was considered a hero for his selfless action and was subject to significant publicity throughout the nation following the assassination attempt.

Among the many articles concerning the event was a column written by Herb Caen and published by the *San Francisco Chronicle* on September 24, 1975. The article read in part as follows: "One of the heroes of the day, Oliver 'Bill' Sipple, the ex-Marine who grabbed Sara Jane Moore's arm just as her gun was fired and thereby may have saved the President's life, was the center of midnight attention at the Red Lantern, a Golden Gate Ave. bar he favors. The Rev. Ray Broshears, head of Helping Hands, and Gay Politico, Harvey Milk, who claim to be among Sipple's close friends, describe themselves as 'proud—maybe this will help break the stereotype'. Sipple is among the workers in Milk's campaign for Supervisor."

Thereafter, the *Los Angeles Times* and numerous out-of-state newspapers published articles which, referring to the primary source (*i.e.*, the story published in the *San Francisco Chronicle*), mentioned both the heroic act shown by Sipple and the fact that he was a prominent member of the San Francisco gay community. Some of those articles speculated that President Ford's failure to promptly thank Sipple for his heroic act was a result of Sipple's sexual orientation.

Finding the articles offensive to his private life, on September 30, 1975, Sipple filed an action against the California defendants, the Chronicle Publishing Company, Charles de Young Thieriot, the publisher of the *Chronicle*, Herb Caen, a columnist for the *Chronicle*, the Times Mirror Company, the owner and publisher of the *Los Angeles Times*, and Otis Chandler (hereafter together respondents) and numerous out-of-state newspapers. The complaint was predicated upon the theory of invasion of privacy and alleged in essence that defendants without authorization and consent published private facts about plaintiff's life by disclosing that plaintiff was homosexual in his personal and private sexual orientation; that said publications were highly offensive to plaintiff inasmuch as his parents, brothers and sisters learned for the first time of his homosexual orientation; and that as a consequence of disclosure of private facts about his life plaintiff was abandoned by his family, exposed to contempt and ridicule causing him great mental anguish, embarrassment and humiliation. Plaintiff finally alleged that defendants' conduct amounted to malice and oppression calling for both compensatory and punitive damages.

. . .

Appellant's principal contention on appeal is that the trial court prejudicially erred in granting summary judgment in favor of respondents. More precisely, appellant argues that the individual elements of the invasion of privacy (*i.e.*, public disclosure of private facts; the offensiveness of the public disclosure; and the newsworthiness of the publication as an exception to tort liability) constituted a factual determination which could not be resolved or adjudicated by way of summary procedure.

Before discussing appellant's contentions on the merit, as an initial matter we set out the legal principles governing the case. It is well settled that there are three elements of a cause of action predicated on tortious invasion of privacy. First, the disclosure of the private facts must be a *public disclosure*. Second, the facts disclosed must be *private facts*, and not public ones. Third, the matter made public must be one which would be *offensive* and objectionable to a reasonable person of ordinary sensibilities. It is likewise recognized, however, that due to the supreme mandate of the constitutional protection of freedom of the press even a tortious invasion of one's privacy is exempt from liability if the publication of private facts is truthful and newsworthy. The latter proposition finds support primarily in Restatement Second of Torts section 652D which provides that "One who gives publicity to a matter concerning the private life of another is subject to liability to the other for invasion of his privacy, if the matter publicized is of a kind that (a) would be highly offensive to a reasonable person, and (b) is not of legitimate concern to the public."

In interpreting the cited section, the cases and authorities emphasize that the privilege to publicize newsworthy matters incorporated in section 652D is not only immunity accorded by the common law, but also one of constitutional dimension based upon the First Amendment of the United States Constitution. As tersely stated in comment d to section 652D: "When the subject-matter of the publicity is of legitimate public concern, there is no invasion of privacy. This has now become a rule not just of common law of torts, but of the Federal Constitution as well." *(Accord Cox Broadcasting Corp. v. Cohn* (1975) 420 U.S. 469 [43 L.Ed.2d 328, 95 S.Ct. 1029]; *Time, Inc. v. Hill* (1967) 385 U.S. 374, 383 [17 L.Ed.2d 456, 464, 87 S.Ct. 534]).

As an additional preliminary matter, it also bears emphasis that a motion for summary judgment in First Amendment cases is an approved procedure because unnecessarily protracted litigation would have a chilling effect upon the exercise of First Amendment rights and because speedy resolution of cases involving free speech is desirable. While the crucial test as to whether to grant a motion for summary judgment remains the same in free speech cases (*i.e.*, whether there is a triable issue of fact presented in the case), the courts impose more stringent burdens on one who opposes the motion and require a showing of high probability that the plaintiff will ultimately prevail in the case. In the absence of such showing the courts are inclined to grant the motion and do not permit the case to proceed beyond the summary judgment stage.

When viewed in light of the aforegoing principles, the summary judgment in this case must be upheld on two grounds. First, as appears from the record properly considered for the purposes of summary judgment, the facts disclosed by the articles were not private facts within the meaning of the law. Second, the record likewise reveals on its face that the publications in dispute were newsworthy and thus constituted a protective shield from liability based upon invasion of privacy.

(A) The facts published were not private.

As pointed out earlier, a crucial ingredient of the tort premised upon invasion of one's privacy is a public disclosure of *private facts,* that is, the unwarranted publication of intimate details of one's private life which are outside the realm of legitimate public interest. In elaborating on the notion, the cases explain that there can be no privacy with respect to a matter which is already public or which has previously become part of the "public domain." Moreover, it is equally underlined that there is no liability when the defendant merely gives further publicity to information about the plaintiff which is already public or when the further publicity relates to matters which the plaintiff leaves open to the public eye.

The case at bench falls within the aforestated rules. The undisputed facts reveal that prior to the publication of the newspaper articles in question appellant's homosexual orientation and participation in gay community activities had been known by hundreds of people in a variety of cities, including New York, Dallas, Houston, San Diego, Los Angeles and San Francisco. Thus, appellant's deposition shows that prior to the assassination attempt appellant spent a lot of time in "Tenderloin" and "Castro," the well-known gay sections of San Francisco; that he frequented gay bars and other homosexual gatherings in both San Francisco and other cities; that he marched in gay parades on several occasions; that he supported the campaign of Mike Caringi for the election of "Emperor"; that he participated in the coronation of the "Emperor" and sat at Caringi's table on that occasion; that his friendship with Harvey Milk, another prominent gay, was well-known and publicized in gay newspapers; and that his homosexual association and name had been reported in gay magazines (such as *Data Boy*, *Pacific Coast Times*, *Male Express*, etc.) several times before the publications in question. In fact, appellant quite candidly conceded that he did not make a secret of his being a homosexual and that if anyone would ask, he would frankly admit that he was gay. In short, since appellant's sexual orientation was already in public domain and since the articles in question did no more than to give further publicity to matters which appellant left open to the eye of the public, a vital element of the tort was missing rendering it vulnerable to summary disposal.

Although the conclusion reached above applies with equal force to all respondents, we cannot help observing that respondents *Times Mirror* and its editor are exempt from liability on the additional ground that the *Los Angeles Times* only republished the *Chronicle* article which implied that appellant was gay. It is, of course, axiomatic that no right of privacy attaches to a matter of general interest that has already been publicly released in a periodical or in a newspaper of local or regional circulation.

(B) The publication was newsworthy.

But even aside from the aforegoing considerations, the summary judgment dismissing the action against respondents was justified on the additional, independent basis that the publication contained in the articles in dispute was newsworthy.

As referred to above, our courts have recognized a broad privilege cloaking the truthful publication of all newsworthy matters. Thus, our Supreme Court stated that a truthful publication is protected if (1) it is newsworthy and (2) it does not reveal facts so offensive as to shock the community notions of decency. While it has been said that the general criteria for determining newsworthiness are (a) the social value of the facts published; (b) the depth of the article's intrusion into ostensibly private affairs; and (c) the extent to which the individual voluntarily acceded to a position of public notoriety, the cases and authorities further explain that the paramount test of newsworthiness is whether the matter is of legitimate public interest which in turn must be determined according to the community mores. As pointed out in *Virgil v. Time, Inc., supra*, 527 F.2d at page 1129: "In determining what is a matter of legitimate public interest, account must be taken of the customs and conventions of the community; and in the last analysis what is proper becomes a matter of the community mores. *The line is to be drawn when the publicity ceases to be the giving of information to which the public is entitled, and becomes a morbid and sensational prying into private lives for its own sake*, with which a reasonable member of the public, with decent standards, would say that he had no concern." (Italics added.) (Accord Rest. 2d Torts, § 652D, com. h.)

In the case at bench the publication of appellant's homosexual orientation which had already been widely known by many people in a number of communities was not so offensive even at the time of the publication as to shock the community notions of decency. Moreover, and perhaps even more to the point, the record shows that the publications were not motivated by a morbid and sensational prying into appellant's private life but rather were prompted by legitimate political considerations, *i.e.*, to dispel the false public opinion that gays were timid, weak and unheroic figures and to raise the equally important political question whether the President of the United States entertained a discriminatory attitude or bias against a minority group such as homosexuals. Thus appellant's case squarely falls within the language of *Kapellas* in which the California Supreme Court emphasized that "when, [as here] the legitimate public interest in the published information is substantial, a much greater intrusion into an individual's private life will be sanctioned, especially if the individual willingly entered into the public sphere." (*Kapellas v. Kofman, supra*, 1 Cal.3d at p. 36.)

Appellant's contention that by saving the President's life he did not intend to enter into the limelight and become a public figure can be easily answered. In elaborating on involuntary public figures, Restatement Second of Torts section 652D, comment f, sets out in part as follows: "There are other individuals who have not sought publicity or consented to it, but through their own conduct or otherwise have become a legitimate subject of public interest. They have, in other words, become 'news.' . . . These persons are regarded as properly subject to the public interest, and publishers are permitted to satisfy the curiosity of the public as to its heroes, leaders, villains and victims, and those who are closely associated with them. As in the case of the voluntary public figure, the authorized publicity is not limited to the event that itself arouses the public interest, and to some reasonable extent includes publicity given to facts about the individual that would otherwise be purely private."

In summary, appellant's assertion notwithstanding, the trial court could determine as a matter of law that the facts contained in the articles were not private facts within the purview of the law and also that the publications relative to the appellant were newsworthy. Since the record thus fails to present any triable issue of fact, the trial court was justified (if not mandated) in granting summary judgment and dismissing the case against respondents by way of summary procedure.

The purported appeal from the order denying a motion for new trial is dismissed as the order is not an appealable order.

The judgment is affirmed.

DISCUSSION

The following story about Oliver ("Billy") Sipple suggests some of the darker potential consequences of outing. Does the story change your perspective? How do you think Professor Mohr would respond?

SORROW TRAILED A VETERAN*

The circumstances of Billy Sipple's death came as no surprise to his friends.

Sometime around Jan. 19, Sipple turned on his television and lay on his bed, half-gallon bottles of cheap bourbon and 7–Up within reach, and fell asleep.

Two weeks later, Wayne Friday stopped by Reflections, a Polk Street bar that was one of Sipple's daily stops. The bartender, worried that Sipple had not been by for days, asked Friday to check up on him.

Without even opening the door of Sipple's apartment, Friday, an investigator for the San Francisco District Attorney, knew that his friend was dead.

"People shouldn't die like that, alone," Friday said.

Sipple's $334–a month apartment looked like a junk store gone to seed. Mementos of value only to their owner were arranged in no order. Bad paintings covered chipped plaster. His most prized possession, a framed letter, hung on a corner wall.

"Dear Mr. Sipple," the letter began.

"I want you to know how much I appreciated your selfless actions last Monday. The events were a shock to us all, but you acted quickly and without fear for your own safety. By doing so, you helped to avert danger to me and to others in the crowd. You have my heartfelt appreciation."

Signed, Jerry Ford.

The letter was dated Sept. 25, 1975. Three days earlier, Oliver (Billy) Sipple, a disabled Vietnam Marine veteran, happened to be at Union Square when Sara Jane Moore aimed a .38 caliber revolver at then-President Gerald Ford. Sipple lunged and knocked away the gun. The bullet went wild. The President was whisked away, safely.

Anyone would have done the same thing, Sipple told his friends. It was no big deal.

Others saw it differently. Not only was he a hero, he was gay, and actively involved in gay politics and in causes—a fact known widely here but not elsewhere.

---

* Dan Morain, *Sorrow Trailed a Veteran Who Saved a President and Then Was Cast in an Unwanted Spotlight*, LOS ANGELES TIMES, Feb. 13, 1989, 1.

In San Francisco in 1975, gays were seeking political power—and there were many who thought Sipple's heroic act could go a long way toward dispelling myths and stereotypes about gays here and across the nation.

Sipple was about to become famous. In the process, he would suffer. His story was news, but it forever estranged him from his parents. He knew he had problems before the fame but he also maintained that the problems became far worse after: he became more nervous, drank more, considered suicide and thought people were following him.

"I have a lot of stress and I take it out on booze," he said in a 1979 deposition, describing what his flash of fame had brought.

Sipple's story is retold in journalism schools and discussions about the right to privacy. There was even mention of it in the movie, "Absence of Malice." The reporter portrayed by Sally Field wrote a story that prompted the subject to commit suicide. The editor tried to console her by telling about "the guy in the crowd" who "saved the President's life."

"Turned out he was also gay. That's news, right? Now the whole country knows that too," the editor in the movie said.

Billy Sipple died of natural causes, according to a coroner's spokeswoman, although the exact cause of death remains unknown. But his friends say he had been suffering from pneumonia. He had a pacemaker and had ballooned to 298 pounds, long ago losing his square-jawed good looks.

Sipple was 47, but many believed him when, for some reason, he announced that he was 59 at a birthday party he threw for himself at Reflections three months ago—and said it would be his last.

About two weeks before his body was discovered, Sipple stopped in at the New Bell Saloon where he told bartender Frank Hagan that he had been by the Veterans Administration hospital, but was told to go home. A hospital spokesman said no record exists of such a visit.

"I'm not a doctor, but I could tell he couldn't breathe," Hagan said. The bartender called him a cab and told him to phone a doctor when he got home. Sipple promised he would.

"I believe that was the last anyone saw him," Hagan said.

"The guy died in pain, with a bottle by his bed. That's pain. That's need for anesthetic," John Wahl said after Sipple's funeral, a simple affair last week attended by 30 people.

Wahl was the lawyer who brought an unsuccessful invasion-of-privacy suit on Sipple's behalf against several newspapers, among them *The [Los Angeles] Times*.

Back in 1975, another client of Wahl's, political activist Harvey Milk, a long-time friend of Sipple's, was making a name for himself by making a serious run for the Board of Supervisors, trying to organize gays and urging that they emerge from their closets.

"Bill was part of that outreach. He was a guy who would do anything we asked—cook, walk precincts," recalled Bob Ross, publisher of the weekly *Bay Area Reporter*.

"Harvey's whole attitude was to show people that not everyone who was gay runs around with lipstick, high heels and a dress," Ross said. Sipple, the ex-Marine, seemed the perfect one to break down the myths. "This was an ordinary American citizen, and he was a gay man."

The first press mention of Sipple's sexual orientation appeared on Sept. 24, 1975, two days after the attempt on Ford's life. *San Francisco Chronicle* columnist Herb Caen reported that Milk and another gay man "who claim to be among Sipple's close friends, describe themselves as 'proud—maybe this will help break the stereotype.' " The item also noted that Sipple worked in Milk's supervisorial campaign.

"In the gay press," recalled Ross, "we were happy to have a hero."

But there was a problem. "Bill didn't want to be a hero," Ross said.

Once the item appeared in Caen's column, the ramifications of Sipple's sexuality added a new twist for other reporters. When President Ford did not immediately thank Sipple, Milk told reporters that Sipple was being ignored because he was gay.

Still, Sipple was evasive when reporters called. When headlines about his homosexuality reached his hometown of Detroit, the reason for Sipple's reluctance became apparent. His parents were shocked that he was being called a prominent member of San Francisco's gay community.

"My father was too old, too stubborn. He couldn't change," said George Sipple, Bill's brother, a Detroit auto worker who came to San Francisco to arrange Bill's burial and clean his apartment.

The estrangement between Sipple and his father was so deep that when his mother died in 1979, his father made it clear that he was not welcome. He could go to the funeral home or the cemetery, but not when his father was there, George Sipple recalled. Sipple stayed in San Francisco.

"His personal life never should have made it back to Detroit," Sipple's brother added.

In the years after he grabbed Moore, Sipple rarely discussed the incident, and downplayed his role when he did. He told his brother that he wasn't even thinking about the President when he grabbed the would-be assassin. He thought that for some reason she was going to shoot him.

In his later years, however, several of his friends would say that when the liquor got him to talking, Sipple would boast about his heroism and inflate his service rank, telling people who would listen that he retired as a Marine colonel. The highest rank he attained was corporal. He was discharged as a private first-class.

Though Sipple believed his notoriety led him to drink more heavily and ruined his life, his life apparently had long been troubled.

He was a high-school drop-out, dyslexic and had been a drinker for years, he said. He was wounded twice in Vietnam, including once in the head, and lived on a 100% veteran's disability pension since his release from the Marines in 1970. The disability was for both psychological and physical reasons. The coroner's report noted that he was diagnosed as a paranoid schizophrenic.

But although he lived on a veteran's pension, he never stopped being generous, his friends said. He would give at least $50 to any worthy charity, or help a Tenderloin derelict.

"I have watched him split his last two dollars. Give one dollar to someone who needed a meal, and use the rest to buy himself a drink," Ross said.

Sipple had come to San Francisco in 1970 knowing that he would be accepted as he never could be back home. But he never envisioned that word of his life style would travel back to his hometown, attorney Wahl said in explaining why Sipple decided to file suit after the publicity that followed his act of heroism.

"There was a principle," Wahl said. "If someone is gay and wants to keep that fact private, then who the hell is Herb Caen or anyone else to say it's not a private fact?"

Sipple's suit was thrown out by a superior court judge in San Francisco. The case dragged on until 1984 when a state court of appeal held that Sipple had indeed become news, and that his sexual orientation was part of the story.

Although the papers won the suit, the Sipple story weighs on Daryl Lembke, then a reporter for *The Times* whose article was among the first to appear after Caen's column item.

"It is a source of concern that will stay with me—that I attempted to make Oliver Sipple a gay hero," Lembke said. "Instead, I helped estrange him from his mother.... If I had it to do it over again, I wouldn't."

Caen doesn't have such second thoughts. In a brief phone conversation, he said: "It was a good item. Members of the gay community wanted it published to show they weren't all a bunch of wimps."

Sipple nonetheless left a mark and that pleased him, said George Sipple, taking a break from cleaning his brother's apartment. George recalled that his brother once said that long after he died, "somebody will pick up a book and see Oliver Sipple saved President Ford's life."

George Sipple felt sorry, however, that he could not honor his brother's wish that he be buried at Arlington National Cemetery. He was buried Wednesday at Golden Gate National Cemetery south of San Francisco.

His brother also wondered why there had been no message of condolence from former President Ford.

Penny Circle, Ford's chief of staff at his Palm Springs office, said the former President had been traveling since she learned of Sipple's death.

"I couldn't get a hold of the President," she said, "and it just fell through the cracks."

DISCUSSION

The Sipple *case intimates an interesting theory: What happens in the gay community stays in the gay community. Is there an unwritten code of silence or privacy in the gay community? Should there be? For example, what if a gay student sees a fellow male student, previously presumed straight, kissing another male in the darkened corner of a gay bar. Is it ethically permissible for him to relay what he saw to others?*

II. DEFAMATION

In a climate of general hostility to homosexuality, accusations of homosexuality can be damaging to the putative homosexual's livelihood and social standing. Traditional tort law holds that publicly naming someone as a homosexual is defamation *per se*. In a real sense, traditional defamation law reinforces the secrecy of "the closet" by underscoring the stigma attached to homosexual identification. Notice how these factors influence the judges' decision in the following case.

HAYES v. SMITH

832 P.2d 1022 (Colo. Ct. App. 1991)

Opinion: JUDGE DUBOFSKY, SMITH and ROTHENBERG, JJ., concur

. . . Plaintiff and defendants were active participants in a conservative Christian community. Plaintiff is a high school teacher, lecturer, and writer. She and Samantha Smith jointly created a corporation to further business ideas related to their common religious outlook. Over time, the relationship between the plaintiff and defendants deteriorated resulting in harassment and verbal accusations.

In May 1986, defendants met with plaintiff's school superintendent with the ostensible purpose of obtaining the superintendent's help in stopping plaintiff from harassing them. Plaintiff alleged that, during the meeting between defendants and the superintendent, defendants defamed her by, inter alia, stating that: (1) plaintiff had tried to establish a homosexual relationship with Samantha Smith; (2) plaintiff had "proposed marriage" to Samantha Smith; and (3) plaintiff had in the past been discharged from a teaching position.

Thereafter, based primarily on these statements to the superintendent, plaintiff filed this defamation action. The jury returned a verdict in favor of the plaintiff and awarded $1,000 in actual damages and $26,000 in special damages.

I.

Defendants argue that the trial court erred in determining that the statements accusing plaintiff of homosexual conduct were slanderous per se and in, therefore, instructing the jury on that basis. We agree.

Cases in various jurisdictions have reached different conclusions in deciding whether statements which falsely accuse a person of being a homosexual or engaging in homosexual activity constitute slander per se. Our analysis of the present state of the law leads us to conclude that the per se classification is inappropriate for the statements at issue here.

Historically, defamation was actionable per se only if the defamatory remark imputed a criminal offense; a venereal or loathsome and communicable disease; improper conduct of a lawful business; or unchastity by a woman. *See* Restatement (First) of Torts § 569 (1938) and *Gertz v. Robert Welch, Inc.*, 418 U.S. 323, 94 S.Ct. 2997, 41 L.Ed.2d 789 (1974).

However, the Restatement (Second) of Torts reflects a trend toward limiting the per se category of slander to those instances in which the defamatory remark is apparent from the publication itself without reference to extrinsic facts. *See* Restatement (Second) of Torts §§ 571–574 (1977); *Gertz, supra* (White, J., dissenting). As to the specific matter at issue here, the Restatement (Second) of Torts expressly left open the issue whether an accusation of homosexuality fell into the per se category.

The primary advantage to a plaintiff claiming slander per se is that certain damages are presumed if the statement is so categorized, *e.g.*, loss of reputation, and therefore, need not be proved. This presumption has been considered desirable because injuries such as loss of reputation can be difficult to prove since the recipients of the information may be reluctant to testify that the publication affected their relationship with the plaintiff and because the words may affect the recipients' view of the relationship in subtle ways of which the recipient is not necessarily aware.

Another advantage to a per se classification is that the plaintiff need not prove the statements were defamatory within the context in which they were made. In *Gertz*, the court was also concerned that per se classifications inhibit and punish freedom of speech by making it too easy to prove defamation and damages.

In *Gertz, supra,* the majority indicated that per se classifications and presumed damages, even where constitutional, are not favored. Indeed, the *Gertz* court held that, as to a public official or public figure, a presumed damage award without proof of reckless or malicious conduct violates the First Amendment rights of the publisher of the false statement.

Thus, the right to presumed damages no longer depends entirely on the nature of the accusation; rather, it also depends on whether the statements were made about a public official or public figure with malice or recklessness as defined in *New York Times v. Sullivan*, 376 U.S. 254, 84 S.Ct. 710, 11 L.Ed.2d 686 (1964).

Furthermore, here, the trial court determined, without objection, that plaintiff was a public official. Peter S. Crane, Note, Defamation of Teachers: Behind the Times?, 56 Fordham L. Rev. 1191 (1988). Thus, the First Amendment constitutional protections of *New York Times v. Sullivan* and its progeny, including *Gertz,* are applicable here. Moreover, defamatory statements to the superintendent may have been of a public concern. . . .

In *Gertz,* however, the court emphasized that, even though presumed damages may be unavailable, plaintiff can recover for any actual injuries caused by the defamation. The *Gertz* court stated:

> Suffice it to say that actual injury is not limited to out-of-pocket loss. Indeed the more customary types of actual harm inflicted by defamatory falsehood include impairment of reputation and standing in the community, personal humiliation, and mental anguish and suffering.

These non-economic and non-reputation damages can be awarded without an initial or predicate determination awarding damages because of either harm to reputation or economic loss.

In many instances, it is easier for a person injured by defamatory comments to prove personal humiliation and mental anguish and suffering than to prove economic loss or reputation damage. Since these non-economic damages do not require predicate or initial proof of reputation or economic loss, a person who has been slandered will be compensated even if there is a failure of proof as to the reputation or economic loss claims.

Furthermore, this approach brings the damages in libel and slander cases more in line with the damages provided for other types of tort action.

Moreover, in this modern era, new methods exist for proving economic and reputational damages in a defamation case, including testimony by economists, psychologists, and other expert witnesses. These factors lessen the need for per se classifications before plaintiffs can recover damages.

We, therefore, interpret the import of *Gertz*, *Firestone*, and *Walker* as furthering an earlier trend to limit and not expand the use of per se characterizations and presumed damages in defamation cases.

There are also several other factors which bear on our decision to conclude that accusations of homosexuality are not slanderous per se.

First, the fact that sexual activities between consenting adults of the same sex are no longer illegal in Colorado tends to indicate that an accusation of being a homosexual is not of such a character as to be slanderous per se.

Second, if a person is falsely accused of belonging in a category of persons considered deserving of social approbation, *i.e.*, thief, murderer, prostitute, etc., it is generally the court's determination as to whether such accusation is considered slander per se so that damages are presumed. *Inter–State Detective Bureau, Inc. v. Denver Post, Inc.*, 29 Colo.App. 313, 484 P.2d 131 (1971). A court should not classify homosexuals with those miscreants who have engaged in actions that deserve the reprobation and scorn which is implicitly a part of the slander/libel per se classifications. *See Shelley v. Kraemer*, 334 U.S. 1, 68 S.Ct. 836, 92 L.Ed. 1161 (1948).

For a characterization of a person to warrant a per se classification, it should, without equivocation, expose the plaintiff to public hatred or contempt. However, there is no empirical evidence in this record demonstrating that homosexuals are held by society in such poor esteem. Indeed, it appears that the community view toward homosexuals is mixed.

Furthermore, as previously indicated, in the *Gertz* holding, the United States Supreme Court has indicated that per se damages, even if constitutional, are not favored. The thrust of that holding is that a court should use caution in expanding categories in which per se classifications are made and presumed damages are awarded.

Although we agree that, in light of plaintiff's showing of malicious or reckless conduct by defendants, there is no constitutional prohibition against these false accusations of homosexuality being treated as slander per se, we, nevertheless, are unwilling to do so. We reach this conclusion because of the *Gertz* hostility to expanding the scope of defamation per se and because there are serious doubts whether homosexuality meets the criteria for such a classification. We, therefore, reverse the trial court on this issue.

II.

Plaintiff implicitly argues that, even if the statements made here would not be slanderous per se outside her employment context, since they were made to her supervisor in an employment context, they did injure her in her profession as a teacher and on that basis, are slanderous per se. We do not agree.

We recognize that teachers' reputations are very vulnerable to injury when they are the subject of false accusations. We conclude, however, for the reasons stated above, that false statements concerning homosexuality are not slander per se even though they arise in an employment context and are directed at plaintiff's business reputation.

In this regard, we further note the availability of proven actual damages to compensate an injured plaintiff in this setting. Plaintiff is entitled to receive compensation not only for economic damages and loss of reputation, but also for other proven damages, *i.e.*, humiliation, mental suffering. Thus, even though the statements are not accorded slander per se status, plaintiff, on retrial, may receive compensation for those damages proven to have resulted from the statements.

DISCUSSION

The court in Hayes v. Smith *follows the trend of abolishing per se defamation categorization for imputations of homosexuality. Considering the underlying rationale for per se defamation (that certain accusations virtually always result in harm) is the court's decision right? Wouldn't the accusations leveled in* Hayes *against a public school employee in a conservative community almost certainly damage her? Do you agree with the court's ultimate conclusion? Why or why not?*

Despite a trend to the contrary, per se categorization persists in some jurisdictions. See, e.g., Yonaty v. Mincolla *31 Misc.3d 1238(A), 2011 NY Slip Op. 51037(U);* Robinson v. Radio One, Inc., *695 F. Supp. 2d 425 (2010).*

III. SPEECH AND ASSOCIATION

The right of expression—the right to speak, to name, to accuse, to advocate—has been central to the development of gay identity. In a very real sense, gays and lesbians do not exist in any materially appreciable way to many heterosexuals until we "come out," that is, until we claim our identity as gay or lesbian. Often such identification is attended by significant negative consequences. Additionally, the Supreme Court has long recognized the right to associate with others for the purpose of like-minded expression as constitutionally protected, and yet many gays and lesbians have had to struggle to do just that. The following cases explore these, often complex, issues.

A. COLLEGE STUDENTS

GAY LESBIAN BISEXUAL ALLIANCE v. PRYOR

110 F.3d 1543 (11th Cir. 1997)

DUBINA, CIRCUIT JUDGE:

Appellant Attorney General Bill Pryor ("the Attorney General") appeals the district court's judgment that ALA.CODE, § 16–1–28, (1995), violates the First Amendment to the United States Constitution both facially and as applied to Appellee Gay and Lesbian Bisexual Alliance ("GLBA"). *Gay Lesbian Bisexual Alliance v. Sessions,* 917 F.Supp. 1548 (M.D.Ala.1996). Based upon our review of the record, we affirm the judgment of the district court.

I.

Statement of the Case

A. Background

Ala. Code § 16–1–28 provides:

(a) No public funds or public facilities shall be used by any college or university to, directly or indirectly, sanction, recognize, or support the activities or existence of any organization or group that fosters or promotes a lifestyle or actions prohibited by the sodomy and sexual misconduct laws of §§ 13A–6–63 to 13A–6–65, inclusive.

(b) No organization or group that receives public funds or uses public facilities, directly or indirectly, at any college or university shall permit or encourage its members or encourage other persons to engage in any such unlawful acts or provide information or materials that explain how such acts may be engaged in or performed.

(c) This section shall not be construed to be a prior restraint of the first amendment protected speech. It shall not apply to any organization or group whose activities are limited solely to the political advocacy of a change in the sodomy and sexual misconduct laws of this state.

The statutes referenced in part (a) criminalize sodomy or "deviate sexual intercourse," which Alabama law defines as "any act of sexual gratification between persons not married to each other involving the sex organs of one person and the mouth or anus of another." Ala. Code § 13A–6–60(2) (1994).

The University of South Alabama ("USA") encourages a wide variety of student activities on campus and has an established procedure for the formation and registration of student organizations. USA has over 100 registered student organizations. These organizations are eligible for certain benefits, including use of campus meeting rooms, on-campus banking services, and funding from the USA Student Government Association ("SGA"). GLBA is an officially recognized student organization whose purpose, according to its constitution, is to provide a foundation for unification for homosexual and nonhomosexual people of the student population, in order to draw support to further our efforts in educating all members of the university community on the fears and dangers of homophobia and to provide a support system for the University of South Alabama's homosexual students. *Gay Lesbian Bisexual Alliance,* 917 F.Supp. at 1551 n. 18.

This case arises from two incidents. First, the district court found that USA effectively denied on-campus banking privileges to GLBA. Following the passage of § 16–1–28, GLBA requested an on-campus bank account to avoid commercial banking fees. Dean Adams of USA advised GLBA that in light of § 16–1–28, USA could freeze GLBA funds placed in an on-campus account. GLBA therefore opened an account off-campus with a commercial bank.

Second, USA denied funding to GLBA based on § 16–1–28. The district court based this conclusion on three events. In the fall of 1992, GLBA requested funds to purchase posters publicizing "World AIDS Day" activities. Dean Adams refused to fund GLBA until he received an opinion from the Attorney General on § 16–1–28's application. In an effort to accommodate GLBA without violating § 16–1–28, Dean Adams instructed the SGA to buy the World AIDS Day posters. In the winter of 1993, GLBA requested funds to bring a guest speaker to campus. Dean Adams instructed the SGA to table the request because USA could not fund GLBA until it received an opinion from the Attorney General interpreting § 16–1–28. In the spring of 1993, GLBA again requested funds for a speaker. This time the SGA approved the request. However, Dean Adams refused to approve final payment of this money. In July 1993, the Attorney General issued a letter opinion stating that GLBA could not receive funds. The Attorney General's opinion did not specify how or why GLBA violated § 16–1–28. It is clear from the record that USA officials made efforts to accommodate GLBA without violating § 16–1–28. However, it is also clear that USA officials felt compelled, by virtue of § 16–1–28, to deny funding to GLBA on the three occasions mentioned above.

. . .

II.

Issues

A. Whether the district court's factual findings are clearly erroneous.

B. Whether § 16–1–28 violates the First Amendment as applied to GLBA.

C. Whether § 16–1–28 violates the First Amendment on its face.

III.

Standards of Review

The constitutionality of a statute is a question of law subject to *de novo* review. *United States v. Harden,* 37 F.3d 595, 602 (11th Cir.1994). We review the district court's underlying factual findings for clear error. Fed. R. Civ. P. 52(a); *Anderson v. Blue Cross/Blue Shield of Ala.,* 907 F.2d 1072, 1075 (11th Cir.1990).

IV.

. . .

B. Whether § 16–1–28 Violates The First Amendment As Applied To GLBA.

1. § 16–1–28 Implicates First Amendment Protected Speech

Appellant argues that the expression affected by § 16–1–28 is not constitutionally protected speech because the statute only outlaws speech advocating violation of the sodomy or sexual misconduct laws. We disagree. It is well-established that the First Amendment protects advocacy to violate a law. *Brandenburg v. Ohio,* 395 U.S. 444, 448–49, 89 S.Ct. 1827, 1830–31, 23 L.Ed.2d 430 (1969). That protection is limited in one important respect: The First Amendment does not "permit a State to forbid or proscribe advocacy of the use of force or of law violation except where such advocacy is directed to *inciting or producing imminent lawless action and is likely to incite or produce such action.*" *Id.* at 447, 89 S.Ct. at 1829 (emphasis added); *see also Healy v. James,* 408 U.S. 169, 188–89, 92 S.Ct. 2338, 2350, 33 L.Ed.2d 266 (1972); *Noto v. United States,* 367 U.S. 290, 297–98, 81 S.Ct. 1517, 1520–21, 6 L.Ed.2d 836 (1961).

The Attorney General argues that we should interpret § 16–1–28 to fit within *Brandenburg*'s narrow exception to the general rule that advocacy to violate the law is protected speech. According to the Attorney General, speech that falls within *Brandenburg*'s incitement of imminent lawless action exception is not constitutionally protected. We have serious doubts about this argument in light of *R.A.V. v. City of St. Paul, Minnesota,* 505 U.S. 377, 112 S.Ct. 2538, 120 L.Ed.2d 305 (1992). *R.A.V.* involved the constitutionality of St. Paul's hate speech ordinance. In striking down the statute, Justice Scalia, writing for the Court, rejected the notion that expressive activity could be devoid of constitutional protection.

> We have sometimes said that these categories of expression [obscenity, defamation, fighting words] are not within the area of constitutionally protected speech or that the protection of the First Amendment does not extend to them. Such statements must be taken in context . . . What they mean is that these areas of speech can, consistently with the First Amendment, be regulated *because of their constitutionally proscribable content* (obscenity, defamation, etc.)—not that they are categories of speech entirely invisible to the Constitution, so that they may be made the vehicles for content discrimination unrelated to their distinctively proscribable content. *Id.* at 383–84, 112 S.Ct. at 2543. Thus, incitement of imminent lawless action is not bereft of constitutional protection and regulation of such speech must be related to its constitutionally proscribable content. Nevertheless, we need not consider whether § 16–1–28 appropriately regulates speech falling within the *Brandenburg* exception, as the Attorney General suggests, because the statute is not capable of such a narrow interpretation.

. . .

2. § 16–1–28 Constitutes Viewpoint Discrimination

The government's power to restrict First Amendment activities depends on "the nature of the relevant forum." *Cornelius v. NAACP Legal Defense & Educ. Fund,* 473 U.S. 788, 800, 105 S.Ct. 3439, 3448, 87 L.Ed.2d 567 (1985); *Ethredge v. Hail,* 56 F.3d 1324, 1326–27 (11th Cir. 1995). The Supreme Court has recognized three types of forums: nonpublic forums, traditional public forums, and limited public forums. *See, e.g., Perry Educ. Assoc. v. Perry Local Educators' Assoc.,* 460 U.S. 37, 45–46, 103 S.Ct. 948, 954–55, 74 L.Ed.2d 794 (1983); *Searcey v. Harris,* 888 F.2d 1314, 1318–19 (11th Cir. 1989). Nonpublic forums are areas that are not traditionally public forums and that the government has not opened for public use. *Perry,* 460 U.S. at 46, 103 S.Ct. at 955–56. For example, military bases and prisons are nonpublic forums. The government's power to regulate speech is strongest in these areas. *M.N.C. of Hinesville v. U.S. Dept. of Defense,* 791 F.2d 1466, 1472 (11th Cir. 1986). Traditional public forums are areas such as streets and parks. *Hague v. CIO,* 307 U.S. 496, 515, 59 S.Ct. 954, 964, 83 L.Ed. 1423 (1939). The government's power to limit speech is weakest in these areas. *Perry,* 460 U.S. at 45, 103 S.Ct. at 954–55. Limited public forums are those areas that the government has created for use by the public as places for expressive activity. *Perry,* 460 U.S. at 45, 103 S.Ct. at 954–55. Although the government is not required to create such forums, once it does so the Constitution constrains its power to regulate speech within the forum. *M.N.C. of Hinesville,* 791 F.2d at 1472.

The Supreme Court's recent decision in *Rosenberger v. Rector & Visitors of the Univ. of Virginia,* 515 U.S. 819, 115 S.Ct. 2510, 132 L.Ed.2d 700 (1995), makes clear that USA's system for funding student groups created a limited public forum. *Rosenberger* involved the University of Virginia's ("UVA") refusal to fund a student newspaper with a Christian viewpoint. UVA's procedure for funding student groups was very much like the procedure in place at USA in this case. UVA allowed certain qualified student organizations to submit bills from outside contractors to the Student Activities Fund ("SAF"). The purpose of the SAF was to support extracurricular activities related to the educational purpose of UVA. The Student Council disbursed the funds subject to review by a UVA faculty committee. UVA prohibited disbursements to groups which "primarily promote[] or manifest[] a particular belief in or about a deity or an ultimate reality." *Rosenberger,* U.S. at 885, 115 S.Ct. at 2514–15 (citations omitted). Pursuant to this policy, UVA refused funding to a qualified student organization which published a newspaper with a Christian perspective. The Court held that UVA's action constituted viewpoint discrimination in violation of the First Amendment.

Justice Kennedy, writing for the majority, explained that when a university makes funds available to encourage student expression, the university creates a limited public forum. Once it has opened a limited forum, however, the State must respect the lawful boundaries it has itself set. The state may not exclude speech where its distinction is not reasonable in light of the purpose served by the forum, nor may it discriminate against speech on the basis of its viewpoint.

. . . We recognize the malleability of the distinction between content discrimination, which is permissible, and viewpoint discrimination, which is not. *See* Robert C. Post, *Subsidized Speech,* 106 YALE L. J. 151, 166 (1996). Yet *Rosenberger* makes clear that government discrimination against speech because of its message is presumptively unconstitutional, even in public forums created by the state. *Id.* at 115 S.Ct. at 2516. Justice Kennedy wrote:

> When the government targets not subject matter but particular views taken by speakers on a subject, the violation of the First Amendment is all the more blatant. Viewpoint discrimination is thus an egregious form of content discrimination. The government must abstain from regulating speech when the specific motivating ideology or the opinion or perspective of the speaker is the rationale for the restriction. These principles provide the framework forbidding the State from exercising viewpoint discrimination, even when the limited public forum is one of its own creation.

Id. (citations omitted).

Section 16–1–28 as applied to GLBA clearly runs afoul of the above-quoted language from *Rosenberger*. USA's limited public forum does not prohibit discussion of the sodomy or sexual misconduct laws in general. Rather, based on § 16–1–28, USA prohibited funding to GLBA based on the Attorney General's unsupported assumption that GLBA fosters or promotes a *violation* of the sodomy or sexual misconduct laws. The statute discriminates against one particular viewpoint because state funding of groups which foster or promote *compliance* with the sodomy or sexual misconduct laws remains permissible. This is blatant viewpoint discrimination.

. . . Simply put, *Rosenberger* is directly on point with regard to both forum analysis and viewpoint discrimination. The district court therefore properly concluded that § 16–1–28 as applied violates GLBA's First Amendment rights.

C. Whether § 16–1–28 Violates The First Amendment On Its Face

The district court also ruled that § 16–1–28 violates the First Amendment on its face. Facial invalidation of a statute is strong medicine and courts should be cautious in utilizing this drastic remedy. Generally, a statute should "be declared invalid to the extent that it reaches too far, but otherwise left intact." *Brockett v. Spokane Arcades, Inc.,* 472 U.S. 491, 504, 105 S.Ct. 2794, 2802, 86 L.Ed.2d 394 (1985). "The normal rule [is] that partial, rather than facial, invalidation is the required course." *Id.* Facial invalidation is therefore inappropriate unless the court is convinced "that the identified overbreadth is incurable and would taint all possible applications of the statute." *Id.; see also Secretary of State of Maryland v. Joseph H. Munson Co.,* 467 U.S. 947, 964–65, 104 S.Ct. 2839, 2850–51, 81 L.Ed.2d 786 (1984).

Thus, the dispositive question is whether the statute is capable of a narrowing interpretation that would render it constitutionally permissible.

. . . The district court concluded that the key language in the statute—"fosters or promotes a lifestyle or actions prohibited by the sodomy or sexual misconduct laws" and "encourages its members or encourages other persons to engage in [sodomy] or provide information or materials that explain how [sodomy] may be engaged in or performed."—was overbroad and not susceptible to a narrowing interpretation. We agree.

We would have to ignore the Supreme Court's instructions and rewrite the statute for it to pass constitutional muster because advocacy to violate the law is protected speech unless directed to inciting or producing imminent lawless action. *See Brandenburg v. Ohio,* 395 U.S. at 448, 89 S.Ct. at 1830. Therefore, § 16–1–28 is invalid on its face unless it could be interpreted as applying only to speech designed to incite or produce imminent lawless action. Such an interpretation is inconsistent with the plain meaning of the words of the statute. We agree with the district court that the statute is not capable of a narrowing interpretation and is therefore invalid on its face.

Conclusion

Section 16–1–28 on its face and as applied to GLBA results in viewpoint discrimination in violation of the First Amendment. Accordingly, we affirm the judgment of the district court.

AFFIRMED.

DISCUSSION

In Gay Lesbian Bisexual Alliance v. Pryor *the court followed* Rosenberger v. Rector & Visitors of the Univ. of Virginia, *515 U.S. 819, 115 S.Ct. 2510, 132 L.Ed.2d 700 (1995), holding that where a limited public forum is created, access to that forum cannot be denied based on the viewpoint of the speaker. Consider how a different version of this issue is explored in the following case.*

CHRISTIAN LEGAL SOCIETY CHAPTER OF THE UNIVERSITY OF CALIFORNIA, HASTINGS COLLEGE OF THE LAW, A/K/A HASTINGS CHRISTIAN FELLOWSHIP v. MARTINEZ ET AL.

___ U.S. ___, 130 S.Ct. 2971, 177 L.Ed.2d 838 (2010)

JUSTICE GINSBURG delivered the opinion of the Court.

In a series of decisions, this Court has emphasized that the First Amendment generally precludes public universities from denying student organizations access to school-sponsored forums because of the groups' viewpoints. *See Rosenberger v. Rector and Visitors of Univ. of Va.*, 515 U.S. 819, 115 S.Ct. 2510, 132 L.Ed.2d 700 (1995); *Widmar v. Vincent*, 454 U.S. 263, 102 S.Ct. 269, 70 L.Ed.2d 440 (1981); *Healy v. James*, 408 U.S. 169, 92 S.Ct. 2338, 33 L.Ed.2d 266 (1972). This case concerns a novel question regarding student activities at public universities: May a public law school condition its official recognition of a student group-and the attendant use of school funds and facilities-on the organization's agreement to open eligibility for membership and leadership to all students?

In the view of petitioner Christian Legal Society (CLS), an accept-all-comers policy impairs its First Amendment rights to free speech, expressive association, and free exercise of religion by prompting it, on pain of relinquishing the advantages of recognition, to accept members who do not share the organization's core beliefs about religion and sexual orientation. From the perspective of respondent Hastings College of the Law (Hastings or the Law School), CLS seeks special dispensation from an across-the-board open-access requirement designed to further the reasonable educational purposes underpinning the school's student-organization program.

. . .

I

. . .

Through its "Registered Student Organization" (RSO) program, Hastings extends official recognition to student groups. . . .

In exchange for these benefits, RSOs must abide by certain conditions. . . .

The Law School's Policy on Nondiscrimination (Nondiscrimination Policy), which binds RSOs, states:

> [Hastings] is committed to a policy against legally impermissible, arbitrary or unreasonable discriminatory practices. All groups, including administration, faculty, student governments, [Hastings]-owned student residence facilities and pro-grams sponsored by [Hastings], are governed by this policy of nondiscrimination. [Hasting's] policy on nondiscrimination is to comply fully with applicable law.
>
> [Hastings] shall not discriminate unlawfully on the basis of race, color, religion, national origin, ancestry, disability, age, sex or sexual orientation. This nondiscrimination policy covers admission, access and treatment in Hastings-sponsored programs and activities." *Id.*, at 220.
>
> Hastings interprets the Nondiscrimination Policy, as it relates to the RSO program, to mandate acceptance of all comers: School-approved groups must "allow any student to participate, become a member, or seek leadership positions in the organization, regardless of [her] status or beliefs." *Id.*, at 221.[1] Other law schools have adopted similar all-comers policies. . . . From Hastings' adoption of its Nondiscrimination Policy in 1990 until the events stirring this litigation, "no student organization at Hastings . . . ever sought an exemption from the Policy." App. 221.

In 2004, CLS became the first student group to do so. . . . CLS–National, an association of Christian lawyers and law students, charters student chapters at law schools throughout the country. *Id.*, at 225. CLS chapters must adopt bylaws that, inter alia, require members and officers to sign a "Statement of Faith" and to conduct their lives in accord with prescribed principles. *Id.* at 225–226; App. to Pet. for Cert. 101a. Among those tenets is the belief that sexual activity should not occur outside of marriage between a man and a woman; CLS thus interprets its bylaws to exclude from affiliation anyone who engages in "unrepentant homosexual conduct." App. 226. CLS also excludes students who hold religious convictions different from those in the Statement of Faith. *Id.*, at 227.

---

1. So long as all students have the opportunity to participate on equal terms, RSOs may require them, inter alia, to pay dues, maintain good attendance, refrain from gross misconduct, or pass a skill-based test, such as the writing competitions administered by law journals. See ibid. The dissent trumpets these neutral, generally applicable membership requirements, arguing that, in truth, Hastings has a "some-comers," not an all-comers, policy. Post, at 3001, 3004, 3005, 3012–3013, 3017–3018 (opinion of ALITO, J.). Hastings' open-access policy, however, requires only that student organizations open eligibility for membership and leadership regardless of a student's status or beliefs; dues, attendance, skill measurements, and comparable uniformly applied standards are fully compatible with the policy.

On September 17, 2004, CLS submitted to Hastings an application for RSO status, accompanied by all required documents, including the set of bylaws mandated by CLS–National. *Id.*, at 227–228. Several days later, the Law School rejected the application; CLS's bylaws, Hastings explained, did not comply with the Nondiscrimination Policy because CLS barred students based on religion and sexual orientation. *Id.*, at 228.

CLS formally requested an exemption from the Nondiscrimination Policy, *id.*, at 281, but Hastings declined to grant one. . . .

Refusing to alter its bylaws, CLS did not obtain RSO status. It did, however, operate independently during the 2004–2005 academic year. . . .

On October 22, 2004, CLS filed suit against various Hastings officers and administrators under 42 U.S.C. § 1983. Its complaint alleged that Hastings' refusal to grant the organization RSO status violated CLS's First and Fourteenth Amendment rights to free speech, expressive association, and free exercise of religion. The suit sought injunctive and declaratory relief. On cross-motions for summary judgment, the U.S. District Court for the Northern District of California ruled in favor of Hastings. . . . [The ruling was affirmed by the Ninth Circuit Court of Appeals and the United States Supreme Court granted certiorari.]

II

. . .

[The Court first determined that the facts that all parties stipulated to could not be changed.]

In light of the joint stipulation, both the District Court and the Ninth Circuit trained their attention on the constitutionality of the all-comers requirement, as described in the parties' accord. See 319 Fed. Appx., at 645–646; App. to Pet. for Cert. 32a; *Id.*, at 36a. We reject CLS's unseemly attempt to escape from the stipulation and shift its target to Hastings' policy as written. This opinion, therefore, considers only whether conditioning access to a student-organization forum on compliance with an all-comers policy violates the Constitution.

. . .

III

A.

In support of the argument that Hastings' all-comers policy treads on its First Amendment rights to free speech and expressive association, CLS draws on two lines of decisions. First, in a progression of cases, this Court has employed forum analysis to determine when a governmental entity, in regulating property in its charge, may place limitations on speech.[2] Recog-

2. . . . [G]overnmental entities establish limited public forums by opening property "limited to use by certain groups or dedicated solely to the discussion of certain subjects." Ibid. As noted in text, "[i]n such a forum, a govern-mental entity may impose restrictions on speech that are reasonable and view-point-neutral." *Ibid.*

nizing a State's right "to preserve the property under its control for the use to which it is lawfully dedicated," *Cornelius v. NAACP Legal Defense & Ed. Fund, Inc.*, 473 U.S. 788, 800, 105 S.Ct. 3439, 87 L.Ed.2d 567 (1985) (internal quotation marks omitted), the Court has permitted restrictions on access to a limited public forum, like the RSO program here, with this key caveat: Any access barrier must be reasonable and viewpoint neutral, *e.g., Rosenberger*, 515 U.S., at 829, 115 S.Ct. 2510. *See also, e.g., Good News Club v. Milford Central School*, 533 U.S. 98, 106–107, 121 S.Ct. 2093, 150 L.Ed.2d 151 (2001); *Lamb's Chapel v. Center Moriches Union Free School Dist.*, 508 U.S. 384, 392–393, 113 S.Ct. 2141, 124 L.Ed.2d 352 (1993); *Perry Ed. Assn. v. Perry Local Educators' Assn.*, 460 U.S. 37, 46, 103 S.Ct. 948, 74 L.Ed.2d 794 (1983).[3]

Second, as evidenced by another set of decisions, this Court has rigorously reviewed laws and regulations that constrain associational freedom. In the context of public accommodations, we have subjected restrictions on that freedom to close scrutiny; such restrictions are permitted only if they serve "compelling state interests" that are "unrelated to the suppression of ideas"—interests that cannot be advanced "through ... significantly less restrictive [means]." *Roberts v. United States Jaycees*, 468 U.S. 609, 623, 104 S.Ct. 3244, 82 L.Ed.2d 462 (1984). *See also, e.g., Boy Scouts of America v. Dale*, 530 U.S. 640, 648, 120 S.Ct. 2446, 147 L.Ed.2d 554 (2000). "Freedom of association," we have recognized, "plainly presupposes a freedom not to associate." *Roberts*, 468 U.S., at 623, 104 S.Ct. 3244. Insisting that an organization embrace unwelcome members, we have therefore concluded, "directly and immediately affects associational rights." *Dale*, 530 U.S., at 659, 120 S.Ct. 2446.

CLS would have us engage each line of cases independently, but its expressive-association and free-speech arguments merge: Who speaks on its behalf, CLS reasons, colors what concept is conveyed.... It therefore makes little sense to treat CLS's speech and association claims as discrete. *See Citizens Against Rent Control/Coalition for Fair Housing v. Berkeley*, 454 U.S. 290, 300, 102 S.Ct. 434, 70 L.Ed.2d 492 (1981). Instead, three observations lead us to conclude that our limited-public-forum precedents supply the appropriate framework for assessing both CLS's speech and association rights.

First, the same considerations that have led us to apply a less restrictive level of scrutiny to speech in limited public forums as compared to other environments, ..., apply with equal force to expressive association occurring in limited public forums. As just noted, speech and expressive-association rights are closely linked. *See Roberts*, 468 U.S., at 622, 104 S.Ct. 3244 (Associational freedom is "implicit in the right to engage in activities protected by the First Amendment."). When these intertwined rights arise in exactly the same context, it would be anomalous for a

3. Our decisions make clear, and the parties agree, that Hastings, through its RSO program, established a limited public forum. *See Rosenberger v. Rector and Visitors of Univ. of Va.*, 515 U.S. 819, 829, 115 S.Ct. 2510, 132 L.Ed.2d 700 (1995); Tr. of Oral Arg. 24 (counsel for CLS); Brief for Petitioner 25–26; Brief for Hastings 27–28; Brief for Hastings Outlaw 27.

restriction on speech to survive constitutional review under our limited-public-forum test only to be invalidated as an impermissible infringement of expressive association.... That result would be all the more anomalous in this case, for CLS suggests that its expressive-association claim plays a part auxiliary to speech's starring role....

Second, and closely related, the strict scrutiny we have applied in some settings to laws that burden expressive association would, in practical effect, in-validate a defining characteristic of limited public forums-the State may "reserv[e] [them] for certain groups." *Rosenberger*, 515 U.S., at 829, 115 S.Ct. 2510. *See also Perry Ed. Assn.*, 460 U.S., at 49, 103 S.Ct. 948 ("Implicit in the concept" of a limited public forum is the State's "right to make distinctions in access on the basis of ... speaker identity."); *Cornelius*, 473 U.S., at 806, 105 S.Ct. 3439 ("[A] speaker may be excluded from" a limited public forum "if he is not a member of the class of speakers for whose especial benefit the forum was created.").

Third, this case fits comfortably within the limited-public-forum category, for CLS, in seeking what is effectively a state subsidy, faces only indirect pressure to modify its membership policies; CLS may exclude any person for any reason if it forgoes the benefits of official recognition. The expressive-association precedents on which CLS relies, in contrast, involved regulations that compelled a group to include unwanted members, with no choice to opt out. *See, e.g., Dale*, 530 U.S., at 648, 120 S.Ct. 2446 (regulation "forc[ed] [the Boy Scouts] to accept members it [did] not desire" (internal quotation marks omitted))[.] ...

In sum, we are persuaded that our limited-public-forum precedents adequately respect both CLS's speech and expressive-association rights, and fairly balance those rights against Hastings' interests as property owner and educational institution. We turn to the merits of the instant dispute, therefore, with the limited-public-forum decisions as our guide.

B

... [W]e do not write on a blank slate; we have three times before considered clashes between public universities and student groups seeking official recognition or its attendant benefits. [The Court went on to discuss *Healy v. James*, 408 U.S. 169, 92 S. Ct. 2338, 33 L.Ed. 2d 266 (1972), *Widmar v. Vincent*, 454 U.S. 263, 102 S.Ct. 269, 70 L.Ed.2d 440 (1981); and *Rosenberger v. Rector and Visitors of Univ. of Va.*, 515 U.S. 819, 115 S.Ct. 2510, 132 L.Ed.2d 700 (1995).]

In all three cases, we ruled that student groups had been unconstitutionally singled out because of their points of view. "Once it has opened a limited [public] forum," we emphasized, "the State must respect the lawful boundaries it has itself set." *Id.*, at 829, 115 S.Ct. 2510. The constitutional constraints on the boundaries the State may set bear repetition here: "The State may not exclude speech where its distinction is not reasonable in light of the purpose served by the forum, ... nor may it discriminate against speech on the basis of ... viewpoint." *Ibid.* (internal quotation marks omitted).

C

. . .

1

Our inquiry is shaped by the educational context in which it arises: "First Amendment rights," we have observed, "must be analyzed in light of the special characteristics of the school environment." *Widmar*, 454 U.S., at 268, n. 5, 102 S.Ct. 269 (internal quotation marks omitted). This Court is the final arbiter of the question whether a public university has exceeded constitutional constraints, and we owe no deference to universities when we consider that question. *Cf.*... Cognizant that judges lack the on-the-ground expertise and experience of school administrators, however, we have cautioned courts in various contexts to resist "substitut[ing] their own notions of sound educational policy for those of the school authorities which they review." ...

... Schools, we have emphasized, enjoy "a significant measure of authority over the type of officially recognized activities in which their students participate." *Board of Ed. of Westside Community Schools (Dist.66) v. Mergens*, 496 U.S. 226, 240, 110 S.Ct. 2356, 110 L.Ed.2d 191 (1990). We therefore "approach our task with special caution," *Healy*, 408 U.S., at 171, 92 S.Ct. 2338, mindful that Hastings' decisions about the character of its student-group program are due decent respect.

2

With appropriate regard for school administrators' judgment, we review the justifications Hastings offers in defense of its all-comers requirement. First, the open-access policy "ensures that the leadership, educational, and social opportunities afforded by [RSOs] are available to all students." Brief for Hastings 32; *see* Brief for American Civil Liberties Union et al. as Amici Curiae 11. Just as "Hastings does not allow its professors to host classes open only to those students with a certain status or belief," so the Law School may decide, reasonably in our view, "that the ... educational experience is best promoted when all participants in the forum must provide equal access to all students." Brief for Hastings 32. RSOs, we count it significant, are eligible for financial assistance drawn from mandatory student-activity fees, *see supra*, at 2979; the all-comers policy ensures that no Hastings student is forced to fund a group that would reject her as a member.

Second, the all-comers requirement helps Hastings police the written terms of its Nondiscrimination Policy without inquiring into an RSO's motivation for membership restrictions. To bring the RSO program within CLS's view of the Constitution's limits, CLS proposes that Hastings permit exclusion because of belief but forbid discrimination due to status. *See* Tr. of Oral Arg. 18. But that proposal would impose on Hastings a daunting labor. How should the Law School go about determining whether a student organization cloaked prohibited status exclusion in belief-based garb? If a hypothetical Male–Superiority Club barred a female student from running for its presidency, for example, how could the Law School tell whether the group rejected her bid because of her sex or because, by seeking to lead the club, she manifested a lack of belief in its fundamental philosophy?

This case itself is instructive in this regard. CLS contends that it does not exclude individuals because of sexual orientation, but rather "on the basis of a conjunction of conduct and the belief that the conduct is not wrong." . . .

Third, the Law School reasonably adheres to the view that an all-comers policy, to the extent it brings together individuals with diverse backgrounds and beliefs, "encourages tolerance, cooperation, and learning among students." App. 349. And if the policy sometimes produces discord, Hastings can rationally rank among RSO-program goals development of conflict-resolution skills, toleration, and readiness to find common ground.

Fourth, Hastings' policy, which incorporates-in fact, subsumes-state-law proscriptions on discrimination, conveys the Law School's decision "to decline to subsidize with public monies and benefits conduct of which the people of California disapprove." Brief for Hastings 35; *id.*, at 33–34 (*citing* Cal. Educ.Code § 66270 (prohibiting discrimination on various bases)). State law, of course, may not command that public universities take action impermissible under the First Amendment. But so long as a public university does not contravene constitutional limits, its choice to advance state-law goals through the school's educational endeavors stands on firm footing.

In sum, the several justifications Hastings asserts in support of its all-comers requirement are surely reasonable in light of the RSO forum's purposes.

3

The Law School's policy is all the more credit-worthy in view of the "substantial alternative channels that remain open for [CLS-student] communication to take place." *Perry Ed. Assn.*, 460 U.S., at 53, 103 S.Ct. 948. If restrictions on access to a limited public forum are viewpoint discriminatory, the ability of a group to exist outside the forum would not cure the constitutional shortcoming. But when access barriers are viewpoint neutral, our decisions have counted it significant that other available avenues for the group to exercise its First Amendment rights lessen the burden created by those barriers. *See ibid.*; *Cornelius*, 473 U.S., at 809, 105 S.Ct. 3439; *Greer v. Spock*, 424 U.S. 828, 839, 96 S.Ct. 1211, 47 L.Ed.2d 505 (1976); *Pell*, 417 U.S., at 827–828, 94 S.Ct. 2800.

In this case, Hastings offered CLS access to school facilities to conduct meetings and the use of chalkboards and generally available bulletin boards to advertise events. App. 232–233. Although CLS could not take advantage of RSO-specific methods of communication, see supra, at 2979, the advent of electronic media and social-networking sites reduces the importance of those channels. . . .

Private groups, from fraternities and sororities to social clubs and secret societies, commonly maintain a presence at universities without official school affiliation. Based on the record before us, CLS was similarly situated: It hosted a variety of activities the year after Hastings denied it recognition, and the number of students attending those meetings and events doubled. App. 224, 229–230. "The variety and type of alternative modes of access present here," in short, "compare favorably with those in other [limited public] forum cases where we have upheld restrictions on access." *Perry Ed. Assn.*, 460 U.S., at 53–54, 103 S.Ct. 948. It is beyond dissenter's license, we note again, . . ., constantly to maintain that nonrecognition of a student organization is equivalent to prohibiting its members from speaking.

4

CLS nevertheless deems Hastings' all-comers policy "frankly absurd." Brief for Petitioner 49. "There can be no diversity of viewpoints in a forum," it asserts, "if groups are not permitted to form around viewpoints." *Id.*, at 50; *accord post*, at 3013 (ALITO, J., dissenting). This catchphrase confuses CLS's preferred policy with constitutional limitation—the advisability of Hastings' policy does not control its permissibility. *See Wood v. Strickland*, 420 U.S. 308, 326, 95 S.Ct. 992, 43 L.Ed.2d 214 (1975). Instead, we have repeatedly stressed that a State's restriction on access to a limited public forum "need not be the most reasonable or the only reasonable limitation." *Cornelius*, 473 U.S., at 808, 105 S.Ct. 3439.

CLS also assails the reasonableness of the all-comers policy in light of the RSO forum's function by forecasting that the policy will facilitate hostile takeovers; if organizations must open their arms to all, CLS contends, saboteurs will infiltrate groups to subvert their mission and message. This supposition strikes us as more hypothetical than real. CLS points to no history or prospect of RSO-hijackings at Hastings. . . . Students tend to self-sort and presumably will not endeavor en masse to join—let alone seek leadership positions in—groups pursuing missions wholly at odds with their personal beliefs. And if a rogue student intent on sabotaging an organization's objectives nevertheless attempted a takeover, the members of that group would not likely elect her as an officer.

. . .

Hastings, furthermore, could reasonably expect more from its law students than the disruptive behavior CLS hypothesizes—and to build this expectation into its educational approach. . . . If students begin to exploit an all-comers policy by hijacking organizations to distort or destroy their missions, Hastings presumably would revisit and revise its policy. . . .

Finally, CLS asserts (and the dissent repeats, post, at 3015–3016) that the Law School lacks any legitimate interest—let alone one reasonably related to the RSO forum's purposes—in urging "religious groups not to favor co-religionists for purposes of their religious activities." Brief for Petitioner 43; *id.*, at 50. CLS's analytical error lies in focusing on the benefits it must forgo while ignoring the interests of those it seeks to fence out: Exclusion, after all, has two sides. Hastings, caught in the crossfire between a group's desire to exclude and students' demand for equal access, may reasonably draw a line in the sand permitting all organizations to express what they wish but no group to discriminate in membership.[4]

D

We next consider whether Hastings' all-comers policy is viewpoint neutral.

1

Although this aspect of limited-public-forum analysis has been the constitutional sticking point in our prior decisions, as earlier recounted, supra, at 2987–2988, we need not dwell on it here. It is, after all, hard to imagine a more viewpoint-neutral policy than one requiring all student groups to accept all comers. In contrast to *Healy, Widmar*, and *Rosenberger*, in which universities singled out organizations for disfavored treatment because of their points of view, Hastings' all-comers requirement draws no distinction between groups based on their message or perspective. An all-comers condition on access to RSO status, in short, is textbook viewpoint neutral.

2

. . .

Finding Hastings' open-access condition on RSO status reasonable and viewpoint neutral, we reject CLS' free-speech and expressive-association claims.

. . .

For the foregoing reasons, we affirm the Court of Appeals' ruling that the all-comers policy is constitutional and remand the case for further proceedings consistent with this opinion.

It is so ordered.

JUSTICE STEVENS, concurring. [Omitted]

JUSTICE KENNEDY, concurring. [Omitted]

4. In arguing that the all-comers policy is not reasonable in light of the RSO forum's purposes, the dissent notes that Title VII, which prohibits employment discrimination on the basis of religion, among other categories, provides an exception for religious associations. *Post*, at 3015, n. 8. The question here, however, is not whether Hastings could, consistent with the Constitution, provide religious groups dispensation from the all-comers policy by permitting them to re-strict membership to those who share their faith. It is instead whether Hastings must grant that exemption. This Court's decision in *Employment Div., Dept. of Human Resources of Ore. v. Smith*, 494 U.S. 872, 878–882, 110 S.Ct. 1595, 108 L.Ed.2d 876 (1990), unequivocally answers no to that latter question. *See also infra*, at 2995, n. 27.

JUSTICE ALITO, with whom THE CHIEF JUSTICE, JUSTICE SCALIA, and JUSTICE THOMAS join, dissenting.

The proudest boast of our free speech jurisprudence is that we protect the freedom to express "the thought that we hate." *United States v. Schwimmer*, 279 U.S. 644, 654–655, 49 S.Ct. 448, 73 L.Ed. 889 (1929) (Holmes, J., dissenting). Today's decision rests on a very different principle: no freedom for expression that offends prevailing standards of political correctness in our country's institutions of higher learning.

. . .

I

. . .

A

The Court bases all of its analysis on the proposition that the relevant Hastings' policy is the so-called accept-all-comers policy.... Overwhelming evidence, however, shows that Hastings denied CLS's application pursuant to the Nondiscrimination Policy and that the accept-all-comers policy was nowhere to be found until it was mentioned by a former dean in a deposition taken well after this case began.

. . .

When CLS applied for registration, Judy Hansen Chapman, the Director of Hastings' Office of Student Services, sent an e-mail to an officer of the chapter informing him that "CLS's bylaws did not appear to be compliant" with the Hastings Nondiscrimination Policy[.] As far as the record reflects, Ms. Chapman made no mention of an accept-all-applicants policy. A few days later, three officers of the chapter met with Ms. Chapman, and she reiterated that the CLS bylaws did not comply with "the religion and sexual orientation provisions of the Nondiscrimination Policy and that they would need to be amended in order for CLS to become a registered student organization." *Id.*, at 228. About a week later, Hastings sent CLS a letter to the same effect. *Id.*, at 228–229, 293–295. On both of these occasions, it appears that not a word was said about an accept-all-comers policy.

. . .

In its complaint, CLS had alleged that the Nondiscrimination Policy discriminates against religious groups because it prohibits those groups "from selecting officers and members dedicated to a particular set of religious ideals or beliefs" but "permits political, social and cultural student organizations to select officers and members dedicated to their organization's ideals and beliefs." *Id.*, at 79. In response, Hastings admitted that its Nondiscrimination Policy "permits political, social, and cultural student organizations to select officers and members who are dedicated to a particular set of ideals or beliefs." *Id.*, at 93. The Court states that "Hastings interprets the Nondiscrimination Policy, as it relates to the RSO program, to mandate acceptance of all comers." *Ante*, at 2979. But this admission in Hastings' answer shows that Hastings had not adopted this interpretation when its answer was filed.

Within a few months, however, Hastings' position changed. In July 2005, Mary Kay Kane, then the dean of the law school, was deposed, and she stated: "It is my view that in order to be a registered student organization you have to allow all of our students to be members and full participants if they want to." App. 343. In a declaration filed in October 2005, Ms. Chapman provided a more developed explanation, stating: "Hastings interprets the Nondiscrimination Policy as requiring that student organizations wishing to register with Hastings allow any Hastings student to become a member and/or seek a leadership position in the organization." *Id.*, at 349.

Hastings claims that this accept-all-comers policy has existed since 1990 but points to no evidence that the policy was ever put in writing or brought to the attention of members of the law school community prior to the dean's deposition. . . .

Hastings' effort to portray the accept-all-comers policy as merely an interpretation of the Nondiscrimination Policy runs into obvious difficulties. First, the two policies are simply not the same: The Nondiscrimination Policy proscribes discrimination on a limited number of specified grounds, while the accept-all-comers policy outlaws all selectivity. Second, the Nondiscrimination Policy applies to everything that Hastings does, and the law school does not follow an accept-all-comers policy in activities such as admitting students and hiring faculty.

. . .

Third, the record is replete with evidence that, at least until Dean Kane unveiled the accept-all-comers policy in July 2005, Hastings routinely registered student groups with bylaws limiting membership and leadership positions to those who agreed with the groups' viewpoints. [Several specific examples of these were given.]

We are told that, when CLS pointed out these discrepancies during this litigation, Hastings took action to ensure that student groups were in fact complying with the law school's newly disclosed accept-all-comers policy. For example, Hastings asked La Raza to revise its bylaws to allow all students to become voting members. App. to Pet. for Cert. 66a. *See also* Brief for State of Michigan et al. as Amici Curiae 2, n. 1 (relating anecdotally that Hastings recently notified the Hastings Democrats that "to maintain the Club's standing as a student organization," it must "open its membership to all students, regardless of party affiliation"). These belated re-medial efforts suggest, if anything, that Hastings had no accept-all-comers policy until this litigation was well under way.

Finally, when Hastings filed its brief in this Court, its policy, which had already evolved from a policy prohibiting certain specified forms of discrimination into an accept-all-comers policy, underwent yet another transformation. Now, Hastings claims that it does not really have an accept-all-comers policy; it has an accept-some-comers policy. Hastings' current policy, we are told, "does not foreclose neutral and generally applicable membership requirements unrelated to 'status or beliefs.'" Brief for Respondent Hastings College of Law 5. Hastings' brief goes on to note with seeming approval that some registered groups have imposed "even conduct requirements." *Ibid.* Hastings, however, has not told us which "conduct requirements" are allowed and which are not-although presumably requirements regarding sexual conduct fall into the latter category.

When this case was in the District Court, that court took care to address both the Nondiscrimination Policy and the accept-all-comers policy. *See, e.g.*, App. to Pet. for Cert. 8a–9a, 16a–17a, 21a–24a, 26a, 27a, 32a, 44a, 63a. On appeal, however, a panel of the Ninth Circuit, like the Court today, totally ignored the Nondiscrimination Policy....

Like the majority of this Court, the Ninth Circuit relied on the following Joint Stipulation, which the parties filed in December 2005, well after Dean Kane's deposition: "Hastings requires that registered student organizations allow any student to participate, become a member, or seek leadership positions in the organization, regardless of their status or beliefs." App. 221.

Citing the binding effect of stipulations, the majority sternly rejects what it terms "CLS's unseemly attempt to escape from the stipulation and shift its target to [the Nondiscrimination Policy]." *Ante*, at 2984.

I agree that the parties must be held to their Joint Stipulation, but the terms of the stipulation should be respected. What was admitted in the Joint Stipulation filed in December 2005 is that Hastings had an accept-all-comers policy. CLS did not stipulate that its application had been denied more than a year earlier pursuant to such a policy. On the contrary, the Joint Stipulation notes that the reason repeatedly given by Hastings at that time was that the CLS bylaws did not comply with the Nondiscrimination Policy. *See* App. 228–229. Indeed, the parties did not even stipulate that the accept-all-comers policy existed in the fall of 2004. In addition, Hastings itself is now attempting to walk away from this stipulation by disclosing that its real policy is an accept-some-comers policy.

. . .

III

The Court pays little attention to *Healy* and instead focuses solely on the question whether Hastings' registration policy represents a permissible regulation in a limited public forum.... In this case, the forum consists of the RSO program. Once a public university opens a limited public forum, it "must respect the lawful boundaries it has itself set." *Rosenberger v. Rector and Visitors of Univ. of Va.*, 515 U.S. 819, 829, 115 S.Ct. 2510, 132 L.Ed.2d 700 (1995). The university "may not exclude speech where its distinction is not 'reasonable in light of the purpose served by the forum.' " *Ibid.* (*quoting Cornelius v. NAACP Legal Defense & Ed. Fund, Inc.*, 473 U.S. 788, 806, 105 S.Ct. 3439, 87 L.Ed.2d 567 (1985)). And the university must maintain strict viewpoint neutrality. *Board of Regents of Univ. of Wis. System v. Southworth*, 529 U.S. 217, 234, 120 S.Ct. 1346, 146 L.Ed.2d 193 (2000); *Rosenberger, supra*, at 829, 115 S.Ct. 2510.

This requirement of viewpoint neutrality extends to the expression of religious viewpoints. In an un-broken line of decisions analyzing private religious speech in limited public forums, we have made it perfectly clear that "[r]eligion is [a] viewpoint from which ideas are conveyed." *Good News Club v. Milford Central School*, 533 U.S. 98, 112, and n. 4, 121 S.Ct. 2093, 150 L.Ed.2d 151 (2001). *See Rosenberger, supra*, at 831, 115 S.Ct. 2510; *Lamb's Chapel v. Center Moriches Union Free School Dist.*, 508 U.S. 384, 393–394, 113 S.Ct. 2141, 124 L.Ed.2d 352 (1993); *Widmar v. Vincent*, 454 U.S. 263, 277, 102 S.Ct. 269, 70 L.Ed.2d 440 (1981).

We have applied this analysis in cases in which student speech was restricted because of the speaker's religious viewpoint, and we have consistently concluded that such restrictions constitute viewpoint discrimination. *E.g., Rosenberger, supra*, at 845–846, 115 S.Ct. 2510; *Widmar, supra*, at 267, n. 5, 269, 277, 102 S.Ct. 269; *see also Good News Club, supra*, at 106–107, 109–110, 121 S.Ct. 2093; *Lamb's Chapel, supra*, at 392–393, 394, 113 S.Ct. 2141. We have also stressed that the rules applicable in a limited public forum are particularly important in the university setting, where "the State acts against a background of tradition of thought and experiment that is at the center of our intellectual and philosophic tradition." *Rosenberger, supra*, at 835, 115 S.Ct. 2510.

IV

Analyzed under this framework, Hastings' refusal to register CLS pursuant to its Nondiscrimination Policy plainly fails. As previously noted, when Hastings refused to register CLS, it claimed that the CLS bylaws impermissibly discriminated on the basis of religion and sexual orientation. As interpreted by Hastings and applied to CLS, both of these grounds constituted viewpoint discrimination.

Religion. The First Amendment protects the right of " 'expressive association' "—that is, "the right to associate for the purpose of speaking." *Rumsfeld v. Forum for Academic and Institutional Rights, Inc.*, 547 U.S. 47, 68, 126 S.Ct. 1297, 164 L.Ed.2d 156 (2006) (*quoting Boy Scouts of America v. Dale*, 530 U.S. 640, 644, 120 S.Ct. 2446, 147 L.Ed.2d 554 (2000)). And the Court has recognized that "[t]he forced inclusion of an unwanted person in a group infringes the group's freedom of expressive association if the presence of that person affects in a significant way the group's ability to advocate public or private viewpoints." *Dale*, supra, at 648.

With one important exception, the Hastings Nondiscrimination Policy respected that right. As Hastings stated in its answer, the Nondiscrimination Policy "permit[ted] political, social, and cultural student organizations to select officers and members who are dedicated to a particular set of ideals or beliefs." App. 93. But the policy singled out one category of expressive associations for disfavored treatment: groups formed to express a religious message. Only religious groups were required to admit students who did not share their views. An environmentalist group was not required to admit students who rejected global warming. An animal rights group was not obligated to accept students who supported the use of animals to test cosmetics. But CLS was required to admit avowed atheists. This was patent viewpoint discrimination. "By the very terms of the [Nondiscrimination Policy], the University ... select[ed] for disfavored treatment those student [groups] with religious ... viewpoints." *Rosenberger*, 515 U.S., at 831, 115 S.Ct. 2510. It is no wonder that the Court makes no attempt to defend the constitutionality of the Nondiscrimination Policy.

. . .

[...] As our cases have recognized, the right of expressive association permits a group to exclude an applicant for membership only if the admission of that person would "affec[t] in a significant way the group's ability to advocate public or private viewpoints." *Dale*, 530 U.S., at 648, 120 S.Ct. 2446. Groups that do not engage in expressive association have no such right.

Similarly, groups that are dedicated to expressing a viewpoint on a secular topic (for example, a political or ideological viewpoint) would have no basis for limiting membership based on religion because the presence of members with diverse religious beliefs would have no effect on the group's ability to express its views. But for religious groups, the situation is very different....

VI

I come now to the version of Hastings' policy that the Court has chosen to address. This is not the policy that Hastings invoked when CLS was denied registration. Nor is it the policy that Hastings now proclaims-and presumably implements. It is a policy that, as far as the record establishes, was in force only from the time when it was first disclosed by the former dean in July 2005 until Hastings filed its brief in this Court in March 2010. Why we should train our attention on this particular policy and not the other two is a puzzle. But in any event, it is clear that the accept-all-comers policy is not reasonable in light of the purpose of the RSO forum, and it is impossible to say on the present record that it is viewpoint neutral.

A

. . .

Taken as a whole, the regulations plainly contemplate the creation of a forum within which Hastings students are free to form and obtain registration of essentially the same broad range of private groups that nonstudents may form off campus. . . .

The way in which the RSO forum actually developed corroborates this design. As noted, Hastings had more than 60 RSOs in 2004–2005, each with its own independently devised purpose. . . . In short, the RSO forum, true to its design, has allowed Hastings students to replicate on campus a broad array of private, independent, noncommercial organizations that is very similar to those that nonstudents have formed in the outside world.

The accept-all-comers policy is antithetical to the design of the RSO forum for the same reason that a state-imposed accept-all-comers policy would violate the First Amendment rights of private groups if applied off campus. . . . The State of California surely could not demand that all Christian groups admit members who believe that Jesus was merely human. Jewish groups could not be required to admit anti-Semites and Holocaust deniers. Muslim groups could not be forced to admit persons who are viewed as slandering Islam.

While there can be no question that the State of California could not impose such restrictions on all religious groups in the State, the Court now holds that Hastings, a state institution, may impose these very same requirements on students who wish to participate in a forum that is designed to foster the expression of diverse viewpoints. The Court lists four justifications offered by Hastings in defense of the accept-all-comers policy and, deferring to the school's judgment, *ante*, at 2989, the Court finds all those justifications satisfactory, *ante*, at 2989–2991. If we carry out our responsibility to exercise our own in-dependent judgment, however, we must conclude that the justifications offered by Hastings and accepted by the Court are insufficient.

. . .

In sum, Hastings' accept-all-comers policy is not reasonable in light of the stipulated purpose of the RSO forum: to promote a diversity of viewpoints "among "—not within—"registered student organizations." App. 216 (emphasis added).

B

The Court is also wrong in holding that the accept-all-comers policy is viewpoint neutral. . . . The adoption of a facially neutral policy for the purpose of suppressing the expression of a particular viewpoint is viewpoint discrimination. . . . A simple example illustrates this obvious point. Suppose that a hated student group at a state university has never been able to attract more than 10 members. Suppose that the university administration, for the purpose of preventing that group from using the school grounds for meetings, adopts a new rule under which the use of its facilities is restricted to groups with more than 25 members. Although this rule would be neutral on its face, its adoption for a discriminatory reason would be illegal.

Here, CLS has made a strong showing that Hastings' sudden adoption and selective application of its accept-all-comers policy was a pretext for the law school's unlawful denial of CLS's registration application under the Nondiscrimination Policy.

. . .

C

One final aspect of the Court's decision warrants comment. In response to the argument that the accept-all-comers-policy would permit a small and un-popular group to be taken over by students who wish to silence its message, the Court states that the policy would permit a registered group to impose membership requirements "designed to ensure that students join because of their commitment to a group's vitality, not its demise." *Ante*, at 2992. With this concession, the Court tacitly recognizes that Hastings does not really have an accept-all-comers policy—it has an accept-some-dissident-comers policy—and the line between members who merely seek to change a group's message (who apparently must be admitted) and those who seek a group's "demise" (who may be kept out) is hopelessly vague.

. . .

In the end, the Court refuses to acknowledge the consequences of its holding. A true accept-all-comers policy permits small unpopular groups to be taken over by students who wish to change the views that the group expresses. Rules requiring that members attend meetings, pay dues, and behave politely, *see ante*, at 2992, would not eliminate this threat.

The possibility of such takeovers, however, is by no means the most important effect of the Court's holding. There are religious groups that cannot in good conscience agree in their bylaws that they will admit persons who do not share their faith, and for these groups, the consequence of an accept-all-comers policy is marginalization.... This is where the Court's decision leads. I do not think it is an exaggeration to say that today's decision is a serious setback for freedom of expression in this country. Our First Amendment reflects a "profound national commitment to the principle that debate on public issues should be uninhibited, robust, and wide-open." *New York Times Co. v. Sullivan*, 376 U.S. 254, 270, 84 S.Ct. 710, 11 L.Ed.2d 686 (1964). Even if the United States is the only Nation that shares this commitment to the same extent, I would not change our law to conform to the international norm. I fear that the Court's decision marks a turn in that direction. Even those who find CLS's views objectionable should be concerned about the way the group has been treated—by Hastings, the Court of Appeals, and now this Court. I can only hope that this decision will turn out to be an aberration.

B. SPEECH RIGHTS OF GAY PUBLIC EMPLOYEES

WEAVER v. NEBO SCH. DIST.

29 F.Supp.2d 1279 (D. Utah 1998)

JUDGE: BRUCE S. JENKINS

. . .

Factual Background

For the past nineteen years, plaintiff Wendy Weaver has been a teacher at Spanish Fork High School in the Nebo School District. Ms. Weaver, a tenured faculty member since 1982, teaches psychology and physical education. Her reputation as an educator at Spanish Fork is unblemished: she has always been considered an effective and capable teacher, her evaluations range from good to excellent, and she has never been the subject of any disciplinary action.

In addition to her teaching responsibilities, Ms. Weaver has served as the girl's volleyball coach since 1979. She has been effective in this endeavor, leading the team to four state championships.

Unlike her teaching position, however, Ms. Weaver's position as coach was not tenured. Instead, as is the case with all coaching positions at Spanish Fork High School, Ms. Weaver was hired as volleyball coach on a year-to-year basis. For each year she was hired as coach, Ms. Weaver received a stipend, which in her most recent year of coaching was $1,500. The practice of hiring coaches, however, is somewhat informal. It is the policy of the School District that Principal Wadley has final decision-making authority in selecting a coach. Generally, Principal Wadley finds out who has an interest, selects a coach from the interested candidates, and notifies the coach that he or she has the position. No written contract is prepared. In practice, the coach from the previous year is routinely offered the position for the following year, or, as Principal Wadley stated, "you assign them once and they stay assigned until you assign someone else."

During the 1995 and 1996 school years, Ms. Weaver did not coach the volleyball team. With the consent of Principal Wadley, she took a break from her coaching duties to pursue a master's degree at the University of Utah. She did, however, anticipate a return to coaching in 1997, an anticipation she shared with Principal Wadley. In the spring of 1997, after completing her graduate work, Ms. Weaver again met with Principal Wadley and told him that she was prepared to return to coaching.

In the late spring and early summer of 1997, Ms. Weaver began preparing for the upcoming school volleyball season—as she did in the past—by organizing two summer volleyball camps for prospective team players. As usual, these camps were to be held at Spanish Fork High

School in June and July of 1997. Ms. Weaver telephoned prospective volleyball team members to inform them of the camp schedules. One of the calls went to a senior team member. During the conversation, the team member asked Ms. Weaver. "Are you gay?" Ms. Weaver truthfully responded, "Yes." The team member then told Ms. Weaver that she would not play on the volleyball team in the fall. On July 14, 1997, the team member and her parents met with defendants Almon Mosher, Director of Human Resources for the Nebo School District, and Larry Kimball, Director of Secondary Education for the Nebo School District, and told them that Ms. Weaver told them that she is gay and that the team member decided she would not play volleyball.

In April of 1997, Gary Weaver, Ms. Weaver's ex-husband and a school psychologist for the Nebo School District, spoke with Principal Wadley about Ms. Weaver's sexual orientation. In May of 1997, Nedra Call, the Curriculum Coordinator for the School District, received two calls concerning Ms. Weaver's "lifestyle and her actions." She related the substance of these calls to defendant Mosher. Defendant Dennis Poulsen, Superintendent of the Nebo School District, also received calls about Ms. Weaver. In addition, several adults affiliated or formerly affiliated with the school contacted Principal Wadley with comments or questions about Ms. Weaver's sexual orientation. Principal Wadley held a meeting with his two assistant principals to discuss Ms. Weaver's sexual orientation. On May 22, 1997, before the phone conversation with Ms. Weaver, the team member and her mother telephoned Principal Wadley to let him know that the team member would not be playing volleyball because she was uncomfortable playing on the team knowing that Ms. Weaver is gay. On May 22nd, Principal Wadley discussed Ms. Weaver's sexual orientation with defendant Larry Kimball. Even the School Advisory Council wanted to discuss Ms. Weaver's sexual orientation.

In response to these reports, and after meeting again with the team member's family on July 14, 1997, defendants Mosher and Kimball discussed taking some action against Ms. Weaver because they felt Ms. Weaver's comments about her sexual orientation were in "violation of district policy." Several days later, on July 21, 1997, Ms. Weaver met with Principal Wadley, who informed her that she would not be assigned to coach volleyball for the 1997–98 school year. This discussion was memorialized in a letter to Ms. Weaver dated the same day but sent subsequently.

The following day, Ms. Weaver was called to a meeting at the School District office and presented a letter, printed on the School District letterhead, which reads in part:

> The District has received reports that you have made public and expressed to students your homosexual orientation and lifestyle. If these reports are true, we are concerned about the potential disruption in the school community and advise you of the following:

> — You are not to make any comments, announcements or statements to students, staff members, or parents of students regarding your homosexual orientation or lifestyle.
>
> — If students, staff members, or parents of students ask about your sexual orientation or anything concerning the subject, you shall tell them that the subject is private and personal and inappropriate to discuss with them.
>
> — This memo is to place you on notice of the expectations the school district has for you concerning this matter. A violation of these requirements may jeopardize your job and be cause for termination.

The letter was drafted by defendant Mosher, signed by him and Larry Kimball, was reviewed by defendant Dennis Poulsen, delivered to Ms. Weaver, and placed in her personnel file.

On August 8, 1997, a similar letter was issued to Gary Weaver. It reads in part:

> The District has received reports that you have made remarks within the school setting about your ex-wife's sexual orientation. If these reports are true we . . . advise you of the following:
>
> You are not to make comments, announcements or statements to students, staff members, or parents regarding your ex-wife's sexual orientation.
>
> If students, staff members or parents of students ask about your ex-wife's sexual orientation, you shall tell them the subject is private and personal and inappropriate to discuss with them.
>
> This memo is to place you on notice of the expectations the school district has for you concerning this matter. A violation of these requirements may jeopardize your job and be cause for termination.

This letter was delivered to Mr. Weaver and placed in his personnel file.

On October 20, 1997, Ms. Weaver commenced an action in this court under 42 U.S.C. § 1983 challenging the restraints on her speech contained in the July 22 letter as well as her removal as volleyball coach. Nine days after the action was filed, the School District delivered another letter to Ms. Weaver, to "clarify" the July 22 letter. In part, the October 29, 1997 letter reads:

> The District's intent with the July 22 letter was that the foregoing restrictions [contained in the July 22 letter] on your communications apply only while you are acting within the course and scope of your duties as a teacher for the District. Our main areas of concern are situations such as classroom teaching, extracurricular school-sponsored activities and parent-teacher conferences where, we believe, discussion of one's sexual orientation would be inappropriate. We believed that this intent was apparent in the July 22 letter from the fact that it was written on District stationary and addressed the issue of "disruption in the school community."

As further clarification of the July 22 letter, we strongly encourage you to avoid discussions of the foregoing matters at any time with students because we believe that in virtually any interaction you have with a student, including off-campus contacts, you are always perceived by the student as a teacher, authority figure and role model.

The letter, printed on the School District's letterhead, was signed by defendants Mosher and. Kimball, and, like the July 22 letter, placed in Ms. Weaver's personnel file.

Discussion

Ms. Weaver makes the following claims:

1. The letters dated July 22 and October 29 directed to her, and particularly the restrictions on speech contained therein, are vague and overbroad and restrain constitutionally protected speech.

2. Her removal as volleyball coach was based on an impermissible reason—namely sexual orientation—and thus violates the Fourteenth Amendment of the United States Constitution.

Ms. Weaver has moved for summary judgment on these claims. The defendants have cross-moved for summary judgment. In their motion for summary judgment and in their opposition to plaintiff's motion, the defendants assert that there are no issues of material fact that would prevent the court from ruling on either motion. Indeed, the defendants do not contest the operative facts that plaintiff has set forth. Rather, the defendants assert that under those facts they are entitled to summary judgment. Thus, because there is no genuine issue of material fact, the court is in a position to apply the law to the facts as presented in the motions. *See* Fed. R. Civ. P. 56(c); D.U. Civ. R. 56–1(c).

I.

Much of this case is controlled by the interpretation of a phrase drafted some 209 years ago that is the keystone of freedom. In language now famous, the First Amendment states: "Congress shall make no law . . . abridging the freedom of speech. . . ."

. . . The First Amendment, of course, is made applicable to the States by the Due Process Clause of the Fourteenth Amendment. Guided by these general principles, the court turns to the questions presented in this case.

Both sides agree that because of the uniqueness of a high school environment, and the existence of a School District "Healthy Responsible Lifestyles Education" policy, Ms. Weaver may not speak about her sexual orientation in the classroom. Instead, what the dispute centers on is whether the School District's restrictions go beyond the classroom and unconstitutionally infringe on Ms. Weaver's right to speak in public.

Because Ms. Weaver, in her role as teacher and coach, is a public employee, the appropriate measure of whether the School District's restrictions violate the First Amendment is found in a two-step analysis set forth in *Pickering v. Board of Educ. of Township High Sch. Dist. 205*, 391 U.S. 563, 88 S.Ct. 1731, 20 L.Ed.2d 811 (1968). The first step in this analysis is whether the employee's speech or actions, whether inside or outside the workplace, address a matter of public concern or are otherwise protected under the First Amendment. *See Id. at* 568; *Connick v. Myers*, 461 U.S. 138, 146, 75 L.Ed.2d 708, 103 S.Ct. 1684 (1983). If the first step is satisfied, the court must then balance the employee's interest in commenting on matters of public concern with the government's interest, as an employer, in promoting workplace efficiency. *Pickering*, 391 U.S. at 568. If the "government's interests" do not outweigh the "employee's interests," then any restriction on employee speech violates the First Amendment. *See id.* Thus, if Ms. Weaver's speech about her sexual orientation is matter of "public concern," it may not be restricted off the job unless the School District can show that her speech adversely affects the functioning of the school.

Additional High Court guidance on speech restrictions in a school setting is provided by *Tinker v. Des Moines Indep. Sch. Dist.*, 393 U.S. 503, 21 L.Ed.2d 731, 89 S.Ct. 733 (1969). Under *Tinker*, speech made outside a school-sponsored activity, such as a school newspaper, a classroom discussion, or an assembly, may not be restricted unless it is shown that the speech "would materially and substantially interfere with the requirements of appropriate discipline in the operation of the school." 393 U.S. at 509; *see also National Gay Task Force v. Board of Educ. of the City of Oklahoma City*, 729 F.2d 1270, 1274 (10th Cir. 1984) (citing *Tinker* and noting that the state's interest outweigh a teacher's interest in publicly speaking about sexual orientation only "when the expression results in a material or substantial interference or disruption in the normal activities of the school"), *aff'd by an equally divided Court*, 470 U.S. 903 (1985).

Defendants assert that Ms. Weaver's First Amendment claim must fail because she cannot meet the first requirement of *Pickering*—that is, she cannot demonstrate that her sexual orientation is a matter of public concern. Certain issues may be considered "inherently of public concern." *See Connick*, 461 U.S. at 148, n.8. (noting racial discrimination as one example). Several legal authorities have suggested that one's identity as a homosexual—even though it is in essence a private matter—is inherently a matter of public concern because it "necessarily and ineluctably" involves that person in the ongoing public debate regarding the rights of homosexuals. *See, e.g., Rowland v. Mad River Local School District, Montgomery County, Ohio,* 470 U.S. 1009, 1012, 84 L.Ed.2d 392, 105 S.Ct. 1373 (1985) (Brennan, J., dissenting from denial of certiorari). Thus, it could be said that a voluntary "coming out" or an involuntary "outing" of a gay, lesbian, or bisexual teacher would always be a matter of public concern. Indeed, the public reaction in the Nebo School District to the rumors about Ms. Weaver's sexual orientation clearly evidence public concern over her sexual orientation.

Even if Ms. Weaver's statement about her sexual orientation in response to a question is not viewed as a matter of public concern, the actions of the defendants—taken before Ms. Weaver ever spoke on the topic—transmuted what should have been a private issue into a matter of public concern. First, Ms. Weaver's ex-husband began publicly disclosing her sexual orientation in April 1997. He spoke with several of the faculty members of the School District and with Principal Wadley. These comments apparently reached members of the community, who then called Principal Wadley. One community member (who was also a former staff member at Spanish Fork High School) called after purportedly seeing Ms. Weaver and her companion walking arm-in-arm at a community softball game. In addition, Principal Wadley discussed Ms. Weaver's sexual orientation at a meeting with his assistant principals. He also spoke with School District Director Kimball regarding the rumors of Ms. Weaver's sexual orientation. And, finally, the School Advisory Council wanted to discuss Ms. Weaver's sexuality at a public meeting. Each of these events pre-dates the telephone call in June of 1997 when Ms. Weaver first mentioned, in a private conversation, that she was a lesbian. Thus, even if a Utah County public school teacher's status as a lesbian could ever be considered a matter of private concern—as defendants unpersuasively argue—defendants' actions converted this issue to a matter of public concern.

Turning to the second step, the court must next determine whether the School District's "interests" outweigh Ms. Weaver's "interests" in acknowledging her sexual orientation and living her life openly as a lesbian. The School District must demonstrate that allowing Ms. Weaver to speak about her sexual orientation would result in a "material and substantial interference or disruption" in the normal activities of the school. *See Tinker*, 393 U.S. at 509; *National Gay Task Force*, 729 F.2d at 1274.

It is clear to this court that on this record no such showing has been made nor can be made.

The defendants point to the several inquiries and complaints they received from some members of the community regarding Ms. Weaver's sexual orientation as evidence of a sufficient "disruption" to justify its efforts to restrict Ms. Weaver's speech. As the record now stands, however, it cannot be said that "her speech" caused a material or substantial disruption. As counsel for Ms. Weaver aptly noted, one of the duties a school administrator undertakes is the handling of student, faculty, parent, and community complaints. Ms. Weaver continued to teach her classes without any problems. Indeed, the defendants have been unable to point to any actual disruptive events since Ms. Weaver's sexual orientation became public knowledge.

The statement from a student and volleyball team member that she felt uncomfortable about playing for Ms. Weaver, and that she would not play volleyball in her senior year, is just that. While this student's actions may have interrupted her own activities, there is no evidence that the activities of the school were in any way disrupted. It cannot be said that a single student's decision not to take part in a wholly voluntary extracurricular activity can support a showing of a "material and substantial" disruption in the school's activities. *See* National Gay Task Force, 729 F.2d at 1274.

Thus, because the record makes clear that Ms. Weaver's right to express her sexual orientation outside the classroom would not, and indeed did not, result in a material or substantial disruption in the school, to the extent the July 22 and October 29 letters limit her speech in this area, they violate the First Amendment.

Turning first to the July 22 letter. As drafted by defendant Mosher, the letter prohibits Ms. Weaver from discussing her "homosexual orientation and lifestyle." It advises her that she could be terminated from her teaching position if she makes any comments to "students, staff members, or parents of students regarding [her] homosexual orientation or lifestyle." She could also be terminated for responding to questions concerning her "sexual orientation or anything concerning the subject."

The July 22 letter does not limit these restrictions to speech made in the classroom or during any school-sponsored functions—a limitation that all parties' now seem to agree would be reasonable. Instead, these restrictions limit Ms. Weaver's ability to speak on her sexuality outside of the school, as, for example, when meeting a parent of a student in the supermarket, or when speaking at dinner with a friend who may be a staff member at the school, or even when speaking with her own children, who are students in the School District. Moreover, under the broad restrictions contained in the July 22 letter, Ms. Weaver could violate its terms if she is spotted by some student, parent, or staff member while walking hand-in-hand with another in the seclusion of her own yard. By restricting Ms. Weaver's speech outside the classroom, these restrictions are unconstitutionally overbroad. *See* National Gay Task Force, 729 F.2d at 1273–74 (holding that a statute that punished teachers for "advocating," "promoting," or "encouraging" homosexuality outside the classroom was unconstitutionally overbroad).

The School District's October 29 letter that "clarifies" the speech restrictions on Ms. Weaver does not change this result. First, the October 29 letter does not retract the July 22 letter. Both letters remain in Ms. Weaver's personnel file. Nor does the October 29 letter sufficiently narrow the July 22 letter. Rather, the October 29 letter remains overbroad in that it seeks to restrict Ms. Weaver's right to speak "at any time with students" and in "virtually any interaction ... including off-campus contacts...." As with the July 22 letter, the October 29 letter also reaches protected activities, and thus is unconstitutionally overbroad.

Moreover, the restrictions in both letters remain vague. Even the author of the letters, defendant Mosher, was unable to describe with certainty in what situations Ms. Weaver could freely speak and in what situations she could not. Under these circumstances, Ms. Weaver should not be called upon to self-censor her speech so that her speech is limited to that "which is unquestionably safe." *Baggett v. Bullitt*, 377 U.S. 360, 372, 12 L.Ed.2d 377, 84 S.Ct. 1316 (1964). Because Ms. Weaver is left to guess at what speech might subject her to termination, the letters are impermissibly vague. *See Gentile v. State Bar of Nevada*, 501 U.S. 1030, 1048, 115 L.Ed.2d 888, 111 S.Ct. 2720 (1991); *see also Connally v. General Constr. Co.*, 269 U.S. 385, 391, 70 L.Ed. 322, 46 S.Ct. 126 (1926) (declaring that a law will be void for vagueness if persons "of common intelligence must necessarily guess at its meaning and differ as to its application") (citation omitted).

Notably, it was only Ms. Weaver who received a letter restricting her speech. The School District concedes that no other teachers have received such a letter limiting their speech on matters of sexual orientation. The only other School District employee who received a similar restriction was Ms. Weaver's ex-husband. Tellingly, however, his letter prohibited only the discussion of Ms. Weaver's sexual orientation, not his own. Indeed, the School District, via its Healthy Responsible Lifestyles Education policy, recognizes and encourages teachers to speak freely on issues concerning heterosexual lifestyles. (*See* policy at 1 (allowing the curriculum to include, among other things, information "that promotes the importance of marriage and the family" and information that promotes "sexual abstinence before marriage and fidelity within marriage.")). Because the restrictions imposed on Ms. Weaver (and her ex-husband) only targeted speech concerning homosexual orientation and not heterosexual orientation, the restrictions are properly considered viewpoint restrictions. Such a one-sided approach to sexual orientation is classic viewpoint discrimination and is "presumptively invalid." *See R.A.V. v. City of St. Paul, Minn.*, 505 U.S. 377, 382, 120 L.Ed.2d 305, 112 S.Ct. 2538 (1992).

Generally, if a state regulation is viewpoint-based, it will be deemed unconstitutional unless the state can show that it has a compelling state interest in restricting the content of the speech and that the restriction is narrowly tailored to achieve that end. *See Perry Educ. Ass'n v. Perry Local Educators' Ass'n.*, 460 U.S. 37, 45, 74 L.Ed.2d 794, 103 S.Ct. 948 (1983). The absence of such a showing here provides further support for concluding that the July 22 and October 29 letters violate Ms. Weaver's First Amendment rights.

In sum, because both the July 22 and the October 29 letters impermissibly infringe on Ms. Weaver's First Amendment rights, Ms. Weaver is entitled to summary judgment on her First Amendment claim. Moreover, because the letters violate Ms. Weaver's constitutional rights so long as they remain extant and in her personnel file, they are void and must be removed from her personnel file.

II.

Despite mounting evidence that gay males and lesbians suffer from employment discrimination and, as recent events in Wyoming remind us, other more life-threatening expressions of bias,* courts, including the Supreme Court, have not yet recognized a person's sexual orientation as a status that deserves heightened protection. To date, Congress has expressly prohibited employment discrimination on the basis of race, religion, national origin, gender, age, and disability, but not sexual orientation. As of this year, eleven states and the District of Columbia offer statutory protection against discrimination on the basis of sexual orientation; thirty-nine states, including Utah, do not.

Nevertheless, the Fourteenth Amendment of the United States Constitution entitles all persons to equal protection under the law. *See* U.S. Const. amend. XIV. It appears that the plain language of the Fourteenth Amendment's Equal Protection Clause prohibits a state government or agency from engaging in intentional discrimination—even on the basis of sexual orientation—absent some rational basis for so doing.

The Supreme Court has recognized that an "irrational prejudice" cannot provide the rational basis to support a state action against an equal protection challenge.

... More recently, in *Romer v. Evans*, 517 U.S. 620, 134 L.Ed.2d 855, 116 S.Ct. 1620 (1996), the Court ... noted that under the ordinary deferential equal protection standard—that is, rational basis—the Court would "insist on knowing the relation between the classification adopted and the object to be obtained."

... The question then is whether bias concerning Ms. Weaver's sexual orientation furnishes a rational basis for the defendants' decision not to assign her as volleyball coach. The "negative reaction" some members of the community may have to homosexuals is not a proper basis for discriminating against them.... If the community's perception is based on nothing more than unsupported assumptions, outdated stereotypes, and animosity, it is necessarily irrational and under *Romer* and other Supreme Court precedent, it provides no legitimate support for the School District's decisions....

The record now before the court contains no job-related justification for not assigning Ms. Weaver as volleyball coach. Nor have the defendants demonstrated how Ms. Weaver's sexual orientation bears any rational relationship to her competency as teacher or coach, or her job performance as coach—a position she has held for many years with distinction. As mentioned earlier, it is undisputed that she was an excellent coach and apparently, up until the time her sexual orientation was revealed, the likely candidate for the position. Principal Wadley's decision not to assign Ms. Weaver (a decision reached after consulting with the other defendants) was based solely on her sexual orientation. Absent some rational relationship to job performance, a decision not to assign Ms. Weaver as coach because of her sexual orientation runs afoul of the Fourteenth Amendment's equal protection guarantee.

---

* Here the court refers to the torture murder of Matthew Shepard in Laramie, Wyoming in 1998.

Although the Constitution cannot control prejudices, neither this court nor any other court should, directly or indirectly, legitimize them. *See City of Cleburne*, 473 U.S. at 448; *Palmore v. Sidoti*, 466 U.S. 429, 433, 80 L.Ed.2d 421, 104 S.Ct. 1879 (1984).... Because a community's animus towards homosexuals can never serve as a legitimate basis for state action, the defendants' actions based on that animus violate the Equal Protection Clause. *See Romer*, 517 U.S. at 634; *City of Cleburne*, 473 U.S. at 448–50; *Stemler*, 126 F.3d at 874.

... The defendants have failed to advance any justification for not assigning Ms. Weaver as volleyball coach other than that there was "negative" reaction in the community. Because this perceived negative reaction arose solely from Ms. Weaver's sexual orientation, and not from her abilities as coach, it does not furnish a rational job-related basis for the defendants' decision. Therefore, Ms. Weaver's Motion for Summary Judgment is granted as to this claim.

III.

In Ms. Weaver's second equal protection claim, she asserts that the defendants violated her rights to equal protection by imposing a viewpoint and content-based restriction on her speech. She argues that she was prohibited from discussing her sexual orientation only because she would have discussed her homosexuality, and points out that other teachers were free to discuss their heterosexual orientations.

Ms. Weaver was threatened with disciplinary action for discussing her intimate associations and sexual orientation. At the same time, no other teacher in the School District was prohibited from discussing these topics. Indeed, as the School District conceded at the hearing, no similar restriction was placed on heterosexual teachers at all. Clearly then, the School District wanted to silence Ms. Weaver's speech because of its expected pro-homosexual viewpoint. Such viewpoint-based restriction is constitutionally impermissible.

Simple as it may sound, as a matter of fairness and evenhandedness, homosexuals should not be sanctioned or restricted for speech that heterosexuals are not likewise sanctioned or restricted for. Because the School District has not restricted other teachers in speaking out on their sexual orientation, the School District has not only violated the First Amendment, but also the Fourteenth Amendment's Equal Protection Clause. In such an instance, when an equal protection claim is based on a person's exercise of a fundamental constitutional right, the proper standard of review is strict scrutiny—that is, is the restriction supported by a compelling state interest? *See City of Cleburne*, 473 U.S. at 440; *Plyler v. Doe*, 457 U.S. 202, 217 n.15, 72 L.Ed.2d 786, 102 S.Ct. 2382 (1982). Because the Court has concluded that the School District's actions cannot be supported on any rational basis, the District's actions obviously fail the strict scrutiny test. Ms. Weaver is granted summary judgment on this claim as well.

IV. WHEN DOES FREEDOM OF EXPRESSION GO TOO FAR?

Westboro Baptist Church, founded by Fred Phelps in 1955, is well known for its protests of gay and military funerals, as well as its slogan, "God Hates Fags." To date, Westboro has a total congregation of Pastor Fred W. Phelps, nine of his 13 children (along with their children and spouses), and a small number of other families. Despite being small in number, Westboro is vocal and adroit at using the print and television media to disseminate its message. Interestingly, five of Phelps's children are attorneys, and Phelps himself is a lawyer, although he was disbarred in 1979.

In 1991, Westboro began its "picketing ministry," in which church members travel to the funerals of openly gay people and picket with signs bearing inflammatory slogans. On October 12, 1998, college student Matthew Shepard died of injuries sustained in a vicious hate crime that shocked the nation. The openly gay Shepard was tied to a crude fence in rural Wyoming, beaten into a coma, and left to die. Westboro came to national prominence when its members picketed Shepard's funeral, carrying signs saying, "God Hates Fags" and "AIDS Kills Fags Dead." The group further attempted to erect a monument "commemorating Shepard's entry into hell," and maintains a virtual "memorial" to Shepard on their website, which depicts Shepard burning in hell.

In order to gain wider exposure for their message, Westboro began picketing the funerals of U.S. soldiers killed in the Afghanistan and Iraq wars, carrying inflammatory signs that say, for example, "Thank God for Dead Soldiers." Westboro congregants maintain that what they see as America's acceptance of homosexuality has condemned the United States to God's wrath. When a father sued Phelps and Westboro for picketing his son's funeral, the case made it to the United States Supreme Court. Phelps was represented at oral argument by one of his daughters.

SNYDER v. PHELPS, ET AL.

562 U.S. ___, 131 S.Ct. 1207, 179 L.Ed.2d 172 (2011)

CHIEF JUSTICE ROBERTS delivered the opinion of the Court.

A jury held members of the Westboro Baptist Church liable for millions of dollars in damages for picketing near a soldier's funeral service. The picket signs reflected the church's view that the United States is overly tolerant of sin and that God kills American soldiers as punishment. The question presented is whether the First Amendment shields the church members from tort liability for their speech in this case.

I

A

Fred Phelps founded the Westboro Baptist Church in Topeka, Kansas, in 1955. The church's congregation believes that God hates and punishes the United States for its tolerance of homosexuality, particularly in America's military. The church frequently communicates its views by picketing, often at military funerals. . . .

Marine Lance Corporal Matthew Snyder was killed in Iraq in the line of duty. . . .

Phelps became aware of Matthew Snyder's funeral and decided to travel to Maryland with six other Westboro Baptist parishioners (two of his daughters and four of his grandchildren) to picket. On the day of the memorial service, the Westboro congregation members picketed on public land adjacent to public streets near the Maryland State House, the United States Naval Academy, and Matthew Snyder's funeral. The Westboro picketers carried signs that were largely the same at all three locations. They stated, for instance: "God Hates the USA/Thank God for 9/11," "America is Doomed," "Don't Pray for the USA," "Thank God for IEDs," "Thank God for Dead Soldiers," "Pope in Hell," "Priests Rape Boys," "God Hates Fags," "You're Going to Hell," and "God Hates You."

The church had notified the authorities in advance of its intent to picket at the time of the funeral, and the picketers complied with police instructions in staging their demonstration. . . .

B

Snyder filed suit against Phelps, Phelps's daughters, and the Westboro Baptist Church (collectively Westboro or the church) in the United States District Court for the District of Maryland under that court's diversity jurisdiction. Snyder alleged five state tort law claims: defamation, publicity given to private life, intentional infliction of emotional distress, intrusion upon seclusion, and civil conspiracy. Westboro moved for summary judgment contending, in part, that the church's speech was insulated from liability by the First Amendment. *See* 533 F.Supp.2d 567, 570 (Md.2008).

The District Court awarded Westboro summary judgment on Snyder's claims for defamation and publicity given to private life, concluding that Snyder could not prove the necessary elements of those torts. *Id.*, at 572–573. A trial was held on the remaining claims. At trial, Snyder described the severity of his emotional injuries. . . .

A jury found for Snyder on the intentional infliction of emotional distress, intrusion upon seclusion, and civil conspiracy claims, and held Westboro liable for $2.9 million in compensatory damages and $8 million in punitive damages. . . .

In the Court of Appeals, Westboro's primary argument was that the church was entitled to judgment as a matter of law because the First Amendment fully protected Westboro's speech. The Court of Appeals agreed. 580 F.3d 206, 221 (C.A.4 2009). . . .

We granted certiorari. 559 U.S. ___, 130 S.Ct. 1737, 176 L.Ed.2d 211 (2010).

II

To succeed on a claim for intentional infliction of emotional distress in Maryland, a plaintiff must demonstrate that the defendant intentionally or recklessly engaged in extreme and outrageous conduct that caused the plaintiff to suffer severe emotional distress....

Whether the First Amendment prohibits holding Westboro liable for its speech in this case turns largely on whether that speech is of public or private concern, as determined by all the circumstances of the case. "[S]peech on 'matters of public concern' ... is 'at the heart of the First Amendment's protection.' " ...

" '[N]ot all speech is of equal First Amendment importance,' " however, and where matters of purely private significance are at issue, First Amendment protections are often less rigorous. *Hustler*, *supra*, at 56, 108 S.Ct. 876 (*quoting Dun & Bradstreet*, *supra*, at 758, 105 S.Ct. 2939); *see Connick, supra*, at 145–147, 103 S.Ct. 1684. That is because restricting speech on purely private matters does not implicate the same constitutional concerns as limiting speech on matters of public interest: "[T]here is no threat to the free and robust debate of public issues; there is no potential interference with a meaningful dialogue of ideas"; and the "threat of liability" does not pose the risk of "a reaction of self-censorship" on matters of public import. *Dun & Bradstreet, supra*, at 760, 105 S.Ct. 2939 (internal quotation marks omitted).

We noted a short time ago, in considering whether public employee speech addressed a matter of public concern, that "the boundaries of the public concern test are not well defined." *San Diego v. Roe,* 543 U.S. 77, 83, 125 S.Ct. 521, 160 L.Ed.2d 410 (2004) (per curiam). Although that remains true today, we have articulated some guiding principles, principles that accord broad protection to speech to ensure that courts themselves do not become inadvertent censors.

Speech deals with matters of public concern when it can "be fairly considered as relating to any matter of political, social, or other concern to the community," *Connick*, supra, at 146, 103 S.Ct. 1684, or when it "is a subject of legitimate news interest; that is, a subject of general interest and of value and concern to the public," *San Diego, supra*, at 83–84, 125 S.Ct. 521....

. . .

The "content" of Westboro's signs plainly relates to broad issues of interest to society at large, rather than matters of "purely private concern." ... The placards read "God Hates the USA/Thank God for 9/11," "America is Doomed," "Don't Pray for the USA," "Thank God for IEDs," "Fag Troops," "Semper Fi Fags," "God Hates Fags," "Maryland Taliban," "Fags Doom Nations," "Not Blessed Just Cursed," "Thank God for Dead Soldiers," "Pope in Hell," "Priests Rape Boys," "You're Going to Hell," and "God Hates You." App. 3781–3787. While these messages may fall short of refined social or political commentary, the issues they highlight—the political and moral conduct of the United States and its citizens, the fate of our Nation, homosexuality in the military, and scandals involving the Catholic clergy—are matters of public import. The signs certainly convey Westboro's position on those issues, in a manner designed, . . ., to reach as broad a public audience as possible. And even if a few of the signs—such as "You're Going to Hell" and "God Hates You"—were viewed as containing messages related to Matthew Snyder or the Snyders specifically, that would not change the fact that the overall thrust and dominant theme of Westboro's demonstration spoke to broader public issues.

Apart from the content of Westboro's signs, Snyder contends that the "context" of the speech—its connection with his son's funeral—makes the speech a matter of private rather than public concern. The fact that Westboro spoke in connection with a funeral, however, cannot by itself transform the nature of Westboro's speech. Westboro's signs, displayed on public land next to a public street, reflect the fact that the church finds much to condemn in modern society. Its speech is "fairly characterized as constituting speech on a matter of public concern," *Connick*, 461 U.S., at 146, 103 S.Ct. 1684, and the funeral setting does not alter that conclusion.

. . .

Snyder goes on to argue that Westboro's speech should be afforded less than full First Amendment protection "not only because of the words" but also because the church members exploited the funeral "as a platform to bring their message to a broader audience." Brief for Petitioner 44, 40. There is no doubt that Westboro chose to stage its picketing at the Naval Academy, the Maryland State House, and Matthew Snyder's funeral to increase publicity for its views and because of the relation between those sites and its views—in the case of the military funeral, because Westboro believes that God is killing American soldiers as punishment for the Nation's sinful policies.

Westboro's choice to convey its views in conjunction with Matthew Snyder's funeral made the expression of those views particularly hurtful to many, especially to Matthew's father. The record makes clear that the applicable legal term—"emotional distress"—fails to capture fully the anguish Westboro's choice added to Mr. Snyder's already incalculable grief. But Westboro conducted its picketing peacefully on matters of public concern at a public place adjacent to a public street. Such space occupies a "special position in terms of First Amendment protection." *United States v. Grace*, 461 U.S. 171, 180, 103 S.Ct. 1702, 75 L.Ed.2d 736 (1983). "[W]e have repeatedly referred to public streets as the archetype of a traditional public forum," noting that " '[t]ime out of mind' public streets and sidewalks have been used for public assembly and debate." *Frisby v. Schultz*, 487 U.S. 474, 480, 108 S.Ct. 2495, 101 L.Ed.2d 420 (1988).

That said, "[e]ven protected speech is not equally permissible in all places and at all times. . . . Maryland now has a law imposing restrictions on funeral picketing, Md.Crim. Law Code Ann. § 10–205 (Lexis Supp.

2010), as do 43 other States and the Federal Government. See Brief for American Legion as Amicus Curiae 18–19, n. 2 (listing statutes). To the extent these laws are content neutral, they raise very different questions from the tort verdict at issue in this case. Maryland's law, however, was not in effect at the time of the events at issue here, so we have no occasion to consider how it might apply to facts such as those before us, or whether it or other similar regulations are constitutional.

. . .

Simply put, the church members had the right to be where they were. Westboro alerted local authorities to its funeral protest and fully complied with police guidance on where the picketing could be staged. The picketing was conducted under police supervision some 1,000 feet from the church, out of the sight of those at the church. The protest was not unruly; there was no shouting, profanity, or violence.

The record confirms that any distress occasioned by Westboro's picketing turned on the content and viewpoint of the message conveyed, rather than any interference with the funeral itself. A group of parishioners standing at the very spot where Westboro stood, holding signs that said "God Bless America" and "God Loves You," would not have been subjected to liability. It was what Westboro said that exposed it to tort damages.

Given that Westboro's speech was at a public place on a matter of public concern, that speech is entitled to "special protection" under the First Amendment. Such speech cannot be restricted simply because it is upsetting or arouses contempt. "If there is a bedrock principle underlying the First Amendment, it is that the government may not prohibit the expression of an idea simply because society finds the idea itself offensive or disagreeable." *Texas v. Johnson*, 491 U.S. 397, 414, 109 S.Ct. 2533, 105 L.Ed.2d 342 (1989). Indeed, "the point of all speech protection ... is to shield just those choices of content that in someone's eyes are misguided, or even hurtful." *Hurley v. Irish-American Gay, Lesbian and Bisexual Group of Boston, Inc.*, 515 U.S. 557, 574, 115 S.Ct. 2338, 132 L.Ed.2d 487 (1995).

. . .

For all these reasons, the jury verdict imposing tort liability on Westboro for intentional infliction of emotional distress must be set aside.

III

. . .

Because we find that the First Amendment bars Snyder from recovery for intentional infliction of emotional distress or intrusion upon seclusion—the alleged unlawful activity Westboro conspired to accomplish—we must likewise hold that Snyder cannot recover for civil conspiracy based on those torts.

IV

. . .

Speech is powerful. It can stir people to action, move them to tears of both joy and sorrow, and—as it did here—inflict great pain. On the facts before us, we cannot react to that pain by punishing the speaker. As a Nation we have chosen a different course—to protect even hurtful speech on public issues to ensure that we do not stifle public debate. That choice requires that we shield Westboro from tort liability for its picketing in this case.

The judgment of the United States Court of Appeals for the Fourth Circuit is affirmed.

It is so ordered.

JUSTICE BREYER, concurring.

. . .

As I understand the Court's opinion, it does not hold or imply that the State is always powerless to provide private individuals with necessary protection. Rather, the Court has reviewed the underlying facts in detail, as will sometimes prove necessary where First Amendment values and state-protected (say, privacy-related) interests seriously conflict. *Cf. Florida Star v. B.J. F.*, 491 U.S. 524, 533, 109 S.Ct. 2603, 105 L.Ed.2d 443 (1989); *Bose Corp. v. Consumers Union of United States, Inc.*, 466 U.S. 485, 499, 104 S.Ct. 1949, 80 L.Ed.2d 502 (1984). That review makes clear that Westboro's means of communicating its views consisted of picketing in a place where picketing was lawful and in compliance with all police directions. The picketing could not be seen or heard from the funeral ceremony itself. And Snyder testified that he saw no more than the tops of the picketers' signs as he drove to the funeral. To uphold the application of state law in these circumstances would punish Westboro for seeking to communicate its views on matters of public concern without proportionately advancing the State's interest in protecting its citizens against severe emotional harm. Consequently, the First Amendment protects Westboro. As I read the Court's opinion, it holds no more.

JUSTICE ALITO, dissenting.

Our profound national commitment to free and open debate is not a license for the vicious verbal assault that occurred in this case.

Petitioner Albert Snyder is not a public figure. He is simply a parent whose son, Marine Lance Corporal Matthew Snyder, was killed in Iraq. Mr. Snyder wanted what is surely the right of any parent who experiences such an incalculable loss: to bury his son in peace. But respondents, members of the Westboro Baptist Church, deprived him of that elementary right.... As a result, Albert Snyder suffered severe and lasting emotional injury. The Court now holds that the First Amendment protected respondents' right to brutalize Mr. Snyder. I cannot agree.

I

Respondents and other members of their church have strong opinions on certain moral, religious, and political issues, and the First Amendment ensures that they have almost limitless opportunities to express their views....

It does not follow, however, that they may intentionally inflict severe emotional injury on private persons at a time of intense emotional sensitivity by launching vicious verbal attacks that make no contribution to public debate. To protect against such injury, "most if not all jurisdictions" permit recovery in tort for the intentional infliction of emotional distress (or IIED). *Hustler Magazine, Inc. v. Falwell*, 485 U.S. 46, 53, 108 S.Ct. 876, 99 L.Ed.2d 41 (1988).

. . .

Although the elements of the IIED tort are difficult to meet, respondents long ago abandoned any effort to show that those tough standards were not satisfied here. On appeal, they chose not to contest the sufficiency of the evidence.... Instead, they maintained that the First Amendment gave them a license to engage in such conduct. They are wrong.

II

It is well established that a claim for the intentional infliction of emotional distress can be satisfied by speech. Indeed, what has been described as "[t]he leading case" recognizing this tort involved speech.... And although this Court has not decided the question, I think it is clear that the First Amendment does not entirely preclude liability for the intentional infliction of emotional distress by means of speech.

. . .

DISCUSSION

Who do you think had the better argument: the majority or Justice Alito in dissent?

CHAPTER 4

SEXUAL IDENTITY AND THE CONSTITUTION

■ ■ ■

This section deals with constitutional substantive due process and equal protection doctrines. In a constitutional law textbook, these subjects would be dealt with separately and, understandably, at great length. For purposes of understanding the struggle for gay and lesbian rights, however, the two doctrines, though operating quite differently, are often compressed and, as *Lawrence v. Texas* shows us, intertwined.

I. SUBSTANTIVE DUE PROCESS AND EQUAL PROTECTION

A. DUE PROCESS

The Fourteenth Amendment ensures that the states, like the federal government, are bound to provide due process before they may deprive citizens of life, liberty, or property. The narrowest reading of the Fourteenth Amendment ensures the imposition of *procedural due process*, that is, that the state may deprive you of life, liberty, or property only so long as a sufficient set of procedures are consistently followed. (*e.g.*, that you be charged and indicted, allowed to defend yourself, allowed to challenge your accuser, etc.)

But to this procedural due process, the Court has added a complement: substantive due process. By giving the word "liberty" in the Clause a substantive dimension, the Court has offered us the challenge of defining and prioritizing our less textually explicit rights, and a mechanism to determine the extent to which public policy and the common good may impair them.

The flexibility of a word like "liberty" puts substantive due process squarely into the crossfire of the debate over whether the Constitution is a document to be construed only historically, or whether it is a document intended to change as our society evolves. Is it to be construed or expanded to accommodate changes in technology, culture, and social mores, or even interpreted in the light of global trends in jurisprudence?

To be sure, there is no one right answer to settle that debate, and the prevailing consensus has shifted and varied over the life of our country.

Substantive due process is, at its heart, often vague and changeable. Where the Constitution is specific and unambiguous, a substantive due process question under the Fourteenth Amendment does not arise. May women vote? The Nineteenth Amendment clearly states that the right of citizens to vote shall not be abridged or denied on account of sex. The Thirteenth Amendment abolished slavery. What constraints may be placed upon the nature of the servitude of convicts? Should it be limited to public works, such as litter cleanup, roadwork, or the manufacture of vehicle license plates? Or, may a correctional institution "rent" inmates as contract labor for private consumption? Would it make a difference if their services are offered at rates below prevailing labor market rates? These are the sorts of questions, among others, that may raise the issue of substantive due process.

Substantive due process encompasses the domain of legal theory between *Positive Law* and *Natural Law*. The ideological conflict between positive law theorists and natural law theorists was far from settled at the drafting of the Constitution, and continues unabated today. Positive law theory holds that the people are entitled only to the rights explicitly enumerated by the government.

In stark contrast, natural law theory purports that there exist abstractions of Right and Wrong, both of which may be discovered through reasoned analysis. Such is the basis of our common law system, wherein judges are charged with constantly defining and redefining the boundaries and spirit of both previously-established judge-made law and legislative enactment. Judicial interpretation of legislative acts is subject, of course, to subsequent legislative amendment, except insofar as the interpretation is grounded in constitutional limitations on the power of the legislative body. Likewise, the legislature may enact laws that constrain, void, or expand judicial precedent.

With the powers vested in judges to declare a law unconstitutional, our constitutional system is a system with an incredible potential for dynamism. This dynamism is tempered by judicial restraint, precedent and *res judicata*. How much dynamism ought to be allowed, and how closely the law ought to follow social change—if at all—is the heart of the controversy over "activist judges."

On the scales of justice, opposite the inalienable rights espoused by the Declaration of Independence, we have the power of the government to enact laws. The Constitution clearly establishes legislative powers, but just as clearly limits them. Because no constitution can address every question that can or will arise in the evolution of a society, we are left to define and redefine the margin between these powers and their limitations, and the relationship between these positive laws and the rights they seek to constrain.

When a plaintiff complains that a right has been violated by the government, a court will first determine the nature of that right. Is it, in the parlance of the courts, a *fundamental* right or liberty? We look to the Constitution to assess whether the asserted right is explicit in the text, implied by historical context or tradition, or analogous to another right previously established. Rights have historically been declared to exist along a continuum of certitude, from the most certain fundamental liberties, to the more vaguely defined implied rights found to arise from other more explicitly defined rights. The vague end of the continuum is the subject of much heated controversy.

Once the Court has established a place for the asserted right along this continuum, it tests the extent to which the *end* (the stated purpose of the limiting legislation) justifies the *means* by which its stated goal is achieved. The locus on the continuum will dictate how closely the end and means must *fit*, and the level of scrutiny the Court will employ in assessing that fit. A more fundamental, established right will receive stricter scrutiny, and will require a much closer fit (*narrow tailoring*) between the stated goal of the legislation and the precision with which the legislation seeks to achieve that goal.

B. EQUAL PROTECTION

The Equal Protection Clause declares, "No State shall ... deny to any person within its jurisdiction the equal protection of the laws." U.S. Const. amend XIV, § 1. Not all unequal treatment, however, is unlawful. In its broadest sense, "discrimination" simply means treating people differently according to some classification. The states (and the federal government) *do* discriminate in extending privileges and opportunities, and imposing burdens on citizens. Military veterans are offered services not available to non-veterans. Married persons receive different treatment under federal tax law than unmarried persons. Males must register for the draft, while females need not. Clearly, *equal protection* does not mean universally uniform treatment. When *is* discrimination acceptable?

Equal protection analysis of legislation begins by identifying the *class* singled out by the legislation. A class is identified by the *trait* that distinguishes those members in the class from those not included. The trait may be gender, as noted, where the selective service law requires that males register, but females are excluded. Persons who have been convicted of a felony represent another class, the trait being their felony status, and based on this trait, they might be denied the right to vote.

A court then examines the extent to which the group disadvantaged or burdened by the legislation is different from those not burdened, or the extent to which the members and non-members of the class are *similarly situated*. This factor is perhaps the most susceptible of variation according to cultural standards and trends. It was once felt that women were fundamentally different from men, or that race created fundamental class distinctions. These views are less widely held today, and this is reflected in the elimination of many laws that discriminated based on gender and race.

The trait that distinguishes the class will determine the level of scrutiny the court applies in analyzing the legislation. Certain traits have been extensively considered by the Supreme Court for their relevance to legitimate government purposes, and these traits are subjected to established levels of scrutiny. Race, almost never relevant to a legitimate government purpose, is subject to *strict scrutiny*. Classifications based on race, alienage, and national origin are almost always subjected to strict scrutiny and have been defined by the Court as suspect classifications (suspect class). Gender, usually irrelevant, is subject to *intermediate scrutiny* (quasi-suspect class), as is legitimacy. The Court seems unwilling to expand these classifications, and specifically refused to create new suspect or quasi-suspect classes on the basis of mental handicap, poverty, and sexual orientation. Legislation that does not impact one of the suspect or quasi-suspect classes is generally subjected only to *rational basis* review.

A court will then consider the purpose or goal of the legislation, and how it seeks to achieve this goal. Where the Court has established a standard of strict scrutiny, the purpose of the legislation must be constitutionally permissible and *compelling*, and the means for achieving this end must be *necessary* or *narrowly tailored*. For intermediate scrutiny, the purpose must be *important*, and the means must be *substantially related*. For low-level rational basis review, the Court requires only a *legitimate purpose* and arguably *rational means*. In a small subset to these latter cases, the Court has applied a somewhat higher standard of rationality, resulting in a standard sometimes known as *rational basis with bite*.

As with other constitutional analysis, the legislation is subject to evaluation for fit—that is, whether the classification is carefully aligned with the purpose of the legislation. A statute may be found unconstitutional if the classification is overinclusive, underinclusive, or both. If a statute imposes a burden on more people than the purpose of the legislation requires, it is overinclusive. Likewise, if it imposes a burden or extends a benefit, but fails to achieve its stated or intended purpose because the classification put forth embraces some, but not substantially all of those it should have reached, it is underinclusive. If a plaintiff is similarly situated with those who benefit from a statute, but fails to benefit herself, this indicates that the statute is underinclusive. In undertaking such an analysis, it is generally presumed that a trait is relevant to the purpose, and the plaintiff bears the burden of proving unjust discrimination. A higher level of scrutiny will drive the extent to which the state bears the burden of proving that the purpose of the statute and the classification applied are tightly aligned, most notably with race and gender.

Even where a trait has been established as generally irrelevant, this does not mean that all classification based on this trait is illegitimate.

Instead, it simply raises the standard to which the statute under scrutiny must comply. Race, for instance, may be a valid basis for extending a health benefit, or the burden of specific health screening, when a particular disease is found to be genetically limited to persons of a particular race.

C. EQUAL PROTECTION AND SEXUALITY

For purposes of generally-accepted federal constitutional analysis, a suspect class is a discrete and insular minority, subject to a history of invidious discrimination based on an immutable trait, and which is politically impotent. Race is the archetypal suspect class. Applying this definition of a suspect class to sexual minorities poses unique problems. In particular, the question of immutability remains unresolved. While sexual orientation has been held to be an immutable trait by some lower courts, appellate courts have been hesitant to give any imprimatur to this reasoning, and the mounting scientific evidence suggesting a biological "cause" for sexual orientation still has many vocal detractors. Further complications derive from the fluidity of the definitions for sexuality and the variety of the statutes challenged as unfair to gays.

The broad umbrella of *sexuality* encompasses numerous subsets, intersecting and insular to varying degrees. *Homosexual*, *transsexual*, *transgender*, *bisexual*, and *gay* all mean different things to different people. Some people equate *gay* and *homosexual*, while for some, *gay* refers to *affective orientation*, a psychosocial trait; *homosexual* to *sexual orientation*, a primarily behavioral construct. While this distinction might seem immaterial, it comes to bear in answering the question of mutability, among others. An emotional state or emotional relationship cannot be legislated, but the behaviors by which it is manifested may be. Similarly, if the behavior is merely a private expression between consenting adults, we are confronted with the need to explain how and why such a private expression ought to relate to public rights, such as property rights, parenting rights, or financial rights and privileges (taxes, social security benefits, inheritance). Gender identity poses similar dilemmas.

Finally, it is not always clear how best to characterize discrimination against gays, lesbians, bisexuals, and transgender persons. The best approach to analysis may depend on the nature of the benefit or burden, and different modes of analysis will often yield contradictory conclusions. If we consider, for instance, that many states prohibit gay marriage, we could characterize this as barring a man's right to marry a man and a woman's right to marry a woman, but allowing a man to marry a woman, or vice versa, is a question of equal protection based on gender. The Supreme Court held in *Loving v. Virginia* that *equal application* did not provide equal protection under the law. Thus, were one to argue that the prohibition survives gender-based analysis, men and women being equally barred from marriage to a partner of the same gender, *Loving* would defeat that reasoning. Where gay marriage has been upheld at a state level, it has been on grounds similar to federal Equal Protection.

While the Supreme Court's decision in *Lawrence v. Texas* might appear to signal a trend toward greater enforcement of equal protection for gays, the Court did not declare gays a suspect class and purportedly decided the case on substantive due process grounds.

II. THE DEBATE ABOUT SODOMY: BENTHAM v. BLACKSTONE*

William Blackstone's magisterial *Commentaries on the Laws of England* (1765–1769) is a work whose influence on English and American law can hardly be overestimated.... Portentously, Blackstone called sodomy a crime "of so dark a nature that the accusation if false deserves a punishment inferior only to the crime itself." Then he added: "I will not act so disagreeable a part, to my readers as well as myself, as to dwell any longer on a subject, the very mention of which is a disgrace to human nature. It will be more eligible to imitate in this respect the delicacy of our English law, which treats it, in its very indictments, as a crime not fit to be named: '*peccatum illud horribile, inter christianos non nominandum.*' " As to punishment, Blackstone was resolutely theological: "This [offense] the voice of nature and of reason and the express law of God, determine to be capital. Of which we have a signal instance, long before the Jewish dispensation [that is, Leviticus] by the destruction of two cities by fire from heaven, so that this is an universal, not merely a provincial, precept."

Blackstone's great antagonist was the utilitarian philosopher Jeremy Bentham, who did not share his uncritical admiration for British law as largely beyond improvement. Indeed, reform of Britain's lethal and archaic penal code was a prime concern throughout Bentham's long life (1748–1832). In his early twenties he had already begun to draft a new criminal code, but the hostile reaction to the French Revolution in the 1790s paralyzed all reform in Britain.... Finally, with the fading of anti-French feeling and the passage of the Reform Bill in 1832, the influence of Bentham's ideas was also enormous in Britain and America; he was by far the most important reformer England ever produced.

Unfortunately, Bentham's views on sodomy law reform law lay hidden in unpublished writings which amply testify to the strength of British homophobia.

. . .

As early as 1774, Bentham had sketched out some notes on homosexual law reform, citing classical antiquity and Enlightenment principles. A decade later he wrote an essay on "pederasty" which argued powerfully

* Reprinted by permission of the publisher from "The Enlightenment 1730–1810" in HOMOSEXUALITY AND CIVILIZATION by Lewis Crompton, pp. 531–534, Cambridge, Mass. The Belknap Press of Harvard University Press, © 2003 by the President and Fellows of Harvard College.

for a change in legal and social attitudes. Same-sex relations, Bentham maintained, give pleasure to those who engage in them and cause no harm to others. To counter Montesquieu's argument that they impart to men the "weakness" of women, he cited famous Greek and Roman generals. To Voltaire's contention that homosexuality threatened the very existence of the human race, he replied that ancient Greece, despite the popularity of male love, suffered from over-rather than under-population. Nor would Bentham tolerate the epithet "unnatural." Those who use it mean only that a sexual act is non-procreative. But if we call all pleasurable activities that are not physiologically necessary unnatural, we would have, for instance, to apply the term to a taste for music.

Bentham was prepared to do battle on a remarkable number of fronts, and even to take the offensive. Though he lacks the word, Bentham has a clear conception of what we now call homophobia....

Even in France or Italy, Bentham's passionate defense would have been exceptional. In Georgian England the public airing of such views was unthinkable. In a page of minute jottings he agonized over the risks: "To other subjects it is expected that you sit down cool, but on this subject if you let it be seen that you have not sat down in a rage you have given judgment against yourself at once." When a man attempts to search this subject it is with a halter around his neck. On this subject a man may indulge his spleen without control. Cruelty and intolerance, the most odious and most mischievous passions in human nature, screen themselves behind a mask of virtue. On one occasion Bentham encountered prejudice face-to-face in a British judge who had just sentenced two men to hang for "an offense of the sort in question." Bentham was deeply shocked by his demeanor. "Delight and exultation," he tells us, "glistened in his countenance; his looks called for applause and congratulations at the hands of the surrounding audience."

. . .

Bentham especially protested the use of traditional pejorative language. Such terms as "abomination" and "perversion," he complains, hopelessly prejudice debate. "It is by the power of names, of signs originally arbitrary and insignificant," he notes, "that the course of imagination has in great measure been guided." To avoid such pitfalls Bentham did what German sexologists did at the end of the nineteenth century when they first attempted to write about homosexuality from a scientific point of view. He tried to create a neutral vocabulary, coining such expressions as "the improlific appetite" and (echoing Beccaris) "the Attic mode."

Bentham wrote assiduously but with deepening despair. "Never did work appear," he declared, "from which at the hand of public opinion a man found so much to fear, so little to hope." Indeed, English popular feeling against sodomites had grown ever stronger during the period when Bentham wrote on the subject. It attained a kind of hysteria during the regency (1810–1820) when brutal pilloryings in the heart of London drew enormous crowds seething with hostility and all but shut down city business. Between 1806 and 1835 over sixty men were hanged in England and another twenty in the navy, a much greater number than in any earlier century. Indeed, this punitiveness reached its peak at a time when executions had ceased elsewhere in Europe. (The last known execution on the Continent occurred in the small town of Schiedam, near Rotterdam, in 1803.) Given these conditions, it is not surprising that none of Bentham's writings on the subject saw print until well into the twentieth century.

The Enlightenment and the cataclysm it provoked had varying effects in Europe. In revolutionary France, anti-clerical feeling was strong enough to sweep away sodomy laws, and those Catholic lands on the Continent that came under the anti-feudal and anti-ecclesiastical influence of the Napoleonic Code shared in this liberalization. Police surveillance continued, however, with little to check arbitrary enforcement, since few men dared complain of entrapment, bribery, or police brutality. In Protestant countries, where the tyranny of the church had been less severe, there was no general reaction against statutes that were religious in origin. After Frederick the Great's death, laws against consensual relations continued to be enforced in Prussia. With German unification, they were extended in 1871 to jurisdictions such as Catholic Bavaria, where they had been dropped under the influence of Napoleonic law. As a result, Germany, Britain, and the United States retained their statutes on sodomy until late in the twentieth century, a pattern that had a curious consequence in Nazi Germany. In a treatise designed to provide a rationale for more severe laws, the jurist Rudolf Kläre gave a racial interpretation to European traditions. Kläre argued that Teutonic jurisdictions (such as Germany, England, and the forty-eight American states that followed English law) were morally superior to decadent Latin countries (such as France, Spain, Italy, and Poland) which no longer punished homosexual acts. With some revisions that widened its scope, the historical Article 175 of the German Imperial Code became a potent instrument of Nazi policy. It is estimated that over 50,000 homosexuals were convicted during Hitler's regime and that as many as 15,000 may have died in death camps. The law was not abolished until 1969. In England, the death penalty survived until 1861, when it was changed to life imprisonment. Thus amended, the statute of Elizabeth remained in force for another century until 1967, when parliament abolished it after a decade of debate spurred by the Wolfenden Report.

In the United States matters took a different turn. The American Revolution fostered no campaign to get rid of church-inspired laws similar to that waged by the philosophers. Nevertheless, in the nineteenth century the death penalty for sodomy was abandoned state by state, although South Carolina kept it on the books until after the Civil War. Not until the publication of the Kinsey Report in 1948 and the subsequent recommendation of the American Bar Association (1961) that laws on private consenting sexual relations between adults be dropped did the decriminalization of homosexuality move ahead. A wave of law reform in the 1960s and 1970s wiped sodomy laws from the books of most northern, western, and Midwestern states. In half a dozen other states, supreme courts declared sodomy laws unconstitutional. Unfortunately, the United States Supreme Court, alarmed at the controversy over its decisions on school prayer and abortion, failed to follow suit. In *Bowers v. Hardwick* (1986) it upheld the constitutionality of sodomy statutes by a vote of five to four, though Justice Lewis Powell, who cast the deciding vote, later admitted that he had "made a mistake." As a result, sixteen American states entered the third millennium with laws that a moderate reformer like Montesquieu thought archaic a generation before the French Revolution. Then, on June 26, 2003, the United States Supreme Court, ruling on a Texas law, overturned *Bowers*.

III. HISTORICAL DEVELOPMENTS IN THE UNITED STATES

The sexual practice of sodomy came with the colonists to the New World. The Reverend Francis Higgeson recorded during his 1629 voyage to New England:

> *This day we examined 5 beastly Sodomiticall boyes, which confessed their wickedness not to bee named. The fact was so fowl we reserved them to bee punished by the governor when we came to new England, who afterward sent them backe to the company to bee punished in ould England, as the crime deserved.*[1]

The link between sodomy and peril to marriage and procreation is also an old rationale. In the *History of New England*, John Winthrop, first governor of Massachusetts Bay Colony, writes of the execution of William Plaine. Plaine, a married man, was accused of and executed for committing sodomy, encouraging masturbation, and voicing atheistic ideas. In Winthrop's words, *"he is a monster in human shape, exceeding all human rules and examples that ever had been heard of, and it tended to the frustrating of the ordinance of marriage and the hindering the generation of mankind."*

Of course, the biblical roots of the condemnation of sodomy are not disputed and, in many cases, they are included in the court proceedings and sentences of accused. On June 25, 1646, Jan Creoli, listed in the Calendar of [Dutch] Historical Manuscripts as a negor, was convicted of the crime *"condemned of God (Gen., c. 19; Levit., c. 18: 22, 29) as an abomination"* and sentenced to death by choking. His body was then burned. His ten year-old victim,[2] was taken to the place of Creoli's execution, tied to a stake, with faggots piled around him, presumably to scare him, and flogged.

1. When the perpetrator was over the age of 14, punishment for the crime of sodomy was death by hanging.

2. I refer to Congo as "victim." But the court of the New Netherland Colony did not. Creoli (and Congo) were punished specifically for sodomy. Pederasty is not mentioned.

The liberty-minded Americans who replaced their colonial ancestors began to abandon death as punishment for sodomy in favor of "milder" forms of punishment. In a sweeping 1776 draft revision of Virginia law, Thomas Jefferson recommended that the punishment for sodomy be changed from death to castration (nostril slitting, in the case of lesbianism).

IV. MODERN SODOMY LAWS

When *Lawrence v. Texas* was decided in 2003, fourteen states had laws prohibiting anal and/or oral sex.[3] Some state laws prohibited such sex acts for both heterosexual and homosexual actors. Other laws targeted only homosexual sex. Following are examples of sodomy laws in force in 2003.

North Carolina

If any person shall commit the crime against nature, with mankind or beast, he shall be punished as a Class I felon.

N.C. Gen. Stat. § 14–177 (2005).

Texas

(a) A person commits an offense if he engages in deviate sexual intercourse with another individual of the same sex.

(b) An offense under this section is a Class C misdemeanor.

Tex. Penal Code Ann. § 21.06 (Vernon 2005).

Oklahoma

Every person who is guilty of the detestable and abominable crime against nature, committed with mankind or with a beast, is punishable by imprisonment in the penitentiary not exceeding ten (10) years.

Okla. Stat Ann. tit. 21 § 886 (West 2005).

V. THE PROGRESSION FROM *BOWERS TO LAWRENCE*

A. AN INTERVIEW WITH MICHAEL HARDWICK*

Michael Hardwick was working in a gay bar in Atlanta when he was given a ticket for drinking in public. Hardwick insists that he threw a beer

3. Ala. Code § 13A–6–65 (2003); Fla. Stat. Ann. § 800.02 (West 2003); Idaho Code § 18–6605; Kan. Stat. Ann. § 21–3505 (2003); La. Rev. Stat. Ann. § 14:89 (West 2003); Mich. Comp. Laws. § 750.158 (2003); Miss. Code Ann. § 97–29–59 (2003); Mo. Rev. Stat. § 566.090; N.C. Gen. Stat. § 14–177 (2003); Okla. Stat. Ann. tit. 21, § 886 (West 2003); S.C. Code Ann. § 16–15–120 (2003); Tex. Pen. Code Ann. § 21.06 (Vernon 2003); Utah Code Ann. § 76–5–403 (2003); Va. Code Ann. § 18.2–361 (Michie 2003).

* Excerpted from PETER IRONS, THE COURAGE OF THEIR CONVICTIONS: SIXTEEN AMERICANS WHO FOUGHT THEIR WAY TO THE SUPREME COURT (© 1988 by Peter Irons).

bottle into the trash next to the entrance of the bar as he was leaving work in the early morning hours. A police officer, Officer Torick, issued the citation, but wrote the improper court date on the ticket. When Hardwick missed his court date, Officer Torick went to Hardwick's residence with a warrant for his arrest. Torick showed up at Hardwick's residence a mere two hours after the missed court appearance; the typical time to process a warrant was forty-eight hours. Hardwick wasn't at home when Torick arrived. When Hardwick returned later, his roommate told him about Torick and the warrant. At that point, Hardwick phoned the court clerk, explained the discrepancy in dates, and paid his fine.

Three weeks later, Hardwick was assaulted in front of his home by three men in civilian clothes. The men knew his name. They tore the cartilage from his nose, kicked him in the face, and cracked six of his ribs.

Shortly thereafter, Hardwick and a friend were engaged in oral sex in Hardwick's bedroom. Another friend, too intoxicated to drive home, had fallen asleep on the sofa and had inadvertently left the front door open. Officer Torick arrived with the three-week-old, invalid warrant and entered Hardwick's home at about 8:30 in the morning.

Hardwick summarized the ensuing events in an interview:

> Officer Torick then came to my bedroom. The door was cracked, and the door opened up and I looked up and there was nobody there. I just blew it off as the wind and went back to what I was involved in, which was mutual oral sex. About thirty-five seconds went by and I heard another noise and looked up, and this officer is standing in my bedroom. He identified himself when he realized I had seen him. He said, "My name is Officer Torick. Michael Hardwick, you are under arrest." I said, "For what? What are you doing in my bedroom?" He said, "I have a warrant for your arrest." I told him the warrant isn't any good. He said, "It doesn't matter, because I [am] acting under good faith."
>
> I asked Torick if he would leave the room so we could get dressed and he said, "There's no reason for that, because I have already seen you in your most intimate aspect." He stood there and watched us get dressed, and then he brought us over to a substation. We waited in the car for about twenty-five minutes, handcuffed to the back floor. Then he brought us in and made sure everyone in the holding cells and guards and people who were processing us knew I was in there for "cocksucking" and that I should be able to get what I was looking for. The guards were having a real good time with that.

Although the district attorney decided not to prosecute him, Michael Hardwick challenged the constitutionality of Georgia's sodomy law. The 11th Circuit Court of Appeals held in Hardwick's favor, but the U.S. Supreme Court reversed in *Bowers v. Hardwick*, below (the Georgia Supreme Court subsequently declared the law unconstitutional when applied to consenting adults in private).

B. BOWERS v. HARDWICK, 478 U.S. 186, 106 S.Ct. 2841, 92 L.Ed.2d 140 (1986)

JUDGES: WHITE, J., delivered the opinion of the Court, in which BURGER, C. J., and POWELL, REHNQUIST, and O'CONNOR, JJ., joined. BURGER, C. J., post, p. 196, and POWELL, J., post, p. 197, filed concurring opinions. BLACKMUN, J., filed a dissenting opinion, in which BRENNAN, MARSHALL, and STEVENS, JJ., joined, post, p. 199. STEVENS, J., filed a dissenting opinion, in which BRENNAN and MARSHALL, JJ., joined, post, p. 214.

In August 1982, respondent Hardwick (hereafter respondent) was charged with violating the Georgia statute criminalizing sodomy[1] by committing that act with another adult male in the bedroom of respondent's home. After a preliminary hearing, the District Attorney decided not to present the matter to the grand jury unless further evidence developed.

Respondent then brought suit in the Federal District Court, challenging the constitutionality of the statute insofar as it criminalized consensual sodomy.[2] He asserted that he was a practicing homosexual, that the Georgia sodomy statute, as administered by the defendants, placed him in imminent danger of arrest, and that the statute for several reasons violates the Federal Constitution. The District Court granted the defendants' motion to dismiss for failure to state a claim, . . .

A divided panel of the Court of Appeals for the Eleventh Circuit reversed. 760 F.2d 1202 (1985). . . . Relying on our decisions in *Griswold v. Connecticut*, 381 U.S. 479 (1965); *Eisenstadt v. Baird*, 405 U.S. 438 (1972); *Stanley v. Georgia*, 394 U.S. 557 (1969); and *Roe v. Wade*, 410 U.S. 113 (1973), the court went on to hold that the Georgia statute violated respondent's fundamental rights because his homosexual activity is a private and intimate association that is beyond the reach of state regulation by reason of the Ninth Amendment and the Due Process Clause of the Fourteenth Amendment. The case was remanded for trial, at which, to prevail, the State would have to prove that the statute is supported by a compelling interest and is the most narrowly drawn means of achieving that end.

---

1. Georgia Code Ann. § 16–6–2 (1984) provides, in pertinent part, as follows:

"(a) A person commits the offense of sodomy when he performs or submits to any sexual act involving the sex organs of one person and the mouth or anus of another. . . .

"(b) A person convicted of the offense of sodomy shall be punished by imprisonment for not less than one nor more than 20 years. . . ."

2. John and Mary Doe were also plaintiffs in the action. They alleged that they wished to engage in sexual activity proscribed by § 16–6–2 in the privacy of their home, App. 3, and that they had been "chilled and deterred" from engaging in such activity by both the existence of the statute and Hardwick's arrest. *Id.* at 5. of Appeals affirmed the District Court's judgment dismissing the Does' claim for lack of standing, 760 F.2d 1202, 1206–1207 (CA11 1985), and the Does do not challenge that holding in this Court.

The only claim properly before the Court, therefore, is Hardwick's challenge to the Georgia statute as applied to consensual homosexual sodomy. We express no opinion on the constitutionality of the Georgia statute as applied to other acts of sodomy.

Because other Courts of Appeals have arrived at judgments contrary to that of the Eleventh Circuit in this case, we granted the Attorney General's petition for certiorari questioning the holding that the sodomy statute violates the fundamental rights of homosexuals. We agree with petitioner that the Court of Appeals erred, and hence reverse its judgment.

. . . The issue presented is whether the Federal Constitution confers a fundamental right upon homosexuals to engage in sodomy and hence invalidates the laws of the many States that still make such conduct illegal and have done so for a very long time. The case also calls for some judgment about the limits of the Court's role in carrying out its constitutional mandate.

We first register our disagreement with the Court of Appeals and with respondent that the Court's prior cases have construed the Constitution to confer a right of privacy that extends to homosexual sodomy and for all intents and purposes have decided this case. The reach of this line of cases was sketched in *Carey v. Population Services International*, 431 U.S. 678, 685 (1977). *Pierce v. Society of Sisters*, 268 U.S. 510 (1925), and *Meyer v. Nebraska*, 262 U.S. 390 (1923), were described as dealing with child rearing and education; *Prince v. Massachusetts*, 321 U.S. 158 (1944), with family relationships; *Skinner v. Oklahoma ex rel. Williamson*, 316 U.S. 535 (1942), with procreation; *Loving v. Virginia*, 388 U.S. 1 (1967), with marriage; *Griswold v. Connecticut, supra*, and *Eisenstadt v. Baird, supra*, with contraception; and *Roe v. Wade*, 410 U.S. 113 (1973), with abortion. The latter three cases were interpreted as construing the Due Process Clause of the Fourteenth Amendment to confer a fundamental individual right to decide whether or not to beget or bear a child. *Carey v. Population Services International, supra* at 688–689.

Accepting the decisions in these cases and the above description of them, we think it evident that none of the rights announced in those cases bears any resemblance to the claimed constitutional right of homosexuals to engage in acts of sodomy that is asserted in this case. No connection between family, marriage, or procreation on the one hand and homosexual activity on the other has been demonstrated, either by the Court of Appeals or by respondent. Moreover, any claim that these cases nevertheless stand for the proposition that any kind of private sexual conduct between consenting adults is constitutionally insulated from state proscription is unsupportable. Indeed, the Court's opinion in *Carey* twice asserted that the privacy right, which the *Griswold* line of cases found to be one of the protections provided by the Due Process Clause, did not reach so far.

Precedent aside, however, respondent would have us announce, as the Court of Appeals did, a fundamental right to engage in homosexual sodomy. This we are quite unwilling to do. It is true that despite the language of the Due Process Clauses of the Fifth and Fourteenth Amendments, which appears to focus only on the processes by which life, liberty, or property is taken, the cases are legion in which those Clauses have been interpreted to have substantive content, subsuming rights that to a great extent are immune from federal or state regulation or proscription. Among such cases are those recognizing rights that have little or no textual support in the constitutional language. *Meyer, Prince*, and *Pierce* fall in this category, as do the privacy cases from *Griswold* to *Carey*.

Striving to assure itself and the public that announcing rights not readily identifiable in the Constitution's text involves much more than the imposition of the Justices' own choice of values on the States and the Federal Government, the Court has sought to identify the nature of the rights qualifying for heightened judicial protection. In *Palko v. Connecticut*, 302 U.S. 319, 325, 326 (1937), it was said that this category includes those fundamental liberties that are "implicit in the concept of ordered liberty," such that "neither liberty nor justice would exist if [they] were sacrificed." A different description of fundamental liberties appeared in *Moore v. East Cleveland*, 431 U.S. 494, 503 (1977) (opinion of POWELL, J.), where they are characterized as those liberties that are "deeply rooted in this Nation's history and tradition." *Id.* at 503 (POWELL, J.). *See also Griswold v. Connecticut*, 381 U.S. at 506.

It is obvious to us that neither of these formulations would extend a fundamental right to homosexuals to engage in acts of consensual sodomy. Proscriptions against that conduct have ancient roots. *See generally Survey on the Constitutional Right to Privacy in the Context of Homosexual Activity*, 40 U. Miami L. Rev. 521, 525 (1986). Sodomy was a criminal offense at common law and was forbidden by the laws of the original 13 States when they ratified the Bill of Rights. In 1868, when the Fourteenth Amendment was ratified, all but 5 of the 37 States in the Union had criminal sodomy laws. In fact, until 1961,[3] all 50 States outlawed sodomy, and today, 24 States and the District of Columbia continue to provide criminal penalties for sodomy performed in private and between consenting adults. *See* Survey, U. Miami L. Rev., *supra* at 524. Against this background, to claim that a right to engage in such conduct is "deeply rooted in this Nation's history and tradition" or "implicit in the concept of ordered liberty" is, at best, facetious.

Nor are we inclined to take a more expansive view of our authority to discover new fundamental rights imbedded in the Due Process Clause. The Court is most vulnerable and comes nearest to illegitimacy when it deals with judge-made constitutional law having little or no cognizable roots in the language or design of the Constitution. That this is so was painfully demonstrated by the face-off between the Executive and the Court in the 1930's, which resulted in the repudiation of much of the substantive gloss that the Court had placed on the Due Process Clauses of

3. In 1961, Illinois adopted the American Law Institute's Model Penal Code, which decriminalized adult, consensual, private, sexual conduct. Criminal Code of 1961, §§ 11–2, 11–3, 1961 Ill. Laws, pp. 1985, 2006 (codified as amended at Ill. Rev. Stat., ch. 38, paras. 11–2, 11–3 (1983) (repealed 1984)). *See* American Law Institute, Model Penal Code § 213.2 (Proposed Official Draft 1962).

the Fifth and Fourteenth Amendments. There should be, therefore, great resistance to expand the substantive reach of those Clauses, particularly if it requires redefining the category of rights deemed to be fundamental. Otherwise, the Judiciary necessarily takes to itself further authority to govern the country without express constitutional authority. The claimed right pressed on us today falls far short of overcoming this resistance.

Respondent, however, asserts that the result should be different where the homosexual conduct occurs in the privacy of the home. He relies on *Stanley v. Georgia*, 394 U.S. 557 (1969), where the Court held that the First Amendment prevents conviction for possessing and reading obscene material in the privacy of one's home: "If the First Amendment means anything, it means that a State has no business telling a man, sitting alone in his house, what books he may read or what films he may watch." *Id.* at 565.

Stanley did protect conduct that would not have been protected outside the home, and it partially prevented the enforcement of state obscenity laws; but the decision was firmly grounded in the First Amendment. The right pressed upon us here has no similar support in the text of the Constitution, and it does not qualify for recognition under the prevailing principles for construing the Fourteenth Amendment. Its limits are also difficult to discern. Plainly enough, otherwise illegal conduct is not always immunized whenever it occurs in the home. Victimless crimes, such as the possession and use of illegal drugs, do not escape the law where they are committed at home. *Stanley* itself recognized that its holding offered no protection for the possession in the home of drugs, firearms, or stolen goods. *Id.* at 568, n. 11. And if respondent's submission is limited to the voluntary sexual conduct between consenting adults, it would be difficult, except by fiat, to limit the claimed right to homosexual conduct while leaving exposed to prosecution adultery, incest, and other sexual crimes even though they are committed in the home. We are unwilling to start down that road.

Even if the conduct at issue here is not a fundamental right, respondent asserts that there must be a rational basis for the law and that there is none in this case other than the presumed belief of a majority of the electorate in Georgia that homosexual sodomy is immoral and unacceptable. This is said to be an inadequate rationale to support the law. The law, however, is constantly based on notions of morality, and if all laws representing essentially moral choices are to be invalidated under the Due Process Clause, the courts will be very busy indeed. Even respondent makes no such claim, but insists that majority sentiments about the morality of homosexuality should be declared inadequate. We do not agree, and are unpersuaded that the sodomy laws of some 25 States should be invalidated on this basis.

Accordingly, the judgment of the Court of Appeals is *Reversed.*

CHIEF JUSTICE BURGER, concurring

I join the Court's opinion, but I write separately to underscore my view that in constitutional terms there is no such thing as a fundamental right to commit homosexual sodomy.

As the Court notes, *ante* at 192, the proscriptions against sodomy have very "ancient roots." Decisions of individuals relating to homosexual conduct have been subject to state intervention throughout the history of Western civilization. Condemnation of those practices is firmly rooted in Judeao–Christian moral and ethical standards. Homosexual sodomy was a capital crime under Roman law. *See* Code Theod. 9.7.6; Code Just. 9.9.31. *See also* D. Bailey, Homosexuality and the Western Christian Tradition 70–81 (1975). During the English Reformation when powers of the ecclesiastical courts were transferred to the King's Courts, the first English statute criminalizing sodomy was passed. 25 Hen. VIII, ch. 6. Blackstone described "the infamous *crime against nature*" as an offense of "deeper malignity" than rape, a heinous act "the very mention of which is a disgrace to human nature," and "a crime not fit to be named." 4 W. Blackstone, Commentaries. The common law of England, including its prohibition of sodomy, became the received law of Georgia and the other Colonies. In 1816 the Georgia Legislature passed the statute at issue here, and that statute has been continuously in force in one form or another since that time. To hold that the act of homosexual sodomy is somehow protected as a fundamental right would be to cast aside millennia of moral teaching.

This is essentially not a question of personal "preferences" but rather of the legislative authority of the State. I find nothing in the Constitution depriving a State of the power to enact the statute challenged here.

JUSTICE POWELL, concurring.

I join the opinion of the Court. I agree with the Court that there is no fundamental right—*i.e.*, no substantive right under the Due Process Clause—such as that claimed by respondent Hardwick, and found to exist by the Court of Appeals. . . . The Georgia statute at issue in this case, Ga. Code Ann. § 16–6–2 (1984), authorizes a court to imprison a person for up to 20 years for a single private, consensual act of sodomy. In my view, a prison sentence for such conduct—certainly a sentence of long duration—would create a serious Eighth Amendment issue. . . .

In this case, however, respondent has not been tried, much less convicted and sentenced. Moreover, respondent has not raised the Eighth Amendment issue below. For these reasons this constitutional argument is not before us.

JUSTICE BLACKMUN, with whom JUSTICE BRENNAN, JUSTICE MARSHALL, and JUSTICE STEVENS join, dissenting.

This case is no more about "a fundamental right to engage in homosexual sodomy," as the Court purports to declare, *ante* at 191, than *Stanley v. Georgia*, 394 U.S. 557 (1969), was about a fundamental right to watch obscene movies, or *Katz v. United States*, 389 U.S. 347 (1967), was about a fundamental right to place interstate bets from a telephone booth. Rather, this case is about "the most comprehensive of rights and the right most valued by civilized men," namely, "the right to be let alone." *Olmstead v. United States*, 277 U.S. 438, 478 (1928) (Brandeis, J., dissenting).

The statute at issue, Ga. Code Ann. § 16–6–2 (1984), denies individuals the right to decide for themselves whether to engage in particular forms of private, consensual sexual activity. The Court concludes that § 16–6–2 is valid essentially because "the laws of . . . many States . . . still make such conduct illegal and have done so for a very long time." *Ante* at 190. But the fact that the moral judgments expressed by statutes like § 16–6–2 may be "natural and familiar . . . ought not to conclude our judgment upon the question whether statutes embodying them conflict with the Constitution of the United States." *Roe v. Wade*, 410 U.S. 113, 117 (1973), quoting *Lochner v. New York*, 198 U.S. 45, 76 (1905) (Holmes, J., dissenting). Like Justice Holmes, I believe that "[it] is revolting to have no better reason for a rule of law than that so it was laid down in the time of Henry IV. It is still more revolting if the grounds upon which it was laid down have vanished long since, and the rule simply persists from blind imitation of the past." Holmes, The Path of the Law, 10 Harv. L. Rev. 457, 469 (1897). I believe we must analyze respondent Hardwick's claim in the light of the values that underlie the constitutional right to privacy. If that right means anything, it means that, before Georgia can prosecute its citizens for making choices about the most intimate aspects of their lives, it must do more than assert that the choice they have made is an "abominable crime not fit to be named among Christians." *Herring v. State*, 119 Ga. 709, 721, 46 S.E. 876, 882 (1904).

I.

In its haste to reverse the Court of Appeals and hold that the Constitution does not "[confer] a fundamental right upon homosexuals to engage in sodomy," *ante* at 190, the Court relegates the actual statute being challenged to a footnote and ignores the procedural posture of the case before it. A fair reading of the statute and of the complaint clearly reveals that the majority has distorted the question this case presents.

First, the Court's almost obsessive focus on homosexual activity is particularly hard to justify in light of the broad language Georgia has used. Unlike the Court, the Georgia Legislature has not proceeded on the assumption that homosexuals are so different from other citizens that their lives may be controlled in a way that would not be tolerated if it limited the choices of those other citizens. *Cf. ante* at 188, n. 2. Rather, Georgia has provided that "[a] person commits the offense of sodomy when he performs or submits to any sexual act involving the sex organs of one person and the mouth or anus of another." Ga. Code Ann. § 16–6–2(a) (1984). The sex or status of the persons who engage in the act is irrelevant as a matter of state law. In fact, to the extent I can discern a legislative purpose for Georgia's 1968 enactment of § 16–6–2, that purpose seems to have been to broaden the coverage of the law to reach heterosexual as well as homosexual activity.[4] I therefore see no basis for the Court's decision to treat this case as an "as applied" challenge to § 16–6–2, *see ante* at 188, n. 2, or for Georgia's attempt, both in its brief and at oral argument, to defend § 16–6–2 solely on the grounds that it prohibits homosexual activity. Michael Hardwick's standing may rest in significant part on Georgia's apparent willingness to enforce against homosexuals a law it seems not to have any desire to enforce against heterosexuals. *See* Tr. of Oral Arg. 4–5; *Cf.* 760 F.2d 1202, 1205–1206 (CA11 1985). But his claim that § 16–6–2 involves an unconstitutional intrusion into his privacy and his right of intimate association does not depend in any way on his sexual orientation.

. . .

II.

"Our cases long have recognized that the Constitution embodies a promise that a certain private sphere of individual liberty will be kept largely beyond the reach of government." *Thornburgh v. American College of Obstetricians & Gynecologists*, 476 U.S. 747, 772 (1986). In construing the right to privacy, the Court has proceeded along two somewhat distinct, albeit complementary, lines. First, it has recognized a privacy interest with reference to certain *decisions* that are properly for the individual to make. *E.g., Roe v. Wade*, 410 U.S. 113 (1973); *Pierce v. Society of Sisters*, 268 U.S. 510 (1925). Second, it has recognized a privacy interest with reference to certain *places* without regard for the particular activities in which the individuals who occupy them are engaged. *E.g., United States v. Karo*, 468 U.S. 705 (1984); *Payton v. New York*, 445 U.S. 573 (1980); *Rios v. United States*, 364 U.S. 253 (1960). The case before us implicates both the decisional and the spatial aspects of the right to privacy.

A

The Court concludes today that none of our prior cases dealing with various decisions that individuals are entitled to make free of governmental interference "bears any resemblance to the claimed constitutional right of homosexuals to engage in acts of sodomy that is asserted in this case." *Ante* at 190–191. While it is true that these cases may be characterized by their connection to protection of the family, *see Roberts v. United States Jaycees*, 468 U.S. 609, 619 (1984), the Court's conclusion that they extend no further than this boundary ignores the warning in *Moore v. East Cleveland*, 431 U.S. 494, 501 (1977) (plurality opinion), against "[closing] our eyes to the basic reasons why certain rights associated with

4. Until 1968, Georgia defined sodomy as "the carnal knowledge and connection against the order of nature, by man with man, or in the same unnatural manner with woman." Ga. Crim. Code § 26–5901 (1933). In *Thompson v. Aldredge*, 187 Ga. 467, 200 S.E. 799 (1939), the Georgia Supreme Court held that § 26–5901 did not prohibit lesbian activity. And in *Riley v. Garrett*, 219 Ga. 345, 133 S.E.2d 367 (1963), the Georgia Supreme Court held that § 26–5901 did not prohibit heterosexual cunnilingus. Georgia passed the act-specific statute currently in force "perhaps in response to the restrictive court decisions such as *Riley*," Note, The Crimes Against Nature, 16 J. Pub. L. 159, 167, n. 47 (1967).

the family have been accorded shelter under the Fourteenth Amendment's Due Process Clause." We protect those rights not because they contribute, in some direct and material way, to the general public welfare, but because they form so central a part of an individual's life. "[The] concept of privacy embodies the 'moral fact that a person belongs to himself and not others nor to society as a whole.' " *Thornburgh v. American College of Obstetricians & Gynecologists*, 476 U.S. at 777, n. 5 (STEVENS, J., concurring), *quoting* Fried, Correspondence, 6 Phil. & Pub. Affairs 288–289 (1977). And so we protect the decision whether to marry precisely because marriage "is an association that promotes a way of life, not causes; a harmony in living, not political faiths; a bilateral loyalty, not commercial or social projects." *Griswold v. Connecticut*, 381 U.S. at 486. We protect the decision whether to have a child because parenthood alters so dramatically an individual's self-definition, not because of demographic considerations or the Bible's command to be fruitful and multiply. *Cf. Thornburgh v. American College of Obstetricians & Gynecologists, supra* at 777, n. 6 (STEVENS, J., concurring). And we protect the family because it contributes so powerfully to the happiness of individuals, not because of a preference for stereotypical households. *Cf. Moore v. East Cleveland*, 431 U.S. at 500–506 (plurality opinion). The Court recognized in *Roberts*, 468 U.S. at 619, that the "ability independently to define one's identity that is central to any concept of liberty" cannot truly be exercised in a vacuum; we all depend on the "emotional enrichment from close ties with others." *Ibid.*

Only the most willful blindness could obscure the fact that sexual intimacy is "a sensitive, key relationship of human existence, central to family life, community welfare, and the development of human personality," *Paris Adult Theatre I v. Slaton*, 413 U.S. 49, 63 (1973); *see also Carey v. Population Services International*, 431 U.S. 678, 685 (1977). The fact that individuals define themselves in a significant way through their intimate sexual relationships with others suggests, in a Nation as diverse as ours, that there may be many "right" ways of conducting those relationships, and that much of the richness of a relationship will come from the freedom an individual has to *choose* the form and nature of these intensely personal bonds. *See* Karst, The Freedom of Intimate Association, 89 Yale L. J. 624, 637 (1980); *cf. Eisenstadt v. Baird*, 405 U.S. 438, 453 (1972); *Roe v. Wade*, 410 U.S. at 153.

In a variety of circumstances we have recognized that a necessary corollary of giving individuals freedom to choose how to conduct their lives is acceptance of the fact that different individuals will make different choices. For example, in holding that the clearly important state interest in public education should give way to a competing claim by the Amish to the effect that extended formal schooling threatened their way of life, the Court declared: "There can be no assumption that today's majority is 'right' and the Amish and others like them are 'wrong.' A way of life that is odd or even erratic but interferes with no rights or interests of others is not to be condemned because it is different." *Wisconsin v. Yoder*, 406 U.S.

205, 223–224 (1972). The Court claims that its decision today merely refuses to recognize a fundamental right to engage in homosexual sodomy; what the Court really has refused to recognize is the fundamental interest all individuals have in controlling the nature of their intimate associations with others.

B

The behavior for which Hardwick faces prosecution occurred in his own home, a place to which the Fourth Amendment attaches special significance. The Court's treatment of this aspect of the case is symptomatic of its overall refusal to consider the broad principles that have informed our treatment of privacy in specific cases. Just as the right to privacy is more than the mere aggregation of a number of entitlements to engage in specific behavior, so too, protecting the physical integrity of the home is more than merely a means of protecting specific activities that often take place there. Even when our understanding of the contours of the right to privacy depends on "reference to a 'place,' " *Katz v. United States*, 389 U.S. at 361 (Harlan, J., concurring), "the essence of a Fourth Amendment violation is 'not the breaking of [a person's] doors, and the rummaging of his drawers,' but rather is 'the invasion of his indefeasible right of personal security, personal liberty and private property.' " *California v. Ciraolo*, 476 U.S. 207, 226 (1986) (POWELL, J., dissenting), *quoting Boyd v. United States*, 116 U.S. 616, 630 (1886).

III.

. . .

... [Freedom] to differ is not limited to things that do not matter much. That would be a mere shadow of freedom. The test of its substance is the right to differ as to things that touch the heart of the existing order." *See also* Karst, 89 Yale L. J. at 627. It is precisely because the issue raised by this case touches the heart of what makes individuals what they are that we should be especially sensitive to the rights of those whose choices upset the majority.

The assertion that "traditional Judeo–Christian values proscribe" the conduct involved, Brief for Petitioner 20, cannot provide an adequate justification for § 16–6–2. That certain, but by no means all, religious groups condemn the behavior at issue gives the State no license to impose their judgments on the entire citizenry. The legitimacy of secular legislation depends instead on whether the State can advance some justification for its law beyond its conformity to religious doctrine. *See, e.g., McGowan v. Maryland*, 366 U.S. 420, 429–453 (1961); *Stone v. Graham*, 449 U.S. 39 (1980). Thus, far from buttressing his case, petitioner's invocation of Leviticus, Romans, St. Thomas Aquinas, and sodomy's heretical status during the Middle Ages undermines his suggestion that § 16–6–2 represents a legitimate use of secular coercive power.[5] A State can no more

5. The theological nature of the origin of Anglo–American antisodomy statutes is patent. It was not until 1533 that sodomy was made a secular offense in England. 25 Hen. VIII, ch. 6. Until

punish private behavior because of religious intolerance than it can punish such behavior because of racial animus. "The Constitution cannot control such prejudices, but neither can it tolerate them. Private biases may be outside the reach of the law, but the law cannot, directly or indirectly, give them effect." *Palmore v. Sidoti*, 466 U.S. 429, 433 (1984). No matter how uncomfortable a certain group may make the majority of this Court, we have held that "[mere] public intolerance or animosity cannot constitutionally justify the deprivation of a person's physical liberty." *O'Connor v. Donaldson*, 422 U.S. 563, 575 (1975). *See also Cleburne v. Cleburne Living Center, Inc.*, 473 U.S. 432 (1985); *United States Dept. of Agriculture v. Moreno*, 413 U.S. 528, 534 (1973).

Nor can § 16–6–2 be justified as a "morally neutral" exercise of Georgia's power to "protect the public environment," *Paris Adult Theatre I*, 413 U.S. at 68–69. Certainly, some private behavior can affect the fabric of society as a whole. Reasonable people may differ about whether particular sexual acts are moral or immoral, but "we have ample evidence for believing that people will not abandon morality, will not think any better of murder, cruelty and dishonesty, merely because some private sexual practice which they abominate is not punished by the law." H. L. A. Hart, Immorality and Treason, reprinted in The Law as Literature 220, 225 (L. Blom–Cooper ed. 1961). Petitioner and the Court fail to see the difference between laws that protect public sensibilities and those that enforce private morality. Statutes banning public sexual activity are entirely consistent with protecting the individual's liberty interest in decisions concerning sexual relations: the same recognition that those decisions are intensely private which justifies protecting them from governmental interference can justify protecting individuals from unwilling exposure to the sexual activities of others. But the mere fact that intimate behavior may be punished when it takes place in public cannot dictate how States can regulate intimate behavior that occurs in intimate places. *See Paris Adult Theatre I*, 413 U.S. at 66, n. 13 ("marital intercourse on a street corner or a theater stage" can be forbidden despite the constitutional protection identified in *Griswold v. Connecticut*, 381 U.S. 479 (1965)).[6]

that time, the offense was, in Sir James Stephen's words, "merely ecclesiastical." 2 J. Stephen, A History of the Criminal Law of England 429–430 (1883). Pollock and Maitland similarly observed that "[the] crime against nature . . . was so closely connected with heresy that the vulgar had but one name for both." 2 F. Pollock & F. Maitland, The History of English Law 554 (1895). The transfer of jurisdiction over prosecutions for sodomy to the secular courts seems primarily due to the alteration of ecclesiastical jurisdiction attendant on England's break with the Roman Catholic Church, rather than to any new understanding of the sovereign's interest in preventing or punishing the behavior involved. *Cf.* 6 E. Coke, Institutes, ch. 10 (4th ed. 1797).

6. At oral argument a suggestion appeared that, while the Fourth Amendment's special protection of the home might prevent the State from enforcing § 16–6–2 against individuals who engage in consensual sexual activity there, that protection would not make the statute invalid. *See* Tr. of Oral Arg. 10–11. The suggestion misses the point entirely. If the law is not invalid, then the police *can* invade the home to enforce it, provided, of course, that they obtain a determination of probable cause from a neutral magistrate. One of the reasons for the Court's holding in *Griswold v. Connecticut*, 381 U.S. 479 (1965), was precisely the possibility, and repugnancy, of permitting searches to obtain evidence regarding the use of contraceptives. *Id.* at 485–486. Permitting the kinds of searches that might be necessary to obtain evidence of the sexual activity

This case involves no real interference with the rights of others, for the mere knowledge that other individuals do not adhere to one's value system cannot be a legally cognizable interest, *cf. Diamond v. Charles*, 476 U.S. 54, 65–66 (1986), let alone an interest that can justify invading the houses, hearts, and minds of citizens who choose to live their lives differently.

. . .

JUSTICE STEVENS, with whom JUSTICE BRENNAN and JUSTICE MARSHALL join, dissenting.

. . .

Because the Georgia statute expresses the traditional view that sodomy is an immoral kind of conduct regardless of the identity of the persons who engage in it, I believe that a proper analysis of its constitutionality requires consideration of two questions: First, may a State totally prohibit the described conduct by means of a neutral law applying without exception to all persons subject to its jurisdiction? If not, may the State save the statute by announcing that it will only enforce the law against homosexuals? The two questions merit separate discussion.

I.

Our prior cases make two propositions abundantly clear. First, the fact that the governing majority in a State has traditionally viewed a particular practice as immoral is not a sufficient reason for upholding a law prohibiting the practice; neither history nor tradition could save a law prohibiting miscegenation from constitutional attack.[7] Second, individual decisions by married persons, concerning the intimacies of their physical relationship, even when not intended to produce offspring, are a form of "liberty" protected by the Due Process Clause of the Fourteenth Amendment. *Griswold v. Connecticut*, 381 U.S. 479 (1965). Moreover, this protection extends to intimate choices by unmarried as well as married persons. *Carey v. Population Services International*, 431 U.S. 678 (1977); *Eisenstadt v. Baird*, 405 U.S. 438 (1972).

In consideration of claims of this kind, the Court has emphasized the individual interest in privacy, but its decisions have actually been animated by an even more fundamental concern. As I wrote some years ago:

> "These cases do not deal with the individual's interest in protection from unwarranted public attention, comment, or exploitation. They deal, rather, with the individual's right to make certain unusually important decisions that will affect his own, or his family's, destiny. The Court has referred to such decisions as implicating 'basic values,' as being 'fundamental,' and as being dignified by history and tradi-

---

banned by § 16–6–2 seems no less intrusive, or repugnant. *Cf. Winston v. Lee*, 470 U.S. 753 (1985); *Mary Beth G. v. City of Chicago*, 723 F.2d 1263, 1274 (CA7 1983).

7. *See Loving v. Virginia*, 388 U.S. 1 (1967). Interestingly, miscegenation was once treated as a crime similar to sodomy. *See* Hawley & McGregor, The Criminal Law at 287 (discussing crime of sodomy); *id.* at 288 (discussing crime of miscegenation).

tion. The character of the Court's language in these cases brings to mind the origins of the American heritage of freedom—the abiding interest in individual liberty that makes certain state intrusions on the citizen's right to decide how he will live his own life intolerable. Guided by history, our tradition of respect for the dignity of individual choice in matters of conscience and the restraints implicit in the federal system, federal judges have accepted the responsibility for recognition and protection of these rights in appropriate cases." *Fitzgerald v. Porter Memorial Hospital*, 523 F.2d 716, 719–720 (CA7 1975) (footnotes omitted), cert. denied, 425 U.S. 916 (1976).

Society has every right to encourage its individual members to follow particular traditions in expressing affection for one another and in gratifying their personal desires. It, of course, may prohibit an individual from imposing his will on another to satisfy his own selfish interests. It also may prevent an individual from interfering with, or violating, a legally sanctioned and protected relationship, such as marriage. And it may explain the relative advantages and disadvantages of different forms of intimate expression. But when individual married couples are isolated from observation by others, the way in which they voluntarily choose to conduct their intimate relations is a matter for them—not the State—to decide.[8] The essential "liberty" that animated the development of the law in cases like *Griswold, Eisenstadt*, and *Carey* surely embraces the right to engage in nonreproductive, sexual conduct that others may consider offensive or immoral.

Paradoxical as it may seem, our prior cases thus establish that a State may not prohibit sodomy within "the sacred precincts of marital bedrooms," *Griswold*, 381 U.S. at 485, or, indeed, between unmarried heterosexual adults. *Eisenstadt*, 405 U.S. at 453. In all events, it is perfectly clear that the State of Georgia may not totally prohibit the conduct proscribed by § 16–6–2 of the Georgia Criminal Code.

II.

If the Georgia statute cannot be enforced as it is written—if the conduct it seeks to prohibit is a protected form of liberty for the vast majority of Georgia's citizens—the State must assume the burden of justifying a selective application of its law. Either the persons to whom Georgia seeks to apply its statute do not have the same interest in "liberty" that others have, or there must be a reason why the State may be permitted to apply a generally applicable law to certain persons that it does not apply to others.

The first possibility is plainly unacceptable. Although the meaning of the principle that "all men are created equal" is not always clear, it surely

8. Indeed, the Georgia Attorney General concedes that Georgia's statute would be unconstitutional if applied to a married couple. *See* Tr. of Oral Arg. 8 (stating that application of the statute to a married couple "would be unconstitutional" because of the "right of marital privacy as identified by the Court in Griswold"). Significantly, Georgia passed the current statute three years after the Court's decision in *Griswold*.

must mean that every free citizen has the same interest in "liberty" that the members of the majority share. From the standpoint of the individual, the homosexual and the heterosexual have the same interest in deciding how he will live his own life, and, more narrowly, how he will conduct himself in his personal and voluntary associations with his companions. State intrusion into the private conduct of either is equally burdensome.

The second possibility is similarly unacceptable. A policy of selective application must be supported by a neutral and legitimate interest—something more substantial than a habitual dislike for, or ignorance about, the disfavored group. Neither the State nor the Court has identified any such interest in this case. . . .

Nor, indeed, does the Georgia prosecutor even believe that all homosexuals who violate this statute should be punished. This conclusion is evident from the fact that the respondent in this very case has formally acknowledged in his complaint and in court that he has engaged, and intends to continue to engage, in the prohibited conduct, yet the State has elected not to process criminal charges against him. As Justice Powell points out, moreover, Georgia's prohibition on private, consensual sodomy has not been enforced for decades. The record of nonenforcement, in this case and in the last several decades, belies the Attorney General's representations about the importance of the State's selective application of its generally applicable law.

Both the Georgia statute and the Georgia prosecutor thus completely fail to provide the Court with any support for the conclusion that homosexual sodomy, *simpliciter*, is considered unacceptable conduct in that State, and that the burden of justifying a selective application of the generally applicable law has been met.

III.

The Court orders the dismissal of respondent's complaint even though the State's statute prohibits all sodomy; even though that prohibition is concededly unconstitutional with respect to heterosexuals; and even though the State's *post hoc* explanations for selective application are belied by the State's own actions. At the very least, I think it clear at this early stage of the litigation that respondent has alleged a constitutional claim sufficient to withstand a motion to dismiss.

I respectfully dissent.

DISCUSSION

What is the narrow holding of Bowers v. Hardwick*? Does it differ from the question Michael Hardwick brought to the Court? What clause of the Constitution does the Court purport to consider?*

What is the basis for the dissenting claim that the conduct at issue in Hardwick *was, in fact, protected by the constitutional right to privacy?*

What methods and tests are used by the majority in Hardwick *in its examination of the claim of a fundamental right to sexual privacy?*

Following his retirement from the Supreme Court, Justice Powell indicated: "I think I probably made a mistake in that one [Hardwick]. I do think it was inconsistent in a general way with Roe [v. Wade]. *When I had the opportunity to reread the opinions a few months later, I thought the dissent had the better of the arguments." Do you agree?*

C. ROMER v. EVANS, 517 U.S. 620, 116 S.Ct. 1620, 134 L.Ed.2d 855 (1996)

JUSTICE KENNEDY delivered the opinion of the Court.

One century ago, the first Justice Harlan admonished this Court that the Constitution "neither knows nor tolerates classes among citizens." *Plessy v. Ferguson*, 163 U.S. 537, 559, 16 S.Ct. 1138, 41 L.Ed. 256 (1896) (dissenting opinion). Unheeded then, those words now are understood to state a commitment to the law's neutrality where the rights of persons are at stake. The Equal Protection Clause enforces this principle and today requires us to hold invalid a provision of Colorado's Constitution.

I

The enactment challenged in this case is an amendment to the Constitution of the State of Colorado, adopted in a 1992 statewide referendum. The parties and the state courts refer to it as "Amendment 2," its designation when submitted to the voters. The impetus for the amendment and the contentious campaign that preceded its adoption came in large part from ordinances that had been passed in various Colorado municipalities. For example, the cities of Aspen and Boulder and the city and County of Denver each had enacted ordinances which banned discrimination in many transactions and activities, including housing, employment, education, public accommodations, and health and welfare services. Denver Rev. Municipal Code, Art. IV, §§ 28–91 to 28–116 (1991); Aspen Municipal Code § 13–98 (1977); Boulder Rev. Code §§ 12–1–1 to 12–1–11 (1987). What gave rise to the statewide controversy was the protection the ordinances afforded to persons discriminated against by reason of their sexual orientation. *See* Boulder Rev. Code § 12–1–1 (defining "sexual orientation" as "the choice of sexual partners, i.e., bisexual, homosexual or heterosexual"); Denver Rev. Municipal Code, Art. IV, § 28–92 (defining "sexual orientation" as "the status of an individual as to his or her hetero-sexuality, homosexuality or bisexuality"). Amendment 2 repeals these ordinances to the extent they prohibit discrimination on the basis of "homosexual, lesbian or bisexual orientation, conduct, practices or relationships."

Yet Amendment 2, in explicit terms, does more than repeal or rescind these provisions. It prohibits all legislative, executive or judicial action at any level of state or local government designed to protect the named class, a class we shall refer to as homosexual persons or gays and lesbians. The amendment reads:

> No Protected Status Based on Homosexual, Lesbian or Bisexual Orientation. Neither the State of Colorado, through any of its branches or departments, nor any of its agencies, political subdivisions, municipalities or school districts, shall enact, adopt or enforce any statute, regulation, ordinance or policy whereby homosexual, lesbian or bisexual orientation, conduct, practices or relationships shall constitute or otherwise be the basis of or entitle any person or class of persons to have or claim any minority status, quota preferences, protected status or claim of discrimination. This Section of the Constitution shall be in all respects self-executing.

Soon after Amendment 2 was adopted, this litigation to declare its invalidity and enjoin its enforcement was commenced in the District Court for the City and County of Denver. Among the plaintiffs (respondents here) were homosexual persons, some of them government employees. They alleged that enforcement of Amendment 2 would subject them to immediate and substantial risk of discrimination on the basis of their sexual orientation. Other plaintiffs (also respondents here) included the three municipalities whose ordinances we have cited and certain other governmental entities which had acted earlier to protect homosexuals from discrimination but would be prevented by Amendment 2 from continuing to do so. Although Governor Romer had been on record opposing the adoption of Amendment 2, he was named in his official capacity as a defendant, together with the Colorado Attorney General and the State of Colorado.

The trial court granted a preliminary injunction to stay enforcement of Amendment 2, and an appeal was taken to the Supreme Court of Colorado. Sustaining the interim injunction and remanding the case for further proceedings, the State Supreme Court held that Amendment 2 was subject to strict scrutiny under the Fourteenth Amendment because it infringed the fundamental right of gays and lesbians to participate in the political process. *Evans v. Romer*, 854 P.2d 1270 (Colo. 1993) *(Evans I)*. . . . On remand, the State advanced various arguments in an effort to show that Amendment 2 was narrowly tailored to serve compelling interests, but the trial court found none sufficient. It enjoined enforcement of Amendment 2, and the Supreme Court of Colorado, in a second opinion, affirmed the ruling. 882 P.2d 1335 (1994) *(Evans II)*. We granted certiorari, 513 U.S. 1146 (1995), and now affirm the judgment, but on a rationale different from that adopted by the State Supreme Court.

II

The State's principal argument in defense of Amendment 2 is that it puts gays and lesbians in the same position as all other persons. So, the State says, the measure does no more than deny homosexuals special rights. This reading of the amendment's language is implausible. We rely not upon our own interpretation of the amendment but upon the authoritative construction of Colorado's Supreme Court. The state court, deeming it unnecessary to determine the full extent of the amendment's reach, found it invalid even on a modest reading of its implications. The critical discussion of the amendment, set out in *Evans I*, is as follows:

> The immediate objective of Amendment 2 is, at a minimum, to repeal existing statutes, regulations, ordinances, and policies of state and local entities that barred discrimination based on sexual orientation. *See* Aspen, Colo., Mun. Code § 13–98 (1977) (prohibiting discrimination in employment, housing and public accommodations on the basis of sexual orientation); Boulder, Colo., Rev. Code §§ 12–1–2 to–4 (1987) (same); Denver, Colo., Rev. Mun. Code art. IV, §§ 28–91 to–116 (1991) (same); Executive Order No. D0035 (December 10, 1990) (prohibiting employment discrimination for "all state employees, classified and exempt" on the basis of sexual orientation); Colorado Insurance Code, § 10–3–1104, 4A C. R. S. (1992 Supp.) (forbidding health insurance providers from determining insurability and premiums based on an applicant's, a beneficiary's, or an insured's sexual orientation); and various provisions prohibiting discrimination based on sexual orientation at state colleges.
>
> The "ultimate effect" of Amendment 2 is to prohibit any governmental entity from adopting similar, or more protective statutes, regulations, ordinances, or policies in the future unless the state constitution is first amended to permit such measures. 854 P.2d at 1284–1285, and n. 26.

Sweeping and comprehensive is the change in legal status effected by this law. So much is evident from the ordinances the Colorado Supreme Court declared would be void by operation of Amendment 2. Homosexuals, by state decree, are put in a solitary class with respect to transactions and relations in both the private and governmental spheres. The amendment withdraws from homosexuals, but no others, specific legal protection from the injuries caused by discrimination, and it forbids reinstatement of these laws and policies.

The change Amendment 2 works in the legal status of gays and lesbians in the private sphere is far reaching, both on its own terms and when considered in light of the structure and operation of modern antidiscrimination laws. That structure is well illustrated by contemporary statutes and ordinances prohibiting discrimination by providers of public accommodations. "At common law, innkeepers, smiths, and others who 'made profession of a public employment,' were prohibited from refusing, without good reason, to serve a customer." *Hurley v. Irish–American Gay, Lesbian and Bisexual Group of Boston, Inc.*, 515 U.S. 557, 571, 115 S.Ct. 2338, 132 L.Ed.2d 487 (1995). The duty was a general one and did not specify protection for particular groups. The common-law rules, however, proved insufficient in many instances, and it was settled early that the Fourteenth Amendment did not give Congress a general power to prohibit discrimination in public accommodations, *Civil Rights Cases*, 109 U.S. 3, 25, 3 S.Ct. 18, 27 L.Ed. 835 (1883). In consequence, most States have chosen to counter discrimination by enacting detailed statutory schemes. . . .

Colorado's state and municipal laws typify this emerging tradition of statutory protection and follow a consistent pattern. The laws first enumerate the persons or entities subject to a duty not to discriminate. The list goes well beyond the entities covered by the common law. The Boulder ordinance, for example, has a comprehensive definition of entities deemed places of "public accommodation." They include "any place of business engaged in any sales to the general public and any place that offers services, facilities, privileges, or advantages to the general public or that receives financial support through solicitation of the general public or through governmental subsidy of any kind." Boulder Rev. Code § 12–1–1(j) (1987). The Denver ordinance is of similar breadth, applying, for example, to hotels, restaurants, hospitals, dental clinics, theaters, banks, common carriers, travel and insurance agencies, and "shops and stores dealing with goods or services of any kind," Denver Rev. Municipal Code, Art. IV, § 28–92 (1991).

These statutes and ordinances also depart from the common law by enumerating the groups or persons within their ambit of protection. Enumeration is the essential device used to make the duty not to discriminate concrete and to provide guidance for those who must comply. In following this approach, Colorado's state and local governments have not limited antidiscrimination laws to groups that have so far been given the protection of heightened equal protection scrutiny under our cases. . . . Rather, they set forth an extensive catalog of traits which cannot be the basis for discrimination, including age, military status, marital status, pregnancy, parenthood, custody of a minor child, political affiliation, physical or mental disability of an individual or of his or her associates—and, in recent times, sexual orientation.

Amendment 2 bars homosexuals from securing protection against the injuries that these public-accommodations laws address. That in itself is a severe consequence, but there is more. Amendment 2, in addition, nullifies specific legal protections for this targeted class in all transactions in housing, sale of real estate, insurance, health and welfare services, private education, and employment. . . .

Not confined to the private sphere, Amendment 2 also operates to repeal and forbid all laws or policies providing specific protection for gays or lesbians from discrimination by every level of Colorado government. The State Supreme Court cited two examples of protections in the governmental sphere that are now rescinded and may not be reintroduced. The first is Colorado Executive Order D0035 (1990), which forbids employment discrimination against " 'all state employees, classified and exempt' on the basis of sexual orientation." 854 P.2d at 1284. Also repealed, and now forbidden, are "various provisions prohibiting discrimination based on sexual orientation at state colleges." *Id.* at 1284, 1285. The repeal of these measures and the prohibition against their future reenactment demonstrate that Amendment 2 has the same force and effect in Colorado's governmental sector as it does elsewhere and that it applies to policies as well as ordinary legislation.

Amendment 2's reach may not be limited to specific laws passed for the benefit of gays and lesbians. It is a fair, if not necessary, inference from the broad language of the amendment that it deprives gays and lesbians even of the protection of general laws and policies that prohibit arbitrary discrimination in governmental and private settings. *See, e.g.*, Colo. Rev. Stat. § 24–4–106(7) (1988) (agency action subject to judicial review under arbitrary and capricious standard); § 18–8–405 (making it a criminal offense for a public servant knowingly, arbitrarily, or capriciously to refrain from performing a duty imposed on him by law); § 10–3–1104(1)(f) (prohibiting "unfair discrimination" in insurance); 4 Colo. Code of Regulations 801–1, Policy 11–1 (1983) (prohibiting discrimination in state employment on grounds of specified traits or "other non-merit factor"). At some point in the systematic administration of these laws, an official must determine whether homosexuality is an arbitrary and, thus, forbidden basis for decision. Yet a decision to that effect would itself amount to a policy prohibiting discrimination on the basis of homosexuality, and so would appear to be no more valid under Amendment 2 than the specific prohibitions against discrimination the state court held invalid.

If this consequence follows from Amendment 2, as its broad language suggests, it would compound the constitutional difficulties the law creates. The state court did not decide whether the amendment has this effect, however, and neither need we. In the course of rejecting the argument that Amendment 2 is intended to conserve resources to fight discrimination against suspect classes, the Colorado Supreme Court made the limited observation that the amendment is not intended to affect many antidiscrimination laws protecting nonsuspect classes, *Romer II*, 882 P.2d at 1346, n. 9. In our view that does not resolve the issue. In any event, even if, as we doubt, homosexuals could find some safe harbor in laws of general application, we cannot accept the view that Amendment 2's prohibition on specific legal protections does no more than deprive homosexuals of special rights. To the contrary, the amendment imposes a special disability upon those persons alone. Homosexuals are forbidden the safeguards that others enjoy or may seek without constraint. They can obtain specific protection against discrimination only by enlisting the citizenry of Colorado to amend the State Constitution or perhaps, on the State's view, by trying to pass helpful laws of general applicability. This is so no matter how local or discrete the harm, no matter how public and widespread the injury. We find nothing special in the protections Amendment 2 withholds. These are protections taken for granted by most people either because they already have them or do not need them; these are protections against exclusion from an almost limitless number of transactions and endeavors that constitute ordinary civic life in a free society.

III

The Fourteenth Amendment's promise that no person shall be denied the equal protection of the laws must coexist with the practical necessity that most legislation classifies for one purpose or another, with resulting disadvantage to various groups or persons. *Personnel Administrator of Mass. v. Feeney*, 442 U.S. 256, 271–272, 99 S.Ct. 2282, 60 L.Ed.2d 870 (1979); *F. S. Royster Guano Co. v. Virginia*, 253 U.S. 412, 415, 40 S.Ct. 560, 64 L.Ed. 989 (1920). We have attempted to reconcile the principle with the reality by stating that, if a law neither burdens a fundamental right nor targets a suspect class, we will uphold the legislative classification so long as it bears a rational relation to some legitimate end. *See, e.g., Heller v. Doe*, 509 U.S. 312, 319–320, 113 S.Ct. 2637, 125 L.Ed.2d 257 (1993).

Amendment 2 fails, indeed defies, even this conventional inquiry. First, the amendment has the peculiar property of imposing a broad and undifferentiated disability on a single named group, an exceptional and, as we shall explain, invalid form of legislation. Second, its sheer breadth is so discontinuous with the reasons offered for it that the amendment seems inexplicable by anything but animus toward the class it affects; it lacks a rational relationship to legitimate state interests.

Taking the first point, even in the ordinary equal protection case calling for the most deferential of standards, we insist on knowing the relation between the classification adopted and the object to be attained. The search for the link between classification and objective gives substance to the Equal Protection Clause; it provides guidance and discipline for the legislature, which is entitled to know what sorts of laws it can pass; and it marks the limits of our own authority. In the ordinary case, a law will be sustained if it can be said to advance a legitimate government interest, even if the law seems unwise or works to the disadvantage of a particular group, or if the rationale for it seems tenuous.... By requiring that the classification bear a rational relationship to an independent and legitimate legislative end, we ensure that classifications are not drawn for the purpose of disadvantaging the group burdened by the law. *See Railroad Retirement Bd. v. Fritz*, 449 U.S. 166, 181, 101 S.Ct. 453, 66 L.Ed.2d 368 (1980) (STEVENS, J., concurring) ("If the adverse impact on the disfavored class is an apparent aim of the legislature, its impartiality would be suspect").

Amendment 2 confounds this normal process of judicial review. It is at once too narrow and too broad. It identifies persons by a single trait and then denies them protection across the board. The resulting disqualification of a class of persons from the right to seek specific protection from the law is unprecedented in our jurisprudence. The absence of precedent for Amendment 2 is itself instructive; "discriminations of an unusual character especially suggest careful consideration to determine whether they are obnoxious to the constitutional provision." *Louisville Gas & Elec. Co. v. Coleman*, 277 U.S. 32, 37–38, 48 S.Ct. 423, 72 L.Ed. 770 (1928).

It is not within our constitutional tradition to enact laws of this sort. Central both to the idea of the rule of law and to our own Constitution's guarantee of equal protection is the principle that government and each of its parts remain open on impartial terms to all who seek its assistance. "Equal protection of the laws is not achieved through indiscriminate imposition of inequalities." *Sweatt v. Painter*, 339 U.S. 629, 635, 70 S.Ct. 848, 94 L.Ed. 1114 (1950) (quoting *Shelley v. Kraemer*, 334 U.S. 1, 22, 68 S.Ct. 836, 92 L.Ed. 1161 (1948)). Respect for this principle explains why laws singling out a certain class of citizens for disfavored legal status or general hardships are rare. A law declaring that in general it shall be more difficult for one group of citizens than for all others to seek aid from the government is itself a denial of equal protection of the laws in the most literal sense. "The guaranty of 'equal protection of the laws is a pledge of the protection of equal laws.' " *Skinner v. Oklahoma ex rel. Williamson*, 316 U.S. 535, 541, 62 S.Ct. 1110, 86 L.Ed. 1655 (1942) (*quoting Yick Wo v. Hopkins*, 118 U.S. 356, 369, 6 S.Ct. 1064, 30 L.Ed. 220 (1886)).

Davis v. Beason, 133 U.S. 333, 10 S.Ct. 299, 33 L.Ed. 637 (1890), not cited by the parties but relied upon by the dissent, is not evidence that Amendment 2 is within our constitutional tradition, and any reliance upon it as authority for sustaining the amendment is misplaced. In *Davis*, the Court approved an Idaho territorial statute denying Mormons, polygamists, and advocates of polygamy the right to vote and to hold office because, as the Court construed the statute, it "simply excludes from the privilege of voting, or of holding any office of honor, trust or profit, those who have been convicted of certain offences, and those who advocate a practical resistance to the laws of the Territory and justify and approve the commission of crimes forbidden by it." *Id.* at 347. To the extent *Davis* held that persons advocating a certain practice may be denied the right to vote, it is no longer good law. *Brandenburg v. Ohio*, 395 U.S. 444, 89 S.Ct. 1827, 23 L.Ed.2d 430 (1969) *(per curiam)*. To the extent it held that the groups designated in the statute may be deprived of the right to vote because of their status, its ruling could not stand without surviving strict scrutiny, a most doubtful outcome. *Dunn v. Blumstein*, 405 U.S. 330, 337, 92 S.Ct. 995, 31 L.Ed.2d 274 (1972); *cf. United States v. Brown*, 381 U.S. 437, 85 S.Ct. 1707, 14 L.Ed.2d 484 (1965); *United States v. Robel*, 389 U.S. 258, 88 S.Ct. 419, 19 L.Ed.2d 508 (1967). To the extent *Davis* held that a convicted felon may be denied the right to vote, its holding is not implicated by our decision and is unexceptionable. *See Richardson v. Ramirez*, 418 U.S. 24, 94 S.Ct. 2655, 41 L.Ed.2d 551 (1974).

A second and related point is that laws of the kind now before us raise the inevitable inference that the disadvantage imposed is born of animosity toward the class of persons affected. "If the constitutional conception of 'equal protection of the laws' means anything, it must at the very least mean that a bare . . . desire to harm a politically unpopular group cannot constitute a *legitimate* governmental interest." *Department of Agriculture v. Moreno*, 413 U.S. 528, 534, 93 S.Ct. 2821, 37 L.Ed.2d 782 (1973). Even laws enacted for broad and ambitious purposes often can be explained by reference to legitimate public policies which justify the incidental disadvantages they impose on certain persons. Amendment 2, however, in making a general announcement that gays and lesbians shall not have any particular protections from the law, inflicts on them immediate, continuing, and real injuries that outrun and belie any legitimate justifications that may be claimed for it. We conclude that, in addition to the far-reaching deficiencies of Amendment 2 that we have noted, the principles it offends, in another sense, are conventional and venerable; a law must bear a rational relationship to a legitimate governmental purpose, *Kadrmas v. Dickinson Public Schools*, 487 U.S. 450, 462, 108 S.Ct. 2481, 101 L.Ed.2d 399 (1988), and Amendment 2 does not.

The primary rationale the State offers for Amendment 2 is respect for other citizens' freedom of association, and in particular the liberties of landlords or employers who have personal or religious objections to homosexuality. Colorado also cites its interest in conserving resources to fight discrimination against other groups. The breadth of the Amendment is so far removed from these particular justifications that we find it impossible to credit them. We cannot say that Amendment 2 is directed to any identifiable legitimate purpose or discrete objective. It is a status-based enactment divorced from any factual context from which we could discern a relationship to legitimate state interests; it is a classification of persons undertaken for its own sake, something the Equal Protection Clause does not permit. "Class legislation ... [is] obnoxious to the prohibitions of the Fourteenth Amendment...." *Civil Rights Cases*, 109 U.S. at 24.

We must conclude that Amendment 2 classifies homosexuals not to further a proper legislative end but to make them unequal to everyone else. This Colorado cannot do. A State cannot so deem a class of persons a stranger to its laws. Amendment 2 violates the Equal Protection Clause, and the judgment of the Supreme Court of Colorado is affirmed.

It is so ordered.

JUSTICE SCALIA, with whom THE CHIEF JUSTICE and JUSTICE THOMAS join, dissenting.

The Court has mistaken a *Kulturkampf* for a fit of spite. The constitutional amendment before us here is not the manifestation of a "bare ... desire to harm" homosexuals, *ante* at 634, but is rather a modest attempt by seemingly tolerant Coloradans to preserve traditional sexual mores against the efforts of a politically powerful minority to revise those mores through use of the laws. That objective, and the means chosen to achieve it, are not only unimpeachable under any constitutional doctrine hitherto pronounced (hence the opinion's heavy reliance upon principles of righteousness rather than judicial holdings); they have been specifically approved by the Congress of the United States and by this Court.

In holding that homosexuality cannot be singled out for disfavorable treatment, the Court contradicts a decision, unchallenged here, pronounced only 10 years ago, *see Bowers v. Hardwick*, 478 U.S. 186, 106 S.Ct. 2841, 92 L.Ed.2d 140 (1986), and places the prestige of this institution behind the proposition that opposition to homosexuality is as reprehensible as racial or religious bias. Whether it is or not is *precisely* the cultural debate that gave rise to the Colorado constitutional amendment (and to the preferential laws against which the amendment was directed). Since the Constitution of the United States says nothing about this subject, it is left to be resolved by normal democratic means, including the democratic adoption of provisions in state constitutions. This Court has no business imposing upon all Americans the resolution favored by the elite class from which the Members of this institution are selected, pronouncing that "animosity" toward homosexuality, *ante* at 634, is evil. I vigorously dissent.

I

Let me first discuss Part II of the Court's opinion, its longest section, which is devoted to rejecting the State's arguments that Amendment 2 "puts gays and lesbians in the same position as all other persons," and "does no more than deny homosexuals special rights," *ante* at 626. The Court concludes that this reading of Amendment 2's language is "implausible" under the "authoritative construction" given Amendment 2 by the Supreme Court of Colorado. *Ibid.*hat dispute, because the Supreme Court of Colorado has resolved it for us. In the case below, 882 P.2d 1335 (1994), the Colorado court stated:

"It is significant to note that Colorado law currently proscribes discrimination against persons who are not suspect classes, including discrimination based on age, § 24–34–402(1)(a), 10A C. R. S. (1994 Supp.); marital or family status, § 24–34–502(1)(a), 10A C. R. S. (1994 Supp.); veterans' status, § 28–3–506, 11B C. R. S. (1989); and for any legal, off-duty conduct such as smoking tobacco, § 24–34–402.5, 10A C. R. S. (1994 Supp.). *Of course Amendment 2 is not intended to have any effect on this legislation, but seeks only to prevent the adoption of anti-discrimination laws intended to protect gays, lesbians, and bisexuals.*" *Id.* at 1346, n. 9 (emphasis added).

The Court utterly fails to distinguish this portion of the Colorado court's opinion. Colorado Rev. Stat. § 24–34–402.5 (Supp. 1995), which this passage authoritatively declares *not* to be affected by Amendment 2, was respondents' primary example of a generally applicable law whose protections would be unavailable to homosexuals under Amendment 2. The clear import of the Colorado court's conclusion that it is not affected is that "general laws and policies that prohibit arbitrary discrimination" would continue to prohibit discrimination on the basis of homosexual conduct as well. This analysis, which is fully in accord with (indeed, follows inescapably from) the text of the constitutional provision, lays to rest such horribles, raised in the course of oral argument, as the prospect that assaults upon homosexuals could not be prosecuted. The amendment prohibits *special treatment* of homosexuals, and nothing more. It would not affect, for example, a requirement of state law that pensions be paid to all retiring state employees with a certain length of service; homosexual employees, as well as others, would be entitled to that benefit. But it would prevent the State or any municipality from making death-benefit payments to the "life partner" of a homosexual when it does not make such payments to the long-time roommate of a nonhomosexual employee. Or again, it does not affect the requirement of the State's general insurance laws that customers be afforded coverage without discrimination unrelated to anticipated risk. Thus, homosexuals could not be denied coverage, or charged a greater premium, with respect to auto collision insurance; but neither the State nor any municipality could require that distinctive health insurance risks associated with homosexuality (if there are any) be ignored.

Despite all of its hand wringing about the potential effect of Amendment 2 on general antidiscrimination laws, the Court's opinion ultimately does not dispute all this, but assumes it to be true. *See ante* at 630. The only denial of equal treatment it contends homosexuals have suffered is this: They may not obtain *preferential* treatment without amending the state constitution. That is to say, the principle underlying the Court's opinion is that one who is accorded equal treatment under the laws, but cannot as readily as others obtain *preferential* treatment under the laws, has been denied equal protection of the laws. If merely stating this alleged "equal protection" violation does not suffice to refute it, our constitutional jurisprudence has achieved terminal silliness.

The central thesis of the Court's reasoning is that any group is denied equal protection when, to obtain advantage (or, presumably, to avoid disadvantage), it must have recourse to a more general and hence more difficult level of political decision-making than others. The world has never heard of such a principle, which is why the Court's opinion is so long on emotive utterance and so short on relevant legal citation. And it seems to me most unlikely that any multilevel democracy can function under such a principle. For *whenever* a disadvantage is imposed, or conferral of a benefit is prohibited, at one of the higher levels of democratic decision-making (*i.e.*, by the state legislature rather than local government, or by the people at large in the state constitution rather than the legislature), the affected group has (under this theory) been denied equal protection. To take the simplest of examples, consider a state law prohibiting the award of municipal contracts to relatives of mayors or city councilmen. Once such a law is passed, the group composed of such relatives must, in order to get the benefit of city contracts, persuade the state legislature—unlike all other citizens, who need only persuade the municipality. It is ridiculous to consider this a denial of equal protection, which is why the Court's theory is unheard of.

The Court might reply that the example I have given is *not* a denial of equal protection only because the same "rational basis" (avoidance of corruption) which renders constitutional the *substantive discrimination* against relatives (*i.e.*, the fact that they alone cannot obtain city contracts) also automatically suffices to sustain what might be called the *electoral-procedural discrimination* against them (*i.e.*, the fact that they must go to the state level to get this changed). This is of course a perfectly reasonable response, and would explain why "electoral-procedural discrimination" has not hitherto been heard of: A law that is valid in its substance is automatically valid in its level of enactment. But the Court cannot afford to make this argument, for as I shall discuss next, there is no doubt of a rational basis for the substance of the prohibition at issue here. The Court's entire novel theory rests upon the proposition that there is something *special*—something that cannot be justified by normal "rational basis" analysis—in making a disadvantaged group (or a nonpreferred group) resort to a higher decision-making level. That proposition finds no support in law or logic.

II

I turn next to whether there was a legitimate rational basis for the substance of the constitutional amendment—for the prohibition of special protection for homosexuals. It is unsurprising that the Court avoids discussion of this question, since the answer is so obviously yes. The case most relevant to the issue before us today is not even mentioned in the Court's opinion: In *Bowers v. Hardwick*, 478 U.S. 186, 106 S.Ct. 2841, 92 L.Ed.2d 140 (1986), we held that the Constitution does not prohibit what virtually all States had done from the founding of the Republic until very recent years—making homosexual conduct a crime. That holding is unassailable, except by those who think that the Constitution changes to suit current fashions. But in any event it is a given in the present case: Respondents' briefs did not urge overruling *Bowers*, and at oral argument respondents' counsel expressly disavowed any intent to seek such overruling, Tr. of Oral Arg. 53. If it is constitutionally permissible for a State to make homosexual conduct criminal, surely it is constitutionally permissible for a State to enact other laws merely *disfavoring* homosexual conduct. (As the Court of Appeals for the District of Columbia Circuit has aptly put it: "If the Court [in *Bowers*] was unwilling to object to state laws that criminalize the behavior that defines the class, it is hardly open ... to conclude that state sponsored discrimination against the class is invidious. After all, there can hardly be more palpable discrimination against a class than making the conduct that defines the class criminal." *Padula v. Webster*, 261 U.S. App. D.C. 365, 822 F.2d 97, 103 (1987).) And *a fortiori* it is constitutionally permissible for a State to adopt a provision *not even* disfavoring homosexual conduct, but merely prohibiting all levels of state government from bestowing *special protections* upon homosexual conduct. Respondents (who, unlike the Court, cannot afford the luxury of ignoring inconvenient precedent) counter *Bowers* with the argument that a greater-includes-the-lesser rationale cannot justify Amendment 2's application to individuals who do not engage in homosexual acts, but are merely of homosexual "orientation." Some Courts of Appeals have concluded that, with respect to laws of this sort at least, that is a distinction without a difference. *See Equality Foundation of Greater Cincinnati, Inc. v. Cincin-*

nati, 54 F.3d 261, 267 (CA6 1995) ("For purposes of these proceedings, it is virtually impossible to distinguish or separate individuals of a particular *orientation* which predisposes them toward a particular sexual conduct from those who actually *engage* in that particular type of sexual conduct"); *Steffan v. Perry*, 309 U.S. App. D.C. 281, 41 F.3d 677, 689–690 (CADC 1994). The Supreme Court of Colorado itself appears to be of this view. *See* 882 P.2d at 1349–1350 ("Amendment 2 targets this class of persons based on four characteristics: sexual orientation; conduct; practices, and relationships. Each characteristic provides a potentially different way of identifying that class of persons who are gay, lesbian, or bisexual. These four characteristics are not truly severable from one another because each provides nothing more than a different way of identifying *the same class of persons*") (emphasis added).

But assuming that, in Amendment 2, a person of homosexual "orientation" is someone who does not engage in homosexual conduct but merely has a tendency or desire to do so, *Bowers* still suffices to establish a rational basis for the provision. If it is rational to criminalize the conduct, surely it is rational to deny special favor and protection to those with a self-avowed tendency or desire to engage in the conduct. Indeed, where criminal sanctions are not involved, homosexual "orientation" is an acceptable stand-in for homosexual conduct. A State "does not violate the Equal Protection Clause merely because the classifications made by its laws are imperfect," *Dandridge v. Williams*, 397 U.S. 471, 485, 90 S.Ct. 1153, 25 L.Ed.2d 491 (1970)....

Moreover, even if the provision regarding homosexual "orientation" *were* invalid, respondents' challenge to Amendment 2—which is a facial challenge—must fail. "A facial challenge to a legislative Act is, of course, the most difficult challenge to mount successfully, since the challenger must establish that no set of circumstances exists under which the Act would be valid." *United States v. Salerno*, 481 U.S. 739, 745, 107 S.Ct. 2095, 95 L.Ed.2d 697 (1987). It would not be enough for respondents to establish (if they could) that Amendment 2 is unconstitutional as applied to those of homosexual "orientation"; since, under *Bowers*, Amendment 2 is unquestionably constitutional as applied to those who engage in homosexual conduct, the facial challenge cannot succeed. Some individuals of homosexual "orientation" who do not engage in homosexual acts might successfully bring an as-applied challenge to Amendment 2, but so far as the record indicates, none of the respondents is such a person. *See* App. 4–5 (complaint describing each of the individual respondents as either "a gay man" or "a lesbian").

III

The foregoing suffices to establish what the Court's failure to cite any case remotely in point would lead one to suspect: No principle set forth in the Constitution, nor even any imagined by this Court in the past 200 years, prohibits what Colorado has done here. But the case for Colorado is much stronger than that. What it has done is not only unprohibited, but eminently reasonable, with close, congressionally approved precedent in earlier constitutional practice.

First, as to its eminent reasonableness. The Court's opinion contains grim, disapproving hints that Coloradans have been guilty of "animus" or "animosity" toward homosexuality, as though that has been established as un-American. Of course it is our moral heritage that one should not hate any human being or class of human beings. But I had thought that one could consider certain conduct reprehensible—murder, for example, or polygamy, or cruelty to animals—and could exhibit even "animus" toward such conduct. Surely that is the only sort of "animus" at issue here: moral disapproval of homosexual conduct, the same sort of moral disapproval that produced the centuries-old criminal laws that we held constitutional in *Bowers*. The Colorado amendment does not, to speak entirely precisely, prohibit giving favored status to people who are *homosexuals;* they can be favored for many reasons—for example, because they are senior citizens or members of racial minorities. But it prohibits giving them favored status *because of their homosexual conduct*—that is, it prohibits favored status *for homosexuality*.

But though Coloradans are, as I say, *entitled* to be hostile toward homosexual conduct, the fact is that the degree of hostility reflected by Amendment 2 is the smallest conceivable. The Court's portrayal of Coloradans as a society fallen victim to pointless, hate-filled "gay-bashing" is so false as to be comical. Colorado not only is one of the 25 States that have repealed their antisodomy laws, but was among the first to do so. *See* 1971 Colo. Sess. Laws, ch. 121, § 1. But the society that eliminates criminal punishment for homosexual acts does not necessarily abandon the view that homosexuality is morally wrong and socially harmful; often, abolition simply reflects the view that enforcement of such criminal laws involves unseemly intrusion into the intimate lives of citizens....

There is a problem, however, which arises when criminal sanction of homosexuality is eliminated but moral and social disapprobation of homosexuality is meant to be retained. The Court cannot be unaware of that problem; it is evident in many cities of the country, and occasionally bubbles to the surface of the news, in heated political disputes over such matters as the introduction into local schools of books teaching that homosexuality is an optional and fully acceptable "alternative life style." The problem (a problem, that is, for those who wish to retain social disapprobation of homosexuality) is that, because those who engage in homosexual conduct tend to reside in disproportionate numbers in certain communities, ... and, of course, care about homosexual-rights issues much more ardently than the public at large, they possess political power much greater than their numbers, both locally and statewide. Quite understandably, they devote this political power to achieving not merely a grudging social toleration, but full social acceptance, of homosexuality....

By the time Coloradans were asked to vote on Amendment 2, their exposure to homosexuals' quest for social endorsement was not limited to newspaper accounts of happenings in places such as New York, Los Angeles, San Francisco, and Key West. Three Colorado cities—Aspen, Boulder, and Denver—had enacted ordinances that listed "sexual orientation" as an impermissible ground for discrimination, equating the moral disapproval of homosexual conduct with racial and religious bigotry. *See* Aspen Municipal Code § 13–98 (1977); Boulder Rev. Municipal Code §§ 12–1–1 to 12–1–11 (1987); Denver Rev. Municipal Code, Art. IV, §§ 28–91 to 28–116 (1991). The phenomenon had even appeared statewide: The Governor of Colorado had signed an executive order pronouncing that "in the State of Colorado we recognize the diversity in our pluralistic society and strive to bring an end to discrimination in any form," and directing state agency heads to "ensure non-discrimination" in hiring and promotion based on, among other things, "sexual orientation." Executive Order No. D0035 (Dec. 10, 1990). I do not mean to be critical of these legislative successes; homosexuals are as entitled to use the legal system for reinforcement of their moral sentiments as is the rest of society. But they are subject to being countered by lawful, democratic counter-measures as well.

That is where Amendment 2 came in. It sought to counter both the geographic concentration and the disproportionate political power of homosexuals by (1) resolving the controversy at the statewide level, and (2) making the election a single-issue contest for both sides. It put directly, to all the citizens of the State, the question: Should homosexuality be given special protection? They answered no. The Court today asserts that this most democratic of procedures is unconstitutional....

. . .

As I have noted above, this is proved false every time a state law prohibiting or disfavoring certain conduct is passed, because such a law prevents the adversely affected group—whether drug addicts, or smokers, or gun owners, or motorcyclists—from changing the policy thus established in "each of [the] parts" of the State. What the Court says is even demonstrably false at the constitutional level. The Eighteenth Amendment to the Federal Constitution, for example, deprived those who drank alcohol not only of the power to alter the policy of prohibition *locally* or through *state legislation*, but even of the power to alter it through *state constitutional amendment* or *federal legislation*. The Establishment Clause of the First Amendment prevents theocrats from having their way by converting their fellow citizens at the local, state, or federal statutory level; as does the Republican Form of Government Clause prevent monarchists.

But there is a much closer analogy, one that involves precisely the effort by the majority of citizens to preserve its view of sexual morality statewide, against the efforts of a geographically concentrated and politically powerful minority to undermine it. The constitutions of the States of Arizona, Idaho, New Mexico, Oklahoma, and Utah *to this day* contain provisions stating that polygamy is "forever prohibited." Polygamists, and those who have a polygamous "orientation," have been "singled out" by these provisions for much more severe treatment than merely denial of favored status; and that treatment can only be changed by achieving amendment of the state constitutions. The Court's disposition today suggests that these provisions are unconstitutional, and that polygamy must be permitted in these States on a state-legislated, or perhaps even local option, basis—unless, of course, polygamists for some reason have fewer constitutional rights than homosexuals.

. . .

... In *Davis v. Beason*, 133 U.S. 333, 10 S.Ct. 299, 33 L.Ed. 637 (1890), Justice Field wrote for a unanimous Court:

> "In our judgment, § 501 of the Revised Statutes of Idaho Territory, which provides that 'no person ... who is a bigamist or polygamist or who teaches, advises, counsels, or encourages any person or persons to become bigamists or polygamists, or to commit any other crime defined by law, or to enter into what is known as plural or celestial marriage, or who is a member of any order, organization or association which teaches, advises, counsels, or encourages its members or devotees or any other persons to commit the crime of bigamy or polygamy, or any other crime defined by law ... is permitted to vote at any election, or to hold any position or office of honor, trust, or profit within this Territory,' *is not open to any constitutional or legal objection.*" *Id.* at 346–347 (emphasis added).

To the extent, if any, that this opinion permits the imposition of adverse consequences upon mere abstract advocacy of polygamy, it has, of course, been overruled by later cases. *See Brandenburg v. Ohio*, 395 U.S. 444, 89 S.Ct. 1827, 23 L.Ed.2d 430 (1969) *(per curiam)*. But the proposition that polygamy can be criminalized, and those engaging in that crime deprived of the vote, remains good law. *See Richardson v. Ramirez*, 418 U.S. 24, 53, 94 S.Ct. 2655, 41 L.Ed.2d 551 (1974). *Beason* rejected the argument that "such discrimination is a denial of the equal protection of the laws." Brief for Appellant in *Davis v. Beason*, O. T. 1889, No. 1261, p. 41. Among the Justices joining in that rejection were the two whose views in other cases the Court today treats as equal protection lodestars—Justice Harlan, who was to proclaim in *Plessy v. Ferguson*, 163 U.S. 537, 559, 16 S.Ct. 1138, 41 L.Ed. 256 (1896) (dissenting opinion), that the Constitution "neither knows nor tolerates classes among citizens," quoted *ante* at 623, and Justice Bradley, who had earlier declared that "class legislation ... [is] obnoxious to the prohibitions of the Fourteenth Amendment," *Civil Rights Cases*, 109 U.S. 3, 24, 3 S.Ct. 18, 27 L.Ed. 835 (1883), quoted *ante* at 635.[1]

1. The Court labors mightily to get around *Beason*, *see ante* at 634, but cannot escape the central fact that this Court found the statute at issue—which went much further than Amendment 2, denying polygamists not merely special treatment but the right *to vote*—"not open to any constitutional or legal objection," rejecting the appellant's argument (much like the argument of respondents today) that the statute impermissibly "singled him out," Brief for Appellant in *Davis v. Beason*, O. T. 1889, No. 1261, p. 41. The Court adopts my conclusions that (a) insofar as *Beason*

This Court cited *Beason* with approval as recently as 1993, in an opinion authored by the same Justice who writes for the Court today. That opinion said: "Adverse impact will not always lead to a finding of impermissible targeting. For example, a social harm may have been a legitimate concern of government for reasons quite apart from discrimination.... *See, e.g.,* ... *Davis v. Beason*, 133 U.S. 333, 10 S.Ct. 299, 33 L.Ed. 637 (1890)." *Church of Lukumi Babalu Aye, Inc. v. Hialeah*, 508 U.S. 520, 535, 113 S.Ct. 2217, 124 L.Ed.2d 472 (1993). It remains to be explained how § 501 of the Idaho Revised Statutes was not an "impermissible targeting" of polygamists, but (the much more mild) Amendment 2 is an "impermissible targeting" of homosexuals. Has the Court concluded that the perceived social harm of polygamy is a "legitimate concern of government," and the perceived social harm of homosexuality is not?

IV

I strongly suspect that the answer to the last question is yes, which leads me to the last point I wish to make: The Court today, announcing that Amendment 2 "defies ... conventional [constitutional] inquiry," and "confounds [the] normal process of judicial review," *ante* at 633, employs a constitutional theory heretofore unknown to frustrate Colorado's reasonable effort to preserve traditional American moral values....

. . .

... To suggest, for example, that this constitutional amendment springs from nothing more than " 'a bare ... desire to harm a politically unpopular group,' " is nothing short of insulting. (It is also nothing short of preposterous to call "politically unpopular" a group which enjoys enormous influence in American media and politics, and which, as the trial court here noted, though composing no more than 4% of the population had the support of 46% of the voters on Amendment 2, *see* App. to Pet. for Cert. C–18.)

When the Court takes sides in the culture wars, it tends to be with the knights rather than the villains—and more specifically with the Templars, reflecting the views and values of the lawyer class from which the Court's Members are drawn. How that class feels about homosexuality will be evident to anyone who wishes to interview job applicants at virtually any of the Nation's law schools. The interviewer may refuse to

---

permits the imposition of adverse consequences based upon mere advocacy, it has been overruled by subsequent cases, and (b) insofar as *Beason* holds that convicted felons may be denied the right to vote, it remains good law. To these conclusions, it adds something new: the claim that "to the extent [*Beason*] held that the groups designated in the statute may be deprived of the right to vote because of their status, its ruling could not stand without surviving strict scrutiny, a most doubtful outcome." *ante* at 634. But if that is so, it is only because we have declared the right *to vote* to be a "fundamental political right," *see, e.g., Dunn v. Blumstein*, 405 U.S. 330, 336, 92 S.Ct. 995, 31 L.Ed.2d 274 (1972), deprivation of which triggers strict scrutiny. Amendment 2, of course, does not deny the fundamental right to vote, and the Court rejects the Colorado court's view that there exists a fundamental right to participate in the political process. Strict scrutiny is thus not in play here. *See ante* at 631. Finally, the Court's suggestion that § 501 of the Revised Statutes of Idaho, and Amendment 2, deny rights on account of "status" (rather than conduct) opens up a broader debate involving the significance of *Bowers* to this case, a debate which the Court is otherwise unwilling to join.

offer a job because the applicant is a Republican; because he is an adulterer; because he went to the wrong prep school or belongs to the wrong country club; because he eats snails; because he is a womanizer; because she wears real-animal fur; or even because he hates the Chicago Cubs. But if the interviewer should wish not to be an associate or partner of an applicant because he disapproves of the applicant's homosexuality, *then* he will have violated the pledge which the Association of American Law Schools requires all its member schools to exact from job interviewers: "assurance of the employer's willingness" to hire homosexuals.... This law-school view of what "prejudices" must be stamped out may be contrasted with the more plebeian attitudes that apparently still prevail in the United States Congress, which has been unresponsive to repeated attempts to extend to homosexuals the protections of federal civil rights laws, *see*, *e.g.*, Employment Non–Discrimination Act of 1994, S. 2238, 103d Cong., 2d Sess. (1994); Civil Rights Amendments of 1975, H. R. 5452, 94th Cong., 1st Sess. (1975), and which took the pains to exclude them specifically from the Americans with Disabilities Act of 1990, *see* 42 U.S.C. § 12211(a) (1988 ed., Supp. V).

. . .

Today's opinion has no foundation in American constitutional law, and barely pretends to. The people of Colorado have adopted an entirely reasonable provision which does not even disfavor homosexuals in any substantive sense, but merely denies them preferential treatment. Amendment 2 is designed to prevent piecemeal deterioration of the sexual morality favored by a majority of Coloradans, and is not only an appropriate means to that legitimate end, but a means that Americans have employed before. Striking it down is an act, not of judicial judgment, but of political will. I dissent.

DISCUSSION

The Romer *majority purports to apply a rational basis standard. Are they? Is this the "more searching review" advocated by Justice O'Connor in her* Lawrence *concurrence (infra)?*

In Romer v. Evans, *Justice Scalia complains in his dissent that the decision in* Hardwick *forecloses the decision arrived at by the majority in* Romer*? Is he right? Why or why not?*

D. LAWRENCE v. TEXAS, 539 U.S. 558, 123 S.Ct. 2472, 156 L.Ed.2d 508 (2003)

JUDGES: Kennedy, J., delivered the opinion of the Court, in which Stevens, Souter, Ginsburg, and Breyer, JJ., joined. O'Connor, J., filed an opinion concurring in the judgment. Scalia, J., filed a dissenting opinion, in which Rehnquist, C. J., and Thomas, J., joined. Thomas, J., filed a dissenting opinion.

Liberty protects the person from unwarranted government intrusions into a dwelling or other private places. In our tradition the State is not omnipresent in the home. And there are other spheres of our lives and existence, outside the home, where the State should not be a dominant presence. Freedom extends beyond spatial bounds. Liberty presumes an autonomy of self that includes freedom of thought, belief, expression, and certain intimate conduct. The instant case involves liberty of the person both in its spatial and more transcendent dimensions.

I.

The question before the Court is the validity of a Texas statute making it a crime for two persons of the same sex to engage in certain intimate sexual conduct.

In Houston, Texas, officers of the Harris County Police Department were dispatched to a private residence in response to a reported weapons disturbance. They entered an apartment where one of the petitioners, John Geddes Lawrence, resided. The right of the police to enter does not seem to have been questioned. The officers observed Lawrence and another man, Tyron Garner, engaging in a sexual act. The two petitioners were arrested, held in custody over night, and charged and convicted before a Justice of the Peace.

The complaints described their crime as "deviate sexual intercourse, namely anal sex, with a member of the same sex (man)." App. to Pet. for Cert. 127a, 139a. The applicable state law is Tex. Penal Code Ann. § 21.06(a) (2003). It provides: "A person commits an offense if he engages in deviate sexual intercourse with another individual of the same sex." The statute defines "deviate sexual intercourse" as follows:

> "(A) any contact between any part of the genitals of one person and the mouth or anus of another person; or
>
> (B) the penetration of the genitals or the anus of another person with an object." § 21.01(1).

The petitioners exercised their right to a trial *de novo* in Harris County Criminal Court. They challenged the statute as a violation of the Equal Protection Clause of the Fourteenth Amendment and of a like provision of the Texas Constitution. Tex. Const., Art. 1, § 3a. Those contentions were rejected. The petitioners, having entered a plea of *nolo contendere*, were each fined $200 and assessed court costs of $141.25. App. to Pet. for Cert. 107a–110a.

The Court of Appeals for the Texas Fourteenth District considered the petitioners' federal constitutional arguments under both the Equal Protection and Due Process Clauses of the Fourteenth Amendment. After hearing the case en banc the court, in a divided opinion, rejected the constitutional arguments and affirmed the convictions. 41 S.W.3d 349 (Tex. App. 2001). The majority opinion indicates that the Court of Appeals considered our decision in *Bowers v. Hardwick,* 478 U.S. 186, 106 S.Ct. 2841, 92 L.Ed.2d 140 (1986), to be controlling on the federal due process aspect of the case. *Bowers* then being authoritative, this was proper.

We granted certiorari, 537 U.S. 1044, 123 S.Ct. 661, 154 L.Ed.2d 514 (2002), to consider three questions:

> 1. Whether Petitioners' criminal convictions under the Texas "Homosexual Conduct" law—which criminalizes sexual intimacy by same-sex couples, but not identical behavior by different-sex couples—violate the Fourteenth Amendment guarantee of equal protection of laws?
>
> 2. Whether Petitioners' criminal convictions for adult consensual sexual intimacy in the home violate their vital interests in liberty and privacy protected by the Due Process Clause of the Fourteenth Amendment?
>
> 3. Whether *Bowers v. Hardwick*, 478 U.S. 186, 106 S.Ct. 2841, 92 L.Ed.2d 140 (1986), should be overruled?" Pet. for Cert. i.
>
> The petitioners were adults at the time of the alleged offense. Their conduct was in private and consensual.

II.

We conclude the case should be resolved by determining whether the petitioners were free as adults to engage in the private conduct in the exercise of their liberty under the Due Process Clause of the Fourteenth Amendment to the Constitution. For this inquiry we deem it necessary to reconsider the Court's holding in *Bowers*.

There are broad statements of the substantive reach of liberty under the Due Process Clause in earlier cases, including *Pierce v. Society of Sisters,* 268 U.S. 510, 45 S.Ct. 571, 69 L.Ed. 1070 (1925), and *Meyer v. Nebraska,* 262 U.S. 390, 43 S.Ct. 625, 67 L.Ed. 1042 (1923); but the most pertinent beginning point is our decision in *Griswold v. Connecticut,* 381 U.S. 479, 85 S.Ct. 1678, 14 L.Ed.2d 510 (1965).

In *Griswold* the Court invalidated a state law prohibiting the use of drugs or devices of contraception and counseling or aiding and abetting the use of contraceptives. The Court described the protected interest as a right to privacy and placed emphasis on the marriage relation and the protected space of the marital bedroom. *Id. at* 485, 85 S.Ct. 1678, 14 L.Ed.2d 510.

After *Griswold* it was established that the right to make certain decisions regarding sexual conduct extends beyond the marital relationship. In *Eisenstadt v. Baird,* 405 U.S. 438, 92 S.Ct. 1029, 31 L.Ed.2d 349 (1972), the Court invalidated a law prohibiting the distribution of contraceptives to unmarried persons. The case was decided under the Equal Protection Clause, *id. at* 454, 92 S.Ct. 1029, 31 L.Ed.2d 349; but with respect to unmarried persons, the Court went on to state the fundamental proposition that the law impaired the exercise of their personal rights, *ibid.* It quoted from the statement of the Court of Appeals finding the law to be in conflict with fundamental human rights, and it followed with this statement of its own:

It is true that in *Griswold* the right of privacy in question inhered in the marital relationship.... If the right of privacy means anything, it is the right of the *individual*, married or single, to be free from unwarranted governmental intrusion into matters so fundamentally affecting a person as the decision whether to bear or beget a child." *Id. at* 453, 92 S.Ct. 1029, 31 L.Ed.2d 349.

. . .

The facts in *Bowers* had some similarities to the instant case. A police officer, whose right to enter seems not to have been in question, observed Hardwick, in his own bedroom, engaging in intimate sexual conduct with another adult male. The conduct was in violation of a Georgia statute making it a criminal offense to engage in sodomy. One difference between the two cases is that the Georgia statute prohibited the conduct whether or not the participants were of the same sex, while the Texas statute, as we have seen, applies only to participants of the same sex. Hardwick was not prosecuted, but he brought an action in federal court to declare the state statute invalid. He alleged he was a practicing homosexual and that the criminal prohibition violated rights guaranteed to him by the Constitution. The Court, in an opinion by Justice White, sustained the Georgia law. Chief Justice Burger and Justice Powell joined the opinion of the Court and filed separate, concurring opinions. Four Justices dissented. 478 U.S. at 199, 106 S.Ct. 2841, 92 L.Ed.2d 140 (opinion of Blackmun, J., joined by Brennan, Marshall, and Stevens, JJ.); *id.* at 214, 106 S.Ct. 2841, 92 L.Ed.2d 140 (opinion of Stevens, J., joined by Brennan and Marshall, JJ.).

The Court began its substantive discussion in *Bowers* as follows: "The issue presented is whether the Federal Constitution confers a fundamental right upon homosexuals to engage in sodomy and hence invalidates the laws of the many States that still make such conduct illegal and have done so for a very long time." *Id. at* 190, 106 S.Ct. 2841, 92 L.Ed.2d 140. That statement, we now conclude, discloses the Court's own failure to appreciate the extent of the liberty at stake. To say that the issue in *Bowers* was simply the right to engage in certain sexual conduct demeans the claim the individual put forward, just as it would demean a married couple were it to be said marriage is simply about the right to have sexual intercourse. The laws involved in *Bowers* and here are, to be sure, statutes that purport to do no more than prohibit a particular sexual act. Their penalties and purposes, though, have more far-reaching consequences, touching upon the most private human conduct, sexual behavior, and in the most private of places, the home. The statutes do seek to control a personal relationship that, whether or not entitled to formal recognition in the law, is within the liberty of persons to choose without being punished as criminals.

This, as a general rule, should counsel against attempts by the State, or a court, to define the meaning of the relationship or to set its boundaries absent injury to a person or abuse of an institution the law protects. It suffices for us to acknowledge that adults may choose to enter upon this relationship in the confines of their homes and their own private lives and still retain their dignity as free persons. When sexuality finds overt expression in intimate conduct with another person, the conduct can be but one element in a personal bond that is more enduring. The liberty protected by the Constitution allows homosexual persons the right to make this choice.

Having misapprehended the claim of liberty there presented to it, and thus stating the claim to be whether there is a fundamental right to engage in consensual sodomy, the *Bowers* Court said: "Proscriptions against that conduct have ancient roots." *Id.* at 192, 106 S.Ct. 2841, 92 L.Ed.2d 140. In academic writings, and in many of the scholarly *amicus* briefs filed to assist the Court in this case, there are fundamental criticisms of the historical premises relied upon by the majority and concurring opinions in *Bowers*. Brief for Cato Institute as *Amicus Curiae* 16–17; Brief for American Civil Liberties Union et al. as *Amici Curiae* 15–21; Brief for Professors of History et al. as *Amici Curiae* 3–10. We need not enter this debate in the attempt to reach a definitive historical judgment, but the following considerations counsel against adopting the definitive conclusions upon which *Bowers* placed such reliance.

At the outset it should be noted that there is no longstanding history in this country of laws directed at homosexual conduct as a distinct matter. Beginning in colonial times there were prohibitions of sodomy derived from the English criminal laws passed in the first instance by the Reformation Parliament of 1533. The English prohibition was understood to include relations between men and women as well as relations between men and men. . . . The absence of legal prohibitions focusing on homosexual conduct may be explained in part by noting that according to some scholars the concept of the homosexual as a distinct category of person did not emerge until the late 19th century. . . . Thus early American sodomy laws were not directed at homosexuals as such but instead sought to prohibit nonprocreative sexual activity more generally. This does not suggest approval of homosexual conduct. It does tend to show that this particular form of conduct was not thought of as a separate category from like conduct between heterosexual persons.

Laws prohibiting sodomy do not seem to have been enforced against consenting adults acting in private. A substantial number of sodomy prosecutions and convictions for which there are surviving records were for predatory acts against those who could not or did not consent, as in the case of a minor or the victim of an assault. . . .

To the extent that there were any prosecutions for the acts in question, 19th-century evidence rules imposed a burden that would make a conviction more difficult to obtain even taking into account the problems always inherent in prosecuting consensual acts committed in private. Under then-prevailing standards, a man could not be convicted of sodomy based upon testimony of a consenting partner, because the partner was considered an accomplice. A partner's testimony, however, was admissible if he or she had not consented to the act or was a minor, and therefore incapable of consent.... The rule may explain in part the infrequency of these prosecutions. In all events that infrequency makes it difficult to say that society approved of a rigorous and systematic punishment of the consensual acts committed in private and by adults. The longstanding criminal prohibition of homosexual sodomy upon which the *Bowers* decision placed such reliance is as consistent with a general condemnation of nonprocreative sex as it is with an established tradition of prosecuting acts because of their homosexual character.

... Despite the absence of prosecutions, there may have been periods in which there was public criticism of homosexuals as such and an insistence that the criminal laws be enforced to discourage their practices. But far from possessing "ancient roots," *Bowers*, 478 U.S. at 192, 106 S.Ct. 2841, 92 L.Ed.2d 140, American laws targeting same-sex couples did not develop until the last third of the 20th century. The reported decisions concerning the prosecution of consensual, homosexual sodomy between adults for the years 1880–1995 are not always clear in the details, but a significant number involved conduct in a public place....

It was not until the 1970's that any State singled out same-sex relations for criminal prosecution, and only nine States have done so. *See* 1977 Ark. Gen. Acts no. 828; 1983 Kan. Sess. Laws p 652; 1974 Ky. Acts p 847; 1977 Mo. Laws p 687; 1973 Mont. Laws p 1339; 1977 Nev. Stats. p 1632; 1989 Tenn. Pub. Acts ch. 591; 1973 Tex. Gen. Laws ch. 399; *see also Post v. State*, 1986 OK CR 30, 715 P.2d 1105 (Okla. Crim. App. 1986) (sodomy law invalidated as applied to different-sex couples). Post–*Bowers* even some of these States did not adhere to the policy of suppressing homosexual conduct. Over the course of the last decades, States with same-sex prohibitions have moved toward abolishing them. *See, e.g., Jegley v. Picado*, 349 Ark. 600, 80 S.W.3d 332 (2002); *Gryczan v. State*, 283 Mont. 433, 942 P.2d 112 (1997); *Campbell v. Sundquist*, 926 S.W.2d 250 (Tenn. App. 1996); *Commonwealth v. Wasson*, 842 S.W.2d 487 (Ky. 1992); *see also* 1993 Nev. Stats. p 518 (repealing Nev. Rev. Stat. § 201.193).

In summary, the historical grounds relied upon in *Bowers* are more complex than the majority opinion and the concurring opinion by Chief Justice Burger indicate. Their historical premises are not without doubt and, at the very least, are overstated.

It must be acknowledged, of course, that the Court in *Bowers* was making the broader point that for centuries there have been powerful voices to condemn homosexual conduct as immoral. The condemnation has been shaped by religious beliefs, conceptions of right and acceptable behavior, and respect for the traditional family. For many persons these are not trivial concerns but profound and deep convictions accepted as ethical and moral principles to which they aspire and which thus determine the course of their lives. These considerations do not answer the question before us, however. The issue is whether the majority may use the power of the State to enforce these views on the whole society through operation of the criminal law. "Our obligation is to define the liberty of all, not to mandate our own moral code." *Planned Parenthood of Southeastern Pa. v. Casey,* 505 U.S. 833, 850, 112 S.Ct. 2791, 120 L.Ed.2d 674 (1992).

Chief Justice Burger joined the opinion for the Court in *Bowers* and further explained his views as follows: "Decisions of individuals relating to homosexual conduct have been subject to state intervention throughout the history of Western civilization. Condemnation of those practices is firmly rooted in Judeao–Christian moral and ethical standards." 478 U.S. at 196, 106 S.Ct. 2841, 92 L.Ed.2d 140. As with Justice White's assumptions about history, scholarship casts some doubt on the sweeping nature of the statement by Chief Justice Burger as it pertains to private homosexual conduct between consenting adults. *See, e.g.,* Eskridge, Hardwick and Historiography, 1999 U. Ill. L. Rev. 631, 656. In all events we think that our laws and traditions in the past half century are of most relevance here. These references show an emerging awareness that liberty gives substantial protection to adult persons in deciding how to conduct their private lives in matters pertaining to sex. "History and tradition are the starting point but not in all cases the ending point of the substantive due process inquiry." *County of Sacramento v. Lewis,* 523 U.S. 833, 857, 118 S.Ct. 1708, 140 L.Ed.2d 1043 (1998) (Kennedy, J., concurring).

This emerging recognition should have been apparent when *Bowers* was decided. In 1955 the American Law Institute promulgated the Model Penal Code and made clear that it did not recommend or provide for "criminal penalties for consensual sexual relations conducted in private." ALI, Model Penal Code § 213.2, Comment 2, p 372 (1980). It justified its decision on three grounds: (1) The prohibitions undermined respect for the law by penalizing conduct many people engaged in; (2) the statutes regulated private conduct not harmful to others; and (3) the laws were arbitrarily enforced and thus invited the danger of blackmail. ALI, Model Penal Code, Commentary 277–280 (Tent. Draft No. 4, 1955). In 1961 Illinois changed its laws to conform to the Model Penal Code. Other States soon followed. Brief for Cato Institute as *Amicus Curiae* 15–16.

In *Bowers* the Court referred to the fact that before 1961 all 50 States had outlawed sodomy, and that at the time of the Court's decision 24 States and the District of Columbia had sodomy laws. 478 U.S. at 192–193, 106 S.Ct. 2841, 92 L.Ed.2d 140. Justice Powell pointed out that these prohibitions often were being ignored, however. Georgia, for instance, had not sought to enforce its law for decades. *Id.* at 197–198, n. 2, 106 S.Ct. 2841, 92 L.Ed.2d 140 ("The history of nonenforcement suggests the moribund character today of laws criminalizing this type of private, consensual conduct").

The sweeping references by Chief Justice Burger to the history of Western civilization and to Judeo–Christian moral and ethical standards did not take account of other authorities pointing in an opposite direction.

A committee advising the British Parliament recommended in 1957 repeal of laws punishing homosexual conduct. The Wolfenden Report: Report of the Committee on Homosexual Offenses and Prostitution (1963). Parliament enacted the substance of those recommendations 10 years later. Sexual Offences Act 1967, § 1.

Of even more importance, almost five years before *Bowers* was decided the European Court of Human Rights considered a case with parallels to *Bowers* and to today's case. An adult male resident in Northern Ireland alleged he was a practicing homosexual who desired to engage in consensual homosexual conduct. The laws of Northern Ireland forbade him that right. He alleged that he had been questioned, his home had been searched, and he feared criminal prosecution. The court held that the laws proscribing the conduct were invalid under the European Convention on Human Rights. *Dudgeon* v *United Kingdom*, 45 Eur. Ct. H. R. (1981) P 52. Authoritative in all countries that are members of the Council of Europe (21 nations then, 45 nations now), the decision is at odds with the premise in *Bowers* that the claim put forward was insubstantial in our Western civilization.

In our own constitutional system the deficiencies in *Bowers* became even more apparent in the years following its announcement. The 25 States with laws prohibiting the relevant conduct referenced in the *Bowers* decision are reduced now to 13, of which 4 enforce their laws only against homosexual conduct. In those States where sodomy is still proscribed, whether for same-sex or heterosexual conduct, there is a pattern of nonenforcement with respect to consenting adults acting in private. The State of Texas admitted in 1994 that as of that date it had not prosecuted anyone under those circumstances. *State v. Morales*, 869 S.W.2d 941, 943, 37 Tex. Sup. Ct. J. 390.

Two principal cases decided after *Bowers* cast its holding into even more doubt. In *Planned Parenthood of Southeastern Pa. v. Casey,* 505 U.S. 833, 112 S.Ct. 2791, 120 L.Ed.2d 674 (1992), the Court reaffirmed the substantive force of the liberty protected by the Due Process Clause. The *Casey* decision again confirmed that our laws and tradition afford constitutional protection to personal decisions relating to marriage, procreation, contraception, family relationships, child rearing, and education. *Id.* at 851, 112 S.Ct. 2791, 120 L.Ed.2d 674. In explaining the respect the Constitution demands for the autonomy of the person in making these choices, we stated as follows:

"These matters, involving the most intimate and personal choices a person may make in a lifetime, choices central to personal dignity and autonomy, are central to the liberty protected by the Fourteenth Amendment. At the heart of liberty is the right to define one's own concept of existence, of meaning, of the universe, and of the mystery of human life. Beliefs about these matters could not define the attributes of personhood were they formed under compulsion of the State." *Ibid.*

Persons in a homosexual relationship may seek autonomy for these purposes, just as heterosexual persons do. The decision in *Bowers* would deny them this right.

The second post-*Bowers* case of principal relevance is *Romer v. Evans,* 517 U.S. 620, 116 S.Ct. 1620, 134 L.Ed.2d 855 (1996). There the Court struck down class-based legislation directed at homosexuals as a violation of the Equal Protection Clause. *Romer* invalidated an amendment to Colorado's constitution which named as a solitary class persons who were homosexuals, lesbians, or bisexual either by "orientation, conduct, practices or relationships," *Id. at* 624, 116 S.Ct. 1620, 134 L.Ed.2d 855 (internal quotation marks omitted), and deprived them of protection under state antidiscrimination laws. We concluded that the provision was "born of animosity toward the class of persons affected" and further that it had no rational relation to a legitimate governmental purpose. *Id. at* 634, 116 S.Ct. 1620, 134 L.Ed.2d 855.

As an alternative argument in this case, counsel for the petitioners and some *amici* contend that *Romer* provides the basis for declaring the Texas statute invalid under the Equal Protection Clause. That is a tenable argument, but we conclude the instant case requires us to address whether *Bowers* itself has continuing validity. Were we to hold the statute invalid under the Equal Protection Clause some might question whether a prohibition would be valid if drawn differently, say, to prohibit the conduct both between same-sex and different-sex participants.

Equality of treatment and the due process right to demand respect for conduct protected by the substantive guarantee of liberty are linked in important respects, and a decision on the latter point advances both interests. If protected conduct is made criminal and the law which does so remains unexamined for its substantive validity, its stigma might remain even if it were not enforceable as drawn for equal protection reasons. When homosexual conduct is made criminal by the law of the State, that declaration in and of itself is an invitation to subject homosexual persons to discrimination both in the public and in the private spheres. The central holding of *Bowers* has been brought in question by this case, and it should be addressed. Its continuance as precedent demeans the lives of homosexual persons.

The stigma this criminal statute imposes, moreover, is not trivial. The offense, to be sure, is but a class C misdemeanor, a minor offense in the Texas legal system. Still, it remains a criminal offense with all that imports for the dignity of the persons charged. The petitioners will bear on their record the history of their criminal convictions. Just this Term we rejected various challenges to state laws requiring the registration of sex offenders. *Smith v. Doe*, 538 U.S. 84, 123 S.Ct. 1140, 155 L.Ed.2d 164 (2003); *Connecticut Dept. of Public Safety v. Doe*, 538 U.S. 1, 123 S.Ct. 1160, 155 L.Ed.2d 98 (2003). We are advised that if Texas convicted an adult for private, consensual homosexual conduct under the statute here in question the convicted person would come within the registration laws of at least four States were he or she to be subject to their jurisdiction. Pet. for Cert. 13, and n 12 (citing Idaho Code §§ 18–8301 to 18–8326 (Cum. Supp. 2002); La. Code Crim. Proc. Ann., §§ 15:540–15:549 (West 2003); Miss. Code Ann. §§ 45–33–21 to 45–33–57 (Lexis 2003); S. C. Code Ann. §§ 23–3–400 to 23–3–490 (West 2002)). This underscores the consequential nature of the punishment and the state-sponsored condemnation attendant to the criminal prohibition. Furthermore, the Texas criminal conviction carries with it the other collateral consequences always following a conviction, such as notations on job application forms, to mention but one example.

The foundations of *Bowers* have sustained serious erosion from our recent decisions in *Casey* and *Romer*. When our precedent has been thus weakened, criticism from other sources is of greater significance. In the United States criticism of *Bowers* has been substantial and continuing, disapproving of its reasoning in all respects, not just as to its historical assumptions. *See, e.g.,* C. Fried, Order and Law: Arguing the Reagan Revolution—A Firsthand Account 81–84 (1991); R. Posner, Sex and Reason 341–350 (1992). The courts of five different States have declined to follow it in interpreting provisions in their own state constitutions parallel to the Due Process Clause of the Fourteenth Amendment, *see Jegley v. Picado*, 349 Ark. 600, 80 S.W.3d 332 (2002); *Powell v. State*, 270 Ga. 327, 510 S.E.2d 18, 24 (1998); *Gryczan v. State*, 283 Mont. 433, 942 P.2d 112 (1997); *Campbell v. Sundquist*, 926 S.W.2d 250 (Tenn. App. 1996); *Commonwealth v. Wasson*, 842 S.W.2d 487 (Ky. 1992).

To the extent *Bowers* relied on values we share with a wider civilization, it should be noted that the reasoning and holding in *Bowers* have been rejected elsewhere. The European Court of Human Rights has followed not *Bowers* but its own decision in *Dudgeon* v *United Kingdom*. *See P. G. & J. H.* v *United Kingdom*, App. No. 00044787/98, P 56 (Eur. Ct. H. R., Sept. 25, 2001); *Modinos* v *Cyprus*, 259 Eur. Ct. H. R. (1993); *Norris* v *Ireland*, 142 Eur. Ct. H. R. (1988). Other nations, too, have taken action consistent with an affirmation of the protected right of homosexual adults to engage in intimate, consensual conduct. *See* Brief for Mary Robinson et al. as *Amici Curiae* 11–12. The right the petitioners seek in this case has been accepted as an integral part of human freedom in many other countries. There has been no showing that in this country the governmental interest in circumscribing personal choice is somehow more legitimate or urgent.

. . .

The rationale of *Bowers* does not withstand careful analysis. In his dissenting opinion in *Bowers* Justice Stevens came to these conclusions:

> Our prior cases make two propositions abundantly clear. First, the fact that the governing majority in a State has traditionally viewed a particular practice as immoral is not a sufficient reason for upholding a law prohibiting the practice; neither history nor tradition could save a law prohibiting miscegenation from constitutional attack. Second,

> individual decisions by married persons, concerning the intimacies of their physical relationship, even when not intended to produce offspring, are a form of "liberty" protected by the Due Process Clause of the Fourteenth Amendment. Moreover, this protection extends to intimate choices by unmarried as well as married persons.

478 U.S. at 216, 106 S.Ct. 2841, 92 L.Ed.2d 140 (footnotes and citations omitted).

Justice Stevens' analysis, in our view, should have been controlling in *Bowers* and should control here.

Bowers was not correct when it was decided, and it is not correct today. It ought not to remain binding precedent. *Bowers v. Hardwick* should be and now is overruled.

The present case does not involve minors. It does not involve persons who might be injured or coerced or who are situated in relationships where consent might not easily be refused. It does not involve public conduct or prostitution. It does not involve whether the government must give formal recognition to any relationship that homosexual persons seek to enter. The case does involve two adults who, with full and mutual consent from each other, engaged in sexual practices common to a homosexual lifestyle. The petitioners are entitled to respect for their private lives. The State cannot demean their existence or control their destiny by making their private sexual conduct a crime. Their right to liberty under the Due Process Clause gives them the full right to engage in their conduct without intervention of the government. "It is a promise of the Constitution that there is a realm of personal liberty which the government may not enter." *Casey*, *supra* at 847, 112 S.Ct. 2791, 120 L.Ed.2d 674. The Texas statute furthers no legitimate state interest which can justify its intrusion into the personal and private life of the individual.

Had those who drew and ratified the Due Process Clauses of the Fifth Amendment or the Fourteenth Amendment known the components of liberty in its manifold possibilities, they might have been more specific. They did not presume to have this insight. They knew times can blind us to certain truths and later generations can see that laws once thought necessary and proper in fact serve only to oppress. As the Constitution endures, persons in every generation can invoke its principles in their own search for greater freedom.

The judgment of the Court of Appeals for the Texas Fourteenth District is reversed, and the case is remanded for further proceedings not inconsistent with this opinion.

It is so ordered.

JUSTICE O'CONNOR, concurring in the judgment.

The Court today overrules *Bowers v. Hardwick,* 478 U.S. 186, 106 S.Ct. 2841, 92 L.Ed.2d 140 (1986). I joined *Bowers*, and do not join the Court in overruling it. Nevertheless, I agree with the Court that Texas' statute banning same-sex sodomy is unconstitutional. *See* Tex. Penal Code

Ann. § 21.06 (2003). Rather than relying on the substantive component of the Fourteenth Amendment's Due Process Clause, as the Court does, I base my conclusion on the Fourteenth Amendment's Equal Protection Clause.

The Equal Protection Clause of the Fourteenth Amendment "is essentially a direction that all persons similarly situated should be treated alike." *Cleburne v. Cleburne Living Center, Inc.,* 473 U.S. 432, 439, 105 S.Ct. 3249, 87 L.Ed.2d 313 (1985); *see also Plyler v. Doe,* 457 U.S. 202, 216, 102 S.Ct. 2382, 72 L.Ed.2d 786 (1982). Under our rational basis standard of review, "legislation is presumed to be valid and will be sustained if the classification drawn by the statute is rationally related to a legitimate state interest." *Cleburne v. Cleburne Living Center, supra* at 440, 105 S.Ct. 3249, 87 L.Ed.2d 313; *see also Department of Agriculture v. Moreno,* 413 U.S. 528, 534, 93 S.Ct. 2821, 37 L.Ed.2d 782 (1973); *Romer v. Evans,* 517 U.S. 620, 632–633, 116 S.Ct. 1620, 134 L.Ed.2d 855 (1996); *Nordlinger v. Hahn,* 505 U.S. 1, 11–12, 112 S.Ct. 2326, 120 L.Ed.2d 1 (1992).

The statute at issue here makes sodomy a crime only if a person "engages in deviate sexual intercourse with another individual of the same sex." Tex. Penal Code Ann. § 21.06(a) (2003). Sodomy between opposite-sex partners, however, is not a crime in Texas. That is, Texas treats the same conduct differently based solely on the participants. Those harmed by this law are people who have a same-sex sexual orientation and thus are more likely to engage in behavior prohibited by § 21.06.

And the effect of Texas' sodomy law is not just limited to the threat of prosecution or consequence of conviction. Texas' sodomy law brands all homosexuals as criminals, thereby making it more difficult for homosexuals to be treated in the same manner as everyone else. Indeed, Texas itself has previously acknowledged the collateral effects of the law, stipulating in a prior challenge to this action that the law "legally sanctions discrimination against [homosexuals] in a variety of ways unrelated to the criminal law," including in the areas of "employment, family issues, and housing." *State v. Morales*, 826 S.W.2d 201, 203 (Tex. App. 1992).

Texas attempts to justify its law, and the effects of the law, by arguing that the statute satisfies rational basis review because it furthers the legitimate governmental interest of the promotion of morality. In *Bowers*, we held that a state law criminalizing sodomy as applied to homosexual couples did not violate substantive due process. We rejected the argument that no rational basis existed to justify the law, pointing to the government's interest in promoting morality. 478 U.S. at 196, 106 S.Ct. 2841, 92 L.Ed.2d 140. The only question in front of the Court in *Bowers* was whether the substantive component of the Due Process Clause protected a right to engage in homosexual sodomy. *Id. at* 188, n. 2, 106 S.Ct. 2841, 92 L.Ed.2d 140. *Bowers* did not hold that moral disapproval of a group is a rational basis under the Equal Protection Clause to criminalize homosexual sodomy when heterosexual sodomy is not punished.

This case raises a different issue than *Bowers:* whether, under the Equal Protection Clause, moral disapproval is a legitimate state interest to justify by itself a statute that bans homosexual sodomy, but not heterosexual sodomy. It is not. Moral disapproval of this group, like a bare desire to harm the group, is an interest that is insufficient to satisfy rational basis review under the Equal Protection Clause. *See, e.g., Department of Agriculture v. Moreno, supra* at 534, 93 S.Ct. 2821, 37 L.Ed.2d 782; *Romer v. Evans*, 517 U.S. at 634–635, 116 S.Ct. 1620, 134 L.Ed.2d 855. Indeed, we have never held that moral disapproval, without any other asserted state interest, is a sufficient rationale under the Equal Protection Clause to justify a law that discriminates among groups of persons.

Moral disapproval of a group cannot be a legitimate governmental interest under the Equal Protection Clause because legal classifications must not be "drawn for the purpose of disadvantaging the group burdened by the law." *Id. at* 633, 116 S.Ct. 1620, 134 L.Ed.2d 855. Texas' invocation of moral disapproval as a legitimate state interest proves nothing more than Texas' desire to criminalize homosexual sodomy. But the Equal Protection Clause prevents a State from creating "a classification of persons undertaken for its own sake." *Id. at* 635, 116 S.Ct. 1620, 134 L.Ed.2d 855. And because Texas so rarely enforces its sodomy law as applied to private, consensual acts, the law serves more as a statement of dislike and disapproval against homosexuals than as a tool to stop criminal behavior. The Texas sodomy law "raises the inevitable inference that the disadvantage imposed is born of animosity toward the class of persons affected." *Id. at* 634, 116 S.Ct. 1620, 134 L.Ed.2d 855.

. . .

Indeed, Texas law confirms that the sodomy statute is directed toward homosexuals as a class. In Texas, calling a person a homosexual is slander *per se* because the word "homosexual" "imputes the commission of a crime." *Plumley v. Landmark Chevrolet, Inc.*, 122 F.3d 308, 310 (CA5 1997) (applying Texas law); *see also Head v. Newton*, 596 S.W.2d 209, 210 (Tex. App. 1980). The State has admitted that because of the sodomy law, *being* homosexual carries the presumption of being a criminal. *See State v. Morales*, 826 S.W.2d at 202–203 ("The statute brands lesbians and gay men as criminals and thereby legally sanctions discrimination against them in a variety of ways unrelated to the criminal law"). Texas' sodomy law therefore results in discrimination against homosexuals as a class in an array of areas outside the criminal law. *See ibid.* In *Romer* v. *Evans,* we refused to sanction a law that singled out homosexuals "for disfavored legal status." 517 U.S. at 633, 116 S.Ct. 1620, 134 L.Ed.2d 855. The same is true here. The Equal Protection Clause "neither knows nor tolerates classes among citizens." *Id. at* 623, 116 S.Ct. 1620, 134 L.Ed.2d 855 (quoting *Plessy v. Ferguson,* 163 U.S. 537, 559, 16 S.Ct. 1138, 41 L.Ed. 256 (1896) (Harlan, J. dissenting)).

. . .

Whether a sodomy law that is neutral both in effect and application, *see Yick Wo v. Hopkins,* 118 U.S. 356, 6 S.Ct. 1064, 30 L.Ed. 220 (1886), would violate the substantive component of the Due Process Clause is an issue that need not be decided today. I am confident, however, that so long as the Equal Protection Clause requires a sodomy law to apply equally to the private consensual conduct of homosexuals and heterosexuals alike, such a law would not long stand in our democratic society. . . .

That this law as applied to private, consensual conduct is unconstitutional under the Equal Protection Clause does not mean that other laws distinguishing between heterosexuals and homosexuals would similarly fail under rational basis review. Texas cannot assert any legitimate state interest here, such as national security or preserving the traditional institution of marriage. Unlike the moral disapproval of same-sex relations—the asserted state interest in this case—other reasons exist to promote the institution of marriage beyond mere moral disapproval of an excluded group.

A law branding one class of persons as criminal solely based on the State's moral disapproval of that class and the conduct associated with that class runs contrary to the values of the Constitution and the Equal Protection Clause, under any standard of review. I therefore concur in the Court's judgment that Texas' sodomy law banning "deviate sexual intercourse" between consenting adults of the same sex, but not between consenting adults of different sexes, is unconstitutional.

JUSTICE SCALIA, with whom the CHIEF JUSTICE and JUSTICE THOMAS join, dissenting.

"Liberty finds no refuge in a jurisprudence of doubt." *Planned Parenthood of Southeastern Pa. v. Casey*, 505 U.S. 833, 844, 112 S.Ct. 2791, 120 L.Ed.2d 674 (1992). That was the Court's sententious response, barely more than a decade ago, to those seeking to overrule *Roe v. Wade*, 410 U.S. 113, 93 S.Ct. 705, 35 L.Ed.2d 147 (1973). The Court's response today, to those who have engaged in a 17–year crusade to overrule *Bowers v. Hardwick*, 478 U.S. 186, 106 S.Ct. 2841, 92 L.Ed.2d 140 (1986), is very different. The need for stability and certainty presents no barrier.

Most of the rest of today's opinion has no relevance to its actual holding—that the Texas statute "furthers no legitimate state interest which can justify" its application to petitioners under rational-basis review. *Ante* at 156 L. Ed. 2d at 526 (overruling *Bowers* to the extent it sustained Georgia's anti-sodomy statute under the rational-basis test). Though there is discussion of "fundamental propositions," *ante* at 156 L. Ed. 2d at 517, and "fundamental decisions," *ibid.,* nowhere does the Court's opinion declare that homosexual sodomy is a "fundamental right" under the Due Process Clause; nor does it subject the Texas law to the standard of review that would be appropriate (strict scrutiny) if homosexual sodomy *were* a "fundamental right." Thus, while overruling the *outcome* of *Bowers*, the Court leaves strangely untouched its central legal conclusion: "Respondent would have us announce . . . a fundamental right to engage in homosexual sodomy. This we are quite unwilling to do." 478 U.S. at 191, 106 S.Ct. 2841, 92 L.Ed.2d 140. Instead the Court simply describes petitioners' conduct as "an exercise of their liberty"—which it undoubtedly is—and proceeds to apply an unheard-of form of rational-basis review that will have far-reaching implications beyond this case. *Ante* at 156 L. Ed. 2d at 516.

. . .

II.

Having decided that it need not adhere to *stare decisis*, the Court still must establish that *Bowers* was wrongly decided and that the Texas statute, as applied to petitioners, is unconstitutional.

Texas Penal Code Ann. § 21.06(a) (2003) undoubtedly imposes constraints on liberty. So do laws prohibiting prostitution, recreational use of heroin, and, for that matter, working more than 60 hours per week in a bakery. But there is no right to "liberty" under the Due Process Clause, though today's opinion repeatedly makes that claim. *Ante* at 156 L. Ed. 2d at 518–519 ("The liberty protected by the Constitution allows homosexual persons the right to make this choice"); *ante* at 156 L. Ed. 2d at 523 ("These matters . . . are central to the liberty protected by the Fourteenth Amendment"); *ante* at 156 L. Ed. 2d at 525–526 ("Their right to liberty under the Due Process Clause gives them the full right to engage in their conduct without intervention of the government"). The Fourteenth Amendment *expressly allows* States to deprive their citizens of "liberty," *so long as "due process of law" is provided:*

> No state shall . . . deprive any person of life, liberty, or property, *without due process of law.*

Amend. 14 (emphasis added).

Our opinions applying the doctrine known as "substantive due process" hold that the Due Process Clause prohibits States from infringing *fundamental* liberty interests, unless the infringement is narrowly tailored to serve a compelling state interest. *Washington v. Glucksberg*, 521 U.S. at 721, 117 S.Ct. 2258, 138 L.Ed.2d 772. We have held repeatedly, in cases the Court today does not overrule, that *only* fundamental rights qualify for this so-called "heightened scrutiny" protection—that is, rights which are " 'deeply rooted in this Nation's history and tradition,' " *ibid. See Reno v. Flores*, 507 U.S. 292, 303, 113 S.Ct. 1439, 123 L.Ed.2d 1 (1993) (fundamental liberty interests must be "so rooted in the traditions and conscience of our people as to be ranked as fundamental" (internal quotation marks and citations omitted)); *United States v. Salerno*, 481 U.S. 739, 751, 107 S.Ct. 2095, 95 L.Ed.2d 697 (1987) (same). *See also Michael H. v. Gerald D.*, 491 U.S. 110, 122, 109 S.Ct. 2333, 105 L.Ed.2d 91 (1989) ("We have insisted not merely that the interest denominated as a 'liberty' be 'fundamental' . . . but also that it be an interest traditionally protected by our society"); *Moore v. East Cleveland*, 431 U.S. 494, 503, 97

S.Ct. 1932, 52 L.Ed.2d 531 (1977) (plurality opinion); *Meyer v. Nebraska*, 262 U.S. 390, 399, 43 S.Ct. 625, 67 L.Ed. 1042 (1923) (Fourteenth Amendment protects "those privileges *long recognized at common law* as essential to the orderly pursuit of happiness by free men" (emphasis added)). All other liberty interests may be abridged or abrogated pursuant to a validly enacted state law if that law is rationally related to a legitimate state interest.

Bowers held, first, that criminal prohibitions of homosexual sodomy are not subject to heightened scrutiny because they do not implicate a "fundamental right" under the Due Process Clause, 478 U.S. at 191–194, 106 S.Ct. 2841, 92 L.Ed.2d 140. Noting that "[p]roscriptions against that conduct have ancient roots," *id.* at 192, 106 S.Ct. 2841, 92 L.Ed.2d 140, that "sodomy was a criminal offense at common law and was forbidden by the laws of the original 13 States when they ratified the Bill of Rights," *ibid.*, and that many States had retained their bans on sodomy, *id.* at 193, 106 S.Ct. 2841, 92 L.Ed.2d 140, *Bowers* concluded that a right to engage in homosexual sodomy was not " 'deeply rooted in this Nation's history and tradition,' " *id.* at 192, 106 S.Ct. 2841, 92 L.Ed.2d 140.

The Court today does not overrule this holding. Not once does it describe homosexual sodomy as a "fundamental right" or a "fundamental liberty interest," nor does it subject the Texas statute to strict scrutiny. Instead, having failed to establish that the right to homosexual sodomy is " 'deeply rooted in this Nation's history and tradition,' " the Court concludes that the application of Texas's statute to petitioners' conduct fails the rational-basis test, and overrules *Bowers'* holding to the contrary, *see id.* at 196, 106 S.Ct. 2841, 92 L.Ed.2d 140. "The Texas statute furthers no legitimate state interest which can justify its intrusion into the personal and private life of the individual." *Ante* at 156 L.Ed.2d at 526.

I shall address that rational-basis holding presently. First, however, I address some aspersions that the Court casts upon *Bowers'* conclusion that homosexual sodomy is not a "fundamental right"—even though, as I have said, the Court does not have the boldness to reverse that conclusion.

III.

. . .

After discussing the history of antisodomy laws, *ante* at 156 L. Ed. 2d at 519–521, the Court proclaims that, "it should be noted that there is no longstanding history in this country of laws directed at homosexual conduct as a distinct matter," *ante* at 156 L. Ed. 2d at 519. This observation in no way casts into doubt the "definitive [historical] conclusion," *id.*, on which *Bowers* relied: that our Nation has a longstanding history of laws prohibiting *sodomy in general*—regardless of whether it was performed by same-sex or opposite-sex couples:

> "It is obvious to us that neither of these formulations would extend a fundamental right to homosexuals to engage in acts of consensual sodomy. Proscriptions against that conduct have ancient roots. *Sod-*

omy was a criminal offense at common law and was forbidden by the laws of the original 13 States when they ratified the Bill of Rights. In 1868, when the Fourteenth Amendment was ratified, all but 5 of the 37 States in the Union had *criminal sodomy laws.* In fact, until 1961, all 50 States outlawed *sodomy*, and today, 24 States and the District of Columbia continue to provide criminal penalties for *sodomy* performed in private and between consenting adults. Against this background, to claim that a right to engage in such conduct is 'deeply rooted in this Nation's history and tradition' " or " 'implicit in the concept of ordered liberty' is, at best, facetious." 478 U.S. at 192–194, 106 S.Ct. 2841, 92 L.Ed.2d 140 (citations and footnotes omitted; emphasis added).

It is (as *Bowers* recognized) entirely irrelevant whether the laws in our long national tradition criminalizing homosexual sodomy were "directed at homosexual conduct as a distinct matter." *Ante* at 156 L.Ed.2d at 519. Whether homosexual sodomy was prohibited by a law targeted at same-sex sexual relations or by a more general law prohibiting both homosexual and heterosexual sodomy, the only relevant point is that it *was* criminalized—which suffices to establish that homosexual sodomy is not a right "deeply rooted in our Nation's history and tradition." The Court today agrees that homosexual sodomy was criminalized and thus does not dispute the facts on which *Bowers actually* relied.

. . .

Realizing that fact, the Court instead says: "We think that our laws and traditions in the past half century are of most relevance here. These references show *an emerging awareness* that liberty gives substantial protection to adult persons in deciding how to conduct their private lives *in matters pertaining to sex.*" *Ante* at 156 L.Ed.2d at 521 (emphasis added). Apart from the fact that such an "emerging awareness" does not establish a "fundamental right," the statement is factually false. States continue to prosecute all sorts of crimes by adults "in matters pertaining to sex": prostitution, adult incest, adultery, obscenity, and child pornography. Sodomy laws, too, have been enforced "in the past half century," in which there have been 134 reported cases involving prosecutions for consensual, adult, homosexual sodomy. . . .

In any event, an "emerging awareness" is by definition not "deeply rooted in this Nation's history and traditions," as we have said "fundamental right" status requires. Constitutional entitlements do not spring into existence because some States choose to lessen or eliminate criminal sanctions on certain behavior. Much less do they spring into existence, as the Court seems to believe, because *foreign nations* decriminalize conduct. The *Bowers* majority opinion *never* relied on "values we share with a wider civilization," *ante* at 156 L.Ed.2d at 524, but rather rejected the claimed right to sodomy on the ground that such a right was not " 'deeply rooted in *this Nation's* history and tradition,' " 478 U.S. at 193–194, 106 S.Ct. 2841, 92 L.Ed.2d 140 (emphasis added). *Bowers'* rational-basis holding is likewise devoid of any reliance on the views of a "wider civilization," *see id.* at 196, 106 S.Ct. 2841, 92 L.Ed.2d 140. The Court's discussion of these foreign views (ignoring, of course, the many countries that have retained criminal prohibitions on sodomy) is therefore meaningless dicta. Dangerous dicta, however, since "this Court ... should not impose foreign moods, fads, or fashions on Americans." *Foster v. Florida*, 537 U.S. 990, 123 S.Ct. 470, 154 L.Ed.2d 359 (2002) (Thomas, J., concurring in denial of certiorari).

IV.

I turn now to the ground on which the Court squarely rests its holding: the contention that there is no rational basis for the law here under attack. This proposition is so out of accord with our jurisprudence—indeed, with the jurisprudence of *any* society we know—that it requires little discussion.

The Texas statute undeniably seeks to further the belief of its citizens that certain forms of sexual behavior are "immoral and unacceptable," *Bowers*, *supra* at 196, 106 S.Ct. 2841, 92 L.Ed.2d 140—the same interest furthered by criminal laws against fornication, bigamy, adultery, adult incest, bestiality, and obscenity. *Bowers* held that this *was* a legitimate state interest. The Court today reaches the opposite conclusion. The Texas statute, it says, "furthers *no legitimate state interest* which can justify its intrusion into the personal and private life of the individual," *ante* at 156 L.Ed.2d at 526 (emphasis added). The Court embraces instead Justice Stevens' declaration in his *Bowers* dissent, that "the fact that the governing majority in a State has traditionally viewed a particular practice as immoral is not a sufficient reason for upholding a law prohibiting the practice," *ante* at 156 L.Ed.2d at 525. This effectively decrees the end of all morals legislation. If, as the Court asserts, the promotion of majoritarian sexual morality is not even a *legitimate* state interest, none of the above-mentioned laws can survive rational-basis review.

V.

Finally, I turn to petitioners' equal-protection challenge, which no Member of the Court save Justice O'Connor, *ante* at 156 L.Ed.2d at 526 (opinion concurring in judgment), embraces: On its face § 21.06(a) applies equally to all persons. Men and women, heterosexuals and homosexuals, are all subject to its prohibition of deviate sexual intercourse with someone of the same sex. To be sure, § 21.06 does distinguish between the sexes insofar as concerns the partner with whom the sexual acts are performed: men can violate the law only with other men, and women only with other women. But this cannot itself be a denial of equal protection, since it is precisely the same distinction regarding partner that is drawn in state laws prohibiting marriage with someone of the same sex while permitting marriage with someone of the opposite sex.

The objection is made, however, that the antimiscegenation laws invalidated in *Loving v. Virginia*, 388 U.S. 1, 8, 87 S.Ct. 1817, 18 L.Ed.2d

1010 (1967), similarly were applicable to whites and blacks alike, and only distinguished between the races insofar as the *partner* was concerned. In *Loving*, however, we correctly applied heightened scrutiny, rather than the usual rational-basis review, because the Virginia statute was "designed to maintain White Supremacy." *Id.* at 6, 11, 87 S.Ct. 1817, 18 L.Ed.2d 1010. A racially discriminatory purpose is always sufficient to subject a law to strict scrutiny, even a facially neutral law that makes no mention of race. *See Washington v. Davis*, 426 U.S. 229, 241–242, 96 S.Ct. 2040, 48 L.Ed.2d 597 (1976). No purpose to discriminate against men or women as a class can be gleaned from the Texas law, so rational-basis review applies. That review is readily satisfied here by the same rational basis that satisfied it in *Bowers*—society's belief that certain forms of sexual behavior are "immoral and unacceptable," 478 U.S. at 196, 106 S.Ct. 2841, 92 L.Ed.2d 140. This is the same justification that supports many other laws regulating sexual behavior that make a distinction based upon the identity of the partner—for example, laws against adultery, fornication, and adult incest, and laws refusing to recognize homosexual marriage.

Justice O'Connor argues that the discrimination in this law which must be justified is not its discrimination with regard to the sex of the partner but its discrimination with regard to the sexual proclivity of the principal actor.

> While it is true that the law applies only to conduct, the conduct targeted by this law is conduct that is closely correlated with being homosexual. Under such circumstances, Texas' sodomy law is targeted at more than conduct. It is instead directed toward gay persons as a class.

Ante at 156 L.Ed.2d at 529.

Of course the same could be said of any law. A law against public nudity targets "the conduct that is closely correlated with being a nudist," and hence "is targeted at more than conduct"; it is "directed toward nudists as a class." But be that as it may. Even if the Texas law *does* deny equal protection to "homosexuals as a class," that denial *still* does not need to be justified by anything more than a rational basis, which our cases show is satisfied by the enforcement of traditional notions of sexual morality.

. . .

Today's opinion is the product of a Court, which is the product of a law-profession culture, that has largely signed on to the so-called homosexual agenda, by which I mean the agenda promoted by some homosexual activists directed at eliminating the moral opprobrium that has traditionally attached to homosexual conduct. . . .

One of the most revealing statements in today's opinion is the Court's grim warning that the criminalization of homosexual conduct is "an invitation to subject homosexual persons to discrimination both in the public and in the private spheres." *Ante* at 156 L.Ed.2d at 523. It is clear from this that the Court has taken sides in the culture war, departing from its role of assuring, as neutral observer, that the democratic rules of engagement are observed. Many Americans do not want persons who openly engage in homosexual conduct as partners in their business, as scoutmasters for their children, as teachers in their children's schools, or as boarders in their home. They view this as protecting themselves and their families from a lifestyle that they believe to be immoral and destructive. The Court views it as "discrimination" which it is the function of our judgments to deter. So imbued is the Court with the law profession's anti-anti-homosexual culture, that it is seemingly unaware that the attitudes of that culture are not obviously "mainstream"; that in most States what the Court calls "discrimination" against those who engage in homosexual acts is perfectly legal; that proposals to ban such "discrimination" under Title VII have repeatedly been rejected by Congress, *see* Employment Non–Discrimination Act of 1994, S. 2238, 103d Cong., 2d Sess. (1994); Civil Rights Amendments, H. R. 5452, 94th Cong., 1st Sess. (1975); that in some cases such "discrimination" is *mandated* by federal statute, *see* 10 U.S.C. § 654(b)(1) [10 USCS § 654(b)(1)] (mandating discharge from the armed forces of any service member who engages in or intends to engage in homosexual acts); and that in some cases such "discrimination" is a constitutional right, *see Boy Scouts of America v. Dale*, 530 U.S. 640, 120 S.Ct. 2446, 147 L.Ed.2d 554 (2000).

Let me be clear that I have nothing against homosexuals, or any other group, promoting their agenda through normal democratic means. Social perceptions of sexual and other morality change over time, and every group has the right to persuade its fellow citizens that its view of such matters is the best. That homosexuals have achieved some success in that enterprise is attested to by the fact that Texas is one of the few remaining States that criminalize private, consensual homosexual acts. But persuading one's fellow citizens is one thing, and imposing one's views in absence of democratic majority will is something else. I would no more *require* a State to criminalize homosexual acts—or, for that matter, display *any* moral disapprobation of them—than I would *forbid* it to do so. What Texas has chosen to do is well within the range of traditional democratic action, and its hand should not be stayed through the invention of a brand-new "constitutional right" by a Court that is impatient of democratic change. It is indeed true that "later generations can see that laws once thought necessary and proper in fact serve only to oppress," *ante* at 156 L.Ed.2d at 526; and when that happens, later generations can repeal those laws. But it is the premise of our system that those judgments are to be made by the people, and not imposed by a governing caste that knows best.

One of the benefits of leaving regulation of this matter to the people rather than to the courts is that the people, unlike judges, need not carry things to their logical conclusion. The people may feel that their disapprobation of homosexual conduct is strong enough to disallow homosexual marriage, but not strong enough to criminalize private homosexual acts—and may legislate accordingly. The Court today pretends that it possesses a similar freedom of action, so that we need not fear judicial imposition of homosexual marriage, as has recently occurred in Canada (in a decision that the Canadian Government has chosen not to appeal).... At the end of its opinion—after having laid waste the foundations of our rational-basis jurisprudence—the Court says that the present case "does not involve whether the government must give formal recognition to any relationship that homosexual persons seek to enter." *Ante* at 156 L.Ed.2d at 525. Do not believe it. More illuminating than this bald, unreasoned disclaimer is the progression of thought displayed by an earlier passage in the Court's opinion, which notes the constitutional protections afforded to "personal decisions relating to *marriage*, procreation, contraception, family relationships, child rearing, and education," and then declares that "persons in a homosexual relationship may seek autonomy for these purposes, just as heterosexual persons do." *Ante* at 156 L.Ed.2d at 523 (emphasis added). Today's opinion dismantles the structure of constitutional law that has permitted a distinction to be made between heterosexual and homosexual unions, insofar as formal recognition in marriage is concerned. If moral disapprobation of homosexual conduct is "no legitimate state interest" for purposes of proscribing that conduct, *ante* at 156 L.Ed.2d at 526; and if, as the Court coos (casting aside all pretense of neutrality), "when sexuality finds overt expression in intimate conduct with another person, the conduct can be but one element in a personal bond that is more enduring," *ante* at 156 L.Ed.2d at 518; what justification could there possibly be for denying the benefits of marriage to homosexual couples exercising "the liberty protected by the Constitution," *ibid.*? Surely not the encouragement of procreation, since the sterile and the elderly are allowed to marry. This case "does not involve" the issue of homosexual marriage only if one entertains the belief that principle and logic have nothing to do with the decisions of this Court. Many will hope that, as the Court comfortingly assures us, this is so.

The matters appropriate for this Court's resolution are only three: Texas's prohibition of sodomy neither infringes a "fundamental right" (which the Court does not dispute), nor is unsupported by a rational relation to what the Constitution considers a legitimate state interest, nor denies the equal protection of the laws. I dissent.

JUSTICE THOMAS, dissenting.

[Omitted]

DISCUSSION

Do you agree with Justice Scalia's argument that all morals legislation has been vanquished by Romer *and* Lawrence*? Must we now legalize pedophilia, bestiality, polygamy? See* Utah v. Holm, *137 P.3d 726 (Utah 2006) (upholding anti-bigamy laws against a Lawrence challenge). For a discussion, see Shannon Gilreath,* Some Penetrating Observations on the Fifth Anniversary of Lawrence v. Texas, *30* WOMEN'S RIGHTS LAW REPORTER *442–478 (2009).*

The Lawrence *dissenters are angered at the majority's brief discussion of international legal norms. After* Lawrence, *some Republicans in Congress called for the impeachment of federal judges who cite foreign precedents in their decisions. Do you agree with these criticisms?*

VI. THE AFTERMATH OF *LAWRENCE*

State and lower federal courts had to grapple with exactly what *Lawrence v. Texas* meant for a host of sex-based regulations. Some courts have taken a very narrow view of *Lawrence*, reading Justice Kennedy's explanation of what the case was *not* about as the ceiling of what it could be about. For example, even after *Lawrence*, some states continue to punish oral and/or anal sex more harshly than vaginal intercourse when the oral/anal sex occurs for hire (*see, e.g., State v. Thomas*, 891 So.2d 1233 (La. 2005)); between minors (*see, e.g., Wilson v. State*, 279 Ga.App. 459, 631 S.E.2d 391 (2006), where acts between minors took place in a motel room) or in public (*see, e.g., In re R.L.C.*, 361 N.C. 287, 643 S.E.2d 920 (2007), where acts between minors happened in a car in a public parking lot. The discussion note after *State v. Limon* analyzes *In re R.L.C.* further). In the following decision, the Kansas Supreme Court considers the *Lawrence* decision's impact on a statutorily-mandated inequity in punishment for unlawful sexual conduct between members of the same-sex, when one partner is a minor.

STATE v. LIMON

280 Kan. 275, 122 P.3d 22 (2005)

The opinion was delivered by LUCKERT, J.:

The principal issue presented in this case is whether the Kansas unlawful voluntary sexual relations statute, K.S.A.2004 Supp. 21–3522, violates the equal protection provision of the Fourteenth Amendment to the United States Constitution. Matthew Limon argues that the United States Supreme Court decision in *Lawrence v. Texas*, 539 U.S. 558, 123 S.Ct. 2472, 156 L.Ed.2d 508 (2003), requires this court to find the statute unconstitutional because it results in a punishment for unlawful voluntary sexual conduct between members of the opposite sex that is less harsh than the punishment for the same conduct between members of the same sex.

The statute subject to this challenge, commonly referred to as the Romeo and Juliet statute, applies to voluntary sexual intercourse, sodomy, or lewd touching when, at the time of the incident, (1) the victim is a child of 14 or 15; (2) the offender is less than 19 years of age and less than 4 years older than the victim; (3) the victim and offender are the only ones involved; and(4) the victim and offender are members of the opposite sex. Limon's conduct meets all of the elements of the Romeo and Juliet statute except the one limiting application to acts between members of the opposite sex.

When the Romeo and Juliet statute applies, prison terms are shorter. Because these disparities are based upon the homosexual nature of Limon's conduct, he argues the Romeo and Juliet statute creates a classification which violates the equal protection principles announced by the United States Supreme Court.

We agree that the United States Supreme Court's decision in *Lawrence* controls our analysis and, when considered in conjunction with several equal protection decisions of the United States Supreme Court, requires us to hold that the State does not have a rational basis for the statutory classification created in the Romeo and Juliet statute. . . .

FACTUAL AND PROCEDURAL BACKGROUND

Limon was convicted of criminal sodomy pursuant to K.S.A. 21–3505(a)(2) after a bench trial on stipulated facts. The stipulation established that on February 16, 2000, Limon had consensual oral contact with the genitalia of M.A.R. Both Limon and M.A.R. are male. Limon turned 18 years of age just 1 week before the incident; his date of birth is February 9, 1982. He was less than 4 years older than M.A.R., who turned 15 years of age the month following the incident. M.A.R.'s date of birth is March 17, 1985.

The contact occurred at a school for developmentally disabled children where Limon and M.A.R. were residents. Although there is a discrepancy between Limon's and M.A.R.'s functioning, the difference is minor. . . .

The trial court rejected Limon's equal protection argument and denied the motion for downward durational departure. The trial court found that Limon's criminal history category was B because of two prior juvenile adjudications for aggravated criminal sodomy. Limon was sentenced to 206 months' imprisonment, which was the mitigated term under the Kansas sentencing guidelines for a severity level 3 crime where the defendant has a criminal history falling in category B. As a consequence of Limon's conviction, he is subject to 60 months' of postrelease supervision and is required to register as a persistent sexual offender. By contrast, had Limon been convicted of sodomy under the unlawful sexual relations statute, the presumptive sentence at the time of the offense (and now) would have been only 13, 14, or 15 months' imprisonment. K.S.A.1999 Supp. 21–4704. Moreover, those sentenced under the unlawful sexual relations statute are not subject to the provisions regarding sentencing of persistent sexual offenders or required to register as a sex offender . . .

Limon sought this court's review of the Court of Appeals' decision; his petition was denied. Limon then filed a petition for writ of certiorari to the United States Supreme Court. While his petition was pending, the Supreme Court issued its decision in *Lawrence v. Texas* . . . .

. . .

ANALYSIS

In this appeal, Limon primarily argues that to punish criminal voluntary sexual conduct between teenagers of the same sex more harshly than criminal voluntary sexual conduct between teenagers of the opposite sex is a violation of the equal protection provision of the United States Constitution....

. . .

Traditionally, when analyzing an equal protection claim, the United States and Kansas Supreme Courts employ three levels of scrutiny: strict scrutiny, intermediate scrutiny, and the rational basis test. The level of scrutiny applied by the court depends on the nature of the legislative classification and the rights affected by that classification. *Romer v. Evans*, (1996). The general rule is that a law will be subject to the rational basis test unless the legislative classification targets a suspect class or burdens a fundamental right.

Thus, when an equal protection claim is made, the first step of the analysis is to determine the nature of the legislative classification and the rights which are affected by the classification. That determination will dictate the level of scrutiny which applies. The final step of the analysis requires determining whether the classification withstands the scrutiny.

CLASSIFICATION

In the first step, we must examine the nature of the classification created by the Romeo and Juliet statute. The State argues that the statute applies only to conduct and does not discriminate against any class of individual, in particular against homosexual persons.

Indeed, there is no per se classification of homosexuals, bisexuals, or heterosexuals in the statute, nor do we know which classification applies to *Limon* or *M.A.R.* However, that does not mean that Limon's argument fails.... The majority in *Lawrence* similarly noted that making homosexual conduct criminal and not legislating against "deviate sexual intercourse" committed by persons of different sexes "in and of itself is an invitation to subject homosexual persons to discrimination both in the public and in the private spheres." Throughout the *Lawrence* opinion, the majority refers to the stigmatizing and demeaning effect of criminalizing conduct commonly engaged in by homosexuals and concludes that a state may not "demean their existence or control their destiny." ...

This case is different from *Lawrence*, where homosexual conduct was criminal and heterosexual conduct was not. The *Lawrence* Court focused upon the "stigma" the criminal statute imposed which it characterized as "not trivial." Here, both types of conduct are criminalized and, thus, stigma attaches to the heterosexual conduct covered by the Romeo and Juliet statute. However, there is an enormous escalation in the severity of punishment for those punished under the general rape, sodomy, and lewd act statutes. The Kansas Sentencing Guidelines impose a presumptive sentence of prison upon all defendants, including those with no prior criminal history, who are convicted of a severity level 3 felony, the severity level applying to Limon's conviction. In contrast, a presumption of probation applies to all sentences, except those for defendants with criminal histories of "A" or "B," who are sentenced for a severity level 9 crime, which would be the applicable severity level for sodomy if the Romeo and Juliet statute applied.

Additionally, the presumptive terms of imprisonment for a severity level 3 felony, as noted earlier, are approximately 15 times that of a severity level 9 felony. . . .

There is also the distinction that Limon faces the stigma of sex offender registration; those convicted under the Romeo and Juliet statute do not. K.S.A. 22–4902.

Furthermore, the demeaning and stigmatizing effect upon which the *Lawrence* Court focused is at least equally applicable to teenagers, both the victim and the offender, as it is to adults and, according to some, the impact is greater upon a teen.

Based upon these considerations we conclude there is a discriminatory classification requiring us to examine the level of scrutiny to be applied in testing the constitutionality of the classification.

LEVEL OF SCRUTINY

The next step of our analysis is to determine the appropriate level of scrutiny to apply. Limon argues that under the holding in *Lawrence* the highest level of scrutiny should apply because the statute creates a classification of homosexuals which the *Lawrence* Court recognized as suspect. Contrary to this argument, the United States Supreme Court has not recognized homosexuals as a suspect classification. . . . Thus, strict scrutiny does not apply to our analysis of whether the Romeo and Juliet provision unconstitutionally discriminates based upon sexual orientation.

. . .

Despite not deciding the case on equal protection grounds and never explicitly identifying the standard utilized for its due process analysis, the *Lawrence* majority, by approvingly citing and discussing the equal protection analysis in *Romer*, at least implied that the rational basis test is the appropriate standard when a statute is attacked because of its classification of homosexual conduct. . . . In *Lawrence*, the Court summarized the *Romer* decision, noting that the amendment named a "solitary class . . . and deprived them of protection under state antidiscrimination laws. We concluded that the provision was 'born of animosity toward the class of persons affected' and further that it had no rational relation to a legitimate governmental purpose."

The *Lawrence* opinion contains another oblique indication that the rational basis test would apply, stating: "The Texas statute furthers no legitimate state interest which can justify its intrusion into the personal and private life of the individual." Typically, a search for a legitimate interest signifies a rational basis analysis.

Hence, we apply the rational basis test to determine whether the Romeo and Juliet statute is unconstitutional because of its exclusion of homosexual conduct.

RATIONAL BASIS TEST

. . .

In explaining the test, the United States Supreme Court has said that, although the rational basis test is "the most deferential of standards, we insist on knowing the relation between the classification adopted and the object obtained." *Romer*. . . . "If the adverse impact on the disfavored class is an apparent aim of the legislature, its impartiality would be suspect."

. . .

LEGISLATIVE HISTORY

Although the legislature need not have articulated the basis for the classification the State relies upon when the classification is challenged, we begin with an examination of the legislative record to determine if a purpose for the classification is suggested therein. . . .

. . .

Although the legislative history does not suggest the State's interest in including the phrase "and are members of the opposite sex," the State argues several possibilities. In addition, we must consider the rationales utilized by the Court of Appeals majority [upholding Limon's conviction]. These various possible State interests can be categorized as: (1) the protection and preservation of the traditional sexual mores of society; (2) preservation of the historical notions of appropriate sexual development of children; (3) protection of teenagers against coercive relationships; (4) protection of teenagers from the increased health risks that accompany sexual activity; (5) promotion of parental responsibility and procreation; and (6) protection of those in group homes.

TRADITIONAL SEXUAL MORES AND DEVELOPMENT

Limon counters this theoretical justification by arguing that the State's moral disapproval of homosexuality is an illegitimate justification for discrimination.

The *Lawrence* decision rejected a morality-based rationale as a legitimate State interest. . . .

. . .

Thus, when Texas argued that its anti-sodomy law furthered the promotion of morality the Court in *Lawrence* rejected the argument and adopted the following reasoning from Justice Stevens' dissent in *Bowers*: "[T]he fact that the governing majority in a State has traditionally viewed a particular practice as immoral is not a sufficient reason for upholding a law prohibiting the practice."

This holding followed the precedent of *Casey, Eisenstadt, Romer*, and other cases. The Court in *Romer* explained that our laws are often morality-based which, in and of itself, is not objectionable if the laws are applied fairly to all. However, the right to equal protection of those laws is offended when legal classifications are drawn for the purpose of invoking moral disapproval with "the purpose of disadvantaging the group burdened by the law." *Romer*.

The Court of Appeals majority would dismiss this analysis in *Lawrence* because of the due process context in which the discussion was made. The *Lawrence* majority, however, signaled application of the principles to equal protection analysis: "Equality of treatment and the due process right to demand respect for conduct protected by the substantive guarantee of liberty are linked in important respects, and a decision on the latter point advances both interests." In essence, the *Lawrence* decision recognized that the substantive due process analysis at issue in that case and the equal protection analysis necessary in this case are inevitably linked....

Thus, we are directed in our equal protection analysis by the United States Supreme Court's holding in *Lawrence* that moral disapproval of a group cannot be a legitimate governmental interest.

HISTORICAL NOTIONS OF APPROPRIATE SEXUAL DEVELOPMENT OF CHILDREN

The Court of Appeals also determined the *Lawrence* holding did not apply to this case because *Lawrence* involved adults and this case involved an adult in a relationship with a minor. Likewise, the State focuses its argument on the State's interest in the moral and sexual development of children.

Undoubtedly, the State has broad powers to protect minors....

However, [the Supreme Court in] *Carey* [*Carey v. Population Services Int'l*, 431 U. S. 678 (1977)] held that "the right to privacy in connection with decisions affecting procreation extends to minors as well as adults" and invalidated the prohibition in question. The Court noted that "State restrictions inhibiting privacy rights of minors are valid only if they serve 'any significant state interest ... that is not present in the case of an adult.' "

. . .

We conclude, as the United States Supreme Court stated in *Romer,* the "status-based enactment [is so] divorced from any factual context" we cannot "discern a relationship" to the espoused State interest that the law preserves the sexual development of children consistent with traditional sexual mores. Additionally, we again recognize the Lawrence Court's conclusion that moral disapproval of a group cannot be a legitimate governmental interest.

COERCIVE EFFECT UPON MINORS

The State at various times refers to the coercive effect often existing in a relationship between an adult and a child. Certainly, the State has a significant interest in prohibiting sex between adults and minors, not only because of the potentially coercive effect of an adult's influence but also because of concern regarding the minor's ability to arrive at an informed consent. These concerns are addressed by and form the fundamental policy rationale of statutory rape provisions. Limon's argument accepts and supports this State interest; he agrees he deserves punishment. He simply disputes that he should be punished more severely for having sex with a member of the same sex.

Additionally, the policy decision made by the legislature in enacting the Romeo and Juliet statute undercuts this argument. The legislature determined, at least as to those in a heterosexual relationship, that a mutual relationship between teenagers is less likely to involve the same coercion that a relationship between an older adult and a child might and is more likely to be one where the minor's participation is voluntary, although not legally consensual.

This, however, begs the question of whether there is a rational basis to distinguish between a class of those 18 years old and younger who engage in voluntary sex with minors aged 14 or 15 who are of the same sex and a class of those 18 years old and younger who engage in voluntary sex with such minors of the opposite sex. We see no basis to determine that as a class one group or the other would have a higher tendency to be coercive. A distinction on this basis has no factual support . . .

NO RATIONAL BASIS

We conclude that K.S.A.2004 Supp. 21–3522, the Kansas unlawful voluntary sexual relations statute, does not pass rational basis scrutiny under the United States Constitution Equal Protection Clause or, because we traditionally apply the same analysis to our state constitution, under the Kansas Constitution Equal Protection Clause. The Romeo and Juliet statute suffers the same faults as found by the United States Supreme Court in *Romer* and *Eisenstadt*; adding the phrase "and are members of the opposite sex" created a broad, overreaching, and undifferentiated status-based classification which bears no rational relationship to legitimate State interests. Paraphrasing the United States Supreme Court's decision in *Romer*, the statute inflicts immediate, continuing, and real injuries that outrun and belie any legitimate justification that may be claimed for it. Furthermore, the State's interests fail under the holding in *Lawrence* that moral disapproval of a group cannot be a legitimate governmental interest. As Justice Scalia stated: "If, as the [United States Supreme] Court asserts, the promotion of majoritarian sexual morality is not even a legitimate state interest," the statute cannot "survive rational-basis review."

CONCLUSION OF EQUAL PROTECTION ANALYSIS

We hold K.S.A.2004 Supp. 21–3522 unconstitutional as violating the equal protection provisions of the United States and Kansas Constitutions and strike from the statute the words "and are members of the opposite sex." We further hold that Limon's conviction and sentence for criminal sodomy pursuant to K.S.A. 21–3505(a)(2) violate his right to equal protection of the laws.

We further grant Limon's requested remedy of imposing a time limit upon further proceedings in this case and order that the State will have 30 days in which to: (1) charge Limon under the provisions of K.S.A.2004 Supp. 21–3522 without the words "members of the opposite sex" or (2) take other action. . . .

DISCUSSION

Review the application of the Lawrence *holding in the* Limon *case. Now consider:*

Two minors (a 12 year-old girl and 14 year-old boy) engage in oral sex in North Carolina in 2006. The North Carolina legislature has decriminalized "sex acts" between minors when the minor actors are both below the age of 16 and are separated by less than 3 years in age. The boy is charged and adjudicated delinquent for violating North Carolina's "crime against nature" statute, which criminalized oral and anal sex. The North Carolina Supreme Court affirmed, stating that Lawrence *does not apply to situations involving minors and, thus, the "crime against nature" statute is still operable under the circumstances.* In re R.L.C., *179 N.C.App. 311, 635 S.E.2d 1 (2006), aff'd, 361 N.C. 287, 643 S.E.2d 920 (2007). Do you agree that this outcome is consistent with Lawrence? For a thorough analysis of* In re R.L.C., *see Michael Kent Curtis and Shannon Gilreath,* Transforming Teenagers into Oral Sex Felons: The Persistence of the Crime Against Nature after Lawrence v. Texas, 42 WAKE FOREST L. REV. *155–221 (2008). Compare* Leung v. Sec. for Justice, *CACB 317/2005 (Court of Appeal for Hong Kong voids age differential in a statute setting 21 as the age of consent for anal sex when 16 was the age of consent for vaginal intercourse).*

CHAPTER 5

EMPLOYMENT DISCRIMINATION

■ ■ ■

This chapter examines discrimination faced by gays and lesbians in the workplace. For organizational purposes, the cases are divided into units on discrimination in private employment and discrimination in public employment, in which the employer is a government entity. Private employees generally have fewer protections against discrimination based on sexual orientation than do public employees. Their employment relationships are often "employment at will," in which employees can essentially be fired for any reason at all, unless their dismissal violates some specific statutory protection.

Sexual orientation is not one of the categories included in Congress's most direct attempts to curb employment discrimination, namely Title VII of the Civil Rights Act of 1964.[1] Title VII outlaws, in virtually every employment setting, discrimination based on race, color, religion, sex, or national origin. The Age Discrimination in Employment Act[2] and the Americans with Disabilities Act[3] further expand federal protections against discrimination based on age and disability respectively. Efforts to extend federal antidiscrimination protections to sexual orientation (most recently the Employment Non–Discrimination Act or "ENDA") have been pending in Congress since 1974. In recent years, gender identity has also been included in proposed legislation.

A 2007 report produced by The Williams Institute entitled "Bias in the Workplace: Consistent Evidence of Sexual Orientation and Gender Identity Discrimination" found that since the mid 1990s, "15% to 43% of LGB respondents experienced discrimination in the workplace. When asked more specific questions about the type of discrimination experienced, LGB respondents reported the following experiences that were related to their sexual orientation: 8%–17% were fired or denied employment, 10%–28% were denied a promotion or given negative performance evaluations, 7%–41% were verbally/physically abused or had their workplace vandalized, and 10%–19% reported receiving unequal pay or bene-

1. 42 U.S.C.A. §§ 2000e–2000e(17).

2. 29 U.S.C.A §§ 621–634.

3. 42 U.S.C.A. §§ 12101–12213.

fits. Fifteen to 57% of transgender people also report experiencing employment discrimination." The report also found that "[w]hen surveyed, many heterosexual co-workers report witnessing sexual orientation discrimination in the workplace." The studies which the report analyzed, although based on various methods, contexts and time periods, ultimately demonstrated a pattern of sexual discrimination as a common occurrence in many workplaces across the country.

Though polls show that a majority of Americans, regardless of party affiliation, religion or age, support employment antidiscrimination legislation that would cover sexual orientation, such efforts have not been without staunch opposition. It is nearly impossible to protect one group's right to equal employment opportunity without interfering with another group's desire to discriminate. During debate over ENDA efforts in 2002, a spokesman for the *Family Research Council* (a Fundamentalist Christian organization) stated that "ENDA will require Americans to hire people they believe to be committing immoral acts, precisely because they commit those acts. It violates employers' and employees' freedom of religion, of speech, and association." Equal employment opportunity for gays and lesbians is often cast as a push for "special rights." But in reality, for example, ENDA would give no more rights to persons with a homosexual orientation than it would to a person with a heterosexual or bisexual orientation. A heterosexual who was refused a job as a bartender in a gay bar on the basis of his sexual orientation could sue for damages, just as a homosexual could sue if she or he were refused a manufacturing job in a widget factory on the basis of sexual orientation.

In any event, absent important federal protections, GLBT employees have most often sought protection through state laws and local ordinances that provide some protection. Consequently, materials in this chapter dealing with private employment discrimination generally focus on state-law-based litigation.

Public employees are somewhat better protected, because constitutional safeguards apply. In addition, civil service policies generally maintain that as long as a person's sexual orientation does not negatively affect the function or reputation of the service, then discrimination on the basis of sexual orientation is prohibited. Consequently, as the following case law shows, litigation tends to center on what constitutes a negative impact on the function or reputation of the government entity. Put another way, the cases center on how "out" a public employee can really be.

I. OUT AT WORK

*The following excerpt describes the ordeal that Ron Woods, a United Auto Workers electrician faced as he came out of the closet at Chrysler. The piece also details some of the advocacy that led to better working conditions at Chrysler and elsewhere.**

---

* Reprinted from, James B. Stewart, *Coming Out at Chrysler*, THE NEW YORKER, July 21, 1997, pp. 38–49. Reprinted by permission of International Creative Management, Inc.

Trenton Engine is one of the largest machine-tool factories in the world—a three-square block complex south of Detroit that employs thirty-five hundred workers and builds the engines for most Chrysler, Dodge, Jeep, and Eagle products. The Trenton assembly line operates twenty-four hours a day, in three shifts, and life there, dominated by the United Auto Workers, is rigidly hierarchical—based on union job classification and seniority. The U.A.W. leadership has historically embraced social change, notably during the civil-rights struggles of the sixties, but the rank and file have traditionally been socially conservative, suspicious, even hostile, toward blacks, war protesters, women—anyone thought of as different—and that conflict has often been played out on the factory floor.

... After Ron Woods reported for work there as an electrician, in 1987, he was often able to work seven days a week, twelve hours a day. During one stint in 1989, Woods worked eighty-three days straight. That year, he earned fifty-five thousand dollars, at $14.82 an hour....

Woods, who is now thirty-seven, is clean-cut and trim—about five feet nine and a hundred and thirty-five pounds—and he says his size distinguishes him from many of his more burly colleagues on the factory floor. He has two junior-college degrees—one in commerce and one in electronics—and these also set him apart from most of his co-workers, for whom high-school diplomas are the rule. From the day Woods arrived at Chrysler, he tried his best to fit in. From time to time, he bought doughnuts for his co-workers on the way to his shift, which began at midnight.... Woods was eager to please his superiors, and he earned a string of sterling job-performance evaluations, which he has proudly saved

But for all his friendliness Woods evaded personal questions. "You laugh at the queerest things," a co-worker once observed, and the reference to "queer" in the otherwise innocuous comment made Woods nervous. There was no doubt in Woods's mind that anyone who was gay would be ostracized. There had been an uproar at the plant when a forklift operator had a sex-change operation, and then began to use the women's bathroom. (She was relegated to another women's bathroom, used by office workers.) Another co-worker was attacked and beaten one night after leaving a gay bar. When the man returned to work after being hospitalized for reconstructive surgery, Woods overheard comments like "He would have been better off if he died."

The first time Woods asked for a week's vacation, he explained that his girlfriend had won a trip to the Bahamas. "Way to go, take the time off," his supervisor said, slapping him on the back. In truth, it was a man he met at a gay bar who had invited him on the trip.

As months passed and his fictitious girlfriend never materialized, Woods could sense a subtle shift in attitude. Co-workers grew more distant. Then, in April, 1990, after three years at the plant, Woods spent hours one hot day finding and installing a part needed to get one of the assembly lines back in operation. Afterward, Woods recalls, he sought refuge from the heat in the air-conditioned office of the foreman, Tony

Neubecker, where he and Neubecker were joined by Mack MacDonald, a toolmaker on the line. Neubecker weighs more than three hundred pounds, and MacDonald weighs about two hundred and ninety. "What took you so long?" MacDonald asked, in an angry tone. "What kind of electrician are you?"

Woods was bewildered. "I couldn't find a part," he stammered, but MacDonald kept badgering him. Woods looked to Neubecker for support, then said, "Why don't you leave me alone?"

With that, MacDonald jumped up from his chair and backhanded Woods hard across the face.

Woods was stunned, angry. "Did you hit me?"

"If I wanted to hit you, you'd be dead," MacDonald replied, according to a grievance Woods later filed detailing the incident. "I can take you outside this office, bend you over, and fuck you in the ass if I want. Or I can wait for you after work and fuck you up."

Woods turned to the foreman. "Could you call security?"

"You don't tell me what to do," Neubecker replied.

"You saw him attack me and you won't call?" Woods asked, incredulous.

"I didn't see anything."

MacDonald has disputed Woods's account, but also agreed to leave him alone. Since then, Woods says, he has been physically attacked four times, received threats on his life, endured countless taunts and insults, and had to be transferred from Trenton Engine on account of increasing hostility. He is still employed by Chrysler—in the company's Technology Center, at corporate headquarters, in Auburn Hills, Michigan—but the experience has transformed him from passive conformist to determined reformer to angry activist. He is now doing something that no one has done before: leading a crusade to secure job protection for gay employees at Chrysler. In that way, he is in the vanguard of a remarkable emergence of gay people within the auto industry. He has picketed Chrysler's headquarters, blitzed its chairman, Robert J. Eaton, with letters and complaints, and founded an organization called the Campaign for Equal Rights at Chrysler, which this past May picketed Chrysler's annual shareholders' meeting, in Seattle. His most notable success has been advocating his cause within the United Auto Workers. Last spring, Woods delivered a rousing address against job discrimination at the union's triennial bargaining convention, and succeeded in adding protection against job discrimination on the basis of sexual orientation to the union's final contract-negotiating planks.

Ron Woods's visibility, if not always his confrontational tactics, has encouraged others.

Chrysler now has another gay employees' organization, People of Diversity. Composed mostly of non-union, managerial employees, it was modeled on a similar organization that had been formed recently at Ford. Perhaps most startling was the decision of a much admired vice-chairman of Ford, Allan Gilmour, to disclose his homosexuality in an interview last winter with *Between the Lines,* a Detroit monthly. . . .

Many people in Detroit are astounded that gay ferment has reached the auto industry. Car and truck manufacturing is "probably the most conservative industry in the country," says Jeff Montgomery, whose father, a Chrysler executive, warned him that being gay could ruin his career. Montgomery heads the Triangle Foundation, a lesbian-and-gay civil rights group in Michigan. . . .

Nevertheless, most gay and lesbian autoworkers remain in the closet, for fear of discrimination and even violence on the factory floor, if not in executive suites. Michigan is one of thirty-nine states with no job protection for gays and lesbians; federal legislation to extend job protection to gays and lesbians failed in the Senate last year by a single vote. Despite Woods's success in obtaining union support, Chrysler refused to include sexual orientation as a protected category in a new three-year contract it entered into with the U.A.W. last year, and the U.A.W. capitulated. Though People of Diversity has adopted a policy of non-confrontation, Chrysler has yet to sanction the group as an official employee organization—a sanction that would entitle members to meet on company property and use company resources such as bulletin boards. (Its counterpart at Ford has company sanction.)

Even as Chrysler earlier this year issued several statements pledging non-discrimination, the company got caught up in two public controversies that brought into question the company's stance. *Esquire* cancelled publication of a short story by David Leavitt planned for the April issue—a story that contained explicit gay material—after its publisher warned the editor that Chrysler would withdraw its advertising. In March, Chrysler cancelled its previously scheduled advertising on an episode of the ABC series "Ellen" in which the main character would reveal that she is a lesbian.

. . .

Last month, I flew to Detroit, rented a black Dodge Intrepid, and visited Woods at his home, in Huntington Woods. . . . Woods was quick to volunteer that he had dreamed all his life of living in a house this nice, and was grateful to Chrysler and his union for making it possible.

Beneath his polite and somewhat self-deprecating manner, I sensed both anger and determination—and growing despair. . . . In recent months, his continuing complaints of gay bias have cost him the support even of his most loyal friends at work, who charge that Woods is using his sexual orientation to demand, and get, preferential treatment. Once seen as a rising star within the U.A.W, he has now lost the support of his union local. Just before I arrived, he told me, he had received a letter informing him that his union membership had been suspended for two years. "My being gay makes regular guys insane," he says. "I don't know why. I was being backstabbed constantly. A coworker finally pulled me aside. 'Don't you understand? Everything you do is wrong. People talk about you all the time. They give me a hard time for working with you. You have no support.' "

Woods at first had tried to ignore the antipathy he felt, but he could not forget the incident with MacDonald in the foreman's office. . . .

Then, a few months later, he read in the newspaper that Cracker Barrel, a Tennessee-based restaurant chain, was opening a branch in the Detroit area. It was also firing gay and lesbian employees for failing to "demonstrate normal heterosexual values," according to a company memo (a policy it has since reversed). Woods was furious. "I said, 'Oh, yeah?' This is U.A.W country, this is workplace-rights country." . . .

So Woods organized a protest on his own. He persuaded a gay-and-lesbian restaurant to provide meeting space. . . . He handed out thousands of flyers at gay bars. The day of the grand opening of Cracker Barrel, Woods walked into the Trenton Engine plant and saw his picture in someone's Detroit *Free Press* along with an article about the protest, to be held that afternoon.

. . .

As Woods walked through the plant, he saw numerous copies of the paper, but no one called out to him. In the employee staging area, he saw a fellow-electrician, Jim Sloan, reading the article. Sloan looked at it, he looked at Woods, he looked down at the article again. "Ron," he finally asked, "did you know your picture and name would be in the paper?"

"Yeah," Woods said. When Sloan didn't reply, Woods added, "Thanks for mentioning it." Sloan said nothing further.

. . . The next day, when Woods arrived at work, a large poster had been taped up above his usual chair. It showed a muscular man—Woods thinks it may have been a Calvin Klein model—wearing nothing but bikini briefs. Not long after that, a pipe fitter tried to pick a fight with Woods on the factory floor. Work rules on the floor, encrusted by years of ritual and collective-bargaining restrictions, provided ample opportunity for disputes, and now Woods seemed constantly embroiled in them.

About seven months after his picture appeared in the paper, a janitor, Robert Thompson, threw a pail of water over Woods's feet while he was sitting in the staging area reading a newspaper. "Get out of here," Thompson said, preparing to mop the floor.

Woods complied, but later, when he returned to his seat, he said to Thompson, "Is there any way you could be a little more polite?"

"I don't have to be," Thompson replied.

"No, but you could be," Woods said.

With that, Thompson, who was about Woods's height but much stockier, grabbed Woods by the neck, as if he were trying to strangle him, and then threw him backward. Woods interviewed a couple of the witnesses to the incident, including his fellow-electrician Jim Sloan, and they said they would give statements supporting Woods to labor relations. Still angry, he reported the incident to the local police when his shift ended. The police report was picked up in a local newspaper, but the paper didn't mention Woods by name. "A 32-year-old Huntington Woods man walked into the Police Station on Wednesday afternoon and said he had been assaulted that morning," the story began. The next day, when Woods arrived at the staging area, someone had posted the news report. Scrawled above it were the words "Ron Woods, faggot."

No action was taken against Thompson. When questioned by union representatives, the witnesses to the event, including Sloan, said they hadn't seen anything....

Woods had never been taunted at school or in previous jobs. He says he was psychologically unprepared for what now seemed like an unrelenting stream of abuse, and he sought psychiatric treatment for depression at the Henry Ford Medical Center. In a report to Chrysler's workers' compensation department, Woods's doctor and social worker there stated that after rumors spread that Woods was homosexual "it appears that Mr. Woods began to be the object of harassment by many co-workers," which ranged in form from "lack of support from management to outright physical violence and threats of severe violence." They found Woods to be "stressed and distraught," and concluded that his condition was "likely" to be related to his employment.

Woods approached his union representative to file a formal grievance detailing various incidents. Woods's union committeeman, Mike Harrald, one of about ten black union members in Woods's unit, was one of the few who seemed sympathetic.... He filed the grievance on Woods's behalf.

Before it could be acted upon, however, Harrald concluded that it was unsafe for Woods to keep working at Trenton Engine, and in August, 1992, he was transferred to the Technology Center Auburn Hills....

Chrysler's corporate headquarters was a different world from Trenton, one dominated by managerial, white-collar workers rather than by the assembly-line. Woods's work shifted from production to construction and repair; additions and renovations at the complex were constant. In general, levels of education were higher, and co-workers more sophisticated.

Unbeknownst to Woods, though, virtually everyone at his new job had already been told he was gay, and that disclosure had triggered a wave of revulsion. A fellow-electrician, Bill Witmer, recalls being told even before Woods arrived that he was gay and being advised not to work with him. Of many fellow-workers, Witmer says, "They're one step from the Klan, if not in the Klan. They're hostile, against gays. People went crazy over this." In 1993, the Secret Service was called in to Chrysler's corporate headquarters after a worker there threatened to kill President Clinton if he followed through on his promise to permit gays in military.

Initially, Woods was shunned. Suspecting that a picture of the Cracker Barrel protest which had run in *Solidarity, U.A.W* magazine, had tipped off his co-workers, he spoke to the editors there about his plight. The conversation led to an article on Woods in the January/February, 1993, issue, which identified Woods as gay and praised his efforts to fight discrimination. "We were trying to say that what was happening to Ron was wrong," says Michael Funke, the *Solidarity* reporter who wrote the article.

. . .

This sort of tolerance was slow to spread among Woods's co-workers. One afternoon when Terry Kremkow, who had been friendly with Woods, came into the lunchroom, he was confronted by Malen Marcum, an air-conditioning repairman and former head of the union in Woods's work unit. "How are you and your little faggot buddy Ron Woods?" Marcum asked in a loud voice, which brought conversation in the room to a stop. "Has he given you head lately?" A fight between the three-hundred-pound Marcum, who rides a Harley–Davidson and wears steel-toed boots, and Kremkow, a serious bodybuilder, seemed imminent, but Kremkow defused the situation by saying, "You're the one with the earring and the pony-tail."

Kremkow's car was vandalized in the Chrysler parking lot on a number of occasions. After work one day, Marcum tried to kick [Bill] Witmer [who had become Woods's friend] in the groin, leaving bruises on Witmer's leg. Witmer filed a police complaint over the incident, and Marcum later pleaded no contest to assault and battery. He was suspended by Chrysler for six months without pay.

. . .

Anti-gay sentiment wasn't confined to hourly workers. One of Woods's supervisors, Michael Conlon, who was in charge of handing out work assignments, mocked Woods to his co-workers with limp-wristed gestures. According to Woods, another supervisor, Mark Hardy, often criticized Woods's work, made threatening gestures, and was overheard by another worker denouncing Woods's gay activism. As his union steward, Kremkow filed a grievance against Hardy on Woods's behalf and Woods was transferred, unwillingly, to another work area. As a result of a subsequent incident, Hardy and Woods were instructed not to speak to each other.

Woods says that he tried to ignore all this and do his job, but that he worried about other gay employees suffering in the plants—people like Martha Grevatt, a lesbian, who was a tool-and-die maker at a Chrysler plant near Cleveland, and Dave Reckinger, a procurement analyst in Chrysler's Service and Parts Division, both of whom had got in touch with Woods after reading the article about him in *Solidarity*. One of five women tool-and-die makers in a three-hundred-person department, Grevatt told Woods she'd been the victim of a stream of antigay harassment at work. Among other incidents, a co-worker kept a spray can on his workbench labeled "Dyke Repellent"; crude poems and pornography regularly appeared at Grevatt's workstation. The union took up her complaints, but Chrysler management argued that it could do nothing, because it couldn't prove who was responsible. Angered by the inaction, Grevatt filed charges with the Equal Employment Opportunity Commission in 1990 alleging sex discrimination, a category covered by federal law. The E.E.O.C. declined to proceed, however, when Chrysler argued successfully that Grevatt was being harassed for being gay and for her political views—neither of which is protected by law—rather than for being female.

Reckinger told Woods he'd concealed his sexual orientation since the early seventies, when a co-worker forced him at gunpoint to perform oral sex. Reckinger called the police, who advised him not to press charges; Reckinger, shaken, agreed. The next workday, he reported the incident to Chrysler management and to his union representative, but both said there was nothing they could do because the incident hadn't occurred on Chrysler premises....

These and other stories, and Woods's own experience, spurred him to act, and he focused, for the first time, on his own employer and industry. In August, 1994, he wrote the first of several letters to Chrysler's chairman, Robert Eaton. In it he said, "I realize that I am indeed fortunate to have been transferred to C.T.C. This is a good place to work. I often ask myself if I should just be silent and ignore the fact that others are still at risk of intense harassment and discrimination. I have decided that I will not be silent. On moral grounds and partly because I now realize that even here at C.T.C. I am not properly protected, as sexual orientation is not included in any Chrysler policies."

Woods received a polite letter from Nancy Rae, then the manager of workforce diversity at Chrysler, stressing the point that Chrysler "encourages and values diversity, mutual respect, trust, and integrity." Woods interpreted this as a rebuff.

Woods's complaints were also referred to Monica Emerson, a twenty-one-year Chrysler veteran who is the current manager of workforce diversity. Woods and Kremkow met with Emerson and, according to Kremkow, the interview got off to a bad start.... Woods recalls, "Monica sat across the table and told me we don't need protection, we don't need it in writing, because Chrysler won't tolerate discrimination. Give me a break. I've been attacked five times."

The next year, Woods shifted his focus from Chrysler management to the union. In April, 1995, in what initially seemed a hopeless quest, he ran for the office of delegate to June's United Auto Workers' constitutional convention, in Anaheim, and to a special bargaining convention the following year, which would determine proposed contract provisions. Woods threw himself into the effort, printing campaign flyers, developing a seven-plank platform, and giving monthly speeches at the union hall. He emphasized his devotion to the union, noted that his father and two older brothers were union men, and declared that he wanted the union to be more politically active. Terry Kremkow campaigned on his behalf, and was instrumental in swaying many voters. None of Woods's literature mentioned any gay issues, but when the inevitable question came he was prepared. "I hope it doesn't matter, because I care about these issues," he said, referring to his platform.

One of Woods's opponents in the race was the openly homophobic Marcum, who had recently returned to work after his suspension, and he tried to make Woods's sexual orientation an issue. He filed a complaint with Chrysler management, which he then made public: in it he alleged that Woods had leaned over a partition in the men's room to stare at Marcum's penis. No one seriously believed that Woods would provoke someone like Marcum, and the allegation backfired by stirring sympathy for Woods. . . .

The election result reflected a remarkable transformation from the days when no one wanted to work with Woods. When the votes were tallied, Woods received eighty, to seventy-three for his closest opponent, who was a longtime Chrysler employee. Marcum got only thirty-one votes-a humiliating defeat. . . .

Despite this electoral success, little would have happened without support from the president of Woods's local, Derek Thiery, whom Woods called immediately after the election to say that he wanted to add two words—"sexual orientation"—to the contract. Like many members of the U.A.W. leadership, Thiery has championed civil rights and progressive social causes to a much greater degree than the rank and file have done. He was impressed by Woods's election. "For him to run for delegate, with his background, and win, that made me proud," Thiery says. He was sympathetic, but urged Woods to gain the support of the local's civil-rights committee first.

The committee had been fending off Woods's proposals for some time, but now, with Thiery's encouragement, it approved his resolution by a vote of five to one, with one abstention.

That summer, the National Gay and Lesbian Task Force held its annual conference in Detroit, and there Woods met Shelley Alpern, a research analyst at the Franklin Research & Development Corporation, in Boston, and told her about his campaign. Alpern, who is thirty-two, is a former human-rights fund-raiser who has shifted her focus from Central America to corporate America. Franklin Research & Development describes itself as North America's largest money-management firm devoted solely to socially responsible investing, and has about five hundred million dollars under management, including some shares of Chrysler stock. While the position is relatively modest, it gives Franklin's clients the right to mount proxy challenges. Alpern was then negotiating with Johnson & Johnson, the pharmaceutical manufacturer, and was threatening to mount a proxy fight unless the company banned discrimination against gays and lesbians (which it ultimately did), so she was keenly interested in Woods's progress at Chrysler. He seemed optimistic that the U.A.W would prevail.

Passage of Wood's sexual-orientation resolution sent it to the next step—the joint council—and there Thiery himself spoke in support. It passed without opposition. Woods addressed the special bargaining convention in Detroit the following spring, the first openly gay person ever to speak at a national convention of the U.A.W. ... Martha Grevatt traveled to Detroit from Cleveland to lend him moral support. At the end of his speech, many of the delegates stood in support. The resolution passed by voice acclamation.

As word of the talks' progress trickled down to the rank and file, however, Woods began to worry that the sexual-orientation plank wouldn't end up in the final contract....

[A]t a meeting to discuss the new contract, he managed to talk to Jack Laskowski, the U.A.W. vice-president in charge of the Chrysler negotiations. Laskowski broke the news that Woods's provision had been rejected and would not be part of the new contract. Laskowski told Woods that he had personally taken to Robert Eaton three final demands that could not be resolved at the negotiating-subcommittee level. Two were what Laskowski called "economic" issues, meaning that they would cost Chrysler hundreds of millions of dollars. The chairman accepted those. Then Laskowski raised the issue of sexual orientation.... Yet Eaton refused to accept the U.A.W. position, according to Laskowski, arguing that Chrysler had no intention of discriminating, so such a provision was unnecessary. Laskowski "negotiated hard" on the issue, but "they were dug in on it," he says. "To me, their position didn't make any sense. I can't give a rational answer for why they took the position they did." ... Thiery, who bargained at the committee level, says Chrysler management argued vehemently that gays should not be a 'special group' with 'special privileges.'" ...

Woods was dejected. "My rights in the workplace were given away," he said. When the heads of the various locals met to vote on the contract, Woods showed up and argued that without an antidiscrimination clause it should be rejected. The contract was nonetheless unanimously approved....

... Alpern, the shareholder activist in Boston, was dismayed when Woods told her that his bargaining initiative had failed.

She wrote to Robert Eaton on October 4th, saying that "we are greatly concerned that Chrysler does not include sexual orientation in its nondiscrimination policy and has recently rejected the U.A.W's demand that it do so." She argued that nondiscrimination simply makes good business sense for Chrysler, not only in that it boosts gay and lesbian employee morale but in that negative publicity hurts sales to gay customers. (Alpern noted that, Toyota, Subaru, and G.M.'s Saturn are marketed aggressively to the gay community; Subaru acts as a corporate sponsor for the Rainbow Card, a credit card that donates a percentage of its revenues to gay and lesbian community groups.)

Alpern's letter triggered a flurry of negotiations. "At first, they were very hesitant," she recalls. "I couldn't get any clear answers." She told Chrysler in November that she was encouraged by their discussions, but she also said that she felt she had no choice but to file a shareholder resolution, to be included in proxy statements, calling for steps designed to end discrimination on the basis of sexual orientation at Chrysler. Chrysler's response was to try to block the resolution at the Securities and Exchange Commission.

Nevertheless, even while opposing Alpern at the S.E.C., Chrysler issued a series of letters and statements to employees which addressed her concerns. On November 11th, Chrysler mailed a statement from Eaton to each employee stating that sexual orientation was to be included within the company's policies promoting tolerance for diversity. Alpern's response to the move was that she wanted to see something more concrete. In January of this year, Chrysler's vice-president for employee relations, Tom Gallagher, and the U.A.W's Laskowski signed a letter acknowledging that Eaton's letter was "consistent," with the collective-bargaining agreement. Finally, Chrysler revised its Standards of Conduct and its Code of Ethical Behavior to include sexual orientation. Alpern agreed to withdraw the proposed shareholder resolution. She calls the measures "a good first step."

. . . Woods denounces them as a sham meant to divert attention from the real problem of virulent homophobia at Chrysler. . . .

Monica Emerson says that, apart from Woods's highly visible protest, she has received few complaints from gay employees at Chrysler. While she says she cannot discuss Woods's situation, K.C. Hortop, a lawyer for Chrysler, said, "We do, in general, deny his allegations of mistreatment by Chrysler." Emerson continues, "I can't discuss specific numbers, but complaints about gay discrimination are very, very few. Of course, even one is too many." She says that all disciplinary actions are confidential, so she can't give any examples of investigations undertaken or punishment meted out for anti-gay harassment. "We recognize that in a company the size of Chrysler there may be incidents of inappropriate behavior," she says. "We do take swift and severe corrective action when we find it is warranted and appropriate." Other than Marcum, none of the people Woods has complained about have been demoted or suspended, though a few were told not to bother Woods.

One reason that there haven't been many complaints from gay employees may be that few employees are willing to identify themselves as gay. A contract worker at Chrysler was told that his contract had expired the day after he registered a sexual-harassment complaint with Chrysler's diversity department. (Chrysler says his departure had nothing to do with the fact that he's gay or that he filed a complaint.) I spoke with a number of gay Chrysler employees, from various levels of the company, and was told of more employees who believe that they or people they know have suffered from anti-gay bias but would not identify themselves as being gay, out of fear of even worse repercussions.

Some gay employees at Chrysler have made use of a Web site that Woods created. He has received messages from about twenty people citing incidents of what they felt was discrimination on the basis of sexual orientation, but many of those who responded to the site have also asked not to be named, no doubt out of fear.

Allan Gilmour, the former Ford vice-chairman, told me that he wouldn't have revealed his homosexuality if he had still been employed at Ford. "I would not have come out at the company. That would not have been appropriate. I was aware of a few other gay executives. They thought it would be inappropriate, dangerous to their careers." Even though Gilmour himself had remained in the closet and, as vice-chairman, had long been viewed as the heir apparent to Ford's chairman, Harold Poling, he was passed over for the top job when Poling retired, in 1993. Gilmour says he was told "he lacked the breadth of operating experience" needed for the job. Others in the Detroit business community, however, believe that the Ford family would not accept a gay chairman....

Whatever their personal feelings about gay rights and workplace issues, Chrysler executives repeatedly say that their only goal is to sell as many cars and trucks as possible. In this effort, Chrysler, like many other large consumer companies, uses its enormous advertising clout to make sure its ads don't appear in contexts that might alienate potential buyers.... Homosexuality falls into the same category. Even as the company was issuing its statements pledging non-discrimination, reports that Ellen DeGeneres, the star of "Ellen," was a lesbian and that her character might come out of the closet on national television caused consternation in Chrysler's marketing department, since Chrysler is a major sponsor of "Ellen" and had committed to advertising on a number of episodes.

... Chrysler's concern about controversy was borne out on March 27th, when Robert Eaton received a letter from Jerry Falwell demanding that Chrysler cancel its ads and never advertise on "Ellen" again or face a consumer boycott.

. . .

While Chrysler's [decision to drop the ads] seemed to placate the religious right—the company heard nothing further from Falwell—the negative reaction from gays, lesbians, and their supporters came as a surprise. Chrysler was flooded with calls, both against and in support of their action regarding "Ellen." According to [Megan] Giles, [a Chrysler spokeswoman] Chrysler has had to reconsider the long-held notion that religious conservatives are better organized, more likely to call for a boycott, and pose a more serious threat to sales than other special-interest groups. The gay-rights advocates "appear to be equally well organized," Giles says. "Once they got their bearings, they were prolific. They're prepared to do battle." Caught between gay advocates and the religious right, she says, "We don't want to pick a fight with either one."

Chrysler resumed advertising on "Ellen" shortly after the controversial episode aired, even though subsequent episodes continued to explore gay themes. While Chrysler hasn't yet decided about next season, it is continuing to advertise this summer. "We like the demographic we're getting," Giles says. "That's what we're interested in, not anybody's life style."

The "Ellen" [controversy] reinforced Woods's suspicions about Chrysler's intentions. But they also seemed remote. "Managing a bookstore in Southern California"—what TV's Ellen does for a living—"is worlds removed from working in a factory. It's dreamland," he told me.

The depth of his personal struggle had been clear since May of 1996, just a month after his successful speech at the U.A.W. convention: he decided to run for shop steward, even though that meant running against Terry Kremkow, who considered himself Woods's best friend at the plant. Kremkow was hurt and angered. This time, Woods had trouble mustering support. According to Kremkow, "People figured out that everything he ran for was strictly for the gay movement." Woods was asked frequently about what some coworkers now referred to as his "gay rights shit." He, in turn, accused co-workers of homophobia. Bill Witmer tried to warn Woods. "Not everyone is against you," he said. "Some people are hurt. They never did anything to you. Be careful. The people who do accept you for being gay—you're going to turn them against you."

The evening of the vote, Woods called the union hall where the votes were being posted. "Give me the bad news," he remembers asking.

"Well, let's put it this way," replied the man who was tallying the votes. "Did you vote for yourself?"

Woods was stunned. "Don't tell me I only got one vote."

After hanging up, Woods cried.

Woods's friendship with Kremkow quickly deteriorated. That November, while continuing his picketing, he reported for work, and his supervisor confronted him with a computerized list of incidents of alleged tardiness. Woods concedes that the picketing made him three to five minutes late on several occasions, but says such delays were common. He expected Kremkow, as his shop steward, to back him up, but when Kremkow was summoned, Woods says, he sided with the supervisor. Kremkow says that such lists were routine and that Woods was not being treated any differently from others. Woods asked to speak to Kremkow alone, so the two went out into the hallway.

Both Kremkow and Woods were highly agitated and shouted at each other. Woods says that Kremkow shoved him hard against a drinking fountain. Kremkow claims that Woods tried to taunt him, saying, "You want to hit me, don't you?" Each denies the other's account. After the altercation, the two returned to the conference room, where Woods's supervisor and security personnel were waiting. "Ron, are you O.K.? You don't seem right, you're acting bizarre," Woods recalls the supervisor saying. Security asked Woods if he required medical assistance and he said, "Yes." He was taken to the hospital, observed for six hours, and released.

Woods, now bereft of both management and union support, compounded the problem by filing a grievance against Kremkow alleging "conduct unbecoming a union member." After a one-day trial in January, a tribunal of union members found Kremkow "obviously innocent" of Woods's charges. But the internal rift and the trial traumatized Woods's local. Kremkow says, "People are paralyzed. There's now more fear of Ron than vice versa. They're afraid he's going to make an allegation. I was afraid for my job." He continues, "I don't care if someone is black, green, or gay. I resent that he's hiding behind his sexual orientation. That's what everyone else feels after the trial."

Kremkow then charged Woods with maliciously filing charges against another union member. Woods was found guilty. For this reason, he explained the day I visited him, he had just been suspended from his union for two years. "It breaks my heart," he said. . . .

Woods now seems blinded by his sense of injustice, and his effectiveness at Chrysler and in the D.A.W. is waning. He says he feels lonely and isolated, is having trouble sleeping, and has begun taking antidepressant medication. In early May, he arranged an extended medical leave, and is getting counseling. He says he has trouble believing that it has come to this. "I never meant to be an activist," he says. "I grew up poor. My father worked fourteen-hour days and lost his business in the 1980 recession. We lost everything. I wanted a car that would work, a house. I just wanted a decent life."

His colleagues, even former supporters, see things differently. "Ron could have been a national advocate, depending on how he handled himself," Thiery says.

"He still could be. But instead he just went over the edge." Woods's co-workers on the second shift were recently asked to attend diversity training, in which they were told not to make anti-gay comments or gestures. "Some people made fun of it," according to Witmer. "A lot of guys were pissed off. They think Ron should quit his bellyaching." Witmer says that even he is distancing himself from Woods to stay out of the controversy. "I've got to work with these guys, too," he explains.

Still, Woods's activism, by the standards of corporate America, has already brought about significant change at Chrysler, and his presence in their midst has made his co-workers some of the most gay-aware factory workers in the country. Everyone I spoke to in Woods's unit described a shift from ignorance about gays and lesbians and overt hostility toward Woods to at least grudging acceptance. . . .

NOTE

As bad as things were for Ron Woods, things were and are worse for many gays who work in states without comprehensive employment nondiscrimination laws and where workers cannot rely on the bargaining power and relative employment security afforded by unions.

As for Chrysler in particular, the company joined Ford and General Motors in extending medical benefits to the partners of their same-sex employees in 2000. In the words of a recent Fortune Magazine article, the workplace activism of people like Ron Woods turned a "trickle of corporate support for gay and lesbian workers into a flood."

But that change did not come without a heavy price. When interviewed by documentary filmmaker Tami Gold, Woods would say:

> I was very alone, very isolated. In the middle of winter, which is a very depressing time for me, my mother asked me to change and started crying. And I started crying. I lost everyone. But I wouldn't give up.... And I went in there all the time and did the best I could, and I realized it wasn't going to work, that until the day I retire and the day I die, that I would always be that faggot people hated.

Nevertheless, there is evidence that committed activism is changing circumstances for the better for many of America's gay workers. The 2011 "Corporate Equality Index," a report published by the Human Rights Campaign which rates the gay-friendliness of U.S. companies, gave 337 major U.S. companies a perfect 100 percent score for providing equal benefits to gay, lesbian, bisexual and transgender workers. When the Human Rights Campaign's Corporate Equality Index was launched in 2002 only 13 companies received 100%. No Fortune 500 company offered health benefits to the domestic partners of gay and lesbian employees prior to 1992. Over half of Fortune 500 companies offered those benefits in 2011. Chrysler was among those companies receiving a perfect score in 2011.

II. DISCRIMINATION IN PRIVATE EMPLOYMENT

PRICE WATERHOUSE v. HOPKINS

490 U.S. 228, 109 S.Ct. 1775, 104 L.Ed.2d 268 (1989)

BRENNAN, J., announced the judgment of the Court and delivered an opinion, in which MARSHALL, BLACKMUN, and STEVENS, JJ., joined.

Ann Hopkins was a senior manager in an office of Price Waterhouse when she was proposed for partnership in 1982. She was neither offered nor denied admission to the partnership; instead, her candidacy was held for reconsideration the following year. When the partners in her office later refused to repropose her for partnership, she sued Price Waterhouse under Title VII of the Civil Rights Act of 1964, 78 Stat. 253, as amended, 42 U. S. C. § 2000e et seq., charging that the firm had discriminated against her on the basis of sex in its decisions regarding partnership ...

Ann Hopkins had worked at Price Waterhouse's Office of Government Services in Washington, D. C., for five years when the partners in that office proposed her as a candidate for partnership. Of the 662 partners at the firm at that time, 7 were women. Of the 88 persons proposed for partnership that year, only 1—Hopkins—was a woman. Forty-seven of these candidates were admitted to the partnership, 21 were rejected, and 20—including Hopkins—were "held" for reconsideration the following year. Thirteen of the 32 partners who had submitted comments on Hopkins supported her bid for partnership. Three partners recommended that her candidacy be placed on hold, eight stated that they did not have an informed opinion about her, and eight recommended that she be denied partnership.

In a jointly prepared statement supporting her candidacy, the partners in Hopkins' office showcased her successful 2–year effort to secure a $25 million contract with the Department of State, labeling it "an outstanding performance" and one that Hopkins carried out "virtually at the partner level." . . .

The partners in Hopkins' office praised her character as well as her accomplishments, describing her in their joint statement as "an outstanding professional" who had a "deft touch," a "strong character, independence and integrity." Clients appear to have agreed with these assessments. At trial, one official from the State Department described her as "extremely competent, intelligent," "strong and forthright, very productive, energetic and creative." Tr. 150. Another high-ranking official praised Hopkins' decisiveness, broadmindedness, and "intellectual clarity"; she was, in his words, "a stimulating conversationalist." Evaluations such as these led Judge Gesell to conclude that Hopkins "had no difficulty dealing with clients and her clients appear to have been very pleased with her work" and that she "was generally viewed as a highly competent project leader who worked long hours, pushed vigorously to meet deadlines and demanded much from the multidisciplinary staffs with which she worked."

On too many occasions, however, Hopkins' aggressiveness apparently spilled over into abrasiveness. Staff members seem to have borne the brunt of Hopkins' brusqueness. Long before her bid for partnership, partners evaluating her work had counseled her to improve her relations with staff members. Although later evaluations indicate an improvement, Hopkins' perceived shortcomings in this important area eventually doomed her bid for partnership. Virtually all of the partners' negative remarks about Hopkins—even those of partners supporting her—had to do with her "inter-personal skills." Both "[s]upporters and opponents of her candidacy," stressed Judge Gesell, "indicated that she was sometimes overly aggressive, unduly harsh, difficult to work with, and impatient with staff."

There were clear signs, though, that some of the partners reacted negatively to Hopkins' personality because she was a woman. One partner described her as "macho"; another suggested that she "overcompensated for being a woman"; a third advised her to take "a course at charm school." Several partners criticized her use of profanity; in response, one partner suggested that those partners objected to her swearing only "because it's a lady using foul language." Another supporter explained that Hopkins "ha[d] matured from a tough-talking somewhat masculine hard-nosed mgr to an authoritative, formidable, but much more appealing lady ptr candidate." But it was the man who, as Judge Gesell found, bore responsibility for explaining to Hopkins the reasons for the Policy Board's decision to place her candidacy on hold who delivered the coup de grace: in order to improve her chances for partnership, Thomas Beyer advised, Hopkins should "walk more femininely, talk more femininely, dress more femininely, wear make-up, have her hair styled, and wear jewelry."

Dr. Susan Fiske, a social psychologist and Associate Professor of Psychology at Carnegie–Mellon University, testified at trial that the partnership selection process at Price Waterhouse was likely influenced by sex stereotyping. Her testimony focused not only on the overtly sex-based comments of partners but also on gender-neutral remarks, made by partners who knew Hopkins only slightly, that were intensely critical of her. One partner, for example, baldly stated that Hopkins was "universally disliked" by staff, and another described her as "consistently annoying and irritating," yet these were people who had had very little contact with Hopkins. According to Fiske, Hopkins' uniqueness (as the only woman in the pool of candidates) and the subjectivity of the evaluations made it likely that sharply critical remarks such as these were the product of sex stereotyping—although Fiske admitted that she could not say with certainty whether any particular comment was the result of stereotyping. Fiske based her opinion on a review of the submitted comments, explaining that it was commonly accepted practice for social psychologists to reach this kind of conclusion without having met any of the people involved in the decision-making process.

In previous years, other female candidates for partnership also had been evaluated in sex-based terms. As a general matter, Judge Gesell concluded, "[c]andidates were viewed favorably if partners believed they maintained their femin[in]ity while becoming effective professional managers"; in this environment, "[t]o be identified as a 'women's lib[b]er' was regarded as [a] negative comment." In fact, the judge found that in previous years "[o]ne partner repeatedly commented that he could not consider any woman seriously as a partnership candidate and believed that women were not even capable of functioning as senior managers—yet the firm took no action to discourage his comments and recorded his vote in the overall summary of the evaluations."

Judge Gesell found that Price Waterhouse legitimately emphasized interpersonal skills in its partnership decisions, and also found that the firm had not fabricated its complaints about Hopkins' interpersonal skills as a pretext for discrimination. Moreover, he concluded, the firm did not give decisive emphasis to such traits only because Hopkins was a woman;

although there were male candidates who lacked these skills but who were admitted to partnership, the judge found that these candidates possessed other, positive traits that Hopkins lacked.

The judge went on to decide, however, that some of the partners' remarks about Hopkins stemmed from an impermissibly cabined view of the proper behavior of women, and that Price Waterhouse had done nothing to disavow reliance on such comments. He held that Price Waterhouse had unlawfully discriminated against Hopkins on the basis of sex by consciously giving credence and effect to partners' comments that resulted from sex stereotyping. Noting that Price Waterhouse could avoid equitable relief by proving by clear and convincing evidence that it would have placed Hopkins' candidacy on hold even absent this discrimination, the judge decided that the firm had not carried this heavy burden.

. . .

II

. . .

B

In deciding as we do today, we do not traverse new ground. We have in the past confronted Title VII cases in which an employer has used an illegitimate criterion to distinguish among employees, and have held that it is the employer's burden to justify decisions resulting from that practice. When an employer has asserted that gender is a BFOQ within the meaning of § 703(e), for example, we have assumed that it is the employer who must show why it must use gender as a criterion in employment. *See Dothard v. Rawlinson*, 433 U.S. 321, 332–337, 97 S.Ct. 2720, 2728–2730, 53 L.Ed.2d 786 (1977). In a related context, although the Equal Pay Act expressly permits employers to pay different wages to women where disparate pay is the result of a "factor other than sex," *see* 29 U.S.C. § 206(d)(1), we have decided that it is the employer, not the employee, who must prove that the actual disparity is not sex linked. *See Corning Glass Works v. Brennan*, 417 U.S. 188, 196, 94 S.Ct. 2223, 2229, 41 L.Ed.2d 1 (1974). Finally, some courts have held that, under Title VII as amended by the Pregnancy Discrimination Act, it is the employer who has the burden of showing that its limitations on the work that it allows a pregnant woman to perform are necessary in light of her pregnancy. *See, e.g., Hayes v. Shelby Memorial Hospital*, 726 F.2d 1543, 1548 (CA11 1984); *Wright v. Olin Corp.*, 697 F.2d 1172, 1187 (CA4 1982). As these examples demonstrate, our assumption always has been that if an employer allows gender to affect its decision-making process, then it must carry the burden of justifying its ultimate decision. We have not in the past required women whose gender has proved relevant to an employment decision to establish the negative proposition that they would not have been subject to that decision had they been men, and we do not do so today.

. . .

C

In saying that gender played a motivating part in an employment decision, we mean that, if we asked the employer at the moment of the decision what its reasons were and if we received a truthful response, one of those reasons would be that the applicant or employee was a woman. In the specific context of sex stereotyping, an employer who acts on the basis of a belief that a woman cannot be aggressive, or that she must not be, has acted on the basis of gender.

Although the parties do not overtly dispute this last proposition, the placement by Price Waterhouse of "sex stereotyping" in quotation marks throughout its brief seems to us an insinuation either that such stereotyping was not present in this case or that it lacks legal relevance. We reject both possibilities. As to the existence of sex stereotyping in this case, we are not inclined to quarrel with the District Court's conclusion that a number of the partners' comments showed sex stereotyping at work. As for the legal relevance of sex stereotyping, we are beyond the day when an employer could evaluate employees by assuming or insisting that they matched the stereotype associated with their group, for "[i]n forbidding employers to discriminate against individuals because of their sex, Congress intended to strike at the entire spectrum of disparate treatment of men and women resulting from sex stereotypes." *Los Angeles Dept. of Water and Power* v. *Manhart*, 435 U.S. 702, 707, n. 13 (1978), *quoting Sprogis v. United Air Lines, Inc.*, 444 F.2d 1194, 1198 (CA7 1971). An employer who objects to aggressiveness in women but whose positions require this trait places women in an intolerable and impermissible catch 22: out of a job if they behave aggressively and out of a job if they do not. Title VII lifts women out of this bind.

Remarks at work that are based on sex stereotypes do not inevitably prove that gender played a part in a particular employment decision. The plaintiff must show that the employer actually relied on her gender in making its decision. In making this showing, stereotyped remarks can certainly be evidence that gender played a part. In any event, the stereotyping in this case did not simply consist of stray remarks. On the contrary, Hopkins proved that Price Waterhouse invited partners to submit comments; that some of the comments stemmed from sex stereotypes; that an important part of the Policy Board's decision on Hopkins was an assessment of the submitted comments; and that Price Waterhouse in no way disclaimed reliance on the sex-linked evaluations. This is not, as Price Waterhouse suggests, "discrimination in the air"; rather, it is, as Hopkins puts it, "discrimination brought to ground and visited upon" an employee. By focusing on Hopkins' specific proof, however, we do not suggest a limitation on the possible ways of proving that stereotyping played a motivating role in an employment decision, and we refrain from deciding here which specific facts, "standing alone," would or would not establish a plaintiff's case, since such a decision is unnecessary in this case.

As to the employer's proof, in most cases, the employer should be able to present some objective evidence as to its probable decision in the absence of an impermissible motive. Moreover, proving "that the same decision would have been justified ... is not the same as proving that the same decision would have been made." *Givhan*, 439 U.S. at 416, *quoting Ayers* v. *Western Line Consolidated School District*, 555 F.2d 1309, 1315 (CA5 1977). An employer may not, in other words, prevail in a mixed-motives case by offering a legitimate and sufficient reason for its decision if that reason did not motivate it at the time of the decision. Finally, an employer may not meet its burden in such a case by merely showing that at the time of the decision it was motivated only in part by a legitimate reason. The very premise of a mixed-motives case is that a legitimate reason was present, and indeed, in this case, Price Waterhouse already has made this showing by convincing Judge Gesell that Hopkins' interpersonal problems were a legitimate concern. The employer instead must show that its legitimate reason, standing alone, would have induced it to make the same decision.

. . .

IV

The District Court found that sex stereotyping "was permitted to play a part" in the evaluation of Hopkins as a candidate for partnership. Price Waterhouse disputes both that stereotyping occurred and that it played any part in the decision to place Hopkins' candidacy on hold. In the firm's view, in other words, the District Court's factual conclusions are clearly erroneous. We do not agree.

In finding that some of the partners' comments reflected sex stereotyping, the District Court relied in part on Dr. Fiske's expert testimony. Without directly impugning Dr. Fiske's credentials or qualifications, Price Waterhouse insinuates that a social psychologist is unable to identify sex stereotyping in evaluations without investigating whether those evaluations have a basis in reality. This argument comes too late. At trial, counsel for Price Waterhouse twice assured the court that he did not question Dr. Fiske's expertise and failed to challenge the legitimacy of her discipline. Without contradiction from Price Waterhouse, Fiske testified that she discerned sex stereotyping in the partners' evaluations of Hopkins, and she further explained that it was part of her business to identify stereotyping in written documents. We are not inclined to accept petitioner's belated and unsubstantiated characterization of Dr. Fiske's testimony as "gossamer evidence" based only on "intuitive hunches" and of her detection of sex stereotyping as "intuitively divined." Nor are we disposed to adopt the dissent's dismissive attitude toward Dr. Fiske's field of study and toward her own professional integrity.

Indeed, we are tempted to say that Dr. Fiske's expert testimony was merely icing on Hopkins' cake. It takes no special training to discern sex stereotyping in a description of an aggressive female employee as requiring "a course at charm school." Nor, turning to Thomas Beyer's memorable advice to Hopkins, does it require expertise in psychology to know that, if an employee's flawed "interpersonal skills" can be corrected by a soft-hued suit or a new shade of lipstick, perhaps it is the employee's sex and not her interpersonal skills that has drawn the criticism.

Price Waterhouse also charges that Hopkins produced no evidence that sex stereotyping played a role in the decision to place her candidacy on hold. As we have stressed, however, Hopkins showed that the partnership solicited evaluations from all of the firm's partners; that it generally relied very heavily on such evaluations in making its decision; that some of the partners' comments were the product of stereotyping; and that the firm in no way disclaimed reliance on those particular comments, either in Hopkins' case or in the past. Certainly a plausible—and, one might say, inevitable—conclusion to draw from this set of circumstances is that the Policy Board in making its decision did in fact take into account all of the partners' comments, including the comments that were motivated by stereotypical notions about women's proper deportment.

Price Waterhouse concedes that the proof in *Transportation Management,* adequately showed that the employer there had relied on an impermissible motivation in firing the plaintiff. Brief for Petitioner 45. But the only evidence in that case that a discriminatory motive contributed to the plaintiff's discharge was that the employer harbored a grudge toward the plaintiff on account of his union activity; there was, contrary to Price Waterhouse's suggestion, no direct evidence that that grudge had played a role in the decision, and, in fact, the employer had given other reasons in explaining the plaintiff's discharge. *See* 462 U.S. at 396, 103 S.Ct. at 2471. If the partnership considers that proof sufficient, we do not know why it takes such vehement issue with Hopkins' proof.

Nor is the finding that sex stereotyping played a part in the Policy Board's decision undermined by the fact that many of the suspect comments were made by supporters rather than detractors of Hopkins. A negative comment, even when made in the context of a generally favorable review, nevertheless may influence the decision maker to think less highly of the candidate; the Policy Board, in fact, did not simply tally the "yes's" and "no's" regarding a candidate, but carefully reviewed the content of the submitted comments. The additional suggestion that the comments were made by "persons outside the decision-making chain" (Brief for Petitioner 48)—and therefore could not have harmed Hopkins—simply ignores the critical role that partners' comments played in the Policy Board's partnership decisions.

Price Waterhouse appears to think that we cannot affirm the factual findings of the trial court without deciding that, instead of being overbearing and aggressive and curt, Hopkins is, in fact, kind and considerate and patient. If this is indeed its impression, petitioner misunderstands the theory on which Hopkins prevailed. The District Judge acknowledged that Hopkins' conduct justified complaints about her behavior as a senior manager. But he also concluded that the reactions of at least some of the partners were reactions to her as a *woman* manager. Where an evaluation is based on a subjective assessment of a person's strengths and weaknesses, it is simply not true that each evaluator will focus on, or even mention, the same weaknesses. Thus, even if we knew that Hopkins had "personality problems," this would not tell us that the partners who cast their evaluations of Hopkins in sex-based terms would have criticized her as sharply (or criticized her at all) if she had been a man. It is not our job to review the evidence and decide that the negative reactions to Hopkins were based on reality; our perception of Hopkins' character is irrelevant. We sit not to determine whether Ms. Hopkins is nice, but to decide whether the partners reacted negatively to her personality because she is a woman.

V.

We hold that when a plaintiff in a Title VII case proves that her gender played a motivating part in an employment decision, the defendant may avoid a finding of liability only by proving by a preponderance of the evidence that it would have made the same decision even if it had not taken the plaintiff's gender into account. Because the courts below erred by deciding that the defendant must make this proof by clear and convincing evidence, we reverse the Court of Appeals' judgment against Price Waterhouse on liability and remand the case to that court for further proceedings.

JOSEPH ONCALE v. SUNDOWNER OFFSHORE SERVICES

523 U.S. 75, 118 S.Ct. 998, 140 L.Ed.2d 201 (1998)

SCALIA, J., delivered the opinion for a unanimous Court. THOMAS, J., filed a concurring opinion.

This case presents the question whether workplace harassment can violate Title VII's prohibition against "discrimination ... because of ... sex," 42 U.S.C. § 2000e–2(a)(1), when the harasser and the harassed employee are of the same sex.

I

The District Court having granted summary judgment for respondent, we must assume the facts to be as alleged by petitioner Joseph Oncale. The precise details are irrelevant to the legal point we must decide, and in the interest of both brevity and dignity we shall describe them only generally. In late October 1991, Oncale was working for respondent Sundowner Offshore Services on a Chevron U.S.A., Inc., oil platform in the Gulf of Mexico. He was employed as a roustabout on an eight-man crew which included respondents John Lyons, Danny Pippen, and Brandon Johnson. Lyons, the crane operator, and Pippen, the driller, had supervisory authority, App. 41, 77, 43. On several occasions, Oncale was forcibly subjected to sex-related, humiliating actions against him by Lyons,

Pippen and Johnson in the presence of the rest of the crew. Pippen and Lyons also physically assaulted Oncale in a sexual manner, and Lyons threatened him with rape.

Oncale's complaints to supervisory personnel produced no remedial action; in fact, the company's Safety Compliance Clerk, Valent Hohen, told Oncale that Lyons and Pippen "picked [on] him all the time too," and called him a name suggesting homosexuality. *Id.* at 77. Oncale eventually quit—asking that his pink slip reflect that he "voluntarily left due to sexual harassment and verbal abuse." *Id.* at 79. When asked at his deposition why he left Sundowner, Oncale stated "I felt that if I didn't leave my job, that I would be raped or forced to have sex." *Id.* at 71.

Oncale filed a complaint against Sundowner in the United States District Court for the Eastern District of Louisiana, alleging that he was discriminated against in his employment because of his sex. Relying on the Fifth Circuit's decision in *Garcia v. Elf Atochem North America*, 28 F.3d 446, 451–452 (CA5 1994), the district court held that "Mr. Oncale, a male, has no cause of action under Title VII for harassment by male co-workers." App. 106. On appeal, a panel of the Fifth Circuit concluded that Garcia was binding Circuit precedent, and affirmed. 83 F.3d 118 (1996). We granted certiorari. 117 S.Ct. 2430, 138 L.Ed.2d 192 (1997).

II

Title VII of the Civil Rights Act of 1964 provides, in relevant part, that "it shall be an unlawful employment practice for an employer ... to discriminate against any individual with respect to his compensation, terms, conditions, or privileges of employment, because of such individual's race, color, religion, sex, or national origin." 78 Stat. 255, as amended, 42 U.S.C. § 2000e–2(a)(1). We have held that this not only covers "terms" and "conditions" in the narrow contractual sense, but "evinces a congressional intent to strike at the entire spectrum of disparate treatment of men and women in employment." *Meritor Savings Bank, FSB v. Vinson*, 477 U.S. 57, 64, 91 L.Ed.2d 49, 106 S.Ct. 2399 (1986) (citations and internal quotation marks omitted). "When the workplace is permeated with discriminatory intimidation, ridicule, and insult that is sufficiently severe or pervasive to alter the conditions of the victim's employment and create an abusive working environment, Title VII is violated." *Harris v. Forklift Systems, Inc.*, 510 U.S. 17, 21, 126 L.Ed.2d 295, 114 S.Ct. 367 (1993) (citations and internal quotation marks omitted).

Title VII's prohibition of discrimination "because of ... sex" protects men as well as women, *Newport News Shipbuilding & Dry Dock Co. v. EEOC*, 462 U.S. 669, 682, 77 L.Ed.2d 89, 103 S.Ct. 2622 (1983), and in the related context of racial discrimination in the workplace we have rejected any conclusive presumption that an employer will not discriminate against members of his own race. "Because of the many facets of human motivation, it would be unwise to presume as a matter of law that human beings of one definable group will not discriminate against other members of that group." *Castaneda v. Partida*, 430 U.S. 482, 499, 51 L.Ed.2d 498, 97 S.Ct.

1272 (1977). See also 430 U.S. 482, 51 L.Ed.2d 498 at 515–516 n. 6, 97 S.Ct. 1272 (Powell, J., joined by Burger, C. J., and Rehnquist, J., dissenting). In *Johnson v. Transportation Agency, Santa Clara Cty.*, 480 U.S. 616, 94 L.Ed.2d 615, 107 S.Ct. 1442 (1987), a male employee claimed that his employer discriminated against him because of his sex when it preferred a female employee for promotion. Although we ultimately rejected the claim on other grounds, we did not consider it significant that the supervisor who made that decision was also a man. *See id.* at 624–625. If our precedents leave any doubt on the question, we hold today that nothing in Title VII necessarily bars a claim of discrimination "because of . . . sex" merely because the plaintiff and the defendant (or the person charged with acting on behalf of the defendant) are of the same sex.

Courts have had little trouble with that principle in cases like Johnson, where an employee claims to have been passed over for a job or promotion. But when the issue arises in the context of a "hostile environment" sexual harassment claim, the state and federal courts have taken a bewildering variety of stances. Some, like the Fifth Circuit in this case, have held that same-sex sexual harassment claims are never cognizable under Title VII. *See also, e.g., Goluszek v. H. P. Smith*, 697 F.Supp. 1452 (ND Ill. 1988). Other decisions say that such claims are actionable only if the plaintiff can prove that the harasser is homosexual (and thus presumably motivated by sexual desire). *Compare McWilliams v. Fairfax County Board of Supervisors*, 72 F.3d 1191 (CA4 1996), with *Wrightson v. Pizza Hut of America*, 99 F.3d 138 (CA4 1996). Still others suggest that workplace harassment that is sexual in content is always actionable, regardless of the harasser's sex, sexual orientation, or motivations. *See Doe v. Belleville*, 119 F.3d 563 (CA7 1997).

We see no justification in the statutory language or our precedents for a categorical rule excluding same-sex harassment claims from the coverage of Title VII. As some courts have observed, male-on-male sexual harassment in the workplace was assuredly not the principal evil Congress was concerned with when it enacted Title VII. But statutory prohibitions often go beyond the principal evil to cover reasonably comparable evils, and it is ultimately the provisions of our laws rather than the principal concerns of our legislators by which we are governed. Title VII prohibits "discrimination . . . because of . . . sex" in the "terms" or "conditions" of employment. Our holding that this includes sexual harassment must extend to sexual harassment of any kind that meets the statutory requirements.

. . . Courts and juries have found the inference of discrimination easy to draw in most male-female sexual harassment situations, because the challenged conduct typically involves explicit or implicit proposals of sexual activity; it is reasonable to assume those proposals would not have been made to someone of the same sex. The same chain of inference would be available to a plaintiff alleging same-sex harassment, if there were credible evidence that the harasser was homosexual. But harassing conduct need not be motivated by sexual desire to support an inference of discrimination on the basis of sex. A trier of fact might reasonably find such discrimination, for example, if a female victim is harassed in such sex-specific and derogatory terms by another woman as to make it clear that the harasser is motivated by general hostility to the presence of women in the workplace. A same-sex harassment plaintiff may also, of course, offer direct comparative evidence about how the alleged harasser treated members of both sexes in a mixed-sex workplace. Whatever evidentiary route the plaintiff chooses to follow, he or she must always prove that the conduct at issue was not merely tinged with offensive sexual connotations, but actually constituted "discrimination . . . because of . . . sex."

. . . The prohibition of harassment on the basis of sex requires neither asexuality nor androgyny in the workplace; it forbids only behavior so objectively offensive as to alter the "conditions" of the victim's employment. "Conduct that is not severe or pervasive enough to create an objectively hostile or abusive work environment—an environment that a reasonable person would find hostile or abusive—is beyond Title VII's purview." *Harris*, 510 U.S. at 21, citing *Meritor*, 477 U.S. at 67. We have always regarded that requirement as crucial, and as sufficient to ensure that courts and juries do not mistake ordinary socializing in the workplace—such as male-on-male horseplay or intersexual flirtation—for discriminatory "conditions of employment."

We have emphasized, moreover, that the objective severity of harassment should be judged from the perspective of a reasonable person in the plaintiff's position, considering "all the circumstances." *Harris, supra* at 23. In same-sex (as in all) harassment cases, that inquiry requires careful consideration of the social context in which particular behavior occurs and is experienced by its target. A professional football player's working environment is not severely or pervasively abusive, for example, if the coach smacks him on the buttocks as he heads onto the field—even if the same behavior would reasonably be experienced as abusive by the coach's secretary (male or female) back at the office. The real social impact of workplace behavior often depends on a constellation of surrounding circumstances, expectations, and relationships which are not fully captured by a simple recitation of the words used or the physical acts performed. Common sense, and an appropriate sensitivity to social context, will enable courts and juries to distinguish between simple teasing or roughhousing among members of the same sex, and conduct which a reasonable person in the plaintiff's position would find severely hostile or abusive.

III

Because we conclude that sex discrimination consisting of same-sex sexual harassment is actionable under Title VII, the judgment of the Court of Appeals for the Fifth Circuit is reversed, and the case is remanded for further proceedings consistent with this opinion.

It is so ordered.

JUSTICE THOMAS, concurring.

I concur because the Court stresses that in every sexual harassment case, the plaintiff must plead and ultimately prove Title VII's statutory requirement that there be discrimination "because of . . . sex."

NOTE

The previous cases notwithstanding, a review of case law shows that private employees turn almost exclusively to state or local non-discrimination law for protection. As of 2011, Minnesota, Rhode Island, New Mexico, California, the District of Columbia, Illinois, Maine, Hawaii, New Jersey, Washington, Iowa, Oregon, Vermont, Colorado, Connecticut and Nevada ban discrimination based on sexual orientation and gender identity. Wisconsin, Massachusetts, New Hampshire, Maryland, New York and Delaware ban discrimination based on sexual orientation.

HYMAN v. THE CITY OF LOUISVILLE

132 F.Supp.2d 528 (W.D. Ky. 2001)

CHARLES R. SIMPSON III, CHIEF JUDGE

In February of 1999, the City of Louisville amended its Code of Ordinances so as to prohibit, in connection with employment, discrimination "because of ... sexual orientation or gender identity ..."[59] In October of that same year, Jefferson County, Kentucky, which is comprised of the City of Louisville as well as other cities and unincorporated areas, amended its Code of Ordinances somewhat more broadly, prohibiting discrimination on the basis of gender identity or sexual orientation not only in connection with employment, but also with access to housing and public accommodations.[60]

In addition to the general prohibitions set forth above, both ordinances contain provisions which prohibit employers from, inter alia, publishing any advertisement relating to employment which indicates a preference based upon gender identity or sexual orientation. *See* Lou. Code Ord. § 98.17(D); Jeff. Co. Code Ord. § 92.06(E). Both ordinances also prohibit any person from inciting another to violate the substantive provisions of the ordinances. *See* Lou. Code Ord. § 98.17(F)(2); Jeff. Co. Code Ord. § 92.16(B). Finally, both ordinances contain identical exemptions which state that the ordinances "in regard to sexual orientation or gender identity shall not apply to a religious institution, or to an organization operated for charitable or educational purposes, which is operated, supervised, or controlled by a religious corporation, association or society." Lou. Code Ord. § 98.00; Jeff. Co. Code Ord. § 92.07(B).

The plaintiff, J. Barrett Hyman, M.D. ("Dr. Hyman") is a physician whose medical practice is said to be located in the City of Louisville. Thus, both the City and the County Ordinances may apply to him in the conduct

59. *See generally* Lou. Code Ord. §§ 98.00, .15–.21 ("the City Ordinance").

60. *See* Jeff. Co. Code Ord. §§ 92.01–.25 ("the County Ordinance").

of the employment function of his business as a medical practitioner.[61] Contending that his religious beliefs so conflict with the ordinances' proscriptions that he will not comply with them and that he thus risks prosecution on account of his religion, Dr. Hyman filed this action seeking to have the ordinances declared invalid insofar as they pertain to employment discrimination on the basis of sexual orientation and gender identity.

The Fairness Campaign, a political action group, advocated the adoption of the changes to the ordinances and conducted a public campaign in support of its position at the times the City and the County legislative bodies were considering the amendments they eventually enacted. It, together with Dan Ferrell and Diane Moten, two self-described homosexuals, were allowed to intervene permissively. *See* DN 19. The United States, by its Department of Justice, was granted amicus curiae status. *See* DN 46. All parties have moved for summary judgment. We now address these motions.[62]

. . .

Dr. Hyman's Contentions

Dr. Hyman alleges that he "believes that acts of homosexuality, bisexuality, transgenderism and other departures from monogamous heterosexual relations are sinful and grievously offensive to God." Am. Compl. at P 10. He contends that his beliefs are inconsistent with the requirements of both the City and the County Ordinances and that because of his religious beliefs, he "will deny employment and discharge certain persons on the basis of sexual orientation and/or gender identity...." Am. Compl. at P 20. Therefore, Dr. Hyman claims that he is faced with the "Hobson's choice" of either obeying the laws of Louisville and Jefferson County or obeying the laws of his conscience.

Dr. Hyman further states that in recent months he attempted to place in the *Courier–Journal*, a Louisville newspaper, an advertisement which purportedly violates both ordinances. He asserts that the newspaper would not allow his ad to be placed because of its "discriminatory"

61. The City of Louisville and Jefferson County are currently litigating the issue of which ordinance applies within the Louisville city limits. By order entered on March 13, 2000, Judge Stephen Ryan of the Jefferson Circuit Court held that the County Ordinance "is valid and enforceable throughout the unincorporated portions of Jefferson County, but is not enforceable within the incorporated portions of Jefferson County." However, Judge Ryan's decision is currently before the Kentucky Court of Appeals. Because the challenged portions of both ordinances are not materially different, and because with respect to conduct related to employment such as advertising, there may be some boundary line overlap, we will address both the City and the County Ordinances.

62. For the sake of convenience, the City of Louisville, David Armstrong in his official capacity as the Mayor of the City of Louisville, the Louisville and Jefferson County Human Relations Commission, and Phyllis Atiba Brown in her official capacity as the Executive Director of the Louisville and Jefferson County Human Relations Commission will be referred to collectively herein as the "City Defendants." Jefferson County and Rebecca Jackson in her official capacity as Jefferson County Judge/Executive will be referred to as the "County Defendants." Finally, the Fairness Campaign, Dan Farrell, and Diane Moten will be referred to collectively as the "Intervenor–Defendants."

content. *See* Pl.'s Mot. Supplement R., Ex. A (DN 52) ("Hyman Affidavit").

Finally, Dr. Hyman indicates that he is in the process of hiring a new employee. *See id.* As a part of the hiring process, Dr. Hyman is said to have inquired into two applicants' sexual orientation intending to take this fact into account in reaching an employment decision.

Dr. Hyman claims that the ordinances deprive him of rights protected by the United States Constitution in violation of 42 U.S.C. § 1983. *See* Am. Compl. at P 29–55. In addition, he contends that the ordinances violate the Kentucky Constitution and several statutes of the Commonwealth of Kentucky. *See id.* at PP 56–85. He seeks, inter alia, declaratory relief pursuant to 28 U.S.C. §§ 2201, 2202.

Each of these contentions, as well as the defendants' responses thereto, will be discussed below.

Discussion

. . .

II. Free Exercise of Religion

Dr. Hyman makes a unique argument in support of his Free Exercise Clause claim. The basis of his challenge is that the ordinances allegedly prefer religious institutions over individuals. Dr. Hyman claims that the ordinances violate both the First Amendment of the U.S. Constitution and § 5 of the Kentucky Constitution.

A. U.S. Const. Amend. I

The First Amendment states that "Congress shall make no law respecting an establishment of religion, or prohibiting the free exercise thereof...." U.S. Const. amend. I. This clause is made applicable to the states and their instrumentalities by the Fourteenth Amendment. *See Cantwell v. Connecticut*, 310 U.S. 296, 303, 60 S.Ct. 900, 84 L.Ed. 1213 (1940). Dr. Hyman claims that his right to the free exercise of his religion is violated by the ordinances he challenges. *See* Am. Compl. at P 32. Specifically, he argues that the ordinances impermissibly distinguish between individuals who, based on their religious beliefs, seek to make employment decisions on the basis of sexual orientation or gender identity and religious institutions with the same intentions.[63] *See* Pl.'s Mot. Summ. J. at 20 (DN 31) (hereinafter the "Hyman MSJ"). While the ordinances make no denominational distinctions, Dr. Hyman contends that provisions which exempt religious institutions and fail to exempt individuals with comparable religious convictions are at odds with the Free Exercise Clause of the First Amendment.

---

63. Both the City and the County Ordinances contain identical exemptions which state that the ordinances "in regard to sexual orientation or gender identity shall not apply to a religious institution, or to an organization operated for charitable or educational purposes, which is operated, supervised, or controlled by a religious corporation, association or society." Lou. Code Ord. § 98.00; Jeff. Co. Code Ord. § 92.07 (B).

In *Employment Div., Dept. of Human Resources of Oregon v. Smith*, 494 U.S. 872, 110 S.Ct. 1595, 108 L.Ed.2d 876 (1990), the Supreme Court set forth a framework for the analysis of free exercise claims such as this. Smith requires a court to determine as a threshold matter whether the challenged regulation is "a 'valid and neutral law of general applicability[.]' "[64] *Smith*, 494 U.S. at 879 (*quoting United States v. Lee*, 455 U.S. 252, 263 n.3, 102 S.Ct. 1051, 71 L.Ed.2d 127 (1982) (Stevens, J., concurring in judgment)). If the challenged regulation is religion-neutral and generally applicable, then it does not violate the Free Exercise Clause even if its enforcement results in an incidental burden on a particular religious practice. *See Smith* at 884–85, 886 n.3. However, regulations found to be either nonneutral or not generally applicable are further scrutinized by courts.[65] These regulations "must be justified by a compelling governmental interest and must be narrowly tailored to advance that interest." *Church of the Lukumi Babalu Aye, Inc.*, 508 U.S. 520, 531–32, 113 S.Ct. 2217, 124 L.Ed.2d 472. *See also Kissinger v. Board of Trustees of Ohio State University, College of Veterinary Medicine*, 5 F.3d 177, 179 (6th Cir. 1993).

Both the City and the County Ordinances generally prohibit employment discrimination on account of gender identity or sexual orientation.[66] However, as noted above, both ordinances contain exemptions which do not prohibit religious institutions from discriminating on the same bases. Dr. Hyman contends that the distinction between religious institutions and individuals destroy the neutrality and general applicability of the ordinances just as surely as would an exemption with a denominational preference. *See* Hyman MSJ at 20–21. In support of this contention, Dr. Hyman argues that the ordinances are facially discriminatory.

The Supreme Court has stated that a law is not neutral if its purpose "is to infringe upon or restrict practices because of their religious motivation." *Lukumi*, 508 U.S. at 533. Evidence of a law's neutrality may come from several sources. *See id.* At a minimum, the text of a statute must not be discriminatory. As the *Lukumi* Court stated, "[a] law lacks facial neutrality if it refers to a religious practice without a secular meaning

64. In *Smith*, the Court analyzed the Free Exercise Clause implications of the enforcement of a criminal statute which prohibited the use of peyote. However, subsequent lower court decisions have made clear that the *Smith* framework applies in both the civil and criminal contexts. *See, e.g., Vandiver v. Hardin County Bd. of Educ.*, 925 F.2d 927, 932 (6th Cir. 1991); *Salvation Army v. Department of Community Affairs of N.J.*, 919 F.2d 183, 195 (3rd Cir. 1990).

65. The Court has held that "neutrality and general applicability are interrelated, and ... failure to satisfy one requirement is a likely indication that the other has not been satisfied." *Church of the Lukumi Babalu Aye, Inc. v. City of Hialeah*, 508 U.S. 520, 531, 113 S.Ct. 2217, 124 L.Ed.2d 472 (1993).

66. The City Ordinance defines "gender identity" as either "(A) Having a gender identity as a result of a sex change surgery; or (B) Manifesting, for reasons other than dress, an identity not traditionally associated with one's biological maleness or femaleness." Lou. Code Ord. § 98.16. It defines "sexual orientation" as "an individual's actual or imputed heterosexuality, homosexuality, or bisexuality." *Id.*

The County Ordinance defines "gender identity" as "manifesting an identity not traditionally associated with one's biological maleness or femaleness." Jeff. Co. Code Ord. § 92.02. It defines "sexual orientation" as "an individual's actual or imputed heterosexuality, homosexuality or bisexuality." *Id.*

discernable from the language or context." *Lukumi* at 533. For example, in *Lukumi*, the Court addressed a situation in which a series of local ordinances effectively outlawed the ritual of animal sacrifice practiced by followers of Santeria. While the Court ultimately found the statutes to be facially neutral, it noted that the use of words like "sacrifice" and "ritual" in the ordinances was consistent with a claim of facial discrimination. *See id.*

We cannot agree with Dr. Hyman that the purpose of the ordinances' exemptions which he challenges is to "restrict practices because of their religious motivation." *See Lukumi, supra* at 533. The record does not support such a conclusion. The policy statements which accompany each ordinance weigh against it as well. *See* Lou. Code Ord. § 98.15; Jeff. Co. Code Ord. § 92.01. Also, neither the ordinances nor their accompanying exemptions refer to "religious practice." *Lukumi, supra* at 533. While discrimination against individuals on account of their sexual orientation or gender identity may be a religious practice for Dr. Hyman, the ordinances' prohibitions are textually and contextually secular.

Finally, the Supreme Court has consistently held that, while an individual's religious principles may be accommodated to a certain extent, it is necessary that "some religious practices yield to the common good." *U. S. v. Lee*, 455 U.S. 252, 259, 102 S.Ct. 1051, 71 L.Ed.2d 127 (1982). *See also Reynolds v. United States*, 98 U.S. 145, 166–67, 8 Otto 145, 25 L.Ed. 244 (1878) ("Laws are made for the government of actions, and while they cannot interfere with mere religious belief and opinions, they may with practices."). Therefore, the ordinances may not, and do not, regulate the beliefs of Dr. Hyman. Rather, they merely seek to regulate the conduct of all individuals who are engaged in the employment of others. We believe that such a religion-neutral, generally applicable regulation is consistent with the mandate of the Free Exercise Clause of the First Amendment. *See United States v. Lee*, 455 U.S. at 261 ("When followers of a particular sect enter into commercial activity as a matter of choice, the limits they accept on their own conduct as a matter of conscience and faith are not to be superimposed on the statutory schemes which are binding on others in that activity.").

Having determined that the ordinances at issue are neutral laws of general applicability, we need not address whether they are justified by a compelling government interest and whether they are narrowly tailored to advance that interest. *See Smith*, 494 U.S. at 886 n.3. Rather, we must only be satisfied that the ordinances are rationally related to a legitimate government interest. *See Walz v. Tax Comm'n of City of New York*, 397 U.S. 664, 696, 90 S.Ct. 1409, 25 L.Ed.2d 697 (1970).

... There is ample authority for the proposition that the elimination of discrimination on the basis of sexual orientation or gender identity is within the purview of legitimate legislative interests. *See, e.g., Hurley v. Irish–American Gay, Lesbian and Bisexual Group of Boston*, 515 U.S. 557, 572, 115 S.Ct. 2338, 132 L.Ed.2d 487 (1995) (holding that laws which prohibit discrimination on the basis of sexual orientation in the provision of public accommodations are "well within the State's usual power to enact when a legislature has reason to believe that a given group is the target of discrimination ..."). With respect to these ordinances, the record indicates that the legislative branches of the Louisville and Jefferson County governments have chosen to balance the goal of nondiscrimination against a similarly valid goal of noninterference with religious institutions. We believe that the essential "link" between "the classification adopted and the object to be attained" is sufficient to justify our conclusion that the ordinances are rationally related to a legitimate government interest. *See Romer v. Evans*, 517 U.S. at 632.

We conclude that the ordinances do not violate the Free Exercise Clause of the First Amendment of the U.S. Constitution.

III. Free Speech

Dr. Hyman contends that two provisions of the ordinances he challenges infringe upon his free speech rights. First, Dr. Hyman takes issue with the ordinances' prohibition against publishing any advertisement relating to employment which indicates a preference based upon gender identity or sexual orientation. *See* Lou. Code Ord. § 98.17 (D); Jeff. Co. Code Ord. § 92.06 (E). Second, he challenges those portions of the ordinances which prohibit any person from inciting another to violate the substantive provisions of the ordinances. *See* Lou. Code Ord. § 98.17 (F)(2); Jeff. Co. Code Ord. § 92.16 (B). We will address each of these arguments in turn.

A. The Advertising Restrictions

In future solicitations for employees, Dr. Hyman desires to articulate an intention to discriminate based upon gender identity and sexual orientation and an intention to not honor the ordinances. *See* Hyman Dep. (DN 27) at 49–50. He argues that the ordinances' prohibition on his ability to advertise his preferences violates his right to free speech.[67]

In his brief, Dr. Hyman acknowledges that the Supreme Court, in *Pittsburgh Press Co. v. Pittsburgh Commission on Human Relations*, 413 U.S. 376, 93 S.Ct. 2553, 37 L.Ed.2d 669 (1973), upheld a similar ordinance prohibiting gender-biased employment advertising in the face of a First Amendment challenge. *Pittsburgh Press*, therefore, appears to foreclose Dr. Hyman's challenge to the ordinances. However, he argues that we should hold otherwise for two reasons: (1) the advertisements at issue in *Pittsburgh Press* are distinguishable from his proposed advertisements; and (2) the ordinances are unconstitutionally overbroad. We find Dr.

67. Dr. Hyman claims to have attempted to place an ad in the *Courier–Journal* which read, "Pro–Life and Traditional Pro–Family office worker for billing, collections, and medical assistant. Fax résumé to (502)587–6535 or call (502)583–5524." However, he alleges that he omitted the phrase "Pro–Life and Traditional Pro–Family" from the ad upon the Courier–Journal's refusal to print the original version. *See* Hyman Affidavit at PP 6–8.

Hyman's arguments unpersuasive and that *Pittsburgh Press* requires us to grant summary judgment in favor of the defendants.

1. Commercial Speech

The ordinance at issue in *Pittsburgh Press* forbade an employer from publishing "any notice or advertisement relating to 'employment' ... which indicates any discrimination because of ... sex." *Pittsburgh Press*, 413 U.S. at 378. The Pittsburgh Commission on Human Relations found that the Pittsburgh Press had aided employers in violating the ordinance by publishing help wanted ads in separate columns titled "Male Help Wanted" and "Female Help Wanted." *See id.* at 379. The Pittsburgh Press appealed the case to the Supreme Court claiming that the ordinance infringed upon its First Amendment rights. The case turned, principally, on whether the speech involved constituted commercial speech. The Court noted that the critical test for commercial speech was whether it "did no more than propose a commercial transaction...." *Pittsburgh Press* at 385. The Court found that the advertisements in the Pittsburgh Press were merely proposals of possible employment, and therefore, were "classic examples of commercial speech." *Id.* at 385.

Dr. Hyman argues that his advertisements are different in that he proposes "to make known his 'stand' " on the ordinances, although it is clear that he intends to do so in the context of soliciting applications from prospective employees. *See* Hyman MSJ at 30; Hyman Dep. at 48. His proposed advertisements, he argues, would express his political and moral opinion on important public issues. He concludes, therefore, that they are larger than mere commercial speech and are worthy of the broadest protection available under the First Amendment.

However, commercial speech is not worthy of broader First Amendment protection simply because it coexists with speech addressing important public issues. *See Central Hudson*, 447 U.S. at 563 n.5. Instead, advertisements can "constitute commercial speech notwithstanding the fact that they contain discussions of important public issues...." *Bolger*, 463 U.S. at 67–68. According to the Court, this conclusion is apt when the commercial speech and political statement are not "inextricably intertwined." *Board of Trustees of the State University of New York v. Fox*, 492 U.S. 469, 474, 109 S.Ct. 3028, 106 L.Ed.2d 388 (1989).

In *Fox*, the Court explained that "no law of man or of nature makes it impossible to sell housewares without teaching home economics, or to teach home economics without selling housewares." *Fox*, 492 U.S. at 474. The same is true of Dr. Hyman's proposed advertisements. Nothing requires him to express his opinions in his advertisements for employment. Including Dr. Hyman's political and moral views in his "Help Wanted" advertisements does no more to turn them into political speech than "opening sales presentations with a prayer or a Pledge of Allegiance would convert them into religious or political speech." *Id.* at 475. Because at their essence, Dr. Hyman's advertisements are proposals of possible employment, we hold that they constitute commercial speech. The language Dr. Hyman proposes to use is, accordingly, not shielded by the First Amendment.

. . .

IV. Freedom of Association

Dr. Hyman claims that his freedom of association, as guaranteed by the First Amendment, is violated by the ordinances. *See* Am. Compl. at pp. 41–45. The Intervenor—Defendants have moved for summary judgment on this claim, arguing that pursuant to *Roberts v. United States Jaycees*, 468 U.S. 609, 104 S.Ct. 3244, 82 L.Ed.2d 462 (1984), Dr. Hyman's medical practice is not entitled to this sort of First Amendment protection. For the reasons set forth below, we agree.

In *Roberts*, the Supreme Court held that two types of relationships are entitled to protection under the Freedom of Association Clause of the First Amendment. First, the Court held that "certain intimate human relationships" such as those that "attend the creation and sustenance of a family" are to be afforded constitutional protection. *Roberts*, 468 U.S. at 618–19. The second type of constitutionally protected relationship is one's "right to associate for the purpose of engaging in those activities protected by the First Amendment-speech, assembly, petition for the redress of grievances, and the exercise of religion." *Id.* at 618. This "freedom of expressive association" is protected in order to preserve "political and cultural diversity" and to shield "dissident expression from suppression by the majority." *Roberts*, 468 U.S. at 618, 622.

The ordinances in question do not violate Dr. Hyman's "freedom of intimate association." Dr. Hyman's ability to enter into the sort of "highly personal relationships" contemplated by the *Roberts* Court is in no way impaired by either ordinance. *See Roberts*, 468 U.S. at 618. The record indicates that Dr. Hyman's medical practice is simply a commercial enterprise. *See, e.g.,* Hyman Affidavit; Hyman Dep. at 21,–22, Ex. 3. The Supreme Court has interpreted the First Amendment to provide little protection under the Freedom of Association Clause to commercial enterprises. *See Roberts, supra* at 620.

. . .

V. Equal Protection

The Equal Protection Clause of the Fourteenth Amendment essentially states that "all persons similarly situated should be treated alike." *City of Cleburne, Tex. v. Cleburne Living Center*, 473 U.S. 432, 439, 105 S.Ct. 3249, 87 L.Ed.2d 313 (1985) (*citing Plyler v. Doe*, 457 U.S. 202, 216, 102 S.Ct. 2382, 72 L.Ed.2d 786 (1982)). A statute which draws a distinction between those to whom it applies will normally be upheld if that distinction is rationally related to a legitimate government interest. *See* 473 U.S. at 440. However, as Dr. Hyman correctly points out, if a statute "impinge[s] on personal rights protected by the Constitution," then strict scrutiny review is applied, and the statute will be upheld only if it is narrowly tailored to serve a compelling government interest. *See id.*

As we have noted above, neither the City nor the County Ordinance impinges on Dr. Hyman's First Amendment rights. Therefore, the proper inquiry is whether or not the exemptions in the ordinances are rationally related to a legitimate state interest.

. . .

We find the Supreme Court's decision in *Amos, supra*, to be instructive on this point. In *Amos*, the Court was faced with a challenge to Title VII's religious exemption which permitted religious employers to discriminate on the basis of religion. While the challenge in Amos was based on the Establishment Clause, the Court addressed the issue of equal protection, as well. The Court held that Title VII's religious exemption was "rationally related to the legitimate purpose of alleviating significant governmental interference with the ability of religious organizations to define and carry out their religious missions." *Amos*, 483 U.S. at 339. Because we believe that the facts which confronted the Supreme Court in Amos are analogous to those with which we are now faced, and because we conclude that the exemptions included in the ordinances challenged by Dr. Hyman are intended to alleviate similar interference with religious institutions, we find that the exemptions contained in both the City and the County Ordinances are rationally related to the same purpose of alleviating governmental interference with the activities of religious institutions. Therefore, Dr. Hyman's challenge, to the extent it is based on the Equal Protection Clause of the Fourteenth Amendment, must fail.

VI. Due Process

Dr. Hyman next claims that the terms "sexual orientation" and "gender identity," as used in the ordinances, are unconstitutionally vague in violation of the Due Process Clauses of the Fifth and Fourteenth Amendments. As such, Dr. Hyman urges this court to invalidate the ordinances to the extent they prohibit discrimination because of "sexual orientation" and "gender identity."

A statute may be found to be void for vagueness for one of two reasons. First, a statute that "fails to provide people of ordinary intelligence a reasonable opportunity to understand what conduct it prohibits" may be found to be unconstitutionally vague. *Hill v. Colorado*, 530 U.S. 703, 120 S.Ct. 2480, 2498, 147 L.Ed.2d 597 (2000). Second, a statute will be struck down under the void-for-vagueness doctrine "if it authorizes or even encourages arbitrary and discriminatory enforcement." *Id.* . . .

The term "sexual orientation" is defined by both the City and the County Ordinances as "an individual's actual or imputed heterosexuality, homosexuality or bisexuality." Lou. Code Ord. § 98.16; Jeff. Co. Code Ord. § 92.02. "Gender identity" is also defined by the ordinances. The City Ordinance defines "gender identity" as either "(A) Having a gender identity as a result of a sex change surgery; or (B) Manifesting, for reasons other than dress, an identity not traditionally associated with one's biological maleness or femaleness." Lou. Code Ord. § 98.16. The term is defined by the County Ordinance as "manifesting an identity not traditionally associated with one's biological maleness or femaleness." Jeff. Co. Code Ord. § 92.02.

... While "gender identity" is less commonly addressed by courts, those that have attempted to define the term have done so consistently. *Compare Smith v. Palmer*, 24 F.Supp.2d 955, 959 n.3 (N.D. Iowa 1998) with *Farmer v. Brennan*, 511 U.S. 825, 829, 114 S.Ct. 1970, 128 L.Ed.2d 811 (1994), and *Powell v. Schriver*, 175 F.3d 107, 111 (2d Cir. 1999).

Second, the use of the terms "sexual orientation" and "gender identity" in many statutes, ordinances, and regulations is consistent with their use in the ordinances challenged by Dr. Hyman.

... Finally, an abbreviated survey of contemporary reference materials indicates that the ordinances' definitions are consistent with the terms' common meanings. *See* Black's Law Dictionary 1379 (7th ed. 1999) (defining "sexual orientation" as "[a] person's predisposition or inclination toward a particular type of sexual activity or behavior; heterosexuality, homosexuality, or bisexuality"); The New Encyclopaedia Britannica, 5 Micropaedia 172 (15th ed. 1994) (defining "gender identity" as "an individual's self-conception as being male or female, as distinguished from actual biological sex").

... We believe the level of certainty that Dr. Hyman seeks is unattainable in this instance. The definitions of "sexual orientation" and "gender identity" are consistent with the meanings attributed to those terms by common usage. Therefore, we find that neither those terms nor their definitions are unconstitutionally vague.

Conclusion

For the foregoing reasons, the plaintiff's motion for summary judgment will be denied. The defendants' motions for summary judgment will be denied with respect to the issues of standing and ripeness. The defendants' motions will be granted in all other respects. A separate order will be entered this date in accordance with this opinion.

NOTE

The judgment in this case was subsequently vacated by the 6th Circuit, in *Hyman v. City of Louisville*, 53 Fed. Appx. 740 (6 Cir. 2002). The court held that Dr. Hyman lacked standing.

DISCUSSION

A lesbian employee of the Billy Graham Evangelistic Association, fired because of her sexual orientation, sued under the Minnesota Human Rights law banning discrimination based on sexual orientation. During her more than 30 years of employment at the Billy Graham Evangelistic Association, she was a mail room clerk and held other positions that did not directly link her to the production of any evangelistic media. The Billy Graham Evangelistic Association sought to have her suit dismissed. How should the court rule? See Thorson v. Billy Graham Evangelistic Association, *687 N.W.2d 652 (Minn. App. 2004), review denied.*

III. DISCRIMINATION IN PUBLIC EMPLOYMENT

HIGH TECH GAYS v. DEFENSE INDUSTRIAL SECURITY CLEARANCE OFFICE

895 F.2d 563 (9th Cir. 1990)

OPINION: BRUNETTI, CIRCUIT JUDGE:

. . .

I.

. . .

B.

The plaintiffs brought this action in district court claiming that DISCO's policy and practice of refusing to grant industrial security clearances to Gay persons because of their sexual orientation, private practice thereof with consenting adults, and related social and political activities, including membership in Gay organizations, and of subjecting them to unjustifiable and time-consuming investigations because of their sexual orientation and related matters violates their Constitutional rights to freedom of speech and association and to equal protection and due process of law.

The suit proceeded as a class action in the district court with three individually named plaintiffs: Timothy Dooling, Joel Crawford, and Robert Weston.

Plaintiff Dooling is a homosexual who applied for a Secret industrial clearance on May 2, 1983. On March 22, 1984, DISCO issued a memorandum recommending that Dooling be considered ineligible for a security clearance and forwarded the case to DISCR. DISCR eventually granted Dooling a Secret clearance in May 1984.

Plaintiff Crawford is a homosexual who applied for Secret clearance in December 1981. After DISCO recommended that Crawford be considered ineligible for a Secret clearance, DISCR denied Crawford's application for a Secret clearance based on evidence of past drug abuse.

Plaintiff Weston, a homosexual, has a Secret clearance and in 1984 submitted an application for Top Secret clearance as required for his job at Lockheed Missiles & Space Co. Lockheed never forwarded his application to the DoD because his application revealed he belonged to a gay organization.

The plaintiffs sought an order: declaring unconstitutional and enjoining the DISCO policy of refusing to grant Secret clearances to gay people who have participated in homosexual activity within the past fifteen years and requiring that applications of gay people be forwarded to DISCR for adjudication; declaring unconstitutional and enjoining the DIS practice of subjecting gay applicants to in-depth and time-consuming investigations (required by DIS Manual for Personnel Security Investigations); declaring unconstitutional the five reasons DISCO used to recommend denial of plaintiff Dooling's clearance; and declaring unconstitutional DISCR's processing of plaintiff Crawford's application subsequent to the filing of this lawsuit.

The plaintiffs and the DoD each moved for summary judgment and upon considering the cross-motions, the district court denied the DoD's motion for summary judgment and granted the plaintiffs' motion.

The DoD then filed a motion for reconsideration and a motion for a stay pending appeal. The motion for reconsideration was based on new evidence from several sources indicating that hostile intelligence agencies target persons who are especially vulnerable, and that among others, persons who are homosexuals are considered vulnerable by these agencies. The district court denied the motion for reconsideration but granted the DoD's motion for a stay pending appeal. The DoD contends that its motion should have been granted and asks that we reverse the district court's grant of the plaintiffs' motion.

. . .

III.

Equal Protection

"The Equal Protection Clause of the Fourteenth Amendment commands that no State shall deny to any person within its jurisdiction the equal protection of the laws, which is essentially a direction that all persons similarly situated should be treated alike." *City of Cleburne v. Cleburne Living Center*, 473 U.S. 432, 439, 87 L.Ed.2d 313, 105 S.Ct. 3249 (1985) (quotation omitted).

In *Bolling v. Sharpe*, 347 U.S. 497, 74 S.Ct. 693, 98 L.Ed. 884 (1954), the Supreme Court held that while the Equal Protection Clause of the Fourteenth Amendment prohibited states from maintaining racially segregated public schools, see Brown v. Board of Education, 347 U.S. 483, 74 S.Ct. 686, 98 L.Ed. 873 (1954), only the Fifth Amendment, not the Fourteenth, was applicable in the District of Columbia. *Bolling*, 347 U.S. at 499, 74 S.Ct. at 694. The Court noted that the Fifth Amendment "does not contain an equal protection clause as does the Fourteenth Amendment which applies only to the states," and held that racial segregation in the District of Columbia public schools violated the Due Process Clause of the Fifth Amendment. The Court believed that in light of their decision in Brown that the Constitution prohibits states from maintaining racially segregated schools, "it would be unthinkable that the same Constitution would impose a lesser duty on the Federal Government." *Id.* at 499–500, 74 S.Ct. at 694–95 (footnote omitted). The Court also noted that the concepts of equal protection and due process, both stemming from our American ideal of fairness, are not mutually exclusive. The "equal protection of the laws" is a more explicit safeguard of prohibited unfairness than "due process of law," and, therefore, we do not imply that the two are always interchangeable phrases. [However], discrimination may be so unjustifiable as to be violative of due process. *id.* (footnote omitted).

It is thus clear that there is an equal protection component of the Due Process Clause of the Fifth Amendment which applies to the federal government.

In this case, the plaintiffs challenge the validity of the DoD Security Clearance Regulations under the equal protection component of the Fifth Amendment; specifically, that the DoD security clearance regulations discriminate against gay people.

. . . It is well established that there are three standards we may apply in reviewing the plaintiffs' equal protection challenge to the DoD Security Clearance Regulations: strict scrutiny, heightened scrutiny, and rational basis review. See *Cleburne*, 473 U.S. at 440–41. The plaintiffs assert that homosexuality should be added to the list of suspect or quasi-suspect classifications requiring strict or heightened scrutiny. We disagree and hold that the district court erred in applying heightened scrutiny to the regulations at issue and that the proper standard is rational basis review. *Accord Ben–Shalom v. Marsh*, 881 F.2d 454, 464 (7th Cir. 1989), *cert. denied*, 494 U.S. 1004, 110 S.Ct. 1296, 108 L.Ed.2d 473 (1990); *Woodward v. United States*, 871 F.2d 1068, 1076 (Fed. Cir. 1989), *cert. denied*, 494 U.S. 1003, 110 S.Ct. 1295, 108 L.Ed.2d 473 (1990); *Padula v. Webster*, 261 U.S. App. D.C. 365, 822 F.2d 97, 103 (D.C. Cir. 1987).

The Supreme Court has ruled that homosexual activity is not a fundamental right protected by substantive due process and that the proper standard of review under the Fifth Amendment is rational basis review. *Bowers v. Hardwick*, 478 U.S. 186, 194–96, 92 L.Ed.2d 140, 106 S.Ct. 2841 (1986). The Court explained that the right to privacy inheres only in family relationships, marriage and procreation, and does not extend to all private sexual conduct between consenting adults. *Id.* at 190–91. The Court specifically characterized "fundamental liberties" under the Constitution "as those liberties that are deeply rooted in this Nation's history and tradition." *Id.* at 192 (quotation omitted). In holding that the Constitution does not confer a fundamental right upon homosexuals to engage in consensual sodomy, the Court stated:

> There should be, therefore, great resistance to expand the substantive reach of [the Due Process Clauses of the Fifth and Fourteenth Amendments], particularly if it requires redefining the category of rights deemed to be fundamental. Otherwise, the Judiciary necessarily takes to itself further authority to govern the country without express constitutional authority.

Id. at 195.

There has been a repudiation of much of the substantive gloss that the Court has placed on the Due Process Clauses of the Fifth and Fourteenth Amendments. See id. at 194–95. If for federal analysis we must reach equal protection of the Fourteenth Amendment by the Due Process Clause of the Fifth Amendment, *see Bolling*, 347 U.S. at 499, and if there is no fundamental right to engage in homosexual sodomy under the Due Process Clause of the Fifth Amendment, *see Hardwick*, 478 U.S. at 194, it would be incongruous to expand the reach of equal protection to find a fundamental right of homosexual conduct under the equal protection component of the Due Process Clause of the Fifth Amendment. *See Bolling*, 347 U.S. at 500.

Other circuits are in accord and have held that although the Court in *Hardwick* analyzed the constitutionality of the sodomy statute on a due process rather than equal protection basis, by the *Hardwick* majority holding that the Constitution confers no fundamental right upon homosexuals to engage in sodomy, and because homosexual conduct can thus be criminalized, homosexuals cannot constitute a suspect or quasi-suspect class entitled to greater than rational basis review for equal protection purposes. *See Ben–Shalom*, 881 F.2d at 464–65; *Woodward*, 871 F.2d at 1076; *Padula*, 822 F.2d at 103. . . .

It is apparent that while the Supreme Court has identified that legislative classifications based on race, alienage, or national origin are subject to strict scrutiny and that classifications based upon gender or illegitimacy call for a heightened standard, the Court has never held homosexuality to a heightened standard of review.

To be a "suspect" or "quasi-suspect" class, homosexuals must (1) have suffered a history of discrimination; (2) exhibit obvious, immutable, or distinguishing characteristics that define them as a discrete group; and (3) show that they are a minority or politically powerless, or alternatively show that the statutory classification at issue burdens a fundamental right. *Bowen v. Gilliard*, 483 U.S. 587, 602–03, 97 L.Ed.2d 485, 107 S.Ct. 3008 (1987) (due to a lack of these characteristics, the statutory classifications of the Federal Aid to Families with Dependent Children Program were subject to only a rational basis review) (*citing Lyng v. Castillo*, 477 U.S. 635, 638, 91 L.Ed.2d 527, 106 S.Ct. 2727 (1986) (due to a lack of these characteristics, the statutory classifications of the Federal Food Stamp Program were subject to only a rational basis review)).

While we do agree that homosexuals have suffered a history of discrimination, we do not believe that they meet the other criteria. Homosexuality is not an immutable characteristic; it is behavioral and hence is fundamentally different from traits such as race, gender, or alienage, which define already existing suspect and quasi-suspect classes. *Accord Woodward*, 871 F.2d at 1076. The behavior or conduct of such already recognized classes is irrelevant to their identification. *Id.*

Moreover, legislatures have addressed and continue to address the discrimination suffered by homosexuals on account of their sexual orientation through the passage of anti-discrimination legislation.[81] Thus, homosexuals are not without political power; they have the ability to and do "attract the attention of the lawmakers," as evidenced by such legislation. *See Cleburne*, 473 U.S. at 445. *Accord Ben–Shalom*, 881 F.2d at 466. Lastly, as previously noted, homosexual conduct is not a fundamental right. *Hardwick*, 478 U.S. at 194.

Our review compels us to agree with the other circuits that have ruled on this issue and to hold that homosexuals do not constitute a suspect or quasi-suspect class entitled to greater than rational basis scrutiny under the equal protection component of the Due Process Clause of the Fifth Amendment.

Because the district court erred in granting the plaintiffs' motion for summary judgment by applying heightened scrutiny in its equal protection analysis, we now review the plaintiffs' and defendants' cross-motions for summary judgment applying rational basis scrutiny.[82]

IV.

Cross–Motions for Summary Judgment

A.

The moving party has the burden of demonstrating the absence of a genuine issue of fact for trial. *Anderson v. Liberty Lobby, Inc.*, 477 U.S. 242, 256, 106 S.Ct. 2505, 2514, 91 L.Ed.2d 202 (1986). If the moving party satisfies this burden, the opponent must set forth specific facts showing that there remains a genuine issue for trial. Fed. R. Civ. P. 56(e). However, no defense to an insufficient showing is required. *Great Hawaiian Fin. Corp. v. Aiu*, 863 F.2d 617, 619 (9th Cir.1988) (per curiam).

If the burden of persuasion at trial would be on the nonmoving party, the party moving for summary judgment may satisfy its burden of production under Rule 56 by submitting affirmative evidence that negates an essential element of the nonmoving party's claim or by demonstrating to the court that the nonmoving party's evidence is insufficient to estab-

---

81. For example: Wisconsin has a comprehensive statute barring employment discrimination on the basis of sexual orientation, Wis. Stat. Ann. §§ 111.31–.395 (West 1988); California has barred violence against persons or property based on sexual orientation, Cal. Civ. Code § 51.7 (West 1984); and Michigan has barred the denial of care in health facilities on the basis of sexual orientation, Mich. Comp. Laws Ann. § 333.20201(2)(a) (West 1984). Executive Orders in other states prohibit such discrimination. *See e.g.*, N.Y. Comp. Codes R. & Regs. tit. 4, § 28 (1983) (barring discrimination in state employment or in the provision of state services and benefits on the basis of sexual orientation). Many cities and counties have also enacted anti-discrimination regulations, including New York, Los Angeles, Chicago, Washington D.C., Atlanta, Boston, Philadelphia, Seattle, and San Francisco. Developments in the Law, *Sexual Orientation and the Law*, 102 Harv. L. Rev. 1509, 1667–68, n. 49–51 (citations omitted).

82. We recognize that the denial of DoD's motion for summary judgment is not a final decision of the district court and thus, under normal circumstances, would not be appealable. However, because we have jurisdiction to decide DoD's appeal from the granting of plaintiffs' motion for summary judgment, we exercise our discretion to decide their claim of error in the denial of their summary judgment motion as well. *See Barhold v. Rodriguez*, 863 F.2d 233, 237 (2nd Cir. 1988).

lish an essential element of the nonmoving party's claim. *Celotex Corp. v. Catrett*, 477 U.S. 317, 331, 106 S.Ct. 2548, 2557, 91 L.Ed.2d 265 (1986) (Brennan, J., dissenting, agreeing with the majority).

We view the materials on file in the light most favorable to the nonmoving party. *Ashton v. Cory*, 780 F.2d 816, 818 (9th Cir.1986). "This is true even though the court was presented with cross-motions for summary judgment; each movant has the burden of presenting evidence to support its motion that would allow the district court, if appropriate, to direct a verdict in its favor." *Barhold v. Rodriguez*, 863 F.2d 233, 236 (2d Cir.1988) (citation omitted).

The DoD contends that the district court improperly granted the plaintiffs' motion for summary judgment. We agree. The plaintiffs' affidavits and evidence fail to make a sufficient showing that the DoD does not have a rational basis for its expanded security investigation of homosexuals or that there is a genuine issue of material fact for trial. *Celotex*, 477 U.S. at 322–23. Nor have the plaintiffs offered "any significant probative evidence tending to support [their] complaint." *Anderson*, 477 U.S. at 256 (quotation omitted).

The plaintiff's first point to the inability of the DoD to find any evidence tending to show that homosexual applicants for clearances have "succumbed to blackmail," "failed to safeguard classified information," or that as a class are a "worse security risk" than heterosexual applicants. Plaintiffs' Brief Supporting Motion for Summary Judgment at 3.

Under a rational basis review as promulgated by the Supreme Court in *Cleburne*, the DoD is not required to conclusively establish that homosexuals have transmitted classified information for its policy of subjecting homosexual applicants to expanded investigations to be constitutional. The DoD need only show a rational basis for its policy and that its policy is rationally related to the legitimate governmental interest of protecting classified material for it to be constitutional. *Cleburne*, 473 U.S. at 440.

Next, the plaintiffs suggest that other "governmental evidence" conclusively demonstrates that homosexuals do not pose a security risk. Relying on the April 1985 hearings before the Senate Permanent Subcommittee on Investigations, the plaintiffs point out that of forty espionage cases, only two involved homosexuals, neither of which involved a blackmail attempt.

The report the plaintiffs refer to consists of unclassified summaries of a limited number of espionage cases involving individuals who have been convicted of compromising United States classified information. Federal Government Security Programs, 1985: Hearings Before the Permanent Subcomm. on Investigations of the Senate Comm. on Governmental Affairs, 99th Cong., 1st Sess. 99–166 (1985) (DIA report). Although these case studies involve actual circumstances where DoD and DoD-related classified information was compromised, the report is not a study of all the significant espionage cases involving homosexuals. Moreover, one of the reported cases points out that homosexuals are targeted by the KGB:

> [He] was a homosexual and this fact interested the KGB handlers since the homosexual frequently is shunned by society and made to feel like a social outcast. Such a personality may seek to retaliate against a society that has placed him in this unenviable position. [He] was such a person and one of his first assignments on behalf of Soviet Intelligence was to spot other homosexuals in the American Community.

Id. at 916.

The plaintiffs' next contention is that their "factual study," illustrating that only two of the nineteen homosexual applicants for security clearance subjected to the expanded investigations were denied security clearances, conclusively establishes that homosexuals who limit their sexual activity to consenting adults in private are a good security risk. This contention is meritless. The plaintiffs' "factual study" of nineteen applications is not a large enough sample of homosexual applicants for security clearances to be able to draw such a broad conclusion. Even if the plaintiffs' contention had merit, it would take an expanded investigation of all homosexual applicants to determine which ones limit their sexual activities to consenting adults.

The plaintiffs' last contention is that the DoD "is more concerned with punishing homosexual clearance applicants than with treating them rationally regarding blackmail." In support, the plaintiffs rely on the deposition of Richard Olinger, former Manager of the Government Security Department at Lockheed Missiles and Space Company, in which Mr. Olinger responded to questions about the subject matter of two conferences he attended during his tenure with Lockheed. According to the plaintiffs, since homosexuality was not discussed at these two conferences on industrial security programs, the DoD has no "real" concern about homosexuals as security risks.

The plaintiffs' conclusion is without merit. A review of the deposition reveals that one of the conferences attended by Mr. Olinger concerned a specific espionage case and the other conference involved a discussion of statistical matters on processing security clearances. Given the limited agenda of these two conferences, it is apparent that the security risk of homosexuals would not be discussed.

We are convinced the DoD has met its burden of persuasion under *Celotex* by demonstrating that its investigatory policies and procedures for homosexuals are rationally related to permissible ends, and that the plaintiffs have failed to submit affirmative evidence to negate DoD's evidence. The DoD's justification for their policy of subjecting homosexual applicants to expanded investigations involves a two-step analyses: First, the DoD sought to establish that counterintelligence agencies target homosexuals; and, second, because homosexuals are targeted, the DoD subjects a homosexual applicant to an expanded investigation to determine if the applicant is susceptible to coercion or blackmail or otherwise vulnerable to counterintelligence efforts.

To establish that homosexuals are targeted by counterintelligence agencies, the DoD presented the following evidence. John Donnelly, Assistant Deputy Under Secretary of Defense for Counterintelligence and Security, who is directly responsible for ensuring that the Department's personnel security program remains responsive to the threats posed by hostile intelligence agencies, concluded that the recruitment of individuals by hostile intelligence agencies often involves the "exploitation of what those agencies consider to be human weaknesses, indiscretions and vices," and that with great consistency sexuality is considered a "potentially exploitable vulnerability." He states that hostile intelligence agencies attempt to segregate those with alcohol or drug problems, financial problems, a known disregard for security, and/or those who can be exploited sexually; and that although blackmail may sometimes be used after the person is already compromised, "generally the initial efforts of exploitation centers around enticing the targeted individual with money, sexual favors, treatment for alcoholism, etc." While he notes that this does not mean that hostile intelligence agencies always seek out homosexuals as targets, they usually spot individuals with the desired access and then assess them in order to determine the most effective approach.

Major Francis R. Short, USMC, Judge Advocate in the United States Marine Corps, who served as assistant trial counsel in the court-martial of Sergeant Clayton J. Lonetree, a marine convicted of espionage, stated that at the trial of Sergeant Lonetree, the court accepted Mr. John Barron of Annandale, Virginia as an expert in the field of the methods and operations of the Soviet Intelligence Service (the KGB), and that Mr. Barron testified as to KGB recruitment of homosexuals. Major Francis R. Short's Declaration in Support of DoD's Motion for New Trial.

Mr. Barron's testimony addressed the area of homosexuality on two occasions. While discussing the characteristics the KGB looks for in identifying potential targets for recruitment, he testified:

> *The KGB will attempt to identify those who are* ideologically sympathetic, experiencing career difficulties, unsuccessful in social relationships, *or experiencing problems with* narcotics, alcohol, *homosexuality*, or marital difficulties ... no one trait may be sufficient, and ... *the KGB is encouraged when these traits are found in combination.*

Barron also specifically cited an example of just such an entrapment operation, in which the KGB entrapped a Canadian ambassador to the Soviet Union through the exploitation of a homosexual relationship. The DoD also relies on Barron's book, *KGB: The Secret Work of Soviet Secret Agents* (1974), which states that "the KGB is not primarily interested in homosexuals because of their presumed susceptibility to blackmail. In its judgment, homosexuality often is accompanied by personality disorders that make the victim potentially unstable and vulnerable to adroit manipulation." *Id.* at 280.

The DoD also presented extracts of sworn statements of Sergeant Lonetree, provided by Lonetree to Special Agents of the Naval Investigative Service, relating one meeting with his Soviet control Sasha (later identified as Aleksei Yefimou, an officer of the KGB), where Sasha specifically inquired as to homosexuals:

> During a meeting with Sasha *he asked me to tell him who were the homosexuals*, drunks and people who were exploitable who worked in the embassy as civilians. *He also asked for other Marines ... who might be queers*, dopers or drunks.
>
> On at least one other occasion, "Sasha also wanted to know what marines had problems with alcohol or drugs *or those who were homosexual*."

Finally, the DoD relies on both plaintiff Dooling's admission that on one occasion someone attempted to blackmail him because of his sexual orientation, and Richard E. Fay, who described the 1979 Madsen espionage case involving the compromise of classified information by a homosexual.

B.

The DoD has determined what groups are targeted by hostile intelligence efforts. If an applicant falls within a targeted group—like homosexuals—the DoD subjects the applicant to an expanded investigation. The expanded investigation determines whether the applicant is susceptible to coercion or otherwise vulnerable to hostile intelligence efforts. See *Padula*, 822 F.2d at 104 ("criminalization of homosexual conduct coupled with the general public opprobrium toward homosexuality, [subjects] even 'open' homosexuals, to the risk of possible blackmail to protect their partners, if not themselves"); and *McKeand v. Laird*, 490 F.2d 1262 (9th Cir. 1973) (examiner found that McKeand feared disclosure of his homosexuality, thus a target for coercion).

Special deference must be given by the court to the Executive Branch when adjudicating matters involving their decisions on protecting classified information:

> Predictive judgment of this kind must be made by those with the necessary expertise.... The protection of classified information must be committed to the broad discretion of the agency responsible, and this must include broad discretion to determine who may have access to it.... Courts traditionally have been reluctant to intrude upon the authority of the Executive in military and national security affairs.

Department of Navy v. Egan, 484 U.S. 518, 108 S.Ct. 818, 825, 98 L.Ed.2d 918 (1988).

No one has the "right" to a security clearance. *Id.* at 824. We recognize that "the attempt to define not only the individual's future actions, but those of outside and unknown influences renders the 'grant or denial of security clearance ... an inexact science at best.' " *Id.* at 825 (*quoting Adams v. Laird*, 136 U.S. App. D.C. 388, 420 F.2d 230, 239 (D.C. Cir. 1969), *cert. denied*, 397 U.S. 1039, 25 L.Ed.2d 650, 90 S.Ct. 1360

(1970)). Inexact science or not the DoD has articulated a rational relationship between their policy of subjecting homosexual applicants to expanded investigations and its compelling interest in national security.[83] *id.* at 825 ("an agency head who must bear the responsibility for the protection of classified information committed to his custody should have the final say in deciding whether to repose his trust in an employee who has access to such information") (quotation omitted).

Since the DoD has met its initial burden of production, by negating an essential element of the plaintiffs' claim, the burden of production shifted to the plaintiffs to "produce evidentiary materials that demonstrate the existence of a 'genuine issue' for trial." *Celotex*, 477 U.S. at 331 (Brennan, J., dissenting). Thus, it was up to the plaintiffs to meet the issue that the expanded investigations were not, in fact, rationally related to national security concerns.

We conclude that the plaintiffs' affidavits do not raise genuine issues as to any fact material to the alleged constitutional violation, but merely raise an issue as to the alleged irrationality of the KGB's opinion on homosexual behavior. The plaintiffs' evidence is not material to the DoD's basis for expanded investigations of homosexual applicants—that homosexuals are targeted by counterintelligence agencies. *See Anderson*, 477 U.S. at 248 (only disputes over the outcome of the suit under the governing law will properly preclude entry of summary judgment).

For example, the plaintiffs rely on a resolution of the American Psychological Association which states that homosexuality "implies no impairment in judgment, stability, reliability or general social or vocational capabilities." Resolution of American Psychological Association (January 1975). According to the plaintiffs, the "KGB's obsolete opinions on homosexual behavior" should be rejected in favor of adopting the position of the American Psychological Association. However, the counterintelligence agencies' reasons for targeting homosexuals—even if based on continuing ignorance or prejudice—are irrelevant. If hostile intelligence efforts are directed at homosexuals, the DoD must be assured that because of the targeting, the individual will not compromise national secrets.

The Preliminary Joint Staff Study on Protection of National Secrets (October 25, 1985) relied upon by the plaintiffs also fails to raise a genuine issue for trial. The paper outlines an alternative approach to the current national security procedures and does not discuss the current operations of hostile intelligence efforts.

Accordingly, the district court erred in denying the DoD's motion for summary judgment.

. . .

83. The DoD advances other justifications for its policy: a homosexual may be emotionally unstable and homosexual conduct may be criminal. Because we conclude that the targeting of homosexuals by hostile intelligence agencies is a legitimate if not compelling justification for the expanded investigations, we need not address these additional justifications.

VI.

Conclusion

We reverse the part of the district court's order granting summary judgment to the plaintiffs, vacate the part denying summary judgment to the DoD, and remand to the District Court for the entry of summary judgment in favor of the DoD, and for reversal of the district court's award of attorneys' fees to the plaintiffs.

QUINN v. NASSAU COUNTY POLICE DEP'T

53 F.Supp.2d 347 (E.D.N.Y. 1999)

HON. ARTHUR D. SPATT, UNITED STATES DISTRICT JUDGE.

The plaintiff, a homosexual man and a former Nassau County police officer, claims that his fellow police officers and supervisors embarked on a vicious campaign of harassment against him because of his sexual orientation, in violation of 42 U.S.C. Sections 1983 and 1985. During a three-week jury trial, the plaintiff testified that approximately a year after he joined the police force in 1986, other officers learned he was gay and over a nine-year period, tormented him with pornographic cartoons and photographs, anti-gay remarks, and barbaric "pranks." The plaintiff further testified that his supervisors at the police department knew of the harassment but did nothing to stop it, and that some supervisors even joined in the harassment. The jury awarded him the total sum of $380,000 in compensatory and punitive damages.

. . .

While this opinion addresses several issues, the central question confronting the Court is whether government employees who are homosexual may be singled out for discrimination and abuse in the workplace because of their sexual orientation. In the Court's view, the United States Constitution and the provisions of 42 U.S.C. § 1983, combined with logic, common sense, and fairness dictate the answer: individuals have a constitutional right under the Equal Protection Clause to be free from sexual orientation discrimination causing a hostile work environment in public employment.

I.

Background

... The plaintiff, James M. Quinn ("Quinn" or the "plaintiff"), a former Nassau County Police Officer, initiated this action under 42 U.S.C. Sections 1983 and 1985 against the Nassau County Police Department (the "Police Department"), Nassau County Police Commissioner Donald Kane ("Kane" or the "Commissioner"), his former supervisors Lieutenant Edward Gonzalez ("Gonzalez"), Deputy Chief Daniel Lishansky ("Lishansky''), Sergeant John Ryan (''Ryan''), Lieutenant Joseph Allen (''Allen''), and his former coworker, Police Officer Phillip Rice (''Rice'').

Quinn began working as a police officer for the Nassau County Police Department in 1986. Quinn testified that he learned to keep his sexual orientation to himself during his first days of training at the Police Academy, after his supervisors ''snickered'' when discussing homosexuals during a ''sensitivity training'' workshop. From then on, Quinn vowed to keep his sexual orientation hidden from his colleagues.

However, his secret was revealed on July 4, 1987, when police officers from the First Precinct, where Quinn was assigned, arrested an assistant district attorney for engaging in homosexual sex in public. The assistant district attorney told the arresting officers that Quinn, too, was gay. Following this revelation, and until he left the force in 1996, Quinn testified that he was ridiculed, humiliated, abused and, singled-out because of his sexual orientation.

For example, fellow officers regularly and frequently posted cartoons about Quinn from the time he was unwillingly ''outed'' through January 1995, when he was transferred to another precinct. At least 19 of these cartoons were put into evidence at the trial. In the cartoons, Quinn is depicted and labeled a homosexual, a child-molester, a transvestite and a sadomasochist. On repeated occasions, Quinn found such cartoons slipped into the pages of the Police Car Book, a book which the officers maintained in the patrol cars for the purpose of leaving official messages and advice for their colleagues.

These cartoons were posted prominently on the bulletin board located in the ''32 Room,'' which many witnesses described as the central hub of the First Precinct. At trial, defendant Rice admitted that he created many of these cartoons. In Rice's opinion, the cartoons were just ''silly stuff'' he created to try and relieve the ''stress and tension'' of being a police officer. Rice attempted to defend himself by explaining that he treated everyone unfairly, and that ''everyone'' was made ''fun of'' on the 32 Room bulletin board.

In addition to the cartoons, Quinn testified about other anti-gay incidents at the First Precinct. Fellow officers hid his uniform and equipment. His colleagues put rocks in the hub caps of his police car so that criminals would hear his noisy approach. On one occasion, Quinn found a night stick in his patrol car with the words ''P.O. Quinn's dildo'' carved into the stick.

Quinn testified that his supervising officers were aware of this harassment, ignored it, and refused to take any action to discourage future occurrences. Rice supported Quinn's testimony in this respect, and told the jury that no supervisor ever asked him to stop making the cartoons about Quinn or to remove these items from the 32 Room bulletin board, even though supervisors ''probably'' saw them and laughed at them. Rice agreed that his cartoons about Quinn were an accepted practice at the precinct.

... Quinn also told the jury that he was treated differently from his fellow officers with regard to the manner in which his superiors "over-supervised" him. Specifically, Quinn alleged that supervisors such as Ryan and Allen would unfairly criticize him, nit-pick his work, and direct him to rewrite his paperwork without any valid reason. Sergeant Ryan also would "ride" many of Quinn's calls, meaning that he would personally follow and observe Quinn responding to calls and performing his official duties. Lishansky testified that this was uncommon. According to Ryan and Allen, they treated Quinn in this manner because of his work performance and repeated lateness.

There was evidence of actual knowledge of this systematic harassment by Quinn's supervisors. On several occasions, Quinn complained to Precinct Commander Lishansky about Ryan and Allen "over-supervising" him. In response, Lishansky asked the supervisors to "cut him some slack," and at one point changed Quinn's squad so that he would only periodically have to work with Allen. In addition, Quinn wrote a letter to Police Commissioner Kane complaining of "unfair treatment and harassment." The Commissioner concededly took no action with regard to the plaintiff's complaint.

Quinn told the jury that the harassment accelerated when, on or about January 20, 1995, he became the target of a baseless investigation by the Internal Affairs Unit of the Nassau County Police Department, resulting in his involuntary transfer to the Fourth Precinct, the furthest precinct from his home. During this investigation, Quinn's car was followed by shifts of unmarked police cars. Notwithstanding this intensive investigation, to this date, no formal charges ever were filed against Quinn.

According to Quinn, soon after his transfer, members of the First Precinct spread the word to the Fourth Precinct officers that they should "watch out for Quinn." Quinn alleges that his mistreatment continued at the Fourth Precinct.

On about May 29, 1995, Quinn was involuntarily transferred on a "temporary" basis—and eventually on a permanent basis—from the Fourth Precinct to the less proactive Court Liaison Office. The plaintiff eventually left the police force in December 1996, due to a line-of-duty back injury. When the plaintiff ended his employment, the Police Department refused to grant him termination pay, which is provided to officers upon completion of employment. He was not given his termination pay because of the pending "charges" against him. As stated above, these "charges" are still pending, and may never be resolved.

Based on this factual scenario, substantially conceded by the defendants, Quinn raised the following causes of action: (1) Section1983/Equal Protection; (2) Section 1983/First Amendment; and (3) Section 1985/Conspiracy. The Court dismissed the Section 1983 First Amendment claim and submitted the Section 1983 Equal Protection claim and the 1985

Conspiracy claim to the jury. The jury returned a special verdict, with the following express findings:

> The plaintiff proved that, after June 6, 1994 (within the statute of limitations period): (1) the members and supervisors of the Nassau County Police Department committed discriminatory acts demonstrating an ongoing policy or practice of sexual orientation discrimination against the plaintiff; and (2) the members and supervisors of the Nassau County Police Department committed specific and related instances of sexual orientation discrimination against the plaintiff, condoned by the supervisors of the Nassau County Police Department.
>
> The plaintiff proved that in the Nassau County Police Department during the period in question, there was a custom, policy or decision to permit sexual orientation harassment.
>
> The plaintiff proved that he was subjected to severe or pervasive unwelcome harassment by members and/or supervisors of the Nassau County Police Department, that the harassment complained of was based on his sexual orientation, and that the claimed harassment had the effect of unreasonably interfering with his work performance and created an intimidating, hostile, or offensive work environment for him.
>
> The plaintiff did not prove that Police Commissioner Donald Kane and Daniel Lishansky knew of the sexual orientation harassment of the plaintiff but did nothing to stop it.
>
> The plaintiff did not prove that the defendant Lieutenant Joseph Allen participated in the sexual orientation harassment of the plaintiff, but did prove that Allen knew of the sexual orientation harassment of the plaintiff and did nothing to stop it.
>
> The plaintiff did not prove that defendant Edward Gonzalez, a Lieutenant in the Fourth Precinct, participated in the sexual orientation harassment of the plaintiff.
>
> The plaintiff proved that defendant Sergeant John Ryan participated in the sexual orientation harassment of the plaintiff, and that he knew of the sexual orientation harassment of the plaintiff but did nothing to stop it.
>
> The plaintiff proved that two or more of the individual defendants in this case were involved in a conspiracy with a purpose to harass the plaintiff because of his sexual orientation; that the action of the defendants in the conspiracy were motivated, in whole or in part, by a disliking or hateful discriminatory attitude toward homosexuals; and that Rice, Allen and Ryan were knowing members of the conspiracy.
>
> The jury awarded Quinn the following: (1) $250,000 for emotional distress; $60,000 for loss of termination pay; (2) $30,000 in punitive damages against defendant Rice; (3) $20,000 in punitive damages

against defendant Allen; and (4) $20,000 in punitive damages against defendant Ryan.

II.

Discussion

. . .

B. Section 1983/Equal Protection

Section 1983 provides, in relevant part:

> Every person who, under color [of law] ... subjects, or causes to be subjected, any citizen of the United States ... to the deprivation of any rights, privileges, or immunities secured by the Constitution and laws, shall be liable to the party injured in an action at law, suit in equity, or other proper proceeding for redress.

42 U.S.C. § 1983. This statute furnishes a cause of action for the violation of federal rights created by the Constitution. See *Chapman v. Houston Welfare Rights Org.*, 441 U.S. 600, 617, 60 L.Ed.2d 508, 99 S.Ct. 1905 (1979). Therefore, a Section 1983 claim has two essential elements: (1) the defendant acted under color of state law; and (2) as a result of the defendant's actions, the plaintiff suffered a denial of his federal statutory rights, or his constitutional rights or privileges....

1. "Under Color of State Law" Element of a Section 1983 Claim

As a threshold issue, the Court must address the first of the two elements of a Section 1983 claim, namely, whether the individual defendants acted "under color of state law."

In the Court's view, "there can be no question that defendants [Donald Kane, the Commissioner of the Nassau County Police Department; Lieutenant Edward Gonzalez; Deputy Chief Daniel Lishansky; Sergeant John Ryan; and Lieutenant Joseph Allen] are, in their personal capacities, amenable to suit under [§ 1983], inasmuch as they were conducting themselves as supervisors for a public employer and thus were acting under color of state law." *Annis v. County of Westchester*, 36 F.3d 251, 253–55 (2d Cir. 1994)(*citing Carrero v. New York City Hous. Auth.*, 890 F.2d 569, 577 [2d Cir. 1989]).

The more difficult question arises with respect to Police Officer Rice, the self-anointed "roaster" who takes credit for creating many of the abusive and harassing materials at issue. Rice asserts that he was not acting "under color of state law" in creating these materials but, rather, was merely "making fun of homosexuals on a non-official bulletin board located at the Precinct." (Defendant Rice's Unpaginated Mem. of Law dated May 12, 1999 at 1). He maintains that his harassment of Quinn, no matter how crude and constant, was "a private act." The Court is constrained to agree.

The Supreme Court has stated that the traditional definition of acting under color of state law requires that the defendant in a § 1983 action have exercised power "possessed by virtue of state law and made possible only because the wrongdoer is clothed with the authority of state law." *West v. Atkins*, 487 U.S. 42, 49, 101 L.Ed.2d 40, 108 S.Ct. 2250 (1988) (*quoting United States v. Classic*, 313 U.S. 299, 326, 85 L.Ed. 1368, 61 S.Ct. 1031 [1941]).

... Turning to the facts of this case, the Court finds, as a matter of law, that Rice was only a co-employee of the plaintiff and was not acting "under color of state law." Quinn has not alleged or proven that Rice had any supervisory role or authority over his employment. Accordingly, Quinn fails to state a claim against Rice under 42 U.S.C. § 1983, and Rice's motion for a judgment as a matter of law dismissing the Section 1983 cause of action as against him is granted.

2. *Denial of Equal Protection Element of a Section 1983 Claim*

Having addressed the "color of state law" element of a Section 1983 claim, the Court addresses the second element, namely, the showing that as a result of the defendants' actions, the plaintiff suffered a denial of his Equal Protection rights.

a. Elements of an Equal Protection Violation

Generally speaking, the Equal Protection Clause of the Fourteenth Amendment directs state actors to treat similarly situated people alike. To establish an Equal Protection violation, a plaintiff must prove purposeful discrimination directed at an identifiable or suspect class. *See Giano v. Senkowski*, 54 F.3d 1050, 1057 (2d Cir. 1995). As the Second Circuit explained in *FSK Drug Corp. v. Perales*, 960 F.2d 6, 10 (2d Cir. 1992)("FSK"), an Equal Protection violation based upon selective application of a facially lawful state regulation is properly found when: (1) the person, compared with others similarly situated, was selectively treated; and (2) the selective treatment was motivated by an intention to discriminate on the basis of impermissible considerations, such as race or religion, to punish or inhibit the exercise of constitutional rights, or by a malicious or bad faith intent to injure the person....

b. Harassment in the Public Workplace as an Equal Protection Violation

One manifestation of impermissible selective treatment is employment discrimination in the public workplace. For example, it is well-settled in this Circuit that "sex discrimination [by a government employer] is covered by § 1983 [as an Equal Protection violation]." *Annis*, 36 F.3d at 254.

... In *Annis* and subsequent cases, the Second Circuit provided guidance regarding the extent to which sexual harassment equals sex discrimination for purposes of Section 1983, and looked to Title VII for guidance in resolving such claims.... The Second Circuit instructed in *Annis*, a case involving sex discrimination involving a female police officer, that "while we do not subscribe to a categorical view that sexual harassment equals sex discrimination, we do agree that harassment that transcends coarse, hostile, and boorish behavior can rise to the level of a constitutional tort."

... With respect to sexual harassment, a District Court in this Circuit has noted that "creating abusive conditions for female employees and not for male employees is discrimination [under § 1983.]" *Osier v. Broome County*, 47 F.Supp.2d 311, 1999 U.S. Dist., 1999 WL 304683, (N.D.N.Y. 1999)(*quoting Bohen v. City of East Chicago*, Indiana, 799 F.2d at 1185). The District Court remarked that a plaintiff can make an ultimate showing of sex discrimination either by showing that sexual harassment that is attributable to the employer under § 1983 amounted to intentional sex discrimination or by showing that the conscious failure of the employer to protect the plaintiff from the abusive conditions created by fellow employees amounted to intentional discrimination." *Id.* (*citing Bohen*, 799 F.2d at 1187; Gierlinger v. New York State Police, 15 F.3d at 34). In this context, Section 1983 liability can be imposed upon individual employers, or responsible supervisors, for failing properly to investigate and address allegations of sexual harassment when through this failure, the conduct becomes an accepted custom or practice of the employer." *Gierlinger v. New York State Police,* 15 F.3d at 34 (*citing Bohen v. City of East Chicago, Ind.*, 799 F.2d at 1189).

c. *Sexual Orientation Harassment as an Equal Protection Violation*

In the Court's view, harassment in the public workplace against homosexuals based on their sexual orientation falls within the ambit of *Annis* and its progeny. Just as *Annis* recognized that harassment of women in the public workplace that transcends coarse, hostile, and boorish behavior can rise to the level of a constitutional tort, so too, in the Court's view, does a hostile work environment directed against homosexuals based on their sexual orientation constitute an Equal Protection violation.

In so finding, the Court notes that in 1996, the Supreme Court struck down, on Equal Protection Clause grounds, a state constitutional amendment categorically prohibiting gay men and lesbians from obtaining state or local legal protection from discrimination based on their sexual orientation. *See Romer v. Evans*, 517 U.S. 620, 134 L.Ed.2d 855, 116 S.Ct. 1620 (1996). The *Romer* Court established that government discrimination against homosexuals, in and of itself, violates the Equal Protection Clause. *Romer,* 517 U.S. at 633–34.

In *Romer,* the issue before the Supreme Court was whether an amendment to Colorado's state constitution, which prohibited any legislation or judicial action designed to protect the status of a person based on sexual orientation, violated the Fourteenth Amendment's Equal Protection Clause. The Supreme Court had little difficulty finding that it did. The Court noted that under the ordinary deferential Equal Protection standard—that is, the "rational basis standard"—the Court would "insist on knowing the relation between the classification adopted and the object to be obtained." *Id.* at 632.

... Under the above cases, and viewing the proof in a light most favorable to Quinn, the plaintiff has introduced more than sufficient evidence to support a claim for an Equal Protection violation based on a workplace environment that transcended hostile, coarse, and boorish behavior, and which was motivated by an invidious, irrational fear and prejudice towards homosexuals. Section 1983 liability can be imposed upon the employer, the Nassau County Police Department, and the remaining defendant supervisors, for failing to properly investigate and address Quinn's complaints, and permitting the acts of harassment which the supervisors either observed or themselves perpetrated. In this case, a jury reasonably could find all of these facts. A jury of reasonable persons could conclude that "through the [supervisors'] failures and actions, the [harassing] conduct [became] an accepted custom or practice of the employer." *Gierlinger v. New York State Police*, 15 F.3d at 34 (citing *Bohen v. City of East Chicago, Ind.*, 799 F.2d at 1189). Like the enactment at issue in *Romer*, conduct by police department officers, supervisors and policy makers contributing to, failing to address, and outright condoning harassment of homosexuals amounts to impermissible "status-based [conduct and policy] divorced from any factual context from which we could discern a relationship to legitimate state interests." *Romer*, 517 U.S. at 635. Such harassment by Nassau County Police Department personnel cannot survive a rational basis review when it is motivated by irrational fear and prejudice towards homosexuals. *See, e.g., Able*, 155 F.3d at 634–35 (*citing City of Cleburne*, 473 U.S. at 448). The "inevitable inference" from Quinn's mistreatment is that it was "born of animosity toward the class of persons affected," *Romer*, 517 U.S. at 634, namely, homosexuals.

The Court disagrees with the defendants' contention that Quinn's claims are barred under the recent opinion by a Judge in this District in *Simonton v. Runyon*, 50 F.Supp.2d 159, 1999 WL 345956 (E.D.N.Y. 1999). In *Simonton*, the District Court granted the defendants' motion to dismiss the Title VII complaint of a former employee of the United States Postal Service, who alleged a hostile work environment stemming from mistreatment he allegedly received from co-workers and supervisors based upon his sexual orientation. The District Court held that Title VII does not provide a cause of action for harassment or discrimination based upon sexual orientation, reasoning that such conduct is not discrimination "based upon sex," is not otherwise included in the statute, and therefore, does not state a claim under Title VII. *Simonton*, 1999 WL 345956.

... In this Court's view, the District Court's decision in *Simonton*, while well-written and thoughtful, is not controlling, because it was in the context of Title VII, not Section 1983. Title VII expressly defines those classes of people which fall under its protection, and states that discrimination in employment is prohibited against "any individual ... because of such individual's race, color, religion, sex or national origin." 42 U.S.C. § 2000e–2(a)(1). This Court need not address the issue whether discrimination "because of sex" under Title VII encompasses discrimination "because of sexual orientation." The Equal Protection Clause of the Fourteenth Amendment is not so limited by express category. On the contrary, as noted above, the Equal Protection Clause protects similarly situated individuals from invidious and irrational discrimination based on sexual orientation.

Accordingly, the Court denies the remaining defendants' motions for judgment as a matter of law dismissing the Section 1983/Equal Protection claim. . . .

IV. DISCRIMINATION INVOLVING TRANSGENDERED PERSONS

GLENN v. BRUMBY

724 F. Supp. 2d. 1284 (N.D. Ga. 2010)*

RICHARD W. STORY, DISTRICT JUDGE.

[Parties on both sides made various summary judgment motions.]

Background

Plaintiff's Gender Identity Disorder

Plaintiff Vandiver Elizabeth Glenn was born a biological male [hereafter, Glenn is referred to as she or her based on her gender identification]. Since puberty, Glenn has had a deep persistent awareness that she is a woman. In early 2005, Glenn was diagnosed with gender identity disorder ("GID"). . . .

The World Professional Association for Transgender Health ("WPATH") recommends a triadic therapeutic protocol for the treatment of GID, which includes: 1) hormone therapy; 2) a real-life experience ("RLE") by living full-time as a member of the new gender; and 3) sex reassignment surgeries. Starting in 2005, Glenn began to take steps to transition from male to female under the supervision of health care providers. Plaintiff underwent electrolysis to remove facial hair, began hormone therapy to make her body more feminine and suppress testosterone, and also began living as a woman outside of the workplace. In April 2006, Plaintiff underwent surgical procedures, including a brow lift, liposuction, and narrowing of her jaw line in order to appear more feminine.

In the Spring of 2006, Plaintiff began a therapist-client relationship with Dr. Erin Swenson, a licensed marriage and family therapist with a Ph.D. in psychological services. In 2006, Glenn was also diagnosed by Dr. Swenson as having GID. In her expert report she states that in the years leading up to Glenn's therapy for GID, Glenn experienced clinical depression, at times severe enough to put her at risk of suicide. Dr. Swenson is

* Note: Throughout this edited opinion, citations to the court record have been omitted.

of the opinion that if Glenn were unable to secure treatment for GID the depression would reemerge and significantly impair her ability to work or properly function socially.

During the course of therapy, Dr. Swenson recommended that it would be appropriate for Glenn to commence the real-life experience by living full-time as a woman. Dr. Swenson's report notes that the successful completion of RLE is a prerequisite to sex reassignment surgery. Dr. Swenson states that RLE is central to the treatment of individuals with severe GID and requires at least a year of living full time in the preferred gender expression. RLE would ideally provide the individual with psychological relief, and Dr. Swenson observed that Glenn's transition to this point has provided her with significant psychological relief. Plaintiff has not, as of yet, undergone sex reassignment surgery.

Plaintiff's Employment

In October 2005, Plaintiff, then known as Glenn Morrison and presenting as a man, was hired as an editor by the Georgia General Assembly's Office of Legislative Counsel ("OLC"). In order to be hired as an editor in the OLC, Glenn had to take a test on grammar, spelling, proofreading, and vocabulary. She did very well on the test and was recommended for the position by Beth Yinger, the senior editor. The OLC is responsible for drafting bills for legislators, code revision, and publication of the Georgia session laws. The staff of the OLC, at all times relevant to this action, included approximately eleven attorneys, eight computer terminal operators, five editors, an office manager, an assistant office manager, and an administrative assistant. Defendant Sewell Brumby is the head of the OLC and the chief legal counsel for the Georgia legislature. Brumby has worked in the OLC continuously since 1978 and in his current position is responsible for OLC personnel decisions.

In 2006, Glenn informed her direct supervisor, Beth Yinger, that she was transgender and was in the process of becoming a woman. However, during the time that Plaintiff worked at OLC she presented as a man on every day but one. On October 31, 2006 (Halloween), Glenn came to work presenting as a woman. When Brumby saw her, he told her that her appearance was not appropriate and asked her to leave the office. Brumby deemed her appearance inappropriate "[b]ecause he was a man dressed as a woman and made up as a woman." Brumby stated that "it's unsettling to think of someone dressed in women's clothing with male sexual organs inside that clothing," and that a male in women's clothing is "unnatural." Following this incident, Brumby met with Yinger to discuss Glenn's appearance on Halloween 2006 and was informed by Yinger that Glenn intended to undergo a gender transition. Brumby took no adverse employment action against Glenn at that time, and in the months following Halloween 2006, Glenn came to work presenting as a man.

In the fall of 2007, Glenn informed Yinger that she was ready to proceed with gender transition and would begin coming to work as a woman and was also changing her legal name. She gave Yinger written materials about GID and photographs of herself presenting as a woman. Yinger notified Brumby of Plaintiff's intent and provided him with the written materials and photographs that Glenn had given her. Brumby read the written materials and stated that they "were supportive of the proposition that people should be able to change their sex within the workplace ... and advocated for that proposition and included what I guess you might say are talking points about how such a transition might best be facilitated." Brumby subsequently informed Yinger that he was going to fire Glenn because she was transitioning from a man to a woman.

III. *Plaintiff's Termination*

Brumby believed that Glenn's intent to transition while employed at OLC could potentially cause adverse consequences. At the time of the termination Brumby was aware that gender transition was considered to be a form of medical treatment for a health condition and that counseling was a component of the transition. He also understood that gender transition entailed assuming the dress and grooming habits of the opposite sex. Before terminating Glenn, Brumby conducted legal research to determine the legality of firing her based upon her gender transition and also had another OLC attorney, Marie Story, do the same. He concluded that some authority indicated that terminating an employee for undergoing gender transition was illegal, but some authority indicated that such firings are permissible.

Brumby also contacted a few legislators and employees of OLC to solicit their opinions on the matter. He spoke with Glenn Richardson, then Speaker of the Georgia House of Representatives. Speaker Richardson told Brumby that it should be Brumby's decision on how to handle the situation. Brumby also spoke with Lieutenant Governor Casey Cagle's Chief of Staff, Bradley Alexander, who shared the information with Lieutenant Governor Cagle. Brumby also asked Story and another OLC attorney what they and their fellow OLC employees would think about working with an individual undergoing a gender transition, but neither offered an opinion.

In their pre-termination conversation, Alexander asked Brumby if Glenn had any job performance issues or whether she was being let go for "the transgender reason." Brumby responded that the termination was not performance-based and was because of the gender transition. Yinger, Glenn's immediate supervisor, found Glenn's work product to be "about average" and did not think she should be fired.

On October 16, 2007, Brumby called Glenn to his office. Once Glenn arrived, Brumby asked her if she "had formed a fixed intention to [become] a woman." She answered that she had. Brumby then informed her that she was being terminated. Brumby told Glenn that the reasons for her termination were that Glenn's intended gender transition was inappropriate, that it would be disruptive, that some people would view it as a moral issue, and that it would make Glenn's coworkers uncomfortable. Brumby was not concerned about whether Glenn's presentation as a woman would appear professional. Further, he stated that some legislators would view the transition as immoral and unnatural, and might lose confidence in the OLC if he did not fire her. Other concerns that Brumby states he had at the time include potential lawsuits resulting from Glenn's restroom usage and that her transition, as it evidenced instability in her life, might cause Glenn to violate the confidentiality of the OLC's work.

Brumby stated during the meeting that he would explore any compromises that Glenn might suggest. Plaintiff contends that such an offer was illusory because Brumby had identified Plaintiff's gender transition as the reason for her termination and therefore Plaintiff did not feel that there was any accommodation she could offer. Plaintiff maintains that Brumby did not think Plaintiff could transition and continue to work at OLC. Brumby stated that "the sheer fact of [Glenn's gender] transition ... seemed to me impossible to accomplish in our workplace in an appropriate manner. And since the sheer fact of it seemed impossible to achieve to me, I did not give consideration to how to best facilitate that which I believed to be impossible."

Plaintiff contends that Brumby's reasons for terminating her were either post hoc justifications or lack support in the record. Brumby has stated that he was concerned about lawsuits resulting from Plaintiff's restroom usage. Plaintiff maintains that Brumby never mentioned a concern about her bathroom use to her or anyone else at or before the time he fired her. Additionally, the OLC has four single-occupancy unisex bathrooms. Defendants note, however, that despite the presence of single-occupancy restrooms in the OLC, Glenn had access to the public multi-person women's restrooms on the first, second, and third floors of the Georgia Capitol Building, in which the OLC is located. Defendants also note that when presenting as a woman, Glenn uses women's restrooms. Plaintiff objects that this assertion is misleading because it relies on Plaintiff's response to an either/or deposition question that did not include the option of a single-occupancy restroom.

IV. *Plaintiff's Complaint*

Plaintiff filed a Complaint seeking declaratory and injunctive relief against Brumby, Richardson, Cagle, Eric Johnson, and Robyn J. Underwood, all in their official capacities. Plaintiff brings the action pursuant to 42 U.S.C. § 1983 for alleged violations of her rights under the Fourteenth Amendment of the U.S. Constitution. The Complaint asserts that "[o]n information and belief, Brumby consulted with Defendants Richardson, Cagle, and Johnson concerning Glenn's continued employment and a decision jointly was made to terminate her." The Complaint also asserts that Underwood signed the termination notice given to Glenn.

Plaintiff's first claim for relief is premised upon discrimination on the basis of sex. The Complaint alleges that by virtue of Plaintiff's sex, Plaintiff is a member of a particular and clearly identifiable group of people. Plaintiff contends that she did not conform to Defendants' sex stereotypes regarding males because of her appearance and behavior at the time of her employment with OLC and because of her intended future appearance and behavior and was terminated for this reason. Plaintiff asserts that in being discriminated against on the basis of sex, she was denied equal protection of the laws, was treated differently from other similarly situated individuals, and her firing bore no substantial relationship to any important government interest.

[Plaintiff's second claim for relief alleged that her constitutional rights under the Fourteenth Amendment were violated due to discrimination based on a medical condition.]

Discussion

I. Plaintiff's Motion for Dismissal

[After granting plaintiff's motion to dismiss the action with regard to Defendants Richardson, Cagle, Johnson, and Underwood, and dismissing these defendant's individual summary judgment motions as moot, the court turned to the remaining claims.] . . .

III. Remaining Motions for Summary Judgment

[A]ll of the Defendants filed a separate Motion for Summary Judgment. The Four Defendants have been dismissed, but the All Defendants' Motion is still before the Court because Defendant Brumby remains a party to this action. Also pending, is Plaintiff's Motion for Summary Judgment against Defendant Brumby. The Court now addresses these cross-motions for summary judgment. [The court laid out the standard for summary judgment.]

. . .

B. *Section 1983 and the Equal Protection Clause*

Plaintiff's claims are brought under 42 U.S.C. § 1983. Section 1983 is a statutory vehicle for addressing the violation of civil rights. It provides as follows:

> Every person who, under color of any statute, ordinance, regulation, custom, or usage, of any State or Territory or the District of Columbia, subjects, or causes to be subjected, any citizen of the United States or other person within the jurisdiction thereof to the deprivation of any rights, privileges, or immunities secured by the Constitution and laws, shall be liable to the party injured in an action at law, suit in equity, or other proper proceeding for redress . . . 42 U.S.C. § 1983. In a § 1983 action, a court must determine "whether the plaintiff has been deprived of a right secured by the Constitution and laws." *Baker v. McCollan,* 443 U.S. 137, 140, 99 S.Ct. 2689, 2692, 61 L.Ed.2d 433 (1979).

Plaintiff's two claims for relief are both based upon alleged violations of the Equal Protection Clause of the Fourteenth Amendment. Her first claim is for discrimination on the basis of sex, while her second claim is for discrimination on the basis of medical condition. The Equal Protection

Clause provides that "[n]o State shall ... deny to any person within its jurisdiction the equal protection of laws." U.S. Const. amend. XIV, § 1. "The central mandate of the equal protection guarantee is that '[t]he sovereign may not draw distinctions between individuals based solely on differences that are irrelevant to a legitimate governmental objective.' " *Lofton v. Sec'y of Dept. of Children and Family Svcs.*, 377 F.3d 1275, 1277 (11th Cir.2004) (*quoting Lehr v. Robertson,* 463 U.S. 248, 265, 103 S.Ct. 2985, 77 L.Ed.2d 614 (1983)). . . .

An equal protection claim must allege that the plaintiff is a member of an identifiable group, was subjected to differential treatment from others similarly situated, and the difference in treatment was based on his or her membership in that group. *See Pers. Adm'r of Mass. v. Feeney,* 442 U.S. 256, 279, 99 S.Ct. 2282, 60 L.Ed.2d 870 (1979). The purpose of this analysis is "[t]o maintain the focus on discrimination and to avoid constitutionalizing every state ... dispute." *Griffin Indus. v. Irvin,* 496 F.3d 1189, 1207 (11th Cir.2007). Plaintiff is a member of an identifiable group. For her sex discrimination claims she is a member of an identifiable group based upon her sex and for her second claim, she is a member of an identifiable group based upon her medical condition-GID. Plaintiff also alleges that she was similarly situated to the other employees of OLC, particularly the other editors, but that she was singled out for termination because of her sex and her medical condition.

In evaluating a claim based upon the Equal Protection Clause, the Supreme Court has applied three different levels of scrutiny, depending upon the basis of the classification. *Clark v. Jeter,* 486 U.S. 456, 461, 108 S.Ct. 1910, 100 L.Ed.2d 465 (1988). The Supreme Court noted that at a minimum, classifications must be rationally related to a legitimate government purpose. *Id.* Intermediate scrutiny is applied to classifications based upon sex or illegitimacy. *Id.* In order to withstand intermediate scrutiny, the classification must be substantially related to an important government objective. *Id.* The most exacting scrutiny is applied to classifications based on race or national origin and those affecting fundamental rights. *Id.* The Court now turns to the application of these principles to Plaintiff's claims.

C. *Plaintiff's Sex Discrimination Claim*

The Supreme Court has recognized that individuals have a right, protected by the Equal Protection Clause, to be free from discrimination on the basis of sex in public employment. *Davis v. Passman,* 442 U.S. 228, 234–35, 99 S.Ct. 2264, 60 L.Ed.2d 846 (1979). To establish a sex discrimination claim, a plaintiff must prove that he or she suffered purposeful or intentional discrimination on the basis of sex. *See Village of Arlington Heights v. Metro. Hous. Dev. Corp.,* 429 U.S. 252, 264–65, 97 S.Ct. 555, 50 L.Ed.2d 450 (1977) (proof of intent or purpose is required to show violation of Equal Protection Clause). The parties disagree as to whether firing Plaintiff for seeking to come to work presenting as a woman constitutes discrimination on the basis of sex.

i. Sex stereotyping

Plaintiff's claim is based upon sex stereotyping, as recognized by the Supreme Court in *Price Waterhouse v. Hopkins,* 490 U.S. 228, 109 S.Ct. 1775, 104 L.Ed.2d 268 (1989). In that case, Ann Hopkins, a senior manager in one of Price Waterhouse's offices, sued her employer after her candidacy for partnership was held for reconsideration and she was later not reproposed for partnership. *Id.* at 231–2, 109 S.Ct. 1775. She alleged that Price Waterhouse had discriminated against her on the basis of sex in its decision regarding partnership. *Id.* at 232, 109 S.Ct. 1775. Hopkins was denied partnership in the firm, in part, because she was considered "macho," and "overcompensated for being a woman." *Id.* at 235, 109 S.Ct. 1775. She was advised that she could improve her chances of becoming a partner if she would take "a course at charm school," "walk more femininely, talk more femininely, dress more femininely, wear make-up, have her hair styled, and wear jewelry." *Id.* Six members of the Supreme Court agreed that such comments were indicative of gender discrimination, holding that Title VII barred not just discrimination because of biological sex, but also sex stereotyping-that is failing to conform to stereotypes associated with one's biological sex. *Id.* at 250–51, 109 S.Ct. 1775 (plurality opinion of four Justices); *id.* at 258–61, 109 S.Ct. 1775 (White, J., concurring); *id.* at 272–73, 109 S.Ct. 1775 (O'Connor, J., concurring). The Court noted that "[a]s for the legal relevance of sex stereotyping, we are beyond the day when an employer could evaluate employees by assuming or insisting that they matched the stereotypes associated with their group." "A number of courts have relied on *Price Waterhouse* to expressly recognize a Title VII cause of action for discrimination based on an employee's failure to conform to stereotypical gender norms." *Etsitty v. Utah Transit Auth.,* 502 F.3d 1215, 1223 (10th Cir. 2007)....

This action is not the first in which an individual with GID has relied upon the sex-stereotyping theory of *Price Waterhouse* to assert a claim resulting from an adverse employment action. Several courts have recognized that a transsexual who alleges that he or she was subject to an adverse employment action for failing to conform to sex stereotypes concerning how an individual of that biological sex should look and behave have sufficiently plead claims of sex stereotyping and gender discrimination.... The Tenth Circuit assumed, without deciding, that such a claim is available, but determined that Plaintiff could not demonstrate that the stated reason for her termination was pretext. *Etsitty,* 502 F.3d at 1224.

In contrast, the court in *Oiler* explicitly rejected the theory that a transsexual can bring an employment discrimination claim based upon sex stereotyping resulting from their presentation as a member of the opposite sex. *Oiler v. Winn–Dixie La., Inc.,* No. Civ. A. 00–3114, 2002 WL 31098541 (E.D.La. Sept. 16, 2002). In reaching this conclusion, the court in *Oiler* relied upon a pre-*Price Waterhouse* Seventh Circuit case, and a series of similar cases that stand for the proposition that individuals discharged because they are transsexuals do not have cognizable claims under Title

VII for sex discrimination. *Oiler,* 2002 WL 31098541 at *3–4, *4 n. 51. This Court has also previously held that transsexuals are not a suspect classification. *Rush v. Johnson,* 565 F.Supp. 856, 868 (N.D.Ga.1983). The line of cases relied upon by the court in *Oiler* and this Court in *Rush* were addressed by the Sixth Circuit in its decision in *Smith.*

The Sixth Circuit noted that, "the approach in *Holloway, Sommers,* and *Ulane* ... has been eviscerated by *Price Waterhouse.*" *Smith,* 378 F.3d at 573 (citing *Schwenk,* 204 F.3d at 1201 ("The initial judicial approach taken in cases such as *Holloway* has been overruled by the logic and language of *Price Waterhouse.*")); *see also Kastl,* 325 Fed.Appx. at 493 (stating that post *Price Waterhouse* and *Schwenk* it is unlawful to discriminate against a transgender for failing to behave in accordance with an employer's expectations for men or women). The Sixth Circuit noted that this earlier jurisprudence denied transsexuals Title VII protection because they were considered victims of "gender" rather than "sex" discrimination. *Smith,* 378 F.3d at 573. However, the Supreme Court in *Price Waterhouse* "established that Title VII's reference to 'sex' encompasses both the biological differences between men and women, and gender discrimination, that is, discrimination based on a failure to conform to stereotypical gender norms." *Id.*

This Court concurs with the majority of courts that have addressed this issue, finding that discrimination against a transgendered individual because of their failure to conform to gender stereotypes constitutes discrimination on the basis of sex. The two circuits that have definitively addressed this question have reached the same conclusion. *See Kastl,* 325 Fed.Appx. at 493; *Smith,* 378 F.3d at 572, 575. This conclusion is not at odds with this Court's earlier decision in *Rush* that transsexuals are not a suspect class, and is the result of the logical application of the Supreme Court's reasoning in *Price Waterhouse.* While transsexuals are not members of a protected class based on sex, those who do not conform to gender stereotypes are members of a protected class based on sex. *See Price Waterhouse,* 490 U.S. at 251, 109 S.Ct. 1775 (stating "we are beyond the day when an employer could evaluate employees by assuming or insisting that they matched the stereotype associated with their group"). In reaching the same conclusion as this Court does today, the Sixth Circuit noted that some courts improperly "superimpose classifications such as 'transsexual' on a plaintiff, and then legitimize discrimination based on plaintiff's gender nonconformity by formalizing the non-conformity into an ostensibly unprotected classification." *Smith,* 378 F.3d at 577; *see also Lopez,* 542 F.Supp.2d at 653 ("[T]ranssexuality is not a bar to [a] sex stereotyping claim. Title VII is violated when an employer discriminates against any employee, transsexual or not, because he or she has failed to act or appear sufficiently masculine or feminine enough for an employer."). While Plaintiff has successfully asserted a claim based on sex, she must still demonstrate that Brumby's actions fail to survive the appropriate level of scrutiny.

ii. The merits of Plaintiff's sex discrimination claim.

To effectively make out an equal protection claim, Plaintiff must prove that she suffered purposeful or intentional discrimination on the basis of gender. *See Vill. of Arlington Heights,* 429 U.S. at 264–65, 97 S.Ct. 555. Discrimination based on gender, once proven, can only be tolerated if the state "demonstrate[s] an 'exceedingly persuasive justification' for that action." *United States v. Virginia,* 518 U.S. 515, 524, 116 S.Ct. 2264, 135 L.Ed.2d 735 (1996).

The overarching framework for this Court's analysis of Plaintiff's claim is the familiar one articulated by the Supreme Court in *McDonnell Douglas Corp. v. Green,* 411 U.S. 792, 93 S.Ct. 1817, 36 L.Ed.2d 668 (1973).... As the Eleventh Circuit has explained:

> Under the *McDonnell Douglas* framework, a plaintiff first must show an inference of discriminatory intent, and thus carries the initial burden of establishing a prima facie case of discrimination. The plaintiff's successful assertion of a prima facie case "creates a rebuttable presumption that the employer unlawfully discriminated against her." Second, if the plaintiff successfully demonstrates a prima facie case, the burden then shifts to the employer to produce evidence that its action was taken for a legitimate, non-discriminatory reason. We proceed to the third step of the analysis once the employer meets its burden of production by proffering a legitimate, non-discriminatory reason, thereby rebutting the presumption of discrimination, and "[our] inquiry 'proceeds to a new level of specificity,' in which the plaintiff must show that the proffered reason really is a pretext for unlawful discrimination." "Although the intermediate burdens of production shift back and forth, the ultimate burden of persuading the trier of fact that the employer intentionally discriminated against the employee remains at all times with the plaintiff."

Brooks v. County Comm'n of Jefferson County, Ala., 446 F.3d 1160, 1162 (11th Cir. 2006).

The Plaintiff has established a prima facie case of discrimination by showing an inference of discriminatory intent in her termination....

Plaintiff asserts that "[i]t is an undisputed fact that Brumby fired [her] not because of her work performance but because of her intention to begin presenting herself as a woman in the workplace." Brumby told Glenn that her termination was not performance-based, but was a result of her gender transition. Brumby stated in his deposition that the thought of someone with male sexual organs in women's clothing was "unsettling" to him, was "something I don't like to think about," and was something he viewed as "unnatural." Furthermore, he only fired Plaintiff after first confirming that she had reached a fixed decision to present as a woman in the workplace. Defendant argues that Plaintiff was terminated for undergoing a gender transition, not for a failure to conform to stereotypes of how a male should look or behave. First, Brumby has failed to identify any concerns that existed at the time of Plaintiff's termination not related to her intention to come to work as a woman. Second, in his Response to Plaintiff's Motion for Summary Judgment, Defendant appears to concede that Plaintiff's appearance was at least in part, a motivating factor behind her termination. This evidence is more than sufficient to establish a prima facie case of discriminatory intent. Plaintiff's desire to present as a woman at work did not comport with Brumby's stereotype of how a biological male should dress or behave. The burden now shifts to Brumby to produce evidence that his action was taken for a legitimate, nondiscriminatory reason.

Plaintiff having shown a prima facie case of discrimination, Defendant must "demonstrate an 'exceedingly persuasive justification'" for her termination. *Virginia,* 518 U.S. at 524, 116 S.Ct. 2264. Defendant may only satisfy the burden of intermediate scrutiny by "showing at least that the classification serves 'important governmental objectives and that the discriminatory means employed' are 'substantially related to the achievement of those objectives.'" *Miss. Univ. for Women v. Hogan,* 458 U.S. 718, 724, 102 S.Ct. 3331, 73 L.Ed.2d 1090 (1982) (citation omitted). Yet Defendant in its briefing does not even argue in the alternative that its actions survive intermediate scrutiny. Defendant based his entire defense on the argument that Plaintiff was not a member of a protected class and therefore his actions must only survive the rational relationship test. However, as discussed in Section III.C.i., Plaintiff has successfully asserted a claim for discrimination on the basis of sex, and sex is a suspect class entitled to intermediate scrutiny review. Defendant has failed to argue that its actions meet the appropriate standard. Nonetheless, because this action is currently before the Court on cross-motions for summary judgment, the Court will explore whether any of Defendants asserted reasons for terminating Plaintiff are substantially related to an important government interest.

Defendant asserts that one legitimate government purpose is the avoidance of lawsuits against the government. Defendant argues that Plaintiff's continued employment at OLC while presenting as a woman without undergoing genital reassignment surgery, could expose the government to suits for invasion of privacy or sexual harassment. Defendant argues that although there were single-occupancy restrooms available in the OLC office, Plaintiff was not required to use these and may have used the multi-person restrooms located elsewhere in the Georgia Capitol Building. When applying heightened scrutiny to sex discrimination claims, the government's "exceedingly persuasive" justification for gender classifications "must be genuine, not hypothesized or invented *post hoc* in response to litigation." *Virginia,* 518 U.S. at 533, 116 S.Ct. 2264. Additionally, "a tenable justification must describe actual state purposes, not rationalizations for actions in fact differently grounded." *Id.* at 535–36, 116 S.Ct. 2264. Brumby has not drawn the Court's attention to any evidence that he was concerned with Plaintiff's restroom usage, or discussed Plaintiff's restroom usage with her or anyone else before her termination. Therefore, since there is no evidence that this was an actual concern of Brumby in terminating Plaintiff, this asserted reason cannot survive the heightened scrutiny applicable to Plaintiff's sex discrimination claim.

The facts of this case are distinguishable from those present in *Etsitty* and *Kastl.* In *Etsitty,* the plaintiff, a bus driver for the transit authority and a biological male, was using female restrooms while on her bus route. 502 F.3d at 1219. Her supervisors expressed concern that the transit authority could incur liability if an employee with male genitalia was observed using a female restroom. *Id.* The transit authority felt that it was unable to accommodate plaintiff's restroom needs because she typically used restrooms along her routes rather than those at the transit authority facility. *Id.* The plaintiff was told that her termination "was based solely on her intent to use women's public restrooms while wearing a UTA uniform . . ." *Id.* at 1224. The Tenth Circuit found this to be a legitimate, nondiscriminatory reason for the plaintiff's termination under Title VII. *Id.* While the Tenth Circuit assumed that the plaintiff had shown a prima facie case of discrimination, it found that plaintiff did not present any evidence that the defendant's asserted rationale for the termination was pretext for discrimination. *Id.* at 1226. Similarly, in *Kastl,* the defendant had received complaints that a man was using the women's restroom and terminated the plaintiff for safety reasons. 325 Fed.Appx. at 493, 494. The Sixth Circuit found that the plaintiff had failed to satisfy the third prong of the *McDonnell Douglas* analysis because she could not show that the defendant's rationale for her termination was merely pretext.

In the present action, there is no evidence that Brumby was concerned about Plaintiff's restroom usage before he terminated her. This fact alone is enough to dismiss this asserted reason as a substantial government interest sufficient to withstand intermediate scrutiny. . . . Additionally, however, there is no evidence that Plaintiff ever used the female restrooms located within the Capitol Building while presenting as a woman, or ever intended to. There is also no evidence of any complaints concerning Plaintiff's restroom use. The facts of this action are more akin to the facts of *Lopez,* than either *Etsitty* or *Kastl.* The court in *Lopez* noted that there was no evidence that the plaintiff's bathroom use was a concern that motivated the defendant's decision to rescind the job offer. 542 F.Supp.2d at 664 n. 15. As is the case with the OLC office, the defendant in *Lopez* admitted "that the facility in which Lopez would have worked was equipped with a unisex restroom that she could have used with 'absolute privacy.'" *Id.* Brumby's asserted concern over Plaintiff's restroom usage does not survive intermediate scrutiny.

Avoiding lawsuits resulting from Plaintiff's restroom usage was the only government interest identified by Defendant in his response to Plaintiff's Motion for Summary Judgment. Defendant did briefly identify two other concerns in his own Motion for Summary Judgment, stating, in totality:

In addition [to concerns resulting from Plaintiff's restroom use], Sewell Brumby's concern regarding the operation of the Office of Legislative Counsel and the Office having the confidence of the legislators of the State of Georgia, the Defendants have presented several conceivable sets of facts that serve as a rational basis for Plaintiff's termination.

However, neither concerns regarding the operation of the OLC nor concerns about preserving the confidence of state legislators presents an "exceedingly persuasive justification" for Plaintiff's termination. The record in this case does not indicate that Plaintiff's transition would have affected the operation of the OLC. Plaintiff's immediate supervisor did not believe that she should be fired. Further, when Brumby asked two OLC attorneys what they thought of working with an individual who was undergoing a gender transition, neither expressed concerns. In regards to Georgia legislators, the record indicates that Brumby communicated his intent to fire Plaintiff to the Speaker of the Georgia House of Representative, the Lieutenant Governor, and the President Pro Tempore of the State Senate, and the record does not indicate that any of the three expressed concern that their confidence in the OLC would diminish if Plaintiff remained employed. To the extent that the record contains any evidence that legislators would lose "confidence" in the OLC, it is in the form of Brumby's statement that some legislators would believe that Glenn's gender transition was immoral, unnatural, and "ultraliberal." Even if this were the case, avoiding the anticipated negative reactions of others cannot serve as a sufficient basis for discrimination and does not constitute an important government interest. . . .

As noted, Plaintiff has properly stated a violation of the Equal Protection Clause based upon sex stereotyping. Such a claim is subject to intermediate scrutiny review. The record demonstrates that Plaintiff's desire to come to work dressed as a woman did not comport with how Defendant Brumby believed a biological male should act and that served as a basis for her termination. The record also indicated that Brumby was concerned about negative reactions from others, including state legislators, if he allowed Plaintiff to do so. Neither is an "exceedingly persuasive justification," and neither explanation is sufficient to survive intermediate scrutiny review. *See Hogan,* 458 U.S. at 724, 102 S.Ct. 3331. Therefore, Plaintiff is entitled to summary judgment for her claim of discrimination based on sex.

. . .

[The court then addressed Plaintiff's medical condition discrimination claim.]

Defendant's Motion for Summary Judgment as to Plaintiff's [Medical Condition Discrimination Claim] is GRANTED and Plaintiff's Motion for Summary Judgment as to that claim is DENIED.

DISCUSSION

The Brumby *case illustrates how one court addressed the issue of transgender discrimination. How should discrimination against transsexuals be properly analyzed? Should they be covered by Title VII's ban on "sex" discrimination? The 6th Circuit in* Smith v. City of Salem, *378 F.3d 566 (6th Cir. 2004) and* Barnes v. Cincinnati, *401 F.3d 729 (6th Cir.), cert. denied, 546 U.S. 1003, 126 S.Ct. 624, 163 L.Ed.2d 506 (2005) concluded that, under a sex stereotyping theory, transsexuals' claims under Title VII could proceed. A district judge in the 3rd Circuit has followed that reasoning. See* Mitchell v. Axcan Scandipharm, *Inc., 2006 WL 456173 (W.D. Pa. 2006). Another district judge has concluded that discrimination against a transsexual is sex discrimination simpliciter, without applying the stereotyping theory, holding that "sex" in Title VII should be construed broadly to encompass transsexuals.*

CHAPTER 6

THE MILITARY

■ ■ ■

For a while the issue of gays in the military occupied the sort of central place in American policy debate that gay marriage now occupies. President Bill Clinton promised to lift the ban on gays in the military in his campaign for the 2002 election. But the ensuing firestorm surrounding the subject caused him to compromise with Congress on what would become known as the "Don't Ask, Don't Tell" policy. The new law became effective in 1994 and marked the first substantial change in policy regarding gays in the military since 1940. "Don't Ask, Don't Tell" was almost immediately challenged as unconstitutional. The policy was eventually repealed by legislative initiative in a bill passed in December 2010, which included a delayed implementation to begin after a certification from the President, the Secretary of Defense, and the Joint Chiefs of Staff that the military was ready to begin the process. All certifications were sent to Congress on July 22, 2011, setting an official end to "Don't Ask, Don't Tell" on September 20, 2011.

Despite repeal, the scars of "Don't Ask, Don't Tell" remain. Additionally, the policy is worth remembering and analyzing because arguments for exclusion of openly gay people from the military are perhaps stronger than any argument for exclusion of gays in any other area. Consequently, if those arguments fail with respect to the military—if they are unpersuasive in this "special" environment—then they should be unpersuasive elsewhere, where such "special" concerns are not present; thus, the possibility of comprehensive nondiscrimination protections is strengthened. (For a discussion of the defense of "Don't Ask, Don't Tell" on the ground that the military is a special environment in which antidiscrimination protections cannot be expected to apply, *see* Shannon Gilreath, *Sexually Speaking: "Don't Ask, Don't Tell" and the First Amendment after* Lawrence v. Texas, 14 DUKE JOURNAL OF GENDER LAW & POLICY, 953–976 (2007)). This chapter presents debate on the military's treatment of gay servicemembers, as well as cases representative of the primary legal claims made in opposition to its enforcement. These materials are followed by the recent repeal and its aftermath.

I. ARGUMENTS FOR AND AGAINST "DON'T ASK, DON'T TELL"

A. MAKE WAR, NOT LOVE*

If homosexuality is incompatible with military service, it should be prohibited outright. Other behavior "incompatible with military service," such as drug abuse and sexual harassment, is not tolerated in private; there is simply no reason why homosexuality should be dealt with differently. Looking the other way when homosexuals seek to join the armed forces sends the message that they are welcome so long as they remain celibate or do not get caught. Such a policy is disingenuous and unrealistic. Even worse, by encouraging deception by homosexuals and self-deception by their commanders, it directly undermines the personal integrity so vital to sustaining the moral authority of command.

Banning homosexuals from the military is both wise and just. It is wise because it accounts for real people functioning in the real world and recognizes that despite their best intentions, heterosexuals and homosexuals are above all human. It is just because it can be defended without recourse to any criticism of homosexuality on moral grounds; indeed, the only moral basis for the ban is the assertion that preventing unnecessary loss of life is more important than sexuality of any variety. Thus, a ban against homosexuals in the military is neither judgmental nor ideological. It is based on the recognition that military life cannot provide for different individual lifestyles and that distractions in combat, sexual or otherwise, get people killed.

It is difficult to foresee a time when homosexuals and heterosexuals no longer see each other as different in a fundamental way. With the slightest introspection, the reasonable person quickly realizes that bonds of trust will be difficult to create within a group of men if there is sexuality beneath the surface. The thought that your comrade might have sexual feelings for you—*even if he is suppressing those feelings*—will make such trust impossible. The slightest inkling that a commander is influenced by his sexuality—even to the extent that he must resist that influence—will destroy his effectiveness as a leader. Soldiers must trust each other, and their commanders, if they are to risk their lives in causes our nation deems appropriate. When trust is absent among civilians, society, although demeaned, still survives. But breaking trust within the military will cause our soldiers to die, our battles to be lost, and our interests to be threatened.

Access to the military is not a right enjoyed by all Americans. It is not guaranteed in the Constitution or anywhere else. Indeed, to build effective units, the armed forces routinely deny the privilege of military service to

* Reprinted from John Luddy, *Make War, Not Love: The Pentagon's Ban Is Wise and Just*, POLICY REVIEW (Spring 1993) pp. 68–71, reprinted in John Corvino (ed.), Same Sex: Debating the Ethics, Science, and Culture of Homosexuality (1997).

patriotic Americans who are too tall, too short, too fat, color-blind, flat-footed, and mentally or physically handicapped in any way. Single parents are not allowed to enlist, nor are chronic bed wetters. This is not a judgment of the inherent worth of these people as human beings; indeed, each of these individuals properly enjoys numerous civil rights. It is simply a determination that they are not suited for military service. . . .

What would be the effect of mixing homosexuals and heterosexuals in combat? Begin by making two assumptions: first, that homosexuality is viewed as entirely normal, natural, and otherwise acceptable throughout the population; and second, that the order has been given to admit open homosexuals and that every military person attempts to execute it in good faith. Even under these highly unlikely conditions, the presence of homosexuals in a military unit would still be an invitation for disaster.

Military leaders are responsible for the training, morale, and physical well-being of each member of their unit. They must first mold a group of individuals into a cohesive team and then lead them into battle. To their men, they must appear capable, physically and mentally tough, brave, and, above all, fair. Their typical responsibilities include, but are not limited to: planning a mission; navigating and otherwise controlling the movement of their troops; maintaining communication with their commander; directing aircraft and artillery fire to support their attack; arranging for resupply of food and ammunition; coordinating with other ground units; and seeing that casualties are treated and evacuated if necessary. They often do all of this in darkness, miserable weather, or both, and always with an enemy trying to kill them. They must continually make decisions that may cost one man's life and spare another's, such as choosing who is assigned a dangerous mission and which of the wounded is treated and evacuated first. Should they be asked to contend with human sexual emotions as well? . . .

A heterosexual lieutenant must order one of his squads to attack a machine gun position that has taken his platoon under fire. Two squads are in position to attack: one is led by a homosexual sergeant. The lieutenant must decide: if he sends the homosexual sergeant, and the sergeant is killed, will the platoon's other homosexual troops think that the lieutenant sent the sergeant because he dislikes homosexuals? Will they trust him with their lives in the future? If the lieutenant were homosexual, and found himself attracted to the sergeant—he is, of course, only human—would he spare that sergeant from dangerous missions and send the other squad instead? What would be the effect on the platoon's morale if he were even perceived as doing so? Above all, would weighing these issues cause him to hesitate while the lives of his men hang in the balance?

If every decision is made, and reacted to, with even the slightest chance that sexual attraction or revulsion played a part in it, how could those decisions be trusted? If a man does not trust his leaders or those around him, will he willingly put his life in their hands?

In this scenario, no heterosexual is an irrational bigot, no homosexual is either compulsive or perverse, and no sexual advance or contact takes place: in short, no stereotypes are present. Indeed, society's view as to which type of sexual activity is or is not acceptable is irrelevant: were the proportion of homosexuals and heterosexuals in society reversed, this argument rightly would continue to be used to ban homosexuals from the armed forces. The clearest and strongest reason for the ban is to remove the influence of sexuality—not heterosexuality, not homosexuality, just sexuality, period—from an environment where the stakes are literally life and death.

DISCUSSION

Some of the arguments Luddy makes could reasonably be made in the context of racial integration of the military as well. For example, isn't Luddy's concern that gay soldiers might question the motivation of a commander who orders a squad led by a gay man on a dangerous mission equally a concern if a white commander ordered a squad led by a black man on a dangerous mission? Are tensions rooted in sexuality somehow qualitatively different that racial tensions? Consider the statement by General Colin Powell, then Chairman of the Joint Chiefs of Staff, testifying in favor of "Don't Ask, Don't Tell," suggesting that preventing gay servicemembers from serving openly was unproblematic and rejecting analogies between sexuality segregation and racial segregation of the armed services. Powell stated that while race was a "benign" characteristic, sexual orientation was "perhaps the most profound of human behavioral characteristics." [Over a decade after he made this statement, Powell reversed position and publicly supported "Don't Ask, Don't Tell" repeal efforts.] How would you respond?

B. "DON'T ASK, DON'T TELL" AS "SECOND-HAND" PREJUDICE*

. . .

Advocates seeking to justify a continuation of the gay ban find it necessary to argue that many privacy issues accruing to the military are unique to that setting. Thus, for example, Congressman John Doolittle (R–CA) testified in front of the Republican Research Committee's Task Force about his recently having visited the Naval Academy at Annapolis for the first time:

> It's truly impressive to see the caliber of young people that serve there in the Academy. It also was driven home to me the conditions in which they live. They're close quarters.... It's two to a room. I understand at West Point it's three to a room.

Professor David Schlueter of the St. Mary's School of Law echoed this sentiment in his testimony before the Nunn committee:

* Excerpted from Paul Siegel, *Second Hand Prejudice and the Military*, 9 Notre Dame J. L. Ethics & Pol'y 185 (1995).

> It is critical that it be understood—the potential importance of this issue. Unlike most civilian jobs, service members typically do not leave the installation at the end of the work day to return to civilian life. The service members' home is often a small two-person tent, a cramped berth in a submarine, or an open-bay barracks where a large number of individuals share not only a common sleeping area but a common shower and restroom facilities as well. What little physical privacy exists in such conditions is highly treasured.

It is precisely because of the close quarters in which some categories of military personnel must serve that our policy has been to separate living and bathing facilities for men and women. Several participants in the gay military debate argued that the same reasoning would mandate separating gays from straights. Congressman Henry Hyde (R–IL) chided his colleagues:

> Anyone who has a daughter has to imagine your daughter living in a barracks with a bunch of men and dressing and showering. You'd say that's unconscionable, that's wrong. I am unable to distinguish the difference between having to do that with people whose sexual orientation and arousal level is exactly the same and maybe more, for all I know . . .

Congressman Hyde's reference to sexual "arousal levels" carries with it the presumption that the main reason we segregate males and females in military settings is to avoid sexual mingling. This is a sentiment that several senators emphasized time and again. . . . Consider this exchange between Senator William Cohen and Lawrence Korb, former Assistant Secretary of Defense:

Cohen: Let me just ask you: Should there be separate facilities for women on board submarines or aircraft carriers?

Korb: I think there already are separate facilities . . .

Cohen: But, should there be?

Korb: I think there should be.

Cohen: Why?

Korb: Well, because of the way in which society expects us to separate people.

Cohen: No, no. But, why? What would be the rational basis for society demanding a separation of the sexes?

Korb: I think it's based upon the moral values that we have.

Cohen: Does it have to do with sexual attraction of male and female?

Korb: Certainly. That's one component of it.

At another point in the hearings, Senator Dan Coats is questioning William Dale Henderson, former commander of the Army Research Institute:

Henderson: So, sex does have a negative effect on military activities.

Coats: Is that then the basis essentially for segregating men and women in close living situations?

Henderson: Well, you have other issues too. You have the privacy issues.

Coats: But it's the sexual attraction, tension, that could either undermine or destroy the unit. That is the basis for separate living quarters?

Senator Coats clearly wished to elicit a response to the effect that the main reason for segregating men and women in the armed forces is the desire to dampen heterosexual attractions. Sexual modesty, however, is not simply the opposite of sexual lasciviousness. The genders shield their bodies from each other for reasons far more complex than to avoid signaling a desire for sexual commingling.

Sexual modesty, especially women from men, is often a very physical manifestation of a much larger phenomenon. Our society's long history of complementary sex roles assigns males and females to separate spheres. Our genders define which doors we are permitted to enter and which are closed to us, which conversations we will be privy to, and which will be denied us....

The societal norm against exposure of the naked body to the opposite sex is applied asymmetrically. We are far more concerned with protecting women from having to reveal their naked bodies to men than vice versa. We do this out of a recognition of the difference in power between men and women. Thus, while many police departments have established policies dictating that strip searches of suspects will be conducted only by officers of the same gender, the rules are seen as a means of protecting female suspects. When hospitals debate whether or not to employ mixed-sex wards as a cost-cutting move, it is the privacy of their female patients that weighs more heavily on the side of sex segregation. Similarly, the California Fair Employment and Housing Commission recently held that a hospital which forbade male nurses to care for pregnant women during labor and delivery was not in violation of that state's employment discrimination statutes. Even at such venues as swimsuit-optional beaches, women are often quite reluctant to expose their naked bodies.

Men and women experience nakedness differently. It is no surprise, then, that Congressman Hyde asked us to imagine the horror of his *daughter* being forced to share close quarters in the military with members of the opposite sex. Indeed, it would have seemed quite odd for him to have expressed a parallel concern about his son. We seek to protect our daughters and women in general, because of their perceived powerlessness. We should feel no corresponding need to protect heterosexual servicemen and women from their lesbian and gay counterparts because the *latter* groups wield the lesser power.

The analogy between gender segregation and the posited need for segregation based on sexual orientation is at best an imperfect one. There is no history of segregating lesbians from heterosexual females, or gay males from heterosexual ones, that corresponds to the long history of segregating the sexes themselves. As Congressman Barney Frank explained in a debate with Senator Dan Coats on a *Face the Nation* broadcast:

> I have to point out to people that gay men and straight men have been sharing dormitories, showers, health clubs for a very long time. I mean, gay men and lesbians throughout this country join health clubs, they live in college dormitories. We don't have ourselves dry-cleaned. We've been taking showers for a long time.

Thus far we have treated the shared showers analogy as if it were on all fours; it ended as an argument for the need to provide separate bathrooms and living spaces for openly gay soldiers. But the analogy was always intended instead as an argument in support of maintaining the ban against openly gay soldiers altogether. Segregated barracks of heterosexual males and of heterosexual females would presumably be devoid of sexual tensions. By the same reasoning, lesbian and especially gay male barracks would be hotbeds of orgiastic expression. . . .

DISCUSSION

Professor Siegel's argument is a class-based one about power. Basically, he suggests that the flap about the vulnerability of heterosexual servicemembers to homosexual advances is a red herring, a dynamic wholly inconsistent with the vulnerability of women soldiers in close proximity to their male counterparts, because gay servicemembers lack the social power to use their sexuality as a weapon of repression or harassment in the way that heterosexual males use their sexual inclination to target and subordinate women. What do you make of this argument?

Now consider Siegel's reasoning in conjunction with the following argument that, irrespective of the official policy, gays should eschew military service as a matter of principle. How do power and domination play into this call for gays to resist military service? Do you find it persuasive?

C. EQUALITY: ANOTHER PERSPECTIVE*

. . .

. . . Personally, I would like to see every gay person leave the military; perhaps then the military establishment would see just how essential gays

* © Shannon Gilreath. Reprinted from *PRIDE and Equality Magazine* (Jan./Feb. 2006).

have been to the security of our nation—not to mention how many gay lives have been sacrificed for the foreign policy of more than one American potentate.

And what exactly are these policies, foreign and otherwise, that gays are lining up to defend? I can't argue that the Afghan people are better off rid of the Taliban. Yet I couldn't help wondering why as [President] Bush outlined the human rights abuses in both Afghanistan and Iraq—violence against women, torture, murder, religious enslavement—he never once mentioned the fact that gays were being routinely buried alive.

Perhaps it is because the gay soldiers liberating Afghanis and Iraqis (and I use "liberating" loosely since I seriously doubt that the lives of gays will be much improved under the replacement regimes) aren't even allowed to acknowledge their own sexuality. Perhaps it is because Bush's Justice Department argued that American gays should be punished as felons for engaging in consensual adult sex. Gays in Iraq . . . will hardly experience a blooming of civil liberties in the new American-backed government.

In the laundry list of abominations that might merit U.S. sanctions of Iran, not once are the post–1979 executions of over 4,000 gays mentioned. Or let us consider our supposed ally, Saudi Arabia, where Condoleezza Rice sees democratic "improvement." There, convicted gays are routinely beheaded, as was the case just this March when a gay couple was publicly beheaded. Often, the headless bodies of sodomy offenders are then crucified. Hundreds of gays have been rounded up in Saudi Arabia in recent months, and it is curious to note the spike in such executions in the years since the American military, with its voiceless gay soldiers, saved the Arabian Peninsula from Saddam's megalomania.

Back in the Land of the Free, even minor efforts to protest the military's draconian policies have been met with an iron fist from the W. administration. In August of 2002, the United States military was allowed to recruit at Harvard Law School's Office of Career Services for the first time since the school instituted a ban on military recruitment over 20 years before to protest the military's anti-gay hiring policies. Previously, the school had complied with the Solomon Amendment, by which federal funds can be denied to schools that openly disrupt military recruitment, by allowing the military to recruit through a student organization. But with the advent of the Bush administration, and especially given heightened military recruitment activities in the wake of 9/11, the United States Air Force threatened to institute proceedings against the law school that could result in the loss of $328 million in federal funding to the university if the Department of Defense found them in violation.

And, anyway, what exactly is the purpose of the ban on gays in the military? You can be sure that it's about something a lot more important to the hetero-establishment than merely preserving the decorum of the communal shower. It seems to me that within the military there is a fear of a shifting in the traditional dominance of machismo, which has heretofore reigned supreme in the Armed Forces just as it has in most of society. The gay man, as traditional wisdom goes, is puny, weak, and girlish—not fit for armed service. The straight man, by contrast, is strong and robust, an engineered warrior.

Already having been forced to include women, the Armed Forces is not about to lose more ground by giving in on the gay issue. The ban on gays is a defensive action on the part of the insecure person; in the case of opposition to women or gays in the military, it is overwhelmingly an action of the straight male, who sees his masculinity threatened if women and gays assume a position of equality with him. If gays should rise from their traditional positions of passivity and weakness to a place on par with his, he fears that his own strength will somehow be diminished.

Moral reasons have been routinely proffered as cause enough to exclude gays from the military, but the whole of bigotry has little to do with morality. If it were really a question of morality, as the ban supporters suggest, wouldn't these same "concerned citizens" be equally, if not more, concerned over the violation of the rights of women in the military?

Why did comparable outrage not burst from the mouths of every serviceman in the wake of the Tailhook scandal? The results of a Department of Defense study leaked to the press showed that almost a quarter of the female cadets who graduated from the United States Military Academy in 2003 were sexually assaulted during their matriculation at the academy. The primary reasons given by the cadets surveyed for not reporting the abuse were fear of ostracism by peers and fear of punishment if they came forward. If sexual morality is an honest concern for the average serviceman, or of his administrators, why does the sexual violation of women continue to occur in the military and its schools? Perhaps it is because the very kind of man who so fears being sexually desired or subjugated by the gay man is exactly the kind of man who would affirm his own masculinity by forcing himself on a woman who would not invite him. Perhaps the greatest fear of the protestors of military integration of gays is the fear that the treatment they have reserved for women will be visited on them.

The position of the United States government on the issue is such an absurd contradiction that it borders on the grotesque. In 1987, during the Reagan Administration, a group of military personnel sued the United States government when they realized they had been the subjects of certain experimental testing without their knowledge or consent. The government argued that soldiers give up their rights to privacy, even to bodily autonomy, when they enter the military, and that neither their knowledge nor consent was necessary for the government to use them effectively as guinea pigs. Today, the government argues that if out gays were allowed in the military, straight soldiers would "lose the freedom of association" that they enjoy in civilian life. The gap in logic in a position that would have a soldier enjoy such a diminished right to privacy that he could be made the subject of secret, dangerous testing without his knowledge or consent and the position that worries about the compromise of the soldier's "freedom of association" if he is forced to share barracks with a gay soldier is staggering.

Now, I fully support the gay person who chooses to tackle any challenge that comes his or her way, but I still cannot fathom why a gay person would wish to lend support—let alone his or her life—to an institution so inimical to gays' interests and in the service of a government that wastes no opportunity to inform gays that they contribute nothing to their country and that their country has little regard for them. True enough, the military needs gay people. It needs the tenacity of a people who have been kicked in the teeth more times than history can record but who have arisen and gone on. The question should be: "Do we need the military?" Perhaps our energies would be better spent fighting for our rights on the domestic front, rather than fighting phantoms abroad.

Bush tells us that the Islamic world "hates our freedoms" and that our invigorated militarism is to defend those freedoms. I'll come closer to believing that when I see a few more straight men knowingly loading a gay man's gun. We do ourselves or our country little service by acquiescing in the tyranny of any institution, particularly one designed for the defense of our freedoms. What we must fight is the real enemy—HOMOPHOBIA—and let us not stop until the enemy is vanquished.

NOTE

Since the above excerpt was published, reports by various human rights activists and groups have reported deteriorating conditions for gays in both Afghanistan and Iraq. In Iraq, gays who enjoyed some freedom under the Saddam Hussein regime are at the mercy of marauding militias that routinely torture and execute suspected gays in the name of Islam. Since the U.S. invasion of Iraq and the subsequent replacement of the Saddam regime with a U.S.-backed government, sustained by U.S. military presence, thousands of gays, generally young men, have simply disappeared. Their friends and families suspect they are the victims of anti-gay violence to which the new Iraqi government refuses to respond and, in some cases, has actively endorsed. *See* Shannon Gilreath: *Why Gays Should Not Serve in the Armed Forces: A Gay Liberationist Statement of Principle*, 18 WILLIAM AND MARY JOURNAL OF WOMEN AND THE LAW ___ (2011) (forthcoming).

II. WHAT CONSTITUTES "TELLING" UNDER THE REGULATIONS?

McVEIGH v. COHEN

983 F.Supp. 215 (D.D.C. 1998)

OPINION: SPORKIN

This matter comes before the Court on Plaintiff's Motion for a Preliminary Injunction. Plaintiff Timothy R. McVeigh, who bears no relation to the Oklahoma City bombing defendant, seeks to enjoin the United States Navy from discharging him under the statutory policy colloquially known as "Don't Ask, Don't Tell, Don't Pursue." *See* 10 U.S.C. § 654 ("new policy"). In the course of investigating his sexual orientation, the Plaintiff contends that the Defendants violated his rights under the Electronic Communications Privacy Act ("ECPA"), 18 U.S.C. § 2701 *et seq.*, the Administrative Procedure Act ("APA") 5 U.S.C. § 706, the Department's own policy, and the Fourth and Fifth Amendments of the U.S. Constitution. Absent an injunction, the Plaintiff avers that he will suffer irreparable injury from the discharge, even if he were ultimately to prevail on the merits of his claims.

Statement of Facts

The Plaintiff, Senior Chief Timothy R. McVeigh, is a highly decorated seventeen-year veteran of the United States Navy who has served honorably and continuously since he was nineteen years old. At the time of the Navy's decision to discharge him, he was the senior-most enlisted man aboard the United States nuclear submarine U.S.S. Chicago.

On September 2, 1997, Ms. Helen Hajne, a civilian Navy volunteer, received an electronic mail ("email") message through the America Online Service ("AOL") regarding the toy-drive that she was coordinating for the Chicago crew members' children. The message box stated that it came from the alias "boysrch," but the text of the email was signed by a "Tim." Administrative Record ("AR") at 110. Through an option available to AOL subscribers, the volunteer searched through the "member profile directory" to find the member profile for this sender. The directory specified that "boysrch" was an AOL subscriber named Tim who lived in Honolulu, Hawaii, worked in the military, and identified his marital status as "gay." *See* AR at 111. Although the profile included some telling interests such as "collecting pics of other young studs" and "boy watching," it did not include any further identifying information such as full name, address, or phone number. However, on other occasions, Hajne had communicated with the Plaintiff about his participation in the drive.

Ms. Hajne proceeded to forward the email and directory profile to her husband, who, like Plaintiff, was also a noncommissioned officer aboard the U.S.S. Chicago. The material eventually found its way to Commander John Mickey, the captain of the ship and Plaintiff's commanding officer. In turn, Lieutenant Karin S. Morean, the ship's principal legal adviser and a member of the Judge Advocate General's ("JAG") Corps was called in to investigate the matter. By this point, the Navy suspected the "Tim" who authored the email might be Senior Chief Timothy McVeigh. Before she spoke to the Plaintiff and without a warrant or court order, Lieutenant Morean requested a Navy paralegal on her staff, Legalman First Class Joseph M. Kaiser, to contact AOL and obtain information from the service that could "connect" the screen name "boysrch" and accompanying user profile to McVeigh. *See* AR at 13. Legalman Kaiser called AOL's toll-free customer service number and talked to a representative at technical services. Legalman Kaiser did not identify himself as a Naval serviceman. According to his testimony at the administrative hearing, he stated that he was "a third party in receipt of a fax sheet and wanted to confirm the profile sheet, [and] who it belonged to." AR at 14. The AOL representative affirmatively identified Timothy R. McVeigh as the customer in question. *See id.* at 11–15.

Upon verification from AOL, Lieutenant Morean notified Senior Chief McVeigh that the Navy had obtained "some indication[ ] that he made a statement of homosexuality" in violation of § 654(b)(2) of "Don't Ask, Don't Tell." AR at 27–28. In light of the Uniform Code of Military Justice prohibition of sodomy and indecent acts, she then advised him of his right to remain silent. *See id.* at 28, 30. Shortly thereafter, in a memorandum dated September 22, 1997, the Navy advised Plaintiff that it was commencing an administrative discharge proceeding (termed by the Navy as an "administrative separation") against him. The reason stated was for "homosexual conduct, as evidenced by your statement that you are a homosexual." AR at 107.

On November 7, 1997, the Navy conducted an administrative discharge hearing before a three-member board.... At the conclusion of the administrative hearing, the board held that the government had sufficiently shown by a preponderance of the evidence that Senior Chief McVeigh had engaged in "homosexual conduct," a dischargeable offense.

. . .

Analysis

. . .

... For the reasons set forth below, this Court concludes that the Plaintiff is entitled to the relief that he seeks at this time, a preliminary injunction barring his discharge.

I. Substantial Likelihood of Success on the Merits

Plaintiff in this case demonstrates a likely success to prevail on the merits. At its core, the Plaintiff's complaint is with the Navy's compliance, or lack thereof, with its new regulations under the "Don't Ask, Don't Tell, Don't Pursue" policy. Plaintiff contends that he did not "tell," as prescribed by the statute, but that nonetheless, the Navy impermissibly "asked" and zealously "pursued."

In short, this case raises the central issue of whether there is really a place for gay officers in the military under the new policy, "Don't Ask, Don't Tell, Don't Pursue."

. . .

In 1993, leaders of Congress and the President reached a compromise designed to recognize the important role that officers who happen to be gay play in the defense of our nation. *See* Policy Concerning Homosexuality in the Armed Forces: Hearings Before the Senate Committee on Armed Services, 103d Cong. 595 *et. seq.* (1993) (statements of General Colin Powell, Chair of the Joint Chiefs of Staff, Admiral David Jeremiah, Navy, and General Merrill McPeak, Air Force). While the heads of the Armed Forces expressed fear that unit cohesion and military preparedness would be compromised by openly gay conduct, they acknowledged that homosexuality itself was not necessarily incompatible with military service. The statute that came to embody this position, "Don't Ask, Don't Tell, Don't Pursue," was specifically drafted to allow members of the military to live private lives as gay men and women, so long as their sexual orientation remained unspoken.

The facts as stated above clearly demonstrate that the Plaintiff did not openly express his homosexuality in a way that compromised this "Don't Ask, Don't Tell" policy. Suggestions of sexual orientation in a private, anonymous email account did not give the Navy a sufficient reason to investigate to determine whether to commence discharge proceedings. In its actions, the Navy violated its own regulations. *See* Guidelines for Fact–Finding Inquiries into Homosexual Conduct, Department of Defense Directive No. 1332.14 ("Guidelines"). An investigation into sexual orientation may be initiated "only when [a commander] has received credible information that there is a basis for discharge," such as when an officer "has said that he or she is a homosexual or bisexual, or made some other statement that indicates a propensity or intent to engage in homosexual acts." *Id.* Yet in this case, there was no such credible information that Senior Chief McVeigh had made such a statement. Under the Guidelines, "credible information" requires more than "just a belief or suspicion" that a Service member has engaged in homosexual conduct. *Id.* In the examples provided, the Guidelines state that "credible information" would exist in this case only if "a reliable person" stated that he or she directly observed or heard a Service member make an oral or written statement that "a reasonable person would believe was intended to convey the fact that he or she engages in or has a propensity or intent to engage in homosexual acts." *Id.*

Clearly, the facts as stated above in this case demonstrate that there was no such "credible information." All that the Navy had was an email message and user profile that it suspected was authored by Plaintiff. Under the military regulation, that information alone should not have triggered any sort of investigation. When the Navy affirmatively took steps to confirm the identity of the email respondent, it violated the very essence of "Don't Ask, Don't Pursue" by launching a search and destroy mission. Even if the Navy had a factual basis to believe that the email message and profile were written by Plaintiff, it was unreasonable to infer that they were necessarily intended to convey a propensity or intent to engage in homosexual conduct. Particularly in the context of cyberspace, a medium of "virtual reality" that invites fantasy and affords anonymity, the comments attributed to McVeigh do not by definition amount to a declaration of homosexuality. At most, they express "an abstract preference or desire to engage in homosexual acts." *See* Guidelines. Yet the regulations specify that a statement professing homosexuality so as to warrant investigation must declare "more than an abstract preference or desire"; they must indicate a likelihood actually to carry out homosexual acts. *Id.*

The subsequent steps taken by the Navy in its "pursuit" of the Plaintiff were not only unauthorized under its policy, but likely illegal under the Electronic Communications Privacy Act of 1986 ("ECPA"). The ECPA, enacted by Congress to address privacy concerns on the Internet, allows the government to obtain information from an online service provider—as the Navy did in this instance from AOL—but only if a) it obtains a warrant issued under the Federal Rules of Criminal Procedure or state equivalent; or b) it gives prior notice to the online subscriber and then issues a subpoena or receives a court order authorizing disclosure of the information in question. *See* 18 U.S.C. § 2073(b)(A)–(B), (c)(1)(B).

. . .

. . . The government knew, or should have known, that by turning over the information without a warrant, AOL was breaking the law. Yet the Navy, in this case, directly solicited the information anyway. What is most telling is that the Naval investigator did not identify himself when he made his request. While the government makes much of the fact that § 2703(c)(1)(B) does not provide a cause of action against the government, it is elementary that information obtained improperly can be suppressed where an individual's rights have been violated. . . .

The government has produced no evidence that would indicate that it would have proceeded without this information from AOL affirmatively linking the email to Senior Chief McVeigh. That the Plaintiff may have made incriminating statements at the subsequent administrative hearing does not bootstrap the Navy out of its legal dilemma of not only violating its own policy, but also a federal statute in its attempt to charge the Plaintiff with homosexuality.

In Plaintiff's case, this Court finds that the Navy has gone too far. The "Don't Ask, Don't Tell, Don't Pursue" policy was clearly aimed at accommodating gay men and women in the military. In effect, it was intended to bring our nation's armed forces in line with the rest of society, which finds discrimination of virtually every form intolerable. It is self-evident that a person's sexual orientation does not affect that individual's performance in the workplace. At this point in history, our society should not be deprived of the many accomplishments provided by people who happen to be gay. The "Don't Ask, Don't Tell, Don't Pursue" policy was a bow to society's growing recognition of this fact. For the policy to be effective, it has to be implemented in a sensitive, balanced manner. Under the policy as it stands today, gay service members must be permitted to serve their country honorably, so long as they are discreet in pursuing their personal lives.

In this case, the Plaintiff has had an exemplary service record for some seventeen years. Indeed, he has risen in the ranks to become the most senior non-commissioned officer on his ship. His evaluations have been of the highest order. Nothing has been produced before this Court which would in any way suggest that his sexual orientation has adversely affected his job performance. Senior Chief McVeigh's place in the Navy might even be characterized by some to be the very essence of what was hoped to be achieved by those who conceived the policy. The Plaintiff is no less an officer today than he was on January 5, 1998, the day before he was told of his imminent discharge from the Navy because of his sexual orientation.

As this Court stated in *Elzie v. Aspin*, 897 F.Supp. 1, 3 (1995), it cannot understand why the Navy would seek to discharge an officer who has served his country in a distinguished manner just because he might be gay. Plaintiff's case "vividly underscores the folly ... of a policy that systematically excludes a whole class of persons who have served this country proudly and in the highest tradition of excellence." *Id.* at 4. Although this case specifically does not reach any of the constitutional issues underscoring the "Don't Ask, Don't Tell, Don't Pursue" policy, *see Able v. United States*, 968 F.Supp. 850 (1997), the Court must note that the defenses mounted against gays in the military have been tried before in our nation's history—against blacks and women. *See Elzie v. Aspin*, 841 F.Supp. 439, 443 (1993). Surely, it is time to move beyond this vestige of discrimination and misconception of gay men and women.

II. Irreparable Harm

Without this Court's immediate intervention, the Plaintiff will lose his job, income, pension, health and life insurance, and all the other benefits attendant with being a Naval officer. Having served honorably for the last seventeen years, Plaintiff will be separated from a position which is central to his life on the sole ground that he has been labeled a "homosexual," and thus by definition unfit for service. The stigma that attaches to such an accusation without substantiation is significant enough that this Court believes it must grant the injunctive relief sought. In cases nearly identical to this, courts have accordingly granted a preliminary injunction, *see Elzie v. Aspin*, 841 F.Supp. 439, 443 (D.D.C. 1993) (loss of benefits and "rights as a Marine" constitute irreparable harm); *May v. Gray*, 708 F.Supp. 716, 719 (E.D.N.C. 1988) (same); *see also Saunders v. George Washington University*, 768 F.Supp. 843, 845 (D.D.C. 1991); *Huynh v. Carlucci*, 679 F.Supp. 61, 67 (D.D.C. 1988).

. . .

... It is accordingly for this reason that a preliminary injunction will issue.

III. CONSTITUTIONAL CHALLENGES

ABLE v. UNITED STATES

155 F.3d 628 (2nd Cir. 1998)

OPINION: WALKER

Defendants United States of America, William S. Cohen and Rodney E. Slater ("the government" or "the United States") appeal from the July 2, 1997 Memorandum and Order of the United States District Court for the Eastern District of New York (Eugene H. Nickerson, Senior District Judge), which found that § 571(b) of the National Defense Authorization Act for the Fiscal Year 1994 (the "Act"), codified at 10 U.S.C. § 654(b), which mandates the termination of a service member of the armed forces for engaging in homosexual conduct, violates the Equal Protection Clause of the Fifth Amendment. *See Able v. United States*, 968 F.Supp. 850, 865 (E.D.N.Y. 1997). The government argues that the district court failed to accord the judgments of Congress and the military the proper deference in deciding the eligibility requirements for military service and that, under the correct standard, § 654(b) is constitutional.

Background

This appeal presents our second encounter with the merits of plaintiffs' constitutional challenge to the military's "don't ask, don't tell" policy toward homosexual members of the United States military. *See Able v. United States*, 88 F.3d 1280 (2d Cir. 1996).

. . .

Plaintiffs filed the instant action on March 7, 1994, in the Eastern District of New York claiming that the Act and the DoD Directives violate their rights under the First and Fifth Amendments to free speech, equal protection, and expressive and intimate association, and violate due process by failing to give adequate notice of what speech or behavior is proscribed.

. . .

Following a four-day trial, the district court held that 10 U.S.C. § 654(b)(2) (the "statements provision"), violated the Free Speech Clause of the First Amendment and the Equal Protection Clause of the Fourteenth Amendment. *See Able*, 880 F.Supp. 968, 980 (E.D.N.Y. 1995). The district court concluded that the plaintiffs, who had not been the subject of discharge or other adverse proceedings, lacked standing to challenge § 654(b)(1) (the "acts prohibition") and dismissed that part of the complaint without prejudice. *See id.* at 970.

The government appealed, and we reversed. We held that the statements provision "substantially furthers the government's interest ... in preventing the occurrence of homosexual acts in the military," *see Able*, 88 F.3d at 1296, and determined that "if the acts prohibition of subsection (b)(1) is constitutional ... the statements presumption of subsection (b)(2) does not violate the First Amendment," *id.*, because the "subsections rise or fall together," *id.* at 1292. We also found that plaintiffs had standing to challenge § 654(b)(1), reinstated the acts provision claim and remanded to the district court to determine whether the acts provision violates the Equal Protection Clause.

On remand, the district court held that the acts provision violates the Equal Protection Clause. *See Able v. United States*, 968 F.Supp. at 865. The United States appealed, arguing that the district court failed to accord Congress the deference required in cases involving the military and that under the correct standard § 654 is constitutional.

Discussion

The Due Process Clause of the Fifth Amendment assures every person the equal protection of the laws, "which is essentially a direction that all persons similarly situated should be treated alike." *City of Cleburne v. Cleburne Living Ctr., Inc.*, 473 U.S. 432, 439, 87 L.Ed.2d 313, 105 S.Ct. 3249 (1985). Of course, the government can treat persons differently if they are not "similarly situated." As a general rule, the equal protection guarantee of the Constitution is satisfied when the government differentiates between persons for a reason that bears a rational relationship to an appropriate governmental interest. *See Heller v. Doe*, 509 U.S. 312, 320, 125 L.Ed.2d 257, 113 S.Ct. 2637 (1993). However, in limited circumstances when the subject of the different treatment is a member of a class that historically has been the object of discrimination, the Supreme Court has required a higher degree of justification than a rational basis, either strict or intermediate scrutiny. Under the strict scrutiny test the government must demonstrate a compelling need for the different treatment and that the provision in question is narrowly tailored to achieve its objective. *See McLaughlin v. Florida*, 379 U.S. 184, 192, 13 L.Ed.2d 222, 85 S.Ct. 283 (1964). Under intermediate scrutiny, the government must at least demonstrate that the classification is substantially related to an important governmental objective. *See United States v. Virginia,* 518 U.S. 515, 533, 135 L.Ed.2d 735, 116 S.Ct. 2264 (1996). The suspect or quasi-suspect classes that are entitled to heightened scrutiny have been limited to groups generally defined by their status, such as race, national ancestry or ethnic origin, alienage, gender and illegitimacy, and not by the conduct in which they engage.

The government argues that the Act in this case proscribes homosexual conduct and that, since any governmental differentiation is based on conduct, not status, no heightened scrutiny is required. The government adds, moreover, that even if, as plaintiffs contend, the Act targets homosexuals based on status, heightened scrutiny still would not be appropriate because other circuits reviewing the Act have not recognized homosexuals as a suspect class and have applied a rational basis test. *See, e.g., Richenberg v. Perry*, 97 F.3d 256, 260–61 (8th Cir. 1996), *cert. denied*, 139 L.Ed.2d 12, 118 S.Ct. 45 (1997); *Thomasson v. Perry*, 80 F.3d 915, 928

(4th Cir.), *cert. denied*, 519 U.S. 948, 136 L.Ed.2d 250, 117 S.Ct. 358 (1996).

In striking down the Act as failing to bear even a rational relationship to a legitimate governmental interest, the district court strongly suggested that in reviewing statutes that discriminate on the basis of homosexuality heightened scrutiny would be appropriate. *See Able*, 968 F.Supp. at 861–64. We need not decide this question because at oral argument plaintiffs asserted that they were not seeking any more onerous standard than the rational basis test. Accordingly, the sole question before us is whether the Act survives rational basis review.

In a long series of cases, the Supreme Court has narrowly defined the concept of rational basis review. In *Heller*, 509 U.S. at 319 (*quoting FCC v. Beach Communications, Inc.*, 508 U.S. 307, 313, 124 L.Ed.2d 211, 113 S.Ct. 2096 (1993)), the Supreme Court held that "rational-basis review in equal protection analysis 'is not a license for courts to judge the wisdom, fairness, or logic of legislative choices.' " Rather, "a classification neither involving fundamental rights nor proceeding along suspect lines is accorded a strong presumption of validity," 509 U.S. at 319, which " 'must be upheld against equal protection challenge if there is any reasonably conceivable state of facts that could provide a rational basis for the classification,' " *id.* at 320 (*quoting Beach Communications*, 508 U.S. at 313). Under the rational basis test, the government "has no obligation to produce evidence to sustain the rationality of a statutory classification." 509 U.S. at 320. We will assume that a statute is constitutional and "the burden is on the one attacking the legislative arrangement to negative every conceivable basis which might support it, whether or not the basis has a foundation in the record." *Id.* at 320–21 (citations and internal quotations omitted).

In the military setting, the Supreme Court has narrowed our review in a further respect. ... *See Able*, 88 F.3d at 1293–94. The Supreme Court has instructed that " 'judicial deference ... is at its apogee when legislative action under the congressional authority to raise and support armies and make rules and regulations for their governance is challenged.' " *Goldman v. Weinberger*, 475 U.S. 503, 508, 89 L.Ed.2d 478, 106 S.Ct. 1310 (1986) (*quoting Rostker v. Goldberg*, 453 U.S. 57, 70, 69 L.Ed.2d 478, 101 S.Ct. 2646 (1981)). This is especially the case where, as here, the challenged restriction was the result of exhaustive inquiry by Congress in hearings, committee and floor debate. *See Rostker*, 453 U.S. at 64, 72.

. . .

In full recognition that within the military individual rights must of necessity be curtailed lest the military's mission be impaired, courts have applied less stringent standards to constitutional challenges to military rules, regulations and procedures than they have in the civilian context. Thus, "our review of military regulations ... is far more deferential than constitutional review of similar laws or regulations designed for civilian society." *Goldman*, 475 U.S. at 507.

Justice is afforded on different terms than is found in civilian life because the military is a "specialized community governed by a separate discipline." *Parker*, 417 U.S. at 744 (quoting *Orloff*, 345 U.S. at 94). Before a military tribunal, a defendant's constitutional rights are diminished. There is no right to a trial by ajury of one's peers. *See Kahn v. Anderson*, 255 U.S. 1, 8–9, 65 L.Ed. 469, 41 S.Ct. 224 (1921). The right of appeal from a criminal conviction is restricted. *See* 28 U.S.C. § 1259 (defining terms for writ of certiorari to the Supreme Court from Court of Appeals for the Armed Forces).

Furthermore, courts have deferred to military judgments that restrict First Amendment privileges including ... restricting political speeches and distribution of political leaflets on military bases, *see Greer v. Spock*, 424 U.S. 828, 838, 47 L.Ed.2d 505, 96 S.Ct. 1211 (1976).

The free exercise of religion is also limited in the military setting....

The conclusion that we draw from these pronouncements is that, while we are not free to disregard the Constitution in the military context....

In this litigation, the United States has justified § 654's prohibition on homosexual conduct on the basis that it promotes unit cohesion, enhances privacy and reduces sexual tension. The plaintiffs have attacked each of these rationales as simply masking irrational prejudice against homosexuals....

First, plaintiffs rely on *Romer v. Evans*, 517 U.S. 620, 134 L.Ed.2d 855, 116 S.Ct. 1620 (1996); *Cleburne Living Ctr.*, 473 U.S. at 448; and *Palmore v. Sidoti*, 466 U.S. 429, 80 L.Ed.2d 421, 104 S.Ct. 1879 (1984), for the proposition that the Act cannot survive even rational basis review because it is motivated by irrational fear and prejudice toward homosexuals. In these cases, the Supreme Court held that the accommodation of an individual's bias or animosity can never serve as a legitimate government interest; "mere negative attitudes, or fear, unsubstantiated by factors which are properly cognizable in [the circumstances], are not permissible bases" for differential treatment by the government. *Cleburne Living Ctr.*, 473 U.S. at 448.

. . .

In this case, plaintiffs' reliance on *Romer, Cleburne Living Ctr.* and *Palmore* is misplaced. Those cases did not arise in the military setting. In the civilian context, the Court was willing to examine the benign reasons advanced by the government to consider whether they masked an impermissible underlying purpose. In the military setting, however, constitutionally-mandated deference to military assessments and judgments gives the judiciary far less scope to scrutinize the reasons, legitimate on their face, that the military has advanced to justify its actions.

Moreover, in this case the military's justifications are based on factors which are unique to military life. The military argues that the prohibition on homosexual conduct is necessary for military effectiveness because it maintains unit cohesion, reduces sexual tension and promotes personal privacy. These concerns distinguish the military from civilian life and go directly to the military's need to foster "instinctive obedience, unity, commitment, and esprit de corps." *Goldman*, 475 U.S. at 507.

. . .

The prohibition against homosexual conduct is a longstanding element of military law that continues to be necessary in the unique circumstances of military service.

. . .

UNITED STATES v. MARCUM

60 M.J. 198 (C.A.A.F. 2004)

JUDGES: BAKER, J., delivered the opinion of the Court, in which GIERKE, EFFRON, and ERDMANN, JJ., joined. CRAWFORD, C.J., filed a separate opinion concurring in the result in part and dissenting in part.

Contrary to his pleas, Appellant was convicted by officer members of dereliction of duty by providing alcohol to individuals under the age of 21, non-forcible sodomy, forcible sodomy, assault consummated by a battery, indecent assault, and three specifications of committing indecent acts in violation of Articles 92, 125, 128, and 134, Uniform Code of Military Justice [hereinafter UCMJ], 10 U.S.C. §§ 892, 925, 928, and 934 (2000), respectively. Appellant was sentenced to confinement for 10 years, a dishonorable discharge, total forfeitures, and reduction to the lowest enlisted grade. The convening authority reduced the confinement to six years, but otherwise approved the findings and sentence.

The case was reviewed by the Air Force Court of Criminal Appeals, which affirmed the findings and sentence. *United States v. Marcum*, No. ACM 34216, slip op. (A.F. Ct. Crim. App. July 25, 2002). This Court granted review of the following issues:

[Issues I and II, being evidentiary and procedural only, have been omitted]

Issue III

WHETHER APPELLANT'S CONVICTION FOR VIOLATING ARTICLE 125, UCMJ, BY ENGAGING IN CONSENSUAL SODOMY (CHARGE II, SPECIFICATION 1) MUST BE SET ASIDE IN LIGHT OF THE UNITED STATES SUPREME COURT'S HOLDING IN *LAWRENCE V. TEXAS*, 539 U.S. 558, 156 L.Ed.2d 508, 123 S.Ct. 2472 (2003).

... [W]e hold that *Article 125*, UCMJ, is constitutional as applied to Appellant.

Constitutional rights generally apply to members of the armed forces unless by their express terms, or the express language of the Constitution, they are inapplicable. However, Appellant's actions in the military context fell outside the zone of autonomy identified by the Supreme Court as a protected liberty interest. Among other things, Appellant was convicted of non-forcible sodomy with a subordinate airman within his chain of command. An Air Force instruction prohibits such sexual conduct between service members in differing pay-grades and within the same chain of command. This instruction provides for potential criminal sanctions through operation of *Article 92*. This instruction evidences that Senior Airman Harrison, Appellant's subordinate, was in a military position where "consent might not easily be refused." *Lawrence v. Texas,* 539 U.S. 558, 578, 156 L.Ed.2d 508, 123 S.Ct. 2472 (2003).

. . .

I. Issue III Article 125

Facts

. . .

... The charges in this case resulted from allegations by some of these subordinate airmen that Appellant engaged in consensual and nonconsensual sexual activity with them.

Among other offenses, Appellant was charged with the forcible sodomy of Senior Airman (SrA) Harrison (E–4). Specifically, Specification 1 of Charge II alleged that Appellant "did, at or near Omaha, Nebraska, between on or about 1 September 1998 and on or about 16 October 1998, commit sodomy with Senior Airman Robert O. Harrison by force and without consent of the said Senior Airman Robert O. Harrison."

With regard to the charged offense, SrA Harrison testified that after a night of drinking with Appellant he stayed at Appellant's apartment and slept on the couch. SrA Harrison further testified that at some point he woke up to find Appellant orally sodomizing him. Although Appellant testified that he "did not perform oral sex on [SrA Harrison] at all," he testified to "kissing [SrA Harrison's] penis twice." When asked "did you, at any time, use any force, coercion, pressure, intimidation or violence?" Appellant responded, "No, sir, I did not and neither did Airman Harrison." Moreover, Appellant testified that the activity that occurred between Appellant and SrA Harrison was "equally participatory."

According to SrA Harrison's testimony, he did not say anything to Appellant at the time of the charged incident, but grabbed the covers, pulled them up over his torso, and turned away from Appellant into the couch. SrA Harrison left the apartment soon after this incident took place. SrA Harrison testified that he didn't protest at the time because he didn't know how Appellant would react. SrA Harrison also testified that Appellant's actions made him scared, angry, and uncomfortable.

According to SrA Harrison, he later confronted Appellant about this incident. He told Appellant, "I just want to make it clear between us that this sort of thing doesn't ever happen again." Nevertheless, SrA Harrison forgave Appellant and continued their friendship. SrA Harrison testified that he considered his relationship with Appellant like that of "a father type son relationship or big brother, little brother type relationship[.]"

Subsequent to this incident, SrA Harrison explained how he and Appellant salsa danced together and kissed each other in the "European custom of men." SrA Harrison also told Appellant that he loved him, bought him a t-shirt as a souvenir, and sent numerous e-mails to Appellant expressing his continued friendship.

Appellant and SrA Harrison also provided testimony regarding an incident that occurred prior to the charged offense. SrA Harrison testified that during the incident he woke up in the morning and he was on top of Appellant with his face near Appellant's stomach. Appellant testified, "I was laying on my side, actually almost on top of the couch, with my belly on the couch but turned a little bit like this towards, with my face towards the rest of the living room. Airman Harrison was [on] top of me with, facing me. Airman Harrison was moving his pelvis area against my butt which is what woke me up. He had an erection, he had his arm around me, around the part that was actually touching the couch."

At the time of the charged conduct in question, Appellant and SrA Harrison were both subject to Dep't of the Air Force, Instruction 36–2909 (May 1, 1996). This instruction addresses professional and unprofessional relationships within the Air Force. Dep't of the Air Force, Instruction 36–2909 is subject to criminal sanction through operation of *Article 92* (Failure to obey order or regulation). Although this instruction was not admitted into evidence at trial, Appellant admitted during cross-examination that he was "aware of an Air Force policy" and that through his actions he had "broken more than an Air Force policy."

A panel of officers and enlisted members found Appellant "not guilty of forcible sodomy but guilty of non-forcible sodomy" in violation of *Article 125*. He was convicted on May 21, 2000. The convening authority approved his sentence except for the term of confinement on September 6, 2000.

Subsequent to the trial, action by the convening authority, and the Air Force Court of Criminal Appeals' review in this case, the Supreme Court granted certiorari in *Lawrence v. Texas*, a case challenging the constitutionality of a Texas statute criminalizing same sex sodomy. *Lawrence* was argued on March 26, 2003, and decided on June 26, 2003. Appellant petitioned this Court for review on September 23, 2002. This Court granted his petition on March 10, 2003. Appellant's supplemental issue regarding the Supreme Court's ruling in *Lawrence* was granted by this Court on August 29, 2003.

Discussion

A. *Article 125 Text*

Article 125 states:

> (a) Any person subject to this chapter who engages in unnatural carnal copulation with another person of the same or opposite sex or with an animal is guilty of sodomy. Penetration, however slight, is sufficient to complete the offense.

> (b) Any person found guilty of sodomy shall be punished as a court-martial may direct.

As we stated in *United States v. Scoby*,

> By its terms, *Article 125* prohibits every kind of unnatural carnal intercourse, whether accomplished by force or fraud, or with consent. Similarly, the article does not distinguish between an act committed in the privacy of one's home, with no person present other than the sexual partner, and the same act committed in a public place in front of a group of strangers, who fully apprehend in the nature of the act.

5 M.J. 160, 163 (C.M.A. 1978). Thus, *Article 125* forbids sodomy whether it is consensual or forcible, heterosexual or homosexual, public or private.

B. Arguments

Appellant challenges his conviction on the ground that *Lawrence* recognized a constitutional liberty interest in sexual intimacy between consenting adults in private. Appellant argues that *Article 125* suffers from the same constitutional deficiencies as the Texas statute in *Lawrence* because both statutes criminalize private consensual acts of sodomy between adults. Appellant further contends that in light of the Supreme Court's rejection of *Bowers v. Hardwick,* 478 U.S. 186, 92 L.Ed.2d 140, 106 S.Ct. 2841 (1986), Appellant's conviction violates the *Due Process Clause*. As a result, Appellant argues that *Article 125* is either unconstitutional on its face or unconstitutional as applied to his conduct.

. . .

The Government argues that *Lawrence* is not applicable in the military environment due to the distinct and separate character of military life from civilian life as recognized by the Supreme Court in *Parker v. Levy,* 417 U.S. 733, 41 L.Ed.2d 439, 94 S.Ct. 2547 (1974).

The Government further argues that because the Supreme Court did not expressly state that engaging in homosexual sodomy is a fundamental right, this Court should analyze *Article 125* using the rational basis standard of review. Utilizing this standard, the Government contends *Article 125* is constitutional because it is rationally related to a legitimate state interest. Specifically, the Government maintains that *Article 125* criminalizes conduct that "creates an unacceptable risk to the high standards of morale, good order and discipline, and unit cohesion" within the military as recognized by Congress in 10 U.S.C. § 654(a)(15).

. . .

C. The Lawrence Decision

. . .

The amici, in their primary argument, contend that strict scrutiny should apply to this Court's review of *Article 125* because the Article impinges on a fundamental constitutional liberty interest. This follows from the amici's conclusion that "the Supreme Court overruled *Bowers*

. . ., and held the Texas sodomy prohibition unconstitutional because the Due Process Clause of the Fourteenth Amendment protects a fundamental right of adults to make decisions regarding private, consensual sexual conduct, including sodomy." As a result, the amici maintain that *Article 125* is unconstitutional because it is not narrowly tailored to achieve a compelling government interest.

In contrast, the Government contends the Supreme Court did not find a fundamental right to engage in homosexual sodomy by overruling *Bowers* because the Supreme Court applied the rational basis standard of review in *Lawrence*. "Rather, by applying a 'rational basis standard of review' to reach their determination that the Texas statute 'furthers no legitimate state interest which can justify its intrusion into the personal and private life of the individual,' the Supreme Court reaffirmed that the right to engage in homosexual sodomy is not a fundamental right."

Although particular sentences within the Supreme Court's opinion may be culled in support of the Government's argument, other sentences may be extracted to support Appellant's argument. On the one hand, the opinion incorporates some of the legal nomenclature typically associated with the rational basis standard of review. For example, as the Government notes, the Supreme Court declared "the Texas statute furthers no legitimate state interest." *See Lawrence,* 539 U.S. at 578. This is the counter-weight applied in the rational basis analysis. Moreover, the Supreme Court did not apply the nomenclature associated with strict scrutiny, *i.e.*, identification of a compelling state interest and narrow tailoring of the statute to accomplish that interest.

On the other hand, the Supreme Court placed *Lawrence* within its liberty line of cases resting on the *Griswold* foundation. *See id.* at 564–65. These cases treated aspects of liberty and privacy as fundamental rights, thereby, subjecting them to the compelling interest analysis. *See Griswold,* 381 U.S. at 485; *Carey,* 431 U.S. at 686. With regard to the Supreme Court's use of language attributed to the rational basis review, Appellant and the amici argue the Supreme Court is simply stating that the Texas statute does not even accomplish a legitimate interest, let alone a compelling one.

Indeed, in response to the Supreme Court's decision in *Lawrence*, some courts have applied the rational basis standard of review while other courts have applied strict scrutiny. For example, the Court of Appeals of Arizona determined that "the Court applied without explanation the rational basis test, rather than the strict scrutiny review utilized when fundamental rights are impinged, to hold the Texas statute unconstitutional." *Standhardt v. Superior Court of Arizona,* 206 Ariz. 276, 77 P.3d 451, 457 (Ariz. Ct. App. 2003). Whereas the court in *Fields v. Palmdale School District,* 271 F.Supp.2d 1217, 1221 n. 7 (C.D. Cal. 2003), concluded, "Many of these fundamental rights, especially those relating to marital activities and family relationships, have been classified by the Supreme

Court under a broader 'right to privacy' that is implicit in the Fourteenth Amendment[.]".

The focus by the Government and Appellant on the nature of the Supreme Court's constitutional test in *Lawrence* is understandable. Utilization of either the rational basis test or strict scrutiny might well prove dispositive of a facial challenge to *Article 125*. On the one hand, the interests in military readiness, combat effectiveness, or national security arguably would qualify as either rational or compelling governmental interests. On the other hand, it is less certain that *Article 125* is narrowly tailored to accomplish these interests.

The Supreme Court did not expressly state which test it used. The Court did place the liberty interest in *Lawrence* within the *Griswold* line of cases. *See Lawrence,* 539 U.S. at 564–65. *Griswold* and *Carey* address fundamental rights. However, the Supreme Court has not determined that all liberty or privacy interests are fundamental rights. In *Lawrence*, the Court did not expressly identify the liberty interest as a fundamental right. Therefore, we will not presume the existence of such a fundamental right in the military environment when the Supreme Court declined in the civilian context to expressly identify such a fundamental right.

What *Lawrence* requires is searching constitutional inquiry. This inquiry may require a court to go beyond a determination as to whether the activity at issue falls within column A—conduct of a nature to bring it within the liberty interest identified in *Lawrence*, or within column B—factors identified by the Supreme Court as outside its *Lawrence* analysis. The Court's analysis reached beyond the immediate facts of the case presented. This is reflected by the Court's decision to rule on the grounds of due process as opposed to equal protection. "Were we to hold the statute invalid under the *Equal Protection Clause*," the Supreme Court noted, "some might question whether a prohibition would be valid if drawn differently, say, to prohibit the conduct both between same-sex and different-sex participants." 539 U.S. at 575. The Supreme Court also acknowledged "an emerging awareness that liberty gives substantial protection to adult persons in deciding how to conduct their private lives in matters pertaining to sex." *Id.* at 572.

At the same time the Court identified factors, which it did not delimit, that might place conduct outside the *Lawrence* zone of liberty. Thus, the door is held open for lower courts to address the scope and nature of the right identified in *Lawrence*, as well as its limitations, based on contexts and factors the Supreme Court may not have anticipated or chose not to address in *Lawrence*. In our view, this framework argues for contextual, as applied analysis, rather than facial review. This is particularly apparent in the military context.

(2) Lawrence in the Military Context

The Supreme Court and this Court have long recognized that "men and women in the Armed Forces do not leave constitutional safeguards and judicial protection behind when they enter military service." *United States v. Mitchell,* 39 M.J. 131, 135 (C.M.A. 1994) (*quoting Weiss v. United States,* 510 U.S. 163, 194, 127 L.Ed.2d 1, 114 S.Ct. 752 (1994) (Ginsburg, J., concurring)). "Our citizens in uniform may not be stripped of basic rights simply because they have doffed their civilian clothes." *Goldman v. Weinberger,* 475 U.S. 503, 507, 89 L.Ed.2d 478, 106 S.Ct. 1310 (1986) (citations omitted). As a result, this Court has consistently applied the *Bill of Rights* to members of the Armed Forces, except in cases where the express terms of the Constitution make such application inapposite. *See United States v. Jacoby,* 11 C.M.A. 428, 430–31, 29 C.M.R. 244, 246–47, (1960) ("It is apparent that the protections in the *Bill of Rights*, except those which are expressly or by necessary implication inapplicable, are available to members of our armed forces.").

At the same time, these constitutional rights may apply differently to members of the armed forces than they do to civilians. *See Parker,* 417 U.S. at 743. "The military is, by necessity, a specialized society." *Id.* Thus, when considering how the *First Amendment* and *Fourth Amendment* apply in the military context, this Court has relied on Supreme Court civilian precedent, but has also specifically addressed contextual factors involving military life. *See United States v. Priest,* 21 C.M.A. 564, 570, 45 C.M.R. 338, 344 (1972) ("The right of free speech in the armed services is not unlimited and must be brought into balance with the paramount consideration of providing an effective fighting force for the defense of our Country."); *see also United States v. McCarthy,* 38 M.J. 398 (C.M.A. 1993) (warrantless entry into military barracks room to effectuate apprehension did not violate *Fourth Amendment*). In light of the military mission, it is clear that service members, as a general matter, do not share the same autonomy as civilians. *See Parker,* 417 U.S. at 758.

While the Government does not contest the general proposition that the Constitution applies to members of the Armed Forces, it argues that *Lawrence* only applies to civilian conduct. Moreover, with respect to the military, the Government contends that Congress definitively addressed homosexual sodomy by enacting 10 U.S.C. § 654 (2000). According to the Government, pursuant to Congress's Article I authority to make rules and regulations for the Armed Forces, Congress not only prohibited sodomy through *Article 125*, but with *Article 125* as a backdrop, determined in 1993 through 10 U.S.C. § 654 that homosexuality, and, therefore, sodomy was incompatible with military service. In enacting § 654, Congress determined that "the presence in the armed forces of persons who demonstrate a propensity or intent to engage in homosexual acts would create an unacceptable risk to the high standards of morale, good order and discipline, and unit cohesion that are the essence of military capability." 10 U.S.C. § 654(a)(15). Thus, according to the Government, this Court should apply traditional principles of deference to Congress's exercise of its Article I authority and not apply *Lawrence* to the military.

The military landscape, however, is less certain than the Government suggests. The fog of constitutional law settles on separate and shared powers where neither Congress nor the Supreme Court has spoken authoritatively. Congress has indeed exercised its Article I authority to address homosexual sodomy in the Armed Forces, but this occurred prior to the Supreme Court's constitutional decision and analysis in *Lawrence* and at a time when *Bowers* served as the operative constitutional backdrop. Moreover, the Supreme Court did not accept the Government's present characterization of the right as one of homosexual sodomy. The Court stated, "To say that the issue in *Bowers* was simply the right to engage in certain sexual conduct demeans the claim the individual put forward." *Lawrence,* 539 U.S. at 567. "The State cannot demean their existence or control their destiny by making their private sexual conduct a crime." *Id.* at 578. Nor did the Supreme Court define the liberty interest in *Lawrence* in a manner that on its face would preclude its application to military members.

Constitutional rights identified by the Supreme Court generally apply to members of the military unless by text or scope they are plainly inapplicable. Therefore, we consider the application of *Lawrence* to Appellant's conduct. However, we conclude that its application must be addressed in context and not through a facial challenge to *Article 125*. . . .

Thus, this case presents itself to us as a challenge to a discrete criminal conviction based on a discrete set of facts. The question this Court must ask is whether *Article 125* is constitutional as applied to Appellant's conduct. This as-applied analysis requires consideration of three questions. First, was the conduct that the accused was found guilty of committing of a nature to bring it within the liberty interest identified by the Supreme Court? Second, did the conduct encompass any behavior or factors identified by the Supreme Court as outside the analysis in *Lawrence*? 539 U.S. at 578. Third, are there additional factors relevant solely in the military environment that affect the nature and reach of the *Lawrence* liberty interest?

D. *Is Article 125 Constitutional as Applied to Appellant?*

. . . As part of Appellant's contested trial, the following additional facts surrounding his conduct were elicited: The act of sodomy occurred in Appellant's off-base apartment during off-duty hours; no other members of the military were present at the time of the conduct; Appellant was an E–6 and the supervising noncommissioned officer in his flight. His duties included training and supervising airmen. SrA Harrison, an E–4, was one of the airmen Appellant supervised. As a result, SrA Harrison was subordinate to, and directly within, Appellant's chain of command.

The first question we ask is whether Appellant's conduct was of a nature to bring it within the *Lawrence* liberty interest. Namely, did Appellant's conduct involve private, consensual sexual activity between adults? In the present case, the members determined Appellant engaged in non-forcible sodomy. This sodomy occurred off-base in Appellant's apartment and it occurred in private. We will assume without deciding that the jury verdict of non-forcible sodomy in this case satisfies the first question of our as applied analysis.

The second question we ask is whether Appellant's conduct nonetheless encompassed any of the behavior or factors that were identified by the Supreme Court as not involved in *Lawrence*. For instance, did the conduct involve minors? Did it involve public conduct or prostitution? Did it involve persons who might be injured or coerced or who are situated in relationships where consent might not easily be refused? *See id.*

. . .

As the supervising noncommissioned officer, Appellant was in a position of responsibility and command within his unit with respect to his fellow airmen. He supervised and rated SrA Harrison. Appellant also testified that he knew he should not engage in a sexual relationship with someone he supervised. Under such circumstances, which Appellant acknowledged was prohibited by Air Force policy, SrA Harrison, a subordinate airman within Appellant's chain of command, was a person "who might be coerced" or who was "situated in [a] relationship[ ] where consent might not easily be refused." *Lawrence,* 539 U.S. at 578. Thus, based on this factor, Appellant's conduct fell outside the liberty interest identified by the Supreme Court. As a result, we need not consider the third step in our *Lawrence* analysis. . . .

Appellant's conduct was outside the protected liberty interest recognized in *Lawrence*; it also was contrary to *Article 125*. As a result, *Article 125* is constitutional as applied to Appellant.

DISCUSSION

The Marcum *court indicates that the liberty interest explicated in* Lawrence *extends to sodomy conduct in private (absent coercion) when such conduct is engaged in by military personnel. See also* United States v. Humphreys, *2005 WL 3591140 (N.M. Ct. Crim. App.2005) (unpublished) in which the Navy–Marine Corps Court of Criminal Appeals reversed a sodomy court martial, holding that* Lawrence *precluded the prosecution of a navy member for consensual anal sex with a female navy member in a barracks bedroom. Do you agree with this reading of* Lawrence, *or are you persuaded by arguments that the military context is simply too different from civilian life to be governed by the* Lawrence *rationale?*

NOTE

In 2008, the 9th Circuit Court of Appeals held in *Witt v. United States Air Force*, 527 F.3d 806, that *Lawrence v. Texas* required that an as applied substantive due process challenge to "Don't Ask, Don't Tell" brought by a gay litigant be adjudicated under intermediate scrutiny. The Obama administration did not appeal the decision, leaving it as binding precedent in the 9th Circuit. On remand the trial judge held that Witt's constitutional rights had indeed been violated by DADT. In a settlement, the Air Force agreed to remove the discharge, allowing Witt (a decorated flight nurse) to retire with full benefits. *Witt* was cited as precedent in a 2010 trial court decision declaring "Don't Ask, Don't Tell" unconstitutional; *see Log Cabin Republicans v. United States*, 716 F. Supp. 2d 884.

CHAPTER 7

PUBLIC ACCOMMODATION

■ ■ ■

I. INTRODUCTION: *ROBERTS v. UNITED STATES JAYCEES*

This chapter considers discrimination against LGBT people in places of public accommodation. Previous chapters have focused on government actors attempting to exclude gays and lesbians from some otherwise available activity. This chapter examines what happens when private (*i.e.*, nongovernmental) actors attempt to deny LGBT people equal opportunity or participation in a privately sponsored organization or activity. Because constitutional prohibitions against discrimination are only applicable to governmental actors, gays must seek recourse in anti-discrimination legislation or ordinances. The private parties seeking to exclude gays, however, may, and often do, invoke constitutional provisions, like the First Amendment, claiming that forced inclusion of LGBT people violates their constitutional rights. For comparison purposes, the chapter begins with *Roberts v. United States Jaycees*, a case in which the U.S. Supreme Court considered the constitutionality of the Jaycees' exclusion of women.

ROBERTS v. UNITED STATES JAYCEES

468 U.S. 609, 104 S.Ct. 3244, 82 L.Ed.2d 462 (1984)

BRENNAN, J., delivered the opinion of the Court, in which WHITE, MARSHALL, POWELL, and STEVENS, JJ., joined, and in Parts I and III of which O'CONNOR, J., joined. O'CONNOR, J., filed an opinion concurring in part and concurring in the judgment, *post*, p. 631. REHNQUIST, J., concurred in the judgment. BURGER, C. J., and BLACKMUN, J., took no part in the decision of the case.

This case requires us to address a conflict between a State's efforts to eliminate gender-based discrimination against its citizens and the constitutional freedom of association asserted by members of a private organization. In the decision under review, the Court of Appeals for the Eighth Circuit concluded that, by requiring the United States Jaycees to admit women as full voting members, the Minnesota Human Rights Act violates the First and Fourteenth Amendment rights of the organization's members. We noted probable jurisdiction, *Gomez–Bethke v. United States Jaycees*, 464 U.S. 1037 (1984), and now reverse.

. . .

Our decisions have referred to constitutionally protected "freedom of association" in two distinct senses. In one line of decisions, the Court has concluded that choices to enter into and maintain certain intimate human relationships must be secured against undue intrusion by the State because of the role of such relationships in safeguarding the individual freedom that is central to our constitutional scheme. In this respect, freedom of association receives protection as a fundamental element of personal liberty. In another set of decisions, the Court has recognized a right to associate for the purpose of engaging in those activities protected by the First Amendment—speech, assembly, petition for the redress of grievances, and the exercise of religion. The Constitution guarantees freedom of association of this kind as an indispensable means of preserving other individual liberties.

The intrinsic and instrumental features of constitutionally protected association may, of course, coincide. In particular, when the State interferes with individuals' selection of those with whom they wish to join in a common endeavor, freedom of association in both of its forms may be implicated. The Jaycees contend that this is such a case. Still, the nature and degree of constitutional protection afforded freedom of association may vary depending on the extent to which one or the other aspect of the constitutionally protected liberty is at stake in a given case. We therefore find it useful to consider separately the effect of applying the Minnesota statute to the Jaycees on what could be called its members' freedom of intimate association and their freedom of expressive association.

A

The Court has long recognized that, because the Bill of Rights is designed to secure individual liberty, it must afford the formation and preservation of certain kinds of highly personal relationships a substantial measure of sanctuary from unjustified interference by the State.... Moreover, the constitutional shelter afforded such relationships reflects the realization that individuals draw much of their emotional enrichment from close ties with others. Protecting these relationships from unwarranted state interference therefore safeguards the ability independently to define one's identity that is central to any concept of liberty....

The personal affiliations that exemplify these considerations, and that therefore suggest some relevant limitations on the relationships that might be entitled to this sort of constitutional protection, are those that attend the creation and sustenance of a family[.] ... Family relationships, by their nature, involve deep attachments and commitments to the necessarily few other individuals with whom one shares not only a special community of thoughts, experiences, and beliefs but also distinctively personal aspects of one's life. Among other things, therefore, they are distinguished by such attributes as relative smallness, a high degree of selectivity in decisions to begin and maintain the affiliation, and seclusion from others in critical aspects of the relationship. As a general matter, only relationships with these sorts of qualities are likely to reflect the considerations that have led to an understanding of freedom of association as an intrinsic element of personal liberty. Conversely, an association lacking these qualities—such as a large business enterprise—seems remote from the concerns giving rise to this constitutional protection. Accordingly, the Constitution undoubtedly imposes constraints on the State's power to control the selection of one's spouse that would not apply to regulations affecting the choice of one's fellow employees. Compare *Loving v. Virginia*, 388 U.S. 1, 12 (1967), with *Railway Mail Assn. v. Corsi*, 326 U.S. 88, 93–94 (1945).

Between these poles, of course, lies a broad range of human relationships that may make greater or lesser claims to constitutional protection from particular incursions by the State.... We need not mark the potentially significant points on this terrain with any precision. We note only that factors that may be relevant include size, purpose, policies, selectivity, congeniality, and other characteristics that in a particular case may be pertinent. In this case, however, several features of the Jaycees clearly place the organization outside of the category of relationships worthy of this kind of constitutional protection.

The undisputed facts reveal that the local chapters of the Jaycees are large and basically unselective groups. At the time of the state administrative hearing, the Minneapolis chapter had approximately 430 members, while the St. Paul chapter had about 400. Apart from age and sex, neither the national organization nor the local chapters employ any criteria for judging applicants for membership, and new members are routinely recruited and admitted with no inquiry into their backgrounds. In fact, a local officer testified that he could recall no instance in which an applicant had been denied membership on any basis other than age or sex. Furthermore, despite their inability to vote, hold office, or receive certain awards, women affiliated with the Jaycees attend various meetings, participate in selected projects, and engage in many of the organization's social functions. Indeed, numerous nonmembers of both genders regularly participate in a substantial portion of activities central to the decision of many members to associate with one another, including many of the organization's various community programs, awards ceremonies, and recruitment meetings.

In short, the local chapters of the Jaycees are neither small nor selective.... Accordingly, we conclude that the Jaycees chapters lack the distinctive characteristics that might afford constitutional protection to the decision of its members to exclude women. We turn therefore to consider the extent to which application of the Minnesota statute to compel the Jaycees to accept women infringes the group's freedom of expressive association.

B

An individual's freedom to speak, to worship, and to petition the government for the redress of grievances could not be vigorously protected from interference by the State unless a correlative freedom to engage in group effort toward those ends were not also guaranteed. *See, e.g., Citizens Against Rent Control/Coalition for Fair Housing v. Berkeley*, 454 U.S. 290, 294 (1981). According protection to collective effort on behalf of shared goals is especially important in preserving political and cultural diversity and in shielding dissident expression from suppression by the majority. *See, e.g., Gilmore v. City of Montgomery*, 417 U.S., at 575; *Griswold v. Connecticut*, 381 U.S., at 482–485; *NAACP v. Button*, 371 U.S. 415, 431 (1963); *NAACP v. Alabama ex rel. Patterson*, 357 U.S., at 462. Consequently, we have long understood as implicit in the right to engage in activities protected by the First Amendment a corresponding right to associate with others in pursuit of a wide variety of political, social, economic, educational, religious, and cultural ends. *See, e.g., NAACP v. Claiborne Hardware Co.*, 458 U.S. 886, 907–909, 932–933 (1982); *Larson v. Valente*, 456 U.S. 228, 244–246 (1982); *In re Primus*, 436 U.S. 412, 426 (1978); *Abood v. Detroit Board of Education*, 431 U.S. 209, 231 (1977). In view of the various protected activities in which the Jaycees engages, *see infra*, at 626–627, that right is plainly implicated in this case.

Government actions that may unconstitutionally infringe upon this freedom can take a number of forms. Among other things, government may . . . try to interfere with the internal organization or affairs of the group, *e.g., Cousins v. Wigoda*, 419 U.S. 477, 487–488 (1975). By requiring the Jaycees to admit women as full voting members, the Minnesota Act works an infringement of . . . [this] type. There can be no clearer example of an intrusion into the internal structure or affairs of an association than a regulation that forces the group to accept members it does not desire. Such a regulation may impair the ability of the original members to express only those views that brought them together. Freedom of association therefore plainly presupposes a freedom not to associate. *See Abood v. Detroit Board of Education, supra*, at 234–235.

The right to associate for expressive purposes is not, however, absolute. Infringements on that right may be justified by regulations adopted to serve compelling state interests, unrelated to the suppression of ideas, that cannot be achieved through means significantly less restrictive of associational freedoms. We are persuaded that Minnesota's compelling interest in eradicating discrimination against its female citizens justifies the impact that application of the statute to the Jaycees may have on the male members' associational freedoms.

. . .

On its face, the Minnesota Act does not aim at the suppression of speech, does not distinguish between prohibited and permitted activity on the basis of viewpoint, and does not license enforcement authorities to administer the statute on the basis of such constitutionally impermissible criteria. *See also infra*, at 3255–3257. Nor does the Jaycees contend that the Act has been applied in this case for the purpose of hampering the organization's ability to express its views. Instead, as the Minnesota Supreme Court explained, the Act reflects the State's strong historical commitment to eliminating discrimination and assuring its citizens equal access to publicly available goods and services. *See* 305 N.W.2d, at 766–768. That goal, which is unrelated to the suppression of expression, plainly serves compelling state interests of the highest order.

. . .

Nor is the state interest in assuring equal access limited to the provision of purely tangible goods and services. A State enjoys broad authority to create rights of public access on behalf of its citizens. *Prune Yard Shopping Center v. Robins*, 447 U.S. 74, 81–88 (1980). Like many States and municipalities, Minnesota has adopted a functional definition of public accommodations that reaches various forms of public, quasi-commercial conduct. This expansive definition reflects a recognition of the changing nature of the American economy and of the importance, both to the individual and to society, of removing the barriers to economic advancement and political and social integration that have historically plagued certain disadvantaged groups, including women Thus, in explaining its conclusion that the Jaycees local chapters are "[places] of public accommodations" within the meaning of the Act, the Minnesota court noted the various commercial programs and benefits offered to members and stated that "[leadership] skills are 'goods,' [and] business contacts and employment promotions are 'privileges' and 'advantages'. . . ." Assuring women equal access to such goods, privileges, and advantages clearly furthers compelling state interests.

In applying the Act to the Jaycees, the State has advanced those interests through the least restrictive means of achieving its ends. Indeed, the Jaycees has failed to demonstrate that the Act imposes any serious burdens on the male members' freedom of expressive association. To be sure, as the Court of Appeals noted, a "not insubstantial part" of the Jaycees' activities constitutes protected expression on political, economic, cultural, and social affairs. Over the years, the national and local levels of the organization have taken public positions on a number of diverse issues, and members of the Jaycees regularly engage in a variety of civic, charitable, lobbying, fundraising, and other activities worthy of constitutional protection under the First Amendment. There is, however, no basis in the record for concluding that admission of women as full voting members will impede the organization's ability to engage in these protected activities or to disseminate its preferred views. The Act requires no change in the Jaycees' creed of promoting the interests of young men, and it imposes no restrictions on the organization's ability to exclude individuals with ideologies or philosophies different from those of its existing members. Moreover, the Jaycees already invites women to share the group's views and philosophy and to participate in much of its training and community activities. Accordingly, any claim that admission of women as full voting members will impair a symbolic message conveyed by the very fact that women are not permitted to vote is attenuated at best.

... In the absence of a showing far more substantial than that attempted by the Jaycees, we decline to indulge in the sexual stereotyping that underlies appellee's contention that, by allowing women to vote, application of the Minnesota Act will change the content or impact of the organization's speech.

In any event, even if enforcement of the Act causes some incidental abridgment of the Jaycees' protected speech, that effect is no greater than is necessary to accomplish the State's legitimate purposes. As we have explained, acts of invidious discrimination in the distribution of publicly available goods, services, and other advantages cause unique evils that government has a compelling interest to prevent—wholly apart from the point of view such conduct may transmit. Accordingly, like violence or other types of potentially expressive activities that produce special harms distinct from their communicative impact, such practices are entitled to no constitutional protection. In prohibiting such practices, the Minnesota Act therefore "responds precisely to the substantive problem which legitimately concerns" the State and abridges no more speech or associational freedom than is necessary to accomplish that purpose.

JUSTICE O'CONNOR, concurring. [Omitted].

JUSTICE REHNQUIST, concurring. [Omitted].

DISCUSSION

How do you feel about the idea of "public accommodation" generally? Is it justified as a means to alleviate class-based discrimination, or is it legal overreaching?

II. GAY PEOPLE AND PUBLIC ACCOMMODATION

As you read the following cases, ask yourself whether these cases mark a departure from *Roberts* as precedent. How does *Roberts* figure in *Hurley*? In *Dale*? For example, is the message in either *Hurley* or *Dale* somehow more discernible, more definite, than the message the Jaycees suggested they had a constitutional interest in protecting? Is there an implicit message in the progression from *Roberts* to *Dale* that a state's interest in the elimination of discrimination based on sexual orientation is simply not as important in the eyes of the justices as is an interest in eliminating gender discrimination?

HURLEY v. IRISH–AMERICAN GAY, LESBIAN & BISEXUAL GROUP OF BOSTON

515 U.S. 557, 115 S.Ct. 2338, 132 L.Ed.2d 487 (1995)

SOUTER, J., delivered the opinion for a unanimous Court.

The issue in this case is whether Massachusetts may require private citizens who organize a parade to include among the marchers a group imparting a message the organizers do not wish to convey. We hold that such a mandate violates the First Amendment.

I

March 17 is set aside for two celebrations in South Boston. As early as 1737, some people in Boston observed the feast of the apostle to Ireland, and since 1776 the day has marked the evacuation of royal troops and Loyalists from the city, prompted by the guns captured at Ticonderoga and set up on Dorchester Heights under General Washington's command. Washington himself reportedly drew on the earlier tradition in choosing "St. Patrick" as the response to "Boston," the password used in the colonial lines on evacuation day. Although the General Court of Massachusetts did not officially designate March 17 as Evacuation Day until 1938, the City Council of Boston had previously sponsored public celebrations of Evacuation Day, including notable commemorations on the centennial in 1876, and on the 125th anniversary in 1901, with its parade, salute, concert, and fireworks display.

The tradition of formal sponsorship by the city came to an end in 1947, however, when Mayor James Michael Curley himself granted authority to organize and conduct the St. Patrick's Day–Evacuation Day Parade to the petitioner South Boston Allied War Veterans Council, an unincorporated association of individuals elected from various South Boston veterans groups. Every year since that time, the Council has applied for and received a permit for the parade, which at times has included as many as 20,000 marchers and drawn up to 1 million watchers. No other applicant has ever applied for that permit. Through 1992, the city allowed the Council to use the city's official seal, and provided printing services as well as direct funding.

In 1992, a number of gay, lesbian, and bisexual descendants of the Irish immigrants joined together with other supporters to form the respondent organization, GLIB, to march in the parade as a way to express pride in their Irish heritage as openly gay, lesbian, and bisexual individuals, to demonstrate that there are such men and women among those so descended, and to express their solidarity with like individuals who sought to march in New York's St. Patrick's Day Parade. Although the Council denied GLIB's application to take part in the 1992 parade, GLIB obtained a state-court order to include its contingent, which marched "uneventfully" among that year's 10,000 participants and 750,000 spectators.

In 1993, after the Council had again refused to admit GLIB to the upcoming parade, the organization and some of its members filed this suit against the Council, the individual petitioner John J. "Wacko" Hurley, and the city of Boston, alleging violations of the State and Federal Constitutions and of the state public accommodations law, which prohibits "any distinction, discrimination or restriction on account of ... sexual orientation ... relative to the admission of any person to, or treatment in any place of public accommodation, resort or amusement." After finding that "for at least the past 47 years, the Parade has traveled the same basic route along the public streets of South Boston, providing entertainment, amusement, and recreation to participants and spectators alike," the state trial court ruled that the parade fell within the statutory definition of a public accommodation, which includes "any place ... which is open to and accepts or solicits the patronage of the general public and, without limiting the generality of this definition, whether or not it be ... (6) a boardwalk or other public highway [or] ... (8) a place of public amusement, recreation, sport, exercise or entertainment." The court found that the Council had no written criteria and employed no particular procedures for admission, voted on new applications in batches, had occasionally admitted groups who simply showed up at the parade without having submitted an application, and did "not generally inquire into the specific messages or views of each applicant." The court consequently rejected the Council's contention that the parade was "private" (in the sense of being exclusive), holding instead that "the lack of genuine selectivity in choosing participants and sponsors demonstrates that the Parade is a public event." It found the parade to be "eclectic," containing a wide variety of "patriotic, commercial, political, moral, artistic, religious, athletic, public service, trade union, and eleemosynary themes," as well as conflicting messages. While noting that the Council had indeed excluded the Ku Klux Klan and ROAR (an antibusing group), it attributed little significance to these facts, concluding ultimately that "the only common theme among the participants and sponsors is their public involvement in the Parade."

The court rejected the Council's assertion that the exclusion of "groups with sexual themes merely formalized [the fact] that the Parade expresses traditional religious and social values," *id.*, at B3, and found the Council's "final position [to be] that GLIB would be excluded because of its values and its message, *i.e.*, its members' sexual orientation." This position, in the court's view, was not only violative of the public accommodations law but "paradoxical" as well, since "a proper celebration of St. Patrick's and Evacuation Day requires diversity and inclusiveness." The court rejected the notion that GLIB's admission would trample on the Council's First Amendment rights since the court understood that constitutional protection of any interest in expressive association would "require focus on a specific message, theme, or group" absent from the parade. "Given the [Council's] lack of selectivity in choosing participants and failure to circumscribe the marchers' message," the court found it "impossible to discern any specific expressive purpose entitling the Parade to protection under the First Amendment." It concluded that the parade is "not an exercise of [the Council's] constitutionally protected right of expressive association," but instead "an open recreational event that is subject to the public accommodations law."

The court held that because the statute did not mandate inclusion of GLIB but only prohibited discrimination based on sexual orientation, any infringement on the Council's right to expressive association was only "incidental" and "no greater than necessary to accomplish the statute's legitimate purpose" of eradicating discrimination. *Id.,* at B25, citing *Roberts v. United States Jaycees,* 468 U.S. 609, 628–629, 82 L.Ed.2d 462, 104 S.Ct. 3244 (1984). Accordingly, it ruled that "GLIB is entitled to participate in the Parade on the same terms and conditions as other participants."

The Supreme Judicial Court of Massachusetts affirmed, seeing nothing clearly erroneous in the trial judge's findings that GLIB was excluded from the parade based on the sexual orientation of its members, that it was impossible to detect an expressive purpose in the parade, that there was no state action, and that the parade was a public accommodation within the meaning of § 272:92A.

Turning to petitioners' First Amendment claim that application of the public accommodations law to the parade violated their freedom of speech (as distinguished from their right to expressive association, raised in the trial court), the court's majority held that it need not decide on the particular First Amendment theory involved "because, as the [trial] judge found, it is 'impossible to discern any specific expressive purpose entitling the Parade to protection under the First Amendment.' " *Id.*, at 249, 636 N.E.2d, at 1299 (footnote omitted). The defendants had thus failed at the trial level "to demonstrate that the parade truly was an exercise of ... First Amendment rights," *id.*, at 250, 636 N.E.2d, at 1299, citing *Clark v. Community for Creative Non–Violence*, 468 U.S. 288, 293, n. 5, 104 S.Ct. 3065, 3069, n. 5, 82 L.Ed.2d 221 (1984), and on appeal nothing indicated to the majority of the Supreme Judicial Court that the trial judge's assessment of the evidence on this point was clearly erroneous, 418 Mass., at 250, 636 N.E.2d, at 1299. The court rejected petitioners' further challenge to the law as overbroad, holding that it does not, on its face, regulate speech, does not let public officials examine the content of speech, and would not be interpreted as reaching speech. *Id.*, at 251–252, 636 N.E.2d, at 1300. Finally, the court rejected the challenge that the public accommodations law was unconstitutionally vague, holding that this case did not present an issue of speech and that the law gave persons of ordinary intelligence a reasonable opportunity to know what was prohibited. *Id.*, at 252, 636 N.E.2d, at 1300–1301.

... We granted certiorari to determine whether the requirement to admit a parade contingent expressing a message not of the private organizers' own choosing violates the First Amendment. 513 U.S. 1071 (1995). We hold that it does and reverse.

II

Given the scope of the issues as originally joined in this case, it is worth noting some that have fallen aside in the course of the litigation, before reaching us. Although the Council presents us with a First Amendment claim, respondents do not. Neither do they press a claim that the Council's action has denied them equal protection of the laws in violation of the Fourteenth Amendment. While the guarantees of free speech and equal protection guard only against encroachment by the government and "erect no shield against merely private conduct," *Shelley v. Kraemer,* 334 U.S. 1, 13, 92 L.Ed. 1161, 68 S.Ct. 836 (1948); respondents originally argued that the Council's conduct was not purely private, but had the character of state action. The trial court's review of the city's involvement led it to find otherwise, however, and although the Supreme Judicial Court did not squarely address the issue, it appears to have affirmed the trial court's decision on that point as well as the others. In any event, respondents have not brought that question up either in a cross-petition for certiorari or in their briefs filed in this Court. When asked at oral argument whether they challenged the conclusion by the Massachusetts' courts that no state action is involved in the parade, respondents' counsel answered that they "do not press that issue here." In this Court, then, their claim for inclusion in the parade rests solely on the Massachusetts public accommodations law.

There is no corresponding concession from the other side, however, and certainly not to the state courts' characterization of the parade as lacking the element of expression for purposes of the First Amendment. Accordingly, our review of petitioners' claim that their activity is indeed in the nature of protected speech carries with it a constitutional duty to conduct an independent examination of the record as a whole, without deference to the trial court. *See Bose Corp. v. Consumers Union of United States, Inc.,* 466 U.S. 485, 499, 80 L.Ed.2d 502, 104 S.Ct. 1949 (1984). The "requirement of independent appellate review ... is a rule of federal constitutional law," which does not limit our deference to a trial court on matters of witness credibility, *Harte–Hanks Communications, Inc. v. Connaughton,* 491 U.S. 657, 688, 105 L.Ed.2d 562, 109 S.Ct. 2678 (1989), but which generally requires us to "review the finding of facts by a State court ... where a conclusion of law as to a Federal right and a finding of fact are so intermingled as to make it necessary, in order to pass upon the Federal question, to analyze the facts," *Fiske v. Kansas,* 274 U.S. 380, 385–386, 71 L.Ed. 1108, 47 S.Ct. 655 (1927). This obligation rests upon us simply because the reaches of the First Amendment are ultimately defined by the facts it is held to embrace, and we must thus decide for ourselves whether a given course of conduct falls on the near or far side of the line of constitutional protection. Even where a speech case has originally been tried in a federal court, subject to the provision of Federal Rule of Civil Procedure 52(a) that "findings of fact ... shall not be set aside unless clearly erroneous," we are obliged to make a fresh examination of crucial facts. Hence, in this case, though we are confronted with the state courts' conclusion that the factual characteristics of petitioners' activity place it within the vast realm of non-expressive conduct, our obligation is to " 'make an independent examination of the whole record,' . . . so as to assure ourselves that this judgment does not constitute a forbidden intrusion on the field of free expression." *New York Times Co. v. Sullivan,* 376 U.S. 254, 285, 11 L.Ed.2d 686, 84 S.Ct. 710 (1964) (footnote omitted), *quoting Edwards v. South Carolina,* 372 U.S. 229, 235, 9 L.Ed.2d 697, 83 S.Ct. 680 (1963).

III

A

If there were no reason for a group of people to march from here to there except to reach a destination, they could make the trip without expressing any message beyond the fact of the march itself. Some people might call such a procession a parade, but it would not be much of one. Real "parades are public dramas of social relations, and in them performers define who can be a social actor and what subjects and ideas are available for communication and consideration." S. Davis, Parades and Power: Street Theatre in Nineteenth–Century Philadelphia 6 (1986). Hence, we use the word "parade" to indicate marchers who are making some sort of collective point, not just to each other but to bystanders along the way. Indeed, a parade's dependence on watchers is so extreme that nowadays, as with Bishop Berkeley's celebrated tree, "if a parade or demonstration receives no media coverage, it may as well not have happened." *Id.,* at 171. Parades are thus a form of expression, not just motion, and the inherent expressiveness of marching to make a point explains our cases involving protest marches. . . .

The protected expression that inheres in a parade is not limited to its banners and songs, however, for the Constitution looks beyond written or spoken words as mediums of expression. Noting that "symbolism is a primitive but effective way of communicating ideas," *West Virginia Bd. of Ed. v. Barnette,* 319 U.S. 624, 632, 87 L.Ed. 1628, 63 S.Ct. 1178 (1943), our cases have recognized that the First Amendment shields such acts as saluting a flag (and refusing to do so), wearing an armband to protest a war, *Tinker v. Des Moines Independent Community School Dist.,* 393 U.S. 503, 505–506, 21 L.Ed.2d 731, 89 S.Ct. 733 (1969), displaying a red flag, *Stromberg v. California,* 283 U.S. 359, 369, 75 L.Ed. 1117, 51 S.Ct. 532 (1931), and even "marching, walking or parading" in uniforms displaying the swastika, *National Socialist Party of America v. Skokie,* 432 U.S. 43, 53 L.Ed.2d 96, 97 S.Ct. 2205 (1977). As some of these examples show, a narrow, succinctly articulable message is not a condition of constitutional protection, which if confined to expressions conveying a "particularized message," *cf. Spence v. Washington,* 418 U.S. 405, 411, 41 L.Ed.2d 842, 94 S.Ct. 2727 (1974) *(per curiam),* would never reach the unquestionably shielded painting of Jackson Pollock, music of Arnold Schoenberg, or Jabberwocky verse of Lewis Carroll.

Not many marches, then, are beyond the realm of expressive parades, and the South Boston celebration is not one of them. Spectators line the streets; people march in costumes and uniforms, carrying flags and banners with all sorts of messages (*e.g.,* "England get out of Ireland," "Say no to drugs"); marching bands and pipers play; floats are pulled along; and the whole show is broadcast over Boston television. To be sure, we agree with the state courts that in spite of excluding some applicants, the Council is rather lenient in admitting participants. But a private speaker does not forfeit constitutional protection simply by combining multifarious voices, or by failing to edit their themes to isolate an exact message as the exclusive subject matter of the speech. Nor, under our precedent, does First Amendment protection require a speaker to generate, as an original matter, each item featured in the communication. Cable operators, for example, are engaged in protected speech activities even when they only select programming originally produced by others. *Turner Broadcasting System, Inc. v. FCC,* 512 U.S. 622, 636, 129 L.Ed.2d 497, 114 S.Ct. 2445 (1994). For that matter, the presentation of an edited compilation of speech generated by other persons is a staple of most newspapers' opinion pages, which, of course, fall squarely within the core of First Amendment security, *Miami Herald Publishing Co. v. Tornillo,* 418 U.S. 241, 258, 41 L.Ed.2d 730, 94 S.Ct. 2831 (1974), as does even the simple selection of a paid noncommercial advertisement for inclusion in a daily paper, *see New York Times,* 376 U.S. at 265–266. The selection of contingents to make a parade is entitled to similar protection.

Respondents' participation as a unit in the parade was equally expressive. GLIB was formed for the very purpose of marching in it, as the trial court found, in order to celebrate its members' identity as openly gay, lesbian, and bisexual descendants of the Irish immigrants, to show that there are such individuals in the community, and to support the like men and women who sought to march in the New York parade. The organization distributed a fact sheet describing the members' intentions, App. A51, and the record otherwise corroborates the expressive nature of GLIB's participation. In 1993, members of GLIB marched behind a shamrock-strewn banner with the simple inscription "Irish American Gay, Lesbian and Bisexual Group of Boston." GLIB understandably seeks to communicate its ideas as part of the existing parade, rather than staging one of its own.

B

The Massachusetts public accommodations law under which respondents brought suit has a venerable history. . . .

. . . As with many public accommodations statutes across the Nation, the legislature continued to broaden the scope of legislation, to the point that the law today prohibits discrimination on the basis of "race, color, religious creed, national origin, sex, sexual orientation . . ., deafness, blindness or any physical or mental disability or ancestry" in "the admission of any person to, or treatment in any place of public accommodation, resort or amusement." Provisions like these are well within the State's usual power to enact when a legislature has reason to believe that a given group is the target of discrimination, and they do not, as a general matter, violate the First or Fourteenth Amendments. Nor is this statute unusual in any obvious way, since it does not, on its face, target speech or discriminate on the basis of its content, the focal point of its prohibition being rather on the act of discriminating against individuals in the provision of publicly available goods, privileges, and services on the proscribed grounds.

C

In the case before us, however, the Massachusetts law has been applied in a peculiar way. Its enforcement does not address any dispute about the participation of openly gay, lesbian, or bisexual individuals in various units admitted to the parade. Petitioners disclaim any intent to exclude homosexuals as such, and no individual member of GLIB claims to have been excluded from parading as a member of any group that the Council has approved to march. Instead, the disagreement goes to the admission of GLIB as its own parade unit carrying its own banner. Since every participating unit affects the message conveyed by the private organizers, the state courts' application of the statute produced an order essentially requiring petitioners to alter the expressive content of their parade. Although the state courts spoke of the parade as a place of public accommodation, once the expressive character of both the parade and the marching GLIB contingent is understood, it becomes apparent that the state courts' application of the statute had the effect of declaring the sponsors' speech itself to be the public accommodation. Under this approach any contingent of protected individuals with a message would have the right to participate in petitioners' speech, so that the communication produced by the private organizers would be shaped by all those protected by the law who wished to join in with some expressive demonstration of their own. But this use of the State's power violates the fundamental rule of protection under the First Amendment, that a speaker has the autonomy to choose the content of his own message.

"Since *all* speech inherently involves choices of what to say and what to leave unsaid," *Pacific Gas & Electric Co. v. Public Utilities Comm'n of Cal.,* 475 U.S. 1, 11, 89 L.Ed.2d 1, 106 S.Ct. 903 (1986) (plurality opinion) (emphasis in original), one important manifestation of the principle of free speech is that one who chooses to speak may also decide "what not to say," Although the State may at times "prescribe what shall be orthodox in commercial advertising" by requiring the dissemination of "purely factual and uncontroversial information," *Zauderer v. Office of Disciplinary Counsel of Supreme Court of Ohio,* 471 U.S. 626, 651, 85 L.Ed.2d 652, 105 S.Ct. 2265 (1985); outside that context it may not compel affirmance of a belief with which the speaker disagrees, *see Barnette,* 319 U.S. at 642. Indeed this general rule, that the speaker has the right to tailor the speech, applies not only to expressions of value, opinion, or endorsement, but equally to statements of fact the speaker would rather avoid, subject, perhaps, to the permissive law of defamation. Nor is the rule's benefit restricted to the press, being enjoyed by business corporations generally and by ordinary people engaged in unsophisticated expression as well as by professional publishers. Its point is simply the point of all speech protection, which is to shield just those choices of content that in someone's eyes are misguided, or even hurtful.

Petitioners' claim to the benefit of this principle of autonomy to control one's own speech is as sound as the South Boston parade is expressive. Rather like a composer, the Council selects the expressive units of the parade from potential participants, and though the score may not produce a particularized message, each contingent's expression in the Council's eyes comports with what merits celebration on that day. Even if this view gives the Council credit for a more considered judgment than it actively made, the Council clearly decided to exclude a message it did not like from the communication it chose to make, and that is enough to invoke its right as a private speaker to shape its expression by speaking on one subject while remaining silent on another. The message it disfavored is not difficult to identify. Although GLIB's point (like the Council's) is not wholly articulate, a contingent marching behind the organization's banner would at least bear witness to the fact that some Irish are gay, lesbian, or bisexual, and the presence of the organized marchers would suggest their view that people of their sexual orientations have as much claim to unqualified social acceptance as heterosexuals and indeed as members of parade units organized around other identifying characteristics. The parade's organizers may not believe these facts about Irish sexuality to be so, or they may object to unqualified social acceptance of gays and lesbians or have some other reason for wishing to keep GLIB's message out of the parade. But whatever the reason, it boils down to the choice of a speaker not to propound a particular point of view, and that choice is presumed to lie beyond the government's power to control.

Respondents argue that any tension between this rule and the Massachusetts law falls short of unconstitutionality, citing the most recent of our cases on the general subject of compelled access for expressive purposes, *Turner Broadcasting System, Inc. v. FCC,* 512 U.S. 622, 129 L.Ed.2d 497, 114 S.Ct. 2445 (1994). There we reviewed regulations requiring cable operators to set aside channels for designated broadcast signals, and applied only intermediate scrutiny. Respondents contend on this authority that admission of GLIB to the parade would not threaten the core principle of speaker's autonomy because the Council, like a cable operator, is merely "a conduit" for the speech of participants in the parade "rather than itself a speaker." But this metaphor is not apt here, because GLIB's participation would likely be perceived as having resulted from the Council's customary determination about a unit admitted to the parade, that its message was worthy of presentation and quite possibly of support as well. A newspaper, similarly, "is more than a passive receptacle or conduit for news, comment, and advertising," and we have held that "the choice of material ... and the decisions made as to limitations on the size and content ... and treatment of public issues ... —whether fair or unfair—constitute the exercise of editorial control and judgment" upon which the State can not intrude. *Tornillo,* 418 U.S. at 258. Indeed, in *Pacific Gas & Electric,* we invalidated coerced access to the envelope of a private utility's bill and newsletter because the utility "may be forced either to appear to agree with [the intruding leaflet] or to respond." 475 U.S. at 15 (plurality opinion) (citation omitted). The plurality made the further point that if "the government [were] freely able to compel ... speakers to propound political messages with which they disagree, ... protection [of a speaker's freedom] would be empty, for the government could require speakers to affirm in one breath that which they deny in the next." Thus, when dissemination of a view contrary to one's own is forced upon a speaker intimately connected with the communication advanced, the speaker's right to autonomy over the message is compromised.

In *Turner Broadcasting,* we found this problem absent in the cable context, because "given cable's long history of serving as a conduit for broadcast signals, there appears little risk that cable viewers would assume that the broadcast stations carried on a cable system convey ideas or messages endorsed by the cable operator." We stressed that the viewer is frequently apprised of the identity of the broadcaster whose signal is being received via cable and that it is "common practice for broadcasters to disclaim any identity of viewpoint between the management and the speakers who use the broadcast facility."

Parades and demonstrations, in contrast, are not understood to be so neutrally presented or selectively viewed. Unlike the programming offered on various channels by a cable network, the parade does not consist of individual, unrelated segments that happen to be transmitted together for individual selection by members of the audience. Although each parade unit generally identifies itself, each is understood to contribute something to a common theme, and accordingly there is no customary practice whereby private sponsors disavow "any identity of viewpoint" between themselves and the selected participants. Practice follows practicability here, for such disclaimers would be quite curious in a moving parade. Without deciding on the precise significance of the likelihood of misattribution, it nonetheless becomes clear that in the context of an expressive parade, as with a protest march, the parade's overall message is distilled from the individual presentations along the way, and each unit's expression is perceived by spectators as part of the whole.

An additional distinction between *Turner Broadcasting* and this case points to the fundamental weakness of any attempt to justify the state-court order's limitation on the Council's autonomy as a speaker. A cable is not only a conduit for speech produced by others and selected by cable operators for transmission, but a franchised channel giving monopolistic opportunity to shut out some speakers. This power gives rise to the Government's interest in limiting monopolistic autonomy in order to allow for the survival of broadcasters who might otherwise be silenced and consequently destroyed. The Government's interest in *Turner Broadcasting* was not the alteration of speech, but the survival of speakers. In thus identifying an interest going beyond abridgment of speech itself, the defenders of the law at issue in *Turner Broadcasting* addressed the threshold requirement of any review under the Speech Clause, whatever the ultimate level of scrutiny, that a challenged restriction on speech serve a compelling, or at least important, governmental object.

In this case, of course, there is no assertion comparable to the *Turner Broadcasting* claim that some speakers will be destroyed in the absence of the challenged law. True, the size and success of petitioners' parade makes it an enviable vehicle for the dissemination of GLIB's views, but that fact, without more, would fall far short of supporting a claim that petitioners enjoy an abiding monopoly of access to spectators. Considering that GLIB presumably would have had a fair shot (under neutral criteria developed by the city) at obtaining a parade permit of its own, respondents have not shown that petitioners enjoy the capacity to "silence the voice of competing speakers," as cable operators do with respect to program providers who wish to reach subscribers. Nor has any other legitimate interest been identified in support of applying the Massachusetts statute in this way to expressive activity like the parade.

The statute is a piece of protective legislation that announces no purpose beyond the object both expressed and apparent in its provisions, which is to prevent any denial of access to (or discriminatory treatment in) public accommodations on proscribed grounds, including sexual orientation. On its face, the object of the law is to ensure by statute for gays and lesbians desiring to make use of public accommodations what the old common law promised to any member of the public wanting a meal at the inn, that accepting the usual terms of service, they will not be turned away merely on the proprietor's exercise of personal preference. When the law is applied to expressive activity in the way it was done here, its apparent object is simply to require speakers to modify the content of their expression to whatever extent beneficiaries of the law choose to alter it with messages of their own. But in the absence of some further, legitimate end, this object is merely to allow exactly what the general rule of speaker's autonomy forbids.

It might, of course, have been argued that a broader objective is apparent: that the ultimate point of forbidding acts of discrimination toward certain classes is to produce a society free of the corresponding biases. Requiring access to a speaker's message would thus be not an end in itself, but a means to produce speakers free of the biases, whose expressive conduct would be at least neutral toward the particular classes, obviating any future need for correction. But if this indeed is the point of applying the state law to expressive conduct, it is a decidedly fatal objective. Having availed itself of the public thoroughfares "for purposes of assembly [and] communicating thoughts between citizens," the Council is engaged in a use of the streets that has "from ancient times, been a part of the privileges, immunities, rights, and liberties of citizens." *Hague v. Committee for Industrial Organization,* 307 U.S. 496, 515, 83 L.Ed. 1423, 59 S.Ct. 954 (1939) (opinion of Roberts, J.). Our tradition of free speech commands that a speaker who takes to the street corner to express his views in this way should be free from interference by the State based on the content of what he says. The very idea that a noncommercial speech restriction be used to produce thoughts and statements acceptable to some groups or, indeed, all people, grates on the First Amendment, for it amounts to nothing less than a proposal to limit speech in the service of orthodox expression. The Speech Clause has no more certain antithesis. While the law is free to promote all sorts of conduct in place of harmful behavior, it is not free to interfere with speech for no better reason than promoting an approved message or discouraging a disfavored one, however enlightened either purpose may strike the government.

Far from supporting GLIB, then, *Turner Broadcasting* points to the reasons why the present application of the Massachusetts law can not be sustained. So do the two other principal authorities GLIB has cited. In *PruneYard Shopping Center v. Robins, supra*, to be sure, we sustained a state law requiring the proprietors of shopping malls to allow visitors to solicit signatures on political petitions without a showing that the shopping mall owners would otherwise prevent the beneficiaries of the law from reaching an audience. But we found in that case that the proprietors were running "a business establishment that is open to the public to come and go as they please," that the solicitations would "not likely be identified with those of the owner," and that the proprietors could "expressly disavow any connection with the message by simply posting signs in the area where the speakers or handbillers stand." 447 U.S., at 87, 100 S.Ct., at 2044. Also, in *Pacific Gas & Electric*, supra, at 12, 106 S.Ct., at 909, we noted that *PruneYard* did not involve "any concern that access to this area might affect the shopping center owner's exercise of his own right to speak: the owner did not even allege that he objected to the content of the pamphlets...." The principle of speaker's autonomy was simply not threatened in that case.

New York State Club Assn. is also instructive by the contrast it provides. There, we turned back a facial challenge to a state antidiscrimination statute on the assumption that the expressive associational character of a dining club with over 400 members could be sufficiently attenuated to permit application of the law even to such a private organization, but we also recognized that the State did not prohibit exclusion of those whose views were at odds with positions espoused by the general club memberships. *See also Roberts,* 468 U.S. at 627. In other words, although the association provided public benefits to which a State could ensure equal access, it was also engaged in expressive activity; compelled access to the benefit, which was upheld, did not trespass on the organization's message itself. If we were to analyze this case strictly along those lines, GLIB would lose. Assuming the parade to be large enough and a source of benefits (apart from its expression) that would generally justify a mandated access provision, GLIB could nonetheless be refused admission as an expressive contingent with its own message just as readily as a private club could exclude an applicant whose manifest views were at odds with a position taken by the club's existing members.

IV

Our holding today rests not on any particular view about the Council's message but on the Nation's commitment to protect freedom of speech. Disapproval of a private speaker's statement does not legitimize use of the Commonwealth's power to compel the speaker to alter the message by including one more acceptable to others. Accordingly, the judgment of the Supreme Judicial Court is reversed and the case remanded for proceedings not inconsistent with this opinion.

It is so ordered.

BOY SCOUTS OF AM. v. DALE

530 U.S. 640, 120 S.Ct. 2446, 147 L.Ed.2d 554 (2000)

REHNQUIST, C. J., delivered the opinion of the Court, in which O'CONNOR, SCALIA, KENNEDY, and THOMAS, JJ., joined. STEVENS, J., filed a dissenting opinion, in which SOUTER, GINSBURG, and BREYER, JJ., joined. SOUTER, J., filed a dissenting opinion, in which GINSBURG and BREYER, JJ., joined.

Petitioners are the Boy Scouts of America and the Monmouth Council, a division of the Boy Scouts of America (collectively, Boy Scouts). The Boy Scouts is a private, not-for-profit organization engaged in instilling its system of values in young people. The Boy Scouts asserts that homosexual conduct is inconsistent with the values it seeks to instill. Respondent is James Dale, a former Eagle Scout whose adult membership in the Boy Scouts was revoked when the Boy Scouts learned that he is an avowed homosexual and gay rights activist. The New Jersey Supreme Court held that New Jersey's public accommodations law requires that the Boy Scouts admit Dale. This case presents the question whether applying New Jersey's public accommodations law in this way violates the Boy Scouts' First Amendment right of expressive association. We hold that it does.

I.

James Dale entered scouting in 1978 at the age of eight by joining Monmouth Council's Cub Scout Pack 142. Dale became a Boy Scout in 1981 and remained a Scout until he turned 18. By all accounts, Dale was an exemplary Scout. In 1988, he achieved the rank of Eagle Scout, one of Scouting's highest honors.

Dale applied for adult membership in the Boy Scouts in 1989. The Boy Scouts approved his application for the position of assistant scoutmaster of Troop 73. Around the same time, Dale left home to attend Rutgers University. After arriving at Rutgers, Dale first acknowledged to himself and others that he is gay. He quickly became involved with, and eventually became the copresident of, the Rutgers University Lesbian/Gay Alliance. In 1990, Dale attended a seminar addressing the psychological and health needs of lesbian and gay teenagers. A newspaper covering the event interviewed Dale about his advocacy of homosexual teenagers' need for gay role models. In early July 1990, the newspaper published the interview and Dale's photograph over a caption identifying him as the copresident of the Lesbian/Gay Alliance.

Later that month, Dale received a letter from Monmouth Council Executive James Kay revoking his adult membership. Dale wrote to Kay requesting the reason for Monmouth Council's decision. Kay responded by letter that the Boy Scouts "specifically forbid membership to homosexuals." App. 137.

In 1992, Dale filed a complaint against the Boy Scouts in the New Jersey Superior Court. The complaint alleged that the Boy Scouts had violated New Jersey's public accommodations statute and its common law by revoking Dale's membership based solely on his sexual orientation. New Jersey's public accommodations statute prohibits, among other things, discrimination on the basis of sexual orientation in places of public accommodation. N. J. Stat. Ann. §§ 10:5–4.

The New Jersey Superior Court's Chancery Division granted summary judgment in favor of the Boy Scouts. The court held that New Jersey's public accommodations law was inapplicable because the Boy Scouts was not a place of public accommodation, and that, alternatively, the Boy Scouts is a distinctly private group exempted from coverage under New Jersey's law. The court rejected Dale's common-law claim holding that New Jersey's policy is embodied in the public accommodations law.

... The New Jersey Superior Court's Appellate Division affirmed the dismissal of Dale's common-law claim, but otherwise reversed and remanded for further proceedings. 308 N.J. Super. 516, 706 A.2d 270 (1998).

... The New Jersey Supreme Court affirmed the judgment of the Appellate Division. It held that the Boy Scouts was a place of public accommodation subject to the public accommodations law, that the organization was not exempt from the law under any of its express exceptions, and that the Boy Scouts violated the law by revoking Dale's membership based on his avowed homosexuality.

... We granted the Boy Scouts' petition for certiorari to determine whether the application of New Jersey's public accommodations law violated the First Amendment. 528 U.S. 1109 (2000).

II.

In *Roberts v. United States Jaycees,* 468 U.S. 609, 622, 82 L.Ed.2d 462, 104 S.Ct. 3244 (1984), we observed that "implicit in the right to engage in activities protected by the First Amendment" is "a corresponding right to associate with others in pursuit of a wide variety of political, social, economic, educational, religious, and cultural ends." This right is crucial in preventing the majority from imposing its views on groups that would rather express other, perhaps unpopular, ideas. *See ibid.* (stating that protection of the right to expressive association is "especially important in preserving political and cultural diversity and in shielding dissident expression from suppression by the majority"). Government actions that may unconstitutionally burden this freedom may take many forms, one of which is "intrusion into the internal structure or affairs of an association" like a "regulation that forces the group to accept members it does not desire." 468 U.S. at 623. Forcing a group to accept certain members may impair the ability of the group to express those views, and only those views, that it intends to express. Thus, "[f]reedom of association ... plainly presupposes a freedom not to associate." *Ibid.*

The forced inclusion of an unwanted person in a group infringes the group's freedom of expressive association if the presence of that person affects in a significant way the group's ability to advocate public or private viewpoints. *New York State Club Assn., Inc. v. City of New York,* 487 U.S. 1, 13, 101 L.Ed.2d 1, 108 S.Ct. 2225 (1988). But the freedom of expressive association, like many freedoms, is not absolute. We have held that the freedom could be overridden "by regulations adopted to serve compelling state interests, unrelated to the suppression of ideas, that cannot be achieved through means significantly less restrictive of associational freedoms." *Roberts, supra,* at 623.

To determine whether a group is protected by the First Amendment's expressive associational right, we must determine whether the group engages in "expressive association." The First Amendment's protection of expressive association is not reserved for advocacy groups. But to come within its ambit, a group must engage in some form of expression, whether it be public or private.

Because this is a First Amendment case where the ultimate conclusions of law are virtually inseparable from findings of fact, we are obligated to independently review the factual record to ensure that the state court's judgment does not unlawfully intrude on free expression. *See Hurley,* 515 U.S. at 567–568. The record reveals the following. The Boy Scouts is a private, nonprofit organization. According to its mission statement:

> It is the mission of the Boy Scouts of America to serve others by helping to instill values in young people and, in other ways, to prepare them to make ethical choices over their lifetime in achieving their full potential.
>
> The values we strive to instill are based on those found in the Scout Oath and Law:
>
> **Scout Oath**
>
> On my honor I will do my best
>
> To do my duty to God and my country and to obey the Scout Law;
>
> To help other people at all times;

To keep myself physically strong, mentally awake, and morally straight.

Scout Law

A Scout is:
Trustworthy Obedient
Loyal Cheerful
Helpful Thrifty
Friendly Brave
Courteous Clean
Kind Reverent.

App. 184.

Thus, the general mission of the Boy Scouts is clear: "To instill values in young people." *Ibid.* The Boy Scouts seeks to instill these values by having its adult leaders spend time with the youth members, instructing and engaging them in activities like camping, archery, and fishing. During the time spent with the youth members, the scoutmasters and assistant scoutmasters inculcate them with the Boy Scouts' values—both expressly and by example. It seems indisputable that an association that seeks to transmit such a system of values engages in expressive activity. *See Roberts, supra,* at 636 (O'CONNOR, J., concurring) ("Even the training of outdoor survival skills or participation in community service might become expressive when the activity is intended to develop good morals, reverence, patriotism, and a desire for self-improvement").

Given that the Boy Scouts engages in expressive activity, we must determine whether the forced inclusion of Dale as an assistant scoutmaster would significantly affect the Boy Scouts' ability to advocate public or private viewpoints. This inquiry necessarily requires us first to explore, to a limited extent, the nature of the Boy Scouts' view of homosexuality.

The values the Boy Scouts seeks to instill are "based on" those listed in the Scout Oath and Law. App. 184. The Boy Scouts explains that the Scout Oath and Law provide "a positive moral code for living; they are a list of 'do's' rather than 'don'ts.' " Brief for Petitioners 3. The Boy Scouts asserts that homosexual conduct is inconsistent with the values embodied in the Scout Oath and Law, particularly with the values represented by the terms "morally straight" and "clean."

Obviously, the Scout Oath and Law do not expressly mention sexuality or sexual orientation. *See supra,* at 6–7. And the terms "morally straight" and "clean" are by no means self-defining. . . .

The New Jersey Supreme Court analyzed the Boy Scouts' beliefs and found that the "exclusion of members solely on the basis of their sexual orientation is inconsistent with Boy Scouts' commitment to a diverse and 'representative' membership . . . [and] contradicts Boy Scouts' overarching objective to reach 'all eligible youth.' " 160 N.J. at 618, 734 A.2d at 1226. The court concluded that the exclusion of members like Dale "appears antithetical to the organization's goals and philosophy." *Ibid.* But our cases reject this sort of inquiry; it is not the role of the courts to reject a group's expressed values because they disagree with those values or find them internally inconsistent. *See Democratic Party of United States v. Wisconsin ex rel. La Follette,* 450 U.S. 107, 124, 67 L.Ed.2d 82, 101 S.Ct. 1010 (1981) ("As is true of all expressions of First Amendment freedoms, the courts may not interfere on the ground that they view a particular expression as unwise or irrational"); *see also Thomas v. Review Bd. of Indiana Employment Security Div.,* 450 U.S. 707, 714, 67 L.Ed.2d 624, 101 S.Ct. 1425 (1981) ("Religious beliefs need not be acceptable, logical, consistent, or comprehensible to others to merit First Amendment protection").

The Boy Scouts asserts that it "teaches that homosexual conduct is not morally straight," Brief for Petitioners 39, and that it does "not want to promote homosexual conduct as a legitimate form of behavior," Reply Brief for Petitioners 5. We accept the Boy Scouts' assertion. We need not inquire further to determine the nature of the Boy Scouts' expression with respect to homosexuality. But because the record before us contains written evidence of the Boy Scouts' viewpoint, we look to it as instructive, if only on the question of the sincerity of the professed beliefs.

A 1978 position statement to the Boy Scouts' Executive Committee, signed by Downing B. Jenks, the President of the Boy Scouts, and Harvey L. Price, the Chief Scout Executive, expresses the Boy Scouts' "official position" with regard to "homosexuality and Scouting":

> Q. May an individual who openly declares himself to be a homosexual be a volunteer Scout leader?
>
> A. No. The Boy Scouts of America is a private, membership organization and leadership therein is a privilege and not a right. We do not believe that homosexuality and leadership in Scouting are appropriate. We will continue to select only those who in our judgment meet our standards and qualifications for leadership."

App. 453–454.

> . . . For example, a 1993 position statement, the most recent in the record, reads, in part:
>
> The Boy Scouts of America has always reflected the expectations that Scouting families have had for the organization. We do not believe that homosexuals provide a role model consistent with these expectations. Accordingly, we do not allow for the registration of avowed homosexuals as members or as leaders of the BSA.

Id. at 461.

. . . We must then determine whether Dale's presence as an assistant scoutmaster would significantly burden the Boy Scouts' desire to not "promote homosexual conduct as a legitimate form of behavior." Reply Brief for Petitioners 5. As we give deference to an association's assertions regarding the nature of its expression, we must also give deference to an association's view of what would impair its expression. *See, e.g., La Follette,* 450 U.S. at 123–124 (considering whether a Wisconsin law burdened the National Party's associational rights and stating that "a State, or a court, may not constitutionally substitute its own judgment for that of the Party"). That is not to say that an expressive association can erect a shield against antidiscrimination laws simply by asserting that mere acceptance of a member from a particular group would impair its message. But here Dale, by his own admission, is one of a group of gay Scouts who have "become leaders in their community and are open and honest about their sexual orientation." App. 11. Dale was the copresident of a gay and lesbian organization at college and remains a gay rights activist. Dale's presence in the Boy Scouts would, at the very least, force the organization to send a message, both to the youth members and the world, that the Boy Scouts accepts homosexual conduct as a legitimate form of behavior.

Hurley is illustrative on this point. There we considered whether the application of Massachusetts' public accommodations law to require the organizers of a private St. Patrick's Day parade to include among the marchers an Irish–American gay, lesbian, and bisexual group, GLIB, violated the parade organizers' First Amendment rights. We noted that the parade organizers did not wish to exclude the GLIB members because of their sexual orientations, but because they wanted to march behind a GLIB banner. . . .

Here, we have found that the Boy Scouts believes that homosexual conduct is inconsistent with the values it seeks to instill in its youth members; it will not "promote homosexual conduct as a legitimate form of behavior." Reply Brief for Petitioners 5. As the presence of GLIB in Boston's St. Patrick's Day parade would have interfered with the parade organizers' choice not to propound a particular point of view, the presence of Dale as an assistant scoutmaster would just as surely interfere with the Boy Scout's choice not to propound a point of view contrary to its beliefs.

The New Jersey Supreme Court determined that the Boy Scouts' ability to disseminate its message was not significantly affected by the forced inclusion of Dale as an assistant scoutmaster because of the following findings:

> Boy Scout members do not associate for the purpose of disseminating the belief that homosexuality is immoral; Boy Scouts discourages its leaders from disseminating *any* views on sexual issues; and Boy Scouts includes sponsors and members who subscribe to different views in respect of homosexuality.

160 N.J. at 612, 734 A.2d at 1223.

We disagree with the New Jersey Supreme Court's conclusion drawn from these findings.

First, associations do not have to associate for the "purpose" of disseminating a certain message in order to be entitled to the protections of the First Amendment. An association must merely engage in expressive activity that could be impaired in order to be entitled to protection. For example, the purpose of the St. Patrick's Day parade in *Hurley* was not to espouse any views about sexual orientation, but we held that the parade organizers had a right to exclude certain participants nonetheless.

Second, even if the Boy Scouts discourages Scout leaders from disseminating views on sexual issues—a fact that the Boy Scouts disputes with contrary evidence—the First Amendment protects the Boy Scouts' method of expression. If the Boy Scouts wishes Scout leaders to avoid questions of sexuality and teach only by example, this fact does not negate the sincerity of its belief discussed above.

Third, the First Amendment simply does not require that every member of a group agree on every issue in order for the group's policy to be "expressive association." The Boy Scouts takes an official position with respect to homosexual conduct, and that is sufficient for First Amendment purposes.

... Having determined that the Boy Scouts is an expressive association and that the forced inclusion of Dale would significantly affect its expression, we inquire whether the application of New Jersey's public accommodations law to require that the Boy Scouts accept Dale as an assistant scoutmaster runs afoul of the Scouts' freedom of expressive association. We conclude that it does.

State public accommodations laws were originally enacted to prevent discrimination in traditional places of public accommodation—like inns and trains. *See, e.g., Hurley,* 515 U.S. at 571–572 (explaining the history of Massachusetts' public accommodations law); *Romer v. Evans,* 517 U.S. 620, 627–629, 134 L.Ed.2d 855, 116 S.Ct. 1620 (1996) (describing the evolution of public accommodations laws). Over time, the public accommodations laws have expanded to cover more places. New Jersey's statutory definition of "[a] place of public accommodation" is extremely broad. The term is said to "include, but not be limited to," a list of over 50 types of places. N.J. Stat. Ann. § 10:5–5(*l*) (West Supp. 2000); *see* Appendix, *infra,* at 18–19. Many on the list are what one would expect to be places where the public is invited. For example, the statute includes as places of public accommodation taverns, restaurants, retail shops, and public libraries. But the statute also includes places that often may not carry with them open invitations to the public, like summer camps and roof gardens. In this case, the New Jersey Supreme Court went a step further and applied its public accommodations law to a private entity without even attempting to tie the term "place" to a physical location. n3 As the definition of "public accommodation" has expanded from clearly commercial entities, such as restaurants, bars, and hotels, to membership organizations such as the Boy Scouts, the potential for conflict between state public accommodations laws and the First Amendment rights of organizations has increased.

... In *Hurley,* we applied traditional First Amendment analysis to hold that the application of the Massachusetts public accommodations law to a parade violated the First Amendment rights of the parade organizers. Although we did not explicitly deem the parade in *Hurley* an expressive association, the analysis we applied there is similar to the analysis we apply here. We have already concluded that a state requirement that the Boy Scouts retain Dale as an assistant scoutmaster would significantly burden the organization's right to oppose or disfavor homosexual conduct. The state interests embodied in New Jersey's public accommodations law do not justify such a severe intrusion on the Boy Scouts' rights to freedom of expressive association. That being the case, we hold that the First Amendment prohibits the State from imposing such a requirement through the application of its public accommodations law.

... We are not, as we must not be, guided by our views of whether the Boy Scouts' teachings with respect to homosexual conduct are right or wrong; public or judicial disapproval of a tenet of an organization's expression does not justify the State's effort to compel the organization to accept members where such acceptance would derogate from the organization's expressive message. "While the law is free to promote all sorts of conduct in place of harmful behavior, it is not free to interfere with speech for no better reason than promoting an approved message or discouraging a disfavored one, however enlightened either purpose may strike the government." *Hurley,* 515 U.S. at 579.

The judgment of the New Jersey Supreme Court is reversed, and the cause remanded for further proceedings not inconsistent with this opinion.

It is so ordered.

. . .

DISSENT: JUSTICE STEVENS, with whom JUSTICE SOUTER, JUSTICE GINSBURG and JUSTICE BREYER join, dissenting.

... The majority holds that New Jersey's law violates BSA's right to associate and its right to free speech. But that law does not "impose any serious burdens" on BSA's "collective effort on behalf of [its] shared goals," *Roberts v. United States Jaycees,* 468 U.S. 609, 622, 626–627, 82 L.Ed.2d 462, 104 S.Ct. 3244 (1984), nor does it force BSA to communicate any message that it does not wish to endorse. New Jersey's law, therefore, abridges no constitutional right of the Boy Scouts.

I.

... In this case, Boy Scouts of America contends that it teaches the young boys who are Scouts that homosexuality is immoral. Consequently, it argues, it would violate its right to associate to force it to admit homosexuals as members, as doing so would be at odds with its own shared goals and values. This contention, quite plainly, requires us to look at what, exactly, are the values that BSA actually teaches.

BSA's mission statement reads as follows: "It is the mission of the Boy Scouts of America to serve others by helping to instill values in young people and, in other ways, to prepare them to make ethical choices over their lifetime in achieving their full potential." *Id.* at 184. Its federal charter declares its purpose is "to promote, through organization, and cooperation with other agencies, the ability of boys to do things for themselves and others, to train them in scoutcraft, and to teach them patriotism, courage, self-reliance, and kindred values, using the methods which were in common use by Boy Scouts on June 15, 1916." 36 U.S.C. § 23; *see also* App. 315–316. BSA describes itself as having a "representative membership," which it defines as "boy membership [that] reflects proportionately the characteristics of the boy population of its service area." *Id.* at 65. In particular, the group emphasizes that "neither the charter nor the bylaws of the Boy Scouts of America permits the exclusion of any boy.... To meet these responsibilities we have made a commitment that our membership shall be representative of *all* the population in every community, district, and council." *Id.* at 66–67 (emphasis in original).

... The Boy Scout Handbook defines "morally straight," as such:

> To be a person of strong character, guide your life with honesty, purity, and justice. Respect and defend the rights of all people. Your relationships with others should be honest and open. Be clean in your speech and actions, and faithful in your religious beliefs. The values you follow as a Scout will help you become virtuous and self-reliant. *Id.* at 218 (emphasis deleted).

The Scoutmaster Handbook emphasizes these points about being "morally straight":

> In any consideration of moral fitness, a key word has to be 'courage.' A boy's courage to do what his head and his heart tell him is right. And the courage to refuse to do what his heart and his head say is wrong. Moral fitness, like emotional fitness, will clearly present opportunities for wise guidance by an alert Scoutmaster.

Id. at 239–240.

As for the term "clean," the Boy Scout Handbook offers the following:

> A Scout is CLEAN. A Scout keeps his body and mind fit and clean. He chooses the company of those who live by these same ideals. He helps keep his home and community clean.
>
> You never need to be ashamed of dirt that will wash off. If you play hard and work hard you can't help getting dirty. But when the game is over or the work is done, that kind of dirt disappears with soap and water.
>
> There's another kind of dirt that won't come off by washing. It is the kind that shows up in foul language and harmful thoughts.
>
> Swear words, profanity, and dirty stories are weapons that ridicule other people and hurt their feelings. The same is true of racial slurs and jokes making fun of ethnic groups or people with physical or mental limitations. A Scout knows there is no kindness or honor in

> such mean-spirited behavior. He avoids it in his own words and deeds. He defends those who are targets of insults.

Id. at 225–226 (emphasis in original); *see also id.* at 189.

It is plain as the light of day that neither one of these principles—"morally straight" and "clean"—says the slightest thing about homosexuality. Indeed, neither term in the Boy Scouts' Law and Oath expresses any position whatsoever on sexual matters.

BSA's published guidance on that topic underscores this point. Scouts, for example, are directed to receive their sex education at home or in school, but not from the organization: "Your parents or guardian or a sex education teacher should give you the facts about sex that you must know." Boy Scout Handbook (1992) (reprinted in App. 211). To be sure, Scouts are not forbidden from asking their Scoutmaster about issues of a sexual nature, but Scoutmasters are, literally, the last person Scouts are encouraged to ask: "If you have questions about growing up, about relationships, sex, or making good decisions, ask. Talk with your parents, religious leaders, teachers, or Scoutmaster." *Ibid.* Moreover, Scoutmasters are specifically directed to steer curious adolescents to other sources of information:

> If Scouts ask for information regarding . . . sexual activity, answer honestly and factually, but stay within your realm of expertise and comfort. If a Scout has serious concerns that you cannot answer, refer him to his family, religious leader, doctor, or other professional.

Scoutmaster Handbook (1990) (reprinted in App. 264).

More specifically, BSA has set forth a number of rules for Scoutmasters when these types of issues come up:

> You may have boys asking you for information or advice about sexual matters. . . .
>
> How should you handle such matters?
>
> Rule number 1: *You do not undertake to instruct Scouts, in any formalized manner, in the subject of sex and family life. The reasons are that it is not construed to be Scouting's proper area*, and that you are probably not well qualified to do this.
>
> Rule number 2: If Scouts come to you to ask questions or to seek advice, you would give it within your competence. A boy who appears to be asking about sexual intercourse, however, may really only be worried about his pimples, so it is well to find out just what information is needed.
>
> Rule number 3: You should refer boys with sexual problems to persons better qualified than you [are] to handle them. If the boy has a spiritual leader or a doctor who can deal with them, he should go there. If such persons are not available, you may just have to do the best you can. But don't try to play a highly professional role. And at the other extreme, avoid passing the buck.

Scoutmaster Handbook (1972) (reprinted in App. 546–547) (emphasis added).

In light of BSA's self-proclaimed ecumenism, furthermore, it is even more difficult to discern any shared goals or common moral stance on homosexuality. Insofar as religious matters are concerned, BSA's bylaws state that it is "absolutely nonsectarian in its attitude toward ... religious training." App. 362. "The BSA does not define what constitutes duty to God or the practice of religion. This is the responsibility of parents and religious leaders." *Id.* at 76. In fact, many diverse religious organizations sponsor local Boy Scout troops. Brief for Petitioners 3. Because a number of religious groups do not view homosexuality as immoral or wrong and reject discrimination against homosexuals, it is exceedingly difficult to believe that BSA nonetheless adopts a single particular religious or moral philosophy when it comes to sexual orientation.

. . .

II.

The Court seeks to fill the void by pointing to a statement of "policies and procedures relating to homosexuality and Scouting" signed by BSA's President and Chief Scout Executive in 1978 and addressed to the members of the Executive Committee of the national organization. *Ante*, at 9. The letter says that the BSA does "not believe that homosexuality and leadership in Scouting are appropriate." App. 454. But when the *entire* 1978 letter is read, BSA's position is far more equivocal:

> 4. Q. May an individual who openly declares himself to be a homosexual be employed by the Boy Scouts of America as a professional or non-professional?
>
> A. Boy Scouts of America does not knowingly employ homosexuals as professionals or non-professionals. We are unaware of any present laws which would prohibit this policy.
>
> 5. Q. Should a professional or non-professional individual who openly declares himself to be a homosexual be terminated?
>
> A. Yes, *in the absence of any law to the contrary*. At the present time we are unaware of any statute or ordinance in the United States which prohibits discrimination against individual's employment upon the basis of homosexuality. *In the event that such a law was applicable, it would be necessary for the Boy Scouts of America to obey it, in this case as in Paragraph 4 above.* It is our position, however, that homosexuality and professional or non-professional employment in Scouting are not appropriate.

Id. at 454–455 (emphasis added).

Four aspects of the 1978 policy statement are relevant to the proper disposition of this case. First, at most this letter simply adopts an exclusionary membership policy. But simply adopting such a policy has never been considered sufficient, by itself, to prevail on a right to associate claim. *See infra*, at 18–23.

Second, the 1978 policy was never publicly expressed—unlike, for example, the Scout's duty to be "obedient." It was an internal memorandum, never circulated beyond the few members of BSA's Executive Committee. It remained, in effect, a secret Boy Scouts policy. Far from claiming any intent to express an idea that would be burdened by the presence of homosexuals, BSA's *public* posture—to the world and to the Scouts themselves—remained what it had always been: one of tolerance, welcoming all classes of boys and young men. In this respect, BSA's claim is even weaker than those we have rejected in the past. *See infra*, at 18–23.

Third, it is apparent that the draftsmen of the policy statement foresaw the possibility that laws against discrimination might one day be amended to protect homosexuals from employment discrimination. Their statement clearly provided that, in the event such a law conflicted with their policy, a Scout's duty to be "obedient" and "obey the laws," even if "he thinks [the laws] are unfair" would prevail in such a contingency. . . .

Fourth, the 1978 statement simply says that homosexuality is not "appropriate." It makes no effort to connect that statement to a shared goal or expressive activity of the Boy Scouts. Whatever values BSA seeks to instill in Scouts, the idea that homosexuality is not "appropriate" appears entirely unconnected to, and is mentioned nowhere in, the myriad of publicly declared values and creeds of the BSA. That idea does not appear to be among any of the principles actually taught to Scouts. Rather, the 1978 policy appears to be no more than a private statement of a few BSA executives that the organization wishes to exclude gays—and that wish has nothing to do with any expression BSA actually engages in.

The majority also relies on four other policy statements that were issued between 1991 and 1993. All of them were written and issued *after* BSA revoked Dale's membership. Accordingly, they have little, if any, relevance to the legal question before this Court. In any event, they do not bolster BSA's claim.

In 1991, BSA issued two statements both stating: "We believe that homosexual conduct is inconsistent with the requirement in the Scout Oath that a Scout be morally straight and in the Scout Law that a Scout be clean in word and deed, and that homosexuals do not provide a desirable role model for Scouts." App. 457–458. A third statement issued in 1992 was substantially the same. *Id.* at 459. By 1993, however, the policy had changed:

> *BSA Position*
>
> The Boy Scouts of America has always reflected the expectations that Scouting families have had for the organization.

> We do not believe that homosexuals provide a role model consistent with these expectations. Accordingly, we do not allow for the registration of avowed homosexuals as members or as leaders of the BSA.

Id. at 461.

Aside from the fact that these statements were all issued after Dale's membership was revoked, there are four important points relevant to them. First, while the 1991 and 1992 statements tried to tie BSA's exclusionary policy to the meaning of the Scout Oath and Law, the 1993 statement abandoned that effort. Rather, BSA's 1993 homosexual exclusion policy was based on its view that including gays would be contrary to "the expectations that Scouting families have had for the organization...."

Second, even during the brief period in 1991 and 1992, when BSA tried to connect its exclusion of homosexuals to its definition of terms found in the Oath and Law, there is no evidence that Scouts were actually taught anything about homosexuality's alleged inconsistency with those principles.

... Third, BSA never took any clear and unequivocal position on homosexuality. Though the 1991 and 1992 policies state one interpretation of "morally straight" and "clean," the group's published definitions appearing in the Boy Scout and Scoutmaster Handbooks take quite another view. And BSA's broad religious tolerance combined with its declaration that sexual matters are not its "proper area" render its views on the issue equivocal at best and incoherent at worst. We have never held, however, that a group can throw together any mixture of contradictory positions and then invoke the right to associate to defend any one of those views. At a minimum, a group seeking to prevail over an antidiscrimination law must adhere to a clear and unequivocal view.

Fourth, at most the 1991 and 1992 statements declare only that BSA believed "homosexual *conduct* is inconsistent with the requirement in the Scout Oath that a Scout be morally straight and in the Scout Law that a Scout be clean in word and deed." *Id.* at 457 (emphasis added). But New Jersey's law prohibits discrimination on the basis of sexual *orientation*. And when Dale was expelled from the Boy Scouts, BSA said it did so because of his sexual orientation, not because of his sexual conduct.

It is clear, then, that nothing in these policy statements supports BSA's claim. The only policy written before the revocation of Dale's membership was an equivocal, undisclosed statement that evidences no connection between the group's discriminatory intentions and its expressive interests. The later policies demonstrate a brief—though ultimately abandoned—attempt to tie BSA's exclusion to its expression, but other than a single sentence, BSA fails to show that it ever taught Scouts that homosexuality is not "morally straight" or "clean," or that such a view was part of the group's collective efforts to foster a belief. Furthermore, BSA's policy statements fail to establish any clear, consistent, and unequivocal position on homosexuality. Nor did BSA have any reason to think Dale's sexual *conduct*, as opposed to his orientation, was contrary to the group's values.

. . .

III.

BSA's claim finds no support in our cases. We have recognized "a right to associate for the purpose of engaging in those activities protected by the First Amendment—speech, assembly, petition for the redress of grievances, and the exercise of religion." *Roberts,* 468 U.S. at 618. And we have acknowledged that "when the State interferes with individuals' selection of those with whom they wish to join in a common endeavor, freedom of association ... may be implicated." *Ibid.* But "the right to associate for expressive purposes is not ... absolute"; rather, "the nature and degree of constitutional protection afforded freedom of association may vary depending on the extent to which ... the constitutionally protected liberty is at stake in a given case." 468 U.S. at 623, 618. Indeed, the right to associate does not mean "that in every setting in which individuals exercise some discrimination in choosing associates, their selective process of inclusion and exclusion is protected by the Constitution." *New York State Club Assn., Inc. v. City of New York,* 487 U.S. 1, 13, 101 L.Ed.2d 1, 108 S.Ct. 2225 (1988). For example, we have routinely and easily rejected assertions of this right by expressive organizations with discriminatory membership policies, such as private schools, law firms, and labor organizations. In fact, until today, we have never once found a claimed right to associate in the selection of members to prevail in the face of a State's antidiscrimination law. To the contrary, we have squarely held that a State's antidiscrimination law does not violate a group's right to associate simply because the law conflicts with that group's exclusionary membership policy.

... The evidence before this Court makes it exceptionally clear that BSA has, at most, simply adopted an exclusionary membership policy and has no shared goal of disapproving of homosexuality. BSA's mission statement and federal charter say nothing on the matter; its official membership policy is silent; its Scout Oath and Law—and accompanying definitions—are devoid of any view on the topic; its guidance for Scouts and Scoutmasters on sexuality declare that such matters are "not construed to be Scouting's proper area," but are the province of a Scout's parents and pastor; and BSA's posture respecting religion tolerates a wide variety of views on the issue of homosexuality. Moreover, there is simply no evidence that BSA otherwise teaches anything in this area, or that it instructs Scouts on matters involving homosexuality in ways not conveyed in the Boy Scout or Scoutmaster Handbooks. In short, Boy Scouts of America is simply silent on homosexuality. There is no shared goal or collective effort to foster a belief about homosexuality at all—let alone one that is significantly burdened by admitting homosexuals.

As in *Jaycees*, there is "no basis in the record for concluding that admission of [homosexuals] will impede the [Boy Scouts'] ability to engage in [its] protected activities or to disseminate its preferred views" and New Jersey's law "requires no change in [BSA's] creed." 468 U.S. at 626–627. And like *Rotary Club*, New Jersey's law "does not require [BSA] to abandon or alter any of" its activities. 481 U.S. at 548. The evidence relied on by the Court is not to the contrary. The undisclosed 1978 policy certainly adds nothing to the actual views disseminated to the Scouts. It simply says that homosexuality is not "appropriate." There is no reason to give that policy statement more weight than Rotary International's assertion that all-male membership fosters the group's "fellowship" and was the only way it could "operate effectively." As for BSA's post-revocation statements, at most they simply adopt a policy of discrimination, which is no more dispositive than the openly discriminatory policies held insufficient in *Jaycees* and *Rotary Club*; there is no evidence here that BSA's policy was necessary to—or even a part of—BSA's expressive activities or was ever taught to Scouts.

Equally important is BSA's failure to adopt any clear position on homosexuality. BSA's temporary, though ultimately abandoned, view that homosexuality is incompatible with being "morally straight" and "clean" is a far cry from the clear, unequivocal statement necessary to prevail on its claim. Despite the solitary sentences in the 1991 and 1992 policies, the group continued to disclaim any single religious or moral position as a general matter and actively eschewed teaching any lesson on sexuality. It also continued to define "morally straight" and "clean" in the Boy Scout and Scoutmaster Handbooks without any reference to homosexuality. As noted earlier, nothing in our cases suggests that a group can prevail on a right to expressive association if it, effectively, speaks out of both sides of its mouth. A State's antidiscrimination law does not impose a "serious burden" or a "substantial restraint" upon the group's "shared goals" if the group itself is unable to identify its own stance with any clarity.

IV.

The majority pretermits this entire analysis. It finds that BSA in fact "teaches that homosexual conduct is not morally straight." *Ante*, at 9. This conclusion, remarkably, rests entirely on statements in BSA's briefs. *See ibid.* (citing Brief for Petitioners 39; Reply Brief for Petitioners 5). Moreover, the majority insists that we must "give deference to an association's assertions regarding the nature of its expression" and "we must also give deference to an association's view of what would impair its expression." *Ante*, at 10. So long as the record "contains written evidence" to support a group's bare assertion, "we need not inquire further." *Ante*, at 9. Once the organization "asserts" that it engages in particular expression, *ibid.*, "we cannot doubt" the truth of that assertion, *ante*, at 10.

This is an astounding view of the law. I am unaware of any previous instance in which our analysis of the scope of a constitutional right was determined by looking at what a litigant asserts in his or her brief and inquiring no further. It is even more astonishing in the First Amendment area, because, as the majority itself acknowledges, "we are obligated to independently review the factual record." *Ante*, at 6. It is an odd form of independent review that consists of deferring entirely to whatever a litigant claims. But the majority insists that our inquiry must be "limited," *ante*, at 7, because "it is not the role of the courts to reject a group's expressed values because they disagree with those values or find them internally inconsistent." *Ante*, at 8; *see also* Brief for Petitioners 25 ("The Constitution protects [BSA's] ability to control its own message").

But nothing in our cases calls for this Court to do any such thing. An organization can adopt the message of its choice, and it is not this Court's place to disagree with it. But we must inquire whether the group is, in fact, expressing a message (whatever it may be) and whether that message (if one is expressed) is significantly affected by a State's antidiscrimination law. More critically, that inquiry requires our *independent* analysis, rather than deference to a group's litigating posture. Reflection on the subject dictates that such an inquiry is required.

Surely there are instances in which an organization that truly aims to foster a belief at odds with the purposes of a State's antidiscrimination laws will have a First Amendment right to association that precludes forced compliance with those laws. But that right is not a freedom to discriminate at will, nor is it a right to maintain an exclusionary membership policy simply out of fear of what the public reaction would be if the group's membership were opened up. It is an implicit right designed to protect the enumerated rights of the First Amendment, not a license to act on any discriminatory impulse. To prevail in asserting a right of expressive association as a defense to a charge of violating an antidiscrimination law, the organization must at least show it has adopted and advocated an unequivocal position inconsistent with a position advocated or epitomized by the person whom the organization seeks to exclude. If this Court were to defer to whatever position an organization is prepared to assert in its briefs, there would be no way to mark the proper boundary between genuine exercises of the right to associate, on the one hand, and sham claims that are simply attempts to insulate nonexpressive private discrimination, on the other hand. Shielding a litigant's claim from judicial scrutiny would, in turn, render civil rights legislation a nullity, and turn this important constitutional right into a farce. Accordingly, the Court's prescription of total deference will not do. . . .

There is, of course, a valid concern that a court's independent review may run the risk of paying too little heed to an organization's sincerely held views. But unless one is prepared to turn the right to associate into a free pass out of antidiscrimination laws, an independent inquiry is a necessity. Though the group must show that its expressive activities will be substantially burdened by the State's law, if that law truly has a significant effect on a group's speech, even the subtle speaker will be able to identify that impact.

In this case, no such concern is warranted. It is entirely clear that BSA in fact expresses no clear, unequivocal message burdened by New Jersey's law.

V.

Even if BSA's right to associate argument fails, it nonetheless might have a First Amendment right to refrain from including debate and dialogue about homosexuality as part of its mission to instill values in Scouts. It can, for example, advise Scouts who are entering adulthood and have questions about sex to talk "with your parents, religious leaders, teachers, or Scoutmaster," and, in turn, it can direct Scoutmasters who are asked such questions "not undertake to instruct Scouts, in any formalized manner, in the subject of sex and family life" because "it is not construed to be Scouting's proper area." *See supra*, at 7–8. Dale's right to advocate certain beliefs in a public forum or in a private debate does not include a right to advocate these ideas when he is working as a Scoutmaster. And BSA cannot be compelled to include a message about homosexuality among the values it actually chooses to teach its Scouts, if it would prefer to remain silent on that subject.

. . . In its briefs, BSA implies, even if it does not directly argue, that Dale would use his Scoutmaster position as a "bully pulpit" to convey immoral messages to his troop, and therefore his inclusion in the group would compel BSA to include a message it does not want to impart. Brief for Petitioners 21–22. Even though the majority does not endorse that argument, I think it is important to explain why it lacks merit, before considering the argument the majority does accept.

BSA has not contended, nor does the record support, that Dale had ever advocated a view on homosexuality to his troop before his membership was revoked. Accordingly, BSA's revocation could only have been based on an assumption that he would do so in the future. But the only information BSA had at the time it revoked Dale's membership was a newspaper article describing a seminar at Rutgers University on the topic of homosexual teenagers that Dale attended. The relevant passage reads:

> James Dale, 19, co-president of the Rutgers University Lesbian Gay Alliance with Sharice Richardson, also 19, said he lived a double life while in high school, pretending to be straight while attending a military academy.
>
> He remembers dating girls and even laughing at homophobic jokes while at school, only admitting his homosexuality during his second year at Rutgers.
>
> "I was looking for a role model, someone who was gay and accepting of me,' Dale said, adding he wasn't just seeking sexual experiences, but a community that would take him in and provide him with a support network and friends.

App. 517.

Nothing in that article, however, even remotely suggests that Dale would advocate any views on homosexuality to his troop. The Scoutmaster Handbook instructs Dale, like all Scoutmasters, that sexual issues are not their "proper area," and there is no evidence that Dale had any intention of violating this rule. Indeed, from all accounts Dale was a model Boy Scout and Assistant Scoutmaster up until the day his membership was revoked, and there is no reason to believe that he would suddenly disobey the directives of BSA because of anything he said in the newspaper article.

... The majority, though, does not rest its conclusion on the claim that Dale will use his position as a bully pulpit. Rather, it contends that Dale's mere presence among the Boy Scouts will itself force the group to convey a message about homosexuality—even if Dale has no intention of doing so. The majority holds that "the presence of an avowed homosexual and gay rights activist in an assistant scoutmaster's uniform sends a distinct ... message," and, accordingly, BSA is entitled to exclude that message. *Ante*, at 13. In particular, "Dale's presence in the Boy Scouts would, at the very least, force the organization to send a message, both to the youth members and the world, that the Boy Scouts accepts homosexual conduct as a legitimate form of behavior." *Ante*, at 11; *see also* Brief for Petitioners 24 ("By donning the uniform of an adult leader in Scouting, he would 'celebrate [his] identity' as an openly gay Scout leader").

It is true, of course, that some acts are so imbued with symbolic meaning that they qualify as "speech" under the First Amendment. *See United States v. O'Brien,* 391 U.S. 367, 376, 20 L.Ed.2d 672, 88 S.Ct. 1673 (1968). At the same time, however, "we cannot accept the view that an apparently limitless variety of conduct can be labeled 'speech' whenever the person engaging in the conduct intends thereby to express an idea." *Ibid.* Though participating in the Scouts could itself conceivably send a message on some level, it is not the kind of act that we have recognized as speech. *See Dallas v. Stanglin,* 490 U.S. 19, 24–25, 104 L.Ed.2d 18, 109 S.Ct. 1591 (1989). Indeed, if merely joining a group did constitute symbolic speech; and such speech were attributable to the group being joined; and that group has the right to exclude that speech (and hence, the right to exclude that person from joining), then the right of free speech effectively becomes a limitless right to exclude for every organization, whether or not it engages in *any* expressive activities. That cannot be, and never has been, the law.

The only apparent explanation for the majority's holding, then, is that homosexuals are simply so different from the rest of society that their presence alone—unlike any other individual's—should be singled out for special First Amendment treatment. Under the majority's reasoning, an openly gay male is irreversibly affixed with the label "homosexual." That label, even though unseen, communicates a message that permits his exclusion wherever he goes. His openness is the sole and sufficient justification for his ostracism. Though unintended, reliance on such a justification is tantamount to a constitutionally prescribed symbol of inferiority. As counsel for the Boy Scouts remarked, Dale "put a banner around his neck when he ... got himself into the newspaper.... He created a reputation.... He can't take that banner off. He put it on himself and, indeed, he has continued to put it on himself." *See* Tr. of Oral Arg. 25.

... Furthermore, it is not likely that BSA would be understood to send any message, either to Scouts or to the world, simply by admitting someone as a member. Over the years, BSA has generously welcomed over 87 million young Americans into its ranks. In 1992 over one million adults were active BSA members. 160 N.J. 562, 571, 734 A.2d 1196, 1200 (1999). The notion that an organization of that size and enormous prestige implicitly endorses the views that each of those adults may express in a non-Scouting context is simply mind-boggling. Indeed, in this case there is no evidence that the young Scouts in Dale's troop, or members of their families, were even aware of his sexual orientation, either before or after his public statements at Rutgers University. It is equally farfetched to assert that Dale's open declaration of his homosexuality, reported in a local newspaper, will effectively force BSA to send a message to anyone simply because it allows Dale to be an Assistant Scoutmaster. For an Olympic gold medal winner or a Wimbledon tennis champion, being "openly gay" perhaps communicates a message—for example, that openness about one's sexual orientation is more virtuous than concealment; that a homosexual person can be a capable and virtuous person who should be judged like anyone else; and that homosexuality is not immoral—but it certainly does not follow that they necessarily send a message on behalf of the organizations that sponsor the activities in which they excel. The fact that such persons participate in these organizations is not usually construed to convey a message on behalf of those organizations any more than does the inclusion of women, African–Americans, religious minorities, or any other discrete group. Surely the organizations are not forced by antidiscrimination laws to take any position on the legitimacy of any individual's private beliefs or private conduct.

The State of New Jersey has decided that people who are open and frank about their sexual orientation are entitled to equal access to employment as school teachers, police officers, librarians, athletic coaches, and a host of other jobs filled by citizens who serve as role models for children and adults alike. Dozens of Scout units throughout the State are sponsored by public agencies, such as schools and fire departments, that employ such role models. BSA's affiliation with numerous public agencies that comply with New Jersey's law against discrimination cannot be understood to convey any particular message endorsing or condoning the activities of all these people.

VI.

... That such prejudices are still prevalent and that they have caused serious and tangible harm to countless members of the class New Jersey seeks to protect are established matters of fact that neither the Boy Scouts nor the Court disputes. That harm can only be aggravated by the creation of a constitutional shield for a policy that is itself the product of a habitual way of thinking about strangers. As Justice Brandeis so wisely advised, "we must be ever on our guard, lest we erect our prejudices into legal principles."

If we would guide by the light of reason, we must let our minds be bold. I respectfully dissent.

JUSTICE SOUTER, with whom JUSTICE GINSBURG and JUSTICE BREYER join, dissenting.

I join Justice Stevens' dissent but add this further word on the significance of Part VI of his opinion. There, Justice Stevens describes the changing attitudes toward gay people and notes a parallel with the decline of stereotypical thinking about race and gender. The legitimacy of New Jersey's interest in forbidding discrimination on all these bases by those furnishing public accommodations is, as Justice Stevens indicates, acknowledged by many to be beyond question. The fact that we are cognizant of this laudable decline in stereotypical thinking on homosexuality should not, however, be taken to control the resolution of this case.

Boy Scouts of America (BSA) is entitled, consistently with its own tenets and the open doors of American courts, to raise a federal constitutional basis for resisting the application of New Jersey's law. BSA has done that and has chosen to defend against enforcement of the state public accommodations law on the ground that the First Amendment protects expressive association: individuals have a right to join together to advocate opinions free from government interference. *See Roberts v. United States Jaycees,* 468 U.S. 609, 622, 82 L.Ed.2d 462, 104 S.Ct. 3244 (1984). BSA has disclaimed any argument that Dale's past or future actions, as distinct from his unapologetic declaration of sexual orientation, would justify his exclusion from BSA. *See* Tr. of Oral Arg. 12–13.

The right of expressive association does not, of course, turn on the popularity of the views advanced by a group that claims protection. Whether the group appears to this Court to be in the vanguard or rearguard of social thinking is irrelevant to the group's rights. I conclude that BSA has not made out an expressive association claim, therefore, not because of what BSA may espouse, but because of its failure to make sexual orientation the subject of any unequivocal advocacy, using the channels it customarily employs to state its message. As Justice Stevens explains, no group can claim a right of expressive association without identifying a clear position to be advocated over time in an unequivocal way. To require less, and to allow exemption from a public accommodations statute based on any individual's difference from an alleged group ideal, however expressed and however inconsistently claimed, would convert the right of expressive association into an easy trump of any antidiscrimination law.

If, on the other hand, an expressive association claim has met the conditions Justice Stevens describes as necessary, there may well be circumstances in which the antidiscrimination law must yield, as he says.

It is certainly possible for an individual to become so identified with a position as to epitomize it publicly. When that position is at odds with a group's advocated position, applying an antidiscrimination statute to require the group's acceptance of the individual in a position of group leadership could so modify or muddle or frustrate the group's advocacy as to violate the expressive associational right. While it is not our business here to rule on any such hypothetical, it is at least clear that our estimate of the progressive character of the group's position will be irrelevant to the First Amendment analysis if such a case comes to us for decision.

III. PERSONAL COSTS: A SCOUT'S STORY*

My name is Chris. I'm nineteen years old. I joined the Cub Scouts when I was eight, and then continued into the Boy Scouts. By the time I was sixteen, being in the Scouts was the most important thing in my life. Most of my friends were in the Scouts, and many of my happiest moments were spent with them at Scouting activities.

It was also at the age of sixteen, that I had come to the realization that I might be gay. This was something that I had been thinking about since I was twelve, and I felt I needed to talk to someone about it. I thought the person I could trust was my Assistant Scoutmaster. I told him about my feelings hoping he would understand. I told him I was afraid of losing my friends and being rejected by everyone. I guess I just wanted to be reassured that everything would be O.K.

Later that night, I received a call from my Scoutmaster telling me that *"my personal preferences were in conflict with the Scouting principle."* I will never forget those words and the way I felt when he said them to me. A meeting with the local Council Executive was immediately arranged. At this meeting, people I had never met before and who didn't know me, told me that I had no place in Scouting. They told me I could no longer participate in any way, and that I could never wear my uniform again. Then they ordered me not to come onto the premises of the Council Office or the Scout Store.

I had gone to them because I thought I could trust them. They had promised me that they would keep what I had told them confidential. Two weeks later my best friend returned from a Scout Camporee. He had heard Scout leaders from other towns talking about me being gay. Then my Scoutmaster called another of my longtime friends over to his house. He told my friend not to associate with me because others might suspect *him* of being gay, thereby jeopardizing his graduation to Eagle. I was forbidden from attending his Eagle Ceremony, even though he had personally invited me to be his guest. Most of my other friends in Scouts had heard that I had been kicked out for being gay. Many of them deserted me; some by their own choice and some because their parents made them.

* Anonymous, *The Personal Story of an Ousted Boy Scout,* YALE DAILY NEWS, APR. 5, 1993.

Not only did the Scoutmasters want to keep Scouting out of my life, it felt like they wanted to keep my friends out of my life as well.

Things have been very rough for me over the past three years. When they kicked me out of the Scouts I felt like everything had come to an end; it didn't seem like there was anything left. I ran away from home, I ended up homeless on the streets of San Francisco and I seriously considered suicide.

Today, as I sort things out, I can't help but notice several ironies about what happened to me. First of all, I'm not even sure if I'm gay. Secondly, the Scouts may talk about being trustworthy, but they sure didn't come through in my case. Thirdly, it was my association with Forgotten Scouts (a group of mostly gay Scouters) that has enabled me to get off the streets and get a job. They don't care whether I'm gay or not. It seems to me the people I've met in Forgotten Scouts could teach some of the Boy Scout leaders a lot about trust.

I am not writing this to say that the Boy Scouts are bad. Most of what they do is very good. But some of what they do really hurts. And it's not just me. This has happened to others before me, and it's happened since. When they throw out kids and adults who are gay, they are sending the message to young people like me that we have no future. Throwing people away and condemning them to an empty future is not what the Boy Scouts should be about.

A lot of people in Scouting have told me they know this policy is wrong. Most of you are saying, "It's BSA national policy and I can't do anything about it." But you can. There are lots of ways to let the national leaders of the Scouts know that you think this policy is wrong and that you want it to be changed. You can write a letter, or make a phone call, or start a petition. That is what the Scout Handbook says we should do. It is part of the duty of being a Scout. Please. If you agree that the Boy Scouts should be for all boys, and that people should be judged by their conduct, not their status, help find a way to change this policy so that others don't have to go through what I went through.

NOTE

From the perspective of gay rights proponents, what are the advantages and disadvantages of the holding in *Dale*? *See, e.g., Evans v. Berkeley*, 38 Cal.4th 1, 40 Cal.Rptr.3d 205, 129 P.3d 394 (2006), *cert. denied*, 549 U.S. 987, 127 S.Ct. 434, 166 L.Ed.2d 330 (2006). In *Evans*, the California Supreme Court held that it was constitutional for the City to disallow free use of a city marina because the requesting group, the Sea Scouts, an affiliate of the Boy Scouts, would not agree to abide by the City's nondiscrimination policy with regard to sexual orientation. The Sea Scouts argued unsuccessfully that the decision violated their rights of freedom of speech and association.

CHAPTER 8

PARENTING

■ ■ ■

Despite surviving stereotypes describing gays as pedophiles or as otherwise unfit to raise (or in many cases even to be in contact with) children, lesbians and gays routinely do have and raise children. Some such families result from prior heterosexual relationships, but also increasingly through adoption, alternative insemination methods, and surrogacy. The battle for gay marriage has in large part been motivated by the desire of gay parents to provide some legal protections for their families. This chapter examines the legal issues concomitant with gay and lesbian parenting, including custody disputes between biological parents and between gay parents and third parties.

I. CHILDREN OF LESBIAN AND GAY PARENTS: SUMMARY OF RESEARCH FINDINGS THROUGH 2002*

In addition to judicial concerns about lesbian and gay parents themselves, courts have voiced three major fears about the influence of lesbian and gay parents on children. The first of these fears is that development of sexual identity will be impaired among children of lesbian and gay parents. For instance, one such concern is that children brought up by lesbian mothers or gay fathers will show disturbances in gender identity and/or in gender role behavior (Falk, 1989, 1994; Hitchens & Kirkpatrick, 1985; Kleber, Howell, & Tibbits–Kleber, 1986; Patterson et al., 2002; Patterson & Redding, 1996). It has also been suggested that children brought up by lesbian mothers or by gay fathers will themselves become lesbian or gay (Patterson & Redding, 1996; Patterson et al., 2002).

A second category of concerns involves aspects of children's personal development other than sexual identity (Falk, 1989, 1994; Patterson & Redding, 1996; Patterson et al., 2002). For example, courts have expressed fears that children in the custody of gay or lesbian parents will be more vulnerable to mental breakdown, will exhibit more adjustment difficulties

* Excerpted from Charlotte Patterson, *Lesbian and Gay Parenting: A Resource for Psychologists* (AMERICAN PSYCHOLOGICAL ASSOCIATION).

and behavior problems, and will be less psychologically healthy than other children.

A third category of specific fears expressed by the courts is that children of lesbian and gay parents may experience difficulty in social relationships (Falk, 1989, 1994; Patterson & Redding, 1996; Patterson et al., 2002). For example, judges have repeatedly expressed concern that children living with lesbian mothers or gay fathers may be stigmatized, teased, or otherwise victimized by peers. Another common fear is that children living with gay or lesbian parents may be more likely to be sexually abused by the parent or by the parent's friends or acquaintances. In the following I will address each of these areas of concern.

Sexual Identity

Three aspects of sexual identity are considered in the research: gender identity, which concerns a person's self-identification as male or female; gender-role behavior, which concerns the extent to which a person's activities, occupations, and the like are regarded by the culture as masculine, feminine, or both; and sexual orientation, which refers to a person's choice of sexual partners, who may be homosexual, heterosexual, or bisexual (Money & Ehrhardt, 1972; Stein, 1993). Research relevant to each of these three major areas of concern is summarized below.

Gender Identity. In studies of children ranging in age from 5 to 14, results of projective testing and related interview procedures have revealed that development of gender identity among children of lesbian mothers follows the expected pattern (Green, 1978; Green, Mandel, Hotvedt, Gray, & Smith, 1986; Kirkpatrick, Smith & Roy, 1981). More direct assessment techniques to assess gender identity have been used by Golombok, Spencer, & Rutter (1983) with the same result: All children in this study reported that they were happy with their gender and that they had no wish to be a member of the opposite sex. There was no evidence in any of the studies of gender identity of any difficulties among children of lesbian mothers. No data have been reported in this area for children of gay fathers.

Gender–Role Behavior. A number of studies have reported that gender-role behavior among children of lesbian mothers fell within typical limits for conventional sex roles (Brewaeys et al., 1997; Golombok et al., 1983; Gottman, 1990; Green, 1978; Green et al., 1986; Hoeffer, 1981; Kirkpatrick et al., 1981; Kweskin & Cook, 1982; Patterson, 1994a). For instance, Kirkpatrick and her colleagues (1981) found no differences between children of lesbian versus heterosexual mothers in toy preferences, activities, interests, or occupational choices.

Rees (1979) administered the Bem Sex Role Inventory (BSRI) to 24 adolescents, half of whom had divorced lesbian and half of whom had divorced heterosexual mothers. The BSRI yields scores on masculinity and femininity as independent factors and an androgyny score based on the ratio of masculinity to femininity. Children of lesbian and heterosexual mothers did not differ on masculinity or on androgyny, but children of lesbian mothers reported greater psychological femininity than did those of heterosexual mothers. This result would seem to run counter to expectations based on stereotypes of lesbians as lacking in femininity, both in their own demeanor and in their likely influences on children.

Gender-role behavior of children was also assessed by Green and his colleagues (1986). In interviews with the children, no differences between the 56 children of lesbian and 48 children of heterosexual mothers were found with respect to favorite television programs, favorite television characters, or favorite games or toys. There was some indication in interviews with children themselves that the offspring of lesbian mothers had less sex-typed preferences for activities at school and in their neighborhoods than did children of heterosexual mothers. Consistent with this result, lesbian mothers were also more likely than heterosexual mothers to report that their daughters often participated in rough-and-tumble play or occasionally played with "masculine" toys such as trucks or guns, but they reported no differences in these areas for sons. Lesbian mothers were no more and no less likely than heterosexual mothers to report that their children often played with "feminine" toys such as dolls. In both family types, however, children's sex-role behavior was seen as falling within the expected range.

More recently, Brewaeys and her colleagues (1997) assessed gender-role behavior among 30, 4– to 8–year–old children who had been conceived via donor insemination by lesbian couples, and compared it to that of 30 same-aged children who had been conceived via donor insemination by heterosexual couples, and to that of 30 same-aged children who had been naturally conceived by heterosexual couples. They used the Pre–School Activities Inventory (Golombok & Rust, 1993), a maternal report questionnaire designed to identify "masculine" and "feminine" behavior among boys and girls within unselected samples of schoolchildren. They found no significant differences between children of lesbian and children of heterosexual parents on preferences for gendered toys, games, and activities (Brewaeys et al., 1997).

In summary, the research suggests that children of lesbian mothers develop patterns of gender-role behavior that are much like those of other children. No data are available regarding gender-role behavior for children of gay fathers.

Sexual Orientation. A number of investigators have also studied a third component of sexual identity, sexual orientation (Bailey, Bobrow, Wolfe, & Mickach, 1995; Bozett, 1980, 1987, 1989; Gottman, 1990; Golombok & Tasker, 1996; Green, 1978; Huggins, 1989; Miller, 1979; Paul, 1986; Rees, 1979; Tasker & Golombok, 1997). In all studies, the great majority of offspring of both lesbian mothers and gay fathers described themselves as heterosexual. Taken together, the data does not suggest elevated rates of homosexuality among the offspring of lesbian or gay parents. For instance, Huggins (1989) interviewed 36 adolescents, half of whom had lesbian mothers and half of whom had heterosexual mothers. No children of lesbian mothers identified themselves as lesbian or gay, but one child of a heterosexual mother did; this difference was not statistically significant. In another study, Bailey and his colleagues (1995) studied adult sons of gay fathers and found more than 90% of the sons to be heterosexual.

Golombok and Tasker (1996, 1997) studied 25 young adults reared by divorced lesbian mothers and 21 young adults reared by divorced heterosexual mothers. They reported that offspring of lesbian mothers were no more likely than those of heterosexual mothers to describe themselves as feeling attracted to same-sex sexual partners. If they were attracted in this way, however, young adults with lesbian mothers were more likely to report that they would consider entering into a same-sex sexual relationship, and they were more likely to have actually participated in such a relationship. They were not, however, more likely to identify themselves as non-heterosexual (*i.e.*, as lesbian, gay, or bisexual). These results were based on a small sample, and they must be interpreted with caution. At the same time, the study is the first to follow children of divorced lesbian mothers into adulthood, and it offers a detailed and careful examination of important issues.

Other Aspects of Personal Development

Studies of other aspects of personal development among children of lesbian and gay parents have assessed a broad array of characteristics. Among these have been separation-individuation (Steckel, 1985, 1987), psychiatric evaluations (Golombok et al., 1983; Kirkpatrick et al., 1981), behavior problems (Brewaeys et al., 1997; Chan, Raboy et al., 1998; Flaks, et al., 1995; Gartrell, Deck, Rodas, Peyser, & Banks, 2005; Golombok et al., 1983, 1997; Patterson, 1994a; Tasker & Golombok, 1995, 1997; Wainright et al., 2004), personality (Gottman, 1990; Tasker & Golombok, 1995, 1997), self-concept (Golombok, Tasker, & Murray, 1997; Gottman, 1990, Huggins, 1989; Patterson, 1994a; Puryear, 1983; Wainright et al., 2004), locus of control (Puryear, 1983; Rees, 1979), moral judgment (Rees, 1979), school adjustment (Wainright et al., 2004), and intelligence (Green et al., 1986). Research suggests that concerns about difficulties in these areas among children of lesbian mothers are unwarranted (Patterson, 1997, 2000; Parks, 1998; Perrin, 1998, 2002; Stacey & Biblarz, 2001; Tasker, 1999). As was the case for sexual identity, studies of these aspects of personal development have revealed no major differences between children of lesbian versus heterosexual mothers. One statistically significant difference in self-concept emerged in Patterson's (1994a) study: Children of lesbian mothers reported greater symptoms of stress but also a greater overall sense of well-being than did children in a comparison group (Patterson, 1994a); but this result has yet to be replicated. Overall, the belief that children of lesbian and gay parents suffer deficits in personal development has no empirical foundation.

Social Relationships

Studies assessing potential differences between children of lesbian and gay parents, on the one hand, and children of heterosexual parents, on the other, have sometimes included assessments of children's social relationships. The most common focus of attention has been on peer relations, but some information about children's relationships with adults has also been collected. Research findings that address the likelihood of sexual abuse are also summarized in this section.

Research on peer relations among children of lesbian mothers has been reported by Golombok and her colleagues (1983, 1997), by Green and his colleagues (1978, 1986), and by Patterson (1994a). Reports by both parents and children suggest typical patterns of development of peer relationships. For example, as would be expected, most school-aged children reported same-sex best friends and predominantly same-sex peer groups (Golombok et al., 1983; Green, 1978; Patterson, 1994a). The quality of children's peer relations was described, on average, in positive terms by researchers (Golombok et al., 1983) as well as by mothers and their children (Green et al., 1986; Golombok et al., 1997). Although some children have described encounters with anti-gay remarks from peers (Gartrell et al., 2005), young adult offspring of divorced lesbian mothers did not recall being the targets of any more childhood teasing or victimization than did the offspring of divorced heterosexual mothers (Tasker & Golombok, 1995, 1997). The number and quality of adolescents' and young adults' romantic relationships has also been found to be unrelated to maternal sexual orientation (Tasker & Golombok, 1997; Wainright et al., 2004). No data on the children of gay fathers have been reported in this area.

Studies of the relationships with adults among the children of lesbian and gay parents have also resulted in a generally positive picture (Brewaeys et al., 1997; Golombok et al., 1983; Harris & Turner, 1985/86; Kirkpatrick et al., 1981; Wainright et al., 2004). For example, adolescent relationships with their parents have been described as equally warm and caring, regardless of whether parents have same-or opposite-sex partners (Wainright et al., 2004). Golombok and her colleagues (1983) found that children of divorced lesbian mothers were more likely to have had recent contact with their fathers than were children of divorced heterosexual mothers. Another study, however, found no differences in this regard (Kirkpatrick et al., 1981). Harris and Turner (1985/86) studied the children of gay fathers, as well as those of lesbian mothers, and reported that parent-child relationships were described in positive terms. One significant difference was that heterosexual parents were more likely than lesbian and gay parents to say that their children's visits with the other parent presented problems for them (Harris & Turner, 1985/86). Another significant difference was that young adult offspring of divorced lesbian mothers described themselves as communicating more openly with their mothers and with their mothers' current partners than did adult children of divorced heterosexual parents (Tasker & Golombok, 1997).

Research has also focused on children's contacts with members of the extended family, especially grandparents. Parents are often facilitators and gatekeepers of contact between generations in families. Because grandparents are generally seen as supportive of their grandchildren, any strains in parents' relationships with grandparents might have adverse effects on the frequency of children's contacts with grandparents, and hence also have a negative impact on grandchildren's development. Patterson and her colleagues have evaluated these possibilities in two separate studies (Fulcher, Chan, Raboy, & Patterson, 2002; Patterson et al., 1998). Their findings revealed that most children of lesbian mothers were described as being in regular contact with grandparents (Patterson et al., 1998). In a recent study based on a systematic sampling frame in which lesbian and heterosexual parent families were well-matched on demographic characteristics, there were no differences in the frequency of contact with grandparents as a function of parental sexual orientation (Fulcher et al., 2002). Gartrell and her colleagues (2000) have also reported that grandparents were very likely to acknowledge the children of lesbian daughters as grandchildren. Thus, available evidence suggests that, contrary to popular concerns, intergenerational relationships in lesbian mother families are satisfactory.

Children's contacts with adult friends of their lesbian mothers have also been assessed (Fulcher et al., 2002; Golombok et al., 1983; Patterson et al., 1998). All of the children were described as having contact with adult friends of their mothers, and most lesbian mothers reported that their adult friends were a mixture of homosexual and heterosexual individuals. Children of lesbian mothers were no less likely than those of heterosexual mothers to be in contact with adult men who were friends of their mothers (Fulcher et al., 2002).

Concerns that children of lesbian or gay parents are more likely than children of heterosexual parents to be sexually abused have also been addressed. Results of work in this area reveal that the great majority of adults who perpetrate sexual abuse are male; sexual abuse of children by adult women is extremely rare (Finkelhor & Russell, 1984; Jones & McFarlane, 1980; Sarafino, 1979). Moreover, the overwhelming majority of child sexual abuse cases involve an adult male abusing a young female (Jenny, Roesler, & Poyer, 1994; Jones & McFarlane, 1980). Available evidence reveals that gay men are no more likely than heterosexual men to perpetrate child sexual abuse (Groth & Birnbaum, 1978; Jenny et al., 1994; Sarafino, 1979). There are few published reports relevant to the issue of sexual abuse of children living in custody of lesbian or gay parents. A recent study did, however, find that none of the lesbian mothers participating in a longitudinal study had abused their children (Gartrell et al., 2005). Fears that children in custody of lesbian or gay parents might be at heightened risk for sexual abuse are without basis in the research literature.

II. RECENT STUDIES REGARDING GAY AND LESBIAN ADOPTION AND PARENTING*

In recent years, various articles and studies have continued to address adoption and parenting in the gay and lesbian community. There are unquestionably "unique and complex challenges" facing same-gender couples interested in adopting children within the United States (Pawelski et al. 349). Even in a modern day progressive society, the subject of gay and lesbian adoption remains a highly controversial issue (Farr, Forssell, and Patterson 164). In 2007, Congress noted "that there were 'serious shortages' of qualified adoptive parents" in the United States (Averett, Nalavany, and Ryan 130). There are over two million gay and lesbian individuals, both single and partnered, that are interested in adopting. (Averett, Nalavany, and Ryan 130). Nevertheless, policies of U.S. adoption agencies, state laws, and the general social stigma of homophobia continue to "limit or prohibit adoptions by lesbian or gay prospective adoptive parents, either explicitly or by banning unmarried couples from adopting children" (Farr, Forssell, and Patterson 165). While questions continue concerning the validity of same-sex couples as parents, 2000 Census figures and other demographic research indicate that "parenting by same-gender couples is an established and growing part of the diverse structure of families in the United States" (Pawelski et al. 351). The 2010 Census figures continue to bear out this trend.

As noted previously, numerous researchers, scientists, and experts (particularly in the fields of child psychology and social work) have continuously supported the view that lesbian and gay adults are well-equipped to serve as capable and effective parents. (Averett, Nalavany, and Ryan 130; Farr, Forssell, and Patterson 165). While the research literature on this topic is growing, it is still considered relatively scarce. (Averett, Nalavany, and Ryan 131). In addition, much less research has focused on families with gay fathers than on those with lesbian parents, so knowledge about children reared by gay fathers is even more scarce. (Farr, Forssell, and Patterson 166).

Despite the showing that research evidence has suggested that lesbian and gay individuals are suitable parents and "that their children are generally happy and healthy, this literature has been subject to several criticisms." One of the criticisms is that studies involving lesbian or gay parents and their children have employed convenience samples, relied entirely on self-reported data, or have not included comparison groups. (Farr, Forssell, and Patterson 166). Utilizing multiple informants is paramount to increasing the validity and reliability of "child behavior prob-

* Rachel H. Farr, Stephen L. Forssell & Charlotte J. Patterson, *Parenting and Child Development in Adoptive Families: Does Parental Sexual Orientation Matter?*, Applied Developmental Science, 14(3), 164–178 (2010); Paige Averett, Blace Nalavany & Scott Ryan, *An Evaluation of Gay/Lesbian and Heterosexual Adoption*, Adoption Quarterly, 12, 129–151 (2009); and James G. Pawelski et al., *The Effects of Marriage, Civil Union, and Domestic Partnership Laws on the Health and Well–Being of Children*, Pediatrics, 118, 349–364 (2006).

lems and psychiatric symptoms'' assessments because children may act differently when placed in different environments (Farr, Forssell, and Patterson 166). Thus, obtaining information from teachers, in addition to parents, may ''facilitate a more complete picture of children's behavior'' (Farr, Forssell, and Patterson 166).

Articles from 2010 and 2009 (Farr, Forssell and Patterson; Averett, Nalavany, and Ryan) include data on studies the authors conducted that investigated how the sexual orientation of parents affected the development of their adopted children (a 2006 article by Pawelski is a collective analysis of several other studies). While both studies compared samples of gay and lesbian adoptive parents to heterosexual adoptive parents, each study used a slightly different methodology and design to collect and analyze data. While one study recruited adoptive families from only private adoption agencies, another utilized information stemming from Florida's public child welfare system (Farr, Forssell, and Patterson 167; Averett, Nalavany, and Ryan 134). Each study acquired data directly from the adoptive parents. Only one study obtained data concerning the children that was provided by ''teachers or outside caregivers'' (Farr, Forssell, and Patterson 168). Although not entirely universal to each study, the general types of data that were collected included information regarding: (1) children gender role behavior and activity; (2) child behavior adjustment (internalizing behavior, externalizing behavior, and total behavior); (3) parental disciplinary techniques; (4) parenting stress; and (5) parental relationship satisfaction (meaning the ''satisfaction, consensus, cohesion, and affection within one's current romantic relationship'') (Farr, Forssell, and Patterson 169–70). In each study, single adoptive parents were not included.

In general, the findings in these articles bore out the findings in the earlier literature. The articles concluded that children with gay or lesbian parents were found to develop normal relationships with other children and ''to maintain social relationships appropriate for their developmental levels'' (Pawelski et al. 359). The articles also found that children adopted by both homosexual and heterosexual parents displayed typical patterns of gender development (Farr, Forssell, and Patterson 175). One study noted that children growing up with same-sex parents may actually experience some advantages; these children have been described as ''more tolerant of diversity and more nurturing toward younger children than children whose parents are heterosexual'' (Pawelski et al. 359). Another common finding throughout all of the studies was that parental sexual orientation had no effect on individual spousal relationships or interaction. (Farr, Forssell, and Patterson 174). However, higher levels of parenting stress were associated with child behavior problems (Farr, Forssell, and Patterson 174). Each of the studies essentially reported that ''[r]egardless of parental sexual orientation, parents who reported less parenting stress, use of more effective disciplinary techniques, and greater happiness in their couple relationships had children who were described as well-adjusted'' (Farr, Forssell, and Patterson 175). Finally, an important product from one study was its findings on the association between gay fathers and their children, given (as noted earlier) that work in this area of research has been limited (Farr, Forssell, and Patterson 175). As predicted, the study discovered that "gay fathers and their children appeared to be faring as well as were lesbian and heterosexual parents and their children" (Farr, Forssell, and Patterson 175). Overall, gay and lesbian parents, as well as both their biological and adopted children, were found to exhibit no significant differences from their heterosexual counterparts.

An increasing number of gay and lesbian individuals are adding children into their long-term partnerships "through adoption, alternative insemination, and surrogacy" (Pawelski et al. 358). In 2006, same-gender couples were raising children in approximately "96% of all the counties in the United States" (Pawelski et al. 358). These figures should be viewed positively given this growing body of evidence indicating that children reared by same-gender parents are no different than children raised by heterosexual parents (Pawelski et al. 361).

Summary

Results of research to date suggest that children of lesbian and gay parents have both positive relationships with peers and satisfactory relationships with adults of both sexes. The picture of lesbian mothers' children that emerges is one of general engagement in social life with peers, with fathers, with grandparents, and with mothers' adult friends—both male and female, both heterosexual and homosexual. Fears about children of lesbians and gay men being sexually abused by adults, ostracized by peers, or isolated in single-sex lesbian or gay communities have received no support from the results of existing research.

III. CUSTODY

BOTTOMS v. BOTTOMS

18 Va.App. 481, 444 S.E.2d 276 (1994)

OPINION: JUDGE SAM W. COLEMAN III

. . .

I.

THE EVIDENCE

In 1989, Sharon Bottoms married Dennis Doustou. They separated when Sharon was pregnant with their son, who was born in 1991. The 1991 divorce decree awarded custody of the child to Sharon Bottoms. Doustou has not been actively involved in his son's life since the divorce. During the three years following the divorce, Sharon Bottoms dated another man, lived with her cousin, lived with two lesbians, and in 1992, began living with April Wade. During this time, Sharon Bottoms had legal custody of her son, but she frequently relied on her mother, Kay Bottoms, to keep and care for the child. Kay Bottoms estimated that she had kept the child most of the time after his birth.

In January 1993, Sharon Bottoms informed her mother that her son would be spending less time at her mother's house because of Tommy Conley's presence there. Tommy Conley was Kay Bottoms' live-in male companion. The two had lived together and reared Sharon Bottoms from the time Sharon was a child. Sharon Bottoms explained to her mother that she was taking her son out of the household because while she, Sharon, was growing up, Tommy Conley had sexually abused her over 800 times. Kay Bottoms was shocked and upset by the accusations, but she later decided that the accusations were not altogether unfounded.

Shortly after the conversation between Sharon and Kay Bottoms, Kay filed a petition with the juvenile and domestic relations district court seeking custody of her grandson. She asked Tommy Conley to move out of the house during the custody dispute because her lawyer "thought it would be best." The circuit court ultimately granted Kay Bottoms custody of her grandson, and this appeal followed.

Sharon Bottoms acknowledges that she is a lesbian and that she shares a residence with April Wade, her lesbian companion. Sharon Bottoms admits that she and April Wade engage in consensual sexual acts in the privacy of their residence. She testified that they share the same bed and engage in oral sex once or twice a week. For a period of time, when the child was very young, the child's crib was in the bedroom where they slept. Sharon Bottoms testified that she and April Wade have never engaged in any type of sexual activity in her son's presence, nor has she exposed him to sexual conduct of any type. She admits that she and April Wade have displayed some affection in the child's presence by hugging, kissing, or patting one another on the bottom. All the psychological evidence introduced on this issue was to the effect that Sharon Bottoms' open lesbian relationship has had no visible or discernible effect on her son.

While the child has spent considerable time with his grandmother, Kay Bottoms, the evidence proved that he and his mother, Sharon Bottoms, have had a close, loving mother-child relationship. Sharon Bottoms has adequately provided him with the basic necessities of life, including food, clothing, and shelter.

On two occasions, Sharon Bottoms spanked the child on the leg "too hard." The evidence did not show that the spankings bruised or injured the child. The evidence showed that Sharon Bottoms had punished the child by making him stand in a corner and had on occasion cursed in the child's presence. However, she has not physically abused the child, neglected him, or endangered or threatened his life, physical safety, or well-being. The psychological evaluations stated that Sharon Bottoms is "warm" and "responsive" with her son, and that he "behaves as if entirely secure and at ease with his mother, it being a very familiar and comfortable situation for him."

Kay Bottoms testified that on one occasion, Sharon Bottoms left the child at Kay's home for a week without telling her how she could be reached. No evidence showed that Sharon Bottoms had ever left the child with an irresponsible person or unattended. Until recently, Sharon Bottoms had been unemployed. She has been receiving Aid to Dependent Children benefits. The evidence shows that April Wade is a recovering alcoholic. The child's father, Dennis Doustou, pays no child support.

II.

THE TRIAL COURT RULING

The trial court ruled that because Sharon Bottoms lives in a sexually active lesbian relationship and engages in illegal sexual acts, she is an unfit parent as a matter of law

... The trial judge granted custody to Kay Bottoms and visitations on Mondays and Tuesdays to Sharon Bottoms, provided that no visitations be in the home shared with April Wade or in April Wade's presence.

III.

THE LEGAL PRINCIPLES

... The custody dispute between Sharon and Kay Bottoms is not governed by the same principles that control a dispute between two parents. When natural parents are contesting for custody of their child, the court balances the equities between the parents and determines with which parent will the child's best interests be served. *See Roe v. Roe*, 228 Va. 722, 723, 324 S.E.2d 691, 691 (1985). The court determines which parent will be the more fit and suitable custodian to care for the child's needs based on the current and foreseeable circumstances.

However, unlike parental custody disputes wherein the parents stand on equal legal footing, when a third party attempts to divest custody of a child from a natural parent, the presumption of parental fitness must be rebutted before a court may consider whether a third party would be a fit or proper custodian. *Wilkerson v. Wilkerson*, 214 Va. 395, 397–98, 200 S.E.2d 581, 583 (1973). Thus, unless a parent, by his or her conduct or condition, is unfit or is unable and unwilling to provide or care for a child, a court is not entitled to consider whether a third party might be better able to care for a child. Unfortunately, and all too frequently, foster parents or third parties would be more willing and better able to provide a loving and nurturing environment for a child than would the child's parents; however, custody of a child may not be taken from a parent on that basis. Even when the parental level of care may be marginally satisfactory, courts may not take custody of a child from his or her parents simply because a third party may be willing and able to provide better care for the child. *Id.*

... The proof of parental unfitness or that continued custody with the natural parent will be harmful to the child must be clear and convincing. *Bailes*, 231 Va. at 100, 340 S.E.2d at 827.

The most that can be said against Sharon Bottoms, insofar as her parenting is concerned, is that on two occasions she spanked her son "too hard," on occasion she swore in his presence, she had him stand in a corner, and on occasion she had failed to change his diaper as soon as conditions required. Sharon Bottoms had lived in four different residences in different relationships in a three-year period, and she had not been regularly employed. On one occasion, Sharon Bottoms had left her son with Kay Bottoms, the grandmother, for a week without informing the grandmother how she could be reached.

Although Sharon Bottoms' parenting during this three-year period was far from ideal, she was not indifferent to her child's well-being. Her disciplining of the child, even if by some standards considered intemperate or inappropriate, was not abusive. Her lifestyle in moving several times in a short period, in being unemployed for a time, and in failing to inform her mother of her whereabouts for a week were not acts of neglect or abuse sufficient to render her an unfit custodian. At all times, Sharon Bottoms either cared for the child or ensured that proper care was provided for the child. No evidence suggested that any of Sharon Bottoms' actions resulted in psychological, emotional, or physical harm to the child or that her actions constituted neglect or abuse.

The psychological evaluations admitted into evidence indicated that Sharon Bottoms' son is a "happy, well-adjusted youngster" with an "outgoing, engaging manner ... capable of forming and sustaining both emotional and social attachments to others." The psychological reports concluded that Sharon Bottoms is "warm" and "responsive" with her son and that "[he] behaves as if entirely secure and at ease with his mother, [being with her is] ... very familiar and comfortable ... for him."

The trial judge based his finding of Sharon Bottoms' parental unfitness on the fact that she is living in an open lesbian relationship with April Wade and that the two engage in sodomy, an illegal sexual act, in the home where the child would reside. Certainly, those facts, which define the nature of the relationship between a custodial parent and a resident of the household where the child would reside, are the most critical and significant factors in this case for determining whether this parent is unfit or whether continued parental custody will be harmful or deleterious to the child. All factors must be considered, but in this instance, the open lesbian relationship and illegality of the mother's sexual activity are the only significant factors that the court considered in finding Sharon Bottoms to be an unfit parent.

We agree with the trial court that the nature of the relationship between a parent and the parent's live-in companion where the child resides may affect the type of conduct and behavior to which a child will be exposed and, thus, profoundly affect the child. The Supreme Court of Virginia has expressly said that a lesbian "lifestyle" is one factor "to [be] ... considered in determining [a woman's] fitness as a mother." *Doe v. Doe*, 222 Va. 736, 748, 284 S.E.2d 799, 806 (1981). A parent's behavior and conduct in the presence of a child influences and affects the child's values and views as to the type of behavior and conduct that the child will find acceptable.

The fact that a parent is homosexual does not per se render a parent unfit to have custody of his or her child. Thus, the fact that a mother is a lesbian and has engaged in illegal sexual acts does not alone justify taking custody of a child from her and awarding the child to a non-parent, even though an award of custody may be only temporary. The fact that a parent has committed a crime does not render a parent unfit, unless such criminal conduct impacts upon or is harmful to the child, or unless other special circumstances exist aside from the parent's conduct that would render continued custody with the parent deleterious to the child.

... In *Mason v. Moon*, we reversed the trial court's decision to award custody of a child to her grandmother instead of her parent. In that case, clear and convincing evidence was not presented that the child would be adversely affected by living in the residence with her stepfather, who had killed the child's father in her presence. 9 Va.App. at 222–23, 385 S.E.2d at 245–46. In *Ferris v. Underwood*, 3 Va.App. 25, 28, 348 S.E.2d 18, 20 (1986), we found the evidence insufficient to rebut the presumption favoring a parent, even though a prostitute, who was the mother's sister, frequently visited in the home where the child lived. *See also Phillips v. Kiraly*, 200 Va. 345, 105 S.E.2d 855 (1958) (aunt and uncle denied custody because evidence that the father was irresponsible, took pictures of nude women, and had been a "peeping tom" did not rebut parental presumption).

Even when a natural parent falls short of society's accepted standards of behavior, such as the parents in the Mason, Ferris and Phillips, unless proof of harm to the child or evidence of neglect or abuse is shown, the state will not intervene to take custody of a child from its natural parent.

In Sharon Bottoms' case, the trial court found that Sharon Bottoms engaged in illegal sexual activity[86] and that her open lesbian relationship rendered her an unfit parent "as a matter of law." The trial court erroneously adopted a per se approach in finding Sharon Bottoms to be an unfit parent without finding that she engaged in conduct or exposed her son to conduct that would be harmful to him. In declaring as a matter of law that Sharon Bottoms is an unfit parent, the trial court misapplied the Supreme Court's decision in *Roe v. Roe*, 228 Va. 722, 324 S.E.2d 691 (1985).

---

86. The trial court noted that Sharon Bottoms' admission that she engaged weekly in oral sex with April Wade violated Code § 18.2–361 ("crimes against nature"), which makes sodomy a Class 6 felony.

In *Sutherland*, we permitted a mother living in an adulterous relationship to retain custody of her children over the natural father's objections, despite the fact that adultery is a crime in Virginia. *See* Code § 18.2–365. 14 Va.App. at 43, 414 S.E.2d at 618. *See Brinkley v. Brinkley*, 1 Va.App. 222, 224, 336 S.E.2d 901, 902 (1985) (an adulterous relationship, "without more, is an insufficient basis upon which to find that a parent is an unfit custodian of his or her child").

First, the *Roe* case does not stand for the proposition that a homosexual parent is per se unfit to have custody of a child. The Court stated in *Roe*, "although we decline[] to hold that every lesbian mother or homosexual father is per se an unfit parent . . . [this] father's continuous exposure of the child to his immoral and illicit relationship renders him an unfit and improper custodian as a matter of law." *Id.* at 727, 324 S.E.2d at 694; *see also Doe*, 222 Va. at 748, 284 S.E.2d at 806.

Second, the *Roe* decision has little or no application to this case because Roe involved a dispute between two parents over which was the preferred custodian. In *Roe*, the presumption of parental fitness had no application. In *Roe*, the court was only required to determine that, as between the parents, the child's best interests would be best served by granting custody of the child to the mother rather than to the father, who was engaged in a homosexual relationship to which the child was openly exposed. *Id.* at 727–28, 324 S.E.2d at 693–94. Although aspects of Sharon Bottoms' behavior were similar to the father's conduct in *Roe* because Sharon Bottoms had hugged and kissed and displayed some affection toward her lesbian partner in the presence of her child, the father in *Roe* had exposed his daughter to more intimate behavior of a sexual nature, which had an impact upon the child. In *Roe*, the nine-year-old daughter was visibly distressed by her father's homosexual relationship after she witnessed the two men "hugging and kissing and sleeping in bed together." *Id.* at 724, 324 S.E.2d at 692. In *Roe*, the father had parties at his house where other homosexuals would "engage in similar behavior in the child's presence." *Id.* Although Sharon Bottoms resides with April Wade in an open lesbian relationship, no evidence showed that they engaged in illegal sexual behavior in the child's presence. No evidence showed that the child has or will suffer any emotional or psychological distress as a result of the relationship. Where a parent exposes a child to an illicit sexual relationship, as in *Roe*, the Supreme Court has upheld denying a parent custody; however, where parents have shielded the child from illegal heterosexual adultery, as in the *Ford* and *Sutherland* cases, we have held the parents not to be unfit.

By applying *Roe* to a custody dispute between a parent and a third party, the trial court extended *Roe* beyond its precedential boundaries. Applying the holding in *Roe* to a custody dispute with a non-parent would allow a third party who may be better able or more fit or suitable to care for a child to be preferred for custody of the child over its natural parent solely because the parent is involved in a homosexual relationship. If we were to so hold, social service agencies would have the duty to take children from parents solely because a parent is homosexual and is living in a homosexual relationship.

The Supreme Court of Virginia has held that adverse effects of a parent's homosexuality on a child cannot be assumed without specific proof. *See Doe*, 222 Va. at 746, 284 S.E.2d at 805. "There is no evidence that children who are raised with a loving couple of the same sex are any more disturbed, unhealthy, or maladjusted than children raised with a loving couple of mixed sex." *Id.* at 748, 284 S.E.2d at 806 (quoting *Bezio v. Patenaude*, 381 Mass. 563, 410 N.E.2d 1207, 1215–16 (Mass. 1980)). The psychological testimony presented in this case was to the effect that a parent's homosexual relationship alone does not harm a child emotionally or psychologically or make the parent an unfit custodian. The social science evidence showed that a person's sexual orientation does not strongly correlate with that person's fitness as a parent. No evidence was presented to refute these studies. No evidence was presented that tended to prove that Sharon Bottoms' living arrangement with April Wade and their lesbian relationship have harmed or will harm Sharon Bottoms' son.

For these reasons, we hold that the trial court erred in finding that Sharon Bottoms' lesbian relationship alone constituted clear and convincing evidence of parental unfitness. The trial court erred in holding that the evidence "of the cursing [and] . . . of the child standing in the corner" and the fact that Sharon Bottoms is a lesbian who lives with her lesbian companion are "of such an extraordinary nature as to rebut the presumption [of parental fitness]."

Because we hold that the presumption favoring Sharon Bottoms in this case was not rebutted, we do not decide whether the grandmother, Kay Bottoms, could best provide for the child's needs. *See Wilkerson*, 214 Va. at 397, 200 S.E.2d at 583. Accordingly, we hold that Sharon Bottoms is not to be deprived of custody of her son upon the present record. We reverse and vacate the circuit court's order and remand the case with directions that the circuit court enter an order effectuating the resumption of custody by the mother of her son.

BOTTOMS v. BOTTOMS

249 Va. 410, 457 S.E.2d 102 (1995)

OPINION BY: A. CHRISTIAN COMPTON

"In all child custody cases, including those between a parent and a non-parent, 'the best interests of the child are paramount and form the lodestar for the guidance of the court in determining the dispute.' " In a custody dispute between a parent and non-parent, "the law presumes that the child's best interests will be served when in the custody of its parent."

Although the presumption favoring a parent over a non-parent is strong, it is rebutted when certain factors, such as parental unfitness, are established by clear and convincing evidence. *Bailes*, 231 Va. at 100, 340 S.E.2d at 827. The term "clear and convincing evidence" is defined as the measure or degree of proof that will produce in the mind of the trier of facts a firm belief or conviction upon the allegations sought to be established. It is intermediate, being more than a mere preponderance, but not to the degree of proof beyond a reasonable doubt as in criminal cases; it does not mean clear and unequivocal. 249 Va. 410, 215 Va. 535 at 540. The burden to show unfitness is upon the one seeking to alter the parent's right to custody.

In custody cases, the welfare of the child takes precedence over the rights of the parent. But, when the contest is between parent and non-parent, this rule is conditioned upon the principle that a parent's rights "are to be respected if at all consonant with the best interests of the child...."

When the trial court hears the evidence ore tenus, its findings are entitled to the weight accorded a jury verdict, and these findings should not be disturbed by an appellate court unless they are plainly wrong or without evidence to support them. A reviewing court should never redetermine the facts on appeal. Absent clear evidence to the contrary in the record, the judgment of a trial court comes to an appellate court with a presumption that the law was correctly applied to the facts. And, the appellate court should view the facts in the light most favorable to the party prevailing before the trial court. Accordingly, we shall summarize the facts in the light most favorable to the grandmother, resolving all conflicts in the evidence in her favor.

This child's mother, born in February 1970, "dropped out" of school in the twelfth grade. Until she was 18 years of age, she resided at home with her mother, who is a divorcee, and her mother's boyfriend.

Upon leaving home, the child's mother was supported by and lived with a cousin, a friend, and a sister respectively. In December 1989, the child's mother married Dennis Doustou, whom she had been dating for several years. She left Doustou after eight months of marriage, and resumed living with the cousin for a while. The child was born during the separation in July 1991. The parties were divorced, and the mother was awarded custody of her child. The child's father has expressed little interest in his son and pays no child support.

The maternal grandmother, born in January 1951, resides in the Richmond area. Her boyfriend ceased living with her shortly before the juvenile court hearing, and has not returned. The grandmother did not complete her high school education, and has worked as a nurse's aide and manager of a shoe store. She currently is employed as a "nanny," taking care of two children.

During the two-year period before the trial court hearing, the child had spent 70 percent of the time with the grandmother and 30 percent with his mother. The grandmother has kept the child for "weeks at a time" and during "every weekend since he's been born." On at least three occasions during that period, the mother left the child with the grandmother without informing her of the mother's whereabouts or how she could be reached "in the event something happened to the child."

Following the mother's separation from Doustou, she continued a "relationship" with another man that had begun during her marriage. She contracted a venereal disease during this relationship that prevents her from having additional children. During the child's first year, the mother "slept with two or three different guys, maybe four, in the same room" with the child "where his crib was." At the time, the mother "lived two blocks away" from the grandmother, and the mother kept the child's "suitcase packed" for visits to the grandmother's home. The mother said that she has "had trouble" with her temper, and that when the child was about "a year" old, she "popped him on his leg too hard a couple of times," and left her fingerprints there. She has had "counseling" in an effort to control her temper.

At "some point subsequent to" the child's birth, the mother lived in a dwelling with yet another man who supported her for more than a year. After the mother "left" this man, she "lived with" a lesbian "couple."

Except for brief employment as a grocery store cashier, the mother had been unemployed during most of the three-year period prior to the trial court hearing. She was receiving "welfare money" which often was spent to "do her fingernails before the baby would get any food."

During May 1992, ten months before the juvenile court hearing, 16 months before the trial court hearing, and when her son was ten months old, the mother met April Wade, a lesbian. Wade, born in April 1966, had been discharged from the U.S. Army in 1986. Wade is a "recovering alcoholic."

The mother and Wade "moved in together" in September 1992. From that time, with the exception of a two-week period, the mother and Wade have lived in "a lesbian relationship." According to the mother, the relationship involves hugging and kissing, patting "on the bottom," sleeping in the same bed, "fondling," and "oral sex." The mother testified that she loves Wade and that they "have a lifetime commitment."

At the time of the juvenile court hearing, the mother, the child, and Wade were living in a two-bedroom apartment with "Evelyn," another lesbian. "At one time," the child's bed was in the room where the mother and Wade slept, having "sex in the same bed." At one point in her testimony, however, when asked "how many times did you do it when the child was sleeping in the same bedroom," the mother responded, "None." She said that she and Wade displayed other signs of affection "in front of" the child.

Wade, employed as a gift shop manager, supports the mother. The pair lives in an apartment complex in Western Henrico County. Wade has become "a parent figure" to the child, who calls Wade "Da Da."

Two months before the petition for custody was filed, the mother revealed her lesbian relationship to the grandmother. This disclosure alienated the two.

During the period after the juvenile court hearing, when regimented visitation with the mother began, the child demonstrated certain traits. For example, when the child returned to the grandmother from being with the mother, he would "stomp" his foot, tell himself to "go to the corner," and then would stand in the corner of a room, facing the wall. He curses, saying "shit" and "damn," language never used in the grandmother's home. On one occasion, when the mother and Wade "came to pick him up," the child "held his breath, turned purple He didn't want to go with her," according to the grandmother. During a period in mid–1993, each time the mother "would come pick him up," the child would scream and cry.

Wade has admitted she "hit" the child. Also, on one occasion, when an argument developed between the mother and Wade, on the one hand, and the grandmother, on the other, about the timing of the exchange of the child for visitation, Wade said during the quarrel, "I might end up killing somebody." According to the grandmother, the child is "always neglected." For example, when the child returns to the grandmother's home, she testified that he "can't even sit down in the bathtub. That's neglect from changing his diaper. He is so red."

... The trial judge, announcing his decision from the bench at the conclusion of the hearing, said the dispute "presents the question ... whether the child's best interest is served by a transfer of the custody of the child from [his] mother to [his] maternal grandmother." Stating that the mother's conduct is "illegal," and constitutes a felony under the Commonwealth's criminal laws, and that "her conduct is immoral," the court recognized the "presumption in the law in favor of the custody being with the natural parent."

Mentioning the evidence of lesbianism and specified "other evidence" in the case not involving homosexual conduct, the trial court concluded from "all the facts and circumstances ... of the case," that "the custody will be with the grandmother."

... The Court of Appeals failed to give proper deference upon appellate review to the trial court's factual findings, and misapplied the law to the facts viewed from a proper appellate perspective.

The evidence plainly is sufficient, when applying the clear and convincing standard and when viewing the facts from the correct appellate perspective, to support the trial court's findings that the parental presumption has been rebutted, that the mother is an unfit custodian at this time, and that the child's best interests would be promoted by awarding custody to the grandmother.

Among the factors to be weighed in determining unfitness are the parent's misconduct that affects the child, neglect of the child, and a demonstrated unwillingness and inability to promote the emotional and physical well-being of the child. Other important considerations include the nature of the home environment and moral climate in which the child is to be raised. We have held, however, that a lesbian mother is not per se an unfit parent. *Doe v. Doe*, 222 Va. 736, 748, 284 S.E.2d 799, 806 (1981). Conduct inherent in lesbianism is punishable as a Class 6 felony in the Commonwealth, Code § 18.2–361; thus, that conduct is another important consideration in determining custody.

And, while the legal rights of a parent should be respected in a custody proceeding, those technical rights may be disregarded if demanded by the interests of the child.

In the present case, the record shows a mother who, although devoted to her son, refuses to subordinate her own desires and priorities to the child's welfare. For example, the mother disappears for days without informing the child's custodian of her whereabouts. She moves her residence from place to place, relying on others for support, and uses welfare funds to "do" her fingernails before buying food for the child. She has participated in illicit relationships with numerous men, acquiring a disease from one, and "sleeping" with men in the same room where the child's crib was located. To aid in her mobility, the mother keeps the child's suitcase packed so he can be quickly deposited at the grandmother's.

The mother has difficulty controlling her temper and, out of frustration, has struck the child when it was merely one year old with such force as to leave her fingerprints on his person. While in her care, she neglects to change and cleanse the child so that, when he returns from visitation with her, he is "red" and "can't even sit down in the bathtub."

Unlike *Doe*, 222 Va. at 747, 284 S.E.2d at 805, relied on by the mother, there is proof in this case that the child has been harmed, at this young age, by the conditions under which he lives when with the mother for any extended period. For example, he has already demonstrated some disturbing traits. He uses vile language. He screams, holds his breath until he turns purple, and becomes emotionally upset when he must go to visit the mother. He appears confused about efforts at discipline, standing himself in a corner facing the wall for no apparent reason.

And, we shall not overlook the mother's relationship with Wade, and the environment in which the child would be raised if custody is awarded the mother. We have previously said that living daily under conditions stemming from active lesbianism practiced in the home may impose a burden upon a child by reason of the "social condemnation" attached to such an arrangement, which will inevitably afflict the child's relationships with its "peers and with the community at large." *Roe v. Roe*, 228 Va. 722, 728, 324 S.E.2d 691, 694 (1985). We do not retreat from that statement; such a result is likely under these facts. Also, Wade has struck the child and, when there was a dispute over visitation, she has threatened violence when her views were not accepted.

... Accordingly, we hold that the trial court, based on all the facts and circumstances, correctly ruled on the custody question. And, the study of the grandmother's home by the Chesterfield–Colonial Heights Department of Social Services determined there was "no reason" why she should not be awarded custody should the trial court make such a ruling.

Reversed and remanded.

PULLIAM v. SMITH

348 N.C. 616, 501 S.E.2d 898 (1998)

MITCHELL, CHIEF JUSTICE.

The overriding question presented for review is whether there was sufficient evidence to support the trial court's finding of a substantial change of circumstances affecting the welfare of two minor children which would warrant a change of custody. The Court of Appeals held that there was not. Since we conclude that the trial court's judgment modifying a prior order placing custody of the children with their father is supported by adequate findings of fact based on substantial evidence, we also conclude that the trial court's judgment was free of error. We therefore reverse the decision of the Court of Appeals.

As a preliminary matter, we address that portion of the Court of Appeals' decision which concluded that the party seeking modification of custody must show "that the change [in circumstances] has had an *adverse* effect on the child or will likely or probably have such an effect unless custody is altered." *Pulliam v. Smith*, 124 N.C.App. 144, 147, 476 S.E.2d 446, 449 (1996) (emphasis added). This Court has never required the party moving for a modification of custody to show that the change in circumstances has had or will have an *adverse* consequence upon the child's well-being, and we decline to do so now.

The controlling statute provides that, when an order for custody of a minor child has been entered by a court of another state, a court of this state may, upon a showing of changed circumstances, enter a new order for custody. N.C.G.S. § 50–13.7(b) (1995). In *Blackley v. Blackley*, 285 N.C. 358, 204 S.E.2d 678 (1974), we interpreted N.C.G.S. § 50–13.7(b) which mandates a "showing of changed circumstances." In that decision, we held:

> The modification of a custody decree must be supported by findings of fact based on competent evidence that there has been a substantial change of circumstances affecting the welfare of the child, and the party moving for such modification assumes the burden of showing such change of circumstances.

Id. at 362, 204 S.E.2d at 681. In *Blackley*, we held that the trial court erred in modifying a prior order awarding custody because the evidence was insufficient to show a substantial change of circumstances affecting the welfare of the child; we neither held nor implied that to establish a change of circumstances which would justify a modification of custody, it must always be shown that the change of circumstances adversely affects or will adversely affect the child.

The welfare of the child has always been the polar star which guides the courts in awarding custody. *Shepherd v. Shepherd*, 273 N.C. 71, 75, 159 S.E.2d 357, 361 (1968). In reviewing a request for modification of custody, courts may not limit the inquiry as to what constitutes the best interests of the child solely to a consideration of those changes in circumstances which it has found to exist and which may *adversely* affect that child. It is true that we have stated in one case that, "We cannot forecast the future, but if there should be a change of circumstances adversely affecting the welfare of these children, the court is empowered to act. . . ." *Thomas v. Thomas*, 259 N.C. 461, 467, 130 S.E.2d 871, 876 (1963). However, this statement in the form of *obiter dictum* should not be read to indicate that a court's consideration of changed circumstances should be limited to those having adverse consequences for the child. The facts in *Thomas* involved a situation in which the children were affected adversely if at all, and our statement there merely reflected those facts. Further, our statement that a change of circumstances adversely affecting children would empower the court to act is not equal to, and should not be read as, a holding that a court could not change custody where a substantial change of circumstances had occurred which would beneficially affect the child if custody should be modified. Rather, courts must consider and weigh all evidence of changed circumstances which affect or will affect the best interests of the child, both changed circumstances which will have salutary effects upon the child and those which will have adverse effects upon the child. In appropriate cases, either may support a modification of custody on the ground of a change in circumstances.

. . . We emphasize that an adverse effect upon a child as the result of a change in circumstances is and remains an acceptable factor for the courts to consider and will support a modification of a prior custody order. However, a showing of a change in circumstances that is, or is likely to be, beneficial to the child may also warrant a change in custody. We conclude this analysis by noting that, in either situation, it must always be remembered that

> [a] decree of custody is entitled to such stability as would end the vicious litigation so often accompanying such contests, unless it be found that some change of circumstances has occurred affecting the welfare of the child so as to require modification of the order. To hold otherwise would invite constant litigation by a dissatisfied party so as to keep the involved child constantly torn between parents and in a resulting state of turmoil and insecurity. This in itself would destroy the paramount aim of the court, that is, that the welfare of the child be promoted and subserved.

Shepherd, 273 N.C. at 75, 159 S.E.2d at 361. Having resolved the foregoing questions of law, we turn to the evidence presented and the issue raised by the parties in this case.

Uncontroverted evidence before the trial court tended to show that plaintiff Carol J. Pulliam and defendant Frederick J. Smith are the mother and father of two boys, Frederick Joseph Smith, II (Joey) and Kenneth August Smith (Kenny). Plaintiff-mother and defendant-father were married in California in November 1982. They separated in 1990 when plaintiff went to live in Kansas with William Pulliam. Plaintiff and defendant were divorced in November 1991. At that time, Joey was six years old, and Kenny was three years old. The parties entered into a consent decree regarding the custody of the children. Pursuant to the decree, the parties had joint legal custody, and defendant-father had physical custody of the children. Until August 1994, the children lived with defendant and his grandmother in North Carolina. In February 1993, plaintiff married Mr. Pulliam, and they have since resided in Wichita, Kansas. Plaintiff-mother had the boys with her for two months during the summer and at Christmas each year. In August 1994, Tim Tipton moved into defendant's home, and defendant's grandmother moved out a month later. Defendant-father and Mr. Tipton are homosexuals.

The trial court made findings of fact supported by evidence, which included, *inter alia*, the following:

> 27. That Tim Tipton first moved into the home located on 9 Roberts Street in Fletcher, North Carolina around March of 1994.
>
> 28. That Tim Tipton and the Defendant often kiss on the check [sic] and sometimes on the lips in front of the two minor children. That Tim Tipton and the Defendant would often hold hands in front of the two minor children.
>
> 29. Tim Tipton and the Defendant both testified that they engaged in oral sex, in that Tim Tipton would about once a week place his mouth on the penis of the Defendant. The Defendant would also place his mouth on the penis of Tim Tipton. The Court accordingly makes this as a finding of fact.
>
> . . .
>
> 32. That Tim Tipton and the Defendant engaged in the acts described in paragraph 29 above while the minor children were present in the home. That the minor children share the same bedroom and the said bedroom of the minor children is directly across the hall from the bedroom occupied by the Defendant and Tipton. That the Defendant and Tipton would engage in the acts described in paragraph 29 above while the children were a short distance away.
>
> 33. The Defendant and Mr. Tipton on at least one (1) occasion had a party for homosexuals at the home located at 9 Roberts Road in Fletcher, North Carolina. That the occasion was an anniversary party marking the first year since the Defendant and Tim Tipton meet [sic] at a homosexual bar in Asheville, North Carolina.
>
> 34. The Defendant and Mr. Tipton on at least three (3) occasions since first meeting have gone to an establishment that caters to homosexuals.
>
> 35. Mr. Tipton keeps in the bedroom he shares with the Defendant pictures of "drag queens." These are pictures of men dressed like women. These pictures are not under a lock, and it is possible for the children to gain access to the pictures.

36. Mr. Tipton testified that these materials (photographs of "drag queens") were not something that a child should be subjected to, and the Court finds this as a fact.

37. That the minor child Joey on one or more occasions observed the Defendant and Tipton in bed together.

38. That the two minor children never have friends stay over night while they are residing with the Defendant.

. . .

43. Uncontroverted evidence was presented that on at least two (2) occasions the Defendant struck the minor child Joey on or about the head, and accordingly the Court makes this as a finding of fact.

44. That on the 27th day of February, 1993, the Plaintiff married William Pulliam.

. . .

49. Defendant's conduct is not fit and proper and will expose the (2) minor male children to unfit and improper influences . . .

. . .

53. The activity of the Defendant will likely create emotional difficulties for the two minor children. That evidence was presented that the minor child Joey cried when he was told by the Defendant that he (Defendant) was homosexual. This evidence leads the Court to find that the minor child Joey may already be experiencing emotional difficulties because of the active homosexuality of the Defendant. Furthermore the Court finds that it is likely that the minor child Kenny will also experience emotional difficulties because of the active homosexuality of the Defendant.

54. That the active homosexuality of the Defendant and his involvement with Tim Tipton by bringing Tim Tipton into the home of the two minor children is detrimental to the best interest and welfare of the two minor children.

55. The Plaintiff is presently in a position to provide an environment more suitable to the two minor children's physical and emotional needs.

Based on such findings of fact, the trial court entered conclusions of law which included, *inter alia*, the following:

2. That since the entry of the California Judgment the Defendant is exposing the two minor children to conduct which is not fit and proper.

3. That since the California Judgment the Defendant is not providing a fit and proper environment in which to rear the two minor children.

4. That there has been a substantial change of circumstances since the entry of the California Judgment adversely affecting the two

minor children or that will likely or probably adversely affect the two minor children.

5. That Plaintiff is a fit and proper person to exercise the exclusive care, custody, and control of the said two minor children. That it is in the minor children's best interest that the Plaintiff have exclusive[] care, custody and control of the minor children, subject to reasonable visitation privileges being awarded to the Defendant as hereinafter set out.

Based upon its findings of fact and conclusions of law, the trial court ordered that plaintiff-mother be awarded the exclusive care, custody and control of the two minor children. Defendant-father was granted one month of visitation during the summers and was directed by the trial court not to allow the boys to live in the same house with Mr. Tipton.

Defendant-father appealed to the Court of Appeals, which held that the findings upon which the trial court based its determination that there had been a change in circumstances adversely affecting the welfare of the children were either speculative or not supported by evidence in the record. The Court of Appeals reversed the trial court. For the reasons stated herein, we reverse the decision of the Court of Appeals.

... With regard to findings of fact 49 and 54, uncontroverted evidence was presented that defendant-father and Mr. Tipton engaged in oral sex approximately once a week in the home with the children present. Defendant-father and Mr. Tipton intended to continue such homosexual activity in the home. Defendant-father saw nothing wrong with such conduct and would not counsel the two minor children that such conduct was improper.

Evidence was also presented tending to show that the children had seen the two men demonstrate physical affection, including kissing each other on the lips. This activity took place in the home in front of the children as the "provider" of this couple prepared to leave for work. The minor child Joey had observed his father and Mr. Tipton in bed together.

The evidence further tended to show that the door of the bedroom occupied by defendant-father and Mr. Tipton was directly across the hall and approximately three feet from the door to the children's bedroom. Defendant-father and Mr. Tipton testified that both their bedroom door and the children's bedroom door were open at all times, except when the two men engaged in sexual activity. Further, testimony tended to show that the children went in and out of the two men's bedroom at will, often during the night when the two men were in bed together.

Defendant testified that he had told the children that society was not accepting of such a homosexual relationship. There was also evidence that Mr. Tipton kept photographs of "drag queens" in the home, despite his admission that the children should not be exposed to such material. Further, evidence was presented that Mr. Tipton had, on at least one occasion, taken the children away from the home without defendant's knowledge of their whereabouts.

The foregoing evidence was admitted by the trial court and was not disputed by defendant. This evidence was substantial evidence and clearly supports findings of fact 49 and 54. We conclude that activities such as the regular commission of sexual acts in the home by unmarried people, failing and refusing to counsel the children against such conduct while acknowledging this conduct to them, allowing the children to see unmarried persons known by the children to be sexual partners in bed together, keeping admittedly improper sexual material in the home, and Mr. Tipton's taking the children out of the home without their father's knowledge of their whereabouts support the trial court's findings of "improper influences" which are "detrimental to the best interest and welfare of the two minor children."

We do not agree with the conclusion of Justice Webb's dissent that the only basis upon which the trial court changed custody was that the defendant is a "practicing homosexual." Instead, we conclude that the trial court could and did order a change in custody *based in part* on proper findings of fact to the effect that defendant-father was regularly engaging in sexual acts with Mr. Tipton in the home while the children were present and upon other improper conduct by these two men. The trial court did not rely on the mere fact that defendant is a homosexual or a "practicing homosexual." Nor does this Court hold that the mere homosexual status of a parent is sufficient, taken alone, to support denying such parent custody of his or her child or children. That question is not presented by the facts of this case. Although the trial court might have worded findings 49 and 54 better or more fully, they are nonetheless supported by substantial uncontroverted evidence. Therefore, they were binding on the Court of Appeals and are binding on this Court.

With regard to finding of fact 53, evidence was presented that when Joey was told that defendant-father was involved in a homosexual relationship, Joey was emotionally distraught, covering his face with his hands and running into the bathroom. Later, Joey cried, grasped onto his mother, and asked his mother to get him out of defendant's home. Evidence was also presented that sometime thereafter, Joey told his stepfather, William Pulliam, that he wanted his mother to come and get him and take him to Wichita where she lived. Further, evidence was presented that Joey expressed confusion over defendant's homosexual relationship with Mr. Tipton by asking Mr. Tipton if he was Joey's stepfather.

The trial court could reasonably find from this substantial evidence, as well as the other evidence discussed above, that "the activity of the Defendant will likely create emotional difficulties for the two minor children." Although the trial court might have worded finding of fact 53 differently, it is nonetheless supported by substantial evidence and is binding on the Court of Appeals and this Court.

Substantial evidence supports all of the above-quoted findings of the trial court. Because these findings are sufficient to support the trial court's conclusions, which in turn justify a change of custody, we conclude that the trial court did not err.

The judgment of the trial court was proper, and the decision of the Court of Appeals to the contrary was in error. The decision of the Court of Appeals must be and is reversed, and this case is remanded to that court for its further remand to the District Court, Henderson County, for reinstatement of the judgment of the trial court.

REVERSED AND REMANDED.

JUSTICE WEBB dissenting.

I dissent. I do not believe the evidence supports a finding that there had been a substantial change in circumstances affecting the welfare of the children so that the custody could be changed.

. . . The majority relies first on findings of fact 49 and 54 to hold that the district court found facts sufficient to justify a change in custody. In these two findings, the district court found only that the defendant is a practicing homosexual and this creates an unfit and improper environment for the children. I do not believe the fact, standing alone, that defendant is a practicing homosexual, is sufficient to support a conclusion that this shows an improper environment which justifies a change in custody.

The majority also relies on finding of fact 53, in which the district court speculated on the possibility that their father's homosexuality will likely create emotional difficulties for the two children. The only evidence that the children actually suffered emotional difficulties was testimony that the older child, when he was told his father was homosexual, cried and asked his mother to remove him from his father's home. This child said at the hearing that he had no preference as to which of the parties was given custody. All the evidence showed the children were well adjusted. They had good attendance records in school and maintained average to above average grades. There was not substantial evidence to support a finding of fact that the defendant's homosexuality will likely create emotional difficulties for the two children.

The difficulty with the majority opinion for me is that it recites actions by the defendant which the majority considers to be distasteful, immoral, or even illegal and says this evidence supports findings of fact which allow a change in custody. There is virtually no showing that these acts by the defendant have adversely affected the two children. The test should be how the action affects the children and not whether we approve of it. I believe the evidence shows only that the defendant is a practicing homosexual without showing any harm has been inflicted on the children by this practice. I do not believe we should allow a change in custody on evidence which shows only that the defendant is a practicing homosexual.

JACOBY v. JACOBY

763 So.2d 410 (Fla. App. 2000)

OPINION BY: NORTHCUTT

The circuit court dissolved the marriage of Julie and David Jacoby in November 1998. Mrs. Jacoby challenges several aspects of the final judgment, including the court's designation of Mr. Jacoby as primary residential parent of the parties' children. We agree with Mrs. Jacoby on the custody issue, and reverse on that point. We also remand for reconsideration of her application for an award of attorney's fees and costs.

PRIMARY RESIDENTIAL CUSTODY OF THE CHILDREN.

Two daughters were born during the marriage, one in August 1989 and the other in October 1992. In November 1996, Mrs. Jacoby informed her husband that she had fallen in love with a longstanding family friend who is a lesbian. The parties separated. Mrs. Jacoby and the children moved into the home of her lesbian partner; Mr. Jacoby stayed in the marital home. After the separation, the children began to visit Mr. Jacoby.

Both parties sought primary residential custody of the two girls. Mrs. Jacoby proposed that they live with her and her partner in the home they had shared since the separation. The father became engaged while the divorce was pending. He intended to marry and move into a home owned by his new wife when the dissolution was final. If he were awarded custody, the girls would live with him, his new wife and her teenaged children. They would attend public school in the neighborhood of his new home, which was in the same county as the marital home, but not nearby.

Numerous witnesses testified at trial, including the mother, her partner, the father, his fiancée and a court appointed psychologist. The mother had been the children's primary caretaker during the marriage and the initial period of separation, and the father admitted she was a great parent. But the father, too, had become a better and more involved parent during the rotating custody. The psychologist confirmed that both parties were good parents, but he concluded that Mrs. Jacoby had an edge in parenting skills. She was more adept at demonstrating affection, he said. In addition, the children had stronger emotional ties to her, and she could provide a fine home environment. The psychologist also believed that Mrs. Jacoby would be the custodial parent more likely to encourage contact with the noncustodial parent. He recommended that she be assigned primary residential responsibility for the children.

As often happens in child custody cases, each parent attempted to prove examples of the other's lapses in parental judgment. The court wisely refused to consider a number of these minor conflicts in deciding which parent should have primary residential responsibility for the girls. At the same time, however, the court's remarks during the final hearing and in the final judgment demonstrate that it succumbed to the father's attacks on the mother's sexual orientation, which were the primary feature of this case.

For a court to properly consider conduct such as Mrs. Jacoby's sexual orientation on the issue of custody, the conduct must have a direct effect or impact upon the children. *See Maradie v. Maradie*, 680 So.2d 538 (Fla. 1st DCA 1996). "The mere possibility of negative impact on the child is not enough." *Id.* at 543. The connection between the conduct and the harm to the children must have an evidentiary basis; it cannot be assumed. *See id.* We have reviewed the court's comments concerning the negative impact of the mother's sexual orientation on the children, and have found them to be conclusory or unsupported by the evidence.

For example, the final judgment stated that "there is no doubt that the husband feels the current living arrangement of the wife is immoral and an inappropriate place in which to rear their children.... Obviously, this opinion is shared by others in the community." But the latter is not obvious to us from this record. In fact, there was no evidence addressing "the community's" beliefs about the morality of homosexuals or their child rearing abilities.

The order then addressed the community's reaction to homosexuals, by paraphrasing the psychologist's testimony: "Dr. Merin testified that a strong stigma attaches to homosexuality and that while being reared in a homosexual environment does not appear to alter sexual preference, it does affect social interaction and that it is likely that the children's peers or their parents will have negative words or thoughts about this." (emphasis supplied). The court mischaracterized Dr. Merin's testimony. In response to the question "and it's your understanding that you say times are changing ..., but there is still a stigma socially attached with homosexual lifestyles in our society?" Dr. Merin responded "yes." He did not quantify the degree. He did remark that "in our society it is now the likelihood that there would be words spoken or thoughts, negative thoughts or concerns by children's peers or the parent of their peers...." Dr. Merin's actual testimony about social interaction was: "research would indicate that the considerations would be given more to their social interaction than to the great degree of probability that they would themselves, you know, develop homosexual characteristics."

But even if the court's comments about the community's beliefs and possible reactions were correct and supported by the evidence in this record, the law cannot give effect to private biases. *See Palmore v. Sidoti*, 466 U.S. 429, 433, 80 L.Ed.2d 421, 104 S.Ct. 1879 (1984); *cf. Department of Health and Rehabilitative Services v. Cox*, 627 So.2d 1210 (Fla. 2d DCA 1993) (stating that private biases against homosexuality are not a permissible rational basis to support statute banning homosexuals from adopting), approved in part, quashed in part, 656 So.2d 902 (Fla. 1995). Moreover, even if the law were to permit consideration of the biases of others, and even if we were to accept the assumption that such would necessarily harm the children, the bias and ensuing harm would flow not from the fact that the children were living with a homosexual mother, but from the fact that she is a homosexual. *See Conkel v. Conkel*, 31 Ohio App.3d 169, 509 N.E.2d 983 (Ohio App. 1987); *M.P. v. S.P.*, 169 N.J.Super. 425, 404 A.2d 1256 (N.J. Super. A.D. 1979). The circuit court's reliance on perceived biases was an improper basis for a residential custody determination.

The final judgment also contained unsupported findings concerning the effect on the children of religious teachings about homosexuality. The judgment stated: "Dr. Merin testified that once the children learn about homosexuality and religious teachings, real confusion and conflict will arise for them." (Emphases supplied.) Again, the order does not accurately reflect Dr. Merin's views. Concerning a possible conflict between religious teachings and homosexuality, Dr. Merin opined that as the children get older, they may become confused, but that their level of comfort would be affected by how the situation was handled. This was the only testimony about the possible effects of religious teaching on the children, and it did not support a finding that the mother's sexual orientation will harm the children.

Moreover, the record contains no competent evidence about what, if any, religious teaching the children were exposed to. Yet the judge criticized Mrs. Jacoby's decision to keep the children in the church-affiliated school they had been attending, stating he "[could not] determine if [the mother] is naive or simply blasé, but she has made absolutely no effort to determine how her current lifestyle might adversely impact the children in their current school environment." These words are disquieting for several reasons. First, ironically, they betray the influence of religious stereotyping. Several witnesses testified about the Baptists' beliefs without ever explaining the sources of their knowledge. When Mr. Jacoby's attorney asked Dr. Merin if he knew the Baptists' position on homosexuality, the doctor responded that they were strongly opposed to it. Mr. Jacoby also testified he had learned that the Baptist religion was against homosexuality. At one point, the trial court itself questioned Mrs. Jacoby directly, asking whether she was aware that "the Baptists" had boycotted Disney World. None of this was competent evidence; nothing in the record suggested that the psychologist, Mr. Jacoby, or the trial court was qualified to expound on Baptist doctrine.

Second, no evidence was presented to show to what degree, how, or even whether this supposed Baptist doctrine of anti-homosexuality was espoused at the children's school or, for that matter, at the church with which it was affiliated. Indeed, the only evidence with any bearing on these questions suggested an atmosphere of tolerance; Mr. and Mrs. Jacoby both testified that the school employed a teacher who was widely known to be homosexual. The court's question about "Disney World" presumably referred to the 1996 and 1997 votes by attendees at the Southern Baptist Convention to boycott the Walt Disney Company in part because it extended health benefits to employees in same-sex relationships. But there was no evidence in this record about that boycott. The court's implication either that Baptists were unanimous in that position or that the Southern Baptist Convention wields some sort of hierarchal authority over Baptist churches and schools had no evidentiary support.

Third, while criticizing Mrs. Jacoby for failing to investigate Baptist teachings on homosexuality, the court chose to ignore Mr. Jacoby's own similar failings. Mr. Jacoby testified that he intended to convert to Catholicism after his remarriage, and he had been taking the girls to a Catholic church. But he conceded that he did not know the Catholic tenets on homosexuality.

In short, there was no evidence to show that the children were being harmed or would be harmed by their continued enrollment in the school they had attended during the parties' marriage. Nor does the record disclose that Mrs. Jacoby's decision to keep the children in that school was any less informed than Mr. Jacoby's desire to take them out of it.

Mrs. Jacoby's sexual orientation found its way into the final judgment in other ways. The judgment referred to the father's fiancée's house as "a very appropriate home" and a "very nice home." It went on to state that "the preference of this home to the one proposed by the wife is obvious...." Again, although we are confident that the court accurately assessed Mr. Jacoby's new home, the obviousness of its preference is not apparent from the evidence. Nothing in the record suggested that Mrs. Jacoby's house was physically inappropriate for raising children; that is, that it was too small or in an unsavory neighborhood, or some such. In fact, the evidence showed it was a three bedroom home, that the girls shared their own bedroom, and that they had a computer complete with children's games.

The court also found that when the Jacoby children have spent time with the father in the company of his fiancée and her children "there has been absolutely nothing inappropriate in the presence of the children or during the time they may have spent the night in the home." We have no quarrel with this finding, which is amply supported by the evidence. But Mr. Jacoby's counsel has endeavored to contrast this fact with a charge that Mrs. Jacoby and her partner were not so circumspect in their behavior. In his written closing argument to the circuit court, in his brief on appeal, and at oral argument the father's counsel repeatedly intoned that the evidence proved the two women allowed the children in their bed when the adults were topless. After carefully reviewing the record, we dismiss this accusation as specious innuendo, intended to imply that the women engaged in sexual conduct in the children's presence. The record citation tendered for this assertion was the father's testimony that one of the girls, upon seeing him working in the yard shirtless, commented "that [he] was topless and [he] slept topless like mommy does." While the mother acknowledged that she and her companion slept together, and that sometimes the children were allowed into their mother's bed to snuggle, these facts simply do not support the inference the father promotes. For its part, the trial court made no finding that Mrs. Jacoby had ever engaged in sexual conduct in the children's presence. We are satisfied that it was no more taken in by this canard than we are.

In summary, when making this custody determination the circuit court penalized the mother for her sexual orientation without evidence that it harmed the children. Accordingly, we reverse the court's appointment of the father as primary residential parent, and remand with directions to enter a new custody order. Because we are remanding, we further note that a number of the court's other findings under the custody factors set out in section 61.13(3), Florida Statutes (1997), were not supported by the evidence, and in some cases were contrary to the undisputed evidence. In reaching a new custody decision, the court must reconsider these factors.

Section 61.13(3)(d) requires that a court consider "the length of time the child has lived in a stable, satisfactory environment and the desirability of maintaining continuity." The final judgment found "that due to the rotating custody, there has been no stable environment favoring one parent over the other...." Similarly, section 61.13(3)(h) directs the court to weigh "the home, school and community record of the child." Again, the court found this factor did not favor either parent because of the rotating custody.

The court appropriately assessed these factors in light of the rotating custody, which had been in effect for a year or more. But its findings ignored the father's stated intention to move the children from the former marital home, which was his residence during the rotation and was the children's residence before the separation, to a new home located in a neighborhood where they were not accustomed to living. Additionally, they would be attending a new school. The mother testified without contradiction that she had continued the children in their prior school, over the husband's objections, because she wanted them to have some continuity after the parties' separation. Finally, the husband's proposed residence included his new wife and teenaged stepchildren. While even the mother testified that the children seemed to like the husband's fiancée, this woman was a relatively new figure in their lives. In contrast, the court overlooked the evidence that the mother's partner, who was her employer and had been a family friend before the separation, had known the children since their births. The psychologist testified that the children's artwork was very positive concerning their mother and her partner. He believed the father's fiancée was an "unknown quantity." The court's conclusory finding that, because of the rotating custody arrangement, the factors in sections 61.13(3)(d) and (h) had no bearing on this case was not supported by the evidence.

In its finding concerning the permanence of the proposed custodial homes, section 61.13(3)(e), the court focused on the psychologist's speculation that the mother might not, in fact, be homosexual. If that turned out to be true, the court ventured, "the permanence of her home becomes quite suspect." But, such conjecture aside, the fact was that the mother had been living with her partner for two years. Moreover, when weighing this factor the court was not free simply to disregard undisputed facts which called into doubt the permanence of the father's home. As had the mother, the father had been married once before this marriage. As was the mother, the father was embarking on a new relationship, and proposing to move the children into his third marital home.

Finally, the court noted that the legislature must have believed that the fostering of a relationship between the children and the noncustodial parent was very important because it addressed this issue twice, in sections 61.13(3)(a) and (j). *See Adair v. Adair*, 720 So.2d 316 (Fla. 4th DCA 1998). The final judgment found that while the father "does not wish the children to reside overnight with their mother while she is actively engaged in a homosexual relationship . . . this can be softened by counseling or court fiat." As we previously discussed, the court also found that Mr. Jacoby felt Mrs. Jacoby's living arrangement was "immoral" and an "inappropriate place in which to rear their children." As for the mother, the court found she had little respect for the father. Indeed, Mrs. Jacoby's testimony showed, and Dr. Merin's confirmed, that she was somewhat rigid and that she tended to pester Mr. Jacoby over relatively minor details associated with visitation.

We are taken aback, though, by the court's declaration that the father's deep-seated animosity toward the mother's homosexuality could be softened, and by its clear implication that the mother's inflexibility could not—and we have searched in vain for record evidence to support either view. Again, the language of the order is discomfiting: "While testifying that the children are the focus of her life, [the mother's] conduct in adamantly refusing to make minor changes in scheduling which would result in her seeing the children for greater periods of time would seem to speak volumes about how she really feels." The court's speculation flew in the face of Dr. Merin's testimony, in which he opined that the children were, indeed, Mrs. Jacoby's primary focus, and in which he concluded that, her rigidness notwithstanding, she was the parent who was most likely to encourage a relationship with the noncustodial parent. Again, the evidence did not support the court's findings on this statutory factor.

THREADGILL, ACTING CHIEF JUDGE, Dissenting.

I respectfully dissent from that portion of the majority opinion that reverses the award of primary residential responsibility for the children to Mr. Jacoby.

In reviewing a true discretionary act, such as an award of child custody, an appellate court must fully recognize the superior vantage point of the trial court and apply a test of reasonableness to determine whether the trial court abused its discretion. *See Canakaris v. Canakaris*, 382 So.2d 1197 (Fla. 1980). If reasonable men could differ as to the propriety of the trial court's action, then it cannot be said the trial court abused its discretion. *See id.* at 1203.

In this case, I believe the trial court gave thorough consideration to the criteria set forth in section 61.13(3), Florida Statutes (1997). I am convinced that the trial court limited its consideration of Mrs. Jacoby's sexual orientation to the effect it would have on the best interests of the children. Unlike the majority, I believe there is competent, substantial evidence in the record to support the relevant findings of the trial court. Under such circumstances, I conclude that the trial court did not abuse its discretion in awarding primary residential responsibility to Mr. Jacoby. I would affirm on that issue. Otherwise, I concur in the majority opinion.

IV. DE FACTO PARENTING AND ADOPTION

WHITE v. THOMPSON

11 S.W.3d 913 (Tenn. Ct. App. 1999)

OPINION: HIGHERS

This consolidated appeal stems from two separate cases, each involving a nonparent's claim to visitation where the nonparent and the child's biological mother previously maintained a same-sex relationship and where the nonparent previously provided care and support to the child. In *White v. Thompson*, Patricia Teresa Thompson is the biological mother to a son, who will be hereafter referred to by his first and last initials, "J.T.," and Pamela Kay White is the nonparent who previously provided care and support to J.T. White commenced the action by filing a Petition for Visitation, which was ultimately dismissed by the trial court. In *Coke v. Looper*, Debbie Coke is the biological mother to a daughter, who will hereafter be designated by her first and last initials, "J.C.," Donald Dooley is the biological father to J.C., and Mary Helen Looper is the nonparent who previously provided care and support to J.C. Although Coke and Dooley originally commenced the action by filing a "Complaint for Permanent Restraining Order and for Damages," Looper filed a "counter-complaint" that asserted, among other things, visitation rights. This claim to visitation was ultimately dismissed by the trial court, and Coke's and Dooley's claims were voluntarily nonsuited. On appeal, White's and Looper's jointly filed brief states the following:

There is a single issue presented for review in this consolidated appeal: Whether a petition for visitation may be brought by a woman who, in the context of a long-term relationship, planned for, participated in the conception and birth of, provided financial assistance for, and until foreclosed from doing so by the biological mother, acted as a parent to the child ultimately borne by her partner.

Based upon the following, we affirm the trial court in each case.

FACTS AND PROCEDURAL HISTORY

I. White v. Thompson

On June 20, 1996, White filed a "Petition for Visitation" against Thompson in the Shelby County Circuit Court. In the petition, White alleged that she and Thompson "were involved in a committed intimate relationship beginning in 1987," and that "throughout the course of the relationship the parties discussed having a child together." According to White's petition, Thompson successfully underwent artificial insemination on November 2, 1992, and White contributed to Thompson's support both during and after Thompson's pregnancy. Thompson's son, J.T., was born July 10, 1993. J.T.'s first name was based upon White's brother, and his middle name was based upon Thompson's father. After J.T.'s birth, both Thompson and White provided care and support to J.T. In June of 1994, however, the relationship between Thompson and White ended, and they ceased living together in August 1994. After the termination of these parties' relationship, however, White continued to provide care and support to J.T. until Thompson began "to interfere with [White's] relationship with the minor child by refusing and/or interfering with visitation and denying [White] the opportunity to talk with the minor child on the telephone." White's petition seeking visitation alleged, "It is in the best interest of the minor child ... that [White] have regular and ongoing visitation with the minor child."

On October 4, 1996, Thompson filed a response to White's Petition for Visitation, wherein she asserted that White "lacks standing to assert visitation rights." She further asserted that White had not alleged any threat of substantial harm to J.T. so as to overcome Thompson's constitutionally protected parental rights.

... Ultimately, on January 9, 1998, the trial court entered an order which granted Thompson's motion to dismiss and which stated, in part, the following:

In light of the Court's ruling, the Court will not address the "best interest of the child" argument. [Furthermore], the Court declines to address the "substantial harm" question.

. . .

The Court ... finds that [White] lacks standing to bring the Petition for Visitation....

. . .

[...] II. Coke (and Dooley) v. Looper

On August 15, 1996, Coke and Dooley jointly filed a "Complaint for Permanent Restraining Order and for Damages" against Looper in the Shelby County Chancery Court. Thereafter Looper filed an Answer and Counter Complaint for Breach of Contract, Permanent Restraining Order and for Damages." Looper's answer admitted that Coke and Dooley are the natural parents of J.C., who was born September 18, 1992, and that J.C. had been legitimated by order of the Shelby County Juvenile Court on July 30, 1996. In Looper's counter-complaint, she alleged that J.C. "was born as the result of artificial insemination after two years of joint efforts by ... Coke and ... Looper to produce a child that they would raise together...." According to Looper's counter-complaint, on April 30, 1993,

Coke and Looper entered a "co-parenting agreement," which provided in part the following:

> 3. Each party acknowledges and agrees that both parties will share in providing [J.C.] with the necessary food, clothing, shelter, medical or any other remedial care that may be needed by the child until the time [J.C.] is 18 years of age."
>
> . . .
>
> 7. Each party acknowledges and agrees that if Debbie Lynn Coke and Mary Helen Looper are no longer living together in the family home they will both continue to provide for [J.C.] in the manner described below:
>
> a. Legal custody of the child would remain in the biological parent, Debbie Lynn Coke;
>
> b. Mary Helen Looper would have reasonable visitation;
>
> c. Mary Helen Looper would have no financial obligations to [J.C.];

. . . Looper's counter-complaint further alleged that Looper and Coke ceased living together in December 1995, and that these parties voluntarily implemented a visitation arrangement that was followed each week until Coke and Dooley commenced this action. Looper's counter-complaint sought damages based upon breach of contract and tort claims. Looper's counter-complaint also requested, however, that Coke and Dooley "be permanently enjoined from interfering with [Looper's] relationship and visitation with the minor child and establish a visitation schedule."

On March 24, 1997, Dooley individually filed a motion for judgment on the pleadings pursuant to Rule 12.03 of the Tennessee Rules of Civil Procedure, wherein he asserted that Looper had failed to allege any actions by Dooley that would support any breach of contract or tort claim against him. Dooley further asserted that Looper failed "to state any legally cognizable interest . . . as to the minor child, who is not the child of [Looper] either by blood or adoption, such as would support a claim for rights to the child or for visitation with such child." On November 7, 1997, Coke filed a separate motion to dismiss, which sought dismissal of Looper's claims as against Coke.

After a November 14, 1997 hearing, the chancery court entered an order providing "That the Motion for Judgment on the Pleadings as to the Counter–Complaint against Donald Dooley is hereby granted, and the Counter–Complaint filed by Mary Helen Looper against Donald Dooley is hereby dismissed, with prejudice." (Ill R. at 64.) The chancery court also entered a separate order that provided, "The Motion to Dismiss filed by . . . Coke is granted as to . . . Looper's claim for visitation. . . ." This order reflected the following statements made by the chancellor at the November 14, 1997 hearing:

But insofar as Ms. Looper is concerned, especially with Ms. Coke, the natural mother, objecting to her visitation, it's this Court's ruling that Ms. Looper just has no claim or interest in that child and the Court so rules.

... ANALYSIS

We find it appropriate to begin our analysis by reviewing the meaning of the term "parent" under Tennessee law. Title 36 of our state's statutory code, titled "Domestic Relations," includes six separate chapters that govern: (1) adoption; (2) paternity; (3) marriage; (4) divorce and annulment; (5) alimony and child support; and (6) child custody and visitation. Tennessee Code Annotated section 36–1–102 defines the terms "legal parent" and "parent," and, while the terms of this statute make these definitions expressly applicable only to part 1 of chapter 1 in title 36 (*i.e.*, sections 36–1–101 *et seq.*, which set forth general provision relating to adoption), "statutes 'in pari materia'—those relating to the same subject or having a common purpose—are to be construed together." *Owens v. State*, 908 S.W.2d 923, 926 (Tenn. 1995). Accordingly, we find that section 36–1–102 provides guidance as to the legislature's meaning of the term "parent." Section 36–1–102 (26) states that a "legal parent" may be any of the following:

(A) The biological mother of a child;

(B) A man who is or has been married to the biological mother of the child if the child was born during the marriage or within three hundred (300) days after the marriage was terminated for any reason, or if the child was born after a decree of separation was entered by a court;

(C) A man who attempted to marry the biological mother of the child before the child's birth by a marriage apparently in compliance with the law, even if the marriage is declared invalid, if the child was born during the attempted marriage or within three hundred (300) days after the termination of the attempted marriage for any reason;

(D) A man who has been adjudicated to be the legal father of the child by any court or administrative body of this state or any other state or territory or foreign country or who has signed, pursuant to §§ 24–7–118, 68–3–203(g), 68–3–302 and 68–3–305(b), an unrevoked and sworn acknowledgment of paternity under the provisions of Tennessee law, or who has signed such a sworn acknowledgment pursuant to the law of any other state, territory, or foreign country; or

(E) An adoptive parent of a child or adult.

TENN. CODE. ANN. 36–1–102(26) (Supp. 1998). Moreover, section 36–1–102(34) provides a somewhat similar, but broader definition of the looser term "parent" by stating: " 'Parent(s)' means any biological, legal, adoptive parent(s) or, for purpose of §§ 36–1–127—36–1–141, stepparents." *Id.* § 36–1–102(34). In the consolidated cases before this Court, neither White nor Looper is a parent as is contemplated by our legislature, despite each parties' characterizations whereby each refers to herself as a "parent" of the child. While it may be true that in our society the term "parent" has become used at times to describe more loosely a person who shares mutual love and affection with a child and who supplies care and support to the child, we find it inappropriate to legislate judicially such a broad definition of the term "parent" as relating to legal rights relating to child custody and/or visitation. Just as a grandparent who provides care and support to a child does not become recognized as being a parent (absent adoption) under Tennessee law, other persons are not recognized as being a parent under Tennessee law based only upon prior care and support of a child. These other persons include any unmarried persons who maintain a close intimate relationship with a child's natural parent, whether they are of the same or opposite sex of that natural parent.

In the absence of some statutory right or proceeding to the contrary, our state legislature has expressly given parents, whether they are biological parents or adoptive parents, the statutory right of custody and control of their minor children.

As one court from another jurisdiction correctly observed, "To allow the courts to award visitation—a limited form of custody—to a third person would necessarily impair the parents' right to custody and control." *Alison D. v. Virginia M.*, 77 N.Y.2d 651, 572 N.E.2d 27, 29, 569 N.Y.S.2d 586 (N.Y. 1991). Accordingly, we conclude that, based upon the statutory right of parents to custody and control of their minor children, Tennessee law does not provide for any award of custody or visitation to a nonparent except as may be otherwise provided by our legislature.

. . . While we recognize that other jurisdictions that have been faced with the issue that is presently before this Court have reached differing results, with some seemingly contrary to our conclusion, several such jurisdictions have reached a similar result to our conclusion. In *Kathleen C. v. Lisa W.*, 71 Cal.App.4th 524, 84 Cal.Rptr. 2d 48 (Cal. App. 1999), Kathleen C., who was a former lesbian partner of Lisa W., sought visitation rights with Lisa W.'s biological children based upon the contention that she was a de facto parent of the children. 84 Cal. Rptr. 2d at 49. Though Lisa W. already had one three year old daughter when the parties began living together, Lisa W. also became pregnant by artificial insemination and had another child during the parties' relationship, and the parties gave the child Kathleen C.'s surname as a middle name. *Id.* Kathleen C. was regularly involved in the care and support of both children until the parties separated. The California Court of Appeal summarized that state's applicable law by stating the following:

> The courts of appeal have previously decided that a lesbian partner who is not a biological or adoptive parent is not entitled to custody of children conceived during a same sex bilateral relationship. In *Curiale v. Reagan*, [222 Cal.App.3d 1597, 272 Cal.Rptr. 520 (1990),] the court held that a nonparent had no standing to assert a claim for custody or visitation as against a child's natural mother upon termination of the

lesbian relationship. The court explained that "jurisdiction to adjudicate custody depends upon some proceeding properly before the court in which custody is at issue such as dissolution, guardianship, or dependency.... The Legislature has not conferred upon one in plaintiff's position, a nonparent in a same-sex bilateral relationship, any right of custody or visitation upon termination of the relationship." Similarly, the court in *West v. Superior Court* [, 59 Cal.App.4th 302, 309 (1997),] held that the courts have no jurisdiction to entertain the petition of a nonparent in a lesbian relationship for custody and visitation rights. Finally, in *Nancy S. v. Michele G.*, [228 Cal.App.3d 831, 836, 279 Cal.Rptr. 212 (1991),] Division One of this court held that a lesbian partner who was not the adoptive or biological parent of children conceived during a lesbian relationship was not entitled to seek custody or visitation of the children under the Uniform Parentage Act.

Finally, [Kathleen C.] cannot prevail on her argument that she is entitled to visitation rights because she is a de facto parent of the children. The term, de facto parent, has its genesis in the juvenile dependency system and generally has been used to refer to foster parents caring for dependent children.... As the California Supreme Court has explained, "the de facto parenthood doctrine simply recognizes that persons who have provided a child with daily parental concern, affection, and care over substantial time may develop legitimate interests and perspectives, and may also present a custodial alternative, which should not be ignored in a juvenile dependency proceeding. The standing accorded de facto parents has no basis independent of these concerns.

In *Titchenal v. Dexter*, 166 Vt. 373, 693 A.2d 682 (Vt. 1997), Chris Titchenal and Diane Dexter were involved in an intimate same-sex relationship during which they decided to raise a child. 693 A.2d at 683. Though their attempts to conceive via a sperm donor failed, they jointly decided that Dexter would adopt a child. *Id.* A newborn baby was adopted by Dexter, and was given the last name "Dexter–Titchenal." *Id.* For several years, both parties provided care and support for the child. *Id.* Eventually, the parties' relationship ended, after which Titchenal "filed a complaint requesting that the superior court exercise its equitable jurisdiction to establish and enforce regular, unsupervised parent-child contact...." *Id.* Titchenal asserted, among other things, that the doctrines of in loco parentis and de facto parenthood allowed the court to exercise such equitable authority. *Id.* The Vermont Supreme Court, however, held, "absent statutory authority extending jurisdiction to adjudicate third-party visitation requests, ... legal parents retain the right to determine whether third-party visitation is in their children's best interest." *Titchenal*, 693 A.2d at 690.

In *Music v. Rachford*, 654 So.2d 1234 (Fla. Dist. Ct. App. 1995), Brenda Music was involved in a lesbian relationship with Tara Rachford, during which the parties decided to raise a child together. 654 So.2d at

1234. As Music was unable to have a child, Rachford was artificially inseminated. *Id.* After birth of the child, the child was given Music's surname, and the parties cohabitated together for several years. *Id.* After the parties' relationship ended and Rachford terminated Music's access to the child, Music filed suit seeking shared parental responsibility and visitation. *Music*, 654 So.2d at 1234–35. She based her claim upon the contention that she was a de facto parent of the child. *Id.* at 1235. The Florida District Court of Appeal, however, rejected her claim and cited prior Florida precedent for the proposition that "visitation rights are, with regard to a non-parent, statutory, and the court has no inherent authority to award visitation." *Id.* (citing *Meeks v. Garner*, 598 So.2d 261 (Fla. Dist. Ct. App. 1992)).

In *Alison D. v. Virginia M.*, 77 N.Y.2d 651, 572 N.E.2d 27, 569 N.Y.S.2d 586 (N.Y. 1991), Alison D. and Virginia M., while living together, decided to raise a child and that Virginia M. would be artificially inseminated. 572 N.E.2d at 28. A child was thereafter born and given Alison D.'s surname as his middle name. *Id.* Afterwards, both parties jointly provided care and support to the child until the parties' relationship ended. *Id.* Though the parties initially agreed to certain specified visitation, Virginia M. eventually terminated all contact between Alison D. and the child. *Id.* Thereafter, Alison D. filed suit to obtain visitation rights, contending that she had standing to assert her claim because she acted as a de facto parent and/or she should be viewed as a parent "by estoppel." *Alison D.*, 572 N.E.2d at 29. The New York Court of Appeals, however, rejected Alison D.'s claims and determined that, because Alison D. was not a "parent" under New York's Domestic Relations Law, she "had no right . . . to seek visitation and, thereby, limit or diminish the right of the . . . parent to choose with whom her child associates."[87] *Id.*

. . . Our conclusion in the instant case is consistent with those cases discussed immediately above. While Tennessee's legislature has generally conferred upon parents the right of custody and control of their children, it has not conferred upon one in either White's or Looper's position (a nonparent who is not and has not been married to either of the children's parents, but who previously maintained an intimate relationship with

87. Subsequent New York cases have similarly held that, in the absence of a statutory proceeding, a nonparent lacks standing to seek visitation of a child. In *Lynda A.H. v. Diane T.O.*, 243 A.D.2d 24, 673 N.Y.S.2d 989 (N.Y. App. Div. 1998), Diane T.O and Lynda A.H. decided to raise a child and that Lynda A.H. would be artificially inseminated. 673 N.Y.S.2d at 990. The child was given Diane T.O.'s last name as her middle name, and both parties provided care and support in rearing the child. *Id.* After the parties' relationship ended, Diane T.O. sought custody an/or visitation with the child. *Id.* After the New York Supreme Court, Appellate Division, first disposed of the issue of custody (ruling against Diane T.O.), the court held that Diane T.O., who was neither a biological nor adoptive parent, lacked standing to seek visitation of the child. *Lynda A.H.*, 673 N.Y.S.2d at 991.

Similarly, in *Bessette v. Saratoga County Comm'r of Soc. Servs.*, 209 A.D.2d 838, 619 N.Y.S.2d 359 (N.Y. App. Div. 1994), "former foster parents sought visitation because they had established significant and long-term parental-like relations with foster children." 619 N.Y.S.2d at 359. On appeal, the New York Supreme Court, Appellate Division, noted that there is no New York statute which expressly gives former foster parents the right to maintain a proceeding for visitation. *Id.* The court held "that, in the absence of any statutory grant of standing to former foster parents, [such persons] have no right to seek visitation. . . ." *Bassette*, 619 N.Y.S.2d at 360.

such a parent and who previously provided care and support to the children) any right of visitation. *Cf.* Kathleen C., 84 Cal. Rptr. 2d at 50. Absent statutory authority establishing such a third-party's right to visitation, parents retain the right to determine with whom their children associate. *Cf. Titchenal,* 693 A.2d at 690; Alison D., 572 N.E.2d at 29. Accordingly, both White and Looper lacked standing to assert their claims to visitation, and the trial courts were correct in dismissing the same.

CONCLUSION

... In accordance with the foregoing, we hereby affirm the trial court's dismissal of the asserted claims to visitation in both *White v. Thompson* and *Coke v. Looper*. Costs on appeal are taxed to White and Looper, for which execution may issue if necessary.

MASON v. DWINNELL

190 N.C.App. 209, 660 S.E.2d 58 (2008)

GEER, JUDGE.

Defendant Irene Dwinnell appeals from the trial court's order awarding permanent joint legal and physical custody of her minor child to Dwinnell and her former domestic partner, plaintiff Joellen Mason. It is important to first observe that the factual context of this case—involving same sex domestic partners—is immaterial to the proper analysis of the legal issues involved. The fundamental question presented by this appeal is whether the district court's findings of fact are sufficient to support its conclusion of law that it should apply the "best interest of the child" standard in determining whether Mason—who is not a legal parent of the child—should be awarded custody of the child, including visitation. We hold that the trial court properly applied the controlling authority of *Price v. Howard,* 346 N.C. 68, 484 S.E.2d 528 (1997), and, accordingly, we affirm the trial court's order.

. . .

Facts and Procedural History

The district court made the following pertinent findings of fact. Mason and Dwinnell were domestic partners for eight years. At some point during that relationship, Dwinnell learned that, for medical reasons, she would need to pursue a pregnancy at that time if she wanted biological children. Although Mason had no plans to bear a biological child, she wanted to have a family with Dwinnell. Subsequently, on 25 November 1995, Mason and Dwinnell held a commitment ceremony attended by their families and friends.

Mason and Dwinnell together researched and discussed their options for conceiving a child, including use of an anonymous or known donor and the various sperm donation programs available. Ultimately, they mutually chose an anonymous sperm donor who had physical characteristics resembling those of Mason. Dwinnell and Mason together attended all of Dwinnell's inseminations and, after she became pregnant, all of her prenatal care appointments, sessions at the hospital, and childbirth classes. They also planned and prepared the child's nursery together.

A birth plan was developed that included Mason's participating in the birth of the child. Mason in fact attended the child's birth on 11 January 1997 and cut his umbilical cord. Combining their surnames, Dwinnell and Mason named the child Mason Dwinnell. Although Dwinnell's name was the only name listed as a parent on the child's birth certificate, evidence was presented that the parties mutually desired to include both Mason and Dwinnell on the birth certificate, but the hospital refused to do so.

Dwinnell and Mason discussed and agreed upon the godparents of the child. They held a baptismal ceremony for the child at which they publicly presented themselves to family and friends as the child's two parents. The women explained how they derived the child's name by combining their last names, and both Mason's parents and Dwinnell's parents were recognized as the child's grandparents.

Dwinnell has stipulated that following the child's birth, "he lived with both parties who were acting as a family unit." Dwinnell and Mason shared caretaking responsibilities for the child with Mason normally caring for him during weekday mornings. Although the women shared paying household expenses and the child's individual expenses, Dwinnell and Mason agreed that Mason would claim the child as a dependent for all income tax purposes.

On 22 March 2000, when the child was three years old, Dwinnell and Mason signed before a notary public a "Parenting Agreement" prepared by an attorney. Each woman had received a draft and had an opportunity to review it prior to signing it. According to the district court, Dwinnell and Mason both wished to enter into an agreement that gave Mason all of the rights and responsibilities of an equal parent.

. . .

Also in 2000, Dwinnel executed a minor health care power of attorney authorizing Mason to obtain medical care for the child. Mason would take the child to the doctor if he needed medical attention while she was caring for him. Mason also went with Dwinnel to the majority of the child's annual pediatric appointments.

. . .

Consistent with the Parenting Agreement, Dwinnell and Mason discussed the child's education and mutually agreed for him to attend private school at Carolina Friends School. Both Dwinnell and Mason attended parent-teacher conferences for the child. In addition, until this litigation, Dwinnell and Mason discussed and mutually agreed upon all of the child's extracurricular activities.

Dwinnell has stipulated that Mason paid the majority of daycare and preschool expenses; all of the child's school tuition for four years and one semester, with a fifth year's tuition paid by a trust funded by Mason's parents; and all of the child's before-and-after-care from 2000 through June 2004. Dwinnell has further stipulated that Mason's parents established an irrevocable trust for the minor child, as they had for all of their grandchildren, with Dwinnell and Mason executing documents in which they agreed to serve as co-trustees. Mason established a college savings account for the child funded by Mason and her parents.

When completing forms relating to the child, Dwinnell marked through "Husband," "Father," or "Guardian" and inserted "co-parent," followed by Mason's name. Such forms admitted at trial included the application for enrollment at Carolina Friends School and a contract with the school completed by Dwinnell and Mason jointly, as well as a consent form signed by both Dwinnell and Mason for the child to have therapeutic intervention at Developmental Therapy Associates. In addition, in 2001, Dwinnell executed a will designating Mason as the child's guardian if she died.

In May 2001, Dwinnell and Mason decided to cease living together, and, in September 2001, Mason moved one block away. From that date until 2004, Dwinnell and Mason exercised parental responsibilities for the child in their respective homes, including overnight stays. Dwinnell has stipulated that on most mornings from October 2001 through much of 2003, after the child had spent the night with her, she would drop the child off at Mason's house, and Mason would take the child to daycare.

Although the parties did not at first have a set custody schedule, beginning in early 2003, Dwinnell would have the child for two days, followed by two days with Mason, with the parties alternating weekends. In early 2004, however, Dwinnell changed the schedule.... Beginning in October 2004, Dwinnell would only allow her child to visit Mason every other weekend and one evening each week for dinner. Dwinnell also removed Mason's name from the school pick-up list.

On 18 October 2004, Mason filed a complaint for custody....

. . .

... As our Supreme Court stated in *Price:* "The question now before us is whether, under the facts of this case, the trial court was required to hold that defendant's constitutionally protected interest in the companionship, custody, care, and control of her child must prevail or whether the statutorily prescribed 'best interest of the child' test should have been applied to determine custody." *Id.* at 74, 484 S.E.2d at 531.

. . .

In *Petersen v. Rogers,* 337 N.C. 397, 445 S.E.2d 901 (1994), our Supreme Court first addressed the impact of *Stanley v. Illinois,* 405 U.S. 645, 92 S.Ct. 1208, 31 L.Ed.2d 551 (1972), on custody determinations in North Carolina. The Court noted *Stanley's* holding, based on the Due Process Clause, that " '[i]t is cardinal with us that the custody, care and nurture of the child reside first in the parents, whose primary function and freedom include preparation for obligations the state can neither supply nor hinder.' " 337 N.C. at 400–01, 445 S.E.2d at 903 (emphasis omitted) (quoting *Stanley,* 405 U.S. at 651, 92 S.Ct. at 1213, 31 L.Ed.2d at 559).

. . .

Our Supreme Court revisited legal parents' constitutional rights in *Price.* The Court noted that "[i]t was unnecessary in *Petersen* to articulate anything more than general constitutional principles." *Price,* 346 N.C. at 73, 484 S.E.2d at 531. The Court explained that "[i]n *Petersen,* this Court held that natural parents have a constitutionally protected interest in the companionship, custody, care, and control of their children" and that "this interest must prevail in a custody dispute with a nonparent, absent a showing of unfitness or neglect." *Id.* at 72, 484 S.E.2d at 530. *Price,* however, addressed "whether other circumstances can require that interest to yield to the 'best interest of the child' test prescribed by N.C.G.S. § 50–13.2(a)." *Id.*

The Court began its discussion of those "other circumstances" by noting that "[a] natural parent's constitutionally protected paramount interest in the companionship, custody, care, and control of his or her child is a counterpart of the parental responsibilities the parent has assumed and is based on a presumption that he or she will act in the best interest of the child." *Id.* at 79, 484 S.E.2d at 534 (citing *Lehr v. Robertson,* 463 U.S. 248, 103 S.Ct. 2985, 77 L.Ed.2d 614 (1983)). Based on this principle, the Court articulated the following test: [T]he parent may no longer enjoy a paramount status if his or her conduct is inconsistent with this presumption or if he or she fails to shoulder the responsibilities that are attendant to rearing a child. If a natural parent's conduct has not been inconsistent with his or her constitutionally protected status, application of the "best interest of the child" standard in a custody dispute with a nonparent would offend the Due Process Clause. *Id.*

. . .

As in *Price,* we are, therefore, required to consider whether the trial court's findings, to the extent based on clear and convincing evidence, support its conclusion of law that Dwinnell "has acted inconsistent with her paramount parental right," making the "best interest of the child" standard applicable. In doing so, we must follow the Supreme Court's mandate that "[s]uch conduct would, of course, need to be viewed on a case-by-case basis. . . ." *Price,* 346 N.C. at 83, 484 S.E.2d at 537.

We note that because this case involves questions of custody only, it does not present the issue whether a former domestic partner may acquire the status of a legal parent. Therefore, we decline to address the doctrine of parent by estoppel adopted in other jurisdictions.

Likewise, we find immaterial Dwinnell's arguments that she and Mason could not marry, and Mason could not adopt the child under North Carolina law. We cannot improve on the Pennsylvania Supreme Court's explanation as to why "the nature of the relationship" has no legal significance to the issues of custody and visitation: "The ability to marry the biological parent and the ability to adopt the subject child have never been and are not now factors in determining whether the third party assumed a parental status and discharged parental duties. *What is relevant, however, is the method by which the third party gained authority to do so.*" *T.B. v. L.R.M.*, 567 Pa. 222, 232, 786 A.2d 913, 918–19 (2001) (emphasis added).

Standing

. . .

As this Court explained in *Ellison v. Ramos,* 130 N.C.App. 389, 392, 502 S.E.2d 891, 893, *appeal dismissed and disc. review denied,* 349 N.C. 356, 517 S.E.2d 891 (1998), despite the statute's "broad language, in the context of a third party seeking custody of a child from a natural (biological) parent, our Supreme Court has indicated that there are limits on the 'other persons' who can bring such an action." A conclusion otherwise " 'would conflict with the constitutionally-protected paramount right of parents to custody, care, and control of their children.' " *Id.* at 393, 502 S.E.2d at 893 (quoting *Petersen,* 337 N.C. at 406, 445 S.E.2d at 906). Applying *Petersen,* this Court concluded that "the relationship between the third party and the child is the relevant consideration for the standing determination." *Id.* at 394, 502 S.E.2d at 894. As a result, "a third party who has no relationship with a child does not have standing under N.C. Gen.Stat. § 50–13.1 to seek custody of a child from a natural parent." *Id.* On the other hand, the Court held "that a relationship in the nature of a parent and child relationship, even in the absence of a biological relationship, will suffice to support a finding of standing." *Id. See also id.* at 395, 502 S.E.2d at 895 (declining to draw a bright line, but rather "confin[ing] our holding to an adjudication of the facts of the case before us: where a third party and a child have an established relationship in the nature of a parent-child relationship, the third party does have standing as an 'other person' under N.C. Gen.Stat. § 50–13.1(a) to seek custody").

. . .

No reasonable basis exists to contend that Mason fails to meet the standard set forth in *Ellison.*

. . .

Dwinnell's Constitutionally–Protected Interest

We next turn to the question whether the district court's findings of fact are sufficient to support its conclusion of law that Dwinnell acted in a manner inconsistent with her constitutionally-protected paramount interest in the companionship, custody, care, and control of her child.

. . .

The district court made findings of fact unchallenged on appeal that Dwinnell and Mason jointly decided to create a family and *intentionally* took steps to identify Mason as a parent of the child, including attempting to obtain sperm with physical characteristics similar to Mason, using both parties' surnames to derive the child's name, allowing Mason to participate in the pregnancy and birth, holding a baptismal ceremony at which Mason was announced as a parent and her parents as grandparents, and designating Mason as a parent of the child on forms and to teachers. Indeed, Dwinnell has stipulated that "[a]fter the child's birth, he lived with both parties who were acting as a family unit." They remained together as a family for four years. Even after Dwinnell and Mason's relationship ended, Dwinnell allowed Mason to have the functional equivalent of joint custody for a three-year period.

The findings of fact also reveal that Dwinnell and Mason functioned as if both were parents, with Dwinnell agreeing to allow Mason to declare the child as a dependent on her tax returns and the parties sharing caretaking and financial responsibilities for the child. The court found, without challenge by Dwinnell, that Dwinnell "encouraged, fostered, and facilitated the emotional and psychological bond between the minor child and [Mason]" and that "[t]hroughout the child's life, [Mason] has provided care for him, financially supported him, and been an integral part of his life such that the child has benefited from her love and affection, caretaking, emotional and financial support, guidance, and decision-making." As a result, Mason became "the only other adult whom the child considers a parent . . ." Although Dwinnell assigned error to this latter finding of fact, it is supported by clear and convincing evidence and, therefore, is binding.

Moreover, the trial court found-again, in findings not challenged on appeal-that Dwinnell chose to share her decision-making authority with Mason, including decisions on godparents, the child's name, whether the child should attend private school, and the child's extracurricular activities. Further, Dwinnell granted Mason a medical power of attorney, allowing Mason to participate in medical decisions regarding the child and, indeed, both Dwinnell and Mason signed a "consent form for the child to have therapeutic intervention at Developmental Therapy Associates." In the "Parenting Agreement," Dwinnell even agreed that Mason should participate in making "all major decisions regarding their child."

The findings of fact also establish that Dwinnell intended that this parent-like relationship be a permanent relationship for her child. The district court, in reaching its decision, pointed to the Parenting Agreement signed by Dwinnell and Mason when the child was three years old. The district court found that Dwinnell had an opportunity to review the agreement and executed it before a notary public. Although Dwinnell points to her testimony that she did not voluntarily enter into the agreement, it was for the district court to decide what credibility and weight to give that testimony. *Phelps v. Phelps,* 337 N.C. 344, 357, 446 S.E.2d 17, 25 (1994). In that document, Dwinnell asserted that she and Mason had committed to "jointly parent" the child; that Dwinnell would consent to Mason's adoption of the child if allowed by North Carolina law; that "although [Mason] is not the biological mother, she is a *de facto* parent who has and will provide the parties' child with a stable environment and she has formed a psychological parenting relationship with the parties' child;" that the child's relationship with Mason "should be protected and promoted to preserve the strong emotional ties that exist between them;" and that the purpose of the document was to make provisions for the continuation of the relationship should Dwinnell and Mason cease to live together.

While Dwinnell argues vigorously that the Parenting Agreement is unenforceable, the district court was not required to address that issue and did not do so. Thus, the issue is also not before this Court. Dwinnell mistakes the significance of the document. The district court was not enforcing any agreement, but rather relied upon the agreement as a manifestation of Dwinnell's intent to create a permanent family unit involving two parents and a child that would continue even if the relationship between Dwinnell and Mason did not. Phrased differently, the assertions in the document constitute admissions by Dwinnell regarding her intentions and conduct in creating a permanent parent-like relationship between Mason and her biological child.

. . .

We believe these circumstances are analogous to those in *Price,* in which the plaintiff, a man who had previously lived with the child's mother, sought custody. In *Price,* the biological mother represented to her child and others, including the plaintiff, that he was the child's father even though he was not. 346 N.C. at 83, 484 S.E.2d at 537. According to the Supreme Court, "[s]he chose to rear the child in a family unit with [the] plaintiff being the child's *de facto* father." *Id.* She thus "created" a "family unit" that included a third person and the child. *Id.*

In contrast to this case, however, the mother in *Price* relinquished all custody to the plaintiff for a period of time. The parties disputed "whether defendant's voluntary relinquishment of custody to plaintiff was intended to be temporary or indefinite and whether she informed plaintiff and the child that the relinquishment of custody was temporary." *Id.* The Court explained:

This is an important factor to consider, for, if [the mother] had represented that [the plaintiff] was the child's natural father and voluntarily had given him custody of the child for an indefinite period of time with no notice that such relinquishment of custody would be temporary, *[the mother] would have not only created the family unit that plaintiff and the child have established, but also induced them to allow that family unit to flourish in a relationship of love and duty with no expectations that it would be terminated. Id.* (emphasis added). If, however, the parties agreed that the plaintiff would have custody for only a temporary period of time, the mother "would still enjoy a constitutionally protected status absent other conduct inconsistent with that status." *Id.* The Court, therefore, remanded for further findings of fact.

While this case does not involve the biological mother's leaving the child in the care of a third person, we still have the circumstances of Dwinnell's intentionally creating a family unit composed of herself, her child and, to use the Supreme Court's words, a "*de facto* parent." *Id.* Indeed, as occurred in *Price* for a period of time, they all lived together as a family and Dwinnell led her child to believe that Mason was one of his parents. Even though Dwinnell did not completely relinquish custody, she fully shared it with Mason, including sharing decision-making, caretaking, and financial responsibilities for the child. And, in contrast to *Price,* the findings establish that Dwinnell intended—during the creation of this family unit—that this parent-like relationship would be permanent, such that she "induced [Mason and the child] to allow that family unit to flourish in a relationship of love and duty with no expectations that it would be terminated." *Id.* Ultimately, Dwinnell succeeded: the district court found that Mason and the child forged a strong parent-child bond.

As the South Carolina Court of Appeals has recognized: "[W]hen a legal parent invites a third party into a child's life, and that invitation alters a child's life by essentially providing him with another parent, *the legal parent's rights to unilaterally sever that relationship are necessarily reduced.*" *Middleton v. Johnson,* 369 S.C. 585, 597, 633 S.E.2d 162, 169 (S.C. Ct. App. 2006) (emphasis added). "A parent has the absolute control and ability to maintain a zone of privacy around his or her child. However, a parent cannot maintain an absolute zone of privacy if he or she voluntarily invites a third party to function as a parent to the child." *Id.*

Similarly, the New Jersey Supreme Court has held: "[A] parent has the absolute ability to maintain a zone of autonomous privacy for herself and her child. However, if she wishes to maintain that zone of privacy she cannot invite a third party to function as a parent to her child and cannot cede over to that third party parental authority the exercise of which may create a profound bond with the child." *V.C. v. M.J.B.,* 163 N.J. 200, 224, 748 A.2d 539, 552, *cert. denied,* 531 U.S. 926, 121 S.Ct. 302, 148 L.Ed.2d 243 (2000).

Thus, like all parents, Dwinnell had the constitutionally-protected right to "maintain a zone of privacy" around her and her child. *Id.* Indeed, since no biological father was present, Dwinnell exercised exclusive and autonomous parental authority in relation to her child. She nonetheless voluntarily chose to invite Mason into that relationship and function as a parent from birth on, thereby materially altering her child's life. She gave up her right to unilaterally exclude Mason (or unilaterally limit contact with Mason) by choosing to cede to Mason a sufficiently significant amount of parental responsibility and decision-making authority to create a permanent parent-like relationship with her child.

. . .

In sum, we conclude that the district court's findings of fact establish that Dwinnell, after choosing to forego as to Mason her constitutionally-protected parental rights, cannot now assert those rights in order to unilaterally alter the relationship between her child and the person whom she transformed into a parent. Her choice does not mean that Mason is entitled to the rights of a legal parent, but only that a trial court may apply the "best interest of the child" standard in considering Mason's request for custody, including visitation. *See, e.g., id.* at 599–600, 633 S.E.2d at 170 (holding third party entitled to visitation when mother invited him "to act as a father," child lived with third party at least half of the week for most of his life, and mother ceded over large part of parental responsibilities, thereby fostering parent-child bond between third party and child).

. . .

Conclusion

Although this appeal arises in the context of a same-sex domestic partnership, it involves only the constitutional standards applicable to all custody disputes between legal parents and third parties. We simply apply the law as set forth by our Supreme Court in *Price,* consistent with the holdings of the United States Supreme Court. Courts do not violate a parent's constitutionally-protected interest by respecting the parent-child relationships that the legal parent-in accordance with her constitutional rights-voluntarily chose to create.

We hold, under the circumstances of this case, as found by the district court, that Dwinnell made the choice, with respect to Mason's relationship to her child, to act in a manner inconsistent with her constitutionally-protected right to custody, care, and control of her child and her right to exclusively make decisions concerning the care, custody, and control of that child. The district court, therefore, properly concluded it should apply the "best interest of the child" standard. At that point, it was up to the parties to establish the best interests of the child. Since Dwinnell has failed to demonstrate that the district court's "best interests" determination was an abuse of discretion, we affirm.

Affirmed.

DISCUSSION

What factors did the court consider in allowing custody in Mason v. Dwinnell? *When is the evidence not compelling enough? Compare* Estroff v. Chatterjee, *190 N.C.App. 61, 660 S.E.2d 73 (2008), decided by the North Carolina Court of Appeals the same day as* Mason v. Dwinnell.

ADOPTION OF TAMMY

416 Mass. 205, 619 N.E.2d 315 (1993)

GREANEY, J. In this case, two unmarried women, Susan and Helen, filed a joint petition in the Probate and Family Court Department under G.L. c. 210, § 1 (1992 ed.) to adopt as their child Tammy, a minor, who is Susan's biological daughter. Following an evidentiary hearing, a judge of the Probate and Family Court entered a memorandum of decision containing findings of fact and conclusions of law. Based on her finding that Helen and Susan "are each functioning, separately and together, as the custodial and psychological parents of [Tammy]," and that "it is the best interest of said [Tammy] that she be adopted by both," the judge entered a decree allowing the adoption. Simultaneously, the judge reserved and reported to the Appeals Court the evidence and all questions of law, in an effort to "secure [the] decree from any attack in the future on jurisdictional grounds." *See* G.L. c. 215, § 13 (1992 ed.). *See also Adoption of Thomas*, 408 Mass. 446 (1990). We transferred the case to this court on our own motion. We conclude that the adoption was properly allowed under G.L. c. 210.[95]

We summarize the relevant facts as found by the judge. Helen and Susan have lived together in a committed relationship, which they consider to be permanent, for more than ten years. In June, 1983, they jointly purchased a house in Cambridge. Both women are physicians specializing in surgery. At the time the petition was filed, Helen maintained a private practice in general surgery at Mount Auburn Hospital and Susan, a nationally recognized expert in the field of breast cancer, was director of the Faulkner Breast Center and a surgical oncologist at the Dana Farber Cancer Institute. Both women also held positions on the faculty of Harvard Medical School.

For several years prior to the birth of Tammy, Helen and Susan planned to have a child, biologically related to both of them, whom they would jointly parent. Helen first attempted to conceive a child through artificial insemination by Susan's brother. When those efforts failed, Susan successfully conceived a child through artificial insemination by Helen's biological cousin, Francis. The women attended childbirth classes together and Helen was present when Susan gave birth to Tammy on April 30, 1988. Although Tammy's birth certificate reflects Francis as her biological father, she was given a hyphenated surname using Susan and Helen's last names.

Since her birth, Tammy has lived with, and been raised and supported by, Helen and Susan. Tammy views both women as her parents, calling

95. The judge also decreed, as an alternative to the adoption ordered under G.L. c. 210, "It would be in the best interest of the child to permit [Helen] to adopt [Tammy] and [Susan] to retain postadoptive parental rights of custody and visitation pursuant to its equitable powers, under G.L. c. 215." Because we conclude that the adoption was properly allowed under G.L. c. 210, we need not consider the alternative equitable ground relied on by the judge in permitting Helen to adopt Tammy and Susan to maintain postadoptive rights.

Helen "mama" and Susan "mommy." Tammy has strong emotional and psychological bonds with both Helen and Susan. Together, Helen and Susan have provided Tammy with a comfortable home, and have created a warm and stable environment which is supportive of Tammy's growth and over-all well being. Both women jointly and equally participate in parenting Tammy, and both have a strong financial commitment to her. During the work week, Helen usually has lunch at home with Tammy, and on weekends both women spend time together with Tammy at special events or running errands. When Helen and Susan are working, Tammy is cared for by a nanny. The three vacation together at least ten days every three to four months, frequently spending time with Helen's and Susan's respective extended families in California and Mexico. Francis does not participate in parenting Tammy and does not support her. His intention was to assist Helen and Susan in having a child, and he does not intend to be involved with Tammy, except as a distant relative. Francis signed an adoption surrender and supports the joint adoption by both women.

Helen and Susan, recognizing that the laws of the Commonwealth do not permit them to enter into a legally cognizable marriage, believe that the best interests of Tammy require legal recognition of her identical emotional relationship to both women. Susan expressed her understanding that it may not be in her own long-term interest to permit Helen to adopt Tammy because, in the event that Helen and Susan separate, Helen would have equal rights to primary custody. Susan indicated, however, that she has no reservation about allowing Helen to adopt. Apart from the emotional security and current practical ramifications which legal recognition of the reality of her parental relationships will provide Tammy, Susan indicated that the adoption is important for Tammy in terms of potential inheritance from Helen. Helen and her living issue are the beneficiaries of three irrevocable family trusts. Unless Tammy is adopted, Helen's share of the trusts may pass to others. Although Susan and Helen have established a substantial trust fund for Tammy, it is comparatively small in relation to Tammy's potential inheritance under Helen's family trusts.

Over a dozen witnesses, including mental health professionals, teachers, colleagues, neighbors, blood relatives and a priest and nun, testified to the fact that Helen and Susan participate equally in raising Tammy, that Tammy relates to both women as her parents, and that the three form a healthy, happy, and stable family unit. Educators familiar with Tammy testified that she is an extremely well-adjusted, bright, creative, cheerful child who interacts well with other children and adults. A priest and nun from the parties' church testified that Helen and Susan are active parishioners, that they routinely take Tammy to church and church-related activities, and that they attend to the spiritual and moral development of Tammy in an exemplary fashion. Teachers from Tammy's school testified that Helen and Susan both actively participate as volunteers in the school community and communicate frequently with school officials. Neighbors testified that they would have no hesitation in leaving their own children in the care of Helen or Susan. Susan's father, brother, and maternal aunt, and Helen's cousin testified in favor of the joint adoption. Members of both women's extended families attested to the fact that they consider Helen and Susan to be equal parents of Tammy. Both families unreservedly endorsed the adoption petition.

The Department of Social Services (department) conducted a home study in connection with the adoption petition which recommended the adoption, concluding that "the petitioners and their home are suitable for the proper rearing of this child." Tammy's pediatrician reported to the department that Tammy receives regular pediatric care and that she "could not have more excellent parents than Helen and Susan." A court-appointed guardian ad litem, Dr. Steven Nickman, assistant clinical professor of psychiatry at Harvard Medical School, conducted a clinical assessment of Tammy and her family with a view toward determining whether or not it would be in Tammy's best interests to be adopted by Helen and Susan. Dr. Nickman considered the ramifications of the fact that Tammy will be brought up in a "non-standard" family. As part of his report, he reviewed and referenced literature on child psychiatry and child psychology which supports the conclusion that children raised by lesbian parents develop normally. In sum, he stated that "the fact that this parent-child constellation came into being as a result of thoughtful planning and a strong desire on the part of these women to be parents to a child and to give that child the love, the wisdom and the knowledge that they possess ... [needs to be taken into account].... The maturity of these women, their status in the community, and their seriousness of purpose stands in contrast to the caretaking environments of a vast number of children who are born to heterosexual parents but who are variously abused, neglected and otherwise deprived of security and happiness." Dr. Nickman concluded that "there is every reason for [Helen] to become a legal parent to Tammy just as [Susan] is," and he recommended that the court so order. An attorney appointed to represent Tammy's interests also strongly recommended that the joint petition be granted.

Despite the overwhelming support for the joint adoption and the judge's conclusion that joint adoption is clearly in Tammy's best interests, the question remains whether there is anything in the law of the Commonwealth that would prevent this adoption. The law of adoption is purely statutory, *Davis v. McGraw*, 206 Mass. 294, 297 (1910), and the governing statute, G.L. c. 210 (1992 ed.), is to be strictly followed in all its essential particulars. *Purinton v. Jamrock*, 195 Mass. 187, 197 (1907). To the extent that any ambiguity or vagueness exists in the statute, judicial construction should enhance, rather than defeat, its purpose. *Hayon v. Coca Cola Bottling Co. of New England*, 375 Mass. 644, 648–649 (1978). *Vallin v. Bondesson*, 346 Mass. 748, 753 (1964). The primary purpose of the adoption statute, particularly with regard to children under the age of fourteen, is undoubtedly the advancement of the best interests of the subject child. *See* G.L. c. 210, §§ 3, 4A, 5A, 5B, 6. *See also Adoption of a Minor*, 343 Mass. 292, 294–296 (1961); *Krakow v. Department of Pub. Welfare*, 326 Mass. 452, 455–456 (1950); *Erickson v. Raspperry*, 320 Mass.

333, 335 (1946); *Merrill v. Berlin*, 316 Mass. 87, 89 (1944); *Bottoms v. Carlz*, 310 Mass. 29 (1941); *Purinton v. Jamrock, supra* at 199 ("It is the right of the children that is protected by this statute.... The first and paramount duty is to consult the welfare of the child"). With these considerations in mind, we examine the statute to determine whether adoption in the circumstances of this case is permitted.

1. The initial question is whether the Probate Court judge had jurisdiction under G.L. c. 210 to enter a judgment on a joint petition for adoption brought by two unmarried cohabitants in the petitioners' circumstances. We answer this question in the affirmative.

There is nothing on the face of the statute which precludes the joint adoption of a child by two unmarried cohabitants such as the petitioners. Chapter 210, § 1, provides that "[a] person of full age may petition the probate court in the county where he resides for leave to adopt as his child another person younger than himself, unless such other person is his or her wife or husband, or brother, sister, uncle or aunt, of the whole or half blood." Other than requiring that a spouse join in the petition, if the petitioner is married and the spouse is competent to join therein, the statute does not expressly prohibit or require joinder by any person. Although the singular "a person" is used, it is a legislatively mandated rule of statutory construction that "words importing the singular number may extend and be applied to several persons" unless the resulting construction is "inconsistent with the manifest intent of the law-making body or repugnant to the context of the same statute." G.L. c. 4, § 6 (1992 ed.). In the context of adoption, where the legislative intent to promote the best interests of the child is evidenced throughout the governing statute, and the adoption of a child by two unmarried individuals accomplishes that goal, construing the term "person" as "persons" clearly enhances, rather than defeats, the purpose of the statute. Furthermore, it is apparent from the first sentence of G.L. c. 210, § 1, that the Legislature considered and defined those combinations of persons which would lead to adoptions in violation of public policy. Clearly absent is any prohibition of adoption by two unmarried individuals like the petitioners.

While the Legislature may not have envisioned adoption by same-sex partners, there is no indication that it attempted to define all possible categories of persons leading to adoptions in the best interests of children. Rather than limit the potential categories of persons entitled to adopt (other than those described in the first sentence of § 1), the Legislature used general language to define who may adopt and who may be adopted. The Probate Court has thus been granted jurisdiction to consider a variety of adoption petitions. *See Adoption of Thomas*, 408 Mass. 446, 449–451 (1990). The limitations on adoption that do exist derive from the written consent requirements contained in § 2, from specific conditions set forth in § 2A, which must be satisfied prior to the adoption of a child under the age of fourteen, and from several statutory and judicial directives which essentially restrict adoptions to those which have been found by a judge to be in the best interests of the subject child. *See Merrill v. Berlin, supra* at

89 (in dismissing elderly grandparents' petition to adopt following death of children's parents, and retaining custody with three female testamentary guardians, the court stated "the only question [to be considered] is whether the best interests of the children would be served by their adoption").

In this case all requirements in §§ 2 and 2A are met, and there is no question that the judge's findings demonstrate that the directives set forth in §§ 5B and 6, and in case law, have been satisfied. Adoption will not result in any tangible change in Tammy's daily life; it will, however, serve to provide her with a significant legal relationship which may be important in her future. At the most practical level, adoption will entitle Tammy to inherit from Helen's family trusts and from Helen and her family under the law of intestate succession (G.L. c. 210, § 6), to receive support from Helen, who will be legally obligated to provide such support (G.L. c. 209C, § 9; G.L. c. 273, § 1 [1992 ed.]), to be eligible for coverage under Helen's health insurance policies, and to be eligible for social security benefits in the event of Helen's disability or death (42 U.S.C. § 402 [d] [1988]).

Of equal, if not greater significance, adoption will enable Tammy to preserve her unique filial ties to Helen in the event that Helen and Susan separate, or Susan predeceases Helen.[96] As the case law and commentary on the subject illustrate, when the functional parents of children born in circumstances similar to Tammy separate or one dies, the children often remain in legal limbo for years while their future is disputed in the courts. Polikoff, This Child Does Have Two Mothers: Redefining Parenthood to Meet the Needs of Children in Lesbian–Mother and Other Nontraditional Families, 78 Geo. J.L. 459, 508–522 (1990); Comment, Second Parent Adoption for Lesbian–Parented Families: Legal Recognition of the Other Mother, 19 U.C. Davis L. Rev. 729, 741–745 (1986). In some cases, children have been denied the affection of a functional parent who has been with them since birth, even when it is apparent at this outcome is contrary to the children's best interests.[97] Adoption serves to establish

---

96. Although Susan has designated Helen guardian of Tammy in her will, Helen's custody of Tammy could conceivably be contested in the event of Susan's death, particularly by Francis, members of his family or members of Susan's family. Absent adoption, Helen would not have a dispositive legal right to retain custody of Tammy, because she would be a "legal stranger" to the child.

97. Cases from other jurisdictions demonstrate the difficulties resulting from the lack of an established legal relationship between a child and its second functional parent. *See, e.g., In re the Interest of Z.J.H.*, 162 Wis.2d 1002, 1033 (1991) (Bablitch, J., dissenting) (former lesbian partner of child's adoptive mother, who had planned on adoption, cultivated "parent-like" relationship with child since his birth, and had A been child's primary caretaker, denied both visitation and custody after partners' separation due to lack of legal relationship with child; court refused to consider issue of child's best interests); *Nancy S. v. Michele G.*, 228 Cal.App.3d 831, 840 & n.8 (1991) (two children conceived by artificial insemination during lesbian couple's relationship deemed legal children of natural mother only, who was granted sole physical and legal custody following the couple's separation; appellate court recognized that adoption would avoid this "unfortunate situation" noting that "we see nothing in [our statutory] provisions [similar to those in Massachusetts] that would preclude a child from being jointly adopted by someone of the same sex as the natural parent"); *In re Pearlman*, 15 Fam. L. Rep. (BNA) 1355 (Fla. Cir. Ct. 1989) (unreported) (custody of child conceived by artificial insemination during lesbian couple's

legal rights and responsibilities so that, in the event that problems arise in the future, issues of custody and visitation may be promptly resolved by reference to the best interests of the child within the recognized framework of the law. *See* G.L. c. 209C, § 10. *See also Adoption of B.L.V.B.*, 628 A.2d 1271, (Vt. 1993) (Vt. Sup. Ct. 92–321). There is no jurisdictional bar in the statute to the judge's consideration of this joint petition. The conclusion that the adoption is in the best interests of Tammy is also well warranted.

2. The judge also posed the question whether, pursuant to G.L. c. 210, § 6 (1992 ed.), Susan's legal relationship to Tammy must be terminated if Tammy is adopted. Section 6 provides that, on entry of an adoption decree, "all rights, duties and other legal consequences of the natural relation of child and parent shall ... except as regards marriage, incest or cohabitation, terminate between the child so adopted and his natural parents and kindred." Although G.L. c. 210, § 2, clearly permits a child's natural parent to be an adoptive parent, § 6 does not contain any express exceptions to its termination provision. The Legislature obviously did not intend that a natural parent's legal relationship to its child be terminated when the natural parent is a party to the adoption petition.

Section 6 clearly is directed to the more usual circumstances of adoption, where the child is adopted by persons who are not the child's natural parents (either because the natural parents have elected to relinquish the child for adoption or their parental rights have been involuntarily terminated). The purpose of the termination provision is to protect the security of the child's newly-created family unit by eliminating involvement with the child's natural parents. Although it is not uncommon for a natural parent to join in the adoption petition of a spouse who is not the child's natural parent, *see, e.g., Adoption of a Minor (No. 1)*, 367 Mass. 907 (1975); *Erickson v. Raspperry*, 320 Mass. 333 (1946), the statute has never been construed to require the termination of the natural parent's legal relationship to the child in these circumstances. Nor has § 6 been construed to apply when the natural mother petitions alone to adopt her child born out of wedlock. *See Curran, petitioner*, 314 Mass. 91 (1943). Reading the adoption statute as a whole, we conclude that the termination provision contained in § 6 was intended to apply only when the natural parents (or parent) are not parties to the adoption petition.[98]

3. We conclude that the Probate Court has jurisdiction to enter a decree on a joint adoption petition brought by the two petitioners when

---

relationship awarded to "de facto" parent after four years of litigation with child's maternal grandparents following death of natural mother; child, who had been separated from her functional parent and suffered anxiety as a result, told the court "for Christmas I don't really want a present. All I want is to live with Neenie ["de facto" parent]").

98. In interpreting a provision similar to *G.L. c. 210, § 6*, the Vermont Supreme Court, citing support from trial courts in other jurisdictions, likewise concluded that the natural or prior adoptive parent's legal relationship to the child does not terminate when the child is adopted by the same-sex partner of the child's legal parent. *See Adoption of B.L.V.B.*, A.2d (Vt. 1993) (Vt. Sup. Ct. 92–321), citing *Matter of Evan*, 153 Misc.2d 844 (N.Y. Sur. Ct. 1992), and *In re Adoption of Minor (T.)*, 60 U.S.L.W. 2191 (D.C. Super. Ct. Sept. 24, 1991) (unreported).

the judge has found that joint adoption is in the subject child's best interests. We further conclude that, when a natural parent is, a party to a joint adoption petition, that parent's legal relationship to the child does not terminate on entry of the adoption decree.

4. So much of the decree as allows the adoption of Tammy by both petitioners is affirmed. So much of the decree as provides in the alternative for the adoption of Tammy by Helen and the retention of rights of custody and visitation by Susan is vacated.

So ordered.

DISSENT BY: NOLAN; LYNCH [omitted]

DISCUSSION

Did the Adoption of Tammy *court reach the right conclusion? Should unmarried opposite-sex couples be able to adopt?*

BOSEMAN v. JARRELL

364 N.C. 537, 704 S.E.2d 494 (2010)

NEWBY, JUSTICE.

In this case we must determine the validity of an adoption decree entered in the Durham County District Court at the request of Wilmington residents. If the decree is invalid, we must also determine whether defendant acted inconsistently with her constitutionally protected, paramount parental status. Because the General Assembly did not vest our courts with subject matter jurisdiction to create the type of adoption attempted here, we hold that the adoption decree at issue is void *ab initio*. However, we also conclude that by intentionally creating a family unit in which defendant permanently shared parental responsibilities with plaintiff, defendant acted inconsistently with her paramount parental status. Thus, the District Court, New Hanover County, ("the trial court") did not err by utilizing the "best interest of the child" standard to make its custody award. As such, we reverse the Court of Appeals' decision that the adoption decree is valid and affirm as modified its conclusion leaving undisturbed the trial court's decision that the parties are entitled to joint custody of the child.

Plaintiff and defendant (collectively, "the parties") met in 1998. At that time, plaintiff lived in Wilmington, North Carolina, and defendant lived in Rhode Island. The first time they met, they "discussed their desires to have children." Roughly one month later, the parties began a romantic relationship. From the outset, the parties continued to voice their desires to have a child. In the spring of 1999, defendant moved from Rhode Island to Wilmington, and the parties began living together as domestic partners.

In May of 2000 the parties initiated the process of having a child. They decided that defendant would actually bear the child, but both parties would otherwise jointly participate in the conception process. The parties agreed to choose an anonymous sperm donor and researched and discussed the available options. They also attended the medical appointments necessary both to impregnate defendant and to address her prenatal care. Plaintiff read to the minor child "in the womb and played music for him." Plaintiff also cared for defendant during the pregnancy and was present for the delivery. Defendant eventually gave birth to the minor child in October of 2002, and the parties jointly selected his first name.

Following the child's birth, the parties held themselves out as the parents of the minor child. They gave the minor child a hyphenated last name composed of both their last names. They also "had a baptismal ceremony for the child at the plaintiff's church during which they publicly presented themselves to family and friends as parents of the child." Further, each of the parties integrated the minor child into their respective families and each family accepted the minor child.

Within the home, the parties shared "an equal role" in parenting. Plaintiff's parenting skills were found to be "very attentive, very loving, hands on and fun." Defendant was found to be "very hands-on and patient in parenting" and to "reprimand[ ] [the minor child] by talking to him in a nice way." As a result of occupational responsibilities, each party was occasionally required to be temporarily away from their home. During such an absence, the party at home would care for the child. Moreover, the minor child treated each of the parties as a parent. The child refers to plaintiff as "Mom" and to defendant as "Mommy." As the trial court stated, the minor child "shows lots of love and respect for both parties." "Each party agrees that the other is and has been a good parent," and defendant even "testified that she thinks it is important for the plaintiff to be in" the minor child's life.

In 2004 the parties discussed the prospect of plaintiff adopting the minor child. The parties sought an adoption by which plaintiff would become a legal, adoptive parent while defendant would remain the minor child's legal, biological parent. According to defendant, in 2005 plaintiff stated "that she had 'found a way' " to adopt the minor child. Plaintiff informed defendant that the type of adoption they sought was "being approved in Durham County, NC."

Shortly thereafter, in June of 2005, the parties asked the District Court, Durham County, ("the adoption court") to make plaintiff an adoptive parent of the minor child while not also terminating defendant's relationship with the child. To accomplish their goal, the parties requested in the petition and accompanying motions that the adoption court not comply with (1) the statutory requirement under N.C.G.S. § 48–3–606(9) that defendant's written consent to the adoption contain an acknowledgment that the adoption decree would terminate her parental rights and (2) the statutory requirement of N.C.G.S. § 48–1–106(c) that an adoption decree "severs the relationship of parent and child between the individual adopted and that individual's biological or previous adoptive parents."

Defendant's consent to the adoption reiterated these conditions and was contingent on the non-enforcement of these statutory provisions.

On 10 August 2005, the adoption court agreed to the parties' request, determined defendant's limited consent was sufficient, and entered an adoption decree. The decree stated that it "effects a complete substitution of families for all legal purposes and establishes the relationship of parent and child ... between ... petitioner and the individual being adopted," while simultaneously "not sever[ing] the relationship of parent and child between the individual adopted and that individual's biological mother." After finding that the Division of Social Services would not index this type of adoption, the adoption court instructed the clerk "not ... to comply with" a statutory requirement that the clerk of court transmit a copy of the adoption decree to the Division, instead ordering that the clerk "securely maintain this file in the clerk's office."

In May of 2006, the parties ceased their relationship. Subsequently, plaintiff, without being ordered to do so, continued to provide "most of the financial support for the partnership" and for the minor child. Nonetheless, defendant limited plaintiff's contact with the minor child following the parties' separation. She did so while admitting "that the plaintiff is a very good parent who loves [the minor child] and that [the minor child] loves [plaintiff]."

Relying in part on the adoption decree, plaintiff filed in the trial court a complaint and an amended complaint seeking custody of the minor child. In response, defendant attacked the adoption decree, arguing that it was void *ab initio,* and contended that plaintiff otherwise could not seek custody of the minor child.

The trial court ultimately awarded the parties joint legal custody of the minor child. That court did not reach the merits of defendant's contention regarding the validity of the Durham County adoption decree. The trial court reasoned that it did "not have jurisdiction to declare void" another District Court Judge's order entered in another judicial district in North Carolina. Thus, the court determined that plaintiff "is a parent of the minor child ... in that the aforementioned Decree of Adoption has not been found to be void by this court or any other court." The court also concluded that "defendant has acted inconsistent with her paramount parental rights and responsibilities." Then, after determining that the "parties are fit and proper persons to have custody of their minor son," the court applied the "best interest of the child" standard to conclude that the parties should have "joint legal custody of the minor child." Defendant appealed.

The Court of Appeals concluded that the adoption decree in this case is valid and left intact the trial court's custody determination. *Boseman v. Jarrell,* 199 N.C.App. 128, 681 S.E.2d 374 (2009). After reviewing Chapter 48 of our General Statutes, the Court of Appeals concluded that the adoption in this case comports with the "intent and purposes" of both our adoption law as a whole and "the specific provisions" of it at issue here.

Id. at 139, 681 S.E.2d at 381. The Court of Appeals stated that N.C.G.S. § 48–2–607(a) prevents defendant from otherwise challenging the adoption decree's propriety, and, therefore, the decree causes plaintiff to be a legal parent of the minor child. *Id.* at 139–40, 681 S.E.2d at 381–82. The Court of Appeals also determined that plaintiff's status as a parent and the trial court's conclusion that the parties "are fit and proper persons for custody of the child, fully support [the trial court's] custody award." *Id.* at 140, 681 S.E.2d at 381. On 28 January 2010, we allowed defendant's petition for discretionary review of the Court of Appeals' decision.

Defendant contends that a court is prohibited from choosing not to enforce the provisions of N.C.G.S. § 48–1–106(c) and N.C.G.S. § 48–3–606(9). Defendant argues that these provisions are mandatory in an adoption proceeding under Chapter 48 of our General Statutes. Because the adoption court crafted a remedy not recognized by the adoption statutes, defendant maintains that the adoption court lacked subject matter jurisdiction to enter the adoption decree at issue in this case, and the decree is, therefore, void *ab initio.* Plaintiff responds that the adoption court "was acting within its subject matter jurisdiction to preside over adoption proceedings" as set forth in N.C.G.S. § 48–2–100. Further, plaintiff asserts that, given the General Assembly's desire to have Chapter 48 "liberally construed and applied to promote its underlying purposes and policies," N.C.G.S. § 48–1–100(d) (2009), these statutory provisions do not have to be enforced in every adoption proceeding because they are designed only to protect the biological parent.

The law governing adoptions in North Carolina is wholly statutory. *Wilson v. Anderson,* 232 N.C. 212, 215, 59 S.E.2d 836, 839 (1950). "Adoption is a status unknown to common law...." *Id.* Thus, to determine whether a court may proceed under Chapter 48 while choosing not to enforce the requirements of N.C.G.S. § 48–1–106(c) and N.C.G.S. § 48–3–606(9), we must examine the text of our adoption statutes.

Through Chapter 48 of our General Statutes, our legislature has provided for three types of adoptions of minor children. The first is referred to as a "direct placement" adoption. N.C.G.S. § 48–3–202(a) (2009). In that type of adoption, our legislature envisioned a complete substitution of families. *Id.* § 48–1–106(a) (2009). A "parent or guardian must personally select a prospective adoptive parent," *id.* § 48–3–202(a), and is required to "execute a consent to the minor's adoption pursuant to [N.C.G.S. §§ 48–3–601 to 48–3–610]," *id.* § 48–3–201(b) (2009), acknowledging that the adoption will terminate the child's relationship with the parent, *id.* § 48–3–606(9) (2009). The second is referred to as an "[a]gency placement" adoption. *Id.* § 48–3–203 (2009). In such an adoption, the "agency may acquire legal and physical custody of a minor for purposes of adoptive placement only by means of a relinquishment pursuant to [N.C.G.S. §§ 48–3–701 to 48–3–707] or by a court order terminating the rights and duties of a parent or guardian of the minor." *Id.* § 48–3–203(a). The agency is then responsible for placing the minor for adoption. *See id.* § 48–3–203(b), (d). The third type is the stepparent adoption. *Id.* § 48–4–

100 (2009). A stepparent is defined as "an individual who is the spouse of a parent of a child, but who is not a legal parent of the child." *Id.* § 48–1–101(18) (2009). Generally speaking, when a stepparent adopts the child of his or her spouse, the child must consent if twelve or more years of age, and the child's parents and any guardian must consent. *Id.* § 48–4–102 (2009). Indicating the comprehensive and limiting nature of this statutory procedure, the General Assembly has also explicitly provided for the adoption of adults, *id.* §§ 48–5–100 to 48–5–103 (2009), and the readoption by former parents of both adults and minors, *id.* §§ 48–6–100 to 48–6–102 (2009). According to plaintiff, the parties here presented a modified direct placement adoption that explicitly omitted the requirements of N.C.G.S. §§ 48–1–106(c) and 48–3–606(9).

In N.C.G.S. § 48–1–106, the General Assembly declared the "[l]egal effect of [a] decree of adoption" in a direct placement adoption. *Id.* § 48–1–106 (2009). That statute provides in pertinent part:

> (a) A decree of adoption effects a complete substitution of families for all legal purposes after the entry of the decree.
>
> (b) A decree of adoption establishes the relationship of parent and child between each petitioner and the individual being adopted. From the date of the signing of the decree, the adoptee is entitled to inherit real and personal property by, through, and from the adoptive parents in accordance with the statutes on intestate succession and has the same legal status, including all legal rights and obligations of any kind whatsoever, as a child born the legitimate child of the adoptive parents.
>
> (c) A decree of adoption severs the relationship of parent and child between the individual adopted and that individual's biological or previous adoptive parents. After the entry of a decree of adoption, the former parents are relieved of all legal duties and obligations due from them to the adoptee, except that a former parent's duty to make past-due payments for child support is not terminated, and the former parents are divested of all rights with respect to the adoptee.

Id. § 48–1–106(a)–(c). With this statute the legislature provided, *inter alia,* that a direct placement adoption decree terminates the adoptee's relationship with his or her former parent or parents. *Id.* § 48–1–106(c).

The provisions of N.C.G.S. § 48–1–106 establish the relief that may be issued by a court in an adoption proceeding. The legislature instructed that in a direct placement adoption the court may issue only an adoption decree that "effects a complete substitution of families." *Id.* § 48–1–106(a). The General Assembly directed our courts to enter adoption decrees that "sever [ ] the [former] relationship of parent and child," *id.* § 48–1–106(c), and "establish [ ] the [new] relationship of parent and child," *id.* § 48–1–106(b). Our legislature expressly required the dictates of N.C.G.S. § 48–1–106 to be stated in a direct placement adoption decree. *Id.* § 48–2–606(a)(6) (2009) ("A decree of adoption *must state* at least ... [t]he effect of the decree of adoption *as set forth in G.S. 48–1–106....*"

(emphasis added)). There is no language in our statutes authorizing the issuance of any other relief. Accordingly, direct placement adoption decrees issued under Chapter 48 must have the effect the General Assembly established in N.C.G.S. § 48–1–106.

Further, the legislature requires that when consenting to the direct placement adoption of their children, parents acknowledge the effect an adoption decree has on their rights and responsibilities. In N.C.G.S. § 48–3–606, titled "Content of consent; *mandatory provisions,*" the legislature provides that a parent's consent to the adoption of her child

> must be in writing and state ... [t]hat the individual executing the consent understands that *when the adoption is final, all rights and obligations of the adoptee's former parents or guardian with respect to the adoptee will be extinguished,* and every aspect of *the legal relationship between the adoptee and the former parent or guardian will be terminated.*

Id. § 48–3–606(9) (emphasis added). Thus, this statute ensures that a parent understands the direct placement adoption will totally sever her relationship with the child being adopted.

If " 'the language of a statute is clear and unambiguous, there is no room for judicial construction and the courts must give the statute its plain and definite meaning, and are without power to interpolate, or superimpose, provisions and limitations not contained therein.' " *In re D.L.H.,* 364 N.C. 214, 221, 694 S.E.2d 753, 757 (2010) (citation omitted). This is especially true in the context of adoption, which is purely a creation of statute. *See Wilson,* 232 N.C. at 215, 59 S.E.2d at 839. With direct placement adoptions, the General Assembly stated in these statutes that an adoption decree must sever the former parent-child relationship. Further, the legislature included no language allowing for the issuance of a decree that does not fulfill this mandate. It did so despite allowing for the alteration of other provisions of Chapter 48. *See, e.g.,* N.C.G.S. § 48–3–501 (2009) ("*Unless the court orders otherwise,* when a parent...." (emphasis added)); *id.* § 48–3–502(a) (2009) ("*Unless the court orders otherwise,* during a proceeding...." (emphasis added)); *id.* § 48–4–101(3) (2009) (allowing a court to dispense with several specific statutory requirements "[f]or cause"). Because the General Assembly's chosen language in these statutes is clear and unambiguous, courts are without power to "liberally construe[ ]," *id.* § 48–1–100(d), that language. Accordingly, a court is without authority to disregard these statutes.

In N.C.G.S. § 48–2–100, titled "Jurisdiction," our General Assembly established prerequisites for our courts to obtain jurisdiction over adoption proceedings. *Id.* § 48–2–100 (2009). At the relevant time, that statute stated in pertinent part:

> (b) Except as provided in subsection (c) of this section, jurisdiction over adoption proceedings commenced under this Chapter exists if, at the commencement of the proceeding:

> (1) The adoptee has lived in this State for at least the six consecutive months immediately preceding the filing of the petition or from birth, and the prospective adoptive parent is domiciled in this State; or
>
> (2) The prospective adoptive parent has lived in or been domiciled in this State for at least the six consecutive months immediately preceding the filing of the petition.

Id. § 48–2–100 (2005). Thus, pursuant to the text of this statute, our courts have subject matter jurisdiction of adoption proceedings "commenced under" Chapter 48 of our General Statutes.

To commence an adoption proceeding under Chapter 48 of our General Statutes, a petitioner must be seeking an adoption available under Chapter 48. *See id.* § 48–2–301(a) (2009); *Wilson,* 232 N.C. at 215, 59 S.E.2d at 839 ("Adoption . . . can be accomplished only in accordance with provisions of statutes enacted by the legislative branch of the State government."). In defining both "[w]ho may adopt" and "[w]ho may be adopted," the legislature emphasized that adoptions may occur only as provided in Chapter 48. N.C.G.S. § 48–1–103 (2009) ("Any adult may adopt another individual *as provided in this Chapter*. . . ." (emphasis added)); *id.* § 48–1–104 (2009) ("Any individual may be adopted *as provided in this Chapter.*" (emphasis added)). Further, under N.C.G.S. § 48–2–301, titled "Petition for adoption; who may file," the legislature provided only that "[a] prospective adoptive parent," someone who is attempting an adoption "provided in" Chapter 48, *id.* § 48–1–103, may file an adoption petition, *id.* § 48–2–301(a).

Plaintiff was not seeking an adoption available under Chapter 48. In her petition for adoption, plaintiff explained to the adoption court that she sought an adoption decree that would establish the legal relationship of parent and child with the minor child, but not sever that same relationship between defendant and the minor child. As we have established, such relief does not exist under Chapter 48. *Id.* §§ 48–1–106, 48–2–606(a)(6), 48–3–606(9). Because plaintiff was seeking relief unavailable under our General Statutes, the adoption proceeding at issue in this case was not "commenced under" Chapter 48 of our General Statutes. *Id.* § 48–2–100 (2005).

A court's subject matter jurisdiction over a particular case is invoked by the pleading. *In re K.J.L.,* 363 N.C. 343, 346–47, 677 S.E.2d 835, 837 (2009). . . . Accordingly, the adoption decree at issue in this case is void *ab initio. Id.* at 590, 636 S.E.2d at 790 (citations omitted).

Plaintiff contends that the legality of the adoption decree notwithstanding, defendant may no longer contest its validity. In support of this contention, plaintiff cites N.C.G.S. § 48–2–607(a), which states in part that "after the final order of adoption is entered, no party to an adoption proceeding nor anyone claiming under such a party may question the validity of the adoption because of any defect or irregularity, jurisdictional or otherwise, in the proceeding, but shall be fully bound by the order." *Id.*

§ 48–2–607(a) (2009). We note that the Court of Appeals rejected this argument in its opinion below, recognizing that this statute does not preclude a challenge to a court's subject matter jurisdiction. *Boseman,* 199 N.C.App. at 134, 681 S.E.2d at 378 ("[T]he only avenue by which [defendant] can contest the adoption is to show that it was void *ab initio,* a legal nullity."). As we have long held, a void judgment has no legal effect; it is a legal nullity that may be challenged at any time. *In re T.R.P.,* 360 N.C. at 590, 636 S.E.2d at 790 (citation omitted); *Stroupe v. Stroupe,* 301 N.C. 656, 662, 273 S.E.2d 434, 438 (1981); *City of Monroe v. Niven,* 221 N.C. 362, 365, 20 S.E.2d 311, 313 (1942) ("The passage of time, however great, does not affect the validity of a judgment; it cannot render a void judgment valid." (citations and quotation marks omitted)); *Casey v. Barker,* 219 N.C. 465, 467–68, 14 S.E.2d 429, 431 (1941) (citations omitted); *Ellis v. Ellis,* 190 N.C. 418, 422, 130 S.E. 7, 9 (1925) (citation omitted); *Clark v. Carolina Homes, Inc.,* 189 N.C. 703, 708, 128 S.E. 20, 23–24 (1925) (citations omitted); *Carter v. Rountree,* 109 N.C. 29, 32, 13 S.E. 716, 717 (1891).

Moreover, the General Assembly intended for N.C.G.S. § 48–2–607 to shield from further review only those decrees entered by courts having subject matter jurisdiction. "It is always presumed that the legislature acted with care and deliberation and with full knowledge of prior and existing law." *State v. Benton,* 276 N.C. 641, 658, 174 S.E.2d 793, 804 (1970) (citations omitted). " 'A universal principle as old as the law is that the proceedings of a court without jurisdiction of the subject matter are a nullity,' " *In re T.R.P.,* 360 N.C. at 590, 636 S.E.2d at 790 (quoting *Burgess ex rel. Burgess v. Gibbs,* 262 N.C. 462, 465, 137 S.E.2d 806, 808 (1964)), and without subject matter jurisdiction, "a court has no power to act," *id.* (citing *Hart v. Thomasville Motors, Inc.,* 244 N.C. 84, 90, 92 S.E.2d 673, 678 (1956)). Because we assume the General Assembly enacted N.C.G.S. § 48–2–607 with full knowledge that subject matter jurisdiction "cannot be conferred upon a court by consent, waiver or estoppel," 360 N.C. at 595, 636 S.E.2d at 793 (citations and quotation marks omitted), the legislature's words "no party," "defect" and "irregularity" indicate that this statute is designed to foreclose challenges other than subject matter jurisdiction. *See* N.C.G.S. § 48–2–607(a). The adoption court in this case had no authority to act in a proceeding seeking relief unknown to Chapter 48. *See State v. Verrier,* 173 N.C.App. 123, 130, 617 S.E.2d 675, 680 (2005) ("It is outside the realm of this Court's function as the judiciary to modify statutory law."). Because the adoption court had no authority to act, N.C.G.S. § 48–2–607 does not apply to its decree.

The argument that the child will lose legal benefits if the adoption is not upheld must also be rejected. The record shows that this new form of judicially-created adoption may have been available only in Durham County and not available in the other counties of North Carolina. If our uniform court system is to be preserved, a new form of adoption cannot be made available in some counties but not all. This Court has the responsibility to ensure that the law is applied uniformly in all our counties. N.C.

Const. art. IV. Accordingly, any best interests evaluation is limited to legal benefits that are equally available under the law to all children. *See State v. Holden,* 64 N.C. 829, 831 (1870) ("The intention of the Legislature and the remedy aimed at are manifest, and under such circumstances it is the duty of Judges to give such an interpretation of the law as shall 'suppress the mischief and advance the remedy, putting down all subtle inventions and evasions for continuance of the mischief . . . and adding force and life to the cure and remedy, according to the true intent of the makers of the act. . . .' " (citation omitted)).

We recognize that many policy arguments have been made to this Court that the adoption in this case ought to be allowed. However, adoption is a statutory creation. *Wilson,* 232 N.C. at 215, 59 S.E.2d at 839. Accordingly, those arguments are appropriately addressed to our General Assembly. Until the legislature changes the provisions of Chapter 48, we must recognize the statutory limitations on the adoption decrees that may be entered. Because the adoption decree is void, plaintiff is not legally recognized as the minor child's parent.

We are now left with a custody dispute between a parent and a third party. The Court of Appeals did not pass upon this issue. The trial court, however, concluded that defendant "has acted inconsistent with her paramount parental rights and responsibilities" before determining that the parties "are fit and proper persons to have custody" of the minor child "and it is in the best interest of the child for the parties to have joint legal custody of him," providing an alternative basis for its custody decision. Defendant contends that the trial court erred by concluding that she has acted inconsistently with her constitutionally protected, paramount parental status. As defendant does not challenge the findings on which this decision is based, we review this conclusion de novo, *see Adams v. Tessener,* 354 N.C. 57, 65, 550 S.E.2d 499, 504 (2001), and determine whether it is supported by "clear and convincing evidence," *id.* at 63, 550 S.E.2d at 503 (citation omitted).

A parent has an "interest in the companionship, custody, care, and control of [his or her children that] is protected by the United States Constitution." *Price v. Howard,* 346 N.C. 68, 73, 484 S.E.2d 528, 531 (1997); *Petersen v. Rogers,* 337 N.C. 397, 400, 445 S.E.2d 901, 903 (1994). So long as a parent has this paramount interest in the custody of his or her children, a custody dispute with a nonparent regarding those children may not be determined by the application of the "best interest of the child" standard. *Price,* 346 N.C. at 79, 484 S.E.2d at 534 (citations omitted).

A parent loses this paramount interest if he or she is found to be unfit or acts inconsistently "with his or her constitutionally protected status." *David N. v. Jason N.,* 359 N.C. 303, 307, 608 S.E.2d 751, 753 (2005). However, there is no bright line beyond which a parent's conduct meets this standard. *See Price,* 346 N.C. at 79, 484 S.E.2d at 534–35. As we explained in *Price,* conduct rising to the "statutory level warranting termination of parental rights" is unnecessary. *Id.* at 79, 484 S.E.2d at 534. Rather, "[u]nfitness, neglect, and abandonment clearly constitute conduct inconsistent with the protected status parents may enjoy. Other types of conduct . . . can also rise to this level so as to be inconsistent with the protected status of natural parents." *Id.* at 79, 484 S.E.2d at 534–35.

As the trial court found, this is not a case in which the natural parent is unfit, or has abandoned or neglected the child. The trial court found that defendant is a fit parent with whom the minor child has a "very loving and respectful relationship." Accordingly, we must determine whether defendant has engaged in some other conduct inconsistent with her paramount parental status. Though determining whether the trial court erred is a fact-sensitive inquiry, we are guided in our analysis by decisions of this Court and the Court of Appeals.

In *Price v. Howard* we observed a custody dispute between a natural mother and a nonparent. The child in that case was born into a family unit consisting of her natural mother and a man who the natural mother said was the child's father. *Id.* at 83, 484 S.E.2d at 537 ("Knowing that the child was her natural child, but not plaintiff's, she represented to the child and to others that plaintiff was the child's natural father."). The mother "chose to rear the child in a family unit with plaintiff being the child's *de facto* father." *Id.*

After illustrating the creation of the family unit in *Price,* we focused our attention on the mother's voluntary grant of nonparent custody. *Id.* We stated:

> This is an important factor to consider, for, if defendant had represented that plaintiff was the child's natural father and voluntarily had given him custody of the child for an indefinite period of time with no notice that such relinquishment of custody would be temporary, defendant would have not only created the family unit that plaintiff and the child have established, but also induced them to allow that family unit to flourish in a relationship of love and duty with no expectations that it would be terminated.
>
> However, if defendant and plaintiff agreed that plaintiff would have custody of the child only for a temporary period of time and defendant sought custody at the end of that period, she would still enjoy a constitutionally protected status absent other conduct inconsistent with that status.

Id. (citation omitted). Thus, under *Price,* when a parent brings a nonparent into the family unit, represents that the nonparent is a parent, and voluntarily gives custody of the child to the nonparent without creating an expectation that the relationship would be terminated, the parent has acted inconsistently with her paramount parental status.

In *Mason v. Dwinnell,* 190 N.C.App. 209, 660 S.E.2d 58 (2008), our Court of Appeals applied our decision in *Price* to facts quite similar to those in the case *sub judice.* In *Mason* the parties "jointly decided to create a family and *intentionally* took steps to identify [the nonparent] as a parent of the child." *Id.* at 222, 660 S.E.2d at 67. These steps included "using both parties' surnames to derive the child's name, allowing [the nonparent] to participate in the pregnancy and birth, [and] holding a baptismal ceremony at which [the nonparent] was announced as a parent." *Id.* at 222–23, 660 S.E.2d at 67. After the child's birth, the parties acted as a family unit. *Id.* at 223, 660 S.E.2d at 67. They shared "caretaking and financial responsibilities for the child." *Id.* As a result of the parties' creation, the nonparent "became the only other adult whom the child considers a parent." *Id.* (internal quotation marks omitted).

The parent in that case also relinquished custody of the minor child to the nonparent with no expectation that the nonparent's relationship with the child would be terminated. *Id.* The parent "chose to share her decision-making authority with [the nonparent]." *Id.* The parent also executed a "Parenting Agreement" in which she "agreed that [the nonparent] should participate in making 'all major decisions regarding their child.'" *Id.* In that document the parent also stated that

> she and [the nonparent] had committed to "jointly parent" the child; that [the parent] would consent to [the nonparent]'s adoption of the child if allowed by North Carolina law; that "although [the nonparent] is not the biological mother, she is a *de facto* parent who has and will provide the parties' child with a stable environment and she has formed a psychological parenting relationship with the parties' child;" that the child's relationship with [the nonparent] "should be protected and promoted to preserve the strong emotional ties that exist between them;" and that the purpose of the document was to make provisions for the continuation of the relationship should [the parties] cease to live together.

190 N.C.App. at 224, 660 S.E.2d at 67–68. As such, the natural parent created along with the nonparent a family unit in which the two acted as parents, shared decision-making authority with the nonparent, and manifested an intent that the arrangement exist indefinitely.

The Court of Appeals recognized that the degree of custody relinquishment in *Mason* differed from that in *Price. Id.* at 225, 660 S.E.2d at 68. In *Price,* though there remained a factual issue regarding whether the relinquishment was intended to be only temporary, the natural parent completely relinquished custody of the child for some period of time. 346 N.C. at 82–83, 484 S.E.2d at 536–37. In *Mason,* on the other hand, the natural parent did not completely relinquish custody. 190 N.C.App. at 225, 660 S.E.2d at 68. However, the natural parent in *Mason* did completely relinquish her paramount parental right to make decisions regarding her child by voluntarily "sharing decision-making" authority with the nonparent. *Id.* at 225, 660 S.E.2d at 68–69. After observing this difference in degree, the Court of Appeals explained, and we think rightly so, that the similarity in both cases is that if a parent cedes paramount decision-making authority, then, so long as he or she creates no expectation that the arrangement is for only a temporary period, that parent has acted inconsistently with his or her paramount parental status. *See id.* at 225–28, 660 S.E.2d at 68–70.

The record in the case *sub judice* indicates that defendant intentionally and voluntarily created a family unit in which plaintiff was intended to act—and acted—as a parent. The parties jointly decided to bring a child into their relationship, worked together to conceive a child, chose the child's first name together, and gave the child a last name that "is a hyphenated name composed of both parties' last names." The parties also publicly held themselves out as the child's parents at a baptismal ceremony and to their respective families. The record also contains ample evidence that defendant allowed plaintiff and the minor child to develop a parental relationship. Defendant even "agrees that [plaintiff] . . . is and has been a good parent."

Moreover, the record indicates that defendant created no expectation that this family unit was only temporary. Most notably, defendant consented to the proceeding before the adoption court relating to her child. As defendant envisioned, the adoption would have resulted in her child having "two legal parents, myself and [plaintiff]." In asking the adoption court to create such a relationship, defendant represented that she and plaintiff "have raised the [minor child] since his birth and have jointly and equally provide[d] said child with care, support and nurturing throughout his life." Defendant explained to the adoption court that she "intends and desires to co-parent with another adult who has agreed to adopt a child and share parental responsibilities." Thus, defendant shared parental responsibilities with plaintiff and, when occurring in the family unit defendant created without any expectation of termination, acted inconsistently with her paramount parental status. The record contains clear and convincing evidence in support of that conclusion.

The Court of Appeals erred in determining that the adoption decree at issue in this case is valid. We hold that the decree is void *ab initio* and that plaintiff is not a legally recognized parent of the minor child. However, because defendant has acted inconsistently with her paramount parental status, the trial court did not err by employing the "best interest of the child" standard to reach its custody decision. Thus, we reverse the Court of Appeals' decision regarding the validity of the adoption decree and affirm as modified its conclusion leaving undisturbed the trial court's custody award. We remand this case to the Court of Appeals for further remand to the trial court for actions not inconsistent with this opinion.

MODIFIED AND AFFIRMED IN PART; REVERSED IN PART AND REMANDED.

JUSTICE TIMMONS-GOODSON dissenting.

> [A]fter the final order of adoption is entered, no party to an adoption proceeding nor anyone claiming under such a party may question the

validity of the adoption because of any defect or irregularity, *jurisdictional or otherwise,* in the proceeding, but shall be fully bound by the order.

N.C.G.S. § 48–2–607(a) (2009) (emphasis added).

Because Melissa Ann Jarrell is statutorily barred from challenging the adoption decree, I dissent.

The legislature identified two narrow situations when challenges are allowed, and neither permits Jarrell's challenge. *Id.* First, Jarrell did not appeal within thirty days of the final adoption decree. *Id.* § 48–2–607(b) (2009). Second, she failed to move to set aside the decree within six months of a discovery that her consent to the adoption was obtained by fraud or duress. *Id.* § 48–2–607(c) (2009). Instead, Jarrell challenged the adoption nearly two years after entry of the final adoption decree. This she cannot do. The plain language of N.C.G.S. § 48–2–607(a) bars her claim.

This Court must respect the statutory limitations imposed by the legislature and should not reach substantive issues not before it. The legislature determined it to be in the best interest of minors that adoptions be final, *see id.* §§ 48–1–100(b)(1) (2009), 48–2–607(a), and allowed challenges in narrow circumstances, none of which are satisfied in this case. The wisdom of these restrictions to adoption challenges is an issue for the legislature to decide, not this Court. And if the members of our General Assembly wish to modify these restrictions, it is their prerogative and role to do so.

JUSTICE HUDSON dissenting.

Today a majority of this Court acts contrary to explicit statutory language and legislative intent in order to achieve this outcome. Because I am not willing to read into statutes language that simply is not there, I dissent.

By its unambiguous language, the General Assembly has emphasized the overriding legislative goals of promoting the finality of adoptions and making primary the best interests of the child when construing Chapter 48. N.C.G.S. § 48–1–100 (2009). To that end, a final adoption decree that was not appealed may be set aside at a date as late as the one here only if the natural parent shows by clear and convincing evidence within six months of the reasonable date of discovery that his or her consent was obtained by fraud or duress. *Id.* § 48–2–607(c) (2009). Defendant Melissa Ann Jarrell has made no such allegations, and indeed, the record plainly shows her active, informed, and voluntary consent to plaintiff Julia Boseman's adoption of the minor child. As such, defendant can present no serious argument that any provision in Chapter 48 would authorize a court to set aside the adoption after the passage of so much time.

Instead, defendant contends that the adoption is void *ab initio,* despite conceding that the jurisdictional requirements set forth in N.C.G.S. § 48–2–100 were fully satisfied here. According to defendant, in reasoning largely adopted by the majority opinion, the trial court stripped itself of subject matter jurisdiction by exceeding its statutory authority under Chapter 48 when it allowed defendant to waive the provisions in N.C.G.S. § 48–1–106(c) (stating that a legal effect of an adoption decree is to sever the relationship between the adoptee and his natural parents) and § 48–3–606(9) (requiring the natural parent's consent to include a recognition that the adoption decree will terminate all parental rights with respect to the minor child). Defendant offers no authority for this approach to subject matter jurisdiction, and I have found none. Instead, the majority opinion today creates an entirely new formulation of the law of subject matter jurisdiction.

The underlying premise of the majority's holding, that the trial court was not authorized under Chapter 48 to waive the provisions of N.C.G.S. § 48–1–106(c) and § 48–3–606(9) concerning termination of defendant's parental rights, at most could amount to an error of law. Our case law makes clear that any such error would neither divest the trial court of, nor even implicate, its subject matter jurisdiction or authority to grant the relief sought by the parties, namely, plaintiff's adoption of the minor child. As such, I conclude that the adoption decree was not void, but merely voidable and subject to the statutory time limits for appeal. Because this challenge is time-barred, I would affirm the Court of Appeals.

When outlining the general adoption procedure in Chapter 48, the General Assembly specifically included a section titled "Jurisdiction," which states in pertinent part:

> (b) Except as provided in subsection (c) of this section, *jurisdiction over adoption proceedings commenced under this Chapter exists* if, at the commencement of the proceeding:
>
>> (1) The adoptee has lived in this State for at least the six consecutive months immediately preceding the filing of the petition or from birth, and the prospective adoptive parent is domiciled in this State; or
>>
>> (2) The prospective adoptive parent has lived in or been domiciled in this State for at least the six consecutive months immediately preceding the filing of the petition.

Id. § 48–2–100 (2005) (emphasis added). These are the only statutory requirements before a North Carolina court may exercise jurisdiction over adoption proceedings. Here the trial court found as fact, properly affirmed by the Court of Appeals, that plaintiff, defendant, and the minor child all fulfilled the North Carolina residency requirements necessary to establish the trial court's subject matter jurisdiction over the adoption under N.C.G.S. § 48–2–100. No party disputes that these statutory requirements were met, or challenges the trial court's personal jurisdiction over the parties.

The majority acknowledges that the General Assembly specifically enacted a section in Chapter 48 entitled "Jurisdiction" and that those requirements were fully met here. The majority then reads into that section an additional requirement that does not actually appear in Chapter 48, to wit: that the trial court may not enter an order waiving certain statutory provisions. Based upon this new requirement, the majority then determines that the district court divested itself of jurisdiction by entering such an order, even though the statutory requirements for jurisdiction were satisfied. As such, reasons the majority, this adoption decree is void *ab initio* rather than potentially voidable for error. This new approach to subject matter jurisdiction—to ignore the statutory requisites and instead create our own—runs counter to the language of N.C.G.S. § 48–2–100, and decades of jurisprudence on subject matter jurisdiction. Indeed, had the General Assembly intended such a requirement, the "Jurisdiction" section makes obvious that legislators are more than capable of drafting it.

The Court's holding today implies that a court may be stripped of subject matter jurisdiction by its own action, a conclusion inconsistent with long-standing case law:

> Once the jurisdiction of a court ... attaches, the general rule is that it will not be ousted by subsequent events.... Jurisdiction is not a light bulb which can be turned off or on during the course of the trial. Once a court acquires jurisdiction over an action it retains jurisdiction over that action throughout the proceeding.... If the converse of this were true, it would be within the power of the defendant to preserve or destroy jurisdiction of the court at his own whim.

See In re Peoples, 296 N.C. 109, 146, 250 S.E.2d 890, 911 (1978) (third alteration in original) (citations and internal quotation marks omitted), *cert. denied,* 442 U.S. 929, 99 S.Ct. 2859, 61 L.Ed.2d 297 (1979). Moreover, if the trial court lacked jurisdiction *ab initio,* then the order defendant now uses to challenge the validity of the adoption must itself be void and of no effect. As such, that order could not serve as the basis for successfully challenging the jurisdiction of the court. In holding that the order does so serve, the majority adopts circular reasoning and has allowed this defendant to "destroy jurisdiction of the court at [her] own whim," by asking the district court to enter the order she now claims deprived it of jurisdiction. *Id.*

In my view, defendant's arguments that the adoption is void *ab initio,* making it "a nullity [which] may be attacked either directly or collaterally," *State v. Sams,* 317 N.C. 230, 235, 345 S.E.2d 179, 182 (1986) (citations omitted), must necessarily fail in light of the long-established rule that "[a]n order is void *ab initio* only when it is issued by a court that does not have jurisdiction," *id.*; *see also Travis v. Johnston,* 244 N.C. 713, 719–20, 95 S.E.2d 94, 99 (1956) ("To have validity a judgment must be rendered by a court which has authority to hear and determine the questions in dispute and control over the parties to the controversy or their interest in the property which is the subject matter of the controversy. When these tests are met, the judgment rendered by the court is not void." (citations omitted)).

A judgment is not rendered void *ab initio,* nor is a trial court divested of subject matter jurisdiction or authority to enter a judgment, because of a failure to follow proper procedure or even because of an error of law. *See Ellis v. Ellis,* 190 N.C. 418, 422, 130 S.E. 7, 9 (1925) (noting "the established principle that where the court has jurisdiction of both the subject-matter and the parties and acts within its power, the binding force and effect of a judgment is not impaired because the same has been erroneously allowed, though the error may be undoubted and apparent on the face of the record" (citations omitted)); *Peoples v. Norwood,* 94 N.C. 167, 172 (1886) ("[W]hen the parties are voluntarily before the [c]ourt, and ... a judgment is entered in favor of one party and against another, such judgment is valid, although not granted according to the orderly course of procedure." (citations omitted)).

While a void judgment "is in legal effect no judgment," as "[i]t neither binds nor bars any one, and all proceedings founded upon it are worthless," *Hart v. Thomasville Motors, Inc.,* 244 N.C. 84, 90, 92 S.E.2d 673, 678 (1956) (citation and quotation marks omitted), "[a]n erroneous judgment should be corrected by appeal or *certiorari,*" *Ellis,* 190 N.C. at 422, 130 S.E. at 9; *see also Daniels v. Montgomery Mut. Ins. Co.,* 320 N.C. 669, 676, 360 S.E.2d 772, 777 (1987) (" 'An irregular order, one issued contrary to the method of practice and procedure established by law, is voidable.' ... An erroneous order may be remedied by appeal; it may not be attacked collaterally." (citations omitted)); *Worthington v. Wooten,* 242 N.C. 88, 92, 86 S.E.2d 767, 770 (1955) (stating that a judgment, "even if irregular or even erroneous was binding on the parties, unless set aside or reversed on appeal ... provided the court had jurisdiction of the person and the subject matter." (citations omitted)); *see also Sawyer v. Slack,* 196 N.C. 697, 146 S.E. 864 (1929) (holding that, partly because of the strong public policy in favor of marriage and maintaining familial relationships and rights, the marriage of an underage female without the parental consent required by statute was not void but voidable).

The time limits for appeal or challenge to this adoption must be read in accordance with the General Assembly's forceful statement of legislative intent in the opening section of Chapter 48, notably not mentioned in the majority opinion:

> **Legislative findings and intent; construction of Chapter**
>
> (a) The General Assembly finds that it is in the public interest to establish a clear judicial process for adoptions, *to promote the integrity and finality of adoptions, to encourage prompt, conclusive disposition of adoption proceedings,* and to structure services to adopted children, biological parents, and adoptive parents that will provide for the needs and protect the interests of all parties to an adoption, particularly adopted minors.

(b) With special regard for the adoption of minors, the General Assembly declares as a matter of legislative policy that:

(1) The *primary purpose* of this Chapter is to advance the welfare of minors by (i) *protecting minors from unnecessary separation from their original parents,* (ii) facilitating the adoption of minors in need of adoptive placement by persons who can give them love, care, security, and support, (iii) protecting minors from placement with adoptive parents unfit to have responsibility for their care and rearing, and (iv) *assuring the finality of the adoption;* and

(2) Secondary purposes of this Chapter are (i) to protect biological parents from ill-advised decisions to relinquish a child or consent to the child's adoption, (ii) to protect adoptive parents from assuming responsibility for a child about whose heredity or mental or physical condition they know nothing, (iii) to protect the privacy of the parties to the adoption, and (iv) to discourage unlawful trafficking in minors and other unlawful placement activities.

N.C.G.S. § 48–1–100 (emphases added); *see also In re Adoption of Anderson,* 360 N.C. 271, 275–76, 624 S.E.2d 626, 628 (2006) (noting that "the General Assembly recognized the public interest in establishing a clear judicial process for adoptions" and "promoting the integrity and finality of adoptions" (citation, internal quotation marks, and brackets omitted)).

Consistent with its legislative intent "to establish a clear judicial process for adoptions," including the "prompt, conclusive disposition of adoption proceedings," *id.* § 48–1–100(a), and its primary purpose of "assuring the finality of" adoptions, *id.* § 48–1–100(b)(1), the General Assembly mandated carefully delineated time limits and circumstances for appeals or challenges to a final adoption. Direct appeal of an adoption decree entered by a district court judge is allowed if filed within thirty days after the adoption becomes final, *id.* § 48–2–607(b) (2009), or within six months of the time a natural parent's consent or relinquishment "was obtained" or "ought reasonably to have been discovered" to have been obtained "by fraud or duress," *id.* § 48–2–607(c). A natural parent may also revoke his or her consent within seven days of a consent to adoption, *id.* § 48–3–608(a) (2009), or within five days after receipt of a preplacement assessment in a direct placement adoption, *id.* § 48–3–608(b) (2009). A consent is void if clear and convincing evidence establishes that it was obtained by fraud or duress, or if the parties mutually agree to set it aside, if the petition to adopt is voluntarily dismissed with prejudice, or if the court dismisses the petition to adopt and either no appeal is taken or the dismissal is affirmed on appeal and all appeals have been exhausted. *Id.* § 48–3–609(a) (2009).

Outside these specific situations, however, the General Assembly explicitly prohibits any challenge after a final order of adoption is entered. Through the unequivocal language of the section of Chapter 48 titled

"Appeals," the legislature has established its preference for the finality of adoptions over correcting procedural irregularities:

> (a) Except as provided in subsections (b) and (c) of this section, *after the final order of adoption is entered, no party to an adoption proceeding nor anyone claiming under such a party may question the validity of the adoption because of any defect or irregularity, jurisdictional or otherwise, in the proceeding, but shall be fully bound by the order.* No adoption may be attacked either directly or collaterally because of any procedural or other defect by anyone who was not a party to the adoption. The failure on the part of the court or an agency to perform duties or acts within the time required by the provisions of this Chapter shall not affect the validity of any adoption proceeding.

Id. § 48–2–607(a) (2009) (emphasis added).[5] This strong preference is further evidenced in provisions that sanction final adoption decrees despite omissions of required information and vesting courts with a certain degree of leeway to determine compliance with statutory requirements. *See, e.g., id.* § 48–2–306(b) (2009) ("After entry of a decree of adoption, omission of any information required [to be in the adoption petition, including consent and/or relinquishments] by G.S. 48–2–304 and G.S. 48–2–305 *does not invalidate the decree.*" (emphasis added)); *id.* § 48–2–603(a)(4) (2009) (providing that, at the hearing on or disposition of a petition to adopt, the court must find that "[e]ach necessary consent, relinquishment, waiver, or judicial order terminating parental rights, has been obtained and filed ... and the time for revocation has expired").

Here, despite the passage of so much time, defendant would have us invalidate the adoption decree, even though she expressly consented to any irregularity, and even though taking such action is contrary to statutory language prioritizing finality over strict procedural compliance. Defendant first sought to challenge plaintiff's adoption of the minor child in a custody proceeding in May 2007, nearly two years after the final adoption decree was entered in August 2005, and well after expiration of the time limits for an appeal specified in N.C.G.S. § 48–2–607. The waivers she now disclaims should fall squarely within the General Assembly's prohibition against untimely appeals claiming "any defect or irregularity, jurisdictional or otherwise." *Id.* § 48–2–607(a). Nothing in the statutory language itself supports defendant's position, or the majority's

---

5. Citing to, but not quoting, this statute, the majority maintains that "the legislature's words 'no party,' 'defect' and 'irregularity' indicate that this statute is designed to foreclose 'waivable' challenges in a court with subject matter jurisdiction." I reiterate that statement here, while including the actual statutory language, to highlight that the majority must necessarily read words (at least the word "waivable") into N.C.G.S. § 48–2–607, while ignoring the words "any" and "fully bound," as well as the lack of a qualifier for "jurisdictional," in order to reach its interpretation of this purported legislative intent.

This approach is at odds with the majority's reliance on *In re D.L.H.*, which states the maxim that when a statute is clear and unambiguous, "there is no room for judicial construction and the courts must give the statute its plain and definite meaning, and are without power to interpolate, or superimpose, provisions and limitations not contained therein." 364 N.C. 214, 221, 694 S.E.2d 753, 757 (2010) (citation omitted).

endorsement of it. Rather, such a holding is contrary to the unequivocally stated primary legislative goal of assuring the finality of adoptions.[6]

The holding here likewise runs afoul of the General Assembly's categorical directive that Chapter 48 be construed in a manner to ensure that "the needs, interests, and rights of minor adoptees are *primary.*" N.C.G.S. § 48–1–100(c) (emphasis added). Moreover, the legislature has instructed that "[a]ny conflict between the interests of a minor adoptee and those of an adult *shall be resolved in favor of the minor,*" *id.* (emphasis added), and Chapter 48 should be "liberally construed and applied to promote its underlying purposes and policies," N.C.G.S. § 48–1–100(d), such as "the integrity and finality of adoptions" and the "prompt, conclusive disposition of adoption proceedings," *id.* § 48–1–100(a).

These provisions are plain and unambiguous, and appear in statutory text. By contrast, there is neither an explicit prohibition against, nor an explicit authorization of, the waivers at issue here. In the absence of any statutory language indicating legislative intent regarding these waivers, we must be guided by the legislative priorities we do know and thus act to safeguard the best interests of this child by barring this late challenge and promoting the finality of this adoption. Reading into Chapter 48 a jurisdictional requirement that is not there, the majority overlooks the interests of this child and promotes defendant's rights over those of the child, in direct contravention of the law as written.

CONCLUSION

The majority decision here is at odds with the timetables and express intent of Chapter 48, as well as prior case law on the finality of adoptions. I would hold that at all pertinent times the trial court had jurisdiction, that this appeal is time-barred, and that the adoption decree must stand. Accordingly, I would affirm the Court of Appeals.

DISCUSSION

1. *Was this ruling a good or bad one for same-sex couples in North Carolina?*

2. *In* Boseman, *Justice Newby mentions that this type of adoption had been allowed for some time in Durham County. What is the effect of this opinion on other adoptions that previously took place in the county?*

3. *Does Justice Hudson make convincing arguments in her dissent that the adoption should have been upheld? How does her dissent differ from the dissent written by Justice Timmons–Goodson?*

---

6. I note as well that this Court has previously considered, and rejected, untimely challenges to final adoption decrees that assert the decree is void for lack of jurisdiction. See Hicks v. Russell, 256 N.C. 34, 40–41, 123 S.E.2d 214, 219 (1961); see also Fakhoury v. Fakhoury, 171 N.C.App. 104, 613 S.E.2d 729 (rejecting as irrelevant due to the un-timeliness of the appeal the argument that "public policy opposes a stepparent adoption when the stepparent, at the time of filing the petition for adoption, does not intend to stay in the marriage with the legal parent"), disc. rev. denied, 360 N.C. 62, 621 S.E.2d 622 (2005).

NOTE

For an in-depth discussion of the decision of the North Carolina Court of Appeals in *Boseman*, see Lavelle, *North Carolina's Continuing Assignment of Responsibility for its Children: Boseman v. Jarrell*, 2 Charlotte L. Rev. 479 (Fall 2010). In the article, Professor Lavelle discusses efforts by the North Carolina legislature and courts to establish responsibility for children of the state by parties in parental roles. She also compares the North Carolina adoption statute with those of similarly situated states.

LOFTON v. SECRETARY OF THE DEP'T OF CHILDREN & FAMILY SERVS.

358 F.3d 804 (11th Cir. 2004)

SUBSEQUENT HISTORY: *Rehearing*, en banc, *denied by Lofton v. Sec'y of the Dep't of Children & Family Servs.*, 377 F.3d 1275, 2004 U.S. App. LEXIS 15056 (11th Cir. Fla., 2004)

US Supreme Court *certiorari denied by*, *Motion granted by Lofton v. Sec'y*, 2005 U.S. LEXIS 285 (U.S., Jan. 10, 2005)

JUDGES: Before BIRCH, CARNES and HUG*, CIRCUIT JUDGES.

OPINION: BIRCH, CIRCUIT JUDGE

In this appeal, we decide the states' rights issue of whether *Florida Statute § 63.042(3)*, which prevents adoption by practicing homosexuals, is constitutional as enacted by the Florida legislature and as subsequently enforced. The district court granted summary judgment to Florida over an equal protection and due process challenge by homosexual persons desiring to adopt. We AFFIRM.

I. BACKGROUND

A. The Challenged Florida Statute

Since 1977, Florida's adoption law has contained a codified prohibition on adoption by any "homosexual" person. 1977 Fla. Laws, ch. 77–140, § 1, Fla. Stat. § 63.042(3) (2002). For purposes of this statute, Florida courts have defined the term "homosexual" as being "limited to applicants who are known to engage in current, voluntary homosexual activity," thus drawing "a distinction between homosexual orientation and homosexual activity." *Fla. Dep't of Health & Rehab. Servs. v. Cox*, 627 So.2d 1210, 1215 (Fla. Dist. Ct. App. 1993), *aff'd in relevant part*, 656 So.2d 902, 903 (Fla. 1995). ... To date, no attempt to overturn the provision has succeeded. We now consider the most recent challenge to the statute.

B. The Litigants

... Steven Lofton, is a registered pediatric nurse who has raised from infancy three Florida foster children, each of whom tested positive for HIV

* Honorable Procter Hug, Jr., United States Circuit Judge for the Ninth Circuit, sitting by designation.

at birth. By all accounts, Lofton's efforts in caring for these children have been exemplary, and his story has been chronicled in dozens of news stories and editorials as well as on national television. We confine our discussion of that story to those facts relevant to the legal issues before us and properly before us in the record. John Doe, also named as a plaintiff-appellant in this litigation, was born on 29 April 1991. Testing positive at birth for HIV and cocaine, Doe immediately entered the Florida foster care system. Shortly thereafter, Children's Home Society, a private agency, placed Doe in foster care with Lofton, who has extensive experience treating HIV patients. At eighteen months, Doe sero-reverted and has since tested HIV negative. In September of 1994, Lofton filed an application to adopt Doe but refused to answer the application's inquiry about his sexual preference and also failed to disclose Roger Croteau, his cohabitating partner, as a member of his household. After Lofton refused requests from the Department of Children and Families ("DCF") to supply the missing information, his application was rejected pursuant to the homosexual adoption provision.... [Plaintiff-appellants Douglas E. Houghton, Jr., Wayne Lame Smith and Daniel Skahen joined Lofton in this action.]

C. Procedural History

Appellants filed suit in the United States District Court for the Southern District of Florida and named as defendants Kathleen A. Kearney and Charles Auslander in their respective official capacities as DCF Secretary and DCF District Administrator for Dade and Monroe Counties. Their complaint alleged that the statute violates appellants' fundamental rights and the principles of equal protection. Jointly, appellants asked the district court to declare Fla. Stat. § 63.042(3) unconstitutional and to enjoin its enforcement. Appellants also sought class certification on behalf of two purported classes: all similarly situated adults and all similarly situated children. The district court denied the request for class certification and granted summary judgment in favor of the state on all counts, thereby upholding the statute. It is from this judgment that appellants now appeal.

Appellants assert three constitutional arguments on appeal. First, appellants argue that the statute violates Lofton, Houghton, Doe, and Roe's rights to familial privacy, intimate association, and family integrity under the Due Process Clause of the Fourteenth Amendment. Second, appellants argue that the Supreme Court's recent decision in *Lawrence v. Texas*, 539 U.S. 558, 123 S.Ct. 2472, 156 L.Ed.2d 508 (2003), recognized a fundamental right to private sexual intimacy and that the Florida statute, by disallowing adoption by individuals who engage in homosexual activity, impermissibly burdens the exercise of this right. Third, appellants allege that, by categorically prohibiting only homosexual persons from adopting children, the statute violates the Equal Protection Clause of the Fourteenth Amendment. Each of these challenges raises questions of first impression in this circuit.

II. DISCUSSION

. . .

B. *Florida's Adoption Scheme*

Appellants' challenge cannot be viewed apart from the context in which it arises. Under Florida law, "adoption is not a right; it is a statutory privilege." *Cox*, 627 So.2d at 1216. Unlike biological parentage, which precedes and transcends formal recognition by the state, adoption is wholly a creature of the state. *Cf. Smith v. Org. of Foster Families for Equal. & Reform*, 431 U.S. 816, 845, 97 S.Ct. 2094, 2110, 53 L.Ed.2d 14 (1977) (noting that, unlike the natural family, which has "its origins entirely apart from the power of the State," the foster parent-child relationship "has its source in state law and contractual arrangements"); *Lindley v. Sullivan*, 889 F.2d 124, 131 (7th Cir. 1989) ("Because of its statutory basis, adoption differs from natural procreation in a most important and striking way.").

In formulating its adoption policies and procedures, the State of Florida acts in the protective and provisional role of in loco parentis for those children who, because of various circumstances, have become wards of the state. Thus, adoption law is unlike criminal law, for example, where the paramount substantive concern is not intruding on individuals' liberty interests, *see, e.g., Lawrence*, 539 U.S. 558, 156 L.Ed.2d 508, 123 S.Ct. 2472; *Roe v. Wade*, 410 U.S. 113, 93 S.Ct. 705, 35 L.Ed.2d 147 (1973), and the paramount procedural imperative is ensuring due process and fairness, *see, e.g., Strickland v. Washington*, 466 U.S. 668, 104 S.Ct. 2052, 80 L.Ed.2d 674 (1984); *Miranda v. Arizona*, 384 U.S. 436, 86 S.Ct. 1602,16 L.Ed.2d 694 (1966); *Gideon v. Wainwright*, 372 U.S. 335, 83 S.Ct. 792, 9 L.Ed.2d 799 (1963). Adoption is also distinct from such contexts as government-benefit eligibility schemes or access to a public forum, where equality of treatment is the primary concern. *See, e.g., Rosenberger v. Rector & Visitors of Univ. of Va.*, 515 U.S. 819, 115 S.Ct. 2510, 132 L.Ed.2d 700 (1995); *Adarand Constructors, Inc. v. Pena*, 515 U.S. 200, 115 S.Ct. 2097, 132 L.Ed.2d 158 (1995). By contrast, in the adoption context, the state's overriding interest is the best interests of the children whom it is seeking to place with adoptive families. *In re Adoption of H.Y.T.*, 458 So.2d 1127, 1128 (Fla. 1984)(noting that, in Florida adoption proceedings, "the court's primary duty is to serve the best interests of the child—the object of the proceeding"). Florida, acting parens patriae for children who have lost their natural parents, bears the high duty of determining what adoptive home environments will best serve all aspects of the child's growth and development.

Because of the primacy of the welfare of the child, the state can make classifications for adoption purposes that would be constitutionally suspect in many other arenas. For example, Florida law requires that, in order to adopt any child other than a special needs child, an individual's primary residence and place of employment must be located in Florida. Fla. Stat.

§ 63.185. In screening adoption applicants, Florida considers such factors as physical and mental health, income and financial status, duration of marriage, housing, and neighborhood, among others. Fla. Admin. Code Ann. r. 65C–16.005(3) (2003). Similarly, Florida gives preference to candidates who demonstrate a commitment to "value, respect, appreciate, and educate the child regarding his or her racial and ethnic heritage." *Id.* Moreover, prospective adoptive parents are required to sign an affidavit of good moral character. *Id.* Many of these preferences and requirements, if employed outside the adoption arena, would be unlikely to withstand constitutional scrutiny. *See, e.g., Troxel v. Granville*, 530 U.S. 57, 68, 120 S.Ct. 2054, 2061, 147 L.Ed.2d 49 (2000) (recognizing that, absent neglect or abuse, the state may not "inject itself into the private realm of the family to further question the ability of that parent to make the best decisions concerning the rearing of that parent's children"); *Supreme Court of Va. v. Friedman*, 487 U.S. 59, 70, 108 S.Ct. 2260, 2267, 101 L.Ed.2d 56 (1988) (invalidating as unconstitutional Virginia's residency requirement for waive-in admission to the state bar).

The decision to adopt a child is not a private one, but a public act. *Cox*, 627 So.2d at 1216. At a minimum, would-be adoptive parents are asking the state to confer official recognition—and, consequently, the highest level of constitutional insulation from subsequent state interference, *see Troxel*, 530 U.S. at 65, 120 S. Ct. at 2060—on a relationship where there exists no natural filial bond. In many cases, they also are asking the state to entrust into their permanent care a child for whom the state is currently serving as in loco parentis. In doing so, these prospective adoptive parents are electing to open their homes and their private lives to close scrutiny by the state. Florida's adoption application requires information on a variety of private matters, including an applicant's physical and psychiatric medical history, previous marriages, arrest record, financial status, and educational history. In this regard, Florida's adoption scheme is like any "complex social welfare system that necessarily deals with the intimacies of family life." *Bowen v. Gilliard*, 483 U.S. 587, 602, 107 S.Ct. 3008, 3017–18, 97 L.Ed.2d 485 (1987) (quoting *Califano v. Jobst*, 434 U.S. 47, 55 n.11, 98 S.Ct. 95, 100 n.11, 54 L.Ed.2d 228 (1977)). Accordingly, such intrusions into private family matters are on a different constitutional plane than those that "seek[] to foist orthodoxy on the unwilling by banning or criminally prosecuting" nonconformity. *Califano*, 434 U.S. at 55 n.11, 98 S. Ct. at 100 n.11; *cf. Lindley*, 889 F.2d at 131 (declining to find a privacy interest in adopting a child because state law "requires adopters to submit their personal lives to intensive scrutiny before the adoption may be approved").

In short, a person who seeks to adopt is asking the state to conduct an examination into his or her background and to make a determination as to the best interests of a child in need of adoption. In doing so, the state's overriding interest is not providing individuals the opportunity to become parents, but rather identifying those individuals whom it deems most capable of parenting adoptive children and providing them with a secure family environment. Indicative of the strength of the state's interest—indeed duty—in this context is the fact that appellants have not cited to us, nor have we found, a single precedent in which the Supreme Court or one of our sister circuits has sustained a constitutional challenge to an adoption scheme or practice by any individual other than a natural parent, and even many challenges by natural parents have failed. *See, e.g.*, *Lehr v. Robertson*, 463 U.S. 248, 103 S.Ct. 2985, 77 L.Ed.2d 614 (1983); *Quilloin v. Walcott*, 434 U.S. 246, 98 S.Ct. 549, 54 L.Ed.2d 511 (1978). Of course, despite their highly sensitive nature, adoption schemes are by no means immune from constitutional scrutiny, and we now consider the constitutionality of the Florida statute. *See, e.g.*, *Caban v. Mohammed*, 441 U.S. 380, 99 S.Ct. 1760, 60 L.Ed.2d 297 (1979) (invalidating on equal protection grounds a state law permitting unwed mothers, but not unwed fathers, to block adoption of their child simply by withholding consent).

C. Appellants' Due Process Challenges

1. Fundamental Right to "Family Integrity"

Neither party disputes that there is no fundamental right to adopt, nor any fundamental right to be adopted. R4–124 at 10 (Joint Pre-trial Stipulation); *see also Mullins v. Oregon*, 57 F.3d 789, 794 (9th Cir. 1995) ("Whatever claim a prospective adoptive parent may have to a child, we are certain that it does not rise to the level of a fundamental liberty interest."); *Lindley*, 889 F.2d at 131 ("We are constrained to conclude that there is no fundamental right to adopt."). Both parties likewise agree that adoption is a privilege created by statute and not by common law. R4–124 at 10. Because there is no fundamental right to adopt or to be adopted, it follows that there can be no fundamental right to apply for adoption.

Nevertheless, appellants argue that, by prohibiting homosexual adoption, the state is refusing to recognize and protect constitutionally protected parent-child relationships between Lofton and Doe and between Houghton and Roe. Noting that the Supreme Court has identified "the interest of parents in the care, custody, and control of their children" as "perhaps the oldest of the fundamental liberty interests recognized by this Court," *Troxel*, 530 U.S. at 65, 120 S. Ct. at 2060, appellants argue that they are entitled to a similar constitutional liberty interest because they share deeply loving emotional bonds that are as close as those between a natural parent and child. They further contend that this liberty interest is significantly burdened by the Florida statute, which prevents them from obtaining permanency in their relationships and creates uncertainty about the future integrity of their families. Only by being given the opportunity to adopt, appellants assert, will they be able to protect their alleged right to "family integrity."

Although the text of the Constitution contains no reference to familial or parental rights, Supreme Court precedent has long recognized that "the Due Process Clause of the Fourteenth Amendment protects the fundamental right of parents to make decisions concerning the care, custody, and control of their children." *Id.* at 66, 120 S. Ct. at 2060. A corollary to this right is the "private realm of family life which the state cannot enter that has been afforded both substantive and procedural protection." *Smith v. Org. of Foster Families for Equal. & Reform*, 431 U.S. 816, 842, 97 S.Ct. 2094, 2108, 53 L.Ed.2d 14 (1977) (internal citation and quotation marks omitted). Historically, the Court's family—and parental—rights holdings have involved biological families *See, e.g., Troxel*, 530 U.S. 57, 120 S.Ct. 2054, 147 L.Ed.2d 49 (2000); *Wisconsin v. Yoder*, 406 U.S. 205, 92 S.Ct. 1526, 32 L.Ed.2d 15 (1972); *Stanley v. Illinois*, 405 U.S. 645, 92 S.Ct. 1208, 31 L.Ed.2d 551 (1972); *Pierce v. Soc'y of Sisters*, 268 U.S. 510, 45 S.Ct. 571, 69 L.Ed. 1070 (1925); *Meyer v. Nebraska*, 262 U.S. 390, 43 S.Ct. 625, 67 L.Ed. 1042 (1923). The Court itself has noted that "the usual understanding of 'family' implies biological relationships, and most decisions treating the relation between parent and child have stressed this element." *Smith*, 431 U.S. at 843, 97 S. Ct. at 2109. Appellants, however, seize on a few lines of dicta from Smith, in which the Court acknowledged that "biological relationships are not [the] exclusive determination of the existence of a family," *id.*, and noted that "adoption, for instance, is recognized as the legal equivalent of biological parenthood," *id.* at 844 n.51, 97 S. Ct. at 2109 & n.51. Extrapolating from Smith, appellants argue that parental and familial rights should be extended to individuals such as foster parents and legal guardians and that the touchstone of this liberty interest is not biological ties or official legal recognition, but the emotional bond that develops between and among individuals as a result of shared daily life.

We do not read *Smith* so broadly. In Smith, the Court considered whether the appellee foster families possessed a constitutional liberty interest in "the integrity of their family unit" such that the state could not disrupt the families without procedural due process. *Id.* at 842, 97 S. Ct. at 2108. Although the Court found it unnecessary to resolve that question, Justice Brennan, writing for the majority, did note that the importance of familial relationships stems not merely from blood relationships, but also from "the emotional attachments that derive from the intimacy of daily association." *Id.* at 844, 97 S. Ct. at 2109. The Smith Court went on, however, to discuss the "important distinctions between the foster family and the natural family," particularly the fact that foster families have their genesis in state law. *Id.* at 845, 97 S. Ct. at 2110. The Court stressed that the parameters of whatever potential liberty interest such families might possess would be defined by state law and the justifiable expectations it created....

Here, we find that under Florida law neither a foster parent nor a legal guardian could have a justifiable expectation of a permanent relationship with his or her child free from state oversight or intervention. Under Florida law, foster care is designed to be a short-term arrangement while the state attempts to find a permanent adoptive home. For instance, Florida law permits foster care as a "permanency option" only for children at least fourteen years of age, Fla. Stat. § 39.623(1), and DCF may remove a foster child anytime that it believes it to be in the child's best interests, *id.* § 409.165(3)(f). Similarly, legal guardians in Florida are subject to ongoing judicial oversight, including the duty to file annual guardianship reports and annual review by the appointing court, *id.* *§§ 744.361–372*, and can be removed for a wide variety of reasons, *id.* *§ 744.474* (permitting removal of a guardian for such causes as incapacity, illness, substance abuse, conviction of a felony, failure to file annual guardianship reports, and failure to fulfill guardianship education requirements). In both cases, the state is not interfering with natural family units that exist independent of its power, but is regulating ones created by it. Lofton and Houghton entered into relationships to be a foster parent and legal guardian, respectively, with an implicit understanding that these relationships would not be immune from state oversight and would be permitted to continue only upon state approval. The emotional connections between Lofton and his foster child and between Houghton and his ward originate in arrangements that have been subject to state oversight from the outset. We conclude that Lofton, Doe, Houghton, and Roe could have no justifiable expectation of permanency in their relationships. Nor could Lofton and Houghton have developed expectations that they would be allowed to adopt, in light of the adoption provision itself. . . .

2. *Fundamental Right to "Private Sexual Intimacy"*

Laws that burden the exercise of a fundamental right require strict scrutiny and are sustained only if narrowly tailored to further a compelling government interest *See, e.g.*, *Zablocki v. Redhail*, 434 U.S. 374, 388, 98 S.Ct. 673, 682, 54 L.Ed.2d 618 (1978); *Shapiro v. Thompson*, 394 U.S. 618, 634, 89 S.Ct. 1322, 1331, 22 L.Ed.2d 600 (1969). Appellants argue that the Supreme Court's recent decision in *Lawrence v. Texas*, 156 L.Ed.2d 508, 539 U.S. 558, 123 S.Ct. 2472 (2003), which struck down Texas's sodomy statute, identified a hitherto unarticulated fundamental right to private sexual intimacy. They contend that the Florida statute, by disallowing adoption to any individual who chooses to engage in homosexual conduct, impermissibly burdens the exercise of this right.

We begin with the threshold question of whether *Lawrence* identified a new fundamental right to private sexual intimacy. *Lawrence*'s holding was that substantive due process does not permit a state to impose a criminal prohibition on private consensual homosexual conduct. The effect of this holding was to establish a greater respect than previously existed in the law for the right of consenting adults to engage in private sexual conduct. 539 U.S. at 567, 123 S. Ct. at 2478. Nowhere, however, did the Court characterize this right as "fundamental." *Cf. id.* at 586, 123 S. Ct. at 2488 (Scalia, J., dissenting) (observing that "nowhere does the Court's opinion declare that homosexual sodomy is a 'fundamental right' under the Due Process Clause"). Nor did the Court locate this right directly in the Constitution, but instead treated it as the by-product of several different constitutional principles and liberty interests.

We are particularly hesitant to infer a new fundamental liberty interest from an opinion whose language and reasoning are inconsistent with standard fundamental-rights analysis. The Court has noted that it must "exercise the utmost care whenever [it is] asked to break new ground" in the field of fundamental rights, *Washington v. Glucksberg*, 521 U.S. 702, 720, 117 S.Ct. 2258, 2268, 138 L.Ed.2d 772 (1997) (citation omitted), which is precisely what the *Lawrence* petitioners and their amici curiae had asked the Court to do. That the Court declined the invitation is apparent from the absence of the "two primary features" of fundamental-rights analysis in its opinion. *Glucksberg*, 521 U.S. at 720, 117 S. Ct. at 2268. First, the *Lawrence* opinion contains virtually no inquiry into the question of whether the petitioners' asserted right is one of "those fundamental rights and liberties which are, objectively, deeply rooted in this Nation's history and tradition and implicit in the concept of ordered liberty, such that neither liberty nor justice would exist if they were sacrificed." *Id.* at 720–21, 117 S. Ct. at 2268 (internal citations and quotation marks omitted). Second, the opinion notably never provides the " 'careful description' of the asserted fundamental liberty interest" that is to accompany fundamental-rights analysis. *Id.* at 721, 117 S. Ct. at 2268 (citation omitted); *see also Reno v. Flores*, 507 U.S. 292, 302, 113 S.Ct. 1439, 1447, 123 L.Ed.2d 1 (1993) (" 'Substantive due process' analysis must begin with a careful description of the asserted right. . . ."). Rather, the constitutional liberty interests on which the Court relied were invoked, not with "careful description," but with sweeping generality. *See, e.g.*, *Lawrence*, 539 U.S. 558, 123 S.Ct. at 2475 ("Liberty protects the person from unwarranted government intrusions into a dwelling or other private places."); *id.* ("The instant case involves liberty of the person both in its spatial and more transcendent dimensions."); *id.* at 562, 123 S. Ct. at 2475 ("There is a realm of personal liberty which the government may not enter.") (citation omitted). Most significant, however, is the fact that the *Lawrence* Court never applied strict scrutiny, the proper standard when fundamental rights are implicated, but instead invalidated the Texas statute on rational-basis grounds, holding that it "furthers no legitimate state interest which can justify its intrusion into the personal and private life of the individual." *Id.* at 578, 123 S. Ct. at 2484 *see also id.* at 586, 123 S. Ct. at 2488 (Scalia, J., dissenting) (observing that the majority opinion did not "subject the Texas law to the standard of review that would be appropriate (strict scrutiny) if homosexual sodomy *were* a 'fundamental right' ").

We conclude that it is a strained and ultimately incorrect reading of *Lawrence* to interpret it to announce a new fundamental right. Accordingly, we need not resolve the second prong of appellants' fundamental-rights argument: whether exclusion from the statutory privilege of adoption because of appellants' sexual conduct creates an impermissible burden on the exercise of their asserted right to private sexual intimacy. *Cf. Lyng v. Castillo*, 477 U.S. 635, 638, 106 S.Ct. 2727, 2729, 91 L.Ed.2d 527 (1986) (only classifications that " 'directly and substantially' interfere" with a fundamental right constitute an impermissible "burden") (citation omitted).

Moreover, the holding of *Lawrence* does not control the present case. Apart from the shared homosexuality component, there are marked differences in the facts of the two cases. The Court itself stressed the limited factual situation it was addressing in *Lawrence*:

> The present case does not involve minors. It does not involve persons who might be injured or coerced or who are situated in relationships where consent might not easily be refused. It does not involve public conduct or prostitution. It does not involve whether the government must give formal recognition to any relationship that homosexual persons seek to enter. The case does involve two adults who, with full and mutual consent from each other, engaged in sexual practices common to a homosexual lifestyle.

Lawrence, 539 U.S. at 578, 123 S. Ct. at 2484. Here, the involved actors are not only consenting adults, but minors as well. The relevant state action is not criminal prohibition, but grant of a statutory privilege. And the asserted liberty interest is not the negative right to engage in private conduct without facing criminal sanctions, but the affirmative right to receive official and public recognition. Hence, we conclude that the *Lawrence* decision cannot be extrapolated to create a right to adopt for homosexual persons.

D. Appellants' Equal Protection Challenge

. . .

2. Florida's Asserted Rational Bases

Cognizant of the narrow parameters of our review, we now analyze the challenged Florida law. Florida contends that the statute is only one aspect of its broader adoption policy, which is designed to create adoptive homes that resemble the nuclear family as closely as possible. Florida argues that the statute is rationally related to Florida's interest in furthering the best interests of adopted children by placing them in families with married mothers and fathers. Such homes, Florida asserts, provide the stability that marriage affords and the presence of both male and female authority figures, which it considers critical to optimal childhood development and socialization. In particular, Florida emphasizes a vital role that dual-gender parenting plays in shaping sexual and gender identity and in providing heterosexual role modeling. Florida argues that disallowing adoption into homosexual households, which are necessarily motherless or fatherless and lack the stability that comes with marriage, is a rational means of furthering Florida's interest in promoting adoption by marital families.

. . .

It is chiefly from parental figures that children learn about the world and their place in it, and the formative influence of parents extends well beyond the years spent under their roof, shaping their children's psychology, character, and personality for years to come. In time, children grow up to become full members of society, which they in turn influence, whether for good or ill. The adage that "the hand that rocks the cradle rules the world" hardly overstates the ripple effect that parents have on the public good by virtue of their role in raising their children. It is hard to conceive an interest more legitimate and more paramount for the state than promoting an optimal social structure for educating, socializing, and preparing its future citizens to become productive participants in civil society—particularly when those future citizens are displaced children for whom the state is standing in loco parentis.

More importantly for present purposes, the state has a legitimate interest in encouraging this optimal family structure by seeking to place adoptive children in homes that have both a mother and father. Florida argues that its preference for adoptive marital families is based on the premise that the marital family structure is more stable than other household arrangements and that children benefit from the presence of both a father and mother in the home. Given that appellants have offered no competent evidence to the contrary, we find this premise to be one of those "unprovable assumptions" that nevertheless can provide a legitimate basis for legislative action. *Paris Adult Theatre I v. Slaton*, 413 U.S. 49, 62–63, 93 S.Ct. 2628, 2638, 37 L.Ed.2d 446 (1973). . . . [I]t is rational for Florida to conclude that it is in the best interests of adoptive children, many of whom come from troubled and unstable backgrounds, to be placed in a home anchored by both a father and a mother. *Paris Adult Theatre I*, 413 U.S. at 63, 93 S. Ct. at 2638.

3. Appellants' Arguments

Appellants offer little to dispute whether Florida's preference for marital adoptive families is a legitimate state interest. Instead, they maintain that the statute is not rationally related to this interest. Arguing that the statute is both overinclusive and underinclusive, appellants contend that the real motivation behind the statute cannot be the best interest of adoptive children.

In evaluating this argument, we note from the outset that "it is entirely irrelevant for constitutional purposes whether the conceived reason for the challenged distinction actually motivated the legislature." *Beach Communications*, 508 U.S. at 315, 113 S. Ct. at 2102; *see also City of Renton v. Playtime Theatres, Inc.*, 475 U.S. 41, 48, 106 S.Ct. 925, 929, 89 L.Ed.2d 29 (1986) ("It is a familiar principle of constitutional law that this Court will not strike down an otherwise constitutional statute on the basis of an alleged illicit legislative motive.") (citation omitted). Instead, the question before us is whether the Florida legislature *could* have reasonably believed that prohibiting adoption into homosexual environments would further its interest in placing adoptive children in homes that will provide them with optimal developmental conditions. *See Panama City Med. Diagnostic Ltd. v. Williams*, 13 F.3d 1541, 1545 (11th Cir. 1994) ("The task is to determine if any set of facts may be reasonably conceived of to justify the legislation."). Unless appellants' evidence, which we view on summary judgment review in the light most favorable to appellants, can negate every plausible rational connection between the statute and Florida's interest in the welfare of its children, we are compelled to uphold the statute. *See Vance v. Bradley*, 440 U.S. 93, 111, 99 S.Ct. 939, 949, 59 L.Ed.2d 171 (1979) ("In an equal protection case of this type, however, those challenging the legislative judgment must convince the court that the legislative facts on which the classification is apparently based could not reasonably be conceived to be true by the governmental decisionmaker."). We turn now to appellants' specific arguments.

a. Adoption by Unmarried Heterosexual Persons

Appellants note that Florida law permits adoption by unmarried individuals and that, among children coming out the Florida foster care system, 25% of adoptions are to parents who are currently single. Their argument is that homosexual persons are similarly situated to unmarried persons with regard to Florida's asserted interest in promoting married-couple adoption. According to appellants, this disparate treatment lacks a rational basis and, therefore, disproves any rational connection between the statute and Florida's asserted interest in promoting adoption into married homes. [By way of argument, the appellants relied on *City of Cleburne v. Cleburne Living Ctr.*, 473 U.S. 432, 105 S.Ct. 3249, 87 L.Ed.2d 313 (1985); the court rejected the argument by distinguishing *City of Cleburne*.]

. . .

b. Current Foster Care Population

Appellants make much of the fact that Florida has over three thousand children who are currently in foster care and, consequently, have not been placed with permanent adoptive families. According to appellants, because excluding homosexuals from the pool of prospective adoptive parents will not create more eligible married couples to reduce the backlog, it is impossible for the legislature to believe that the statute advances the state's interest in placing children with married couples.

We do not agree that the statute does not further the state's interest in promoting nuclear-family adoption because it may delay the adoption of some children. Appellants misconstrue Florida's interest, which is not simply to place children in a permanent home as quickly as possible, but, when placing them, to do so in an optimal home, *i.e.*, one in which there is a heterosexual couple or the potential for one. According to appellants' logic, every restriction on adoptive-parent candidates, such as income, in-state residency, and criminal record—none of which creates more available married couples—are likewise constitutionally suspect as long as Florida has a backlog of unadopted foster children. The best interests of children, however, are not automatically served by adoption into *any* available home merely because it is permanent. Moreover, the legislature could rationally act on the theory that not placing adoptees in homosexual households increases the probability that these children eventually will be placed with married couple families, thus furthering the state's goal of optimal placement. Therefore, we conclude that Florida's current foster care backlog does not render the statute irrational.

c. Foster Care and Legal Guardianship

Noting that Florida law permits homosexuals to become foster parents and permanent guardians, appellants contend that this fact demonstrates that Florida must not truly believe that placement in a homosexual household is not in a child's best interests. We do not find that the fact that Florida has permitted, homosexual foster homes and guardianships defeats the rational relationship between the statute and the state's asserted interest. We have not located and appellants have not cited any precedent indicating that a disparity between a law and its enforcement is a relevant consideration on rational-basis review, which only asks whether the legislature could have reasonably thought that the challenged law would further a legitimate state interest. Thus, to the extent that foster care and guardianship placements with homosexuals are the handiwork of Florida's executive branch, they are irrelevant to the question of the *legislative* rationale for Florida's adoption scheme To the extent that these placements are the product of an intentional legislative choice to treat foster care and guardianships differently than adoption, the distinction is not an irrational one. Indeed, it bears a rational relationship to Florida's interest in promoting the nuclear-family model of adoption since foster care and guardianship have neither the permanence nor the societal, cultural, and legal significance as does adoptive parenthood, which is the legal equivalent of natural parenthood. Fla. Stat. § 63.032(2).

Foster care and legal guardianship are designed to address a different situation than permanent adoption, and "the legislature must be allowed leeway to approach a perceived problem incrementally." *Beach Communications*, 508 U.S. at 316, 113 S. Ct. at 2102. The fact that "the legislature may select one phase of one field and apply a remedy there, neglecting the others," does not render the legislative solution invalid. *Id.* (citation omitted); *Heller*, 509 U.S. at 321, 113 S. Ct. at 2643 ("The problems of government are practical ones and may justify, if they do not require, rough accommodations—illogical, it may be, and unscientific.") (citation omitted). We conclude that the rationality of the statute is not defeated by the fact that Florida permits homosexual persons to serve as foster parents and legal guardians.

d. Social Science Research

Appellants cite recent social science research and the opinion of mental health professionals and child welfare organizations as evidence that there is no child welfare basis for excluding homosexuals from adopting. They argue that the cited studies show that the parenting skills of homosexual parents are at least equivalent to those of heterosexual parents and that children raised by homosexual parents suffer no adverse outcomes. Appellants also point to the policies and practices of numerous adoption agencies that permit homosexual persons to adopt.

In considering appellants' argument, we must ask not whether the latest in social science research and professional opinion *support* the decision of the Florida legislature, but whether that evidence is so well established and so far beyond dispute that it would be irrational for the Florida legislature to believe that the interests of its children are best served by not permitting homosexual adoption. Also, we must credit any conceivable rational reason that the legislature might have for choosing not to alter its statutory scheme in response to this recent social science research. ... Or the legislature might consider, and even credit, the research cited by appellants, but find it premature to rely on a very recent and still developing body of research, particularly in light of the absence of longitudinal studies following child subjects into adulthood and of studies of adopted, rather than natural, children of homosexual parents.

We do not find any of these possible legislative responses to be irrational. Openly homosexual households represent a very recent phenomenon, and sufficient time has not yet passed to permit any scientific study of how children raised in those households fare as adults. Scientific attempts to study homosexual parenting in general are still in their nascent stages and so far have yielded inconclusive and conflicting results. Thus, it is hardly surprising that the question of the effects of homosexual parenting on childhood development is one on which even experts of good faith reasonably disagree. Given this state of affairs, it is not irrational for the Florida legislature to credit one side of the debate over the other. Nor is it irrational for the legislature to proceed with deliberate caution before placing adoptive children in an alternative, but unproven, family structure that has not yet been conclusively demonstrated to be equivalent to the marital family structure that has established a proven track record spanning centuries. Accordingly, we conclude that appellants' proffered social science evidence does not disprove the rational basis of the Florida statute.

e. Romer v. Evans

Finally, we disagree with appellants' contention that *Romer* requires us to strike down the Florida statute. In *Romer*, the Supreme Court invalidated Amendment 2 to the Colorado state constitution, which prohibited all legislative, executive, or judicial action designed to protect homosexual persons from discrimination. 517 U.S. 620, 624, 116 S.Ct. 1620, 1623, 134 L.Ed.2d 855 (1996). The constitutional defect in Amendment 2 was the disjunction between the "sweeping and comprehensive" classification it imposed on homosexuals and the state's asserted bases for the classification—respect for freedom of association and conservation of resources to fight race and gender discrimination. *Id.* at 627, 116 S. Ct. at 1625. The Court concluded that the Amendment's "sheer breadth is so discontinuous with the reasons offered for it that the amendment seems inexplicable by anything but animus toward the class it affects." *Id.* at 632 116 S. Ct. at 1627.

Unlike Colorado's Amendment 2, Florida's statute is not so "sweeping and comprehensive" as to render Florida's rationales for the statute "inexplicable by anything but animus" toward its homosexual residents. Amendment 2 deprived homosexual persons of "protections against exclusion from an almost limitless number of transactions and endeavors that constitute ordinary civic life in a free society." *Id.* at 631, 116 S. Ct. at 1627. In contrast to this "broad and undifferentiated disability," the Florida classification is limited to the narrow and discrete context of access to the statutory privilege of adoption and, more importantly, has a plausible connection with the state's asserted interest. *Id.* at 632, 116 S. Ct. at 1627. Moreover, not only is the effect of Florida's classification dramatically smaller, but the classification itself is narrower. Whereas Amendment 2's classification encompassed both conduct *and* status. *Id.* at 624, 116 S. Ct. at 1623 (quoting the text of Amendment 2, which covered "homosexual, lesbian or bisexual orientation, conduct, practices or relationships"), Florida's adoption prohibition is limited to conduct *see Cox*, 627 So.2d at 1215. Thus, we conclude that *Romer's* unique factual situation and narrow holding are inapposite to this case.

III. CONCLUSION

We exercise great caution when asked to take sides in an ongoing public policy debate, such as the current one over the compatibility of homosexual conduct with the duties of adoptive parenthood. *See Reno*, 507 U.S. at 315, 113 S. Ct. at 1454; *Schall v. Martin*, 467 U.S. 253, 281, 104 S.Ct. 2403, 2419, 81 L.Ed.2d 207 (1984). The State of Florida has made the determination that it is not in the best interests of its displaced children to be adopted by individuals who "engage in current, voluntary homosexual activity," *Cox*, 627 So.2d at 1215, and we have found nothing in the Constitution that forbids this policy judgment. Thus, any argument that the Florida legislature was misguided in its decision is one of legislative policy, not constitutional law. The legislature is the proper forum for this debate, and we do not sit as a superlegislature "to award by judicial decree what was not achievable by political consensus." *Thomasson v. Perry*, 80 F.3d 915, 923 (4th Cir. 1996). The judgment of the district court is

AFFIRMED.

DISCUSSION

On petition for rehearing en banc, six judges voted to rehear Lofton *and six did not vote for rehearing. Because there was no majority, en banc review was denied. Judge Barkett wrote a dissent from the denial of rehearing in which she claimed that the panel of the court of appeals "attempt[ed] to evade the application of* Lawrence.*" She argued that the classification in* Lofton *violated equal protection because it "burdens personal relationships and exudes animus against a politically unpopular group." Judge Barkett applied a "more searching form of rational basis review" (quoting Justice O'Connor's* Lawrence *concurrence) and found that Florida's stated interest (providing adopted children with married couples as parents) failed the equal protection require-*

ment that "all persons similarly situated should be treated alike." She opined, "Here, irrational prejudice can be inferred as the basis for this classification because there is no difference in relevant respects between single heterosexual persons and single homosexual persons with reference to the state's purported justification for the ban in the statute.... Since Florida's rationale is not plausible given that single persons may adopt, the inference is obvious that Florida's decision to single out homosexuals is based solely on anti-gay animus. Unsurprisingly, animus is just what the legislative history of Florida's ban confirms." [Judge Barkett then detailed Anita Bryant's Save Our Children campaign.]

Judge Barkett also argued that Lawrence, *by overruling* Bowers, *extended* Griswold*'s privacy right to cover consensual sodomy. Florida's classification, therefore, burdened the appellants' right to engage in consensual homosexual intimacy, triggering strict scrutiny. Judge Birch authored an opinion concurring in the denial of rehearing en banc, specifically to take issue with Judge Barkett's assessment. Judge Birch argued that, aside from Justice O'Connor's* Lawrence *concurrence, no Supreme Court precedent validating Judge Barkett's heightened rationality review existed. Judge Birch also argued that* Lawrence *had not extended the fundamental right to privacy to cover consensual sodomy. With whom do you agree?*

FLORIDA DEPT. OF CHILDREN AND FAMILIES v. ADOPTION OF X.X.G.

45 So.3d 79 (Fla.App. 2010)

Before COPE, SHEPHERD and SALTER, JJ.

COPE, J.

This is an appeal of a final judgment of adoption, under which F.G. became the adoptive father of two boys, X.X.G. and N.R.G. (collectively, "the children"). The trial court found, and all parties agree, that F.G. is a fit parent and that the adoption is in the best interest of the children.

The question in the case is whether the adoption should have been denied because F.G. is a homosexual. Under Florida law, a homosexual person is allowed to be a foster parent. F.G. has successfully served as a foster parent for the children since 2004. However, Florida law states, "No person eligible to adopt under this statute [the Florida Adoption Act] may adopt if that person is a homosexual." § 63.042(3), Fla. Stat. (2006). According to the judgment, "Florida is the only remaining state to expressly ban all gay adoptions without exception." Judgment at 38. Judge Cindy Lederman, after lengthy hearings, concluded that there is no rational basis for the statute. We agree and affirm the final judgment of adoption.

I.

We begin with three observations. First, there does not appear to be any disagreement between the parties regarding the facts of the case. The parties entered into a lengthy list of stipulated facts. The stipulated facts are attached as an appendix to this opinion. Second, the parties agree that the father is a fit parent and that the adoption is in the best interest of the children. Appendix ¶¶ 44–56. Third, the Department of Children and Families ["Department"] "agrees that gay people and heterosexuals make equally good parents." Appendix ¶ 31.

II.

[The court recited the facts of the case showing that F.G., a licensed foster caregiver, sought to adopt the children, and that he was denied by the Department solely because he was a homosexual.]

In 2007, F.G. filed a petition in the circuit court to adopt the children. F.G. asked the court to find subsection 63.042(3) unconstitutional because it violates his rights to equal protection, privacy, and due process. Independent counsel acting on behalf of the children asserted that the children's rights to equal protection and due process had also been violated. The Department filed a motion to dismiss, but the court only dismissed the privacy claim.

Trial began on October 1, 2008, and continued for four days. F.G. presented fact witnesses as well as expert witnesses who testified regarding homosexual and heterosexual parenting capabilities. In opposition, the Department offered the testimony of two expert witnesses.

The trial court rendered a 53–page judgment declaring subsection 63.042(3) unconstitutional and granting the petition for adoption. The trial court found, among other things, that the statute violates the equal protection rights of F.G. and the children that are guaranteed by Article I, Section 2 of the Florida Constitution.

The Department has appealed.

III.

The Department contends that the trial court erred by finding subsection 63.042(3) unconstitutional. The Department argues that there is a rational basis for the statute and that the trial court misinterpreted the law.

Under the Florida Constitution, each individual person has a right to equal protection of the laws. The constitutional provision states, in part:

> **SECTION 2. Basic rights.**—All natural persons, female and male alike, are equal before the law and have inalienable rights, among which are the right to enjoy and defend life and liberty, to pursue happiness, to be rewarded for industry, and to acquire, possess and protect property....

Art. I, § 2, Fla. Const.

F.G. successfully argued in the trial court that the statute treated him unequally in violation of the constitutional provision because the statute creates an absolute prohibition on adoption by homosexual persons, while allowing all other persons—including those with criminal histories or histories of substance abuse—to be considered on a case-by-case basis.

When this case was pending in the trial court, the parties and trial court agreed that this case does not involve a fundamental right or suspect class, so the case was decided under the rational basis test. That being so, we have considered this appeal only under that test.

Under the rational basis test, "a court must uphold a statute if the classification bears a rational relationship to a legitimate governmental objective." *Warren v. State Farm Mut. Auto. Ins. Co.,* 899 So.2d 1090, 1095 (Fla.2005). The classification must be "based **on a real difference** which is reasonably related to the subject and purpose of the regulation." *State v. Leicht,* 402 So.2d 1153, 1155 (Fla.1981) (emphasis added).

The question now before us—whether there is a rational basis for subsection 63.042(3)—was previously presented to the Supreme Court of Florida with inconclusive results. [The court discussed *Cox v. Florida Department of Health & Rehabilitative Services,* 656 So.2d 902 (Fla.1995).]

IV.

We next consider how the adoption statute works. The statute requires that there be individual studies which the judge must consider in order to decide whether the proposed adoption is in the best interest of the child. § 63.022(2), (4)(c), Fla. Stat.; Fla. Admin. Code R. 56C–16.005(2).

There must be a favorable preliminary home study, § 63.112(2)(b), Fla. Stat., followed by a final home investigation "to ascertain whether the adoptive home is a suitable home for the minor and whether the proposed adoption is in the best interest of the minor." *Id.* § 63.125(1); Fla. Admin. Code R. 65C–16.001(7), (8). "The report of the investigation must contain an evaluation of the placement with a recommendation on the granting of the petition for adoption and any other information the court requires regarding the petitioner or the minor." § 63.125(3), Fla. Stat. This process includes a family social and medical history, in-home visits with the minor and minor's proposed adoptive parent or parents and gathering any other information which may be relevant to the suitability of the intended adoptive home. *Id.* § 63.125(5). If the trial judge concludes that the adoption is in the best interest of the person to be adopted, the Court enters the judgment of adoption. *Id.* § 63.142(4).

Simply put, the statute calls for an individual, case-by-case evaluation to determine if the proposed adoption is in the best interest of the child. Except for homosexual persons, there is no automatic, categorical exclusion of anyone from consideration for adoption.

For example, "[a]doption applicants who have previous verified findings of abuse, neglect or abandonment of a child are subject to a special review before they can be approved to adopt, but are not automatically disqualified from adopting." Appendix ¶ 15. For a child who was privately placed (not placed by the Department or Department's agent), there is no categorical exclusion for adoption by a person with a prior criminal history, although a special review is involved. Appendix ¶¶ 12–15. Where the placement is through the Department, a very serious criminal history is disqualifying. Appendix ¶ 12. There is a five-year preclusion if there is a prior history for assault, battery, or a drug crime, Appendix ¶ 13, and no preclusion for other felonies.

Florida law specifies that a person cannot be "prohibited from adopting solely because such person possesses a physical disability or handicap, unless it is determined by the court or adoption entity that such disability or handicap renders such person incapable of serving as an effective parent." § 63.042(4), Fla. Stat. An individual who is HIV-positive but healthy and able to care for a child is not excluded if, after having a physical, a doctor determines that the applicant is healthy and that the child is not going to go through another loss. Appendix ¶ 11. There is a special review, but no categorical exclusion, for an applicant "with serious or chronic medical conditions that could predictably compromise ... the ability to provide the physical, emotional, social and economic support necessary for a child to thrive." Appendix ¶ 10. "No person shall be denied the opportunity to become an adoptive parent on the basis of race, color or national origin." Fla. Admin. Code R. 65C–16.005(1).

A single adult is specifically allowed to adopt. § 63.042(2)(b), Fla. Stat. Florida "makes over a third of its adoptive placements with single adults." Appendix ¶ 2. "The percentage of adoptions of dependent children in Florida that were by single parents for the year 2006 was 34.47%." Appendix ¶ 2.

The Department or its agents "have placed children in the permanent care of foster parents known by [the Department] and/or its agents to be lesbians or gay men." Appendix ¶ 26. Homosexual persons "are not prohibited by any state law or regulation from being legal guardians of children in Florida." Appendix ¶ 27. The Department or its agents have placed children in the care, including permanent care, of legal guardians known by the Department and/or its agents to be lesbians or gay men, and ceased Department supervision. Appendix ¶¶ 28–29.

However, the Florida Adoption Act categorically excludes a homosexual person from adopting. The question is whether there is a rational basis for the difference in treatment.

V.

Given a total ban on adoption by homosexual persons, one might expect that this reflected a legislative judgment that homosexual persons are, as a group, unfit to be parents.

No one in this case has made, or even hinted at, any such argument. To the contrary, the parties agree "that gay people and heterosexuals make equally good parents." Appendix ¶ 31. "The qualities that make a particular applicant the optimal match for a particular child could exist in a heterosexual or gay person." Appendix ¶ 32. Thus in this case no one attempts to justify the prohibition on homosexual adoption on any theory that homosexual persons are unfit to be parents.

Instead, the Department argues that there is a rational basis for the prohibition on homosexual adoption because children will have better role models, and face less discrimination, if they are placed in non-homosexual households, preferably with a husband and wife as the parents. But that is not what the statute does.

As previously stated, the statute specifically allows adoption by an unmarried adult. § 63.042(2)(b). Single parent adoption has been allowed under the Florida Adoption Act, enacted in 1973, and predecessor statutes. § 63.042(2)(b), Fla. Stat. (1973); ch. 73–159, § 4, Laws of Fla.; § 63.061, Fla. Stat. (1967); § 72.11, Fla. Stat. (1943). One-third of Florida's adoptions are by single adults. Appendix ¶ 2. The Florida Statutes do not restrict adoption to heterosexual married couples.

The statute contains no prohibition on placing children with homosexual persons who are foster parents. The Department has placed children with homosexual foster parents in short-term placements, and long-term placements. Appendix ¶¶ 25–26. The average length of stay in foster care before adoption is thirty months. Appendix ¶ 38.

Florida also has a guardianship statute. Ch. 744, Fla. Stat. Homosexual persons "are not prohibited by any state law or regulation from being legal guardians of children in Florida." Appendix ¶ 27. The Department has placed children in the legal guardianship of homosexual persons. This has included permanent guardianships in which the Department ceased supervision. Appendix ¶ 29.

It is difficult to see any rational basis in utilizing homosexual persons as foster parents or guardians on a temporary or permanent basis, while imposing a blanket prohibition on adoption by those same persons. The Department contends, however, that the basis for this distinction can be found in the social science evidence.

VI.

The trial court heard extensive expert testimony in this case.

. . .

The court concluded as follows:

> The quality and breadth of research available, as well as the results of the studies performed about gay parenting and children of gay parents, is robust and has provided the basis for a consensus in the field. Many well renowned, regarded and respected professionals have [produced] methodologically sound longitudinal and cross-sectional studies into hundreds of reports. Some of the longitudinal studies have tracked children for six, ten and fourteen years. The starting ages of the children in the longitudinal studies has varied from birth, six to ten years old and followed them throughout childhood, adolescence and into adulthood. The studies and reports are published in many

> well respected peer reviewed journals including the Journal of Child Development, the Journal of Family Psychology, the Journal of Child Psychology, and the Journal of Child Psychiatry. Each of the studies and hundreds of reports also withstood the rigorous peer review process and were tested statistically, rationally and methodologically by seasoned professionals prior to publication.
>
> In addition to the volume, the body of research is broad; comparing children raised by lesbian couples to children raised by married heterosexual couples; children raised by lesbian parents from birth to children raised by heterosexual married couples from birth; children raised by single homosexuals to children raised by single heterosexuals; and children adopted by homosexual parents to those raised by homosexual biological parents, to name a few. **These reports and studies find that there are no differences in the parenting of homosexuals or the adjustment of their children.** These conclusions have been accepted, adopted and ratified by the American Psychological Association, the American Psychiatry Association, the American Pediatric Association, the American Academy of Pediatrics, the Child Welfare League of America and the National Association of Social Workers. As a result, based on the robust nature of the evidence available in the field, **this Court is satisfied that the issue is so far beyond dispute that it would be irrational to hold otherwise;** the best interests of children are not preserved by prohibiting homosexual adoption.

Final Judgment at 36–37 (emphasis added). This finding coincides with the Department's agreement "that gay people and heterosexuals make equally good parents." Appendix ¶ 31.

As we understand it, the Department maintains that the trial court should not have conducted an evidentiary hearing. We reject that argument. In the *Cox* decision, which considered the identical constitutional challenge, the Florida Supreme Court ruled that an evidentiary hearing must be held. 656 So.2d at 903.

The Department also appears to say that the trial court should not have made findings about the social science evidence. Again, we disagree. The *Cox* decision called for "a factual completion of the record as to this single constitutional issue and a decision as to this issue based upon the completed record." *Id.*

The Department does not argue that the trial court's judgment lacks support in the evidence.

VII.

Turning now to the remainder of the Department's argument, we understand the Department to assert that if there is an alternative legitimate way to interpret the scientific data, then that alternative view can provide a rational basis for the statute's blanket exclusion of homosexual adoption while allowing homosexual foster case and guardianships.

The Department contends that the alternative views expressed by its experts and F.G.'s experts support the existence of a rational basis for the statute. *See Hamilton v. State,* 366 So.2d 8, 10 (Fla. 1978) (classification will be upheld where there continues to be expert opinion supporting the reasons which prompted the legislature to enact the statute).

We consider first the Department's experts. One of the Department's witnesses was Dr. Schumm. Dr. Schumm is of no assistance to the Department's argument. That is so because Dr. Schumm did **not** agree "that homosexuals should be banned from adopting but rather states that gay parents can be good foster parents, and opines that the decision to permit homosexuals to adopt is best made by the judiciary on a case by case basis." Final Judgment at 24.

The final judgment also states:

> Although Dr. Schumm is not a psychologist, a summary of his testimony is included in this section because he conducted a methodological analysis of the works of psychologists on homosexual parenting. When reanalyzing studies on outcomes of children raised by gay parents, he found some differences in outcomes as a factor of parental sexual orientation where the original researchers reported no differences (the null hypothesis). He suggests that his reanalysis, mostly unpublished, should be accepted over the analyses of well respected researchers in peer reviewed journals. Dr. Schumm admitted that he applies statistical standards that depart from conventions in the field. In fact, Dr. Cochran and Dr. Lamb testified that Dr. Schumm's statistical re-analysis contained a number of fundamental errors. Dr. Schumm ultimately concluded that based on his re-analysis of the data, there are statistically significant differences between children of gay and lesbian parents as compared to children of heterosexual parents. Dr. Schumm understands that much of the scientific community disagrees with his conclusions and concedes to the possibility that some gay parents may be beneficial to some children.
>
> Final Judgment at 23–24.

The testimony of Dr. Schumm does not support the blanket prohibition on homosexual adoption. Dr. Schumm's conclusion was that such decisions should be made on a case-by-case basis. Further, the trial court was entitled to accept the testimony of Dr. Cochran and Dr. Lamb that Dr. Schumm's statistical re-analyses contained fundamental statistical errors.

The Department also called Dr. Rekers to testify as an expert. Dr. Rekers opined that "homosexuals are less able to provide a stable home for children than heterosexuals." Final Judgment at 19. He cited several studies indicating that homosexual adults have a higher lifetime prevalence of major depression, affective disorders, anxiety disorders and substance abuse. For that reason, Dr. Rekers believes that adoption (and foster parenting) should be ruled out for homosexual persons.

Unlike Dr. Schumm, Dr. Rekers sees no role for individual evaluation of the proposed adoptive parent, if that parent is a homosexual. He maintained that performing an individualized study of the proposed adoptive parent, like F.G., is not viable because even if F.G. is found to be entirely appropriate as an adoptive parent at the present time, it is possible that he may develop some sort of a disorder later in life.

By contrast, Dr. Cochran, one of F.G.'s witnesses, testified that the scientific data do not support Dr. Rekers' analysis:

> As a general premise, elevated occurrences of psychiatric disorders and rates of depression and suicidality are associated with demographic characteristics, such as race, gender, age, socioeconomic status and sexual orientation. In terms of the specific demographic characteristic of sexual orientation, the witness [Dr. Cochran] cited to several population-based studies comparing the mental health of gay and heterosexual individuals including the 1996 National Survey on Drug Abuse, the National Co-morbidity Survey (1990–1992), the National Health and Nutrition Examination Survey (1971–1975, 1976–1980, 1988–1994, 1999–2002, 2003–2004, 2005–2006), the National Examination Survey, the Midlife Survey of Adult Development (1995–1996), the Add Health Cohort study (1994–95, 1996, 2001–2002, 2007–2008), the California Quality of Life Survey (2001) and the National Latino and Asian–American Survey (May 2002 and November 2003). **According to the witness [Dr. Cochran], taken as a whole, the research shows that sexual orientation alone is not a proxy for psychiatric disorders, mental health conditions, substance abuse or smoking; members of every demographic group suffer from these conditions at rates not significantly higher than for homosexuals.** Therefore, based on the research, while the average rates of psychiatric conditions, substance abuse and smoking are generally slightly higher for homosexuals than heterosexuals, the rates of psychiatric conditions, substance abuse and smoking are also higher for American–Indians as compared to other races, the unemployed as compared to the employed and non-high school graduates as compared to high school graduates, for example. **Poignantly, Dr. Cochran pointed out that if every demographic group with elevated rates of psychiatric disorders, substance abuse and smoking were excluded from adopting, the only group eligible to adopt under this rationale would be Asian American men.**

Final Judgment at 13–14 (emphasis added) (footnote omitted). Dr. Cochran also testified about errors in scientific methodology and reporting in Dr. Rekers' study, stating that Dr. Rekers had failed to present an objective review of the evidence on those subjects. R. 916–18. Dr. Cochran concluded that Dr. Rekers' work did not meet established standards in the field. R. 916–18. Another expert, Dr. Peplau, testified that Dr. Rekers had omitted in his review of the scientific literature "other published, widely cited studies on the stability of actual relationships over time." R. 822.

Dr. Rekers was questioned about his recent authorship of a law review article entitled *An Empirically Supported Rational Basis for Prohibiting Adoption, Foster Parenting, and Contested Child Custody by Any Person in a Household that Includes a Homosexually–Behaving Member,* 18 St. Thomas L. Rev. 325 (2005). According to the judgment, "the doctor heavily cited to the conclusions of a colleague who is sharply criticized as distorting data and was censured and ousted [or withdrew in lieu of ousting] by the American Psychological Association for misreporting evidence regarding homosexual households." Final Judgment at 20 (footnote omitted). The court concluded that "Dr. Rekers' testimony was far from a neutral and unbiased recitation of the relevant scientific evidence." Final Judgment at 23.

Under applicable law, a legislative classification will be upheld if it is "based on a real difference which is reasonably related to the subject and purpose of the regulation." *Leicht,* 402 So.2d at 1155. The trial judge was entitled to reach the conclusion, which she did, that the Department's experts' opinions were not valid from a scientific point of view.

VIII.

The Department argues that homosexuals should be barred from adopting "because the homes of homosexuals may be less stable and more prone to domestic violence." Initial Brief at 34. The Department maintains that in this part of its argument, it is relying on F.G.'s own experts. The Department has, however, read selectively from the expert testimony and the record does not support the Department's position.

The Department says that there are disturbingly high domestic violence rates among same-sex couples. However, the Department selectively quotes the testimony by Dr. Peplau. In reality, Dr. Peplau testified that gay people or gay couples do not have higher rates of domestic violence than heterosexual couples. R. 811. In the population-based study cited by Dr. Peplau, "the highest rate of domestic violence, defined as physical assault or rape . . . was 20 percent, and that was for women in heterosexual relationships being attacked by their male partner." R. 812. The rates for all other groups was lower. This was consistent with a study by the Centers for Disease Control, which found that over an eighteen-year period, ninety-five percent of female homicide victims were women killed by a male domestic partner. R. 814.

With regard to break-ups of relationships, the Department acknowledges Dr. Peplau's conclusion that unmarried heterosexual couples show break-up rates similar to homosexuals. R. 773. The same predictors for divorce apply to evaluate the likelihood of break-up in unmarried or same-sex couples. R. 769, 780. The predictors include age at marriage, education, family income, race or ethnicity, and religion. Dr. Peplau concluded that sexual orientation is not the strongest predictor of break-up among all the different demographic characteristics. R. 795. Other demographic factors "seem to have as strong or even stronger correlations with break-ups." R. 795.

The Department claims that homosexual parents "support adolescent sexual activity and experimentations." Initial Brief at 32. The Department claims to draw this from the testimony of F.G.'s experts, but the experts did not say this. Dr. Lamb testified that research showed no difference between children of gay parents and heterosexual parents with respect to the age at which they initiated sexual activity. R. 1235.

Dr. Berlin testified that there is no evidence that the environment in which a child is raised, heterosexual or homosexual, would determine the sexual identity of the child who is raised in that environment. R. 1382–83. "[T]he overwhelming majority of homosexual individuals were raised in heterosexual households, suggesting that the environment in which they were raised in those instances certainly wasn't the determining factor of their development. . . ." R. 1383. Similarly, the overwhelming majority of those children raised in a gay environment turned out to be heterosexual, R. 1383, a point with which Department expert Schumm agreed. R. 1863.

The Department argues that placement of children with homosexuals presents a risk of discrimination and societal stigma. Here, too, the argument is misplaced. Florida already allows placement of children in foster care and guardianships with homosexual persons. This factor does not provide an argument for allowing such placements while prohibiting adoption. We reject the Department's remaining arguments for the same reason: they do not provide a reasonable basis for allowing homosexual foster parenting or guardianships while imposing a prohibition on adoption.

In conclusion on the equal protection issue, the legislature is allowed to make classifications when it enacts statutes. *Leicht,* 402 So.2d at 1155. As a general proposition, a classification "will be upheld even if another classification or no classification might appear more reasonable." *Id.* The classifications must, however, be "based on a **real** difference which is reasonably related to the subject and purpose of the regulation." *Id.* (Emphasis added). "The reason for the equal protection clause was to assure that there would be no second class citizens." *Osterndorf v. Turner,* 426 So.2d 539, 545–46 (Fla.1982).

Under Florida law, homosexual persons are allowed to serve as foster parents or guardians but are barred from being considered for adoptive parents. All other persons are eligible to be considered case-by-case to be adoptive parents, but not homosexual persons-even where, as here, the adoptive parent is a fit parent and the adoption is in the best interest of the children.

The Department has argued that evidence produced by its experts and F.G.'s experts supports a distinction wherein homosexual persons may serve as foster parents or guardians, but not adoptive parents. Respectfully, the portions of the record cited by the Department do not support the Department's position. We conclude that there is no rational basis for the statute.

IX.

The trial court held that the statute violated the equal protection rights of the children in addition to violating the equal protection rights of F.G. Because we affirm the judgment on account of the violation of F.G.'s equal protection rights, we need not reach the claim of violation of the children's equal protection rights.

The trial court made an alternative finding that "the statute infringes on the Children's right to permanency pursuant to the Adoption and Safe Families Act of 1997, [42 U.S.C. § 671,] adopted in Chapter 39 of the Florida Statutes." Final Judgment at 38. The Department contends that this ruling was erroneous. Because we affirm the declaration of unconstitutionality on the ground that there is an equal protection violation under the Florida Constitution, we need not reach the trial court's alternative holding.

X.

We affirm the judgment of adoption, which holds subsection 63.042(3), Florida Statutes, violates the equal protection provision found in article I, section 2, of the Florida Constitution.

. . .

SALTER, J. (concurring).

I concur in affirming the judgment of adoption in this case. I write only to emphasize certain parts of the record beyond those detailed by the trial court and my respected colleagues.

. . .

The Department Opposes the Statute; Legal Developments After 1977

The Department, while acknowledging a general obligation to follow Florida law (including § 63.042(3)), believes that the categorical ban against adoptions by homosexuals is not in the best interest of children and is contrary to current standards and best practices recommended by social services and child development professionals. The Department's Tallahassee-based chief of child welfare services and training, as well as the Tallahassee-based adoption program manager reporting to her, both testified that eliminating the categorical ban would promote the best interest of children. Neither of these experienced, caring public servants had seen any instance in which any child was harmed by a homosexual parent or foster parent. These conclusions by the leadership of the agency charged with carrying out state policy regarding abused, neglected, and dependent children are entitled to considerable deference. *Verizon Florida, Inc. v. Jacobs,* 810 So.2d 906, 908 (Fla.2002).

The categorical ban was enacted in haste and reaction in 1977. Those who voted for it in the legislature did not prohibit the placement of children with homosexual foster parents or permanent guardians—only the permanent step of adoption was addressed. Because the Department has approved homosexuals to serve as foster parents and permanent guardians, the Department now has years of experience and observation to inform its position and its testimony in the trial court. Moreover, the placement of children in those households has allowed bonds and relationships to form that are in the best interests of children-steps toward permanency and stability in young lives that have already known too much pain and separation. In short, the categorical ban and the statutory polestar of "best interests of the children" after an extended and very successful foster placement (as here) are inimical.

. . .

When the ban was enacted in 1977, the adoption statute was much shorter. The legislative intent of the "Florida Adoption Act" was summarized at that time in section 63.022(1):

> It is the intent of the legislature to protect and promote the well-being of persons being adopted and their natural and adoptive parents and to provide to all children who can benefit by it a permanent family life.

At that time, section 63.142(4) guided the trial court: "At the conclusion of the hearing, when the court determines that all necessary consents have been obtained and that the adoption is in the best interest of the person to be adopted, a judgment of adoption shall be entered."

The Act was substantially modified in 2001, 24 years after the enactment of the categorical ban. Subsection 63.022(2), part of the 2001 overhaul, states:

> It is the intent of the Legislature that in **every** adoption, the best interest of the child should govern and be of **foremost concern** in the court's determination. The court shall make a specific finding as to the best interest of the child in accordance with the provisions of this chapter. (Emphasis added).

"Foremost concern" must also be evaluated in light of a circumstance that was not considered by the Legislature in 1977 (the successful placement of children with homosexual foster parents and permanent guardians). By the time of the trial below, the application of the statutory ban was contrary to both the professional judgment of the Department and the legislative directive to assure "the best interest of the child" in "every" adoption. Confronted with two irreconcilable provisions, the trial court properly followed the later and "foremost" directive. *See Cable–Vision, Inc. v. Freeman,* 324 So.2d 149, 152 (Fla. 3d DCA 1975) ("any such inconsistency should be resolved in favor of the last expression of the legislative will").

Similarly, in 2009 the Second District accorded full faith and credit to a Washington state judgment of adoption by a same-sex parent, rejecting a claim that the Washington adoption was contrary to Florida public policy under § 63.042(3). *Embry v. Ryan,* 11 So.3d 408 (Fla. 2d DCA 2009). The categorical ban was once again subordinated to post–1977 legal developments—in that case, to developments outside Florida.

Conclusion

In striking the categorical ban of section 63.042(3) on equal protection grounds, we need not address the larger controversy regarding same-sex marriage. . . .

. . .

With these few differences in analysis, I concur in affirming the final judgment of adoption.

DISCUSSION

1. *What is the practical effect of the court's decision in* Florida Dept. of Children and Families v. Adoption of X.X.G.*?*

2. *Are second-parent adoptions granted in one state recognized in a second state when the second state is one where the adoption could not have been granted in the first place? See* Embry v. Ryan, *11 So.3d 408 (Fla.App. 2009) and* Finstuen v. Crutcher, *496 F.3d 1139, 1153–1154 (10th Cir. 2007). How do adoptions differ from recognition of same-sex marriage?*

CHAPTER 9

TREATMENT OF SAME-SEX COUPLES

■ ■ ■

I. EARLY EFFORTS AT MARRIAGE RECOGNITION

The once unthinkable idea of legally recognized same-sex relationships has risen to the forefront of American social and legal debate and now stands on par with the abortion rights controversy as a pivotal issue in United States politics. This chapter sketches the quest for gay marriage in the United States and also examines alternative forms of recognition, namely domestic partnerships and civil unions. The chapter also examines the ongoing debate over constitutional amendments that would prohibit judicial resolution of marriage equality claims.

The battle over gay marriage has been raging for nearly forty years. *Baker v. Nelson* (Minn. 1971) is considered by many to be the "first" gay marriage case. In that case a male couple applied for a marriage license in Minnesota. Ultimately, on a "marriage for procreation" rationale, the Minnesota appellate courts denied the plaintiffs' claims. The Minnesota court also rejected federal Due Process and Equal Protection claims, stating simply, "We do not find support for [these arguments] in any decision of the United States Supreme Court."

In December 1990, two lesbian couples and one gay couple applied for marriage licenses at the Hawaii State Department of Health. The applications were denied, and the plaintiffs sued. In *Baehr v. Lewin* (Ha. 1993), the Supreme Court of Hawaii ruled that the Hawaii legislature must either present a "compelling state interest" for denying same-sex couples marriage licenses or must allow same-sex marriage. On remand in 1996, a trial judge found that the state of Hawaii could not justify its discrimination. While an appeal from the trial judge's ruling was pending, the Hawaii legislature proposed a constitutional amendment providing that "the legislature has the power to reserve marriage to opposite-sex couples." The voters of Hawaii approved that amendment in 1998 by a more than two-to-one margin.

While the Hawaii appeal was pending, in March 1998, an Alaska state trial court ruled that the choice of a marital partner is fundamental and cannot be interfered with by the state absent a compelling reason. In the court's words, "[T]he choice of a life partner is personal, intimate, and subject to the protection of the right of privacy." (*Brause v. Bureau of Vital Statistics* (Alaska Super. Ct., 1998)). As in Hawaii, in November 1998, the Alaska electorate approved a state constitutional amendment requiring that all marriages be "between one man and one woman."

II. DOMESTIC PARTNERSHIPS

During this same time period, an alternative to marriage known as a "domestic partnership" was being created in various settings. Coined in San Francisco in the 1980s, it covered (and continues to cover) a range of relationships conferred by private employers and by ordinance or statute at the municipal and state levels (around 9,400, according to a 2008 survey by the Human Rights Campaign). The following cases illustrate the difficulty in defining the limits of domestic partnerships and in determining to whom they apply.

TANNER v. OREGON HEALTH SCIENCES UNIVERSITY

157 Or. App. 502, 971 P.2d 435 (1998)

OPINION: LANDAU, P. J.

At issue in this case is the lawfulness of Oregon Health Science University's (OHSU) denial of health and life insurance benefits to the unmarried domestic partners of its homosexual employees. Plaintiffs, who are three lesbian employees of OHSU and their domestic partners, initiated this action for judicial review of State Employees' Benefits Board (SEBB) orders affirming the lawfulness of the denial and for declaratory and injunctive relief. Plaintiffs contend that OHSU's actions violate ORS 659.030(1)(b), which prohibits discrimination in employment on the basis of the sex of an employee or the sex of any other person with whom the employee associates, as well as Article I, section 20, of the Oregon Constitution, which prohibits granting privileges or immunities not equally belonging to all citizens. Plaintiffs named as defendants OHSU, the State of Oregon, the State Board of Higher Education, the Executive Department, and SEBB.

The matter was tried to the court. Following the trial, the 1995 Legislative Assembly enacted legislation transforming OHSU from a state university to a nonstate agency public corporation. The trial court ultimately concluded that OHSU's denial of benefits violated both ORS 659.030(1)(b) and Article I, section 20, of the Oregon Constitution and entered an order enjoining the state from denying group insurance benefits to unmarried domestic partners of its homosexual employees.

Defendants appeal, arguing that the trial court erred in concluding that OHSU violated either the statute or the constitution. Plaintiffs contend that the trial court's judgment was correct in all respects. On our own motion, we requested briefing from the parties on the question whether the conversion of OHSU from a state university to a nonstate agency public corporation renders the action moot as to any defendants.

We conclude that the action is moot as to all state agency defendants and that the case must be remanded with instructions to dismiss all claims against those defendants. We conclude that the case is not moot as to OHSU. As to the merits of the controversy, we conclude that the trial court erred in declaring that OHSU violated ORS 659.030(1)(b). The evidence in this record does not support a claim for violation of that statute. We also conclude, however, that the trial court was correct in declaring that OHSU's denial of insurance benefits to domestic partners of homosexual employees violates Article I, section 20, of the Oregon Constitution.

FACTUAL BACKGROUND

The relevant facts are not in dispute. Before this controversy arose, OHSU provided group health insurance benefits to its employees. It provided each employee a certain amount of money and authorized each employee to select insurance benefits within the limits of the money provided. In accordance with SEBB eligibility criteria, OHSU permitted employees to purchase insurance coverage for "family members." Under the SEBB criteria, unmarried domestic partners of employees were not "family members" who were entitled to insurance coverage.

Plaintiffs are three lesbian nursing professionals employed by OHSU and their unmarried domestic partners. Each of the couples has enjoyed a long-term and committed relationship, which each wishes to continue for life. Each of the couples would be married if Oregon law permitted homosexual couples to marry.

All three OHSU employees applied for medical and dental insurance benefits for their domestic partners. The OHSU benefits manager refused to process the applications on the ground that the domestic partners of the employees did not meet the SEBB eligibility criteria. Plaintiffs appealed to SEBB itself, and, in a series of 1991 letters, SEBB's Case Management Committee upheld OHSU's denial of benefits.

. . .

The case was tried to the court in February 1995. At trial, the parties stipulated that OHSU paid the same amount of money for a fringe benefit package to all employees in a given category, without regard to marital status or sexual orientation. The parties further stipulated that, in administering its employee benefits program, OHSU treated heterosexual unmarried couples and homosexual unmarried couples the same. Plaintiffs declined to stipulate that OHSU did not intend its administration of the benefits to discriminate against gay and lesbian employees. In response, OHSU elicited testimony from the State Administrator of the Human Resource Management Division of the Department of Administrative Services that the sex or sexual orientation of employees was not taken into account in any way in the administration of state benefits programs. Plaintiffs offered no contrary testimony.

The court took the matter under advisement. Meanwhile, the 1995 Legislative Assembly enacted legislation declaring that OHSU no longer is part of the State Board of Higher Education, but is instead an independent public corporation. Ore. Laws 1995, ch. 162, §§ 2, 74. The new legislation further declares that the terms and conditions of employment at OHSU are to be determined and administered by the Board of Directors of OHSU.

On June 14, 1996, the trial court issued a letter opinion concluding that the denial of benefits to plaintiffs and their domestic partners violated ORS 659.030(1)(b) and Article I, section 20. The court did not address defendants' request that the case be dismissed as moot. Shortly after that, plaintiffs prepared a proposed form of judgment. Defendants objected to the form of judgment, contending that, among other things, it applied to state agency defendants that no longer had any interest in the controversy.

On August 12, 1996, the court entered its judgment, containing findings of fact and conclusions of law. The judgment enjoined the State of Oregon, OHSU, SEBB, and the State Board of Higher Education from continuing the practice of denying group life, health, and dental insurance coverage to domestic partners of homosexual employees when those benefits are offered to spouses of heterosexual employees. The judgment defines "domestic partners" as homosexual persons not related by blood closer than first cousins who are not legally married, who have continuously lived together in an exclusive and loving relationship that they intend to maintain for the rest of their lives, who have joint financial accounts and joint financial responsibilities, who would be married to each other if Oregon law permitted it, who have no other domestic partners, and who are 18 years of age or older. The judgment awarded plaintiffs their costs and attorney fees.

Defendants appealed. While the appeal was pending, the legislature enacted legislation abolishing SEBB and transferring all of SEBB's duties to a newly created Public Employees' Benefits Board (PEBB). Ore. Laws 1997, ch. 22. The parties submitted a stipulated motion for substitution of PEBB for SEBB and for an order directing the trial court to enter an amended judgment reflecting that change. The motion was allowed, and the trial court amended the judgment accordingly. That legislation otherwise has no effect on this litigation.

Also while the appeal was pending, OHSU adopted an employee benefit plan that now provides fringe benefits for the domestic partners of its employees, whether or not they are married. It continues to take the position, however, that it is not legally obligated to provide such benefits.

... We begin with OHSU. As we have noted, OHSU currently provides precisely the domestic partner benefits that plaintiffs seek in this action. OHSU continues to maintain that it is under no legal obligation to do so, however. The voluntary cessation of a practice that is challenged in an action for declaratory and injunctive relief does not, in itself, render an action moot; if the law were otherwise, wrongdoers could cease their wrongdoing as soon as complaints are filed and resume the wrongdoing as soon as the complaints are dismissed for being moot. *Gates v. McClure*, 284 Ore. 685, 689, 588 P.2d 32 (1978); *Safeway v. OPEU*, 152 Ore. App. 349, 357, 954 P.2d 196 (1998).

We turn to the state agency defendants. In their complaint, plaintiff employees alleged that they were employed by the state and State Board of Higher Education. Before the entry of judgment in the case, however, that was no longer so. The legislature, by that time, had declared that OHSU is no longer a state agency, Ore. Laws 1995, ch. 162, §§ 2, 74, and all OHSU employees had been transferred from their previous employment with the State Board of Higher Education, Ore. Laws 1995, ch. 162, § 43. By the time the trial court entered its judgment, therefore, the state and the State Board of Higher Education no longer had an interest in the outcome of the case and could no longer be bound by any remedy that resulted.

We reach the same conclusion as to SEBB and the Executive Department of which it is a part. Plaintiffs' claim against SEBB pertained solely to the 1991 letters denying their applications for benefits. Before the judgment was entered, however, the legislature declared that OHSU no longer is a state agency and no longer is subject to the administration of its employee benefits by SEBB. The legislature declared that OHSU may elect to adopt its own personnel system. It further declared that, "until such time as an alternative personnel system is adopted, **the university shall exercise exclusive administrative authority and control over the system**." Ore. Laws 1995, ch. 162, § 10 (emphasis added). Thus, after July 1, 1995, the effective date of the new OHSU legislation, SEBB had no authority independent of OHSU to offer benefits to plaintiffs, and its previous orders denying benefits to plaintiffs became moot.

. . .

Plaintiffs' arguments to the contrary are unavailing. First, their argument that the case against the state defendants remains alive and well because plaintiffs sued in a representative capacity is belied by their own complaint, which contains no such allegations. Plaintiffs could have framed their complaint as a class action. ORCP 32. They did not do so, and they cannot attempt to convert it into one for the first time on appeal.

. . .

Second, plaintiffs' argument that the propriety of their judgment for attorney fees requires us to address the merits of the underlying claims is similarly unpersuasive. We assume, for the sake of argument, that plaintiffs are correct that a judgment for attorney fees requires examination of the merits of a case that otherwise has become moot since the entry of the judgment. *Cf. Barcik*, 321 Ore. at 189 n 10 (declining to address whether a prayer for attorney fees prevents claims from becoming moot on appeal).

The fact remains that, in this case, the claims against the state defendants became moot **before** the trial court entered its judgment for attorney fees. Thus, because at the time of the entry of judgment the trial court had no authority to enter **any** judgment against the state defendants, the entire case against those defendants—merits and award of attorney fees—is moot.

ANALYSIS OF THE PARTIES' CLAIMS ON THE MERITS

We turn, then, to the portion of the case that remains a live controversy, that is, the lawfulness of OHSU's denial of insurance benefits to domestic partners of its homosexual employees. Following the traditional "first things first" decisional methodology of Oregon judicial opinions, we begin with the question whether OHSU's denial violated applicable employment statutes and, if not, turn to whether the denial violates the state constitution.

A. Violation of ORS 659.030(1)(b)

Plaintiffs allege, and the trial court held, that OHSU's denial of benefits to domestic partners of OHSU's employees violated ORS 659.030(1)(b). That statute provides, in part:

"(1) ... It is an unlawful employment practice:

. . .

> "(b) For an employer, because of an individual's race, religion, color, sex, national origin, marital status or age if the individual is 18 years of age or older, or because of the race, religion, color, sex, national origin, marital status or age of any other person with whom the individual associates ... to discriminate against such individual in compensation or in terms, conditions or privileges of employment."

ORS 659.030(1)(b). On appeal, OHSU argues that the trial court erred, because its denial of benefits was in no way predicated on the sex of any employee or of any individual with whom an employee associates. OHSU argues that its denial of benefits instead was based on marital status alone, without reference to the sexual orientation of the employees or their domestic partners. OHSU emphasizes that **any** unmarried domestic partners—heterosexual and homosexual alike—were denied insurance benefits.

Plaintiffs acknowledge that, at least on the surface, OHSU denied benefits to unmarried domestic partners of its employees without regard to their sexual orientation. They argue that OHSU's denial of benefits to domestic partners nevertheless violates ORS 659.030(1)(b) because, although OHSU's denials did not facially discriminate against homosexual couples, the denials had the effect of discriminating against homosexual couples. That is so, plaintiffs argue, because homosexual couples cannot marry. Heterosexual couples can marry and thus at least have the option of doing so to avail themselves of the employee benefits; homosexual couples cannot marry and have no such option. Because of the disparate impact on homosexual couples of denying benefits on the otherwise facially neutral basis of marital status, plaintiffs argue, OHSU has discriminated on the basis of the sex of persons with whom employees associate, in violation of ORS 659.030(1)(b).

. . .

Whether OHSU's denial of insurance benefits to domestic partners of its homosexual employees amounts to unlawful discrimination "because of the ... sex ... of any other person with whom the [employee] associates," ORS 659.030(1)(b), involves two subsidiary issues. First, we must determine whether discrimination on the basis of sexual orientation constitutes prohibited discrimination because of the "sex ... of any other person with whom the [employee] associates"; if it does not, then the dispute is at an end. Second, we must determine whether OHSU's denials of insurance benefits in this case constituted discrimination "because of" plaintiffs' sexual orientation.

Whether ORS 659.030(1)(b) encompasses discrimination because of sexual orientation is a matter of first impression. The Supreme Court has suggested that it is at least possible to construe the statute to apply to discrimination on the basis of sexual orientation. *ACLU v. Roberts*, 305 Ore. 522, 752 P.2d 1215 (1988) ...

In our view, the Supreme Court's suggestion in *Roberts* is the only plausible construction of the statutory language. The statute prohibits discrimination on the basis of the "sex ... of any other person with whom an individual associates." ORS 659.030(1)(b). Plaintiffs allege that OHSU discriminated against them by denying them the option of providing their domestic partners insurance benefits because their domestic partners are of the same sex. Discrimination of that sort hinges on the sex of the individual with whom plaintiffs associate. It plainly falls within the wording of the statute.

Whether OHSU's denial of insurance benefits to domestic partners of its homosexual employees amounted to discrimination "because of" their sexual orientation may not be so readily answered. OHSU's denial of benefits to plaintiffs ostensibly was based on the fact that plaintiffs were unmarried. As OHSU contends—and as plaintiffs concede—its practice of denying benefits to domestic partners was based on a definition of eligible family members that applied both to unmarried heterosexual couples and unmarried homosexual couples. Ostensibly, therefore, OHSU did not discriminate "because of" sexual orientation; it discriminated "because of" marital status, without regard to sexual orientation.

. . .

There remains the question whether plaintiffs' claims are subject to the more limited liability described in ORS 659.028, which provides, in part:

> "It is not an unlawful employment practice for an employer, employment agency or labor organization to observe the terms of a ... bona

fide employee benefit plan, such as a retirement, pension or insurance plan, which is not a subterfuge to evade the purposes of this chapter."

The parties do not dispute that the insurance benefits at issue in this case and OHSU's policy of denying benefits to the domestic partners of unmarried employees are part of a "bona fide employee benefit plan." The only question is whether OHSU's denial of benefits was part of a "subterfuge to evade the purposes" of the employment statutes. Answering that question, however, entails addressing three more: First, precisely what does "subterfuge" mean; more specifically, does it require proof of intent? Second, who has the burden of proving the presence or absence of a subterfuge? Third, has the burden of proof been satisfied in this case?

... A "subterfuge" ordinarily refers to "a deception by artifice or stratagem to conceal, escape, avoid or evade." *Webster's Third New Int'l Dictionary* 2281 (unabridged ed. 1993). The term obviously entails intentional conduct; one does not accidentally or negligently deceive by artifice or stratagem. Nothing in the text or context of the statute suggests a contrary definition.

. . .

Regardless of who bears the burden of proof, the fact is that, on the record in this case, it is clear that OHSU did not engage in a subterfuge. Appellate review of the evidence on the issue is de novo. *Wincer v. Ind. Paper Stock Co.*, 48 Ore. App. 859, 862–63, 618 P.2d 15 (1980). Our review of that evidence reveals that there is unrebutted testimony that sexual orientation was not taken into account in the administration of OHSU's employee benefits program and that OHSU did not intend, directly or indirectly, to discriminate on the basis of sexual orientation.

Accordingly, although OHSU's practice of denying insurance benefits to unmarried domestic partners of its homosexual employees had an otherwise unlawful disparate impact on a protected class, because there is no evidence that OHSU engaged in a subterfuge to discriminate against that protected class—and because there is affirmative evidence that it did not—it did not engage in an unlawful employment practice. The trial court erred in reaching a contrary conclusion.

B. *Violation of Article I, section 20*

Finally, we address whether OHSU's denial of insurance benefits to the unmarried domestic partners of its homosexual employees violated Article I, section 20, of the Oregon Constitution, which provides:

> "No law shall be passed granting to any citizen or class of citizens privileges or immunities, which, upon the same terms, shall not equally belong to all citizens."

Plaintiffs allege, and the trial court held, that OHSU's denial of benefits to domestic partners of its employees violated Article I, section 20. On appeal, OHSU argues that the trial court erred because OHSU's denials did not discriminate on the basis of sexual orientation but instead on the basis of marital status, discrimination that is justified by the entirely rational purpose of promoting the institution of marriage. Plaintiffs reply that OHSU's practices have the effect of denying a privilege—insurance benefits—to a class of citizens—homosexuals—without any justification and that the practice runs afoul of the constitution. OHSU acknowledges that its denials have the effect of discriminating against homosexual couples. It contends that such a discriminatory effect is not actionable in the absence of an intentionally discriminatory classification.

. . .

Article I, section 20, prohibits granting privileges or immunities to one citizen or class of citizens that are not equally available to all citizens. That generally is understood to express two separate prohibitions. As the Supreme Court explained in its seminal opinion, *State v. Clark*, 291 Ore. 231, 237, 630 P.2d 810 (1981), the clause "forbids inequality of privileges or immunities not available upon the same terms, first, to any citizen, and second, to any class of citizens." In this case, plaintiffs contend that they are members of a class of citizens—homosexual couples—to whom certain privileges—insurance benefits—are not made available.

As used in the Article I, section 20, case law, the term "class" takes on special meaning; only laws that disparately treat a "true class" may violate that section of the constitution. In attempting to describe precisely what is meant by a "true class," the cases draw a distinction between classes that are created by the challenged law or government action itself and classes that are defined in terms of characteristics that are shared apart from the challenged law or action.

The standard example of a nontrue class, drawn from the Supreme Court's decision in *Clark*, is the classification created by a statute that imposes a filing deadline for filing a petition for review. Such legislation creates two classes of persons: (1) those who timely file petitions for review, and (2) those who do not. Both are "classes" of persons, at least in the colloquial sense of groups having something in common. But in the absence of the statute, they have no identity at all. Legislation that disparately affects such "classes" does not violate Article I, section 20, because of the essentially circular nature of the argument: The legislation cannot disparately affect a class that the legislation itself creates.

. . .

Turning to the facts of this case, there is no question but that plaintiffs are members of a true class. That class—unmarried homosexual couples—is not defined by any statute nor by the practices that are the subject of plaintiffs' challenges. Moreover, the class clearly is defined in terms of ad hominem, personal and social characteristics. The question then is whether plaintiffs are members of a suspect class. Here, too, we have no difficulty concluding that plaintiffs are members of a suspect class. Sexual orientation, like gender, race, alienage, and religious affiliation is widely regarded as defining a distinct, socially recognized group of citizens, and certainly it is beyond dispute that homosexuals in our society have been and continue to be the subject of adverse social and political stereotyping and prejudice.

Because plaintiffs are members of a suspect class to which certain privileges and immunities are not made available, we must determine whether the fact that the privileges and immunities are not available to that class may be justified by genuine differences between the class and those to whom the privileges and immunities are made available. Stated perhaps more plainly, we must determine whether the fact that the domestic partners of homosexual OHSU employees cannot obtain insurance benefits can be justified by their homosexuality. The parties have suggested no such justification, and we can envision none.

OHSU's defense is that it determined eligibility for insurance benefits on the basis of marital status, not sexual orientation. According to OHSU, the fact that such a facially neutral classification has the unintended side effect of discriminating against homosexual couples who cannot marry is not actionable under Article I, section 20. We are not persuaded by the asserted defense. Article I, section 20, does not prohibit only intentional discrimination.

... OHSU has taken action with no apparent intention to treat disparately members of any true class of citizens. Nevertheless, its actions have the undeniable effect of doing just that. As in *Zockert*, OHSU's intentions in this case are not relevant. What is relevant is the extent to which privileges or immunities are not made available to all citizens on equal terms.

OHSU insists that in this case privileges and immunities are available to all on equal terms: All married employees—heterosexual and homosexual alike—are permitted to acquire insurance benefits for their spouses. That reasoning misses the point, however. Homosexual couples may not marry. Accordingly, the benefits are not made available on equal terms. They are made available on terms that, for gay and lesbian couples, are a legal impossibility.

We conclude that OHSU's denial of insurance benefits to the unmarried domestic partners of its homosexual employees violated Article I, section 20, of the Oregon Constitution and that the trial court correctly entered judgment in favor of plaintiffs on that ground.

Reversed as to declaration that Oregon Health Sciences University's benefit program violates ORS 659.030(1)(b); remanded with instructions to enter judgment dismissing the State of Oregon, the State Board of Higher Education, the Executive Department and PEBB; otherwise affirmed.

IRIZARRY v. BOARD OF EDUCATION OF THE CITY OF CHICAGO

251 F.3d 604 (7th Cir. 2001)

OPINION: POSNER

Although Milagros Irizarry has lived with the same man for more than two decades and they have two (now adult) children, they have never married. As an employee of the Chicago public school system, she receives health benefits but he does not, even though he is her "domestic partner" (the term for persons who are cohabiting with each other in a relationship similar to marriage), though he would if he were her husband. In July 1999, the Chicago Board of Education extended spousal health benefits to domestic partners—but only if the domestic partner was of the same sex as the employee, which excluded Irizarry's domestic partner, an exclusion that she contends is unconstitutional.

Besides being of the same sex, applicants for domestic-partner status must be unmarried, unrelated, at least 18 years old, and "each other's sole domestic partner, responsible for each other's common welfare." They must satisfy two of the following four additional conditions as well: that they have been living together for a year; that they jointly own their home; that they jointly own other property of specified kinds; that the domestic partner is the primary beneficiary named in the employee's will. Although the board's purpose in entitling domestic partners so defined to spousal benefits was to extend such benefits to homosexual employees, homosexual marriage not being recognized by Illinois, 750 ILCS 5/212, 5/213.1, entitlement to the benefits does not require proof of sexual orientation.

Irizarry's domestic partner satisfies all the conditions for domestic-partner benefits except being of the same sex. She argues that the board's policy denies equal protection and, secondarily, due process. The district court dismissed her suit for failure to state a claim.

The board of education makes two arguments for treating homosexual couples differently from unmarried heterosexual couples. First, since homosexual marriage is not possible in Illinois (or anywhere else in the United States, though it is now possible in the Netherlands), and heterosexual marriage of course is, the recognition of a domestic-partnership surrogate is more important for homosexual than for heterosexual couples, who can obtain the benefits simply by marrying. Second, the board wants to attract homosexual teachers in order to provide support for homosexual students. *Cf. Crawford v. City of Chicago*, 304 Ill. App. 3d 818, 710 N.E.2d 91, 98–99, 237 Ill. Dec. 668 (Ill. App. 1999). According to its brief, the board "believes that lesbian and gay male school personnel who have a healthy acceptance of their own sexuality can act as role models and provide emotional support for lesbian and gay students.... They can support students who are questioning their sexual identities or who are feeling alienated due to their minority sexual orientation. They can also encourage all students to be tolerant and accepting of lesbians and gay males, and discourage violence directed at these groups."

. . .

The efficacy of the policy may be doubted. Although it had been in effect for a year and a half when the appeal was argued, only nine employees out of some 45,000 had signed up for domestic-partner benefits and none of the nine indicated whether he or she was homosexual; they may not all have been, as we shall see—perhaps none were. Nor is there any indication that any of the nine are new employees attracted to teach in the Chicago public schools by the availability of health benefits for same-sex domestic partners. Maybe it's too early, though, to assess the efficacy of the policy. No matter; limited efficacy does not make the policy irrational—not even if we think limited efficacy evidence that the policy is more in the nature of a political gesture than a serious effort to improve the lot of homosexual students—if only because with limited efficacy comes limited cost. Because homosexuals are a small fraction of the population, because the continuing stigma of homosexuality discourages many of them from revealing their sexual orientation, and because nowadays a significant number of heterosexuals substitute cohabitation for marriage in response to the diminishing stigma of cohabitation, extending domestic-partner benefits to mixed-sex couples would greatly increase the expense of the program.

. . .

Irizarry and her domestic partner may, given the unusual duration of their relationship, be an exception to generalizations about the benefits of marriage. We are not aware of an extensive scholarly literature comparing marriage to long-term cohabitation. This may be due to the fact that long-term cohabitation is rare—only ten percent of such relationships last for five years or more, Pamela J. Smock, "Cohabitation in the United States: An Appraisal of Research Themes, Findings, and Implications," 26 Ann. Rev. Sociology 1 (2000). But there is evidence that the widespread substitution of cohabitation for marriage in Sweden has given that country the highest rate of family dissolution and single parenting in the developed world. David Popenoe, Disturbing the Nest: Family Change and Decline in Modern Societies 173–74 (1988). It is well known that divorce is harmful to children (see Jonathan Gruber, "Is Making Divorce Easier Bad for Children? The Long Run Implications of Unilateral Divorce," NBER Working Paper No. 7968 (Oct. 2000), for a survey of the evidence), and presumably the same is true for the dissolution of a cohabitation—and a cohabitation is more likely to dissolve than a marriage. True, Irizarry's cohabitation has not dissolved; but law and policy are based on the general rather than the idiosyncratic, as the Supreme Court noted with reference to other benefits tied to marital status in *Califano v. Jobst,* 434 U.S. 47, 53–54, 54 L.Ed.2d 228, 98 S.Ct. 95 (1977). Nor is it entirely clear that this couple ought to be considered an exception to the general concern with heterosexuals who choose to have a family outside of marriage. For when asked at argument why the couple had never married, Irizarry's counsel replied that he had asked his client that question and she had told him that "it just never came up." There may be good reasons why a particular couple would not marry even after producing children, but that the thought of marriage would not even occur to them is disquieting.

. . .

To the board's argument that it has extended spousal benefits to the domestic partners of homosexual employees because homosexual marriage is not a status available to its employees, Irizarry replies that the argument depends on the board's groundless decision to provide benefits to spouses, rather than domestic partners, of its employees. She says that all the board has to do to purge the constitutional violation is to condition all nonemployee fringe benefits on satisfaction of its domestic-partnership conditions other than that the domestic partner be of the same sex as the employee; and then the "discrimination" in favor of heterosexuals that the extension of spousal benefits to homosexual domestic partners was intended to erase will be eliminated without discrimination against heterosexual domestic partners. She points to Chicago's Human Rights Ordinance, which forbids discrimination on the basis of marital status. But the purpose, at least the primary purpose, of such a prohibition is surely not to dethrone marriage; it is to prevent discrimination against married women, who employers might think have divided loyalties. Such laws are pro-marriage, not anti-as the plaintiff suggests.

All other considerations to one side, the board reaps cost savings by basing dependent benefits on marital status—savings distinct from those discussed earlier that depend simply on the much smaller number of homosexuals than heterosexuals likely to seek or qualify for domestic-partner benefits. It is easier to determine whether the claimant is married to an employee than to determine whether the claimant satisfies the multiple criteria for domestic partnership. Earlier we took for granted that cost is an admissible consideration in evaluating the rationality of a classification; here we add that the cases so hold. *Bankers Life & Casualty Co. v. Crenshaw*, 486 U.S. 71, 83–84, 100 L.Ed.2d 62, 108 S.Ct. 1645 (1988); *LaGuerre v. Reno*, 164 F.3d 1035, 1041 (7th Cir. 1998); *DeSousa v. Reno*, 190 F.3d 175, 185 (3d Cir. 1999); *Silver v. Baggiano*, 804 F.2d 1211, 1218–19 (11th Cir. 1986). And we do not understand the plaintiff to be arguing that the board of education must have anything more than a rational basis for its action in order to defeat the plaintiff's equal protection claim. Only when the plaintiff in an equal protection case is complaining of a form of discrimination that is suspect because historically it was irrational or invidious is there a heavier burden of justifying a difference in treatment than merely showing that it is rational. *E.g.*, *Kimel v. Florida Bd. of Regents*, 528 U.S. 62, 83–84, 145 L.Ed.2d 522, 120 S.Ct. 631 (2000); *Milner v. Apfel*, 148 F.3d 812, 815–16 (7th Cir. 1998); *Miller v. United States*, 73 F.3d 878, 881–82 (9th Cir. 1995); *Disabled American Veterans v. Dept. of Veterans Affairs*, 962 F.2d 136, 141–42 (2d Cir. 1992).

Heterosexuals cohabiting outside of marriage are not such a class. There is a history of disapproval of (nonmarital) cohabitation, and some states still criminalize it. *See, e.g.*, Ariz. Rev. Stat. Ann. § 13–1409; Mich. Comp. Laws Ann. § 750.355; N.D. Cent. Code § 12.1–20–10—as indeed Illinois did until 1990. *United States v. Nichols*, 937 F.2d 1257, 1263 (7th Cir. 1991). But the disapproval is not necessarily irrational or invidious, *Doe v. Duling*, 782 F.2d 1202, 1207 (4th Cir. 1986), given the benefits of marriage discussed earlier. It was rational for the board to refuse to extend domestic-partnership benefits to persons who can if they wish marry and by doing so spare the board from having to make a factual inquiry into the nature of their relationship.

The least rational feature of the board's policy, though not emphasized by the plaintiff, is that although-domestic-partner benefits are confined to persons of the same sex, the partners need not be homosexual. They could be roommates who have lived together for a year and own some property jointly and for want of relatives are each other's "sole domestic partner," and if so they would be entitled to domestic-partner benefits under the board of education's policy. To distinguish between roommates of the same and of different sexes, as the policy implicitly does, cannot be justified on the ground that the latter but not the former could marry each other!

So the policy does not make a very close fit between end and means. But it doesn't have to, provided there is a rational basis for the loose fit. *See, e.g.*, *Kimel v. Florida Bd. of Regents*, *supra*, 528 U.S. 62 at 83–84; *Vance v. Bradley*, 440 U.S. 93, 108–109, 59 L.Ed.2d 171, 99 S.Ct. 939 (1979); *Zehner v. Trigg*, 133 F.3d 459, 463 (7th Cir. 1997); *Wedderburn v. INS*, 215 F.3d 795, 800 (7th Cir. 2000). This follows from our earlier point that cost is a rational basis for treating people differently. Economy is one of the principal reasons for using rules rather than standards to govern conduct. Rules single out one or a few facts from the welter of possibly relevant considerations and make that one or those few facts legally determinative, thus dispensing with inquiry into the other considerations. A standard that takes account of all relevant considerations will produce fewer arbitrary differences in outcome, but at a cost in uncertainty, administrative burden, and sometimes even—as here—in invading people's privacy. It is easy to see why the board of education does not want to put applicants to the proof of their sexual preference. That would be resented. The price of avoiding an inquiry that would be costly because it would be obnoxious is that a few roommates may end up with windfall benefits. We cannot say that the board is being irrational in deciding to pay that price rather than snoop into people's sex lives. *Cf. Califano v. Jobst*, *supra*, 434 U.S. at 53–54.

If the result is, as it may be, that none of the nine employees who have opted for domestic-partner benefits is homosexual (or at least that none is willing to acknowledge his homosexuality publicly, for that is not required by the board's policy though it would seem implicit in the board's desire to attract homosexuals who have "a healthy acceptance of their own sexuality"), this would lend a note of irony to the board's policy and would reinforce our earlier conjecture that the purpose is to make a statement rather than to confer actual monetary benefits. But "making a statement" is a common purpose of legislation and does not condemn it as irrational.

. . .

Affirmed.

III. THE FIRST BACKLASH TO THE MARRIAGE MOVEMENT

Between 1995 and 2001, after the Hawaii and Alaska litigation, 34 states enacted laws expressly providing that marriage be limited to one man and one woman and also providing that those states would not recognize same-sex marriages from other states.

In 1996, Congress passed the Defense of Marriage Act ("DOMA"), which provided that no state was obliged to recognize a same-sex marriage from another state. Following is the text of DOMA as well as Senatorial debate about the legislation.

A. THE DEFENSE OF MARRIAGE ACT

The Defense of Marriage Act provides:

> No State, territory, or possession of the United States, or Indian tribe, shall be required to give effect to any public act, record, or judicial proceeding of any other State, territory, possession, or tribe respecting a relationship between persons of the same sex that is treated as a marriage under the laws of such other State, territory, possession, or tribe, or a right or claim arising from such relationship.
>
> In determining the meaning of any Act of Congress, or of any ruling, regulation, or interpretation of the various administrative bureaus and agencies of the United States, the word 'marriage' means only a legal union between one man and one woman as husband and wife, and the word 'spouse' refers only to a person of the opposite sex who is a husband or a wife.

(Codified at 28 U.S.C. sec. 1738C (1996) and 1 U.S.C. sec. 7 (1996).)

B. THE DOMA DEBATE

HON. HENRY A. WAXMAN IN OPPOSITION (EXTENSION OF REMARKS—JULY 17, 1996)

The House in Committee of the Whole House on the State of the Union had under consideration the bill (H.R. 3396) to define and protect the institution of marriage:

Mr. Waxman. Mr. Chairman, I rise in strong opposition to H.R. 3396, the so-called Defense of Marriage Act, and ask my colleagues to reject this mean-spirited legislation.

The proponents of H.R. 3396 would have us believe that this legislation is necessary to save the institution of marriage. The real purpose of H.R. 3396 is to create a wedge issue for Republicans for the upcoming elections.

In a shameless attempt to divide the American public, the Republican Party is espousing official bigotry. It is promoting discrimination against individuals who seek the same responsibilities and opportunities other Americans seek when they form a lifelong union with someone they love. It is scapegoating a segment of our society to fan the flames of intolerance and prejudice. And it is doing this to try to improve its standings in the polls.

Discrimination against people who are gay and committed to one another does nothing to defend marriage or to strengthen family values. It does, however, continue to deny them legal rights that married couples simply take for granted—inclusion in a spouse's health insurance plan, pension and tax benefits, the ability to participate in medical decisions, and the right to visit a dying spouse in the hospital.

Our nation's families deserve better from their leaders than this cynical effort to raise fears and create divisions for political gain. They need leaders who will recognize the true needs of families and who are willing to work for adequate healthcare, access to educational opportunities, a decent wage, and a livable environment.

Let's work together on the real challenges we face as a nation. Let's not allow our Republican leaders to create scapegoats to distract the public's attention from the failure of this Congress to address issues the American public cares about.

I urge my colleagues to stand up to bigotry and discrimination. I urge you to vote against this mean-spirited legislation.

HON. JESSE HELMS IN SUPPORT (SEPTEMBER 9, 1996)

Mr. HELMS. Mr. President, during my years in the Senate I have been privileged on many occasions to work with a substantial number of ministers whose Washington churches today are referred to as "African–American."

The day before the Senate adjourned for the August recess, I ran into one of these fine ministers over in the Russell Building. His church is Baptist. He has a booming, cheerful voice. And when I heard that voice, I knew who it was. He was saying, "Are you going home tomorrow?" And I told him I thought I was since the Senate probably would recess for the month of August.

I asked him, Mr. President, if he had a message for the folks back home. And he said, "I sure do. Tell them that God created Adam and Eve—not Adam and Steve."

Some may chuckle at this good-natured minister's humor. But he meant exactly what he was saying. In fact, it was a sort of sermonette. The truth is, he was hitting the nail on the head, if you want to use that cliché, or telling it like it is. However one may choose to describe this minister's getting down to the nitty-gritty, it was no mere cliché, Mr. President. There could not have been, as a matter of fact, a better way to begin this debate in favor of the Defense of Marriage Act, which is H.R. 3396. The formal debate will begin tomorrow morning in this Chamber, the U.S. Senate.

Now, then, let there be no mistake about it, this bill in no way, to any degree, is the kind of legislation which homosexual and lesbian leaders have disdainfully described as a, to use their words, "hate-driven bill."

In fact, it is precisely the critics of H.R. 3396 who are demanding that homosexuality be considered as just another lifestyle—these are the people who seek to force their agenda upon the vast majority of Americans who reject the homosexual lifestyle.

Indeed, Mr. President, the pending bill—the Defense of Marriage Act—will safeguard the sacred institutions of marriage and the family from those who seek to destroy them and who are willing to tear apart America's moral fabric in the process.

Isn't it disheartening, Mr. President, that Congress must clarify the traditional definition of marriage? But inch by inch, little by little, the homosexual lobby has chipped away at the moral stamina of some of America's courts and some legislators, in order to create the shaky ground that exists today that prompts this legislation being the subject of debate tomorrow morning in the U.S. Senate.

Just think, the prospect of a sovereign state's being compelled to recognize same-sex marriages sanctioned in another state is incredibly stark. If Hawaii's Supreme Court legalizes same-sex marriages in Hawaii, does the full faith and credit clause of the Constitution compel the other forty-nine states to recognize the new marriage law within their jurisdictions? I say no.

Such a suggestion, Mr. President, is a cockeyed interpretation of the Constitution, and this is one of so many times that I have wished the late, great Senator Sam J. Ervin, Jr., were here to cut it down to size. Homosexuals and lesbians boast that they are close to realizing their goal—legitimizing their behavior.

Mr. President, Bill Bennett has championed the cause of preserving America's culture; he contends that we are already reaping the consequences of the devaluation of marriage. And he warns that "it is exceedingly imprudent to conduct a radical, untested, and inherently flawed social experiment on an institution that is the keystone and the arch of civilization."

Bill Bennett is everlastingly right, and I believe the American people in the majority understand that the Defense of Marriage Act is vitally important. It will establish a simple, clear federal definition of marriage as the legal union of one man and one woman, and it will exempt sovereign states from being compelled by a half-baked interpretation of the U.S. Constitution to recognize same-sex marriages wrongfully legalized in another state.

If the Senate, tomorrow, makes the mistake of approving the Employment Nondiscrimination Act proposed by the senator from Massachusetts,* it will pave the way for liberal judges to threaten the business policies of countless American employers, and, in the long run, put in question the legality of the Defense of Marriage Act. The homosexual lobby knows this and that is why there is such a clamor favoring adoption of the Kennedy bill.

Mr. President, at the heart of this debate is the moral and spiritual survival of this nation. Alexis de Tocqueville said a century and a half ago that America had grown great because America was good. Mr. de Tocqueville also warned that if America made the mistake of ceasing to be good, America would cease to be great.

So, we must confront the question posed long ago: "Quo Vadis, America?" The Senate is about to answer that question. We will decide whither goeth America. It is solely up to us.

C. TRANSCRIPT OF THE MARK-UP RECORD OF THE DEFENSE OF MARRIAGE ACT

House Judiciary Committee, June 12, 1996

Mr. Bono: I, I ... this has been an amazing experience for me because I'm immersed in legal rhetoric that is interpreting the Constitution, and it's staggering how brilliant everyone is and how well they know their craft, and I wouldn't dare venture into their craft.

And it's clear to me, Mr. Chairman, that your job here, or my job here, is to try to interpret the Constitution and then act on that interpretation, representing the people. But it seems like the rhetoric has gone on to a point—sometimes things go way beyond where they should go, and an impasse is an impasse. And if there was ever an obvious impasse, this is it.

And what seems to have occurred here is that this subject is a rough subject because, if you're not a homo-

* Senator Edward Kennedy (D–Mass.).

sexual, you have strong feelings one way; if you are a homosexual, you have strong feelings the other way. But I would just like to go on the record and say this: that when things like this come out, it certainly makes a minority feel like everyone thinks they're less. And I think for someone to defend that is absolutely natural.

And Barney's a good friend of mine—or I consider him a good friend of mine. And I see his point of view, and I appreciate his fight. He's fighting as hard as he can because he's a human being; he has these feelings; he's gay; my daughter's gay. He has to live this way. So society hasn't quite accepted all of this.

So I think we go beyond the Constitution here. I think we go beyond all these brilliant interpretations here, and I think we have hit feelings, and we've hit what people can handle and what they can't handle, and it's that simple. And no matter how you justify what you say legally or whether it represents the Constitution, I think it breaks down to whether you're able to handle something or whether you're not able to handle something. I don't love my daughter any less because she's gay, and I don't dislike Barney any more because he's gay. I have, again, a tremendous respect.

And I want to reiterate that, no matter how strong of a person you are, these kind[s] of bills and this kind of legislation is going to make someone defensive and going to make them feel like other people are trying to make them less, and Barney's not less.

And so I think that sometimes we have to now go beyond the law and get into a sensitivity and just say it like it is, tell the truth, and go on with it. I mean, what is obvious here is the votes are going to be the way they're going to be. And we can talk for hours and hours and hours, and you'll hear both sides brilliantly discussed.

Mr. Gekas: Will the gentleman yield for a moment?

Bono: Let me just finish, and I'll be happy to yield.

I just want to say this; I owe this to Barney, and I want to go on record that I'm not homophobic; I'm not a bigot, and I'm not pandering to hatred, and I like—I like Barney, and I love my daughter. I simply can't handle it yet, Barney. It's nothing—nothing else, but at least I want to honestly say that to you, and throw aside all the legal rhetoric. I wish I was ready, but I can't tell my son it's okay, or I don't think I can yet. So if I could—

Mr. Frank: Would you yield to me?

Bono: Yes.

Frank: I would ask that the gentleman have an additional minute, and I thank the gentleman and I appreciate candor and the decency that motivates it.

I would say two things. It's not that I feel less. This bill says I and many others are less. It says that—and no one is asking for a stamp of approval. What we're saying is, if we pay taxes, if we work, we simply want to be able to get the same financial benefits and the same responses other people do.

And, secondly, in terms of handling it—and I understand that, but no one is asking you or any of the others to do any more than leave us alone and let us have the same rights as anyone else. Let us have the rights in any State that decides, because that's all this amendment says. If the State—if we can persuade a State legislature to do it, if we can win a referendum, if we can have a court decision not be overturned, let us be like anyone else. So no one is asking you to do anything else, and if it bothers people, turn your head, but don't inflict legal disabilities that carry out that feeling.

Bono: I ask for an additional thirty seconds.

Chair: Without objection.

Bono: I hear you. I really do hear you. And my response back to you is, you're absolutely right, but the other side of it is this has taken people to as far as they can go, and then no justifiers—I don't want to justify it because I can't. You just go as far as you can go, and then that's why I want to say to you again, honestly, I can't go this far as you deserve even, but—and I'm sorry, but I think that's the whole situation here, and I think we could argue it legally for hours and days, but that's what it's going to get down to.

IV. THE EMERGENCE OF THE CIVIL UNION

Despite the passage of DOMA, the struggle for gay marriage continued. In 1997 three same-sex couples: Stan Baker and Peter Harrigan; Beck and Stacy Jolles; and Lois Farnham and Holly Puterbaugh, brought suit against the State of Vermont and their towns for denying them marriage licenses.

BAKER v. STATE OF VERMONT

170 Vt. 194, 744 A.2d 864 (1999)

OPINION BY: JEFFREY L. AMESTOY

AMESTOY, C.J. May the State of Vermont exclude same-sex couples from the benefits and protections that its laws provide to opposite-sex married couples? That is the fundamental question we address in this appeal, a question that the Court well knows arouses deeply-felt religious, moral, and political beliefs. Our constitutional responsibility to consider the legal merits of issues properly before us provides no exception for the controversial case. The issue before the Court, moreover, does not turn on the religious or moral debate over intimate same-sex relationships, but rather on the statutory and constitutional basis for the exclusion of same-sex couples from the secular benefits and protections offered married couples.

We conclude that under the Common Benefits Clause of the Vermont Constitution, which, in pertinent part, reads,

> That government is, or ought to be, instituted for the common benefit, protection, and security of the people, nation, or community, and not for the particular emolument or advantage of any single person, family, or set of persons, who are a part only of that community . . .

Vt. Const., ch. I, art 7., plaintiffs may not be deprived of the statutory benefits and protections afforded persons of the opposite sex who choose to marry. We hold that the State is constitutionally required to extend to same-sex couples the common benefits and protections that flow from marriage under Vermont law. Whether this ultimately takes the form of inclusion within the marriage laws themselves or a parallel "domestic partnership" system or some equivalent statutory alternative, rests with the Legislature. Whatever system is chosen, however, must conform with the constitutional imperative to afford all Vermonters the common benefit, protection, and security of the law.

Plaintiffs are three same-sex couples who have lived together in committed relationships for periods ranging from four to twenty-five years. Two of the couples have raised children together. Each couple applied for a marriage license from their respective town clerk, and each was refused a license as ineligible under the applicable state marriage laws. Plaintiffs thereupon filed this lawsuit against defendants—the State of Vermont, the Towns of Milton and Shelburne, and the City of South Burlington—seeking a declaratory judgment that the refusal to issue them a license violated the marriage statutes and the Vermont Constitution.

The State, joined by Shelburne and South Burlington, moved to dismiss the action on the ground that plaintiffs had failed to state a claim for which relief could be granted. The Town of Milton answered the complaint and subsequently moved for judgment on the pleadings. Plaintiffs opposed the motions and cross-moved for judgment on the pleadings. The trial court granted the State's and the Town of Milton's motions, denied plaintiffs' motion, and dismissed the complaint. The court ruled that the marriage statutes could not be construed to permit the issuance of a license to same-sex couples. The court further ruled that the marriage statutes were constitutional because they rationally furthered the State's interest in promoting "the link between procreation and child rearing." This appeal followed.

I. THE STATUTORY CLAIM

Plaintiffs initially contend the trial court erred in concluding that the marriage statutes render them ineligible for a marriage license. It is axiomatic that the principal objective of statutory construction is to discern the legislative intent. *See Merkel v. Nationwide Ins. Co.*, 166 Vt. 311, 314, 693 A.2d 706, 707 (1997). While we may explore a variety of sources to discern that intent, it is also a truism of statutory interpretation that where a statute is unambiguous we rely on the plain and ordinary meaning of the words chosen. *See In re P.S.*, 167 Vt. 63, 70, 702 A.2d 98, 102 (1997). "We rely on the plain meaning of the words because we presume they reflect the Legislature's intent." *Braun v. Board of Dental Examiners*, 167 Vt. 110, 116, 702 A.2d 124, 127 (1997).

. . .

Although it is not necessarily the only possible definition, there is no doubt that the plain and ordinary meaning of "marriage" is the union of one man and one woman as husband and wife. *See* Webster's New International Dictionary 1506 (2d ed. 1955) (marriage consists of state of "being united to a person . . . of the opposite sex as husband or wife"); Black's Law Dictionary 986 (7th ed. 1999) (marriage is "the legal union of a man and woman as husband and wife"). This understanding of the term is well rooted in Vermont common law. . . . The legislative understanding is also reflected in the enabling statute governing the issuance of marriage licenses, which provides, in part, that the license "shall be issued by the clerk of the town where either the bride or groom resides." 18 V.S.A. § 5131(a). "Bride" and "groom" are gender-specific terms. *See* Webster's, *supra*, at 334 (bride defined as "a woman newly married, or about to be married"; bridegroom defined as "a man newly married, or about to be married").

Further evidence of the legislative assumption that marriage consists of a union of opposite genders may be found in the consanguinity statutes, which expressly prohibit a man from marrying certain female relatives, *see* 15 V.S.A. § 1, and a woman from marrying certain male relatives, *see id.* § 2. In addition, the annulment statutes explicitly refer to "husband and wife," *see id.* § 513, as do other statutes relating to married couples. *See, e.g.*, 12 V.S.A. § 1605 ("husband and wife" may not testify about communications to each other under rule commonly known as "marital privilege," *see State v. Wright*, 154 Vt. 512, 525, 581 A.2d 720, 728 (1989)); 14 V.S.A. §§ 461, 465, 470 (referring to interest of "widow" in estate of her "husband"); *id.* § 10 (requiring three witnesses where "husband or wife" are given beneficial interest in other's will); 15 V.S.A. § 102 (legal protections where "married man ... deserts, neglects or abandons his wife").

These statutes, read as a whole, reflect the common understanding that marriage under Vermont law consists of a union between a man and a woman. Plaintiffs essentially concede this fact. They argue, nevertheless, that the underlying purpose of marriage is to protect and encourage the union of committed couples and that, absent an explicit legislative prohibition, the statutes should be interpreted broadly to include committed same-sex couples. Plaintiffs rely principally on our decision in *In re B.L.V.B.*, 160 Vt. 368, 369, 628 A.2d 1271, 1272 (1993). There, we held that a woman who was co-parenting the two children of her same-sex partner could adopt the children without terminating the natural mother's parental rights. Although the statute provided generally that an adoption deprived the natural parents of their legal rights, it contained an exception where the adoption was by the "spouse" of the natural parent. *See id.* at 370, 628 A.2d at 1273 (citing 15 V.S.A. § 448). Technically, therefore, the exception was inapplicable. We concluded, however, that the purpose of the law was not to restrict the exception to legally married couples, but to safeguard the child, and that to apply the literal language of the statute in these circumstances would defeat the statutory purpose and "reach an absurd result." *Id.* at 371, 628 A.2d at 1273. Although the Legislature had undoubtedly not even considered same-sex unions when the law was enacted in 1945, our interpretation was consistent with its "general intent and spirit." *Id.* at 373, 628 A.2d at 1274.

Contrary to plaintiffs' claim, *B.L.V.B.* does not control our conclusion here. We are not dealing in this case with a narrow statutory exception requiring a broader reading than its literal words would permit in order to avoid a result plainly at odds with the legislative purpose. Unlike *B.L.V.B.*, it is far from clear that limiting marriage to opposite-sex couples violates the Legislature's "intent and spirit." Rather, the evidence demonstrates a clear legislative assumption that marriage under our statutory scheme consists of a union between a man and a woman. Accordingly, we reject plaintiffs' claim that they were entitled to a license under the statutory scheme governing marriage.

II. THE CONSTITUTIONAL CLAIM

Assuming that the marriage statutes preclude their eligibility for a marriage license, plaintiffs contend that the exclusion violates their right to the common benefit and protection of the law guaranteed by Chapter I, Article 7 of the Vermont Constitution. They note that in denying them access to a civil marriage license, the law effectively excludes them from a broad array of legal benefits and protections incident to the marital relation, including access to a spouse's medical, life, and disability insurance, hospital visitation and other medical decision-making privileges, spousal support, intestate succession, homestead protections, and many other statutory protections. They claim the trial court erred in upholding the law on the basis that it reasonably served the State's interest in promoting the "link between procreation and child rearing." They argue that the large number of married couples without children, and the increasing incidence of same-sex couples with children, undermines the State's rationale. They note that Vermont law affirmatively guarantees the right to adopt and raise children regardless of the sex of the parents, *see* 15A V.S.A. § 1–102, and challenge the logic of a legislative scheme that recognizes the rights of same-sex partners as parents, yet denies them—and their children—the same security as spouses.

In considering this issue, it is important to emphasize at the outset that it is the Common Benefits Clause of the Vermont Constitution we are construing, rather than its counterpart, the Equal Protection Clause of the Fourteenth Amendment to the United States Constitution. It is altogether fitting and proper that we do so. Vermont's constitutional commitment to equal rights was the product of the successful effort to create an independent republic and a fundamental charter of government, the Constitution of 1777, both of which preceded the adoption of the Fourteenth Amendment by nearly a century. As we explained in *State v. Badger*, 141 Vt. 430, 448–49, 450 A.2d 336, 347 (1982), "our constitution is not a mere reflection of the federal charter. Historically and textually, it differs from the United States Constitution. It predates the federal counterpart, as it extends back to Vermont's days as an independent republic. It is an independent authority, and Vermont's fundamental law."

. . .

Although our decisions over the last few decades have routinely invoked the rhetoric of suspect class favored by the federal courts, *see, e.g.*, *Choquette*, 153 Vt. at 51, 569 A.2d at 458, there are notable exceptions. The principal decision in this regard is the landmark case of *State v. Ludlow Supermarkets, Inc.*, 141 Vt. 261, 448 A.2d 791 (1982). There, Chief Justice Albert Barney, writing for the Court, invalidated a Sunday closing law that discriminated among classes of commercial establishments on the basis of their size. After noting that this Court, unlike its federal counterpart, was not constrained by considerations of federalism and the impact of its decision on fifty varying jurisdictions, the Court declared that Article 7 "only allows the statutory classifications . . . if a case of necessity can be established overriding the prohibition of Article 7 by reference to the common benefit, protection, and security of the people." *Id.* at 268, 448 A.2d at 795. Applying this test, the Court concluded that the State's justifications for the disparate treatment of large and small businesses failed to withstand constitutional scrutiny. *Id.* at 269–70, 448 A.2d at 796.

Ludlow, as we later explained, did not alter the traditional requirement under Article 7 that legislative classifications must "reasonably relate to a legitimate public purpose." *Choquette,* 153 Vt. at 52, 569 A.2d at 459. Nor did it overturn the principle that the justifications demanded of the State may depend upon the nature and importance of the benefits and protections affected by the legislation; indeed, this is implicit in the weighing process. It did establish that Article 7 would require a "more stringent" reasonableness inquiry than was generally associated with rational basis review under the federal constitution. *State v. Brunelle*, 148 Vt. 347, 351, 534 A.2d 198, 201–02 (1987); *see also Hodgeman v. Jard Co.*, 157 Vt. 461, 464, 599 A.2d 1371, 1373 (1991) (citing *Ludlow* for principle that Article 7 "may require this Court to examine more closely distinctions drawn by state government than would the Fourteenth Amendment"). Ludlow did not override the traditional deference accorded legislation having any reasonable relation to a legitimate public purpose. It simply signaled that Vermont courts—having "access to specific legislative history and all other proper resources" to evaluate the object and effect of state laws—would engage in a meaningful, case-specific analysis to ensure that any exclusion from the general benefit and protection of the law would bear a just and reasonable relation to the legislative goals. *Ludlow*, 141 Vt. at 268, 448 A.2d at 795.

. . .

Thus, "labels aside," Vermont case law has consistently demanded in practice that statutory exclusions from publicly-conferred benefits and protections must be "premised on an appropriate and overriding public interest." *Ludlow*, 141 Vt. at 268, 448 A.2d at 795. The rigid categories utilized by the federal courts under the Fourteenth Amendment find no support in our early case law and, while routinely cited, are often effectively ignored in our more recent decisions. As discussed more fully below, these decisions are consistent with the text and history of the Common Benefits Clause which, similarly, yield no rigid categories or formulas of analysis. The balancing approach utilized in *Ludlow* and implicit in our recent decisions reflects the language, history, and values at the core of the Common Benefits Clause. We turn, accordingly, to a brief examination of constitutional language and history.

B. Text

. . .

We first focus on the words of the Constitution themselves, for, as Chief Justice Marshall observed, "although the spirit of an instrument, especially of a constitution, is to be respected not less than its letter, yet the spirit is to be collected chiefly from its words." *Sturges v. Crowninshield,* 17 U.S. (4 Wheat.) 122, 202, 4 L. Ed. 529 (1819). One of the fundamental rights included in Chapter I of the Vermont Constitution of 1777, entitled "A Declaration of Rights of the Inhabitants of the State of Vermont," the Common Benefits Clause as originally written provided:

> That government is, or ought to be, instituted for the common benefit, protection, and security of the people, nation or community; and not for the particular emolument or advantage of any single man, family or set of men, who are a part only of that community; and that the community hath an indubitable, unalienable and indefeasible right, to reform, alter or abolish government, in such manner as shall

be, by that community, judged most conducive to the public weal. Vt. Const. of 1777, ch. I, art. VI.

The first point to be observed about the text is the affirmative and unequivocal mandate of the first section, providing that government is established for the common benefit of the people and community as a whole. Unlike the Fourteenth Amendment, whose origin and language reflect the solicitude of a dominant white society for an historically-oppressed African–American minority (no state shall "deny" the equal protection of the laws), the Common Benefits Clause mirrors the confidence of a homogeneous, eighteenth-century group of men aggressively laying claim to the same rights as their peers in Great Britain or, for that matter, New York, New Hampshire, or the Upper Connecticut River Valley. *See* F. Mahady, *Toward a Theory of State Constitutional Jurisprudence: A Judge's Thoughts*, 13 Vt. L. Rev. 145, 151–52 (1988) (noting distinct eighteenth-century origins of Article 7). The same assumption that all the people should be afforded all the benefits and protections bestowed by government is also reflected in the second section, which prohibits not the denial of rights to the oppressed, but rather the conferral of advantages or emoluments upon the privileged.

The words of the Common Benefits Clause are revealing. While they do not, to be sure, set forth a fully-formed standard of analysis for determining the constitutionality of a given statute, they do express broad principles which usefully inform that analysis. Chief among these is the principle of inclusion. As explained more fully in the discussion that follows, the specific proscription against governmental favoritism toward not only groups or "sets of men," but also toward any particular "family" or "single man," underscores the framers' resentment of political preference of any kind. The affirmative right to the "common benefits and protections" of government and the corollary proscription of favoritism in the distribution of public "emoluments and advantages" reflect the framers' overarching objective "not only that everyone enjoy equality before the law or have an equal voice in government but also that everyone have an equal share in the fruits of the common enterprise." W. Adams, *The First American Constitutions* 188 (1980) (emphasis added). Thus, at its core the Common Benefits Clause expressed a vision of government that afforded every Vermonter its benefit and protection and provided no Vermonter particular advantage.

C. Historical Context

Although historical research yields little direct evidence of the framers' intentions, an examination of the ideological origins of the Common Benefits Clause casts a useful light upon the inclusionary principle at its textual core. Like other provisions of the Vermont Constitution of 1777, the Common Benefits Clause was borrowed verbatim from the Pennsylvania Constitution of 1776, which was based, in turn, upon a similar provision in the Virginia Declaration of Rights of 1776.

. . .

Although aimed at Great Britain, the American Revolution—as numerous historians have noted—also tapped deep-seated domestic antagonisms.

. . .

The powerful movement for "social equivalence" unleashed by the Revolution ultimately found its most complete expression in the first state constitutions adopted in the early years of the rebellion. In Pennsylvania, where social antagonisms were most acute, the result was a fundamental charter that has been described as "the most radical constitution of the Revolution." Wood, *supra*, at 84–85; *see also Shaeffer, supra*, at 35–36. Yet the Pennsylvania Constitution's egalitarianism was arguably eclipsed the following year by the Vermont Constitution of 1777. In addition to the commitment to government for the "common benefit, protection, and security," it contained novel provisions abolishing slavery, eliminating property qualifications for voting, and calling for the governor, lieutenant governor, and twelve councilors to be elected by the people rather than appointed by the legislature. *See Shalhope, supra*, at 171–72. These and other provisions have led one historian to observe that Vermont's first charter was the "most democratic constitution produced by any of the American states." *See id.* at 172.

The historical origins of the Vermont Constitution thus reveal that the framers, although enlightened for their day, were not principally concerned with civil rights for African–Americans and other minorities, but with equal access to public benefits and protections for the community as a whole. The concept of equality at the core of the Common Benefits Clause was not the eradication of racial or class distinctions, but rather the elimination of artificial governmental preferments and advantages. The Vermont Constitution would ensure that the law uniformly afforded every Vermonter its benefit, protection, and security so that social and political preeminence would reflect differences of capacity, disposition, and virtue, rather than governmental favor and privilege.

. . .

E. The Standard Applied

With these general precepts in mind, we turn to the question of whether the exclusion of same-sex couples from the benefits and protections incident to marriage under Vermont law contravenes Article 7. The first step in our analysis is to identify the nature of the statutory classification. As noted, the marriage statutes apply expressly to opposite-sex couples. Thus, the statutes exclude anyone who wishes to marry someone of the same sex.

. . .

Next, we must identify the governmental purpose or purposes to be served by the statutory classification. The principal purpose the State advances in support of excluding same-sex couples from the legal benefits of marriage is the government's interest in "furthering the link between procreation and child rearing." The State has a strong interest, it argues, in promoting a permanent commitment between couples who have children to ensure that their offspring are considered legitimate and receive ongoing parental support. The State contends, further, that the Legislature could reasonably believe that sanctioning same-sex unions "would diminish society's perception of the link between procreation and child rearing ... [and] advance the notion that fathers or mothers ... are mere surplusage to the functions of procreation and child rearing." The State argues that since same-sex couples cannot conceive a child on their own, state-sanctioned same-sex unions "could be seen by the Legislature to separate further the connection between procreation and parental responsibilities for raising children." Hence, the Legislature is justified, the State concludes, "in using the marriage statutes to send a public message that procreation and child rearing are intertwined."

. . .

Thus, with or without the marriage sanction, the reality today is that increasing numbers of same-sex couples are employing increasingly efficient assisted-reproductive techniques to conceive and raise children. *See* L. Ikemoto, *The In/Fertile, the Too Fertile, and the Dysfertile*, 47 Hastings L.J. 1007, 1056 & n.170 (1996). The Vermont Legislature has not only recognized this reality, but has acted affirmatively to remove legal barriers so that same-sex couples may legally adopt and rear the children conceived through such efforts. *See* 15A V.S.A. § 1–102(b) (allowing partner of biological parent to adopt if in child's best interest without reference to sex). The state has also acted to expand the domestic relations laws to safeguard the interests of same-sex parents and their children when such couples terminate their domestic relationship. *See* 15A V.S.A. § 1–112 (vesting family court with jurisdiction over parental rights and responsibilities, parent-child contact, and child support when unmarried persons who have adopted minor child "terminate their domestic relationship").

. . .

The question thus becomes whether the exclusion of a relatively small but significant number of otherwise qualified same-sex couples from the same legal benefits and protections afforded their opposite-sex counterparts contravenes the mandates of Article 7. It is, of course, well settled that statutes are not necessarily unconstitutional because they fail to extend legal protection to all who are similarly situated. *See Benning*, 161 Vt. at 486, 641 A.2d at 764 ("A statute need not regulate the whole of a field to pass constitutional muster."). Courts have upheld underinclusive statutes out of a recognition that, for reasons of pragmatism or administrative convenience, the legislature may choose to address problems incrementally. *See, e.g., City of New Orleans v. Dukes*, 427 U.S. 297, 303, 49 L.Ed.2d 511, 96 S.Ct. 2513 (1976) (legislature may adopt regulations "that only partially ameliorate a perceived evil"); *Williamson v. Lee Optical of Okla., Inc.*, 348 U.S. 483, 489, 99 L.Ed. 563, 75 S.Ct. 461 (1955) ("The legislature may select one phase of one field and apply a remedy there, neglecting the others."). The State does not contend, however, that the same-sex exclusion is necessary as a matter of pragmatism or administrative convenience. We turn, accordingly, from the principal justifications advanced by the State to the interests asserted by plaintiffs.

. . .

While the laws relating to marriage have undergone many changes during the last century, largely toward the goal of equalizing the status of husbands and wives, the benefits of marriage have not diminished in value. On the contrary, the benefits and protections incident to a marriage license under Vermont law have never been greater. They include, for example, the right to receive a portion of the estate of a spouse who dies intestate and protection against disinheritance through elective share provisions, under 14 V.S.A. §§ 401–404, 551; preference in being appointed as the personal representative of a spouse who dies intestate, under 14 V.S.A. § 903; the right to bring a lawsuit for the wrongful death of a spouse, under 14 V.S.A. § 1492; the right to bring an action for loss of consortium, under 12 V.S.A. § 5431; the right to workers' compensation survivor benefits under 21 V.S.A. § 632; the right to spousal benefits statutorily guaranteed to public employees, including health, life, disability, and accident insurance, under 3 V.S.A. § 631; the opportunity to be covered as a spouse under group life insurance policies issued to an employee, under 8 V.S.A. § 3811; the opportunity to be covered as the insured's spouse under an individual health insurance policy, under 8 V.S.A. § 4063; the right to claim an evidentiary privilege for marital communications, under V.R.E. 504; homestead rights and protections, under 27 V.S.A. §§ 105–108, 141–142; the presumption of joint ownership of property and the concomitant right of survivorship, under 27 V.S.A. § 2; hospital visitation and other rights incident to the medical treatment of a family member, under 18 V.S.A. § 1852; and the right to receive, and the obligation to provide, spousal support, maintenance, and property division in the event of separation or divorce, under 15 V.S.A. §§ 751–752. Other courts and commentators have noted the collection of rights, powers, privileges, and responsibilities triggered by marriage. *See generally Baehr v. Lewin*, 74 Haw. 530, 852 P.2d 44, 59 (Haw. 1993); D. Chambers, *What If? The Legal Consequences of Marriage and the Legal Needs of Lesbian and Gay Male Couples*, 95 Mich. L. Rev. 447, passim (1996); J. Robbennolt & M. Johnson, *Legal Planning for Unmarried Committed Partners: Empirical Lessons for a Preventive and Therapeutic Approach*, 41 Ariz. L. Rev. 417, passim (1999); J. Trosino, *American Wedding: Same–Sex Marriage and the Miscegenation Analogy*, 73 B.U. L. Rev. 93, 96 (1993).

While other statutes could be added to this list, the point is clear. The legal benefits and protections flowing from a marriage license are of such significance that any statutory exclusion must necessarily be grounded on public concerns of sufficient weight, cogency, and authority that the justice of the deprivation cannot seriously be questioned. Considered in light of the extreme logical disjunction between the classification and the stated purposes of the law—protecting children and "furthering the link between procreation and child rearing"—the exclusion falls substantially short of this standard. The laudable governmental goal of promoting a commitment between married couples to promote the security of their children and the community as a whole provides no reasonable basis for denying the legal benefits and protections of marriage to same-sex couples, who are no differently situated with respect to this goal than their opposite-sex counterparts. Promoting a link between procreation and childrearing similarly fails to support the exclusion. We turn, accordingly, to the remaining interests identified by the State in support of the statutory exclusion.

The State asserts that a number of additional rationales could support a legislative decision to exclude same-sex partners from the statutory benefits and protections of marriage. Among these are the State's purported interests in "promoting child rearing in a setting that provides both male and female role models," minimizing the legal complications of surrogacy contracts and sperm donors, "bridging differences" between the sexes, discouraging marriages of convenience for tax, housing or other benefits, maintaining uniformity with marriage laws in other states, and generally protecting marriage from "destabilizing changes." The most substantive of the State's remaining claims relates to the issue of childrearing. It is conceivable that the Legislature could conclude that opposite-sex partners offer advantages in this area, although we note that child-development experts disagree and the answer is decidedly uncertain. The argument, however, contains a more fundamental flaw, and that is the Legislature's endorsement of a policy diametrically at odds with the State's claim. In 1996, the Vermont General Assembly enacted, and the Governor signed, a law removing all prior legal barriers to the adoption of children by same-sex couples. *See* 15A V.S.A. § 1–102. At the same time, the Legislature provided additional legal protections in the form of court-ordered child support and parent-child contact in the event that same-sex parents dissolved their "domestic relationship." *Id.* § 1–112. In light of these express policy choices, the State's arguments that Vermont public policy favors opposite-sex over same-sex parents or disfavors the use of artificial reproductive technologies are patently without substance.

Similarly, the State's argument that Vermont's marriage laws serve a substantial governmental interest in maintaining uniformity with other jurisdictions cannot be reconciled with Vermont's recognition of unions, such as first-cousin marriages, not uniformly sanctioned in other states. *See* 15 V.S.A. §§ 1–2 (consanguinity statutes do not exclude first cousins); 1 H. Clark, The Law of Domestic Relations in the United States § 2.9 at 153–54 (2d ed. 1987) (noting states that prohibit first-cousin marriage). In an analogous context, Vermont has sanctioned adoptions by same-sex partners, *see* 15A V.S.A. § 1–102, notwithstanding the fact that many states have not. *See generally* Annotation, Adoption of Child By Same–Sex Partners, 27 A.L.R.5th 54, 68–72 (1995). Thus, the State's claim that Vermont's marriage laws were adopted because the Legislature sought to conform to those of the other forty-nine states is not only speculative, but refuted by two relevant legislative choices which demonstrate that uniformity with other jurisdictions has not been a governmental purpose.

. . .

Thus, viewed in the light of history, logic, and experience, we conclude that none of the interests asserted by the State provides a reasonable and just basis for the continued exclusion of same-sex couples from the benefits incident to a civil marriage license under Vermont law. Accordingly, in the faith that a case beyond the imagining of the framers of our Constitution may, nevertheless, be safely anchored in the values that infused it, we find a constitutional obligation to extend to plaintiffs the common benefit, protection, and security that Vermont law provides opposite-sex married couples. It remains only to determine the appropriate means and scope of relief compelled by this constitutional mandate.

F. Remedy

It is important to state clearly the parameters of today's ruling. Although plaintiffs sought injunctive and declaratory relief designed to secure a marriage license, their claims and arguments here have focused primarily upon the consequences of official exclusion from the statutory benefits, protections, and security incident to marriage under Vermont law. While some future case may attempt to establish that—notwithstanding equal benefits and protections under Vermont law—the denial of a marriage license operates per se to deny constitutionally-protected rights, that is not the claim we address today.

We hold only that plaintiffs are entitled under Chapter I, Article 7, of the Vermont Constitution to obtain the same benefits and protections afforded by Vermont law to married opposite-sex couples. We do not purport to infringe upon the prerogatives of the Legislature to craft an appropriate means of addressing this constitutional mandate, other than to note that the record here refers to a number of potentially constitutional statutory schemes from other jurisdictions. These include what are typically referred to as "domestic partnership" or "registered partnership" acts, which generally establish an alternative legal status to marriage for same-sex couples, impose similar formal requirements and limitations, create a parallel licensing or registration scheme, and extend all or most of the same rights and obligations provided by the law to married partners.

. . .

Further, while the State's prediction of "destabilization" cannot be a ground for denying relief, it is not altogether irrelevant. A sudden change in the marriage laws or the statutory benefits traditionally incidental to marriage may have disruptive and unforeseen consequences. Absent legislative guidelines defining the status and rights same-sex couples, consistent with constitutional requirements, uncertainty and confusion could result. Therefore, we hold that the current statutory scheme shall remain in effect for a reasonable period of time to enable the Legislature to consider and enact implementing legislation in an orderly and expeditious fashion.

. . .

III. CONCLUSION

While many have noted the symbolic or spiritual significance of the marital relation, it is plaintiffs' claim to the secular benefits and protections of a singularly human relationship that, in our view, characterizes this case. The State's interest in extending official recognition and legal protection to the professed commitment of two individuals to a lasting relationship of mutual affection is predicated on the belief that legal support of a couple's commitment provides stability for the individuals, their family, and the broader community. Although plaintiffs' interest in seeking state recognition and protection of their mutual commitment may—in view of divorce statistics—represent "the triumph of hope over experience," the essential aspect of their claim is simply and fundamentally for inclusion in the family of state-sanctioned human relations.

The past provides many instances where the law refused to see a human being when it should have. *See, e.g., Dred Scott*, 60 U.S. at 407 (concluding that African slaves and their descendants had "no rights which the white man was bound to respect"). The future may provide instances where the law will be asked to see a human when it should not. *See, e.g.*, G. Smith, *Judicial Decisionmaking in the Age of Biotechnology*, 13 Notre Dame J. Ethics & Pub. Policy 93, 114 (1999) (noting concerns that genetically engineering humans may threaten very nature of human individuality and identity). The challenge for future generations will be to define what is most essentially human. The extension of the Common Benefits Clause to acknowledge plaintiffs as Vermonters who seek nothing more, nor less, than legal protection and security for their avowed commitment to an intimate and lasting human relationship is simply, when all is said and done, a recognition of our common humanity.

The judgment of the superior court upholding the constitutionality of the Vermont marriage statutes under Chapter I, Article 7 of the Vermont Constitution is reversed. The effect of the Court's decision is suspended, and jurisdiction is retained in this Court, to permit the Legislature to consider and enact legislation consistent with the constitutional mandate described herein.

FOR THE COURT:

Chief Justice

CONCUR BY: DOOLEY (In Part); JOHNSON (In Part)

DOOLEY, J., concurring. I concur in Part I of the majority opinion, the holding of Part II, and the mandate. I do not, however, concur in the reasoning of Part II. I recognize that to most observers the significance of this decision lies in its result and remedy. In the cases that come before us in the future, however, the significance of this case will lie in its rationale—that is, how we interpret and apply Chapter I, Article 7 of the Vermont Constitution. Moreover, in this, the most closely-watched opinion in this Court's history, its acceptability will be based on whether its reasoning and result are clearly commanded by the Constitution and our precedents, and whether it is a careful and necessary exercise of the Court's limited powers. I do not believe that the majority's rationale meets this exacting standard, and I fear how it may be applied—or ignored—in the future.

This is a concurrence and not a dissent. I agree with the majority that the consequence of limiting marriage to a man and woman is the exclusion of these plaintiffs, and many persons similarly situated, from numerous rights, benefits, and duties that government and society provide to—and impose on—married persons. However we might have described marriage in relation to the very limited government that was created by our Constitution, the complexity of the current system of government-created benefits and burdens has made civil marriage a modern-day emolument, a government recognized and supported special status for which these plaintiffs are not eligible.

. . .

The marriage statutes do not facially discriminate on the basis of sexual orientation. There is, however, no doubt that the requirement that civil marriage be a union of one man and one woman has the effect of discriminating against lesbian and gay couples, like the plaintiffs in this case, who are unable to marry the life partners of their choice. The majority proclaims that most decisions have concluded that lesbians and gay men are not a suspect classification, inferring that any conclusion to the contrary is wrong. *See* 170 Vt. at 213, n. 10, 744 A.2d at 878 n.10. On this point, however, I believe the central analysis of *Ludlow* is critical:

> [A] state court reviewing state legislation is in a very different posture from the United States Supreme Court when it undertakes the parallel task. Rather than disposing of a case on the premise that its impact will presumably affect more than fifty varying jurisdictions, a state court reaches its result in the legal climate of the single jurisdiction with which it is associated, if federal proscriptions are not transgressed.

. . .

Since 1992, it has generally been the policy of Vermont to prohibit discrimination based on sexual orientation. *See* 1991, No. 135 (Adj. Sess.). This includes discrimination based on "female or male homosexuality." 1 V.S.A. § 143. Thus, I believe our "legal climate" is vastly different from that in *Bowers*, where, after considering that twenty-four states had criminalized sodomy between consenting adults, the United States Supreme Court concluded that there was no fundamental right, deeply rooted in the Nation's history, to engage in such conduct. My point here is simply that the rationale in federal decisions for withholding a more searching scrutiny does not apply in Vermont. The majority errs in relying on these decisions and the state court decisions applying the same federal analysis.

Although the Oregon Supreme Court has not addressed whether lesbians and gay men are a suspect classification, the Oregon Court of Appeals has recently done so. *See Tanner v. Oregon Health Sciences Univ.*, 157 Ore. App. 502, 971 P.2d 435 (Or. Ct. App. 1998). In *Tanner*, the court held that Article I, Section 20 of the Oregon Constitution requires the Oregon Health Sciences University to extend health and life insurance benefits to the unmarried domestic partners of its homosexual employees. *See* 971 P.2d at 448. The *Tanner* court examined the *Hewitt* two-part test for defining suspect classes and determined that "immutability—in the sense of inability to alter or change—is not necessary" because alienage and religious affiliation—which may be changed—have been held to be suspect classifications. Thus, it held that defining a suspect class depends not on the immutability of a class-defining characteristic, but upon (1) whether the characteristic has historically been regarded as defining a distinct socially-recognized group, and if so (2) whether that group has been the subject of adverse social or political stereotyping. *See id.* at 446.

Applying this test, the court concluded that the class of homosexual couples is clearly defined in terms of stereotyped personal and social characteristics; is widely regarded as a distinct, socially recognized group; and indisputably has "been and continue[s] to be the subject of adverse social and political stereotyping and prejudice." *Id.* at 447. Thus, the court found that the plaintiffs, three lesbian couples, were members of a suspect class.

In this concurrence, I do not detail a suspect-classification analysis, but I can summarize my opinion by saying that I agree with the general framework adopted by the Oregon courts in *Hewitt* and *Tanner*. These decisions concerning Article I, Section 20 of that state's constitution are entirely consistent with the law we have developed under Chapter I, Article 7 of the Vermont Constitution, at least prior to this decision. I find *Hewitt* and *Tanner* far more persuasive than the majority's decision, which backtracks from the established legal framework under Article 7 and fails to provide any guidelines whatsoever for the Legislature, the trial courts, or Vermonters in general to predict the outcome of future cases.

I agree with the majority that the State cannot justify the denial of legal benefits and responsibilities of civil marriage to gay and lesbian couples. And I agree that the appropriate remedy is either to require the State to extend the option of receiving these benefits and associated responsibilities to these couples, or to require that it offer the opportunity for civil marriage on equal terms. I will briefly explain my disagreement with the majority's rationale for reaching the same result.

. . .

The effect of the majority decision is that the State now bears no higher burden to justify discrimination against African–Americans or women than it does to justify discrimination against large retail stores as in *Ludlow*. I doubt that the framers of our Constitution, concerned with preventing the equivalent of British royalty, would believe that the inevitable line-drawing that must occur in economic regulation should be equated with the denial of civil and human rights. I do not believe that the new standard is required by, or even consistent with, the history on which the majority bases it.

. . .

Two points about the new standard are particularly troublesome for me. The majority now requires that legislative classifications be "reasonably necessary to accomplish the State's claimed objectives." *Id.*, Id. at 214, 744 A.2d at 878. In our imperfect world, few legislative classifications are "necessary," and most legislation could be more narrowly tailored to the state's objective. I cannot square this standard with our limited role in constitutional adjudication. As I noted earlier, while language to this effect appears in *Ludlow,* it has never been used as the basis of one of our decisions until today.

More importantly, I cannot endorse, in this vitally important area of constitutional review, a standard that relies wholly on factors and balancing, with no mooring in any criteria or guidelines, however imperfect they may be. On this point, I agree with Justice Johnson. *See* 170 Vt. at 255 n.13, 744 A.2d at 907–08 n.13. I accept the majority's assertion that it has attempted to avoid a standard based on "personal notions," and that all constitutional adjudication requires reasoned judgment, but I do not believe that it has succeeded in properly applying the critical considerations it has identified. *Id.* at 214, 744 A.2d at 879. Instead of mooring its analysis within the framework of fundamental rights and suspect classifications, the majority professes to make its new Article 7 standard "objective and grounded" by requiring courts, in balancing the competing interests, to "look to the history and 'traditions from which [the State] developed' as well as those 'from which it broke.' " *Id.* at 214, 744 A.2d at 879. It is difficult to conceive that any persons sitting on this Court, whatever their philosophical persuasions, would be insensitive to the history and traditions from which Vermont developed, and those from which it broke, but how this standard will be applied to Article 7 challenges is not at all predictable. In the end, the approach the majority has developed relies too much on the identities and personal philosophies of the men and women who fill the chairs at the Supreme Court, too little on ascertainable standards that judges of different backgrounds and philosophies can apply equally, and very little, if any, on deference to the legislative branch.

The final irony in this decision for me is that the balancing and weighing process set forth in the Court's opinion describes exactly the process we would expect legislators to go through if they were facing the question before us. We are judges, not legislators.

For the above reasons, I concur in the mandate, but respectfully disagree with Part II of the Court's decision, the majority's rationale for reaching this mandate.

Associate Justice

DISSENT BY: JOHNSON (In Part)

JOHNSON, J., concurring in part and dissenting in part. Forty years ago, in reversing a decision that had denied injunctive relief for the immediate desegregation of publicly owned parks and recreational facilities in Memphis, Tennessee, a unanimous United States Supreme Court stated:

The basic guarantees of our Constitution are warrants for the here and now and, unless there is an overwhelmingly compelling reason, they are to be promptly fulfilled. *Watson v. City of Memphis*, 373 U.S. 526, 533, 10 L.Ed.2d 529, 83 S.Ct. 1314 (1963).

Plaintiffs come before this Court claiming that the State has unconstitutionally deprived them of the benefits of marriage based solely upon a discriminatory classification that violates their civil rights. They ask the Court to remedy the unlawful discrimination by enjoining the State and its municipalities from denying them the license that serves to identify the persons entitled to those benefits. The majority agrees that the Common Benefits Clause of the Vermont Constitution entitles plaintiffs to obtain the same benefits and protections as those bestowed upon married opposite-sex couples, yet it declines to give them any relief other than an exhortation to the Legislature to deal with the problem. I concur with the majority's holding, but I respectfully dissent from its novel and truncated remedy, which in my view abdicates this Court's constitutional duty to redress violations of constitutional rights. I would grant the requested relief and enjoin defendants from denying plaintiffs a marriage license based solely on the sex of the applicants.

The majority declares that the issue before this Court does not turn on the heated moral debate over intimate same-sex relationships, and further, that this Court has a constitutional responsibility to consider the legal merits of even controversial cases. *See* 170 Vt. at 197, 744 A.2d at 867. Yet, notwithstanding these pronouncements, the majority elects to send plaintiffs to an uncertain fate in the political caldron of that very same moral debate. And to what end? Passing this case on to the Legislature will not alleviate the instability and uncertainty that the majority seeks to avoid, and will unnecessarily entangle this Court in the Legislature's efforts to accommodate the majority's mandate within a "reasonable period of time." *Id.* at 226, 744 A.2d at 887.

. . .

I.

My dissent from the majority's mandate is grounded on the government's limited interest in dictating public morals outside the scope of its police power, and the differing roles of the judicial and legislative branches in our tripartite system of government. I first examine the State's narrow interest in licensing marriages, then contrast that interest with the judiciary's fundamental duty to remedy civil rights violations, and lastly emphasize the majority's failure to adequately explain why it is taking the unusual step of suspending its judgment to allow the Legislature an opportunity to redress the unconstitutional discrimination that we have found.

. . .

While the State's interest in licensing marriages is narrow, the judiciary's obligation to remedy constitutional violations is central to our form of government. Indeed, one of the fundamental principles of our tripartite system of government is that the judiciary interprets and gives effect to the constitution in cases and controversies concerning individual rights. *See Marbury v. Madison*, 5 U.S. (1 Cranch) 137, 163, 177–78, 2 L. Ed. 60 (1803); *see also Shields v. Gerhart*, 163 Vt. 219, 223, 658 A.2d 924, 927–28 (1995) (emphasizing "the preeminence of the Vermont Constitution in our governmental scheme," which includes right of citizens under Chapter I, Article 4 to find a certain remedy promptly and without delay).

. . .

The power of courts to fashion remedies for constitutional violations is well established in both this Court's and the United States Supreme Court's jurisprudence concerning individual rights and equal protection. *See MacCallum v. Seymour's Adm'r*, 165 Vt. 452, 462, 686 A.2d 935, 941 (1996) (holding that statute denying adopted children right to inherit from collateral heirs violated Common Benefits Clause, and declaring plaintiff to be lawful heir of estate of collateral relative); *Medical Ctr. Hosp. v. Lorrain*, 165 Vt. 12, 14–15, 675 A.2d 1326, 1329 (1996) (determining that doctrine making husbands liable to creditors for necessary items provided to wives violated principle of equal protection when applied only to men, and choosing to abolish doctrine rather than to extend it to both men and women); *see also Heckler v. Mathews*, 465 U.S. 728, 740, 79 L.Ed.2d 646, 104 S.Ct. 1387 (1984) (when right invoked is that to equal treatment, "the appropriate remedy is a mandate of equal treatment"); *Davis v. Passman*, 442 U.S. 228, 241–42, 60 L.Ed.2d 846, 99 S.Ct. 2264 (1979) (within "great outlines" of Constitution, "judiciary is clearly discernible as the primary means through which these rights may be enforced"; unless Constitution commits issue to coordinate branch, "we presume that justiciable constitutional rights are to be enforced through the courts"). Particularly in civil rights cases involving discrimination against a disfavored group, "courts do not need specific [legislative] authorization to employ a remedy, at law or in equity, that is tailored to correct a constitutional wrong." *Aguayo v. Christopher*, 865 F.Supp. 479, 487–88 (N.D. Ill. 1994) (finding unconstitutional on its face statute making citizenship available to foreign-born children of citizen fathers, but not citizen mothers, and issuing judgment declaring plaintiff to be citizen).

Accordingly, absent "compelling" reasons that dictate otherwise, it is not only the prerogative but the duty of courts to provide prompt relief for violations of individual civil rights. *See Watson*, 373 U.S. at 532–33 (defendants have heavy burden of showing that delay in desegregating public parks and recreational facilities is "manifestly compelled by constitutionally cognizable circumstances"). This basic principle is designed to assure that laws enacted through the will of the majority do not unconstitutionally infringe upon the rights of a disfavored minority.

. . .

. . . We have held that the Vermont Constitution entitles plaintiffs "to obtain the same benefits and protections afforded by Vermont law to married opposite-sex couples." 170 Vt. at 224, 744 A.2d at 886. Given this holding, the most straightforward and effective remedy is simply to enjoin the State from denying plaintiffs a marriage license, which would designate them as persons entitled to those benefits and protections. No legislation is required to redress the constitutional violation that the Court has found. *Cf. Watson*, 373 U.S. at 532 (desegregation of recreational facilities does not present same kind of cognizable difficulties inherent in desegregating schools). Nor does our paramount interest in vindicating plaintiffs' constitutional rights interfere in any way with the State's interest in licensing marriages. Far from intruding upon the State's narrow interest in its licensing statute, allowing plaintiffs to obtain a license would further the overall goals of marriage, as defined by the majority—to provide stability to individuals, their families, and the broader community by clarifying and protecting the rights of married persons. *See* 170 Vt. at 228, 744 A.2d at 889. *Cf. In re B.L.V.B.*, 160 Vt. 368, 372, 375, 628 A.2d 1271, 1274–75 (1993) (purpose of adoption statute read in its entirety is to clarify and protect legal rights of adopted persons, not to proscribe adoptions by certain combinations of individuals; denying children of same-sex partners security of legally recognized relationship with second parent serves no legitimate state interest).

. . .

The majority declines to provide plaintiffs with a marriage license, however, because a sudden change in the marriage laws "may have disruptive and unforeseen consequences," and "uncertainty and confusion could result." 170 Vt. at 225, 744 A.2d at 887. Thus, within a few pages of rejecting the State's doomsday speculations as a basis for upholding the unconstitutionally discriminatory classification, the majority relies upon those same speculations to deny plaintiffs the relief to which they are entitled as the result of the discrimination. *See* 170 Vt. at 225, 744 A.2d at 887.

. . .

"Groups that have historically been the target of discrimination cannot be expected to wait patiently for the protection of their human dignity and equal rights while governments move toward reform one step at a time." *Rosenberg v. Canada*, Docket No. C22807 (Ontario Court of

Appeals, April 23, 1998 at 17–18 (quoting *Vriend v. Alberta*, [1998] S.C.J. No. 29 (Q.L.) at para. 122). Once a court has determined that a discriminatory classification has deprived plaintiffs of a constitutionally ripe entitlement, the court must decide if the classification "is demonstrably justifiable in a free and democratic society, not whether there might be a more propitious time to remedy it." *Id.* at 18.

Today's decision, which is little more than a declaration of rights, abdicates that responsibility. The majority declares that plaintiffs have been unconstitutionally deprived of the benefits of marriage, but does not hold that the marriage laws are unconstitutional, does not hold that plaintiffs are entitled to the license that triggers those benefits, and does not provide plaintiffs with any other specific or direct remedy for the constitutional violation that the Court has found to exist. By suspending its judgment and allowing the Legislature to choose a remedy, the majority, in effect, issues an advisory opinion that leaves plaintiffs without redress and sends the matter to an uncertain fate in the Legislature. *Cf. In re Williams*, 154 Vt. 318, 318–19, 321, 577 A.2d 686, 686–87 (1990) (statute requiring district court to hold hearings, issue findings, and advise local legislative bodies concerning alleged police misconduct violated separation of powers between judicial and legislative branches by requiring courts to give advisory opinions, upon which municipalities might or might not act). Ironically, today's mandate will only increase "the uncertainty and confusion" that the majority states it is designed to avoid. 170 Vt. at 225, 744 A.2d at 887.

No decision of this Court will abate the moral and political debate over same-sex marriage. My view as to the appropriateness of granting plaintiffs the license they seek is not based on any overestimate (or any estimate) of its effectiveness, nor on a miscalculation (or any calculation) as to its likely permanence, were it to have received the support of a majority of this Court. Rather, it is based on what I believe are the commands of our Constitution.

II.

Although I concur with the majority's conclusion that Vermont law unconstitutionally excludes same-sex couples from the benefits of marriage, I write separately to state my belief that this is a straightforward case of sex discrimination.

. . .

In sum, the State treats similarly situated people—those who wish to marry—differently, on the basis of the sex of the person they wish to marry. The State provides no legally valid rationale for the different treatment. The justifications asserted by the State for the classification are tautological, wholly arbitrary, or based on impermissible assumptions about the roles of men and women. None of the State's justifications meets the rational-basis test under the Common Benefits Clause. Finding no legally valid justification for the sex-based classification, I conclude that the classification is a vestige of the historical unequal marriage relationship that more recent legislative enactments and our own jurisprudence have unequivocally rejected. The protections conferred on Vermonters by the Common Benefits Clause cannot be restricted by the outmoded conception that marriage requires one man and one woman, creating one person—the husband. As this Court recently stated, "equal protection of the laws cannot be limited by eighteenth-century standards." *See Brigham*, 166 Vt. at 267, 692 A.2d at 396.

III.

This case is undoubtedly one of the most controversial ever to come before this Court. Newspaper, radio and television media have disclosed widespread public interest in its outcome, as well as the full spectrum of opinion as to what that outcome should be and what its ramifications may be for our society as a whole. One line of opinion contends that this is an issue that ought to be decided only by the most broadly democratic of our governmental institutions, the Legislature, and that the small group of men and women comprising this Court has no business deciding an issue of such enormous moment. For better or for worse, however, this is simply not so. This case came before us because citizens of the state invoked their constitutional right to seek redress through the judicial process of a perceived deprivation under state law. The Vermont Constitution does not permit the courts to decline to adjudicate a matter because its subject is controversial, or because the outcome may be deeply offensive to the strongly held beliefs of many of our citizens. We do not have, as does the Supreme Court of the United States, certiorari jurisdiction, which allows that Court, in its sole discretion, to decline to hear almost any case. To the contrary, if a case has been brought before us, and if the established procedures have been followed, as they were here, we must hear and decide it.

Moreover, we must decide the case on legal grounds. However much history, sociology, religious belief, personal experience or other considerations may inform our individual or collective deliberations, we must decide this case, and all cases, on the basis of our understanding of the law, and the law alone. This must be the true and constant effort of every member of the judiciary. That effort, needless to say, is not a guarantee of infallibility, nor even an assurance of wisdom. It is, however, the fulfillment of our pledge of office.

NOTE

In response to the *Baker* case, the Vermont legislature created "civil unions" for same-sex couples. The Vermont "Act Relating to Civil Unions" reads as follows:

It is hereby enacted by the General Assembly of the State of Vermont:

Sec. 1. LEGISLATIVE FINDINGS

The General Assembly finds that:

(1) Civil marriage under Vermont's marriage statutes consists of a union between a man and a woman. This interpretation of the state's marriage laws was upheld by the Supreme Court in *Baker v. State*.

(2) Vermont's history as an independent republic and as a state is one of equal treatment and respect for all Vermonters. This tradition is embodied in the Common Benefits Clause of the Vermont Constitution, Chapter I, Article 7th.

(3) The state's interest in civil marriage is to encourage close and caring families, and to protect all family members from the economic and social consequences of abandonment and divorce, focusing on those who have been especially at risk.

(4) Legal recognition of civil marriage by the state is the primary and, in a number of instances, the exclusive source of numerous benefits, responsibilities and protections under the laws of the state for married persons and their children.

(5) Based on the state's tradition of equality under the law and strong families, for at least 25 years, Vermont Probate Courts have qualified gay and lesbian individuals as adoptive parents.

(6) Vermont was one of the first states to adopt comprehensive legislation prohibiting discrimination on the basis of sexual orientation (Act No. 135 of 1992).

(7) The state has a strong interest in promoting stable and lasting families, including families based upon a same-sex couple.

(8) Without the legal protections, benefits and responsibilities associated with civil marriage, same-sex couples suffer numerous obstacles and hardships.

(9) Despite longstanding social and economic discrimination, many gay and lesbian Vermonters have formed lasting, committed, caring and faithful relationships with persons of their same sex. These couples live together, participate in their communities together, and some raise children and care for family members together, just as do couples who are married under Vermont law.

(10) While a system of civil unions does not bestow the status of civil marriage, it does satisfy the requirements of the Common Benefits Clause. Changes in the way significant legal relationships are established under the constitution should be approached carefully, combining respect for the community and cultural institutions most affected with a commitment to the constitutional rights involved. Granting benefits and protections to same-sex couples through a system of civil unions will provide due respect for tradition and long-standing social institutions, and will permit adjustment as unanticipated consequences or unmet needs arise.

(11) The constitutional principle of equality embodied in the Common Benefits Clause is compatible with the freedom of religious belief and worship guaranteed in Chapter I, Article 3rd of the state constitution. Extending the benefits and protections of marriage to same-sex couples through a system of civil unions preserves the fundamental constitutional

right of each of the multitude of religious faiths in Vermont to choose freely and without state interference to whom to grant the religious status, sacrament or blessing of marriage under the rules, practices or traditions of such faith.

Sec. 2. PURPOSE

(a) The purpose of this act is to respond to the constitutional violation found by the Vermont Supreme Court in Baker *v.* State, and to provide eligible same-sex couples the opportunity to "obtain the same benefits and protections afforded by Vermont law to married opposite-sex couples" as required by Chapter I, Article 7th of the Vermont Constitution.

(b) This act also provides eligible blood-relatives and relatives related by adoption the opportunity to establish a reciprocal beneficiaries relationship so they may receive certain benefits and protections and be subject to certain responsibilities that are granted to spouses.

Sec. 3. 15 V.S.A. chapter 23 is added to read:

PARTIES TO A CIVIL UNION

(a) Parties to a civil union shall have all the same benefits, protections and responsibilities under law, whether they derive from statute, administrative or court rule, policy, common law or any other source of civil law, as are granted to spouses in a marriage.

(b) A party to a civil union shall be included in any definition or use of the terms "spouse," "family," "immediate family," "dependent," "next of kin," and other terms that denote the spousal relationship, as those terms are used throughout the law.

(c) Parties to a civil union shall be responsible for the support of one another to the same degree and in the same manner as prescribed under law for married persons.

(d) The law of domestic relations, including annulment, separation and divorce, child custody and support, and property division and maintenance shall apply to parties to a civil union.

(e) The following is a nonexclusive list of legal benefits, protections and responsibilities of spouses, which shall apply in like manner to parties to a civil union:

(1) laws relating to title, tenure, descent and distribution, intestate succession, waiver of will, survivorship, or other incidents of the acquisition, ownership, or transfer, inter vivos or at death, of real or personal property, including eligibility to hold real and personal property as tenants by the entirety (parties to a civil union meet the common law unity of person qualification for purposes of a tenancy by the entirety);

(2) causes of action related to or dependent upon spousal status, including an action for wrongful death, emotional distress, loss of consortium, dramshop, or other torts or actions under contracts reciting, related to, or dependent upon spousal status;

(3) probate law and procedure, including nonprobate transfer;

(4) adoption law and procedure;

(5) group insurance for state employees under 3 V.S.A. § 631, and continuing care contracts under 8 V.S.A. § 8005;

(6) spouse abuse programs under 3 V.S.A. § 18;

(7) prohibitions against discrimination based upon marital status;

(8) victim's compensation rights under 13 V.S.A. § 5351;

(9) workers' compensation benefits;

(10) laws relating to emergency and nonemergency medical care and treatment, hospital visitation and notification, including the Patient's Bill of Rights under 18 V.S.A. chapter 42 and the Nursing Home Residents' Bill of Rights under 33 V.S.A. chapter 73;

(11) terminal care documents under 18 V.S.A. chapter 111, and durable power of attorney for health care execution and revocation under 14 V.S.A. chapter 121;

(12) family leave benefits under 21 V.S.A. chapter 5, subchapter 4A;

(13) public assistance benefits under state law;

(14) laws relating to taxes imposed by the state or a municipality other than estate taxes;

(15) laws relating to immunity from compelled testimony and the marital communication privilege;

(16) the homestead rights of a surviving spouse under 27 V.S.A. § 105 and homestead property tax allowance under 32 V.S.A. § 6062;

(17) laws relating to loans to veterans under 8 V.S.A. § 1849;

(18) the definition of family farmer under 10 V.S.A. § 272;

(19) laws relating to the making, revoking and objecting to anatomical gifts by others under 18 V.S.A. § 5240;

(20) state pay for military service under 20 V.S.A. § 1544;

(21) application for absentee ballot under 17 V.S.A. § 2532;

(22) family landowner rights to fish and hunt under 10 V.S.A. § 4253;

(23) legal requirements for assignment of wages under 8 V.S.A. § 2235; and

(24) affirmance of relationship under 15 V.S.A. § 7.

(f) The rights of parties to a civil union, with respect to a child of whom either becomes the natural parent during the term of the civil union, shall be the same as those of a married couple, with respect to a child of whom either spouse becomes the natural parent during the marriage.

§ 1206. DISSOLUTION OF CIVIL UNIONS

The family court shall have jurisdiction over all proceedings relating to the dissolution of civil unions. The dissolution of civil unions shall follow the same procedures and be subject to the same substantive rights and obligations that are involved in the dissolution of marriage in accordance with chapter 11 of this title, including any residency requirements.

DISCUSSION

Did the Vermont civil union scheme constitute legal equality?

V. MARRIAGE

A. IS THERE A FUNDAMENTAL RIGHT TO MARRY?

As a preliminary to the cases that follow, this section looks at one commentator's view of the way the United States Supreme Court has addressed the fundamental right to marry.*

. . .

The Court's fundamental right to marry cases fall into two categories. The first category consists of what I will here call the "interference with marriage" cases. In these cases, the parties bringing the constitutional challenges claimed that the state was impermissibly interfering with their *already existing* marital relationships. The second group consists of the "failure to recognize" cases. These challenges were brought by individuals after the state refused to recognize their relationships as marital.

The first time the Court described marriage as a fundamental right in a way that played a role in the outcome of the case was in *Skinner v. Oklahoma. Skinner* was neither explicitly about marriage nor was it a due process case. In *Skinner,* an Oklahoma statute that called for the sterilization of some habitual criminals (such as burglars) but not others (such as embezzlers) was the subject of an equal protection challenge. The Court was troubled by the equal protection implications of a statute that treated differently individuals who were similarly situated. Those who habitually stole from strangers, for example, were subject to sterilization while those who habitually embezzled money from their employers were not. The Court was also, however, concerned about the impact of the sterilization statute on fundamental rights. In striking down the law, the Court noted that "[w]e are dealing here with legislation which involves one of the basic civil rights of man. Marriage and procreation are fundamental to the very existence and survival of the race."

It is not surprising that the Court, in assessing the constitutionality of the Oklahoma statute, raised the issue of its impact on marriage. The traditional view of marriage links the institution of marriage to the capabilities of spouses to procreate. One of the traditional purposes of marriage, in fact, has been to organize and channel reproductive capabilities. A statute that takes away the ability of some individuals to reproduce also takes away their ability to carry out what has traditionally been understood to be one of the primary functions of marriage. We do not

* This discussion is excerpted from Carlos A. Ball, *The Positive in the Fundamental Right to Marry: Same-Sex Marriage in the Aftermath of* Lawrence v. Texas, 88 Minn. L. Rev. 1184 (2003–04).

know from the facts presented in the case whether Mr. Skinner was married. But given the broad scope of the statute (it could be applied to any habitual criminal who engaged in crimes of moral turpitude with only a few exceptions), the Court's concern about its impact on marital relationships was an understandable one.

Skinner, then, can be viewed as the first "interference with marriage" case. The Oklahoma statute was constitutionally problematic, in part, because it interfered with the ability of already married prisoners to engage in procreative activities (presumably after release from prison). The statute also represented a threat to the procreative abilities of unmarried inmates who might marry after being released from prison.

The second "interference with marriage" case to reach the Supreme Court was *Poe v. Ullman.* The plaintiffs in *Poe* challenged the constitutionality of a Connecticut statute that prohibited the use of contraceptives. The plurality in *Poe* held that the controversy did not present a justiciable question that was ripe for review and therefore did not reach the merits of the case. Justice Harlan, writing in dissent, concluded that the case did present a justiciable question and, as a result, proceeded to address the constitutional claim. Justice Harlan's opinion has become an important one because it presaged much of what the Court itself would do in the area of substantive due process in the years to come.

Justice Harlan in *Poe* did not question the general right of the state to enforce morality through the criminal law. He noted, for example, that laws forbidding adultery, fornication, and homosexuality were legitimate laws, in part because they involved "the State's rightful concern for its people's moral welfare." What troubled Justice Harlan was that the Connecticut contraception law intruded into the marital relationship and the marital home. It was this intrusion that entailed an unacceptable infringement on the right to privacy. It was the value and importance of marriage that allowed the privacy rights of spouses to trump the state's interests in promoting its view of morality. As Justice Harlan saw it, the Due Process Clause imposes on the state the obligation to respect the sexual intimacy that accompanies a particular kind of relationship: namely, the intimate one.

Interestingly, Justice Harlan in his dissent argued that "the intimacy of husband and wife is necessarily an essential and accepted feature of the institution of marriage, *an institution which the State not only must allow,* but which always and in every age it has fostered and protected." The italicized portion of this sentence is intriguing because it suggests that the state cannot simply abolish the institution of marriage altogether. This position is consistent with Justice Harlan's understanding of the fundamental right at issue in the case because that right, as he saw it, emerged directly from the marital relationship, a relationship that must exist in order for the right to attach. If the state cannot *interfere* with the right to marital privacy by prohibiting married couples from using contraceptives, it would seem at least plausible that the state cannot *abolish* the institution that gives rise to that right.

. . . Justice Harlan's opinion, in what is primarily an "interference with marriage" case, nonetheless suggests that the right at issue is not entirely a negative one, but is one that, at the very least, presumes that the state is allowing the institution of marriage to continue to exist. Although the issue of which relationships should be recognized as marital was not before the Court in *Poe,* and although we can safely surmise that the possibility that the state might abolish marriage never occurred to Justice Harlan, the right to privacy that he articulated in *Poe* depends on the assumption that the state makes available the institution of marriage to interested citizens.

The connection between a right to privacy and the institution of marriage is also present in *Griswold v. Connecticut.* In *Griswold,* unlike in *Poe,* the full Court reached the merits of the constitutionality of the Connecticut statute that prohibited the use of contraceptives. Although the majority opinion in *Griswold* found the bases for the fundamental right at stake in the penumbras of several provisions of the Bill of Rights (including the First, Fourth, Fifth, and Ninth Amendments) rather than, as Justice Harlan did in *Poe,* exclusively in the liberty interests protected by the Due Process Clause of the Fourteenth Amendment, it is clear that what led the *Griswold* Court to strike down the statute was the burden it placed on marital relationships. The Court noted that by prohibiting the use of contraceptives, as opposed to their sale or manufacture, the State "seeks to achieve its goals by means having a maximum destructive impact upon th[e] [marital] relationship." "The marital relationship," the Court added, in what has become a famous passage, "is older than our political parties, older than our school system. Marriage is a coming together for better or for worse, hopefully enduring, and intimate to the degree of being sacred. It is an association that promotes a way of life, not causes; a harmony in living, not political faiths; a bilateral loyalty, not commercial or social projects. Yet it is an association for as noble a purpose as any involved in our prior decisions."

The Court in *Griswold,* like Justice Harlan in *Poe,* linked the negative rights of individuals not to be interfered with by the state to the existence of the institution of marriage. According to the reasoning of *Griswold,* the absence of the institution of marriage would have meant the absence of the right to privacy as recognized by the Court in that case. Although the Court, since *Griswold,* has made it clear that fundamental rights involving sexual intimacy (and its consequences in terms of procreation and the begetting of children) extend beyond the marital relationship, the important point for our purposes is that the "interference with marriage" opinions *(Skinner, Griswold,* and Justice Harlan's dissent in *Poe)* operate under the assumption that the state is making the institution available to interested citizens. In other words, even the "interference with marriage" cases, which are primarily (and necessarily) focused on the negative obligations of the state, depend, if only implicitly, on the prior positive steps taken by the state to recognize certain relationships as marital. This would suggest that the state's negative obligations with respect to marriage are not wholly separable from its positive steps of recognition.

The "interference with marriage" cases, then, are important, not because they clearly stand for the proposition that the state has a positive constitutional obligation to recognize at least certain relationships as marital, but because they suggest a link between the state's obligation of noninterference and its (prior) affirmative steps of recognition. The former would be inapplicable (and irrelevant) in the absence of the latter. Whether the recognition of marriages is constitutionally mandated, however, does not become clear until we shift from the "interference with marriage" cases to the "failure to recognize" cases.

Griswold, decided almost forty years ago, was the last "interference with marriage" case to reach the Supreme Court. The three marriage cases that the Court has decided since then have all been "failure to recognize" cases. The first such case was *Loving v. Virginia,* which challenged the constitutionality of Virginia's antimiscegenation law. *Loving* is primarily thought of as an equal protection case because the law prohibiting interracial marriages classified individuals on the basis of race. *Loving,* however, is also an important due process marriage case because in it the Court for the first time addressed the significance of the marital relationship from the perspective of due process *in the absence of considerations of privacy and the right to be left alone.* The crux of the constitutional claim in *Griswold* was that the state should leave married couples alone so that they can make important decisions, such as those that relate to the use of contraceptives, about the intimate components of their relationships. The claimants in *Loving,* on the other hand, were not asking that the state leave them alone; instead, they were seeking state recognition (and by implication, state regulation) of their relationship. The Court concluded that the denial of that recognition, that is, the *failure* of the state to act, violated the claimants' fundamental right to marry.

Loving, then, stands for two important propositions that are relevant to a due process argument on behalf of same-sex marriage. First, the liberty protected by the Due Process Clause in the context of marriage goes beyond privacy concerns that are limited to notions of noninterference and the right to be left alone.... Second, the failure of the state to act can constitute a violation of the fundamental right to marry.

If *Loving* were the only "failure to recognize" case decided by the Supreme Court, its holding could be limited to instances where the state, for race-based reasons, fails to recognize some relationships as marital. But *Loving* is only the first such case. The second case is *Zablocki v. Redhail. Zablocki* involved an equal protection and due process challenge to a Wisconsin statute that prohibited individuals who owed child support from marrying. The Court in *Zablocki* decided the case on equal protection grounds, focusing on the classification (made up of individuals who owed child support) created by the Wisconsin statute. The Court applied strict scrutiny because the classification burdened the fundamental right to marry. In discussing marriage cases such as *Skinner, Griswold,* and *Loving,* the Court pointed out that:

> [i]t is not surprising that the decision to marry has been placed on the same level of importance as decisions relating to procreation, childbirth, child rearing, and family relationships. As the facts of this case illustrate, it would make little sense to recognize a right of privacy with respect to other matters of family life and not with respect to the decision to enter the relationship that is the foundation of the family.

The classification created by the Wisconsin statute, the Court argued, significantly interfered with the fundamental right to marry because those who "lack the financial means to meet their support obligations or cannot prove that their children will not become public charges . . . are absolutely prevented from getting married. The Court then concluded that the state's purported interests in support of the statute were insufficient to justify the interference with the right to marry."

Although the Court in *Zablocki* explained the right to marry as being a part of a broader right to privacy, *Zablocki* (like *Loving)* can be distinguished from *Griswold* in that it did not implicate the right to privacy in the traditional sense of demanding that the state leave individuals alone. The constitutional problem in *Zablocki* was not what the state did in terms of actions (such as in *Griswold,* where the state's goal was to punish those who used contraceptives), but in terms of its omission, that is, its refusal to recognize the plaintiffs' relationship as marital. The harm alleged in *Zablocki* did not, in the end, arise from state *interference* with an intimate relationship; instead, the harm arose from the state's *indifference* toward that relationship. If we view the right to marry only in terms of negative liberty, therefore, we are unable to explain fully the kind of affirmative obligation of recognition that the state is under as a result of the Court's ruling in *Zablocki.*

I want to pause for a moment to make it clear that I am not denying that the *Zablocki* Court's understanding of the fundamental right to marry contained a negative component to it. I am arguing instead that that understanding also included within it a limitation in the ability of the state to be indifferent toward at least some intimate relationships.

If *Loving* and *Zablocki* were the only "failure to recognize" cases decided by the Supreme Court, it could be argued that whatever positive obligation on the state to recognize marriage that can be gleaned from them is primarily based on equal protection considerations rather than on substantive due process grounds. *Zablocki,* after all, was decided on equal protection grounds and *Loving* was primarily (though as we have seen, not exclusively) an equal protection case. It is for this reason that *Turner v. Safley,* the third (and last) "failure to recognize" case, is in many ways the most important Supreme Court case for the purpose of determining whether the Due Process Clause imposes on the state obligations to recognize at least some intimate relationships as marital. *Turner* involved a class action suit brought by prisoners living in Missouri correctional facilities who challenged a regulation that prohibited inmates from marrying unless the prison authorities first approved.

The inmates in *Turner* argued that the Missouri regulation impermissibly interfered with their fundamental right to marry, without (unlike the plaintiff in *Zablocki)* adding an equal protection claim to their substantive due process argument. Although the inmates *could* have raised equal protection objections to the regulation (given that Missouri law singled out prisoners and imposed on them a restriction on marriage that was not placed on the general population), they did not do so. None of the three courts, including the Supreme Court, that issued opinions in the case addressed equal protection issues. Instead, they all viewed the case solely from the perspective of due process and fundamental rights. For this reason, I believe *Turner* is the case that most clearly supports the proposition that the state has a due process obligation to recognize at least some relationships as marital independently of equal protection considerations that go to the issue of whether the state, once it recognizes some relationships as marital, has an equality-based obligation to recognize others in the same way.

The government in *Turner* did not argue that there was no fundamental right to marry (an untenable position after *Zablocki);* it argued instead that prisoners, because of their unique circumstances, could not avail themselves of that right. The Supreme Court rejected the state's attempt to exclude prisoners from the scope of the right to marry by noting the ways in which "[m]any important attributes of marriage remain ... after taking into account the limitations imposed by prison life." Those attributes include the "expressions of emotional support and public commitment [that] are an important and significant aspect of the marital relationship" and that survive imprisonment. The Court also pointed out that "many religions recognize marriage as having spiritual significance" and that as a result "for some inmates and their spouses ... the commitment of marriage may be an exercise of religious faith as well as an expression of personal dedication." Finally, the Court noted that marriage brings with it a panoply of legal privileges, such as Social Security benefits and inheritance rights, which are not affected by imprisonment. All of these elements of marriage, the Court concluded, "are sufficient to form a constitutionally protected marital relationship in the prison context."

Although the Court, prior to *Turner,* had explained that the right to marry was part of a broader fundamental right to privacy, it is important to note that *Turner* by necessity delinks marriage from privacy. This is so because prisoners do not enjoy constitutionally protected privacy rights. If prisoners do not enjoy constitutionally protected rights to privacy, then their liberty interests in marriage must flow from considerations other than privacy. Furthermore, the fundamental right to marry applied in *Turner,* even though there is no corresponding right of married individuals to engage in sexual intimacy while in prison. The right to marry that arises from *Turner,* therefore, cannot be grounded in an understanding of liberty that protects privacy interests through the enforcement of negative rights of noninterference. The right instead is better understood as a positive right that places on the state an affirmative obligation to recognize the relationships at issue in the case as marital.

The *Turner* Court's discussion of the importance of the marital relationship did not include *any* mention of negative liberty and the right to be left alone. *Turner* decouples marriage from the understanding of liberty that we see in *Griswold,* namely, liberty as protected by the right to be left alone to make important decisions about sexual intimacy within the marital relationship. The constitutionally protected liberty at issue in *Turner,* rather than driven by considerations of non interference in the private sphere, was instead driven by the *public* components of marriage: the public expression of commitment by the partners to each other, the recognition and support on the part of the community for the partners' relationship, and the legal rights and benefits that accompany marriage. These are the elements of marriage that survive imprisonment and that were crucial to the *Turner* Court's determination that the Missouri prison regulations impermissibly interfered with the fundamental right to marry.

LOVING v. VIRGINIA

388 U.S. 1, 87 S.Ct. 1817, 18 L.Ed.2d 1010 (1967)

OPINION: CHIEF JUSTICE WARREN

This case presents a constitutional question never addressed by this Court: whether a statutory scheme adopted by the State of Virginia to prevent marriages between persons solely on the basis of racial classifications violates the Equal Protection and Due Process Clauses of the Fourteenth Amendment. For reasons which seem to us to reflect the central meaning of those constitutional commands, we conclude that these statutes cannot stand consistently with the Fourteenth Amendment.

In June 1958, two residents of Virginia, Mildred Jeter, a Negro woman, and Richard Loving, a white man, were married in the District of Columbia pursuant to its laws. Shortly after their marriage, the Lovings returned to Virginia and established their marital abode in Caroline County. At the October Term, 1958, of the Circuit Court of Caroline County, a grand jury issued an indictment charging the Lovings with violating Virginia's ban on interracial marriages. On January 6, 1959, the Lovings pleaded guilty to the charge and were sentenced to one year in jail; however, the trial judge suspended the sentence for a period of 25 years on the condition that the Lovings leave the State and not return to Virginia together for 25 years. He stated in an opinion that:

> Almighty God created the races white, black, yellow, malay [sic] and red, and he placed them on separate continents. And but for the interference with his arrangement there would be no cause for such

marriages. The fact that he separated the races shows that he did not intend for the races to mix.

After their convictions, the Lovings took up residence in the District of Columbia. On November 6, 1963, they filed a motion in the state trial court to vacate the judgment and set aside the sentence on the ground that the statutes which they had violated were repugnant to the Fourteenth Amendment. The motion not having been decided by October 28, 1964, the Lovings instituted a class action in the United States District Court for the Eastern District of Virginia requesting that a three-judge court be convened to declare the Virginia antimiscegenation statutes unconstitutional and to enjoin state officials from enforcing their convictions. On January 22, 1965, the state trial judge denied the motion to vacate the sentences, and the Lovings perfected an appeal to the Supreme Court of Appeals of Virginia. . . .

The Supreme Court of Appeals upheld the constitutionality of the antimiscegenation statutes and, after modifying the sentence, affirmed the convictions.

The two statutes under which appellants were convicted and sentenced are part of a comprehensive statutory scheme aimed at prohibiting and punishing interracial marriages. The Lovings were convicted of violating § 20–58 of the Virginia Code:

> *Leaving State to evade law.*—If any white person and colored person shall go out of this State, for the purpose of being married, and with the intention of returning, and be married out of it, and afterwards return to and reside in it, cohabiting as man and wife, they shall be punished as provided in § 20–59, and the marriage shall be governed by the same law as if it had been solemnized in this State. The fact of their cohabitation here as man and wife shall be evidence of their marriage.

Section 20–59, which defines the penalty for miscegenation, provides:

> *Punishment for marriage.*—If any white person intermarry with a colored person, or any colored person intermarry with a white person, he shall be guilty of a felony and shall be punished by confinement in the penitentiary for not less than one nor more than five years. Other central provisions in the Virginia statutory scheme are § 20–57, which automatically voids all marriages between "a white person and a colored person" without any judicial proceeding,[101] and §§ 20–54 and 1–14 which, respectively, define "white persons" and "colored persons and Indians" for purposes of the statutory prohibitions.[102]

101. Section 20–57 of the Virginia Code provides:

"*Marriages void without decree.*—All marriages between a white person and a colored person shall be absolutely void without any decree of divorce or other legal process." Va. Code Ann. § 20–57 (1960 Repl. Vol.).

102. Section 20–54 of the Virginia Code provides:

"*Intermarriage prohibited; meaning of term 'white persons.'*—It shall hereafter be unlawful for any white person in this State to marry any save a white person, or a person with no other

The Lovings have never disputed in the course of this litigation that Mrs. Loving is a "colored person" or that Mr. Loving is a "white person" within the meanings given those terms by the Virginia statutes.

Virginia is now one of 16 States which prohibit and punish marriages on the basis of racial classifications.[103] Penalties for miscegenation arose as an incident to slavery and have been common in Virginia since the colonial period. The present statutory scheme dates from the adoption of the Racial Integrity Act of 1924, passed during the period of extreme nativism which followed the end of the First World War. The central features of this Act, and current Virginia law, are the absolute prohibition of a "white person" marrying other than another "white person," a prohibition against issuing marriage licenses until the issuing official is satisfied that the applicants' statements as to their race are correct, certificates of "racial composition" to be kept by both local and state registrars, and the carrying forward of earlier prohibitions against racial intermarriage.

---

admixture of blood than white and American Indian. For the purpose of this chapter, the term 'white person' shall apply only to such person as has no trace whatever of any blood other than Caucasian; but persons who have one-sixteenth or less of the blood of the American Indian and have no other non-Caucasic blood shall be deemed to be white persons. All laws heretofore passed and now in effect regarding the intermarriage of white and colored persons shall apply to marriages prohibited by this chapter." Va. Code Ann. § 20–54 (1960 Repl. Vol.).

The exception for persons with less than one-sixteenth "of the blood of the American Indian" is apparently accounted for, in the words of a tract issued by the Registrar of the State Bureau of Vital Statistics, by "the desire of all to recognize as an integral and honored part of the white race the descendants of John Rolfe and Pocahontas. . . ." Plecker, The New Family and Race Improvement, 17 Va. Health Bull., Extra No. 12 at 25–26 (New Family Series No. 5, 1925), cited in Wadlington, The *Loving* Case: Virginia's Anti–Miscegenation Statute in Historical Perspective, 52 Va. L. Rev. 1189, 1202, n. 93 (1966).

Section 1–14 of the Virginia Code provides:

"*Colored persons and Indians defined.*—Every person in whom there is ascertainable any Negro blood shall be deemed and taken to be a colored person, and every person not a colored person having one fourth or more of American Indian blood shall be deemed an American Indian; except that members of Indian tribes existing in this Commonwealth having one fourth or more of Indian blood and less than one sixteenth of Negro blood shall be deemed tribal Indians." Va. Code Ann. § 1–14 (1960 Repl. Vol.).

103. After the initiation of this litigation, Maryland repealed its prohibitions against interracial marriage, Md. Laws 1967, c. 6, leaving Virginia and 15 other States with statutes outlawing interracial marriage: Alabama, Ala. Const., Art. 4, § 102, Ala. Code, Tit. 14, § 360 (1958); Arkansas, Ark. Stat. Ann. § 55–104 (1947); Delaware, Del. Code Ann., Tit. 13, § 101 (1953); Florida, Fla. Const., Art. 16, § 24, Fla. Stat. § 741.11 (1965); Georgia, Ga. Code Ann. § 53–106 (1961); Kentucky, Ky. Rev. Stat. Ann. § 402.020 (Supp. 1966); Louisiana, La. Rev. Stat. § 14:79 (1950); Mississippi, Miss. Const., Art. 14, § 263, Miss. Code Ann. § 459 (1956); Missouri, Mo. Rev. Stat. § 451.020 (Supp. 1966); North Carolina, N. C. Const., Art. XIV, § 8, N. C. Gen. Stat. § 14–181 (1953); Oklahoma, Okla. Stat., Tit. 43, § 12 (Supp. 1965); South Carolina, S. C. Const., Art. 3, § 33, S. C. Code Ann. § 20–7 (1962); Tennessee, Tenn. Const., Art. 11, § 14, Tenn. Code Ann. § 36–402 (1955); Texas, Tex. Pen. Code, Art. 492 (1952); West Virginia, W. Va. Code Ann. § 4697 (1961).

Over the past 15 years, 14 States have repealed laws outlawing interracial marriages: Arizona, California, Colorado, Idaho, Indiana, Maryland, Montana, Nebraska, Nevada, North Dakota, Oregon, South Dakota, Utah, and Wyoming.

The first state court to recognize that miscegenation statutes violate the Equal Protection Clause was the Supreme Court of California. *Perez v. Sharp*, 32 Cal.2d 711, 198 P.2d 17 (1948).

I.

In upholding the constitutionality of these provisions in the decision below, the Supreme Court of Appeals of Virginia referred to its 1955 decision in *Naim v. Naim*, 197 Va. 80, 87 S.E.2d 749, as stating the reasons supporting the validity of these laws. In *Naim*, the state court concluded that the State's legitimate purposes were "to preserve the racial integrity of its citizens," and to prevent "the corruption of blood," "a mongrel breed of citizens," and "the obliteration of racial pride," obviously an endorsement of the doctrine of White Supremacy. The court also reasoned that marriage has traditionally been subject to state regulation without federal intervention, and, consequently, the regulation of marriage should be left to exclusive state control by the Tenth Amendment.

While the state court is no doubt correct in asserting that marriage is a social relation subject to the State's police power, *Maynard v. Hill*, 125 U.S. 190 (1888), the State does not contend in its argument before this Court that its powers to regulate marriage are unlimited notwithstanding the commands of the Fourteenth Amendment. Nor could it do so in light of *Meyer v. Nebraska*, 262 U.S. 390 (1923), and *Skinner v. Oklahoma*, 316 U.S. 535 (1942). Instead, the State argues that the meaning of the Equal Protection Clause, as illuminated by the statements of the Framers, is only that state penal laws containing an interracial element as part of the definition of the offense must apply equally to whites and Negroes in the sense that members of each race are punished to the same degree. Thus, the State contends that, because its miscegenation statutes punish equally both the white and the Negro participants in an interracial marriage, these statutes, despite their reliance on racial classifications, do not constitute an invidious discrimination based upon race. The second argument advanced by the State assumes the validity of its equal application theory. The argument is that, if the Equal Protection Clause does not outlaw miscegenation statutes because of their reliance on racial classifications, the question of constitutionality would thus become whether there was any rational basis for a State to treat interracial marriages differently from other marriages. On this question, the State argues, the scientific evidence is substantially in doubt and, consequently, this Court should defer to the wisdom of the state legislature in adopting its policy of discouraging interracial marriages.

Because we reject the notion that the mere "equal application" of a statute containing racial classifications is enough to remove the classifications from the Fourteenth Amendment's proscription of all invidious racial discriminations, we do not accept the State's contention that these statutes should be upheld if there is any possible basis for concluding that they serve a rational purpose. The mere fact of equal application does not mean that our analysis of these statutes should follow the approach we have taken in cases involving no racial discrimination where the Equal Protection Clause has been arrayed against a statute discriminating between the kinds of advertising which may be displayed on trucks in New York City, *Railway Express Agency, Inc. v. New York*, 336 U.S. 106 (1949), or an exemption in Ohio's ad valorem tax for merchandise owned by a nonresident in a storage warehouse, *Allied Stores of Ohio, Inc. v. Bowers*, 358 U.S. 522 (1959). In these cases, involving distinctions not drawn according to race, the Court has merely asked whether there is any rational foundation for the discriminations, and has deferred to the wisdom of the state legislatures. In the case at bar, however, we deal with statutes containing racial classifications, and the fact of equal application does not immunize the statute from the very heavy burden of justification which the Fourteenth Amendment has traditionally required of state statutes drawn according to race.

The State argues that statements in the Thirty-ninth Congress about the time of the passage of the Fourteenth Amendment indicate that the Framers did not intend the Amendment to make unconstitutional state miscegenation laws. Many of the statements alluded to by the State concern the debates over the Freedmen's Bureau Bill, which President Johnson vetoed, and the Civil Rights Act of 1866, 14 Stat. 27, enacted over his veto. While these statements have some relevance to the intention of Congress in submitting the Fourteenth Amendment, it must be understood that they pertained to the passage of specific statutes and not to the broader, organic purpose of a constitutional amendment. As for the various statements directly concerning the Fourteenth Amendment, we have said in connection with a related problem, that although these historical sources "cast some light" they are not sufficient to resolve the problem; "[at] best, they are inconclusive. The most avid proponents of the post-War Amendments undoubtedly intended them to remove all legal distinctions among 'all persons born or naturalized in the United States.' Their opponents, just as certainly, were antagonistic to both the letter and the spirit of the Amendments and wished them to have the most limited effect." *Brown v. Board of Education*, 347 U.S. 483, 489 (1954). *See also Strauder v. West Virginia*, 100 U.S. 303, 310 (1880). We have rejected the proposition that the debates in the Thirty-ninth Congress or in the state legislatures which ratified the Fourteenth Amendment supported the theory advanced by the State, that the requirement of equal protection of the laws is satisfied by penal laws defining offenses based on racial classifications so long as white and Negro participants in the offense were similarly punished. *McLaughlin v. Florida*, 379 U.S. 184 (1964).

The State finds support for its "equal application" theory in the decision of the Court in *Pace v. Alabama*, 106 U.S. 583 (1883). In that case, the Court upheld a conviction under an Alabama statute forbidding adultery or fornication between a white person and a Negro which imposed a greater penalty than that of a statute proscribing similar conduct by members of the same race. The Court reasoned that the statute could not be said to discriminate against Negroes because the punishment for each participant in the offense was the same. However, as recently as the 1964 Term, in rejecting the reasoning of that case, we stated "*Pace* represents a limited view of the Equal Protection Clause which has not withstood analysis in the subsequent decisions of this

Court." *McLaughlin v. Florida, supra*, at 188. As we there demonstrated, the Equal Protection Clause requires the consideration of whether the classifications drawn by any statute constitute an arbitrary and invidious discrimination. The clear and central purpose of the Fourteenth Amendment was to eliminate all official state sources of invidious racial discrimination in the States. *Slaughter–House Cases*, 16 Wall. 36, 71 (1873); *Strauder v. West Virginia*, 100 U.S. 303, 307–308 (1880); *Ex parte Virginia*, 100 U.S. 339, 344–345 (1880); *Shelley v. Kraemer*, 334 U.S. 1 (1948); *Burton v. Wilmington Parking Authority*, 365 U.S. 715 (1961).

There can be no question but that Virginia's miscegenation statutes rest solely upon distinctions drawn according to race. The statutes proscribe generally accepted conduct if engaged in by members of different races. Over the years, this Court has consistently repudiated "distinctions between citizens solely because of their ancestry" as being "odious to a free people whose institutions are founded upon the doctrine of equality." *Hirabayashi v. United States*, 320 U.S. 81, 100 (1943). At the very least, the Equal Protection Clause demands that racial classifications, especially suspect in criminal statutes, be subjected to the "most rigid scrutiny," *Korematsu v. United States*, 323 U.S. 214, 216 (1944), and, if they are ever to be upheld, they must be shown to be necessary to the accomplishment of some permissible state objective, independent of the racial discrimination which it was the object of the Fourteenth Amendment to eliminate. Indeed, two members of this Court have already stated that they "cannot conceive of a valid legislative purpose . . . which makes the color of a person's skin the test of whether his conduct is a criminal offense." *McLaughlin v. Florida, supra*, at 198 (STEWART, J., joined by DOUGLAS, J., concurring).

There is patently no legitimate overriding purpose independent of invidious racial discrimination which justifies this classification. The fact that Virginia prohibits only interracial marriages involving white persons demonstrates that the racial classifications must stand on their own justification, as measures designed to maintain White Supremacy.[104] We have consistently denied the constitutionality of measures which restrict the rights of citizens on account of race. There can be no doubt that restricting the freedom to marry solely because of racial classifications violates the central meaning of the Equal Protection Clause.

II.

These statutes also deprive the Lovings of liberty without due process of law in violation of the Due Process Clause of the Fourteenth Amend-

104. Appellants point out that the State's concern in these statutes, as expressed in the words of the 1924 Act's title, "An Act to Preserve Racial Integrity," extends only to the integrity of the white race. While Virginia prohibits whites from marrying any nonwhite (subject to the exception for the descendants of Pocahontas), Negroes, Orientals, and any other racial class may intermarry without statutory interference. Appellants contend that this distinction renders Virginia's miscegenation statutes arbitrary and unreasonable even assuming the constitutional validity of an official purpose to preserve "racial integrity." We need not reach this contention because we find the racial classifications in these statutes repugnant to the Fourteenth Amendment, even assuming an even-handed state purpose to protect the "integrity" of all races.

ment. The freedom to marry has long been recognized as one of the vital personal rights essential to the orderly pursuit of happiness by free men.

Marriage is one of the "basic civil rights of man," fundamental to our very existence and survival. *Skinner v. Oklahoma*, 316 U.S. 535, 541 (1942). *See also Maynard v. Hill*, 125 U.S. 190 (1888). To deny this fundamental freedom on so unsupportable a basis as the racial classifications embodied in these statutes, classifications so directly subversive of the principle of equality at the heart of the Fourteenth Amendment, is surely to deprive all the State's citizens of liberty without due process of law. The Fourteenth Amendment requires that the freedom of choice to marry not be restricted by invidious racial discriminations. Under our Constitution, the freedom to marry, or not marry, a person of another race resides with the individual and cannot be infringed by the State.

These convictions must be reversed.

It is so ordered.

MR. JUSTICE STEWART, concurring.

I have previously expressed the belief that "it is simply not possible for a state law to be valid under our Constitution which makes the criminality of an act depend upon the race of the actor." *McLaughlin v. Florida*, 379 U.S. 184, 198 (concurring opinion). Because I adhere to that belief, I concur in the judgment of the Court. . . .

B. THE BEGINNING OF SAME-SEX MARRIAGES

In 2003, the Massachusetts Supreme Judicial Court decided the landmark case of *Goodridge v. Department of Public Health*.

GOODRIDGE v. DEPARTMENT OF PUBLIC HEALTH

440 Mass. 309, 798 N.E.2d 941 (2003)

OPINION: MARSHALL

Marriage is a vital social institution. The exclusive commitment of two individuals to each other nurtures love and mutual support; it brings stability to our society. For those who choose to marry, and for their children, marriage provides an abundance of legal, financial, and social benefits. In return it imposes weighty legal, financial, and social obligations. The question before us is whether, consistent with the Massachusetts Constitution, the Commonwealth may deny the protections, benefits, and obligations conferred by civil marriage to two individuals of the same sex who wish to marry. We conclude that it may not. The Massachusetts Constitution affirms the dignity and equality of all individuals. It forbids the creation of second-class citizens. In reaching our conclusion we have given full deference to the arguments made by the Commonwealth. But it has failed to identify any constitutionally adequate reason for denying civil marriage to same-sex couples.

We are mindful that our decision marks a change in the history of our marriage law. Many people hold deep-seated religious, moral, and ethical convictions that marriage should be limited to the union of one man and one woman, and that homosexual conduct is immoral. Many hold equally strong religious, moral, and ethical convictions that same-sex couples are entitled to be married, and that homosexual persons should be treated no differently than their heterosexual neighbors. Neither view answers the question before us. Our concern is with the Massachusetts Constitution as a charter of governance for every person properly within its reach. "Our obligation is to define the liberty of all, not to mandate our own moral code." *Lawrence v. Texas*, 539 U.S. 558, 156 L.Ed.2d 508, 123 S.Ct. 2472, 2480 (2003) (*Lawrence*), quoting *Planned Parenthood of Southeastern Pa. v. Casey*, 505 U.S. 833, 850, 120 L.Ed.2d 674, 112 S.Ct. 2791 (1992).

Whether the Commonwealth may use its formidable regulatory authority to bar same-sex couples from civil marriage is a question not previously addressed by a Massachusetts appellate court. It is a question the United States Supreme Court left open as a matter of Federal law in *Lawrence, supra* at 2484, where it was not an issue. There, the Court affirmed that the core concept of common human dignity protected by the Fourteenth Amendment to the United States Constitution precludes government intrusion into the deeply personal realms of consensual adult expressions of intimacy and one's choice of an intimate partner. The Court also reaffirmed the central role that decisions whether to marry or have children bear in shaping one's identity. *Id.* at 2481. The Massachusetts Constitution is, if anything, more protective of individual liberty and equality than the Federal Constitution; it may demand broader protection for fundamental rights; and it is less tolerant of government intrusion into the protected spheres of private life.

Barred access to the protections, benefits, and obligations of civil marriage, a person who enters into an intimate, exclusive union with another of the same sex is arbitrarily deprived of membership in one of our community's most rewarding and cherished institutions. That exclusion is incompatible with the constitutional principles of respect for individual autonomy and equality under law.

I.

The plaintiffs are fourteen individuals from five Massachusetts counties. As of April 11, 2001, the date they filed their complaint, the plaintiffs Gloria Bailey, sixty years old, and Linda Davies, fifty-five years old, had been in a committed relationship for thirty years; the plaintiffs Maureen Brodoff, forty-nine years old, and Ellen Wade, fifty-two years old, had been in a committed relationship for twenty years and lived with their twelve year old daughter; the plaintiffs Hillary Goodridge, forty-four years old, and Julie Goodridge, forty-three years old, had been in a committed relationship for thirteen years and lived with their five year old daughter; the plaintiffs Gary Chalmers, thirty-five years old, and Richard Linnell, thirty-seven years old, had been in a committed relationship for thirteen years and lived with their eight year old daughter and Richard's mother; the plaintiffs Heidi Norton, thirty-six years old, and Gina Smith, thirty-six years old, had been in a committed relationship for eleven years and lived with their two sons, ages five years and one year; the plaintiffs Michael Horgan, forty-one years old, and Edward Balmelli, forty-one years old, had been in a committed relationship for seven years; and the plaintiffs David Wilson, fifty-seven years old, and Robert Compton, fifty-one years old, had been in a committed relationship for four years and had cared for David's mother in their home after a serious illness until she died.

The plaintiffs include business executives, lawyers, an investment banker, educators, therapists, and a computer engineer. Many are active in church, community, and school groups. They have employed such legal means as are available to them—for example, joint adoption, powers of attorney, and joint ownership of real property—to secure aspects of their relationships. Each plaintiff attests a desire to marry his or her partner in order to affirm publicly their commitment to each other and to secure the legal protections and benefits afforded to married couples and their children.

The Department of Public Health (department) is charged by statute with safeguarding public health. *See* G.L.c. 17. Among its responsibilities, the department oversees the registry of vital records and statistics (registry), which "enforces all laws" relative to the issuance of marriage licenses and the keeping of marriage records, *see* G.L.c. 17, § 4, and which promulgates policies and procedures for the issuance of marriage licenses by city and town clerks and registers. *See, e.g.*, G.L.c. 207, §§ 20, 28A, and 37. The registry is headed by a registrar of vital records and statistics (registrar), appointed by the Commissioner of Public Health (commissioner) with the approval of the public health council and supervised by the commissioner. *See* G.L.c. 17, § 4.

In March and April, 2001, each of the plaintiff couples attempted to obtain a marriage license from a city or town clerk's office. As required under G.L.c. 207, they completed notices of intention to marry on forms provided by the registry, *see* G.L.c. 207, § 20, and presented these forms to a Massachusetts town or city clerk, together with the required health forms and marriage license fees. *See* G.L.c. 207, § 19. In each case, the clerk either refused to accept the notice of intention to marry or denied a marriage license to the couple on the ground that Massachusetts does not recognize same-sex marriage. n4, n5 Because obtaining a marriage license is a necessary prerequisite to civil marriage in Massachusetts, denying marriage licenses to the plaintiffs was tantamount to denying them access to civil marriage itself, with its appurtenant social and legal protections, benefits, and obligations.

On April 11, 2001, the plaintiffs filed suit in the Superior Court against the department and the commissioner seeking a judgment that "the exclusion of the plaintiff couples and other qualified same-sex couples from access to marriage licenses, and the legal and social status of civil marriage, as well as the protections, benefits and obligations of marriage, violates Massachusetts law." *See* G.L.c. 231A. The plaintiffs alleged violation of the laws of the Commonwealth, including but not limited to their rights under arts. 1, 6, 7, 10, 12, and 16, and Part II, c. 1, § 1, art. 4, of the Massachusetts Constitution.

The department, represented by the Attorney General, admitted to a policy and practice of denying marriage licenses to same-sex couples. It denied that its actions violated any law or that the plaintiffs were entitled to relief. The parties filed cross motions for summary judgment.

A Superior Court judge ruled for the department. In a memorandum of decision and order dated May 7, 2002, he dismissed the plaintiffs' claim that the marriage statutes should be construed to permit marriage between persons of the same sex, holding that the plain wording of G.L.c. 207, as well as the wording of other marriage statutes, precluded that interpretation. Turning to the constitutional claims, he held that the marriage exclusion does not offend the liberty, freedom, equality, or due process provisions of the Massachusetts Constitution, and that the Massachusetts Declaration of Rights does not guarantee "the fundamental right to marry a person of the same sex." He concluded that prohibiting same-sex marriage rationally furthers the Legislature's legitimate interest in safeguarding the "primary purpose" of marriage, "procreation." The Legislature may rationally limit marriage to opposite-sex couples, he concluded, because those couples are "theoretically . . . capable of procreation," they do not rely on "inherently more cumbersome" noncoital means of reproduction, and they are more likely than same-sex couples to have children, or more children.

After the complaint was dismissed and summary judgment entered for the defendants, the plaintiffs appealed. Both parties requested direct appellate review, which we granted.

II.

Although the plaintiffs refer in passing to "the marriage statutes," they focus, quite properly, on G.L.c. 207, the marriage licensing statute, which controls entry into civil marriage. As a preliminary matter, we summarize the provisions of that law.

General Laws c. 207 is both a gatekeeping and a public records statute. It sets minimum qualifications for obtaining a marriage license and directs city and town clerks, the registrar, and the department to keep and maintain certain "vital records" of civil marriages. The gatekeeping provisions of G.L.c. 207 are minimal. They forbid marriage of individuals within certain degrees of consanguinity, §§ 1 and 2, and polygamous marriages. *See* G.L.c. 207, § 4. *See also* G.L.c. 207, § 8 (marriages solemnized in violation of §§ 1, 2, and 4, are void ab initio). They prohibit marriage if one of the parties has communicable syphilis, *see* G.L.c. 207, § 28A, and restrict the circumstances in which a person under eighteen years of age may marry. *See* G.L.c. 207, §§ 7, 25, and 27. The statute requires that civil marriage be solemnized only by those so authorized. *See* G.L.c. 207, §§ 38–40.

The record-keeping provisions of G.L.c. 207 are more extensive. Marriage applicants file standard information forms and a medical certificate in any Massachusetts city or town clerk's office and tender a filing fee. G.L.c. 207, §§ 19–20, 28A. The clerk issues the marriage license, and when the marriage is solemnized, the individual authorized to solemnize the marriage adds additional information to the form and returns it (or a copy) to the clerk's office. G.L.c. 207, §§ 28, 30, 38–40 (this completed form is commonly known as the "marriage certificate"). The clerk sends a copy of the information to the registrar, and that information becomes a public record. *See* G.L.c. 17, § 4; G.L.c. 66, § 10.

In short, for all the joy and solemnity that normally attend a marriage, G.L.c. 207, governing entrance to marriage, is a licensing law. The plaintiffs argue that because nothing in that licensing law specifically prohibits marriages between persons of the same sex, we may interpret the statute to permit "qualified same sex couples" to obtain marriage licenses, thereby avoiding the question whether the law is constitutional. *See School Comm. of Greenfield v. Greenfield Educ. Ass'n*, 385 Mass. 70, 79, 431 N.E.2d 180 (1982), and cases cited. This claim lacks merit.

We interpret statutes to carry out the Legislature's intent, determined by the words of a statute interpreted according to "the ordinary and approved usage of the language." *Hanlon v. Rollins*, 286 Mass. 444, 447, 190 N.E. 606 (1934). The everyday meaning of "marriage" is "the legal union of a man and woman as husband and wife," Black's Law Dictionary 986 (7th ed. 1999), and the plaintiffs do not argue that the term "marriage" has ever had a different meaning under Massachusetts law. *See, e.g., Milford v. Worcester*, 7 Mass. 48, 52 (1810) (marriage "is an engagement, by which a single man and a single woman, of sufficient discretion, take each other for husband and wife"). This definition of marriage, as both the department and the Superior Court judge point out, derives from the common law. *See Commonwealth v. Knowlton*, 2 Mass. 530, 535 (1807) (Massachusetts common law derives from English common law except as otherwise altered by Massachusetts statutes and Constitution). *See also Commonwealth v. Lane*, 113 Mass. 458, 462–463 (1873) ("when the statutes are silent, questions of the validity of marriages are to be determined by the jus gentium, the common law of nations"); C.P. Kindregan, Jr., & M.L. Inker, Family Law and Practice § 1.2 (3d ed. 2002). Far from being ambiguous, the undefined word "marriage," as used in G.L.c. 207, confirms the General Court's intent to hew to the term's common-law and quotidian meaning concerning the genders of the marriage partners.

The intended scope of G.L.c. 207 is also evident in its consanguinity provisions. *See Chandler v. County Comm'rs of Nantucket County*, 437 Mass. 430, 435, 772 N.E.2d 578 (2002) (statute's various provisions may offer insight into legislative intent). Sections 1 and 2 of G.L.c. 207 prohibit marriages between a man and certain female relatives and a woman and certain male relatives, but are silent as to the consanguinity of male-male or female-female marriage applicants. *See* G.L.c. 207, §§ 1–2. The only reasonable explanation is that the Legislature did not intend that same-sex couples be licensed to marry. We conclude, as did the judge, that G.L.c. 207 may not be construed to permit same-sex couples to marry.

III.

A

The larger question is whether, as the department claims, government action that bars same-sex couples from civil marriage constitutes a legitimate exercise of the State's authority to regulate conduct, or whether, as the plaintiffs claim, this categorical marriage exclusion violates the Massachusetts Constitution. We have recognized the long-standing statutory understanding, derived from the common law, that "marriage" means the lawful union of a woman and a man. But that history cannot and does not foreclose the constitutional question.

The plaintiffs' claim that the marriage restriction violates the Massachusetts Constitution can be analyzed in two ways. Does it offend the Constitution's guarantees of equality before the law? Or do the liberty and due process provisions of the Massachusetts Constitution secure the plaintiffs' right to marry their chosen partner? In matters implicating marriage, family life, and the upbringing of children, the two constitutional concepts frequently overlap, as they do here.

. . .

We begin by considering the nature of civil marriage itself. Simply put, the government creates civil marriage. In Massachusetts, civil marriage is, and since pre-Colonial days has been, precisely what its name implies: a wholly secular institution. *See Commonwealth v. Munson*, 127 Mass. 459, 460–466 (1879) (noting that "in Massachusetts, from very early times, the requisites of a valid marriage have been regulated by statutes of the Colony, Province, and Commonwealth," and surveying marriage statutes from 1639 through 1834). No religious ceremony has ever been required to validate a Massachusetts marriage. *Id.* In a real sense, there are three partners to every civil marriage: two willing spouses and an approving State. *See DeMatteo v. DeMatteo*, 436 Mass. 18, 31, 762 N.E.2d 797 (2002) ("Marriage is not a mere contract between two parties but a legal status from which certain rights and obligations arise"); *Smith v. Smith*, 171 Mass. 404, 409, 50 N.E. 933 (1898) (on marriage, the parties "assume[] new relations to each other and to the State"). *See also French v. McAnarney*, 290 Mass. 544, 546, 195 N.E. 714 (1935). While only the parties can mutually assent to marriage, the terms of the marriage—who may marry and what obligations, benefits, and liabilities attach to civil marriage—are set by the Commonwealth. Conversely, while only the parties can agree to end the marriage (absent the death of one of them or a marriage void ab initio), the Commonwealth defines the exit terms. *See* G.L.c. 208.

Civil marriage is created and regulated through exercise of the police power. *See Commonwealth v. Stowell,* 389 Mass. 171, 175, 449 N.E.2d 357 (1983) (regulation of marriage is properly within the scope of the police power). "Police power" (now more commonly termed the State's regulatory authority) is an old-fashioned term for the Commonwealth's lawmaking authority, as bounded by the liberty and equality guarantees of the Massachusetts Constitution and its express delegation of power from the people to their government. In broad terms, it is the Legislature's power to enact rules to regulate conduct, to the extent that such laws are "necessary to secure the health, safety, good order, comfort, or general welfare of the community" (citations omitted). Opinion of the Justices, 341 Mass. 760, 785, 168 N.E.2d 858 (1960).[108] *See Commonwealth v. Alger,* 61 Mass. 53, 7 Cush. 53, 85 (1851).

Without question, civil marriage enhances the "welfare of the community." It is a "social institution of the highest importance." *French v. McAnarney, supra.* Civil marriage anchors an ordered society by encouraging stable relationships over transient ones. It is central to the way the Commonwealth identifies individuals, provides for the orderly distribution of property, ensures that children and adults are cared for and supported whenever possible from private rather than public funds, and tracks important epidemiological and demographic data.

Marriage also bestows enormous private and social advantages on those who choose to marry. Civil marriage is at once a deeply personal commitment to another human being and a highly public celebration of the ideals of mutuality, companionship, intimacy, fidelity, and family. "It is an association that promotes a way of life, not causes; a harmony in living, not political faiths; a bilateral loyalty, not commercial or social projects." *Griswold v. Connecticut,* 381 U.S. 479, 486, 14 L.Ed.2d 510, 85 S.Ct. 1678 (1965). Because it fulfils yearnings for security, safe haven, and connection that express our common humanity, civil marriage is an esteemed institution, and the decision whether and whom to marry is among life's momentous acts of self-definition.

Tangible as well as intangible benefits flow from marriage. The marriage license grants valuable property rights to those who meet the entry requirements, and who agree to what might otherwise be a burdensome degree of government regulation of their activities. *See Leduc v. Commonwealth,* 421 Mass. 433, 435, 657 N.E.2d 755 (1995), *cert. denied,* 519 U.S. 827, 136 L.Ed.2d 47, 117 S.Ct. 91 (1996) ("The historical aim of licensure generally is preservation of public health, safety, and welfare by extending the public trust only to those with proven qualifications"). The Legislature has conferred on "each party [in a civil marriage] substantial

108. "The term public welfare has never been and cannot be precisely defined. Sometimes it has been said to include public convenience, comfort, peace and order, prosperity, and similar concepts, but not to include 'mere expediency.' " Opinion of the Justices, 333 Mass. 773, 778, 128 N.E.2d 557 (1955).

rights concerning the assets of the other which unmarried cohabitants do not have." *Wilcox v. Trautz*, 427 Mass. 326, 334, 693 N.E.2d 141 (1998). *See Collins v. Guggenheim*, 417 Mass. 615, 618, 631 N.E.2d 1016 (1994) (rejecting claim for equitable distribution of property where plaintiff cohabited with but did not marry defendant); *Feliciano v. Rosemar Silver Co.*, 401 Mass. 141, 142, 514 N.E.2d 1095 (1987) (government interest in promoting marriage would be "subverted" by recognition of "a right to recover for loss of consortium by a person who has not accepted the correlative responsibilities of marriage"); *Davis v. Misiano*, 373 Mass. 261, 263, 366 N.E.2d 752 (1977) (unmarried partners not entitled to rights of separate support or alimony). *See generally Attorney Gen. v. Desilets*, 418 Mass. 316, 327–328, 636 N.E.2d 233 & nn. 10, 11 (1994).

The benefits accessible only by way of a marriage license are enormous, touching nearly every aspect of life and death. The department states that "hundreds of statutes" are related to marriage and to marital benefits. With no attempt to be comprehensive, we note that some of the statutory benefits conferred by the Legislature on those who enter into civil marriage include, as to property: joint Massachusetts income tax filing (G.L.c. 62C, § 6); tenancy by the entirety (a form of ownership that provides certain protections against creditors and allows for the automatic descent of property to the surviving spouse without probate) (G.L.c. 184, § 7); extension of the benefit of the homestead protection (securing up to $300,000 in equity from creditors) to one's spouse and children (G.L.c. 188, § 1); automatic rights to inherit the property of a deceased spouse who does not leave a will (G.L.c. 190, § 1); the rights of elective share and of dower (which allow surviving spouses certain property rights where the decedent spouse has not made adequate provision for the survivor in a will) (G.L.c. 191, § 15, and G.L.c. 189); entitlement to wages owed to a deceased employee (G.L.c. 149, § 178A [general] and G.L.c. 149, § 178C [public employees]); eligibility to continue certain businesses of a deceased spouse (*e.g.*, G.L.c. 112, § 53 [dentist]); the right to share the medical policy of one's spouse (*e.g.*, G.L.c. 175, § 108, Second [a] [3] [defining an insured's "dependent" to include one's spouse), *see Connors v. Boston*, 430 Mass. 31, 43, 714 N.E.2d 335 (1999) [domestic partners of city employees not included within the term "dependent" as used in G.L.c. 32B, § 2]); thirty-nine week continuation of health coverage for the spouse of a person who is laid off or dies (*e.g.*, G.L.c. 175, § 110G); preferential options under the Commonwealth's pension system (*see* G.L.c. 32, § 12 [2] ["Joint and Last Survivor Allowance"]); preferential benefits in the Commonwealth's medical program, MassHealth (*e.g.*, 130 Code Mass. Regs. § 515.012 [A] prohibiting placing a lien on long-term care patient's former home if spouse still lives there); access to veterans' spousal benefits and preferences (*e.g.*, G.L.c. 115, § 1 [defining "dependents"] and G.L.c. 31, § 26 [State employment] and § 28 [municipal employees]); financial protections for spouses of certain Commonwealth employees (fire fighters, police officers, prosecutors, among others) killed in the performance of duty (*e.g.*, G.L.c. 32, §§ 100–103); the equitable division of marital property on divorce (G.L.c. 208, § 34); temporary and permanent alimony rights (G.L.c. 208, §§ 17 and 34); the right to separate support on separation of the parties that does not result in divorce (G.L.c. 209, § 32); and the right to bring claims for wrongful death and loss of consortium, and for funeral and burial expenses and punitive damages resulting from tort actions (G.L.c. 229, §§ 1 and 2; G.L.c. 228, § 1. *See Feliciano v. Rosemar Silver Co., supra*).

Exclusive marital benefits that are not directly tied to property rights include the presumptions of legitimacy and parentage of children born to a married couple (G.L.c. 209C, § 6, and G.L.c. 46, § 4B); and evidentiary rights, such as the prohibition against spouses testifying against one another about their private conversations, applicable in both civil and criminal cases (G.L.c. 233, § 20). Other statutory benefits of a personal nature available only to married individuals include qualification for bereavement or medical leave to care for individuals related by blood or marriage (G.L.c. 149, § 52D); an automatic "family member" preference to make medical decisions for an incompetent or disabled spouse who does not have a contrary health care proxy, *see Shine v. Vega*, 429 Mass. 456, 466, 709 N.E.2d 58 (1999); the application of predictable rules of child custody, visitation, support, and removal out-of-State when married parents divorce (*e.g.*, G.L.c. 208, § 19 [temporary custody], § 20 [temporary support], § 28 [custody and support on judgment of divorce], § 30 [removal from Commonwealth], and § 31 [shared custody plan]; priority rights to administer the estate of a deceased spouse who dies without a will, and requirement that surviving spouse must consent to the appointment of any other person as administrator (G.L.c. 38, § 13 [disposition of body], and G.L.c. 113, § 8 [anatomical gifts]); and the right to interment in the lot or tomb owned by one's deceased spouse (G.L.c. 114, §§ 29–33).

Where a married couple has children, their children are also directly or indirectly, but no less auspiciously, the recipients of the special legal and economic protections obtained by civil marriage. Notwithstanding the Commonwealth's strong public policy to abolish legal distinctions between marital and nonmarital children in providing for the support and care of minors, *see Department of Revenue v. Mason M.*, 439 Mass. 665, 790 N.E.2d 671 (2003); *Woodward v. Commissioner of Social Sec.*, 435 Mass. 536, 546, 760 N.E.2d 257 (2002), the fact remains that marital children reap a measure of family stability and economic security based on their parents' legally privileged status that is largely inaccessible, or not as readily accessible, to nonmarital children. Some of these benefits are social, such as the enhanced approval that still attends the status of being a marital child. Others are material, such as the greater ease of access to family-based State and Federal benefits that attend the presumptions of one's parentage.

It is undoubtedly for these concrete reasons, as well as for its intimately personal significance, that civil marriage has long been termed a "civil right." *See, e.g., Loving v. Virginia*, 388 U.S. 1, 12, 18 L.Ed.2d 1010, 87 S.Ct. 1817 (1967) ("Marriage is one of the 'basic civil rights of man,' fundamental to our very existence and survival"), quoting *Skinner v. Oklahoma*, 316 U.S. 535, 541, 86 L.Ed. 1655, 62 S.Ct. 1110 (1942); *Milford v. Worcester*, 7 Mass. 48, 56 (1810) (referring to "civil rights incident to marriages"). *See also Baehr v. Lewin*, 74 Haw. 530, 561, 852 P.2d 44 (1993) (identifying marriage as a "civil right[]"); *Baker v. State*, 170 Vt. 194, 242, 744 A.2d 864 (1999) (Johnson, J., concurring in part and dissenting in part) (same). The United States Supreme Court has described the right to marry as "of fundamental importance for all individuals" and as "part of the fundamental 'right of privacy' implicit in the Fourteenth Amendment's Due Process Clause." *Zablocki v. Redhail*, 434 U.S. 374, 384, 54 L.Ed.2d 618, 98 S.Ct. 673 (1978). *See Loving v. Virginia*, *supra* ("The freedom to marry has long been recognized as one of the vital personal rights essential to the orderly pursuit of happiness by free men").

Without the right to marry—or more properly, the right to choose to marry—one is excluded from the full range of human experience and denied full protection of the laws for one's "avowed commitment to an intimate and lasting human relationship." *Baker v. State*, *supra* at 229. Because civil marriage is central to the lives of individuals and the welfare of the community, our laws assiduously protect the individual's right to marry against undue government incursion. Laws may not "interfere directly and substantially with the right to marry." *Zablocki v. Redhail*, *supra* at 387. *See Perez v. Sharp*, 32 Cal.2d 711, 714, 198 P.2d 17 (1948) ("There can be no prohibition of marriage except for an important social objective and reasonable means").

. . .

The individual liberty and equality safeguards of the Massachusetts Constitution protect both "freedom from" unwarranted government intrusion into protected spheres of life and "freedom to" partake in benefits created by the State for the common good. *See Bachrach v. Secretary of the Commonwealth*, 382 Mass. 268, 273, 415 N.E.2d 832 (1981); *Dalli v. Board of Educ.*, 358 Mass. 753, 759, 267 N.E.2d 219 (1971). Both freedoms are involved here. Whether and whom to marry, how to express sexual intimacy, and whether and how to establish a family—these are among the most basic of every individual's liberty and due process rights. *See, e.g.*, *Lawrence, supra* at 2481; *Planned Parenthood of Southeastern Pa. v. Casey,* 505 U.S. 833, 851, 120 L.Ed.2d 674, 112 S.Ct. 2791 (1992); *Zablocki v. Redhail*, 434 U.S. 374, 384, 54 L.Ed.2d 618, 98 S.Ct. 673 (1978); *Roe v. Wade,* 410 U.S. 113, 152–153, 35 L.Ed.2d 147, 93 S.Ct. 705 (1973); *Eisenstadt v. Baird*, 405 U.S. 438, 453, 31 L.Ed.2d 349, 92 S.Ct. 1029 (1972); *Loving v. Virginia*, *supra*. And central to personal freedom and security is the assurance that the laws will apply equally to persons in similar situations. "Absolute equality before the law is a fundamental principle of our own Constitution." Opinion of the Justices, 211 Mass. 618, 619, 98 N.E. 337 (1912). The liberty interest in choosing whether and whom to marry would be hollow if the Commonwealth could, without sufficient justification, foreclose an individual from freely choosing the person with whom to share an exclusive commitment in the unique institution of civil marriage.

The Massachusetts Constitution requires, at a minimum, that the exercise of the State's regulatory authority not be "arbitrary or capricious." *Commonwealth v. Henry's Drywall Co.*, 366 Mass. 539, 542, 320 N.E.2d 911 (1974). Under both the equality and liberty guarantees, regulatory authority must, at very least, serve "a legitimate purpose in a rational way"; a statute must "bear a reasonable relation to a permissible legislative objective." *Rushworth v. Registrar of Motor Vehicles*, 413 Mass. 265, 270, 596 N.E.2d 340 (1992). *See, e.g.*, *Massachusetts Fed'n of Teachers v. Board of Educ.*, 436 Mass. 763, 778, 767 N.E.2d 549 (2002) (equal protection); *Coffee–Rich, Inc. v. Commissioner of Pub. Health,* 348 Mass. 414, 422, 204 N.E.2d 281 (1965) (due process). Any law failing to satisfy the basic standards of rationality is void.

The plaintiffs challenge the marriage statute on both equal protection and due process grounds. With respect to each such claim, we must first determine the appropriate standard of review. Where a statute implicates a fundamental right or uses a suspect classification, we employ "strict judicial scrutiny." *Lowell v. Kowalski,* 380 Mass. 663, 666, 405 N.E.2d 135 (1980). For all other statutes, we employ the " 'rational basis' test." *English v. New England Med. Ctr.*, 405 Mass. 423, 428, 541 N.E.2d 329 (1989). For due process claims, rational basis analysis requires that statutes "bear[] a real and substantial relation to the public health, safety, morals, or some other phase of the general welfare." *Coffee–Rich, Inc. v. Commissioner of Pub. Health*, *supra*, quoting *Sperry & Hutchinson Co. v. Director of the Div. on the Necessaries of Life*, 307 Mass. 408, 418, 30 N.E.2d 269 (1940). For equal protection challenges, the rational basis test requires that "an impartial lawmaker could logically believe that the classification would serve a legitimate public purpose that transcends the harm to the members of the disadvantaged class." *English v. New England Med. Ctr., supra* at 429, quoting *Cleburne v. Cleburne Living Ctr., Inc.*, 473 U.S. 432, 452, 87 L.Ed.2d 313, 105 S.Ct. 3249 (1985) (Stevens, J., concurring).

The department argues that no fundamental right or "suspect" class is at issue here, and rational basis is the appropriate standard of review. For the reasons we explain below, we conclude that the marriage ban does not meet the rational basis test for either due process or equal protection. Because the statute does not survive rational basis review, we do not consider the plaintiffs' arguments that this case merits strict judicial scrutiny.

The department posits three legislative rationales for prohibiting same-sex couples from marrying: (1) providing a "favorable setting for procreation"; (2) ensuring the optimal setting for child rearing, which the department defines as "a two-parent family with one parent of each sex"; and (3) preserving scarce State and private financial resources. We consider each in turn.

The judge in the Superior Court endorsed the first rationale, holding that "the state's interest in regulating marriage is based on the traditional concept that marriage's primary purpose is procreation." This is incorrect. Our laws of civil marriage do not privilege procreative heterosexual intercourse between married people above every other form of adult intimacy and every other means of creating a family. General Laws c. 207 contains no requirement that the applicants for a marriage license attest to their ability or intention to conceive children by coitus. Fertility is not a condition of marriage, nor is it grounds for divorce. People who have never consummated their marriage, and never plan to, may be and stay married. *See Franklin v. Franklin*, 154 Mass. 515, 516, 28 N.E. 681 (1891) ("The consummation of a marriage by coition is not necessary to its validity"). People who cannot stir from their deathbed may marry. *See* G.L.c. 207, § 28A. While it is certainly true that many, perhaps most, married couples have children together (assisted or unassisted), it is the exclusive and permanent commitment of the marriage partners to one another, not the begetting of children, that is the sine qua non of civil marriage.

. . .

The "marriage is procreation" argument singles out the one unbridgeable difference between same-sex and opposite-sex couples, and transforms that difference into the essence of legal marriage. Like "Amendment 2" to the Constitution of Colorado, which effectively denied homosexual persons equality under the law and full access to the political process, the marriage restriction impermissibly "identifies persons by a single trait and then denies them protection across the board." *Romer v. Evans*, 517 U.S. 620, 633, 134 L.Ed.2d 855, 116 S.Ct. 1620 (1996). In so doing, the State's action confers an official stamp of approval on the destructive stereotype that same-sex relationships are inherently unstable and inferior to opposite-sex relationships and are not worthy of respect.

The department's first stated rationale, equating marriage with unassisted heterosexual procreation, shades imperceptibly into its second: that confining marriage to opposite-sex couples ensures that children are raised in the "optimal" setting. Protecting the welfare of children is a paramount State policy. Restricting marriage to opposite-sex couples, however, cannot plausibly further this policy. "The demographic changes of the past century make it difficult to speak of an average American family. The composition of families varies greatly from household to household." *Troxel v. Granville*, 530 U.S. 57, 63, 147 L.Ed.2d 49, 120 S.Ct. 2054 (2000). Massachusetts has responded supportively to "the changing realities of the American family," *Id.* at 64, and has moved vigorously to strengthen the modern family in its many variations. *See, e.g.*, G.L.c. 209C (paternity statute); G.L.c. 119, § 39D (grandparent visitation statute); *Blixt v. Blixt*, 437 Mass. 649, 774 N.E.2d 1052 (2002), *cert. denied*, 537 U.S. 1189, 123 S.Ct. 1259, 154 L.Ed.2d 1022 (2003) (same); *E.N.O. v. L.M.M.*, 429 Mass. 824, 711 N.E.2d 886, *cert. denied*, 528 U.S. 1005, 145 L.Ed.2d 386, 120 S.Ct. 500 (1999) (de facto parent); *Youmans v. Ramos*, 429 Mass. 774, 782, 711 N.E.2d 165 (1999) (same); and *Adoption of Tammy,* 416 Mass. 205,

619 N.E.2d 315 (1993) (coparent adoption). Moreover, we have repudiated the common-law power of the State to provide varying levels of protection to children based on the circumstances of birth. *See* G.L.c. 209C (paternity statute); *Powers v. Wilkinson*, 399 Mass. 650, 661, 506 N.E.2d 842 (1987) ("Ours is an era in which logic and compassion have impelled the law toward unburdening children from the stigma and the disadvantages heretofore attendant upon the status of illegitimacy"). The "best interests of the child" standard does not turn on a parent's sexual orientation or marital status. *See e.g.*, *Doe v. Doe*, 16 Mass. App. Ct. 499, 503, 452 N.E.2d 293 (1983) (parent's sexual orientation insufficient ground to deny custody of child in divorce action). *See also E.N.O. v. L.M.M.*, *supra* at 829–830 (best interests of child determined by considering child's relationship with biological and de facto same-sex parents); *Silvia v. Silvia*, 9 Mass. App. Ct. 339, 341, 400 N.E.2d 1330 & n.3 (1980) (collecting support and custody statutes containing no gender distinction).

The department has offered no evidence that forbidding marriage to people of the same sex will increase the number of couples choosing to enter into opposite-sex marriages in order to have and raise children. There is thus no rational relationship between the marriage statute and the Commonwealth's proffered goal of protecting the "optimal" child rearing unit. Moreover, the department readily concedes that people in same-sex couples may be "excellent" parents. These couples (including four of the plaintiff couples) have children for the reasons others do—to love them, to care for them, to nurture them. But the task of child rearing for same-sex couples is made infinitely harder by their status as outliers to the marriage laws. While establishing the parentage of children as soon as possible is crucial to the safety and welfare of children, *see Culliton v. Beth Israel Deaconess Med. Ctr.*, 435 Mass. 285, 292, 756 N.E.2d 1133 (2001), same-sex couples must undergo the sometimes lengthy and intrusive process of second-parent adoption to establish their joint parentage. While the enhanced income provided by marital benefits is an important source of security and stability for married couples and their children, those benefits are denied to families headed by same-sex couples. *See, e.g.*, note 6, *supra*. While the laws of divorce provide clear and reasonably predictable guidelines for child support, child custody, and property division on dissolution of a marriage, same-sex couples who dissolve their relationships find themselves and their children in the highly unpredictable terrain of equity jurisdiction. *See E.N.O. v. L.M.M.*, *supra*. Given the wide range of public benefits reserved only for married couples, we do not credit the department's contention that the absence of access to civil marriage amounts to little more than an inconvenience to same-sex couples and their children. Excluding same-sex couples from civil marriage will not make children of opposite-sex marriages more secure, but it does prevent children of same-sex couples from enjoying the immeasurable advantages that flow from the assurance of "a stable family structure in which children will be reared, educated, and socialized." *Post* at 381 (Cordy, J., dissenting).

. . .

The third rationale advanced by the department is that limiting marriage to opposite-sex couples furthers the Legislature's interest in conserving scarce State and private financial resources. The marriage restriction is rational, it argues, because the General Court logically could assume that same-sex couples are more financially independent than married couples and thus less needy of public marital benefits, such as tax advantages, or private marital benefits, such as employer-financed health plans that include spouses in their coverage.

An absolute statutory ban on same-sex marriage bears no rational relationship to the goal of economy. First, the department's conclusory generalization—that same-sex couples are less financially dependent on each other than opposite-sex couples—ignores that many same-sex couples, such as many of the plaintiffs in this case, have children and other dependents (here, aged parents) in their care. The department does not contend, nor could it, that these dependents are less needy or deserving than the dependents of married couples. Second, Massachusetts marriage laws do not condition receipt of public and private financial benefits to married individuals on a demonstration of financial dependence on each other; the benefits are available to married couples regardless of whether they mingle their finances or actually depend on each other for support.

It has been argued that, due to the State's strong interest in the institution of marriage as a stabilizing social structure, only the Legislature can control and define its boundaries. Accordingly, our elected representatives legitimately may choose to exclude same-sex couples from civil marriage in order to assure all citizens of the Commonwealth that (1) the benefits of our marriage laws are available explicitly to create and support a family setting that is, in the Legislature's view, optimal for child rearing, and (2) the State does not endorse gay and lesbian parenthood as the equivalent of being raised by one's married biological parents. These arguments miss the point. The Massachusetts Constitution requires that legislation meet certain criteria and not extend beyond certain limits. It is the function of courts to determine whether these criteria are met and whether these limits are exceeded. In most instances, these limits are defined by whether a rational basis exists to conclude that legislation will bring about a rational result. The Legislature in the first instance, and the courts in the last instance, must ascertain whether such a rational basis exists. To label the court's role as usurping that of the Legislature, *see, e.g., post* at 364 (Cordy, J., dissenting), is to misunderstand the nature and purpose of judicial review. We owe great deference to the Legislature to decide social and policy issues, but it is the traditional and settled role of courts to decide constitutional issues.

. . .

The marriage ban works a deep and scarring hardship on a very real segment of the community for no rational reason. The absence of any reasonable relationship between, on the one hand, an absolute disqualification of same-sex couples who wish to enter into civil marriage and, on the other, protection of public health, safety, or general welfare, suggests that the marriage restriction is rooted in persistent prejudices against persons who are (or who are believed to be) homosexual. "The Constitution cannot control such prejudices but neither can it tolerate them. Private biases may be outside the reach of the law, but the law cannot, directly or indirectly, give them effect." *Palmore v. Sidoti*, 466 U.S. 429, 433, 80 L.Ed.2d 421, 104 S.Ct. 1879 (1984) (construing Fourteenth Amendment). Limiting the protections, benefits, and obligations of civil marriage to opposite-sex couples violates the basic premises of individual liberty and equality under law protected by the Massachusetts Constitution.

. . .

IV

We consider next the plaintiffs' request for relief. We preserve as much of the statute as may be preserved in the face of the successful constitutional challenge. *See Mayor of Boston v. Treasurer & Receiver Gen.*, 384 Mass. 718, 725, 429 N.E.2d 691 (1981); *Dalli v. Board of Educ.*, 358 Mass. 753, 759, 267 N.E.2d 219 (1971). *See also* G.L.c. 4, § 6, Eleventh.

Here, no one argues that striking down the marriage laws is an appropriate form of relief. Eliminating civil marriage would be wholly inconsistent with the Legislature's deep commitment to fostering stable families and would dismantle a vital organizing principle of our society. We face a problem similar to one that recently confronted the Court of Appeal for Ontario, the highest court of that Canadian province, when it considered the constitutionality of the same-sex marriage ban under Canada's Federal Constitution, the Charter of Rights and Freedoms (Charter). *See Halpern v.* Toronto (City), 172 O.A.C. 276 (2003). Canada, like the United States, adopted the common law of England that civil marriage is "the voluntary union for life of one man and one woman, to the exclusion of all others." *Id.* at par. (36), quoting *Hyde v. Hyde*, [1861–1873] All E.R. 175 (1866). In holding that the limitation of civil marriage to opposite-sex couples violated the Charter, the Court of Appeal refined the common-law meaning of marriage. We concur with this remedy, which is entirely consonant with established principles of jurisprudence empowering a court to refine a common-law principle in light of evolving constitutional standards. *See Powers v. Wilkinson*, 399 Mass. 650, 661–662, 506 N.E.2d 842 (1987) (reforming common-law rule of construction of "issue"); *Lewis v. Lewis*, 370 Mass. 619, 629, 351 N.E.2d 526 (1976) (abolishing common-law rule of certain interspousal immunity).

We construe civil marriage to mean the voluntary union of two persons as spouses, to the exclusion of all others. This reformulation redresses the plaintiffs' constitutional injury and furthers the aim of marriage to promote stable, exclusive relationships. It advances the two legitimate State interests the department has identified: providing a stable setting for child rearing and conserving State resources. It leaves intact the Legislature's broad discretion to regulate marriage. *See Commonwealth v. Stowell,* 389 Mass. 171, 175, 449 N.E.2d 357 (1983).

In their complaint the plaintiffs request only a declaration that their exclusion and the exclusion of other qualified same-sex couples from access to civil marriage violates Massachusetts law. We declare that barring an individual from the protections, benefits, and obligations of civil marriage solely because that person would marry a person of the same sex violates the Massachusetts Constitution. We vacate the summary judgment for the department. We remand this case to the Superior Court for entry of judgment consistent with this opinion. Entry of judgment shall be stayed for 180 days to permit the Legislature to take such action as it may deem appropriate in light of this opinion. *See, e.g., Michaud v. Sheriff of Essex County*, 390 Mass. 523, 535–536, 458 N.E.2d 702 (1983).

So ordered.

CONCUR BY: GREANEY

I agree with the result reached by the court, the remedy ordered, and much of the reasoning in the court's opinion. In my view, however, the case is more directly resolved using traditional equal protection analysis.

(a) Article 1 of the Declaration of Rights, as amended by art. 106 of the Amendments to the Massachusetts Constitution, provides:

> All people are born free and equal and have certain natural, essential and unalienable rights; among which may be reckoned the right of enjoying and defending their lives and liberties; that of acquiring, possessing and protecting property; in fine, that of seeking and obtaining their safety and happiness. Equality under the law shall not be denied or abridged because of sex, race, color, creed or national origin.

This provision, even prior to its amendment, guaranteed to all people in the Commonwealth—equally—the enjoyment of rights that are deemed important or fundamental. The withholding of relief from the plaintiffs, who wish to marry, and are otherwise eligible to marry, on the ground that the couples are of the same gender, constitutes a categorical restriction of a fundamental right. The restriction creates a straightforward case of discrimination that disqualifies an entire group of our citizens and their families from participation in an institution of paramount legal and social importance. This is impermissible under art. 1.

Analysis begins with the indisputable premise that the deprivation suffered by the plaintiffs is no mere legal inconvenience. The right to marry is not a privilege conferred by the State, but a fundamental right that is protected against unwarranted State interference. *See Zablocki v. Redhail*, 434 U.S. 374, 384, 54 L.Ed.2d 618, 98 S.Ct. 673 (1978) ("the right to marry is of fundamental importance for all individuals"); *Loving v. Virginia*, 388 U.S. 1, 12, 18 L.Ed.2d 1010, 87 S.Ct. 1817 (1967) (freedom to marry is "one of the vital personal rights essential to the orderly pursuit of happiness by free men" under due process clause of Fourteenth

Amendment); *Skinner v. Oklahoma*, 316 U.S. 535, 541, 86 L.Ed. 1655, 62 S.Ct. 1110 (1942) (marriage is one of "basic civil rights of man"). *See also Turner v. Safley*, 482 U.S. 78, 95–96, 96 L.Ed.2d 64, 107 S.Ct. 2254 (1987) (prisoners' right to marry is constitutionally protected). This right is essentially vitiated if one is denied the right to marry a person of one's choice. *See Zablocki v. Redhail, supra* at 384 (all recent decisions of United States Supreme Court place "the decision to marry as among the personal decisions protected by the right of privacy").

. . .

A classification may be gender based whether or not the challenged government action apportions benefits or burdens uniformly along gender lines. This is so because constitutional protections extend to individuals and not to categories of people. Thus, when an individual desires to marry, but cannot marry his or her chosen partner because of the traditional opposite-sex restriction, a violation of art. 1 has occurred. *See Commonwealth v. Chou*, 433 Mass. 229, 237–238, 741 N.E.2d 17 (2001) (assuming statute enforceable only across gender lines may offend Massachusetts equal rights amendment). I find it disingenuous, at best, to suggest that such an individual's right to marry has not been burdened at all, because he or she remains free to choose another partner, who is of the opposite sex.

. . .

With these two propositions established (the infringement on a fundamental right and a sex-based classification), the enforcement of the marriage statutes as they are currently understood is forbidden by our Constitution unless the State can present a compelling purpose furthered by the statutes that can be accomplished in no other reasonable manner. *See Blixt v. Blixt*, 437 Mass. 649, 655–656, 774 N.E.2d 1052 (2002), *cert. denied*, 537 U.S. 1189, 154 L.Ed.2d 1022, 123 S.Ct. 1259 (2003); *Lowell v. Kowalski*, 380 Mass. 663, 667–669, 405 N.E.2d 135 (1980). This the State has not done. The justifications put forth by the State to sustain the statute's exclusion of the plaintiffs are insufficient for the reasons explained by the court, to which I add the following observations.

The rights of couples to have children, to adopt, and to be foster parents, regardless of sexual orientation and marital status, are firmly established. *See E.N.O. v. L.M.M.*, 429 Mass. 824, 829, 711 N.E.2d 886, *cert. denied*, 528 U.S. 1005, 145 L.Ed.2d 386, 120 S.Ct. 500 (1999); *Adoption of Tammy*, 416 Mass. 205, 210–211, 619 N.E.2d 315 (1993). As recognized in the court's opinion, and demonstrated by the record in this case, however, the State's refusal to accord legal recognition to unions of same-sex couples has had the effect of creating a system in which children of same-sex couples are unable to partake of legal protections and social benefits taken for granted by children in families whose parents are of the opposite sex. The continued maintenance of this caste-like system is irreconcilable with, indeed, totally repugnant to, the State's strong interest in the welfare of all children and its primary focus, in the context of family law where children are concerned, on "the best interests of the child." The issue at stake is not one, as might ordinarily be the case, that can be unilaterally and totally deferred to the wisdom of the Legislature. "While the State retains wide latitude to decide the manner in which it will allocate benefits, it may not use criteria which discriminatorily burden the exercise of a fundamental right." *Moe v. Secretary of Admin. & Fin.*, 382 Mass. 629, 652, 417 N.E.2d 387 (1981). Nor can the State's wish to conserve resources be accomplished by invidious distinctions between classes of citizens. *See Plyler v. Doe*, 457 U.S. 202, 216–217, 227, 102 S.Ct. 2382, 72 L.Ed.2d 786 (1982).

. . .

(b) I am hopeful that our decision will be accepted by those thoughtful citizens who believe that same-sex unions should not be approved by the State. I am not referring here to acceptance in the sense of grudging acknowledgment of the court's authority to adjudicate the matter. My hope is more liberating. The plaintiffs are members of our community, our neighbors, our coworkers, our friends. As pointed out by the court, their professions include investment advisor, computer engineer, teacher, therapist, and lawyer. The plaintiffs volunteer in our schools, worship beside us in our religious houses, and have children who play with our children, to mention just a few ordinary daily contacts. We share a common humanity and participate together in the social contract that is the foundation of our Commonwealth. Simple principles of decency dictate that we extend to the plaintiffs, and to their new status, full acceptance, tolerance, and respect. We should do so because it is the right thing to do. The union of two people contemplated by G.L.c. 207 "is a coming together for better or for worse, hopefully enduring, and intimate to the degree of being sacred. It is an association that promotes a way of life, not causes; a harmony in living, not political faiths; a bilateral loyalty, not commercial or social projects. Yet it is an association for as noble a purpose as any involved in our prior decisions." *Griswold v. Connecticut*, 381 U.S. 479, 486, 14 L.Ed.2d 510, 85 S.Ct. 1678 (1965). Because of the terms of art. 1, the plaintiffs will no longer be excluded from that association.

DISSENT BY: SPINA; SOSMAN; CORDY

What is at stake in this case is not the unequal treatment of individuals or whether individual rights have been impermissibly burdened, but the power of the Legislature to effectuate social change without interference from the courts, pursuant to art. 30 of the Massachusetts Declaration of Rights. The power to regulate marriage lies with the Legislature, not with the judiciary. *See Commonwealth v. Stowell*, 389 Mass. 171, 175, 449 N.E.2d 357 (1983). Today, the court has transformed its role as protector of individual rights into the role of creator of rights, and I respectfully dissent.

1. Equal protection. Although the court did not address the plaintiffs' gender discrimination claim, G.L.c. 207 does not unconstitutionally discriminate on the basis of gender. A claim of gender discrimination will

lie where it is shown that differential treatment disadvantages one sex over the other. *See Attorney Gen. v. Massachusetts Interscholastic Athletic Ass'n*, 378 Mass. 342, 349–352, 393 N.E.2d 284 (1979). *See also United States v. Virginia,* 518 U.S. 515, 135 L.Ed.2d 735, 116 S.Ct. 2264 (1996). General Laws c. 207 enumerates certain qualifications for obtaining a marriage license. It creates no distinction between the sexes, but applies to men and women in precisely the same way. It does not create any disadvantage identified with gender, as both men and women are similarly limited to marrying a person of the opposite sex. *See Commonwealth v. King*, 374 Mass. 5, 15–22, 372 N.E.2d 196 (1977) (law prohibiting prostitution not discriminatory based on gender because of equal application to men and women).

Similarly, the marriage statutes do not discriminate on the basis of sexual orientation. As the court correctly recognizes, constitutional protections are extended to individuals, not couples. *Ante* n.15. The marriage statutes do not disqualify individuals on the basis of sexual orientation from entering into marriage. All individuals, with certain exceptions not relevant here, are free to marry. Whether an individual chooses not to marry because of sexual orientation or any other reason should be of no concern to the court.

The court concludes, however, that G.L.c. 207 unconstitutionally discriminates against the individual plaintiffs because it denies them the "right to marry the person of one's choice" where that person is of the same sex. *Ante.* To reach this result the court relies on *Loving v. Virginia*, 388 U.S. 1, 12, 18 L.Ed.2d 1010, 87 S.Ct. 1817 (1967), and transforms "choice" into the essential element of the institution of marriage. The *Loving* case did not use the word "choice" in this manner, and it did not point to the result that the court reaches today. In *Loving*, the Supreme Court struck down as unconstitutional a statute that prohibited Caucasians from marrying non-Caucasians. It concluded that the statute was intended to preserve white supremacy and invidiously discriminated against non-Caucasians because of their race. *See id.* at 11–12. The "choice" to which the Supreme Court referred was the "choice to marry," and it concluded that with respect to the institution of marriage, the State had no compelling interest in limiting the choice to marry along racial lines. *Id.* The Supreme Court did not imply the existence of a right to marry a person of the same sex. To the same effect is *Perez v. Sharp*, 32 Cal.2d 711, 198 P.2d 17 (1948), on which the court also relies.

Unlike the *Loving* and *Sharp* cases, the Massachusetts Legislature has erected no barrier to marriage that intentionally discriminates against anyone. Within the institution of marriage, anyone is free to marry, with certain exceptions that are not challenged. In the absence of any discriminatory purpose, the State's marriage statutes do not violate principles of equal protection. *See Washington v. Davis*, 426 U.S. 229, 240, 48 L.Ed.2d 597, 96 S.Ct. 2040 (1976) ("invidious quality of a law claimed to be ... discriminatory must ultimately be traced to a ... discriminatory purpose"); *Dickerson v. Attorney Gen.*, 396 Mass. 740, 743, 488 N.E.2d 757

(1986) (for purpose of equal protection analysis, standard of review under State and Federal Constitutions is identical). *See also Attorney Gen. v. Massachusetts Interscholastic Athletic Ass'n, supra.* This court should not have invoked even the most deferential standard of review within equal protection analysis because no individual was denied access to the institution of marriage.

2. Due process. The marriage statutes do not impermissibly burden a right protected by our constitutional guarantee of due process implicit in art. 10 of our Declaration of Rights. There is no restriction on the right of any plaintiff to enter into marriage. Each is free to marry a willing person of the opposite sex. *Cf. Zablocki v. Redhail,* 434 U.S. 374, 54 L.Ed.2d 618, 98 S.Ct. 673 (1978) (fundamental right to marry impermissibly burdened by statute requiring court approval when subject to child support order).

Substantive due process protects individual rights against unwarranted government intrusion. *See Aime v. Commonwealth,* 414 Mass. 667, 673, 611 N.E.2d 204 (1993). The court states, as we have said on many occasions, that the Massachusetts Declaration of Rights may protect a right in ways that exceed the protection afforded by the Federal Constitution. *Ante. See Arizona v. Evans,* 514 U.S. 1, 8, 131 L.Ed.2d 34, 115 S.Ct. 1185 (1995) (State courts afforded broader protection of rights than granted by United States Constitution). However, today the court does not fashion a remedy that affords greater protection of a right. Instead, using the rubric of due process, it has redefined marriage.

. . . Although this court did not state that same-sex marriage is a fundamental right worthy of strict scrutiny protection, it nonetheless deemed it a constitutionally protected right by applying rational basis review. Before applying any level of constitutional analysis there must be a recognized right at stake. Same-sex marriage, or the "right to marry the person of one's choice" as the court today defines that right, does not fall within the fundamental right to marry. Same-sex marriage is not "deeply rooted in this Nation's history," and the court does not suggest that it is. Except for the occasional isolated decision in recent years, *see, e.g., Baker v. State,* 170 Vt. 194, 744 A.2d 864 (1999), same-sex marriage is not a right, fundamental or otherwise, recognized in this country. Just one example of the Legislature's refusal to recognize same-sex marriage can be found in a section of the legislation amending G.L.c. 151B to prohibit discrimination in the workplace on the basis of sexual orientation, which states: "Nothing in this act shall be construed so as to legitimize or validate a 'homosexual marriage'. . . ." St. 1989, c. 516, § 19. In this Commonwealth and in this country, the roots of the institution of marriage are deeply set in history as a civil union between a single man and a single woman. There is no basis for the court to recognize same-sex marriage as a constitutionally protected right.

. . .

SOSMAN, J. (dissenting, with whom SPINA and CORDY, JJ., join). In applying the rational basis test to any challenged statutory scheme, the issue is not whether the Legislature's rationale behind that scheme is persuasive to us, but only whether it satisfies a minimal threshold of rationality. Today, rather than apply that test, the court announces that, because it is persuaded that there are no differences between same-sex and opposite-sex couples, the Legislature has no rational basis for treating them differently with respect to the granting of marriage licenses. Reduced to its essence, the court's opinion concludes that, because same-sex couples are now raising children, and withholding the benefits of civil marriage from their union makes it harder for them to raise those children, the State must therefore provide the benefits of civil marriage to same-sex couples just as it does to opposite-sex couples. Of course, many people are raising children outside the confines of traditional marriage, and, by definition, those children are being deprived of the various benefits that would flow if they were being raised in a household with married parents. That does not mean that the Legislature must accord the full benefits of marital status on every household raising children. Rather, the Legislature need only have some rational basis for concluding that, at present, those alternate family structures have not yet been conclusively shown to be the equivalent of the marital family structure that has established itself as a successful one over a period of centuries. People are of course at liberty to raise their children in various family structures, as long as they are not literally harming their children by doing so. *See Blixt v. Blixt*, 437 Mass. 649, 668–670, 774 N.E.2d 1052 (2002) (Sosman, J., dissenting), *cert. denied*, 537 U.S. 1189, 154 L.Ed.2d 1022, 123 S.Ct. 1259 (2003). That does not mean that the State is required to provide identical forms of encouragement, endorsement, and support to all of the infinite variety of household structures that a free society permits.

Based on our own philosophy of child rearing, and on our observations of the children being raised by same-sex couples to whom we are personally close, we may be of the view that what matters to children is not the gender, or sexual orientation, or even the number of the adults who raise them, but rather whether those adults provide the children with a nurturing, stable, safe, consistent, and supportive environment in which to mature. Same-sex couples can provide their children with the requisite nurturing, stable, safe, consistent, and supportive environment in which to mature, just as opposite-sex couples do. It is therefore understandable that the court might view the traditional definition of marriage as an unnecessary anachronism, rooted in historical prejudices that modern society has in large measure rejected and biological limitations that modern science has overcome.

It is not, however, our assessment that matters. Conspicuously absent from the court's opinion today is any acknowledgment that the attempts at scientific study of the ramifications of raising children in same-sex couple households are themselves in their infancy and have so far produced inconclusive and conflicting results. Notwithstanding our belief that gender and sexual orientation of parents should not matter to the success of the child rearing venture, studies to date reveal that there are still some observable differences between children raised by opposite-sex couples and children raised by same-sex couples. *See post* at 337–38 (Cordy, J., dissenting). Interpretation of the data gathered by those studies then becomes clouded by the personal and political beliefs of the investigators, both as to whether the differences identified are positive or negative, and as to the untested explanations of what might account for those differences. (This is hardly the first time in history that the ostensible steel of the scientific method has melted and buckled under the intense heat of political and religious passions.) Even in the absence of bias or political agenda behind the various studies of children raised by same-sex couples, the most neutral and strict application of scientific principles to this field would be constrained by the limited period of observation that has been available. Gay and lesbian couples living together openly, and official recognition of them as their children's sole parents, comprise a very recent phenomenon, and the recency of that phenomenon has not yet permitted any study of how those children fare as adults and at best minimal study of how they fare during their adolescent years. The Legislature can rationally view the state of the scientific evidence as unsettled on the critical question it now faces: Are families headed by same-sex parents equally successful in rearing children from infancy to adulthood as families headed by parents of opposite sexes? Our belief that children raised by same-sex couples should fare the same as children raised in traditional families is just that: a passionately held but utterly untested belief. The Legislature is not required to share that belief but may, as the creator of the institution of civil marriage, wish to see the proof before making a fundamental alteration to that institution.

Although ostensibly applying the rational basis test to the civil marriage statutes, it is abundantly apparent that the court is in fact applying some undefined stricter standard to assess the constitutionality of the marriage statutes' exclusion of same-sex couples. While avoiding any express conclusion as to any of the proffered routes by which that exclusion would be subjected to a test of strict scrutiny—infringement of a fundamental right, discrimination based on gender, or discrimination against gays and lesbians as a suspect classification—the opinion repeatedly alludes to those concepts in a prolonged and eloquent prelude before articulating its view that the exclusion lacks even a rational basis. *See, e.g., ante* at 360 (noting that State Constitution is "more protective of individual liberty and equality," demands "broader protection for fundamental rights," and is "less tolerant of government intrusion into the protected spheres of private life" than Federal Constitution); *ante* at 360 (describing decision to marry and choice of marital partner as "among life's momentous acts of self-definition"); *ante* at 360 (repeated references to "right to marry" as "fundamental"); *ante* at 360 (repeated comparisons to statutes prohibiting interracial marriage, which were predicated on suspect classification of race); *ante* at 360 (characterizing ban on same-sex marriage as "invidious" discrimination that "deprives individuals of access to an institution of fundamental legal, personal, and social significance'' and again noting that Massachusetts Constitution ''protects matters of personal liberty against government incursion'' more zealously than Federal Constitution); *ante* at 365 (characterizing ''whom to marry, how to express sexual intimacy, and whether and how to establish a family'' as ''among the most basic of every individual's liberty and due process rights''); *id.* (''liberty interest in choosing whether and whom to marry would be hollow'' if Commonwealth could ''foreclose an individual from freely choosing the person'' to marry); *ante* at 333 (opining that in ''overlapping realms of personal autonomy, marriage, family life, and child rearing,'' characterized as ''fundamentally private areas of life,'' court uses ''integrated'' analysis instead of ''narrow focus''). *See also ante* at 337 n.29 (suggesting that prohibition on same-sex marriage ''imposes limits on personal beliefs''); *ante* 339 at n.31 (suggesting that ''total deference'' to Legislature in this case would be equivalent to ''stripping'' judiciary ''of its constitutional authority to decide challenges'' in such areas as forced sterilization, antimiscegenation statutes, and abortion, even though all cited examples pertain to fundamental rights analyzed under strict scrutiny, not under rational basis test); *ante* at 345 (civil marriage as ''a right of fundamental importance''); *ante* at 341 (noting State policy of ''preventing discrimination on the basis of sexual orientation''); *id.* (prohibition against same-sex marriage inconsistent with ''gender-neutral laws promoting stable families,'' and ''rooted in persistent prejudices against'' homosexuals); *ante* at 342 (prohibition against same-sex marriage ''violated the basic premises of individual liberty''). In short, while claiming to apply a mere rational basis test, the court's opinion works up an enormous head of steam by repeated invocations of avenues by which to subject the statute to strict scrutiny, apparently hoping that that head of steam will generate momentum sufficient to propel the opinion across the yawning chasm of the very deferential rational basis test.

. . .

More importantly, it is not our confidence in the lack of adverse consequences that is at issue, or even whether that confidence is justifiable. The issue is whether it is rational to reserve judgment on whether this change can be made at this time without damaging the institution of marriage or adversely affecting the critical role it has played in our society. Absent consensus on the issue (which obviously does not exist), or unanimity amongst scientists studying the issue (which also does not exist), or a more prolonged period of observation of this new family structure (which has not yet been possible), it is rational for the Legislature to postpone any redefinition of marriage that would include same-sex couples until such time as it is certain that that redefinition will not have unintended and undesirable social consequences. Through the political process, the people may decide when the benefits of extending civil marriage to same-sex couples have been shown to outweigh whatever risks—be they palpable or ephemeral—are involved. However minimal the risks of that redefinition of marriage may seem to us from our vantage point, it is not up to us to decide what risks society must run, and it is inappropriate for us to arrogate that power to ourselves merely because we are confident that "it is the right thing to do." *Ante* at 350 (Greaney, J., concurring).

As a matter of social history, today's opinion may represent a great turning point that many will hail as a tremendous step toward a more just society. As a matter of constitutional jurisprudence, however, the case stands as an aberration. To reach the result it does, the court has tortured the rational basis test beyond recognition. I fully appreciate the strength of the temptation to find this particular law unconstitutional—there is much to be said for the argument that excluding gay and lesbian couples from the benefits of civil marriage is cruelly unfair and hopelessly outdated; the inability to marry has a profound impact on the personal lives of committed gay and lesbian couples (and their children) to whom we are personally close (our friends, neighbors, family members, classmates, and co-workers); and our resolution of this issue takes place under the intense glare of national and international publicity. Speaking metaphorically, these factors have combined to turn the case before us into a "perfect storm" of a constitutional question. In my view, however, such factors make it all the more imperative that we adhere precisely and scrupulously to the established guideposts of our constitutional jurisprudence, a jurisprudence that makes the rational basis test an extremely deferential one that focuses on the rationality, not the persuasiveness, of the potential justifications for the classifications in the legislative scheme. I trust that, once this particular "storm" clears, we will return to the rational basis test as it has always been understood and applied. Applying that deferential test in the manner it is customarily applied, the exclusion of gay and lesbian couples from the institution of civil marriage passes constitutional muster. I respectfully dissent.

DISCUSSION

Contrast the Vermont (and later New Jersey) court's handling of the issue (allowing the legislature to craft a remedy short of civil marriage) with that of the court in Goodridge v. Dept. of Health and Human Services *(in an opinion to the Massachusetts senate, the Supreme Judicial Court specifically rejected the senate's proposed civil union scheme). Which court got it right?*

On May 17, 2004, the fiftieth anniversary of *Brown v. Board of Education*, Cambridge, Massachusetts issued the first legally authorized marriage license to a same-sex couple. Thousands of gay couples have married and continue to marry legally in Massachusetts. Gays also sought to open marriage across the country and a number of locales complied. San Francisco, California, Sandoval, New Mexico, and New Paltz, New York all began issuing licenses. Oregon's Multnomah County (which includes Portland), granted some three thousand marriage licenses. State courts halted all of these efforts to expand marriage.

VI. THE NEXT WAVE OF BACKLASH—THE AMENDMENT EFFORT

As noted, successful efforts for gay marriage have often been followed by a backlash, and that was so after the Massachusetts decision as well. The forward march of the marriage equality movement, coupled with concerns about the constitutionality of DOMA, led to a push for state constitutional amendments banning gay marriage, as well as a federal amendment. Twenty-four states amended their constitutions expressly to ban same-sex marriage or were considering such a move in the wake of *Goodridge*. In the November 2004 elections, constitutional amendments to ban same-sex marriage passed in every state (11 total) in which they appeared on the ballot. Some went beyond prohibiting "marriage" and prohibited granting rights to gay couples on par with those enjoyed by married couples—which might arguably include even domestic partner health benefits granted by private firms. Five of these constitutional amendments follow in this reading.

In the 2006 mid-term elections, seven more states added amendments banning same-sex marriage. Arizona became the first state in which a proposed amendment banning same-sex marriage was defeated by voters, 51% to 49%. However, in November 2008, a new attempt to add a same-sex marriage ban amendment in Arizona succeeded. State amendments have been challenged under federal due process and equal protection arguments. (*See, e.g., Citizens for Equal Protection v. Bruning* (8th Cir., 2006). For a general discussion see SHANNON GILREATH, SEXUAL POLITICS: THE GAY PERSON IN AMERICA TODAY (2006)).

A. REPRESENTATIVE STATE AMENDMENTS

The Ohio Amendment (passed by voters, 62–38% (2004))

Article XV, Section 11. Only a union between one man and one woman may be a marriage valid in or recognized by this state and its political subdivisions. This state and its political subdivisions shall not create or recognize a legal status for relationships of unmarried individuals that intends to approximate the design, qualities, significance or effect of marriage.

The Georgia Amendment (passed by voters, 77–23% (2004))

Article I of the Constitution is amended by adding a new Section IV to read as follows:

(a) This state shall recognize as marriage only the union of man and woman. Marriages between persons of the same sex are prohibited in this state.

(b) No union between persons of the same sex shall be recognized by this state as entitled to the benefits of marriage. This state shall not give effect to any public act, record, or judicial proceeding of any other state or jurisdiction respecting a relationship between persons of the same sex that is treated as a marriage under the laws of such other state or jurisdiction. The courts of this state shall have no jurisdiction to grant a divorce or separate maintenance with respect to any such relationship or otherwise to consider or rule on any of the parties respective rights arising as a result of or in connection with such relationship." (Voting provisions omitted.)

The Utah Amendment (passed by voters, 66–34% (2004))

Article I, Section 29. [Marriage.]

(1) Marriage consists only of the legal union between a man and a woman.

(2) No other domestic union, however denominated, may be recognized as a marriage or given the same or substantially equivalent legal effect.

The Oregon Amendment, passed by voters 57–43% (2004)

It is the policy of Oregon, and its subdivisions, that only a marriage between one man and one woman shall be valid or legally recognized as a marriage.

The Oklahoma Amendment (passed by voters, 76–24% (2004))

Section 35. A. Marriage in this state shall consist only of the union of one man and one woman. Neither this Constitution nor any other provision of law shall be construed to require that marital status or the legal incidents thereof be conferred upon unmarried couples or groups.

B. A marriage between persons of the same gender performed in another state shall not be recognized as valid and binding in this state as of the date of the marriage.

C. Any person knowingly issuing a marriage license in violation of this section shall be guilty of a misdemeanor.

B. AN ARGUMENT FOR A FEDERAL CONSTITUTIONAL AMENDMENT

The following are remarks by President George W. Bush (February 24, 2004) regarding a federal marriage amendment.

Eight years ago, Congress passed, and President Clinton signed the Defense of Marriage Act, which defined marriage, for purposes of federal law, as the legal union between one man and one woman as husband and wife. The act passed the House of Representatives by a vote of 342 to 6 and the Senate by a vote of 85 to 14. Those Congressional votes and the passage of similar defense of marriage laws in 38 states express an overwhelming consensus in our country for protecting the institution of marriage.

In recent months, however, some activist judges and local officials have made an aggressive attempt to redefine marriage. In Massachusetts, four judges on the highest court have indicated they will order the issuance of marriage licenses to applicants of the same gender in May of this year.

In San Francisco, city officials have issued thousands of marriage licenses to people of the same gender, contrary to the California Family Code. That code, which clearly defines marriage as the union of a man and a woman, was approved overwhelmingly by the voters of California.

A county in New Mexico has also issued marriage licenses to applicants of the same gender. And unless action is taken, we can expect more arbitrary court decisions, more litigation, more defiance of the law by local officials, all of which adds to uncertainty.

After more than two centuries of American jurisprudence and millennia of human experience, a few judges and local authorities are presuming to change the most fundamental institution of civilization. Their actions have created confusion on an issue that requires clarity.

On a matter of such importance, the voice of the people must be heard. Activist courts have left the people with one recourse. If we are to prevent the meaning of marriage from being changed forever, our nation must enact a constitutional amendment to protect marriage in America. Decisive and democratic action is needed, because attempts to redefine marriage in a single state or city could have serious consequences throughout the country.

The Constitution says that full faith and credit shall be given in each state to the public acts and records and judicial proceedings of every other state. Those who want to change the meaning of marriage will claim that this provision requires all states and cities to recognize same-sex marriages performed anywhere in America.

Congress attempted to address this problem in the Defense of Marriage Act by declaring that no state must accept another state's definition of marriage.

My administration will vigorously defend this act of Congress. Yet there is no assurance that the Defense of Marriage Act will not itself be struck down by activist courts. In that event, every, state would be forced to recognize any relationship that judges in Boston or officials in San Francisco choose to call a marriage.

Furthermore, even if the Defense of Marriage Act is upheld, the law does not protect marriage within any state or city. For all these reasons, the defense of marriage requires a constitutional amendment.

An amendment to the Constitution is never to be undertaken lightly. The amendment process has addressed many serious matters of national concern, and the preservation of marriage rises to this level of national importance.

The union of a man and woman is the most enduring human institution, honored and encouraged in all cultures and by every religious faith. Ages of experience have taught humanity that the commitment of a husband and wife to love and to serve one another promotes the welfare of children and the stability of society. Marriage cannot be severed from its cultural, religious arid natural roots without weakening the good influence of society.

Government, by recognizing protecting marriage, serves the interests of all. Today, I call upon the Congress to promptly pass and to send to the states for ratification an amendment to our Constitution defining and protecting marriage as a union of a man and woman as husband and wife. The amendment should fully protect marriage while leaving the state legislatures free to make their own choices in defining legal arrangements other than marriage.

America's a free society which limits the role of government in the lives of our citizens. This commitment of freedom, however, does not require the redefinition of one of our most basic social institutions. Our government should respect every person and protect the institution of marriage.

There is no contradiction between these responsibilities.

We should also conduct this difficult debate in a manner worthy of our country, without bitterness or anger. In all that lies ahead, let us match strong convictions with kindness and good will and decency.

C. AN ARGUMENT AGAINST CONSTITUTIONAL AMENDMENTS

The following is a transcript of remarks by Professor Shannon Gilreath at the 2005 North Carolina March for Marriage Equality, a faith-based initiative organized to oppose pending legislation to add an antigay amendment to the North Carolina constitution and held at the state capitol.

Looking out on this crowd of faces, I am reminded that President Bush has said that "all religious faiths condemn same-sex marriage." You are testament to the graveness of that overstatement. Thank you. And thanks to the North Carolina Religious Coalition for Marriage Equality and its important work teaching people that belief in fairness does not equate to secularism.

But let us not muddy the waters. We may be here as people of Faith, but what we are talking about is a wholly civic matter. Let me be clear to anyone who can hear my remarks: We are not, today, talking about forcing churches to marry gay and lesbian couples. That cannot and will not happen in our present-day constitutional order. What we are talking about is opening a civil institution to gay and lesbian couples—making available, as a matter of equity, a civil marriage license to gays and lesbians just as it is available to heterosexual couples. It is axiomatic in a democracy that all citizens similarly situated should have the same rights. The marriage amendment efforts at both the federal and state levels are the antitheses of that principle. Today, I was asked to speak specifically about the North Carolina amendment effort, which sadly resembles more a fit of spite than it does legitimate legislation.

Our opponents are being dishonest with us and with their constituencies. The amendment they have crafted goes far beyond their stated goal of "protecting" marriage. There are some important things you should know about the amendment. We all know that it is designed to define marriage as a union between one man and one woman and to prohibit any other. In that respect, it is ridiculously unnecessary, since neither the North Carolina legislature nor our courts are poised to tinker with that definition in any way. But you may not know that the amendment, as written, would also preclude the possibility of civil unions for gay and lesbian couples. Perhaps most troubling is the provision of the proposed amendment that would invalidate domestic partnerships. So, the municipal benefits that gays, lesbians, and their allies fought so long and hard for in neighboring Durham would be impossible because of this amendment. In fact, so broad is the language of the proposal that it could potentially invalidate even private domestic partnership plans offered by employers, like my employer, Wake Forest University, to their employees as a matter of equity. The one silver lining is that the amendment's broad reach may be its ultimate downfall. For if the citizens of this state don't recognize it for the hatefulness that it is, there is United States Supreme Court precedent that declares unconstitutional laws that burden entire classes of people purely based on a larger group's distaste for the minority.

You must make people realize that this amendment goes far beyond its stated goal of "protecting" marriage. It interferes with private employer/employee relationships and chills our freedom to contract. It will also doubtlessly discourage talented scholars and scientists, not to mention beneficial corporations, who are fair-minded, from locating in our state. The legislators and the people they represent have got to see that this thing is a very bad idea.

But beyond statutory interpretation and economics, it is important to note that North Carolinians were the first Americans to stand against the tyranny of conscience that spurred the Revolutionary War and American liberty. It is my hope and my conviction that our citizens, and the men and women in this building behind me who represent them, will once again be guided by those yearnings for liberty. It is my hope that they will recognize that we truly protect marriage when we realize that we do so, to paraphrase a U.S. Supreme Court justice, not because it contributes to the general public welfare or because the Bible commands us to be fruitful and multiply, but because it is an intimate association that promotes a way of life, not causes; a harmony in living, not politics or faiths, a bilateral loyalty, not commercial or social projects. We protect marriage not because it contributes, in some direct and material way, to society, but because it forms so central a part of an individual's life. And we protect the family because it contributes so powerfully to the happiness of individuals, not because of a preference for stereotypical households.

Our American liberty cannot be exercised in a vacuum; we all depend on emotional enrichment from close ties with others. That is all that gay and lesbian North Carolinians are asking for: the right to have their ties recognized like those of their fellow citizens. The proposed North Carolina marriage amendment unconscionably denies them that right, and we are right to oppose it.

Lastly, we must remember that North Carolina's history is marred by painful episodes of laws that protected slavery, silenced abolitionist voices, condemned interracial marriage, and supported segregation—and in every case, supporters of these atrocities professed to find their mandate in the Word of God. My friend, Maya Angelou, has said that "history, while it cannot be unlived, if faced with courage, need not be lived again." I hope that North Carolinians, my fellow citizens, will choose, sooner rather than later, to place themselves on the right side of history with regard to this important human rights issue.

VII. CONTINUED PROGRESS

Despite setbacks, progress continued. On April 20, 2005, the Connecticut legislature became the first state legislature to provide civil union rights for gay citizens in the absence of a judicial mandate. Prompted by its state Supreme Court in *Lewis v. Harris*, 188 N.J. 415, 908 A.2d 196 (2006), the New Jersey legislature passed a statute creating civil unions, effective in 2007. New Hampshire did likewise, effective 2008. Oregon allowed domestic partnerships, effective 2007. The next two states to allow marriage by case law were California (2008) and Iowa (2009), although same-sex couples may no longer marry in California (a legal timeline of same-sex partner rights in California follows *Varnum v. Brien* in this chapter.) Same-sex marriages began in Iowa on April 27, 2009.

Also in April, 2009, Vermont was again a leader (having enacted the first civil union law in the nation in 2000), this time successfully enacting marriage equality by legislative initiative and without a judicial mandate. The law was enacted by a legislative supermajority override of a veto by Republican governor Jim Douglas, and same-sex marriages began in Vermont on September 1, 2009.

Connecticut enacted a marriage equality law in 2008 in direct response to the Connecticut Supreme Court's decision in *Kerrigan v. Commissioner of Public Health*, 289 Conn. 135, 957 A.2d 407 (2008), holding that state laws restricting marriage qua marriage to opposite-sex couples violated state constitutional equal protection guarantees (Connecticut had created civil unions for same-sex couples by legislative initiative in 2005). The law also converted existing civil unions into marriages as of October 1, 2010.

VARNUM v. BRIEN

763 N.W.2d 862 (Iowa 2009).

CADY, JUSTICE.

In this case, we must decide if our statute limiting civil marriage to a union between a man and a woman violates the Iowa Constitution, as the district court ruled. On our review, we hold the Iowa marriage statute violates the *equal protection clause* of the Iowa Constitution. Therefore, we affirm the decision of the district court.

I. Background Facts and Proceedings.

This lawsuit is a civil rights action by twelve individuals who reside in six communities across Iowa. Like most Iowans, they are responsible, caring, and productive individuals. They maintain important jobs, or are retired, and are contributing, benevolent members of their communities. They include a nurse, business manager, insurance analyst, bank agent, stay-at-home parent, church organist and piano teacher, museum director, federal employee, social worker, teacher, and two retired teachers. Like many Iowans, some have children and others hope to have children. Some are foster parents. Like all Iowans, they prize their liberties and live within the borders of this state with the expectation that their rights will be maintained and protected—a belief embraced by our state motto.[1]

Despite the commonality shared with other Iowans, the twelve plaintiffs are different from most in one way. They are sexually and romantically attracted to members of their own sex. The twelve plaintiffs compromise six same-sex couples who live in committed relationships. Each maintains a hope of getting married one day, an aspiration shared by many throughout Iowa.

Unlike opposite-sex couples in Iowa, same-sex couples are not permitted to marry in Iowa. The Iowa legislature amended the marriage statute in 1998 to define marriage as a union between only a man and a woman.[2]

. . .

IV. Equal Protection.

A. Background Principles. The primary constitutional principle at the heart of this case is the doctrine of equal protection. The concept of equal protection is deeply rooted in our national and state history, but that history reveals this concept is often expressed far more easily than it is practiced. For sure, our nation has struggled to achieve a broad national consensus on equal protection of the laws when it has been forced to apply

1. The state motto of Iowa is: "Our liberties we prize and our rights we will maintain." It is inscribed on the Great Seal of Iowa and on our state flag. *See Iowa Code §§ 1A.1, 1B.1* (2009).

2. *Iowa Code section 595.2(1)* provides "[o]nly a marriage between a male and a female is valid." All statutory references are to the 2009 Code of Iowa. While some statutes referenced here have been amended since this lawsuit originated, none of the amendments dictate the outcome of this case.

that principle to some of the institutions, traditions, and norms woven into the fabric of our society. This observation is important today because it reveals equal protection can only be defined by the standards of each generation. *See* Cass R. Sunstein, *Sexual Orientation and the Constitution: A Note on the Relationship Between Due Process and Equal Protection,* 55 U. Chi. L. Rev. 1161, 1163 (1988) ("[T]he *Equal Protection Clause* looks forward, serving to invalidate practices that were widespread at the time of its ratification and that were expected to endure.").

The process of defining equal protection, as shown by our history as captured and told in court decisions, begins by classifying people into groups. A classification persists until a new understanding of equal protection is achieved. The point in time when the standard of equal protection finally takes a new form is a product of the conviction of one, or many, individuals that a particular grouping results in inequality and the ability of the judicial system to perform its constitutional role free from the influences that tend to make society's understanding of equal protection resistant to change. As Justice Oliver Wendell Holmes poignantly said, "It is revolting to have no better reason for a rule of law than that so it was laid down in the time of Henry IV. It is still more revolting if the grounds upon which it was laid down have vanished long since, and the rule simply persists from blind imitation of the past." Oliver Wendell Holmes, Justice, Supreme Judicial Court of Massachusetts, *The Path of the Law,* address dedicating new hall at Boston University School of Law (January 8, 1897), *in* 10 Harv. L. Rev. 457, 469 (1897). This concept is evident in our past cases.

In the first reported case of the Supreme Court of the Territory of Iowa, *In re Ralph, Morris 1,* 1 Morris 1 (Iowa 1839), we refused to treat a human being as property to enforce a contract for *slavery and held our laws must extend equal protection to persons of all races and conditions. 1 Morris at 7.* This decision was seventeen years before the United States Supreme Court infamously decided *Dred Scott v. Sandford,* 60 U.S. (19 How.) 393, 15 L. Ed. 691 (1856), which upheld the rights of a slave owner to treat a person as property. Similarly, in *Clark v. Board of Directors,* 24 Iowa 266 (1868), and *Coger v. North West. Union Packet Co.,* 37 Iowa 145 (1873), we struck blows to the concept of segregation long before the United States Supreme Court's decision in *Brown v. Board of Education,* 347 U.S. 483, 74 S. Ct. 686, 98 L. Ed. 873 (1954). Iowa was also the first state in the nation to admit a woman to the practice of law, doing so in 1869. *Admission of Women to the Bar,* 1 Chicago Law Times 76, 76 (1887). Her admission occurred three years before the United States Supreme Court affirmed the State of Illinois' decision to *deny* women admission to the practice of law, *see Bradwell v. Illinois,* 83 U.S. (16 Wall.) 130, 139, 21 L. Ed. 442, 445 (1873), and twenty-five years before the United States Supreme Court affirmed the refusal of the Commonwealth of Virginia to admit women into the practice of law, *see Ex parte Lockwood,* 154 U.S. 116, 118, 14 S. Ct. 1082, 1083, 38 L. Ed. 929, 930 (1894). In each of those instances, our state approached a fork in the road toward fulfillment of our constitution's ideals and reaffirmed the "absolute equality of all" persons before the law as "the very foundation principle of our government." *See Coger*, 37 Iowa at 153.

. . .

So, today, this court again faces an important issue that hinges on our definition of equal protection. This issue comes to us with the same importance as our landmark cases of the past. The same-sex-marriage debate waged in this case is part of a strong national dialogue centered on a fundamental, deep-seated, traditional institution that has excluded, by state action, a particular class of Iowans. This class of people asks a simple and direct question: How can a state premised on the constitutional principle of equal protection justify exclusion of a class of Iowans from civil marriage?

. . .

B. Legal Tests to Gauge Equal Protection. The foundational principle of equal protection is expressed in *article I, section 6 of the Iowa Constitution*, which provides: "All laws of a general nature shall have a uniform operation; the general assembly shall not grant to any citizen or class of citizens, privileges or immunities, which, upon the same terms shall not equally belong to all citizens." *See also Iowa Const. art. I, § 1* ("All men and women are, by nature, free and equal...."); *id. art. I, § 2* (recognizing "[a]ll political power is inherent in the people" and "[g]overnment is instituted for the protection, security, and benefit of the people"). Like the Federal *Equal Protection Clause* found in the *Fourteenth Amendment to the United States Constitution*, Iowa's constitutional promise of equal protection " 'is essentially a direction that all persons similarly situated should be treated alike.' " *Racing Ass'n of Cent. Iowa v. Fitzgerald*, 675 N.W.2d 1, 7 (Iowa 2004) [hereinafter *RACI II*] (quoting *City of Cleburne v. Cleburne Living Ctr.*, 473 U.S. 432, 439, 105 S. Ct. 3249, 3254, 87 L. Ed. 2d 313, 320 (1985)).

. . .

Even in the zealous protection of the constitution's mandate of equal protection, courts must give respect to the legislative process and presume its enactments are constitutional. We understand that Iowa's tripartite system of government requires the legislature to make difficult policy choices, including distributing benefits and burdens amongst the citizens of Iowa. In this process, some classifications and barriers are inevitable. As a result, courts pay deference to legislative decisions when called upon to determine whether the Iowa Constitution's mandate of equality has been violated by legislative action. More specifically, when evaluating challenges based on the *equal protection clause*, our deference to legislative policy-making is primarily manifested in the level of scrutiny we apply to review legislative action.

In most cases, we apply a very deferential standard known as the "rational basis test." *Id.* Under the rational basis test, "[t]he plaintiff has the heavy burden of showing the statute unconstitutional and must negate every reasonable basis upon which the classification may be sustained." *Bierkamp v. Rogers,* 293 N.W.2d 577, 579–80 (Iowa 1980). In deference to the legislature, a statute will satisfy the requirements of the *equal protection clause.*

. . .

The constitutional guarantee of equal protection, however, demands certain types of statutory classifications must be subjected to closer scrutiny by courts. *See, e.g., Plyler v. Doe,* 457 U.S. 202, 216, 102 S. Ct. 2382, 2394, 72 L. Ed. 2d 786, 799 (1982) ("[W]e would not be faithful to our obligations under the *Fourteenth Amendment* if we applied so deferential a standard to every classification."). Thus, courts apply a heightened level of scrutiny under equal protection analysis when reasons exist to suspect "prejudice against discrete and insular minorities . . . which tends seriously to curtail the operation of those political processes ordinarily to be relied upon to protect minorities." *United States v. Carolene Prods. Co.,* 304 U.S. 144, 152 n.4, 58 S. Ct. 778, 783 n.4, 82 L. Ed. 1234, 1242 n.4 (1938).

Under this approach, classifications based on race, alienage, or national origin and those affecting fundamental rights are evaluated according to a standard known as "strict scrutiny." *Sherman v. Pella Corp.,* 576 N.W.2d 312, 317 (Iowa 1998). Classifications subject to strict scrutiny are presumptively invalid and must be narrowly tailored to serve a compelling governmental interest. *In re S.A.J.B.,* 679 N.W.2d 645, 649 (Iowa 2004).

A middle tier of analysis exists between rational basis and strict scrutiny. This intermediate tier has been applied to statutes classifying on the basis of gender or illegitimacy and requires the party seeking to uphold the statute to demonstrate the challenged classification is substantially related to the achievement of an important governmental objective. *Sherman,* 576 N.W.2d at 317. It is known as "intermediate scrutiny" or "heightened scrutiny," and groups entitled to this tier of review are often called "quasi-suspect" groups. *See Cleburne Living Ctr.,* 473 U.S. at 445, 105 S. Ct. at 3258, 87 L. Ed. 2d at 324. To survive intermediate scrutiny, the law must not only further an important governmental interest and be substantially related to that interest, but the justification for the classification must be genuine and must not depend on broad generalizations. *United States v. Virginia,* 518 U.S. 515, 533, 116 S. Ct. 2264, 2275, 135 L. Ed. 2d 735, 751 (1996).

. . .

D. Similarly Situated People. The County seeks to undercut the plaintiffs' equal protection claim by asserting the plaintiffs are not similarly situated to heterosexuals. We consider this threshold argument before proceeding to the application of our equal protection test.

. . .

The County references this threshold test in this case and asserts the plaintiffs are not similarly situated to opposite-sex couples so as to necessitate further equal protection analysis because the plaintiffs cannot "procreate naturally." In other words, the County argues the statute does not treat similarly situated persons differently, but merely treats dissimilar persons differently.

In considering whether two classes are similarly situated, a court cannot simply look at the trait used by the legislature to define a classification under a statute and conclude a person without that trait is not similarly situated to persons with the trait. *See Racing Ass'n of Cent. Iowa v. Fitzgerald,* 648 N.W.2d 555, 559 (Iowa 2002) *(RACI I);* Joseph Tussman & Jacobus tenBroek, *The Equal Protection of the Laws,* 37 Cal. L. Rev. 341, 344–47 (1949) [hereinafter Tussman & tenBroek]. The *equal protection clause* does not merely ensure the challenged statute applies equally to all people in the legislative classification. " '[S]imilarly situated' cannot mean simply 'similar in the possession of the classifying trait.' All members of any class are similarly situated in this respect and consequently, any classification whatsoever would be reasonable by this test." Tussman & tenBroek, 37 Cal. L. Rev. at 345. In the same way, the similarly situated requirement cannot possibly be interpreted to require plaintiffs to be identical in every way to people treated more favorably by the law. No two people or groups of people are the same in every way, and nearly every equal protection claim could be run aground onto the shoals of a threshold analysis if the two groups needed to be a mirror image of one another. Such a threshold analysis would hollow out the constitution's promise of equal protection.

Thus, equal protection before the law demands more than the equal application of the classifications made by the law. The law itself must be equal. *See Fachman,* 255 Iowa at 998, 125 N.W.2d at 215 ("The equal protection of the laws is a pledge of the protection of equal laws. . . .' " (*quoting Yick Wo v. Hopkins,* 118 U.S. 356, 369, 6 S. Ct. 1064, 1070, 30 L. Ed. 220, 226 (1886))). In other words, to truly ensure equality before the law, the equal protection guarantee requires that laws treat all those who are similarly situated *with respect to the purposes of the law* alike. *RACI II,* 675 N.W.2d at 7. This requirement makes it "impossible to pass judgment on the reasonableness of a [legislative] classification without taking into consideration, or identifying, the purpose of the law." Tussman & tenBroek, 37 Cal. L. Rev. at 347. The purposes of the law must be referenced in order to meaningfully evaluate whether the law equally protects all people similarly situated with respect to those purposes. For these reasons, the trait asserted by the County is insufficient to support its threshold argument.

Nevertheless, we have said our marriage laws "are rooted in the necessity of providing an institutional basis for defining the fundamental relational rights and responsibilities of persons in organized society." *Laws v. Griep,* 332 N.W.2d 339, 341 (Iowa 1983); *see also Baehr v. Lewin,* 74 Haw. 530, 852 P.2d 44, 58 (Haw. 1993) (stating civil marriage is " 'a partnership to which both partners bring their financial resources as well as their individual energies and efforts' " (*quoting Gussin v. Gussin,* 73 Haw. 470, 836 P.2d 484, 491 (Haw. 1992))). These laws also serve to recognize the status of the parties' committed relationship. *See Madison v. Colby,* 348 N.W.2d 202, 206 (Iowa 1984) (stating " 'the marriage state is not one entered into for the purpose of labor and support alone,' " but also includes " 'the comfort and happiness of the parties to the marriage contract' " (*quoting Price v. Price, 91* Iowa 693, 697–98, 60 N.W. 202, 203 (Iowa 1894)) (emphasis added)); *Hamilton v. McNeill*, 150 Iowa 470, 478, 129 N.W. 480, 482 (1911) ("The marriage to be dissolved is not a mere contract, but is a status."); *Turner v. Hitchcock,* 20 Iowa 310, 325 (1866) (Lowe, C.J., concurring) (observing that marriage changes the parties' "legal and social status").

Therefore, with respect to the subject and purposes of Iowa's marriage laws, we find that the plaintiffs are similarly situated compared to heterosexual persons.

. . .

E. Classification Undertaken in *Iowa Code Section 595.2.*

. . .

By purposefully placing civil marriage outside the realistic reach of gay and lesbian individuals, the ban on same-sex civil marriages differentiates implicitly on the basis of sexual orientation. *See Kerrigan*, 957 A.2d at 431 n.24; *Conaway v. Deane,* 401 Md. 219, 932 A.2d 571, 605 (Md. 2007). Thus, we proceed to analyze the constitutionality of the statute based on sexual orientation discrimination.

F. Framework for Determining Appropriate Level of Judicial Scrutiny. Our determination that the marriage statute employs a sexual-orientation-based classification does not, of course, control the outcome of our equal protection inquiry. Most statutes, one way or the other, create classifications. *Clements v. Fashing*, 457 U.S. 957, 967, 102 S. Ct. 2836, 2845, 73 L. Ed. 2d 508, 518 (1982) ("Classification is the essence of all legislation, and only those classifications which are invidious, arbitrary, or irrational offend the *Equal Protection Clause* of the Constitution."). To determine if this particular classification violates constitutional principles of equal protection, we must next ask what level of scrutiny applies to classifications of this type. The County argues the more deferential rational basis test should apply, while plaintiffs argue closer scrutiny is appropriate.

Although neither we nor the United States Supreme Court has decided which level of scrutiny applies to legislative classifications based on sexual orientation, numerous Supreme Court equal protection cases provide a general framework to guide our analysis under the Iowa Constitution. To say a general framework exists is not to say the Supreme Court has provided a precise formula for determining when legislative action is subject to a heightened form of scrutiny. *See Cleburne Living Ctr.,* 473

U.S. at 472 n.24, 105 S. Ct. at 3272 n.24, 87 L. Ed. 2d at 341 n.24 (Marshall, J., concurring in part and dissenting in part) ("No single talisman can define those groups likely to be the target of classifications offensive to the *Fourteenth Amendment* and therefore warranting heightened or strict scrutiny; experience, not abstract logic, must be the primary guide."); *Conaway,* 932 A.2d at 606 ("There is no brightline diagnostic, annunciated by ... the U.S. Supreme Court, by which a suspect or quasi-suspect class may be readily recognized."). Instead, the Supreme Court has expressed a number of general principles to assist in identifying the appropriate level of scrutiny.

. . .

Classifications based on factors like race, alienage, national origin, sex, or illegitimacy are "so seldom relevant to achievement of any legitimate state interest that laws grounded in such considerations are deemed to reflect prejudice and antipathy." *Cleburne Living Ctr.*, 473 U.S. at 440, 105 S. Ct. at 3254, 87 L. Ed. 2d at 320. Rather than bearing some relationship to the burdened class's ability to contribute to society, such classifications often reflect irrelevant stereotypes. *Id.* at 440–41, 105 S. Ct. at 3254–55, 87 L. Ed. 2d at 320–21. "For these reasons and because such discrimination is unlikely to be soon rectified by legislative means," laws based on these types of classifications must withstand more intense judicial scrutiny than other types of classifications. *Id.*

Instead of adopting a rigid formula to determine whether certain legislative classifications warrant more demanding constitutional analysis, the Supreme Court has looked to four factors. *Conaway,* 932 A.2d at 606 (discussing factors examined by Supreme Court in considering use of heightened scrutiny). The Supreme Court has considered: (1) the history of invidious discrimination against the class burdened by the legislation; (2) whether the characteristics that distinguish the class indicate a typical class member's ability to contribute to society; (3) whether the distinguishing characteristic is "immutable" or beyond the class members' control; and (4) the political power of the subject class. In considering whether sexual orientation is a suspect class, a number of our sister jurisdictions have referenced similar factors. *See In re Marriage Cases,* 183 P.3d at 442–43; *Kerrigan,* 957 A.2d at 426; *Conaway,* 932 A.2d at 606–07; *Andersen v. King County,* 158 Wn.2d 1, 138 P.3d 963, 974 (Wash. 2006).

. . .

Both parties recognize the relevance of these factors. They disagree, however, over how the factors should be applied to decide whether sexual orientation is a suspect or quasi-suspect class. The County essentially views the factors as elements, asserting each must be fulfilled before we may abandon our deferential level of scrutiny. To this end, the County argues the immutability and political powerlessness "elements" are not satisfied in this case.

In its effort to treat the factors as essential elements, the County overlooks the flexible manner in which the Supreme Court has applied the four factors in the past. For purposes of state constitutional analysis, we likewise refuse to view all the factors as elements or as individually demanding a certain weight in every case. Instead, we analyze each of the four factors and assess how each bears on the question of whether the Iowa Constitution requires a more searching scrutiny be applied to the specific classification at issue. We note the first two factors-history of intentional discrimination and relationship of classifying characteristic to a person's ability to contribute-have always been present when heightened scrutiny has been applied.

They have been critical to the analysis and could be considered as prerequisites to concluding a group is a suspect or quasi-suspect class. However, we consider the last two factors—immutability of the characteristic and political powerlessness of the group—to supplement the analysis as a means to discern whether a need for heightened scrutiny exists.

. . .

G. Determination of Appropriate Level of Scrutiny. Guided by the established framework, we next consider each of the four traditional factors and assess how each bears on the question of whether the constitution demands a more searching scrutiny be applied to the sexual-orientation-based classification in Iowa's marriage statute.

1. *History of discrimination against gay and lesbian people.* The first consideration is whether gay and lesbian people have suffered a history of purposeful unequal treatment because of their sexual orientation. The County does not, and could not in good faith, dispute the historical reality that gay and lesbian people as a group have long been the victim of purposeful and invidious discrimination because of their sexual orientation. The long and painful history of discrimination against gay and lesbian persons is epitomized by the criminalization of homosexual conduct in many parts of this country until very recently. *See Lawrence,* 539 U.S. at 578–79, 123 S. Ct. 2483–84, 156 L. Ed. 2d at 520 (invalidating criminalization of homosexual sodomy in 2003).

Additionally, only a few years ago persons identified as homosexual were dismissed from military service regardless of past dedication and demonstrated valor. Public employees identified as gay or lesbian have been thought to pose security risks due to a perceived risk of extortion resulting from a threat of public exposure. School-yard bullies have psychologically ground children with apparently gay or lesbian sexual orientation in the cruel mortar and pestle of school-yard prejudice. At the same time, lesbian and gay people continue to be frequent victims of hate crimes. *See* Criminal Justice Information Servs. Div., FBI, *Hate Crime Statistics 2007,* http://www.fbi.gov/ucr/hc2007/victims.htm (according to FBI-collected data, the only hate crimes occurring more frequently than sexual-orientation-motivated hate crimes are crimes based on race or religious bias).

The Iowa General Assembly has recognized the need to address sexual-orientation-based discrimination by including sexual orientation as a characteristic protected in the Iowa Civil Rights Act, by defining hate crimes to include certain offenses committed because of the victim's sexual orientation, and by prohibiting "harassing or bullying" behavior in schools based on sexual orientation. *See Iowa Code §§ 216.2–.18A* (Iowa Civil Rights Act) (sexual-orientation-based discrimination); *id.* § *280.28* (school harassment and bullying); *id.* § *729A.2* (hate crimes committed because of the victim's sexual orientation). These statutory enactments demonstrate a legislative recognition of the need to remedy historical sexual-orientation-based discrimination. and gay people as a class "are more likely than others to reflect deep-seated prejudice rather than legislative rationality in pursuit of some legitimate objective." *Plyler*, 457 U.S. at 216 n.14, 102 S. Ct. at 2394 n.14, 72 L. Ed. 2d at 799 n.14. This observation favors an elevated scrutiny to uncover any such prejudice.

2. *Sexual orientation and the ability to contribute to society.* A second relevant consideration is whether the characteristic at issue—sexual orientation—is related to the person's ability to contribute to society. Heightened scrutiny is applied when the classification bears no relationship to a person's ability to contribute to society. The existence of this factor indicates the classification is likely based on irrelevant stereotypes and prejudice. *Kerrigan,* 957 A.2d at 453. A classification unrelated to a person's ability to perform or contribute to society typically reflects "prejudice and antipathy—a view that those in the burdened class are not as worthy or deserving as others" or "reflect[s] outmoded notions of the relative capabilities of persons with the characteristic." *Cleburne Living Ctr.,* 473 U.S. at 440–41, 105 S. Ct. at 3254–56, 87 L. Ed. 2d at 320–21.

Not surprisingly, none of the same-sex marriage decisions from other state courts around the nation have found a person's sexual orientation to be indicative of the person's general ability to contribute to society. *See, e.g., In re Marriage Cases,* 183 P.3d at 442; *Kerrigan,* 957 A.2d at 434–36; *Dean v. District of Columbia,* 653 A.2d 307, 345 (D.C. 1995); *Conaway,* 932 A.2d at 609. More importantly, the Iowa legislature has recently declared as the public policy of this state that sexual orientation is not relevant to a person's ability to contribute to a number of societal institutions other than civil marriage. *See Iowa Code* § *216.6* (employment); *id.* § *216.7* (public accommodations); *id.* § *216.8* (housing); *id.* § *216.9* (education); *id.* § *216.10* (credit practices). Significantly, we do not construe Iowa Code chapter 216 to allow marriage between persons of the same sex, a construction expressly forbidden in the Iowa Code. *See id.* § *216.18A* ("[Chapter 216] shall not be construed to allow marriage between persons of the same sex, in accordance with chapter 595."). Rather, we merely highlight the reality that chapter 216 and numerous other statutes and regulations demonstrate sexual orientation is broadly recognized in Iowa to be irrelevant to a person's ability to contribute to society. Those statutes and regulations reflect at least some measure of legislative and executive awareness that discrimination based on sexual orientation is often predicated on prejudice and stereotype and further express a desire to remove sexual orientation as an obstacle to the ability of gay and lesbian people to achieve their full potential. Therefore, we must scrutinize more closely those classifications that suggest a law may be based on prejudice and stereotype because laws of that nature are "incompatible with the constitutional understanding that each person is to be judged individually and is entitled to equal justice under the law." *Plyler,* 457 U.S. at 217 n.14, 102 S. Ct. at 2394 n.14, 72 L. Ed. 2d at 799 n.14. Thus, although we do not interpret chapter 216 to allow same-sex marriage, we rely on the legislative judgment underlying chapter 216 to determine the appropriate level of scrutiny when sexual orientation is the basis for a statutory classification. Based on Iowa statutes and regulations, it is clear sexual orientation is no longer viewed in Iowa as an impediment to the ability of a person to contribute to society.

. . .

3. *Immutability of sexual orientation.* The parties, consistent with the same-sex-marriage scholarship, opinions, and jurisprudence, contest whether sexual orientation is immutable or unresponsive to attempted change. The County seizes on this debate to argue the summary judgment granted by the district court in this case was improper because plaintiffs could not prove, as a matter of fact, that sexuality is immutable. This argument, however, essentially limits the constitutional relevance of mutability to those instances in which the trait defining the burdened class is absolutely impervious to change. To evaluate this argument, we must first consider the rationale for using immutability as a factor.

A human trait that defines a group is "immutable" when the trait exists "solely by the accident of birth," *Frontiero v. Richardson,* 411 U.S. 677, 686, 93 S. Ct. 1764, 1770, 36 L. Ed. 2d 583, 591 (1973) (Brennan, J., plurality opinion), or when the person with the trait has no ability to change it, *Regents of Univ. of Cal. v. Bakke,* 438 U.S. 265, 360, 98 S. Ct. 2733, 2784, 57 L. Ed. 2d 750, 815 (1978). Immutability is a factor in determining the appropriate level of scrutiny because the inability of a person to change a characteristic that is used to justify different treatment makes the discrimination violative of the rather " 'basic concept of our system that legal burdens should bear some relationship to individual responsibility.' " *Frontiero,* 411 U.S. at 686, 93 S. Ct. at 1770, 36 L. Ed. 2d at 591 (Brennan, J., plurality opinion) (quoting *Weber v. Aetna Cas. & Sur. Co.,* 406 U.S. 164, 175, 92 S. Ct. 1400, 1407, 31 L. Ed. 2d 768, 779 (1972)); *accord Plyler,* 457 U.S. at 217 n.14, 102 S. Ct. at 2394 n.14, 72 L. Ed. 2d at 799 n.14 ("Legislation imposing special disabilities upon groups disfavored by virtue of circumstances beyond their control suggests the kind of 'class or caste' treatment that the *Fourteenth Amendment* was designed to abolish."). Put another way, when a characteristic is immutable, different treatment based on this characteristic seems "all the more invidious and unfair." Nan D. Hunter, *The Sex Discrimination Argument in Gay Rights Cases,* 9 J.L. & Pol'y 397, 403 (2001). Additionally, immutability can relate to the scope and permanency of the barrier imposed on the group. Temporary barriers tend to be less burdensome on a group and more likely to actually advance a legitimate governmental interest. Consequently, such barriers normally do not warrant heightened scrutiny. *See Sosna v. Iowa,* 419 U.S. 393, 406, 95 S. Ct. 553, 561, 42 L. Ed. 2d 532, 544–45 (1975) (one-year residency requirement for divorce permitted in part because the constraint was only temporary); *Vlandis v. Kline,* 412 U.S. 441, 453, 93 S. Ct. 2230, 2236, 37 L. Ed. 2d 63, 72 (1973) (bona fide state resident requirement for college tuition permissible when students are provided an opportunity to prove they have become residents). The permanency of the barrier also depends on the ability of the individual to change the characteristic responsible for the discrimination. This aspect of immutability may separate truly victimized individuals from those who have invited discrimination by changing themselves so as to be identified with the group. As implied by Justice Ferren, in dissent, in *Dean:*

> The degree to which an individual controls, or cannot avoid, the acquisition of the defining trait, and the relative ease or difficulty with which a trait can be changed, are relevant to whether a classification is "suspect" or "quasi-suspect" because this inquiry is one way of asking whether someone, rather than being victimized, has voluntarily joined a persecuted group and thereby invited the discrimination.

653 A.2d at 346 (Ferren, J., dissenting).

Importantly, this background reveals courts need not definitively resolve the nature-versus-nurture debate currently raging over the origin of sexual orientation in order to decide plaintiffs' equal protection claims. The constitutional relevance of the immutability factor is not reserved to those instances in which the trait defining the burdened class is absolutely impossible to change. *Compare Sherman,* 576 N.W.2d at 317 (suggesting heightened scrutiny is applicable to gender classifications), *with Iowa Code § 144.23* (providing legal procedure to obtain new birth certificate indicating change in gender). That is, we agree with those courts that have held the immutability "prong of the suspectness inquiry surely is satisfied when ... the identifying trait is 'so central to a person's identity that it would be abhorrent for government to penalize a person for refusing to change [it].'" *Kerrigan,* 957 A.2d at 438 (*quoting Watkins v. U.S. Army,* 875 F.2d 699, 726 (9th Cir. 1989) (Norris, J., concurring in the judgment)); *see also In re Marriage Cases,* 183 P.3d at 442 ("Because a person's sexual orientation is so integral an aspect of one's identity, it is not appropriate to require a person to repudiate or change his or her sexual orientation in order to avoid discriminatory treatment.").

In this case, the County acknowledges sexual orientation is highly resistant to change. Additionally, "sexual orientation 'forms a significant part of a person's identity.'" *Kerrigan,* 957 A.2d at 438 (*quoting Able v. United States,* 968 F. Supp. 850, 863 (E.D.N.Y. 1997), *rev'd on other grounds,* 155 F.3d 628 (2d Cir. 1998)). Sexual orientation influences the formation of personal relationships between all people—heterosexual, gay, or lesbian—to fulfill each person's fundamental needs for love and attachment. Accordingly, because sexual orientation is central to personal identity and " 'may be altered [if at all] only at the expense of significant damage to the individual's sense of self,' " classifications based on sexual orientation "are no less entitled to consideration as a suspect or quasi-suspect class than any other group that has been deemed to exhibit an immutable characteristic." *Id.* at 438–39 (*quoting Jantz v. Muci,* 759 F. Supp. 1543, 1548 (D. Kan. 1991), *rev'd on other grounds,* 976 F.2d 623 (10th Cir. 1992)). Sexual orientation is not the type of human trait that allows courts to relax their standard of review because the barrier is temporary or susceptible to self-help.

4. *Political powerlessness of lesbian and gay people.* As observed, the political power of the burdened class has been referenced repeatedly in Supreme Court cases determining the level of scrutiny to be applied to a given piece of legislation. Unfortunately, the Court has never defined what it means to be politically powerless for purposes of this analysis, nor has it quantified a maximum amount of political power a group may enjoy while still receiving the protection from unfair discrimination accompanying heightened scrutiny. The County points to the numerous legal protections gay and lesbian people have secured against discrimination, and the County argues those protections demonstrate gay and lesbian people are not a politically powerless class. The County's argument implies gay and lesbian people must be characterized by a complete, or nearly complete, lack of political power before courts should subject sexual-orientation-based legislative burdens to a heightened scrutiny.

Notwithstanding the lack of a mathematical equation to guide the analysis of this factor, a number of helpful general principles related to the political power of suspect classes can be culled from the Supreme Court's cases. First, these cases show absolute political powerlessness is not necessary to subject legislative burdens on a certain class to heightened scrutiny. For example, females enjoyed at least some measure of political power when the Supreme Court first heightened its scrutiny of gender classifications. *See Frontiero,* 411 U.S. at 685–88 & n.17, 93 S. Ct. at 1769–72 & n.17, 36 L. Ed. 2d at 591–92 & n.17 (Brennan, J., plurality opinion) (subjecting gender classifications to heightened scrutiny after observing Civil Rights Act of 1964 and Equal Pay Act of 1963 prohibited sex discrimination and noting "the position of women in America [had] improved markedly" by 1973 such that "women [did] not constitute a small and powerless minority").

Second, Supreme Court jurisprudence establishes that a group's current political powerlessness is not a prerequisite to enhanced judicial protection. "[I]f a group's *current* political powerlessness [was] a prerequisite to a characteristic's being considered a constitutionally suspect basis for differential treatment, it would be impossible to justify the numerous decisions that continue to treat sex, race, and religion as suspect classifications." *In re Marriage Cases,* 183 P.3d at 443. Race continues to be a suspect classification, *Grutter v. Bollinger,* 539 U.S. 306, 326, 123 S. Ct. 2325, 2337, 156 L. Ed. 2d 304, 331 (2003), even though racial minorities enjoy growing political power. Likewise, gender classifications receive various forms of heightened scrutiny, even though women continue to gain political power. *See, e.g., Virginia,* 518 U.S. at 532–33, 116 S. Ct. at 2275, 135 L. Ed. 2d at 751–52 (applying intermediate scrutiny).

. . .

While a more in-depth discussion of the history of the political-power factor is possible, *see Kerrigan,* 957 A.2d at 439–44, we are satisfied, for the purpose of analyzing the Iowa Constitution, the political powerlessness factor of the level-of-scrutiny inquiry does not require a showing of absolute political powerlessness. Rather, the touchstone of the analysis should be "whether the group lacks sufficient political strength to bring a prompt end to the prejudice and discrimination through traditional political means." *Id.* at 444.

It is also important to observe that the political power of gays and lesbians, while responsible for greater acceptance and decreased discrimination, has done little to remove barriers to civil marriage. Although a small number of state legislatures have approved civil *unions* for gay and lesbian people without judicial intervention, no legislature has secured the right to civil *marriage* for gay and lesbian people without court order. The myriad statutes and regulatory protections against discrimination based on sexual orientation in such areas as employment, housing, public accommodations, and education have not only been absent in the area of marriage, but legislative bodies have taken affirmative steps to shore up the concept of traditional marriage by specifically excluding gays and lesbians. Like Iowa, over forty other states have passed statutes or constitutional amendments to ban same-sex marriages. *See* Ben Schuman, Note, *Gods & Gays: Analyzing the Same–Sex Marriage Debate From a Religious Perspective,* 96 Geo. L.J. 2103, 2107–08 (2008) (recognizing forty-two states with laws prohibiting same-sex marriage as of November 8, 2007) [hereinafter Schuman]; Human Rights Campaign, *Statewide Marriage Prohibitions* (2008), *available at* http://www.hrc.org/documents/marriage_prohibitions.pdf (mapping states' enactment of marriage prohibitions). Thus, although equal rights for gays and lesbians have been increasingly recognized in the political arena, the right to civil marriage is a notable exception to this trend. Consequently, the specific right sought in this case has largely lacked any extensive political support and has actually experienced an affirmative backlash.

. . .

We are convinced gay and lesbian people are not so politically powerful as to overcome the unfair and severe prejudice that history suggests produces discrimination based on sexual orientation. Gays and lesbians certainly possess no more political power than women enjoyed four decades ago when the Supreme Court began subjecting gender-based legislation to closer scrutiny. Additionally, gay and lesbian people are, as a class, currently no more powerful than women or members of some racial minorities. These facts demonstrate, at the least, the political-power factor does not weigh against heightened judicial scrutiny of sexual-orientation-based legislation.

5. *Classifications based on sexual orientation demand closer scrutiny.* In summarizing the rationale supporting heightened scrutiny of legislation classifying on the basis of sexual orientation, it would be difficult to improve upon the words of the Supreme Court of Connecticut:

> Gay persons have been subjected to and stigmatized by a long history of purposeful and invidious discrimination that continues to manifest itself in society. The characteristic that defines the members of this group—attraction to persons of the same sex—bears no logical relationship to their ability to perform in society, either in familial relations or otherwise as productive citizens. Because sexual orientation is such an essential component of personhood, even if there is some possibility that a person's sexual preference can be altered, it would be wholly unacceptable for the state to require anyone to do so. Gay persons also represent a distinct minority of the population. It is true, of course, that gay persons recently have made significant advances in obtaining equal treatment under the law. Nonetheless, we conclude that, as a minority group that continues to suffer the enduring effects of centuries of legally sanctioned discrimination, laws singling them out for disparate treatment are subject to heightened judicial scrutiny to ensure that those laws are not the product of such historical prejudice and stereotyping.

Kerrigan, 957 A.2d at 432.

. . .

H. Application of Heightened Scrutiny. Plaintiffs argue sexual-orientation-based statutes should be subject to the most searching scrutiny. The County asserts Iowa's marriage statute, *section 595.2,* may be reviewed, at most, according to an intermediate level of scrutiny. Because we conclude Iowa's same-sex marriage statute cannot withstand intermediate scrutiny, we need not decide whether classifications based on sexual orientation are subject to a higher level of scrutiny. Thus, we turn to a discussion of the intermediate scrutiny standard.

. . .

1. *Intermediate scrutiny standard.* "To withstand intermediate scrutiny, a statutory classification must be substantially related to an important governmental objective." *Clark v. Jeter,* 486 U.S. 456, 461, 108 S. Ct. 1910, 1914, 100 L. Ed. 2d 465, 472 (1988). In applying an intermediate standard to review gender-based classifications, the Supreme Court has stated: "Focusing on the differential treatment or denial of opportunity for which relief is sought, the reviewing court must determine whether the proffered justification is 'exceedingly persuasive.' " *Virginia,* 518 U.S. at 532–33, 116 S. Ct. at 2275, 135 L. Ed. 2d at 751. To this end, courts evaluate whether the proffered governmental objectives are important and whether the statutory classification is " 'substantially related to the

achievement of those objectives.' " *Id.* at 533, 116 S. Ct. at 2275, 135 L. Ed. 2d at 751 *(quoting Miss. Univ. for Women v. Hogan,* 458 U.S. 718, 724, 102 S. Ct. 3331, 3336, 73 L. Ed. 2d 1090, 1098 (1982)).

2. *Statutory classification: exclusion of gay and lesbian people from civil marriage.* To identify the statutory classification, we focus on the "differential treatment or denial of opportunity for which relief is sought." *Id.* at 532–33, 116 S. Ct. at 2275, 135 L. Ed. 2d at 751 (considering "categorical exclusion" of women from institution of higher education). Plaintiffs bring this lawsuit complaining of their exclusion from the institution of civil marriage. In response, the County offers support for the legislature's decision to statutorily establish *heterosexual* civil marriage. Because the relevant focal point is the opportunity sought by the plaintiffs, the issue presented by this lawsuit is whether the state has "exceedingly persuasive" reasons for denying civil marriage to same-sex couples, not whether state-sanctioned, heterosexual marriage is constitutional. *See id.* at 531, 116 S. Ct. at 2274, 135 L. Ed. 2d at 751. Thus, the question we must answer is whether excluding gay and lesbian people from civil marriage is substantially related to any important governmental objective.

3. *Governmental objectives.*

. . .

The first step in scrutinizing a statutory classification can be to determine whether the objectives purportedly advanced by the classification are important. "The burden of justification is demanding and it rests entirely on the State." *Id.* at 533, 116 S. Ct. at 2275, 135 L. Ed. 2d at 751. Where we find, or can assume, the proffered governmental interests are sufficiently weighty to be called "important," the critical inquiry is whether these governmental objectives can fairly be said to be advanced by the legislative classification. *See, e.g., Fed. Land Bank v. Arnold,* 426 N.W.2d 153, 156 (Iowa 1988) ("First we must examine the legitimacy of the end to be achieved; we then scrutinize the means used to achieve that end."). In this analysis, we drill down to analyze the "link between classification and objective." *Romer*, 517 U.S. at 632, 116 S. Ct. at 1627, 134 L. Ed. 2d at 866.

a. Maintaining traditional marriage. First, the County argues the same-sex marriage ban promotes the "integrity of traditional marriage" by "maintaining the historical and traditional marriage norm ([as] one between a man and a woman)." This argument is straightforward and has superficial appeal. A specific tradition sought to be maintained cannot be an important governmental objective for equal protection purposes, however, when the tradition is nothing more than the historical classification currently expressed in the statute being challenged. When a certain tradition is used as both the governmental objective and the classification to further that objective, the equal protection analysis is transformed into the circular question of whether the classification accomplishes the governmental objective, which objective is to maintain the classification. In other words, the *equal protection clause* is converted into a " 'barren form of words' " when " 'discrimination . . . is made an end in itself.' " Tussman & tenBroek, 37 Cal. L. Rev. at 357 (*quoting Truax v. Raich,* 239 U.S. 33, 41, 36 S. Ct. 7, 10, 60 L. Ed. 131, 135 (1915)).

This precise situation is presented by the County's claim that the statute in this case exists to preserve the traditional understanding of marriage. The governmental objective identified by the County—to maintain the traditional understanding of marriage—is simply another way of saying the governmental objective is to limit civil marriage to opposite-sex couples.

. . .

This approach is, of course, an empty analysis. It permits a classification to be maintained " 'for its own sake.' " *Kerrigan,* 957 A.2d at 478 (*quoting Romer,* 517 U.S. at 635, 116 S. Ct. at 1629, 134 L. Ed. 2d at 868). Moreover, it can allow discrimination to become acceptable as tradition and helps to explain how discrimination can exist for such a long time. If a simple showing that discrimination is traditional satisfies equal protection, previous successful equal protection challenges of invidious racial and gender classifications would have failed. Consequently, qual protection demands that " 'the classification ([that is], the exclusion of gay [persons] from civil marriage) must advance a state interest that is separate from the classification itself.' " *Id.*

. . .

Because the County offers no particular *governmental* reason underlying the tradition of limiting civil marriage to heterosexual couples, we press forward to consider other plausible reasons for the legislative classification.

. . .

b. Promotion of optimal environment to raise children. Another governmental objective proffered by the County is the promotion of "child rearing by a father and a mother in a marital relationship which social scientists say with confidence is the optimal milieu for child rearing."

. . .

Plaintiffs presented an abundance of evidence and research, confirmed by our independent research, supporting the proposition that the interests of children are served equally by same-sex parents and opposite-sex parents. On the other hand, we acknowledge the existence of reasoned opinions that dual-gender parenting is the optimal environment for children. These opinions, while thoughtful and sincere, were largely unsupported by reliable scientific studies.[3]

3. The research appears to strongly support the conclusion that same-sex couples foster the same wholesome environment as opposite-sex couples and suggests that the traditional notion that children need a mother and a father to be raised into healthy, well-adjusted adults is based more on stereotype than anything else. In any event, we do not address whether there is a

Even assuming there may be a rational basis at this time to believe the legislative classification advances a legitimate government interest, this assumed fact would not be sufficient to survive the equal protection analysis applicable in this case. In order to ensure this classification based on sexual orientation is not borne of prejudice and stereotype, intermediate scrutiny demands a closer relationship between the legislative classification and the purpose of the classification than mere rationality. Under intermediate scrutiny, the relationship between the government's goal and the classification employed to further that goal must be "substantial." *Clark,* 486 U.S. at 461, 108 S. Ct. at 1914, 100 L. Ed. 2d at 472. In order to evaluate that relationship, it is helpful to consider whether the legislation is over-inclusive or under-inclusive. *See* RACI II, 675 N.W.2d at 10 (considering under-inclusion and over-inclusion even in the rational basis context).

. . .

We begin with the County's argument that the goal of the same-sex marriage ban is to ensure children will be raised only in the optimal milieu. In pursuit of this objective, the statutory exclusion of gay and lesbian people is both under-inclusive and over-inclusive. The civil marriage statute is under-inclusive because it does not exclude from marriage other groups of parents—such as child abusers, sexual predators, parents neglecting to provide child support, and violent felons—that are undeniably less than optimal parents. Such under-inclusion tends to demonstrate that the sexual-orientation-based classification is grounded in prejudice or "overbroad generalizations about the different talents, capacities, or preferences" of gay and lesbian people, rather than having a substantial relationship to some important objective. *See Virginia,* 518 U.S. at 533, 116 S. Ct. at 2275, 135 L. Ed. 2d at 751 (rejecting use of overbroad generalizations to classify). If the marriage statute was truly focused on optimal parenting, many classifications of people would be excluded, not merely gay and lesbian people.

. . .

While a statute does not automatically violate equal protection merely by being under-inclusive, the degree of under-inclusion nonetheless indicates the substantiality of the relationship between the legislative means and end.

. . .

The ban on same-sex marriage is substantially over-inclusive because not all same-sex couples choose to raise children. Yet, the marriage statute denies civil marriage to all gay and lesbian people in order to discourage the limited number of same-sex couples who desire to raise children. In doing so, the legislature includes a consequential number of "individuals within the statute's purview who are not afflicted with the evil the statute

rational basis for the marriage statute, as the sexual-orientation classification made by the statute is subject to a heightened standard of scrutiny.

seeks to remedy." *Conaway*, 932 A.2d at 649 (Raker, J., concurring in part and dissenting).

At the same time, the exclusion of gay and lesbian people from marriage is under-inclusive, even in relation to the narrower goal of improving child rearing by limiting same-sex parenting. Quite obviously, the statute does not prohibit same-sex couples from raising children. Same-sex couples currently raise children in Iowa, even while being excluded from civil marriage, and such couples will undoubtedly continue to do so. Recognition of this under-inclusion puts in perspective just how minimally the same-sex marriage ban actually advances the purported legislative goal. A law so simultaneously over-inclusive and under-inclusive is not substantially related to the government's objective. In the end, a careful analysis of the over-and under-inclusiveness of the statute reveals it is less about using marriage to achieve an optimal environment for children and more about merely precluding gay and lesbian people from civil marriage.

. . .

c. Promotion of procreation. The County also proposes that government endorsement of traditional civil marriage will result in more procreation. It points out that procreation is important to the continuation of the human race, and opposite-sex couples accomplish this objective because procreation occurs naturally within this group. In contrast, the County points out, same-sex couples can procreate only through assisted reproductive techniques, and some same-sex couples may choose not to procreate. While heterosexual marriage does lead to procreation, the argument by the County fails to address the real issue in our required analysis of the objective: whether *exclusion* of gay and lesbian individuals from the institution of civil marriage will result in *more* procreation? If procreation is the true objective, then the proffered classification must work to achieve that objective.

Conceptually, the promotion of procreation as an objective of marriage is compatible with the inclusion of gays and lesbians within the definition of marriage. Gay and lesbian persons are capable of procreation. Thus, the sole conceivable avenue by which exclusion of gay and lesbian people from civil marriage could promote more procreation is if the unavailability of civil marriage for same-sex partners caused homosexual individuals to "become" heterosexual in order to procreate within the present traditional institution of civil marriage. The briefs, the record, our research, and common sense do not suggest such an outcome. Even if possibly true, the link between exclusion of gay and lesbian people from marriage and increased procreation is far too tenuous to withstand heightened scrutiny. Specifically, the statute is significantly under-inclusive with respect to the objective of increasing procreation because it does not include a variety of groups that do not procreate for reasons such as age, physical disability, or choice. In other words, the classification is not substantially related to the asserted legislative purpose.

d. Promoting stability in opposite-sex relationships. A fourth suggested rationale supporting the marriage statute is "promoting stability in opposite sex relationships." While the institution of civil marriage likely encourages stability in opposite-sex relationships, we must evaluate whether *excluding* gay and lesbian people from civil marriage encourages stability in opposite-sex relationships. The County offers no reasons that it does, and we can find none. The stability of opposite-sex relationships is an important governmental interest, but the exclusion of same-sex couples from marriage is not substantially related to that objective.

e. Conservation of resources. The conservation of state resources is another objective arguably furthered by excluding gay and lesbian persons from civil marriage. The argument is based on a simple premise: couples who are married enjoy numerous governmental benefits, so the state's fiscal burden associated with civil marriage is reduced if less people are allowed to marry. In the common sense of the word, then, it is "rational" for the legislature to seek to conserve state resources by limiting the number of couples allowed to form civil marriages. By way of example, the County hypothesizes that, due to our laws granting tax benefits to married couples, the State of Iowa would reap less tax revenue if individual taxpaying gay and lesbian people were allowed to obtain a civil marriage. Certainly, Iowa's marriage statute causes numerous government benefits, including tax benefits, to be withheld from plaintiffs. Thus, the ban on same-sex marriages may conserve some state resources. Excluding any group from civil marriage—African–Americans, illegitimates, aliens, even red-haired individuals—would conserve state resources in an equally "rational" way. Yet, such classifications so obviously offend our society's collective sense of equality that courts have not hesitated to provide added protections against such inequalities.

. . .

As observed in our analysis of the other reasons offered in support of the marriage statute, significant degrees of over-inclusion and under-inclusion shed light on the true relationship between exclusion of gay and lesbian people from civil marriage and the goal of conserving governmental resources. Exclusion of all same-sex couples is an extremely blunt instrument for conserving state resources through limiting access to civil marriage. In other words, the exclusion of same-sex couples is over-inclusive because many same-sex couples, if allowed to marry, would not use more state resources than they currently consume as unmarried couples. To reference the County's example, while many heterosexual couples who have obtained a civil marriage do not file joint tax returns—or experience any other tax benefit from marital status—many same-sex couples may not file a joint tax return either. The two classes created by the statute—opposite-sex couples and same-sex couples—may use the same amount of state resources. Thus, the two classes are similarly situated for the purpose of conserving state resources, yet the classes are treated differently by the law. In this way, sexual orientation is a flawed indicator of resource usage.

Just as exclusion of same-sex couples from marriage is a blunt instrument, however, it is also significantly undersized if the true goal is to conserve state resources. That is to say, the classification is under-inclusive. The goal of conservation of state resources would be equally served by excluding any similar-sized group from civil marriage. Indeed, under the County's logic, more state resources would be conserved by excluding groups more numerous than Iowa's estimated 5800 same-sex couples (for example, persons marrying for a second or subsequent time). Importantly, there is also no suggestion same-sex couples would use *more* state resources if allowed to obtain a civil marriage than heterosexual couples who obtain a civil marriage.

. . .

This tenuous relationship between the classification and its purpose demonstrates many people who are similarly situated with respect to the purpose of the law are treated differently. As a result, the sexual-orientation-based classification does not substantially further the suggested governmental interest, as required by intermediate scrutiny.

4. *Conclusion.* Having examined each proffered governmental objective through the appropriate lens of intermediate scrutiny, we conclude the sexual-orientation-based classification under the marriage statute does not substantially further any of the objectives.

. . .

Religious Opposition to Same–Sex Marriage. Now that we have addressed and rejected each specific interest advanced by the County to justify the classification drawn under the statute, we consider the reason for the exclusion of gay and lesbian couples from civil marriage left unspoken by the County: religious opposition to same-sex marriage. The County's silence reflects, we believe, its understanding this reason cannot, under our Iowa Constitution, be used to justify a ban on same-sex marriage. While unexpressed, religious sentiment most likely motivates many, if not most, opponents of same-sex civil marriage and perhaps even shapes the views of those people who may accept gay and lesbian unions but find the notion of same-sex marriage unsettling.[4] Consequently, we address the religious undercurrent propelling the same-sex marriage debate as a means to fully explain our rationale for rejecting the dual-gender requirement of the marriage statute.

It is quite understandable that religiously motivated opposition to same-sex civil marriage shapes the basis for legal opposition to same-sex

4. A survey in the Des Moines Register in 2008 found 28.1% of individuals surveyed supported same-sex marriage, 30.2% opposed same-sex marriage but supported civil unions, and thirty-two percent of respondents opposed both same-sex marriage and civil unions. Erin Jordan, About 6 in 10 Iowans back same-sex unions, poll finds, Des Moines Register, Nov. 26, 2008, at 4B. The Des Moines Register survey is consistent with a national survey by the PEW Research Center in 2003. This PEW survey found that fifty-nine percent of Americans oppose same-sex marriage, and thirty-two percent favor same-sex marriage. Schuman, 96 Geo. L.J. at 2108. However, opposition to same-sex marriage jumped to eighty percent for people "with a high level of religious commitment," with only twelve percent of such people in favor of same-sex marriage. *Id.*

marriage, even if only indirectly. Religious objections to same-sex marriage are supported by thousands of years of tradition and biblical interpretation.[5] The belief that the "sanctity of marriage" would be undermined by the inclusion of gay and lesbian couples bears a striking conceptual resemblance to the expressed secular rationale for maintaining the tradition of marriage as a union between dual-gender couples, but better identifies the source of the opposition. Whether expressly or impliedly, much of society rejects same-sex marriage due to sincere, deeply ingrained—even fundamental—religious belief. Yet, such views are not the only religious views of marriage. As demonstrated by amicus groups, other equally sincere groups and people in Iowa and around the nation have strong religious views that yield the opposite conclusion.[6]

This contrast of opinions in our society largely explains the absence of any religion-based rationale to test the constitutionality of Iowa's same-sex marriage ban. Our constitution does not permit any branch of government to resolve these types of religious debates and entrusts to courts the task of ensuring government *avoids* them. *See Iowa Const. art. I, § 3* ("The general assembly shall make no law respecting an establishment of religion. . . ."). The statute at issue in this case does not prescribe a definition of marriage for religious institutions. Instead, the statute declares, "Marriage is a civil contract" and then regulates that civil contract. *Iowa Code § 595.1A.* Thus, in pursuing our task in this case, we proceed as civil judges, far removed from the theological debate of religious clerics, and focus only on the concept of civil marriage and the state licensing system that identifies a limited class of persons entitled to secular rights and benefits associated with civil marriage.

. . .

In the final analysis, we give respect to the views of all Iowans on the issue of same-sex marriage—religious or otherwise—by giving respect to our constitutional principles. These principles require that the state recognize both opposite-sex and same-sex civil marriage. Religious doctrine and views contrary to this principle of law are unaffected, and people can continue to associate with the religion that best reflects their views. A religious denomination can still define marriage as a union between a man and a woman, and a marriage ceremony performed by a minister, priest, rabbi, or other person ordained or designated as a leader of the person's religious faith does not lose its meaning as a sacrament or other religious institution. The sanctity of all religious marriages celebrated in the future

5. Schuman, 96 Geo. L.J. at 2109–12 (discussing the religious arguments against same-sex marriage found in both the Old and New Testaments of the Bible, supporting a conclusion that homosexuality is considered to be a sin and same-sex marriage to be an extension of that sin).

6. Many religions recognize same-sex marriage, such as Buddhists, Quakers, Unitarians, and Reform and Reconstructionist Jews. Schuman, 96 Geo. L.J. at 2108. Amicus curiae Iowa and National Faith Leaders, Communities, and Scholars point out the United Church of Christ encourages, but does not require, its local congregations to adopt wedding policies that do not discriminate between heterosexual, gay, and lesbian couples, while the Episcopal Church permits priests to perform liturgies and blessings at same-sex weddings as a matter of pastoral care. Additionally, many groups and clergy within various religions are working to achieve inclusion of same-sex marriage. *Id.* at 2108–09.

will have the same meaning as those celebrated in the past. The only difference is *civil* marriage will now take on a new meaning that reflects a more complete understanding of equal protection of the law. This result is what our constitution requires.

J. Constitutional Infirmity. We are firmly convinced the exclusion of gay and lesbian people from the institution of civil marriage does not substantially further any important governmental objective. The legislature has excluded a historically disfavored class of persons from a supremely important civil institution without a constitutionally sufficient justification. There is no material fact, genuinely in dispute, that can affect this determination.

We have a constitutional duty to ensure equal protection of the law. Faithfulness to that duty requires us to hold Iowa's marriage statute, *Iowa Code section 595.2*, violates the Iowa Constitution. To decide otherwise would be an abdication of our constitutional duty. If gay and lesbian people must submit to different treatment without an exceedingly persuasive justification, they are deprived of the benefits of the principle of equal protection upon which the rule of law is founded. *Iowa Code section 595.2* denies gay and lesbian people the equal protection of the law promised by the Iowa Constitution.

. . .

V. Remedy.

Because our civil marriage statute fails to provide equal protection of the law under the Iowa Constitution, we must decide how to best remedy the constitutional violation. The sole remedy requested by plaintiffs is admission into the institution of civil marriage. The County does not suggest an alternative remedy. The high courts of other jurisdictions have remedied constitutionally invalid bans on same-sex marriage in two ways. Some courts have ordered gay and lesbian people to be allowed to access the institution of civil marriage. *See In re Marriage Cases,* 183 P.3d at 453; *Kerrigan,* 957 A.2d at 480 ("definition of marriage necessarily must be expanded" to include same-sex couples); *Opinions of the Justices to the Senate,* 440 Mass. 1201, 802 N.E.2d 565, 571 (Mass. 2004). Other courts have allowed their state legislatures to create parallel civil institutions for same-sex couples. *See Lewis v. Harris,* 188 N.J. 415, 908 A.2d 196, 221 (N.J. 2006); *Baker v. State,* 170 Vt. 194, 744 A.2d 864, 887 (Vt. 1999).

Iowa Code section 595.2 is unconstitutional because the County has been unable to identify a constitutionally adequate justification for excluding plaintiffs from the institution of civil marriage. A new distinction based on sexual orientation would be equally suspect and difficult to square with the fundamental principles of equal protection embodied in our constitution. This record, our independent research, and the appropriate equal protection analysis do not suggest the existence of a justification for such a legislative classification that substantially furthers any governmental objective. Consequently, the language in *Iowa Code section 595.2* limiting civil marriage to a man and a woman must be stricken from the statute, and the remaining statutory language must be interpreted and applied in a manner allowing gay and lesbian people full access to the institution of civil marriage.

AFFIRMED.

All justices concur.

DISCUSSION

1. *In 2009, by a unanimous vote, the Iowa Supreme Court became the second court to rule in favor of same-sex marriage. In 2010, a removal campaign led by unhappy voters resulted in the ouster of the three Supreme Court justices who were up for their retention elections. What do you think this says about the effectiveness of retention elections and the political process? Do you believe the Iowa Supreme Court decided prematurely to address this issue?*

2. *Compare the Iowa marriage decision with the Massachusetts marriage decision. What are the differences between the two? Which one do you think best articulates the argument for same-sex marriage?*

VIII. THE CALIFORNIA SAGA

In 2008, in the landmark *In re Marriage Cases*, the California Supreme Court held that California's bifurcated system of partnership recognition (marriage for straights, domestic partnerships for gays) affronted a fundamental right to marry found in the privacy and due process provisions of the state constitution. The court held that designation of same-sex relationships by a different name than straight relationships denied same-sex partners "one of the core elements" of the right to marry: the right to the "same dignity, respect, and stature as that accorded to all other officially recognized family relationships" in California. The court also held that the state's dual system violated equal protection under the California constitution. In so doing, the court for the first time declared sexual orientation a suspect classification under California law. Gay couples began legally marrying in California in June, 2008.

However, in *Strauss v. Horton,* 46 Cal.4th 364, 93 Cal. Rptr. 3d 591, 207 P.3d 48 (2009), the California Supreme Court upheld Proposition 8, the measure approved by voters in November 2008 to alter the California constitution to define marriage as a union of a man and woman and effectively to overturn *In re Marriage Cases*. The court, however, upheld the validity of all same-sex marriages performed after *In Re Marriage Cases* and before the passage of Proposition 8.

Prop. 8 was then litigated in the case of *Perry v. Schwarzenegger* (2010) by the legal team of Theodore B. Olson and David Boies, adversaries in *Bush v. Gore* years earlier, but on the same side in this undertaking.

A. THE CONSERVATIVE CASE FOR GAY MARRIAGE: WHY SAME-SEX MARRIAGE IS AN AMERICAN VALUE*

Together with my good friend and occasional courtroom adversary David Boies, I am attempting to persuade a federal court to invalidate California's Proposition 8—the voter-approved measure that overturned California's constitutional right to marry a person of the same sex.

My involvement in this case has generated a certain degree of consternation among conservatives. How could a politically active, lifelong Republican, a veteran of the Ronald Reagan and George W. Bush administrations, challenge the "traditional" definition of marriage and press for an "activist" interpretation of the Constitution to create another "new" constitutional right?

My answer to this seeming conundrum rests on a lifetime of exposure to persons of different backgrounds, histories, viewpoints, and intrinsic characteristics, and on my rejection of what I see as superficially appealing but ultimately false perceptions about our Constitution and its protection of equality and fundamental rights.

Many of my fellow conservatives have an almost knee-jerk hostility toward gay marriage. This does not make sense, because same-sex unions promote the values conservatives prize. Marriage is one of the basic building blocks of our neighborhoods and our nation. At its best, it is a stable bond between two individuals who work to create a loving household and a social and economic partnership. We encourage couples to marry because the commitments they make to one another provide benefits not only to themselves but also to their families and communities. Marriage requires thinking beyond one's own needs. It transforms two individuals into a union based on shared aspirations, and in doing so establishes a formal investment in the well-being of society. The fact that individuals who happen to be gay want to share in this vital social institution is evidence that conservative ideals enjoy widespread acceptance. Conservatives should celebrate this, rather than lament it.

Legalizing same-sex marriage would also be a recognition of basic American principles, and would represent the culmination of our nation's commitment to equal rights. It is, some have said, the last major civil-rights milestone yet to be surpassed in our two-century struggle to attain the goals we set for this nation at its formation.

This bedrock American principle of equality is central to the political and legal convictions of Republicans, Democrats, liberals, and conservatives alike. The dream that became America began with the revolutionary concept expressed in the Declaration of Independence in words that are among the most noble and elegant ever written: "We hold these truths to

* Excerpted from, Theodore B. Olson, *Newsweek*, January 09, 2010 (used with permission).

be self-evident, that all men are created equal, that they are endowed by their Creator with certain unalienable Rights, that among these are Life, Liberty and the pursuit of Happiness."

Sadly, our nation has taken a long time to live up to the promise of equality. In 1857, the Supreme Court held that an African–American could not be a citizen. During the ensuing Civil War, Abraham Lincoln eloquently reminded the nation of its founding principle: "our fathers brought forth on this continent, a new nation, conceived in liberty and dedicated to the proposition that all men are created equal."

At the end of the Civil War, to make the elusive promise of equality a reality, the 14th Amendment to the Constitution added the command that "no State shall deprive any person of life, liberty or property, without due process of law; nor deny to any person the equal protection of the laws."

Subsequent laws and court decisions have made clear that equality under the law extends to persons of all races, religions, and places of origin. What better way to make this national aspiration complete than to apply the same protection to men and women who differ from others only on the basis of their sexual orientation? I cannot think of a single reason—and have not heard one since I undertook this venture—for continued discrimination against decent, hardworking members of our society on that basis.

Various federal and state laws have accorded certain rights and privileges to gay and lesbian couples, but these protections vary dramatically at the state level, and nearly universally deny true equality to gays and lesbians who wish to marry. The very idea of marriage is basic to recognition as equals in our society; any status short of that is inferior, unjust, and unconstitutional.

The United States Supreme Court has repeatedly held that marriage is one of the most fundamental rights that we have as Americans under our Constitution. It is an expression of our desire to create a social partnership, to live and share life's joys and burdens with the person we love, and to form a lasting bond and a social identity. The Supreme Court has said that marriage is a part of the Constitution's protections of liberty, privacy, freedom of association, and spiritual identification. In short, the right to marry helps us to define ourselves and our place in a community. Without it, there can be no true equality under the law.

It is true that marriage in this nation traditionally has been regarded as a relationship exclusively between a man and a woman, and many of our nation's multiple religions define marriage in precisely those terms. But while the Supreme Court has always previously considered marriage in that context, the underlying rights and liberties that marriage embodies are not in any way confined to heterosexuals.

Marriage is a civil bond in this country as well as, in some (but hardly all) cases, a religious sacrament. It is a relationship recognized by governments as providing a privileged and respected status, entitled to the state's support and benefits. The California Supreme Court described marriage as a "union unreservedly approved and favored by the community." Where the state has accorded official sanction to a relationship and provided special benefits to those who enter into that relationship, our courts have insisted that withholding that status requires powerful justifications and may not be arbitrarily denied.

What, then, are the justifications for California's decision in Proposition 8 to withdraw access to the institution of marriage for some of its citizens on the basis of their sexual orientation? The reasons I have heard are not very persuasive.

The explanation mentioned most often is tradition. But simply because something has always been done a certain way does not mean that it must always remain that way. Otherwise we would still have segregated schools and debtors' prisons. Gays and lesbians have always been among us, forming a part of our society, and they have lived as couples in our neighborhoods and communities. For a long time, they have experienced discrimination and even persecution; but we, as a society, are starting to become more tolerant, accepting, and understanding. California and many other states have allowed gays and lesbians to form domestic partnerships (or civil unions) with most of the rights of married heterosexuals. Thus, gay and lesbian individuals are now permitted to live together in state-sanctioned relationships. It therefore seems anomalous to cite "tradition" as a justification for withholding the status of marriage and thus to continue to label those relationships as less worthy, less sanctioned, or less legitimate.

The second argument I often hear is that traditional marriage furthers the state's interest in procreation—and that opening marriage to same-sex couples would dilute, diminish, and devalue this goal. But that is plainly not the case. Preventing lesbians and gays from marrying does not cause more heterosexuals to marry and conceive more children. Likewise, allowing gays and lesbians to marry someone of the same sex will not discourage heterosexuals from marrying a person of the opposite sex. How, then, would allowing same-sex marriages reduce the number of children that heterosexual couples conceive?

This procreation argument cannot be taken seriously. We do not inquire whether heterosexual couples intend to bear children, or have the capacity to have children, before we allow them to marry. We permit marriage by the elderly, by prison inmates, and by persons who have no intention of having children. What's more, it is pernicious to think marriage should be limited to heterosexuals because of the state's desire to promote procreation. We would surely not accept as constitutional a ban on marriage if a state were to decide, as China has done, to discourage procreation.

Another argument, vaguer and even less persuasive, is that gay marriage somehow does harm to heterosexual marriage. I have yet to meet anyone who can explain to me what this means. In what way would allowing same-sex partners to marry diminish the marriages of heterosexual couples? Tellingly, when the judge in our case asked our opponent to identify the ways in which same-sex marriage would harm heterosexual marriage, to his credit he answered honestly: he could not think of any.

The simple fact is that there is no good reason why we should deny marriage to same-sex partners. On the other hand, there are many reasons why we should formally recognize these relationships and embrace the rights of gays and lesbians to marry and become full and equal members of our society.

No matter what you think of homosexuality, it is a fact that gays and lesbians are members of our families, clubs, and workplaces. They are our doctors, our teachers, our soldiers (whether we admit it or not), and our friends. They yearn for acceptance, stable relationships, and success in their lives, just like the rest of us.

Conservatives and liberals alike need to come together on principles that surely unite us. Certainly, we can agree on the value of strong families, lasting domestic relationships, and communities populated by persons with recognized and sanctioned bonds to one another. Confining some of our neighbors and friends who share these same values to an outlaw or second-class status undermines their sense of belonging and weakens their ties with the rest of us and what should be our common aspirations. Even those whose religious convictions preclude endorsement of what they may perceive as an unacceptable "lifestyle" should recognize that disapproval should not warrant stigmatization and unequal treatment.

When we refuse to accord this status to gays and lesbians, we discourage them from forming the same relationships we encourage for others. And we are also telling them, those who love them, and society as a whole that their relationships are less worthy, less legitimate, less permanent, and less valued. We demean their relationships and we demean them as individuals. I cannot imagine how we benefit as a society by doing so.

I understand, but reject, certain religious teachings that denounce homosexuality as morally wrong, illegitimate, or unnatural; and I take strong exception to those who argue that same-sex relationships should be discouraged by society and law. Science has taught us, even if history has not, that gays and lesbians do not choose to be homosexual any more than the rest of us choose to be heterosexual. To a very large extent, these characteristics are immutable, like being left-handed. And, while our Constitution guarantees the freedom to exercise our individual religious convictions, it equally prohibits us from forcing our beliefs on others. I do not believe that our society can ever live up to the promise of equality, and the fundamental rights to life, liberty, and the pursuit of happiness, until we stop invidious discrimination on the basis of sexual orientation.

If we are born heterosexual, it is not unusual for us to perceive those who are born homosexual as aberrational and threatening. Many religions and much of our social culture have reinforced those impulses. Too often, that has led to prejudice, hostility, and discrimination. The antidote is understanding, and reason. We once tolerated laws throughout this nation that prohibited marriage between persons of different races. California's Supreme Court was the first to find that discrimination unconstitutional. The U.S. Supreme Court unanimously agreed 20 years later, in 1967, in a case called Loving v. Virginia. It seems inconceivable today that only 40 years ago there were places in this country where a black woman could not legally marry a white man. And it was only 50 years ago that 17 states mandated segregated public education—until the Supreme Court unanimously struck down that practice in Brown v. Board of Education. Most Americans are proud of these decisions and the fact that the discriminatory state laws that spawned them have been discredited. I am convinced that Americans will be equally proud when we no longer discriminate against gays and lesbians and welcome them into our society.

Reactions to our lawsuit have reinforced for me these essential truths. I have certainly heard anger, resentment, and hostility, and words like "betrayal" and other pointedly graphic criticism. But mostly I have been overwhelmed by expressions of gratitude and good will from persons in all walks of life, including, I might add, from many conservatives and libertarians whose names might surprise. I have been particularly moved by many personal renditions of how lonely and personally destructive it is to be treated as an outcast and how meaningful it will be to be respected by our laws and civil institutions as an American, entitled to equality and dignity. I have no doubt that we are on the right side of this battle, the right side of the law, and the right side of history.

Some have suggested that we have brought this case too soon, and that neither the country nor the courts are "ready" to tackle this issue and remove this stigma. We disagree. We represent real clients—two wonderful couples in California who have longtime relationships. Our lesbian clients are raising four fine children who could not ask for better parents. Our clients wish to be married. They believe that they have that constitutional right. They wish to be represented in court to seek vindication of that right by mounting a challenge under the United States Constitution to the validity of Proposition 8 under the equal-protection and due-process clauses of the 14th Amendment. In fact, the California attorney general has conceded the unconstitutionality of Proposition 8, and the city of San Francisco has joined our case to defend the rights of gays and lesbians to be married. We do not tell persons who have a legitimate claim to wait until the time is "right" and the populace is "ready" to recognize their equality and equal dignity under the law.

Citizens who have been denied equality are invariably told to "wait their turn" and to "be patient." Yet veterans of past civil-rights battles found that it was the act of insisting on equal rights that ultimately sped acceptance of those rights. As to whether the courts are "ready" for this case, just a few years ago, in Romer v. Evans, the United States Supreme Court struck down a popularly adopted Colorado constitutional amendment that withdrew the rights of gays and lesbians in that state to the protection of anti-discrimination laws. And seven years ago, in Lawrence v. Texas, the Supreme Court struck down, as lacking any rational basis, Texas laws prohibiting private, intimate sexual practices between persons of the same sex, overruling a contrary decision just 20 years earlier.

These decisions have generated controversy, of course, but they are decisions of the nation's highest court on which our clients are entitled to rely. If all citizens have a constitutional right to marry, if state laws that withdraw legal protections of gays and lesbians as a class are unconstitutional, and if private, intimate sexual conduct between persons of the same sex is protected by the Constitution, there is very little left on which opponents of same-sex marriage can rely. As Justice Antonin Scalia, who dissented in the Lawrence case, pointed out, "[W]hat [remaining] justification could there possibly be for denying the benefits of marriage to homosexual couples exercising '[t]he liberty protected by the Constitution'?" He is right, of course. One might agree or not with these decisions, but even Justice Scalia has acknowledged that they lead in only one direction.

California's Proposition 8 is particularly vulnerable to constitutional challenge, because that state has now enacted a crazy-quilt of marriage regulation that makes no sense to anyone. California recognizes marriage between men and women, including persons on death row, child abusers, and wife beaters. At the same time, California prohibits marriage by loving, caring, stable partners of the same sex, but tries to make up for it by giving them the alternative of "domestic partnerships" with virtually all of the rights of married persons except the official, state-approved status of marriage. Finally, California recognizes 18,000 same-sex marriages that took place in the months between the state Supreme Court's ruling that upheld gay-marriage rights and the decision of California's citizens to withdraw those rights by enacting Proposition 8.

So there are now three classes of Californians: heterosexual couples who can get married, divorced, and remarried, if they wish; same-sex couples who cannot get married but can live together in domestic partnerships; and same-sex couples who are now married but who, if they divorce, cannot remarry. This is an irrational system, it is discriminatory, and it cannot stand.

Americans who believe in the words of the Declaration of Independence, in Lincoln's Gettysburg Address, in the 14th Amendment, and in the Constitution's guarantees of equal protection and equal dignity before the law cannot sit by while this wrong continues. This is not a conservative or liberal issue; it is an American one, and it is time that we, as Americans, embraced it.

B. THE FEDERAL DISTRICT COURT DECISION

PERRY v. SCHWARZENEGGER

704 F.Supp.2d 921 (N.D.Cal. 2010)

PROPOSITION 8 IS UNCONSTITUTIONAL BECAUSE IT DENIES PLAINTIFFS A FUNDAMENTAL RIGHT WITHOUT A LEGITIMATE (MUCH LESS COMPELLING) REASON

Because plaintiffs seek to exercise their fundamental right to marry, their claim is subject to strict scrutiny. *Zablocki,* 434 U.S. at 388. That the majority of California voters supported Proposition 8 is irrelevant, as "fundamental rights may not be submitted to [a] vote; they depend on the outcome of no elections." *West Virginia State Board of Education v. Barnette,* 319 U.S. 624, 638 (1943). Under strict scrutiny, the state bears the burden of producing evidence to show that Proposition 8 is narrowly tailored to a compelling government interest. *Carey v. Population Services International,* 431 U.S. 678, 686, 97 S.Ct. 2010, 52 L.Ed.2d 675 (1977). Because the government defendants declined to advance such arguments, proponents seized the role of asserting the existence of a compelling California interest in Proposition 8.

As explained in detail in the equal protection analysis, Proposition 8 cannot withstand rational basis review. Still less can Proposition 8 survive the strict scrutiny required by plaintiffs' due process claim. The minimal evidentiary presentation made by proponents does not meet the heavy burden of production necessary to show that Proposition 8 is narrowly tailored to a compelling government interest. Proposition 8 cannot, therefore, withstand strict scrutiny. Moreover, proponents do not assert that the availability of domestic partnerships satisfies plaintiffs' fundamental right to marry; proponents stipulated that "[t]here is a significant symbolic disparity between domestic partnership and marriage." Doc #159–2 at 6. Accordingly, Proposition 8 violates the Due Process Clause of the Fourteenth Amendment.

EQUAL PROTECTION

The Equal Protection Clause of the Fourteenth Amendment provides that no state shall "deny to any person within its jurisdiction the equal protection of the laws." US Const Amend XIV, § 1. Equal protection is "a pledge of the protection of equal laws." *Yick Wo v. Hopkins,* 118 U.S. 356, 369, 6 S.Ct. 1064, 30 L.Ed. 220 (1886). The guarantee of equal protection coexists, of course, with the reality that most legislation must classify for some purpose or another. See *Romer v. Evans,* 517 U.S. 620, 631, 116 S.Ct. 1620, 134 L.Ed.2d 855 (1996). When a law creates a classification but neither targets a suspect class nor burdens a fundamental right, the court presumes the law is valid and will uphold it as long as it is rationally related to some legitimate government interest. See, for example, *Heller v. Doe,* 509 U.S. 312, 319–320, 113 S.Ct. 2637, 125 L.Ed.2d 257 (1993).

The court defers to legislative (or in this case, popular) judgment if there is at least a debatable question whether the underlying basis for the classification is rational. *Minnesota v. Clover Leaf Creamery Co.,* 449 U.S. 456, 464, 101 S.Ct. 715, 66 L.Ed.2d 659 (1980). Even under the most deferential standard of review, however, the court must "insist on knowing the relation between the classification adopted and the object to be attained." *Romer,* 517 U.S. at 632; *Heller,* 509 U.S. at 321 (basis for a classification must "find some footing in the realities of the subject addressed by the legislation"). The court may look to evidence to determine whether the basis for the underlying debate is rational. *Plyler v. Doe,* 457 U.S. 202, 228, 102 S.Ct. 2382, 72 L.Ed.2d 786 (1982) (finding an asserted interest in preserving state resources by prohibiting undocumented children from attending public school to be irrational because "the available evidence suggests that illegal aliens underutilize public services, while contributing their labor to the local economy and tax money to the state fisc"). The search for a rational relationship, while quite deferential, "ensure[s] that classifications are not drawn for the purpose of disadvantaging the group burdened by the law." *Romer,* 517 U.S. at 633. The classification itself must be related to the purported interest. *Plyler,* 457 U.S. at 220 ("It is difficult to conceive of a rational basis for penalizing [undocumented children] for their presence within the United States," despite the state's interest in preserving resources.).

Most laws subject to rational basis easily survive equal protection review, because a legitimate reason can nearly always be found for treating different groups in an unequal manner. *See Romer,* 517 U.S. at 633. Yet, to survive rational basis review, a law must do more than disadvantage or otherwise harm a particular group. *United States Department of Agriculture v. Moreno,* 413 U.S. 528, 534, 93 S.Ct. 2821, 37 L.Ed.2d 782 (1973).

SEXUAL ORIENTATION OR SEX DISCRIMINATION

Plaintiffs challenge Proposition 8 as violating the Equal Protection Clause because Proposition 8 discriminates both on the basis of sex and on the basis of sexual orientation. Sexual orientation discrimination can take the form of sex discrimination. Here, for example, Perry is prohibited from marrying Stier, a woman, because Perry is a woman. If Perry were a man, Proposition 8 would not prohibit the marriage. Thus, Proposition 8 operates to restrict Perry's choice of marital partner because of her sex. But Proposition 8 also operates to restrict Perry's choice of marital partner because of her sexual orientation; her desire to marry another woman arises only because she is a lesbian.

The evidence at trial shows that gays and lesbians experience discrimination based on unfounded stereotypes and prejudices specific to sexual orientation. Gays and lesbians have historically been targeted for discrimination because of their sexual orientation; that discrimination continues to the present. FF 74–76. As the case of Perry and the other plaintiffs illustrates, sex and sexual orientation are necessarily interrelated, as an individual's choice of romantic or intimate partner based on sex is a large part of what defines an individual's sexual orientation. See FF 42–43. Sexual orientation discrimination is thus a phenomenon distinct from, but related to, sex discrimination.

Proponents argue that Proposition 8 does not target gays and lesbians because its language does not refer to them. In so arguing, proponents seek to mask their own initiative. FF 57. Those who choose to marry someone of the opposite sex—heterosexuals—do not have their choice of marital partner restricted by Proposition 8. Those who would choose to marry someone of the same sex—homosexuals—have had their right to marry eliminated by an amendment to the state constitution. Homosexual conduct and identity together define what it means to be gay or lesbian. See FF 42–43. Indeed, homosexual conduct and attraction are constitutionally protected and integral parts of what makes someone gay or lesbian. *Lawrence,* 539 U.S. at 579; FF 42–43; *see also Christian Legal Society v. Martinez,* 561 U.S. ___, 130 S.Ct. 2971, 177 L.Ed.2d 838, No 08–1371 Slip Op at 23 ("Our decisions have declined to distinguish between status and conduct in [the context of sexual orientation].") (June 28, 2010) (*citing Lawrence,* 539 U.S. at 583 (O'Connor, J, concurring)).

Proposition 8 targets gays and lesbians in a manner specific to their sexual orientation and, because of their relationship to one another, Proposition 8 targets them specifically due to sex. Having considered the evidence, the relationship between sex and sexual orientation and the fact that Proposition 8 eliminates a right only a gay man or a lesbian would exercise, the court determines that plaintiffs' equal protection claim is based on sexual orientation, but this claim is equivalent to a claim of discrimination based on sex.

STANDARD OF REVIEW

As presently explained in detail, the Equal Protection Clause renders Proposition 8 unconstitutional under any standard of review. Accordingly, the court need not address the question whether laws classifying on the basis of sexual orientation should be subject to a heightened standard of review.

Although Proposition 8 fails to possess even a rational basis, the evidence presented at trial shows that gays and lesbians are the type of minority strict scrutiny was designed to protect. *Massachusetts Board of Retirement v. Murgia,* 427 U.S. 307, 313, 96 S.Ct. 2562, 49 L.Ed.2d 520 (1976) (noting that strict scrutiny may be appropriate where a group has experienced a " 'history of purposeful unequal treatment' or been subjected to unique disabilities on the basis of stereotyped characteristics not truly indicative of their abilities" (quoting *San Antonio School District v. Rodriguez,* 411 U.S. 1, 28, 93 S.Ct. 1278, 36 L.Ed.2d 16 (1973)). See FF 42–43, 46–48, 74–78. Proponents admit that "same-sex sexual orientation does not result in any impairment in judgment or general social and vocational capabilities." PX0707 at RFA No 21.

The court asked the parties to identify a difference between heterosexuals and homosexuals that the government might fairly need to take into account when crafting legislation. Doc #677 at 8. Proponents pointed only to a difference between same-sex couples (who are incapable through sexual intercourse of producing offspring biologically related to both parties) and opposite-sex couples (some of whom are capable through sexual intercourse of producing such offspring). Doc #687 at 32–34. Proponents did not, however, advance any reason why the government may use sexual orientation as a proxy for fertility or why the government may need to take into account fertility when legislating. Consider, by contrast, *City of Cleburne v. Cleburne Living Center,* 473 U.S. 432, 444, 105 S.Ct. 3249, 87 L.Ed.2d 313 (1985) (Legislation singling out a class for differential treatment hinges upon a demonstration of "real and undeniable differences" between the class and others); see also *United States v. Virginia,* 518 U.S. 515, 533, 116 S.Ct. 2264, 135 L.Ed.2d 735 (1996) ("Physical differences between men and women ... are enduring."). No evidence at trial illuminated distinctions among lesbians, gay men and heterosexuals amounting to "real and undeniable differences" that the government might need to take into account in legislating.

The trial record shows that strict scrutiny is the appropriate standard of review to apply to legislative classifications based on sexual orientation. All classifications based on sexual orientation appear suspect, as the evidence shows that California would rarely, if ever, have a reason to categorize individuals based on their sexual orientation. FF 47. Here, however, strict scrutiny is unnecessary. Proposition 8 fails to survive even rational basis review.

PROPOSITION 8 DOES NOT SURVIVE RATIONAL BASIS

Proposition 8 cannot withstand any level of scrutiny under the Equal Protection Clause, as excluding same-sex couples from marriage is simply not rationally related to a legitimate state interest. One example of a legitimate state interest in not issuing marriage licenses to a particular group might be a scarcity of marriage licenses or county officials to issue them. But marriage licenses in California are not a limited commodity, and the existence of 18,000 same-sex married couples in California shows that the state has the resources to allow both same-sex and opposite-sex couples to wed. See Background to Proposition 8 above.

Proponents put forth several rationales for Proposition 8, see Doc #605 at 12–15, which the court now examines in turn:

Proponents first argue that Proposition 8 is rational because it preserves: (1) "the traditional institution of marriage as the union of a man and a woman"; (2) "the traditional social and legal purposes, functions, and structure of marriage"; and (3) "the traditional meaning of marriage as it has always been defined in the English language." Doc #605 at 12–13. These interests relate to maintaining the definition of marriage as the union of a man and a woman for its own sake.

Tradition alone, however, cannot form a rational basis for a law. *Williams v. Illinois,* 399 U.S. 235, 239, 90 S.Ct. 2018, 26 L.Ed.2d 586 (1970). The "ancient lineage" of a classification does not make it rational. *Heller,* 509 U.S. at 327. Rather, the state must have an interest apart from the fact of the tradition itself.

The tradition of restricting marriage to opposite-sex couples does not further any state interest. Rather, the evidence shows that Proposition 8 harms the state's interest in equality, because it mandates that men and women be treated differently based only on antiquated and discredited notions of gender. See FF 32, 57.

The evidence shows that the state advances nothing when it adheres to the tradition of excluding same-sex couples from marriage. Proponents' asserted state interests in tradition are nothing more than tautologies and do not amount to rational bases for Proposition 8.

Proponents next argue that Proposition 8 is related to state interests in: (1) "[a]cting incrementally and with caution when considering a radical transformation to the fundamental nature of a bedrock social institution"; (2) "[d]ecreasing the probability of weakening the institution of marriage"; (3) "[d]ecreasing the probability of adverse consequences that could result from weakening the institution of marriage"; and (4) "[d]ecreasing the probability of the potential adverse consequences of same-sex marriage." Doc #605 at 13–14.

Instead, the evidence shows beyond debate that allowing same-sex couples to marry has at least a neutral, if not a positive, effect on the institution of marriage and that same-sex couples' marriages would benefit the state. Id. Moreover, the evidence shows that the rights of those opposed to homosexuality or same-sex couples will remain unaffected if the state ceases to enforce Proposition 8. FF 55, 62.

The process of allowing same-sex couples to marry is straightforward, and no evidence suggests that the state needs any significant lead time to integrate same-sex couples into marriage. The evidence shows that allowing same-sex couples to marry will be simple for California to implement because it has already done so; no change need be phased in.

Because the evidence shows same-sex marriage has and will have no adverse effects on society or the institution of marriage, California has no interest in waiting and no practical need to wait to grant marriage licenses to same-sex couples. Proposition 8 is thus not rationally related to proponents' purported interests in proceeding with caution when implementing social change. Proponents' largest group of purported state interests relates to opposite-sex parents. Proponents argue Proposition 8: (1) promotes "stability and responsibility in naturally procreative relationships"; (2) promotes "enduring and stable family structures for the responsible raising and care of children by their biological parents"; (3) increases "the probability that natural procreation will occur within stable, enduring, and supporting family structures"; (4) promotes "the natural and mutually beneficial bond between parents and their biological children"; (5)

increases "the probability that each child will be raised by both of his or her biological parents"; (6) increases "the probability that each child will be raised by both a father and a mother"; and (7) increases "the probability that each child will have a legally recognized father and mother." Doc #605 at 13–14.

The evidence supports two points which together show Proposition 8 does not advance any of the identified interests: (1) same-sex parents and opposite-sex parents are of equal quality, FF 69–73, and (2) Proposition 8 does not make it more likely that opposite-sex couples will marry and raise offspring biologically related to both parents, FF 43, 46, 51.

Moreover, Proposition 8 has nothing to do with children, as Proposition 8 simply prevents same-sex couples from marrying. FF 57. Same-sex couples can have (or adopt) and raise children. When they do, they are treated identically to opposite-sex parents under California law. FF 49. Even if California had an interest in preferring opposite-sex parents to same-sex parents—and the evidence plainly shows that California does not—Proposition 8 is not rationally related to that interest, because Proposition 8 does not affect who can or should become a parent under California law. FF 49, 57.

To the extent California has an interest in encouraging sexual activity to occur within marriage (a debatable proposition in light of *Lawrence,* 539 U.S. at 571) the evidence shows Proposition 8 to be detrimental to that interest. Because of Proposition 8, same-sex couples are not permitted to engage in sexual activity within marriage. FF 53. Domestic partnerships, in which sexual activity is apparently expected, are separate from marriage and thus codify California's encouragement of non-marital sexual activity. Cal Fam Code §§ 297–299.6. To the extent proponents seek to encourage a norm that sexual activity occur within marriage to ensure that reproduction occur within stable households, Proposition 8 discourages that norm because it requires some sexual activity and child-bearing and child-rearing to occur outside marriage. The inability to marry denies same-sex couples the benefits, including stability, attendant to marriage. FF 50. Proponents failed to put forth any credible evidence that married opposite-sex households are made more stable through Proposition 8. FF 55. The only rational conclusion in light of the evidence is that Proposition 8 makes it less likely that California children will be raised in stable households. See FF 50, 56.

None of the interests put forth by proponents relating to parents and children is advanced by Proposition 8; instead, the evidence shows Proposition 8 disadvantages families and their children.

Proponents next argue that Proposition 8 protects the First Amendment freedom of those who disagree with allowing marriage for couples of the same sex. Proponents argue that Proposition 8: (1) preserves "the prerogative and responsibility of parents to provide for the ethical and moral development and education of their own children"; and (2) accommodates "the First Amendment rights of individuals and institutions that oppose same-sex marriage on religious or moral grounds." Doc #605 at 14.

These purported interests fail as a matter of law. Proposition 8 does not affect any First Amendment right or responsibility of parents to educate their children. See *In re Marriage Cases,* 76 Cal.Rptr.3d 683, 183 P.3d at 451–452. Californians are prevented from distinguishing between same-sex partners and opposite-sex spouses in public accommodations, as California antidiscrimination law requires identical treatment for same-sex unions and opposite-sex marriages. *Koebke v. Bernardo Heights Country Club,* 36 Cal.4th 824, 31 Cal.Rptr.3d 565, 115 P.3d 1212, 1217–1218 (Cal 2005). The evidence shows that Proposition 8 does nothing other than eliminate the right of same-sex couples to marry in California. See FF 57, 62. Proposition 8 is not rationally related to an interest in protecting the rights of those opposed to same-sex couples because, as a matter of law, Proposition 8 does not affect the rights of those opposed to homosexuality or to marriage for couples of the same sex. FF 62.

Proponents argue that Proposition 8 advances a state interest in treating same-sex couples differently from opposite-sex couples by: (1) "[u]sing different names for different things"; (2) "[m]aintaining the flexibility to separately address the needs of different types of relationships"; (3) "[e]nsuring that California marriages are recognized in other jurisdictions"; and (4) "[c]onforming California's definition of marriage to federal law." Doc #605 at 14. Here, proponents assume a premise that the evidence thoroughly rebutted: rather than being different, same-sex and opposite-sex unions are, for all purposes relevant to California law, exactly the same. FF 47–50. The evidence shows conclusively that moral and religious views form the only basis for a belief that same-sex couples are different from opposite-sex couples. See FF 48, 76–80. The evidence fatally undermines any purported state interest in treating couples differently; thus, these interests do not provide a rational basis supporting Proposition 8. In addition, proponents appear to claim that Proposition 8 advances a state interest in easing administrative burdens associated with issuing and recognizing marriage licenses. Under precedents such as *Craig v. Boren,* "administrative ease and convenience" are not important government objectives. 429 U.S. 190, 198, 97 S.Ct. 451, 50 L.Ed.2d 397 (1976). Even assuming the state were to have an interest in administrative convenience, Proposition 8 actually creates an administrative burden on California because California must maintain a parallel institution for same-sex couples to provide the equivalent rights and benefits afforded to married couples.

Finally, proponents assert that Proposition 8 advances "[a]ny other conceivable legitimate interests identified by the parties, amici, or the court at any stage of the proceedings." Doc #605 at 15. But proponents, amici and the court, despite ample opportunity and a full trial, have failed to identify any rational basis Proposition 8 could conceivably advance. Proponents, represented by able and energetic counsel, developed a full trial record in support of Proposition 8. The resulting evidence shows that

Proposition 8 simply conflicts with the guarantees of the Fourteenth Amendment.

In the absence of a rational basis, what remains of proponents' case is an inference, amply supported by evidence in the record, that Proposition 8 was premised on the belief that same-sex couples simply are not as good as opposite-sex couples. FF 78–80. Whether that belief is based on moral disapproval of homosexuality, animus towards gays and lesbians or simply a belief that a relationship between a man and a woman is inherently better than a relationship between two men or two women, this belief is not a proper basis on which to legislate. *See Romer,* 517 U.S. at 633; *Moreno,* 413 U.S. at 534; *Palmore v. Sidoti,* 466 U.S. 429, 433, 104 S.Ct. 1879, 80 L.Ed.2d 421 (1984) ("[T]he Constitution cannot control [private biases] but neither can it tolerate them.").

The evidence shows that Proposition 8 was a hard-fought campaign and that the majority of California voters supported the initiative. See Background to Proposition 8 above, FF 17–18, 79–80. The arguments surrounding Proposition 8 raise a question similar to that addressed in *Lawrence,* when the Court asked whether a majority of citizens could use the power of the state to enforce "profound and deep convictions accepted as ethical and moral principles" through the criminal code. 539 U.S. at 571. The question here is whether California voters can enforce those same principles through regulation of marriage licenses. They cannot. California's obligation is to treat its citizens equally, not to "mandate [its] own moral code." *Id. (citing Planned Parenthood of Southeastern Pa. v. Casey,* 505 U.S. 833, 850, 112 S.Ct. 2791, 120 L.Ed.2d 674, (1992)). "[M]oral disapproval, without any other asserted state interest," has never been a rational basis for legislation. *Lawrence,* 539 U.S. at 582 (O'Connor, J, concurring). Tradition alone cannot support legislation. *See Williams,* 399 U.S. at 239; *Romer,* 517 U.S. at 635; *Lawrence,* 539 U.S. at 579.

Proponents' purported rationales are nothing more than post-hoc justifications. While the Equal Protection Clause does not prohibit post-hoc rationales, they must connect to the classification drawn. Here, the purported state interests fit so poorly with Proposition 8 that they are irrational, as explained above. What is left is evidence that Proposition 8 enacts a moral view that there is something "wrong" with same-sex couples. See FF 78–80.

The evidence at trial regarding the campaign to pass Proposition 8 uncloaks the most likely explanation for its passage: a desire to advance the belief that opposite-sex couples are morally superior to same-sex couples. FF 79–80. The campaign relied heavily on negative stereotypes about gays and lesbians and focused on protecting children from inchoate threats vaguely associated with gays and lesbians. FF 79–80; See PX0016 Video, *Have You Thought About It?* (video of a young girl asking whether the viewer has considered the consequences to her of Proposition 8 but not explaining what those consequences might be).

At trial, proponents' counsel attempted through cross-examination to show that the campaign wanted to protect children from learning about same-sex marriage in school. See PX0390A Video, Ron Prentice Addressing Supporters of Proposition 8, Excerpt; Tr 132:25–133:3 (proponents' counsel to Katami: "But the fact is that what the Yes on 8 campaign was pointing at, is that kids would be taught about same-sex relationships in first and second grade; isn't that a fact, that that's what they were referring to?"). The evidence shows, however, that Proposition 8 played on a fear that exposure to homosexuality would turn children into homosexuals and that parents should dread having children who are not heterosexual. FF 79; PX0099 Video, *It's Already Happened* (mother's expression of horror upon realizing her daughter now knows she can marry a princess).

The evidence at trial shows those fears to be completely unfounded. FF 47–49, 68–73, 76–80. Because Proposition 8 disadvantages gays and lesbians without any rational justification, Proposition 8 violates the Equal Protection Clause of the Fourteenth Amendment.

REMEDIES

Because Proposition 8 is unconstitutional under both the Due Process and Equal Protection Clauses, the court orders entry of judgment permanently enjoining its enforcement; prohibiting the official defendants from applying or enforcing Proposition 8 and directing the official defendants that all persons under their control or supervision shall not apply or enforce Proposition 8.

. . .

NOTE

As the opinion above indicates, on August 4, 2010, Judge Walker ruled that Proposition 8 was unconstitutional. Two groups that had intervened as defendants, ProtectMarriage.com and the Campaign for California Families, tried the case (then Attorney General Jerry Brown and Governor Arnold Schwarzenegger chose not to defend the lawsuit). On August 16, 2010, the judgment was stayed, pending appeal, to the Ninth Circuit Court of Appeals. On January 4, 2011, the Ninth Circuit certified a question to the California Supreme Court, specifically asking if the defendant-intervenors had a "particularized interest in the initiative's validity" such that they should be permitted to defend the lawsuit, when state officials had refused to do so. The California Supreme Court agreed to consider the matter, and heard arguments on the issue in September 2011.

IX. MARRIAGE—MOST RECENT DEVELOPMENTS

In June 2009, the governor of New Hampshire signed a law opening marriage to same-sex couples in that state as well. Same sex marriages began in New Hampshire on January 1, 2010. In December 2009, the

Council of the District of Columbia approved a same-sex marriage bill, and it was signed days later by the mayor. Same-sex marriage is now permitted in Washington, D.C. as of March 3, 2010. On June 24, 2011, a same-sex marriage law was passed in New York, in an instant more than doubling the number of Americans living in states covered by same-sex marriage laws. New York became the sixth state to legalize gay marriage.

Steps short of full marriage equality have been taken in several jurisdictions. The state of Washington expanded its Domestic Partnership Law, purportedly to extend all the rights and responsibilities of marriage (but not the name) to same-sex couples who register as domestic partners under state law. Colorado has enacted a Designated Beneficiary Agreement Act, which took effect July 1, 2009. The law provides a limited set of rights to unmarried Coloradans (both same-sex and opposite-sex) who designate each other as beneficiaries.

Many of these legislative victories were hard-won, but elsewhere there were setbacks. For example, in May 2009, the Maine legislature enacted and the governor signed a bill legalizing same-sex marriage in that state. However, before same-sex marriage began in Maine, the law was repealed by a People's Veto referendum on November 3, 2009. And General Assemblies in states such as Maryland have debated the issue with no success. In addition, Florida voters passed an anti-marriage amendment on the November '08 ballot in their state. Twenty-nine states (Alabama, Alaska, Arizona, Arkansas, California, Colorado, Florida, Georgia, Idaho, Kansas, Kentucky, Louisiana, Michigan, Mississippi, Missouri, Montana, Nebraska, Nevada, North Dakota, Ohio, Oklahoma, Oregon, South Carolina, South Dakota, Tennessee, Texas, Utah, Virginia and Wisconsin) currently have constitutional amendments specifically defining marriage as a union between a man and a woman. Hawaii's state constitutional amendment has the same effect, although it does not technically define marriage, reading instead that the Hawaii legislature has "the power to reserve marriage to opposite-sex couples." Thirty-seven states have legislation banning same-sex marriage: Alabama, Alaska, Arizona, Arkansas, Colorado, Delaware, Florida, Georgia, Hawaii, Idaho, Illinois, Indiana, Kansas, Kentucky, Louisiana, Maine, Maryland, Michigan, Minnesota, Mississippi, Missouri, Montana, North Carolina, North Dakota, Ohio, Oklahoma, Pennsylvania, South Carolina, South Dakota, Tennessee, Texas, Utah, Virginia, Washington, West Virginia, Wisconsin and Wyoming.

Recent gay rights victories on the partnership front have made the question of interstate recognition of same-sex relationships more pressing and complicated. The attorney general of Rhode Island opined that same-sex marriages would be recognized as valid for purposes of state benefits. The New Jersey attorney general opined that same-sex relationships that are the legal equivalent of New Jersey's civil union would be recognized as a civil union in that state. In October 2009, California recognized out-of-state same-sex marriages, and in a February 2010 opinion, the Attorney General of Maryland required the state to recognize out-of-state same-sex marriages.

Ten other nations now recognize gay marriage: The Netherlands (2000), Belgium (2003), Canada (2005), Spain (2005), South Africa (2006), Norway (2008), Sweden (2009), Portugal (2010) Iceland (2010) and Argentina (2010). Other nations, including Australia, Austria, Brazil, Columbia, Croatia, Denmark, Finland, France, Germany, Greenland, Hungary, Ireland, Israel, Luxembourg, New Zealand, Switzerland and the United Kingdom provide varying degrees of legal recognition for same-sex couples, including partnership registration, civil unions, and common law marriage status.

Thirty-five million Americans now live in states where same-sex couples can marry. Several national polls conducted between 2009–2011 show that a growing majority (52%) of Americans now support the right of same-sex couples to marry.

X. DOMA UPDATE

In two DOMA related cases, *Gill et al. v. Office of Personnel Management*, 699 F.Supp.2d 374 (D.Mass. 2010, appeal pending) and *Commonwealth of Massachusetts v. United States Department of Health and Human Services* 698 F.Supp.2d 234 (D.Mass. 2010, appeal pending), a federal judge found Section 3 of DOMA (which defines marriage for federal purposes as only between a man and a woman) unconstitutional.

Late in 2010, two more lawsuits challenging DOMA were filed. *Pedersen v. OPM* was filed in the United States District Court for the District of Connecticut and *Windsor v. United States* was filed in the United States District Court for the Southern District of New York. These lawsuits also challenged Section 3 of DOMA. After these lawsuits were filed, the Attorney General of the United States sent the following letter to House Speaker John Boehner on behalf of President Barack Obama (This letter is reprinted from the Attorney General's Office pursuant to the Freedom of Information Act).

The Honorable John A. Boehner
Speaker
U.S. House of Representatives
Washington, DC 20515

Re: Defense of Marriage Act

Dear Mr. Speaker:

After careful consideration, including review of a recommendation from me, the President of the United States has made the determination that Section 3 of the Defense of Marriage Act ("DOMA"), 1 U.S.C. § 7,[1] as applied to same-sex couples who are legally married under state law,

1. DOMA Section 3 states: "In determining the meaning of any Act of Congress, or of any ruling, regulation, or interpretation of the various administrative bureaus and agencies of the United States, the word 'marriage' means only a legal union between one man and one woman as husband and wife, and the word 'spouse' refers only to a person of the opposite sex who is a husband or a wife."

violates the equal protection component of the Fifth Amendment. Pursuant to 28 U.S.C. § 530D, I am writing to advise you of the Executive Branch's determination and to inform you of the steps the Department will take in two pending DOMA cases to implement that determination.

While the Department has previously defended DOMA against legal challenges involving legally married same-sex couples, recent lawsuits that challenge the constitutionality of DOMA Section 3 have caused the President and the Department to conduct a new examination of the defense of this provision. In particular, in November 2010, plaintiffs filed two new lawsuits challenging the constitutionality of Section 3 of DOMA in jurisdictions without precedent on whether sexual-orientation classifications are subject to rational basis review or whether they must satisfy some form of heightened scrutiny. *Windsor v. United States*, No. 1:10–cv–8435 (S.D.N.Y.); *Pedersen v. OPM*, No. 3:10–cv–1750 (D. Conn.). Previously, the Administration has defended Section 3 in jurisdictions where circuit courts have already held that classifications based on sexual orientation are subject to rational basis review, and it has advanced arguments to defend DOMA Section 3 under the binding standard that has applied in those cases.[2]

These new lawsuits, by contrast, will require the Department to take an affirmative position on the level of scrutiny that should be applied to DOMA Section 3 in a circuit without binding precedent on the issue. As described more fully below, the President and I have concluded that classifications based on sexual orientation warrant heightened scrutiny and that, as applied to same-sex couples legally married under state law, Section 3 of DOMA is unconstitutional.

Standard of Review

The Supreme Court has yet to rule on the appropriate level of scrutiny for classifications based on sexual orientation. It has, however, rendered a number of decisions that set forth the criteria that should inform this and any other judgment as to whether heightened scrutiny applies: (1) whether the group in question has suffered a history of discrimination; (2) whether individuals "exhibit obvious, immutable, or distinguishing characteristics that define them as a discrete group"; (3) whether the group is a minority or is politically powerless; and (4) whether the characteristics distinguishing the group have little relation to legitimate policy objectives or to an individual's "ability to perform or contribute to society." *See Bowen v. Gilliard*, 483 U.S. 587, 602–03 (1987); *City of Cleburne v. Cleburne Living Ctr.*, 473 U.S. 432, 441–42 (1985).

Each of these factors counsels in favor of being suspicious of classifications based on sexual orientation. First and most importantly, there is, regrettably, a significant history of purposeful discrimination against gay

---

2. *See, e.g., Dragovich v. U.S. Department of the Treasury*, 2011 WL 175502 (N.D. Cal. Jan. 18, 2011); *Gill v. Office of Personnel Management*, 699 F. Supp. 2d 374 (D. Mass. 2010); *Smelt v. County of Orange*, 374 F. Supp. 2d 861, 880 (C.D. Cal.,2005); *Wilson v. Ake*, 354 F.Supp.2d 1298, 1308 (M.D. Fla. 2005); *In re Kandu*, 315 B.R. 123, 145 (Bkrtcy. W.D. Wash. 2004); *In re Levenson*, 587 F.3d 925, 931 (9th Cir. E.D.R. Plan Administrative Ruling 2009).

and lesbian people, by governmental as well as private entities, based on prejudice and stereotypes that continue to have ramifications today. Indeed, until very recently, states have "demean[ed] the[] existence" of gays and lesbians "by making their private sexual conduct a crime." *Lawrence v. Texas*, 539 U.S. 558, 578 (2003).[3]

Second, while sexual orientation carries no visible badge, a growing scientific consensus accepts that sexual orientation is a characteristic that is immutable, *see* Richard A. Posner, Sex and Reason 101 (1992); it is undoubtedly unfair to require sexual orientation to be hidden from view to avoid discrimination, *see* Don't Ask, Don't Tell Repeal Act of 2010, Pub. L. No. 111–321, 124 Stat. 3515 (2010).

Third, the adoption of laws like those at issue in *Romer v. Evans,* 517 U.S. 620 (1996), and *Lawrence*, the longstanding ban on gays and lesbians in the military, and the absence of federal protection for employment discrimination on the basis of sexual orientation show the group to have limited political power and "ability to attract the [favorable] attention of the lawmakers." *Cleburne*, 473 U.S. at 445. And while the enactment of the Matthew Shepard Act and pending repeal of Don't Ask, Don't Tell indicate that the political process is not closed *entirely* to gay and lesbian people, that is not the standard by which the Court has judged "political powerlessness." Indeed, when the Court ruled that gender-based classifications were subject to heightened scrutiny, women already had won major political victories such as the Nineteenth Amendment (right to vote) and protection under Title VII (employment discrimination).

Finally, there is a growing acknowledgment that sexual orientation "bears no relation to ability to perform or contribute to society." *Frontiero v. Richardson*, 411 U.S. 677, 686 (1973) (plurality). Recent evolutions in legislation (including the pending repeal of Don't Ask, Don't Tell), in community practices and attitudes, in case law (including the Supreme Court's holdings in *Lawrence* and *Romer*), and in social science regarding sexual orientation all make clear that sexual orientation is not a characteristic that generally bears on legitimate policy objectives. *See, e.g.,* Statement by the President on the Don't Ask, Don't Tell Repeal Act of 2010 ("It is time to recognize that sacrifice, valor and integrity are no

---

3. While significant, that history of discrimination is different in some respects from the discrimination that burdened African–Americans and women. *See Adarand Constructors, Inc. v. Pena*, 515 U.S. 200, 216 (1995) (classifications based on race "must be viewed in light of the historical fact that the central purpose of the Fourteenth Amendment was to eliminate racial discrimination emanating from official sources in the States," and "[t]his strong policy renders racial classifications 'constitutionally suspect.' "); *United States v. Virginia*, 518 U.S. 515, 531 (1996) (observing that " 'our Nation has had a long and unfortunate history of sex discrimination' " and pointing out the denial of the right to vote to women until 1920). In the case of sexual orientation, some of the discrimination has been based on the incorrect belief that sexual orientation is a behavioral characteristic that can be changed or subject to moral approbation. *Cf. Cleburne*, 473 U.S. at 441 (heightened scrutiny may be warranted for characteristics "beyond the individual's control" and that "very likely reflect outmoded notions of the relative capabilities of" the group at issue); *Boy Scouts of America v. Dale*, 530 U.S. 640 (2000) (Stevens, J., dissenting) ("Unfavorable opinions about homosexuals 'have ancient roots.' " (quoting *Bowers*, 478 U.S. at 192)).

more defined by sexual orientation than they are by race or gender, religion or creed.")

To be sure, there is substantial circuit court authority applying rational basis review to sexual-orientation classifications. We have carefully examined each of those decisions. Many of them reason only that if consensual same-sex sodomy may be criminalized under *Bowers v. Hardwick*, then it follows that no heightened review is appropriate–a line of reasoning that does not survive the overruling of *Bowers* in *Lawrence v. Texas*, 538 U.S. 558 (2003).[4] Others rely on claims regarding "procreational responsibility" that the Department has disavowed already in litigation as unreasonable, or claims regarding the immutability of sexual orientation that we do not believe can be reconciled with more recent social science understandings.[5] And none engages in an examination of all the factors that the Supreme Court has identified as relevant to a decision about the appropriate level of scrutiny. Finally, many of the more recent decisions have relied on the fact that the Supreme Court has not recognized that gays and lesbians constitute a suspect class or the fact that the Court has applied rational basis review in its most recent decisions addressing classifications based on sexual orientation, *Lawrence* and *Romer*.[6] But neither of those decisions reached, let alone resolved, the level of scrutiny issue because in both the Court concluded that the laws could not even survive the more deferential rational basis standard.

Application to Section 3 of DOMA

In reviewing a legislative classification under heightened scrutiny, the government must establish that the classification is "substantially related to an important government objective." *Clark v. Jeter*, 486 U.S. 456, 461 (1988). Under heightened scrutiny, "a tenable justification must describe actual state purposes, not rationalizations for actions in fact differently grounded." *United States v. Virginia*, 518 U.S. 515, 535–36 (1996). "The justification must be genuine, not hypothesized or invented post hoc in response to litigation." *Id.* at 533.

In other words, under heightened scrutiny, the United States cannot defend Section 3 by advancing hypothetical rationales, independent of the

---

4. *See Equality Foundation v. City of Cincinnati*, 54 F.3d 261, 266–67 & n. 2. (6th Cir. 1995); *Steffan v. Perry*, 41 F.3d 677, 685 (D.C. Cir. 1994); *Woodward v. United States*, 871 F.2d 1068, 1076 (Fed. Cir. 1989); *Ben–Shalom v. Marsh*, 881 F.2d 454, 464 (7th Cir. 1989); *Padula v. Webster*, 822 F.2d 97, 103 (D.C. Cir. 1987).

5. *See, e.g., Lofton v. Secretary of the Dep't of Children & Family Servs.*, 358 F.3d 804, 818 (11th Cir. 2004) (discussing child-rearing rationale); High Tech Gays v. Defense Indust. Sec. Clearance Office, 895 F.2d 563, 571 (9th Cir. 1990) (discussing immutability). As noted, this Administration has already disavowed in litigation the argument that DOMA serves a governmental interest in "responsible procreation and child-rearing." H.R. Rep. No. 104–664, at 13. As the Department has explained in numerous filings, since the enactment of DOMA, many leading medical, psychological, and social welfare organizations have concluded, based on numerous studies, that children raised by gay and lesbian parents are as likely to be well-adjusted as children raised by heterosexual parents.

6. *See Cook v. Gates*, 528 F.3d 42, 61 (1st Cir. 2008); *Citizens for Equal Prot. v. Bruning*, 455 F.3d 859, 866 (8th Cir. 2006); *Johnson v. Johnson*, 385 F.3d 503, 532 (5th Cir. 2004); *Veney v. Wyche*, 293 F.3d 726, 732 (4th Cir. 2002); *Equality Foundation of Greater Cincinnati, Inc. v. City of Cincinnati*, 128 F.3d 289, 292–94 (6th Cir. 1997).

legislative record, as it has done in circuits where precedent mandates application of rational basis review. Instead, the United States can defend Section 3 only by invoking Congress' actual justifications for the law.

Moreover, the legislative record underlying DOMA's passage contains discussion and debate that undermines any defense under heightened scrutiny. The record contains numerous expressions reflecting moral disapproval of gays and lesbians and their intimate and family relationships–precisely the kind of stereotype-based thinking and animus the Equal Protection Clause is designed to guard against.[7] *See Cleburne*, 473 U.S. at 448 ("mere negative attitudes, or fear" are not permissible bases for discriminatory treatment); *see also Romer*, 517 U.S. at 635 (rejecting rationale that law was supported by "the liberties of landlords or employers who have personal or religious objections to homosexuality"); *Palmore v. Sidoti*, 466 U.S. 429, 433 (1984) ("Private biases may be outside the reach of the law, but the law cannot, directly or indirectly, give them effect.").

Application to Second Circuit Cases

After careful consideration, including a review of my recommendation, the President has concluded that given a number of factors, including a documented history of discrimination, classifications based on sexual orientation should be subject to a heightened standard of scrutiny. The President has also concluded that Section 3 of DOMA, as applied to legally married same-sex couples, fails to meet that standard and is therefore unconstitutional. Given that conclusion, the President has instructed the Department not to defend the statute in *Windsor* and *Pedersen*, now pending in the Southern District of New York and the District of Connecticut. I concur in this determination.

Notwithstanding this determination, the President has informed me that Section 3 will continue to be enforced by the Executive Branch. To that end, the President has instructed Executive agencies to continue to comply with Section 3 of DOMA, consistent with the Executive's obligation to take care that the laws be faithfully executed, unless and until Congress repeals Section 3 or the judicial branch renders a definitive verdict against the law's constitutionality. This course of action respects the actions of the prior Congress that enacted DOMA, and it recognizes the judiciary as the final arbiter of the constitutional claims raised.

---

7. *See, e.g.,* H.R. Rep. at 15–16 ("judgment [opposing same-sex marriage] entails both moral disapproval of homosexuality and a moral conviction that heterosexuality better comports with traditional (especially Judeo–Christian) morality"); *id.* at 16 (same-sex marriage "legitimates a public union, a legal status that most people ... feel ought to be illegitimate" and "put[s] a stamp of approval ... on a union that many people ... think is immoral"); *id.* at 15 ("Civil laws that permit only heterosexual marriage reflect and honor a collective moral judgment about human sexuality"); *id.* (reasons behind heterosexual marriage—procreation and child-rearing—are "in accord with nature and hence have a moral component"); *id.* at 31 (favorably citing the holding in *Bowers* that an "anti-sodomy law served the rational purpose of expressing the presumed belief ... that homosexual sodomy is immoral and unacceptable"); *id.* at 17 n.56 (favorably citing statement in dissenting opinion in *Romer* that "[t]his Court has no business ... pronouncing that 'animosity' toward homosexuality is evil").

As you know, the Department has a longstanding practice of defending the constitutionality of duly-enacted statutes if reasonable arguments can be made in their defense, a practice that accords the respect appropriately due to a coequal branch of government. However, the Department in the past has declined to defend statutes despite the availability of professionally responsible arguments, in part because the Department does not consider every plausible argument to be a "reasonable" one. "[D]ifferent cases can raise very different issues with respect to statutes of doubtful constitutional validity," and thus there are "a variety of factors that bear on whether the Department will defend the constitutionality of a statute." Letter to Hon. Orrin G. Hatch from Assistant Attorney General Andrew Fois at 7 (Mar. 22, 1996). This is the rare case where the proper course is to forgo the defense of this statute. Moreover, the Department has declined to defend a statute "in cases in which it is manifest that the President has concluded that the statute is unconstitutional," as is the case here. Seth P. Waxman, *Defending Congress*, 79 N.C. L.Rev. 1073, 1083 (2001).

In light of the foregoing, I will instruct the Department's lawyers to immediately inform the district courts in *Windsor* and *Pedersen* of the Executive Branch's view that heightened scrutiny is the appropriate standard of review and that, consistent with that standard, Section 3 of DOMA may not be constitutionally applied to same-sex couples whose marriages are legally recognized under state law. If asked by the district courts in the Second Circuit for the position of the United States in the event those courts determine that the applicable standard is rational basis, the Department will state that, consistent with the position it has taken in prior cases, a reasonable argument for Section 3's constitutionality may be proffered under that permissive standard. Our attorneys will also notify the courts of our interest in providing Congress a full and fair opportunity to participate in the litigation in those cases. We will remain parties to the case and continue to represent the interests of the United States throughout the litigation.

Furthermore, pursuant to the President's instructions, and upon further notification to Congress, I will instruct Department attorneys to advise courts in other pending DOMA litigation of the President's and my conclusions that a heightened standard should apply, that Section 3 is unconstitutional under that standard and that the Department will cease defense of Section 3.

A motion to dismiss in the *Windsor* and *Pedersen* cases would be due on March 11, 2011. Please do not hesitate to contact us if you have any questions.

Sincerely yours,

Eric H. Holder, Jr.
Attorney General

DISCUSSION

What is the effect of Attorney General Holder's letter? Is this an unusual course of action for the President to take?

NOTE

Property, inheritance, and tort law rights are affected by the advent of partnership and marriage laws that now include same-sex couples when these collide with DOMA. Consider the following questions:

1. The effect of state recognition of same-sex domestic partnership schemes (and marriage) on property rights in the interstate context is unclear. Suppose that same-sex domestic partners living in Hawaii purchase some personal property as tenants by the entirety. They then move, taking their property with them, to State X, which recognizes tenancy by the entirety in personalty but does not recognize the validity of a Hawaii "reciprocal beneficiary" partnership. The couple splits. Will State X's courts distribute the property as though it was held in a tenancy by the entirety?

2. What effect would DOMA have on your resolution of problem 1?

3. Further consider DOMA's effect on the following situation. Suppose that A and B, two partners of the same gender, marry in Massachusetts. Driver, a resident of Texas, who is visiting Massachusetts on vacation, strikes A and kills him. B, as surviving spouse, sues Driver in Massachusetts for wrongful death and wins a substantial money judgment. Driver flees to Texas. B pursues with his judgment. What result? Must the Texas court enforce the Massachusetts judgment? *See* Andrew Koppelman, *Dumb and DOMA: Why the Defense of Marriage Act is Unconstitutional*, 83 IOWA L. REV. 1 (1998).

4. Let us suppose further that the defendant Driver files a counterclaim for declaratory judgment and re-litigates the liability question in Texas's courts, which hold that no wrongful death suit lies because no marriage ever existed under Texas law. Can this happen?

5. Is DOMA's denial of Full Faith and Credit in the context of interstate portability of judgments constitutionally problematic?

6. A and B, a same-sex couple, lived together for 25 years. They entered a civil union in New Jersey. The couple resides in Virginia, which does not recognized civil unions or gay marriage. A is struck by a motorist, sustaining minor injuries and a broken leg, which required routine surgery. Because of complication resulting from the surgery, A dies. B sues the hospital where the surgery was performed, seeking damages for A's wrongful death. The hospital moves for summary judgment on the grounds that only a "spouse" can recover for wrongful death. Applying an equal protection analysis, how should the court rule? *See Langan v. St. Vincent's Hosp. of N.Y.*, 196 Misc.2d 440, 765 N.Y.S.2d 411 (2003), *rev'd by Langan v. St. Vincent's Hosp. of N.Y.*, 25 A.D.3d 90, 802 N.Y.S.2d 476, 2005 N.Y. Slip Op. 07495 (N.Y.A.D. 2005). The appellate decision gives an alternative equal protection analysis.

CHAPTER 10

TREATMENT OF TRANSGENDER AND INTERSEXUAL PEOPLE

■ ■ ■

The cases and materials in this section deal with the legal treatment of "transgender" individuals. There is recurring criticism of the inclusion of transgender people in the fight for gay rights. Transgender people do not usually identify as gay or lesbian. Rather, they feel that their psychological gender does not comport with their physiological gender. Nevertheless, transgender rights have been included within the greater gay rights struggle. Professor Taylor Flynn asserts that "[t]ransgender" is an umbrella term that, in fact, includes gay men, lesbians, and bisexuals within its scope: "It applies to persons whose appearance, behavior, or other personal characteristics differ from traditional gender norms."[1] Indeed, we have seen the roles gender norms play in the treatment of gay youth and, perhaps most powerfully, in the employment discrimination arena. Many gay rights organizations have refused to endorse employment nondiscrimination legislation that does not include protection for transgender people.

While there is still a paucity of case law concerning transgender individuals, the following materials give a view of the socio-legal status of transgender Americans.

I. LEGAL EVOLUTION*

. . .

Dicta from an 1845 South Carolina bigamy decision indicates that the state would not allow a hermaphrodite to marry *at all,* implying that such persons were incapable of being the opposite sex of either males or females.

. . .

1. Taylor Flynn, *Transforming the Debate: Why We Need to Include Transgender Rights in the Struggles for Sex and Sexual Orientation Equality*, 101 COLUM. L. REV. 392 (2001).

* Reprinted from Katrina C. Rose, *A History of Gender Variance in Pre-20th Century Anglo-American Law*, 14 TEX. J. WOMEN & L. 77 (2004–2005) (original headings and subheadings have been modified and/or removed for our format).

However, the early English law treatise, *Bracton* from the mid-Thirteenth century, addressed the status of hermaphrodites in one passage appearing to totally set them apart from non-hermaphrodites, but in the other bringing them back into the gender-binary. After a passage including language indicating that a "monster" could not be classified as a person's child, the treatise provides: "Mankind may also be classified in another way: male, female *or hermaphrodite.* Women differ from men in many respects, for their position is inferior to that of men."

The following passage, however, lessens the permanency of the otherness of hermaphrodites by noting: "A hermaphrodite is classed with male or female according to the predominance of the sexual organs." Significantly, the word did not disappear after the thirteenth century.

Sir Edward Coke addressed the topic in the first of his *Institutes,* which was his commentaries on the *post–Bracton* treatise, *Littleton.* J.H. Baker observes that Coke

> delighted in wandering off at tangents, and in doing so covered many aspects of the common law which Littleton's text never hinted at. Coke seems to have been oblivious to the disorder, but the reader can easily forgive him. He wrote like a helpful old wizard, anxious to pass on all his secrets before he died, but not quite sure where to begin or end. The comment on the first section of Littleton provides a typical foretaste. The text itself is a definition of "fee simple"; but the commentary wanders through such disparate topics as etymology, alien status, misnomer in grants, interest rates and usury, the precedence of earth over the other elements, the correct Latin words for ponds, marshes, rushes, willows, elders, and boileries of salt, the Domesday Book, the eight parts of a deed, the styles and titles of the kings of England, the ownership of the Isle of Man, and *the legal status of monsters and hermaphrodites.*

Although perhaps a tangent to the early English *Littleton's* thoughts on fee simple, Coke's thoughts on hermaphrodites (as well as monsters) reflect Bracton—though at least in one passage with the air of an afterthought: "And note that an hermaphrodite may purchase land according to that sex which prevails." Later, one can find: "Every heir is either a male, or female, or an hermaphrodite, that is both male and female. And an hermaphrodite (which is also called *Androgynus)* shall be heir, either male or female, according to that kind of sex which prevails." Nothing specifically is said about "sexual organs."

This passage from Coke was referenced in a section of an early post-Revolution legal manual: "A bastard is excluded from being heir; and a monster without human shape cannot be heir to a person; but an hermaphrodite, if there be any such, may take lands, etc. as heir according to that sex which is most prevalent."

Interestingly, it is the existence of hermaphrodites, not monsters, which appears to have been questioned. Medical treatises of the day, however, indicate that hermaphroditism among humans was indeed known. Some dictionary definitions clearly indicate that the concept in humans was understood, though others speak in more general terms of "an animal uniting two sexes." Dreger's primarily nineteenth-century study notes approximately 300 case studies (involving around 200 persons) on hermaphrodites in France and the United Kingdom from 1860–1915.

TODAY

Somewhat strangely, the current version of *Black's Law Dictionary* contains definitions for "sex reassignment" and "transsexual" but not for "intersex" or "hermaphrodite" (and, despite copious amounts of arcane Latin terminology, not even *hermaphrodita).*

But the inclusion of hermaphrodites in the formation of the common law is not forgotten.

As recently as 2003, in the American sex declaration case *In re Heilig*,[1] attorneys representing a male-to-female transsexual reached back beyond Coke to *Bracton* in order to reach back *even further* to construct the argument that the law, even prior to *Bracton,* was cognizant *and accommodating* of "what we now call transgendered individuals, then described as hermaphrodites." Notably, a part of this argument was the setting forth of the emerging realization that transsexualism is *not* something *apart* from what was in Bracton's time (and even Coke's and on forward) called hermaphroditism but, in reality, a *subset of* what is now known as intersexuality. Specifically cited was ancient Jewish law, the Mishnas, which provided that "one of doubtful sex" was "at times a man and at times a woman" and further provided specific penalties for maltreatment of such persons. Together with an observation from Plucknett's Concise History of the common law:

> However remote the date at which we start, it will always be necessary to admit that much of the still remoter past that lies behind [the Common Law of England] will have to be considered as directly bearing upon the later history.... But behind the Roman system were others still more ancient—Greek, Semetic ...
>
> . . .
>
> For purposes of this concise history we can begin with the advent of Christianity. Itself, the culmination of several centuries of religious and ethical thinking in Judaea....

Despite the invitation to go deep into the history of the common law, the Maryland Court of Appeals confined itself in *Heilig* to the narrow question of whether the state's courts, irrespective of the state having a statute that specifically allows *Maryland-born* transsexuals to conform their Maryland birth certificates to post-gender-transition reality have jurisdiction to declare a change of legal gender for transsexual residents of Maryland who may have been born *elsewhere.*

1. 816 A.2d 68 (Md. 2003).

In a unanimous opinion, which stands as part of a triumvirate of groundbreaking, modern-thinking, pro-recognition decisions issued on both sides of the globe during a ten-day period in early 2003, the court decided in favor of such jurisdiction and offered an extensive look at the medical issues inherent in transsexualism as well as an extensive look at American transsexual birth certificate statutes but did not cite the extensive legal history included in the party's brief. Still, not surprisingly, *Heilig,* along with the background that it contains, has been totally ignored by [some] American appellate courts that have issued antirecognition decisions since.

THREE HISTORICAL CASES

A. THE *HALL* CASE OF 1629

Of the three cases that I look at in depth, somewhat strangely the oldest is from North America. It involves the General Court of the Colony of Virginia's 1629 attempt to ascertain and declare the sex of a person alternately known as Thomas Hall or Thomasine Hall (or, as referred to in portions of the analysis of the case by Mary Beth Norton, simply T. Hall or T). A marriage was not at issue, although there were questions about relationships that Hall had while in Virginia. Apart from the outcome—a declaration that Hall was "a man *and* a woeman," a conclusion seemingly unique in Anglo–American law outside of one 1979 Australian decision, and in opposition to *Bracton* and Coke—the case is also unusual in that, contrary to almost all modern transsexual and intersex cases where transsexual or intersexed persons have, at the time of litigation, a consistent gender presentation (though perhaps simply different than presupposed by the sex designation at birth), the surviving documents related to the case indicate that Hall apparently had a habit of going back and forth between a male identity and a female identity. Norton theorizes that part of Hall's willingness to adopt a male identity on occasion was for its advantages of autonomy—particularly travel.

The General Court's record of the matter is available in a volume of the records from the era which survived the burning of the state court building during the closing days of the Civil War in April 1865. Here, however, for purposes of language simplicity, I summarize the case history via citations to the work of Mary Beth Norton, whose look at the case in her 1996 book, *Founding Mothers & Fathers,* has been the most extensive of the few analyses of it.

Hall was born in England in the vicinity of Newcastle–Upon–Tyne and, at birth, was christened Thomasine Hall. At the age of twelve, she moved to London to stay with her aunt. In 1625, her brother entered the army and served in an expedition against Cadiz. At some point shortly thereafter, Hall adopted a male identity and also entered the military, serving in France and, upon returning, settled in Plymouth. There, however, Hall resumed a female identity, though remaining in it only for a short time. Upon learning of a ship about to leave for Virginia, Hall reverted to a male identity to make the journey to the Chesapeake as an indentured servant. By January 21, 1628, Hall appears to have been in Virginia and possibly convicted of receiving stolen property, though Norton acknowledges that the records are not clear as to whether the Thomas Hall who was convicted in that instance was the gender-ambiguous Hall.

Whatever involvement Hall may have had in that court proceeding, it is clear that at some point after getting to Virginia, Hall adopted a *female* identity, though ultimately questions arose among those with whom she associated as to her sex (and Norton points out that exactly why these questions began to be asked is unclear). Hall was examined by three women as well as by John Tyos, to whom Hall was then indentured, who disagreed as to whether Hall was male or female, the former saying male and the latter female. During this encounter, Hall refused to choose male or female for an identity, but Capt. Nathaniel Basse, the commander for the region, chose female. This did not quell the questions, and subsequent examinations were conducted by between three and five women, once "covertly" while Hall was asleep—and their conclusion was that Hall was male. Hall's new master, John Atkins, ordered Hall to dress according to *that* determination.

As Norton notes, "By this time not only Hall but also everyone else was undoubtedly confused." After a subsequent forcible examination by Roger Rodes, a final resolution was sought from the General Court, which took testimony from Hall and considered depositions from two male witnesses. "Remarkably, the court accepted T's own self-definition and, although using the male personal pronoun, declared that Hall was 'a man and a woman, that all the inhabitants there may take notice thereof and that hee shall goe clothed in man's apparel, only his head to be attired in a Coyfe and Crosecloth with an apron before him.' "

. . .

Taking into account all of the known aspects of Hall's life, Norton concludes that the concept of sex in seventeenth century Virginia was far removed from the arbitrary standards that have been adopted in various modern forums.

> [F]or these colonists, sex had two possible determinants. One was physical: the nature of one's genitalia. The other was cultural: the character of one's knowledge and one's manner of behaving.
>
> Hall acted like a woman and physically resembled a man. Thus in T's case the results of the two independent criteria clashed, and that was the source of the confusion.

Additionally, she surmises that, beyond anything that may have been regarded as sex and/or gender transgressions or rebelliousness by Hall, the dual-gender outcome represented a rebellion of sorts by the women of the colony who refused to accept the philosophy that women were simply sexually inferior men, a philosophy that apparently was the root of the earlier determinations that Hall was female.

. . .

B. *HUNT V. POULTER*

[T]he case that actually involves a marriage is from 1680. Patricia Crawford and Sara Mendelson refer to it as a marriage between two women: Arabella Hunt and Amy Poulter. However, Poulter had adopted a male identity by the time of the marriage, going by the name of James Howard. Consequently, the situation could well be analogous to relationships from other eras involving "passing women," some of whom, had they lived in modern times, might have identified as transsexual or transgendered, though others might have identified as lesbian. The court action in which the legal sex question became an issue was one for annulment by Hunt, brought in the London Consistory Court, though, as Crawford and Mendelson point out, the case "turned on two inherently contradictory legal issues: bigamy and nullity."

Additionally, some question existed as to whether Poulter/Howard, who had been married to a man, was a hermaphrodite—or, as per the unique phraseology of the case, "of a double gender." Moreover, Crawford and Mendelson acknowledge that the documents are susceptible to at least two readings—one indeed of a lesbian relationship but another in which Amy "deceived" Arabella, with deception being a common derogatory description even of modern relationships involving transsexuals, particularly those in which the relationship comes to light after the transsexual is murdered.

The marriage ceremony took place on September 12, 1680, in the London parish church of St. Mary Le Bone.

> Dressed as a man, Amy Poulter signed the marriage register "James Howard," a name she had been using for several months for her masculine persona. The church ceremony was witnessed by Elizabeth Hunt, Arabella's widowed mother, and at least two of Mrs. Hunt's friends, Sarah Cunningham and Phoebe Horton. Afterwards, the wedding party went to Kensall Green, where the bride and groom submitted to the usual nuptial ritual of being put into bed together. For the next six months, Arabella and Amy cohabited as "man and wife" in Elizabeth Hunt's London house in the Haymarket.

Crawford and Mendelson surmise that this relationship would have never come to light had Arabella not filed a suit for annulment in the London Consistory Court.

> As plaintiff, Arabella Hunt presented her case to the Consistory Court in the form of a Libel, or written allegation composed of numbered statements. She also exhibited affidavits and produced witnesses who testified before the Court in June, 1682, to support statements contained in the Libel. In examining the truth of Arabella's claims, the Court interrogated Amy Poulter, who supplied Personal Answers in response to the numbered statements of the plaintiff's Libel.
>
> The prosecution's key argument was the assertion that Amy Poulter had already been legally married, with a husband still living, when

> Amy went through a form of marriage with Arabella Hunt in 1680. The Libel also claimed that Amy had represented herself to be a man named James Howard, having dressed sometimes as a man and sometimes as a woman. Finally, Arabella intimated in the fifth article of the Libel that Amy was "of a double gender" or an hermaphrodite.
>
> In her Personal Answers, recorded and signed on 15 July 1682, Amy Poulter acknowledged that she had been legally married to Arthur Poulter in 1672, and had been collecting a jointure of £300 per annum settled on her by the Poulter family ever since Arthur's death in January, 1681. Amy confessed she had courted Arabella Hunt while dressed sometimes in men's and sometimes in women's apparel. She also admitted she had gone through a marriage ceremony with Arabella while Arthur was still alive. Amy told court officials, however, that both the courtship and marriage to Arabella had been a mere frolicsome prank; consequently she agreed that the marriage ought to be annulled. Amy denied the "slanderous" insinuation that she was an hermaphrodite, professing herself [to be] a "perfect woman."

Like the Hall case, there was an examination of the person whose sexual status was disputed.

Unlike the initial informal and impromptu examinations which took place in *Hall*, a jury of five midwives was ordered to examine Poulter. The midwives

> made a careful inspection disquisition and examination into the body, privities, and other parts of . . . Amy Poulter on the one and twentieth day of November 1682 and do hereby certify and report upon the oath by us severally taken, that in our best judgement, skill and knowledge . . . Amy Poulter is a perfect woman in all her parts, by us inspected, and that she doth not at all partake either inwardly or outwardly of the masculine sex.

On December 16, 1682, the court declared the marriage to be null and void—and that each was free to marry again, though only to men. Crawford and Mendelson note that, although she never married, Hunt lived for twenty years after the case. She became a famous lutenist and soprano at the court of Queen Mary II. Poulter/Howard, however, died shortly after the conclusion of the case, with records indicating that she was buried only five weeks after the decision.

. . .

Exactly how many cases similar to *Hunt v. Poulter* transpired in England is unclear, though Crawford and Mendelson mention that of Mary Hamilton, who, in 1746, was "severely punished" under vagrancy laws for marrying another woman. Rudolf Dekker and Lotte van de Pol, in a study of 119 cases of women who lived as men during the seventeenth and eighteenth centuries in the Netherlands, noted that "a far from exhaustive investigation into the literature resulted in fifty authentic cases of female transvestism" in Great Britain during that time, a period encompassing *Hunt v. Poulter*. Notably, one of the Dutch cases they highlight, that of Maria van Antwerpen, they list in the category of transsexualism, not merely transvestism or even hermaphroditism/ intersexuality.

C. *THE QUEEN V. BOULTON* AND OTHERS

Of the three cases, arguably the most extensively examined to date has been the Boulton and Park matter from 1870–71, which began with a charge essentially based solely on cross-dressing but developed into a prosecution for conspiracy to commit buggery. Of course, even with having been written about extensively, it has not achieved the notoriety of [Oscar] Wilde's trials, which occurred a quarter-century later.

Ernest Boulton was the son of a London stockbroker and Frederick Park was the son of a superior court officer, and the major case in which they were involved played out in the English courts, but had a connection to America, albeit an indirect one. The appointment of John Safford Fiske as American consul to Scotland in 1867 began the series of events which led to the pair (and two others in addition to Fiske) being tried for conspiracy to commit buggery in 1871. Boulton and Park met Fiske on a trip to Edinburgh. As Jonathan Katz describes the result: "Fiske became enamored of the British Boulton, and when Boulton returned to London, fascinated Fiske attempted to sustain the romance by mail. Fiske's letters proved fateful for all concerned." Katz's analysis delves more into the language utilized in the surviving correspondence, concluding that the "distinctive, still secret, subcultural mode of speech now known as 'camp' " was developing among a group of men in England and, more specifically, was already using a particular now well-known term, "drag," to refer to men dressing as women.

One reason that transgender terminology had occasion to appear in these letters was that Boulton and Park had somewhat well-known femme personas, Boulton being known as Lady Stella Clinton (the title and surname not being frivolous camp but, rather, derived from Boulton's companion—not Park, but Lord Arthur Clinton, a member of Parliament), and Park as Fanny Winifred. On April 28, 1870, the cross-dressed Boulton and Park were, as they were leaving the Strand Theatre, arrested on charges of outraging public decency. Per William Cohen's rather straightforward summary:

> The police had been trailing the two drag debutantes for the preceding year, from their legitimate appearances playing women's parts in amateur theatrical performances to their frequent cross-dressed promenades through public markets and arcades, restaurants, public houses, balls, and theaters. After being arrested for appearing publicly in women's attire, they were taken into the police station at Bow Street where they were detained overnight. They might have been routinely charged and dismissed the next morning with little commotion, as they had been before, had it not happened that the police

superintendent ran across a friend of his, the divisional police surgeon, in the street the next morning.

Here is where the matter, despite involving two people who, even today, likely would both be regarded as gay male transvestites rather than transsexuals or intersexed people, develops a similarity—one beyond more general issues of gender nonconformity—with *Hall* and *Hunt v. Poulter*. The surgeon was asked to examine Boulton and Park "for the purpose of ascertaining their sex," something Cohen feels was "intended more to harass the prisoners than to determine their sex." "But," Katz notes, "the doctor had been studying French medical writings on 'La Pédérastie.' "

Irrespective of whether it *truly* was for harassment or for sex determination, the physician took the request as a "justification for examining them in any way [he] thought proper," which led him to go beyond an examination of the genitals to conduct a rectal examination: "I do not in my practice ever remember to have seen such an appearance of the anus as those of the two prisoners presented. The insertion of a man's person would cause the appearances I have described." As Cohen notes, the change in direction of the examination marked a "critical transformation" in the matter. "[The issue ceased to be the conflict between the drag queens' costumes and their anatomical gender, and became instead a question of their illicit sexual practice." "With this new charge, the crime of Boulton and Park had escalated from a relatively minor violation of gender norms and laws into a much more serious breach of sexual standards and statutes." Katz further observes that, with this case, "the historical, cultural, and public linking of gender bending with, specifically, sexual deviance" could be observed.

While still in custody, Boulton and Park were examined further—once at the behest of their own counsel and in another instance at Newgate prison "by six of the most prominent physicians and surgeons in the city," including Frederick LeGros Clark, the vice president of the Royal Medical Society—and the resulting opinions differed from that of the initial examination. Clark eventually testified that their appearance "was natural, differing in no respect from hundreds whom I have examined."

The medical evidence, inconclusive and improperly obtained as it was, nevertheless was a major factor in bringing the pair to trial on more serious charges. H. Montgomery-Hyde succinctly summarizes the strengths and the weaknesses that permeated the Crown's case thereafter:

> Although there could be no doubt that all the defendants were homosexuals, the prosecution was unable to prove that any of them had infringed the law. The letters seized by police and read out in court, although most affectionate in tone, did not in any degree suggest that buggery had taken place or been attempted. Nor did the appearance of Boulton and Park in public places dressed as women and visiting the "ladies' room" in various theatres and bars constitute proof that a felony had been committed by any of them. Much

> evidence was given about numerous performances of amateur theatricals in which Boulton and Park had played women's parts, and it was admitted that they often went to parties after the shows in their female costume: their counsel argued strongly that there was no evidence whatever of conspiracy "beyond the mere going about as women." In particular, the letters addressed to Park by Fiske, which appeared [to be] the most compromising, were dismissed as light-hearted notes to "an effeminate lad, a dainty and pleasing boy, who was generally treated as a young girl.' "

. . .

The judge, Alexander Cockburn, Lord Chief Justice of Queen's Bench, indeed had criticized the initial unauthorized physical examination, the police search of the lodgings of Fiske and Louis Hurt (one of the other defendants), and the logic of the legal theory behind the ultimate form of the prosecution.

Nevertheless, it did go to the jury. Still, on May 15, 1871, after less than an hour of deliberation, all were acquitted—prompting cheering in the court. Katz observes: "In London, in the early 1870s, the 'charge that cross-dressing and an unmanly literary style were hallmarks of anal intercourse was found to be unproved.' Within twenty years, however, the link between gender non-conformity and sexual crime would be assumed, customarily."

. . .

Even after Boulton and Park—and even after the infamous Labouchère Amendment, which in 1885 had created the offense of "gross indecency with males in public or private," (the specific offense for which [Oscar] Wilde was prosecuted) cross-dressing was targeted, at least on the surface, with charges other than cross-dressing *per se* or even invocation of the current version of the sodomy statute. In summarizing the societal transformation that was occurring during this time, John Tosh observes:

> During the late Victorian and Edwardian era the components of manliness, while including nothing new, were configured in a different way, with different emphases. The attack on sexual license of young men was taken up with much greater vigour by the Evangelicals in the 1880s, partly due to the feminist campaigning against the Contagious Diseases Acts, and partly due to fears about moral corruption at the heart of the Empire. The new Puritanism also made much greater play of the threat posed by homosexuality—both the male prostitution of the cities and the schoolboy relationships which were such a common feature of boarding school life. The Labouchère Amendment to the Criminal Law Amendment Act of 1885 strengthened the hand of the moralists, and after the trials of Oscar Wilde ten years later vigilance was intensified. Manliness was increasingly seen to be incompatible not only with homosexual relationships, but with intimate friendship between men.

. . .

AMERICA—THE OLD

A. DEFAMATION

. . .

In the U.S., just as there were a number of defamation cases regarding the legal status of a person as tied to that person's race, litigation based on impugned sex status was not unknown. Some states apparently actively disfavored litigation in which the subject would be at issue. According to a 1795 Connecticut law treatise:

> An action upon a contract that wantonly tends to introduce indecent evidence will not be retained in a court of justice. As if a wager were laid that a woman had a particular defect in a particular part of her body, or that such person was an hermaphrodite, or had a particular disorder, or as to the cause why a woman did not breed, or the like.

Of course, that addressed the matter in terms of actions on contract, not defamation.

In Ohio, Olive Stewart alleged that Elizabeth Malone was a hermaphrodite and, as a result, Malone sued Stewart and her husband for slander. A common pleas court sustained a demurrer entered by the Stewarts because specific damages were not alleged. The Ohio Supreme Court, however, held that an allegation of hermaphroditism was actionable *even without* alleging special damages. Justice Read, as part of an exceedingly short opinion stated:

> It is said that the charge imports neither crime, guilt, nor moral turpitude. It is a well-established principle of law, that words which impute a charge necessarily tending to injure a man, or his trade, or occupation, or profession, or to exclude him from society, are actionable in themselves. A more gross or indelicate slander could not well have been uttered against a female—especially a young girl—or one more calculated to wound her feelings and do her mischief. It *unsexes* her; makes her a thing to be stared at; converts her into a *monster,* whose very existence is shocking to nature; and would be certain, among the young or thoughtless, to bring her into ridicule and contempt; and excludes her from social intercourse and all hopes of marriage. It is infinitely worse than a charge of incontinence, as to its injurious results, to the feelings and prospects of the female.
>
> To hold that there was no remedy for a case of this sort, would be an utter disgrace to the law and ourselves.

. . .

B. MARRIAGE

Apart from the slander cases, there were at least two reported nineteenth century marriage cases in which an allegation by one spouse of the other being a hermaphrodite was an issue. In *Van Arsdalen v. Van Arsdalen,* from New Jersey, the allegation by the husband of hermaphroditism in the wife appears to have been one of a number of peculiar things said and done by the husband (who was eighty at the time of the marriage; the wife but thirty-five), though he had been quite insistent (at least prior to the suit for maintenance by the wife) that "she is no woman." The court found in favor of the wife, who had testified "that the physical defects imputed to her have never existed, and there is no evidence to the contrary except the defendant's statement." The opinion does not indicate whether a physical examination was conducted to see which spouse was closer to being accurate.

Van Arsdalen was a suit for support, and it is unclear as to whether the husband had attempted to have the marriage declared to be void *ab initio,* as Arthur Corbett sought (successfully) in *Corbett v. Corbett.* In an Illinois case (one which was ongoing at the time of Boulton and Park in England), a husband sought a "divorce for impotency" on the part of the wife. The bulk of the incredibly short per curiam opinion from the Illinois Supreme Court reads:

> Testing the allegations of this bill by this rule, it fails to show that the malformation complained of is such as necessarily to constitute impotency.
>
> In this case no complaint on account of the cause alleged seems to have been made by complainant until in May, 1876; nor was there any election on his part to avoid the marriage contract on that ground until at that time. This was more than thirteen years after the marriage. For near eight years complainant cohabited with appellee, with full knowledge and without complaint of this cause.
>
> In the absence of strong rebutting facts, he must be taken to have accepted the situation, and can not now be heard to complain. Mere motives of delicacy are not a sufficient explanation of such long continued acquiescence.*

The word "hermaphrodite" actually does not appear in the opinion but does in the syllabus—as does a clearer picture of the facts of the case. The couple were married in 1863, shortly before the husband went off to serve in the Union Army during the Civil War. In 1864

> he returned home and lived with the defendant until some time in the month of January, 1872, when she became insane, and was sent to the insane hospital in Jacksonville, where she had since remained; that shortly after his return from the army he discovered that the defendant was an hermaphrodite, and when sexually excited no male could have sexual intercourse with her, and the bill charges that so the defendant was naturally impotent at the time of the marriage.

Given the disturbing willingness of modern courts to judicially legislate marriages involving transsexuals or intersexed persons into being void *ab initio,* perhaps the most remarkable aspect of *Peipho v. Peipho* was the Illinois court's absence of willingness to let the non-gender-variant party, who either had knowledge of the gender variance prior to the marriage or

* *Peipho v. Peipho,* 88 Ill. 438 (1878).

had accepted the condition for a long period of time prior to seeking to end the marriage, get out from under the marriage *at all*, much less in a way that would impugn the legal identities of sex-ambiguous people (and, later, transsexuals) in the jurisdiction.

II. MODERN LAW

LITTLETON v. PRANGE

9 S.W.3d 223 (Tex. App. 1999)

OPINION: HARDBERGER

This case involves the most basic of questions. When is a man a man, and when is a woman a woman? Every schoolchild, even of tender years, is confident he or she can tell the difference, especially if the person is wearing no clothes. These are observations that each of us makes early in life and, in most cases, continue to have more than a passing interest in for the rest of our lives. It is one of the more pleasant mysteries.

The deeper philosophical (and now legal) question is: can a physician change the gender of a person with a scalpel, drugs and counseling, or is a person's gender immutably fixed by our Creator at birth? The answer to that question has definite legal implications that present themselves in this case involving a person named Christie Lee Littleton.

Factual Background

A complete stipulation of the facts was made by the parties in this case.

Christie is a transsexual. She was born in San Antonio in 1952, a physically healthy male, and named after her father, Lee Cavazos. At birth, she was named Lee Cavazos, Jr. (Throughout this opinion Christie will be referred to as "She." This is for grammatical simplicity's sake, and out of respect for the litigant, who wishes to be called "Christie," and referred to as "she." It has no legal implications.)

At birth, Christie had the normal male genitalia: penis, scrotum and testicles. Problems with her sexual identity developed early though. Christie testified that she considered herself female from the time she was three or four years old, the contrary physical evidence notwithstanding. Her distressed parents took her to a physician, who prescribed male hormones. These were taken, but were ineffective. Christie sought successfully to be excused from sports and physical education because of her embarrassment over changing clothes in front of the other boys.

By the time she was 17 years old, Christie was searching for a physician who would perform sex reassignment surgery. At 23, she enrolled in a program at the University of Texas Health Science Center that would lead to a sex reassignment operation. For four years Christie underwent psychological and psychiatric treatment by a number of physicians, some of whom testified in this case.

On August 31, 1977, Christie's name was legally changed to Christie Lee Cavazos. Under doctor's orders, Christie also began receiving various treatments and female hormones. Between November of 1979 and February of 1980, Christie underwent three surgical procedures, which culminated in a complete sex reassignment. Christie's penis, scrotum and testicles were surgically removed, and a vagina and labia were constructed. Christie additionally underwent breast construction surgery.

Dr. Donald Greer, a board certified plastic surgeon, served as a member of the gender dysphoria team at UTHSC in San Antonio, Texas during the time in question. Dr. Paul Mohl, a board certified psychiatrist, also served as a member of the same gender dysphoria team. Both participated in the evaluation and treatment of Christie. The gender dysphoria team was a multi-disciplinary team that met regularly to interview and care for transsexual patients.

The parties stipulated that Dr. Greer and Dr. Mohl would testify that their background, training, education and experience is consistent with that reflected in their curriculum vitaes, which were attached to their respective affidavits in Christie's response to the motions for summary judgment. In addition, Dr. Greer and Dr. Mohl would testify that the definition of a transsexual is someone whose physical anatomy does not correspond to their sense of being or their sense of gender, and that medical science has not been able to identify the exact cause of this condition, but it is in medical probability a combination of neuro-biological, genetic and neonatal environmental factors. Dr. Greer and Dr. Mohl would further testify that in arriving at a diagnosis of transsexualism in Christie, the program at UTHSC was guided by the guidelines established by the Johns Hopkins Group and that, based on these guidelines, Christie was diagnosed psychologically and psychiatrically as a genuine male to female transsexual. Dr. Greer and Dr. Mohl also would testify that true male to female transsexuals are, in their opinion, psychologically and psychiatrically female before and after the sex reassignment surgery, and that Christie is a true male to female transsexual.

On or about November 5, 1979, Dr. Greer served as a principal member of the surgical team that performed the sex reassignment surgery on Christie. In Dr. Greer's opinion, the anatomical and genital features of Christie, following that surgery, are such that she has the capacity to function sexually as a female. Both Dr. Greer and Dr. Mohl would testify that, in their opinions, following the successful completion of Christie's participation in UTHSC's gender dysphoria program, Christie is medically a woman.

Christie married a man by the name of Jonathon Mark Littleton in Kentucky in 1989, and she lived with him until his death in 1996. Christie filed a medical malpractice suit under the Texas Wrongful Death and Survival Statute in her capacity as Jonathon's surviving spouse. The sued doctor, appellee here, filed a motion for summary judgment. The motion challenged Christie's status as a proper wrongful death beneficiary, asserting that Christie is a man and cannot be the surviving spouse of another man.

The trial court agreed and granted the summary judgment.

. . .

The Legal Issue

Can there be a valid marriage between a man and a person born as a man, but surgically altered to have the physical characteristics of a woman?

Overview of Issue

This is a case of first impression in Texas. The underlying statutory law is simple enough. Texas (and Kentucky, for that matter), like most other states, does not permit marriages between persons of the same sex. *See* Tex. Fam. Code Ann. § 2.001(b) (Vernon 1998); Ky. Rev. Stat. Ann. § 402.020 (1)(d) (Banks–Baldwin 1999). In order to have standing to sue under the wrongful death and survival statues, Christie must be Jonathon's surviving spouse. Tex. Civ. Prac. & Rem. Code Ann. §§ 71.004, 71.021 (Vernon 1977). The defendant's summary judgment burden was to prove she is not the surviving spouse. Referring to the statutory law, though, does not resolve the issue. This court, as did the trial court below, must answer this question: Is Christie a man or a woman? There is no dispute that Christie and Jonathon went through a ceremonial marriage ritual. If Christie is a woman, she may bring this action. If Christie is a man, she may not.

Christie is medically termed a transsexual, a term not often heard on the streets of Texas, nor in its courtrooms. If we look at other states or even other countries to see how they treat marriages of transsexuals, we get little help.

... Public antipathy toward same-sex marriages notwithstanding, the question remains: is a transsexual still the same sex after a sex-reassignment operation as before the operation? A transsexual, such as Christie, does not consider herself a homosexual because she does not consider herself a man. Her self-identity, from childhood, has been as a woman. Since her various operations, she does not have the outward physical characteristics of a man either. Through the intervention of surgery and drugs, Christie appears to be a woman. In her mind, she has corrected her physical features to line up with her true gender.

. . .

Case Law

The English case of *Corbett v. Corbett*, 2 All E.R. 33 (P.1970), appears to be the first case to consider the issue, and is routinely cited in later cases, including those cases from the United States. April Ashley, like Christie Littleton, was born a male, and like Christie, had undergone a sex-reassignment operation. *Id.* at 35–36. April later married Arthur

Corbett. *Id.* at 39. Arthur subsequently asked for a nullification of the marriage based upon the fact that April was a man, and the marriage had never been consummated. *Id.* at 34. April resisted the nullification of her marriage, asserting that the reason the marriage had not been consummated was the fault of her husband, not her. *Id.* at 34–35. She said she was ready, willing, and able to consummate the marriage. *Id.*

... Based upon the doctors' testimony, the court came up with four criteria for assessing the sexual identity of an individual. These are:

(1) Chromosomal factors;

(2) Gonadal factors (i.e., presence or absence of testes or ovaries);

(3) Genital factors (including internal sex organs); and

(4) Psychological factors.

Id. at 44.

... The English court stated that "The biological sexual constitution of an individual is fixed at birth (at the latest), and cannot be changed, either by the natural development of organs of the opposite sex, or by medical or surgical means. The respondent's operation, therefore, cannot affect her true sex." *Id.* at 47. The court then reasoned that since marriage is essentially a relationship between man and woman, the validity of the marriage depends on whether April is, or is not, a woman. *Id.* at 48. The court held that the criteria for answering this question must be biological and, having so held, found that April, a transsexual, "is not a woman for the purposes of marriage but is a biological male and has been so since birth," and, therefore, the marriage between Arthur and April was void. *Id.* at 48–49. The court specifically rejected the contention that individuals could "assign" their own sex by their own volition, or by means of an operation. *Id.* at 49. In short, once a man, always a man.

The year after *Corbett* was decided in England, a case involving the validity of a marriage in which one of the partners was transsexual appeared in a United States court. This was the case of *Anonymous v. Anonymous,* 67 Misc.2d 982, 325 N.Y.S.2d 499 (N.Y. Sup. Ct. 1971).

This New York case had a connection with Texas. The marriage ceremony of the transsexual occurred in Belton, while the plaintiff was stationed at Fort Hood. *Anonymous*, 325 N.Y.S.2d at 499. The purpose of the suit was to declare that no marriage could legally have taken place. *Id.* The court pointed out that this was not an annulment of a marriage because a marriage contract must be between a man and a woman. *Anonymous*, 325 N.Y.S.2d at 501. If the ceremony itself was a nullity, there would be no marriage to annul, but the court would simply declare that no marriage could legally have taken place. *Id.* The court had no difficulty in doing so, holding: "The law makes no provision for a 'marriage' between persons of the same sex. Marriage is and always has been a contract between a man and a woman." *Anonymous*, 325 N.Y.S.2d at 500.

Factually, the New York case was less complicated than *Corbett*, and the instant case, because there had been no sexual change operation, and the "wife" still had normal male organs. *Anonymous*, 325 N.Y.S.2d at 499. The plaintiff made this unpleasant discovery on his wedding night. *Id.* The husband in *Anonymous* was unaware that he was marrying a transsexual. *Id.* In both *Corbett* and the instant case, the husband was fully aware of the true state of affairs, and accepted it. In fact, in the instant case, Christie and her husband were married for seven years, and, according to the testimony, had normal sexual relations. This is a much longer period of time than any of the other reported cases.

The next reported transsexual case came from New Jersey. This is the only United States case to uphold the validity of a transsexual marriage. In *M.T. v. J.T.*, 140 N.J.Super. 77, 355 A.2d 204, 205 (1976), a transsexual wife brought an action for support and maintenance growing out of her marriage. The husband interposed a defense that his wife was male, and that their marriage was void (and therefore he owed nothing). *Id.* M.T., the wife, testified she was born a male, but she always considered herself a female. *Id.* M.T. dated men all her life. *Id.* After M.T. met her husband-to-be, J.T., they decided that M.T. would have an operation so she could "be physically a woman." *Id.*

In 1971, M.T. had an operation where her male organs were removed and a vagina was constructed. *Id.* J.T. paid for the operation, and the couple were married the next year. *Id.* M.T. and J.T. lived as husband and wife and had sexual intercourse. *Id.* J.T. supported M.T. for over two years; however, in 1974, J.T. left the home, and his support of M.T. ceased. *Id.* The lawsuit for maintenance and support followed.

. . . The trial court, in ruling for M.T. by finding the marriage valid, stated:

> It is the opinion of the court that if the psychological choice of a person is medically sound, not a mere whim, and irreversible sex reassignment surgery has been performed, society has no right to prohibit the transsexual from leading a normal life. Are we to look upon this person as an exhibit in a circus side show? What harm has said person done to society? The entire area of transsexualism is repugnant to the nature of many persons within our society. However, this should not govern the legal acceptance of a fact.

M.T., 355 A.2d at 207. The appellate court affirmed, holding:

> If such sex reassignment surgery is successful and the postoperative transsexual is, by virtue of medical treatment, thereby possessed of the full capacity to function sexually as male or female, as the case may be, we perceive no legal barrier, cognizable social taboo, or reason grounded in public policy to prevent the persons' identification at least for purposes of marriage to the sex finally indicated.

M.T., 355 A.2d at 210–11. Ohio is the last state that has considered this issue. *See In re Ladrach*, 32 Ohio Misc.2d 6, 513 N.E.2d 828 (Ohio Probate

Ct. 1987). *Ladrach* was a declaratory judgment action brought to determine whether a male who became a post-operative female was permitted to marry a male. *Ladrach*, 513 N.E.2d at 829–30. The court decided she may not. *Ladrach*, 513 N.E.2d at 832.

... The court cited a New York Academy of Medicine study of transsexuals that concluded: "... male to female transsexuals are still chromosomally males while ostensibly females." *Ladrach*, 513 N.E.2d at 831. The court stated that a person's sex is determined at birth by an anatomical examination by the birth attendant, which was done at Elaine's birth. *Ladrach*, 513 N.E.2d at 832.

. . .

Discussion

Christie challenges the trial court's summary judgment on four issues: (1) Prange did not carry his summary judgment burden of proving, as a matter of law, that Christie's marriage was between persons of the same sex; there is no summary judgment evidence that Christie was male at the time of her ceremonial marriage to Jonathon Littleton, the deceased; (2) Prange did not carry his burden of proving, as a matter of law, that Christie was male at the time of her ceremonial marriage to Jonathon Littleton, the deceased; sex at birth is not the test for determining the sex of a true post-operative transsexual for purposes of marriage; (3) Prange did not carry his summary judgment burden of proving, as a matter of law, that Christie's marriage is void; there is no summary judgment evidence that rebuts the presumption of validity of marriage; and (4) the summary judgment should be reversed because, at the very least, Christie produced summary judgment evidence raising a genuine issue of material fact that precludes summary judgment.

... In our system of government it is for the legislature, should it choose to do so, to determine what guidelines should govern the recognition of marriages involving transsexuals. The need for legislative guidelines is particularly important in this case, where the claim being asserted is statutorily-based. The statute defines who may bring the cause of action: a surviving spouse, and if the legislature intends to recognize transsexuals as surviving spouses, the statute needs to address the guidelines by which such recognition is governed. When or whether the legislature will choose to address this issue is not within the judiciary's control.

It would be intellectually possible for this court to write a protocol for when transsexuals would be recognized as having successfully changed their sex. Littleton has suggested we do so, perhaps using the surgical removal of the male genitalia as the test. As was pointed out by Littleton's counsel, "amputation is a pretty important step." Indeed it is. But this court has no authority to fashion a new law on transsexuals, or anything else. We cannot make law when no law exists: we can only interpret the written word of our sister branch of government, the legislature. Our responsibility in this case is to determine whether, in the absence of legislatively-established guidelines, a jury can be called upon to decide the legality of such marriages. We hold they cannot. In the absence of any guidelines, it would be improper to launch a jury forth on these untested and unknown waters.

... Christie was created and born a male. Her original birth certificate, an official document of Texas, clearly so states. During the pendency of this suit, Christie amended the original birth certificate to change the sex and name. Under section 191.029 of the Texas Health and Safety Code she was entitled to seek such an amendment if the record was "incomplete or proved by satisfactory evidence to be inaccurate." Tex. Health & Safety Code Ann. § 191.029 (Vernon 1992). The trial court that granted the petition to amend the birth certificate necessarily construed the term "inaccurate" to relate to the present, and having been presented with the uncontroverted affidavit of an expert stating that Christie is a female, the trial court deemed this satisfactory to prove an inaccuracy. However, the trial court's role in considering the petition was a ministerial one. It involved no fact-finding or consideration of the deeper public policy concerns presented. No one claims the information contained in Christie's original birth certificate was based on fraud or error. We believe the legislature intended the term "inaccurate" in section 191.028 to mean inaccurate as of the time the certificate was recorded; that is, at the time of birth. At the time of birth, Christie was a male, both anatomically and genetically. The facts contained in the original birth certificate were true and accurate, and the words contained in the amended certificate are not binding on this court.

There are some things we cannot will into being. They just are.

Conclusion

We hold, as a matter of law, that Christie Littleton is a male. As a male, Christie cannot be married to another male. Her marriage to Jonathon was invalid, and she cannot bring a cause of action as his surviving spouse.

We affirm the summary judgment granted by the trial court.

CONCUR BY: ANGELINI

I concur in the judgment.... According to Chief Justice Hardberger, such biological considerations are preferable to psychological factors as tools for making the decision we must make. In this case, I must agree.

I note, however, that "real difficulties ... will occur if these three criteria [chromosomal, gonadal and genital tests] are not congruent." *Corbett v. Corbett*, 2 All E.R. 33, 48 (P.1970). We must recognize the fact that, even when biological factors are considered, there are those individuals whose sex may be ambiguous. *See* Julie A. Greenberg, *Defining Male and Female: Intersexuality and the Collision Between Law and Biology*, 41 ARIZ. L. REV. 265 (1999). Having recognized this fact, I express no opinion as to how the law would view such individuals with regard to marriage. We are, however, not presented with such a case at this time. *See Corbett*, 2 All E.R. at 48–49.

. . . Thus, in the case of Christie Lee Littleton, it appears that all biological and physical factors were congruent and were consistent with those of a typical male at birth. The only pre-operative distinction between Christie Lee Littleton and a typical male was her psychological sense of being a female. Under these facts, I agree that Texas law will not recognize her marriage to a male.

DISSENT: LOPEZ

Although the standard for reviewing a trial court's order for summary judgment is well-settled in this state, that standard is not addressed in the majority's opinion. To prevail on a motion for summary judgment, the movant must show that no genuine issue of material fact exists and that the movant is entitled to judgment as a matter of law. *Nixon v. Mr. Property Management Co.*, 690 S.W.2d 546, 548–49 (Tex. 1985). In the instant case, this standard required Dr. Prange to prove that Christie Littleton was not the surviving spouse of Jonathon Littleton. To disprove this element of the plaintiff's cause of action, Dr. Prange produced only Christie's original birth certificate. This evidence, the majority concludes, is enough to prove as a matter of law that Christie Littleton is a male and that, as a result, Christie is not Jonathon's surviving spouse.

While a birth certificate would ordinarily establish a person's gender conclusively, Christie presented significant controverting evidence that indicated she was female. This evidence was so substantial that it raised a genuine issue of material fact about whether she was Jonathon's surviving spouse.

. . . Our state legislature has not determined the guidelines that should govern the recognition of marriages involving transsexuals. Particularly material to this case, the legislature has not addressed whether a transsexual is to be considered a surviving spouse under the Wrongful Death and Survival Statutes. In an ordinary case, the absence of such law would prevent this court from concluding that the movant was entitled to judgment as a matter of law. In the instant case, however, the majority relies on the absence of statutory law to conclude that this case presents a pure question of law that must be decided by this court rather than to allow the case to proceed to trial; that is, whether Christie is male or female.

. . . Texas law recognizes that inaccuracies occur in determining, or at least recording, gender. By permitting the amendment of an original birth certificate upon satisfactory evidence, Texas law allows these inaccuracies to be corrected. TEX. HEALTH & SAFETY CODE ANN. § 191.029 (Vernon 1992). Indeed, Christie's gender was lawfully corrected by an amended birth certificate months before the trial court ruled on Dr. Prange's motion for summary judgment.

... Under the rules of civil procedure, a document that has been replaced by an amended document is considered a nullity. Rule 65 provides that the substituted instrument takes the place of the original.... Although a birth certificate is not a legal pleading, the document is an official state document. Amendment of the state document is certainly analogous to an amended legal pleading. In this case, Christie's amended birth certificate replaced her original birth certificate. In effect, the amended birth certificate nullified the original birth certificate. As a result, summary judgment was issued based on a nullified document.

... Here, the stipulated evidence alone raises a genuine question about whether Christie is Jonathon's surviving spouse. Every case need not be precedential. In this case, the court is required to determine as a matter of law whether Christie is Jonathon's surviving spouse, not to speculate on the legalities of public policies not yet addressed by our legislature. Under a focused review of this case, a birth certificate reflecting the birth of a male child named Lee Cavazos does *not* prove that Christie Littleton is not the surviving spouse of Jonathan Littleton. Having failed to prove that Christie was not Jonathon's surviving spouse, Dr. Prange was not entitled to summary judgment. Because Christie's summary judgment evidence raises a genuine question of material fact about whether she is the surviving spouse of Jonathon Littleton, I respectfully dissent.

IN RE ESTATE OF GARDINER

29 Kan.App.2d 92, 22 P.3d 1086 (2001)

OPINION: GERNON

This is an appeal from an order issued by the district court granting summary judgment to Joseph M. Gardiner, III, (Joe) finding the marriage between Joe's father, Marshall G. Gardiner, and J'Noel Gardiner to be void under Kansas law and denying partial summary judgment to J'Noel. We reverse and remand with instructions.

. . .

I–Marriage Issue

I–A Court Procedural Background

Marshall died intestate on August 12, 1999. He was a resident of Leavenworth County, Kansas.

Joe filed a petition for letters of administration with the District Court of Leavenworth County, Kansas. Joe named himself and J'Noel, Marshall's surviving spouse, as Marshall's heirs. In his petition, Joe argued that J'Noel had waived any rights to Marshall's estate, and, thus, he was the sole heir-at-law to Marshall.

J'Noel filed an objection to Joe's petition. J'Noel also applied for letters of administration. The court then appointed a special administrator to handle the estate. Joe filed an objection to J'Noel's application.

Joe then petitioned the district court to amend his pleadings. In his amended petition, Joe named himself as Marshall's sole heir. Joe denied that Marshall and J'Noel were validly married. He contended that J'Noel was previously known as Jay N. Ball and was born a man. He argued that despite surgery, a name change, and other steps taken by J'Noel to change sex, she remains a man for the purposes of Kansas law relating to the issuance of a marriage license. Joe argued that the marriage between Marshall and J'Noel is void since, pursuant to K.S.A. 2000 Supp. 23–101, marriages between persons of the same sex are prohibited. Therefore, Joe claimed, J'Noel had no right to a share of Marshall's estate as the surviving spouse.

Joe also argued fraud regarding the waiver of J'Noel's rights and fraud in the inducement to marry in that Marshall did not know J'Noel was born a man. Even if the purported marriage was valid, he stated, J'Noel executed a waiver of any interest in Marshall's assets. Joe also alleged that a premarital agreement was entered into by both parties.

J'Noel filed a response to Joe's objection to her petition for issuance of letters. In the response, J'Noel asserted that her marriage to Marshall was valid. J'Noel argued that she is a biological female, and, as such, under K.S.A. 2000 Supp. 23–101, she is not prohibited from marrying Marshall, a biological male. J'Noel also stated that there is no evidence that she, through a memo written to Marshall, intended to waive any interest in Marshall's property and that no premarital agreement was ever entered into by her and Marshall. J'Noel further asserted that she told Marshall about the sex reassignment surgery she had undergone before the marriage.

Joe moved for summary judgment on the basis of waiver and estoppel and the invalidity of the marriage between J'Noel and Marshall under K.S.A. 2000 Supp. 23–101 due to fraud. J'Noel moved for partial summary judgment on the issue of whether she is legally a female and was a female at the time of the marriage to Marshall. In a memorandum in support of her motion, J'Noel argued that the district court is required to give full faith and credit to the Wisconsin court order changing her sex to female on her birth certificate and to the new birth certificate that was issued.

The district court heard oral arguments on the motions. The court denied Joe's motion with respect to the waiver and estoppel, finding disputed facts in that issue. However, the court granted Joe's motion with respect to the issue of the validity of the marriage, finding that J'Noel was born a male and remains a male for purposes of marriage under Kansas law.

The court found that the marriage between J'Noel and Marshall is void under K.S.A. 2000 Supp. 23–101, that J'Noel is not Marshall's surviving spouse, and therefore, that J'Noel is not entitled to a spousal share under the laws of intestate succession.

The court then stated that J'Noel has no interest in or right to Marshall's estate. Accordingly, J'Noel's motion for partial summary judgment was denied. J'Noel appeals.

I–B Personal Background

J'Noel was born in Green Bay, Wisconsin. J'Noel's original birth certificate indicates J'Noel was born a male. The record shows that after sex reassignment surgery, J'Noel's birth certificate was amended in Wisconsin, pursuant to Wisconsin statutes, to state that she was female. J'Noel argued that the order drafted by a Wisconsin court directing the Department of Health and Social Services in Wisconsin to prepare a new birth record must be given full faith and credit in Kansas.

Marshall was a businessman in northeast Kansas who had accumulated some wealth. He had one son, Joe, from whom he was estranged. Marshall's wife had died some time before he met J'Noel. There is no evidence that Marshall was not competent. Indeed, both Marshall and J'Noel possessed intelligence and real world experience. J'Noel had a Ph.D. in finance and was a teacher at Park College.

J'Noel met Marshall while on the faculty at Park College in May 1998. Marshall was a donor to the school. After the third or fourth date, J'Noel testified that Marshall brought up marriage. J'Noel wanted to get to know Marshall better, so they went to Utah for a trip. When asked about when they became sexually intimate, J'Noel testified that on this trip, Marshall had an orgasm. J'Noel stated that sometime in July 1998, Marshall was told about J'Noel's prior history as a male. The two were married in Kansas on September 25, 1998.

There is no evidence in the record to support Joe's suggestion that Marshall did not know about J'Noel's sex reassignment. It had been completed years before Marshall and J'Noel met. Nor is there any evidence that Marshall and J'Noel were not compatible.

Both parties agree that J'Noel has gender dysphoria or is a transsexual. J'Noel agrees that she was born with male genitalia. In a deposition, J'Noel testified that she was born with a "birth defect"—a penis and testicles. J'Noel stated that she thought something was "wrong" even prepuberty and that she viewed herself as a girl but had a penis and testicles.

J'Noel's journey from perceiving herself as one sex to the sex her brain suggests she was, deserves to be detailed. In 1991 and 1992, J'Noel began electrolysis and then thermolysis to remove body hair on the face, neck, and chest. J'Noel was married at the time and was married for 5 years. Also, beginning in 1992, J'Noel began taking hormones, and, in 1993, she had a tracheal shave. A tracheal shave is surgery to the throat to change the voice. All the while, J'Noel was receiving therapy and counseling.

In February 1994, J'Noel had a bilateral orchiectomy to remove the testicles. J'Noel also had a forehead/eyebrow lift at this time and rhinoplasty. Rhinoplasty refers to plastic surgery to alter one's nose. In July 1994, J'Noel consulted with a psychiatrist, who opined that there were no signs of thought disorder or major affective disorder, that J'Noel fully understood the nature of the process of transsexual change, and that her life history was consistent with a diagnosis of transsexualism. The psychiatrist recommended to J'Noel that total sex reassignment was the next appropriate step in her treatment.

In August 1994, J'Noel underwent further sex reassignment surgery. In this surgery, Eugene Schrang, M.D., J'Noel's doctor, essentially cut and inverted the penis, using part of the skin to form a female vagina, labia, and clitoris. Dr. Schrang, in a letter dated October 1994, stated that J'Noel has a "fully functional vagina" and should be considered "a functioning, anatomical female." In 1995, J'Noel also had cheek implants. J'Noel continues to take hormone replacements.

Regardless of whether one agrees with the concept of sex reassignment, one must be impressed with the resolve of, and have compassion for, any human being who undergoes such a demanding set of procedures.

After the surgery in 1994, J'Noel petitioned the Circuit Court of Outagamie County, Wisconsin, for a new birth certificate which would reflect her new name as J'Noel Ball and sex as female. The court issued a report ordering the state registrar to make these changes and issue a new birth certificate. A new birth certificate was issued on September 26, 1994. The birth certificate indicated the child's name as J'Noel Ball and sex as female. J'Noel also has had her driver's license, passport, and health documents changed to reflect her new status. Her records at two universities have also been changed to reflect her new sex designation.

I–C The Statute: K.S.A. 2000 Supp. 23–101

J'Noel argues that the district court erred when it held that her marriage to Marshall violated K.S.A. 2000 Supp. 23–101. J'Noel argues that the legislature, through the language in K.S.A. 2000 Supp. 23–101, intended to prohibit only homosexual marriages and that her marriage to Marshall was not such a marriage.

K.S.A. 2000 Supp. 23–101 states:

> The marriage contract is to be considered in law as a civil contract **between two parties who are of opposite sex. All other marriages are declared to be contrary to the public policy of this state and are void.** The consent of the parties is essential. The marriage ceremony may be regarded either as a civil ceremony or as a religious sacrament, but the marriage relation shall only be entered into, maintained or abrogated as provided by law. (Emphasis added.)

For purposes of marriage under Kansas law, the district court found that J'Noel was born and remains a male. Since the statute requires that a marriage must be between two parties of the opposite sex, the court found that the marriage between J'Noel and Marshall was void because both individuals were males.

There is no dispute that the legislature meant to void any marriage between members of the same sex.

The question here is whether J'Noel should have been considered a female under Kansas law at the time the marriage license was issued. Subparts to that question are the criteria used to determine sex and the timing of the determination. Stated another way: Is this marriage, between a post-operative male-to-female transsexual and a male, prohibited under Kansas law?

The interpretation of a statute is a question of law for which appellate review is unlimited. *Rose & Nelson v. Frank*, 25 Kan.App.2d 22, 24, 956 P.2d 729, rev. denied, 265 Kan. 886, 1998 Kan. LEXIS 482 (1998).

The amendment to 23–101 limiting marriage to two parties of the opposite sex began its legislative history in 1975. The minutes of the Senate Committee on Judiciary for January 21, 1976, state that the amendment would "affirm the traditional view of marriage." The proposed amendment was finally enacted in 1980.

K.S.A. 23–101 was again amended in 1996, when language was added, stating: "All other marriages are declared to be contrary to the public policy of this state and are void." This sentence was inserted immediately after the sentence limiting marriage to two parties of the opposite sex.

In 1996, K.S.A. 23–115 was amended, with language added stating: "It is the strong public policy of this state only to recognize as valid marriages from other states that are between a man and a woman."

The legislative history contains discussions about gays and lesbians, but nowhere is there any testimony that specifically states that marriage should be prohibited by two parties if one is a post-operative male-to-female or female-to-male transsexual. Thus, the question remains: Was J'Noel a female at the time the license was issued for the purpose of the statute?

I–D The Science

It is perhaps well to pause and attempt to define what a transsexual is by stating what a transsexual is not. A transsexual is not a homosexual. A homosexual is one who prefers the same sex for sexual contact. Nor is a transsexual a transvestite. A transvestite is one who remains one sex but gains pleasure from dressing like the other sex. A transsexual is one who experiences himself or herself as being of the opposite sex, despite having some biological characteristics of one sex, or one whose sex has been changed externally by surgery and hormones. A transsexual might be a homosexual or a transvestite also, but one does not define the other.

The scientific literature relating to studies of transsexuals is limited both in scope and history. Serious inquiry is limited to approximately the last 30 years. To state that we know everything about this issue is wrong. To state that we know more and more every year about this complex issue is more accurate. This case has the benefit of some research which preceding cases on this issue did not.

A recent study that autopsied the brains of transsexuals and others supports a conclusion that there is a scientific basis for J'Noel's assertion that she was born with a condition—specifically that she had a penis and testicles, which was evidence that she was male, but in most other senses of the word, she was female. The same science which allows us to map the genome and explore our DNA requires us to recognize these discoveries in all aspects of our lives, including the legal ramifications. We can no longer be permitted to conclude who is male or who is female by the amount of facial hair one has or the size of one's feet.

A study in the respected medical journal, The Journal of Clinical Endocrinology & Metabolism, analyzed the brains of homosexual males, heterosexual males, heterosexual females, and male-to-female transsexuals. It concluded:

> Regardless of sexual orientation, men had almost twice as many somatostatin neurons as women. The number of neurons in . . . male-to-female transsexuals was similar to that of the females. . . . In contrast, the neuron number of female-to-male transsexual was found to be in the male range. . . . The present findings of somatostatin neuronal sex differences in the BSTc (a part of the brain) and its sex reversal in the transsexual brain clearly support the paradigm that in transsexuals sexual differentiation of the brain and genitals may go into opposite directions and point to a neurobiological basis of gender identity disorder.

Kruijver, Zhou, Pool, Hofman, Gooren, and Swaab, Male-to-Female Transsexuals Have Female Neuron Numbers in a Limbic Nucleus, 85 The Journal of Clinical Endocrinology & Metabolism 2034 (2000).

We would be remiss if we did not recognize and mention other medical and scientific information which underscores the complexity of these issues and requires our introspection.

If one concludes that chromosomes are all that matter and that a person born with "male" chromosomes is and evermore shall be male, then one must confront every situation which does not conform with such a rigid framework of thought. There are situations of ambiguity in which certain individuals have chromosomes that differ from the typical pattern. The questions which must be asked, if not answered, are: "Are these people male or female?" and, "Should they be allowed to get married?" Professor Julie A. Greenberg, writing in the Summer 1999 issue of the Arizona Law Review, states:

> Medical experts recognize that many factors contribute to the determination of an individual's sex. According to medical professionals, the typical criteria of sex include:
>
> 1. Genetic or chromosomal sex—XY or XX;
> 2. Gonadal sex (reproductive sex glands)—testes or ovaries;

3. Internal morphologic sex (determined after three months gestation)—seminal vesicles/prostrate [**sic**] or vagina/uterus/fallopian tubes;
4. External morphologic sex (genitalia)—penis/scrotum or clitoris/labia;
5. Hormonal sex—androgens or estrogens;
6. Phenotypic sex (secondary sexual features)—facial and chest hair or breasts;
7. Assigned sex and gender of rearing; and
8. Sexual identity.

For most people, these factors are all congruent, and one's status as a man or woman is uncontroversial. For intersexuals, some of these factors may be incongruent, or an ambiguity within a factor may exist.

The assumption is that there are two separate roads, one leading from XY chromosomes at conception to manhood, the other from XX chromosomes at conception to womanhood. The fact is that there are not two roads, but one road with a number of forks that turn in the male or female direction. Most of us turn in the same direction at each fork.

The bodies of the millions of intersexed people have taken a combination of male and female forks and have followed the road less traveled. These individuals have noncongruent sexual attributes. For these individuals, the law must determine which of the eight sexual factors will determine their sex and whether any one factor should be dispositive for all legal purposes.

Because the law has typically looked to biology and the medical community for guidance in determining how an individual's sex should be legally established, the complex nature of sexual differentiation must be understood.

A. Sexual Differentiation—The Typical Path

During the first seven weeks after conception, all human embryos are sexually undifferentiated. At seven weeks, the embryonic reproductive system consists of a pair of gonads that can grow into either ovaries (female) or testes (male). The genital ridge that exists at this point can develop either into a clitoris and labia (female) or a penis and a scrotum (male). Two primordial duct systems also exist at this stage. The female ducts are called Mullerian ducts and develop into the uterus, fallopian tubes and the upper part of the vagina if the fetus follows a female path. The male ducts are called Wolffian ducts and are the precursors of the seminal vesicles, vas deferens and epididymis.

At eight weeks, the fetus typically begins to follow one sex path. If the fetus has one X and one Y chromosome (46XY), it will start down the male path. At eight weeks, a 'master switch' on the Y chromosome, called the testis-determining factor, signals the embryonic gonads to form into testes. The testes begin to produce male hormones. These male hormones prompt the gonads and genitalia to develop male features. Additionally, the testes produce a substance called Mullerian inhibiting factor that causes the female Mullerian ducts to atrophy and be absorbed by the body, so that a female reproductive system is not created.

Because the typical female fetus is 46XX and does not have a Y chromosome, the master switch that leads to the development of male organs is not turned on. The fetus continues on what is considered the default path and in the thirteenth week the gonads start to transform into ovaries. Because no testes exist to produce male hormones, the remainder of the sexual system develops along a female path. During this time, the Wolffian (male) ducts shrivel up. In other words, unless the body is triggered by hormonal production to follow the male path, the fetus will normally develop as a female. Therefore, although chromosomes generally control the hormones that are produced, it is actually the hormones that directly affect sexual development."

B. Sexual Differentiation—Intersexuals: The Paths Less Followed

Two circumstances may lead to an intersexual condition: (1) failure to meet the typical criteria within any one factor; or (2) one or more factors may be incongruent with the other factors.

1. Ambiguity within a Factor

a. Chromosomal Ambiguity—Certain individuals have chromosomes that differ from the typical pattern of either XY or XX. Doctors have discovered people with a variety of combinations including: XXX, XXY, XXXY, XYY, XYYY, XYYYY, and XO.

b. Gonadal Ambiguity—Some intersexuals do not have typical ovaries or testes. Instead, they have 'streak' gonads that do not appear to function as either ovaries or testes. Others have ovotestes, a combination of both male and female gonads. Still others have one ovary and one testis.

c. External Morphologic Sex—Some individuals' external genitalia are neither clearly male nor clearly female. In addition, some women have clitoral hypertrophy, a clitoris that is larger than the typical clitoris, may more closely resemble a penis, and is sometimes accompanied by an internal vagina.

d. Internal Morphologic Sex—Some individuals have incomplete internal sex organs or a complete absence of an internal sex organ. In addition, some individuals are born with a combination of male and female internal organs.

e. Hormonal Sex—The male hormones are referred to as androgens. The female hormones are estrogen and progesterone. Although they are referred to as male and female hormones, all human sex hormones are shared by men and women. Typically, men and women have hormones of each type, but the levels of production and reception of each hormone are highly variable among all individuals. Different medical disorders further influence levels of hormone production and/or reception.

f. Phenotypic Sex—Individuals may have a variety of combinations of incongruent phenotypic characteristics. In other words, an individual may have characteristics that are typically associated with a male (heavy facial hair) and characteristics that are typically associated with a female (developed breasts).

g. Assigned Sex/Gender of Rearing—Although it occurs rarely, some parents have raised their child as a gender other than the sex that was assigned by the medical attendant at birth. In addition, in some circumstances, doctors have recommended that a child be raised as the sex different from the one assigned at birth.

h. Sexual Identity—Sexual identity refers to how individuals would identify themselves; gender identity refers to how society would identify an individual. Some individuals do not consider themselves to be either male or female; they identify themselves as a third sex.

2. Ambiguity Among Factors

Some individuals have an incongruence among the eight factors due to a sexual differentiation disorder. In other words, some factors may be clearly male, some may be clearly female, and others may be a mixture of male and female. Incongruity among factors can result from a number of disorders and circumstances including:

a. Chromosomal sex disorders;

b. Gonadal sex disorders;

c. Internal organ anomalies;

d. External organ anomalies;

e. Hormonal disorders;

f. Gender identity disorders; and

g. Surgical creation of an intersexed condition.

These conditions are described in detail below. . . .

a. Chromosomal Sex Disorders

Klinefelter Syndrome

Approximately one in 500 to 1000 'males' is affected by Klinefelter Syndrome, a condition in which a mostly phenotypic male does not fall neatly into the XY chromosome complement. Individuals with Klinefelter Syndrome will typically have two or more X chromosomes. The testes, and often the penis, are smaller than in unaffected XY males.

A diagnosis of Klinefelter Syndrome is typically not made before puberty because no easily identifiable sign exists prior to the onset of puberty. The swelling of the breasts (gynecomastia) that occurs in adolescence is typically the first sign of the existence of this intersexual condition. Most individuals with Klinefelter Syndrome report a male psychosexual orientation. Many take supplemental testosterone, which further results in a male phenotype (e.g. facial hair).

Turner Syndrome

Disorders of chromosomal sex also appear in phenotypic females. Turner Syndrome is a condition that affects approximately one in 5000 newborn females. Individuals with Turner Syndrome will typically have an XO chromosomal pattern, not falling neatly into the XX, XY binary system. Individuals with Turner Syndrome typically have bilateral 'streak' gonads (unformed and non-functioning gonads) instead of clearly defined ovaries or testes. The absence of complete ovaries or testes in-utero means that the fetus has little exposure to either female or male hormones. In the absence of male hormones, the fetus will follow the female path.

Individuals with Turner Syndrome are typically shorter than XX females. They have female appearing genitalia, but little breast development in the absence of exogenous estrogen administration.

b. Gonadal Sex Disorders—Swyer Syndrome

Pure gonadal dysgenesis is a condition sometimes referred to as Swyer Syndrome. This syndrome is similar to Turner Syndrome in that individuals with this syndrome will have only streak gonads. In contrast to Turner Syndrome, in which a chromosome is missing (XO), individuals with Swyer Syndrome have XY (male) chromosomes. Although Swyer Syndrome individuals have a Y chromosome, the chromosome may be missing the sex-determining segment. Without this segment, the embryo cannot develop testes and as a result, the masculinizing hormones are also missing. In the absence of the masculinizing hormones, the fetus will take the 'default' female path and will develop a uterus but will not have any ovaries.

This condition is not apparent at birth and the child will be raised as a girl. The syndrome is generally diagnosed at puberty when the absence of a menstruation and breast enlargement causes suspicion.

c. Internal Organ Anomalies—Persistent Mullerian Duct Syndrome

Individuals with Persistent Mullerian Duct Syndrome have the internal organs typical of males as well as females. These individuals have a male chromosomal pattern (XY) and therefore develop testes which secrete androgen but for some reason fail to secrete anti-Mullerian hormones. The androgens cause the fetus to follow the male path and develop the external appearance and internal organs of a male. However, fallopian tubes and a uterus are also formed because the anti-Mullerian hormones are not acting to stop this development. This condition is generally not diagnosed at birth. Individuals with this syndrome are reared as males and have a male identity.

d. External Organ Anomalies: Hermaphroditism

Individuals who have ambiguous external genitalia (neither clearly male nor female) are commonly referred to as hermaphrodites. Hermaphrodites are often classified into three categories: true hermaphrodites, male pseudo-hermaphrodites, and female pseudo-hermaphrodites. A 'true hermaphrodite' has some ovarian and some testicular tissue. So-called 'true hermaphrodites' have either one ovary and one testis, two ovotestes (a combination of an ovary and testis in a single gonad) or some combination thereof (e.g. one ovotestes and one ovary). True hermaphroditic conditions are more rare than many of the other intersex conditions described in this section. A male pseudo-hermaphrodite has testes and no ovaries but some aspect of female genitalia. A female pseudo-hermaphrodite has ovaries and no testes and some aspect of male genitalia.

A variety of disorders can lead to hermaphroditic conditions. Hermaphroditic conditions are named according to their etiology (e.g. Partial Androgen Insensitivity Syndrome ['PAIS'] or Congenital Adrenal Hyperplasia ['CAH']) unless the etiology of the condition remains unknown.

True hermaphroditism is rare and the exact incidence is unknown. The chromosome count may vary but is predominantly 46XX.

e. Hormonal Disorders

Androgen Insensitivity Syndrome

Androgen Insensitivity Syndrome ("AIS") affects approximately 1 out of every 20,000 genetic males. AIS can be either complete ("CAIS") or partial (PAIS). Individuals with AIS are born with XY chromosomes and normally-functioning testes, which would otherwise suggest a normal male fetus. Individuals with CAIS, however, have a receptor defect and are unable to process the androgens produced by the testes.

Because the body cannot process the androgens, the fetus will follow the default path of female development. External female genitalia will form. No internal reproductive organs will form because the Mullerian inhibiting factor produced by the testes will inhibit the growth of the uterus and fallopian tubes. The vagina will be shorter than in the typical woman (or may only be a dimple) and will end blindly because there are no female internal reproductive organs with which to connect.

Unlike several other intersex conditions, individuals with CAIS almost always are identified as 'normal' females at birth because externally they are indistinguishable from XX females. The disorder is sometimes diagnosed in infancy because of inguinal hernias that contain the testes. Often, however, CAIS is not diagnosed until after the onset of puberty as a result of a failure to menstruate. At puberty, breasts will form because of the estrogen that is produced by the testes. Until puberty, many CAIS women have no inkling that they are other than normal XX women.

In PAIS, an XY individual with testes will be partially receptive to androgens. Unlike individuals with CAIS, individuals with PAIS may fall anywhere along a spectrum from an almost completely male external appearance and male sexual identity to a completely female external appearance and female sexual identity. The degree to which the individual has male features depends upon the degree to which the receptors are able to process the male hormones the testes produce.

The external phenotype of PAIS individuals will initially be determined by the degree of androgen reception in the body. Thus, a PAIS individual may have genitalia resembling either a clitoris or a penis, the labia may be fused, and during adolescence there may be breast development due to the conversion of testosterone produced by the gonads to estradiol, an estrogen compound.

5–Alpha–Reductase Deficiency

This condition is similar to the androgen resistance syndromes. Individuals with 5–Alpha–Reductase Deficiency have XY chromosomes and testes but appear phenotypically female at birth. This condition results from the body's failure to convert testosterone to dihydrotestosterone, the more powerful form of androgen responsible for the development of male external genitalia. Despite a female appearance during childhood, by the onset of puberty, the body will masculinize. The testes descend, the voice deepens, muscle mass substantially increases, and a 'functional' penis that is capable of ejaculating develops from what was thought to be the clitoris. The prostate, however, remains small and beard growth is scanty. Although the individual is typically raised as a girl, at puberty, psychosexual orientation typically becomes male. In other words, virilization will occur at puberty in the absence of medical intervention.

5–Alpha–Reductase Deficiency is an inheritable condition, and has resulted in a large group of affected individuals in some communities in the Dominican Republic. In some cases, a diagnosis is made in early puberty, male external development is arrested, and the individual will take exogenous female hormones to simulate a female puberty. In these cases, the individual will often have a female sexual identity. Other individuals with 5–Alpha–Reductase Deficiency will develop a masculine appearance in conformity with their genotype and will also develop a male psychosexual identification.

Congenital Adrenal Hyperplasia

Some individuals with XX chromosomes, ovaries, and other female internal structures have a more masculinized external appearance and/or demeanor due to an abundance of androgen production in-utero. Typical of this category is 21–Hydroxylase Deficiency Congenital Adrenal Hyperplasia ('CAH'). It occurs in approximately one out of 5000 to 15,000 births.

Both the chromosomes and gonads of CAH individuals are indistinguishable from unaffected females. The genitals, however, may be ambiguous and may more closely resemble male genitalia.

Some CAH individuals have been identified as males at birth and are reared as boys despite the presence of XX chromosomes and ovaries. In other cases, the masculinization of prenatal life is interrupted at birth, and the child is surgically and hormonally treated and reared as a girl. These girls often have characteristics that are popularly stereotyped as masculine. In addition, many CAH individuals identify themselves as lesbians.

Progestin–Induced Virilization

Similar to CAH is Progestin–Induced Virilization ('PIV'), which results from an abundance of male hormones in an otherwise normal XX female. PIV is caused by exposure in-utero to progestin that has been taken by the mother during pregnancy. Like individuals with CAH, PIV women will frequently have clitoral hypertrophy. In all other respects, however, they have completely female gonads.

f. Gender Identity Disorder

Some individuals may be seemingly harmonious in all of the first six factors, but do not identify themselves with the sex associated with these factors. These individuals may be said to have gender dysphoria or gender identity disorder ('GID'). Often these individuals are called transsexuals. Science has yet to definitely isolate a biological common denominator that causes these individuals to feel transgendered. A recent study, however, has determined that a section of the brain area that is essential for sexual behavior is larger in men than in women and that the brain structure of genetically male transsexuals is more similar to female brains than to male brains. Some transgendered individuals choose to undergo hormonal treatment and/or surgery so that their bodies comport with their sexual identity while other transsexuals do not choose to undergo such treatment.

Transsexualism is not necessarily related to sexual orientation. Some transsexuals identify themselves as gays or lesbians while others identify themselves as heterosexuals. In other words, a male-to-female transsexual who has undergone surgery to acquire female genitalia may still prefer to have sex with another female, and a female-to-male transsexual may still prefer to have sex with another male.

g. Surgical Creation of an Intersexed Condition

In addition to cases in which intersexed individuals may be assigned a sex that does not comport with their own sexual identity, some persons have had their sexual features altered either accidentally or purposefully. For instance, some individuals have had their penises removed at a young age because they were mistakenly identified as females and the penis was considered an oversized clitoris that required reduction. Although these cases are rare, they are illustrative of the complex nature of sexual identity.

The most famous surgical alteration case involves a male whose penis was accidentally ablated when he was eight months old. The doctors recommended that his genitals be reconstructed to have a female appearance and that he be raised as a girl even though all other sexual factors were congruent and were male. The doctors also recommended that his 'history' as a male be hidden from him.

This surgical alteration case made headlines in 1973. Because the doctors involved in the surgical alteration reported that the child and the parents had successfully adapted to the sex/gender alteration, sociology, psychology, and women's study texts were rewritten to argue, 'This dramatic case ... provides strong support ... that conventional patterns of masculine and feminine behavior can be altered. It also casts doubt on the theory that major sex differences, psychological as well as anatomical, are immutably set by the genes at conception.'

For more than twenty years, the scientific literature continued to report that the surgical alteration was successful and the child's sexual identity was female. This case made headlines again in 1997 when Milton Diamond and Keith Sigmundson reported in the Archives of Pediatric & Adolescent Medicine that the boy who was turned into a girl was now living as a man.

According to the Diamond and Sigmundson report, John (a pseudonym) had always thought of himself as different from other girls. As a child, he preferred 'boy' type toys and preferred to mimic his father's rather than his mother's behavior. He also preferred to urinate in a standing position although he had no penis. Because of the cognitive dissonance, Joan (a pseudonym used by the authors to describe John while he lived a female life) often had thoughts of suicide.

At twelve, Joan was put on an estrogen regimen. She rebelled against the regimen and often refused to take the medication. At fourteen, Joan confessed to a doctor that she had suspected that she was a boy since second grade. At that point, the doctors agreed with Joan that she should be remasculinized and become John once more. At age fourteen, Joan/John returned to living as a male. He received male hormone shots and a mastectomy. He underwent surgery to reconstruct a phallus at ages fifteen and sixteen. John was eventually accepted as a boy by his peers. He is now married and helping to raise his wife's children.

John was not born an intersexual. He became an intersexual when doctors removed his penis, constructed external female genitalia and

> administered female hormones. Despite this intervention, John always felt that he was not a female.
>
> In another recently reported similar case, a child's penis was severely damaged during a circumcision that was performed when the child was two months old. A decision was made to 'turn' the child into a girl. At seven months, surgery was performed to remove the remainder of the male genitalia and from that point on the child was raised as a girl. She was interviewed by a psychiatrist at ages sixteen and twenty-six. The results of these interviews indicate that she self identifies as a bi-sexual female whose recreational and occupational interests are more typically identified with males.
>
> The significance of these two reports is that they exemplify the difficulty law and medicine must confront in defining sex. At birth, these infants' sex factors were congruent and were male. After the original intervention, they were turned into intersexuals but were treated by society as if they were females. They had male chromosomes, ambiguous genitalia, and female gender assignment. As adults, one person self-identifies as a heterosexual male while the other self-identifies as a bi-sexual female.
>
> These studies and other reports about intersexuals have forced the medical and psychiatric communities to question their long-held beliefs about sex and sexual identity. Just as current scientific studies have caused the scientific communities to question their beliefs about sex and sexual identity, the legal community must question its long-held assumptions about the legal definitions of sex, gender, male, and female.

Greenberg, Defining Male and Female: Intersexuality and the Collision Between Law and Biology, 41 Ariz. L. Rev. 265, 278–92 (1992).

I–E Case Law

This is a case of first impression in Kansas. A discussion of case law on transsexualism from other jurisdictions, including another nation, may prove helpful.

The cases generally fall into three categories: cases dealing with the amendment of identification records, usually birth certificate name and/or sex changes; cases dealing with discrimination, most pointedly in the workplace; and cases dealing with marriage between a transsexual and a nontranssexual.... The analysis will follow the cases chronologically.

The first case in the United States to deal with transsexualism involved a petition for a change of sex on a birth certificate. In *Mtr. of Anonymous v. Weiner*, 50 Misc.2d 380, 270 N.Y.S.2d 319 (1966), a post-operative transsexual who had assumed the name and role of a female applied to the Bureau of Vital Statistics in the New York City Health Department for a new birth certificate. The Bureau requested guidance from the Board of Health, who, in turn, called on a committee on public health of the New York Academy of Medicine to investigate the issue and make recommendations. The group called on to assist included gynecologists, endocrinologists, cytogeneticists, psychiatrists, and a lawyer.

The committee, after a detailed analysis and taking into account that at the time 10 states permitted such a change, concluded that male-to-female transsexuals are "still chromosomally males while ostensibly females." 50 Misc.2d at 382. Further, it was concluded that "it is questionable whether laws and records such as the birth certificate should be changed and thereby used as a means to help psychologically ill persons in their social adaption." 50 Misc.2d at 382. Therefore, the committee found that it was opposed to a change on birth certificates in transsexualism cases.

... In examining this issue, the New York appellate court looked at the New York City Health Code provisions. The code provided for a change in birth certificate only if the Commissioner of Public Health was satisfied that the evidence shows true facts and that an error was made at the time of preparing and filing of the certificate. 50 Misc.2d at 383. The court found that based on the code provision, the Board did not act arbitrarily, capriciously, or in an otherwise illegal manner. The decision of the Board to deny the transsexual's request was affirmed. 50 Misc.2d at 385. By upholding the Board, the court then, indirectly, adopted the Academy's position.

However, a civil court in New York, in 1968 and then again in 1970, granted an application for a change of name to a post-operative transsexual. *Matter of Anonymous*, 57 Misc.2d 813, 293 N.Y.S.2d 834 (1968); *Matter of Anonymous*, 64 Misc.2d 309, 314 N.Y.S.2d 668 (1970). In the 1968 case of Anonymous, a male-to-female transsexual petitioned the court to order the Bureau of Vital Statistics of the Department of Health of the City of New York to change his birth certificate to reflect a name and sex change. Based on New York law, the civil court lacked jurisdiction to change the sex on the birth certificate. 57 Misc.2d at 813–14. Even so, the court still criticized the findings of the Academy.

The court noted that all male organs had been removed and that the petitioner could no longer have sex as a male. The court stated that where, with or without medical intervention, the psychological sex and the anatomical sex are "harmonized," then the social sex or gender of the individual should conform to the harmonized status of the individual, and if such conformity requires a change in statistical information, the changes should be made. 57 Misc. 2d at 816.

Later, in *Mtr. of Hartin v. Dir. of Bur. of Recs.*, 75 Misc. 2d 229, 232, 347 N.Y.S.2d 515 (1973), the appellate court reaffirmed the decision in Weiner. We can conclude that as of the filing date of Hartin, New York was stating that its birth records should reflect the sex of an individual as determined at birth.

... A change in thinking can perhaps be observed beginning in 1975 in *Darnell v. Lloyd,* 395 F. Supp. 1210 (D. Conn. 1975). The petitioner, called a male at birth, had a sex change operation and later requested that the Commissioner of Health change the sex on his birth certificate from male to female. The Commissioner refused to make such a change. The transsexual sued to have the Commissioner ordered to make this change, and the Commissioner moved for summary judgment.

The court denied the motion for summary judgment, finding that the Commissioner of Health must show some substantial state interest in his policy of refusing to change a birth certificate to reflect current sexual status unless that was also the status at birth. 395 F. Supp. at 1214. The court found that this heightened level of scrutiny exists because the court felt that the fundamental right to marry could be implicated by the Commissioner's decision. 395 F. Supp. at 1214.

... The case of *M.T. v. J.T.*, 140 N.J. Super. 77, 355 A.2d 204, cert. denied, 71 N.J. 345, 364 A.2d 1076 (1976), deserves greater attention, in our view, than *Corbett, Hartin*, or *Darnell*.

In *M.T.*, a husband and wife were divorcing, and the issue was support and maintenance. The husband argued that he should not have to pay support to his wife because she was a male, making the marriage void. The issue before the court, similar to that before this court, was whether the marriage of a post-operative male-to-female transsexual and a male was a lawful marriage between a man and a woman. The court found that it was a valid marriage. 140 N.J. Super. at 90.

... Since the court found that the wife's gender and genitalia were no longer "discordant" and had been harmonized by medical treatment, the court held that the wife was a female at the time of her marriage and that her husband, then, was obligated to support her. 140 N.J. Super. at 89–90.

The importance of the holding in *M.T.* is that it replaces the biological sex test with dual tests of anatomy and gender, where "for marital purposes if the anatomical or genital features of a genuine transsexual are made to conform to the person's gender, psyche or psychological sex, then identity by sex must be governed by the congruence of these standards." 140 N.J. Super. at 87.

The *M.T.* court further stated

> In this case the transsexual's gender and genitalia are no longer discordant; they have been harmonized through medical treatment. Plaintiff has become physically and psychologically unified and fully capable of sexual activity consistent with her reconciled sexual attributes of gender and anatomy. Consequently, plaintiff should be considered a member of the female sex for marital purposes. It follows that such an individual would have the capacity to enter into a valid marriage relationship with a person of the opposite sex and did so here. In so ruling we do no more than give legal effect to a *fait accompli*, based upon medical judgment and action which are irreversible. Such recognition will promote the individual's quest for inner peace and personal happiness, while in no way disserving any societal interest, principle of public order or precept of morality.

140 N.J. Super. at 89–90.

In *M.T.*, the husband was arguing that he did not owe any support because his wife was a man. However, in the record, it was stated that the wife had a sex reassignment operation after meeting the husband. Her husband paid for the operation. The husband later deserted the wife and then tried to get out of paying support to someone he had been living with since 1964 and had been married to for over 2 years.

... In 1984, the United States Court of Appeals, Seventh Circuit, analyzed an issue concerning transsexualism and workplace discrimination. In *Ulane v. Eastern Airlines, Inc.*, 742 F.2d 1081 (7th Cir. 1984), cert. denied 471 U.S. 1017, 85 L.Ed.2d 304, 105 S.Ct. 2023 (1985), a post-operative male-to-female transsexual who was a pilot for Eastern Airlines was fired in 1981, shortly after sex reassignment surgery. The transsexual sued the airline, alleging that the employer violated Title VII by discharging her from her position as a pilot. A federal district court agreed with the transsexual, finding discrimination against this person as both a female and a transsexual, and the airline appealed. 742 F.2d at 1082.

The Seventh Circuit disagreed with the district court. The court stated that while it does not condone discrimination in any form, it must hold that Title VII does not protect transsexuals. 742 F.2d at 1084. First, the court stated: "It is a maxim of statutory construction that, unless otherwise defined, words should be given their ordinary, common meaning." 742 F.2d at 1085. The court explained that the words of Title VII do not outlaw discrimination against a person who has a sexual identity disorder. It noted that the law clearly prohibits discrimination against women because they are women or men because they are men; it does not protect a person born with a male body who believes himself to be female or a person born with a female body who believes herself to be male. 742 F.2d at 1085.

... The two most recent decisions in the United States in the area of transsexualism have dealt with the precise issue before this court, that is, whether two individuals, biologically and legally of the same sex at birth, may contract to marry each other.

In 1987, a probate court in Ohio addressed the question in the case of *In re Ladrach*, 32 Ohio Misc.2d 6, 513 N.E.2d 828 (1987). In *Ladrach*, a post-operative male-to-female transsexual and the transsexual's fiancé, a biological male, applied for a marriage license. The application indicated that the transsexual had been married two times before to spouses of the female gender and that both marriages had ended in divorce.

After reading the application, the clerk at the license bureau called a judge who reviewed the application. The judge also reviewed a signed letter by a physician indicating that the transsexual had undergone sex reassignment surgery. After reviewing the marriage statute in Ohio, the judge concluded that the application must be denied. Later, the transsexual also filed a petition to have the sex corrected on the transsexual's birth certificate to state "Girl" instead of "Boy." This application was dismissed, and the transsexual filed a complaint for declaratory judgment to have the birth certificate changed and the marriage license issued.

The Ohio Probate Court found that the birth certificate, based on Ohio law, should not be changed. The court stated that its statute is a "correction" type statute, which permits a court to correct errors such as spelling of names, dates, race and sex, if in fact there was an error. 32 Ohio Misc.2d at 8. Since there was no error in the designation of the transsexual as a boy, the application, the court stated, must be dismissed as to the birth certificate change. 32 Ohio Misc.2d at 8. The court concluded, after a review of prior case law, law review articles, and the posthearing brief of the applicant, that no authority existed in Ohio for the issuance of a marriage license to a post-operative male-to-female transsexual and a male person. 32 Ohio Misc.2d at 10. If it is to be the public policy of the state of Ohio to issue marriage license in such cases, the court stated, "it is this court's opinion that the legislature should change the statutes." 32 Ohio Misc.2d at 10.

The most recent decision in the United States regarding transsexualism was decided by the Texas Court of Appeals in *Littleton v. Prange*, 9 S.W.3d 223 (Tex. Civ. App. 1999), cert. denied 531 U.S. 872, 148 L.Ed.2d 119, 121 S.Ct. 174 (2000).

I–F Other Laws, Cases, Regulations, and Considerations

Kansas law allows individuals to change the sex designation on their birth certificates "with a medical certificate substantiating that a physiological or anatomical change occurred." K.A.R. 28–17–20(b)(1)(A)(i).

K.S.A. 2000 Supp. 65–2416(a) states that a birth certificate is "prima facie evidence of the facts therein stated."

Kansas does not require proof of one's sex to obtain a marriage license. K.S.A. 2000 Supp. 23–106.

The Kansas Supreme Court has stated that the "public policy relating to marriage is to foster and protect it, to make it a permanent and public institution, to encourage the parties to live together and to prevent separation." *Ranney v. Ranney,* 219 Kan. 428, 431, 548 P.2d 734 (1976).

Transsexual issues have or will arise in situations involving penal institutions, schools, sports, employment, and every other situation in which perceived gender is important.

I–G Summary Judgment

. . .

The district court found that J'Noel was a male at the time she obtained her license and married, for purposes of K.S.A. 2000 Supp. 23–101. There is no dispute between the parties that J'Noel was born a male with male genitalia, that J'Noel's original birth certificate stated that J'Noel was a male, or that J'Noel suffers from gender dysphoria, which is characterized by a strong desire to be the opposite sex. The question really is whether J'Noel was a male or a female, for the purpose of the statute, at the time the marriage license was issued. Inherent in that question is the question of what criteria are to be used to determine the sex of an applicant at the time of the application process. Both parties agree that J'Noel's original birth certificate has been amended to state that J'Noel is a female.

The district court was provided with J'Noel's deposition and affidavits that give opinions as to whether what J'Noel has undergone indeed transformed J'Noel into a female. The affidavits are material, and they contradict each other. The district court was required to interpret K.S.A. 2000 Supp. 23–101 as to what the legislature intended when it is stated that marriage must be between two parties "who are of opposite sex." The court had to decide whether the legislature intended a marriage between a post-operative male-to-female transsexual and a male to be valid for purposes of the statute.

. . .

Conclusion

This court rejects the reasoning of the majority in the *Littleton* case as a rigid and simplistic approach to issues that are far more complex than addressed in that opinion.

We conclude that a trial court must consider and decide whether an individual was male or female at the time the individual's marriage license was issued and the individual was married, not simply what the individual's chromosomes were or were not at the moment of birth.

The court may use chromosome makeup as one factor, but not the exclusive factor, in arriving at a decision. Aside from chromosomes, we adopt the criteria set forth by Professor Greenberg. On remand, the trial court is directed to consider factors in addition to chromosome makeup, including: gonadal sex, internal morphologic sex, external morphologic sex, hormonal sex, phenotypic sex, assigned sex and gender of rearing, and sexual identity. The listed criteria we adopt as significant in resolving the case before us should not preclude the consideration of other criteria as science advances.

... This matter is reversed and remanded for a full hearing, with the opportunity for each side to present evidence on at least the factors enumerated in the Greenberg article and with directions to consider the conclusions of this court and the legal and scientific research we rely upon.

NOTE

The Court of Appeals' decision in *Gardiner* validating J'Noel's marriage was reversed by the Kansas Supreme Court (273 Kan. 191, 42 P.3d 120 (2002)). The Court held that

> ... The district court granted summary judgment, finding the marriage void under K.S.A. 2001 Supp. 23–101. Summary judgment is appropriate

when there is no genuine issue of material fact. *Bergstrom v. Noah*, 266 Kan. 847, 871, 974 P.2d 531 (1999). Here, the parties have supplied and agreed to the material facts necessary to resolve this issue. There are no disputed material facts. We disagree with the decision reached by the Court of Appeals. We view the issue in this appeal to be one of law and not fact. The resolution of this issue involves the interpretation of K.S.A. 2001 Supp. 23–101. The interpretation of a statute is a question of law, and this court has unlimited appellate review. *State v. Lewis*, 263 Kan. 843, 847, 953 P.2d 1016 (1998).

The fundamental rule of statutory construction is that the intent of the legislature governs. In determining legislative intent, courts are not limited to consideration of the language used in the statute, but may look to the historical background of the enactment, the circumstances attending its passage, the purpose to be accomplished, and the effect the statute may have under the various constructions suggested. *Sowers v. Tsamolias*, 23 Kan.App.2d 270, 273, 929 P.2d 188 (1996). Words in common usage are to be given their natural and ordinary meaning. *State v. Heffelman*, 256 Kan. 384, 886 P.2d 823 (1994). When a statute is plain and unambiguous, the court must give effect to the intention of the legislature as expressed, rather than determine what the law should or should not be. *In re Marriage of Killman*, 264 Kan. 33, 42–43, 955 P.2d 1228 (1998).

The words "sex," "male," and "female" are words in common usage and understood by the general population. Black's Law Dictionary, 1375 (6th ed. 1999) defines "sex" as "the sum of the peculiarities of structure and function that distinguish a male from a female organism; the character of being male or female." Webster's New Twentieth Century Dictionary (2nd ed. 1970) states the initial definition of sex as "either of the two divisions of organisms distinguished as male or female; males or females (especially men or women) collectively." "Male" is defined as "designating or of the sex that fertilizes the ovum and begets offspring: opposed to *female*." "Female" is defined as "designating or of the sex that produces ova and bears offspring: opposed to *male*." [Emphasis added.] According to Black's Law Dictionary, 972 (6th ed. 1999) a marriage "is the legal status, condition, or relation of one man and one woman united in law for life, or until divorced, for the discharge to each other and the community of the duties legally incumbent on those whose association is founded on the distinction of sex."

The words "sex," "male," and "female" in everyday understanding do not encompass transsexuals. The plain, ordinary meaning of "persons of the opposite sex" contemplates a biological man and a biological woman and not persons who are experiencing gender dysphoria. A male-to-female post-operative transsexual does not fit the definition of a female. The male organs have been removed, but the ability to "produce ova and bear offspring" does not and never did exist. There is no womb, cervix, or ovaries, nor is there any change in his chromosomes. As the *Littleton* court noted, the transsexual still "inhabits . . . a male body in all aspects other than what the physicians have supplied." 9 S.W.3d at 231. J'Noel does not fit the common meaning of female.

That interpretation of K.S.A. 2001 Supp. 23–101 is supported by the legislative history of the statute. That legislative history is set out in the Court of Appeals decision:

> "The amendment to 23–101 limiting marriage to two parties of the opposite sex began its legislative history in 1975. The minutes of the Senate Committee on Judiciary for January 21, 1976, state that the amendment would 'affirm the traditional view of marriage.' The proposed amendment was finally enacted in 1980.
>
> "K.S.A. 23–101 was again amended in 1996, when language was added, stating: 'All other marriages are declared to be contrary to the public policy of this state and are void.' This sentence was inserted immediately after the sentence limiting marriage to two parties of the opposite sex.
>
> "In 1996, K.S.A. 23–115 was amended, with language added stating: 'It is the strong public policy of this state only to recognize as valid marriages from other states that are between a man and a woman.' " 29 Kan.App.2d at 99.

The Court of Appeals then noted:

> "The legislative history contains discussions about gays and lesbians, but nowhere is there any testimony that specifically states that marriage should be prohibited by two parties if one is a post-operative male-to-female or female-to-male transsexual. Thus, the question remains: Was J'Noel a female at the time the license was issued for the purpose of the statute?" 29 Kan.App.2d at 100.

We do not agree that the question remains. We view the legislative silence to indicate that transsexuals are not included. If the legislature intended to include transsexuals, it could have been a simple matter to have done so. We apply the rules of statutory construction to ascertain the legislative intent as expressed in the statute. We do not read into a statute something that does not come within the wording of the statute. *Joe Self Chevrolet, Inc. v. Board of Sedgwick County Comm's*, 247 Kan. 625, 633, 802 P.2d 1231 (1990).

In *Ulane v. Eastern Airlines, Inc.*, 742 F.2d 1081 (7th Cir. 1984), the federal district court, like the Court of Appeals here, held sex identity was not just a matter of chromosomes at birth, but was in part a psychological, self-perception, and social question. In reversing the district court, the Seventh Circuit stated:

> In our view, to include transsexuals within the reach of Title VII far exceeds mere statutory interpretation. Congress had a narrow view of sex in mind when it passed the Civil Rights Act, and it has rejected subsequent attempts to broaden the scope of its original interpretation. For us to now hold that Title VII protects transsexuals would take us out of the realm of interpreting and reviewing and into the realm of legislating. *See Gunnison v. Commissioner*, 461 F.2d 496, 499 (7th Cir. 1972) (it is for the legislature, not the courts, to expand the class of people protected by a statute). This we must not and will not do.

> Congress has a right to deliberate on whether it wants such a broad sweeping of the untraditional and unusual within the term 'sex' as used in Title VII. Only Congress can consider all the ramifications to society of such a broad view. We do not believe that the interpretation of the word 'sex' as used in the statute is a mere matter of expert medical testimony or the credibility of witnesses produced in court. Congress may, at some future time, have some interest in testimony of that type, but it does not control our interpretation of Title VII based on the legislative history or lack thereof. If Congress believes that transsexuals should enjoy the protection of Title VII, it may so provide. Until that time, however, we decline in behalf of the Congress to judicially expand the definition of sex as used in Title VII beyond its common and traditional interpretation. 742 F.2d at 1086.

We agree with the Seventh Circuit's analysis in *Ulane*. It is well reasoned and logical. Although *Ulane* involves sex discrimination against Ulane as a transsexual and as a female under Title VII, the similarity of the basic issue and facts to the present case make it both instructive and persuasive. As we have previously noted, the legislature clearly viewed "opposite sex" in the narrow traditional sense. The legislature has declared that the public policy of this state is to recognize only the traditional marriage between "two parties who are of the opposite sex," and all other marriages are against public policy and void. We cannot ignore what the legislature has declared to be the public policy of this state. Our responsibility is to interpret K.S.A. 2001 Supp. 23–101 and not to rewrite it. That is for the legislature to do if it so desires. If the legislature wishes to change public policy, it is free to do so; we are not. To conclude that J'Noel is of the opposite sex of Marshall would require that we rewrite K.S.A. 2001 Supp. 23–101.

Finally, we recognize that J'Noel has traveled a long and difficult road. J'Noel has undergone electrolysis, thermolysis, tracheal shave, hormone injections, extensive counseling, and reassignment surgery. Unfortunately, after all that, J'Noel remains a transsexual, and a male for purposes of marriage under K.S.A. 2001 Supp. 23–101. We are not blind to the stress and pain experienced by one who is born a male but perceives oneself as a female. We recognize that there are people who do not fit neatly into the commonly recognized category of male or female, and to many life becomes an ordeal. However, the validity of J'Noel's marriage to Marshall is a question of public policy to be addressed by the legislature and not by this court.

BEGER v. ACTING COMM'R, DIV. OF MED. ASSISTANCE

11 Mass. L. Rptr. 745 (Mass. Super. Ct. 2000)

MARIA I. LOPEZ

MEMORANDUM OF DECISION ON PLAINTIFF'S MOTION FOR JUDGMENT ON THE PLEADINGS

Plaintiff Germaine Beger ("Ms. Beger") claims that the Defendant, Division of Medical Assistance ("Division"), wrongfully denied her breast reconstruction surgery after her defective breast implants were removed. Count I of the complaint seeks judicial review of the Division's decision under *G.L.c. 30A, 14*.... Ms. Beger filed this motion for summary judgment on Count I, which shall be treated as a motion for judgment on the pleadings. For the following reasons, the Division's decision is *REVERSED*.

Background

The following facts are undisputed. Ms. Beger is a 49–year–old Medicaid recipient who for the past 25 years has lived as a woman. In 1975, Ms. Beger received breast implants as part of her sex-reassignment transition. In December 1998, on a referral by her doctor Dr. Jeffrey Korff ("Korff"), Ms. Beger sought treatment for a possible cyst in her right breast. After that evaluation, an MRI was conducted on January 12, 1999 by Dr. Laurie Loiacana ("Loiacana"), who determined that both of Ms. Beger's breast implants needed to be removed, one due to calcification and the other due to leakage. On March 26, 1999, Surgeon Kristin Steuber ("Steuber") submitted a Prior Authorization Request to the Division stating that surgery to remove the implants and reconstruct the breasts was medically necessary.

Dr. Linda Clayton ("Clayton"), a doctor for the Division, approved the Prior Request for removal of the breast implants but denied the request for reconstruction, and wrote in the space for reason: "see regulation 130 CMR 433.404(B)."[2] On March 29, 1999, the Division authorized the removal of the implants but denied the insertion of saline breast implants to reconstruct the breasts citing both 130 CMR 450.204 and 130 CMR 433.404(B). On April 7, 1999, Ms. Beger filed a Request for a Fair Hearing to review the Division's decision. On June 25, 1999, the Board of Hearings held a hearing to review the Division's decision. On August 25, 1999, the Division's hearing officer denied Ms. Beger's appeal and affirmed the Division's decision to deny Ms. Beger's request for breast reconstruction surgery. Ms. Beger filed this action on September 24, 1999.

Discussion

The question before this Court is whether the Division's action denying Ms. Beger's breast reconstruction surgery is arbitrary, capricious, or contrary to law under G.L.c. 30A, 14(7). The Division, as a recipient of federal funding, must comply with the requirements of Title XIX of the Social Security Act and the implementing regulations. *See Haley v. Commissioner of Public Welfare,* 394 Mass. 466, 467, 476 N.E.2d 572 (1985).

2. Under "nonreimbursable circumstances," 130 CMR 433.404(B) states:

The Division will not pay a physician for performing, administering, or dispensing any experimental, unproven, cosmetic, or otherwise medically unnecessary procedure or treatment, specifically including but not limited to, sex-reassignment surgery, thyroid cartilage reduction surgery, and any other related surgeries and treatments, including pre-and post-sex-reassignment surgery hormone therapy. Notwithstanding the preceding sentence, the Division will continue to pay for post-sex-reassignment surgery hormone therapy for which it had been paying immediately prior to May 15, 1993.

Medicaid "confers broad discretion on the States to adopt standards for determining the extent of medical assistance, requiring only that such standards be 'reasonable' and 'consistent with the objectives of the Act.' " *Norfolk County Hospital v. Commonwealth,* 25 Mass. App. Ct. 586, 587, 521 N.E.2d 406, rev. denied 402 Mass. 1104, 524 N.E.2d 400 (1988), quoting *Beal v. Doe,* 432 U.S. 438, 444, 53 L.Ed.2d 464, 97 S.Ct. 2366 (1977). The Court shall "give due weight to the experience, technical competence, and specialized knowledge of the agency, as well as to the discretionary authority conferred upon it." G.L.c. 30A, 14 (7). An agency's interpretation of its own regulation is generally entitled to great weight and should be overturned only if it is arbitrary or unreasonable. *See Norwood Hospital v. Commissioner of Public Welfare,* 417 Mass. 54, 58, 627 N.E.2d 914 (1994).

As the decision to deny Ms. Beger's breast reconstruction surgery was based on a question of law, the court reviews the interpretation *de novo*. *See Hogan v. Labor Relations Commission,* 430 Mass. 611, 613, 722 N.E.2d 446 (2000); *Haverhill Municipal Hospital v. Commissioner of the Division of Medical Assistance, 45 Mass. App. Ct.* 386, 390, 699 N.E.2d 1, *rev. denied* 428 Mass. 1107, 705 N.E.2d 278 (1998). The court may compel any action unlawfully withheld or unreasonably delayed if it determines that the substantial rights of any party have been prejudiced when the agency decision is: 1) based upon an error of law; 2) arbitrary or capricious; or 3) unsupported by substantial evidence. *See* G.L.c. 30A, 14(7)(c), (e), (g).

At the hearing, Clayton testified that the breast reconstruction surgery could not be performed on Ms. Beger because the Division did not cover surgeries related to sex-reassignment under 130 CMR 433.404(B). Clayton stated that in making her recommendation she relied completely on a legal interpretation of the regulation. Because of that regulation, Clayton asserted, a determination of whether the procedure was a medical necessity was unnecessary.

The hearing officer determined that the Division's decision to deny Ms. Beger's breast reconstruction surgery was correct because the "the present need for replacement implants arises in fact because the appellant underwent sex-reassignment in the first place and this fact makes the requested surgical procedure related to the previous sex-reassignment surgery." Recognizing a difference between the two, the hearing officer stated that the removal of defective implants presents a situation where the absence of such removal poses a medical threat to the appellant's continued health. I find nothing incompatible with the removal of defective implants and the regulatory prohibition for replacement implants related to post sex-reassignment surgery.

I. *The Division's Decision is Incorrect as a Matter of Law.* The hearing officer affirmed the Division's denial of breast reconstruction surgery for Ms. Beger under *130 CMR 433.404(B),* finding that the regulation "was meant to encompass all procedures and treatments related to sex-reassignment surgery without regard to time elapsed." The Court finds that construction of the regulation incorrect as a matter of law for two reasons. First, the construction of the words "related to" sweeps too broadly. Under the Division's interpretation any treatments available to females would have to be denied to Ms. Beger. That, however, is not how the Division applies its regulations. The record indicates that Ms. Beger is entitled to receive routine gynecological care. Removal of Ms. Beger's breast implants has been authorized by the Division. These treatments are clearly related to her sex-reassignment surgery. In addition, the Division's reading of "related to" would include miscellaneous medical issues that only a woman might encounter, such as allergic reactions to female hygiene products. The words "related to" have to be given a narrower scope. Reading the regulation in context with the entire regulatory scheme, the regulation at issue is meant to apply only to those surgeries and treatments that accomplish sex-reassignment.

Second, the Division's finding that 103 CMR 433.404(B) applies without regard to time elapsed from sex-reassignment surgery is in error. The only reference to a time frame in the regulation grandfathers in individuals who were receiving post-surgery hormone therapy prior to May 15, 1993. Thus, contrary to the Division's interpretation, the regulation contemplates time elapsed from sex-reassignment surgery. The Division's argument that the exception for post-surgery hormone therapy is the only one allowed by the regulation ignores the reference in the exception to the preceding sentence which denies payment for sex-reassignment surgery "including pre-and post-sex-reassignment hormone therapy." Thus, the exception for post-surgery hormone therapy specifically modifies the prior sentence and is not, as the Division contends, a limitation on the treatment available for individuals who have completed their transition. Indeed, as this case shows, the Division provides a number of medical treatments to individuals who have completed their transition.

This Court finds that 103 CMR 433.404(B) is meant to cover only those surgeries and treatments intended to accomplish sex-reassignment and not to surgeries and treatments needed by individuals who have completed their transition. In this case, Ms. Beger's breast reconstruction is not intended to accomplish a sex-reassignment. Ms. Beger has been a woman for 25 years. Ms. Beger's request does not fall within 103 CMR 433.404(B). Ms. Beger was entitled to be considered for breast reconstruction only under 130 CMR 433.451(B)(3).[5]

II. *The Division's Decision is Arbitrary*. The hearing officer found that because replacement breast implants are related to Ms. Beger's [*10] sex-reassignment surgery, "medical necessity" did not need to be consid-

---

5. 103 CMR 433.451(B)(3) states:

Reconstructive surgery is reimbursable only when determined by the Division pursuant to a request for prior authorization to be medically necessary to correct, repair or ameliorate the physical effects of physical disease or defect, or traumatic injury.

ered in this case.[6] The Court finds this conclusion illogical and arbitrary. Clearly, both the removal and the replacement of the failed implants are related to Ms. Beger's sex-reassignment surgery. Here, the Division applied medical necessity to the removal of the implants. It is only logical and reasonable to apply medical necessity to their replacement. It is arbitrary and capricious for the Division to find that it will pay for the removal of Ms. Beger's implants but will not even consider the medical necessity of replacing the implants it will pay to remove. The Division's action in this case simply punishes Ms. Beger because her implants failed after 25 years.

III. *The Division's Decision is Unsupported by Substantial Evidence.* An administrative agency's decision must be supported by substantial evidence, defined as "such evidence as a reasonable mind might accept as adequate to support a conclusion." *Pyfrom v. Commissioner of Public Welfare,* 39 Mass. App. Ct. 621, 624, 659 N.E.2d 1206 (1996), quoting G.L.c. 30A, 1. "In order to determine if an agency's decision is supported by substantial evidence, one must examine the entire administrative record and take into account whatever detracts from its weight." *Pyfrom,* 39 Mass. App. Ct. at 624–25, citing *New Boston Garden Corp. v. Assessors of Boston,* 383 Mass. 456, 466, 420 N.E.2d 298 (1981). If the evidence points to an overwhelming probability to the contrary, the agency's decision may be set aside. *Pyfrom,* 39 Mass. App. Ct. at 625, quoting *New Boston Garden,* 383 Mass. at 466.

The Division's denial of breast reconstruction surgery is not supported by substantial evidence. The Division introduced no evidence showing that the breast reconstruction was not medically necessary. The surgery sought here is reconstructive surgery. Reconstructive surgery is defined as "a surgical procedure that is performed to correct, repair, or ameliorate the physical effects of physical disease or defect (for example, correction of cleft palate), or traumatic injury." 130 CMR 433.401. In its surgical services section, the Division states that reconstructive surgery is reimbursable to physicians when it is medically necessary to correct the physical effects of a defect, or traumatic injury. *See* 130 CMR 433.451(B)(3). Ms. Beger introduced uncontroverted evidence that the breast replacement surgery was sought to correct the physical effects of the removal of the defective breast implants.

Clayton testified that Ms. Beger successfully completed her sex-reassignment surgery in 1975 and has lived as a woman for 25 years.

6. 103 CMR 450.204(A) defines a service as "medically necessary" if:

(1) it is reasonably calculated to prevent, diagnose, prevent the worsening of, alleviate, correct, or cure conditions in the member that endanger life, cause suffering or pain, cause physical deformity or malfunction, threaten to cause or to aggravate a handicap, or result in illness or infirmity; and

(2) there is no other medical service or site of service, comparable in effect, available, and suitable for the member requesting the service, that is more conservative or less costly to the Division. Services that are less costly to the Division include, but are not limited to, health care reasonably known by the provider, or identified by the Division pursuant to a prior authorization request, to be available to the member through sources described in 130 CMR 450.317(C), 503.007, or 517.007.

Clayton also testified that the Division provides breast reconstruction surgery for women who have lost their breast due to congenital deformity, injury, or mutilating surgery. In addition, Clayton testified that the decision to provide a woman with breast reconstruction would largely be made on an individual basis between a patient and her doctor. There was substantial evidence, in the form of testimony and letters from doctors showing that Ms. Beger's breast reconstruction surgery was medically necessary under 130 CMR 450.204(A).[8] The evidence presented by Ms. Beger demonstrated that the surgery "is reasonably calculated to ... correct ... conditions ... that ... cause suffering or pain, [or] cause physical deformity" and that because of Ms. Beger's allergic reaction to hormone treatments, there exists "no other medical service ... comparable in effect, ... available, and suitable ... that is more conservative or less costly to the Division."[9] 130 CMR 450.204(A)(1) & (2). The evidence presented by Ms. Beger which was not rebutted by the Division should have been credited by the hearing officer. As the Division failed to provide any evidence that the surgery is not medically necessary, the decision by the hearing officer is not supported by the record.

---

8. The request by Steuber stated that "because of the patient's status, it is felt medically necessary to replace the implants with saline implants." On June 17, 1999, Steuber wrote the Division a letter stating "there is no question that new implants are medically necessary.... As with any other woman, Ms. Beger has suffered injury to her breasts which needs medical attention. Implant replacement is not merely cosmetic ... Replacement will thus alleviate, correct and cure Ms. Beger's suffering and pain, and it will also prevent a physical deformity which would result from the removal of implants were there not a corresponding replacement."

Doctors Margaret Harak (a licensed psychologist and Ms. Beger's current therapist) and Martha Woodard (licensed psychologist) and Florence Mayer (a licensed marriage and family therapist) wrote a letter to Massachusetts Health Insurance on March 10, 1999, stating that "as Ms. Beger had a sex change operation over twenty years ago and clearly identifies herself as a woman, her breast implants do not serve a merely cosmetic purpose. Rather, she views her implants as an integral part of her identity. Therefore, we strongly believe that psychologically, it is in Ms. Beger's best interests to have her implants replaced."

Dr. Kevin Epstein (Ms. Beger's primary care provider since June 1997) wrote to the Division of Medical Assistance on June 23, 1999 stating that "failure to cosmetically reaugment her breast(s) would likely contribute to an exacerbation of the many psychological issues that she deals with on a daily basis. Overall it is safe to say that failure to provide breast reconstruction at this point will likely have a long lasting psychological impact which would be devastating to her."

Nurse Bette Kisner (an advance practice nurse who is a clinical specialist in psychiatric and mental health nursing, specializing in the treatment of patients with cancer, especially women with breast cancer) wrote a letter to the Division of Medical Assistance on June 24, 1999, stating that the breast replacement is medically necessary since "the breast implants are integral to her sense of identity as a woman. Because Ms[.] Beger's breasts are a core part of her identity, their pending removal can be compared to the experience that a mastectomy provides for the woman with breast cancer ... like a woman who loses a breast to mastectomy, Ms. Beger would experience depression, lowered self esteem, a sense of bodily deformity, diminished feelings of attractiveness, and feelings of being viewed as less than feminine ... because she is transsexual, with the associated discrimination that has accompanied that identity, Ms[.] Beger's vulnerability to rejection and loneliness is that much greater than that experienced by a non-transsexual female mastectomy patient. The medical necessity for replacing Germaine Beger's breast implants is without question."

9. A letter from Korff on March 16, 1999 states "she has been intolerant to 2 courses of transdermal estrogen in the past due to a rash which will limit our ability to replace her with estrogen and thereby stimulate endogenous breast development. I would therefore recommend, if possible, that following removal of her encapsulated breast implants that you consider reimplantation of new breast prosthesis."

IV. *Conclusion*. The Court finds that the Division's decision is based on an error of law, is arbitrary and is not supported by substantial evidence. As a result, Ms. Beger's right to breast reconstruction, which is a substantial right, has been unlawfully withheld and unreasonably delayed.

Order

For the foregoing reasons, the decision by the Division of Medical Assistance denying Germaine Beger breast reconstruction surgery is hereby *REVERSED*. The Division of Medical Assistance is directed to authorize payment for Germaine Beger's breast reconstruction surgery.

KOSILEK v. MALONEY

221 F. Supp. 2d 156 (D. Mass. 2002)

WOLF, D.J.

I. Summary

Plaintiff Michelle Kosilek is serving a life sentence, without the possibility of parole, for murdering his wife. Kosilek is also suffering from a severe form of a rare, medically recognized, major mental illness—gender identity disorder ("GID"). Kosilek is a transsexual. Since at least age three, Kosilek has believed that he is actually a female who has been cruelly trapped in a male's body.[1] This belief has caused Kosilek to suffer constant mental anguish and, at times, abuse. While incarcerated, it has also caused Kosilek to attempt twice to kill himself, and to try to castrate himself as well.

The Harry Benjamin Standards of Care (the "Standards of Care") are protocols used by qualified professionals in the United States to treat individuals suffering from gender identity disorders. According to the Standards of Care, psychotherapy with a qualified therapist is sufficient treatment for some individuals. In other cases psychotherapy and the administration of female hormones provide adequate relief. There are, however, some cases in which sex reassignment surgery is medically necessary and appropriate.

Since being incarcerated in 1990, Kosilek has sought but not received any of the forms of treatment described in the Standards of Care. In 1992, Kosilek filed a pro se lawsuit, pursuant to 42 U.S.C. § 1983, against the Sheriff of Bristol County, David R. Nelson, and others. Kosilek generally alleged that he was being denied adequate medical care for his serious medical need in violation of the Eighth Amendment of the United States Constitution. Kosilek sought both damages and an injunction requiring

1. The court recognizes that it is painful for Kosilek to be referred to as "he" and that courts have, at times, referred to male transsexuals as "she." *See, e.g., Farmer v. Perrill*, 275 F.3d 958 n.1 (10th Cir. 2001); *Schwenk v. Hartford*, 204 F.3d 1187, 1192 n.1 (9th Cir. 2000). However, this court finds that referring to Kosilek by the male pronoun is necessary to make this Memorandum as clear as possible.

that he be provided sex reassignment surgery. After his conviction and transfer to the Massachusetts Department of Corrections (the "DOC") in 1992, Kosilek amended his complaint to seek the same relief from the DOC.

Defendant Michael Maloney became the Commissioner of the DOC in 1997. In 1999, he became a defendant in this case.

. . .

The court granted the motions of Nelson and Maloney to dismiss the claims for damages against them individually based on qualified immunity, and granted Nelson's motion for summary judgment on the claims against him in his official capacity. Maloney's motion for summary judgment on Kosilek's claim for injunctive relief was denied. A non-jury trial concerning that claim was conducted in February 2002.

At trial, counsel for Kosilek represented that Kosilek is now requesting that the court issue an injunction requiring that he be provided with treatment in prison for gender identity disorder consistent with the Standards of Care. More specifically, Kosilek requests that the court order that Maloney: retain a doctor who specializes in treating gender identity disorders to evaluate Kosilek; authorize that doctor to prescribe any treatment deemed appropriate; and provide the treatment prescribed by that doctor. The court is not now being asked to order that Kosilek be administered female hormones or provided sex reassignment surgery. These are, however, forms of treatment that are provided to some, but not all, transsexuals pursuant to the Standards of Care. Thus, the injunction that Kosilek requests could ultimately require the administration of female hormones and, a year or more lately, sex reassignment surgery.

Ordinarily, the Commissioner of the DOC would not be the appropriate defendant in a case involving an inmate's claim alleging a denial of medical care. As Commissioner, Maloney does not usually make decisions concerning medical care. It is his policy and usual practice to rely on the social workers and medical professionals employed by the DOC, and the outside experts they often consult, to determine whether an inmate has a serious medical need and, if so, what is necessary to treat it adequately.

Kosilek, however, has been dealt with differently. Because of Kosilek's lawsuit Maloney, as a practical matter, has made the major decisions relating to Kosilek's medical care.

As a result of this case, in consultation with attorneys and doctors employed by the DOC, in 2000 Maloney adopted a blanket policy concerning the treatment the DOC would provide to the several transsexual prisoners in its custody. That policy is aimed at "freezing" a transsexual in the condition he was in when incarcerated. It contemplates the administration of female hormones for inmates for whom they were prescribed prior to incarceration. The policy strictly prohibits providing hormones to inmates like Kosilek who have taken only "black market" hormones previously. Maloney's policy also categorically excludes the possibility that an inmate will receive sex reassignment surgery. Because Maloney removed from the professionals employed by the DOC their usual discretion concerning Kosilek's medical needs and care, Maloney's conduct is properly the focus of this case.

Kosilek's claims involve facts that are unusual, but not unprecedented. In view of the general lack of public knowledge and understanding of gender identity disorders, the idea that an imprisoned male murderer may ever have a right to receive female hormones and sex reassignment surgery may understandably strike some people as bizarre. However, Kosilek's claims raise issues involving substantial jurisprudence concerning the application of the Eighth Amendment to inmates with serious medical needs. This case requires the neutral application of the principles that emerge from that jurisprudence to the facts established by the evidence in this case.

The Eighth Amendment prohibits Cruel and Unusual Punishment. The Supreme Court has explained that "the Amendment embodies broad and idealistic concepts of dignity, civilized standards, humanity, and decency...." *Estelle v. Gamble,* 429 U.S. 97, 50 L.Ed.2d 251, 102, 97 S.Ct. 285 (1976) (internal quotation and citation omitted).

Among other things, the Eighth Amendment does not permit the unnecessary infliction of pain on a prisoner, either intentionally or because of the deliberate indifference of the responsible prison official. Any such infliction of pain is deemed "wanton." The wanton infliction of pain on an inmate violates the Eighth Amendment.

Prisoners in the United States have a right to humane treatment, including a right to adequate care for their serious medical needs. The Constitution does not protect this right because we are a nation that coddles criminals. Rather, we recognize and respect this right because we are, fundamentally, a decent people, and decent people do not allow other human beings in their custody to suffer needlessly from serious illness or injury.

Nevertheless, because the Eighth Amendment prohibits only certain punishments, to establish a violation when a prisoner's health is at issue, it is not sufficient for an inmate to prove only that he has not received adequate medical care. Rather, he must also prove that the official responsible for his care has intentionally ignored a serious medical need or been deliberately indifferent to it.

Accordingly, the Eighth Amendment standard has an objective and subjective component. With regard to the objective prong, it must be proven that there is a serious medical need and that adequate care has not been provided. A serious medical need is one that involves a substantial risk of serious harm if it is not adequately treated. Typically, it is a need that has been diagnosed by a physician as mandating treatment or one that is so obvious that even a lay person would easily recognize the necessity for a doctor's attention.

Adequate care requires treatment by qualified personnel, who provide services that are of a quality acceptable when measured by prudent professional standards in the community. Adequate care is tailored to an inmate's particular medical needs and is based on medical considerations.

An inmate is not entitled to the care of his choice. Courts must defer to the decisions of prison officials concerning what form of adequate care to provide an inmate. However, courts must decide if the care being provided is minimally adequate.

The subjective prong of the deliberate indifference test also has two parts. The responsible official must be aware of facts from which the inference could be drawn that a substantial risk of serious harm exists. He must also draw that inference.

Because the Eighth Amendment proscribes the unnecessary infliction of pain on a prisoner, the practical constraints imposed by the prison environment are relevant to whether the subjective component of the Eighth Amendment test has been satisfied. The duty of prison officials to protect the safety of inmates and prison personnel is a factor that may properly be considered in prescribing medical care for a serious medical need. It is conceivable that a prison official, acting reasonably and in good faith, might perceive an irreconcilable conflict between his duty to protect safety and his duty to provide an inmate adequate medical care. If so, his decision not to provide that care might not violate the Eighth Amendment because the resulting infliction of pain on the inmate would not be unnecessary or wanton. Rather, it might be reasonable and reasonable conduct does not violate the Eighth Amendment.

It is not, however, permissible to deny an inmate adequate medical care because it is costly. In recognition of this, prison officials at times authorize CAT scans, dialysis, and other forms of expensive medical care required to diagnose or treat familiar forms of serious illness.

If deliberate indifference to a serious medical need is proven, in order to obtain an injunction, an inmate must also prove that it is likely to continue in the future.

Thus, to prevail in this case, Kosilek is required to prove that: (1) he has a serious medical need; (2) which has not been adequately treated; (3) because of Maloney's deliberate indifference; and (4) that deliberate indifference is likely to continue in the future.

Kosilek has proven the first two elements of his claim, but not the last two. Kosilek has a serious medical need. He has not been offered adequate medical treatment for it. Indeed, he has been offered no real treatment at all. Therefore, the objective component of the Eighth Amendment standard has been proven.

Kosilek has not, however, satisfied the subjective component of the test. Maloney knew many facts from which it could have been inferred that Kosilek was at substantial risk of serious harm if he did not receive adequate treatment. Maloney did not, however, actually draw that inference.

Because of this litigation and the unusual issues it involves, Kosilek's medical needs have not been addressed in a manner consistent with the DOC's usual policy and practice. Qualified physicians have never evaluated Kosilek for the primary purpose of prescribing treatment. Rather, they have been employed as potential expert witnesses in this case.

Because of the pendency of this case, Maloney as a practical matter removed from the medical personnel the DOC employs their usual authority to diagnose and treat Kosilek. Maloney, who is not qualified to make medical judgments, was prompted by this case to adopt a rigid, freeze-frame policy. This policy effectively prohibits DOC doctors and social workers from considering for Kosilek hormone therapy and sex reassignment surgery, which are forms of treatment prescribed by qualified professionals in the community for some, but not all, individuals suffering from severe gender identity disorders. As a result of that policy, no individualized medical evaluation has been done for the purpose of prescribing treatment for Kosilek's serious medical need.

Maloney, however, did not adopt his policy with the intent to inflict pain on Kosilek or as a result of deliberate indifference. Maloney did not focus on Kosilek's medical needs. He acted as a defendant with a legal problem. He has been reluctant to allow Kosilek to receive hormones or sex reassignment surgery unless he was legally required to do so. His reluctance has been rooted in sincere security concerns, and in a fear of public and political criticism as well. Maloney has not been influenced by the possibility that treatment for Kosilek might be expensive. Rather, he has been concerned that any expenditure for hormones or sex reassignment surgery might be an inappropriate use of taxpayers' money.

As stated earlier, security is a legitimate consideration for Eighth Amendment purposes. A concern about political or public criticism for discharging a constitutional duty is not.

State and local officials, like judges, have a duty to obey the Constitution. The Bill of Rights provides citizens, including those who are incarcerated, with certain rights that even a majority of their contemporaries cannot properly decide to violate. Prison officials share with the courts the duty to protect those rights, even if they believe that it may be unpopular to do so.

This court's decision puts Maloney on notice that Kosilek has a serious medical need which is not being properly treated. Therefore, he has a duty to respond reasonably to it. The court expects that he will.

In essence, the court expects that Maloney will allow qualified medical professionals to recommend treatment for Kosilek. At a minimum, psychotherapy with, or under the direction of, a professional with training and experience concerning individuals with severe gender identity disorder is required. Such therapy should raise no security concerns.

If hormones or sex reassignment surgery are recommended, Maloney may properly consider whether security issues make it impossible to provide adequate medical care in prison for Kosilek's serious medical need. The court expects that any such consideration will include the following facts.

Kosilek is already living largely as a woman in a medium security male prison. This has not presented a security problem. The policy Maloney adopted contemplates continuing female hormones for transsexuals for whom they have been prescribed prior to incarceration. Maloney expects that he would keep such inmates in the general population of a male prison. This has, evidently, been done safely in several states, in the United States Bureau of Prisons system, and in Canada.

If Maloney, in good faith, reasonably decides that there is truly no way that he can discharge both his duty to protect safety and his duty to provide Kosilek with adequate medical care, and concludes that security concerns must trump the recommendations of qualified medical professionals, a court will have to decide whether the Eighth Amendment has been violated. That question is not now before this court. If, however, concerns about cost or controversy prompt Maloney to deny Kosilek adequate care for his serious medical need, Maloney will have violated the Eighth Amendment. Kosilek will then likely be entitled to the injunction that he has unsuccessfully sought in this case.

II. Findings of Fact

The following facts are proven by a preponderance of the credible evidence.

It is not disputed that Kosilek has a genuine gender identity disorder. A gender identity disorder is defined by the Diagnostic and Statistical Manual of Mental Disorders, Fourth Edition–Text Revision ("DSM–IV–TR") as a major mental illness. Generally, and in this case, a person suffering from a gender identity disorder has the anatomy of a male, but a brain that in effect tells him that he is a female.

Individuals suffering from a gender identity disorder are sometimes referred to as "transsexuals." Ex. 7, at 3–4. The Supreme Court has accurately described a transsexual as a person who has:

> "[a] rare psychiatric disorder in which a person feels persistently uncomfortable about his or her anatomical sex," and who typically seeks medical treatment, including hormone therapy and surgery, to bring about a permanent sex change."

Farmer v. Brennan, 511 U.S. 825, 829, 128 L.Ed.2d 811, 114 S.Ct. 1970 (quoting American Medical Association, Encyclopedia of Medicine 1006 (1989)).

The consensus of medical professionals is that transsexualism is biological and innate. It is not a freely chosen "sexual preference" or produced by an individual's life experience.

The DSM–IV–TR includes four diagnostic criteria for a gender identity disorder:

> A. A strong and persistent cross-gender identification (not merely a desire for any perceived cultural advantages of being the other sex)
>
> . . .
>
> B. Persistent discomfort with his or her sex or sense of inappropriateness in the gender role of that sex
>
> . . .
>
> C. The disturbance is not concurrent with an intersex condition [meaning sexually ambiguous genitalia]
>
> . . .
>
> D. The disturbance causes clinically significant distress or impairment in social, occupational, or other important areas of functioning.

Ex. 6A, at 581.

Kosilek is now fifty-three years old. Kosilek has long held a strong and persistent belief that he is a woman trapped in a man's body. The severity of Kosilek's gender identity disorder is evidenced, in part, by Kosilek's history of drug abuse and use of female hormones.

At the age of three, Kosilek was left by his mother in an orphanage, where he was frequently punished for dressing as a female. Beginning at the age of ten, he was reunited with his mother, repeatedly raped by his grandfather, and stabbed by his stepfather for his announced desire to live as a girl.

As a teenager, Kosilek ran away from home, often dressed as a woman, engaged in prostitution, and abused illegal drugs. From 1967 to 1968, Kosilek received female hormones prescribed by a physician in exchange for sex. He also took hormones for several months in 1971 and 1972. While on hormones, Kosilek "felt normal" for the first time in his life.

As a result of taking hormones in 1971 and 1972, Kosilek developed breasts. When imprisoned in Chicago in this condition, Kosilek was gang raped in 1971 and 1972. He was also assaulted outside a gay bar by two men who said they resented his effort to become a girl. Kosilek was beaten so badly that he stopped taking hormones.

Although he had dropped out of high school, Kosilek managed to earn a college degree and to work productively for periods of time. Despite his painful belief that he was truly a female, Kosilek did not seek treatment for his gender identity disorder.

After relapsing into drug abuse, Kosilek entered a drug rehabilitation facility. There he met Cheryl McCaul, who was working as a volunteer counselor. McCaul told Kosilek that his transsexualism would be cured by "a good woman," and married him. However, Kosilek's distress did not abate. In 1990, Kosilek murdered McCaul.

Kosilek was incarcerated at the Bristol County Jail pending trial. Kosilek's case immediately received a great deal of publicity, in part because he was wearing female clothing when arrested. Later, when Kosilek's efforts to obtain treatment for his gender identity disorder at his own expense failed, Kosilek engaged in a publicized campaign to be elected Sheriff. He also initiated a pro se lawsuit against the Sheriff and others, claiming a denial of necessary medical care.

While detained pending trial at the Bristol County Jail, Kosilek again took female hormones in the form of birth control pills. The pills were illegally provided by a guard.

Bristol County Jail officials allowed Kosilek, at his own expense, to consult an expert in gender identity disorders. Dr. Nancy Strapko, in preparation for his trial. Dr. Strapko was not, however, permitted to provide any treatment to Kosilek. The Sheriff also did not follow Dr. Strapko's recommendation that Kosilek begin psychotherapy with a qualified specialist to address his gender identity disorder.

Kosilek twice tried to commit suicide while awaiting trial. One attempt occurred when he was taking the antidepressant Prozac. In addition, Kosilek attempted to castrate himself.

Kosilek was convicted of murder and sentenced in 1992 to life in prison without the possibility of parole. In January 1993 he was placed in the custody of the Commissioner of the DOC.

When Kosilek was transferred to the custody of the DOC, an intake form noted that he had "minor breast development." Ex. 10, at 3. This breast development evidently resulted from the hormones that Kosilek had been taking at the Bristol County Jail.

Since 1994, Kosilek has been incarcerated in the general population at MCI–Norfolk, a medium-security male prison. There, Kosilek has attempted to live as a woman to the maximum extent possible. Kosilek had his name legally changed from Robert to Michelle. Virtually all of the inmates and guards now call Kosilek "Michelle." Kosilek has grown his fingernails and hair long, modulated his voice to sound more feminine, had his clothing tailored to appear more feminine, and used various products as makeup.

Kosilek has not been assaulted sexually while at MCI–Norfolk. Nor does the evidence indicate that Kosilek has voluntarily had sexual relations with any other inmate.

Kosilek has demanded that prison officials at MCI–Norfolk provide treatment for his gender identity disorder. When his demands were not met, Kosilek amended his complaint to add allegations concerning his treatment by the DOC and many motions. Kosilek's case against Nelson and the present suit have provided Kosilek with hope. As a result, Kosilek has behaved well in prison and has been properly perceived by prison officials as not presenting a high risk of imminent harm to him.

However, Kosilek has repeatedly expressed his intention to kill himself if he does not obtain relief in this case. The court concludes that there is a high risk that Kosilek will harm himself if he does not receive adequate treatment for his severe mental illness. Kosilek's stated intention to kill himself is not merely a threat made to manipulate the DOC or the court. As Dr. Marshall Forstein persuasively put it, he has never known a "heterosexual man want to voluntarily give us his penis to get something like hormones." The court concludes that Kosilek's gender identity disorder is causing him severe emotional distress.

Dr. George Brown opined that if Kosilek does not receive hormone treatments, "the likelihood is exceedingly close to one hundred percent that she will kill herself." The DOC is committed to trying to prevent this. However, the court finds that absent adequate treatment, there is a significant risk that Kosilek will again attempt suicide and may, like some other inmates, succeed.[4]

. . .

At trial Kosilek, through counsel, requested that the court issue an injunction requiring that he be provided with treatment in prison for gender identity disorder consistent with the Standards of Care. The Standards of Care are developed and published by international experts who specialize in the treatment of gender identity disorders. As explained by Kosilek's experts, Drs. Forstein and Brown, as well as by Dr. Appelbaum, the Standards of Care describe the generally accepted treatment for individuals with gender identity disorders in the community.

The following provisions of the Standards of Care are pertinent to this case. The eligibility requirements for certain treatments are "meant to be minimum requirements." Ex. 7, at 2. Clinical departures from the guidelines may be justified by a patient's "unique ... social ... situation," among other things. *Id.*

The Standards of Care establish a "triadic treatment sequence." This triadic sequence is comprised of: (1) hormone therapy; (2) a real-life experience of living as a member of the opposite sex; and (3) sex reassignment surgery. *Id.* at 3. According to the Standards of Care:

> Many adults with gender identity disorder find comfortable, effective ways of living that do not involve all the components of the triadic treatment sequence. While some individuals manage to do this on their own, psychotherapy can be very helpful in bringing about the discovery and maturational processes that enable self-comfort.

Id. at 11 (emphasis added). However, "psychotherapy is not intended to cure the gender identity disorder." *Id.* at 12.

4. The court notes that the DOC employees who are most directly responsible for Kosilek, Dr. Ira Packer, Gregory Hughes, and Mark Burrowes, agree with Kosilek's experts, Drs. Forstein and Brown, that there is a high risk that Kosilek will attempt suicide if he does not receive adequate treatment as a result of this case.

The Standards of Care state that cross-sex hormones are "often medically necessary" "for properly selected adults with gender identity disorders." *Id.* at 13. "They improve the quality of life and limit the psychiatric co-morbidity, which often accompanies lack of treatment." *Id.* In lay terms, this means that the administration of hormones to a transsexual typically diminishes co-existing serious psychological problems such as depression and suicidality. As the Standards of Care explain:

> Hormone therapy can provide significant comfort to gender patients who do not wish to cross live or undergo surgery, or who are unable to do so. In some patients, hormone therapy alone may provide sufficient symptomatic relief to obviate the need for cross living or surgery.

Id. at 14 (emphasis added).[5]

Pursuant to the Standards of Care, in order to be eligible for hormones, an individual must, among other things, have a documented real life experience of living as a member of the opposite sex for three months or at least three months of psychotherapy. Ex. 7, at 13.

The Standards of Care expressly address the issue of hormone therapy for certain prisoners:

> Hormone Therapy and Medical Care for Incarcerated Persons. Persons who are receiving treatment for gender identity disorders should continue to receive appropriate treatment following these Standards of Care after incarceration. For example, those who are receiving psychotherapy and/ or cross-sex hormonal treatments should be allowed to continue this medically necessary treatment to prevent or limit emotional liability, undesired regression of hormonally-induced physical effects and the sense of desperation that may lead to depression, anxiety and suicidality. Prisoners who are subject to rapid withdrawal of cross-sex hormones are particularly at risk for psychiatric symptoms and self-injurious behaviors. Medical monitoring of hormonal treatment as described in these Standards should also be provided. Housing for transgendered prisoners should take into account their transition status and their personal safety.

Ex. 7, at 14. Dr. Brown wrote this part of the Standards of Care. He persuasively explained that this statement does not mean that the Standards of Care intend to suggest that hormone therapy and other treatment need not be provided to prisoners who were not receiving such treatment prior to their incarceration. Rather, this is an issue not specifically addressed in, or resolved by, the Standards of Care.

If hormone therapy does not adequately alleviate a transsexual's distress, the Standards of Care generally contemplate a "real life experience" in which the person "fully adopt[s] a new or evolving gender role or gender presentation in everyday life." *Id.* at 17. Hormones are important

---

5. Dr. Forstein testified that, in recognition of the medical necessity of hormones for some transsexuals, Massachusetts now pays for hormones prescribed for indigent individuals being treated for gender identity disorders.

to this effort. Ordinarily, the real life experience includes functioning in school, at work, or in the community as a member of the opposite sex, and being regarded as a person of that gender. *Id.* at 17–18. As Drs. Forstein and Brown convincingly testified, however, Kosilek's "real life" is prison. The fact that he is incarcerated does not mean that he could not have a real life experience within the meaning of the Standards of Care, which are expressly intended to be applied flexibly to accommodate a patient's unique social situation. *Id.* at 1.

Pursuant to the Standards of Care, after at least one year of a real life experience, including hormones, some individuals are candidates for sex reassignment surgery. *Id.* at 20. The Standards of Care state that:

> Sex Reassignment is Effective and Medically Indicated in Severe GID. In persons diagnosed with transsexualism or profound GID, sex reassignment surgery, along with hormone therapy and real-life experience, is a treatment that has proven to be effective. Such a therapeutic regimen, when prescribed or recommended by qualified practitioners, is medically indicated and medically necessary. Sex reassignment is not "experimental," "investigational," "elective," cosmetic," or optional in any meaningful sense. It constitutes very effective and appropriate treatment for transsexualism or profound GID.

Id. at 18 (emphasis added).

The DOC has published policies concerning medical services for inmates. Among other things, it is the DOC's policy that, "access to health care is an inmate's right and not a privilege" and that "all health care services shall be comparable in quality to that available in the community." Ex. 13, at § 630.01. This policy expressly applies to mental health services. Under the relevant contract, the private medical contractor is to have full responsibility for decisions concerning the type, timing and level of medical, dental and health services to be provided to inmates. Consistent with this, decisions concerning an inmate's health care are made by medical professionals, social workers employed by the DOC, and the specialists they often choose to consult.

Kosilek, however, has been dealt with differently, in part because of his lawsuit relating to his medical care....

[T]he decision on how to deal with Kosilek and any other prisoner suffering from a gender identity disorder was, as a practical matter, made by Maloney in his capacity as the Commissioner of the DOC, in consultation with his attorneys, mental health professionals, and several members of his staff. Therefore, Maloney is the person on whom the court must focus in determining whether the deliberate indifference required to establish a violation of the Eighth Amendment has been proven in this case.

Maloney previously served as the head social worker for the DOC. Maloney testified, however, that he was not qualified to make medical judgments. Rather, he has to seek advice from the medical professionals, particularly in this matter Drs. Appelbaum and Packer of the University of Massachusetts Medical School. That institution has a three-year, $18,000,000 contract to provide mental health services to inmates in the custody of the DOC.[7]

In about April 2000, a meeting to discuss this case and the possible issuance of guidelines for dealing with inmates with gender identity disorders was planned. In anticipation of that meeting, Dr. Packer spoke with the attorneys for the DOC and others who worked for Maloney. As a result, he understood "from the get go" (meaning "immediately") that Maloney did not want to provide Kosilek or any other inmate hormones or sex reassignment surgery.

Dr. Packer had no experience with gender identity disorders. To prepare for the meeting with Maloney, he did a search of the medical literature. He found a 1996 article by Dr. Robert Dickey and others in Canada, "Transsexuals within the Prison System: An International Survey of Correctional Services Policies," which had been published in Peterson, et al., 14 Behavioral Sciences and the Law 219–29 (1996).

On April 18, 2000, Dr. Packer sent a memorandum to Dr. Appelbaum and several members of Maloney's staff, but not to Maloney himself. In that memorandum, Dr. Packer distilled what he characterized as "the gist of the article." Ex. 12. He wrote that the authors had conducted a survey of sixty-four prison programs from Europe, Canada, Australia, and the United States, and reported that "none had a policy that allowed for sex reassignment surgery and 'the vast majority of respondents indicated that there were no circumstances whereby sex reassignment would be considered for an already incarcerated transsexual.' " *Id.* Dr. Packer also wrote that in Dr. Dickey's view: "The best principle in management of transsexuals is to 'freeze-frame' the inmate at the state he or she was at on the date of their arrival in the system, i.e., maintain the status quo." *Id.* According to Dr. Packer's memorandum, "pursuant to this approach: Inmates should be maintained on hormones only if they had previously been a candidate for sex reassignment surgery and if they were prescribed by a recognized expert in treating gender disorders." *Id.*

. . .

Maloney announced at [a] April 28, 2000 meeting that he would adopt a freeze-frame policy for inmates having gender identity disorders. The DOC would provide hormones to any inmate who had previously been prescribed hormones, probably place that person in the general population of the prison, and deal with any security issues that might arise. The DOC would not, however, initiate hormones for an inmate for whom hormones had not been prescribed prior to his incarceration. . . .

As directed by Maloney at the April 28, 2000 meeting, Dr. Packer drafted "Guidelines for Mental Health Treatment of Inmates with Gender

7. The DOC contract for health services states that the provider is not obligated to pay for "sex change surgery or treatment," but does not prohibit such payments. Ex. 9, at 73.

Identity Disorder" (the "Guidelines") to implement Maloney's decision concerning transsexual prisoners. As Dr. Packer testified, he was not then knowledgeable about individuals with gender identity disorders. At the time he drafted the Guidelines, Dr. Packer was still not aware of the Standards of Care.

Maloney approved the Guidelines. Drs. Appelbaum and Packer issued them on May 15, 2000. The Guidelines expressly apply only to inmates who were not on prescribed hormones prior to being incarcerated. Ex. 3 at 1. They state that they would need to be modified for individuals who were receiving hormones previously. *Id.* The Guidelines prohibit hormones and/ or sex reassignment surgery from being provided for inmates who were not receiving hormones prior to incarceration because the "Department of Corrections has determined that [opportunities for the Real Life Experience that is recommended prior to sex reassignment surgery] cannot be afforded inmates since security and operational concerns do not allow inmates to dress and function as members of the opposite sex." *Id.*

The Guidelines permit Kosilek, as an individual who has not received prescribed hormones prior to incarceration, and others similarly situated, to receive "supportive therapy" to help "the inmate cope with the distress and stress associated with the desire to be of the opposite sex and the inability to change within the prison environment." *Id.*

In essence, the Guidelines provide that DOC personnel should try to help Kosilek and any other inmate having a gender identity disorder to cope with his plight, but categorically preclude the forms of treatment generally provided in the community in this country—no matter how severe and painful the inmate's mental illness may be—if the inmate was not receiving prescribed hormones prior to his incarceration. . . .

After the Guidelines were issued, Maloney sought additional information concerning how other jurisdictions dealt with inmates with gender identity disorders. He contacted officials in Nebraska and New York, and was told that they do not have separate units for inmates with gender identity disorders.

Maloney also caused his staff to send out a survey to other jurisdictions. With one exception, however, he did not read the results or the somewhat misleading summary of them that was prepared. . . .

There is no psychiatrist at MCI–Norfolk. In October 2001, Mark Burrowes was the social worker assigned to work with Kosilek. At that time, Burrowes had no training or experience working with individuals having gender identity disorders. He and several colleagues received about two hours of training on gender identity disorders prior to trial.

According to Burrowes, it was "strange" that a treatment plan for Kosilek was prepared without his participation. This was the only time that Burrowes was not involved in developing the treatment plan for an inmate for whom he was responsible. Burrowes has met with Kosilek since the plan was issued in October 2001. In his opinion, the Revised Treatment Plan is not adequate to keep Kosilek from attempting suicide if he loses this case. In Burrowes' view, the Revised Treatment Plan is deficient because it makes no provision for therapy with anyone with expertise in gender identity disorders or for hormones. *Id.* at 54, 56. Burrowes also testified that because the Revised Treatment Plan "does not include treatment via hormonal therapy, this plan is basically nothing." *Id.* at 56.

. . .

As DeWees and Burrows, the DOC employees responsible for dealing directly with Kosilek, as well as Drs. Forstein and Brown testified, the DOC's treatment plans for Kosilek have not been adequate to treat his condition. As indicated earlier, those plans have not been developed pursuant to the DOC's usual procedures. The Revised Treatment Plan did not result from a clinical decision by a doctor or social worker concerning Kosilek's condition and particular medical needs. Rather, it was derived from an administrative decision by Maloney that created a blanket policy prohibiting initiation of hormones for inmates for whom they were not prescribed prior to their incarceration. Even Dr. Dickey agrees with Drs. Forstein and Brown that a rigid blanket policy prohibiting the initiation of hormones in every case is not appropriate. This court concurs.

As a result of that blanket policy, however, no clinical assessment of Kosilek's individual circumstances and medical needs has been made. Rather, major forms of the treatment provided in the community in the United States pursuant to prudent professional standards have been eliminated as options by an administrative decision made by Maloney, who acknowledges that he is not qualified to decide what treatment is medically necessary for a particular inmate.

Maloney did not, however, adopt his policy in order to punish Kosilek. On April 28, 2000, Maloney was not aware of certain critical facts and had not actually inferred that there would be a substantial risk of serious harm to Kosilek—in the form of at least intense psychological pain, and quite possibly suicide or self-mutilation—as a result of the policy he decided to adopt. Although Maloney read Dr. Forstein's report, including the part describing Kosilek's attempts to kill and castrate himself, before approving the Guidelines, he still did not infer that Kosilek's condition created a substantial risk of serious harm to him. Nor did Maloney reach this conclusion prior to testifying at trial.

. . .

In any event, the court finds that the services now being offered to Kosilek are not sufficient to diminish his intense emotional distress, and the related risks of suicide and self-mutilation, to the point at which he would no longer be at a substantial risk of serious harm.

Maloney knows that the DOC medical staff regularly refer inmates to outside specialists if they present problems that are beyond the competence of the professionals who are on staff. The court fully accepts Maloney's testimony that if the doctors from the University of Massachusetts who are engaged to provide mental health care to inmates decided to bring in a specialist to treat Kosilek, he would not interfere. Such medical judgments are "what [he is] paying them for." Feb. 6, 2000 Tr. at 111. Indeed, Maloney sincerely believes that he has "never in [his] career interfered with a doctor's order for treatment and [has] no intention of doing so in the future," with regard to Kosilek or anyone else. *Id.* at 113.

. . .

A decision to prescribe hormones for Kosilek would not be unprecedented. According to Dr. Brown, the federal Bureau of Prisons settled a case in which he participated by agreeing to provide hormones to Yolanda Burt, who had used only "black market" hormones before being incarcerated.

. . .

In any event, the DOC policy contemplates continuing hormones for any inmate for whom they were prescribed prior to incarceration. The DOC is prepared to protect the safety of such an inmate. As described earlier, such an inmate would probably be placed by Maloney in the general population of a male prison.

. . .

IV. Analysis

1. *Kosilek Has a Serious Medical Need*

It is undisputed that Kosilek has a gender identity disorder, which is a rare, medically recognized, major mental illness. A gender identity disorder is not, however, necessarily a serious medical need for which the Eighth Amendment requires treatment. As with other mental illnesses, gender identity disorders have differing degrees of severity. As the Standards of Care explain, some individuals with gender identity disorders manage to find their own comfortable, effective ways of living that do not require psychotherapy, hormone therapy, a real life experience, or sex reassignment surgery. Ex. 7, at 11. Thus, the Court of Appeals for the District of Columbia has correctly stated, "merely because someone is a transsexual, it does not inexorably follow that he or she needs psychotherapy" or any other form of treatment. *Farmer v. Moritsugu,* 333 U.S. App. D.C. 319, 163 F.3d 610, 615 (D.C. Cir. 1998).

However, the evidence in this case demonstrates that Kosilek's gender identity disorder is severe. Kosilek's gender identity disorder, and not any sense of guilt or despair about his life sentence, causes him intense and enduring mental anguish. It has prompted him to attempt suicide twice while incarcerated, and to try to castrate himself as well. There is a significant risk that he will attempt to kill, mutilate, or otherwise harm himself again if he is not afforded adequate treatment for his disorder. Kosilek's good behavior while incarcerated, and the hope that he currently holds, is a result of the litigation that he has initiated. Kosilek's stated intention to commit suicide is not merely a threat to manipulate the DOC or the court, but rather a sincere manifestation of his mental anguish. Kosilek will attempt, and perhaps succeed, in killing himself if he does not receive adequate treatment.

Kosilek's ardent desire for sex reassignment surgery is further evidence of the severity of his mental illness. "Someone eager to undergo this mutilation is plainly suffering from a profound psychiatric disorder." *Maggert v. Hanks,* 131 F.3d 670, 671 (7th Cir. 1997). These facts alone demonstrate that Kosilek has a serious mental health need and will continue to be at a substantial risk of serious harm until he receives adequate treatment. *See, e.g., Torraco,* 923 F.2d at 235 n.4 (attempted suicide in confinement and drug overdose sufficient to prove serious medical need); *Waldrop,* 871 F.2d at 1032 (self-mutilation by manic depressive sufficient to prove a serious medical need); *Steele,* 87 F.3d at 1267, 1260 (inmate subject to severe mood swings, who had twice attempted suicide and was considered a potential suicide risk had a serious medical need).

It is significant that Kosilek has also now been properly diagnosed by two doctors as having a disorder that requires treatment. *See Mahan,* 64 F.3d at 18; *Gaudreault,* 923 F.2d at 208. Dr. Forstein originally made his diagnosis and recommendations while employed by the DOC. Dr. Brown provided a persuasive second opinion to the same effect after being retained by Kosilek's counsel. Their diagnoses and recommendations contribute to establishing that Kosilek has the serious medical need necessary to implicate the protection provided to prisoners by the Eighth Amendment. *See Mahan,* 64 F.3d at 18 (doctor's "prescription indicated that ... Mahan needed and would benefit from [anti-depressant]. The record thus established a serious medical need."); *Cortes–Quinones v. Jimenez–Nettleship,* 842 F.2d 556, 559 (1st Cir. 1988) ("prison system memo stated that [plaintiff] needed treatment with a psychiatrist or a psychologist.")

2. *Kosilek Has Not Been Offered Adequate Treatment For His Serious Medical Need*

. . .

As Kosilek has proven that he has a serious medical need which is not being adequately treated, he has satisfied the objective component of the Eighth Amendment test. Therefore, the court must determine whether the DOC's failure to provide Kosilek with adequate medical care for his serious medical need is a result of deliberate indifference on the part of Maloney.

3. *Maloney's Failure to Provide Kosilek With Adequate Care Has Not Been Due to Deliberate Indifference*

Kosilek has not proven the facts necessary to satisfy the subjective prong of the deliberate indifference test. Once again, as the Supreme Court explained in *Farmer*:

> [A] prison official cannot be held liable under the Eighth Amendment for denying an inmate humane conditions of confinement unless the official knows of and disregards an excessive risk to inmate health or safety: the official must both be aware of facts from which the inference could be drawn and he must also draw the inference.... An official's failure to alleviate a significant risk that he should have perceived but did not, while no cause for commendation, cannot under our cases be condemned as the infliction of punishment.

Farmer, 511 U.S. at 837–38 (emphasis added). This is essentially such a case.

As defendant agreed at the pretrial conference, and as the court now concludes, in this case it is necessary to focus on Maloney's state of mind to determine whether deliberate indifference has been proven. Maloney is not the focus of attention because of his official status as the Commissioner of the DOC. He is the responsible official because he was the "major decisionmaker" concerning Kosilek's medical care. Once again, Maloney issued a policy that prevented those dealing directly with Kosilek from considering forms of care prescribed by prudent professionals in the community for some individuals suffering from gender identity disorder. Thus, the DOC medical personnel were stripped of their usual authority to make an individualized decision concerning the care necessary to address adequately Kosilek's needs.

. . .

As described earlier, Maloney did not decide to adopt a policy that he knew would apply primarily to Kosilek in order to punish him. Nor was Maloney deliberately indifferent to Kosilek's plight. Rather, Maloney had not actually inferred that there would be a substantial risk of serious harm to Kosilek as a result of the policy he had adopted.

As of April 28, 2000, when Maloney made the policy decision that effectively prohibited qualified professionals from considering the full range of options that might be necessary to treat Kosilek adequately, Maloney had not read Dr. Forstein's report. Maloney was not aware that Kosilek had while incarcerated twice attempted suicide and also tried to castrate himself. Maloney did not then know of the severe psychological pain and mental anguish that Kosilek was suffering as a result of his major mental illness.

By May 15, 2000, when the Guidelines developed pursuant to his April 28, 2000 policy decision were issued, Maloney had read Dr. Forstein's report. He knew that there were risks of serious harm associated with the failure to treat a gender identity disorder. He also knew that Dr. Forstein, at least, thought that there was a great risk that Kosilek would again attempt suicide if his gender identity disorder was not adequately addressed as a result of the lawsuit he had instituted. Thus, Maloney was aware of facts from which he could have inferred that there was an excessive risk to Kosilek's health. *See Farmer,* 511 U.S. at 837.

Nevertheless, from April 2000 through the trial of this case Maloney never actually formed the belief that there was a substantial risk of serious harm to Kosilek. Maloney knew that prior to receiving Dr. Forstein's report DOC clinicians did not perceive a risk that Kosilek would commit suicide. In any event, through the time of trial Maloney believed that his policy for prisoners with gender identity disorders would provide minimally adequate care for Kosilek. Moreover, Maloney believed that the DOC's established procedures would prevent Kosilek from killing himself if that risk were real.

Accordingly, Maloney "knew the underlying facts but believed (albeit unsoundly) that the risk to which the facts gave rise was insubstantial or nonexistent." *Id.* at 844. This is not enough to prove deliberate indifference. *Id.*

. . .

4. *Maloney is Not Likely to be Indifferent to Kosilek's Serious Medical Need in the Future*

If Kosilek had proven that Maloney has been deliberately indifferent to his serious medical need, he would have had to prove more to obtain the injunction he is seeking. To obtain an injunction Kosilek would also have had to prove that Maloney would continue in the future to knowingly and unreasonably disregard the significant risk of serious harm that has been proven in this case. *Farmer*, 511 U.S. at 846. Indeed, when a constitutional violation is proven it is at times appropriate for a court to exercise its equitable discretion to give "prison officials time to rectify the situation before issuing an injunction." *Id.* at 847.

The court expects that, educated by the trial record and this decision, Maloney and his colleagues will in the future attempt to discharge properly their constitutional duties to Kosilek. Maloney has not intended to punish Kosilek by denying him necessary medical care. Maloney has previously served as the head social worker for the DOC. He is genuinely concerned about the welfare of the inmates for whom he is ultimately responsible.

Kosilek's case has, however, presented Maloney with what has been for him a highly unusual, if not novel, issue. While concerns about security and public controversy have made him reluctant to do more for Kosilek than the law requires, the court does not expect that Maloney will be recalcitrant in the future.

Rather, the court expects that he will allow medical professionals to decide what would ordinarily be required to treat Kosilek adequately. He may then himself decide if there is a legitimate reason relating to prison administration, such as security, that makes it truly necessary to deny Kosilek that treatment.

More specifically, Maloney is now on notice that Kosilek's severe gender identity disorder constitutes a serious medical need. Therefore, the

DOC has a duty to provide Kosilek adequate treatment. *Estelle*, 429 U.S. at 105–06; *Farmer*, 511 U.S. at 846 n.9.

It is permissible for the DOC to maintain a presumptive freeze-frame policy. However, decisions as to whether psychotherapy, hormones, and/ or sex reassignment surgery are necessary to treat Kosilek adequately must be based on an "individualized medical evaluation" of Kosilek rather than as "a result of a blanket rule." *Allard*, 9 Fed. Appx. 793, 200. Those decisions must be made by qualified professionals. *Waldrop*, 871 F.2d at 1035–36; *Harris*, 941 F.2d at 1509. Such professionals must exercise sound medical judgment, based upon prudent professional standards, particularly the Standards of Care. *Estelle,* 429 U.S. at 104 n.10; *Chance*, 143 F.3d at 704; *DeCologero*, 821 F.2d at 42.

Thus, the court expects that Maloney will follow the DOC's usual policy and practice of allowing medical professionals to assess what is necessary to treat Kosilek. As the DOC does not employ anyone with expertise in treating gender identity disorders, the DOC may decide to follow its regular practice of retaining an outside expert to evaluate Kosilek and to participate in treating, or recommending treatment for, him.

The evidence demonstrates that, at a minimum, Kosilek should receive genuine psychotherapy from, or under the direction of, someone qualified by training and experience to address a severe gender identity disorder. It will be Kosilek's obligation to cooperate in establishing a proper relationship with his therapist(s). The Standards of Care indicate that such therapy, or such therapy and pharmacology, may be sufficient to reduce the anguish caused by Kosilek's gender identity disorder so that it no longer constitutes a serious medical need. Ex. 7, at 11.

If psychotherapy, and possibly psychopharmacology, do not eliminate the significant risk of serious harm that now exists, consideration should be given to whether hormones should be prescribed to treat Kosilek. Administering female hormones to a male prisoner in a male prison could raise genuine security concerns. *Farmer*, 511 U.S. at 848. Maloney would be entitled to consider whether those concerns make it necessary to deny Kosilek care that the medical professionals regard as required to provide minimally adequate treatment for his serious medical need.

If this issue arises, Maloney may wish to consider that Kosilek is already living largely as a female in the general population of a medium security male prison. This has not presented security problems.

Moreover, under the Guidelines, Maloney is prepared to accommodate inmates who enter prison on prescribed hormones, probably by placing them in the general population of a male prison. Other state prison officials have apparently been able to do so safely. *See Phillips v. Mich. Dept. of Corr.*, 731 F.Supp. 792, 792 at n.1 (W.D. Mich. 1990), *aff'd*, 932 F.2d 969 (1991) (issuing preliminary injunction requiring the reinstitution of previously prescribed hormones); *Murray v. United States Bureau of Prisons*, 106 F.3d 401, 1997 WL 34677 at *3–*4 (6th Cir. 1997) (affirming prison decision to reduce dosage, but not eliminate, previously prescribed hormones).

The Bureau of Prisons also evidently addressed security concerns adequately when it settled Burt's litigation by initiating hormones. In addition, "access to hormone therapy is now provided to transsexual inmates under [Correctional Services of Canada's] Health Services policy, on the recommendation of a recognized Gender Identity Disorder Clinic if the inmate was not "on hormone therapy at the time of incarceration." *Kavanagh*, B.C.H.R.T. T505/2298, at 2, 9. In *Kavanagh*, the Canadian Human Rights Tribunal found that Correctional Services of Canada "had failed to establish that it cannot accommodate [transsexuals on hormones or after sex reassignment surgery] within the male prison population without incurring undue hardship." *Id.* at 32.

By making these observations, the court does not intend to denigrate the significance of Maloney's security concerns. Maloney estimates that twenty-five percent of the inmates in his custody are sex offenders. Farmer was a case in which a transsexual prisoner alleged deliberate indifference to his safety after he was beaten and raped while in the general population at a federal penitentiary. 511 U.S. at 830–31. As the Supreme Court noted, however, "penitentiaries are typically higher security prisons that house more troublesome prisoners than federal correctional institutes." *Id.* at 831.

Prison officials must "take reasonable measures to guarantee the safety of inmates," as well as to provide them with adequate medical care. *Id.* at 832 (quoting *Palmer*, 468 U.S. at 526–27). One way to attempt to discharge both of these duties to a transsexual inmate taking hormones is to make reasonable efforts to incarcerate him with a less dangerous population of other prisoners.

As the Standards of Care explain, "hormone therapy alone may provide sufficient symptomatic relief to obviate the need for cross-living or surgery." Ex. 9, at 14. If psychotherapy, hormones, and possibly psychopharmacology are not sufficient to reduce the anguish caused by Kosilek's gender identity disorder to the point that there is no longer a substantial risk of serious harm to him, sex reassignment surgery might be deemed medically necessary. *Id.* at 18. If that occurs, Maloney may consider whether security requirements make it truly necessary to deny Kosilek adequate care for his serious medical need. If and when he makes such a decision, a court may have to determine again whether the Eighth Amendment has been violated . . . . .

DISCUSSION

1. Do you believe that transsexuals should be included in the greater gay rights movement? Does it matter that most transsexuals identify as heterosexuals trapped in the wrong body—not as gay? For a discussion, see SHANNON GILREATH, THE END OF STRAIGHT SUPREMACY: REALIZING GAY LIBERATION (2011) (especially Chapter 8).

2. What about the case of a male-to-female transsexual who is married to a female at the time of his transition and the couple does not divorce? Does the marriage continue to be valid?

CHAPTER 11

LOCAL POLICY AND DECISION-MAKING

■ ■ ■

Although movement has been slow at the federal level for lesbian, gay, bisexual and transgender legal rights, local and state decision-making by policy makers affecting the legal rights of the LGBT community happens every day. These grassroots efforts are the most hands-on, successful ways that change is being effectuated in terms of legal rights for LGBT citizens and their families. How this is accomplished varies from municipality to municipality, depending on the laws of the particular state. The following article gives an overview of the tension of lawmaking between the federal, state and local governments.

I. PROGRESSIVE POLICY-MAKING ON THE LOCAL LEVEL: RETHINKING TRADITIONAL NOTIONS OF FEDERALISM*

In his oft-quoted and famous dissent, Justice Louis Brandeis stated that "[i]t is one of the happy incidents of the federal system that a single courageous State may, if its citizens choose, serve as a laboratory; and try novel social and economic experiments without risk to the rest of the country." ... And while states may indeed be fertile grounds for policy innovation, one must question whether states continue to be the best level of government at which to engage in such experimentation. Instead, local governments may prove even more fruitful agents for social change and policy innovation than the state or federal levels of government. After all, conceptually speaking, the principles underlying federalism seem logically to apply not only to the relationship between the federal government and the states, but also to that between the states and local governments.

. . .

Local governments are not mentioned or even considered in the United States Constitution. Local governments were originally created by states and began as small urban and rural areas, far from the cities and

* Excerpted from Parlow, *Progressive Policy-Making on the Local Level: Re-Thinking Traditional Notions of Federalism*, 17 TEMP. POL. & CIV. RTS. L. REV. 371 (2008). Reprinted with permission.

major metropolitan areas we know and experience today. States created local governments—and, with many forms of local government, still do to this day—to carry out the duties of the state on the local level. Local governments were limited by Dillon's Rule, which permitted localities to exercise only those powers expressly granted to them by the states. In this regard, courts and scholars viewed local governments as mere administrative arms of the state. From this view, local governments would not seem to be promising forums for policy experimentation. However, . . . the home rule movement aimed to empower local governments in a more meaningful way where localities could exercise all powers not expressly reserved by the state—so long as they were not preempted by the state government. This change, as discussed further below, provided hope for policy innovations on the local level the way Justice Brandeis envisioned the states would do in our federalism system.

Local governments have also transformed from the smaller urban and rural centers when originally conceived to include flourishing metropolitan areas. Many cities and counties are now significantly more powerful, socially, economically, and politically than when they were originally created and their powers—or lack thereof—originally devised. In fact, one might even argue that cities' economic strength, large populations, and political importance make them more powerful and influential than some states. . . .

Finally, local governments also warrant our attention because a significant percentage of public goods, services, and regulation occur at the local level. In particular, local governments provide essential services that affect citizens' day-to-day lives: police, fire, library, trash collection, street maintenance, transportation, water and power, education, and others. As one scholar notes, "The services performed by municipalities are those most vital to the preservation of life (police, fire, sanitation, public health), liberty (police, courts, prosecutors), property (zoning, planning, taxing), and public enlightenment (schools, libraries)." In this regard, local governments can be viewed as perhaps the most critical level of government in terms of responding—through regulation, goods, or services—to the needs and wants of its constituents.

Local governments may also have the potential to best embody the values of federalism. Local governments provide opportunities for public participation in the decision-and policy-making processes that are more difficult, if not impossible, at the state and federal levels of government. It is far more likely that average citizens may interact with their city councilmember or mayor than their state legislator or governor, or their congressperson, senator, or President. Congress conducts its sessions in Washington, D.C.—far away from most cities. State legislatures meet in their state capitol, which is often inconvenient for those living outside of that metropolitan area. In this regard, average citizens cannot take advantage of opportunities to voice their opinions at open meetings when Congress or their state legislature considers various regulations and the like. On the other hand, city council meetings are held within the locality—usually at city hall—thus making it convenient for community members to voice their concerns to their local elected officials.

More importantly, perhaps, many local governments offer meaningful opportunities for public participation through various substructures of local governments that aim to engage the public in the local decision-and policy-making process: business improvement districts, neighborhood councils, and the like. Such opportunities allow community stakeholders to dialogue regarding the issues the city faces and then interact with their elected officials to help inform the decision-making process. This type of public participation furthers one of the key values of federalism: democracy.

Because they are smaller in size, local governments are more capable of being responsive to the needs of their respective communities because they are more in touch with their constituents. This leads, in theory, to more responsive and representative policy-making as local government officials make decisions informed by the community's wants and needs. Moreover, because citizens are closer to and more in touch with their local governments, they can better monitor and hold accountable their elected and appointed officials and mitigate against the capture of their local government by special interest groups.

Perhaps the most significant federalism value embodied in local governments is the opportunity to be laboratories of innovation as Justice Brandeis envisioned for the states. In many ways, local governments have led the way in many areas of public policy where the federal and state governments have either failed, avoided issues altogether, or been unable to reach an agreement because of the divergent interests of their constituencies. For example, local governments have been on the forefront of policy areas such as climate change, gay rights and gay marriage, domestic partner benefits, affordable housing, campaign finance and other electoral reforms, health care, and term limits. . . .

[U]nsurprisingly, local innovation is often thwarted by state and federal courts on preemption grounds. . . .

Local governments are critical components of our federal system, particularly because they are the primary provider of the goods and services that affect our day-to-day lives. Moreover, local governments have been more willing to advance innovative laws and/or policies that the federal and state governments are unwilling or unable to effect. Yet, despite their maturation from when they were originally conceived, local governments still have rather limited law-making authority under current law and are thus often preempted by state and federal law when they attempt such local policy experimentation[.] . . . This state-of-affairs seems to run counter to the re-conceptualized notion of local government advanced by the home rule movement.

Prior to 1875, most local governments were subject to Dillon's Rule. Under Dillon's Rule, local governments lack inherent law-making authority. Instead, local governments only exercise those powers expressly delegated by the state. Courts thus view municipalities as mere administrative arms of the state. In this regard, when a conflict arises between state and local law, the state prevails.

In 1875, the home rule movement began when Missouri became the first state to adopt a constitutional provision in its state constitution to allow home rule. Home rule provisions enable cities—usually with a certain minimum population—to set up their own local constitutions, called charters. Forty-eight states provide these home rule powers to cities through either constitutional or statutory provisions. Home rule provisions delegate all legislative power regarding local matters to home rule cities except the authority for those areas of law and policy-making reserved for the state. Home rule thus empowers cities to legislate in areas of local concern, so long as their laws do not conflict with state law. In this regard, home rule provisions were envisioned as "mini-Tenth Amendments designed to cordon off local matters from state intervention." Accordingly, home rule provisions were supposed to provide a constitutional or statutory defense against assertions of state preemptive power. Home rule cities, then, should only be preempted by the state if they legislate in an area reserved for the state, or in an area involving a matter of statewide concern.

However, state courts—after decades of only following Dillon's Rule—continue to give great deference to state governments over local governments when conflicts arise. Most state courts narrowly construe the concept of "local affairs," viewing the language as limiting a local government's power rather than reading it as a grant of power. Moreover, state courts rely heavily on the implied preemption doctrine to strike down innovative local policy-making. In this regard, state courts will invalidate local laws, even when they do not conflict with state law—finding that the state intended to occupy the policy field, even without explicit language suggesting such. To be sure, some state courts have upheld local government innovation as falling within local home rule power, even when such legislation directly conflicted with state law. Nevertheless, such cases tend to be the exception to an otherwise (ironically) state-dominated home rule jurisprudence.

The preceding should not be read as advocating for localities to have the authority to pass laws that directly conflict with federal or state law. However, the narrow construction of home rule powers, coupled with the frequency with which implied preemption is used by state courts to invalidate local laws, raises questions as to whether we are foreclosing a significant opportunity to use local governments as the forums for experimentation as Justice Brandeis once envisioned of the states. . . .

DISCUSSION

Explain your understanding of federalism, Dillon's Rule and Home Rule. How does a state constitution affect these concepts? Research any of our fifty states and explain how your chosen state applies these doctrines.

II. HOME RULE, DILLON'S RULE AND PREEMPTION

Some of the more common LGBT protections that are being addressed at the municipal level include domestic partner benefits and nondiscrimination laws. Following are cases that illustrate attempts by different local jurisdictions concerning these areas of the law. Consider the decision-making authority of the governing boards as you review these cases.

CITY OF CLEVELAND HEIGHTS EX REL. HICKS ET. AL. v. CITY OF CLEVELAND HEIGHTS

162 Ohio App.3d 193, 832 N.E.2d 1275 (2005)

SEAN C. GALLAGHER, JUDGE.

Appellants, city of Cleveland Heights ex rel. Jimmie Hicks Jr. and Charlie Byrne, appeal from the judgment of the Cuyahoga County Court of Common Pleas that denied their request for a statutory injunction enjoining the operation of a domestic-partner-registry ordinance established by appellee, the city of Cleveland Heights. For the reasons stated below, we affirm.

Appellants Hicks and Byrne are residents and taxpayers of the city of Cleveland Heights. In March 2003, Hicks attended a council meeting at which he became aware of an initiative petition for an ordinance that would cause the city to establish a domestic-partner registry. In November 2003, Cleveland Heights voters approved the ordinance by referendum. Pursuant to the ordinance, couples may file a declaration of domestic partnership and be placed in the registry provided they (1) pay a fee, (2) share a common residence, (3) are not married to another individual, (4) are 18 years of age or older, (5) are not related by blood to a certain degree of consanguinity, (6) agree to be in a relationship of mutual interdependence, and (7) agree to file a declaration of domestic partnership with Cleveland Heights.

On January 14, 2004, Hicks, through legal counsel, sent a letter to the city law director requesting that an injunction action be filed. The law director indicated he would review the matter and make a decision within two weeks.

The city commenced administering the registry on January 26, 2004. The following day, the city law director issued a letter declining to bring an injunction action on behalf of the city. Thereafter, Hicks brought this action, which was later amended to include Byrne as a plaintiff. Hicks and Byrne asserted that the ordinance was unconstitutional because it was an abuse of the city's corporate powers conferred by Section 3, Article XVIII of the Ohio Constitution.

The trial court denied appellants' request for a statutory injunction, finding that appellants had not shown any irreparable harm, that the city was within its home-rule authority in enacting and maintaining the domestic-partner registry, and that the registry was not beyond the scope of authority granted by Section 3, Article XVIII of the Ohio Constitution.

Hicks and Byrne have appealed the trial court's decision, raising one assignment of error for our review, which provides:

"The trial court erred in denying Relators' request for a statutory injunction enjoining operation of the City's Domestic Partner Registry Ordinance."

The Home Rule Amendment to the Ohio Constitution, Section 3, Article XVIII, provides:

"Municipalities shall have authority to exercise all powers of local self-government and to adopt and enforce within their limits such local police, sanitary and other similar regulations, as are not in conflict with general laws."

The Supreme Court of Ohio, in *Canton v. Whitman* (1975), 44 Ohio St.2d 62, 65–66, 73 O.O.2d 285, 337 N.E.2d 766, wrote: "This section, adopted in 1912, preserved the supremacy of the state in matters of 'police, sanitary and other similar regulations,' while granting municipalities sovereignty in matters of local self-government, limited only by other constitutional provisions." Thus, the Home Rule Amendment provides municipalities with "full and complete political power in all matters of local self government." *Perrysburg v. Ridgway* (1923), 108 Ohio St. 245, 255, 140 N.E. 595.

It is well settled that the Ohio Constitution grants broad powers of local self-government to municipalities. *See Buckeye Community Hope Found. v. Cuyahoga Falls* (1998), 82 Ohio St.3d 539, 541, 697 N.E.2d 181. In *Benjamin v. Columbus* (1957), 167 Ohio St. 103, 108, 4 O.O.2d 113, 146 N.E.2d 854, the Ohio Supreme Court stated: "The 'powers of local self-government' conferred upon municipalities by this constitutional provision include the power to enact local legislation, except to the extent that limitations upon that legislative power have been set forth in the Constitution." To that end, the Supreme Court of Ohio has been liberal in its application of the home-rule doctrine. Indeed, the court has established that as a general policy, municipalities have the "broadest possible powers of self-government" for local political issues. *State Personnel Bd. of Revision v. Bay Village Civ. Serv. Comm.* (1986), 28 Ohio St.3d 214, 218, 28 OBR 298, 503 N.E.2d 518.

While it has been established that the powers of local self-government are broad, no definitive description exists. As recognized by the Supreme Court of Ohio in *Britt v. Columbus* (1974), 38 Ohio St.2d 1, 6, 67 O.O.2d 1, 309 N.E.2d 412: "This court has never framed an all-inclusive definition of the term 'all powers of local self-government' appearing in Section 3 of Article XVIII. In the context of specific cases before it, the term has been stated to mean '. . . such powers of government as, in view of their nature and the field of their operation, are local and municipal in character'

(*State, ex rel. Toledo, v. Lynch* [1913], 88 Ohio St. 71, 97 [102 N.E. 670]); '... the powers referred to are clearly such as involve the exercise of the functions of government, and they are local in the sense that they relate to the municipal affairs of the particular community' (*Fitzgerald v. Cleveland* [1913], 88 Ohio St. 338, 344 [103 N.E. 512]), 'the phrase "all powers of local self-government" as used ... [in Section 3] means the power of self-government in all matters of a purely local nature' (*State, ex rel. Arey, v. Sherrill* [1944], 142 Ohio St. 574 [53 N.E.2d 501])."

In *Beachwood v. Cuyahoga Cty. Bd. of Elections* (1958), 167 Ohio St. 369, 370–371, 5 O.O.2d 6, 148 N.E.2d 921, the Supreme Court of Ohio explained its test for determining whether municipal legislation is local in nature in the following manner:

"The power of local self-government granted to municipalities by Article XVIII relates solely to the government and administration of the internal affairs of the municipality, and, in the absence of statute conferring a broader power, municipal legislation must be confined to that area. (*See Prudential Co–Operative Realty Co. v. City of Youngstown,* 118 Ohio St. 204, 160 N.E. 695.) Where a proceeding is such that it affects not only the municipality itself but the surrounding territory beyond its boundaries, such proceeding is no longer one which falls within the sphere of local self-government but is one which must be governed by the general law of the state.

"To determine whether legislation is such as falls within the area of local self-government, the result of such legislation or the result of the proceedings thereunder must be considered. If the result affects only the municipality itself, with no extraterritorial effects, the subject is clearly within the power of local self-government and is a matter for the determination of the municipality. However, if the result is not so confined it becomes a matter for the General Assembly."

This analysis brings us to a consideration of the question raised by this appeal as to whether the administration and enforcement of the Cleveland Heights ordinance establishing a domestic-partnership registry falls within the sphere of local self-government. Here, the registry affects only the municipality itself and has no extraterritorial effects. As the trial court found: "The city allows residents and nonresidents alike to register. However, the city of Cleveland Heights confers no benefit, right or obligation upon those registering. The taxpayers of the city incur no cost since the registering couples pay a fee to cover the entire cost of the registry. A nonresident must pay the same fee but obtains no benefit aside from their names on the registry. Foreign jurisdictions are not bound to acknowledge the registry or to confer any rights or obligations. Residents and nonresidents are free to recognize the declaration, but no other city is obligated to take notice. The registry does not create any result, either within the city or outside its territory, other than the mere existence of names on a list. Therefore, the court, applying the territorial test established in *Beachwood,* finds the city of Cleveland Heights' Domestic Registry to be an act of self-governance.''

We agree with the analysis of the trial court. The registry confers no right or obligation upon registrants, is administered exclusively within the city of Cleveland Heights, and has no effect outside the territory of the city. We hold that the domestic-partner-registry ordinance is a matter of local self-government. Although the registry pertains to domestic partners, we would find no distinction had the registry pertained to other citizen groups, such as war veterans. Our holding is consistent with the principle that municipalities are to be given the broadest possible powers of self-government and a liberal application to be applied to the home-rule doctrine.

Because we find that the domestic-partner-registry ordinance is lawful, we decline to address Hicks's arguments pertaining to injunctive relief.

Appellants' first assignment of error is overruled.

Judgment affirmed.

NOTE

In 2008, Cleveland became the third city in Ohio (after Cleveland Heights and Toldeo) to establish a domestic partner registry. In 2011, the council was considering legislation to offer domestic partner benefits to city employees.

ARLINGTON COUNTY v. WHITE

259 Va. 708, 528 S.E.2d 706 (2000)

KOONTZ, JUSTICE.

In this appeal, we consider whether a local governing body acted *ultra vires* [''beyond the powers''] in extending coverage under its self-funded health insurance benefits plan to unmarried ''domestic partners'' of its employees.

On March 12, 1998, Andrew White, Diana White, and Wendell Brown, residents and taxpayers of Arlington County (the Taxpayers), filed a bill of complaint in the trial court against Arlington County and its County Board (collectively, the County). The Taxpayers sought a declaration that the County lacked the authority to extend coverage to the newly defined category of domestic partners under its self-funded health insurance benefits plan. The Taxpayers also sought to enjoin the County from implementing the provision of benefits to domestic partners.

The parties filed cross-motions for summary judgment. Holding that ''Arlington County's coverage for domestic partners in its self-funded health benefit plan for County employees violates the Dillon Rule,'' the trial court granted the Taxpayers' motion for summary judgment and denied the County's motion. We awarded the County this appeal.

The record shows that in an Employee Relations Benefits Newsletter, issued in May 1997, the County announced that, effective July 1, 1997, "[t]he definition of eligible dependents has been expanded under the [County's self-funded] health plan" to allow "for coverage of one adult dependent, who can be [an employee's] spouse, domestic partner, or other adult who is claimed as a dependent on [the employee's] federal income tax return." The Newsletter listed eight criteria in defining an "adult dependent" as "[t]he domestic partner . . . who"

— has resided with the employee for a 1 year period;

— shares with the employee the common necessities of life and basic living expenses;

— is financially interdependent with the employee;

— is involved with the employee in a mutually exclusive relationship of support and commitment;

— is not related by blood to the employee;

— is not married to anyone;

— was mentally competent at time of consent to relationship;

— is 18 years of age or older.

A stipulation entered into by the parties states that "[a] 'domestic partner' eligible for coverage as an adult dependent of a County employee under the County's health benefits plan may be either a same-sex or opposite-sex domestic partner of a County employee," that "[a]n employee applying for domestic partner coverage must certify that the employee and the domestic partner meet the criteria established by the County," and that "[t]here are individuals who currently are covered as domestic partners of County employees under the County's health benefits plan, and who have received benefits under the plan." It was also stipulated that "[f]unds used by Arlington County to provide health benefits coverage for County employees and their adult dependents under the County's self-funded plan include local tax dollars."

Citing Code §§ 15.2–1517(A) and 51.1–801, the County correctly points out that "[t]he General Assembly specifically authorizes a local government to provide self-funded health benefit programs for its employees and their dependents." The County notes that neither statute defines the term "dependent" or refers to other statutory provisions that define the term for different purposes. Continuing, the County further notes that no express statutory provision specifies which employee dependents are eligible to participate in a locality's self-funded health benefits plan or by what method their eligibility is to be determined.

Under these circumstances, the County correctly maintains, "[t]he power to determine who is an employee's dependent . . . is fairly and necessarily implied." Furthermore, the County asserts, "the locality must make [the] determination itself"; indeed, it "could not carry out its authority without exercising its discretion." In the process, the County submits, the term "dependent" should be given its plain and ordinary meaning as one "[r]elying on ... the aid of another for support." The American Heritage Dictionary 501 (2nd College Ed.1985).

In this regard, however, we note that a dependant is also defined as "one not able to exist or sustain oneself without the power or aid of someone else." Black's Law Dictionary 449 (7th edition 1999). Moreover, as a term of art, a "legal dependent" is defined as "[a] person who is dependent according to law; a person who derives principal support from another." *Id.* (emphasis added). Nevertheless, these definitions do not control our resolution of this appeal.

In the end, the County opines, the "appropriate inquiry is whether [its] decision to include domestic partners as dependents in its plan is a reasonable method of implementing its authority." This inquiry, the County concludes, must be answered in the affirmative.

Under Dillon's Rule, [local governing bodies] have only those powers which are expressly granted by the state legislature, those powers fairly or necessarily implied from expressly granted powers, and those powers which are essential and indispensable. Where the state legislature grants a local government the power to do something but does not specifically direct the method of implementing that power, the choice made by the local government as to how to implement the conferred power will be upheld as long as the method selected is reasonable. Any doubt in the reasonableness of the method selected is resolved in favor of the locality. *City of Virginia Beach v. Hay*, 258 Va. 217, 221, 518 S.E.2d 314, 316 (1999) (citations omitted).

In light of these principles, we must decide whether the County's inclusion of domestic partners as defined by the County is a reasonable implementation of the County's authority to define an employee's dependent for purposes of coverage in the County's self-funded health benefits plan pursuant to Code §§ 15.2–1517(A) and 51.1–801. For the reasons that follow and giving the County the benefit of any doubt, we conclude that the County's definition of dependent is not reasonable and, therefore, violates the Dillon Rule.

In 1997, responding to an inquiry from a member of the General Assembly, the Attorney General issued an opinion that the statutory scheme which permits local governments "to provide for their officers and employees [self-funded] group life, accident, and health insurance programs ... [does not] contain any language from which a general legislative intent to extend insurance coverage to persons within the definition of 'domestic partner' may be inferred." 1997 Op. Va. Att'y Gen. 131, 131–32. Citing prior interpretations applying the Dillon Rule and its corollary to the statutes at issue, *Id.* at 131 n. 8, the Attorney General concluded that "[i]n the absence of any statutory authority indicating an intent to permit a local governing body to extend health insurance coverage provided employees to persons other than the spouse, children or dependants [sic] of the employee ... a county lacks the power to provide such coverage."

Id. at 132. In reaching this conclusion, the Attorney General expressly noted that the requirement that the employee be "financially interdependent" with the "domestic partner" was contrary to the established definition of a "dependant" as one who "must receive from the taxpayer over half of his or her support for the calendar year." *Id.*

The County's benefit plan extends coverage to a County employee and one other adult, who may be the employee's spouse, another adult who is properly claimed as a dependent on the employee's federal tax return, or the employee's "domestic partner." The County's definition of "domestic partner" includes eight criteria. Only two of these criteria address financial dependency-sharing expenses and being "financially interdependent." Neither of these criteria is synonymous with "financially dependent."

The inclusion of a spouse as a dependent for the purpose of coverage under the County's benefit plan does not eliminate the significance of this distinction. It is a matter of common knowledge and experience that a spouse may or may not be financially dependent on the employee-spouse. However, including a spouse as a dependent for coverage such as this is of such long standing that, even in the absence of financial dependence, there can be no dispute that the General Assembly contemplated that a spouse would be included for coverage under local benefit plans.

It is, nevertheless, equally clear that the General Assembly in leaving the definition of dependent to the local governing bodies which adopt self-funded health insurance benefit plans did not contemplate adoption of a definition that does not require some aspect of financial dependence rather than mere financial interdependence. This is the essential position of the Attorney General's opinion cited above and, in our view, it is sound.

Considering Code §§ 15.2–1517(A) and 51.1–801 and the Attorney General's opinion, we are of opinion that the expanded definition of dependants eligible to receive coverage under the self-funded health insurance benefits plan adopted by the County is not a reasonable method of implementing its implied authority under those statutes and is, therefore, an *ultra vires* act. Accordingly, the judgment below will be affirmed.

Affirmed.

KINSER, JUSTICE, concurring.

I join the majority opinion. However, I write additionally to point out that the central issue presented in this case is not, as stated in the dissenting opinion, whether "Arlington County [has] the legal authority to recognize common law marriages or 'same-sex unions' by conferring certain health insurance benefits upon domestic partners of County employees who are engaged in these relationships."

. . .

I do not intend in any way to suggest that I condone common law marriages or "same-sex unions." Nor do I question that such relationships do, indeed, violate the public policy of Virginia. However, neither my personal beliefs nor Virginia's public policy make it necessary to decide this appeal on grounds that could call into question other sections of Virginia's laws.

. . .

HASSELL, JUSTICE, with whom CHIEF JUSTICE CARRICO and SENIOR JUSTICE COMPTON join, dissenting in part, and concurring in judgment.

I.

I dissent because the majority ignores the fundamental issue raised in this appeal: Does Arlington County have the legal authority to recognize common law marriages or "same-sex unions" by conferring certain health insurance benefits upon domestic partners of County employees who are engaged in these relationships? Even though a review of the briefs and record filed in this appeal demonstrates that this question is the primary issue raised in this appeal, the majority decides this case on another legal basis....

I respectfully disagree with the majority's decision to ignore the central issue raised in this appeal. This Court has a duty, as well as an obligation, to decide issues of great importance to the citizens of this Commonwealth when, as here, those issues are properly presented to this Court.

. . .

II.

. . .

The primary issue that the taxpayers raised in the circuit court was that the County had violated the Dillon Rule because the General Assembly had not conferred upon the County the power to grant health insurance benefits to domestic partners of County employees. The circuit court entered a judgment in favor of the taxpayers which states in relevant part that "Arlington County's coverage for domestic partners in its self-funded health benefit plan for County employees violates the Dillon Rule." The circuit court, however, did not articulate the precise reasons it relied upon in reaching its conclusion.

On appeal, the County argues that the circuit court erred because the County's health insurance coverage for its employees' domestic partners in its self-funded benefit plan does not violate the Dillon Rule. The County also argues that it has authority to determine which dependents are eligible for coverage and that its decision to include domestic partners of County employees as dependents in the County's self-funded health benefits plan must be approved as long as the County's action is reasonable.

We stated in *City of Chesapeake v. Gardner Enterprises*, 253 Va. 243, 246, 482 S.E.2d 812, 814 (1997), that "[t]he Dillon Rule of strict construction controls our determination of the powers of local governing bodies. This rule provides that municipal corporations have only those powers that are expressly granted, those necessarily or fairly implied from expressly granted powers, and those that are essential and indispensable. *Ticonderoga Farms v. County of Loudoun*, 242 Va. 170, 173–74, 409 S.E.2d 446, 448 (1991); *City of Richmond v. Confrere Club of Richmond*, 239 Va. 77, 79, 387 S.E.2d 471, 473 (1990)."

. . .

Code § 15.2–1517(A), which permits a locality to provide health insurance programs, states in relevant part that "[a]ny locality may provide ... health insurance programs for their officers and employees ... through a program of self-insurance." Code § 51.1–801 provides in relevant part that a "local governing body may, through self-funding ... provide ... sickness insurance coverage for officers and employees ... and their dependents." The General Assembly, however, did not define the word "dependents." The County argues that the "appropriate inquiry is whether [its] decision to include domestic partners as dependents in its plan is a reasonable method of implementing its authority."

We have stated the following principles that we must apply when ascertaining whether a power may be implied from a statutory grant to a county:

"In questions of implied power, the answer is to be found in legislative intent. To imply a particular power from a power expressly granted, it must be found that the legislature intended that the grant of the express also would confer the implied.

"In determining legislative intent, the rule is clear that where a power is conferred and the mode of its execution is specified, no other method may be selected; any other means would be contrary to legislative intent and, therefore, unreasonable. A necessary corollary is that where a grant of power is silent upon its mode of execution, a method of exercise clearly contrary to legislative intent, or inappropriate to the ends sought to be accomplished by the grant, also would be unreasonable.

"Consistent with the necessity to uphold legislative intent, the doctrine of implied powers should never be applied to create a power that does not exist or to expand an existing power beyond rational limits. Always, the test in application of the doctrine is reasonableness, in which concern for what is necessary to promote the public interest is a key element."

Commonwealth v. Arlington County Board, 217 Va. 558, 577, 232 S.E.2d 30, 42 (1977) (citations omitted); *accord Tidewater Ass'n of Homebuilders, Inc. v. City of Virginia Beach*, 241 Va. 114, 119, 400 S.E.2d 523, 526 (1991).

The County's expanded definition of the word "dependents" clearly and unequivocally violates the Dillon Rule. This definition is an unreasonable method of implementing the power granted to the County under Code §§ 15.2–1517(A) and 51.1–801. The County's expanded definition of eligible dependents is nothing more than a disguised effort to confer health benefits upon persons who are involved in either common law marriages or "same-sex unions," which are not recognized in this Commonwealth and are violative of the public policy of this Commonwealth. The General Assembly, by enacting Code § 20–45.2, expressly prohibited marriage between persons of the same sex. This Code provision states in relevant part that "[a] marriage between persons of the same sex is prohibited." Also, we have held that Virginia does not recognize common law marriages. *Murphy v. Holland*, 237 Va. 212, 219–220, 377 S.E.2d 363, 367–68 (1989).

Furthermore, and just as important, the County's expanded definition of dependents is inappropriate because it permits the County to legislate in the area of domestic relations, a prerogative that lies within the exclusive domain of the General Assembly of this Commonwealth. See *Cramer v. Commonwealth*, 214 Va. 561, 564–65, 202 S.E.2d 911, 914, cert. denied, 419 U.S. 875, 95 S.Ct. 137, 42 L.Ed.2d 114 (1974). The General Assembly, not a county, is entrusted with the responsibility of recognizing and defining marital relationships.

Certainly, the General Assembly did not intend, by its enactment of Code §§ 15.2–1517(A) and 51.1–801, to grant counties, like Arlington, the power to recognize common law marriages or "same-sex unions." Even a cursory review of Arlington County's eligibility criteria demonstrates that Arlington County seeks to recognize such relationships because the criteria require that the employee, who seeks to add a non-employee as a dependent in the County's health plan, certify that the employee has resided with his or her domestic partner for a period of one year, "not [be] married to anyone," "[share] with the employee the common necessities of life and basic living expenses," "[be] financially interdependent with the employee," "not [be] related by blood to the employee," and "[be] involved with the employee in a mutually exclusive relationship of support and commitment." There can be no question or doubt that Arlington County seeks to recognize, tacitly, relationships that are violative of the public policy of this Commonwealth.

. . .

The majority holds that Arlington County's decision to provide health benefits to domestic partners of County employees violates the Dillon Rule only be-cause the County's health benefits plan requires that the domestic partner be "financially interdependent with the employee." As I have already stated, the majority's opinion ignores the central issue in this appeal. The majority's decision to do so is troublesome because if the Arlington County Board of Supervisors deletes from its health benefits plan the provision that the majority finds offensive, and implements a health benefits plan that confers benefits upon partners of County employees who are involved in common law marriages or "same-sex unions," the taxpayers will be compelled to file another lawsuit to challenge the legality of the County's actions.

I think that a purpose of the appellate process is to render decisions that will adjudicate the primary principles of an appeal, thereby ending the litigation when possible. Unfortunately, because the majority has chosen to ignore the primary issue in this appeal, the taxpayers and the County may incur additional legal fees to relitigate an issue that is already before the Court. The majority's decision to ignore this issue may also result in a waste of judicial resources because, presumably, the circuit court and this Court will confront this issue again. For these reasons, I cannot join in the opinion of the majority.

COUNCIL OF CITY OF NEW YORK v. BLOOMBERG

6 N.Y.3d 380, 813 N.Y.S.2d 3, 846 N.E.2d 433 (2006)

R.S. SMITH, J.

We hold that New York City's Equal Benefits Law is preempted by state and federal statutes. We therefore affirm the Appellate Division's dismissal of a CPLR article 78 proceeding brought by the New York City Council to compel enforcement of that law.

Facts and Procedural History

The Equal Benefits Law (Administrative Code of City of N.Y. § 6–126) was enacted by the City Council in 2004 over the Mayor's veto. It provides, in substance, that no city agency may enter into contracts having a value of $100,000 or more annually with any person or firm that fails to provide to its employees' domestic partners employment benefits equal to those provided to spouses. "Domestic partners," as defined in the Equal Benefits Law, means people who are registered as having that status under Administrative Code § 3–240(a), or who register with a contractor pursuant to the Equal Benefits Law itself (Administrative Code § 6–126[b][5]). "Employment benefits," as used in the Equal Benefits Law,

> "means benefits including, but not limited to, health insurance, pension, retirement, disability and life insurance, family, medical, parental, bereavement and other leave policies, tuition reimbursement, legal assistance, adoption assistance, dependent care insurance, moving and other relocation expenses, membership or membership discounts, and travel benefits provided by a contractor to its employees" (Administrative Code § 6–126[b] [7]).

Shortly before the Equal Benefits Law's effective date, the Mayor began a declaratory judgment action against the Council, asserting that the law was inconsistent with, and therefore preempted by, provisions of the General Municipal Law and the New York City Charter relating to municipal contracting; that it was also preempted by the federal Employee Retirement Income Security Act of 1974 (29 USC § 1001 et seq. [ERISA]); and that it was invalid because it curtailed the Mayor's powers without a referendum, in violation of the Municipal Home Rule Law and City Charter. After unsuccessfully seeking a temporary restraining order against the law's enforcement, the Mayor, through his counsel, informed Supreme Court that he would withdraw his motion for a preliminary injunction, that he would move promptly for summary judgment, and that in the meanwhile he would "comply with controlling state laws concerning procurement and the Charter"-i.e., that he would not implement the Equal Benefits Law. The next day, the Council began this CPLR article 78 proceeding, in the nature of mandamus to compel, against the Mayor and the City, asking for a judgment requiring them "immediately to implement and enforce the Equal Benefits Law." In response, the Mayor asserted, as he had in the declaratory judgment action, his reasons for considering the law invalid.

Supreme Court granted the petition without addressing the Mayor's arguments, relying on "the presumption of validity." The Appellate Division concluded that the Equal Benefits Law was preempted by both the General Municipal Law and ERISA, and dismissed the proceeding on that basis. We now affirm.

Discussion

I

The Council argues that we should grant its petition and order the Equal Benefits Law enforced without considering the merits of the controversy, on the ground that the validity of a legislative enactment cannot be decided in an article 78 proceeding. The Council's argument is misconceived.

The rule relied on by the Council that "article 78 does not lie to challenge a legislative act" (*New York City Health & Hosps. Corp. v. McBarnette*, 84 N.Y.2d 194, 201, 616 N.Y.S.2d 1, 639 N.E.2d 740 [1994]) means that a petitioner who is challenging the validity of legislation may not use an article 78 proceeding for that purpose; a lawsuit to challenge the validity of legislation should take the form of an action for a declaratory judgment. (*See also Press v. County of Monroe*, 50 N.Y.2d 695, 702, 431 N.Y.S.2d 394, 409 N.E.2d 870 [1980]; *Matter of Kovarsky v. Housing & Dev. Admin. of City of N.Y.*, 31 N.Y.2d 184, 192, 335 N.Y.S.2d 383, 286 N.E.2d 882 [1972].) It does not mean that, when an article 78 proceeding is brought to compel the enforcement of legislation the petitioner claims is valid, the court must grant the petition whether the legislation is valid or not.

On the contrary, article 78 relief in the form of mandamus to compel may be granted only where a petitioner establishes a "clear legal right" to the relief requested (*Matter of Brusco v. Braun*, 84 N.Y.2d 674, 679, 621 N.Y.S.2d 291, 645 N.E.2d 724 [1994]). And we have repeatedly held that an officer against whom a proceeding for a writ of mandamus is brought may defend on the ground that the legislation he or she has been asked to enforce is invalid (*Matter of Carow v. Board of Educ. of City of N.Y.*, 272 N.Y. 341, 345, 6 N.E.2d 47 [1936]; *People ex rel. Balcom v. Mosher*, 163 N.Y. 32, 35, 57 N.E. 88 [1900]). The theory the Council advocates would put the courts in the unacceptable position of directing an officer to violate his or her oath of office by enforcing an un-constitutional law, and would contradict the principle that "mandamus is never granted for the purpose of compelling the performance of an unlawful act" (*Matter of People ex rel. Sherwood v. State Bd. of Canvassers*, 129 N.Y. 360, 370, 29 N.E. 345 [1891]).

Thus we hold that the Appellate Division was correct in concluding that the Mayor was entitled to raise the invalidity of the Equal Benefits Law as a defense in this case. We are not persuaded by our dissenting colleagues' arguments to the contrary.

The dissent asserts, without citation of authority, that the Mayor's duty is to "follow a duly enacted law ... unless and until a court nullifies it" (dissenting op. at 396, 813 N.Y.S.2d at 12, 846 N.E.2d at 442). The assertion has a circular quality, for how can a law be "duly enacted" if the legislature that enacted it had no authority to do so? The Mayor does indeed have a duty to implement valid legislation passed by the City Council, whether over his veto or not, but he also has a duty to comply with valid state and federal legislation, including state competitive bidding laws and ERISA. Where a local law seems to the Mayor to conflict with a state or federal one, the Mayor's obligation is to obey the latter, as the Mayor has done here.

The dissent suggests that the procedural characteristics of an article 78 proceeding make it unsuitable for resolving the Mayor's contention that the Equal Benefits Law is invalid (dissenting op. at 401–402, 813 N.Y.S.2d at 16–17, 846 N.E.2d at 446–447). The suggestion is puzzling. Article 78 proceedings are indeed designed for the prompt resolution of largely legal issues, rather than for discovery, trials and "credibility judgments" (*Id.* at 400, 813 N.Y.S.2d at 15, 846 N.E.2d at 445), but, as we explain below, the validity of the Equal Benefits Law turns entirely on issues of law, not of fact. The dissent says that the likely fiscal impact of the Equal Benefits Law presents an issue of fact (*Id.* at 399, 813 N.Y.S.2d at 14, 846 N.E.2d at 444) but, as the next section of our opinion explains, it is not an issue sufficient to defeat summary judgment in this case. We assume the accuracy of the Council's assertion that the law will "not cost contractors much money" (*Id.* at 400, 813 N.Y.S.2d at 15, 846 N.E.2d at 445). We conclude that the law is nevertheless preempted by the competitive bidding statute.

The dissent seems to shrink, understandably, from following to the limits of its logic the proposition that an executive must implement every law, valid or invalid, that a legislative body enacts until a court determines the law's validity. Certainly, the dissenters would not so hold in an extreme case: If a legislative body enacted a law requiring racial segregation of public schools, the dissenters would not say that it is the duty of police to bar black children from "white" schools until a court orders them let in. And even in this case, the dissent stops short of saying that the relief the Council seeks in this article 78 proceeding-an order requiring implementation of the Equal Benefits Law, issued without considering the law's validity-should be granted. The dissenters say only that they would "reverse the order of the Appellate Division and allow the declaratory judgment action to proceed" (dissenting op. at 403, 813 N.Y.S.2d at 17, 846 N.E.2d at 447)—so that the article 78 proceeding would presumably remain in limbo until the declaratory judgment action is decided. All that means, in this case, is that the parties would make, and the courts would resolve, exactly the same arguments the parties make here, but under a different caption. We decline to order such a purposeless exercise, and we proceed to consider whether the Mayor can be ordered to enforce the Equal Benefits Law.

II

We agree with the Appellate Division that the Council's article 78 proceeding must be dismissed because the Equal Benefits Law conflicts with, and is therefore preempted by, General Municipal Law § 103.

Under section 103(1), "all contracts for public work involving an expenditure of more than twenty thousand dollars and all purchase contracts involving an expenditure of more than ten thousand dollars, shall be awarded ... to the lowest responsible bidder...." The Mayor argues, and we hold, that the Equal Benefits Law violates this requirement by excluding from public contracting any "responsible bidder" that does not provide equal benefits to domestic partners and spouses.

Associated Bldrs. & Contrs. v. City of Rochester, 67 N.Y.2d 854, 501 N.Y.S.2d 653, 492 N.E.2d 781 is the controlling authority. That case involved a City of Rochester ordinance providing that in awarding municipal construction contracts in excess of $100,000, preference must be given to a contractor whose employees participated in a state-approved apprenticeship program. We held that, in view of section 103's predominant purpose of "protection of the public fisc by requiring competitive bidding," the ordinance could not stand (*Id.* at 856, 501 N.Y.S.2d 653, 492 N.E.2d 781). We acknowledged that the apprentice training that the Rochester ordinance sought to promote was "a desirable end," but held it was not one that could "affect the qualification of an otherwise responsible low bidder" (*Id.*). That logic is dispositive in this case. The provision of equal benefits for domestic partners and spouses may be a desirable end, but it is not one that New York City is free to pursue by departing from the requirements of the competitive bidding statute.

The Council argues that the Equal Benefits Law will not undermine the purposes of competitive bidding, because, the Council says, the economic impact of the Equal Benefits Law will be de minimis. The Council asserts, and we assume, that the cost of providing equal benefits to domestic partners and to spouses will be close to zero. But the competitive bidding statute does not become inapplicable when the sums saved by complying with it are immaterial.

Apart from its purely financial effect, competitive bidding serves to prevent "favoritism, improvidence, fraud and corruption in the awarding of public contracts" (*Matter of New York State Ch., Inc., Associated Gen.*

Contrs. of Am. v. New York State Thruway Auth., 88 N.Y.2d 56, 68, 643 N.Y.S.2d 480, 666 N.E.2d 185 [1996]). If municipalities are free to contract only with firms that provide certain benefits to their employees, the door is open at least to favoritism, for the municipality could design its requirements to match the benefit structure of the bidder it favored. No such thing has happened in this case, of course; we have no doubt that the Equal Benefits Law is a good faith effort to make contractors treat the domestic partners of employees in a way that the Council considers fair. But the competitive bidding statute reflects a judgment by the State Legislature that, to avoid among other things the risk of favoritism, municipalities must give business to the lowest responsible bidder, whether the bidder's benefit plans meet the municipality's idea of fairness or not.

The Council says that the validity of the Equal Benefits Law finds support in the New York State Chapter case; in *McMillen v. Browne,* 14 N.Y.2d 326, 251 N.Y.S.2d 641, 200 N.E.2d 546 [1964]; and in the home rule provisions of the State Constitution and implementing legislation. None of these is a sufficient basis for upholding the law.

In New York State Chapter, we held that entities governed by competitive bidding requirements could, under some circumstances, adopt so-called project labor agreements (PLAs), providing that bidders for public construction contracts must sign pre-negotiated labor agreements or be barred from bidding. We did not hold, however, that public entities could enter into PLAs as a means of assuring fair treatment to contractors' employees. Indeed, we said that "PLAs that do have as their purpose social policymaking, such as remedying racial and gender bias, will not be sustained" (88 N.Y.2d at 76, 643 N.Y.S.2d 480, 666 N.E.2d 185). But we recognized that, while PLAs "have an anticompetitive impact on the bidding process," they also brought economic benefits to the contracting authority, in that "the union promises labor peace through the life of the contract" (*Id.* at 65, 643 N.Y.S.2d 480, 666 N.E.2d 185). We held that the resulting "efficiencies to be gained" (*Id.)* might justify a PLA under the competitive bidding laws. We said that a PLA would be upheld only if it "had as its purpose and likely effect the advancement of the interests embodied in the competitive bidding statutes" (*Id.* at 69, 643 N.Y.S.2d 480, 666 N.E.2d 185), which we identified as "prudent use of public moneys and . . . the acquisition of high quality goods and services at the lowest possible cost" (*Id.* at 67, 643 N.Y.S.2d 480, 666 N.E.2d 185).

In other words, under New York State Chapter, PLAs and other procedures having an anticompetitive effect on the bidding process can be justified only by proof that they are designed to save the public money by causing contracts to be performed at smaller cost or without disruption. No such justification can be convincingly claimed for the Equal Benefits Law. The Council says that the cost of the law will be insignificant, and will be outweighed by the benefits to the public that flow from assuring adequate health care to workers' domestic partners, but the Council cannot and does not seriously assert that the "purpose and likely effect" of the law is to make the City's contracts cheaper or their performance more efficient. The law—like the mayoral executive order prohibiting discrimination by city contractors based on sexual preference that was at issue in *Under 21, Catholic Home Bur. for Dependent Children v. City of New York*, 65 N.Y.2d 344, 492 N.Y.S.2d 522, 482 N.E.2d 1 [1985]—is obviously designed as "an enactment of social policy" (*Id.* at 359 n. 5, 492 N.Y.S.2d 522, 482 N.E.2d 1). New York State Chapter gives no support to the view that social policy goals may trump the competitive bidding statute.

The Council relies on *McMillen* because in that case we upheld a local law requiring payment of a minimum wage by city contractors—a law plainly designed, as is the Equal Benefits Law, for the protection of contractors' employees. The flaw in the Council's argument is that *McMillen* had nothing to do with competitive bidding requirements; they are nowhere referred to in the decision. The issue in *McMillen* was whether New York City's minimum wage requirement was preempted by the State's prevailing wage and minimum wage laws. Our resolution of that issue is not relevant to this case.

The home rule provisions of the Constitution and the legislation implementing them list several subjects about which local governments are given the power to legislate. One of those subjects is "[t]he wages or salaries, the hours of work or labor, and the protection, welfare and safety of persons employed by any contractor or sub-contractor performing work, labor or services for [the municipality]" (N.Y. Const., art. IX, § 2[c][ii] [9]; Municipal Home Rule Law § 10[1][ii][a][10]). But this grant of power to municipalities is expressly made subject to contrary state legislation. The Constitution and the statute say that municipalities may adopt laws of the kind described in the language we have quoted "except to the extent that the legislature shall restrict the adoption of such a local law" (N.Y. Const., art. IX, § 2[c][ii]; Municipal Home Rule Law § 10[1][ii]). General Municipal Law § 103 is, as Associated Builders makes clear, just such a restriction. The requirement of section 103 that municipalities contract with the lowest responsible bidder is plainly in tension with the right of a municipality to say that it will contract only with firms that provide certain benefits. Where the two conflict, as they do here, the legislative restriction on the municipality's power prevails.

In short, the Equal Benefits Law conflicts with General Municipal Law § 103. The City Council has not demonstrated a clear legal right to have the Equal Benefits Law enforced.

III

The Equal Benefits Law is also preempted by ERISA, except to the extent that it governs benefits that are outside ERISA's scope. In so holding, we agree with two federal district courts that have addressed the validity under ERISA of local legislation similar to the Equal Benefits Law (*Catholic Charities of Me., Inc. v. City of Portland*, 304 F.Supp.2d 77, 84–

93 [D.Me.2004]; *Air Transp. Assn. of Am. v. City & County of San Francisco*, 992 F.Supp. 1149, 1165–1180 [N.D.Cal.1998]).

ERISA is a federal statute that imposes disclosure and reporting requirements, and establishes standards of conduct, for employee benefit plans and their fiduciaries (see 29 USC § 1001[b]). A consistent, nationwide regulatory scheme was clearly one of Congress's goals, and to that end it provided that "the provisions of [ERISA] shall supersede any and all State laws insofar as they may now or hereafter relate to any employee benefit plan" of the kind governed by ERISA (29 USC § 1144[a]). ERISA plans include, among other things, "any plan, fund, or program ... maintained by an employer ... for the purpose of providing ... medical, surgical, or hospital care or benefits, or benefits in the event of sickness, accident, disability, death or unemployment ..." (29 USC § 1002[1][A]). Clearly, the coverage of ERISA overlaps substantially with the coverage of the Equal Benefits Law, though the Equal Benefits Law may apply to some benefits not governed by ERISA (see Air Transp. Assn. of Am. v. City & County of San Francisco, 992 F.Supp. at 1169 [a law applying to "benefits that ... require no 'ongoing administrative program,' ... does not apply to a 'plan' and thus is not preempted"; also, "(m)oving expenses ... are not even ERISA-covered benefits"]).

The broad preemptive language of 29 USC § 1144(a), superseding all laws that "relate to any employee benefit plan," has been held by the United States Supreme Court to be no less sweeping than it appears on its face: "A law 'relates to' an employee benefit plan, in the normal sense of the phrase, if it has a connection with or reference to such a plan" (*Shaw v. Delta Air Lines, Inc.*, 463 U.S. 85, 96–97, 103 S.Ct. 2890, 77 L.Ed.2d 490 [1983]). In *Shaw*, the Court struck down a New York law that prohibited discrimination in the provision of employee benefits on the basis of pregnancy. *Shaw* holds that states (and, of course, municipalities) cannot regulate the content of ERISA plans. That holding has been left untouched by more recent cases, which hold, in effect, that ERISA does not preempt every state law that has an indirect impact on an ERISA plan (*New York State Conference of Blue Cross & Blue Shield Plans v. Travelers Ins. Co.*, 514 U.S. 645, 115 S.Ct. 1671, 131 L.Ed.2d 695 [1995]; *HMI Mech. Sys., Inc. v. McGowan*, 266 F.3d 142 [2d Cir.2001]).

The Equal Benefits Law seemingly seeks to do exactly what ERISA, as interpreted in Shaw, prohibits-to prescribe the terms of benefit plans. The Council argues, however, that the prohibition is inapplicable because the Equal Benefits Law does not compel any firm to offer domestic partner benefits; it merely provides that the City will not contract with firms that do not do so. Thus, says the Council, the law does not regulate benefit plans, but reflects a decision by the City, as a market participant, to choose the firms it deals with based on the benefits those firms provide their employees. The Council's "market participant" argument is inconsistent with United States Supreme Court precedent.

While the Supreme Court has not addressed the market participant theory in an ERISA preemption case, it recognized a limited market participant exception to federal labor law preemption in the so-called *Boston Harbor* case (*Building & Constr. Trades Council v. Associated Builders & Contractors of Mass./R.I., Inc.*, 507 U.S. 218, 113 S.Ct. 1190, 122 L.Ed.2d 565 [1993]). *Boston Harbor* (like our New York State Chapter case, discussed at pages 391–392, 813 N.Y.S.2d at 8–9, 846 N.E.2d at 438–439 above) involved a public agency's practice of entering into project labor agreements that required its contractors to sign agreements with labor unions, in order to prevent a project from being disrupted by labor disputes. Under the preemptive provisions of federal labor law, a state could not impose such a requirement by statute or regulation, but the Court held in *Boston Harbor* that the requirement could be imposed by a state agency when the state is not regulating, but is acting as an owner or manager of property that "must interact with private participants in the marketplace" (507 U.S. at 227, 113 S.Ct. 1190). The *Boston Harbor* court recognized, as we did in New York State Chapter, that a PLA may produce economic benefits that a public proprietor, like a private proprietor, should be free to seek in the marketplace. The Court thus recognized a distinction "between government as regulator and government as proprietor" (*Id.*).

Boston Harbor does not hold, however, that a state may escape the force of federal preemption by using its power in the marketplace to implement governmental policies. To the contrary, *Boston Harbor* makes clear that a state acts as a regulator, not a proprietor, when it uses its bargaining leverage as a means of attaining policy ends. Thus, the Court in *Boston Harbor* distinguished *Wisconsin Dept. of Industry v. Gould Inc.*, 475 U.S. 282, 106 S.Ct. 1057, 89 L.Ed.2d 223 [1986], which held that certain state activity in the marketplace was preempted.

In *Gould*, the Court held that a Wisconsin statute barring some labor law violators from doing business with the State was preempted by federal labor law. The difference between *Boston Harbor* and *Gould*, the Court explained in *Boston Harbor,* is that in *Gould* the State's reason for its marketplace activity was to deter labor law violations, not to protect the State's proprietary interest in the efficient performance of contracts (507 U.S. at 228–229, 113 S.Ct. 1190). Under *Boston Harbor*, the market participant exception to preemption is limited to the situation where "the State acts as a market participant with no interest in setting policy" (*Id.* at 229, 113 S.Ct. 1190).

The Equal Benefits Law is much more like the statute involved in *Gould* than the contract specification at issue in *Boston Harbor*. In enacting the Equal Benefits Law the Council was obviously "setting policy." As we pointed out above, it was not acting just as a manager or owner of property concerned with assuring the cheap and efficient performance of con-tracts. The Equal Benefits Law, as its name implies, is designed to induce contractors to treat domestic partners and spouses equally, just as the Wisconsin statute in *Gould* was designed to induce contractors to avoid unfair labor practices. Thus the market participant exception does not apply here, and the Equal Benefits Law, except to the extent that the benefits it governs are not provided through ERISA plans, is preempted by ERISA.

Accordingly, the order of the Appellate Division should be affirmed, with costs.

ROSENBLATT, J. (dissenting).

As a threshold matter, the City Council asserts that the Mayor may not challenge the validity of the Equal Benefits Law in this CPLR article 78 case. The majority claims that the Council's approach would put the courts in "the unacceptable position of directing an officer to violate his or her oath of office by enforcing an unconstitutional law" (majority op. at 388, 813 N.Y.S.2d at 6–7, 846 N.E.2d at 436–437). Respectfully, I dissent. Under a separation of powers system it is the job of the legislative branch to enact laws and the executive to carry them out.[1] An executive who believes that a law is unconstitutional is not powerless but must follow a process by which the judiciary-and not the executive-determines the issue in the first instance.

I.

By insisting that the Mayor follow a duly enacted law-unless and until a court nullifies it-the Council is not putting the courts in an "unacceptable position" of directing the Mayor to violate his oath.[2] On the contrary, our system requires that the judiciary preserve its duty as arbiter of a law's constitutionality. An executive is authorized to bring a declaratory judgment action challenging an enactment's constitutionality and the case goes forward until a final judicial declaration is made. That's how the system is supposed to work.

What happened here upended the process. The City Council enacted Local Law No. 27 (2004) (adding Administrative Code of City of N.Y. § 6–126 [the Equal Benefits Law]) by a vote of 43 to 5. The Mayor disapproved the law. By a vote of 41 to 4 the City Council overrode the Mayor's veto, pursuant to New York City Charter § 37(b).[3]

1. The Mayor is "the chief executive officer of the city" (N.Y. City Charter § 3), whereas the City Council is "vested with the legislative power of the city" (N.Y. City Charter § 21).

2. The majority disapproves of my asserting "without citation of authority" that the Mayor has a duty to follow enacted law unless and until a court nullifies it (majority op. at 389, 813 N.Y.S.2d at 7, 846 N.E.2d at 437). It seems to me basic that legislatures pass laws, executives carry them out and courts decide their constitutionality. The Supreme Court has told us as much (see *Marbury v. Madison*, 1 Cranch [5 U.S.] 137, 177, 2 L.Ed. 60 [1803]; *Kendall v. United States ex rel. Stokes*, 12 Pet [37 U.S.] 524, 613, 9 L.Ed. 1181 [1838]; *Youngstown Sheet & Tube Co. v. Sawyer*, 343 U.S. 579, 587–588, 72 S.Ct. 863, 96 L.Ed. 1153 [1952]). If the majority means that there is no authority in the New York jurisprudence for this proposition, that is probably because no one thought to question it and the prospect of a New York executive (governor, mayor or county executive) unilaterally refusing to follow a legislative enactment is virtually unheard of.

3. The Mayor may veto ("disapprove") a local law but, if after reconsideration, "the votes of two-thirds of all the council members be cast in favor of repassing such local law, it shall be deemed adopted, notwithstanding the objections of the mayor" (N.Y. City Charter § 37[b]).

The Mayor then sought a judgment declaring the law invalid and a permanent injunction barring its implementation. He also applied for a temporary restraining order and moved for a preliminary injunction staying implementation. After Supreme Court denied his application for a temporary restraining order, the Mayor announced that his administration would not implement the law. On the day the Equal Benefits Law took effect, the City Council commenced an article 78 proceeding to compel the Mayor to enforce the law. In his verified answer, the Mayor asserted by way of affirmative defense that the law was invalid.

After the legislature enacts a law it should not be necessary for it to start a lawsuit saying, in effect, "We've passed the law and really meant it; now we need a court to direct the executive to enforce it." Passing the law ought to be enough; a legislature should not be forced to go through this second step. By implementing a duly enacted law, the Mayor is violating no oath; he is following precepts fundamental to a system of separation of powers (*see Under 21, Catholic Home Bur. for Dependent Children v. City of New York*, 65 N.Y.2d 344, 356, 492 N.Y.S.2d 522, 482 N.E.2d 1 [1985]). Indeed, an executive's oath of office is honored not by repudiating the law but by carrying it out unless and until the judiciary nullifies it.

Should a piece of legislation appear to be unlawful, the executive may seek its judicial invalidation, using expedited measures as necessary. Were this a clearly unlawful piece of legislation, as the racial segregation example the majority poses (majority op. at 389–390, 813 N.Y.S.2d at 7–8, 846 N.E.2d at 437–438), then no doubt a court would act immediately to block its implementation. Here, the Mayor lost his application for a temporary restraining order but still refuses to comply with the law, conflating the roles of the executive and judicial branches of our government.

II.

Our colleagues in the majority apparently recognize that a petitioner who challenges the validity of legislation may not proceed by article 78 but must bring a declaratory judgment action (see majority op. at 388, 813 N.Y.S.2d at 16, 846 N.E.2d at 436). That is the law. (*New York City Health & Hosps. Corp. v. McBarnette*, 84 N.Y.2d 194, 203–204, 616 N.Y.S.2d 1, 639 N.E.2d 740 [1994].) Cases to this effect are legion. Unless the challenge is directed at the procedures followed in the enactment or at the constitutionality of its application, "an article 78 proceeding may not be used to test the constitutionality of a legislative enactment" (*Board of Educ. of Belmont Cent. School Dist. v. Gootnick*, 49 N.Y.2d at 687, 427 N.Y.S.2d 777, 404 N.E.2d 1318.

. . .

The majority goes on, however, to hold that a constitutional challenge may be employed as a "defense" in an article 78 proceeding (majority op. at 388, 813 N.Y.S.2d at 6, 846 N.E.2d at 436). I disagree and would rule that the executive may not assail the constitutionality of a law in a lawsuit that he, in effect, provoked because he refused to apply the law in the first place. If we approved of that type of executive action, the executive branch could refuse to enforce duly enacted legislation and put lawmakers to the burden of bringing litigation to give life to their laws.

By acting as it did, the executive branch shifted the burden, creating a precedent that, in my view, skews the roles of the legislative and executive branches. The City Charter "provide[s] for distinct legislative and executive branches" and "no matter how well-intentioned his actions may be, the Mayor may not unlawfully infringe upon the legislative powers reserved to the City Council" (*Under 21, Catholic Home Bur. for Dependent Children v. City of New York*, 65 N.Y.2d at 356, 492 N.Y.S.2d 522, 482 N.E.2d 1). This is true whether the executive attempts to "legislate" by action or by inaction, by an unauthorized executive order or by impermissible failure to enforce.

Further, executive action of this type would strip the judiciary of its power to determine, in the first instance, whether a law is valid, and thereby clothe the executive with not only legislative but judicial powers. The Mayor's position that the executive branch can say when a law is unconstitutional equates the powers of executive officials with those of the judiciary (*see Ameron, Inc. v. U.S. Army Corps of Engrs.*, 610 F.Supp. 750, 754 [D.N.J.1985]). "It is emphatically the province and duty of the judicial department to say what the law is." (*Marbury v. Madison*, 1 Cranch [5 U.S.] 137, 177, 2 L.Ed. 60 [1803].)

III.

For these reasons, I would not reach the questions of state or federal preemption but would have the declaratory judgment action go forward. The grounds of that action are that the Equal Benefits Law is preempted by state law and by federal law and that it curtails mayoral powers without providing for a referendum. The Mayor claims state law preemption, asserting that the Equal Benefits Law conflicts with the competitive bidding statute, General Municipal Law § 103. He further claims that the Equal Benefits Law is federally preempted insofar as it directly affects contractors' Employee Retirement Income Security Act of 1974 (ERISA) plans.

Contrary to the majority's statement (majority op. at 389, 813 N.Y.S.2d at 7, 846 N.E.2d at 437), the state and federal law preemption claims do raise questions of fact. The Mayor claims that the Equal Benefits Law impedes competition to bid for contracts with New York City, and that neither its purpose nor its likely effect is to obtain the best work at the lowest possible price. The City Council, on the other hand, asserts the very opposite, quoting New York State Comptroller Alan Hevesi's testimony that the Equal Benefits Law "has the potential to save significant resources for both the city and the state of New York." The federal law preemption claim turns on the nature and extent of the economic effect of the law on the costs of contractors' ERISA plans.

Contradicting the Mayor's position on the Equal Benefits Law, the City Council quotes testimony suggesting that a similar law in San Francisco "works because it does not cost contractors much money to comply with this legislation."

If, as our own jurisprudence mandates, the declaratory judgment action were allowed to run its course, the Mayor's motion for summary judgment and the City Council's response would be accompanied by the submission of evidence pertaining to the intent of the City Council in enacting the Equal Benefits Law and its expected economic effects. Expert testimony would be sought, hearings transcripts would be studied, credibility judgments would be made. Supreme Court would be able to consider the extent to which factual matters were rationally controverted in reaching a conclusion about whether summary judgment was warranted. It would do so with all facts viewed in the light most favorable to the nonmoving City Council.

Instead, the Appellate Division improperly chose to rule on the validity of a duly enacted local law in the context of an article 78 proceeding and therefore made its decision with the benefit only of a verified petition, a verified answer and a handful of accompanying documents and preceding pleadings. Such a ruling implicitly does away with the heavy burden our case law imposes on a party seeking to challenge a duly enacted law. "[P]arties challenging a duly enacted statute face the initial burden of demonstrating the statute's invalidity beyond a reasonable doubt" (*Dalton v. Pataki*, 5 N.Y.3d 243, 255, 802 N.Y.S.2d 72, 835 N.E.2d 1180 [2005] [internal quotation marks and citations omitted]).

In fact, in order to prevail, a challenger has to "prove beyond a reasonable doubt that in any degree and in every conceivable application the [legislative enactment] suffers wholesale constitutional impairment" (*Local Govt. Assistance Corp. v. Sales Tax Asset Receivable Corp.*, 2 N.Y.3d 524, 535, 780 N.Y.S.2d 507, 813 N.E.2d 587 [2004]. . . . Moreover, we have held that this heavy initial burden applies not only to challenges to state laws but also to challenges to municipal ordinances (*Lighthouse Shores v. Town of Islip*, 41 N.Y.2d 7, 11, 390 N.Y.S.2d 827, 359 N.E.2d 337 [1976]; *Twin Lakes Dev. Corp. v. Town of Monroe*, 1 N.Y.3d 98, 106, 769 N.Y.S.2d 445, 801 N.E.2d 821 [2003]).

When a challenge to a law is raised in an article 78 proceeding, whether by one side or the other, the challenger is unfairly relieved of its burden if a court summarily declares the law invalid without benefit of a record assembled with that burden in mind. This distinction between article 78 and declaratory judgment is critical and must be maintained if we are to preserve proper methods of constitutional analysis. This goes to more than form. In the case before us, it implicates separation of powers.

IV.

As a special proceeding, an article 78 proceeding "is as plenary as an action, culminating in a judgment, but is brought on with the ease, speed, and economy of a mere motion" (Siegel, N.Y. Prac. § 547, at 943 [4th ed.]). Since it is "designed to facilitate a 'summary disposition' of the issues presented," its procedures are in keeping with its summary nature (*Davidson v. Capuano*, 792 F.2d 275, 280 [2d Cir.1986]). Although an article 78 respondent may move for summary judgment pursuant to CPLR 409(b), it remains "in the very spirit and purpose of proceedings under article 78 to provide a summary remedy, so summary, indeed, as to dispense with the need or occasion for the application of summary judgment" (*Matter of Rockwell v. Morris*, 12 A.D.2d 272, 275, 211 N.Y.S.2d 25 [1st Dept.1961]).

By contrast, a declaratory judgment action brings with it all the apparatus of an action, proceeding to trial unless the court dismisses the case or grants a motion for summary judgment. Faced with a summary judgment motion, the court must carefully consider the material facts to ascertain whether any are genuinely controverted, before deciding that there is, or is not, a material triable issue of fact (*Glick & Dolleck v. Tri–Pac Export Corp.*, 22 N.Y.2d 439, 441, 293 N.Y.S.2d 93, 239 N.E.2d 725 [1968]; *Zuckerman v. City of New York*, 49 N.Y.2d 557, 562, 427 N.Y.S.2d 595, 404 N.E.2d 718 [1980]). Moreover, in that posture, the facts must be viewed in the light most favorable to the nonmoving party (*Matsushita Elec. Industrial Co. v. Zenith Radio Corp.*, 475 U.S. 574, 587, 106 S.Ct. 1348, 89 L.Ed.2d 538 [1986]).

Whether it is the article 78 petitioner or—as in this case—the opposing side (the Mayor) who seeks to have the courts declare a law invalid, the careful scrutiny of the record in search of triable facts that accompanies an action at the summary judgment stage is too easily bypassed when the validity of a law is summarily and improperly assessed in a manner suited to special proceedings that are strictly limited in scope.

The article 78 proceeding has the quite specific purpose of superseding the common-law writs of mandamus, prohibition and certiorari to review. It is ill fit as a vehicle for constitutional analysis. By contrast, there is no statutory restriction on the kinds of claim that may be brought in the form of a declaratory judgment action and it has traditionally been used to test a law's constitutionality (Siegel, N.Y. Prac. § 437, at 741 [4th ed.]).

V.

The Mayor relies on Matter *of People ex rel. Sherwood v. State Bd. of Canvassers*, 129 N.Y. 360, 29 N.E. 345 [1891]. There, we denied an application for a writ of mandamus compelling the issuance of a certificate of election to a prospective state senator who was constitutionally ineligible for the office because he was already a city government officer. The Court, however, repeatedly stressed the undisputed nature of the facts: the question of the candidate's ineligibility was "a pure legal question, depending upon undisputed facts" (*Id.* at 366, 29 N.E. 345); "upon the undisputed facts, the court [was] able to see that he [was] ineligible" (*Id.* at 373, 29 N.E. 345). At best, *Sherwood* stands for the proposition that an article 78 proceeding may properly be dismissed where, because the facts are undisputed, the court can decide as a matter of law that the petitioner has no legal right to the relief sought. The present litigation is as factually controverted as Sherwood was factually simple.

In *Kendall v United States ex rel. Stokes,* 12 Pet. [37 U.S.] 524, 9 L.Ed. 1181 [1838], the United States Supreme Court affirmed a judgment of the Circuit Court of the District of Columbia ordering a writ of mandamus to compel an executive branch official, the Postmaster General, to implement a law that he refused to enforce. The Court rejected the argument that the executive branch was vested with the power to refuse to enforce a law. "To contend that the obligation imposed on the [executive branch] to see the laws faithfully executed, implies a power to forbid their execution, is a novel construction of the constitution, and entirely inadmissible" (*Id.* at 613).

VI.

Just as a judicial "injunction must be obeyed until modified or dissolved, and its unconstitutionality is no defense to disobedience" (*Metropolitan Opera Assn., Inc. v. Local 100, Hotel Empls. & Rest. Empls. Intl. Union*, 239 F.3d 172, 176 [2d Cir.2001]; *see Walker v. Birmingham*, 388 U.S. 307, 314–321, 87 S.Ct. 1824, 18 L.Ed.2d 1210 [1967]), duly enacted legislation must be enforced by the executive branch and its alleged invalidity is no defense.

By refusing to enforce a duly enacted law of New York City's legislative branch, the Mayor assumes a legislative authority he does not possess. When the executive acts inconsistently with the legislature or usurps its exclusive powers, the doctrine of separation of powers is violated (*Rapp v. Carey*, 44 N.Y.2d 157, 404 N.Y.S.2d 565, 375 N.E.2d 745 [1978]). "The Framers with memories of the tyrannies produced by a blending of executive and legislative power rejected that political arrangement." (*Youngstown Sheet & Tube Co. v. Sawyer*, 343 U.S. 579, 633, 72 S.Ct. 863, 96 L.Ed. 1153 [1952, Douglas, J., concurring].)

I would therefore reverse the order of the Appellate Division and allow the declaratory judgment action to proceed.

DISCUSSION

Compare Hartman v. City of Allentown, 880 A.2d 737 (Pa. 2005), *in which the Pennsylvania appellate court held that Allentown's police powers provided authority for it to enact a local anti-discrimination ordinance that prohibited discrimination in employment, housing and public accommodations as to sexual orientation and gender identity in addition to classifications specifically listed in the Pennsylvania Human Relations Act. The court also held that the ordinance at issue was not* ultra vires *under the authority granted the city by Home Rule.*

III. LOCAL DECISION-MAKING AUTHORITY

Municipalities typically handle decision making in one of two ways. One form is known as the council-manager form of government. This type of governing body is composed of a board of members (council members or alderpersons, for example) who are elected to perform legislative functions, and a city or town manager who is hired by the board to perform administrative functions (similar to a CEO of a large corporation). These administrative functions include preparing the annual budget, hiring and firing department head, and other tasks of this nature. The mayor in this form is somewhat of a figurehead, and can be elected from the citizens at large, or from the board members. Counties typically use a similar form of government.

The second is the mayor-council form of government. This form of government is used more predominantly in larger cities because it is a form that has the ability to give the mayor a large amount of control. Mayors in this form of government not only have pronounced political independence, but they often have total administrative authority, including the preparation of annual budgets and employee hiring and firing responsibility.

As you review the pleading below, consider under what authority the mayor was attempting to act.

IN THE UNITED STATES DISTRICT COURT
FOR THE NORTHERN DISTRICT OF ALABAMA
SOUTHERN DIVISION

Case No. 2:08–cv–1533–KOB

CENTRAL ALABAMA PRIDE, INC.,
an Alabama non-profit corporation,
Plaintiff,
v.
LARRY LANGFORD, in his
individual and official capacities
as Mayor of Birmingham
Defendant.

AMENDED COMPLAINT*

INTRODUCTION AND JURISDICTIONAL STATEMENT

1. This is an action brought pursuant to 42 U.S.C. § 1983 seeking declaratory and injunctive relief, as well as compensatory and punitive damages, to redress violation of the constitutional rights of Plaintiff Central Alabama Pride (''Plaintiff'' or ''C.A.P.'') by Defendant Larry Langford (''Defendant''). This Court has jurisdiction pursuant to that statute as well as 28 U.S.C. § 1331 (federal question) and 28 U.S.C.

* Lambda Legal's amended complaint can be found at their website at http://www.lambdalegal.org/in-court/legal-docs/central-alabama-pride_al_20081222_complaint-amended.html.

§ 1343(a)(3) (redress of civil rights violations under color of state law). Venue is proper in this Court pursuant to 28 U.S.C. § 1391(b) in that Plaintiff was incorporated in Jefferson County, Alabama, in the Northern District of Alabama, Defendant resides there and all actions complained of occurred there.

2. Plaintiff is an Alabama non-profit corporation and is exempt from the payment of taxes under the provisions of 26 U.S.C. § 501(c)(3). Plaintiff incorporated in Jefferson County with the objectives and purposes of promoting pride within the lesbian, gay, bisexual and transgender ("LGBT") community, and understanding between the LGBT community all other communities in central Alabama through education, public forums and organized social and recreational activities. Plaintiff was founded in 1979 and secured its status under 26 U.S.C. § 501(c)(3) in 2007. Plaintiff brings this action on behalf of itself and its members.

3. Defendant is the mayor of the City of Birmingham (the "City" or "Birmingham"). As such, Defendant is the City's chief executive and exercises general supervision and control of all other officers, employees and affairs of the City pursuant to Ala. Code § 11–43D–14 and § 11–43–81. Thus, Defendant is the final decision maker and final policy maker with respect to deciding on and directing the duties of City employees. In making the decisions complained of in this action, Defendant acted in his capacity as the final decision maker and final policy maker for the City. Defendant is sued in his individual and official capacities.

STATEMENT OF FACTS

The History of Central Alabama Pride and Birmingham Pride Celebrations

4. Since June 1989, Plaintiff has organized and sponsored a parade through the Southside area of Birmingham as part of Plaintiff's annual Pride Celebration ("the parade"). The month of June is generally celebrated in LGBT communities across the country in commemoration of the "Stonewall Uprising," when police in New York City raided a gay bar, the Stonewall Inn, on June 28, 1969 and patrons—having endured years of abuse at the hands of police and government authorities—engaged in active resistance to government mistreatment that lasted several days. The Stonewall Uprising is generally considered the beginning of the modern gay liberation movement.

5. Each year from 1989 through 2007, Plaintiff was given a permit for its parade, the City's mayor at the time (initially, Richard Arrington and, following him, Bernard Kincaid) issued a proclamation in honor of the event and Plaintiff's banners were attached to City utility poles by City employees, as part of a custom and tradition within the City that facilitates private expression by temporarily attaching entities' banners and flags recognizing private entities as well as events taking place within the City ("banner forum"). Plaintiff's banners are rainbow flags, universally

recognized as representing gay pride. These banners have been attached in all these years by City employees to four utility poles at one intersection along the parade route.

The City's Banner Forum

6. The City has, over the years, required City employees to attach and detach private entities' flags and banners on City utility poles as part of its banner forum. This practice facilitates speech announcing many diverse events that take place in Birmingham.

7. Generally, the City's Traffic Engineering Department is provided the flags or banners to be attached, and does so safely and efficiently with the use of a bucket truck. Johnathan Quinn (Quinn), Plaintiff's president, and other C.A.P. members are routinely present during the attachment of their banners and celebrate the attachment as the unofficial kick-off of the Pride celebration. The entire process of attaching the banners takes the City's employees approximately 15 minutes.

8. The City utility poles, upon which the four Pride banners regularly have been attached, are positioned inches from the busy "Five Points South" intersection in Birmingham. The attachment posts for flags and banners on City utility poles are more than 30 feet high, and are unreachable without mechanical or other assistance. The attachment posts were specifically designed to hold flags and banners and are permanently attached, if not part of, the City utility poles.

9. One of the private entities and events that has used and otherwise participated in the banner forum is the City Stages music festival, which is reportedly now some $150,000 in debt and has been subsidized by the City. In contrast, Plaintiff's Pride events are an annual source of income for the City and local merchants. Among the many other private entities and events that have utilized the City's banner forum and have had their expressive flags and banners attached to City utility poles by City employees are football games, including the "Magic City Classic," an annual football game sponsored by several large, for-profit corporations, including Food World, Pepsi and McDonald's; cultural festivals; and religious entities.

10. At all times relevant to this action, the City's banner forum was a designated public forum created by the City through a policy, custom and/or practice of allowing private entities to exercise their right to freedom of expression by announcing and publicizing events taking place in the City through having their expressive flags and banners attached by City employees to City utility poles.

Defendant's Efforts to Prevent the 2008 Pride Celebration

11. Defendant was elected mayor of the City of Birmingham in October 2007 and assumed the office on November 13, 2007.

12. In May of 2008, in accordance with Plaintiff's past practice and City policies, Quinn, on behalf of Plaintiff, filed an application for a parade permit, a form requesting a proclamation recognizing Pride, and a form to

have Plaintiff's Pride flags attached to City utility poles along the parade route. The request sought to have the banners attached, as always, beginning one week before the parade, which was scheduled to take place on June 7, 2008.

13. Applications for parade permits in Birmingham are routinely handled through the Birmingham Department of Traffic Engineering which, on information and belief, issues permits in consultation with the City's police department. Plaintiff's Pride parade had, since its inception, been so handled. However, on or about May 24, 2008, Defendant announced that he would not grant a permit for the parade. Defendant's reasons for denying the permit and attempting to prevent the parade was that he did not personally condone the "lifestyle choice" represented by the Plaintiff, the parade and its gay-positive message. According to news reports, "Langford said anyone familiar with his personality and religious views should not be surprised by the denial."

14. Defendant's unilateral and publicly announced intervention into a matter routinely handled by the City's Traffic Engineering and/or police departments resulted in significant local press coverage. A meeting was arranged between Defendant, members of the local LGBT community, including officers of the Plaintiff corporation and Alabama State Representative Patricia Todd (who is Alabama's first openly gay state legislator), as well as the City Councilor representing the Five Points South district. As a consequence of the meeting, Defendant agreed not to interfere with the parade, so long as he did not have to sign the parade permit (which he never would have had to do in the ordinary course of events). Defendant refused, however, to issue the proclamation that had always been issued in previous years.

15. The following day, Defendant announced that he would not allow City employees to attach Plaintiff's expressive banners to the City utility poles. In fact, Defendant demanded that Plaintiff immediately retrieve its banners, which were in the City's possession and ready to be attached and displayed in the banner forum, threatening to have them thrown in the garbage if they were not retrieved.

16. Plaintiff's Pride flags were annually and routinely attached and detached by City employees, as were all other flags and banners of all other entities participating in the banner forum. At Defendant's express direction, however, employees of the City Department of Traffic Engineering were not permitted or authorized to attach Plaintiff's expressive banners by Defendant's intervention, even as those City employees were preparing to do so.

17. On information and belief, City employees have never been prevented from attaching, or refused authorization to attach, the expressive banners or flags of any other organization using the City's banner forum.

18. When confronted with Defendant's refusal to permit or authorize City employees to attach Plaintiff's expressive flags, Quinn requested that C.A.P. be provided the reason. Defendant reiterated his objection to the

banners' gay-positive message and stated that he would not "waste taxpayers" money attaching Plaintiff's banners. Quinn offered to have C.A.P. reimburse the City for any costs associated with having the banners attached and expressly offered to pay the City for twice the amount of time that Defendant claimed would be required, which amount far exceeded the actual time and effort required to hang Plaintiff's banners in every prior year. Defendant refused the offer and steadfastly denied Plaintiff the ability to use the City's banner forum on equal footing as other similarly situated entities.

19. As a result of Defendant's refusal to permit or authorize City employees to attach Plaintiff's Pride flags to City utility poles, members of Plaintiff were forced to go to considerable lengths and expose themselves to significant risks not faced by members of any other similarly situated organization in order to effectuate their speech in a designated public forum. Among the additional expenses and effort required to use the banner forum as a result of Defendant's actions, Plaintiff was forced to purchase a tall ladder and members of Plaintiff were forced to climb to the highest rung of the ladder and extend themselves approximately three stories above a busy intersection in order to attach and detach Plaintiff's banners, an effort that required four members of the organization to accomplish.

20. Based on information and belief, all other flags and banners that use the banner forum are attached and detached to City utility poles by City employees using City resources.

21. Based on information and belief, no other private individuals have been required to expose themselves to risk of personal injury in order to exercise their right of expression via the City's banner forum.

22. Defendant was solely responsible for the decision not to permit or authorize City employees to attach and detach Plaintiff's banners to City utility poles. The only reason Defendant expressed for his decision not to permit or authorize City employees to attach Plaintiff's banners to City property was that he disagreed with Plaintiff's message in that he personally disapproves of the "lifestyle choice" the Pride banners represent. Because he is the City's chief executive and, in this context, final policymaker, Plaintiff alleges that Defendant's unilateral decision concerning the attachment of the banners to City utility poles, specifically, his decision not to permit or authorize City employees to attach and detach Plaintiff's expressive banners, constitutes municipal policy.

23. Defendant unilaterally decided that Plaintiff's message was distasteful to him and therefore denied to Plaintiff City services and a governmental benefit made available to other similarly situated entities.

24. No compelling or even rational or legitimate reason existed to treat Plaintiff unlike other similarly situated entities. Defendant's actions were impermissibly based on animus and/or were wholly arbitrary.

25. While Defendant was not required to sign the proclamation, he violated Plaintiff's constitutional rights by refusing to permit or authorize City employees to provide governmental services the City routinely provide all other similarly situated entities and, in so doing, Defendant infringed upon Plaintiff's fundamental rights to free speech and equal protection without a legitimate governmental interest or reason.

26. Plaintiff is aware of no criteria employed by Defendant in deciding which expressive banners and flags he will permit or authorize to be attached to City utility poles by City employees and those he will not so allow. Thus, each time Defendant makes such a decision, his actions as final policymaker in this area constitutes municipal policy. By exercising his authority in this manner, he provides himself unbridled discretion, based solely on his approval or disapproval of a particular message, in choosing among entities and expressive content.

27. All the actions taken by Defendant were in his capacity as mayor of the City of Birmingham and, therefore, were taken under color of state law. The actions taken by Defendant were constitutional violations of clearly established law.

Plaintiff's Injuries

28. Because Defendant would not permit or authorize City employees to hang Plaintiff's banners, Plaintiff had to have purchased and pay for a 25 foot ladder at a cost of approximately $350.00 in order to hang Plaintiff's banners and thereby use, and otherwise participate in, the City's banner forum.

29. In addition to the cost incurred as a result of Defendant's discriminatory treatment, Plaintiff's expression was significantly delayed and limited to only one day before the parade began contrary to Plaintiff's written requests, intentions and years past.

30. The discriminatory treatment Plaintiff experienced in being denied government resources on equal footing with other similarly situated entities resulted in reputational and dignitary harm to Plaintiff.

31. Plaintiff intends to organize and sponsor Birmingham's Pride celebration in 2009 and to use the banner forum to display its message announcing and commemorating the Pride celebration. Plaintiff seeks to be provided government resources in 2009 in the same manner as other entities using the banner forum and to be treated in the same manner as other entities using the banner forum.

FIRST CAUSE OF ACTION

(Violation of Freedom of Speech)

32. Plaintiff adopts and incorporates by reference all the preceding allegations in this Amended Complaint.

33. As set forth herein, Defendant's actions that infringed upon, delayed, and limited Plaintiff's ability to use a designated public forum of the City, and that denied Plaintiff a governmental benefit based on the content of

Plaintiff's speech, constituted viewpoint and/or content-based discrimination in violation of Plaintiff's rights under the First Amendment to the United States Constitution, as made applicable to the states by the Fourteenth Amendment.

34. Defendant's policy regulating speech within the banner forum, by determining which entities within the forum will be provided benefit of City employees to facilitate their expressions and which entities will be forced to suffer the risks and costs of hanging their own banners to exercise their right to expression in the forum, violates the right of free speech in that it is not justified by any compelling or even rational or legitimate state interest and is arbitrary and, if not enjoined, would provide a single governmental official with unbridled and unappealable authority to decide which entities will receive municipal assistance in expressing their messages and which will be denied such assistance.

SECOND CAUSE OF ACTION

(Equal Protection Violation Burdening Plaintiff's Right to Free Speech Without a Compelling Governmental Interest)

35. Plaintiff adopts and incorporates by reference the preceding allegations.

36. Defendant's actions in refusing to permit or authorize City employees to attach Plaintiff's expressive banners to City utility poles in compliance with the City's customary practice for participants in its banner forum burdened and otherwise infringed upon Plaintiff's fundamental right to free speech within a designated public forum based on the content of Plaintiff's speech.

37. There was no compelling or even rational or legitimate governmental interest justifying the denial of City services to Plaintiff that are routinely provided to other similarly-situated entities.

38. Defendant's actions violated Plaintiff's right to equal protection of the law as protected by the Fourteenth Amendment to the United States Constitution.

THIRD CAUSE OF ACTION

(Equal Protection and Due Process Violation for Arbitrary Action Lacking Any Legitimate Governmental Interest)

39. Plaintiff adopts and incorporates by reference the preceding allegations.

40. Defendant's actions in refusing to permit or authorize City employees to attach Plaintiff's expressive flags to City utility poles in compliance with its customary practice for participants in its banner forum was wholly arbitrary and/or based on animus.

41. There was no rational basis or legitimate governmental interest justifying the denial of City services to Plaintiff that are routinely provided to other similarly situated entities. As a result, Defendant violated

Plaintiff's rights to equal protection and due process not to be treated arbitrarily by the government.

PRAYER FOR RELIEF

WHEREFORE, Plaintiff prays for judgment under all its causes of action and requests that this Court grant the following relief:

i. A declaratory judgment holding that Defendant's actions deprived Plaintiff of its constitutional rights.

ii. A permanent injunction prohibiting Defendant from treating Plaintiff in any way differently from other similarly situated entities, or denying Plaintiff City services made available to such entities.

iii. Judgment against Defendant for nominal damages.

iv. Punitive damages against Defendant in his individual capacity.

v. Judgment against Defendant, in his official and/or individual capacity, for three hundred fifty dollars ($350.00).

vi. Pursuant to 42 U.S.C. § 1988, Plaintiff's costs and reasonable attorneys' fees for pursuing this action.

vii. Such other, further and different relief as to which Plaintiff may be entitled.

This 22nd day of December, 2008.

NOTE

In response to the complaint above, Defendant filed a motion to dismiss in January 2009. First pointing out that the parade was still held and the banners hung as usual, Defendant stated that "[t]he only real difference, and the one that is the basis for the Plaintiff's claims, is that Mayor Langford did not personally approve and celebrate Plaintiff's cause in the way previous mayors had apparently done. Of course, there is no constitutional right to the Mayor's approval of Plaintiff's private agenda. Nor, by Plaintiff's own admission, is there any absolute right to have City workers hang Plaintiff's banners. In short, Plaintiff has not suffered any real and concrete harm; therefore, Plaintiff has failed plead any cause of action that would entitle it to relief in a court of law." Further, Defendant noted that "[a]lthough Mayor Langford did not issue a proclamation, the Birmingham City Council passed a resolution endorsing not only the parade but the entire week's activities regarding Gay Pride Week." Defendant argued that he was entitled to qualified immunity, that he did not engage in viewpoint discrimination, that his actions were purely discretionary; and that Plaintiff's equal protection claim would fail because that Plaintiff did not suffer any loss cognizable under the law and that this claim would fail when applied to this class-of-one, the Defendant. Defendant also stated that Plaintiff's assertion that the Mayor was "the city's chief executive and final policy maker" was incorrect, and that the City Council, not the Mayor, was the final policymaker in Birmingham. In so asserting, the Defendant cited Alabama law (1955 Ala. Act 452 as amended, Mayor Council Act, § 3.07).

According to the Lambda Legal website, in September 2009, a settlement agreement was reached in this lawsuit. Besides paying attorneys' fees and costs in an amount exceeding $40,000, the city agreed to establish non-discriminatory regulations guiding the approval of the hanging of banners on city property by city employees to announce upcoming public events.

Local Acts

Drafting of enabling legislation by decision-makers at the local level requires an understanding of not only federal limitations, but also of those found in one's state constitution, many of which prohibit special or "local" acts of a certain sort.

WILLIAMS v. BLUE CROSS BLUE SHIELD OF N.C.

357 N.C. 170, 581 S.E.2d 415 (2003)

EDMUNDS, JUSTICE.

In this action, we are called upon to determine: (1) whether the North Carolina General Assembly violated Article II, Section 24 of the North Carolina Constitution by ratifying enabling legislation permitting Orange County, the Orange County Board of Commissioners, and the Orange County Human Relations Commission (collectively, counterclaim defendants) to enact and enforce the employment provisions of an antidiscrimination ordinance entitled the Orange County Civil Rights Ordinance (the Ordinance); and (2) whether counterclaim defendants acted illegally in enacting and enforcing the employment provisions of that Ordinance. For the reasons that follow, we affirm the trial court's grant of partial summary judgment to defendant Blue Cross Blue Shield of North Carolina (BCBSNC) and denial of summary judgment to counterclaim defendants.

Pursuant to N.C.G.S. § 160A–492, the Orange County Board of Commissioners (the Board of Commissioners) in 1987 established the Orange County Human Relations Commission (the HRC). *See* N.C.G.S. § 160A–492 (2001) ("[t]he governing body of any city, town, or county is hereby authorized to undertake ... human relations, community action and manpower development programs ... [and] may appoint such human relations, community action and manpower development committees or boards and citizens' committees, as it may deem necessary in carrying out such programs and activities"). The Board of Commissioners' mandate to the HRC was that it

> (1) study and make recommendations concerning problems in the field of human relationships; (2) anticipate and discover practices and customs most likely to create animosity and unrest and to seek solutions to problems as they arise; (3) make recommendations designed to promote goodwill and harmony among groups in the County irrespective of their race, color, creed, religion, ancestry, national origin, sex, affectional preference, disability, age, marital status or status with regard to public assistance; (4) monitor complaints involving discrimination; (5) address and attempt to remedy the violence,

> tensions, polarization, and other harm created through the practices of discrimination, bias, hatred, and civil inequality; and (6) promote harmonious relations within the county through hearings and due process of law. . . .

Orange County Civil Rights Ordinance, art. II, sec. 2.1(a), at 1 (effective 1 January 1995) [hereinafter Ordinance].

Thereafter, the HRC advertised and conducted public hearings on discrimination in the areas of employment, housing, and public accommodation and determined that discrimination in those areas existed in Orange County on the basis of race, color, religion, sex, national origin, age, disability, familial status, marital status, sexual orientation, and veteran status. *See* Ordinance, art. II, sec. 2.1(b), (c). As a result of these findings, the Board of Commissioners requested that the North Carolina General Assembly adopt enabling legislation allowing Orange County to enact a comprehensive civil rights ordinance. [This legislation was passed in 1991.]

On 23 March 1993, the Board of Commissioners adopted a resolution requesting that the Orange County delegation to the General Assembly introduce a rewrite of the 1991 legislation to provide for "local administration of federal and [s]tate laws prohibiting discrimination on the basis of race, color, religion, sex, national origin, age, disability, marital status, familial status, and veteran status." The General Assembly made the requested amendments[.] . . .

After the General Assembly passed this enabling legislation, the Board of Commissioners, on 6 June 1994, adopted the Ordinance. On 18 April 1995, the Board of Commissioners adopted another resolution requesting from the General Assembly an amendment to the enabling legislation authorizing the HRC to serve as a deferral agency for cases deferred by the Equal Employment Opportunity Commission (EEOC) and the Department of Housing and Urban Development (HUD), pursuant to planned "worksharing agreements" with those agencies. These agreements would authorize transfer by the EEOC to Orange County of employment discrimination complaints filed with it originating in the county and transfer by HUD to Orange County of housing discrimination complaints arising in the county. [These laws were passed by the General Assembly in 1995.]

In its current form, the Ordinance is an antidiscrimination law applicable only in Orange County and administered by counterclaim defendants. The employment provisions of the Ordinance provide in pertinent part:

> (a) It is unlawful for an employer:
>
> (1) To fail or refuse to hire or to discharge any individual, or otherwise to discriminate against any individual with respect to that individual's compensation, terms, conditions, or privileges of employ-

> ment, because of such individual's race, color, religion, sex, national origin, age, disability, familial status, or veteran status.

Ordinance, art. IV, sec. 4.1(a)(1), at 9 (effective 1 January 1996). The Ordinance is enforceable by a private cause of action that permits those affected to recover injunctive relief, back pay, and compensatory and punitive damages up to $300,000. Ordinance, art. VIII, sec. 8.3.2, at 50–53; art. X, at 54–55. Different sections of the Ordinance prohibit discrimination in employment, housing, and public accommodations, as well as the infliction of bodily injury or property destruction on account of the factors listed above. The employment discrimination provision of the Ordinance became effective 1 January 1996 and applies to all employers engaged in an industry affecting commerce who have fifteen or more employees in Orange County. Ordinance, art. III, at 4. Specifically excepted employers include the State of North Carolina and the United States. *Id.* at 4–5. The Ordinance provides that when the HRC receives individual complaints of employment discrimination, it may begin its investigation by requesting a statement of the employer's position regarding the allegations. Ordinance, art. VIII, sec. 8.1, at 39–42. HRC may also issue subpoenas to obtain documents and materials from the employer. *Id.* After completing its investigation, the HRC issues either a finding of cause to believe discrimination occurred or a finding that reasonable cause does not exist. Ordinance, art. VIII, sec. 8.2, at 42–46.

If the HRC finds cause to exist, attempts are made to resolve the complaint by conference, conciliation, and/or persuasion. Ordinance, art. VIII, sec. 8.1, at 42. If these efforts fail, the HRC issues a right-to-sue letter, Ordinance, art. VIII, sec. 8.2, at 45, allowing the complainant to litigate the matter in the Superior Court, Orange County, within one year of receipt of the letter, Ordinance, art. X, at 54. As an alternative if cause is found to exist, the HRC itself can instead choose to litigate the employment discrimination claim before a state administrative law judge (ALJ). Ordinance, art. VIII, sec. 8.2(j)(1), at 45. In such a case, the employer has no opportunity to opt out of the administrative process and demand a jury trial in state court. Ordinance, art. VIII, sec. 8.3.1(a), at 46. Any decision by the ALJ is automatically reviewed by a three-member panel of the HRC commissioners. Ordinance, art. VIII, sec. 8.3.1(j)(1), at 48. A reviewing panel has the discretion to review all aspects of the ALJ's findings, including findings of fact, credibility determinations, and legal findings, and may affirm, modify, or reverse the ALJ's recommended decision. *Id.*

In the case at bar, plaintiff Mary Williams filed claims with the HRC and the EEOC alleging discrimination on the grounds that she had been forced to resign from her employment with BCBSNC because of her age and sex, and also alleging that BCBSNC had retaliated against her for filing the discrimination claim. Following an investigation, the HRC found reasonable cause to believe that BCBSNC had discriminated against plaintiff based on her age and gender, and issued a right-to-sue letter.

Plaintiff filed the suit giving rise to the instant appeal in Superior Court, Orange County, on 23 March 1999, claiming that BCBSNC fired her because of her age and also in retaliation for filing a claim of discrimination with the HRC and the EEOC. Specifically, plaintiff alleged four causes of action: (1) that BCBSNC wrongfully discharged plaintiff because of her age, in violation of North Carolina public policy as set forth in the Equal Employment Practices Act (EEPA), N.C.G.S. ch. 143, art. 49A (2001), and the Ordinance; (2) that BCBSNC wrongfully discharged plaintiff because she filed a charge of age discrimination with the HRC and the EEOC, in violation of North Carolina public policy as set forth in the EEPA and the Ordinance; (3) that BCBSNC discharged plaintiff because of her age, in violation of the Ordinance; and (4) that BCBSNC discharged plaintiff in retaliation for filing a complaint with the HRC in violation of the Ordinance.

[BCBSNC removed the case to federal court where it was remanded back to the Superior Court of North Carolina.]

After the trial court on 1 November 1999 approved BCBSNC's motion to add a counterclaim, BCBSNC filed its amended answer and counterclaim. This new filing contained a declaratory judgment action (denominated as the counterclaim), asserting that the enabling legislation and the Ordinance violated Article II, Section 24(1)(j) of the North Carolina Constitution, which prohibits "any local, private, or special act or resolution ... [r]egulating labor, trade, mining, or manufacturing." N.C. Const. art. II, § 24(1)(j). On 31 July 2000, BCBSNC filed a further amended answer and first amended counterclaim, adding a claim that the Ordinance denied BCBSNC equal protection of the law. Beginning on 6 November 2000, the trial court heard cross-motions for summary judgment. BCBSNC's motion was based upon a claim that the Ordinance's employment discrimination provisions were unconstitutional, while counterclaim defendants' motion argued that the Ordinance was constitutional in its entirety but that, even if it were not, BCBSNC was precluded from attacking the Ordinance based on the affirmative defenses of laches and the statute of limitations.

After hearing arguments and reviewing the parties' briefs, the trial court on 13 November 2000 entered an order declaring the employment provisions of the Ordinance to be in violation of Article II, Section 24 of the North Carolina Constitution, and in violation of the equal protection guarantees of the Fourteenth Amendment to the United States Constitution and Article I, Section 19 of the North Carolina Constitution. The trial court also enjoined counterclaim defendants from enforcing the unlawful employment discrimination provisions of the Ordinance as well as any civil rights investigations and civil actions thereunder....

As a preliminary matter, we observe that the only issues before us pertain to the employment provisions of the enabling legislation and the Ordinance. Because the parties had no occasion to brief or argue the constitutionality of the provisions of the enabling legislation and the

Ordinance relating to housing and public accommodation and because the following analysis consequently focuses only on the employment provisions, we express no opinion as to the legality of any aspect of either the enabling legislation or the Ordinance unrelated to employment.

[First, the court addressed and overruled assignments of error that the action was barred by the statute of limitation and that the equitable doctrine of laches should apply in this action.]

We next consider whether the trial court erred in its holding that the employment discrimination provisions of the Ordinance and its enabling legislation violated Article II, Section 24 of the North Carolina Constitution. This section of the Constitution, entitled "Limitations on local, private, and special legislation," provides in pertinent part:

> (1) *Prohibited subjects.* The General Assembly shall not enact any local, private, or special act or resolution:
>
> . . . .
>
> (j) Regulating labor, trade, mining, or manufacturing;
>
> . . . .
>
> (3) *Prohibited acts void.* Any local, private, or special act or resolution enacted in violation of the provisions of this Section shall be void.

N.C. Const. art. II, § 24(1)(j), (3).

Counterclaim defendants argue that neither the enabling legislation nor the Ordinance is a local act under Article II, Section 24. Further, counterclaim defendants contend that even if this Court determines that the enabling legislation and the Ordinance are local acts, they are not prohibited local acts because they seek to regulate *discrimination* (which is not a forbidden purpose) rather than labor or trade.

Our review of counterclaim defendants' argument is two-fold. First, we must determine whether the enabling legislation and the Ordinance are local acts as contended by BCBSNC or whether they are general laws as contended by counterclaim defendants. Second, if they are found to be local acts, we must determine whether the enabling legislation and the Ordinance regulate labor or trade. As we make this determination, we are aware that:

> It is well settled in this State that the courts have the power, and it is their duty in proper cases, to declare an act of the General Assembly unconstitutional—but it must be plainly and clearly the case. If there is any reasonable doubt, it will be resolved in favor of the lawful exercise of their powers by the representatives of the people.

Glenn v. Board of Educ., 210 N.C. 525, 529–30, 187 S.E. 781, 784 (1936).

"A statute is either 'general' or 'local'; there is no middle ground." *High Point Surplus Co. v. Pleasants,* 264 N.C. 650, 656, 142 S.E.2d 697, 702 (1965). We have observed that "no exact rule or formula capable of constant application can be devised for determining in every case whether a law is local, private or special or whether general." *McIntyre v. Clarkson,* 254 N.C. 510, 517, 119 S.E.2d 888, 893 (1961). Consequently, since the enactment of Article II, Section 24 (originally Article II, Section 29, *see Smith v. County of Mecklenburg,* 280 N.C. 497, 506, 187 S.E.2d 67, 73 (1972)), we have set out alternative methods for determining whether a law is general or local. *See City of New Bern v. New Bern–Craven Cty. Bd. of Educ.,* 338 N.C. 430, 435–36, 450 S.E.2d 735, 738–39 (1994). In earlier decisions, we held that if the legislation impacted a majority of the counties, the law was general. *See State v. Dixon,* 215 N.C. 161, 165, 1 S.E.2d 521, 523 (1939). Later, we established what has become known as the "reasonable classification" test. *See McIntyre v. Clarkson,* 254 N.C. at 518–19, 119 S.E.2d at 894–95. This test considers how the law in question classifies the persons or places to which it applies. Pursuant to this test, the "[c]lassification must be reasonable and ... must be based on a reasonable and tangible distinction and operate the same on all parts of the state under the same conditions and circumstances." *Id.* at 519, 119 S.E.2d at 894. A law is deemed local

> where, by force of an inherent limitation, it arbitrarily separates some places from others upon which, but for such limitation, it would operate, where it embraces less than the entire class of places to which such legislation would be necessary or appropriate having regard to the purpose for which the legislation was designed, and where the classification does not rest on circumstances distinguishing the places included from those excluded.

Id. at 518, 119 S.E.2d at 894. On the other hand,

> the constitutional prohibition against local acts simply commands that when legislating in certain specified fields the General Assembly must make rational distinctions among units of local government which are reasonably related to the purpose of the legislation. A law is general if "any rational basis reasonably related to the objective of the legislation can be identified which justifies the separation of units of local government into included and excluded categories."

Adams v. N.C. Dep't. of Natural & Econ. Res., 295 N.C. 683, 691, 249 S.E.2d 402, 407 (1978) (*quoting* Joseph S. Ferrell, *Local Legislation in the North Carolina General Assembly,* 45 N.C. L.Rev. 340, 391 (1967)).

In *Town of Emerald Isle v. State,* 320 N.C. 640, 360 S.E.2d 756 (1987), we departed from the reasonable classification test enunciated in *Adams* where the act in question applied only to a site-specific portion of land on a particular beach. Instead, we applied a test that examined "the extent to which the act in question affects the general public interests and concerns," *Id.* at 651, 360 S.E.2d at 763, because the reasonable classification test was "ill-suited to the question presented in [that] case, since by definition a particular public pedestrian beach access facility must rest in but one location," *Id.* at 650, 360 S.E.2d at 762.

Our review of the various analyses for determining whether an act is local or general satisfies us that the reasonable classification test is most appropriate to the case at bar. While, in this case, the enabling legislation and the Ordinance allowing for the creation of a comprehensive civil rights ordinance apply only to Orange County, this legislation is not site-specific as in *Emerald Isle* because "[s]uch a legislated change could be effected as easily in [Orange County] as in any other [county] in the state." *City of New Bern v. New Bern–Craven Cty. Bd. of Educ.*, 338 N.C. at 436, 450 S.E.2d at 739. Consequently, the *Emerald Isle* analysis is inapplicable to this case.

Under a reasonable classification analysis, "the distinguishing factors between a valid general law and a prohibited local act are the related elements of reasonable classification and uniform application." *Adams v. N.C. Dep't. of Natural & Econ. Res.*, 295 N.C. at 690, 249 S.E.2d at 407. Legislative classification of conditions, persons, places, or things is reasonable when it is "based on [a] rational difference of situation or condition." *High Point Surplus Co. v. Pleasants*, 264 N.C. at 656, 142 S.E.2d at 702.

Based upon our earlier decisions, we must determine in this case whether the legislature had a rational basis to justify singling out Orange County through the enabling legislation, thereby allowing this one county to create its own civil rights ordinance enforcing particular employment rights of Orange County citizens. Phrased differently, we must determine whether the General Assembly should have granted Orange County the power, rationally based upon some situation unique to that county, to create and enforce additional employment rights beyond those accorded any other county in this state. Based upon our thorough review of the record, we determine that neither the enabling legislation passed by the legislature nor the Ordinance suggests any rational basis justifying treatment of Orange County differently from all other North Carolina counties as to those rights.

A history of the promulgation of Article II, Section 24 reveals:

> The organic law of the State was originally drafted and promulgated by a convention which met at Halifax in December, 1776. During the ensuing 140 years, the Legislature of North Carolina possessed virtually unlimited constitutional power to enact local, private, and special statutes. This legislative power was exercised with much liberality, and produced a plethora of local, private, and special enactments. As an inevitable consequence, the law of the State was frequently one thing in one locality, and quite different things in other localities. To minimize the resultant confusion, the people of North Carolina amended their Constitution at the general election of 1916 so as to deprive their Legislature of the power to enact local, private, or special acts or resolutions relating to many of the most common subjects of legislation.
>
> . . . .
>
> In thus amending their organic law, the people were motivated by the desire that the General Assembly should legislate for North Carolina in respect to the subjects specified as a single united commonwealth

> rather than as a conglomeration of innumerable discordant communities. To prevent this laudable desire from degenerating into a mere pious hope, they decreed in emphatic and express terms that "any local, private, or special act or resolution passed in violation of the provisions of this section shall be void."

Idol v. Street, 233 N.C. 730, 732–33, 65 S.E.2d 313, 314–15 (1951) (quoting N.C. Const. of 1868, art. II, sec. 29 (1917)) (now Article II, Section 24, as previously noted); *see also* John V. Orth, *The North Carolina State Constitution: A Reference Guide* 89–90, 166–67 (1993).

A brief comparison of the Ordinance with the employment discrimination law applicable across North Carolina reveals that the enabling legislation and the Ordinance generate different law in one locality from that applicable to other localities within the state. First, the Ordinance creates in Orange County two additional protected categories of employment discrimination apparently found nowhere else in the state. The Ordinance prevents Orange County employers with fifteen or more employees from discriminating because of "familial status" or "veteran status," Ordinance, art. IV, sec. 4.1(a)(1), at 9, classifications that are not found in either the EEPA or section 2000e–2 of title 42 of the United States Code, 42 U.S.C. § 2000e–2 (2000) ("Unlawful employment practices"). Second, a method for enforcing employment discrimination suits has been created in Orange County that exists nowhere else in North Carolina. Thus, in a single dispute involving one employee, an employer in Orange County may be investigated and sued by either the HRC or the EEOC. In other words, as acknowledged in deposition by the Director of the Orange County Department of Human Rights and Relations, such an Orange County employer can be compelled to respond to two different government investigations and suits. By contrast, an employer elsewhere in North Carolina may be subject to investigation by the EEOC or the North Carolina Department of Administration's Human Relations Commission, *see* N.C.G.S. § 143–422.3, but can only be sued through a federal claim brought by the EEOC.

Additionally, an employee working in Orange County may benefit from a longer statute of limitations for the raising of administrative claims than employees working in other counties. Employers in any county other than Orange may raise a statute of limitations defense if an employee fails to file a complaint with the EEOC within 180 days of the alleged unlawful act. *See* 42 U.S.C. § 2000e–5(e) (2000). In Orange County, however, by virtue of the Ordinance, an employer may not raise a statute of limitations defense unless the charge was filed after 300 days of the alleged act. *See Id.; see also* 29 U.S.C. § 626(d)(2) (2000).

Similarly, the statute of limitations period for the filing of discrimination lawsuits differs between Orange County employers and employers elsewhere. A North Carolina employer not in Orange County may assert a statute of limitations defense against an employee who fails to file suit within ninety days of receiving a right-to-sue letter from the EEOC. *See*

42 U.S.C. § 2000e–5(f)(1); 29 U.S.C. § 626(e). In contrast, while the limitations period for EEOC complaints remains the same, an employer in Orange County may not assert a statute of limitations defense for discrimination claims filed under the Ordinance unless the employee fails to file suit one year after receiving a right-to-sue notice from the HRC. Ordinance, art. X, at 54.

In addition, there is no evidence in the record to suggest that employment practices in Orange County differ in any significant way from the employment practices in other North Carolina counties. Consequently, we are unable to conclude that conditions in Orange County alone are suspect to such an extent that the legislature legally could create a separate classification to address employment discrimination in that county only. *See City of New Bern v. New Bern–Craven Cty. Bd. of Educ.,* 338 N.C. at 438, 450 S.E.2d at 740 (no rational basis to separate New Bern from other cities for special legislative attention regarding the designation of an appropriate inspection department); *Smith v. County of Mecklenburg,* 280 N.C. at 507–08, 187 S.E.2d at 74 (no particular features in Mecklenburg and Moore Counties that differentiate them from other counties with reference to the right of their citizens to decide whether to have liquor by the drink); *High Point Surplus Co. v. Pleasants,* 264 N.C. at 657, 142 S.E.2d at 703 (no reasonable distinction to demonstrate that a Sunday observance law is more necessary for the welfare of Wake County than other counties); *Treasure City of Fayetteville, Inc. v. Clark,* 261 N.C. 130, 134–35, 134 S.E.2d 97, 100–01 (1964) (no reasonable basis to exempt certain counties from Sunday closing statute than other counties); *McIntyre v. Clarkson,* 254 N.C. at 524–25, 119 S.E.2d at 898 (no reasonable and distinctive feature to allow certain counties to have different laws regarding the appointment of justices of the peace). Based on all the considerations set out above, we hold that the employment provisions of the enabling legislation and the Ordinance are local laws.

. . . Our role . . . is to determine whether the method employed by Orange County comports with the Constitution of North Carolina. Any local, private, or special act or resolution enacted in violation of Article II, Section 24 shall be void, "no matter how praiseworthy or wise [its provisions] may be." *Idol v. Street,* 233 N.C. at 733, 65 S.E.2d at 315.

> It was the purpose of [Article II, Section 24] to free the General Assembly from the enormous amount of petty detail which had been occupying its attention, to enable it to devote more time and attention to general legislation of statewide interest and concern, to strengthen local self-government by providing for the delegation of local matters by *general laws* to local authorities, and to require uniform and coordinated action under general laws on matters related to the welfare of the whole State.

High Point Surplus Co. v. Pleasants, 264 N.C. at 656, 142 S.E.2d at 702. Therefore, if the General Assembly should undertake to address employment discrimination by means of a state statute, Article II, Section 24 requires that it enact either a statewide law applicable to employers and their employees regardless of where they reside within the state or a general law that makes reasonable classifications based upon rational differences of circumstances. That process was not followed here. Upholding the particularized laws in this case could lead to a balkanization of the state's employment discrimination laws, creating a patchwork of standards varying from county to county. The end result would be the "conglomeration of innumerable discordant communities" that Article II, Section 24 was enacted to avoid. 233 N.C. at 732, 65 S.E.2d at 315.

Having determined that the enabling legislation and the Ordinance are local laws, we next must consider whether they regulate labor or trade. Previously, this Court has adopted the definition of to "regulate" as " 'to govern or direct according to rule; . . . to bring under the control of law or constituted authority.' " *State v. Gulledge,* 208 N.C. 204, 208, 179 S.E. 883, 886 (1935) (quoting *Webster's New International Dictionary* 2099 (2d ed. 1935)), *quoted in Cheape v. Town of Chapel Hill,* 320 N.C. 549, 559, 359 S.E.2d 792, 798 (1987). "Labor" has been defined as "compensated employment," *State v. Chestnutt,* 241 N.C. 401, 403, 85 S.E.2d 297, 299 (1955), and "trade" has been defined as "a business venture for profit and includes any employment or business embarked in for gain or profit," *High Point Surplus Co. v. Pleasants,* 264 N.C. at 655–56, 142 S.E.2d at 702. After reviewing the record, we believe the enabling legislation and the Ordinance regulate labor in Orange County.

As noted above, counterclaim defendants contend that the acts seek only to regulate discrimination, not labor or trade. However, the record demonstrates that while the intent of the enabling legislation and the Ordinance is to prohibit discrimination in the workplace, the effect of these enactments is to govern the labor practices of "person[s] engaged in an industry affecting commerce who has 15 or more employees" in Orange County. Numerous aspects of the employer/employee relationship fall within the ambit of the Ordinance, from hiring through resignation, retirement, or termination. The Ordinance requires covered employers to conduct their internal practices pursuant to the requirements of the Ordinance or face the possibility of civil suit by either an employee or the HRC. By seeking to curb unlawful discrimination by regulating covered employers, the enabling legislation and the Ordinance have the practical effect of regulating labor, as forbidden by Article II, Section 24.

In their briefs and at oral argument, the parties discussed the enabling legislation and the Ordinance in terms of trade. Although our conclusion that the acts regulate labor is dispositive as to this issue, we believe that they regulate trade as well. Most of the employers affected by the Ordinance are businesses operated for gain or profit. Regulation of these employers has the practical effect of regulating trade. *See Smith v. County of Mecklenburg,* 280 N.C. at 509, 187 S.E.2d at 75 (statute authorizing an election in Mecklenburg County to determine whether liquor by the drink could be sold under rules and regulations created by the local county board was determined to be a regulation of trade); *High*

Point Surplus Co. v. Pleasants, 264 N.C. at 656–57, 142 S.E.2d at 702–03 (local ordinance and statute that excepted forty-eight counties from its operation of establishing Sunday sales laws was determined to be a regulation of trade); *Orange Speedway, Inc. v. Clayton,* 247 N.C. 528, 533, 101 S.E.2d 406, 410 (1958) (statute that forbade the holding of motorcycle or automobile races on Sunday in Orange County was determined to be a regulation of trade).

Counterclaim defendants also argue that the enabling legislation does not "directly" regulate trade or labor because the legislation merely gives Orange County the option of adopting an employment discrimination ordinance. Therefore, counterclaim defendants claim that "permissive" legislation, such as the enabling legislation, does not violate Article II, Section 24 in this case. Even though we have concluded that the enabling legislation and the Ordinance regulate labor, we address this argument because its validity is not dependent on the purpose for which the local law was passed. In other words, if the legislation as passed is valid because it is "permissive," it does not matter that the purpose of the act is to regulate labor as opposed to trade.

[The Court then distinguished *High Point Surplus Co. v. Pleasants,* 264 N.C.650, 142 S.E.2d 697.] ... Accordingly, counterclaim defendants' argument that the purportedly permissive nature of the enabling legislation renders it valid is unpersuasive. We hold that this legislation, by giving the power to Orange County to enact the employment legislation, is invalid, whether or not Orange County had chosen to act on that power.

Finally, counterclaim defendants argue that, even if the enabling legislation is unconstitutional, Orange County possesses the inherent authority to pass the employment discrimination Ordinance at bar. They cite section 153A–121(a), which gives a county the power to enact ordinances that "define, regulate, prohibit, or abate acts, omissions, or conditions detrimental to the health, safety, or welfare of its citizens and the peace and dignity of the county," N.C.G.S. § 153A–121(a), and section 160A–174, which provides that "[t]he fact that a State or federal law, standing alone, makes a given act, omission, or condition unlawful shall not preclude city ordinances requiring a higher standard of conduct or condition," N.C.G.S. § 160A–174 (2001). However, under the Ordinance, a citizen is given subpoena power and the right to sue, even in the absence of finding of cause by the HRC. Under the Ordinance, the citizen may seek an injunction against an employer and may recover back pay and compensatory and punitive damages. By creating a civil relationship and concomitant private cause of action by one citizen against another, the Ordinance goes far beyond merely "requiring a higher standard of conduct or condition." Such a new and independent framework for litigation substantially exceeds the leeway permitted to individual counties by these statutes. Consequently, we are satisfied that Orange County's employment discrimination Ordinance is not saved by these statutory provisions.

In this analysis, as before, we are addressing only the employment discrimination provisions of the Ordinance. Aspects of the Ordinance dealing with housing and public accommodation, including such matters as any enforcement mechanisms and remedies available under those portions of the Ordinance, are not before us, and we express no opinion as to whether Orange County possessed inherent authority to address these areas.

These assignments of error are overruled.

Because we hold that the enabling legislation and the Ordinance violate Article II, Section 24 of the North Carolina Constitution, we need not address the additional assignments of error as to whether the acts are violative of equal protection under the federal and state Constitutions. Based upon the foregoing, we hold that the trial court did not err in concluding that the enabling legislation and the Ordinance pertaining to employment discrimination are unconstitutional acts.

AFFIRMED.

DISCUSSION

1. What is a "local act"? Consider what the Orange County Board of Commissioners was trying to do with its Human Relations Board.

2. How is this case relevant to the legal issues discussed in this chapter? Is the Court correct in holding that this attempt violated the North Carolina Constitution?

3. Discuss whether you believe Orange County has the legal authority to address housing and public accommodation claims with this Civil Rights Ordinance.

IV. LOCAL BILLS

In most (if not all) states, attempting to get local bills passed is a political game. Usually, if the proposed bill is not preempted by federal or state law or if there are no other legal concerns such as the constitutionality of the bill, and if the local legislative delegation unanimously supports it, the bill makes its way into law. This is oftentimes not the case, however, with so-called "controversial" bills. Witness the following editorial regarding an attempt by Carrboro, North Carolina to expand housing non-discrimination coverage.

Not in this house*

In Carrboro, we try to play fair with our house rules. We have this silly notion that housing opportunities should be available to everyone. Not so in the big House, where our local bill could not make it intact out of the Local Government II Committee.

* This editorial was written in May of 2009 by Professor Lavelle, who is also an elected member of the Carrboro, North Carolina Board of Aldermen.

Our Town Charter addresses housing discrimination, offering protection to persons based on race, color, religion, sex and national origin. Our Board of Aldermen wanted to update the charter to also extend protection to persons based on familial status, handicap, sexual orientation, gender identification, and gender expression. Since familial status and handicap are now covered under the Fair Housing Act, this was an effort to update this provision so that it was consistent with federal law, as well as to extend this protection to others.

On four occasions, the BOA unanimously supported this bill; not one citizen wrote or spoke against this effort. [State Senator] Ellie Kinnaird and [State Representative] Verla Insko introduced the bill in their respective chambers. The first House committee to address the bill, the one mentioned above, includes Rep. Paul Stam, the House minority leader, as a vice-chair.

I attended this first committee meeting, and heard Rep. Insko make an eloquent, well-reasoned argument in favor of the bill. I pointed out that twenty states, Washington, DC and over 150 municipalities have passed such laws.

Rep. Stam then started remarking about his perception of sexual orientation and gender identity. He asked how one would know if the definition that "these people" have of sexual orientation includes bestiality, and asked what you call a man who has sex with underage boys. He did not understand how a person could not know if they were a man or a woman. Again, Rep. Insko gave thoughtful and sensitive answers to his comments, noting that although this bill would apply only in Carrboro, every community has gay, lesbian, bisexual and transgender residents, and these are our family members, co-workers and friends. [Carrboro] Mayor Mark Chilton was also present at the second meeting to address committee concerns, and stated that Carrboro simply wanted to afford equal protection to everyone. Other committee members offered comments and asked questions about the bill. Rep. Stam warned the other members that this was not just a local bill, but that every person who has rental property in Carrboro would be affected by this. Representatives from advocacy groups spoke for and against the legislation.

When all was said and done, only one member of the committee (Rep. Marvin Lucas) supported the bill with the inclusion of sexual orientation, gender identity and expression. The other fifteen members of the committee did not. I can only surmise that this issue was too controversial for them to support.

Although I was discouraged, Rep. Insko and Mayor Chilton, who have been involved with GLBT issues in Orange County longer than I have, commented that just the fact that this topic was being discussed in a House committee meeting was progress. In the broader context, as I write, the School Violence Prevention Act (which would cover sexual orientation as well as gender identity and expression) is progressing through both the House and the Senate; this bill is another way of educating legislators about other issues that GLBT persons face [this bill passed the month after this editorial was written by a 25–22 Senate vote and a 58–57 House vote].

And so, although this committee sees nothing wrong with denying housing and mortgage opportunities to people solely on the basis of who they are, or who they love, or how they express themselves, I know that I speak for many others when I say that we want to play fair in Carrboro. Someday we will be permitted to do so.

V. RESOLUTIONS

Often, local policy-makers make positions known by passing resolutions about controversial matters.

CATHOLIC LEAGUE FOR RELIGIOUS AND CIVIL RIGHTS v. CITY AND COUNTY OF SAN FRANCISCO

567 F.3d 595 (9th Cir. 2009)

PAEZ, CIRCUIT JUDGE:

Appellants, Catholic League for Religious and Civil Rights, Dr. Richard Sonnenshein, and Valerie Meehan (collectively, "Catholic League" or "the League"), appeal the dismissal of their civil rights action under 42 U.S.C. § 1983 for failure to state a claim. At issue is the constitutionality of a non-binding resolution adopted by the Board of Supervisors of the City and County of San Francisco ("the Board") concerning the adoption of children by same-sex couples and the Catholic Church's position against such adoptions. Catholic League argues that in adopting the resolution the Board expressed disapproval of the Catholic religion in violation of the First Amendment's Establishment Clause. Because we conclude that the resolution passes constitutional scrutiny, we affirm.

I.

In March, 2006, the Board passed a nonbinding resolution, Res. No. 168–06, titled: "Resolution urging Cardinal Levada to withdraw his directive to Catholic Charities forbidding the placement of children in need of adoption with same-sex couples." ("Resolution"). The Resolution provides in full:

Resolution urging Cardinal William Levada, in his capacity as head of the Congregation for the Doctrine of the Faith at the Vatican, to withdraw his discriminatory and defamatory directive that Catholic Charities of the Archdiocese of San Francisco stop placing children in need of adoption with homosexual households.

WHEREAS, It is an insult to all San Franciscans when a foreign country, like the Vatican, meddles with and attempts to negatively influence this great City's existing and established customs and traditions such as the right of same-sex couples to adopt and care for children in need; and

WHEREAS, The statements of Cardinal Levada and the Vatican that "Catholic agencies should not place children for adoption in homosexual households," and "Allowing children to be adopted by persons living in such unions would actually mean doing violence to these children" are absolutely unacceptable to the citizenry of San Francisco; and

WHEREAS, Such hateful and discriminatory rhetoric is both insulting and callous, and shows a level of insensitivity and ignorance which has seldom been encountered by this Board of Supervisors; and

WHEREAS, Same-sex couples are just as qualified to be parents as are heterosexual couples; and

WHEREAS, Cardinal Levada is a decidedly unqualified representative of his former home city, and of the people of San Francisco and the values they hold dear; and

WHEREAS, The Board of Supervisors urges Archbishop Niederauer and the Catholic Charities of the Archdiocese of San Francisco to defy all discriminatory directives of Cardinal Levada; now, therefore, be it

RESOLVED, That the Board of Supervisors urges Cardinal William Levada, in his capacity as head of the Congregation for the Doctrine of the Faith at the Vatican (formerly known as Holy Office of the Inquisition), to withdraw his discriminatory and defamatory directive that Catholic Charities of the Archdiocese of San Francisco stop placing children in need of adoption with homosexual households.

The Board passed this resolution in response to a then-recent directive from Prefect Cardinal William Levada, instructing the Archdiocese of San Francisco that Catholic social services agencies should not place children in need of adoption with gay or lesbian couples. Cardinal Levada is the head of the Congregation for the Doctrine of the Faith-an official body within the Catholic Church that, according to the complaint, is charged with "promot[ing] and safeguard[ing] the doctrine on the faith and morals throughout the Catholic world." The Resolution also quotes a statement in a 2003 document issued by the Congregation, titled "Considerations Regarding Proposals to Give Legal Recognition to Unions Between Homosexual Persons" ("Considerations document"). The Resolution does not name or specifically refer to the Considerations document, but the League alleges that the language "Allowing children to be adopted by persons living in [homosexual] unions would actually mean doing violence to these children" is taken from the 2003 document.

Shortly after the Board adopted the Resolution, Catholic League filed a 42 U.S.C. § 1983 suit in the Northern District of California, alleging that the Resolution violates the Establishment Clause by expressing disapproval of and hostility towards the Catholic Church and Catholic religious tenets. Catholic League sought "nominal damages, a declaration that this anti-Catholic resolution is unconstitutional, and a permanent injunction enjoining this and other official resolutions, pronouncements, or declarations against Catholics and their religious beliefs."

The Defendants–Appellees filed a Federal Rule of Civil Procedure 12(b)(6) motion to dismiss, which the district court granted in a thorough and well-reasoned decision. Applying the three-part Lemon test, the district court determined that the Resolution did not have a purpose secondary to a predominant religious purpose nor a primary effect of expressing hostility towards the Catholic religion and that the resolution did not foster excessive government entanglement with religion. *See Lemon v. Kurtzman*, 403 U.S. 602 (1971); *Catholic League v. City and County of San Francisco*, 464 F.Supp.2d 938 (N.D. Cal. 2006). As a result, the court concluded that Catholic League failed to state a claim under § 1983 for violation of the Establishment Clause and dismissed the complaint. Catholic League timely appealed.

II.

. . .

III.

"[T]he 'First Amendment mandates governmental neutrality between religion and religion and between religion and nonreligion.' " *McCreary County v. ACLU*, 545 U.S. 844, 860, 125 S.Ct. 2722, 162 L.Ed.2d 729 (2005) (*quoting Epperson v. Arkansas*, 393 U.S. 97, 104, 89 S.Ct. 266, 21 L.Ed.2d 228 (1968)). This constitutional mandate requires careful and nuanced consideration in a society like ours where religion has long played a pervasive social role; government conduct towards religion "must be judged in its unique circumstances to determine whether it constitutes an endorsement or disapproval of religion." *Lynch v. Donnelly*, 465 U.S. 668, 694, 104 S.Ct. 1355, 79 L.Ed.2d 604 (1984) (O'Connor, J., concurring).

We apply the three-part Lemon test to determine whether government conduct-either through endorsement of religion or hostility towards it-violates the Establishment Clause. Government action will pass muster if it "(1) has a secular purpose; (2) has a principal or primary effect that neither advances nor disapproves of religion; and (3) does not foster excessive governmental entanglement with religion." *Vasquez*, 487 F.3d at 1255 (citing *Lemon*, 403 U.S. at 612–13, 91 S.Ct. 2105). Failure to satisfy any of these three inquiries condemns government conduct as unconstitutional.

Although the courts have not often had occasion to determine whether government action effects a disapproval of religion, as opposed to an endorsement, the Establishment Clause's neutrality mandate applies here with equal force. We are guided in our analysis by American Family Association, one of only a handful of disapproval cases, which dealt with another set of resolutions adopted by the San Francisco Board of Supervisors. American Family Association treated disapproval and endorsement as flipsides of the same coin-the same legal tests and underlying First

Amendment values apply. We phrased the applicable principle in several ways—the state may not disapprove of religion, express hostility towards religion, nor inhibit religion, *American Family Ass'n*, 277 F.3d at 1121, 1122—and used the three terms interchangeably.

The first step in the *Lemon* analysis is to discern the government's actual purpose in taking the challenged action—in this case, adopting the Resolution. A "predominantly religious purpose" violates the Establishment Clause. *McCreary County*, 545 U.S. at 881, 125 S.Ct. 2722. Government action, however, satisfies the purpose prong if it is "grounded in a secular purpose." *Vasquez*, 487 F.3d at 1255. Furthermore, "[a] legislature's stated reasons will generally get deference, [but] the secular purpose required has to be genuine, not a sham, and not merely secondary to a religious objective." *McCreary County*, 545 U.S. at 864, 125 S.Ct. 2722.

Catholic League argues that it is evident from the face of the Resolution that the City's predominant purpose was to attack Catholic religious beliefs. The League points to the resolution's harsh and forceful language as betraying the Board's true intentions: "discriminatory," "defamatory," "absolutely unacceptable," "hateful and discriminatory," "insulting and callous," and "show[ing] a level of insensitivity and ignorance which has seldom been encountered." The Board counters that, despite the inflammatory language, it passed the resolution for secular purposes.

As we explained in American Family Association, we do not question whether the Board's actions were wise; "rather we determine the constitutionality of those actions." *American Family Ass'n*, 277 F.3d at 1122. *See also Brown v. Woodland Joint Unified School District*, 27 F.3d 1373, 1382 (9th Cir.1994) ("[O]nce the state is free to use a secular means of attaining a goal, it is not required to use an alternative secular means that is less likely to be associated with religion."). To be sure, the Board could have spoken with a gentler tone, but the strength of the Board's language alone does not transform a secular purpose into a religious one. The constitutional question remains whether the Board's purpose in adopting the Resolution was secular in nature. In other words, we must first decide whether the Board's purpose in criticizing the Cardinal's directive was disapproval of religious doctrine, or a call for non-discrimination in the adoption of children, and second whether for Establishment Clause purposes there is a difference between the two.

"The eyes that look to purpose belong to an 'objective observer.'" *McCreary County*, 545 U.S. at 862, 125 S.Ct. 2722 (*quoting Santa Fe Independent School Dist. v. Doe*, 530 U.S. 290, 308, 120 S.Ct. 2266, 147 L.Ed.2d 295 (2000)). The objective observer is "one presumed to be familiar with the history of the government's actions and competent to learn what history has to show." *Id.* at 866, 125 S.Ct. 2722. In so describing the objective observer, the Supreme Court has instructed that we cannot "cut the context" out of the purpose inquiry. *Id.* at 864, 125 S.Ct. 2722. Examining the Board's resolution in context, the district court correctly concluded that the objective observer would ascertain a secular purpose behind the Board's adoption of the non-binding Resolution.

The Board argues that its predominant purpose in adopting the Resolution was to "denounce discrimination against same-sex couples, and to try to preserve for San Francisco children the opportunity to be placed for adoption with qualified families without regard to sexual orientation." That purpose is set out by both the title and preamble of the Resolution. Indeed, the title states: "Resolution urging Cardinal Levada to withdraw his directive to Catholic Charities forbidding the placement of children in need of adoption with same-sex couples." And to emphasize, the preamble declares: "Resolution urging Cardinal William Levada, in his capacity as head of the Congregation for the Doctrine of the Faith at the Vatican, to withdraw his discriminatory and defamatory directive that Catholic Charities of the Archdiocese of San Francisco stop placing children in need of adoption with homosexual households." This theme is born out in the opening paragraph, which places the Resolution in the context of San Francisco's "existing and established customs and traditions such as the right of same-sex couples to adopt and care for children in need," and continues throughout the text, which explains that "[s]ame-sex couples are just as qualified to be parents as are heterosexual couples." It is apparent that the Resolution is about non-discrimination in adoption.

In addition, the timing of the Resolution lends further context and supports the Board's asserted purpose. *See McCreary County*, 545 U.S. at 866, 125 S.Ct. 2722 (*quoting Santa Fe*, 530 U.S. at 315, 120 S.Ct. 2266) ("[R]easonable observers have reasonable memories, and our precedents sensibly forbid an observer 'to turn a blind eye to the context in which [the] policy arose.' " (*quoting Santa Fe*, 530 U.S. at 315, 120 S.Ct. 2266)). The Congregation for the Doctrine of the Faith issued its clarion call against legalization of gay and lesbian unions, as an exposition of religious belief, in 2003. It was not until March 2006, days after Cardinal Levada directed Catholic Charities, a social services agency in the City of San Francisco, to stop placing children for adoption with gay and lesbians couples, that the Board adopted this resolution. Keeping in mind the context in which the Resolution arose, the objective observer would conclude that the Board's purpose in adopting the Resolution was to respond to a public action that would affect both its gay and lesbian constituents, as well as the children in the City and County's jurisdiction. The Board's focus was on same-sex couples, not Catholics.

Moreover, "[a] reviewing court must be 'reluctant to attribute unconstitutional motives' to government actors in the face of a plausible secular purpose." *Kreisner*, 1 F.3d at 782 (*quoting Mueller v. Allen*, 463 U.S. 388, 394–95, 103 S.Ct. 3062, 77 L.Ed.2d 721 (1983)). In light of this proscription, and the Resolution's focus on and stated goal of protecting and promoting adoption by same-sex couples, an objective observer would conclude that the Board's purpose was to champion needy children, gays, lesbians, and same-sex couples within its jurisdiction; not to officially disapprove of the Catholic faith or its religious tenets.

Catholic League maintains, however, that this is a distinction without a difference. It argues that the Board's support for same-sex adoption, and its basic underlying assumption that same-sex couples should be treated no differently than heterosexual couples-and that anything less is discriminatory, defamatory, and hateful-expresses hostility toward their religious beliefs that homosexuality is "deviant," and "intrinsically disordered," homosexual acts are "acts of grave depravity," homosexual unions are "clearly ... immoral," and "[a]llowing children to be adopted by persons living in such unions would actually mean doing violence to these children."

As the district court noted, same-sex adoption is "a secular dimension of the City's culture and tradition that the City believes is threatened by the specific directive issued to the Archdiocese." *Catholic League*, 464 F.Supp.2d at 944. The Board considers its Resolution as a secular message promoting same-sex adoption—a message that is in accord with a bevy of California and San Francisco laws and policies that promote equal rights for gays and lesbians and their families, *see In re Marriage Cases,* 43 Cal.4th 757, 76 Cal.Rptr.3d 683, 183 P.3d 384 (2008) (documenting the City and County of San Francisco's involvement as a plaintiff in the litigation to legalize same-sex marriage); *Lockyer v. City and County of San Francisco*, 33 Cal.4th 1055, 17 Cal.Rptr.3d 225, 95 P.3d 459 (2004) (holding that City and County officials lacked the authority to issue marriage licenses to same-sex couples, a practice they adopted at the Mayor's direction); SF Admin. Code § 62.1 (officially recognizing domestic partnerships); SF Admin. Code § 12B1 (preventing entities that contract with the City from discriminating on the basis of sexual orientation, domestic partner status, or marital status), and resolutions that denounce discrimination against gays and lesbians from all sources, see infra pp. 606–07 (listing San Francisco Board of Supervisors non-binding resolutions). To put it plainly, what the Board considers secular, Catholic League considers hostile to Catholic religious tenets.

This dual characterization is not uncommon. Courts have long recognized that certain secular beliefs, views, and positions coincide with religious beliefs, views, and positions. In such cases, government speech or action with respect to a secular issue is not considered endorsement of religion simply because the government's views are consistent with religious tenets. That is, the same belief can have both religious and secular dimensions; the government is not stripped of its secular purpose simply because the same concept can be construed as religious. *See McGowan v. Maryland*, 366 U.S. 420, 442, 81 S.Ct. 1101, 6 L.Ed.2d 393 (1961) ("[T]he 'Establishment' Clause does not ban federal or state regulation of conduct whose reason or effect merely happens to coincide or harmonize with the tenets of some or all religions. In many instances, the Congress or state legislatures conclude that the general welfare of society, wholly apart from any religious considerations, demands such regulation.... [T]he fact that [a policy] agrees with the dictates of the Judaeo Christian religions while it may disagree with others does not invalidate the regulation."); *Bowen v.*

Kendrick, *487 U.S. 589, 612–13, 108 S.Ct. 2562, 101 L.Ed.2d 520 (1988) ("On an issue as sensitive and important as teenage sexuality, it is not surprising that the Government's secular concerns would either coincide or conflict with those of religious institutions. But the possibility or even the likelihood that some of the religious institutions who receive Adolescent Family Life Act funding will agree with the message that Congress intended to deliver . . . is insufficient to warrant a finding that the statute on its face has the primary effect of advancing religion.");* Id. *at 605, 108 S.Ct. 2562 (noting that "promot[ing] adoption as an alternative [for adolescent parents]" is an approach that is not "inherently religious, although it may coincide with the approach taken by certain religions."); Brown, 27 F.3d at 1381 ("'[M]ere consistency with religious tenets is insufficient to constitute unconstitutional advancement of religion.'"* (quoting Smith v. Bd. of Sch. Comm'rs of Mobile County, *827 F.2d 684, 692 (11th Cir.1987))). In sum, if consistency with religious beliefs is not endorsement of religion, inconsistency is not hostility to it.*

Our opinion in American Family Association is particularly instructive. In 1998, several religious groups sponsored a multimedia advertising campaign titled "Truth in Love." *American Family Ass'n*, 277 F.3d at 1118. The advertisement, printed in the San Francisco Chronicle, stated that "God abhors any form of sexual sin," including homosexuality, and claimed that Jesus Christ could help gays and lesbians "walk[ ] out of homosexuality into sexual celibacy." *Id.* at 1119. The ad also included "statistics" about homosexuality, sexually transmitted infections, and "destructive behavior." *Id.*

In response to the ad campaign, the San Francisco Board of Supervisors sent a letter to the plaintiffs (among other campaign sponsors), stating that "Supervisor Leslie Katz denounces your hateful rhetoric against gays, lesbians and transgendered people," and that "there is a direct correlation between these acts of discrimination, such as when gays and lesbians are called sinful and when major religious organizations say they can change if they tried, and the horrible crimes committed against gays and lesbians," such as the brutal murder of Matthew Shepard. *Id.* The Board then adopted two resolutions—one urging Alabama legislators to include sexual orientation in their hate crimes legislation, and calling on the "Religious Right to take accountability for the impact of their long-standing rhetoric denouncing gays and lesbians," *Id.*; the other addressing the advertisements. The second resolution called the ad's statistical assertions "erroneous and full of lies," and stated that the campaign encouraged maltreatment of and violence against gays and lesbians. *Id.* at 1120.

The plaintiffs, religious organizations, filed a § 1983 action against the Board, claiming that the letter and resolutions violated the Establishment Clause by disapproving of a "particular religion." *Id.* On appeal we concluded that the defendants' actions had a plausible secular purpose and the primary effect of the documents in question was "encouraging equal rights for gays and discouraging hate crimes," *Id.* at 1121–23, not hostility "towards the religious view that homosexuality is sinful or immoral," *Id.*

at 1122 (emphasis added). We recognized the dual nature of views on homosexuality, and determined that San Francisco should not be hamstrung in its public policy simply because its secular position was at odds with certain religious views; that some perspectives on gay and lesbian issues are rooted in religious belief cannot overwhelm the fact that gay and lesbian issues are also secular policy matters. Any other approach would stymie government's ability to take action on all "potentially religious issues, including abortion, alcohol use, [and] other sexual issues." *Id.* at 1123. That is simply not the purpose or function of the Establishment Clause. The government must maintain neutrality among religions and between religion and nonreligion, but it cannot be held hostage to it. It is well within the Board's secular purview to promote adoptions of children by same-sex couples and denounce discrimination for the "general welfare of society." *McGowan*, 366 U.S. at 442, 81 S.Ct. 1101.

B.

Although the Board's purpose was secular, the resolution may still violate the Establishment Clause if it "has the principal or primary effect of advancing or inhibiting religion." *American Family Ass'n*, 277 F.3d at 1122. To ascertain effect, we ask whether "it would be objectively reasonable for the government action to be construed as sending primarily a message of either endorsement or disapproval of religion." *Vernon v. City of Los Angeles*, 27 F.3d 1385, 1398 (9th Cir.1994). This inquiry is conducted "from the perspective of a 'reasonable observer' who is both informed and reasonable," *American Family Ass'n*, 277 F.3d at 1122 (*quoting Kreisner*, 1 F.3d at 784), and who is "familiar with the history of the government practice at issue." *Kreisner*, 1 F.3d at 784.

As discussed above, the Board's unequivocal promotion of non-discrimination against same-sex couples in adoption is secular, regardless of whether the Catholic Church may be opposed to it as a religious tenet. The question is whether promotion of same-sex adoption is reasonably understood as the primary message conveyed by the Resolution. It is not enough that one might " 'infer' " disapproval of Catholic religious tenets; rather, disapproval or inhibition must " 'objectively be construed as the primary focus or effect.' " *American Family Ass'n*, 277 F.3d at 1122 (quoting *Vernon*, 27 F.3d at 1398–99).

The primary message conveyed by the Resolution turns in large part on the scope of the lens through which we view it. We believe that a sufficiently broad lens is essential. We must read the Resolution "as a whole," *American Family Ass'n*, 277 F.3d at 1122; its message can be affected by its context and must be analyzed given its "unique circumstances." *Lynch*, 465 U.S. at 694, 104 S.Ct. 1355 (O'Connor, J., concurring). To be sure, there are statements in the Resolution that, taken in isolation, may be said to convey disparagement towards the Catholic Church. But to be violative of the Establishment Clause, those statements must overwhelm the Resolution's secular dimensions. Considering the

Resolution as a whole, with its focus on the City's tradition of promoting and defending same-sex relationships, they do not.

Again, Catholic League argues that the Board's harsh language conveys a message of disapproval. As we explained above, generally, the Resolution's strong language speaks to its secular message: "denounc[ing] discrimination against same-sex couples" and supporting adoption by such couples of children in need. The Resolution, however, also targets the statement, attributed to Cardinal Levada and the Vatican that "Allowing children to be adopted by persons living in such unions would actually mean doing violence to these children," and calls it, among other things "absolutely unacceptable to the citizenry of San Francisco." That statement comes from the Considerations document, which the complaint explains is an exposition of Catholic religious tenets. Standing alone, therefore, an objective observer might conclude that the Board was expressing disapproval of Catholic religious belief, rather than endorsing a secular position. But the statement does not stand alone. It is embedded in the larger Resolution which is primarily a defense of same-sex adoption. That one statement cannot fairly be said to embody the Resolution's primary message.

The Resolution also urges "Archbishop Niederauer and the Catholic Charities of the Archdiocese of San Francisco to defy all discriminatory directives of Cardinal Levada," and urges "Cardinal William Levada, in his capacity as head of the Congregation for the Doctrine of the Faith at the Vatican (formerly known as Holy Office of the Inquisition), to withdraw his discriminatory and defamatory directive." Catholic League argues that those statements express disapproval of religion/Catholicism, and that they are not incidental to the primary message, but rather they define the message. We agree with the district court's observation that "[t]he fact that the City was commenting on the policy of the Archdiocese in this regard does not violate the Establishment Clause simply because the secular activity [i.e. adoption] was being performed by a religious organization." *Catholic League*, 464 F.Supp.2d at 945 (*citing Bowen*, 487 U.S. at 613, 108 S.Ct. 2562). In any event, however, given the Resolution's primary message of promoting same-sex adoption, any hostility conveyed towards particular Catholic tenets by those statements was secondary at best.

The Board's extensive and persistent practice of passing non-binding resolutions denouncing discrimination against gays and lesbians also shapes the message the Resolution conveys. The Board's secular defense of same-sex couples in all aspects of life is the dominant theme of the Board's actions. See Resolution No. 73–05 ("Resolution urging the Supreme Court of the United States to rescind their refusal and to accept the hearing of a legal challenge to Florida's prohibition of adoption of children by gays and lesbians"); Resolution No. 129–06 ("Resolution urging the IRS to reconsider their ruling on Domestic Partners and Community Property"); Resolution No. 166–06 ("Resolution urging Governor Schwarzenegger to submit amicus brief to New York Supreme Court of Appeals in support of the right of same-sex civil marriage''); Resolution No. 364–06 (''Resolution condemning the government sanctioned violence and chaos which took place during Moscow's first Gay Pride march''); Resolution No. 127–05 (''Resolution urging ... Secretary of Education to publicly apologize to gay, lesbian, bisexual, and transgender community''); Resolution No. 454–05 (''Resolution condemning the offensive and discriminatory training video shown to San Francisco 49er players''); Resolution No. 308–03 (''Resolution urging Senator Rick Santorum to step down from his leadership position in the Republican Party and to apologize for his comments [comparing homosexuality to polygamy, incest, and adultery]''); Resolution No. 199–00 (''Resolution urging Dr. Laura Schlessinger to refrain from making inaccurate statements about gays and lesbians that incite violence and hate''); *see also American Family Ass'n*, 277 F.3d at 1119–23 (concluding that a letter and two resolutions by the San Francisco Board of Supervisors criticizing religious groups for denouncing homosexuality did not violate the Establishment Clause).

Just as the ''overall holiday setting'' can change the message conveyed by a crèche, and a ''typical museum setting, though not neutralizing the religious content of a religious painting, negates any message of endorsement of that content,'' *Lynch*, 465 U.S. at 692, 104 S.Ct. 1355 (O'Connor, J., concurring), the Board's well-established practice of responding whenever the equality of gay and lesbian families is called into question necessarily colors the message conveyed by the Resolution. In adopting the Resolution, consistent with past practice, the Board sought to champion same-sex families and non-discrimination as to gays and lesbians. An objective observer would understand as much.

C.

Last, we consider whether government action ''foster[s] excessive governmental entanglement with religion.'' *Vasquez*, 487 F.3d at 1255. ''Administrative entanglement typically involves comprehensive, discriminating, and continuing state surveillance of religion.'' *Vernon*, 27 F.3d at 1399. Entanglement in the form of ''political divisiveness,'' that is, government actions that cause the public to fracture along religious lines, '' 'has never been relied upon as an independent ground for holding a government practice unconstitutional.' '' *American Family Ass'n*, 277 F.3d at 1123 (*quoting Brown*, 27 F.3d at 1383).

Catholic League's primary argument is that the resolution fosters excessive entanglement by taking ''an official position on religious doctrine,'' and that the Board has attempted to ''improperly influence Church authority and meddle in Church affairs.'' The case cited by Catholic League, *Commack Self–Service Kosher Meats, Inc. v. Weiss*, 294 F.3d 415 (2d Cir. 2002), simply does not support its argument that the Board's non-binding Resolution fosters excessive entanglement.

Commack held that New York's statutes prohibiting fraud in the sale of kosher food violated the Establishment Clause by fostering excessive entanglement. *Id.* at 425. The Second Circuit concluded that the laws "excessively entangle government and religion because they (1) take sides in a religious matter, effectively discriminating in favor of the Orthodox Hebrew view of dietary requirements; [and] (2) require the State to take an official position on religious doctrine...." *Id.*

The laws challenged in *Commack* are different in kind than the Board's Resolution here. New York's kosher fraud laws took sides in a religious matter in that they took one definition of kosher, codified it, and regulated it, to the exclusion of other competing doctrines of kashrut within Judaism. *See Id.* at 426. The laws took an official position on religious doctrine because determining whether each food article met kashrut's requirements, the State had to "either interpret religious doctrine or defer to the interpretations of religious officials." *Id.* at 427. By contrast, the Board's Resolution did not codify one strain of Catholic belief. It did not "take sides in a religious matter," nor an "official position on religious doctrine." The Board expressed its secular view in a non-binding resolution on a matter of public policy.

Nor does the Resolution attempt to influence Church policy in a way that creates excessive entanglement. To be sure, the Establishment Clause prohibits government from intervening in a religious dispute. The federal courts "are not arbiters of scriptural interpretation." *Thomas v. Review Bd.*, 450 U.S. 707, 716, 101 S.Ct. 1425, 67 L.Ed.2d 624 (1981). But the Board has not crossed that line with its non-binding resolution; the resolution enacts no policy or regulation-it is simply a statement of the Board's position on same-sex adoption.

IV.

"[I]t is inevitable that the secular interests of government and the religious interests of various sects and their adherents will frequently intersect, conflict, and combine." *Wallace v. Jaffree*, 472 U.S. 38, 69, 105 S.Ct. 2479, 86 L.Ed.2d 29 (1985) (O'Connor, J., concurring in judgment). Invalidating government action where this incidental overlap is present would create "chaos," *Id.* at 70, 105 S.Ct. 2479, and cripple the government's ability to take "action that affect[s] [all] potentially religious issues, including abortion, alcohol use, [and] other sexual issues." *American Family Ass'n*, 277 F.3d at 1123. The rights of same-sex families are no different.

Properly contextualized, the Resolution does not have the purpose or primary effect of expressing hostility towards Catholic religious beliefs, and it does not foster excessive government entanglement with the Catholic Church. Accordingly, the judgment of the district court is AFFIRMED.

DISCUSSION

1. *Do resolutions of this sort carry any purpose? Are they ever effective?*

2. *Find an example of a resolution passed by a municipality on a matter involving LGBT rights. Critique the wording of the resolution and who the*

policy-makers are trying to influence. Is this an effective use of a board or council's time?

VI. "OUT" POLITICIANS

How much does being an "out" elected official aid in getting legislation drawn, discussed or passed? As more openly gay and lesbian officials are elected across the country, anecdotal evidence shows that openly gay officials not only initiate more gay rights legislation, but serve to educate their heterosexual counterparts on the pros and cons of these policy decisions. According to the Gay and Lesbian Victory Fund, in 1991 only 49 openly LGBT elected officials served in the United States. In 2011, serving at all levels of government, there are more than 500 out elected officials. In addition, in his first two years in office, President Barack Obama appointed more than 200 openly LGBT Americans to his administration.

Tammy Baldwin: Congresswoman from Wisconsin*

This essay is written by Tammy Baldwin, who has been a member of the United States House of Representatives since 1998. She is contemplating a run for the United States Senate in 2012.

My interest in public service was apparent to me much earlier than my sexual orientation. I can date it back to middle school, in my hometown of Madison, Wisconsin, where I first ran for student council in 1974. My love for it continued through high school and college, when I realized I wanted a career in politics. I began asking myself: Would I run for public office? Would I become a lobbyist?

About the same time, I had a dramatic awakening. In my junior year of college, I fell in love with a woman. It hit me like a ton of bricks. I remember thinking, *No wonder there weren't any sparks and it didn't go further with those guys!* Like my girlfriends, I had dated guys in high school. And they were lovely guys. In fact, I recently got together with probably my most serious boyfriend in high school, and I still adore him—but not in the sense of marriage.

Although I was thrilled to be in a relationship that finally felt right, I kept thinking about its effect on my future career. I didn't know any gay politicians. I didn't even know any gay adults. I was absolutely certain I would eventually have to make a choice.

In the supportive atmosphere of Smith College, a women's college in Massachusetts, my girlfriend and I began coming out to friends. We quickly learned there was an active lesbian community on campus. That was one big difference between realizing I was gay in college versus high school: It was much easier to meet gay people my own age.

Another difference was that documentaries about the gay liberation movement were first appearing. I don't know if I'd have been able to see

* Excerpted from MITCHELL GOLD, CRISIS (2008). Reprinted with permission.

them when I was in high school without my family finding out. And it was important for me to see them because they helped me create a context for my new self. I didn't have a gay family to join; so what was I becoming a part of?

While I was thinking about my political future, I was lucky to be learning about gay heroes like Harvey Milk, Frank Kameny, and Del Martin and Phyllis Lyon. It gave me instant role models—not people I could actually talk with, but whose stories helped me realize my world wasn't ending.

At Smith, I felt safe. However, I knew after graduation I'd head home to Wisconsin for law school and to be closer to my recently widowed eighty-year-old grandmother. Even though home is liberal Madison, I was worried. My first girlfriend had a tough time with initial rejection by her family and watching that scared me. Actually, the more I think about it, I remember it terrified me. I hadn't yet told my grandmother, mother, or friends from high school. I kept thinking: *This is big. It's life altering. Sure, I've read about those heroic figures. But what makes me think I could do what they did?*

[Upon returning to Madison, Baldwin came out to her high school friends, mother and grandmother. All were accepting.]

I also spent those years in internal debate over whether I could run for local office. I decided to test the waters by working on local campaigns. Through this, I met real-live role models, including Dick Wagner and Kathleen Nichols of the Dane County Board of Supervisors. An out gay man and an out lesbian had gotten elected in the liberal community of Dane County. I felt my question had been answered. I joined them in working on campaigns and eagerly identified myself to them as gay. Thus, by the time I had the opportunity to run for the Dane County Board myself, it wasn't like I *could* go back in the closet.

I remember a big moment right after the first campaign. When journalists had profiled the candidates, they hadn't asked, "And by the way, what is your sexual orientation?" They simply listed me as a single graduate student (I was in law school). However, after I won the election, our largest-circulation paper, the *Wisconsin State Journal,* decided to write a series on the gay community, with a different focus each day: the gay bar scene, gays and religion, gays in politics. I accepted an invitation to be interviewed.

I was really concerned about the article. I hadn't hidden being a lesbian, but no matter how out I was before, this article would make it public to about fifty thousand people, the paper's circulation at the time. I worried what it would mean; after all, I had a listed address and phone number.

The article was a turning point. Many people who already knew sent messages like, "I'm so proud of you for doing that. You're going to educate lots of people." Some who didn't know had an issue with it, but they were civilized people. The Conservatives kind of grumped. I only had one "hate call" in the middle of the night. But with so much support, it put the negativity in context.

It was a good warm-up for what was to come. I was the county board's third openly gay member; so that barrier had been broken. But when I was elected to the Wisconsin State Legislature, I was its first openly gay member.

And then I ran for Congress. Wisconsin had never elected a woman before, and no state had ever elected a candidate who was out during their campaign. (Gays and lesbians who served before me came out in office and, in most cases, had been elected several times before addressing the issue with their constituencies.)

That's when I started getting some of the hateful stuff—people protesting and sending vitriolic letters and threats. But I didn't feel like it related to me personally or to my coming-out process. It just proved those creeps are out there.

It did, however, have the potential to affect more than me. Being an out public figure also impacts your partner. When I started in politics, I dated a number of women, and depending on factors like whether they were out to their families, it varied as to what risks they felt they could take.

. . .

One way we can make a better future for gay kids is though education—of both the gay and the heterosexual communities. And it should start earlier in life because kids are coming out earlier.

In the 1970s, although I was in one of the country's most progressive public school systems, there was no curriculum that referenced contributions by gays to America or even noted that they were part of society. There still hasn't been enough progress on that front. Yet it could be included in so many ways. We could mention that a famous historical figure was gay or talk about the gay rights movement in discussing other social change movements. We could include it in sex education by at least saying, "These people exist, too." That would tell gay kids they had a place in the rich and diverse history of this country. And it would tell heterosexual students that gay people are accepted and valued. Many parents need this information as much as their kids do because they probably grew up deprived of it.

I grapple with the issue of education in my own work on the Employment Non–Discrimination Act and the struggle to pass a bill that includes protection for transgender people. How do I educate my colleagues about Transgender 101? Many are now comfortable with protecting people based on sexual orientation, but we haven't gone the same distance on transgender issues. When I think of the parents of young children dealing with gender identity issues—something Barbara Walters presented so movingly in a 2007 *20/20* segment—I know we must help ensure that these children are protected as well.

. . .

INDEX

References are to Pages

Note: Index references non-case material.

†